Of Seeds and Salt

A Parable of Judgment

Of Seeds and Salt:

A Parable of Judgment

Volume One — Book One

in the

Aeon Regis Historical Series

Samuel Benjamin Gray

The Wild Olive Press

Oakfield, ME

This edition first published in the United States in 2018 by:
The Wild Olive Press
240 Thompson Settlement Road
Oakfield, Maine 04763
www.thewildolivepress.com

For bulk or special sales, please contact manager@thewildolivepress.com or write to us at the above address.

Most characters and events in this book are fictitious. Relative to those fictional characters, any similarity to real persons, living or dead, is coincidental and not intended by the author. Some characters are historical and represent real people as they existed within the time frame depicted in this work.

All Scripture quotations are taken from the New American Standard Bible, with the exception of those contained in Emma's Journal.

Cataloging-in-Publication Data is available from the Library of Congress.

Book design and type formatting by The Wild Olive Press
Manufactured in the United States of America

ISBN 978-0982474952

For the remnant …

"Listen, O my people, to my instruction; incline your ears to the words of my mouth. I will open my mouth in a parable; I will utter dark sayings of old, which we have heard and known, and our fathers have told us. We will not conceal them from their children, but tell to the generation to come the praises of the Lord, and His strength and His wondrous works that He has done. For He established a testimony in Jacob, and appointed a law in Israel, which He commanded our fathers, that they should teach them to their children, that the generation to come might know, even the children yet to be born, that they may arise and tell them to their children, that they should put their confidence in God, and not forget the works of God, but keep His commandments, and not be like their fathers, a stubborn and rebellious generation, a generation that did not prepare its heart, and whose spirit was not faithful to God."

Psalm 78:1-8

To whom shall I speak and give warning that they may hear? Behold, their ears are closed and they cannot listen. Behold, the word of the Lord has become a reproach to them; they have no delight in it.

Jeremiah 6:10

"You are the salt of the earth; but if the salt has become tasteless, how can it be made salty again? It is no longer good for anything, except to be thrown out and trampled under foot by men."

Matthew 5:13

Moral of the Work

Versus Deception: Truth

Versus Persecution: Trust

Versus Unbelief: Endurance

Versus Flesh: the Cross

From the Author

Dear Reader;

There are a number Christian fictional books that 'preach' a particular version of end-times events. They place their characters in situations that unfold according to the author's particular eschatology. However, this work has no intention of attempting any such eschatological assertions; it is purely a parable.

As you know, parables instruct, admonish, encourage, and enlighten, but while parables wondrously illuminate truth, they are not intended to be taken literally. They are carefully crafted symbols, and as such, this story should be seen as a figurative description—set in a fictional setting—of what happens to people and nations and churches when they turn away from God. I hope it gives you pause to consider where we are as a church, where your nation is before God, and, most importantly, what your responsibilities are as a Believer who must 'endure to the end' and stay true to the God of Abraham, Isaac, and Jacob.

The work has a number of complementary objectives. Of greatest importance, my desire is for readers to gain a clearer picture and a better understanding of the Cross; *the* central, essential feature to our Christian life, and yet one so grievously ignored. I hope readers better understand the need for a full and complete commitment to God; not to a particular denomination or pastor or tradition or culture or social group, but to the Living God and to His inerrant Word as explained through His Holy Spirit. Nothing else will keep us from deception in these days but a great love of the Truth. I hope readers gain a clearer picture of how our enemies in the spirit realm work to undermine and destroy mankind. I hope readers honestly investigate the many heresies that are only lightly touched on in this work, holding them up to comparison with the Word, and lastly I hope readers avoid the dangerous deceptions that suffuse the Body of Christ in the close of the age.

You'll note that there is a fictional author —a warrior poet, one Sartorius Crux Vita, a crusty, grizzled combat veteran from the Roman Legions. *Of Seeds and Salt* is one of a number of intended future works that provide a range of perspectives on the times leading up to the return of Jesus, the Messiah. The Aeon Regis series is simply a literary vehicle designed to present to the church in this day and age perspectives from fictional future observers looking back on the times in which we now live. You could consider this and the following books in the series to be works of 'future history'.

If you have any comments or questions about what is in this book, I would be delighted to talk with you. Please address them to the Managing Director at The Wild Olive Press via the email here:

manager@thewildolivepress.com

CONTENTS

Foreword to the Aeon Regis Historical Series

In the first century of the Age of the King (i.e. 'Aeon Regis' in my language), the Great King directed that a history of the days preceding the advent of His rule be recorded, days in which the usurper was thrown down and despoiled, days in which the Great King assumed His rule over the Earth. He called for this history to be developed from not one but twelve different points of view. Twelve souls, stewards now in various realms, were commanded to compile from various sources their own perspectives of that evil and tremulous time when it seemed that darkness would cover the world—but righteousness was finally, tumultuously upheld. Twelve historians were drawn from many different occupations: a pastor, a prophet, a physician, a stonemason, an artist, an engineer, an olive grower, a shepherd, a fisherman, a horse, a lion, and a warrior poet[1].

***

The King called for us all one day, and we met on top of a green hill near Jerusalem. Reposing in a glade under a warm and pleasant sun, eating oranges (or grass), we looked down upon the sparkling river of life-giving water running out from the throne. He described our task, commissioned each, and directed that we tell of the time in our own way, according to our own nature. And so it has been: two have set their stories to music, with power to stir souls. One has majestically captured the symbology of how the Great King is the Water of Life by building a great stone aqueduct that spans the globe, and ultimately serves its purpose by watering the souls of men and nations. Yet most have chosen to put their stories into words, so that men who remain upon the earth may read and understand the love of the King, so that they may understand what befell them, and too so that they may understand and be warned, for wherever there are men without the Cross, there too is man's nature.

***

The book you hold in your hand is my story. I am Sartorius Crux Vita, the warrior poet. I have chosen to relate this history—which is also a parable—by telling of a few men and women whose lives were marked in ways that, I hope, speak to every soul. I would ask readers to note carefully that the selection of the Ironbridge family was no accident.

As a warrior, I have focused on the strategy and tactics employed by the powers and principalities of the time, and the reader will find herein much of plotting, plans, wrestling, combat, and the horrors of war, both in the natural and supernatural realms. I include only a few instances of the enemy's communications, as they remain almost untranslatable.

I am as well a poet, and so I have chosen also to see this time as a romance—for what was the King's pursuit of His bride if not a romance?

1 See each Contributor's biography at the end of this Volume.

Therefore this story is told as a romance, which readers should take rightly as symbol. And as a poem is to language—words carefully chosen from all the words in a language to distill, display, or examine an experience or a feeling or a thought, each gravid with portent, while words unwritten speak and pierce softly and unendingly to the heart—so can a man's life be to the time in which he lives.

***

There are some who may question the King's inclusion of a warrior's perspective, for as is quite well known now, no one learns the arts of war any longer. He did not explain why I was selected—He did not explain any of His selections. It is His nature to wait for us to seek the wisdom hidden in His ways; our pursuit of Him pleases Him in some way, perhaps in the way a beloved is pleased by the pursuit of a lover. While I cannot say that I have discovered every reason, I can say that my experiences in war have been helpful in understanding how Believers needed to struggle in a world controlled by the enemy at the time, fighting spiritual battles daily. Experience in war gives a man insight that cannot be obtained anywhere else—the horrors of death and slaughter; the screams of pain, fear, and agony; and the indescribable sense of joyous victory when one stands, alive, surrounded by one's friends who also have survived ... all were so very similar to those times just at the closing days of the Age of Man when so many true Believers fought so many vicious battles to fulfill the missions the King had given them—or to just stand in the face of an overwhelming flood of persecution, trial, difficulty, perversion, and deception. And finally, experience in war helps to interpret the motives and actions of those who fought, struggled, died, and triumphed in a time when war was the turbulent sea of blood upon which almost every soul living then was tossed.

***

I have included writings from other Historian Stewards where their perspectives or inputs shed cleaner, brighter light on the subject, or where I thought it necessary to inject editorial comments regarding the application of their work to this particular history.

***

It is no surprise to readers in this Age, the Age of the King (Aeon Regis), that massively powerful spiritual powers and principalities were arrayed against mankind, working behind the scenes, actively obscuring mankind's abilities to perceive their existence, influencing times and events at every conceivable level of action during the Age of Man—from individual lives, to family relationships, to national cultures, to heads of state, to heads of religions. As part of this history, I have chosen to include documentary material produced by a number of those powers or principalities, captured by the King's forces. I do so to provide the reader a perspective from 'the other side of the hill', to borrow a phrase from a prescient British historian, Sir Basil

Liddell Hart, which he used once as the title of a book wherein he described German opinions and perspectives during that conflict men named World War One. Hart perceived his enemy to be other human beings—Germans, in his case. By including these captured documents—termed 'Protocols'— in my history which depict the Adversary's point of view, the view 'from the other side of the hill', I hope to show that mankind's true enemies have been hidden from view throughout much of man's history, and they were not human.

***

Before reading the protocols, it would perhaps be helpful for readers unfamiliar with the dynamics underpinning the Adversary's motions, actions, or power, to learn how the various principalities and powers obtained their strength; how they garnered or generated the ability to exert such compelling influence upon men and nations. Therefore I have included an appendix to this volume titled 'Notes on the Protocols' which describe how the enemy generated and effected so much influence in the world of men. Readers interested in the mind of the enemy would find this appendix of benefit.

Sartorius Crux Vita
Diamond Gate, Jerusalem
AR 40

Theme of the Volume

How America met its end while the church lost its savor and was trampled underfoot in a time when understanding and discernment was dependent only upon faithfulness.

Prelude

Tack & Claire

"For Christ did not send me to baptize, but to preach the gospel, not in cleverness of speech, so that the cross of Christ would not be made void. For the word of the cross is foolishness to those who are perishing, but to us who are being saved it is the power of God. For it is written, 'I will destroy the wisdom of the wise, and the cleverness of the clever I will set aside.'"

1 Corinthians 1:17-19

When Thackeray Ironbridge was twenty-eight, on his second deployment while on active duty as an infantry officer in the U.S. Marine Corps, his Marine Air-Ground Task Force took part in a joint exercise with the Israeli Defense Force while operating off the coast of Israel, near Haifa. Thackeray, or 'Tack', as he'd been known since childhood, was selected as the liaison officer to coordinate schedules, set up a specific command post exercise, and support other training missions with the Israelis.

At dinner one evening ashore celebrating the end of the exercise with a group of Israelis, he met Claire Perrin, then a twenty-seven year old professor of Comparative Religion at the Sorbonne. She was in Israel leading a seminar on the Holy Land, and one of the Israeli officers was something of a distant relative. Claire was Jewish, yet had no affinity for either ethnicity or tribe, and felt herself completely assimilated, far more French than Jewish.

Tack had just recently become a Christian, called from a life of self-centered self-righteousness, and he had the intensity and passion of a new convert. When he learned that the tall, slim, dark-haired Frenchwoman was a professor of comparative religion, he began an intensive discussion about the errors and shortcomings of Islam, Judaism, and other world religions.

Her first impression was that this young American was far too brash, and sorely needed to expand his scholarship regarding the early history of the world's monotheistic religions. But then she happened to look up from her drink and caught the blazing intensity of his gaze. It shook her. She realized this young man wasn't just chatting her up to attempt an evening's conquest. He was consumed with passion about his faith, and she'd never met anyone with such conviction. So she began to engage, seriously, with the power of her intellect fully positioned to slay his every argument. She felt she owed him that much.

And yet, she couldn't. For every rational explanation as to why Islam took a certain position, or why Judaism had every reason to doubt the carpenter who claimed to be their Messiah, he had an explanation that was, it seemed to her at the time, suffused with an irritating spirituality. He would respond to her academic justifications with quotes from his precious Bible, passages that to her just didn't make sense. Soon, though, it dawned on her. She realized that he was dancing upon a different pin—he saw the entire world from a spiritual perspective. To him, religion wasn't just another academic topic, and her recitation of events, great personages, dates, and opinions of some of the world's greatest scholars mattered not one whit. He was drawing his water from a different well. It bothered her, then irritated her, but after forty-five minutes of discussion and professionally heated iteration, the very faintest seed of interest in the American officer began to grow.

They sustained a moderate correspondence over the course of the next few months. Claire was not romantically interested in Tack, because at the time she was dispassionately but with consummate skill maneuvering M. Luc Valencour, a young but very wealthy French banker. While avoiding Luc's somewhat anemic amorous attentions, she intentionally and tantalizingly developed in him a deep attachment, with the object in view that he would eventually propose marriage, solving at a stroke all her materialistic concerns. And while all this was happening, her heart and soul (and body) were passionately enmeshed with a strikingly handsome Lebanese Muslim named Tabouk. He was only a poor starving artist with soulful eyes, but she could no more resist his dark, brooding masculinity than an addict could resist the white powder. She did not know how she could live without Tabouk if she snared Luc, but with typical Gallic aplomb, she was convinced of her own consummate ability to handle *les affaires de l'amour.*

Occasionally during this period, Tack would write and describe where he was and what he was doing. To Claire, his travelogues from different parts of the world were somewhat interesting, but she just did not see him as an object of romance, especially since he would go on at length about one spiritual topic or another in his letters. With intellectual disdain she realized that he was presuming that a professor of Comparative Religion must herself be religious. Fairly soon though, he got the hint. Her return missives were pale, barely touching upon those issues about which he wrote with passion, her prose conveying the very faintest whiff of disinterest, though in the most tactful way. His correspondence became less challenging, more innocuous, less frequent, and less personal. Tack, the prototypical alpha male, was not one to pursue a woman if she expressed no interest. Things would probably have tapered off and ended between them had it not been for two serious events, which like torpedoes blew holes in the ordered and professionally structured ship of Claire's life.

The first of these had to do with the poor, starving, soulful-eyed artist. Claire was in the throes of an ardent passion, all the more intense as she was required to keep her passionate nature subdued when she was with Luc. Claire was drunk with her passion for Tabouk. She couldn't get enough of him, and it was beginning to strain her ability to emotionlessly manipulate the wealthy young banker. And then came the day when she had to suddenly bolt from one of her morning classes to be sick in the ladies' toilette, and soon thereafter learned that she was with child by the artist. Fear struck. All her well-laid plans were threatened. She became wildly emotional, swinging from despair one moment as she considered the ruin of her professional career, to ecstatic, joyful contemplation of life as Tabouk's wife, a mother to his children.

It was in one of her more intense periods of despair and melancholy that a letter from Tack arrived. This one was different. In it, he put a very direct question to her. *"Do you have a personal, ongoing relationship with God? I'm sure you've taught on it to so many people, but I've never heard from you, exactly, about what the cross of Christ means to you."* She snorted derisively at the last question and snapped the sheets together without reading the rest of it. It was just like Americans, everywhere they go, butting into a person's private, personal affairs, proselytizing, trying to make everyone as they were, as if they had the answer to all life's questions. She stuffed the letter back into its envelope and threw it into a drawer, hurling an epithet in after it, resolving never to have anything further to do with such an unsophisticated innocent. God, he was such a prying ass.

And then events began to gather speed, outpacing Claire's ability to manage things on her own. One day at a boulangerie, in a foul mood, picking out a baguette and some pastry while starkly considering the impossibility of balancing motherhood and her teaching position, Luc, her young banker, came into the shop. He startled her; he had stopped in to pick up some bread for a colleague's wife. The colleague's wife was ill, this was where the colleague's wife always bought her bread, Luc had put the colleague, her husband, to work on a critical paper for the firm that required the husband to stay late and, so, well, there he was, trying to help.

She hadn't wanted to see him. His questions, solicitous and kind, only irritated her. He pushed; she didn't look well. Was everything okay? In anger she rounded on him outside the shop, beyond reason, well outside the bounds of her normal constancy. Distraught, unthinking, wildly hormonal, she seized on this chance meeting to vent, to clear the air, and—and yes, *why not?*—to simplify her life.

"Let me tell you something, Luc," she said in gutter French, designed intentionally to express disgust for his high-brow life. "You and I ... we are going nowhere, and I am tired of the game, so let's stop playing." She looked directly into his face as anger grew at the memory of so many emotions, so many feelings pushed down, suppressed, stifled.

He was shocked, stunned ... taken aback. She could see it in his eyes; it was the last thing he expected. Throughout their relationship Claire had taken great pains to appear always steady, unwavering, and unemotional. It was what Luc wanted. Emotion, passion, wild swings of moods—very unsuitable, he would opine, and she dutifully complied. Frustration from years spent bottling up her passionate nature suddenly erupted.

"And what is this game you are playing with the wife of a colleague?" she accused. His eyes widened, not comprehending her baseless accusation. She sliced her hand through the air. "Bah! It's nothing to me anyway, who you play with. You're a dead fish, Luc. You think I look unwell? *Merde*, you *are* an idiot. I am not unwell." She was shaking her baguette in his face now, yelling. "I'm pregnant with another man's child, a *real* man, and if that makes it easier for you to despise me and be gone, then good ... go! Go find some emotionless robot of a woman and raise a collection of cardboard children." She threw her baguette at him and stalked off, wiping tears from her eyes.

Throwing her dinner plans to the winds, she took a taxi and fled to Tabouk's flat. She had to see him. She pounded desperately on his door, scraping tears away with a sleeve, hoping he was home. He was; he opened the door and stood there, bare-chested, a cigarette in his hand, and through the rising smoke she saw another woman in his bed. She was smoking a cigarette as well, and she tossed her hair over her shoulder and shot Claire a dark, disdainful glance. Claire was stunned for a moment. She didn't understand; she couldn't make sense of what her eyes could so plainly see.

Tabouk saw her confusion, looked back at the unclad woman in his bed—the bed he'd shared with Claire so many times—turned back to her, shrugged callously and said, "*Que, chère?* Did you think you were the only one?" He slowly closed the door, snickering softly. She stood transfixed, unable to move until through the door she heard Tabouk and the woman laugh—jagged glass on her soul—and somehow she stumbled home.

The coming days were no kinder. Unhinged now, bereft, not thinking at all, over the edge emotionally, she determined upon a strategy she thought would put things right. She would do away with the *thing* growing within her. She would excise this thing of Tabouk's in her body, and with just a quick procedure her professional career would again be in hand, stretching out before her into a bright green future as it had before this aberration. And once she set things aright medically, she would go and see Luc and take him in hand again—he could be managed, she knew. Some contrite apologies, the right mingling of tears and regret, and he would be again dancing attendance.

As she planned, so she did. Abortions in France at the time were relatively easy to procure, and in the space of twenty minutes in a doctor's office as an outpatient, Claire sacrificed her very tiny unborn child on the altar of her career, on the altar of materialism, the altar of Ba'al, the 'Lord of the Flies', named so because the heathen, seeing how those creatures proliferate, wished their own wealth and material possessions to do likewise. She grieved just one day for her unknown child, but her heart hardened, her eyes steeled, and she picked herself up and set herself to get on with her life's plan, to go again and recapture the guarantor of her future wealthy lifestyle.

But she could not reach Luc. She called his flat dozens of times, left many messages. She was beginning to think that perhaps she had gone too far, that he was not taking her calls, when she hit upon the idea of meeting him at the bank where he worked. She thought this the *bon mot*—there on his own turf, she would confess and beg his forgiveness. So off she went.

She arrived at the bank exactly ten days after she had last seen Luc, late in a rainy fall afternoon. She stepped into the bank, shook the rain from her anorak, and asked the woman behind the counter if she could speak with M. Valencour.

The clerk looked up in some alarm. "I am sorry, madam, but M. Valencour does not work here any longer."

Claire was confused. "But ... but has he taken another position? Could you tell me where he works now?"

The woman looked from left to right, as though worried someone might overhear, and then leaned forward and said a hushed voice, "Madam, I am sorry if you did not know, but M. Valencour committed suicide, oh, let me see, it must have been, I think, eight days ago."

***

For three days Claire lay in her small rented home in a Paris suburb, curled up in a ball on her bed, dead to the world, grieving. She would moan or cry until her eyes ached, and sometimes yell at the world, or scream, or punch the wall. Tabouk's betrayal was painful, yes. That she was the cause of Luc taking his life was clear as well, and that pressed in upon her dreadfully. Yet the most horrible thing, the act which beyond the others crushed her into the dust, was the realization that she herself had taken the life of a little innocent human being simply for her own convenience. Why this grief was assailing her now, she had no idea. The pain was unbearable, and just as she thought that she could take it no longer, when thoughts of ending things as Luc had done began to assault her senses, there came flashing into her mind, like a swallow darting in through a window about to be closed, the remembrance of Tack's letter. She sat bolt upright in bed, gasping, almost blinded by tears, and flew to her dresser. She rummaged through clothes, scattered notes, riffed the pages of an old book, cursing bitterly, and tossed it to the floor, desperately trying to remember where she had put his letter. She found it stuffed in the back of the last drawer she opened. She went back to the bed, tucked her legs under her, wiped her eyes, blew her nose, and began to read.

Claire;

Very nice to get your last letter, although I look forward to hearing more about your thoughts regarding how Mohammed would not be considered a pedophile. Most of what I read tells me that he married at least one of his wives when she was six, and consummated the marriage when the child was nine; and there were others. But hey, you are the Comparative Religion professor, not me.

We are working off the coast of Spain this week with Spanish ground troops. We've been tasked to find some of their military equipment as an exercise; they secreted tanks and artillery pieces and such in the countryside, so it was a great excuse to go running around the Spanish landscape, chasing herds of sheep and flocks of goats. I've eaten some of the best food of my life out here, waiting for some shepherd to clear away his goats from the road before our vehicles can move on.

Claire, something has been nagging at me now for some time and I know in recent months I have not delved too much into anything personal between us, but I am compelled now for some reason to ask you a direct question. I don't know why I feel I need to ask you this; sometimes God moves us in ways we can't understand. So here goes.

Do you have a personal, ongoing relationship with God? I'm sure you've taught on it to so many people, but I've never heard from you, exactly, about what the cross of Christ means to you. For some reason, again, not being clear why, I want to share with you what it has come to mean to me, and why I think that without applying the cross of Christ to our own lives, we cannot consider ourselves Christians, nor is there any hope of true spiritual or eternal life.

The cross of Christ is first and foremost an instrument designed to kill ... to kill our flesh, our human nature. I know you and I have had some disagreements on this, but I am convinced by what I read in God's Word and what I see in the world that human nature is inherently and completely evil. Only by allowing God to put our human nature to death by His cross will we ever really get to the point where we can begin to truly grow spiritually. But ... this death of our own nature is painful. None of us goes to it willingly, and, like crucifixion, it is not a quick or painless death. It is a long, slow, constant, agonizing choking, a suffocation of that dark nature we all possess. We must either undertake this crucifixion—each one of us, on a daily basis—or live a life devoid of any relationship with God and then die unknown by Him, consigned to eternal fire.

The cross applied in a person's life is not an event in which something bad happens to us, like, say, a car accident or the death of a loved one or someone doing something horrible to us. No ... for the cross to be truly applied in our lives requires that we first face and admit the truth that we ourselves are to blame for our failure to live good, holy lives—good lives, I mean, by God's standard. It is voluntarily choosing to put to death one's flawed, sinful nature. Admitting this truth about ourselves and agreeing with God that our natures are sinful is the first step to eternal life. We are sinful creatures, Claire. The cross in our lives is not comprised of bad things happening to us; it is instead we ourselves agreeing with God that we are inherently evil, corrupt, sinful, and that on our own we can do nothing God would consider good, realizing, when you get to the bottom of it, that the choices we make are all based in self-interest, and then asking God for help in voluntarily choking our own human nature to death.

Reading thus far, the thought struck her forcibly: no one had forced her to lay bare her heart to Tabouk, to so totally invest herself emotionally in him and so thereupon to offer him her last favors—it was her choice. And no one had pressured or tricked or coerced her or even suggested to her that she should end her child's life. It was her own choice, springing from her own mind, her own heart ... her own nature. No one had forced her to be cruel and manipulative with Luc. She had treated him that way for her own selfish reasons, and she'd been utterly and completely unaware and heartlessly ignorant about the degree to which Luc had been invested in her. She had betrayed and hurt him so badly that he felt life was no longer worth living, and so dispatched himself, in such grief that he would disdain the most precious gift any person has—life itself. She could do nothing but agree with Tack's depiction of human nature. With clarity and a pain more intense than anything she'd yet encountered, she saw clearly her own vileness. The blood of her murdered child was mute testimonty to the truth. Trembling, she read on.

The 'Good News' is called Good News for a reason. When we truly face the fact that we are wicked and sinful and spiteful, that we think of ourselves naturally before thinking of others, we are faced with an intractable moral dilemma. Knowing God to be completely perfect, and knowing that we are not, it is blindingly obvious therefore that there is absolutely no hope that we could ever be acceptable in His sight; no way we could have any kind of fellowship with Him. When we grasp this truth, it should occassion despair, fear, and even more brokenness. There is blood on our hands; blood that we cannot wash away, and we are doomed to walk through life with that stain ever on us and whatever we touch.

Reading words that called forth her deepest fears by naming that about her which was most true and therefore most powerfully convicting, Claire burst into uncontrollable tears, finally coming to the bottom of her soul and admitting to herself and to God that she, Claire Perrin, had caused the death of two human beings—she was a murderess. After three days of grieving, of wrestling, of looking for and failing to find any excuses for her behavior and living with the tragic, irreversible results in other peoples' lives that she herself had caused, the answer was before her in the words in Tack's letter. She cried out to God in anguish, gasping, admitting first to herself and then to God that it was she who was to blame. She begged forgiveness from a God in whom she had never believed, for alas, there was nothing else she could do. There was no other hope. She could not wake up from this nightmare. The rest of her life stretched out before her like a dark, stench-filled tunnel, and she could not bear it to be so.

But suddenly, there on her bed, wracked with grief, she was granted a precious gift, a flashing celestial epiphany—she saw herself as God saw her: wretched, culpable, full of sin, unworthy, and guilty ... above all, *guilty*. The weight of her guilt bore her down into the folds of the duvet like an unbearable burden, and she could not read for several minutes, fists gripping the coverlet, shaking, nauseous, groaning in agony, at the very end of herself, at the place of no hope, realizing that it was impossible for her to live a life that was in any way good or acceptable to the only real Good in the world. Even more painful was the realization that uncorrected, she would do worse to others. In admitting to herself what she was, she realized what she could not help but become. She shrank in horror from the impact of the monstrosity of her conduct, and the fear of what she might do in the future, which she perceived to be nothing but a horrid blackness. Yet something, some hope when she was beyond hope, some great desperate thought that maybe there was something in the letter that might help made her swipe a sleeve across her eyes and read more ... for there was more.

> *But the 'Good News', Claire, is that if we choose to accept the sacrifice made by God on our behalf—the sacrifice of His Son, put to death on our behalf—and obey Him, to obey what Jesus tells us to do each day, then we have the assurance that God will open eternity to us, because we will in effect be 'covered' by the blood of His sacrifice. We who are guilty of shedding blood (because all sin always, eventually, results in death) are ourselves cleansed by blood shed as a sacrifice for that sin. I am in awe at both the complexity and simplicity of God's most perfect arrangement. Even though we ourselves are wretched, in no way deserving of mercy, He will nonetheless cover us with the blood of His perfectly innocent, blameless, sinless Son and extend to us incredible mercy. We* can *live good, righteous lives. We* can *go to heaven. We can come into God's presence and we can be used by Him to do His work in the world—but only through obeying His Son in everything we do. This, Claire, is why the 'Good News' is good news.*

Here at last a bit of hope, a ray of light, dawned in Claire's heart, and gasping, she read on with a slight awakening. The phrase 'Good News' resonated in her soul like a cathedral bell ringing in a dungeon.

> *Now, when I say 'accept the sacrifice of His Son' I do not mean that one need simply 'accept Jesus in your heart' via some easily mouthed words. No, to 'accept' His sacrifice means that we 'accept and comply with' the terms of the offer—and the terms are that we obey His commandments. And one of His commandments to us is that we 'pick up our cross daily'. Wiser men than me have since ages past understood such to mean that every day we must squarely face the fact that there is nothing good in our flesh and that His nature must have preeminence in what we do, say, think, and feel—that He must rule our hearts, mind, strength, and soul. And this is a constant fight. Our human natures will never completely die until we actually die physically and God gives us new bodies. While we are living in these fleshly bodies, our human natures will still be with us, and the Christian life is among many things a process of learning how every day to ruthlessly choke out our own natures and let the nature of Jesus grow in us instead. I am not talking about suppressing our human nature. No, for that would be our own selves simply putting a mask on our lives, trying (as we Christians say) 'in the flesh'—that is, with our own strength of will and character—to try and appear acceptable. No, that won't work ... and this is why Jesus directs us to the cross. The cross does not*

hide or suppress our human nature. No, it brings it out, puts our nature on public display, and while hanging there for all the world to see, naked and shameful, the cross slowly chokes the life out of it.

You see, Claire, when our natures die ... when we truly put our natures to death on His cross, when we come to the end of ourselves by fully agreeing with God that there is no good in us, and seeing ourselves as He sees us—wretched and sinful and poor and blind and naked—only then can we be raised up in new life. This is what it means to have new life; to be 'born again', or what sometimes people term 'resurrected'. But without a death, Claire, there can be no resurrection. This is what the cross of Christ means—a first death leading to the new birth, and then subsequently, daily deaths leading to spiritual growth, the death of our human natures, and the emergence within us of a character and personality and life habits that pattern the nature and character of Jesus.

Perhaps this is all familiar to you, Claire—you do, after all, teach religion at one of the world's leading universities. Yet for some reason God has had me share with you my thoughts about this most crucial element of the Christian faith. I can get up on my soapbox at times, I admit. But this last week or so I've felt a strange desire to pray that God would bring you to this point of seeing the truth about His cross and about what He wants of you. I know this is sometimes a dangerous prayer, but it is the only hope any of us have of actually dying and being resurrected into new life.

I hope this letter has not offended you, and I hope it explains a little more clearly why I have perhaps labored in our previous correspondence to speak of such things. I place the greatest deal of importance in my relationship with God, and feel that is the only real basis for any future friendship between us.

Best regards;
Tack Ironbridge

Finishing the letter, a great heartrending sob of anguish and hope burst forth from her flayed soul, and she crushed the pages to her bosom and bent over in raw, anguished prayer, the words spilling out in choked sobs.

"O God, I do not know who you are, but please, please, help me. I do not know how you can forgive me, but please, I beg you, I just want to tell you how sorry I am. I have killed two people. It was my fault; they're dead, and I can't bring them back and there is so much blood on my hands and I don't know what to do. Please, God ... help me."

***

A day after Claire's death and resurrection in a rented flat outside of Paris, Tack's ship was unexpectedly diverted into the port of Cannes, in southern France, for emergency repairs. Taking advantage of the situation, the senior Marine officer in the Task Force sent a deputation from one of the infantry battalions to liaison with members of the French Air Force at Base aérienne 217 Brétigny-Sur-Orge, a little over three kilometers southeast of Brétigny-sur-Orge, and about 30 kilometers or so south of Paris, to prepare for a conference on NATO air-ground operational doctrine. Tack was part of this delegation. It was from the officer's club at the base that he placed a call to Claire's flat, just as a courtesy since he was in the area and knew she lived in Paris.

Upon hearing his voice and learning where he was, Claire burst into tears. Things progressed from there.

***

Fourteen years later, Tack and his wife, Claire, retired from the U.S. Marine Corps when Tack was forty-two years of age. Tack realized with some surprise that he didn't know what he wanted to do with his life. Since he'd been three years old, he'd wanted to be a warrior. He'd gone to the Naval Academy, graduated first in his class from the Marine Corps' Basic School, then spent an adventurous career as a Marine infantry officer until, in his late thirties and early forties, the politicized mediocrity, institutionalized immorality, and stultifying military bureaucracy drove him from his beloved service.

So he turned to wondering what God had for him, and he and Claire spent many days and hours praying for God's direction. Miraculously, Claire had given birth to two boys—Marcus, the oldest, and Mace. Claire's abortion had been a rushed, botched affair and the Navy obstetricians were of the opinion that she would never again get pregnant. But God in His mercy prevailed and Claire first brought forth Marcus a little more than two years after they'd been married, and Mace three years later. After that, however, the old sin took its toll, and there could be no more children.

When Tack retired, Marcus was eleven and Mace eight. Tack and Claire both wanted a clean, wholesome environment for their boys, and they both feared and loathed what man had made of the world. The last thing either of them wanted was for Tack to jump on the defense contractor bandwagon and sacrifice time with his family in exchange for a large paycheck.

One of the things Tack and Claire had in common was a love of good food. Being French, it was in Claire's genes, and Tack, after spending time in that country, came to appreciate the good food and wine that came from a man putting his sweat and energy into caring for the land with his own hands. So, with a peace from God about the plan, they decided to buy a farm in a remote area—being remote, the price of land would be within a range they could afford—start a dairy, and make cheese.

Tack and Claire began Eagle's Wings Creamery six months after he retired. Tack had saved up quite a bit of his pay while serving as a Marine officer, and adding a small inheritance Claire received from an uncle, they purchased a unique property literally on the northern border between the U.S. and Canada, in Minnesota—more than a 1000 acres on the Red Rock peninsula, bordering Saganaga Lake. Tack was only able to purchase it because it belonged originally to a timber company that happened to be owned by a man whose son had served with Tack during his Marine Corps career, and in a strange incident, Tack had saved the son's life. Even after so many years, the man's father remembered Tack and carved out almost 1000 acres on the peninsula from this company. The nearest town was over 40 miles away—Granite Sky, Minnesota. Tack and Claire determined that they would do everything together as a family: master the art of making cheese, take care of the livestock, keep up the farm, and Claire would market the product. In the meantime she and Tack would both homeschool the boys.

They designed and built their own barn and creamery from plans they purchased from a Marine Corps Warrant Officer who'd retired in Oregon to start a cheese business. They purchased five Brown Swiss cows and the basic equipment needed to begin making cheese. Tack and Claire learned basic animal husbandry, simple veterinary skills, and the essentials about raising and storing the feed necessary to keep their dairy herd through the harsh Minnesota winters.

The boys responded with eagerness to their parents as they grew. At Tack's insistence Claire spoke French in the home, and Tack spoke English; the boys both grew up bilingual. In some families, there was a division in which one child took after one parent and another child modeled more closely the other, but it was not the case in the Ironbridge home. Both of the boys went out with their father when it came time for the hard physical labor of putting in fences, mucking the stalls, and putting in wood and hay for the winter. The boys would both pitch in to help Claire in the house, cleaning, cooking, and washing. Claire worked alongside the men as well, and at the end of the day, four pairs of muck boots were nestled snugly in the mudroom—tired, well-worn, satisfied, and together.

The entire family together tackled the challenge of crafting artisan cheese. They started with the basics—quick mozzarella, fromage Blanc, cream cheese, and the soft cheeses. But Tack had a particular love for the hard French and Italian cheeses—the Swiss, the Emmental, the Gruyère, the Parmesan. Taking at the very least ten or more months to age before becoming testimonies to the artful skill of a good affineur, he knew they would need to be patient and exact. They built a concrete aging cave with an artistically-curved ceiling and Claire, upon seeing it completed, newly painted, the arching ceiling gracefully curved over the strong wooden shelves, poured forth a stream of rapid French in rapturous delight. She said she felt like some great lady of Normandy in her own castle in a fairytale, and she grasped Marcus and twirled him around, laughing gaily, wonderfully content. Tack enjoyed the spectacle, knowing his wife had not lost her passion for life. Soon, upon maple hardwood shelves in the aging cave there were at first small rounds and then larger wheels of aromatic cheese growing to maturity.

Along with the cheeses, the boys matured, learning discipline, a furiously intense work ethic, and becoming strong in mind, body, and spirit. Marcus, larger in frame than Mace, combined the best of his father's athletic grace and strength with his mother's Gallic passion, a powerful presence, and a fiery temper toward injustice. Mace—Mace was different. He was born with an odd speech defect. Mace did not speak until he was four years old. Tack and Claire would wonder about it, during those times alone when, like all parents, they talked and worried about their children. Claire worried privately that perhaps her old sins had come to account. Mace had been very, very slow to speak, but when he did finally began to utter sounds, his words were always paced much further apart than normal, either in French or English. Claire thought that she had arrested his speech development by forcing another language on him while he was so young, but Tack was reassuring, helping her to realize that Mace was in God's hands and trusting that God would look after the boy. And they soon had proof. Mace saw things at a deeper level than Marcus. One day during a family devotion, when Marcus was nine and Mace six, Tack read to them about Jesus praying in the garden before being crucified. He stopped and asked the boys why they thought Jesus was upset enough so that his sweat became like drops of blood. Marcus spoke up first. "He knew what kind of pain He would be facing," he said.

"I ... think ... " Mace began slowly, but then, to the surprise of his family, his words flowed normally. "I think that He knew He would be taking on the sins of the world, and that would make His Daddy turn His face away, and Jesus had been with His

Daddy for all of time and I think Jesus was sad because His Daddy would turn His face away from Him." Tack and Claire were taken aback at this insight from a six-year old. Mace seemed to know things about the nature of God that many pastors of Tack's age and acquaintance had not yet learned. Neither Tack nor Claire knew where this spiritual sensitivity came from, but they regarded their youngest son with not a little wonder at times.

Their business grew slowly, but within a few years, Eagles' Wings Creamery was renowned for producing some of the finest artisan hard cheeses in America. They built an addition to their barn, expanded their herd of Brown Swiss cows, and with Tack's perfectionist attention to detail and Claire's flare for marketing, helped quite a bit in northern Minnesota by her French accent, they did well.

When they'd first moved to the area, Granite Sky was the closest large town, and there was an extensive school system and even a university. The town was growing exponentially since oil had been discovered under the northern Minnesota lakes. The Governor orchestrated a law through the legislature to legalize its extraction, and many of the world's largest international oil companies moved in and made Granite Sky their headquarters, as it was centrally located.

Granite Sky had numerous churches, and Tack and Claire tried them all. Sadly, not one had any spark of real spiritual life. Some were social clubs, catering to the needs of their flocks with activities and events and coffee bars in the sanctuaries and meetings and conferences and seminars, ignoring each sheep's main need—a direct relationship with the living God preceded by repentance, dying to self, and obedience to God through a strong knowledge of His Word. Others were far along down the road of deception, embracing one new fad or another, some new doctrine, some new 'revelation', or some new 'truth', all of which ran counter to the Word of God.

So Tack and Claire began a small home fellowship. Soon there began a steady stream of families, never a multitude, who met at each other's homes, who wanted to better understand God's Word without the encumbrance of commentaries or 'study guides' marketed by the latest Christian celebrity, without being required to do 'formal church' things. As it was in the parable, there were those who dismissed the Word because they just didn't understand it; they didn't come back. There were others, at first expressing a high level of interest in life in the Spirit, who then encountered the cares of their world, which choked out their enthusiasm; they too stopped coming. And there were others who would bear fruit to one degree or another, usually based on how much they wanted God.

There is a spiritual principle that says each of us will have as much of God as we want, and so it was. As they lived life corporately, as they learned each other's faults and foibles and bore with each other and loved each other, they grew in the Spirit in ways they could not when exercising their faith independently. They would sing and worship and the men would alternate as teachers. They had no need to go into the community and bang on doors out of some sense of tradition-sourced obligation. In the normal stream of their everyday lives, the Lord brought them lost sheep—people who were hurting, anxious, sorrowful, bereft of hope, angry, in pain. They met them in stores, in schools, at work, on the job, wherever they lived their normal lives. And the little fellowship would bring them in, sometimes into one family, sometimes into another, and pour out the love of God in a hundred different practical ways, nourishing and healing and restoring the battered sheep and doing it all because they believed it was what Jesus would have them do—for the love of Him.

This steady and reliable stream of needy people being brought into the fellowship through both mundane and miraculous circumstances and the attendant outpouring of charity made a strong impression on the two Ironbridge boys. They came to believe that the substance of Christian life consisted of showing love, tangibly, for others.

Marcus and Mace made close friends in those early fellowship families. Marcus developed a reputation for defending victims of injustice, bullying, and unrighteousness. During his home schooling sessions, he would argue endlessly with Tack or Claire about various historical events, wondering why ruling governments or kings endured unfairness, or worse, fostered it in their kingdoms. When his parents would try to explain the grievous outworking of man's fallen nature, Marcus would struggle to comprehend. 'But these things are just not right! They shouldn't *be*!' he would exclaim, and they recognized the signs of a budding idealist.

Mace was different. He appeared to be more accepting of the true character of man's fallen human nature, even at his younger age, or perhaps it was that he felt he couldn't do anything about righting injustices or deposing tyrants. Instead, he focused on the individuals themselves, and his parents would find him often sitting tucked away with some poor soul, listening to their sorrows or holding their hand while they poured out endless stories of their miseries. Not able to speak easily, he did not speak often, and so became a good listener. Like flies to honey, those with desperate, hurting hearts naturally gravitated to him. Mace listened and cared, seldom offered criticisms, and never any condemnations. Thus did a prodigious compassion begin to grow from an early age. Where Marcus's eye was hard and bright and fiery and roamed his world to see where he might crush tyranny or injustice or the neighborhood bully, Marcus' nature seemed to reflect more of an awareness of the world's pain, and wherever he went his eyes cast about looking for ways to alleviate sorrow and tears.

When each boy moved out of elementary school subjects, their parents, feeling they had provided them with a solid foundation academically and spiritually, launched them off into the world, giving them the freedom to either continue on with homeschooling through high school or enroll in the public school system. Both boys had their father's innate confidence as well as his aggressiveness, along with their mother's passionate nature, and they both wanted very much to play football. So, one at a time, off they went, bathed in prayer by their parents and those in their fellowship.

The boys did well, for they had been started well. They had both been taught to think for themselves, to depend wholly and utterly on God, looking to Him and His Word as a guide to their conduct. They were less concerned about pleasing other men than taking care to assure their conduct pleased God. They were not 'man-pleasers'; truly a unique, almost unheard-of quality of character in young American teens. Marcus and Mace were two young men with independent minds, respectful yet not easily swayed by worldly opinions uttered by public school authority figures in what was rapidly becoming a cesspool. The brothers would stand up for the downtrodden, the lowly, and the bullied.

Marcus, moving through high school first, made a reputation as one who would brook no bullying in his presence, and the misfits and outcasts in all the grades flocked to him, enjoying an aura of protection they'd never known. Teachers and school administrators watched as Marcus established an environment of safety, kindness, and gentleness first around where he was, but then throughout the school in general. If someone, perhaps new to the school, decided to take up what was elsewhere the common habit of bullying or try to establish some sort of caste system in which some were degraded for the benefit of others, that person was soon visited by Marcus, who would at first conduct an extensive discussion in which he would describe how things ran at 'his' school. If the person was wise, they changed their behavior. Others, not so wise, would forge ahead and apply their old behavior patterns on the weaker or unpopular kids. If Marcus heard about the event (and he always did), the individual had another visit from Marcus, in which Marcus would help the transgressor understand in a visceral way how it felt to be on the other end of being physically bullied.

When Mace appeared as a freshman, he walked into a student body that held the Ironbridge name in great regard, and he only added to its esteem. Where Marcus was a physical enforcer, making sure that no cliques or gangs or groups mistreated others, Mace addressed their souls. He very quickly became the student others sought out to talk about their problems—at home, at school, problems with other kids—and one who would dispense some measure of comfort or wisdom in each session. He would talk with and listen to anyone—honor student or druggie or jock or gear head or geek.

Where Marcus was feared by the unrighteous and appreciated by those he protected, Mace was hated by the wicked and loved by those he helped.

PART 1
Sowers

By smooth words he will turn to godlessness those who act wickedly toward the covenant, but the people who know their God will display strength and take action.

Daniel 11:32

Chapter 1
Zoe

"But He was pierced through for our transgressions, He was crushed for our iniquities; the chastening for our well-being fell upon Him, and by His scourging we are healed."

Isaiah 53:5

"You dirty Jew *whore*!"

She whipped her head around at the ageless verbal slash and froze. They had surprised her, coming around from the other side of the bleachers while she was looking out at the football players. She was between the bleachers and the scraggly remains of a whitish-gray line in the dirt that marked the sideline, holding her books close to her chest. It was a cold afternoon in late fall, with a misting drizzle that threatened to become a full-fledged rainstorm later in the day. Her fingers were beginning to get numb; she had no gloves, and nothing but a thin high-necked pullover. Leaves still clinging to trees lining the horizon beyond the football field were dull and dingy, drained of life and their blaze of color. Practice had just finished, and most of the high school gridiron stalwarts had headed for the locker room twenty minutes ago. She had been looking out at the field, watching the last few players in their raggedy orange practice jerseys running at a full sprint, a coach harassing them down the field with a whistle, or playing catch with each other, or running full speed into blue nylon cylinders that were stuffed and cushioned, yelling all the way until with grunts or growls or roars they collided with the tackling dummy and knocked it to the ground.

Six boys sauntered around the far edge of the faded green bleacher seats, their feet squelching in the mud. Two of them had those oversized jeans that looked they were already halfway off. She noticed one of the boys with the jeans had a chain going from the front of his jeans to his back pocket.

"We don't think that you should be here, Jew *whore*," their leader said coldly, the Middle Eastern accent plain and too familiar, but it was discordant, hearing it now in northern Minnesota. She knew who he was; Fahd al-Hussein. She was as tall as he, which probably made him even angrier. His dull black eyes bored straight at her like a shark, and he was wearing a black, red, and green striped fleece with a crescent moon symbol stitched over the left chest pocket. He sported a few scraggly black hairs that tried to assemble themselves in the form of a goatee around his full mouth. He was rail thin but lethal, and moved like a leopard, full of menace, power, and quickness. His followers—punks, low-life thugs, and hangers-on—were either obese or had the drug-addicts' lean, ropy, starved-looking physique. They followed just behind him, and as he moved toward her, they ranged themselves, one behind each of his shoulders, two swaggering on either side of her, and the last, she sensed, taking up a spot behind her as she edged away from the bleachers onto the field. She was trapped down around the 30-yard line.

After the initial shock, anger flared. Her parents had moved from Russia to get away from this kind of treatment. They'd encountered it in the barren British Columbia wilderness, in Prague, in Mexico, and now here it was again. It made her furious.

"You don't get to say who can be here, Fahd," she answered, using just the right inflection in pronouncing his name so that he would know she could get around in Arabic. The boys surrounding her laughed. Her voice sounded hollow and tremulous.

Fahd moved into her space and poked his finger into her books, hard, pushing her backward. "I get to tell *you* where to go, little Jew bitch," he hissed. "And you don't *ever* speak to me that way."

"You're the big man, gonna tell me what to do?" she replied, leaning back at him, angry, dropping her books, her hands curling into fists, shoulders way back, pushing her face at him, trying to keep her voice from trembling. He leaned back away from her instinctively. She felt the two on either side of her grab her arms like steel bands. It only made her angrier. She looked down at her arms, pinned, and then back up at Fahd. "You need five other goons to make sure you don't get hurt? That's typical. It takes at least six of you to try anything against one Jew, a Jewish *girl* even, just so you don't wet your pants." She threw the words at him with disdain.

He cursed then, in Arabic, and before she could see it coming, the side of her head exploded in stars and pain, and she was in the mud on her face. He had slapped her, hard, with his open hand. His ring opened a deep cut in the skin above her cheekbone, and she felt the sting and then the bite of cold wind on the open wound. She put her hand to her face and it came away smeared in red, silken strands.

It was starting to rain, drizzling steadily, the drops splattering, diluting the pooled blood in her hand. She blinked her eyes and shook her head, trying to clear her vision. She tried to push herself up, but one of the young toughs put a foot in her ribcage and shoved her back down into the mud. She could hear them laughing at her as though from a distance.

"Get her up," Fahd hissed, and then she felt a hand on her head, grasping, clutching, and more pain. She was lifted almost bodily by her long red hair, and against her will she let out a yelp.

"Now let me tell you, Jew—."

"*Hey! What are you people doing?*" There was another voice, strong and confident and strident, indignant, but far off in the distance. Fahd turned to look toward the sound. Her vision was coming back slowly. When she could focus on Fahd's face, she narrowed her eyes, compressed her lips, cleared her throat ... and when he turned back to face her, splattered what spit she could muster into his face. His eyes grew wide in shock, and then with furious anger and fearsome quickness, twisted like a snake and punched her in the solar plexus, hard. She felt his knuckle bones against her cartilage and then the breath left her body and she was on all fours again, hands splayed in the mud, gasping, trying to get air, willing her lungs to work. Black and yellow spots swirled in her eyes, but all she could think of was getting a breath. Finally, with a great heave, she sucked in a lungful of air. More laughter. She felt a kick, the shock of a shoe traveling up through the top of her leg and hip, and she fell flat into the wet mud again.

When she looked up, her face covered in grass clippings and mud, Fahd was squatting in front of her face. "You Jews never know when to quit, do you?" he sneered.

"*Get away from her!*" she heard, and by then her vision had cleared enough to see. Behind Fahd, a few yards from his two bodyguards, someone was moving quickly, and as she watched he broke into a run. Two of the bodyguards, the fat one with a thick neck, the other rail-thin with dreadlocks, turned to face this intruder, posturing with their shoulders. "Hey, punk!" one of them said, "You doan' want none o' this—"

But the intruder suddenly fell to the ground on the run and rolled into their legs and they both fell like bowling pins. The intruder was a young boy, somewhat thin, wearing an oversized gold-colored firehose canvas farm coat. She saw that it was covered in mud now as he leapt up and tackled Fahd like she'd seen the football players hit the blue practice dummies. Fahd and Gold Coat crunched down into the mud just a yard before her eyes, the younger boy driving his shoulder into Fahd's face. And then there was nothing but arms and legs and cursing and blows and the five young punks had Gold Coat down under their combined weight, crushing him, throwing punches furiously.

Fahd stood up, visibly angry that he'd gotten his fancy pullover covered in mud. She could see that before Gold Coat had been taken down, he'd connected. Fahd's cheek was scraped and bleeding.

"Stand him up!" Fahd hissed. His black eyes were flashing in fury. The crowd of arms and legs parted, and she looked up to see a thin, well-formed young boy, one eye swollen shut already, with cuts on his face, being frog-marched up to where Fahd stood.

"Stupid sunnovabitch," Fahd hissed, shaking his head derisively. "You and what army gonna mess with me?" Fahd, chest puffed out, spun around and stuck out a long, thin arm. "What's this Jew bitch to you anyway?" Fahd put his hand to his face, flinched away, saw the blood, and in a split second, whirled and threw a roundhouse swing at the young boy and hit him square in the jaw. She heard the impact of flesh on flesh. The young boy's head snapped around.

"*Leave him alone!*" she screamed, and she vaulted off the ground and went for Fahd's face, arms whirling, fingers curled, flaying wildly in rage. Two of Fahd's toadies easily stepped in front of her and pinned her arms. She kicked out, trying to hurt them any way she could. They laughed at her.

"Jew bitch wants to play, does she?" Fahd sneered, eyebrows raised. "And this is your Mister White Knight?" Fahd looked back at Gold Coat, who was staring at him with cold anger, eyes tearing in the cold wind. "What's up, Mister White Knight? You and she got a little thing goin'? Do you not know, you stupid white boy, you do not want to mess with Jewish women—they're *poison*. Now, here's what I am going to do for you, little boy. I am going to carve up her face a bit and then no person will be wanting to kiss with her, and this will be a good thing for the world and for Allah, hey?" And with that she heard the snick of a knife opening, and Fahd saying, "Stand the bitch up."

It took three boys to hold Gold Coat, struggling fiercely now and apparently much stronger than he looked. The other two lifted her off the ground. They were all looking at Fahd as he came up to her, about a yard away with the knife held in front of him, swaying like a snake, the top of his hand upward, waving the tip of his switchblade at her as he approached. She felt the numbing sensation of fear gripping her stomach.

And then the knife and his hand weren't there anymore. Something had knocked his hand away, the knife splashed into the mud, and she saw a football helmet in a flashing white blur, curving in an upward arc. It struck Fahd on the side of the head and Fahd went down like a poleaxed steer. The two thugs holding her let go in surprise at the sudden attack, and she collapsed in a heap near Fahd. She could see his eyes, open and glazed. Gold Coat suddenly grabbed the arms of the punks holding him and dropped with all his weight to the ground, dragging them down.

Another intruder, bigger, much bigger, and faster still, was swinging a white football helmet like a war club. One of the other punks pulled a knife and went for him. White Helmet caught the blade with some kind of thick padded thing, using it like a shield, and with the other hand swung his helmet down against the punk's arm, now stuck in the padding. The elbow snapped and bent backward at an odd angle, and the punk started screaming. Gold Coat was up now, and while one of the punks let go of him and went for White Helmet, Gold Coat took the other punk down into the mud, rolled around until he was on top of him, and started punching, fierce and hard.

She watched the fight, mouth open, unaware that she was still gasping for breath. White Helmet was faced off against three of the punks. Fahd was down and out. Another was rolling around on the ground, holding his arm, screaming, and Gold Coat was thrashing the other. One punk ran off, frightened, leaving the big intruder to face two—one with the dreadlocks, and the other, the one with those stupid-looking jeans and the chain. White Helmet was wearing nothing but the cut-off t-shirt the football players wore under their pads, and his football pants, and he was holding his helmet like a favored sword. He looked like some fierce medieval warrior, and she could see his stomach muscles; they were heaving, the big kid was breathing hard, but when she looked at his face, she was shocked to see he was smiling.

"What are you sleaze bags waiting for?" he asked derisively. "You need a few more of your buddies to come and even up the odds for you?" Fahd's eyes were now blinking and he was starting to moan. The kid with the broken elbow had stopped screaming and was lying a few yards away, crying in pain, holding his arm to his side.

"You boys want some of that?" White Helmet asked, chiding them.

One of the punks let fly with the ubiquitous f-bomb—the most-used word in their entire eighteen-word vocabulary—and they both rushed White Helmet. Dreadlocks got there first, and with a move quicker than her eye could follow, White Helmet shoved his forearm straight up under the punk's chin. Dreadlocks' feet went out from under him and he went down into the mud. The other kid, the one in the jeans, took a swinging helmet to the side of the head. White Helmet grabbed the kid by the shirt, held him up, and hit him again, this time on the forehead with a backhand stroke. Jean boy went down, his pants down around his knees.

While she was watching this she felt a hand on her hair, her head was yanked back, a crushing weight pressed her down further into the mud, and Fahd's face appeared close to hers. She felt his knife—wherever had that come from?—cold against her skin. It stung, as Fahd wasn't too careful and his knife opened a long cut around her collarbone. "Hey, Jew-lover!" he shouted at White Helmet, standing there bleeding from a small cut on his face. His words were loud in her ear. "Do you want to have some fun? Do you want to have some *real* fun? Why not just you watch while I cut this bitch's throat? Hey? What are you thinking about that?" She could hear Fahd's Arabic accent coming through thickly in his fear as he spoke English, his second language, in a broken cadence.

She felt Fahd's arm tense and her mind froze in fear and terror, thinking that this was impossible, this couldn't be happening, she wasn't meant to die in a muddy football field in Minnesota at the hand of some adolescent Arab. And then another arm slapped around and on top of Fahd's, an arm covered in mud-stained gold firehose canvas. The hand coming out of the coat grabbed Fahd's knife and with amazing power and strength, pulled it away from her neck. Her eyes widened and she would never forget the site of the knife piercing the boy's palm as he struggled to keep Fahd from slicing her throat by putting his hand over the pointed edge of the blade and jamming his hand down onto the steel. The bleeding flesh of his hand now between the knife and her throat, he slowly leveraged Fahd's right arm away from her.

Released, she rolled away, hands clutching at the cut on the side of her throat, gagging. She looked up to see Gold Coat standing behind Fahd, his left hand around Fahd's waist, holding him tightly, the other hand pinioned by Fahd's knife. Gold Coat lifted his right arm away from Fahd's body and in so doing, lifted Fahd's right hand holding the knife—both their arms went up together like a pair of dancers, Gold Coat's hand transfixed by Fahd's blade—and in a grimace of pain, she heard him growl something like, "Now, brother, now." White Helmet, in a rage, roaring like a berserker, with a great sweeping swing caught Fahd under the chin. Fahd's chin split, his head snapped back, his heels lifted off the ground and she heard a crack and in falling, Fahd ripped the knife out of Gold Coat's hand, causing even more damage to the boy's palm. There was a agonized grunt of pain, Gold Coat yanked his hand up and away, blood flying in a silken scarlet arc, hanging suspended in the air in the chopped seconds of her fractured sense of time. After what seemed like an eternity, the liquid red arcing skein fell from its position on the wall of the sky and splattered out and over the muddy grass. Gold Coat fell to his knees, out of breath, cupping his injured hand, looked up at White Helmet and mumbled something she couldn't make out. She noticed then that there was an ugly swelling on the side of his face, and realized Fahd must have hurt him badly.

Gold Coat looked up, straight into her eyes, took a deep breath, put his hand up to his jaw, grimaced in pain, but said, "Are you okay?" He reached out a hand to her—the injured one, without thinking—and she was about to take it when she saw the gaping wound and recoiled. And then the thought struck her with more force than the shock of his violated palm: *this hole in his hand is because of me; he did this to save my life.*

"I'm fine," she said, nodding her head weakly. Yet just that little movement made her dizzy. She was shivering in the cold rain now, and it felt as though the field was tilting crazily. She put out a hand to the ground to steady herself and tried to stand, but she couldn't. She couldn't make her legs work. Gold Coat shuffled closer and put his arm around her to steady her as she knelt on all fours in the mud. Suddenly the full enormity and shock of what had happened and what might have happened caught up with her and the contents of her stomach roiled and rushed upward and she leaned forward and threw up into the muddy grass. He held her while she retched, shaking, heaving, until nothing was left but lines of thin saliva and the burning acid taste on her tongue.

" S'okay," he mumbled. She felt his arms around her, holding her up. His hand brushed strands of hair back and away from her face. She looked at him and spoke the first thing that came into her mind as she wiped the sleeve of her sweater across her mouth.

"Your coat is too big for you."

He smiled slowly, tilted his head back and opened his mouth in silent laughter, and then, in garbled words, his mouth swelling badly, said "It b'longed to m' brudder. Izza hand-me-down." He paused, and then asked in a slurred tone, "Whuzzyer name?"

"Zoe ... Zoe Davidovitch." She could barely sputter the words.

He smiled slowly. "Mace." That was his name.

She nodded much more slowly, not trusting herself to say anything else without getting sick, and instead turned and looked dumbly at the crowd of people now coming from the school building, trotting across the grass, people of authority—teachers, a coach—coming in a trickle, then a growing stream toward them from across the practice field.

"Is there enough room in there for me?" she said to herself, looking at his coat, and realized that she had spoken the words aloud in a croaking voice she did not recognize. Her throat felt lacerated and raw. Gold Coat touched the side of her face with his wounded hand, his blood mingling with her own from the cut on her cheek. In the freezing air, she felt his warmth. He gently turned her face toward him, and it felt to her as if he could look straight through her eyes and into her heart. He nodded and slowly, painfully took one arm out of his coat, draped one side of the big garment over her shoulders, and they sat there, huddled together, one large old torn, blood-stained gold work coat covering the two of them until the arbiters came.

***

They'd both been taken into the school clinic run by the school nurse, and when that worthy saw Mace's hand she immediately called for an ambulance.

"Gonna need surgery, no question, young man. I do not like the look of that hand, no sirree." She was muttering, shaking her head. "What in God's name were you thinking, getting into a scrape like that?" Mace just looked down at his hand, wondering, and then turned to look at Zoe, sitting in a blue plastic chair in the corner, shivering, but still wearing his coat. Her eyes began to fill; she couldn't help it, knowing that he had ruined his hand for her sake. It was something so completely out of the realm of her experience that it overwhelmed her, and she sat there, trembling, tears dripping down onto the lapel of his golden coat.

"And you, missee," the nurse said with more than a touch of irritation in her voice, "have caused enough problems for one day." She went about the little clinic muttering to herself. "Boys cutting each other up over some silly frippet, acting like animals; don't have the sense God gave a rock."

The nurse wrapped Mace's ripped hand with a loose bandage and gave him an icepack to hold on his face with his other hand. A loud siren sounded near the school's entrance, and soon two paramedics with a stretcher came through the door of the nurse's office. One of the paramedics took a look at Mace's hand and wrapped it with something that began to numb his fingers, and then they gently put him on the mobile stretcher and took him away, leaving Zoe with the nurse. Zoe stared after Mace, trembling.

She was beginning to feel nauseous again when White Helmet came in, filling the doorway, still holding his football helmet and the thing with plastic-looking padding. He walked across the linoleum, his cleats making a clip-clopping sound, sat down in another blue plastic chair next to her and held out his hand.

"Hi. I'm Marcus ... Marcus Ironbridge." His voice was deep and full of confidence and strength and she noticed he looked a little like Mace.

"Zoe Davidovitch," she replied, voice trembling. She shook his hand and then winced slightly. Her knuckles were raw.

"Sorry," he said, letting go of her hand gently. "You put up a good fight."

"Who was that kid? Mace, his name was. He saved my life."

Marcus nodded grimly. "Yeah," he said, drawing out the word, and then turned to look at her. "He did that very thing, Zoe. He's pretty amazing sometimes."

"You know him?"

Marcus chuckled. "Yeah, I know him. He's my brother."

Zoe's eyes widened slightly. "Right ... right, of course. You look a lot alike."

Marcus smiled and Zoe could see the resemblance even more clearly. Marcus was older than Mace, broader in the shoulders, with a fuller face, a very masculine jaw, and the same dark hair that Mace had. Mace had bright blue eyes, she recalled. Marcus' eyes were a stormy gray.

"So Zoe, what were you doing out there after practice?"

Zoe thought for a moment, and then suddenly remembered. "Oh," she exclaimed, "that's weird." Marcus raised his eyebrow. "I mean, Mr. Lanahan sent me out to find some kid named ... I think ... yeah, Ironbridge ... Mace Ironbridge. *That was him.* He said he would be finishing up football practice."

"Why did Mr. Lanahan send you to find Mace?" Marcus asked.

"I had questions about a book I've been reading on the side, for a report, and after class I asked Mr. Lanahan about it and he said that this kid Mace would be able to answer my questions better than he could."

"So he sent you to find Mace after practice."

Zoe nodded. "Right. I waited for a couple hours until practice ended and then headed out to the field. I didn't know those ... those people would be there." She started to tremble again, remembering.

The nurse came back into the office after helping the paramedics out to the ambulance and put on a pair of latex gloves. She seemed tense, irritated, and in a hurry. "Your mother is on her way in," she said to Marcus. He nodded, figuring as much. "Your turn, Miss Davids," she said, nodding to the treatment table. Marcus stood and helped Zoe up.

"Davidovitch," Zoe mumbled.

"What?"

"My name is Davidovitch."

"Whatever. Let's have a look at you, now."

Marcus stood behind the nurse but didn't leave, sensing Mrs. Arbuckle was making Zoe nervous.

"You're awfully young to be causing fights like this, young lady," the nurse said, shining a light into her eyes.

"I didn't cause anything," Zoe replied with some asperity. Marcus saw her eyes flash and it amused and encouraged him. This kid was tough.

"How old are you, Zoe?" he asked, trying to distract Zoe from the nurse's obvious dislike.

"She is ... " the nurse replied, looking at the clipboard on which Zoe's particulars were recorded, "all of twelve years old, though she's a tall drink of water for twelve, and what a twelve-year old is doing, running around with that crowd, I'll never know. Your parents would be ashamed of you, young lady."

The nurse was turning Zoe's face to and fro with a medical detachment, examining the laceration on her cheek. "But first, you, young man, need to step outside for a moment. I've some questions for the young lady."

"No!" Zoe blurted out reflexively, grasping at Marcus' hand. "I mean, sure, questions, whatever, but I want him to stay." Her grip on his hand was like iron. She was still in shock from the assault.

Mrs. Arbuckle looked at the girl clenching Marcus' hand in her own. "Marcus, is she some sort of relative of yours?" she asked. Everyone in school knew Marcus.

"He's Mace's brother," Zoe answered. "I need him here."

"I'll stay," Marcus said in a way that let Mrs. Arbuckle know that if she wanted him out she'd have to carry him out physically. She pursed her lips, irritated at the display of male dominance, not wanting to argue with the school's most famous quarterback. And she knew his mother.

"Fine then. So," she said, turning to Zoe, throwing the question at her, "did those boys ... take any ... you know ... advantage?" Zoe looked at the nurse, not comprehending.

"She wants to know if they tried to rape you or anything," Marcus said calmly. The nurse bristled at the bluntness of the question.

"Nope," Zoe replied in a voice of cold steel, shock, disgust, and anger in her eyes. "*Nothing* like that happened."

"So they didn't do anything bad?" the nurse asked.

Zoe's eyes flashed up angrily. "Unless you consider trying to kill me something good."

The nurse made a dismissive noise at the young girl's sarcasm and turned to her examination of Zoe's face. "What else did they do besides this?" she asked, touching Zoe's cheek.

"There's this," she replied, pulling down the collar of her pullover and showing the long cut along her collarbone. "And Fahd punched me ... right here." Zoe put her hand to her sternum.

"Well, let's take a look." The nurse turned around, stared at Marcus and pointed to the door.

***

The nurse opened the door again and Marcus walked back into the office. "She okay?" he asked.

"Nothing's broken, if that's what you mean, ribs are good, but she'll be sore for a week or so. Her face will need stitches," she said, "and so will the cut across her neck. She *says* someone almost killed her. She might have just cut herself, I don't know." She turned back to Zoe. "Looks like you're gonna need a ride to the emergency room as well, missee. We don't do stitches here."

Marcus said quickly, "I can take her, Mrs. Arbuckle."

"I don't know," the nurse replied, hesitating, "school policy ... I should call her parents."

"My parents won't be home yet," Zoe spoke up.

"I'll take her," Marcus said in a voice that brooked no argument, leveraging his recognition that Mrs. Arbuckle wanted to close up her office and go home and didn't particularly like this little freshman anyway—for what reason, Marcus didn't know, but the dislike was palpable.

"Well, let me call her parents at least and let them know where you'll take her. I have their numbers here."

"Granite Sky General ... my truck is right outside. C'mon, Zoe, let's go." Marcus helped Zoe off the table, slipped Mace's coat over her shoulders, grabbed her thin pullover from the blue plastic chair and rushed her out before Mrs. Arbuckle could find any other reason to object.

***

They were in Marcus' truck, an old gold two-tone Dodge with a camper top. It was clean inside for such an old farm truck. Marcus pulled out of the school's parking lot and took the road toward the hospital. Zoe was sitting in the passenger seat holding an icepack on her face. "Zoe, you're kind of young to be in high school, aren't you?" Marcus asked.

"I'm twelve, yeah. I skipped two grades, so I'm a freshman this year."

Marcus looked impressed. "I didn't know they let twelve-year olds start high school. You must be pretty smart, huh?"

"How's Mace," she asked, trembling slightly, ignoring Marcus' question.

"Mace ... yeah, well, he's going to need surgery on his hand, no question." Marcus looked out into the distance, down the road in the gray rain. "It was a pretty brave thing he did, Zoe."

Zoe nodded, eyes watering up again, and she did not trust herself to speak; too many unfamiliar emotions were welling up inside, overwhelming her. "What else?" she asked, barely getting the words out.

"They may have broken his jaw; not sure yet, they'll have to take some x-rays."

"Will they put Fahd in jail?" she asked.

Marcus grunted. Far from it, he thought to himself. Zoe's questions called to mind the session he'd had with the school principal, Mrs. Anniston, in her office just after the fight. She was a short, fat woman who had spent her life being in charge and she tended to use her authority like a battering ram.

"Well, Mister Ironbridge, you've certainly put the fat in the fire now," she had said, putting Marcus somewhat off balance. She asked what had happened, and Marcus described how he had just finished practice and was heading into the locker room and met his girlfriend, Sigrid, and they had been standing by his pickup just talking when he heard a girl's high scream cutting through the wind, coming from near the practice field. When he went to see what it was, he saw two boys holding a young girl by the hair, while another group was surrounding a figure on the ground. "I didn't recognize any of them from that distance, Mrs. Anniston, but it was pretty clear it wasn't a fair fight, and when I saw two guys holding this little girl by the hair and another kid come at her, well, it was time to do something."

"Mmm," she replied, unconvinced. "What then?"

"So I just ran, taking what I had in my hand at the time. I had my helmet and shoulder pads and, well, I sort of just dove in."

"And did you *have* to break Dwayne Ruckle's elbow?" she asked. "And did you *have* to split open al-Husseini's chin, and give him a concussion, and possibly crack one of the vertebrae in his neck?" she asked, pounding the questions at him.

Marcus became defensive. "Hey, Mrs. Anniston, I'm not the one that pulled a knife. I'm not the one that tried to cut up the girl's face."

"What knife? No one told me about any knife. Dwayne or Fahd didn't mention anything about a knife. I talked to those boys before they went to the hospital. They said you just came storming out of the locker room while they were talking to Miss Davido ... Davidovsky ... and just attacked them."

At this point in the conversation, Marcus' mother burst through the door of the Principal's office with a police officer in train. His mother, Claire Ironbridge, was a tall, passionate and at the moment very angry French woman and she'd hadn't even seen Mace yet, Marcus thought. She's going to go through the roof.

"*Ce va, maman,*" Marcus said in French.

"Officer Daggit," the plainclothes officer said, introducing himself.

"What happened?" his mother asked in English, looking at the Principal.

"Marcus was just explaining," Anniston replied sourly, her arms folded across her ample bosom. "Why don't you start over?" So Marcus did, rehashing what had happened up to the point where Dwayne Ruckles had threatened him with a knife.

"What'd he pull a knife on you for?" the policeman asked. "Was he feeling threatened? Were you threatening him in some way?"

"He broke his elbow with a football helmet," the Principal put in angrily. "Of course Dwayne was feeling threatened. We don't need that kind of violence in this school."

"Why, Marcus?" his mother asked, looking at him steadily.

"Because," Marcus replied slowly, "he was probably worried that I would hit him the way I hit his friend Fahd."

"And what did you to do his friend Fahd?" the policeman asked.

"Well, the first time I hit him, I cracked him in the arm to knock the knife out of his hand, and then I hit him in the head." The Principal was shaking her head in disgust. "Yeah," the policeman said, figuring out where this was going. "And why was that?"

"Because, sir, Fahd was threatening to cut the girl's face up with the knife he had."

Anniston interjected harshly. "Are you saying that Mr. al-Husseini had a knife as well? Mr. al-Husseini didn't say anything about any knife. Did everyone have a knife out there or are you just making this up, Ironbridge? Because if you're making this up—"

"Excuse me, Ma'am," Daggit interrupted, "but he's not making anything up. I found this near the scene." The plainclothes police officer held out a muddy, bloody switchblade in a plastic bag. "And I found this stuck in the young man's shoulder pads." The policeman held out another plastic bag containing a black tactical folding knife, extended.

"Whose blood is on the knife?" his mother asked, staring at the switchblade in the bag. Marcus hesitated. "Whose blood is on the knife, Marcus?" she repeated. He told her, and she bolted from the room.

***

Marcus shook himself, made the turn onto the interstate, and considered the young girl sitting across from him, wondering what had possessed Mace, who had finished practice and come out of the locker room earlier than Marcus, to risk his life to defend her. It was like Mace, though. There were things Mace did that Marcus just didn't understand.

"What book were you reading, that Lanahan had to get Mace to answer the questions you had?" he asked.

"The Bible," she replied. "Lanahan said Mace knew it backwards and forwards and if anyone around here was going to make sense of it, he said Mace could."

"Well ... that would be Mace all right," Marcus replied quietly, smiling slowly.

"Will I get to see Mace at the hospital?" she asked, as though she hadn't heard him.

"I don't really know, Zoe, but first you need to get your face and your neck stitched up and your folks need to see you."

Zoe sat there, holding the icepack to her face, and nodded. "I just want to see Mace," she mumbled, still trembling.

When they got to the hospital, Zoe had her cuts stitched by an emergency room physician from Cambodia, and they told her Mace was in surgery and couldn't be seen and sent her home wrapped in Mace's still bloody, mud-stained oversized gold farm coat.

***

When Zoe walked into Mace's hospital room the next day, she saw an older man and a woman, the woman sitting next to the bed. She saw Mace's profile in the older man's face, and there was a sense about the woman that reminded her of Mace as well.

Mace was sleeping, his right hand encased in a large white plaster cast up to his elbow. She stood still in the doorway like a frightened bird, trembling, the site of the cast bringing back memories. She held Mace's golden coat folded in her arms, not sure how his parents would feel about her being there.

The woman saw her standing there first. "Ah, *Mon chère*, come," she said gently, and moved to gently embrace Zoe and lead her into the room. "You must be Zoe. How beautiful you are, my dear. My name is Claire, I am Mace's mother, and now sit here, *Mon petite chère*, here." The woman's warmth set Zoe immediately at ease, and she sat down in the chair next to the hospital bed.

"I ... I came to say thanks, and I ... I brought Mace's coat back," she said tentatively, holding it out.

The older man moved across the room toward her with a fluid grace. "My name is Thackeray Ironbridge," he said. He reminded her of Marcus. "You must be Zoe Davidovitch. I talked to your parents last night. I'm Mace's father. Mace hasn't been able to tell us anything yet, but Marcus has. He said you were very brave."

"Mace was the brave one, sir. Didn't Mace tell you what happened?"

"We talked to Marcus, yes, but Mace's jaw is wired, my dear. It is broken," Claire put in gently, her hand on Zoe's arm, worried that news about Mace's jaw would upset Zoe.

It did; Zoe began to cry. Claire pulled her close and Zoe folded up in her arms. "I'm sorry," she said, sobbing. "I don't normally cry like this."

"*Mon dieu*," cried Claire, "after what you went through yesterday, why, *ma petite colombe*, who would not be crying? We completely understand."

"Can you tell us what happened?" Mace's father asked. "Marcus was a little busy."

Mace's mother said, "No, Tack, not now, look, you can see it is too difficult for her."

"No, no ma'am, I can tell you what happened. I wouldn't mind." Zoe sat up, wiped her eyes, wincing a bit as her sleeve caught the stitches in her face. "But ... how is Mace? Will he be okay?" Claire shot a look over Zoe's head at her husband, who answered Zoe's question.

"He has a very bad injury to his hand, Zoe. The knife cut a number of tendons and ligaments in the palm, and he spent about six hours or so in surgery yesterday."

"Will he ... will he be able to use it?"

Tack Ironbridge hesitated for a moment. A doubtful glance over at his wife, and then: "We hope so, Zoe."

"Of course he will, dear," Claire said. "Don't you worry."

"He has a fractured jaw, and they've wired it shut to make sure it heals properly," Mr. Ironbridge continued. "Besides a few other cuts and bruises, that's about it. But we would really like to know what happened if you could tell us, Zoe."

So she took a deep breath and recounted everything, starting at the first slur that cut across her heart in the cold wind.

"He called me a dirty Jew whore," she began. She paused, looking to see how Mace's parents would react to a twelve-year old throwing around foul language, and at the same time trying out her finely honed anti-Semitic antenna. They were looking back at her with open, compassionate eyes that went flinty at the sound of the racist epithet, and she was encouraged. "So he came up to me and told me I had to leave, and I told him that he wasn't in charge of who could go where. My mother and father had to leave Russia because someone told them Jews had to leave and then they were kicked out of Canada because someone told them Jews couldn't stay there either and I'm tired of being kicked out of places and—I didn't tell him all this but that's what I was thinking—and besides who was he to tell me where I can and can't go. So he hit me in the face." Her hand fluttered nervously toward her cheek.

"And how is that, my dear?" Claire asked.

"I'm fine, ma'am. So then I tried to get up but one of his friends kicked me and I was down in the mud and then Fahd was in front of my face telling me that Jews never know when to quit, and that's when Mace came in and knocked down two of Fahd's punks and tackled Fahd, hit Fahd right in the face and pushed him away from me, and knocked him down and got his brand new pullover all muddy, and that made Fahd really mad. And then all of them began to punch and kick Mace, and he was trying to fight back but there were too many of them, and ... and then they picked him up and Fahd was really angry because Mace had tackled him hard, and so they held Mace up and Fahd hit him really hard in the face. That's probably when they broke his ... when they broke his jaw. And then Fahd pulled out his knife and was going to cut me to keep people from ever wanting to kiss me again, or something like that, and Mace began to really fight and it took three of them to hold him and just when Fahd was going to cut my face, White Helmet ... I mean, Mace's brother came in and knocked the knife out of his hand and hit him in the side of the head and knocked him down again."

Mr. Ironbridge asked in a deep voice that reminded her of Marcus, "What happened to Mace's hand, Zoe?"

"Right. So ... so one of them ran away and another tried to stab Marcus with a knife but Marcus hit him really hard in the arm and I heard a cracking sound and the kid's arm broke, I think, and then he was on the ground yelling, and two other guys went after Marcus, but he knocked both of them down too, and that's when Fahd woke up, found his knife in the mud, and grabbed me by the hair and said he was going to kill me."

"Did he actually threaten to kill you, dear?" Claire asked softly.

"He said, let me think ... he said to Marcus, '*Why not just you watch while I cut this bitch's throat? Hey? What are you thinking about that?*'"

"Perhaps he was just bluffing," Mr. Ironbridge offered quietly. Someone trying to kill this girl in the mud on a football field in northern Minnesota just didn't process. Maybe she was histrionic or flighty or overly emotional.

"He tried to cut my throat, sir," Zoe replied, and tilted her neck, pulled back the collar of her sweater, and showed him the bandage covering a four-inch span across the hollow between her clavicle and throat. Zoe continued. "That's when Mace grabbed Fahd from behind and ... and then Mace jammed his hand down over the point of the knife so Fahd couldn't cut me and while it was stuck in the middle of his hand he pulled it away from my throat." Zoe's eyes filled and she tilted her head back, letting the tears drain down out of her reddened eyes. Claire growled with menace and then took Zoe's hand.

"*Les salauds meurtriers*," Claire gasped, white-faced. Tack Ironbridge looked at the girl and then to his son lying in the bed.

"They are, yes ma'am," Zoe said. "So then Mace was holding Fahd by the waist and pulled him off me and they stood up and Mace pulled his arm back—for some reason Fahd wouldn't let go of the knife—and then Mace said something to ... to Marcus I guess, because Marcus came out of nowhere and hit Fahd under his chin with his helmet and Fahd flew up in the air about a foot and when he came down, he wasn't moving. If he's not dead I hope they put him in jail."

"I hope so too, *ma colombe*," Claire said.

"He's not dead," Tack said grimly. He went over to the side of the bed and put his hand on Mace's head, pushing back the dark hair from his eyes, and bent down and kissed his unconscious son on the forehead. "You did well, my son," he whispered. "Well done."

Claire wiped tears from her own eyes and asked Zoe, "How are your parents taking this, *mon chère*?"

"They're pretty angry, Mrs. Ironbridge. I mean, my parents left Russia because of what they saw happening there to the Jews and then when they told my father he couldn't work in Canada any more, well ... we thought that America would be different. I'm afraid they're beginning to wonder. Their daughter gets attacked like she's on the streets of some Arab city and they begin to wonder."

"No, no, don't let them worry, my dear, no, not at all. This is a different place, and if it takes everything we have we will make sure you are safe here."

"What does your father do, Zoe?" Tack asked, changing the subject.

"He's a chemist, sir ... a petroleum engineer. Clarion Oil brought him here because he invented a new process to refine oil."

"And what about your mother, dear?" Claire asked.

"She's at the University; she's getting her doctorate in Literature, and she teaches sometimes to help out."

"So they are both quite busy," Claire observed.

"If I might ask, what does your Father have to say about ... ah, what happened?" Tack asked. "I know he was extremely angry last night, but he was also very, very complimentary about Mace, which I appreciate."

"I don't know what he wants to do about it, Mr. Ironbridge. The only thing I know is that Mace saved my life."

"Yeah, well ... " Tack didn't say anything else, struck silent by the realization of what *could* have happened. Then he turned back to the young girl. "But Zoe, why would this kid Fahd want to kill you? I mean, did he know you from, well, before, was he ... "

"If you mean was he a previous boyfriend, absolutely not. I just moved here two months ago, and yeah, I've seen him around a couple of times this year at school, but I've had nothing to do with him. But really sir, it doesn't take that much to figure out why. I'm a Jew; he's an Arab. What's not to understand?"

"This isn't the West Bank, Zoe. This is America. Jews, Arabs, Irish, Catholic, Protestant ... everyone is sort of in the same melting pot."

"That may be, sir, but some people don't like to get melted, and they stay separate. And they carry a lot of ugly stuff in their own stew."

"Enough of this," Claire announced briskly, taking Zoe by both hands and looking her squarely in the eye. "Now look here, *ma petite chère*, there is something you should know about Mace ... something you should know before he awakes." Claire looked uncomfortable then, and Zoe wondered what she was going to tell her. "Mace doesn't ... well ... he doesn't speak exactly like everyone else."

Zoe didn't understand. "What do you mean, Mrs. Ironbridge? I didn't notice anything different, except, well, after he got hit in the face, then, but ... "

"No, sweet, that is not what I am talking about. Mace speaks, but ... he ... speaks ... very ... slowly. He didn't talk until he was four, for goodness sake, *Mon Dieu*, he drove us crazy wondering, and when he finally did open his mouth, he could barely get one word out every ten minutes. No, this is a rare condition that he has had since he was born. He makes very good sense, and he is quite intelligent, oh, yes, but he just does not speak as *quickly* as everyone else."

Zoe sat and listened without saying anything, but she could remember exactly what was said and how it was said when Mace and his golden coat showed up and saved her life, and she didn't hear anything like what Mrs. Ironbridge was talking about.

"Well, then ... how does he get along, I mean, in school and everything?" Zoe asked.

Claire reached over to the bedside table and lifted up a thin square of something metallic looking, with a small embedded keyboard. "He types on this, *ma petite chère*. He can type faster than most people can speak, and he types what he wants to say and shows them what he has to say on the screen."

Zoe looked at the small device, looked at Mace lying there on the bed, and in a striking flash suddenly realized that if his hand were permanently injured, he wouldn't be able to communicate. His sacrifice took on even more depth, more meaning, and she realized what it had cost Mace to keep her alive.

"If ... if his hand doesn't get better," she whispered. "O God, he won't be able to ... it's my fault," and she put her face in her hands. Tack and Claire let her alone, waiting until she absorbed the full impact of Mace's injury.

"We trust that God has this situation in His hands, Zoe," said Mr. Ironbridge softly.

"I am *so* sorry," she sobbed, her shoulders shaking. "I didn't know. I didn't know anything about *that*." She made a weak gesture toward Mace's tablet on the stand.

Claire stood and took Zoe in her arms and spoke firmly. "Now, now, *Mon colombe*, look at me. This is nothing of it your fault, my sweet dear, absolutely *not* your fault, do you hear me? Do not think any such thing, I forbid it. Mace knew what he was doing and it was not your fault that these *enfants du diable* chose to act so wickedly. We will trust that God put Mace there to keep you alive. If you want to wonder about anything, wonder why God is taking such an interest in you, hey?" Claire held her at arms length, put her hand under Zoe's chin and smiled at her with wet eyes. "God loves you very much, *Mon petite chère.* Go home and rest in that, okay?"

Zoe nodded, took a handkerchief from Claire, and wiped her eyes. "Yes, you're right. I think ... I think I should go now. My mother doesn't want me out of the house for long; she's getting a little paranoid."

"I can't say I blame her, my dear. You go along now, and we will tell Mace that you stopped by."

"Thank you, Mrs. Ironbridge," Zoe whispered, pain mixed with gratefulness. "*Thank you.* And please thank Mace when he wakes up."

Claire put her hand to Zoe's cheek with such tenderness that her eyes began to fill again. "You come back and thank him yourself tomorrow, love. Go now with God and talk to Him and see what He is asking of you."

Zoe turned to go but stopped at the door of the room, her hand on the hard metal doorjamb. "Would you mind ... would ... do you think Mace would mind if I kept his coat for a while?" She held the golden coat tightly in her arms.

"*Pas problem,* you go ahead and wear it home, *Mon petite chère,* " Claire replied.

Zoe still paused at the door with a curious look on her fact. "Mr. and Mrs. Ironbridge ... "

"*Que voulez-vous ma chère*?" asked Claire.

"Do you know *why* Mace did what he did? *Why* did he risk his life for me?"

Claire looked at her husband, who took a breath and quietly answered, "I think, Zoe, that you should let Mace answer that when he wakes up."

Chapter 2
Marcus

"It is by his deeds that a lad distinguishes himself if his conduct is pure and right."

Proverbs 20:11

A few days after Mace and Marcus had intervened on Zoe's behalf, Tack took a load of cheeses to the weekly farm market sponsored by local farmers. Arriving at his booth, he lined the shelves with paper, unpacked his wares, set the wheels and wedges on display, donned an apron, and prepared to meet the day's customers.

Granite Sky was a not a small town but it wasn't a metropolis either. Many people knew Tack and Claire and the boys, and the altercation at school had been thoroughly bandied about. Opinions varied as to what happened, who was at fault, and what should have transpired. Tack listened with equanimity to most, but when one woman from the town's most prominent church came up to his counter, he knew what would follow.

"Thackeray, how are you today," she asked primly. Stella Pomhausen had been a schoolteacher and a principal in her former life. Now she spent most of her time behind the scenes, subtly directing the men who ostensibly were the leaders of Granite Sky's largest Protestant church.

"Just fine, Stella. And you?"

"Acceptable," she replied, looking over his lower row of thick cheese wedges. She glanced up behind the counter. "Your boys here today?"

"Not today, Stella."

"Hmmm ... right. They wouldn't be, I suppose." There was a pause. "How's that foreign boy doing? I heard he was sent to the hospital."

"Don't really know. Don't really care. It's a shame he went to the hospital, though. Did you want to order something?"

"Why, Thackeray, you say you don't care what happened to that poor young man but you regret he went to the hospital. Isn't that a little ... conflicted? Doesn't quite make sense." She had a superior smile on her face, with eyebrows raised, as though she'd caught him out.

"I don't care what happens to that 'poor young man' as you describe him. He tried to murder a young woman in cold blood. And yes, I regret he went to the hospital. He should have gone to the morgue."

Mrs. Pomhausen's eyes widened, her shoulders drew back, and she put on her 'Principal's' face—slight frown, raised eyebrows, nose tilted upward, and pushed all the moral authority she possessed at Tack. In a tone shaded with denigration and the full weight of offended righteous indignation, she lectured him like a ten-year old boy. "This is not the attitude Jesus would want us to have, Thackeray. We are to love our fellow man. As the father of two boys, you should set the example for your sons. They ought to be suspended. Why it's disgraceful, actually, that—"

"That's enough, Mrs. Pomhausen. You want to lecture someone, go lecture your husband. But don't talk to me about a Jesus you know nothing about."

Mrs. Pomhausen wasn't accustomed to being talked to in such fashion. Men in general listened to her, either from a suspicion that perhaps she was right because they didn't know any better, or withholding comment in accordance with the old proverb about dogs not biting bitches. She unconsciously leveraged this in her dealings with men, and took their gentlemanly forbearance as simply a sign that men acquiesced to her natural authority. With an effort she kept her temper in check.

"We are required to be tolerant of all peoples, Thackeray ... all religions. Who knows but that our patience with them will bear fruit?"

"I disagree, Stella. In fact, that's blasphemy. In what world would a true God be tolerant of false gods? In what universe would a God Who is Himself truth and righteousness approve of falsity, lies, deception, and disgusting behavior?"

"Do you think Christianity has a corner on the truth? Do *you* have a corner on truth, Thackeray? Are you the final judge of what is or isn't good behavior? Would you not even consider that perhaps other faiths might have additional perspectives about God that you haven't yet grasped?"

Tack shook his head. "Listen, Stella. You want to peddle that claptrap to others, go ahead. But you can't show me in the Word that what you're advocating is approved by God."

"And you think your Bible is the sole arbiter of all truth, then?"

By now other customers were gathering, some swimming around the edge of the burgeoning argument, eyes on the wares, but ears tilted like radar dishes toward the discussion.

"There is one truth, Stella, no matter what you think. That truth is in this Word," and here Tack let his hand rest on the Bible that was nearby on the counter.

Pomhausen sniffed and with a superior tone, replied, "Think what you will, Thackeray. If you want to maintain your narrow perspective on life, that's your choice, and I for one will not disabuse you of such an ... an *elementary* value system."

"Elementary? Maybe so ... but the truth of God is simple, at a level even children can understand. Even a child could understand that when Israel chased after other gods, even after God kept their very lives in His hands, God would feel hurt, betrayed, and heartbroken. He considers it akin to adultery—spiritual adultery."

"Ah, now Thackeray, seriously, the Jews? Any reference to Jews in today's world, as a guide for how we should now live ... I mean seriously, isn't it just a little," and here she laughed, "*antediluvian*, wouldn't you say?"

"What Bible are you people reading in that church of yours?"

"The Bible is all very well," Pomhausen replied, now cross, "but in case you are not aware, Thackeray, God gave us all a brain, and specific gifts, and He wants us to use them to further His kingdom. There is some marvelous new teaching out there, which I'm sure you're not aware of. I happen to think He wants us to be relevant to our fellow man, and frankly, well, stories about Jews and prophets and animal sacrifices just don't reach the people of today. We each have gifts that we should use to make the idea of God more relevant to those around us."

Tack felt himself getting angry, and for one moment thought that he ought to check himself, but then a remembrance of Jesus encountering the Pharisees in the temple came to mind. He leaned forward over the counter and looked directly at the stocky woman with her butch haircut.

"Well, my gift is speaking the truth, so let me utilize that gift this morning to make the truth of God more relevant to you. You're a hypocrite, Pomhausen. You should be ashamed to darken the door of a Christian church. That you would even question His Word makes you a heretic. You're a snake, sneaking around behind the scenes, pulling strings and manipulating men, spreading your poisonous agendas and ideas and philosophies. In you is the spirit of the world, arranging things yourself, building things yourself, ordering lives according to how you see things, never just waiting on God to bring things about in His time. You are a stench in God's nostrils. You are most assuredly Jezebel incarnate. Now get yourself gone. You disgust God, and you disgust me."

Brought up short, her dignity assaulted, not accustomed to being accosted in such fashion, and definitely intimidated physically, Pomhausen turned and stalked off in a huff.

In the swirling dust of Pomhausen's wake, a diminutive stooped old man stepped up, wearing a faded brown sweater and a green plaid shirt buttoned all the way up. Bemused, he stared at Pomhausen's retreating form for a moment and then turned to Tack and said, "I wonder if I might have a pound of your Emmentaler, sir? I do wonder what's in it."

***

"It's not important," Sigrid said. "They're just immigrants anyway. And hey, Islam is a religion of peace—your President keeps saying so."

"They're going to cause your country a lot of problems," Marcus replied. "They're going to cause everyone a lot of problems." They were sitting on a bench at Sigrid's home, overlooking Lake Montrose. Marcus stood and picked up a stone and skimmed it across the water. "And Islam is the farthest thing from a religion of peace that I can imagine."

"They can't even run their own countries. Wherever they go, they live like animals. What problems can a bunch of ignorant Muslims cause?"

"They will," Marcus said ominously.

"How do you know?"

"I just know."

Marcus drove Sigrid crazy sometimes. He was tall and strong and the most popular boy in Granite Sky High School and she just couldn't make him do what she wanted. Her brother Leif thought Marcus was the greatest thing since Thor; he would, since Marcus was captain of the football team and Leif one of the star lineman.

"You're not right all the time," she said, eyebrows arching.

"We'll see." That's what he always said; *'We'll see'.*

"You don't have a crystal ball, you know."

"The Bible is clear about what's to come, Sigrid, I wish you'd believe that."

She looked away in frustration. "I know you believe all that ... stuff ... whatever," she waved her hand ethereally in the air, referring to the vast unknown content of this mystical Bible about which he spoke too often. "And hey, that's okay. I say live and let live; if someone wants to believe the moon is made of green cheese, what's the harm, let them."

"The problem with Muslims, Sig, is that they won't let you believe what you want. They won't let anyone believe what they want to believe. They don't 'live and let live.' Either you believe what they tell you to believe, or they kill you. No choice."

"Hmmph. And why is all that important, anyway?" She looked at him directly, invitingly, and traced the fresh scar across his forearm.

"Don't start, Sig. This is serious stuff. It'll affect you and I and whatever future we might have, and it will definitely make an impact on the world's future. And Sig, seriously, if you believe the moon is made of green cheese, and you get there and it turns out it isn't, and where you spend eternity depends on you getting it right—where will you be?"

She would not be dissuaded or turned. "Always so serious; world changer, you are. Come over here and give me a kiss, world changer."

Marcus remained where he was, still staring out over the water. The temptation to just pull the statuesque young woman into his arms was overpowering. He had deep feelings for her, and his parents had warned him about the effects physical passion could have on a man's ability to think clearly. And he wanted to think clearly—about her, about them, and about their future.

"Look, Sig ... you know how I feel about you. You know ... no, now, don't start, really, I want to talk about something." She sat back down again. "Okay, so ... we might have a future, Sig. I know your father is a big global business executive and my father is a cheese maker, but we can overcome that, right?"

She laughed. "*Du er slik et troll*," she said.

"What?" he asked. "What's that?"

"I just said you're such a troll, that's all." She smiled.

"What's a troll?" he asked, eyes sharp and curious.

"Never mind. What were you saying about our future?"

"Yeah, well ... I'm saying that if we are going to have any chance of a life in this world ... I mean, if *anyone* is going to have any chance of a good life in this world, we can't let Islam keep going the way it's going. There are already almost two billion Muslims in the world."

"That's a lot of Muslims, Marcus. You will not be able to hit them all on the head with your helmet."

"Yeah, don't laugh, Sig, but it's going to be a problem. It's like a person has cancer and everyone is either making light of it or telling the person that they should just put up with it, be tolerant, like they tolerate a hangnail or bad breath or an achy joint. Only a hangnail or bad breath or an achy joint won't kill you—they don't seem to get this."

"Marcus, you cannot save the whole world, I don't care what you read in that Bible."

"And as long as we're talking about our future, Sig ... I mean, we need to talk about that too."

She became downcast at this turn of the conversation. She knew the big issue between them was religion. Raised agnostic in powerfully anti-Christian northern Europe, she could not comprehend the American fixation with religion, and it grieved her that the one boy upon whom she'd fixed her heart had a higher priority in his heart than her. Unknowingly, she wanted to be god on the throne of Marcus' life, as she was on the throne of her own.

***

Norway's largest company, Statoil, invested in the recent discovery of oil under the northern Minnesota lakes several years before Tack and Claire Ironbridge ever came to Granite Sky, and over time the investment paid significant dividends. When Marcus and Mace went to Granite Sky High School, Statoil was the reigning company in the state.

Purchasing most of the smaller US-owned oil and gas companies, Statoil soon controlled much of the western half of northern Minnesota's lake fields, and Granite Sky was the Norwegian firm's American headquarters.

Statoil sent one of its best executives to administer their affairs in Minnesota. Johan Jannsen was forty-three when he arrived in Granite Sky. He'd started with Statoil when he was eighteen, working as a wildcatter on one of their oil rigs off the cost of the United Kingdom. Johan was nothing to look twice at, but he was full of determination, drive, persistence, and vigor. While home from the rigs on leave when he was twenty-five, he captured the eye of a tall, stunning young Norwegian heiress and bulling through all obstacles with monumental persistence, married her. Shortly thereafter he worked up to become manager of the UK rig, and when Statoil began to develop their Sverdrup field, he suggested a reorganization of tools, equipment, and offshore helicopter service provision that saved the company several million dollars. The company liked his ideas and made him one of the deputy managers for Sverdrup, controlling all support services to the offshore rigs. After four years at Sverdrup, Statoil transferred him to corporate headquarters in Stavanger. Jannsen excelled at the rough and tumble, hard-nosed corporate-level politics—he was fresh off the rigs, didn't put up with dissembling, and his bosses needed to hear honest input. He made his mark and soon was selected to lead Statoil's development of the Bakken and underlying Three Forks formation in the western half of northern Minnesota. The company wanted a no-nonsense, direct, clear-thinking man up from the fields to interact with Americans (who were still thought by Norwegians to be just a generation removed from Cowboys and Indians). So the hard-nosed, plain speaking Johan Jannsen brought his family to the 'land of a thousand lakes', purchased a large home on Lake Montrose and installed his daughter, Sigrid, and his son, Leif, in Granite Sky High School.

Johan was a short man, stocky, with a barrel chest and a tough countenance. Leif inherited his father's build but his mother's height, and Granite Sky's football coach was overjoyed to see the young man. Sigrid, however, like her mother, was the picture of a Scandinavian princess. Tall, svelte, muscular, white-blonde, stunningly beautiful with long legs and a shapely figure, she was unique even among the internationally eclectic population of Granite Sky. She could have any young man she wanted, and from the day she put her foot across the school's threshold, for some reason, she set her cap for Marcus Ironbridge.

Marcus, for all his strength, could not resist the feminine assault by this statuesque queen from the north. They immediately became a couple. But then Sigrid encountered Marcus' stolid fixation with religion, and it shook her confidence. At first it was dismaying. Marcus stuck doggedly to his priority; he wouldn't sleep with her, which caused her no end of grief, since sex was a woman's main and most powerful means of manipulation. Sigrid worried that if they would ever have a life together, she would not be first in his heart. Yet with the stubborn, dogged persistence she inherited from her father, she set to the challenge of winning Marcus' heart away from his God. She wouldn't have put it that way, but her desire was to be first priority in Marcus' life—which is the same thing.

Marcus had no idea about these currents under their relationship. Being an honest young man, in his naiveté he thought that everyone else was honest as well, not realizing that even where some others might not know that what they wanted was something less than honorable, they were probably even less aware of darker spiritual forces in play.

Sigrid would have been the last person to recognize and admit that any type of spiritual force held sway in her life or heart. From her perspective, she was fully in control of her own life—and the devils were happy to keep her thinking so.

***

"We can't go through life like we are now," Marcus was saying. He was serious, and she realized with a catch in her heart that he really did have feelings for her. It gave her a sudden thrill of renewed hope and strengthened her confidence. She reached up and took his hands in hers.

"We can do anything we set our minds to," she replied intensely, looking into his eyes. A shadow of hesitation crossed his face, and she caught it. "Do you not this believe?" Though her English was superb, in moments of emotion she would restructure her grammar.

"Listen, Sig," he began hesitantly, "I believe that if we do what God says, He will make things right with us. If we run out ahead of Him, we're just asking for trouble."

She put her fingers to his lips and stared into his eyes. "Shhh. I'll give things a try, my world changer. But right now, it is just you and I."

She was *so* beautiful. She took his face in her hands and kissed him, and he responded, wrapping his strong arms around her, pulling her close. They kissed, breathlessly, with the cares of the world flying away like birds rising from a lake.

***

Snow fell in thick wet flakes in an early winter snowstorm, covering the land with a white blanket. The wind was up, threatening to drift snow over field and fence. Marcus and Mace were in the barn, shoveling out cow stalls. Marcus shoveled while Mace drove the four-wheeler towing the manure sled. They worked companionably for an hour or so in silence, each preoccupied with their own thoughts.

Marcus took a break, leaning on the pitchfork, and signaled to Mace to turn off the four-wheeler.

"Mace, why don't you and Zoe come along with Sigrid and I this weekend?"

"Where?" Mace replied slowly.

"Sig picked up four tickets to the *New Times Comin'* concert up near Haskill."

Mace turned to look directly at his brother, a question on his face. Marcus understood. "She's trying, Mace. She wants to find out what Christianity is all about. Where she grew up, there was nothing about Christianity; the place was dead—still is."

"Can't," Mace replied.

"What? Don't you think Zoe will go with you? She follows you everywhere now. Of course she'll go with you."

"Not ... that." Mace couldn't type yet, his hand was still in a cast. He still had a massive bruise on one side of his face, where Fahd had struck him. "Watching ... Hogan's ... farm ... weekend."

"You're farm-sitting for Mr. Hogan this weekend."

Mace nodded.

"Okay ... understand, no worries. Sig can probably find another couple to go."

Mace lifted his hand, still encased in the plaster. "Be ... careful," he said.

Marcus looked down at the floor of the stall, still deep in manure. "Brother, don't I know it. She is one beautiful woman. She's smart, ambitious, strong ... everything you could want in a wife."

Mace, sitting on the four-wheeler, tapped his chest with one hand.

"Yeah, well, that's the rub, isn't it? But I really think she'll try to understand, Mace. She's open, at least. She's actually looking forward to the concert. It was her idea."

Mace got up off the four-wheeler and went into the tack room. He emerged holding two horse collars from the family's harness rigs, one large, and one small. He set them down on the seat of the four-wheeler. Marcus stared at them for a moment, then looked up at Mace. "What?"

Mace picked up the smaller one, then tried to pick up the other, but couldn't.

"Okay, yeah, yeah, Mace, I got it. You're thinking we're unequally yoked, right?" Marcus chuckled and Mace nodded his head, a sober expression on his face.

"Can't argue with you, brother. But where there's life there's hope, right? She could come around."

Mace lifted a cautionary hand. "Be ... careful."

"Yeah, I hear you, little brother." Marcus waved a gloved hand at the stall. "Let's get this done." Marcus picked up another load of manure with his pitchfork.

***

Amos Hogan was in his sixties, struggling to manage a large dairy farm after his much younger wife of fifteen years left him ... for another woman. Irascible, crusty, and by his own admission ornery beyond all salvation, he nonetheless appreciated the help Mace offered. Hogan used Mace often when he needed an extra hand around his farm.

When Hogan had first asked if Mace could help out on the weekend, Mace had his mother call and ask Mr. Hogan if Zoe could come along.

"Zoe ... that's a girl's name, ain't it?" the old farmer asked in his wheezy voice.

"It is, Amos," Claire replied, over the phone. "But she's strong; she keeps up her parents' place. She's no stranger to hard work. And Mace got into a little bit of an accident, Amos, so he's only got one good working hand at the moment."

"Ehh ... yeah, I heard about that. Whatser last name?"

"Davidovitch."

"She that girl they went after, t'other day, at the school?"

"That's her, Amos. She and Mace have become good friends."

"Well ... I guess. Yeah, I suppose. Mace'll look after her though, right? Tell her what's what? I don't have time to go nursemaidin' some little girl all over the farm."

"No, Amos, you don't have to worry about that. Mace will take care of her. You'll be there the whole time, though, I assume, Amos?"

"Yeah, nowhere else for me to go. I'll look after 'em."

"Oh good, Amos, that would be so kind. Mace will need another hand, and Zoe...well, Zoe is a little fragile right now, and she seems to perk up whenever she's around Mace, so it would do them both some good."

"I'm no babysitter, now," the old man warned.

"You're a good man, Amos Hogan."

"Yeah, yeah, don't let it git around. I'll be over t'pick up Mace Friday after school or so. I suppose Miss whatsername'll need a ride, too?"

***

Hogan's white Ford F350 pulled into the Creamery's semi-circular driveway in the dark of the morning, crunching the snow that had fallen on a Thursday and which was now a thick, frozen white crust on the ground. Mace came out of the house, followed by Marcus carrying a large blue camp cooler.

"Amos, I've packed some things for Mace and Zoe and you, for the weekend," Claire said, wiping her hands on her apron.

"We'll make out okay on our own," Hogan growled ... but he didn't say no. He'd tasted Claire's cooking, and he wouldn't say no. "Load it up, younker," he said. "We're burnin' daylight. Got cows to milk."

Mace hopped into the front of the truck and they went over to the Davidovitch place. Zoe came out of the door like a shot, screen door slamming, running down the front porch steps with her coat half on, long red pigtails flying, a brown paper sack in her mouth, before the Ford came to a stop. Mace hopped out, and she clambered up into the middle seat, throwing her brown sack on the dashboard.

"Hey Mr. Hogan! Thanks for letting me come. Mrs. Ironbridge told me to make sure I didn't make you wait, so I'm ready. Lookin' forward to it. Mrs. Ironbridge said you had cows. I *love* cows! Do you like cows, Mace?" Mace smiled noiselessly. "See, Mace loves cows, I *knew* it!" she exclaimed, and instinctively grabbed Mace's left hand. "This'll be great!" She looked at Hogan and then back at Mace, head on a swivel, smiling from ear to ear.

"What's in the sack, young lady?"

"Oh, my mother said I was supposed to take my own food, so she packed me a sandwich. It's tuna fish. You like tuna fish?"

"That all yer gonna eat till Sunday?"

"Don't eat much. Mom says I have a high metabolism."

"Uh huh."

"Mrs. Ironbridge said you had seventy cows. That's a lot of cows. How do you milk them all, and twice a day? That's wild! That's a lot of milk. My mother won't let me drink milk. She says it's bad for you. Is that what you think, Mr. Hogan?"

Mace took his left arm and draped it up along the back edge of the front seat and over Zoe's shoulders. It was like a light switch. As though it was the most natural thing in the world, Zoe unconsciously let out a long sigh, ever so subtly nestled into the crook of his arm, put her head against his chest, and became quiet.

Hogan leaned forward over the steering wheel, sent a significant glance across Zoe to Mace, and put the truck in gear. 'Ain't love grand,' he wheezed to himself.

***

"So are you ready for Annapolis?" Tack asked his son Marcus that Friday evening. Mace had already gone off with Amos Hogan, and Tack and Claire were alone with Marcus, who sat at table, broad shoulders, a rough-cut plaid work shirt open at the neck, the line of his throat leading to a masculine jaw.

"I think so, Pop. They say the first year is pretty tough."

"No tougher than what you do around here, I'm thinking," Tack replied. "You'll do fine."

"Do you have any idea what you'll study?" Claire asked.

"Military history, *Maman*, no question." Marcus had been reading about wars and battles since he could open a book, and he was the acknowledged expert on World War II at school.

"You should do well," she answered. She'd made a *boeuf bourguignon* with a *gratin dauphinois*, and an apple *tart tétin* for dessert. "It is something you enjoy."

"Do you think they'll let me try out for the football team?" Marcus asked. "These days, unless you're recruited, it seems like you don't stand a chance."

"You go try," Tack said. "Don't let those high-powered recruits intimidate you. Most of those kids aren't half as tough as you are. You walk on and let your performance there do the talking."

"Lot of top-drawer talent, Pop," Marcus answered, selecting a large ladleful of stew.

Tack looked at his son. Marcus had gotten the best from both he and his wife—height, strength, rugged good looks, and a burning, passionate idealism. Marcus was a distillation of his own intensity coupled with Claire's drive.

"Marcus, when you're on the field, one on one with these guys, the only thing that matters is the amount of fierceness and determination and guts and intensity each of you brings to each play. Doesn't matter who has a pedigree or who was all-state this or all-American that—when you step on the field, just decide that you'll be better than anyone else there. Give it your best; it's all you can do."

"This game of you Americans, what you call football. Brutal sport."

"It's a game, that's true, Claire, but it teaches young men lessons that are hard to find elsewhere."

"Such as?" she asked, breaking a baguette and wiping her plate. She winked at Marcus, sharing a hidden joke, enjoying leading Tack onto a soapbox.

Tack, oblivious, explained. "Such as carrying on when you're exhausted—what did Jesus say? '*He who endures to the end will be saved.*' Endurance is not something everyone is born with. The game teaches you to endure, to carry on when you're tired, or hurt, or when it doesn't look like there is any hope. It teaches teamwork. The best teams are those with no individual stars, only everyone doing their job to the best of their ability. If the body of Christ worked like that, we'd have much stronger churches. And it teaches setting aside one's own interests for the interests of the larger team. Personal sacrifice, and—"

"*Oui, oui*, I get it," Claire said, smiling. She turned to Marcus. "Are you sure you have the dedication to carry on through this school? It is how many years?"

"*Quatre, maman*."

"So four years. This is a long time. You are sure this is where God wants you?"

"*Oui Maman*. I mean, look at everything I've ever been interested in, my entire life. All I've ever wanted to be was a warrior. You and Dad have always told me that God usually prepares a person by shaping their interests, and He calls them into places that match what He's prepared them for all their lives. Everything seems to point that way."

"Yes, well, sometimes this is a good indicator, *Mon fils*, and sometimes not ... but you have prayed about this, and it seems that God has opened doors. Not many young men from the bricks of Minnesota are selected to attend this school, no?"

Tack and Marcus laughed. "What?" Claire asked.

"Nothing, nothing," Tack answered. "And you're right; Marcus getting an appointment was sort of a minor miracle in itself. God opens doors. We walk through them in faith."

"So ... you will need to be dedicated. This will need to be a high priority, yes?"

"I'll keep my eyes on Jesus, *Maman*, don't worry."

"Well, you are correct that I am worried about where your eyes are, *Mon fils*."

Marcus looked over at his mother, wondering. She leaned back in her chair while he continued to devour his beef. Tack knew what was on her mind.

"You and Sig are very close. What are her thoughts about you going off to become a warrior? Does she wish to be the wife of a warrior?"

"We haven't really talked about it, *Maman*. We're not that serious."

"You mean, *you* are not that serious. She's been to dinner here many times, Marcus. You've been seeing each other most of your last year at this school, *oui*? Are you telling me she is not ... attached?"

"To tell you the truth, we haven't talked much about it."

"A woman like that does not involve herself in a man's life unless she wants something," Claire said, and for a moment Marcus saw a much harder woman sitting across the table. "She's a very beautiful woman, she is very intelligent, and in my opinion I think she has plans for you."

After a long pause, Marcus said, "*Bon boeuf*," with his mouth full, holding up his fork.

"*Vous savez ce que je veux dire*," Claire replied, not to be deterred.

"She is beautiful, *Maman, oui*."

"She is also very dangerous."

"I know that too, *Maman*." Marcus cut into another piece of beef. Claire looked over at Tack, pointing her fork at him, frustrated. "You tell him."

"You're the expert here, my dear. Marcus and I have talked about this issue before."

Marcus put down his knife. "I know what you're going to tell me, and I agree. She's not a believer, she has no inkling of what life in the Spirit is, and I could get in a lot of trouble. But I think I can handle it."

Claire leaned back and put up her hands in frustration. "Men! You, none of you, have any inking of how women think."

"Inkling, *mon cheri*," Tack said quietly.

"Inking, winkling, it doesn't matter." Claire waved one hand in the air, holding a piece of bread. "Bah! This is not something a mother can say to a son," she said, turning to Tack.

Tack finally spoke up. "Marcus, God does not make human beings into robots, He leaves us free will, to make our own choices. Since you've been old enough, we've always let you make your own choices. Others have kept their children from making the hard decisions, but we have always thought that if you boys were going to make good decisions as adults, you needed the practice, and sometimes you needed the consequences of making wrong decisions. I've told you what I think about dating—I think it's a dangerous practice—but I am going to let you make your own decisions about that. You know my advice about that has always been to let God pick your mate. Don't go and try to find your own."

"I know that, Pop, and I appreciate it."

"But here, Marcus ... here, if you make a wrong decision, the consequences are huge, and painful, and not easy to recover from. They're life-changing. And as far as I know, they don't let married men remain at the Academy."

"Pop, we're not going to run away and get married."

Claire smacked Tack on his shoulder. "Mon Dieu, you beat around the tree." She turned to Marcus. "*Toi ... mon fils ... tien toi a l'écarte d'elle!*"

Marcus blushed and lowered his eyes.

"You know what your mother is talking about, Marcus. Big things start with small things. And sometimes when you put your foot along a small path, it tends to funnel the rest of your walk until what you thought was just a little deviation becomes a deep ditch, and you can't get out without some serious pain."

"I know this game from the woman's perspective, my son," Claire said. "I know this woman. She wants to crag you and put you up on her trophy wall."

"'Bag', not 'crag'," Tack corrected.

"Whatever." Claire pointed her finger at her son. "She has weapons against which you have no defense, Marcus. Every woman knows this, and Sigrid knows how to use them better than most."

"But what if through me she can be introduced to real life?" Marcus asked, spreading his hands out, reminiscent of an old Gallic gesture. Claire looked over at Tack, eyebrows passing the question to him.

"It's possible, Marcus. I won't say it isn't—nothing is impossible with God. And I've known in the past where a young believing man pursued an unbelieving woman and led her to Christ." Tack looked significantly at Claire, who reached out and touched his arm. "But ... typically God tends not to work this way."

"How do you mean?" his son asked. "It worked for you."

"Right now she's pursuing you, wouldn't you say?"

"She's chased him since she set foot in this town," Claire put in.

"*Oui, Maman*, you're right. But from what you both have told me, Pop pursued you as well, didn't he?"

"And so we come to the point," Tack answered. "What role has God played in all this? Where have you two given God the opportunity to work, to demonstrate that He is the One bringing this relationship about? When I was 'pursuing' your mother, as you put it, I wasn't actively pursuing her when I sensed there was no interest. I was just praying for her, and God led me to write her a letter, and…"

"And that letter came at a good time," Claire finished. "Can you say that you have prayed about this relationship and committed it to God, Marcus?"

Marcus looked down at his plate. "I can't say that," he replied honestly. "But ... there's no way Sig would either understand or agree to a relationship like that."

"Then doesn't it seem like you are going somewhere God is not leading?" his father asked gently.

Marcus sighed and leaned back from the table. "I don't know, Pop," he said, frustrated. "It's confusing. I mean, I like her—a lot—and I wonder why? Why would God permit me to have this heart for her?"

"You are sure God is the source of these feelings you have?" Tack asked.

"Enough," Claire said, with a Gallic finality. "You are a man, Marcus. Realize that you will always think like a man, and men many times do not know how women think. Do not make my mistake, *Mon fils*. I too once thought I had a heart for a young man, and it was just my own flesh, my own human nature. There was nothing of God in it. It is too so easy to confuse one with the other."

"I know, *Maman*. You told me that story. I'll be careful."

"Your life is in your hands, Marcus. Your mother and I can't live it for you. We can give you the best advice we have, gleaned from living our own lives, but you have to make your own decisions. You alone are accountable to God for your life."

"It would be the same if you were a daughter," Claire put in. "This is not just because you are male."

"True," Tack confirmed. "If you were my daughter, we'd be telling you the same thing, and we'd be giving you the same latitude to make your own decisions."

"I don't think Sig is getting any kind of advice like this," Marcus said grimly.

"No ... and it's her loss," Claire said sharply, swiping her baguette across the remains of sauce on her plate. "She could do with some."

Tack reached out a hand and caressed his wife's shoulder. "It requires a breaking first, my love," he said, "before anyone can hear anything like this."

"That is what I am afraid of," she answered in a whisper.

***

And so there Marcus sat, hands on the wheel of his dependable old Dodge pickup, taking a few deep breaths and running over last night's conversation in his head before going in to pick up Sig.

The Jannsen's home was massive, with a main central unit and wings on each side, arching around to embrace the long semi-circular entrance way. The garage, holding eight bays, stood off in the distance. There was even a butler. Marcus had never seen a butler, but there he was, standing in the open doorway, wondering why a young man in a faded gold Dodge pickup truck was sitting in the Jannsen's driveway. Sitting there, taking things in, Marcus was struck with the disparity between his own upbringing and this opulence. And in so thinking, the disparity in their spiritual backgrounds came to mind, only this time, it was his upbringing that could be considered suffused in opulence—rich in the knowledge of God—compared to Sig's life, impoverished, starved, ignorant of anything to do with the spiritual realm. With that thought motivating him to share what he'd known all his life, he popped open the door and went to meet his date.

The *New Times Comin'* was a popular Christian rock band. Marcus had never heard of them, but Sig had discovered the group doing a search on the web, and she thought they would be interesting to hear. "Maybe it might be a good first introduction to this stuff you are always talking about," she'd said when she first proposed the idea.

Now, tonight, standing in the foyer as she came down the long winding staircase, he wasn't so sure. He wasn't clear how he was going to keep his mind on anything except the tall blonde creature before his eyes. Dressed in an ice-blue turtleneck and a white jacket over black leggings, she smiled at him, blue eyes locking on his from halfway up the stairs.

"Hey, World Changer," she said. It had become her pet name for him, and he felt just then that with her next to him, he *could* change the world.

They went to the concert with another couple, friends of Sig's, who also expressed interest in a 'Christian' rock group. Before they got to the show, the talk was all about what was happening in Europe—Sig's friend Maria was from Italy, her mother an oil company executive for Eni, and her escort that night was a guy Marcus didn't know, from another town. The Italian economy was tilting crazily out of control, but Maria and her date just talked about the most popular soccer players, or what new music videos they'd seen, or what new wardrobe malfunction had happened to the most infamous celebrities they'd heard about. Marcus asked a few questions about the Vatican, since it turned out Maria lived in Rome. Maria was a Catholic—"every Italian is a Catholic, Marcus!" she said, "Didn't you know?" and laughed in a high, giggling voice.

It was quickly apparent that Maria's date had zero interest in Christianity. Marcus found himself a little nervous, because it was obvious Maria's date, and Maria, were both looking forward to the same type of immoral denouement to the evening. He wondered what Sig was getting him into. But the evening went on and Sig was scintillating, and beautiful, and very affectionate. Any thought about the disparity between the nature of his present companions and the subject of the concert soon disappeared in threads of feminine laughter, the smell of Sig's perfume, and something indefinable that gently rocked him into a dulled acceptance of everything around him, as though it was the most natural thing in the world, convincing him that everything would work out.

The music at the concert did nothing for Marcus, though he could see the others enjoyed the beat, even though they couldn't understand the lyrics. Nothing different from the other music they listened to, they said. Marcus couldn't see that they were too far wrong, for try as he might, he couldn't find any reverence or peace or reference to the God he knew. But Sig was there, close on his arm, smiling, laughing, enjoying the music and enjoying him. He found himself confused, exposed to new feelings, a new and different spectrum of life in which there was another person, a woman, tied to him, bonded to him, someone incredibly attractive, and for the first time the surreptitious and powerful nature of the flesh struck deeply into his soul, making him think what life would be like with a woman like this on his arm. God made man to be bonded to woman, and when the nature of such a bonding first makes itself known to a young man, it can be powerful and overwhelming.

After the concert they drove back to Sig's house. Sig's parents were out, and soon Marcus found himself alone with Sig as Maria and her date inevitably disappeared into one of the bedrooms. He could tell Sig was hoping he would have the same idea, and here he put on the brakes.

"Sig ... Sig ... " he was breathless from kissing her, from the intensity of her passion, and he had to hold her out at arm's length. "Sig, this is wonderful, but we don't really want to go further—"

Sig looked at him, eyes bright. "Why not?" she asked in a voice husky with passion. "Don't you want me?" She spread out her arms, threw out a hip, and stood there in all her feminine glory. Still wearing every stitch she'd started the evening with, she was nonetheless overpoweringly sensual. Marcus felt so confused—the lights were soft, the room appointed richly, and he could feel the pull of a life lived in luxury that surrounded him now, but he knew where the line was, and he wasn't going to go past that line. Not tonight.

"I want you, Sig, you know that, but the right way, in the right time. And this," he said, his arms sweeping around to take in the large living room, "this isn't the right place or the right time. I'm leaving for Annapolis soon; you're headed for Georgetown. Both of us have some big challenges in front of us and getting wrapped up physically right now isn't right—and above all that, we're not married."

She resisted the temptation to taunt him yet again about his prudish outlook on life, but instead sighed, turned away, and walked toward the window, folded her arms across her chest and looked out into the cold night, crisp under stars in a clear sky. He went to stand near her.

"It's this religious thing you have, isn't it?" she asked.

He didn't know how to answer her. It wasn't religion—she didn't know the difference between religion and relationship and there wasn't any way he could explain it—not now. He put his arms around her, she leaned her head back against his shoulder, and they both stared out into the dark night sky, neither of them knowing what to say or what to do.

Chapter 3

Mace & Zoe

"For I am not ashamed of the gospel, for it is the power of God for salvation to everyone who believes, to the Jew first and also to the Greek."

Romans 1:16

The farm in winter was like living in a postcard. Snow covered the evergreens; the house and barn and the hills in the distance were all covered in a purifying white blanket. The lake, completely covered in ice and blanketed in snow, stretched out like a huge white comforter. Wisps of smoke from wood cook stoves rose lazily into a steel-gray sky, and the world held its breath, waiting for the birth of spring. When Mace and Zoe went out to milk in the evenings, stumping through the snow with their headlamps on, they would turn their heads toward the woods and everywhere their beams would shine, tiny points of light winked at them—trees covered in frost, the tip of every branch, every twig would sparkle in the cold, crisp, clear night air like tiny diamonds.

Three years ago, Marcus had left for the Naval academy, and now Mace was a senior at Granite Sky High. *Eagles Wings Creamery* was milking ten cows—about 50 to 60 gallons of milk per day, and their automatic milking system could milk four at a time. He and Zoe had taken on most of the milking and cheese preparation tasks. Tack and Claire were getting on in years, and they welcomed help from the two youngsters.

"You get the cows, Zoe. I'll get the stalls." They were out on a Friday night, doing the milking. The stars were stark and clear in a black winter night's sky, and the air was cold and crisp. Mace took a pitchfork and a black plastic manure sled and headed for the stalls while Zoe called the cows. They each had a name, they each knew their own names and the names of the others in the herd, and when Zoe called each individually, the cow would step out of the bunched up group and move toward the gate. It was important that they come through the gate in the right order—an order they decided upon themselves. Zoe opened the gate for each cow and would call the next only after the previous cow moved through. In this way, everything was orderly, organized, and they tended to avoid a mass rush by 800-pound bovine creatures wanting oats. Oats were the incentive; when the cows stood to be milked, Zoe would put a scoop of oats in the feed trough rigged at the front of the milking stand.

Zoe ran the milking system while Mace shoveled manure out of the stalls. After the last cow was connected to the milking system, Zoe walked over to the cow stalls, put her arms up on the top board, and watched Mace shovel manure into the sled. Mace had grown into a solid, broad-shouldered, seventeen-year old young man, muscular, with a lean, sinewy frame and a fine-featured face, dark hair that occasionally fell across his forehead, and a wide mouth that could break into a wistful, heart-rending smile.

"So why do you muck out these stalls each day?" she asked. "Isn't it easier to just come in once in a while with a little front-loader and scoop it out all at once?"

Mace stopped for a bit and leaned on his pitchfork. "Could be," he said, "but then, where does that leave the cows?"

"They don't mind all that crap," she retorted.

"Well, maybe they don't, but what if they do? I think Mom and Dad are thinking of that line in the Bible that talks about the wise man having a care for the life of his beasts."

"Oh," she said. "That's nice, I guess."

"So," Mace said, changing the subject and bending over the manure again, "are they going to let you graduate this year?"

"That's what they say," Zoe answered, picking at a piece of straw. "I've got enough credits and I've already been accepted to Yale, Columbia, and, oh yeah, the University of Chicago."

Mace looked up from shoveling. "Those schools are pretty far away," he said, looking at her significantly.

"I know," she replied, tossing her head. "I can handle it ... I think."

"Well, they'd better let you graduate then, if you have your sights set on schools like those. Otherwise they'd have a whole bunch of college professors down on their heads. Those are some pretty heavyweight schools. Congratulations."

"It's no big deal, Mace. And there's no reason I can't graduate. Nothing in the State legal code says anything about age, fortunately. It just says that you have to complete the required number of credits. If a nine-year old completed the required credits, I suppose he could graduate."

"Well, you're fifteen and you've done it." Mace paused again and looked at her. "You know, Zoe, you're smarter than a lot of people. You know that, right?"

Zoe looked uncertain and distracted. "That's what everyone says. I don't think about it much."

Mace nodded. "That's probably good," he said, partly to himself. "What will you study in college?" He put in the last forkful of manure and before he could get to it, Zoe lunged for the rope to pull the sled.

"I've got it," she said quickly.

"Zoe, the thing weighs more than you do."

"I can do it." She threw her body weight into the rope, leaning back and pulling hard. The sled didn't budge. She pulled again; nothing. Mace moved next to her. "Let me help you," he said, and together they hauled the sled out into the pasture, where they turned it over and dumped the load into the snow.

"Literature," Zoe said, breathing hard. Her breath fogged in the cold night air.

"What?"

"You asked me what I want to study."

"Oh, right." Mace pulled the empty sled and began walking back to the next stall.

"What about you?" Zoe asked, trudging along next to him.

"Well, I think I'd kind of like to study the same thing. You know I want to write one day."

"What kind of things do you want to write?"

Mace stopped just outside the barn, and she could see his breath in the night air as he spoke. He leaned on the pitchfork.

"I want to write things that move people. I want to write stories that touch them and make them think about things they don't normally think about. Everyone we know, all the kids we're at school with—all they think about are just the things that touch their own little world here in Granite Sky, or maybe their favorite television shows, or the rock star that happens to be popular that month. What they think about is what the mainstream media tells them to think about, and today that has nothing to do with the really important questions in life. No one dwells on important things anymore. It's like we've all been lulled to sleep in some giant manufactured dream where everyone gets to live the life they dream about vicariously, through pop stars or sports stars or some reality show. They depend on some new thing they wear, or something they eat, to give them some kind of new attitude, or to help them get through the day. It's crazy! It's like they assume the world will go on as it always has, without any kind of effort on their part. I want to reach these people who are asleep and wake them up."

'Good luck with that,' Zoe said, under her breath.

"I want to write stories that help people get a better picture of who God is and what He's like."

"How will you do *that*?" she asked, with a shade of respectful deference. Whenever Mace talked about God Zoe throttled back her tendency toward brash confidence and listened carefully.

Mace began to shovel again. "I don't know yet," he answered, smiling. "But maybe you can help."

"Me? How can *I* help? I don't know half as much about God as you do. I'm Jewish, remember. Most of us don't even think there *is* a God. I know my folks don't."

Mace laughed at that. "I think there are a lot of Jews who think there's a God. But hey, you're a good writer, aren't you?"

"I guess."

"Well, so many people who try to write about God don't know how to actually write. They think it doesn't matter if they spell words incorrectly, or if their grammar is horrible, or if their sentences run on or aren't complete. It's as if they say to themselves, 'Well, God gave me this jewel of an insight, so it doesn't matter how I express it, people will just have to read it anyway, because it comes directly from God.' As if God doesn't really care about excellence in things. They use Him as an excuse not to work hard and study and master the craft of writing, or whatever it is they're doing—at least, that's what I've heard Dad say. It's why most of Christianity today has a reputation for mediocrity. You can help me write when you're not off studying at college."

"I *hate* mediocrity," Zoe said, picking at a splintering shred of wood. "It's like eating half-cooked chicken."

"Half-cooked chicken can make you pretty sick," Mace said, smiling.

"My point *exactly*."

Mace went on loading the sled, letting his thoughts wander toward what he might like to write about one day, when Zoe, who had been standing off to the side with an introspective look on her face, one hand pulling at the other, shifting her weight from one leg to the other, said "Mace, take off your glove."

He stopped and looked at her for a long moment. He spoke softly, reassuringly. "Zoe, it's been ... it's been a little more than three years. How will you be able to make it at college if you can't—"

"Mace, *please*?" Her hands fluttered in the air. "Every time you talk about God I feel weird, like there's something important I don't know, like I'm going to have a test on something I haven't studied, but I don't know what, and it reminds me of that day." She was twisting her hands together, upset and anxious. "There are some bad things around, Mace."

"I know, Zoe; I understand. It's okay." He set his pitchfork against one wall of the stall and removed the glove on his right hand. The tendons and ligaments had knitted satisfactorily, although he had some trouble in cold weather, and there was still and always would be a large, dark red knurled scar in the center of his palm where the pointed metal had pierced his hand and ripped the flesh while he tried to keep Fahd from cutting Zoe's throat. Every time since then, when Zoe became frightened or anxious, the only thing that would do would be for her to put her eyes on Mace's scarred hand, or better, hold it in her own, and somehow it connected her to the moment and, more importantly, to the fact that she was still alive, that someone had cared enough, had loved her enough, to risk such pain to keep her alive. It was a peculiar malady, and neither Mace nor his parents had ever heard of anything like it. Apparently visible evidence that she could see and touch was enough to drive home the truth that someone cared for her, and so for that reason, seeing Mace's scar seemed to give her a measure of peace.

She stepped closer to Mace and took his wounded hand in hers, put it to the side of her face, and looked up at him, eyes wide and wet. "Why do I get frightened when you talk about God, Mace?"

Mace caressed the side of her face and then folded her in his arms. She pressed up against his chest, trembling. The trauma of that near-death experience had never really faded. "God doesn't want to frighten you, Zoe. I think it's for the same reason that I can talk normally when I'm with you, and that it never happens with anyone else."

She leaned back away from him, still in his arms, and stared at him with eyes wide. "Why *is* that? I've noticed that like, a gazillion times! It's so *weird*! Why is it that you talk normally with me, but if I'm not around, you talk ... slowly?"

Mace looked thoughtfully at her for a moment, and then, pensively, said, "I think these two things are for the same reason, Zoe. It's because He wants us to know something important."

"What, you mean, like, God is trying to tell us the same thing?"

"Sort of. He's trying to get our attention in a way that we'll recognize. I know what he's trying to tell *me*, Zoe."

"I thought God was some big old man with a long white beard who just sat around on clouds and watched what was going on without really getting too involved."

Mace smiled wistfully. "Not exactly. He's talking to us all the time. I'm pretty sure I know what He's saying to me about this."

"What is it?"

"I'm not sure I want to tell you. It's sort of personal." Mace seemed hesitant to say more. He put his hands in the pockets of his gold chore coat.

She snorted derisively, smacked him in the chest again, and looked directly into his eyes. "You tell me what it is, Mace Ironbridge. You have to tell me everything. That's the rule."

Laughing nervously, the seventeen-year old said, "Okay, okay, then. I think what God wants me to know," and he hesitated again, but then dived ahead, "with this ability to only talk normally when you're around is that ... I'm not really complete without you." He put both of his hands on her shoulders and looked into her eyes. "You're my other half, Zoe. I think that's why, when you're with me, I can speak normally. If you're not around, I don't talk easily or well. I don't understand it, but I think ... I think God is telling me that you're the one I'm supposed to spend the rest of my life with." There, he'd gotten it out, finally, after carrying the knowledge around with him for the last three years. He'd known it in his very bones since the day he rescued her, but this was the first time he ever shared with her what he believed about the two of them. He held his breath, waiting to see how she would react.

She forcibly crushed herself against his chest and wrapped her arms around him. "Oh, Mace, that's no secret. I've known *that* since the day you rescued me." They held each other then for a few quiet moments, there in the cold barn, their breath rising together from the center of the cow stall.

"How did you know?" Mace asked with a tinge of wonder.

"I honestly can't say," she whispered softly, into the folds of his chore coat. "I just knew."

"Well, I thought it was my big secret."

"Ha! Not." But she became pensive, and after a moment she said, very softly, "As long as we're telling secrets, I need to tell you something." She paused, looking nervous in his arms. "You probably think this is stupid, but I get the shakes if I'm away from you for too long. Mom thinks it's some kind of mental thing, and she wants me to see a shrink, but I know what it is. As soon as I'm with you, it disappears." It was true. Ever since the assault, Zoe had no peace unless she was close to Mace. They had been inseparable since the day Mace came out of the hospital. On the weekends, Zoe would beg her parents to let her help out at the Creamery so she could be near Mace. At the end of each school day, Mace made it a habit to set aside a few minutes to just sit and talk with Zoe after their classes so she could feel safe again.

"Yeah, Zoe, I knew that. My folks and I figured that out a while ago. We think that's part of what God is trying to talk to you about."

After a time Zoe looked up at him. "But ... I'm not getting it. What is that God wants me to know about? I have no idea."

"Zoe ... it's pretty clear. My Dad told me about this a little after the accident, and I'm surprised I didn't see it sooner."

"Told you about what?"

Mace paused for a moment before he said, "Zoe, how much do you know about how Jesus died?"

"Not much. Jesus isn't a big topic of conversation at home, if you know what I mean."

Mace produced an ironic smile. "Right. I mean, do you know exactly *how* He died?"

"I suppose it had something to do with a cross or something, since that's what's on top of all the churches. I saw Spartacus once—you know, that movie? Didn't Jesus die on some kind of cross thing too?"

"Right. And do you know how people die when they're crucified?"

"Well, I guess they sort of ... what, just tie them up and hang them there, right? Not really."

"Not exactly. What happens is that first they scourge a person before they actually crucify them—"

"That scourging thing is with a whip, right?"

"Right, at the time, the Romans used a whip with leather thongs that had little sharp pieces of bone in them, so that after just a few strokes, the person's back looked like raw hamburger."

"Ughh," the girl exclaimed. "That's gross."

"It gets worse. After they scourge the person, they take two big pieces of wood and make them into a cross, and then they make the person carry it. When they finally get to the place where they'll crucify the person, he drops the cross on the ground so it's laying flat. Then they slam the person down on his back and spread his arms out wide, one arm along one side of the cross, the other along the other, and they stretch out the person's feet down the long side. They don't tie them to the wood. They take big iron nails and they have other people flatten out the person's hands, and they nail their hands into the wood while their arms are spread, and they put one foot on top of another and put one big nail through both of them." Zoe was horror-stricken, but he continued. "Sometimes they drive the nails through the wrist bones, here," he said, pointing to his wrist, and then talking slowly to make a point, "but sometimes they would drive the nails through the palms of their hands." Zoe's eyes widened as she stared again at his injured right palm.

"You mean ... "

"Every time you look at my hand, Zoe, you realize what I did for you, and it makes you feel better, right?" Zoe nodded, speechless. She backed up against one of the walls in the stall and slid to the ground, overcome with emotion as the analogy struck home. He went on. "God permitted this to happen to me because He wanted it to be a reminder to you. He wants you to know that He loves you, and He proved it to you the same way I did, but He did more for you than I did that day, Zoe. He did what I couldn't do. I only got hurt a little, but He died for you."

Zoe's eyes widened. "But *why?* I mean, if you Gentiles are right, and you say that that Jesus guy was the Son of God, then ... then *why* would God let his own Son die? It doesn't make sense."

"Well, it doesn't make sense to us, but it makes perfect sense when you think about it from God's perspective."

"Help me with that. I don't get it. All I have is my perspective, and I'm Jewish, don't forget, so ... help me out here."

"Okay." He leaned the pitchfork up against the wall and sat down next to her.

"Wait ... put your coat around us, Mace. You know, like ... like you did then. I'm getting cold." She would ask him to do this whenever she was feeling nervous or upset or emotional. He would never make fun of her, never complain, but would always stop what he was doing and wrap her up until she felt better. There would be times at school when something in particular would upset her, and she would make a beeline to his classroom, burst in, and look around with wild eyes until she found him. Everyone in school realized that it was something she couldn't control, a byproduct of the trauma of that day, and no one—ever—made fun of her. The teachers understood, and they never complained when the wild-eyed, red-haired, rail-thin girl burst into their classrooms. It was why Mace took his coat with him to every class, winter or summer—he never knew when it might be needed.

Now, in the cold barn, with gentleness, he took off the same old worn golden work coat and draped the left part of it over Zoe. She put her left arm through, and he put the right side over his own shoulders. As his shoulders had broadened, it no longer fit with both of them in the sleeves. They snuggled closer.

"That's better," she sighed, wriggling with relief, and looked up at him. "So, what's God's perspective? How can it make sense for God to put His Son to death?"

"To explain that, we have to understand something about human nature. According to what God says, our nature is so messed up and dirty that unless it's changed, we'll never be able to be near God. But most people believe that human beings are basically good."

"And why not? Why would God make bad people, people He can't be around?"

"Well, okay, let's go back to the beginning. If God is God, then He's perfect, right?"

"Logical," she replied. "Maybe not so poetic, but logical."

"So if He's perfect, He can't have anything around Him that isn't perfect. It's sort of like someone who decides that they will only have perfectly white tablecloths in their restaurant, because the rule is that a restaurant can only be perfect if it has perfectly white tablecloths, and then someone comes along and tries to put a dirty, manure-stained tablecloth on one of the tables. Well, by definition then, it wouldn't be a perfect restaurant anymore, and the owner just won't let that happen—*can't* let that happen. It would destroy the meaning of perfection. You can't have something that isn't perfect and say that it's perfect."

"Okay. Good so far."

"So God says our human nature is not perfect."

"Wait, wait, just a minute. If God is all so perfect, and He made us—the storyline is that He made us, right?" Mace nodded. "Well then, if He made us, why did He make us with such a lousy rotten nature? Doesn't make any sense."

Mace leaned his head back against the wooden stall wall made of pressure-treated 2x6 pine boards. He spread his hands out, and she again caught a glimpse of that gnarled knot of scar tissue in his right hand. "Zoe, oh, it makes so much sense. Look, imagine your parents forced you to tell them each morning that you loved them, or else they would beat you. Imagine if," and Mace hesitated again, but decided to plunge onward, "if I forced you to say you loved me. It wouldn't be real love, because real love is only love that is offered freely, from the heart."

"I ... I know," she said softly, taking his free hand in hers. He knew what her parents were like and he knew this was a sore spot, but he also knew she could easily identify with the analogy. He went on.

"This is what is so amazingly wonderful and awesome about this 'free will' thing. See, God gave each one of us a free will, to make choices, to determine what we do and where we go in life, and so when you think about it, this free will He gave us is the only thing that makes love possible. Without it, we couldn't really love anyone or anything. The nature of love is that it must be given freely, and so we needed a human nature that had free will. But it was also a huge risk, making human beings with the ability to choose, because what if they chose not to love God?"

"Why would they?" she asked.

"Why would they what?"

"Why would they choose to love God?"

Mace thought for a moment. "Why do you ... why do you love me?"

Zoe didn't hesitate. "Because you *saved* me, Mace. And then because every time

I've needed you, you are *always* there—I mean *always*. You're *never* not around, Mace, you're always there, keeping me safe, helping me, doing stuff for me and with me, and you never complain. You never have to run off with the guys, or go off to find your own 'space' or whatever. I *know* you love me—you don't even have to say it. How can a person not love someone like that?"

"So to you it sort of looks like I'm giving up my life for you, right?"

She paused to reflect on that, and then, quietly, said, "Yeah. Yeah, that's it. That's what it feels like."

"Always remember that it was God who sent me out to the field that day, Zoe, and it was God who gave me the courage to intervene, and it was God who made sure things worked out the way they did. And God saved us from something worse than what would have happened to you, Zoe. He is always with us—I mean *always*. He's never not around, He's always there, keeping us safe, helping us, doing stuff for us and, if we let Him, doing stuff with us. He *did* give up His life for us. How can a person not love someone like that?"

She punched him lightly on the shoulder. "Yeah, yeah, okay. Touché. I get it."

"So here we have this free will thing that makes love possible, but also carries with it a risk that we humans might not choose to love God."

"Okay, wait, so, how, *exactly*, do people actually love God?"

"What do you mean?" Mace asked.

"I mean, what kinds of things do people actually do if they want to love God, practically speaking? I know the kind of stuff you do for me—and don't be all macho, you goof, I know you love me."

Mace smiled self-consciously. "Yeah, okay, I do."

"*I knew it,*" she said triumphantly, pumping her fist in the air. "So what do people do when they want to show that they love God?"

"Jesus gave a simple answer to that question. He said, 'If you love me, you'll obey me.' Basically, He said that if we love Him, we'll do what He says."

"Okaaay," she answered hesitantly, "but that means you have to be able to figure out what He says, right?"

"Right. And that's one of the challenging parts of living a Christian life—learning to hear what He says to us."

"Okay, okay, I can see where that would be a challenge, trying to hear what the God of the Universe would be saying to you personally. But let's go back to why God would make us human beings with lousy natures. If He's God, He can do anything, and yeah, I understand the love part, so He had to put in the free will thing so we could actually love and be loved. But why make us with rotten natures in the first place?"

"So what happened is, the first two people He made, Adam and Eve, had free will. They had the choice to obey Him or disobey Him, and they chose to disobey Him, and since you know what He said about loving Him—if you love Him, you'll obey Him—what does that say about the character of Adam and Eve?"

"That they must not have loved Him?" she said, questioning.

"Right. What it boiled down to was that they wanted to be like God—they wanted to have all the knowledge and power and wisdom that they knew God had; they wanted that for themselves. They wanted that more than they wanted to obey Him. They didn't like being dependent on God. So ... they believed the lie Satan told them, lying to them about how they could gain this knowledge and power and wisdom, and by doing so, they made a decision that demonstrated their true nature—which, oh by the way, is the same as *our* true nature. What it really comes down to, then and now, is that each human being has a choice, to either try to become *like* God, or acknowledge that God is God and let Him be God and just do what He says. But it's our nature, every one of us, to try and be a god."

"That's tragic."

"Well, it's human nature. Every two-legged creature since Adam and Eve has sinned. No person ever born—except one—has been perfect."

"So if what you said about being perfect is true, and everyone has sinned, and if the guy with the restaurant can't have any tablecloth that isn't perfectly white, then there's no hope for anyone, except whoever that one person was; Jesus, I suppose you mean. You screw up once, you're done, you're not perfect anymore."

"Exactly."

"But hey, if God is perfect and He knows everything, He would have known that would have happened. He would have known what choice Adam and Eve would make. Why didn't He prevent them from doing that?"

"Back to the free will thing, Zoe. If He had prevented them, it would have meant He would have taken away their free will, and then their love for Him would have been false—"

"And therefore, not perfect, and therefore, not allowed, yeah got it. So He couldn't have forced them to do anything. Yeah, that makes sense."

"Right. Even today, He doesn't force anybody to do anything. Everyone has to make their own choice. You can't depend on your mother or father's relationship with God; it doesn't matter if you're Greek or Jewish or whatever. You can't use anyone else to make an excuse for not facing up to the terms and conditions of that sacrifice."

"I'm piecing this together, Mace. So, let me think about this. I get frightened every time you bring up God. It feels like those dreams you have, you know, where you're going into an exam and you realize you never even took one class during the semester? That's how I feel whenever you talk about God. Like I'm gonna face something terribly important and I've missed the prep for it, or like I've never even learned about some really important thing and I'm going to be held accountable for it anyway. That's scary."

"With our own human nature, Zoe, we're never going to able to be in heaven with God. What He is letting you sense is the natural fear a person will have when they stand before God to be judged, and they haven't made Him God—they haven't obeyed Him."

The fifteen-year old adolescent female realized suddenly that she had been given a supernatural insight into what one possible future might be. She sat stunned for a moment.

"You're not lying. I know it. I sense it. That's what's behind my fear."

Mace nodded quietly.

"So what ... what do I do? What does anyone have to do? We're stuck."

"Well, yes and no. Back to your question about why God would make people with bad natures ... He made them and gave the free will, and as you know, Zoe, our choices actually make us who and what we are, but God knew how things would go, so He made sort of a provision."

"What do you mean, a 'provision'? You mean, like some sort of 'out'?"

"Sort of. You remember that God is perfect, right?"

"Got that—He's perfect, we're not, so we're not allowed into the restaurant, right."

"Everyone *will* live eternally, Zoe, but the problem is, unless we're clean, unless we're perfect, we won't be able to be near a perfectly sinless, holy God. We won't be able to be in heaven; we'll be in the other place—hell. That's a really bad place. If you've even had one bad thought, if you've ever told just one lie, if you've done anything that would be considered not in line with what God would want you to have done, then you've missed the mark—which is what the word 'sin' means. So now you have a situation where everyone is missing the mark all the time, every person ever born, and the only way anyone can be made clean is if a perfectly innocent person is sacrificed in their place—"

"So *that's* what all those sacrifices were about in the Old Testament," she burst out, and smacked her forehead dramatically with her left hand, giving the coat a hard tug, tightening it around both of them. "I remember now ... *that's* what I wanted to ask you about that day ... *I remember!* God, this is so *weird*! I wanted to know why God would set up a religious system with all that blood and sacrifice, and Mr. Lanahan didn't have any idea, and he said, 'Go ask Mace Ironbridge.'"

"—but whoever wants to benefit from that perfect sacrifice needs to accept the terms and conditions of that sacrifice."

Zoe froze, the light of an epiphany dawning across her features. "*That's* what I've been anxious about, isn't it—those terms and conditions? I have no idea what they are, but you're saying that if I don't meet them, I don't get the benefit of that sacrifice. I don't get clean. That's the exam I sense is coming, and I've never even been to the class."

"Right. Your people in the Old Testament called it the 'blood atonement.' God is a God of perfect justice. There are spiritual 'laws' in the world. One of them is that when a person sins, it eventually results or 'calls for' a death. Something happens in the spirit realm when we sin, Zoe. It's like there is some giant account book that keeps a record, and when a sin is committed, a death is put on the account to be paid. To atone for sin then, there needs to be something that fulfills the requirement for a death. I haven't figured it all out, actually—I don't think anyone really has—but God set up the symbolism of animal sacrifice because it was supposed to show us all that sin caused death, and to make atonement for sin, it would cost the sinner a life—luckily for him, not his own life, but something precious to him. I mean, imagine if every time you or I sinned, to get right with God, to be forgiven, we would have to kill one of these cows."

Zoe's eyes widened. "That's terrible!"

"No ... what's worse is a God who would let us continue on in sin without teaching us that sin has consequences, and if we're going to avoid sin, those consequences have to be drastic."

"If what you're saying is true, man, in a pretty short time, you wouldn't have any cows left!"

"Yeah, our family's livelihood would disappear, wouldn't it? So it was back then, when God made that system. Those animals were people's main source of income—they were incredibly important to their lives. But He wanted them to understand how damaging and destructive sin was. And even at that, all those animal sacrifices pointed to the one huge, awesome sacrifice God made for each of us—His only son.

"The reason God sent His only Son, who was also God, to die was because only perfect innocence, perfect holiness would be able to make atonement for every person's sin. But ... again, we would have to accept the terms and conditions of that sacrifice for it to apply to us. One of those terms and conditions is that we obey Him; that we stop sinning."

"So you're saying He tells you to do stuff, like, every day?"

"He does. It's just a matter of being able to hear Him."

"That must be cool," the diminutive girl said softly, with an honest sense of wonder.

"Zoe, the comfort you find in seeing a physical reminder that someone cared enough about you to risk their life for you is something God is arranging for you so that you'll become aware of something greater and more important than what happened to us that day. I believe He let that happen so you could see how much He cares for you."

"Wait, wait, hold up, Mace. How could letting something like what happened that day help me know how much God cares for me?"

Mace tilted his head slightly and said, "Well, Zoe, He sent me as sort of His representative, to risk my life to make sure you were okay. It sort of showed you in a small way what He already did for you in a big way. And it bonded us together, didn't it?"

"It did," she said, suddenly sounding like a much older woman, grasping his hand. "So ... He would do that for me." Her voice was edged with the beginnings of amazement.

"God made us so we could love Him and be loved by Him, Zoe." Mace hesitated, and then added, "And ... so we could love each other the way we should."

Zoe paused to let this sink in. "If that's true," she said slowly, "if people actually believed that, it would change everything—how we treat each other, how we look at things in the world, and the things we would do." She paused and then said, "I ... I never thought of that."

"Of what?"

"That God would actually *love* me."

"He does love you, Zoe. He gave you some tangible evidence, you know. He knew His Son wasn't a big topic of conversation in the Davidovitch household, so He gave you a dramatic demonstration in real life of how much He cares for you."

"He used you to do that, didn't He?" she said in a whisper. She reached out and caressed his right palm. "That's what that day was really all about."

Mace nodded slowly. "Now you're getting it."

She sat quietly for a few minutes, and Mace was content to be quiet as well, just holding her. After a while she looked up at him and asked, "Mace, why haven't you ever kissed me?" She surprised him with the question, seemingly so far off the topic, but after a moment's thought he realized it was perfectly in line with what they were talking about.

"I guess ... I guess because I never felt it was the right time, Zoe. I have this thing in my mind that the first time I kiss you should be after ... after we, um—"

"Come on, Mace, you don't have to get all freaked out about it. We're gonna get married. Just face it. Duh. Just say it." She made a face, tilted her head down, knitted her eyebrows together and in a deep voice imitating his own, and said, "Mace will marry Zoe."

Mace opened his mouth in silent laughter and looked at her. "Ah, Zoe, you're right. Mace *will* marry Zoe," he repeated. She laughed at him with her eyes. "I need to just realize that this whole thing we have is from God," he said, "and He's in it all the way—He made it happen, and so yeah, I guess what I want to say is that I want to wait to kiss you until after we're married. I think that's what He would want, and if He's in the middle of all this, then I'm thinking we better do what He says. Does that make sense?" He touched the tip of her nose gently with his forefinger.

She nestled closer to him inside the old work coat. "I know this is weird, but yeah, it does. It's the same way I feel, and *that's* weird, let me tell you. I mean, most of the other girls my age—man, there aren't even any *virgins* left, never mind just kissing. But this ... this thing we have, Mace. You know I still get frightened, and I need to be around you to feel safe. Somehow that puts our relationship in a different space."

"God is trying to show us that this thing we have between us, this link, this bond, is from Him. He wants us to make sure that we obey Him in everything we do together. He's working this out; He's had His hand in everything between us. He worked out how we met, and what happened, and why nothing worse happened, and He is allowing you to get frightened so that you can find comfort with me. He lets this fear you have occur to sort of lead you to realizing that one day, you need to look to Him for comfort, not me."

"So He's sort of training me?" she asked.

"You could say that," Mace replied.

She wrapped both arms around him, one with a sleeve, the other around his waist inside the coat, and tucked her head into his chest. "So if I learn what He wants me to learn," she mumbled, almost afraid of her own words, "will it mean you and I will be different? Will I not need you anymore?" He could tell she was nervous.

He tightened his arm around her. "No, Zoe, it doesn't. It means you and I will be even closer than we are now. We'll always need each other; we'll be like one person, with one heart."

She let out a long sigh, closed her eyes. "Inside one coat," she whispered. "I would like that." She looked up at him then and asked, "What do I need to do so that can happen?"

Chapter 4

Zoe

"And the peace of God, which surpasses all comprehension, will guard your hearts and your minds in Christ Jesus."

Philippians 4:7

"Zoe Eschet Chayil Davidovitch," the loudspeaker boomed, the announcer butchering the two Hebrew middle names, but no one noticed except Zoe's parents, grimacing politely. The crowd attending the Granite Sky High School graduation ceremony came to their feet and raucously applauded. Zoe was graduating Summa Cum Laude—the highest ranked member of the graduation class. Just fifteen, it had been almost as if an alien with a computer brain was dropped from some strange world into their high school a few short years ago, who without a second thought ripped off correct answers to every question on every test in every class, and then spent the rest of her time trying without much success to learn how to live among the strange beings populating the planet. They knew she hadn't fit in, that most of the teachers didn't like her because she was Jewish, and most of the students—and probably most of the teachers, too—had been jealous because she was so much smarter than they would ever be. But they also knew how she had struggled with the trauma after being attacked a little more than three years ago, here on this very field. Everyone in the school had seen her rushing through the halls or watched with sympathy as she burst into a classroom, looking with wild, desperate eyes to find Mace so she could feel safe again. No one, not even the newest kids in school, after the story was explained to them, ever ridiculed her—not once, ever. It was as if they had front row seats to a minor miracle that occurred regularly in their school, for every time the terrified girl would find Mace, he would gently and miraculously comfort her, allowing her to breath again for another day or so. And now, no matter what anyone thought of her individually, as the fifteen-year old girl strode across the stage, so much smarter and, they all knew, so much more fragile than the others, everyone—supporters and detractors alike—rose in respect and compassion and applauded her triumph.

The young woman took her diploma from the Principal, shook her hand once with an exaggerated gesture, and then turned to face the crowd and raised both hands, smiling. They yelled even louder in response, and she laughed with delight, skipping across the stage with her diploma clutched tightly. But she stopped suddenly, and instead of exiting stage left as she was supposed to do, she caught site of Mace standing in line, down on the ground, close to the steps leading up to the platform, smiling up at her. She ran across center stage and leapt, her arms out like a swan, flying through the air, into his arms. He caught her, held her up as he twirled her around once, set her down gently, and gave her a great hug. The crowd went wild.

The other students, all 137 of them, traipsed across the stage one by one, received their diplomas, switched the tassels on their hats and then together, tossed them in the air. It was all somewhat anticlimactic.

***

"How do you like the party, Rachel?" Claire asked, holding a tray of crackers and cheese.

"It was very kind of you and Tack to do this," Rachel Davidovitch replied. "Murray and I are just so busy, as you know—"

"Nothing to it," Claire replied, forestalling Rachel's apologies. "And you know how we feel about Zoe."

"You're very kind," Rachel replied out of habit. She was a formal woman and Claire's open friendliness was sometimes hard for her to accommodate.

"Will Marcus be here tonight?" she asked, to change the subject. Talking about Zoe made her nervous.

"No, he's in the middle of final exams, and then he's been assigned to a ship for his summer cruise. Bad timing, and he's a little pressed."

"You must be very proud," Rachel said. She darted a furtive look at Mace, standing tall in a corner, talking with some classmates, his dark hair falling across his forehead.

"We love them both, my dear," Claire answered, following her gaze.

Murray Davidovitch came up then with two drinks in his hand, handing one to his wife. He was a short, thin, taciturn man with salt and pepper hair, black-framed glasses, and he wore a sport jacket and a bow tie. He was the prototypical nerdish chemistry professor, except that his formulations and refinement processes for crude oil had enabled his company to leap ahead of global oil competitors and reduce harmful automotive emissions in the world by almost 50%. Among oil business insiders and some of the world's most important politicians, he was something akin to the golden goose. There were two very large, very quiet men with oversized sport jackets who followed him whenever he went anywhere publicly. They stood at a discreet distance behind him now as he awkwardly nodded to Claire. Rachel gave him a significant look, and when he remained silent, she turned to Claire and said, "Claire, this is a good time for both of us to express how much we appreciate what Mace did, and has continued to do for Zoe these past few years."

"Won't pretend we understand," Murray exclaimed, shaking his head and staring at the drink in his hand. His wife put a restraining hand on his arm.

"Of course we don't understand, but we *are* grateful nonetheless," she said again to Claire, an apologetic tone in her voice.

Claire said, "Ah, yes, well, is that not the secret of life? We do not understand so many things, and yet we can be grateful for them nonetheless. Well put, Rachel. And we should congratulate you both," she went on, gushing a little for Rachel's sake, "such an honor, for your Zoe at her age to graduate Summa Cum Laude."

Murray, as though he hadn't heard Claire's last compliment, said, "We don't understand how your boy does what he does with our Zoe, Claire ... but as her father, I've seen my daughter go from a terrified vegetable to a fully functional human being, and it's all due to Mace. I can't see the logic or the science in it, but let me tell you, that boy of yours is different. He almost makes me believe there's a God." Rachel looked embarrassed and smiled weakly at Claire, but Claire was listening closely to Murray, who went on. "And if you or your family, and especially that boy of yours ever needs anything, you just ask, okay?"

Claire saw Rachel's eyes tear over suddenly, wide with surprise and pleasure. Apparently this was quite out of the ordinary for Murray. Rachel was speechless.

Claire, seeing Rachel overcome, put her hand on Murray's jacketed arm and said, "Why, Murray, how thoughtful! Yes, of course we will ask if we should ever need anything."

***

Mace and Zoe sat at one of the card tables on the brick patio, by themselves for the first time that night. The little candle in the glass jar was flickering, and Zoe held Mace's hand.

"So what school will you pick?" he asked.

Zoe sat back in her chair and rubbed her arms with her hands, though it wasn't cold. "Haven't decided yet," she said, "but I'm leaning toward Yale." Mace nodded, wondering how Zoe would function as a fifteen-year old among college students back east. She turned to look at him. "And what about you? What will you do?"

"Well, Mom and Dad sort of sprung a surprise on me yesterday."

"What? A surprise? What?" She was popping up and down in her chair.

"They said they've been putting away money for me since I was a little kid, and now they have enough to send me to the University of Minnesota."

Zoe looked shocked for just a second and then said, "Oh, Mace, that's ... that's wonderful!" She smiled at him and grasped both his hands in hers. "Are you excited? I know I would be! Man, how did your parents keep *that* secret for so long? That would have driven me *crazy*, trying not to spill the beans for eighteen years!"

Mace chuckled softly. "Well, they're good at that kind of thing. They were pretty happy to share the news with me, though. They know how much I want to write, and the chance to learn about the great books of history, about how the great writers thought and what they were trying to say ... it's kind of overwhelming. It's a great gift."

"When ... when will you leave?"

"Well, I have to fill out a formal application, but we called the school last week and they know some of the teachers here and it seems there were some pretty good recommendations, so they told Mom that the application was just a formality and I'll get in, no problem. They say new students should show up on campus sometime in the middle of September. The folks will drive me down and help me get set up."

"Does the school know about ... about your ..."

"You mean, my speech issue? I'll mention it on the application, but they already know about it from the teachers here. They don't think it will be too much of a problem."

"Good." She suddenly became quiet, like a balloon that's lost its air, and settled back in her chair sullenly.

"What about you? When do you leave? I mean, if you pick Yale."

"I dunno yet."

Mace looked at her carefully and put a hand on hers. "Zoe, going to Yale isn't like jumping down the interstate to the University of Minnesota or something. It's a major trip across country. You don't even have a driver's license yet. Your folks will have to take you, right?"

"I guess." Her arms were folded across her chest.

"You *do* want to go, right?"

Pause. Mace could hear crickets out in the field, even through the party noise. "I guess."

"You don't sound like you want to go."

"My Dad wants me to go; so does my Mom. They think it will be important for my *socialization*." She spat out the last word.

"You're doing pretty good with that, you know," Mace said. "You haven't needed the coat in, gee, at least a few months."

"I guess," she replied, unconvincingly.

"I could send it along with you if you need me to," he said, with a little smile.

That got her out of the gully. "Not the same, Mace *Antoine*. And what's all *that* about? *Antoine?!?* Where did *that* come from?" Zoe was referring to Mace's middle name, which had been blared across half of Minnesota by a loudspeaker that morning when the announcer at the podium announced Mace's full name as written on his diploma.

Mace sat back and put an open hand flat on his chest. "Antoine, my dear, is a grand and glorious moniker, which also just happens to be the name of my mother's grandfather. He was a French soldier in World War II, very brave, and since my father gave Marcus both of his names and then insisted that I be named after some powerful, barbarous, and effective medieval war weapon, Mom insisted I have at least a little reminder of her part of the family."

Zoe was struggling to smile, lip trembling. "Antoine ... okay, *Antoine*." She looked at him, eyes searching his, as if she was trying to memorize every feature of his face. Her thin smile lost its struggle and fled. "I like Mace better," she said, her voice breaking. "Sorry." She cried while Mace held her, and the candlelight flickered across them both, huddled there in the darkness.

***

Three days later, Mace went out to the barn after chores that evening and noticed that the grain bin was getting low. He went back into the house.

He picked up his tablet, which he could now use again as well as he could before the accident, and quickly typed a message and held the tablet out to his father. "*Am going for oats—they're low.*"

Tack, in the middle of a history on insurgent warfare, glanced at the tablet and then looked up at Mace and said, "Hey, okay, good idea. Thanks, Mace."

"Back ... to ... your ... book," Mace said softly, smiling, patting his father on the shoulder.

The phone rang. Claire picked it up and then quickly said from upstairs, "Tack, it's Zoe. Is Mace out in the barn?"

"Here ... Mom!" Mace said, and picked up the downstairs extension.

"Hey Zoe."

"Can I come over?" She was tripping over her words, talking so quickly. "Mom and Dad say they're taking me to Yale Monday and I don't know if I want to go then and I don't think anyone will like me there anyway, and if they don't I can't get away, and if I have an episode then where will you be and you won't even be there you'll be in some college dorm probably making out with ten girls before I even get home—"

"Zoe, come over," Mace said quietly. "It'll be okay."

"I know people change when they get older, Mace, I know that, and I don't want you to feel like I'm trapping you or anything like that, you know, and so if you want to make out with ten girls at college go ahead I'll try and understand and I'll probably—"

"Zoe ... Zoe, can you hear me?"

There was a pause in the rush of words. "I can hear you." Zoe, breathless.

"Zoe, the only girl I will ever make out with is you, after we get married. So come on over now. Things will be okay."

"On the way," he heard, and the line clicked dead. Mace went upstairs to get the coat.

Tack saw him come down, saw the coat in his arms, and said, "Zoe?" Mace nodded.

"She okay?"

"She'll ... be ... okay. College ... stuff."

"Right. She coming over on the bike?" Mace again nodded. Zoe's parents had gotten her a dirt bike when she began her senior year, because she could ride the back trails between town and the Creamery without needing a license, and it saved them so much time, driving Zoe over to visit Mace whenever she had one of her 'episodes'. Driving actually seemed to calm her down. Tack put two and two together, closed his book, and got out of his chair.

"Let's see those keys, Mace." Mace flipped him the keys to the pickup. "I need some things in town anyway. Claire!" Tack yelled upstairs. "You want to come into town?"

"*Merci no, Mon Cher*, too many things to do here, but thank you, my love."

"Right." Tack turned to Mace and put his hand on his shoulder. He found he was having to reach higher every year to do that, and it made him both wistful and proud, and he never once put his hand on Mace's shoulder without remembering that day in the hospital, when he saw the wound in his son's hand, and then Zoe had come in and he saw the cut across her neck, and realized what his son had braved. Sometimes he wasn't sure what God was doing in the boy's life, but he was fairly sure that Mace was destined for something beyond anything he could ever hope to accomplish spiritually. It gave him a sense of peace that his boy was surpassing him in the realm of the spirit.

"See you shortly, Mace. You take care of Zoe, okay?"

"Right ... Pop."

***

Tack took the small pickup out of the farm's main gate and down the long winding dirt road leading to the main route into town. The dirt road ran through flat, fenced grass pastures, with a few cows now and again grazing, looking up at his headlights as he drove. It ran over the single-lane bridge that spanned the narrow inlet that separated Red Rock peninsula from the main part of the state. He turned onto the Gunflint Trail road, which was the main highway into town, trundling over bumps and cracks, watching for stray moose. In about half a mile he was approaching the first intersection, where one of the many lonely county roads crossed the main route, when his front left tire blew out. He maintained control of the car with ease—his reflexes were still far beyond normal—and brought it to a stop safely, a little canted to the left, almost in the middle of the intersection. It was dark, there were no streetlights, but he wasn't bothered. It was just another tire change. He pulled the flashlight from the back seat, got out of the car, and went back to check on the spare tire. There it was, sitting where it should be in its cradle under the pickup bed toward the rear of the truck. He thought about calling Claire or Mace, but then just decided to change it himself and get on into town before the feed store closed. He walked forward to the front of the truck to examine the tire and saw something sharp and very hard, with a strangely long point, embedded in the rubber. He picked it out and couldn't believe what he was seeing. It was about four inches in length, with six sharp iron points arranged in different directions, such that however it would lay on the ground, at least one of the points would be upright. He tried to imagine what kind of farm or ranch machinery this item had fallen from as some rancher trundled down the highway behind his tractor. Headlights flashed in the distance. A car was coming along down the county road that intersected the main route. Great, and here he was, in the middle of the intersection. Maybe it was a police officer. They were out and about fairly regularly around Granite Sky. He stood there, though, to make sure the oncoming car saw him in the middle of the intersection. He waved his flashlight back and forth.

***

Mace was waiting on the porch when the phone in the house rang. Claire picked it up. He waited to see if he could discern who was on the phone while watching for Zoe, waiting to see the little headlight on her dirt bike bouncing along their access road.

The screen door slammed and Claire raced out toward the other pickup. "*Allons-y*," she said, her face pale, throwing him a set of keys. "*Ce était Zoe; elle est à l'intersection. Ce est votre père.*" Mace followed his mother as they both ran toward the barn where the larger diesel pickup was stored. "*Elle a déjà appelé l'hôpital.*" Mace didn't waste time asking questions. His mother only spoke French to him when she was nervous or upset.

***

They saw the flashing ambulance lights as they approached the intersection. Mace's hands tightened on the wheel. His mother gave a small sob. As they arrived, they saw two paramedics hunched over a figure on the ground. Mace stopped in the center of the road, effectively blocking it to traffic, kept his headlights shining on the scene to give the paramedics more light, and hopped out of the truck. Zoe stood off to one side, near the front of Tack's ruined truck, arms clutching her sides, looking like a pale, red-haired ghost. They heard the wailing siren and saw the blue twirling lights of a police cruiser screaming at them from town, on its way. A third paramedic was trundling out a stretcher on wheels. Claire ran to her husband. One of the paramedics looked up and stood to address her as well as making sure she didn't come too close to the scene. He put both hands on her shoulders and spoke clearly and firmly, with confidence and optimism.

"He's alive, ma'am, and he's got a steady pulse. We're taking care of his injuries. We're stabilizing him now; we're not treating him for anything. We're taking him to Granite Sky General, so if you can meet us there, the doctors can tell you more." He gave a firm nod to Mace, conveying in no uncertain terms that he wanted Mace to get his mother back in the truck.

Claire, overwrought as she was, stumbled about. She walked over to Zoe, hugged her, and told her to come with them.

One of the paramedics spoke up. "No ma'am, we're sorry, but we need her to come with us. She was first on the scene and we'll need her to describe the first aid she provided."

Claire was momentarily disoriented. The other paramedic said, partly to her, partly to his team, "She probably saved his life with that," and she pointed to something that Claire couldn't see. "It's a side-by-side dual tourniquet." They had Tack up on the stretcher and were wheeling him over to the ambulance.

"Pardon me, Mrs. Ironbridge, but we need to get going. We'll meet you at the hospital." The paramedics gently lifted Tack onto the stretcher—she could see him strapped to some kind of flat board—and put him into the back of the ambulance. One of the paramedics indicated to Zoe that she should ride up front and she jumped into the front seat.

Claire was still not moving, and Mace recognized that she was not processing what was happening. "*Maman ... viens ... avec ... moi.*" He took her firmly by the arm and led her back to the truck. She followed along, stumbling now and again. He put her in the passenger seat gently. "*Faites ... confiance ... à ... Jésus ... d'accord?*" Claire seemed to shake herself, gave Mace a focused look, and nodded. "*Bien,*" she replied, mostly to herself. "*Bien.*"

The ambulance pulled out, lights flashing, siren blaring, as the police cruiser pulled up. Mace waved him over and said they were going to the hospital along with the ambulance. Jimmy Callas, one of the town's police officers, had seen too many traffic accidents, and sent Mace and Clair on, indicating he would get any information he needed from them there while he secured the crash scene.

***

Tack was in surgery for six hours. Claire and Mace and Zoe stayed in the waiting room the entire time. Zoe watched as Mace, solidly composed, held his mother together, praying with her, comforting her, assuring her that God had things under control. Mace needed Zoe close by so he could speak to his mother normally, and while she sat next to his mother she wondered where Mace got the strength. She could see Claire visibly relax as she apprehended what Mace was sharing with her. Mace was telling her that God was sovereign and in control of every little thing that happened, that—and she remembered this part particularly later—'*all things work together for good for those who love God and are called according to His purpose.*' She had to process that, but it seemed to give Claire a great deal of comfort. Zoe felt a rush of deep, almost overpowering affection for Mace as she watched him be so gentle with his mother. Zoe sat next to Claire and now and then Claire would turn to her and Zoe would hold her while Claire cried.

Early on in the wait, Zoe was called in to share with one of the doctors what first aid she'd provided.

"You put a side-by-side tourniquet on," he asked her right away, after asking for her name and age. The doctor on the emergency room shift was around forty or so, from Ireland. "Why?"

"I wanted to control the bleeding and extinguish the distal pulse," she replied.

He looked up sharply from his notepad. "You know what a distal pulse is?" he asked, incredulous.

"Sure ... it's the pulse at the far end of the limbs; the proximal pulse on a limb is the pulse found closest to the torso." He stared at her like she had three eyes.

"I read it in a book once," she explained.

"Why don't you just walk me through the event from the time you came on the scene. And do you mind if I record this?" He pulled out a pocket recorder and set it on the counter.

"Not at all. I was driving over to visit Mace on the Trail out of town, on the side of the road, you know, the dirt path?"

"I know it."

"So as I came up to the intersection, I saw what looked like a pickup truck off to the side, stopped. Didn't look right. It was dark, so I pointed my dirt bike's headlamp at it and saw Mr. Ironbridge lying in the road, by the back passenger door."

"What was his condition?"

"He was lying on his face. There was a lot of blood on the ground. I couldn't see too well, but I did notice a flashlight lying on the ground, so I picked that up and looked him over. That's when I saw a nasty cut on his head, and then I saw his leg, his left leg. There was a big gash in that too, and it was lying sort of crooked, the angle wasn't right. Lots of blood there, too, and it was still bleeding. I was worried about the cut on his head, because there was some bruising, so it could have been that he hit his head or neck, so I ran around to the back of the pickup—it was Mace's pickup, by the way, and he always keeps some spare scrap wood in the back—and got a flat piece of board with some baling twine. I strapped the board to the back of Mr. Ironbridge's head with one string, and then to the small of his back with the other string. It wasn't a very good backboard, but it was all I had. I needed to turn him over to stop the bleeding in his leg. After I turned him over—and I did the best I could to make sure his head stayed aligned with the rest of his body—I took off his belt, ripped away his trousers up and past the wound, and tried a windlass tourniquet just under his knee, but it didn't extinguish the distal pulse. That's why I put another one on; I took off *my* belt and put it just below the first tourniquet, and that finally put a stop to the pulse there. The bones were sticking out, and I rearranged the bottom portion of the leg so it would be more natural, and then put him on his back and raised his right leg. I didn't want to touch his left one."

"Was he conscious when you got there?"

"No, not at all. It looked like he took a wicked hit on the head."

"That he did. Slight skull fracture, concussion; we're waiting on x-rays to see more," the doctor confirmed.

"So I took my water bottle, washed his leg, and ripped part of my shirt to make a pressure bandage on the exposed area."

"That's what the red plaid fabric was."

"Yeah, see?" she said, holding up the remaining shirttail.

"Pretty quick thinking," he replied, staring at her strangely. "What then?"

"I pulled out my cell phone and called 911; they routed me to the hospital and I gave them a report on his injuries."

"You were the one that passed the information about the head wound?"

"Right. It looked pretty bad."

"Well, I guess that answers the question about why there was an ad hoc back board already in place by the time they got there."

"Should I not have rigged that board on his neck?" she asked nervously.

"Oh, absolutely, that was a good precaution, no question," he looked down at a clipboard, "Miss Davidovitch. You had to get the bleeding under control, so you had to turn him, so you did what you had to do, and it was the right thing. He was still bleeding when you got there, right?"

"Badly; there was a lot of blood, all around."

"You probably ... no, you *definitely* saved his life, applying those tourniquets. Good work."

"Doctor, his leg was really bad. Will he lose it?"

"He's still in surgery, and I can't answer that question. You're right, it was pretty bad." He looked preoccupied, and then said, "I've got to get back and give them a report from this. Thanks." The doctor turned and moved back through the double doors, but then stopped and asked, "Hey, now tell me, how did you know to do this stuff?"

"I read a book once," she replied, shrugging her shoulders, and he shook his head, mumbled something about Americans being the truly lucky ones, and stalked back toward the surgery.

A little later, Rachel came through the doors of the waiting room, looking anxiously around for her daughter. Mace had called her on the way to the hospital, slowly sharing over the phone what had happened, knowing she would probably have been worried if for some reason she saw or heard about an ambulance out where her daughter was with the dirt bike.

Rachel at first wanted to take Zoe home immediately, to remove her from this unseemly swirl of pain and tragedy and loss and emotion, all of which was horridly distasteful to her, but when she walked in, Claire was tucked into Zoe's shoulder, sobbing, and Zoe looked up and met her mother's eyes. Something struck Rachel viscerally, and Zoe's mother understood instantly that something beyond her own experience was transpiring, some transference of something that did not exist in their own family, some activity or emotion she herself had never known ... but, she realized with a sudden ache, something she'd always wanted. Standing there watching her daughter comfort another woman, Rachel felt a strangely powerful pull toward Zoe then, a sense of love beyond anything she could remember, and a great deal of pride that her daughter would prove to be so comforting. Any thoughts of taking Zoe home right away vanished when she saw how much Claire seemed to need her daughter.

Claire looked up and wiped her eyes with a tissue. "Thank you for coming, Rachel. I ... they tell me Zoe saved Tack's life. We don't know any more than that, he's still in surgery."

"I just came to see if there is anything I can do," Rachel said.

"It's very kind of you, dear," Claire replied, reaching out her hand. Rachel, unsure of herself in such situations, took it, and Zoe slid over to let her mother sit next to Claire.

***

They were able to see Tack around midnight. The doctor had come out before they would let them in to see Tack to explain the extent of his injuries.

"Mrs. Ironbridge, we're very sorry, but we could not save his leg." Claire seemed to deflate at that, leaning into Mace, who held her up. Zoe stood on the other side of Claire, holding her hand for support.

"There was just too much trauma. Truthfully, he would not have lived if the young lady here hadn't put those tourniquets on; there was an enormous amount of blood loss, and the damage was just too great."

"He's alive, that's the main thing," Claire managed to say. "Thank you, God." Zoe felt the overpowering weight of sincerity in Claire's heartfelt gratefulness. It seemed a strange thing about which to be thanking God, but she sensed Claire's composure beginning to settle.

"Does he know?" Mace asked.

"He does," the doctor replied. "And frankly, we were amazed at how well he took the news."

"What did he say?" Claire asked.

The doctor paused, put both of his hands into his white lab coat, and looked down at the ground. "Strange thing," he replied. "And it makes me a little ashamed at the lack of depth in my own faith, but he said something like 'Praise God' and then "I look forward to this new thing God is doing in my life," or something like that, and then smiled at everyone around the bed there, and thanked us for all the work we'd put in. He said that this was what God wanted and he would be content to stump around for the rest of his life in great happiness if that's how God wanted things to be."

Claire smiled through her tears then, and Zoe was again amazed at what she was seeing. There were no hysterics, no screaming, no railing at the doctors for amputating Tack's leg—just the opposite, it seemed. But while amazed and heartened, she wasn't surprised, for she knew Mace well, and these people were the two most responsible for Mace being what he was. She felt like she wanted to burrow down into their very hearts and remain there for the rest of her life.

Tack was reclining slightly in the bed, groggy but coherent, and smiling at them when they came in. There was a tent of sheets over his left leg. There was a large bandage around his head. He reached out a hand to Claire, who took it, kissed it, and sat down next to the hospital bed.

"How are you, *Mon Cher*?"

"Fine, fine, love. Just a small interruption, and a little weight loss." He looked up at Mace and Zoe. "Hey, son. Sorry, but it seems I didn't get around to picking up those oats. But I am glad it's me here and not you."

Claire tried to laugh but it came out as a great sob, and she threw herself across his chest.

"Hey, hey, it's okay, love, it's okay, I'll be fine, really." He patted her back with his free left hand—the other had an IV attached. Tack looked over Claire's head to Mace. He gave Mace a look that seemed to ask, '*Hey, is she okay?*'

Mace took a quick glance to find Zoe standing next to him and then said, "Hey Dad. We're okay; we're just worried about you. Mom's fine. She just loves you a lot, that's all."

"We all ... love you a lot," Zoe whispered timidly, hiding behind Mace. But Claire heard her, and she lifted her head and reached out a hand for Zoe to come closer. Zoe came close to the bed, and Tack lifted up one hand and Claire reached out for her with another, and Mace's mother and father embraced the woman who would one day be Mace's wife.

***

Rachel sat in her open, lemon-colored kitchen stocked with all the most modern conveniences and appliances, took down a mug from a cabinet and poured coffee for herself. She stared absently at her iPhone—no messages. She had to leave for work in a half hour, but something was pulling at her, slowing her down, and it felt like she was dragging an anchor around and couldn't set it loose. 'Malaise,' she thought to herself, 'the first signs of the onset of depression, probably. Just what I need.' She could not determine what was causing this unease. Perhaps it was the Ironbridge accident, just three days ago. She moved her leg as an unconscious act of sensory gratefulness. Perhaps it was that Zoe was leaving for college; but no, neither of these things seemed to be the main reason for her disquiet, although she seemed to sense in a non-natural way that both elements were related.

Zoe shot into the kitchen, slid on the floor in an imitation of a snowboard move, and did not see her mother in repose, tucked away in the breakfast nook, both hands around her mug of coffee. Zoe snowboarded into the pantry, disappeared, made noises, then reappeared balancing peanut butter and jelly jars and a loaf of bread. She put the jars and the bread down on the counter and began to make two sandwiches, and then saw her mother, sitting in the nook.

"Hey Mom. Not at work?"

"No, Zoe. Don't have to leave quite yet," Rachel replied, somewhat listlessly, as though she really didn't want to go to work. Zoe looked at her strangely. She had never known her mother *not* wanting to go to work.

"Everything okay?" Zoe asked.

"Fine," her mother answered automatically, and then, "well ... perhaps not altogether fine, Zoe, now that you ask."

Zoe set down her knife, stopped making her sandwiches, and went to stand near the breakfast nook. This was a world event—her mother admitting that something was not fine, not settled, not going as planned. She looked at her mother, who at the moment could not meet her eyes, and was staring down into the clouds in her coffee. Zoe sat and waited.

"It's not something I can clearly elucidate," Rachel began, "and that in itself is perplexing, and not a little ... *disturbing*, actually. I am not accustomed to a lack of clarity in my affairs." Zoe just sat quietly, waiting. This was definitely not normal behavior for her mother. Rachel went on. "Take, for example, this ... this *situation* you have with Mace Ironbridge. I understand that, perhaps, a little. You experienced a traumatic event, and he was the one who saved you from something horrible. You naturally identify him with safety. Your father and I, we were so worried about you, and as we've seen you come to find safety and assurance near Mace, well, we realize that he provides you something we can't any longer. Oh, we understand the reasons why, Zoe, but it is still sort of an adjustment for us; well, for *me*, actually, more than your father. And yet you've triumphed, and that has made both your father and I so very proud." She smiled at Zoe, weakly. "But we don't know how long that will go on, or how long you'll need ... you'll need what Mace provides now. Perhaps this need will fade over time, we don't know. But we do know that it will be important for you to get an education, dear, and you must realize that you are quite gifted in certain areas, as is your father and to a smaller degree myself as well. You must not let one incident in your life derail you from what you might possibly achieve in the future." Her mother now sounded as though she was on more familiar ground.

"What's the problem, Mom?"

The question brought Rachel back to contemplating her conundrum, and she looked down into her coffee, confused. "I don't really know, Zoe."

"When did it start?"

Rachel thought for a moment. If she felt it odd that her daughter was playing the role of psychoanalyst to her 'patient on the couch', she gave no indication. "Truthfully it was around the time Mr. Ironbridge had his accident," she answered. "Yes, around then."

In a flash, Zoe, inexplicably, knew exactly what was disturbing her mother's equilibrium. She had seen the earthquake occur in her mother's eyes when she walked into the waiting room and saw her comforting Claire Ironbridge. Her mother would have no conception of the bonds that might exist between the spirits of two people, nor how those bonds might be demonstrated, or strengthened. Zoe, just coming alive in her own spirit, could see that her mother had not yet come to such life. They who are alive in spirit can so easily discern the absence of life in another, while those who are dead do not even know they are dead.

"Did Mr. Ironbridge's injury upset you?" Zoe asked, knowing the answer.

Rachel paused again for a long moment, thinking. "No," she said reflectively, "no, I truly don't think so. I realize accidents happen and he was actually fortunate that you came along when you did. The odds were that the outcome would have been quite worse than how things actually turned out, so ... no, I can't say that his injury is causing this ... disturbance."

Zoe decided not to beat around the bush anymore, or try to lead her mother to see what was obvious to her. "Was it when you saw Claire crying on my shoulder?"

Rachel looked down again at her coffee. Zoe could hear the little second hand ticking away on the clock on the sill above the kitchen sink. A car drove by outside. Zoe's mouth felt dry.

"I ... I wrestle with that," Rachel began, hoarsely, and then, clearing her throat, trying to regain emotional control, said, "I realized that something was happening there, no question. I saw that she was upset, and that you were comforting her. These are normal things during such times, certainly." Rachel's words made sense, but Zoe could sense the emotional turmoil under them. "But something else was passing between the two of you, something I sensed but could not understand, and it is this inability to understand that thing that, I think, is causing this...I don't know, whatever it is that I'm experiencing; this malaise, or disquiet. It's almost as though I'm somehow disoriented, as if ... as if—"

"As if someone has shifted the world under your feet," Zoe put in firmly.

Zoe saw a look of both recognition and fear pass across her mother's face, but then the old habit asserted itself. She chuckled slightly. "Nothing so dramatic as all that, Zoe, certainly. No, it was, more like ... something ..." and her mother's sentence trailed off into nothing, because she could not keep up the pretense and still accurately describe what she had felt, and her mother was nothing if not precise.

"You sensed something pass between Claire and me that you didn't understand," Zoe said. "I felt it too. But it wasn't an '*it*', Mom. You saw, or sensed, a '*Who*'. If Mace were here he would tell you that you sensed the Spirit of the Living God, who lives in Claire—and who lives in me too, Mom. He was there, bearing the grief both of us felt, and that Spirit in me was strengthening Claire, and she could sense Him and He gave her comfort through me." Rachel was looking at her with eyes of fear but with questioning as well, so Zoe plunged on. "I know we don't talk about this kind of stuff, Mom, but it's sort of like someone is thirsty, you know, and you have a pitcher and she has a glass, and in your pitcher you have water, so you pour this water into her glass. Your pitcher isn't giving her comfort, nor does the glass, but the pitcher and the glass are both sort of 'containers' for the water, and the water is what quenches her thirst. And when the pitcher passes water to the glass, something happens; the pitcher and the glass *bond together* somehow. The Spirit is like the water, and you felt Him there when you walked into the waiting room, Mom, because He was being passed from my 'pitcher' to Claire's 'glass', and anytime anyone gets a sense of that Spirit, it will take everything they ever thought about what life is and turn it upside down."

Rachel couldn't speak; her throat closed with a fear she hadn't known since falling asleep one afternoon in a barn and waking to darkness all around her. Her mind, wrestling with Zoe's information, was telling her that it was nonsense. Every fiber in her heart and soul, however, was vibrating to the truth of what Zoe was saying, nonsense though it might be. The dichotomy frightened her to death. "I ... I can't talk about that now," she said in a whisper. "I need to get to work."

Zoe put her hand gently on her mother's wrist. "Mom, Mace doesn't do anything special, you know, when I have my ... events. It's not Mace; it's the *Spirit* that lives in Mace—*the Spirit* is the one Who comforts me. I can't explain how it works, but it does. For some reason God wants me to go to Mace to get that comfort. I'm not sure why yet, but Mace says he thinks it's because God wants us to be together. There is something that bonds two people together when the Spirit is shared between the two of them, and that's what you sensed, or saw, or felt, that day in the waiting room." Zoe paused and then added, "This isn't something we ever talked about at home, I know."

"It's not something your father or I actually believe in," Rachel said, her voice faltering with emotion, struggling to maintain a sense of normality in a rapidly churning reality, and still staring at her coffee. She could not meet her daughter's eyes.

"But you *felt* Him, Mom," Zoe said intensely. "You *know*. It's like getting smacked in the face with a wet fish and then saying you don't believe in fish."

Her mother smiled slightly. "It's ... it's just that it is outside of my field of understanding, Zoe," her mother replied.

"It's *not* natural, Mom. It's *super*natural; it is not going to be in anyone's 'field of understanding'. The Spirit of God transcends our natural understanding in the same way that what you saw transpiring there in the waiting room transcends a handshake between two strangers."

Rachel sighed and looked at her daughter, sitting across from her, eyes shining, alive, intense, passionate. A week ago, she would have privately disdained Zoe's indecipherable and somewhat distasteful analogy. Yet that would have been before she witnessed the bond that had been shared between Zoe and Claire Ironbridge. Unsettled, she wondered at what her daughter had become—still fragile, still tender, yet at times so intense and focused on this new relationship with 'God'. It was foreign to Rachel's intellectual background and upbringing, so outside her experience that it frightened her; it seemed to her sometimes that she didn't know who her daughter was any longer. But then, no one had tried to cut her throat when she was twelve years old, either. Perhaps it was just the trauma of that event. But no ... Zoe's trauma did not explain what she had sensed in the waiting room, passing between Zoe and Claire, and it did not explain why since then something unexplained was nagging mercilessly at her. It was too confusing; she couldn't explain it, it frightened her, and anything she couldn't explain was, after a reasonable period of time, set on the back shelf of her intellectual cupboard, to be stored and, if fortunate, forgotten. But this *thing*, this experience, would not fade away or stay agreeably and decorously forgotten. It nagged and pulled at her, like a desire she had not known existed suddenly emerging to become a consuming passion.

She wanted to have done with this talk of spiritual things and switched subjects, now looking up at her daughter. "We should talk about the trip east, Zoe ... to Yale. There are a hundred details to work out and we need to confirm your accommodations and your schedule for the first semester, and we need to talk about the security plan your father has worked out for your time there—there's a reliable firm he's engaged—and I've some friends in the area who have been kind enough to offer to look in on you now and again. You'll want friends around you your first few months, I would expect." On firmer ground with things she could touch and move and plan, she smiled brightly at Zoe, who was now sitting back in her chair, arms folded.

"Do I have to go?"

"We've been through this, Zoe. You have so much to offer the world; it would be…it would be a travesty not to develop this gift of yours. I realize you have feelings for Mace, but seriously, you are not even twenty-one yet, and you have so much of life to live in front of you, so many new and fascinating experiences to encounter, so many new and different people to meet—giving this future up just for a ... a relationship,"—she had almost said 'a romance', but the word choked in her throat, and she could not get it out—"would be the very height of foolishness, and I know you are not a foolish girl. Be serious, Zoe. *Life* is serious; this is reality."

"I disagree, Mom," Zoe replied, arms still crossed. "You want me to go to school, okay, I'll go. You want me to meet new and different people, sure, okay, I'll meet them. But don't try and tell me all of that is reality." Zoe stood up from the table and looked directly at her mother. "What you saw in the waiting room; what you saw between Claire and I; what happens every day between Mace and I ... *that's* reality. And *that's* where I want to live." She left her mother still sitting, holding her cold coffee, unable to reply, staring sightlessly out the window at the dead grass on the neighbor's lawn.

***

Mace took his tablet into the ground floor master bedroom and sat down next to his father. He smiled, and Tack nodded, just waking. The pain pills were making him groggy, and he was still arguing with Claire about whether he needed them at all, but Claire insisted.

"Hey, son. Grab me a water over there, would you?" Tack pushed himself up on the bed, took the water bottle Mace proffered, and drank, wiping his mouth with his wrist. "Thanks. These pills are putting me down hard. Now what's on your mind?"

Mace held up his tablet, asking for permission to use that instead of trying to speak. "Sure, sure, type away. As long as you don't ask me to follow you around the room trying to read it."

Mace smiled and tapped the keys and held up the tablet. *Want to talk about college.*

Tack sensed Mace was serious. "Okay." Claire walked in, carrying a vase with flowers. She smiled at Tack, who said, "Mace wants to talk about college, Claire. Here, come, sit." He patted the bed next to him, and Claire, setting the vase on his bedside table, sat down.

God shifts things according to His plan, Dad, and I think it would be best for you and Mom if I stayed here, at least for the next year, to make sure the business does okay. Marcus can't come back, and truthfully, now ... I shouldn't go.

"Oh, Mace, how thoughtful, but it's absolutely out of the question, dear," Claire exclaimed at once ... but Tack put a hand on her arm.

"Let's hear him out, *Chéri*." Claire, surprised, darted a look at her husband, but he was serious. "Mace isn't a child any longer, *Chéri*; he's given this some thought, and we need to respect what he has to say."

Mace held up his tablet again. *I'm becoming more convinced God wants me here, not in college. Whatever it is He has for me to do, it requires that I stay here. I'm certain He doesn't want me to spend next few years @ school. It would be a distraction.*

Claire, too shocked to reply, waited for Tack's response.

"What makes you think so, Mace?" Tack asked. He sounded more like a commanding officer asking a subordinate about the logic of an assault plan than a father asking a son to explain a life-changing career choice.

Mace tapped furiously for a few moments. *Timing of accident, business only means of support, customers depending on us ... and what I want to write, won't learn to write at a college. Will come from Him or won't be worth writing.*

"And what about Zoe?" Tack asked, again, like a commander making sure his subordinates were covering everything.

Mace tapped very slowly and then showed them the screen. *Zoe is going to Yale.*

Tack felt his son's pain and knew he would miss Zoe. Tack was confused as well; he had been so convinced God wanted those two together. Mace held up the screen again.

Don't understand that part.

"Neither do I, but let's wait on God for that." Tack gathered himself and said, "Mace, if things were normal, I'd thank you for your offer, but insist that nonetheless you get yourself off to school. But we're not living in normal times. First, let me say I agree with you, and I also feel it will be important for you to remain here. Can't say why, and perhaps this may have something to do with it," he waved distractedly at his missing limb. "I sense with you that you'll be needed here, somehow. Sure, the business will need to go on, but more importantly, I feel that what you have to do needs to be done from here."

Mace tapped again. *Glad you agree.* He flipped the screen to Claire. *What about you, Mom?*

Claire held her hands together tightly. "I ... I am confused. In this country, to get even a moderate position, you need a college education, of this I have read about. I know this, and it seems to put some anxiousness in me, but I also know that you have an ability to hear from God that I do not have, and I also know that positions and jobs are not as important as doing what God wants you to do, and I trust you to know what He is asking of you. So ... I guess I am okay in it."

Tack and Mace smiled together.

"What? What did I say?"

"Nothing, nothing, *Chéri*." Tack turned to Mace. "Have you told Zoe yet?"

She's coming over tonight; I'll tell her then.

"She'll understand too, I think."

I hope.

***

The sun was rising above the distant tree line, an awakening golden-scarlet wash of distant light pushing into a somnambulant morning sky. Mace had finished morning chores and was coming in from the barn when he saw headlights in the early morning dusk, out at the end of the driveway. Zoe had called the previous evening, letting him know that she might stop by and say goodbye one last time before her mother took her to the airport.

Mace stood there in his gold chore coat, wiping his hands on a towel hanging by the pump just off the front porch, wondering why the headlights remained out at the gate, when he saw Zoe come trudging up the driveway toward the house.

She stopped about five yards from him, looking up at the house in the early morning light, and then looking back at him. She wore a very fine gray cashmere traveling coat, complete with a little cloak, and her hair was pulled back into a single French braid—convenient for traveling, he supposed. She was twisting her hands together.

"I came to say goodbye."

He walked toward her slowly. "I'm going to miss you terribly," he said.

"Me too." She paused. Tears were running down her cheeks. "I don't want to go."

"I understand, Zoe." He didn't think she should be going either, but now wasn't the time to say so. He reached out a hand, and she took it.

"You won't forget me?"

"I won't forget you, Zoe. I'll be right here when you get back."

"I'm ... I'm sorry you can't go to college, Mace, but I really think you're doing the right thing."

"I'm at peace with it, Zoe. There is a peace that comes when we do what God wants us to do. It's kind of hard to explain, but—"

"I understand. I don't have any peace about going to Yale, about going anywhere. I've never been so convinced in all my life about anything that I need to stay *right here*."

Mace didn't say anything; he didn't want to contradict Zoe's parents, but felt as she did—leaving wasn't the right thing for her.

Rachel Davidovitch came up then, out of the morning mist, surprising them both. She had left the car running, the headlights on, still shooting into the fading darkness.

"Good morning, Mrs. Davidovitch," Mace said clearly. He kept Zoe's hand in his. Zoe's free hand swiped at her face.

"Good morning, Mace. You're up early." She seemed distracted, or disoriented. She didn't seem impatient, though.

"Yes Ma'am. Life on the farm ... "

Rachel looked over at the barn, then at the house, and then again out at the fields in the distance. She was uncharacteristically quiet, and Mace, surprising himself, put his arm around Zoe and said without a trace of any kind of hesitation, "Forgive me for saying so, Mrs. Davidovitch, but I don't have a peace about Zoe leaving."

Zoe darted a look at Mace. It was a rather bold thing to say to her mother, but Rachel didn't seem to hear him. She looked at Mace standing in the breaking light, Zoe tucked under his arm—obviously Zoe had been crying—and sensed the same strange transference, the same awareness of a flowing, living bond between the two of them that she had felt in the hospital waiting room, only this time the feeling was almost overpowering. It was so strong that it took her breath away, literally, and she could not speak. She put her hand to her chest. She knew, absolutely and without question, that there was a bond between these two that could not be broken, and her fears about Zoe's youth or Mace's handicap or meager professional prospects seemed almost obscene in the presence of such overwhelming, almost scintillating ... *truth*. There—that was it. It struck her then what had confused her so about this experience. It was truth she was sensing, truth she was seeing. She didn't know why the word 'truth' would come to mind, but beyond doubt it was as if truth had become embodied, taken on form or image—the image of these two young people standing near a hand pump on a Minnesota farm.

With Claire in the waiting room, such feelings disquieted her, but here, this morning, now, seeing Mace with Zoe, the experience shook the foundations of her life—it made her question everything she'd ever known or thought to be true, or right, or decent, or 'appropriate'. Such feelings frightened her terribly, and she sensed she would be certain about nothing again in her life until she understood this thing she felt as 'truth'. She felt Mace and Zoe knew something—something crucial, something of eternal significance—about which she was, at her age, still egregiously ignorant. She felt stunned, at a loss, at sea in a tumultuous storm that was her internal life. But her nature struggled against this *foreign* thing, this thing she could not control, and thus emerged fear, and the fear deadened her senses.

"Zoe ... let's ... it's time to go. We'll ... we'll miss our plane. The plane. Your plane." Rachel shook herself. "Come along," she said weakly, turned, and began walking back to the car.

Zoe looked up at Mace, who nodded to her quietly, held up her hand and kissed the inside of her palm. Zoe, weeping, couldn't speak. "You look to Jesus, now, Zoe. He'll keep you." She just nodded, tears pouring, unable to speak. He put his injured palm to hers so she would remember.

Zoe turned and caught up with her mother and they walked down the long lane toward their car, two separate forms fading into the darkness, until he heard the car doors close, the engine accelerate, and the headlights changed their aspect, now turning, turning again, and then pointing off into the darker horizon.

He stood there, watching. "God," he said, "O God, please, please keep her safe. Please be a shield around her." Halfway down the long driveway, the headlights stopped for a moment, pausing for several long seconds. And then he saw them move off again, down the lane toward the highway, and the cloying darkness closed in around them.

He stood, unable to move, leaning on the pump handle, staring off down the lane, feeling as though part of his own heart had been taken. He felt disoriented, sad—his main emotion a deep, tumbling grief.

He was just turning to go back into the house when he saw, out of the gray dawning light, a very slight form. He wiped his eyes once, stared again, and began to run.

When he was close enough for her to see him through the mist, she dropped her suitcase and shot into his arms like a slim, red-topped missile. She was trembling.

"Zoe ... Zoe, it's okay. What? What is it?"

"Mom said I should stay here," Zoe said. She leaned back in his arms and looked at him. "She stopped the car, and she was crying—I don't think I've ever seen my Mom cry before—and I can't explain it, but she just turned to me and said that I was supposed to stay here with you."

She buried her face in his golden coat and sobbed, and when she could speak again, she said, "*Now* I'm at peace."

Chapter 5

Marcus

"Now therefore, my sons, listen to me, and pay attention to the words of my mouth. Do not let your heart turn aside to her ways, Do not stray into her paths. For many are the victims she has cast down, and numerous are all her slain. Her house is the way to Sheol, descending to the chambers of death."

Proverbs 7:24-27

Marcus thrived at the Naval Academy. He easily adjusted to the disciplined way of life in Bancroft Hall, having been raised by his father in a home environment that was almost military in its discipline and structure. Marcus reveled in the military atmosphere, the routine, and the expectation that young officers were to strive for the highest ideals, and felt in his element, submersed in a culture which held up the idea that being an officer in the United States Navy was a noble profession—not a trade, but a profession—and that every officer was expected to exemplify the very best quality of character at all times. Other than forgetting to return a library book on the Battle of Jutland early in his freshman, or 'plebe' year, Marcus went through the four years without a demerit. Majoring in military history, his studies provided him the rewarding experience of learning from some of the best naval historians in the country in a field that fully captured his interest. Very early on during his college years, he realized he wanted to be a Marine Infantry officer like his father. To Marcus, the Marines idealized the best traits in leadership and esprit de corps, and he passionately wanted to be part of a team that did great things. It was his one passion in life, a deep drive he believed came from God, and as he assessed the service options and the geopolitical climate during his years at the Academy, he realized that the Marines would be the service most likely to see combat, and that within the Corps, the Infantry branch would be the most likely branch to see combat.

As his father had predicted, when Marcus stepped foot on the football field during his freshman year and brought his drive, intensity, and desire, no one could hold him back. He slowly but surely moved up on the depth chart, passing the higher-priced recruited talent from larger high schools, the state champions, the prima donnas. Marcus had thought about and dreamed about and prepared to play football at Navy since he was four years old, and he would not be denied. He played clean but hard, out-toughed his competitors, played when he was puking, played when sick with a fever of 104—didn't matter. He was always the first on the practice field and the last one off, and never missed a practice or a game. When he reported as a freshman, the coaches evaluated him. They had an overflow of highly touted recruits from big schools around the country, so they didn't consider Marcus seriously. They made him a receiver. Marcus did well, but he ached to get his hands on the ball and run with it. He wanted the responsibility of carrying the ball, because he felt beyond question that no one else wanted that ball to get down the field more than he did; no one else had the level of desire he did; no one had the commitment to succeeding that he did—and, he would realize later, he craved responsibility. While not blessed with amazing athletic abilities like some of the young men that would come through Navy occasionally and go on to play professional football instead of serving in the military, Marcus' sole desire was to excel for Navy—for the United States Navy, for the service. This is why, when he played against Army or Air Force, he looked at the Army and Air Force players as fellow teammates—yes, for a moment wearing a different uniform—

and felt that like he and his Navy team, they too would be going off to serve the country upon graduation. This was very different from the men he played against from the civilian colleges, who majored in football during their four or five years at college, and upon graduation would in the main not really make any significant contribution to the country except to give them something to watch on Sunday afternoons.

The one thing at his young age he did not expect was that his living faith would come into conflict with the core value systems of American military service. For Marcus, high ideals and noble professions were automatically and implicitly grounded or, as he once penned in an essay he wrote, 'anchored' in the essential fundamentals of the Judeo-Christian faith. Integrity, honesty, truth, justice, compassion, forgiveness, service to others before self—these were all Christian virtues for Marcus first, never realizing that others only perceived them to be 'American' virtues tied to a particular American culture or, more likely, a specific individual. Most officers with whom he served would have said that the source of such value systems was within the individual officers themselves. Marcus believed that these character traits had their origin in the values God established as being right and good, and therefore were unquestionable; they were not relative to specific individuals nor specific social mores or times. He would come to realize only later that when the culture changed, so too would the value systems that underpinned the military's culture. After he graduated and was on active service, when homosexuals were permitted to remain in the military, Marcus was stunned to his very core, and on the heels of that shock came bitter disillusionment as the military fell in line with the various liberal American political administrations and simply adjusted its laws, morals, ethics, and virtues to comply with prevalent American cultural mores. Out the door went integrity, honesty, truth, justice, and morality.

***

"So I guess you did okay today," Sig said, as Marcus folded himself into her car. She picked him up outside of the campus after the Air Force game, where he'd scored a couple of touchdowns. She was driving a shiny black BMW, and as she navigated through the choked Annapolis streets to get out to the highway, Marcus just said, "It went okay, Sig. It's good to see you again. How are things going in your world?"

They had occasionally seen each other over the years while Marcus was at Annapolis. Sig had been accepted at George Washington University the same year Marcus went off to Navy, and while he couldn't date his first year, and his liberty was nothing like civilian college students, they kept up their relationship—but it had definitely changed. With exposure to a much wider variety of men, Sig had blossomed, and she wasn't so clinging or desperate. Riding the fitness craze, Sig had become a long-distance runner, and it toned her long, lean frame until she had the figure of a fashion model. She was drop-dead gorgeous and she knew it. Early on they had come to an understanding that she would see other men, and he was free to see other women, but Annapolis was a pretty tough course of sprouts and football took up what small amount of discretionary time he had, so there wasn't much time or opportunity for Marcus to develop other female relationships. When he needed a date, he called Sig, and if he let her know far enough in advance, she usually cleared her schedule for him.

When she'd been tucked away in Minnesota while her father explored the ramifications of pulling oil out from under ten thousand lakes, a young, handsome, and virile Marcus, soon to go off to become a naval officer, had seemed to be the answer to her every prayer, especially the prayers she offered hoping to escape from her increasingly dreary home. Her father continued his rise up through the executive ranks of his oil company, and her mother, emotionally abandoned, tried to find solace first in alcohol and then in other men and finally in drugs. In her second year at George Washington University, her mother wrapped a Mercedes Benz coupe around a telephone pole driving while drunk, and walked away from it without a scratch. Her father filed for divorce. When Sig heard the news about the divorce, it knocked her for a spin. She spent a day crying, inconsolable, and then that night went on a drunken binge that scared even her, and in fear, she reached out to Marcus the next day by email, asking him to call her as soon as he could.

When he got to a phone, she told him that her parents were splitting up. She was less than coherent and begged him to come visit her, and Marcus wrangled weekend leave and took a bus over to her school and spent the entire next day—fortunately a Saturday, not during the season, before spring training began—walking the streets of the nation's capital while Sig poured out her heart, talking about being left alone most of her life, about her mother's abandonment, about trying without success to please a distant, emotionally aloof father, and at the bottom of it all, never feeling truly loved. Marcus could not identify with that, since his parents had both throughout his life lavished love and affection on him and Mace. He always knew he was loved, because the Spirit of the Living God lived in his parents, and that Spirit could not help but be expressing love to the children. Yet he also knew Sig had never really embraced Christianity, and on their walk that gloomy spring day, he listened and tried to hear her heart, to see where the need was, and to what degree she had been broken. He sensed that not being loved was the sharpest, most painful spear cutting into her heart just then. While it was tempting to try and fill that void with his own love, he knew eventually it wouldn't work. He needed to steer her toward that Love that never fails, and so instead of making a play for her while she was vulnerable, he shared with her that she could have the sense of being loved, of being cared for, of being looked after, through a relationship with Jesus.

Sig listened to Marcus, trying to understand, but her expectations of what life should be kept getting in the way. She kept trying to see how she could get from where she was now, bereft and anguished, to a point where she would feel loved and cared for, but she couldn't see how God could get her from one place to the other.

"I hear what you're saying, Marcus, but look, here I am, alone now, my family is exploding, and there's nothing behind me, no home anymore."

"Sig, there never was a home, if you want to be honest ... at least from what you're telling me. Without the Spirit of God living in us, there will never be any true sense of home."

"Well yeah, you're right now that you say it. I remember looking at you and Mace and wishing I had what you had; I always wished I had parents like yours."

Marcus put his arm around her shoulder and she began to cry again. The wind was whipping up and he turned her into a corner coffee shop. They sat down and Marcus ordered a hot chocolate. Sig ordered a café latte.

"Marcus, I'll be okay, really," she said once the waiter left the table. She wiped her eyes and donned a tough, worldly woman manner. "It's their life, not mine. I don't know what I'm so upset about, really. I mean, look at me. I'm tucked away here at GW, I've got plenty of money, my father buys me a new car every year, and my classes are going great."

Marcus reached across the table and took her hand. "Sig, you know none of that stuff matters. Don't go down that road. Listen to your heart. Love is supposed to last. Jesus lasts—He never gives up on us, He never forsakes us, He never *leaves*. He will always love us. You can have that."

Sig's eyes narrowed. "You can say that, Marcus, because you know what it's like to be loved. I don't, okay? You can't describe the color red to a man blind from birth; he just doesn't have any reference frame. You know what love is, I mean, to me? Really? I'll tell you. It's someone who will hold me, and be there for me, and support me whenever I need it. And now there's no one, do you understand? I have no 'family' any more. It's broken."

Marcus cupped his hands around the chocolate. "I'm not sure I'd define love that way, Sig."

"So what's love, then ... at least according to Marcus Ironbridge?"

"Love is doing what is best for the object of one's love, without worrying about what one gets in return, even though sometimes it might mean doing something they might not like or want."

Sig looked through the quaintly curtained window at the crowds passing by on the street outside. "I ... I don't know anything about that, Marcus. It doesn't make sense to me. My parents always took care of themselves first. It's what we're supposed to do, right? This is how the world works."

"Sig, so ... how is it working out for them? I mean, are they really happy?"

She was about to respond when her phone rang, and she grabbed for it. She saw the number and stood up, holding up a finger to Marcus. "I have to take this," she said, and walked over to the window, out of earshot. He could see her talking, at first her eyes shining, an expression of pleased anticipation on her face. But after a minute, she began to gesture roughly with a hand, slicing it up and down, and he could see her bend over the phone and talk intensely into it, putting her other hand to her head anxiously. Then he watched as she listened while the other party was talking. She tried to interrupt, but the other party apparently rambled on. She began to cry again, silently. He could see her eyes moisten, and she finally snapped the phone shut and stood there for a moment, looking out the window. After a bit, she remembered Marcus was sitting at their table, and she meandered back and sat down.

Sig leaned back and let the tears spill out of her large blue eyes. He sat there without saying a word, waiting for her to share with him about the conversation she'd just had.

But she chose not to. Instead, she said, "What were we talking about, Marcus?"

"Your parents ... I asked you if you thought they were really happy, living their lives for themselves."

She paused, took a sip of her latte, now cold, and said, "They were! I mean, well, I *thought* they were. They had everything you could ask for, Marcus! There was the house on the lake, my father's great job, my mother was a beauty queen—at least, until the bitch started drinking—and they had the world by the tail."

"But they didn't have love," Marcus interjected. Sig twigged her head to one side in a gesture of bitter agreement. She reached for his hands over the little round table and surprised him with a question. "Do you love me?" she asked, hungrily, eagerly, eyes wide and attentive, sharp, looking at him closely.

"If you mean, will I do what is best for you without thinking of myself or what I can get from the relationship, yes, Sig, I do love you."

"Then come home with me and take me to bed and make love to me," she said quickly, leaning forward, clasping his face in her hands. An old woman at a table close by did a double take as the strikingly attractive blonde woman so brazenly propositioned the handsome young naval officer.

Marcus put his hands to hers and slowly lowered them from his face, but held them firmly. "You know we can't do that, Sig, and besides, is that really the best thing for you now? Oh, make no mistake, babe, I'd like to," he said, his voice low and thick with emotion and desire, and then recovering, he looked up at her and continued "but what would it solve, other than to fulfill my selfish desire?"

"Mine too," she said in a husky voice, looking directly into his eyes, squeezing his hands.

"You're making it difficult, Sig," Marcus said.

"Nothing could be easier, Marcus. Come on; my apartment is two blocks away. You said you had leave until Monday morning, right?"

"Sig, you know I can't. Please."

Sig yanked her hands back into her lap. "And why the f—, I mean, why the hell not, *dammit*? Isn't that what love is, giving each other comfort? I *need* you, Marcus. Do you understand that? Does your God understand that? I need you *now*, here, today. I need you to show me that you love me in a tangible way; in a way men have been showing women they love them for a million years. *I need you.* There, I said it." She stood up, threw her napkin down on the table, and looked down at him. "Now either you come home with me, or go find some Daisy May to sit around and read your Bible with, okay? What's it gonna be?"

***

Marcus had not gone back with her to her apartment, and that conversation had been almost two years ago. Since then he had learned from friends they had in common that she was going through men in Washington like a hot knife through butter. Yet two days before the Air Force game in his senior year, she emailed him and asked to meet for dinner after the game.

She pulled up in a new black BMW, blond hair flowing, and the looks she garnered from the assembled midshipmen waiting for rides along with Marcus were enough to feed ten women's egos. She paid it no mind. She was even more beautiful than he remembered. Making small talk during the drive, they went to a local mall, where they walked and Marcus listened while she described the past two years. She told him about her studies in journalism and mass communication.

"We had a class the other day with Dan Rather," she said, gushing. "He told us all about his show, '60 minutes', and some of the stories he had were hilarious. I've met Lesley Stahl, Christiane Amanpour, Morley Safer, and ... let's see, who else ... oh, God, how could I forget, Diane Sawyer and Mike Wallace."

"Did you enjoy that?" he asked.

"Oh yeah," she replied. "They've seen so much of the world. Some of the stories they had to tell about where they've been, who they've seen—I mean, it would be amazing to have that kind of life, don't you think? Traveling around the world, meeting famous people, putting your finger on the pulse of the world, watching global events emerge like chicks out of an egg, you know, seeing things happen before the rest of the world knows about it."

Marcus just sat while she talked, listening. Truthfully, he didn't think much of journalism or journalists, and he distrusted the general inclination that community had toward values, ethics, and morals directly opposed to what God had clearly stated as righteousness. They walked to their own tune.

"It doesn't bother you that sometimes these people put their own spin on things, shaping how people will think of those events?"

Sig looked over at him while she expertly steered the car through traffic. "Actually that's the part I like best," she said with a sly grin. "They tell us in the courses that truth is what you make it," she added. "And I wonder, what's so bad about that? Why can't a person do the very best they can to make the world the way they think it should be?"

"Sort of like playing God a little, isn't it?"

"So what if it is, Marcus? He's not doing such a great job of things from where I sit, so what's wrong with me trying to make it a little better?"

For the hundredth time, Marcus wondered what he was doing, having a relationship with this woman. "The god of this world, Sig, is Satan, and he's running things, in case you hadn't noticed."

"So then why shouldn't we do everything we can to make things better?"

"Sig, Satan runs things in the world, okay? He is the one who decides who gets to be famous. He decides what news stories get aired, what events people get to see, what huge crisis in some black hole of the planet is suddenly shoved into people's living rooms so they worry about it and talk about it and maybe spend their money to fix it, or vote for someone to fix it. And he decides who runs for elections so they can make pretend that they're actually guiding or directing things so that people really believe that man has control over his own destiny."

She looked over at him so long that he began to get nervous. Her eyes darted back to the road, but she said, "God, that's a depressing viewpoint. So you're telling me that all these famous people, with all their talents and intelligence and insights, all of our politicians who give up their lives to govern nations and people, are just tools in the hand of some celestial boogeyman?"

"Couldn't have put it better myself," he said.

"So ... how is it that you're going to be a naval officer? You're going to do what your admirals tell you, right? And they'll do what their political bosses tell them to do, right? And if their political bosses are just tools in Satan's hand, what are you doing, being in the military?"

It was a good question, and one for which he didn't have a ready answer. "It's a good question, Sig. I've asked myself that a lot lately. I keep finding these disconnects between the values and ethics I see in the higher ranks, and the ideals that I always thought underpinned the military."

"But you work there anyway, to try and make it at least a little better place, a little more like what it should be, right?"

He looked at her. "Yeah, maybe ... I guess." There was something he wasn't quite getting in her answer, but he couldn't find the flaw in her argument, so he set it aside as a matter to think about later.

They got to the mall. Sig parked, and as they walked into the entrance, he asked, "So what's been keeping you busy these last couple of years. Any serious candidates to take you away from all this and make you filthy rich?"

Holding on to his arm, she laughed. "I wouldn't be here if that had happened," she said, unthinking. The dart pierced through Marcus' armor more than any other thing she'd said or done since he'd known her. She went on, pulling no punches about her relationships. "I've seen other guys, yeah," she said unapologetically, almost proudly. "Some nice, some not so nice. Nothing serious," she went on, striding through the mall, holding on to Marcus. "Sometimes a girl just wants something from home now and again, something familiar ... safe, if you know what I mean." She glanced coyly at him, but he missed it.

"I'm sorry we haven't talked for so long," Marcus said.

She patted his arm. "Consider that my fault," she answered. "It was me, honestly. I mean, you have to understand though, when a woman invites a man to partake of her last favors ..."

"You don't have to go into it, Sig. I understand it was something you needed, but it was something I couldn't give you. I didn't think it would have been the best for you."

She went quiet then, her face seemed somewhat crestfallen, and he could sense her dredging up a less than pleasurable memory of something. "You were probably right," she said somberly, sadness lacing the reply.

"So what—" he paused as her phone announced an incoming text. She let go of his arm and took it out of her purse. She read it once, then brought it up closer to her face. She stopped walking.

"Everything okay?" he asked.

She looked up, staring straight ahead at nothing. "I ... I think so." He watched her take a deep breath and put a hand to her belly.

"Are you feeling okay, Sig?"

"What? Oh, yeah, yeah, I'm fine, Marcus, just fine. Just something I ate." Two teenage boys walked by the other way, one of them plainly gawking at the tall, stunning blonde on Marcus' arm.

"What was that?" he said, nodding toward her phone.

"Nothing, nothing at all ... nothing," she answered distractedly, and resumed her stroll, again taking his arm, her grip tightening. "Remind me not to eat Mexican food before five in the evening, okay? Now ... um, what were we talking about?" She smiled at him, but he knew her too well.

He slowed down. "Sig, what's up?"

She slowed with him, but didn't stop, pulling him along. "Don't let's talk about that now, Marcus, okay? I don't want to go into it. Something that ... it was just a surprise, that's all. So tell me," she said, trying to muster some bright conversation, "how's your religion thing coming? Still into all that?"

"Sig, it was never about religion, and yes, my relationship with God is coming along."

"Ah, Marcus, I could never understand any of that, really." She dismissed the topic of eternal life with a blithe wave of her perfectly-manicured hand.

"I'm sorry I couldn't explain it better, Sig. He could have helped; He can still help."

She stumbled and drew closer to him, grasping his arm. "Why Marcus, my dear, thanks, and oh, thank Him too, if you like, but I'm doing just fine. Did I tell you I've been accepted into the internship program at Wiley, Chilton, and Soames?"

Marcus shook his head. "Don't know who those guys are; are they some kind of law firm or something?"

"Don't be dense," she said, punching his arm lightly. "Wiley, Chilton, and Soames is only the most exclusive public relations firm in the country. Who do you think handles PR for the Administration now? And who do you think handles PR for 50% of the CEOs from the Fortune 100?"

"So they know about public relations; what will you be doing for them?" he asked, not really wanting to know. A heaviness, something like a sense of sadness or grief was weighing upon his spirit as the conversation wound on, and he wondered at it.

"Well, I won't be running for coffee and donuts, boyo," she said with vigor. "I'll be attached to the International Division—I speak, like, four or five languages, remember? I guess they think this face and figure aren't too bad either, because I'll have airtime as well. I think they'll have me be something like a spokesperson for one of their international clients."

"And that will fulfill your greatest desire?" Marcus asked, letting just a tinge of cynicism show through. As the words left his mouth, the question rose in his mind unbidden, *'Would this woman help you fulfill your greatest desire?'*

Sig shot him a look of blank surprise. "What kind of question is that? Why shouldn't it? I mean, Marcus, this is my career, remember? Did you think I was going to jaunt off to college and then just chuck all the hard work and studying and slaving and find some slob and get married and pump out a passel of kids?"

"There are worse fates for a woman, Sig ... excepting the 'slob' part, that is."

"Oh REALLY?" she replied archly, swooping her last word up into high tones. "Such as?"

"Such as giving herself to whatever guy comes along, and then finding in the end that none of them love her for who she is, but just for what they get from her."

Sig stopped in her tracks and looked at Marcus, and he didn't know if she was going to slap him or cry. She stared at him for a good minute, and her eyes filmed over. "So ... would you make an honest woman out of me, Marcus?" Her voice was quiet and, if he'd been a little more attentive, he would have caught the note of desperation in it.

"Sig, I've longed to make an honest woman out of you even when you were an honest woman, you know that. But until you know Him, until you lay aside your own life and pick up what life He has for you ... well, it just wouldn't work. I'm sorry. And this isn't news to you, Sig. You know this. You knew it when you sent me the email to meet you again."

"Right," she said, smiling, wiping away a tear from her cheek. "I knew that. But I just thought ... I don't know, never mind. But it does bring up a question, Mr. Ironbridge."

"What's that, Sig?"

She looked at him directly, boldly, putting in words the very same question that had been nagging at him for the past year. "Just what exactly are we doing? What's your interest in me?"

He looked down at his hand holding hers, the fingers intertwined, and suddenly Mace's unspoken commentary about being unequally yoked, demonstrated silently but eloquently in the barn one afternoon, came to mind. He thought for a while, wondering how to tell her how much he cared for her, but also how much he was convinced that any relationship they had needed to be on God's terms, not his, and certainly not on hers. He knew it was over then, and he needed to say so, right then, tell her straight out. As he looked up and opened his mouth to try and explain, she put a finger to his lips.

"Maybe we should just take our walk, okay?"

***

"Second lieutenant Marcus Arminius Ironbridge." The announcer at the podium pronounced Marcus' name, and he strode across the stage set up on the 50-yard line of Navy-Marine Corps Memorial Stadium in Annapolis. He wore the gold bars of a second lieutenant in the United States Marine Corps, and the Superintendent of the Naval Academy handed him his diploma and commission, shook his hand, smiled at him briefly. Marcus moved off as the next graduate followed. After four years of hard work, rigorous academic examinations, and a successful football career, Marcus was graduating from the U.S. Naval Academy.

All his life he'd wanted to be in the military, and today was a fulfillment of a dream. But instead of being buoyant, exuberant, or frenetic with excitement, Marcus stood in the crowd of newly-minted ensigns and second lieutenants aloof, unnaturally quiet, somber, and thoughtful. If someone had taken his emotional pulse, they would have discerned a deep, profound sense of satisfaction—a very personal, private, scintillating joy that an idealist feels when a life goal is achieved. The gravity of the accomplishment sat heavily upon him, for he sensed that this step would open to him other, more important opportunities. He was grateful to God for giving him the strength to come this far, and in the tumult of the day, amidst the congratulations from friends and family, it was as if his soul was suffused in thankfulness. He did not forget to constantly thank God for bringing him to this point, and asked Him to help him keep his life's worldly achievements in perspective. 'God,' he said at least ten times that day, 'use me now for whatever purposes you desire. Take me wherever You wish; put me wherever You wish. Do with me whatever You wish. *Whatever* ...' He was so emotional that he could barely breath out the words.

***

He met his parents after the graduation ceremony and they walked back to Bancroft Hall, Tack moving along quite well on his prosthetic leg. After they congratulated him he asked about his brother.

Claire smiled. "Oh, Marcus, you would be so proud of them both. Mace is handling everything outside—the barn, the animals, the business, making the cheese, everything. He *insisted* that we come. And Zoe!" She laughed, "Zoe took over the house before I left. Quite the little mother, that one! She has commanded the kitchen ... is that how you say it?"

"*Vous dites* commandeered," Marcus replied.

"Oh, well, anyway, even before we left she had kicked Mace out of the kitchen, pulled down my Julia Child, and shooed us all away from the table and back to the living room. She started doing the laundry, vacuuming the carpets, and dusting. You'd think the place was a mess before she arrived."

Marcus smiled again, thinking of Zoe's energy. "She wants you to see that she's willing to work hard for you," he said. "She wants to impress you. You could be her future mother-in-law."

"Phfffft," Claire said, shrugging a Gallic shoulder and snapping her fingers in the air, "she has *already* impressed me. I just *know* those two will get married, Marcus, it is the strangest thing. It is like watching two halves of the same person move about the house, let me tell you. Whenever Zoe is with us, I swear it, Mace speaks normally."

"Why is that?" Marcus asked.

"I have no idea of this earth. I asked Mace about that one time."

"And?"

"He said—in his slow way, because Zoe wasn't there, 'I think because God wants me to know that we are supposed to be as one.'"

Marcus nodded, stirred deeply. He felt a strong emotion just then for his brother, and he missed him. "Mace has a sense of God that is ... I don't know, *Maman*, very deep I think. There are times he is beyond me."

"Beyond us all, sometimes, I think," Tack said quietly.

"*Ce est la vérité*," Claire added in a low voice. "*Et moi aussi.* But he did want to be here with you, Marcus, though he knew you would understand."

"Oh, absolutely, no worries, *Maman*. We knew the place couldn't be left vacant when we started the business, and it was God's mercy that Mace and Zoe are able to run it without you two."

Claire asked Marcus where he would be going next, and Tack answered. "The Basic School, *Mon chéri*. It is the first school designed to prepare young Marine officers to lead an infantry platoon."

"*Mon Dieu*, if your great grandfather could see you now," she sighed, looking at her eldest. "He was a *poilus* in France, you know."

"I know, *Maman*. You have told us the story." Claire's grandfather had been on the line in France when the Germans came blasting through in 1940. He had been smacked down by a bullet from an MG42, but fought well enough to stave off an assault by a squad of storm troopers. Eventually his team had exhausted their ammunition, and the Germans rounded them up and put them in a temporary holding facility near Metz. He had escaped three days later, and eventually joined a British unit that ended up on the beach at Dunkirk.

"He would have lost his leg if he hadn't fallen in with the British, you know," Claire said. "I am sure he would approve of you being in the infantry."

"You know it's what I've always wanted," Marcus replied slowly. "And I think he would have, if he was around and saw the world we're living in. This is my *calling*." His voice was heavy with suppressed emotion and a gravity that made everything in the day seem weighted with portent. It was hard for him to make small talk, but he knew his mother was worried about him, and he wanted to tell her as much as he could about what would be happening to him. His father already knew what was in store for him in the near future.

"*Qu'est-ce que cela signifie*, 'calling'?" she asked.

"It means I feel that this is what I was made by God to do ... *le destin*," he answered.

Claire was thoughtful for a moment, and then asked, "What will you learn of them, at this school of basics?"

Tack smiled at his French wife's butchered English, but only from amusement, not scorn, for he knew her French was far better than his own. Marcus replied, "Well, infantry tactics of course; how to lead a platoon of Marines. They'll teach us how to employ small arms— rifles and hand grenades and mortars and machine guns. They'll teach us how to use common communications equipment, how to use supporting arms ... you know, like artillery and air support ... and logistics and martial arts and, well, a whole lot of other things."

"How long is the school?" she asked.

"Twenty-eight weeks," he replied.

"And then?"

"Based on my MOS, I'll go on to another school."

"MOS?"

"Sorry, *Maman* ... it means 'military occupational specialty.' It is what I will specialize in as an officer. Some officers will specialize in flying airplanes, others in tanks, others in artillery, but most will become infantry officers."

"What will you specialize in, Marcus?"

"I want to be an infantry officer, *Maman*. I'm convinced that I should learn how to fight on the ground. I can't tell you why, but that's how I feel."

"*Oui*, Tack felt the same thing. It was what he was supposed to do. We understand."

A newly graduated young ensign walked by with a girl on his arm. She was a tall, willowy blonde in a white summer frock under a broad, striking red summer hat with a wide brim and a feather in the band. Disturbingly, Claire chose that time in the conversation to ask, "Marcus, what about Sigrid? Did you invite her today?"

"No, *Maman*," he replied, "I didn't." Marcus hadn't yet shared the news that he'd broken up with Sigrid. He was beginning to see that it was something he should have done a long time ago. "She's in Belgium. She's hoping to be hired by a high-powered Washington media firm, and one of the company's Vice Presidents asked her to accompany him to Brussels so they could see how she would work out."

Claire held her tongue. Sigrid was a sensitive topic with Marcus, and it sounded to her like the young lady was sleeping her way through whatever glass ceiling there was in her profession. Like most young men when they are enamored of a particular young woman, it appeared that Marcus was blind to things that were blatantly obvious to other women. While she did not know how Marcus stood with Sigrid, she did not want to discuss it on this day. She sensed her son's somber mood, and did not want to put a stick in what could be a hornet's nest of emotion. But Marcus turned that around.

"*Maman*, I know how you feel about Sigrid, and I want to tell you ... you were right ... right about a lot of things. We broke up a few months ago. I finally realized that she's isn't going to see things the way I see things; she's enamored of the world, and doing a good job of making her way through it, and, well, that's not what I want."

Tack and Claire both pulled up short and the graduation crowd flowed around them. They looked at Marcus in surprise. "This is new," Task said, trying for Marcus' sake to hide his pleasure at the news.

"Yes sir ... I can't explain things, but the last time we met it seemed like God was speaking to me ... I mean, really clearly, and I realized that I'd let my own flesh get in the way, and I was misinterpreting what I wanted with what God says we should have."

Claire's eyes misted from a deep sense of relief and a conviction that her son had dodged a dangerous risk in his life. Tack, though, nodded.

"Son, I hear what you're saying, and I agree with you, but I want you to consider that there might be an additional perspective here." They'd started moving again with the crowd, but Marcus could see that Tack's leg was giving him a problem, so he steered them toward one of the benches strewn around the campus, and they sat.

"You're an idealist, Marcus. That means a lot of things, but one of the things it means is that, as a man in your relations with women, you're going to be a rescuer. Yeah, sure, the hormones were working and they kept you circling that wagon when you should have probably ridden on, but one of the other reasons you circled that wagon for so long was because of this desire you have, this hope for Sigrid you had, that somehow you could rescue her. And son," Task said, grasping Marcus' shoulder, "realize that the inclination to rescue is a mark of a child of God; it's in God's character to rescue. He is a redeeming God who ransoms those who have no hope. *Don't ever lose that.*"

Marcus digested this for a moment, sitting there, watching the crowd stream by, happy young men and women, now young naval officers, about to launch off into their careers, surrounded by proud parents, relatives, and sweethearts.

"And let me say this, Marcus," his father went on, and suddenly Marcus felt a strong pull to pay attention. "You will meet the one God wants for you, and you'll rescue her—somehow, some way, mark my words. It was that way with me and it was that way with your brother and for some reason I think it will be that way with you. I know it may have looked like that with Sig, but I never had a good feeling about that relationship, and neither did your mother. But we make mistakes sometimes, Marcus, you know? Though, when we make them trying to do something we think God would want done, He'll redeem the heart's motivation in some way."

Claire was staring at her husband with eyes of love, shining, remembering how the man sitting there with one leg had, so many years ago, rescued her.

"I'll remember, Dad," Marcus answered.

***

Marcus drove his parents back to their hotel and then went back to the Academy and up to his room in the eighth wing of Bancroft Hall. He was almost completely packed; everything he owned in the world fit into the bed of the pickup truck he'd purchased. He planned to drive with his parents back home to Minnesota to spend time home before his life in the Marine Corps began.

As he pulled out of the eighth wing parking lot for what would probably be the last time, he glanced at his officer's cap, placed carefully on his black leather messenger bag in the passenger seat. He took in the eagle, globe, and anchor in gold, and the import of that symbol, representing the attainment of a deeply-held desire to be part of a close-knit group of men who would go into harm's way to defend the innocent, to strike down the wicked, and to uphold righteousness. As he thought about the symbol, the dream he'd had the night prior suddenly shot back into the forefront of his mind, unbidden, unexpected, and as he navigated the thick Graduation Day traffic out to pick up his parents, he replayed it again in his thoughts.

In his dream, he was a guard in full combat rig, complete with an M16, body armor, Kevlar helmet, combat gloves, and desert boots. He was patrolling along a wide board walkway that was placed atop fenced wooden pens. The pens were square, and he looked down on prisoners milling about in them like cattle. The prison camp complex was in the middle of a vast desert. His task was to guard the prisoners in the pens, and he and the other guards would walk along the catwalk above the heads of the prisoners, looking down to make sure things were secure. In the dream, Marcus found himself befriending the prisoners, feeling sorry for them, and then coming to identify with them. The other guards discovered his affinities and in a brutal act of revenge, seized him, took away his combat gear, and butchered him like an animal. He watched it happen as if from a distance. They took his remains a short distance outside the camp and buried him in a shallow sandy grave. As sometimes is the case in dreams, he was conscious throughout the entire event, as though he was watching something happening to himself just a bit removed from the actuality of it. Yet he knew it was his own flesh going into the shallow grave, and he felt the brutal, savage hate of those who had been his brothers, killing him because of his identification with those who had been prisoners. Yet, when in the dream night fell, Marcus' remains rose up, an amorphous mass, floated back over the sand toward the prison, and with a furious, avenging passion, slaughtered the guards who had oppressed the prisoners. And then he awoke.

He wondered why he'd had such a dream the night before he graduated, and with determination, decided to just tuck it away and think about it later. He darted in and out of traffic on the way to pick up his parents, drive home for his first leave as an active-duty Marine, and then begin the rest of his life.

Chapter 6

Billy Rob

"I will give you the treasures of darkness and hidden wealth of secret places, so that you may know that it is I, the Lord, the God of Israel, who calls you by your name. 'For the sake of Jacob My servant, and Israel My chosen one, I have also called you by your name; I have given you a title of honor though you have not known Me."

Isaiah 45:3-4

At the corner of San Felipe Street and River Oaks Boulevard in Houston, Texas, a young man stood hanging from an 1890-style faux gaslight lamppost under an oak tree wearing black trousers with a silk stripe down each leg, a disheveled dinner jacket, and a frilled white dress shirt open to his waist. He held on to the lamppost with one hand and waved a champagne bottle in the other, and was whooping and yelling at the top of his lungs, shouting out to the world that he would be the "undisputed All 'n Gay-us King o' th' *en*-tar world."

A group of partygoers had followed him out of the massive mansion where a raucous party was still rambling on, laughing, as drunk as he was, wondering if he would get himself run down by traffic on River Oaks, a busy street. One of the revelers yelled out at him, "Hey, Billy Rob, is that bottle half-empty or half-full?"

The young man swinging from the lamppost yelled back boisterously, "It's half-full, you negative, pessimistic sumbitch!" The group of dilettantes and sycophants all laughed uproariously, further feeding Billy Rob's inebriated exultation. He let out a shrieking Texas war whoop.

It was one in the morning, the streetlights were glistening in the humid Texas night, and after a while a police cruiser appeared on the scene. Billy Rob just kept swinging around, waving the bottle, now and then taking a pull, and continuing to announce to the world that he would soon be the king of all the world's oil and gas resources. One policeman got out of the cruiser and sauntered over to where Billy Rob was hanging from the light, while the other parked the cruiser to block southbound traffic on River Oaks boulevard.

"Hey Billy Rob," the patrolman said calmly, as though he was encountering Billy Rob during a nice, pleasant stroll down the street—at one in the morning.

"Hey yerself, Tommy John, you sumbitch." Billy Rob and Tommy John were old high school buddies, and had kept up the acquaintance, the meetings usually occurring just after Billy Rob would get drunk, or disorderly, or both.

"Nice night for a concert," Tommy John said, looking around, hands tucked peacefully into his utility belt. He ignored the group of formally dressed young people gathered around Billy Rob as he stood on the base of the street lamp. They had quieted down as the policeman approached the scene.

"Ain't no concert here, you sumbitch," Billy Rob replied at the top of his voice. "This here is what you call a *press conference*, Tommy John. And you can bet a hunnert percent o' that measly salary the city pays you on what ah'm announcin'."

Officer Tommy John Lambert looked up at Billy Rob swinging around the lamppost and asked, "Yeah. Maybe I can finally make some good money. Whaddya got, Billy Rob?"

"Only that ah'm gone be the richest sumbitch in Houston, Tommy John, 'cause ah'm gone take over de fambly all bidness. Whoo hoo!" he yelled. The revelers gathered around the lamppost yelled with him, raising drinks in their hands. The girls were all yelling 'whoo hoo, whoo hoo' in high-pitched squeals. Billy Rob then jumped down from the lamppost and put his arm around the police officer. He stuck his face right up next to Tommy John's, and in what was supposed to be a whisper, blurted out, "Th' ol' man has done croaked his last, Tommy John. Ol' Digger Jack done called up not a hour ago. Th' ol' man was hangin' with one o' his latest babes around some place over with them *Eye*-talians ... 'La Speeziya or sumthin'. Well, Ol' Digger Jack says that Daddy got ta pukin' while he was playin' at some casino, so he headed down to the marina, and by the time he got back on the boat, he was worse'n a gutshot dog. By the time them *Eye*-talians got a doctor to 'im, he was stone dead."

Officer Lambert took off his hat and said, "I'm right sorry to hear that, Billy Rob. Are you sure?"

"Damn right he's sure," a female voice cried happily from the crowd, "don't he look sure?" There was giggling coming from the group of drunken revelers on the grass of the Brewster estate's lawn, just a few yards away from where Billy Rob was standing with his arm around Tommy John, breathing an alcoholic fume into his face.

"Ol' Digger Jack says them *Eye*-ties arrested th' bitch he was with at the *hoe*-tell, Tommy John. Got 'er for poisonin' the old man. Ah *tolt* 'im she was trouble." Billy Rob was shaking his head, and only Officer Lambert, standing up close and personal next to Billy Rob could see the tears on his face.

"You de *man* now, Billy Rob!" one of the young dandies yelled from the grass, whooping loudly. Officer Lambert heard a choked sob, and then Billy Rob rubbed his free hand across his face quickly.

"What's Ol' Digger Jack gonna do?" Tommy John asked, to cover Billy Rob's embarrassment as his friend tried to stand.

Billy Rob paused for a long moment. "For Chrissake," he said almost to himself, but Tommy John could hear him. "Ah'm only twenty-five, the sumbitch. What th' hell ah'm gonna do now?" Billy Rob seemed to shake himself and turned to Tommy John. "What? Yeah, right, well, TJ, we're gonna bring the body back here," he said, weaving a bit. "We'll send 'im up one of his own smokestacks, like he wanted. His ashes'll float out over the Gulf, out there," Billy Rob waved his hand in the general direction of the Gulf of Mexico, from which Jamison Daniel Brewster the Third had drawn forth massive amounts of black oil, which in turn created his massive wealth, and which fueled his ambition to become the richest man in the world. He never achieved that ambition, and left his only son, Billy Rob Brewster, effectively an orphan while trying.

"Well, we'll do what we can to make things go smooth here," Tommy John said quietly. "You need any help with them yahoos over there?" he asked, referring to the unruly group of drunken friends that were now gamboling on Billy Rob's front lawn. One of the younger men had thrown his dinner jacket up into the trees, and another had a half-clad girl on his shoulders, trying to retrieve it.

Billy Rob suddenly could stand up without any help, and he looked at his friend steadily. "You smarter'n you look, Tommy John. How's come you're just a policeman?"

"I guess I like working a high-risk job, getting shot at by angry people, getting paid peanuts, Billy Rob, just so I can come haul your rich ass out of jail whenever you get on the wrong side of the law."

Billy Rob gave him a long look and then said, "Yeah. Right. Well, look, Tommy John, I gotta go back to the party, if you know what I mean."

A clearly feminine voice rose up out of the crowd on the grass. The two men looked together to see a tall, willowy woman with long blonde hair, in a shockingly short evening dress that became even shorter as she stood on tiptoes and lifted a long, elegant arm to wave at Billy Rob. "Billy Rob, it's dang cold out here, honey, now, come on in and let me warm you up!"

Tommy John took a long look at the stunning blonde standing on the grass. She *must* be cold, he thought. Yowies. He turned to Billy Rob, who was now weaving again like a drunken sailor. "You go whup it up, Billy Rob. Just be careful with the ladies."

In a voice that was stone cold sober, Billy Rob replied with caustic irony. "God, don't I know it. Them women'll be the death of me yet."

***

Billy Rob Brewster was the only son of Jamison Daniel Brewster the Third, and Margaret Llewellyn Argent, daughter of Sir Arthur and Dame Jeanine Argent, minor English royalty. Jamison Daniel, or 'JD' as he was known throughout the oil and gas industry, had struck it rich as a young oil company entrepreneur, and after riding the rough and tumble Texas oil market for a few years, he parlayed one small exploration company into a massive oil and gas empire, giving the large international oil companies stiff competition. Once he made his first billion dollars, he said to his faithful Chief Operating Officer, Jack Riker—who from the day they first began working together in his start-up company was called 'Ol' Digger Jack'—that he would be 'headin' over to England to nab him a princess.' Nothin' but royalty for Jamison Daniel Brewster the Third.' Ol' Digger Jack made all the arrangements and lo and behold, was taken aback when eight months later JD returned to the states with Margaret Argent in tow, a tall plain-looking woman with a slim figure and sandy brownish hair and a pleasant, gentlewomanly manner. Ol' Digger Jack, crusty wildcatter that he was, took to her right off, because she treated him in the same polite and considerate way that she treated everyone else—no cheek with her, no 'coming it the nob', as he would often hear her caution herself. But he didn't exactly know how she'd work out in the breakneck environment of being the wife of an oilman, especially an oilman that was trying to break into the cabal of the Seven Sisters—the seven largest oil companies in the world. JD wanted his very own United States Oil Company, or USOCO, to be the eighth member of that distinguished group, and he spent much of his early time in the industry trying to make that happen.

But Margaret was made of tough English stock. A quiet woman, realizing that JD had married her primarily for her pedigree, she nonetheless decided to be a good wife. She bore him a son, Billy Rob, and soon thereafter became pregnant with another child, a daughter. But she lost the daughter in a miscarriage very late in her pregnancy, and the damage done by the emergency dilation and curettage procedure was such that she could never have another child. This crushed her, but she rebounded quickly, realizing that she still had one child who was depending on her. The death of his daughter also struck JD hard, and it caused him to re-evaluate his life and his priorities. For a time he turned his heart back to his wife, and for the majority of Billy Rob's formative years, JD was a devoted husband to his English wife. And then, while being simply a devoted husband, he actually then fell in love with her, and their marriage went from one of convenience, to a pleasant companionship, to a deep romance. Billy Rob was the beneficiary of this, and they were the happiest years of his life.

But when Margaret was thirty-five, they found she had breast cancer, and in four months, she was dead. JD was shattered, and Billy Rob, a young boy of thirteen, felt that his world had come to an end. With all their money, all their work and wealth and privilege, they realized that Margaret had been the most important thing in their lives.

But they had to live; they had to move on. JD threw himself into his work, and in a strange translation of his grief, seemed to tie the success of his company to the feelings he had for his dead wife, and so worked even more intensely to make the firm prosperous. But in his focus on building a corporate monument to Margaret, he didn't realize that Billy Rob was left adrift. Billy Rob had inherited some of his mother's intuition about people, and realized that his father's devotion to work was simply a reaction to his grief at losing the one person he'd ever loved, and so it tempered what could have become bitter feelings toward his absent father. But it still hurt. He tried everything to get his father's attention, and finally figured out that the only thing that worked was getting on the wrong side of the law. He and Tommy John got to know each other well during that phase of Billy Rob's life. Billy Rob never did anything wholly stupid or dangerous, but it was fortunate that Tommy John Lambert knew the backstory and was an understanding law enforcement officer. But after a few scrapes with the law, Billy Rob realized that he didn't want that kind of attention, and so he figured he'd just head down a different trail.

When Billy Rob graduated from Texas A&M, he surprised his father by seeking and obtaining a commission as a second lieutenant in the United States Marine Corps, and went off to The Basic School. Billy was a good officer; better than good, actually. He consistently received top fitness reports wherever he was posted, and no one, if he could help it, ever realized he was richer than probably the Commandant of the Marine Corps and his top ten generals combined. Billy's military occupational specialty was aviation—he became a helicopter pilot. He was first in his flight class, and as such, chose to fly the AH-1W Cobra, the Marine Corps' most advanced attack helicopter at the time. Billy Rob built a reputation within Marine aviation as an intense, aggressive, professional perfectionist, who would lay himself out to make sure his Marines had everything they needed to do their jobs. When he flew, he was known for his willingness to risk his own safety for that of the mud Marines—the Marines on the ground. He had an excellent flight safety record, and his performance in the air was unsurpassed. Off duty, however, Billy Rob was known as the squadron's biggest party animal with a chip on his shoulder the size of Texas.

While Billy Rob was off flying for the Marines, and after a few years of absorption in his work, realizing that work wasn't filling the void left by his wife's death, JD decided to find another wife. By then, JD was perhaps one of the world's most eligible bachelors, and there was no shortage of women waiting in the wings to assuage the poor widower's heart, so to speak. His first try was a Hungarian fashion model; she lasted about two months and took JD for around three or four million. The next was a Swiss heiress who, surprisingly, turned out not to be an heiress at all, but actually a bold, attractive adventuress prowling through Europe, looking for rich men to con. It was purely by happenstance that she encountered JD, who had been skiing in Staad for a week. That one cost JD around eight million and eight months out of his life. About that time, Ol' Digger Jack first sat down with Billy Rob when he was home on leave from his first tour of duty. Ol' Digger Jack had a heart-to-heart with Billy Rob, explaining to the son that his beloved boss was going through 'a phase' and that he shouldn't take this as some kind of slight against his mother.

"It's just something he's gotta do," Ol' Digger Jack began.

"Yeah, yeah, I know, Ol' Digger Jack. It doesn't make me feel any better, but I understand."

"Your momma was a real Princess," Ol' Digger Jack said softly, shaking his head, grinding his leathery hands together.

"She was that, sir," Billy Rob replied, clearing his throat. "They broke the mold when they turned her out. But what're we gonna do about JD?" Billy Rob, like most Texans and other people in the world, referred to his father by his first two initials. "He's costin' the business, like, ah'm figuring around eight or nine hundred thousand a month, averagin' out an' all." Billy Rob's Texas accent came back strong when he was home.

Ol' Digger Jack just shook his head. "It ain't like the business cain't afford it, boy."

"Yeah, Ol' Digger Jack, but it's *bad* business."

Ol' Digger Jack shrugged his shoulders like the weary old man that he was. "Well, maybe he'll find another Princess."

Billy Ray looked at Ol' Digger Jack and he put his hand on his shoulder while Ol' Digger Jack's eyes filled up. "Maybe so, Ol' Digger Jack ... maybe so."

***

JD never did find another Princess. After the faux Swiss heiress, there was a Brazilian fashion model—he hadn't learned his lesson with the Hungarian; a Norwegian shipping company heiress—a real one this time; a Russian diplomat working in Washington at the Soviet embassy; and a young and highly ambitious software developer from Boston who JD met while Billy Rob was doing diligence during the purchase of the company for which she worked. After the software developer engineered USOCO out of five million dollars and a lengthy court battle, JD decided to go fishing in Europe again. Billy Rob and Ol' Digger Jack were at their wits' end, but some instinct told them that they shouldn't try to stop JD. He was trying to find Margaret in the only way he knew how, and they didn't have the heart to kill that in him. Fortunately they had the money to let him keep trying. The company was incredibly successful.

The Italian woman, Giovanna Disarona, at first looked like she was a possibility. She was pretty but not a beauty queen, and in fact she looked a little like Margaret. She seemed a down-to-earth, hard-working woman. She had been trained as a chef, and then turned to become an entrepreneur who started a chain of country restaurants throughout northern Italy and was working to expand her brand into England, where, God knows, they needed good food. She was an experienced world traveler, had tons of her own money—at least, so they thought—and seemed to be comfortable with JD's personality and habits. She would travel with him when she could break free of her own responsibilities, but she didn't strike Billy Rob as being too possessive or clingy. But Ol' Digger Jack never liked her from the start, and Billy Rob couldn't figure that out. JD married her after a whirlwind courtship—JD didn't know how to conduct any other kind—and shortly thereafter, while reveling at a local casino in La Spezia, she dropped a lethal dose of belladonna into JD's drink. JD made it back to his yacht only to die in a rictus of pain. After the autopsy and the investigation conducted by the Italian police and Interpol, they discovered that her vaunted company was in fact on the ropes financially, and she had been turned down by numerous financing sources. JD had been purely a play for financing, and apparently JD had turned her down when she asked him to finance a part of her growing company. He didn't think it was a good investment, and so she decided to just get him out of the way and use the inheritance as bridge financing. Ol' Digger Jack's disparaging nickname for her—'Giovanna Borgia'—had proved eerily prophetic.

Billy Rob Brewster took over his family's business after getting a special dispensation from the Marine Corps to be released from active duty before his period of commitment had expired. It broke his heart to leave the Corps, but he didn't know what else to do. At the time, USOCO was doing around three billion dollars a year, and the employees were like his own family. He felt no one could take care of them better than he could—but it ripped him apart, taking off the uniform for the last time.

He thereupon became known in Texas and in the oil industry, two groups with a propensity to peg their people with outlandish or dramatic monikers, as 'BR'. To his friends though, he was always just Billy Rob. He proved an even more astute businessman than his father, and where JD had the Seven Sisters as the antagonist in his life's story, Billy Rob had to contend with the Organization of Petroleum Exporting Countries, or 'OPEC'. He kept Ol' Digger Jack as his Chief Operating Officer—he couldn't imagine anyone else filling the post. One day soon after Billy Rob took over, they talked about the direction USOCO should take in the future.

"Them Ay-rab sumbitches is gittin' outside their lane, Ol' Digger Jack. Ah'm thinkin' it's time we set 'em back a bit." Billy Rob was sitting in a huge leather chair with his feet up on a huge lacquered wooden desk, smoking a big black cigar.

"Yeah, Billy Rob, but they has got themselves more oil than they got sand, and you know what that means."

"What's that gonna mean?" Billy Rob asked, blowing smoke up toward the ceiling.

"They're gonna have more friends than a filly in a pasture full o' stallions."

Billy Rob laughed out loud, choking on his cigar, and looked at his old friend. "Ol' Digger Jack, you wouldn't know the difference between a filly and a stallion if they ran you over."

"Yeah, but it sounded purty good, didn't it?" Billy Rob laughed again. "But seriously, Billy Rob, the politicians are gonna line up to kiss their table-cloth-covered asses, you know that. Expect all kinds of rules and regulations to make it easy for them to sell their oil all over the world."

"Well, we'll just have to make it easier for them to buy oil from us, don't ya think?"

Ol' Digger Jack ground his hands together for a bit. "Well, hell, why not? We can give it a good run, anyway. But hell, Billy Rob, where we gonna git oil them Ay-rabs can't git cheaper?"

Billy Rob looked at his old friend and smiled. "Well, ah'll tell ya, Ol' Digger Jack, what I hear tell, them Ay-rabs, they just hate cold weather. So ahm a'thinkin' we'll head north."

"To Alaska? Them politicians ain't gonna let you stick a shovel in the ground up there, Billy Rob!"

"Nope, it ain't up in Alaska. Minnesota."

Ol' Digger Jack looked at Billy Rob for a minute. "Minne-what? Is that someplace in Canada, up around the artist circle or somewhere?"

Billy Rob laughed. "Yeah, well, Ol' Digger Jack, it ain't in Canada, it's right here in the ol' U.S. of A. and we're gonna jump all over that action. An' the best part is them politicians up there'll do anything if you bring 'em jobs, so ... let's go bring 'em some jobs!"

So Billy Rob and Ol' Digger Jack took USOCO up to Minnesota and competed head-to-head with OPEC by investing in the new explorations under the lakes in Minnesota, of all places.

***

A young woman in a golden-yellow stretch top and tight black running shorts jogged out of the village of Toussus le Noble, a southwest suburb of Paris, and turned onto the Rue Robert Esnault Pelterie. It was a brilliant June morning, the sky a crystalline blue, and the sun pushed down light and warmth onto her olive skin. She sucked in the scent of jasmine as she ran past the hedgerows. Her feet pounded the asphalt as she came upon the traffic round just east of the little airfield. She circled the airport and picked up the Chemin du Plessis a-Trappes, a dirt road bordering a wood that would take her out toward the golf course. After a short time she turned onto the Chemin de l'Orme Rond, the little lane lined with elm trees that circled the golf course. She was perspiring freely, a thick dark circle on her front and a patch of moisture down the small of her back. Her breathing was controlled and easy, and she felt strong. She was svelte, 1.75 meters tall—her American friends would say 5'9"—with a trim figure and slim hips—almost too thin, if one asked her mother, who, watching her daughter's trajectory in life, despaired of grandchildren. Marie-Clémence had long, muscular legs that would eat up the kilometers whenever she could find the time to get in a run. Her thick black hair was up in a French braid and secured behind her head, and it tapped her back in time with her pace. Her green eyes scanned the terrain around her, taking in the golfers, gracelessly lurching or lunging, or hunched over their little white spheres, or riding in little electric cars making antic gestures. She saw men dressed in pastels, which she found strange and not attractive in the least. 'Men should be strong,' she thought; 'stronger than me, at least.' For some reason she equated pastels with femininity. She picked up her pace, eyes flashing, flushed with her own strength and power and fluidity of movement, disdaining men who would waste time and give up an opportunity for real exercise and instead chase a little white ball around for hours. She felt free and strong, ready to conquer the world, and she would do at least 12 kilometers this morning. As she ran, she took from a compartment in her mind the memory of yesterday and replayed it again like a video, remembering, the joy of the day obliterating the effort of running through the woods, and the kilometers flashed by unnoticed.

Yesterday, Marie-Clémence Genevieve Gabrielle Levinson, only child of Zasha and Rachel Levinson, had graduated magna cum laude from *Ecole Normale Supérieure*, or ENS. Founded in 1794, ENS was renowned throughout France and around the world as one of the most preeminent educational institutions in history, where many of the nation's leading scientists, engineers, and civil servants all began their careers. Jean-Paul Sartre, Michel Foucault, Henri Bergson, Louis Pasteur, Paul Langevin, and Laurent Schwartz graced their graduate list. Thirteen Nobel Prize laureates, including eight in Physics, eleven Fields Medalists, more than half the recipients of the CNRS's Gold Medal (France's highest scientific prize), and several hundred members of the Institut de France had graduated from this school, but what most interested Marie-Clémence, however, was that several Prime Ministers, and many ministers, called this their alma mater. She had competed against more than 9000 applicants to win one of 250 places as an undergraduate.

Working more than 70 hours a week for the last four years, 21-year old Marie-Clémence Levinson was on the intellectual razor's edge—she scintillated with nervous energy, pulsating with the strength of youth and enthusiasm, for her ambition was nothing less than to be the *second* female Prime Minister of France, and its *first* female Jewish Prime Minister; the Golda Meir of France. Her top position among the class had garnered the attention of the Office of the President of the French Republic, since the school was renowned for producing some of France's leading civil servants, and this very afternoon she had an interview with one of staff members of the Minister for Foreign Affairs. She would finish her run, have a shower, dress casually, take a small luncheon at one of the local cafes, and then take the Métro to the 8th arrondissement, where the meeting would take place in the *Place Beauvau*, facing the *Élysée Palace*.

She rounded her course, turned onto the Chemin du Bois des Linots, and headed back to the village to begin the rest of her life.

***

The Métro emptied Marie-Clémence under the street at the Madeleine station, and she purposefully strode toward the address on the thick, cream-colored stationary that had arrived in the mail the week prior. The *Place Beauvau* had housed the French Ministry of the Interior since 1861 in the Hotel Beauvau, and people referred to the '*Place Beauvau*' as a shorthand reference to the Ministry, in much the same way people referred to 'Downing Street' or 'the White House' when referring to those respective governments. She moved through the crowds, taking in the broad avenue, the ever-present traffic, the Eiffel Tower on the skyline across the Seine. She peered into the shops lining the boulevard—Swarovski, Armani, Banana Republic, Gap, Louis Vuitton, H&M, and others, all competing to take her money. For the last three years she had buried herself in her studies, and strolling along one of the world's most fashionable stretches of marketing and materialism was liking coming awake in a strange new world. Marie-Clémence enjoyed fashionable clothes—she liked to be feminine, but her tastes did not run to excess, as did some of her friends. Her tastes ran to simple, classic styles; elegant, usually expensive but timeless, and so far she had received no complaints from the men in her life. This afternoon she wore a simple two-piece suit; a dove gray blazer and slacks over a modest black knit high-collared blouse with a thin gold necklace. Her hair, washed and dried after her run, was now loose, black, and flowing just below her shoulders. Small, comfortable black shoes, a black leather Vuitton messenger bag that had been a gift from her mother upon being accepted at ENS, and a thin gold watch completed the ensemble.

She arrived at the *Place Beauvau* and stood looking up at the ornate black and gold wrought iron gate. French gendarmeries eyed her closely. She held up her card. "I have an appointment." One of the gendarmeries took the card, glanced at it, and opened the gate for her. Another, smelling oddly of grilled onions and tobacco, escorted her down the long walkway toward another entrance, which proved to be a small tunnel into a courtyard, around which stood several discreet doors. She saw two large men who were obviously private security flanking one door in a corner. The gendarmerie nodded to one of the men at the door.

"Mme. Levinson, I presume?" said the taller of the two men.

"Yes. I have an appointment." She held up the card again. The gendarmerie departed. The security man took the invitation, read it slowly, apparently digesting every line, and asked her for some identification with her picture affixed. He looked closely at her passport and then up at her face. She stared back at him to make sure he knew she wasn't intimidated. He held out his hand with a gesture toward her bag. She handed him the messenger bag and he set it down on a small table near the door. He went through it quickly, respectful of her property, but thoroughly. She had a MacBook Air, an iPad, several cords and plugs for her electronics, three pens, her iPhone, some tissue, a makeup case, and her wallet in the bag. After checking the compartment in which she kept her cords and keeping her passport, he gestured for her to follow him in. He did not smile.

They walked up three flights of polished wooden stairs, her hand on the black wrought iron railing that curved around an ancient-looking lift that reached upward through to the top of the building. It was an unnaturally quiet passage up the flight of steps. Her shoes made little sound on the wooden risers, and she noticed the guard was wearing soft-soled tactical boots.

On the third floor, the tall man took her to a door at the end of a long hallway. He knocked once and opened the door, nodding tersely. She went in. There was a man seated at a desk, and another man in a chair against the wall. They both stood. An empty chair sat before the desk. The man from behind the desk came around it to shake her hand.

"Mme. Levinson; thank you for coming. I am Paul Giscard; this is my colleague, Jean-Patrique Gillette. Please have a seat."

The security man who had led her to the room took her messenger bag, lifted a lid on a small square metal container standing in the corner of the room, deposited the bag in the box, and turned and left the room after nodding to the man in a chair against the wall.

They all sat, Giscard behind the desk, while Marie-Clémence and Jean-Patrique pulled their chairs up on the other side of the desk to face the older man. Giscard spoke in a mellifluous and very refined French, and was in his mid-forties, with silver-gray hair about the temples. He wore a dark blue business suit with a red silk tie, cufflinks in a crisply starched cream-colored shirt, gray eyes, and a complexion that called to mind summers in Saint Croix or Cannes. Jean-Patrique was mid-twenty-something, obviously the junior person, but there was a hardness to the young man that was absent in Giscard. Gillette's shoulders strained against the fabric of his gray business suit, tapering to a thin waist. Veins stood out prominently in strong hands, and he sat with an air of expectancy, it seemed to Marie-Clémence, holding himself in waiting should someone or something come crashing through the door. He had short dark hair, a dark complexion, with a lean face and a stubbled, angled jawline. She guessed he was Paul's personal bodyguard.

"So I should begin by saying that we are quite impressed with your performance at ENS, Marie, and we offer our congratulations. We are grateful that you have agreed to meet with us. But forgive me ... may I call you Marie?"

"Marie-Clémence," she corrected, and then added, "thank you."

Paul nodded graciously. "Of course; Marie-Clémence, it is so much prettier, if you will permit me to say so." She smiled demurely. She sensed Giscard was a professional diplomat. He spoke and gestured with fluid grace, and his French was erudite and distinguished. He clasped his hands, leaned forward on the desk, and looked at her. "So then, before we move further, may we first between us come to an agreement that what is spoken about here remains strictly confidential?"

"But of course," Marie-Clémence replied. "I expected it to be so."

"Good," Giscard replied, smiling. "M. Gillette has a few papers for you to sign that will, shall we say, 'formalize' your kind and courteous assertion."

Marie-Clémence looked over at Jean-Patrique, in whose hand suddenly papers had materialized. He stood—average height, she noted—and put them down on the desk.

"Look them over, please, Mme. Levinson, while M. Gillette and I get a coffee. Might we bring you something? Surely a coffee? A croissant?"

"No, thank you, M. Giscard."

The papers were a formal agreement between the Ministry of the Interior for the Republic of France, and Marie-Clémence Genevieve Gabrielle Levinson—they had spelled her entire name correctly, she noticed—regarding the confidentiality of topics discussed during her interactions with that ministry, under pain of not less than five years in prison, and the possibility of charges up to and including treason. She had seen similar agreements in her sessions at ENS; these were typical when undertaking business with the French government, and she was not in any way disturbed. She did notice, however, something she had not seen before—a clause which indicated that she might, in these discussions, and in future activities toward which these discussions might lead, be exposed to interactions with members of the French intelligence community, and may, for one reason or another, become privy to information associated with or in support of these services, and she was to consider herself therefore under constraint regarding the use, publication, or distribution of such knowledge or information, under pain of prison, judicial prosecution, or other such penalties as the Republic might determine.

After seven and a half minutes she put down her pen, having read and signed all four documents. Giscard and Gillette entered a very few seconds afterward—extraordinary timing, she thought—and Gillette gathered the papers wordlessly.

"Thank you so much, Marie-Clémence. Do you have any questions about what you signed?"

"If I may, M. Giscard, any questions I have might be better informed as we move on into our ... discussion."

Giscard smiled, nonplussed, and sat down. "Of course, yes, how percipient. Completely agree." Jean-Patrique sat down in the same chair as he had taken previously, with the same posture, eyes on her closely but, as it were, unobtrusively, giving the impression that he was part of the conversation when in fact he was probably there simply to make sure she didn't pull out a gun or a knife and threaten Giscard's life.

"So, Marie-Clémence, we know you. You were born in Normandy and raised by Zasha and Rachel Levinson—an only child—and your father is one of France's most prominent caterers. You traveled around the world with him as he was assigned to various countries, supporting the development of various agricultural techniques. You are twenty-one years of age, having graduated magna cum laude from ENS, with the world at your feet."

She nodded. She expected the government to know her background. She would have been surprised had they any questions about that.

"Permit me to introduce myself," Giscard was saying. "My position at the

Ministry is somewhat ... recent. You might say that my office has come into being due to an amalgamation of different responsibilities, which together do not fit neatly into any existing portfolio. The President recognizes that we must as a nation accommodate certain trends in the days in which we live, and he has identified one of these trends and charged me with the responsibility to structure France's response to this trend."

Marie-Clémence listened politely, her hands folded demurely in her lap, watching Giscard's gestures accompanying his dialogue. His hand moved gracefully like a conductor orchestrating the smooth words that poured forth. His head tilted this way or that, gently, slightly, inclining to show openness or a hint of self-deprecation. She watched him as she listened, entranced. Jean-Patrique kept his eyes on her hands.

"The trend? Yes, well, as you know, France is seeing a dramatic rise in the number of Muslim citizens. The government is not blind, and can read demographic statistics as well as any man on the street, and these numbers will only increase. And yet, while most French people wish France to be a country that is open and welcoming to all nationalities, to all ethnicities, at the same time most French people still want France to remain French. Would you agree?"

"Most definitely, M. Giscard."

"You have some qualms about the increase in the number of Muslims in France?"

Marie-Clémence hesitated. It was inconceivable that they did not know she was Jewish. "I do, actually, M. Giscard. I agree with most citizens that France should be an open and inviting country, but primarily for those who wish to come and be French, or at least, for those who will choose not to actively work to subdue or destroy French culture in favor of their own. And we know what an increase in the Muslim population in France would do for French Jews, who have made this country their own."

"You are quite frank on this point," Giscard said, but she could see that he was not bothered; on the contrary, she felt that he was leading her, and she was taking the right turns in the conversation.

"You know I am Jewish, M. Giscard." He nodded gently. "Nonetheless, I believe Muslims and Jews can get along, that we can live together in this country in peace, *if* we all agree to live as French men and French women, united in the culture and belief systems and ethics and value systems that have made this country great throughout history. I believe in this passionately, M. Giscard, this is not just hyperbole."

"Yes, I believe you," Giscard said, holding up a preemptory hand. "We've read your thesis on the subject, and it is part of the reason you are here today. You argued very well that future ethnic violence has the potential to do great damage to France's economy and to her position among the nations of the world. And so," he went on, "let us come to the point of our discussion.

"The Minister has determined that two things are very important to France at this time, and we believe you can help us in these areas. The first is that the Ministry believes that there may be segments of the Muslim population in our nation that may not be, well, shall we say, amenable to integrating into French society or French culture. In fact, they may well wish to make France into another Lebanon, or Syria, or Morocco, or like some other nation from which now stream millions of discontented refugees. Unfortunately they have come into France and are integrating into almost every portion of our social infrastructure, and while most of the Muslims in the country are peaceful, we must not ignore the fact that some are not. In fact, some wish to plan nefarious actions against France and against her people. We cannot let such things happen."

Marie-Clémence watched Giscard as he spoke. She sensed that while his words were selected with great care towards diplomacy, he was nonetheless agitated at the inroads Muslim radicals were making in France. He went on.

"I cannot stress this firmly enough, Marie-Clémence. Beyond what the government already does in the context of normal civil protections and maintaining the rule of law, the government must have information about what these people are planning. We must be fully informed about their plans so that we can take steps to prevent them."

Marie-Clémence sat quietly, waiting. "How might I ... assist your portfolio in this, M. Giscard?"

"We shall come to that, but permit me first to pose a question related to the second area." He paused for a moment and sat back in his chair and looked at her. "You speak Arabic, do you not?"

"I do, yes," she replied, hesitant, alert, sitting on the edge of her chair. She had no idea how they knew she spoke Arabic.

"How did you come to the language?" he asked easily, a casual smile on his face.

She thought for a moment of the implications of her answer, but then realized that there was, truly, nothing sinister in it.

"When I was four," she replied in a straightforward fashion, "my father took a position with his firm in Jerusalem. Many of my playmates were Arabs, and I picked it up naturally. We lived in Jerusalem until I was ten."

And then Giscard switched to flawless Arabic, taking Marie-Clémence completely by surprise. "So it would be fair to say that you have a fluent command of, what is the term, 'street' Arabic?"

She gathered her wits and the words in Arabic flowed out in response, automatically. "That is accurate, M. Giscard. I can wax poetic about the beauties of the Arabian desert or blister the paint on the walls of a men's toilet." She stared at him with boldness, hoping that he would see she was unafraid to be direct.

"*Parfait, mademoiselle, parfait*," he replied, chuckling, back again in French, clasping his hands together in a discreet gesture of approval. "This is just what we need." The merest hint of a smile cracked Jean-Patrique's closed visage.

"So ... let us discuss what we would like you to undertake in the first area," Giscard began. He leaned forward over the desk and clasped his hands together. "How would you like to work for the government?"

She took just a moment. "In what capacity, M. Giscard?"

"We would ask you to help the government gather Muslim opinions on issues of governmental concern," he replied.

She was somewhat disconcerted. "M. Giscard, you know so much better than I that as a woman, I will have very little opportunity to access such information, either through social or business lines. Truthfully, especially in their own closed, very male business associations, it will be very difficult for me to, how shall we say…'move in those circles'."

"Yes, we would normally expect such to be the case, Marie-Clémence, but we would like to approach this task somewhat differently. And this brings us to the second part of our discussion."

Giscard stood and walked to the window, pulling back the thick, cream-colored curtain and looking out at the Parisian skyline. Then he turned to look directly at her. "Let me be frank, Marie-Clémence, and it may help if I introduced my associate here. M. Gillette—Jean-Patrique—he is with our friends from the counter-intelligence division."

Marie-Clémence suddenly understood why Jean-Patrique seemed to look somewhat more dangerous than a junior diplomat should appear, and then with a flash of understanding, put together the entire gist of the interview and realized what Giscard was asking of her.

"You want me to do intelligence work?" she blurted.

Giscard, one hand in his jacket pocket, the other still caressing the fold in the curtain, asked with a composed urbanity, "Would that distress you so much, spying for your country?" His eyebrows were raised, his face open with an innocent curiosity.

Marie-Clémence was stunned. This was something she had dared not expect, even when she saw the language in the papers she'd signed about working with intelligence assets; she'd assumed it was just boilerplate. But unknown to anyone—not even her parents—all her life she had harbored a deep, private desire to undertake some dangerous task in support of her people. She had read *The Diary of Anne Frank* as a little girl, and she dreamed of one day swirling through the mists of underground networks, hiding Jews, fighting evil men, and saving precious lives. She had never disclosed this deepest ambition of hers to anyone, ever, and the offer now on the table in front of her was enough to make her think, if such a thought wasn't so ludicrous, that there might be a God. She made a mighty effort not to let her enthusiasm show, but Gillette's eye caught the gleam, the tension, the tightened grip of the hand on the arm of the chair, and he knew. Giscard missed nothing.

"I ... I think that such work would be interesting, M. Giscard ... of course, if you think I can help in this area. I have no experience, you realize?"

"Oh, you should not worry about such things, Marie-Clémence. You have a natural intelligence, you are a quick wit, and you carry yourself well. From initial assessments, it appears your language skills are not inconsiderate. And, of course, we will make sure you are thoroughly trained. You realize of course that our offer is contingent upon you successfully completing the training?"

"I ... I had assumed as much, yes," she replied, still unbalanced, her mind and more critically her heart still darting off into potential futures.

She fleetingly thought about compensation. She suspected the salary they would offer would not be anything like what her fellow graduates would be making in the commercial sector. The government never compensated their people commensurately with the private sector. Yet this opportunity to engage in public service attracted her powerfully. Unlike her father, she was altruistic by nature, and while such an opportunity was not precisely aligned with the life vector she had planned when she determined to attend ENS, she found it hard to resist a call to do battle, even clandestinely, for her country against the encroaching Muslim hordes. The opportunity was that much more enticing because the call to serve the government also enabled an opportunity to serve her own people.

"Where would I be based?" she asked, trying to appear composed, folding her hands so they wouldn't see them trembling with anticipation and eagerness.

Giscard politely turned again to the window and waved out toward the city.

"Here in Paris—at least, after your training is completed. We would arrange for a flat in the 8th arrondissement; comfortable, something on a par with what your colleagues would be able to arrange regarding their own living conditions—we are not without our sensibilities, Marie-Clémence, but not something, you understand, so lavish that it would excite comment ... not something beyond the expected means of an up-and-coming civil servant."

She waved a hand, indicating that her accommodations were the least of her concerns. "M. Giscard, I cannot dissemble, nor will I be coy. The opportunity interests me extremely. Actually, if I might be more accurate, I would say passionately. This is a position I could truly find extremely rewarding." And then, as an afterthought, she said, "You don't really work for the Ministry of Foreign Affairs, do you?"

Giscard chuckled good-naturedly but did not answer her question. "Your particular combination of language skills, intelligence, and a specifically youthful-looking appearance—you could pass for someone five years younger—would be particularly useful for us. We will have need of someone to monitor things within one of our business schools. Having just graduated, I am confident you could put yourself back into the environment and pass for just another graduate student."

"I ... I would find the experience ... productive, if you think I could contribute."

"I have no doubt, Marie-Clémence. We will explain particularly why we would find this service valuable another time, after you have completed your initial training. But overall you would be working for my department. So," he said, arising, stretching out a manicured hand across the desk. Marie-Clémence stood and shook it, once, firmly, the gesture betraying her enthusiasm. Giscard, unable to contain a discrete look of pleasure at how things were eventuating, looked at his watch. "We have a table reserved at *Lé Bougainville*, Marie-Clémence," he said with some small degree of insistence—an elder uncle speaking to a treasured young niece. "This is France, after all, yes? No business arrangement would be complete without a diversion into the delightful and sublime realm of the epicene. Perhaps you would be kind enough to join us for dinner so we might continue to discuss the specifics of this…engagement?"

It was the happiest day of Marie-Clémence 's life.

***

It was the beginning of the happiest days of their lives.

Mace and Zoe were both growing closer to God and, thereby closer to each other. It was becoming evident that Mace's speech defect would be permanent—except when he was with Zoe, or, strangely, when he was moved by the Spirit of God to expound on something, or when he was speaking directly to someone when the Spirit moved him. Zoe realized that, just as Mace's speech defect would probably never go away, neither would the strange effect Mace had on her whenever he was near, and she also suspected that the fear and anxiety she would feel when he wasn't around would also be a permanent part of her life. And, oddly ... she was okay with that.

There was never a question they would marry, and, in a soft and gentle evening in June, this expectation was fulfilled in a quiet and deeply joyous ceremony at the Creamery. There was no music, no cake shoved into each other's mouths, no garter removals or tossing of bouquets—no coarse, burlesque antics that so cheapened most modern wedding ceremonies, lowering the dignity of the event, moving it away from the symbolism it was intended to represent. Not wanting any such foolishness, Mace and Zoe and the family agreed that the marriage would take place on a specific weekend, but Mace didn't say exactly which day. He said simply that he would come for her "sometime during that time."

Beginning forty days before the Friday of the designated weekend, Mace began a fast, consuming no solid food, only drinking water, broth, and some tea with honey. His intention was to weaken himself, to afflict his 'flesh' so as to better hear God, to go before Him and ask for direction, blessing, wisdom, and discernment as he began his life as a husband. Mace wanted to be to his wife as Jesus is to the Church.

Claire put Zoe in the Carriage house—a stone garage with an apartment over the bays—and Mace moved out and stayed in a small cottage in the coastal pasture about a mile from the main house he and Zoe had built the year before, stone by stone, together, as a place to sleep when they were watching over the cows to the coastal pasture in the spring. It was on a small rise in a clearing overlooking the entire pasture—they had problems with wolves going after the newly-born calves, and Mace had spent many a long night with Tack's NVG system mounted on the top of his M1A1 rifle as a guardian, and he'd shot plenty of marauding wolves. He was an excellent marksman.

Zoe waited eagerly that Friday afternoon ... and waited, and waited, attired in her wedding gown, until the sun went down. Claire and Tack stayed up with her. Rachel and Murray were on call in a very nice RV they'd rented for the weekend, parked behind the main house. Both of them were a little confused about this unorthodox approach to a wedding. Rachel, strangely, was most worried about Zoe's choice of husband, even though she knew they loved each other. Rachel's concerns centered, naturally, around her apprehensions regarding Mace's ability to earn a living—a 22-year old dairy farmer with a speech impediment wasn't every Jewish mother's dream pick for a son-in-law. But every time she saw Zoe with Mace, and every time she saw Mace's ugly red, gnarled scar in the center of his palm, her doubts seemed to dissipate. Murray, on the other hand, accepted unquestioningly that Mace was the best thing that could have possibly happened to his crazy, uncontrollable, energetic, emotionally fragile daughter. Murray saw how tender Mace was with Zoe, and he saw how she relaxed whenever she was around him, and for him that settled the issue. He was confident, due to his own earning potential, that his precious only daughter would never lack for funds, no matter what her husband did for a living. So it had been too with the man who planned to tear down his old barns to build new ones.

Zoe stood on the porch that Friday afternoon under an oil lamp (well-filled, with a spare vessel at hand), looking out into the gathering darkness, waiting. By then Zoe was well versed in the symbology Mace was attempting to enact—the Bridegroom, Jesus, coming for his bride, the Church—and she most definitely wanted to be ready for her Bridegroom. Yet he did not come that night.

Saturday dawned and found Zoe again on the porch at first light, waiting. After an hour or so looking into the distance, hoping for Mace to appear, Claire imposed upon her to come into the kitchen and get some nourishment. Zoe, bouncing with nervous energy, zipped into the Carriage house, dodged out of her gown and put on a shirt and jeans, ran back to the main house and wolfed down bacon and eggs, a glass of orange juice in one long gulp, then jumped up and ran back to the Carriage house, donned her gown again, and took up her station on the porch. Her heart pounded with anticipation.

She so very much wanted to be married to the one who had protected her, loved her, strengthened her, and cared for her above all others.

Saturday was a soft, warm day, a gentle breeze blowing, and Claire would occasionally come by and wait with her, talking about the cows, or cheese, or the different parts of the world Zoe had lived, or the increase in anti-Semitism they were seeing in the world, or the things a married woman tells a young maiden before she joins her life with her man. Claire spoke her wisdom to Zoe here and there through the day, but Zoe remained steadfast on the porch, adorned in her gown, settled in one of the rocking chairs, grazing through the Word, looking up every other word, every once in a while going to the railing to look out toward the road down which her Beloved had said he would come. She was alert and waiting eagerly.

About the time the great orange ball of the sun began to think about touching the tops of the trees in the western sky, Zoe looked up for the thousandth time and, catching her breath, saw a small group of people walking up the long driveway. One, two...three men. She could barely make them out, but as they came closer, she saw the tallest, Marcus, on the left, behind the person leading. Then she could make out the older one, Tack, limping slightly behind the leading figure. And finally her eyes fixed on Mace. She hadn't known what he would be wearing. He had talked to her about a long robe, or maybe a tuxedo, or maybe his father's suit. At 22, Mace had become a broad-shouldered man, with a narrow waist and very strong, tough, but tender hands. He could bend a horseshoe or deliver a baby lamb, and all with that deep red scar in the palm of his hand, the mark that would until the day he died proclaim his love for her, and his commitment to protect and cherish her.

As Zoe stood there, hands on the railing, heart beating faster, she saw her Bridegroom coming to her to take her as his Bride, walking between his father and his brother, wearing not a robe or a tuxedo or a suit, but ... coming toward her to begin their new life together with a silent smile in his eyes and his strong hands tucked in the pockets of a golden firehose canvas chore coat.

***

So began their life together. More so than in the years prior to their marriage, they took on most of the real work of the dairy. Mace and Zoe together ran the milking systems morning and night. The farm had graduated to a small skid steer to clean out stalls and lanes, so Mace spent the mornings on that chore while Zoe, working closely under Claire, learned the art of French cheese-making and began to delight in the pure artistry of creating something so pure and rich and nutritious from the lacteal fluid extracted from the female of the bovine species. Every time she cracked the wax on a wheel of cheddar, or opened the cheesecloth on a batch of drying French cream cheese, or mailed out a round of Emmentaler aged more than 15 months with an aroma that spoke to her soul of rich earth and green grass and sweet cream, she marveled at the beauty and wonder and intense pleasures wrapped up in the most delightful packages throughout God's creation.

Mace and Zoe delighted in the work that brought the income to the company Tack and Claire had started, and they worked through the days and weeks and months and years together, happy in what they were doing, fulfilled, growing each day in their relationship with God and with each other. Every morning after the cows were milked and the chores complete, they would come in for a large farm breakfast and then the family would move to the great room for their daily Bible study. Tack would facilitate, but everyone would participate, sharing the insights God gave to each. They would share their fears, their hopes, what God was doing with them personally, and the group would bring out what God gave each of them to contribute to the discussion. Everyone learned from the Spirit of God as the Spirit poured out an insight here, a lesson there, clarified an analogy, explained a portion of Scripture, and worked gently, quietly, persistently, to bring them all closer to a pure knowledge of the living God as He was shown through Jesus.

Soon after they were married, one night after they'd finished cleaning the milking system, they were walking back to the Carriage House, Zoe carrying a baby ewe lamb that had just been born but which had been rejected by its mother. Like she'd done with a number of them before, she intended to bottle feed her and keep her in by the wood stove in their apartment for a few nights. The lambs she would bottle feed ended up thoroughly bonded to her, and would race up to her whenever she appeared in the pasture and follow her around the yard, even after they'd been weaned.

They stopped just outside the door of the Carriage House and Mace turned to her and said, "I think I'd like to write a novel."

Zoe looked up at him with complete confidence, gentling the lamb in her arms. "Of course," she replied. "And I get to read it first." She laughed, and he smiled and pulled her close. "What would it be about?"

Mace thought for a few more steps, and then they halted just outside the door to their little apartment and looked at Zoe. "I want to describe what's happening now in Christianity, this massive departure from true faith. It's like an avalanche, becoming more intense as it gets further along, moving through the world like some flood of deception and darkness, sweeping away so many people like an avalanche sweeps away rocks as it moves down a mountain."

"Is this because of what we're seeing these past few Sundays?" Zoe asked. They'd been doing a reconnaissance of the local churches in the area, just Mace and Zoe, making a wide geographical sweep, driving sometimes a hundred miles one way to find a body of fellow Believers. Mace couldn't explain at the time what drove him to undertake this survey. Tack and Claire had long ago despaired of finding a church that would, no matter what else, at least teach from the Bible via the Spirit. Most of the churches either denied that the Spirit of God was working in the present day, thus standing in the door in their suits and ties and plastered-on smiles, manufacturing a 'Sunday holiness', because if the Spirit was not present, then it was only through their own efforts that they could attain to such holiness. Their self-righteousness prevented Him from doing any work in their precious church facility, as a lack of faith in a hometown many centuries ago prevented Him from doing any great work there as well. Times never change.

Others went the counterfeit route, rolling around on the floor, barking like dogs or some other animal, or hysterically laughing, all the while alleging that this was some sort of 'anointing' from God. The Spirit did not come within a hundred leagues of such cities.

What was even more frightening was the amazing penetration into mainstream Protestant churches made by Catholicism: sure, they expected to see the young and unformed in the faith be pulled off toward candles and rituals and beads, but when they listened to some old farmer, a die-hard Baptist, tell them about how they were 'celebrating Lent' at their little Baptist country church, Mace was stunned.

Zoe was completely content to stay home, worshipping and learning, and everyone could see she was growing in her relationship with God. Mace, always quiet, gentle, loving, never impatient with her, always looking to her needs before his own, was helping her to see the true nature of God, especially now that their physical intimacy was complete. It was as a marriage should be. Tack and Claire glowed with a deep joy for their son and his beloved wife.

No, it was Mace who felt the need to go out among the fields. Neither of them could figure out exactly why, until Zoe, standing there arm-in-arm with Mace outside their apartment, smacked him gently in the chest.

"Well, yeah, I suppose it is."

"Of course ... *that's* why you've felt the need to go looking! It wasn't to find a place to fit in, it was so God could show you what's happening to the church in this country, so you could write about it."

Mace looked at her again, nodding slowly. "You're right, my love, I think that's it. I never felt a need to settle into a place, and that's kind of strange when you think about it. We're supposed to be functioning as Believers with others ... like a body doesn't exist in separate parts."

"Yeah, well, who'd want to be where the Spirit of God isn't? That would just be like hanging around dead people ... worse, dead people who claim they're alive. That's a laugh. But we *are*, Mace, don't you see? I mean, we *are* in a Body. There's Tack and Claire, and you and I, and sometimes other families or couples show up now and again. Jesus said that wherever two or three were gathered together, He'd be there too, right? Hey, we've got more than two or three right now! Church doesn't have to be in a big building with pews and steeples and programs and an organ and a piano and a bulletin and four different Bible studies at once, does it?" The lamb bleated once or twice, and she caressed it until he rested quietly again in her arms.

"No, absolutely not, you're right, Zoe."

"I just wonder what people are looking for, to go to these places," she asked.

Mace shook his head. "I suppose," he said, riffing on the analogy presented by the Son of Man, "where death is, there the vultures will gather."

The week prior they'd been to a church about 70 miles away, arriving early, not knowing anything about the place other that it had a cross stuck up on the roof, and after the obligatory welcome handshakes at the door and the two introductory 'warm-up' songs, the announcements about conferences and meetings and groups and how the ladies would be studying the newest book from some famous female Christian personality, and how the men would be headed off to the men's retreat in the coming days—prefaced by a somewhat off-color remark by the older man reading the announcements that subtly disparaged the marriage state—the pastor ascended the pulpit. At first Mace and Zoe thought the woman stepping up was going to give a special announcement, but no, she opened the Bible and it was clear she was going to teach. Mace checked the bulletin they'd been handed. Well, there it was, in black and white: "Terry Sampson, Pastor."

Mace had turned to Zoe and she had looked at him and yanked her head toward the door. Even though they'd picked seats in the front of the church, they both got up just as Pastor Terry began to expound on a verse somewhere in Corinthians. They knew they were making something of a scene, but sitting under a female pastor wasn't something either of them could reconcile with the Word of God, so ... out they went, and drove the 70 miles home, the prevalent emotion being grief and sadness.

The lamb cried again. "So yeah, Mace, this seems to be where God is leading you. You've always wanted to write. Maybe it's time you start? And hey, let's get inside. This little one is hungry.

Mace nodded, opened the door for her, and then said, "They say the best way to learn to write is, well, just to write."

"Hey, I know! Why don't you start writing a blog? Lots of writers get their start doing that."

Mace thought about that for a few moments. "You know, Zoe ... that's an inspired idea. That's just what I'll do."

"But what will you write about?" She set the lamb down in the little pen that had been prepared beforehand, and while the little creature sniffed around the assembled blankets and put her two front feet in the water dish, Zoe went to warm the small bottle of milk she'd made up earlier in the day.

Mace sat, watching her, and said, "I know exactly what I'll write about. That ... that, right there." He was pointing at the lamb.

"You want to blog about sheep?"

Mace smiled. "No, no, I mean, God talks about sheep all the time in the Word, right? He calls us sheep. He talks to us in parables. That's what I want to do. I'll blog, but I'll blog in parables."

Zoe put the bottle of milk from the refrigerator into a pot of water sitting on the wood stove. She looked at Mace. "Yeah ... some people might get what you write, but I think most won't."

Mace nodded, bent over the railings on the pen, and picked up the lamb. "Those who have, will be given more; those who don't have, even what they have will be taken."

"I guess you're right. Sad, though."

"I don't want to reach everyone, Zoe. I don't expect what I write to be some kind of Christian bestseller."

"I wouldn't think so," she said, shaking the bottle of milk over the pan, "especially if you plan on writing about apostasy during a time of apostasy. It's like complaining about the lack of soap in a land of ten-year old boys."

"If I can just reach one person, maybe wake up two or three, help them see what's coming, but more importantly help them to come to an experiential knowledge of God, then I think it would be worth the time."

"Why a novel, Mace? Why not just write a non-fiction book about what you're seeing, plain and simple?"

Mace took the bottle from her and began to feed the lamb, who suckled greedily. "Because there are truths so important that they can only be told through fiction. Fiction can convey truth more powerfully than the plain recitation of facts. Jesus taught in parables for a reason, I think. Fiction weaves its way through the mind, pushes through the intellect, and strikes deeply into the heart in a way non-fiction cannot. No ... I don't think it will be a bestseller, but for those who might have ears to hear, maybe it will get their attention, or wake them up, or, I don't know, help them maybe get a better sense of the relationship God wants with them. And I think it would be very important to talk about what He wants of us as the times get darker."

Zoe took the lamb from Mace's arms and sat down on their little love seat in their tiny living room. The lamb was drinking steadily now, eyes closed in bliss, tail jerking back and forth occasionally. "I've seen that, you know," she replied quietly, one hand holding the bottle, the other arm holding the lamb. "At least to me, it seems that Christians are either completely unaware of the times in which we're living, or they think we're going to have a massive societal collapse but then come out on the other side and remake American into what the Founding Fathers had intended it to be all along."

"I see the same thing," Mace answered in a quiet voice, deep, pensive, thoughtful. "They're unaware of the times in which we live because they don't have the Spirit of God, and they'll soon find themselves eating and drinking and beating the slaves and their Master will show up when they don't expect Him. They seem to have missed that part where Jesus talks about the fact that 'night is coming when no man can work.' There will be times coming—and soon, I think—when the 'work of the Lord' won't just mean going out and evangelizing. In fact, I'm pretty sure it never did just mean only that, but Christians have, over the years, sort of classified that and that alone as "the Lord's Work" so we don't have to worry about maybe doing His work in other parts of our lives."

"Or we just leave 'the Lord's Work' to the pastor to handle, right?"

Mace smiled grimly. "Sad but true, Zoe, yeah."

"But what should Believers be doing now, though?" she asked, turning to him with questioning eyes. "It seems like we're safe here, on the farm, growing pretty much everything we need to eat. We've got a well with a hand pump and generator and horses and all kinds of horse-drawn implements ..." She stopped when Mace looked at her, and she knew he wanted to interrupt her. So she stopped talking.

"It's you," he said. "He wants us to take care of you."

"*You're* doing that. What does He want for everyone else?"

"No ... no, I mean, I think God is wanting His Believers to help Jews. There is a time coming when Jews will be hunted all over the world, and no one will want to help them. That's what we're supposed to do. I think night is coming, the time of the Gentiles is coming to an end, and it's time for Christians to consider that maybe He has something else for us to do in the days when most people will be actively trying to kill us."

Zoe had heard this before, when Tack had highlighted so many of the passages that spoke of a coming crucible for Jews, but in all the churches they'd been to, she'd never heard it mentioned before.

"Why don't ... why aren't Christians seeing this, Mace?"

"I think because most of the teaching about the end times is all confused, wrapped up with when the Rapture will happen and who the two witnesses are, or who Babylon is, and they miss this key thing that almost every Old Testament prophet spoke about."

She looked somber for a moment, and pushed a copy of C.S. Lewis' works across the edge of the side table. They were going through it together in the evenings.

"You're thinking about your parents," Mace said.

She nodded. "They're so trapped! All their lives, the entire history of the Jews that they know, their culture, their family stories, their ways of life on both sides ... it's always been black and white. Believe in Jesus, or be a Jew, but you can't do both. It's like there's some genetic thing that prevents them from even thinking about the claims Jesus made, about Himself, and worse, about what would happen to people if they ignored Him."

"Well, He did say that they would not see Him again until they said, 'Blessed is

He Who comes in the name of the Lord.' Paul said there's a veil over their eyes."

"Why is that?" Zoe asked. "That's exactly what I sense every time I talk to my mother about Him."

Mace was silent for just a moment, thinking. "It's for our sake," he answered. "I mean, for the Gentiles, for those of us who aren't Jews. Paul said that this blindness that was happening to his people was for our benefit. The Jews as a nation, as a people, as a culture turned away from Him, so God for a time has sort of 'opened the door' for Gentiles to come to Him. It's for our sake that your people have this veil over their heart, Zoe. Which is why, in these last days, especially during the time of Jacob's Trouble, it's even more important for Gentiles to pony up and protect those Jews God brings to us."

"The way you protect me."

"That's the plan," Mace said, smiling.

"What's 'Jacob's Trouble?"

"Jacob's Trouble is a period of time when there will be a persecution upon the Jewish people, Zoe, that will make the Holocaust look like a picnic. Massive numbers of Jews are going to be killed—hunted down, killed, slaughtered, murdered, simply because they're Jews."

"That's horrible!"

"It's God's judgment."

"No, I mean, well, yeah, I understand that, that's not what I mean. I mean, why aren't more Christians realizing this? *That's* what's so horrible."

"Lots of reasons. People calling themselves Christians haven't really died to themselves, so there's been no resurrection, no life, which means there isn't any Spirit that would give them this kind of discernment. Add to that the attachment most people have to the world right now. Things are pretty cozy when you think about it, and why step into a realm of belief that might require you to leave all that luxury behind? Zoe, seriously, Marcus told me one day when he was, I think, a senior in High School that he'd been reading about the Ukrainian famine and what Stalin did to his own people. He starved millions of Ukrainians. They died simply because of where they lived; they were mostly farmers, and they were starved on their own land. We don't have any idea of what something like that was like, living in those times, when people would come down along the road to a farm or village and just kill for the sake of killing, or take all the food, or shoot all the animals. We have no conception of such things happening here. But ... but I think they will. Things are coming here, Zoe. Things will get hard. Most of America's Christians just don't want to face that. And the other thing is, to consider that maybe in these last days Christians won't be the center of focus, the 'main players' on the stage, if you will, doesn't sit right with modern-day Christianity. God is going to turn again to focus on the Jews. "

"Sort of like the Jews getting thrown off center stage when Paul turned to the Gentiles?" she asked.

"Exactly. Well, now the sandal's on the other foot, I suppose, and we Gentiles are proving to be just as stubborn, heard-hearted, and self-centered as the Jews were then. We're proving by our actions, in every church we've seen for the last few years, that if Jesus showed up today, we wouldn't recognize Him. In fact, give it a few years, and I think in this country at least, if Jesus showed up and said what He said in the Bible, they'd at least arrest Him for hate crimes and probably try to kill Him. Nothing changes."

She sighed and got up off the couch to put another log into the wood stove. "You want to write about all this ... to put all this in a novel?"

"I do. Though I don't know how yet."

The lamb emptied the bottle and began to suckle on Zoe's finger. She picked her up and set her down in the little pen, where she very quickly folded her front legs down, toppled over, curled up, and fell asleep among the soft blankets.

Zoe sat back on the couch, tucked in under Mace's arm, feeling the soft scratchiness of his shirt against her face as she put her head on his chest.

"You're not going to be very popular," she said.

"You'll stick with me, though, right?"

"Right here," she replied, pressing herself closer to him. "Forever."

***

As the years rolled by, Mace and Zoe found themselves increasingly loving each other and growing in their love for God. As their trust in Him deepened, so too did their relationship with Him as He worked in each of their lives, drawing them closer to Him in ways tailored to refine each as the need determined.

Mace and Zoe had no children. Though Claire pondered this missing element somewhat wistfully, it never seemed to bother either Mace or, oddly enough, Zoe. As the years progressed and the attack behind the bleachers faded into the past, Zoe was able to function on her own, but everyone could plainly see that when Mace was nearby, she was a different person; energized, alive, peaceful, content, and thoroughly, completely, effervescently the picture of walking joy. It began to dawn on Claire that Zoe's joy stemmed from her relationship with Mace, and perhaps, Claire thought, she would not need children. God, Claire finally decided, knew best. In a very short time, Claire would see the wisdom of God's particular family planning strategy in Mace and Zoe's life.

Chapter 7

Cold Water Parables
A Blog from the Lakes of Minnesota
by Mace Ironbridge

The Wisdom Shop
- FREEDOM -

There once was a great city on a high mountain, and people from every tongue and tribe and nation streamed through its gates to buy all kinds of goods and services in rich, proud, and varied congress.

On a back street of this city, in a decrepit neighborhood, where poverty, affliction, and need stalked and buffeted those who had been rejected or cast aside or turned away from the center of the bright city, a shop was tucked into a corner at a nondescript intersection. The shop was far, far away from the center of the city's great market. The shop's façade was old...older, truth to tell, than the city itself, but this was not generally known nor even suspected. A wooden sign painted with a background of a deep, dark green, with gold letters proclaiming, "Invia, Verum & Vita, Proprietors" hung above the row of shop windows, with a massive wooden and wrought-iron door at their center.

One day a man, his wife, and his daughter came into the center of the city from their luxurious apartment in one of the towering skyscrapers, embarked upon a costly and time-consuming shopping expedition.

The man and his wife had been arguing that morning. She was distressed; he wasn't spending enough time at home with her. He was a slave to his job. He felt she was ungrateful. He was working like a dog, he said with some asperity, so he could keep her and her daughter 'in the style to which they had very definitely become accustomed'. He was about to be promoted and the last thing he needed to do now was to reduce his presence at the firm. He needed to show them he was dedicated; fully bought in—a team player.

Before words became too heated the daughter flounced into the room and petulantly complained that her spring wardrobe was utterly unacceptable and she absolutely *must* complement her closet with some of the latest designs offered in the fashion boutiques profusely spattered throughout the city's main market, or she would not be able to hold her head up at school the following week. Neither husband nor wife thought to question or dissuade the young princess, and so the wife's plans to manipulate her husband that day, bringing him round to adjusting his career plans, and the husband's plans to escape from his wife to the office, were abandoned. They would, it had been decreed, go shopping. In this part of the city, it was the children who were increasingly coming to rule over their parents.

So there they were, coming out of one store encumbered with bags and a yet still dissatisfied daughter, trudging into yet another den of iniquitous merchandisers, when they perceived a commotion in the street. A woman was standing, shouting about some shop or other at which she alleged people could purchase things that would exceed their heart's desires, quell their greatest grief, quench their deepest thirst.

"Dramatic, what?" ventured the husband.

"Ra-*ther*," the wife replied with disdain.

"I saw her at the entrance to the city gates yesterday," the daughter sniffed.

"What was she doing there?" the father asked, craning his neck to get a better view. He wondered if the woman was attractive.

"She was complaining about people not paying attention to her, from what I could gather. Fancy that. She runs about screeching in the square and wonders why people don't pay her any mind."

"What's she on about *now*?" the mother asked, irritated at being distracted from her efforts to manipulate her husband and bothered simultaneously that she did not look as well as she had a few years ago. The major tool she utilized to manipulate her husband was, sadly, deteriorating with age.

"Something ... something about minding what she's saying," her husband replied. "Apparently she's recommending some kind of shop. Here, here's a flyer she's giving out." The husband bent down and retrieved a filmy golden sheet of silken fabric that had floated down and was resting on the marble pavement, on which were printed details of the shop the woman was on about. A logo was ranged across the top of the fabric flyer.

"What's that!" the daughter asked, pointing with a finger at the top of the fabric, which the husband needed to hold with both hands, for there was a slight breeze and the flyer would flutter now and again, almost as if it were alive.

"Why, I believe they're apples."

"Apples, yes, well, of course," his wife sniffed, overriding her husband's attempt at description, tapping the fabric with a dominating finger. "Gold, it looks like, gold threads woven into the fabric in the shape of apples." She had been a jeweler by trade before her husband rescued her from a life in the trades. "And there, see? They're set in a filigree of silver. Quite plain to see, if you've eyes in your head."

"What kind of shop advertises with such finery?" the husband wondered.

"I wonder where it is?" the daughter questioned. "I've never heard of it before. Does it sell clothes?"

"Let me see, yes, here's the address ... why, my goodness," the husband coughed, "Why, ahem, that's in one of the worst parts of the city."

His wife looked over his arm and saw the address. "We certainly wouldn't even consider shopping in such a place!" the mother stated flatly.

"Ewww," the daughter added in disgust, not knowing the location of the shop but simply out of a general need to be disapproving.

"Let go of that disgusting thing directly!" the wife commanded in a harsh tone.

"Yes, well, I suppose if you say so," the husband said, dropping the silky fabric from his hands with a strange and unsettling feeling of regret, wistfully watching the filmy sheath waft back down to the marbled pavement—'*What a waste of gorgeous fabric; I wonder what that shop is like?*' he thought—but his wife was already tugging at his sleeve.

"Come, husband, there's a store we need to visit next. This way. Come along, dear," she said, this to the precious princess, and mother and daughter turned their back on the woman crying out in the street and led the husband into just one more establishment designed to part him from his money and, incidentally, drown out the woman yelling in the square.

Later that day, a mature woman of about thirty-five came into the old shop touted by the woman who'd been proclaiming in the streets of the city. This woman was named Martha Abercrombie. Martha was a maid, employed in cleaning people's houses and apartments. She had heard a woman advertising the shop—strange woman she was, plain looking, nothing pretentious about her to be sure, but there was something that piqued Martha's interest. And who goes around tossing such flyers about? My goodness, well, she'd have that flyer home and sitting as a tea cozy in half a second, wouldn't she just! It was beautiful, all gold silk and silver threading and such. And those little apples, all golden-like, surrounded by silver threads ... just darling.

And so, with a determined logic, Martha thought that she might as well stop off at the shop she saw advertised in the flyer, because it was quite lovely ... and as well, she had a plan. She worked all day, true, but she had a dream of setting herself up with some sort of business, something on the side, so that she might maybe one day have a maid of her own, to clean her own house and do for her now and again.

Martha pushed open the heavy door, which was remarkably easy to move compared to how massive it looked, and stepped into the shop. She stood, frozen, gaping. There, stretched out before her eyes, were aisle after aisle after aisle, shelves that seemed to go up, oh, my, it must have been, why—and here she bent her head to perhaps see a little further upwards—but no, she couldn't see the top shelf from where she was. This curiosity drew her further in a step or two.

"Welcome." An old man stood at her elbow.

"Oh!" she exclaimed, "Why, yes, hello. I've ... I've your flyer here," the woman said, a little flustered, reaching in her purse to pull out the golden fabric, for the old man had appeared somewhat out of nowhere, "and quite a nice flyer it is, if I might say so. This *is* your shop, isn't it?" she asked, holding out the fabric. "I had it from a ... a young woman just yesterday, down near the head of one of the streets in the city."

The old man carefully took out a pair of spectacles from the pocket of a well-starched white shirt, looked at the golden silky fabric, noted the golden apples surrounded by the silver filigree, and said, "Hmmm ... it is, yes, Madam. My daughter, you see. She does our advertising. Please do keep it." The fabric was immediately whisked into the safety of her voluminous purse.

"Well, excellent. Surprising layout you have, I must say," she noted, looking upward to the tops of the shelves, holding her purse close to her chest. "I mean, it certainly doesn't look this big from the outside, I can tell you."

The old man made no reply, but instead spoke. "Mr. Verum!" he said, and a tallish young man appeared, well-constructed, with a fine, clear eye, coming toward them down one of the long aisles.

"My partner, Mr. Verum, will help you find what you are looking for, Madam."

"Oh, well, thank you I'm sure," she replied, and the old man turned back toward the counter ... she supposed, because she could not see any counter anywhere. 'Funny,' she thought to herself, considering the old man and Mr. Verum, who was now walking her way. 'They don't *look* foreign.'

"You wish to start a business." Mr. Verum announced, now by her side, holding what looked like a dust rag and a bottle of some liquid. He saw her looking at it. "Oh, this, yes, we do like to keep the shelves clean, you know."

"Yes of course," she replied, "but here now, how did ... how did you know what I'm here for?"

"It is our specialty, Madam."

"Well, that may be ... but it's disconcerting nonetheless, I can tell you."

"We make no apologies, Madam."

Martha rumbled and murmured out of habit—to herself—and then said, "Well, you're right. I've been a cleaning woman most of my life and I don't want to end my days on my knees, scrubbing some other woman's floors."

"I understand, Madam."

"But I don't know what I might do. I'm no businessperson, you see. I don't know what's what; totally lost. But I know I don't want to be cleaning the rest of my life."

Mr. Verum nodded, listening closely. "Mmmm," he said. "Yes, I see. I think we may have exactly what you need. Come along." He turned and began to navigate his way back through a veritable labyrinth of aisles and passageways and twists and turns and over stacks of books and under ladders reaching up, oh, so high she couldn't see to their tops. He finally stopped in front of one ladder and ascended. "Be so kind as to wait right here, Madam. I'll be back shortly." Up he went; up, up, up, higher and higher. She lost sight of him for a few moments—perhaps it was the dust or the poor light or the fact that he was wearing pearl-gray trousers and he just seemed to blend in with his surroundings. But then he suddenly appeared again at her elbow and she jumped.

"My apologies, Madam, but while there is only one way up, there are many ways down." He proffered a small rectangular box.

"What is this?" she asked, taking it gingerly, turning it over in her hand. It was firmly closed and latched with a little metal catch, and she saw on the box the same logo that had been on the flyer—golden apples in a setting of silver filigree. She ran her fingers softly over the symbol. It gave her a sensation of ... of rightness, of the right thing, of being settled in. How strange.

"Madam, that is Wisdom."

She looked at the box and then looked up at Verum. "Wisdom?"

"Yes, Madam. As in, 'discernment, understanding, knowledge, awareness'."

"Wisdom? In a box?"

"In your very hands, Madam."

"And what ... what am I to do with it?"

"Well, Madam, our customers usually find the most satisfaction from our products by taking them home, opening the box, and following the instructions."

"And what instructions would they be."

"Ah, yes, well, Madam, it is the policy in our shop that customers be permitted to know the instructions only after they have made their purchase."

"And why is that?"

"Because the instructions in the box are different for each customer, Madam."

Martha looked up at the young man with some asperity, one arm akimbo. "You certainly are a strange lot," she said. "So I'm to take your word on things, lay out good money for this—and from what I'm seeing just from the box this'll be a pretty penny, with this silly frippish gold silk and whatnot—and go on home and hope that some list or pamphlet or note will help me arrange a business."

"Not exactly, Madam."

"Well I should hope not exactly!" she replied.

"What we mean, Madam, is that this particular product," and here Verum pointed discretely to the golden-wrapped box, "must be kept close to your person at all times. Yes, we do mean for you to follow the instructions in the package. But we cannot say to you here that the instructions will direct you to start a new business. It may be that the instructions might lead to something else altogether."

Mrs. Abercrombie assumed a look of offended dignity. "Now this is the strangest thing, young man. This is a shop, right? You serve customers, do you not? You told me yourself I'm here to find a way to start a business, right? You heard me with your own ears tell you I don't want to be cleaning all the rest of by life, did you not? You did. And here you stand telling me that these...these *instructions* may result in me getting something else altogether different? You've got some nerve!"

"We can say with certainty, Madam, that if you follow these

instructions," and here he tapped the box in her hands, "you will find yourself most wonderfully satisfied. That may or may not mean that you find a way to start a business, but it does mean you will find the right path in your life."

Martha let out with a somewhat undignified epithet at this last assertion. "Right path? And what's wrong with the path I'm on now? The gall you have, making out that I'm on some kind of wrong path. Here," she said, and shoved the box back into Verum's hand. "Keep it. Keep it and do me the favor of finding the door for me in this ... this infernal rat's nest of ... of *things*!" She waved her hand around in frustration at the shelves and books and boxes and aisles and ladders.

"Madam, I entreat you, reconsider, please. You may not be able to find the shop again; you may not be in the appropriate frame of mind in the future; there are a host of reasons why you should reconsider and accept this product. It *will* meet your need."

Martha stopped in her aggressive stride away from him and turned back. "My need? Wait a minute," she said, in a tone of dawning comprehension. "You just want me to buy this. I've seen your type. So, Mr. Foreign whatever-your-name-is, just how much is this ... this box!" She nodded with disdain at the box of golden-wrapped Wisdom in Verum's hand.

"It will cost everything you have, Madam, although payment terms can be arranged. Some pay all at once, some pay over a certain amount of time."

Martha's eyebrows went up. "Payment terms? All I have?" She laughed derisively. "No surprise there, you bandit! Everything I have! And they don't even require you to wear a mask! I'd have thought you'd be ashamed to even put the terms to your customers. I'd have thought your type to be smoother; a bit more cunning, if you like. But no, greedy is as greedy does, I suppose. I should have seen it the moment I stepped foot in the place. It's the door for me, young man. Now which way is it?"

The door had no sooner closed on the still-muttering form of Mrs. Abercrombie when, just second later, a superbly attired man in his mid-forties ambled into the shop. His name was Adam Rilling, and he was a very prosperous technology consultant. He was visiting the great city from a far-away land, a land in which he was very wealthy and very, very busy. He was wearing a suit and an overcoat that was dripping wet, as it had begun to rain. He was pale, somewhat drained, and as he came through the door, he saw a well-upholstered chair nearby and immediately sat down, taking deep breaths, rubbing his leg in a pained fashion.

An old man approached. "Welcome," he said. "My name is Invia. Take your rest. You're tired, I see."

"Yeah, I suppose I am," the man replied, breathing heavily.

"Would you like a cup of tea?"

"Nah, I'm good, thanks." Rilling waved the old man off. "I was just out walking and it started to rain and I thought I'd duck in here, maybe look around. This a book store, isn't it?"

"We have books, yes," the old man replied.

"I love bookstores," Rilling said, "though I don't get to spend much time looking through 'em. When I take the family shopping, it isn't for books, I can tell you."

"Ah," said Mr. Invia.

"No, usually it's for cars or houses or colleges," Rilling replied, grimacing.

"I see."

"So anyway, I was down here, in this part of town, actually looking for this place." Rilling leaned to one side, grunting in the chair, reached into a pocket of his overcoat, and pulled out a flyer—the same flyer Mrs. Abercrombie had brought in. "Some crazy woman was running around down in our building downtown, I have no idea how she got up to the 20th floor, but there she was in the atrium, yelling about some shop down in this part of town. My team thought she was a hoot, but one of them brought back this flyer she was handing out, and it seemed ... I dunno, it seemed kind of ... strange, I guess. So I thought, hey, I've got the afternoon free, and, well, why not? So I come down here and promptly get lost. You wouldn't know where this place is, would you?"

The old man took the silk flyer from Rilling's hand. "Ah, well, you see, the crazy woman you refer to is my daughter. She handles our advertising, and yes, actually, this is the shop to which she was referring."

Rilling was slightly embarrassed. "Oh man, my bad, sorry, Mister ...?"

"Invia is my name. Welcome to our establishment."

Rilling twisted around in his chair somewhat, trying to get comfortable.

"What kind of name is 'Invia?"

"Ah, well, now, that is a question that would require some time to provide an adequate answer."

"Not from around here, then?"

"Yes and no."

"Yeah," Rilling said, and took another breath while he massaged a knee. "She *is* kinda weird—your daughter, I mean—you gotta admit, running around, yelling about this place everywhere. One of the kids on my team said he'd seen her down near the square one day and near the gates of the city the next."

"She does get around, yes," Mr. Invia replied. "So you would like something." It was a statement, not a question.

"What? Nah, I'm just—" and then Rilling paused and thought for a long moment. "—but now that you mention it ... yeah ... actually ... I *was* looking for something. But honestly, sir, I couldn't for the life of me tell you what it is."

"Well," the old man replied, smiling softly, "you've come to the right shop." He turned. "Mr. Vita, if you please." A broad-shouldered man appeared, dressed in very fine pearl-gray trousers and a crisply starched white shirt under a dove-gray waistcoat encasing a trim and narrow waist.

"Mr. Rilling," Mr. Vita nodded, welcoming Adam.

"Adam Rilling," Adam replied, rising somewhat painfully from his chair, holding out his hand. Vita shook it firmly, and Adam was surprised at Vita's iron grip.

"Mr. Vita can help you find exactly what you need," Invia said, and turned to Vita and nodded.

"Mr. Rilling, if you would, come with me."

Rilling limped after Vita, and they both made their way through aisles and stacks of books and boxes, around and under ladders, until Rilling's breathing became labored. Vita stopped, turned and looked at Rilling for a moment, and then put his hand on Adam's shoulder. He paused for a long moment and then said more than asked, "You are okay now?" and Rilling, suddenly able to breathe better—much better—shook himself. "Whoa! Well, yeah, actually, I am. That's pretty amazing."

"Part of the service," Vita replied. "We've a bit of a way more to go. Follow me."

They finally came to a ladder, the top of which eluded Adam's gaze. Vita turned again and said, "Be so kind as to wait here, Mr. Rilling, thank you. I should be back presently." Up the ladder Vita went, climbing steadily. Adam sat on a chair that happened to be close by the foot of the ladder. The higher Vita went, it seemed, the harder it became for Adam to breathe. He must have walked a long way, he thought to himself. Adam pulled out his phone to check his mail.

Vita came back, not climbing down from the ladder, but appearing from around another aisle, stepping around a stack of books. Adam found he could suddenly breathe easily again.

"There is but one way up, though there are many ways down," Vita said in response to Rilling's questioning glance, "and we do not know sometimes where our search for the customer's product will take us. Here," Vita said, holding out a rectangular box about the size of a box of candy. Rilling stood. The box was wrapped in golden silk, the same fabric as the flyers, and the logo on the box was the same as the logo on the flyer ... apples of gold in settings of silver.

"What's this?" Adam asked.

"Freedom."

"Is that the title? It's a book?"

"No, it is freedom itself. Freedom ... for you."

"Freedom in a box?"

"Yes."

Adam looked at the box or book or whatever and then looked back up at Vita. "Sorry, Vita, but I don't understand."

"You came here looking for freedom, Adam. You are weighed down with the cares of the world, with earning a living, burdened with significant debt, feeling as if you must earn enormous sums of money to ensure your family's comfort and, though you would deny it, their love as well—yes, don't look so surprised, we know, it's quite clear—and what you were looking for when you stepped through our door was this," and he again held out the box. "Freedom."

Adam sat back down in a nearby chair, hard.

"You're losing me. This is a bookstore, right?"

"Not exactly. We do have books, yes. But we offer a very different product than what you are accustomed to see in other parts of the city."

"There was a book called Freedom, wasn't there?"

"There have, I am sure, been many books with that title, yes. But this," Vita said, tapping the box, "this *is* freedom. Freedom itself. Your freedom."

Suddenly Adam's face creased in a knowing smile. "Okay, okay, who put you up to this? Was it McKay? Was it Donalsen, Mary Pat Donalsen? It *was* her, wasn't it! She's the practical joker on the team." Rilling chuckled quietly. "You had me going for a minute there, Vita. Well-played. I have to text her and tell her I busted her plan and she'd better up her game."

Vita looked down at the floor and then back up at Rilling and Rilling's fingers froze in mid-text. Vita spoke slowly, in a rich brown, earth-like voice: "Adam, this ... is ... your ... freedom. Here, in this box." Vita's voice at once made Rilling both deeply ashamed and wildly hopeful.

"You're not kidding about this are you?"

"I am not."

"Donalsen didn't set this up?"

"She did not."

Rilling was nodding. "Yeah, I suppose I knew that. So ... why don't you run this down for me, Mr. Vita. No one sells freedom."

"We do. We offer freedom here, and wisdom, and deliverance, and discretion, and hope, and, truth, and, of interest to some, time."

"Time?" Rilling asked, pulling out his phone to check the time.

"We proffer many things here," Vita replied, "but the policy of the shop is to proffer only what the customer needs. You need freedom."

"Okay, so let's say I'm interested. Hey, I know selling—I'm a salesman by trade. So sell me this thing you're calling freedom."

"Freedom is a power, the power to create a particular state of being in which one has the right to act or think or conduct oneself as one wishes without interference or constraint."

Rilling laughed, a quick, barking, derisive outburst. "Yeah, and the last time I can recall having that kind of power was when I was something like twenty years old."

"You can have it again." Vita raised the box in emphasis.

"And how will what's in that little box there suddenly arrange my life such that I have the freedom to be what I want to be."

"The freedom *to be what you should be*," Vita corrected. "The two are not necessarily the same."

"Yeah, okay, point taken, but you still haven't told me how that little box will make that happen."

"You take it home and you eat it."

"Eat it?"

"That is correct. You eat it, it will enter into you, what is in the box will become part of you, and you will change and then your life will change and, after a time, you will find yourself free, free to do what you should be doing, in the way you should be doing it."

Rilling was shaking his head now, and the thought was running through his mind that he had better begin to back slowly out of the shop—if only he knew how to get out. He glanced around to look for an exit, but decided to keep Vita talking. "And what happens, my friend, when I finish the last bite? Then what? I'm supposed to come back here for refills the rest of my life?"

"This box will last your entire life."

Rilling's eyes widened, his attention gathered fully back to Vita. "My whole life?"

"The one box, yes, it is enough to last your entire life ... and beyond, come to think of it."

Rilling thought for a moment. "Okay, I'll go along. So what's it cost?"

Vita looked at Rilling for a long moment. "It will cost you a number of preconceived ideas about how you raise your family and the things to which you believe they are entitled; it *may* cost you the affection of those you care for, and who you think care for you—perhaps permanently; it will definitely cost you many of the friends you have now; it may cost you your job."

Rilling looked hard at Vita. "I eat what's in this box and you're telling me it might result in me losing my job. Why would I want to do that?"

"Mr. Rilling, what I am telling you is that if you eat what is in that box, it will change who you are, and the people with whom you work or with whom you live may suddenly not find you so appealing. Your bosses might not find your new nature so amenable or malleable, and they may dismiss you. It has been known to happen among those who have purchased this product. Call it a warning label if you wish."

Rilling sat down again. "So let's say I believe you," he said, and Vita could begin to see the grain of hope lighting Adam's eyes. The man was unbelievably burdened, and freedom was his only hope. "The payment terms. I don't carry around preconceived ideas about raising my family in my wallet. How does the transaction take place? What do I give you so I can walk out of the shop with that ... with my ... my *freedom*?"

"We do not deal in transactions, Adam. We deal in transformations."

"And what does that mean?"

"It means that you do not need to give me anything to walk out of here with this box. You keep your wallet in your pocket, take the box, go home, open it, read the instructions, eat of it, and then the costs will begin to appear. You choose then to either pay or not pay the cost. As you pay the cost, you get the product. You don't pay the cost, you'll find you don't get the product."

"And the costs are ..."

"Those items I mentioned."

"Right. So what I'm hearing is that I don't really need to give you anything."

"You are correct. But you do need to do something to actually obtain the product."

"What do I need to do?" Rilling asked warily.

"Simple; you obey the instructions on the package."

"I take this box home, open it, follow the instructions, eat it, and then I begin to obtain my freedom."

"In short, yes."

"What if I have questions about the instructions? What kind of product support is there?" Rilling laughed at the ludicrous nature of his question—at the entire situation, actually—but Vita had an answer.

"You simply call me and I will explain the instructions you're questioning."

"Simple as that?"

"Simple as that."

Rilling looked at Vita for a long moment. "You're really serious about this, aren't you? You're not pulling my leg."

Vita put his hand on Adam's shoulder again and looked straight into his eyes, and Rilling felt a strength coursing through him that he'd all but forgotten existed. He stood up. "You're serious," he said with a first breath of real hope.

"Freedom," Vita said, holding out the box.

Rilling reached out his hand, and then paused. "What about ... what about my wife?"

"What about her?"

"What if ... what if she doesn't like me following the instructions?"

"You must follow them anyway."

"Ahhhyeaahhhhbuttt ... *that's* gonna be an issue. We've got some pretty strong obligations right now. I've got two kids in college and two more to go, and each of them needs a car, each of the kids in college needs an apartment; you have no idea how much that runs a month, and to pay for all that I need the job I've got."

"You are describing reasons which all the more should convince you to take this box home and eat of it ... not to avoid obligations but to ensure you assume obligations you should be taking upon yourself, and discarding those you should not be carrying."

"Yeah, well, and then if one of the kids finds themselves out of a job, who's gonna carry them until they find another one?"

"Again, Adam, the instructions in this box will clarify for you what obligations you should and should not be assuming."

Rilling shook himself mentally for a long, eternal few seconds and then said, "Yeah, well, you know, Mr. Vita, hey, I sincerely appreciate the offer, and maybe some time later in my life it might work, but you know, right now, I'm not sure I could follow the instructions in that box." Adam pointed at the gold-wrapped box in Vita's hand.

Vita looked disappointed; no, more grieved than disappointed. "You are making a mistake."

"Yeah, well, I've heard that before and sometimes they've been right and sometimes they've been wrong, but seriously, if any of the instructions in there require that I terminate funds to my kids, or in some way even threaten to cause me to lose my job, I mean, do you really think my wife would go along with that? No, I'm telling you before you say anything, she wouldn't. Yeah, yeah, I know I'm supposed to be the man of the house, but right now I'm more the 'horse pulling the cart' with the rest of the family in the back with the buggy whip, if you know what I mean. So while I appreciate your offer and all, Mr. Vita, if you could just show me the door, I could get back to the hotel and get some dinner before my next meeting tonight."

Vita realized there was nothing more to say, and so led Rilling back to the door and watched the man, head down, hunched over, trying to text on his phone as he limped off into the rain.

Chapter 8
Emma

"...but whoever causes one of these little ones who believe in Me to stumble, it would be better for him to have a heavy millstone hung around his neck, and to be drowned in the depth of the sea."

Matthew 18:5-6

Dear Miss J;

I was in a hurry to get the next five-gallon bucket of hot water up the ladder this evening when I slipped on the wooden rung and ripped my sock. 'Oh, man, Dad is going to be so angry,' I thought right away. But I didn't stop, because it was Morgan's turn for the shower next and she needed a new bucket of water like, right away, standing there in the shower all soaped up already, shaking from the cold. I dumped the hot water into the holding tank and called down—not too loud, so as not to disturb Dad—that she could start. I heard her step into the closet and pull the chain on the nozzle as I came back down the ladder, trying to walk with my one foot sliding on the floor to hide the gaping hole in my sock that I'm sure will show. Dad was sitting in his chair reading, fortunately.

"Let's get a move on, girls," he said, without looking up. "Dinner's coming up."

"Right, Dad. Almost there," I answered as I ran down the hall toward the stove room. I slid the large cooking pot full of water onto the hottest part of the wood stove and ran outside with the plastic bucket to get five more gallons from the river for Misty's shower—she's making the cornbread for dinner—and I felt the frigid sole of my boot on my bare foot. Oh, man, I must have really ripped that sock. When I got back to our bedroom after coming inside I quick-changed it for another, and yeah, oh man, it's going to take me at least an hour to repair that rip.

Our house has no running water—at least, in the house, though Dad likes to joke that we have running water just ten feet away ... the Black Rock River runs past our homestead. We did cut a nice stairway into the bank on the U.S. side, though, and we rigged an easy lever with a rope, a pulley, and some spare wood from a construction site in town we'd scavenged.

I hooked the bucket handle to the hook on the pulley, swung it out over the river, lifted the handle which lowered the bucket into the river, and waited for just a few seconds while it filled. As I've told you before, Miss J, we have to be careful not to dunk the bucket too far into the river or it will snap the hook on the pulley and we'll lose it downriver. I remember telling you, J, about that one morning last year when the home funds were thin on the ground and I dunked a five-gallon pail too far, and sure enough, *snap*, off it came and off it went, down the river. When I got back in the house and told Dad, he made me go get it. I was lucky; it was summer and the bucket had snagged itself on a branch only about three-quarters of a mile down river. The hardest part was walking back through the brush all the way uphill in my wet clothes, because he made me 'take the same path the bucket took', which meant I had to swim downriver. Then of course I had to pay for the hook and pulley out of my earnings. My Dear Miss J, you should have told me that metal hooks and pulleys cost so much!

Well, we finally got Morgan and Misty through their showers tonight—it's their day of the week for showers—and while they were washing up, Mia and Mandy set the table. Mom somehow had turned up a package of ground beef and we had a nice casserole with elbow noodles, cornbread and gravy. Dad said grace, and like always we waited for him to take the first bite before any of us started in. He was in a good mood, maybe because of the ground beef. We don't have meat often. I suspect Morgan brought it home; she's just been hired by the local community college to teach a course on animal husbandry, and from the way the pantry is stocked, it looks like she's just been paid.

The meal went well, by which you know I mean there were no significant eruptions. Dad seemed pleasant, and apparently he's enjoying his book. He got it from the library in Granite Sky. When he isn't working—and for some reason, J, he hasn't been working often these past years—most of the time he reads or watches movies. We've seen every war movie or science fiction movie made in the last twenty years, I think ... at least four times. And I probably have told you all about each one of them more times than you want to count. Sorry about that!!!

Oh Miss J, there are times when I wonder what the future is for the six of us girls, plus Mom and Dad, in our little homestead here. From what I can see and from what I know and from what Dad says, the future will be just like the past. It stretches out like a straight road, the same day after day, off into the horizon. There are times when that comforts me, especially when times are good in the family and I find myself too busy to think much about it, but there are days—and worse, the nights—when I lay here writing to you and wonder if there is anything else. Is this all God has for us? And then I feel guilty about wanting more than what we have. I should feel grateful, Dad says, for the roof over our heads and the food we have.

Dad says that we girls can't really understand what's written in the Bible—I mean, girls in general, not just us—and I guess he's right—he's Dad, so, well, I guess that goes without saying—but then ... and I know I shouldn't feel this way ... but it makes me feel almost as if God doesn't care about us ... women, I mean ... as much as he does the men. Why is it that men can understand the Bible better than women? Do they have different brains? Is there something in them that helps them know God better? Maybe that's the way things are. I'm so confused sometimes. I just need to trust Dad. He knows what the Bible says and he loves us and won't let anything bad happen to us.

***

Dear Miss J;

You wonder why I call my journal 'Miss J'? Honestly, though, you're my best friend, and just about the only one I can talk to. I'm the youngest one in the family and sometimes I think I'm just different than everyone else. I even have a different name. All the other girls' names start with 'M', but after Dad picking the names of the first five girls, all starting with 'M' because (this is true) he wanted everyone's initials to remind them of his father, who was a doctor, Mom really wanted me to be named after her grandmother, Emma MacFarland. Dad worked out a compromise: my name technically is Meredith Melissa Ann, but everyone calls me by my initials—'MMA', or 'Emma'. So Dad got what he wanted, and Mom sort of did, kind of sideways. I couldn't even pronounce the whole thing until I was five. Yeah, everyone laughs at the story, but I wonder why Dad wouldn't just let Mom name me the way she wanted? I guess he knows what he's doing, though.

Everyone is busy doing what they're doing in their lives, and sometimes I find myself sort of on my own. Sometimes I find myself sort of ending up listening to Dad more than my sisters, and I think that's usually because they're all so busy and he doesn't have anyone else to talk to, so I feel sorry for him. We're learning Greek together. I usually ask most of the questions at Bible study, though I would truthfully say that's because I really want to learn about the Word. And since we're being honest here, Miss J, I think part of the reason I spend time with him is because it tends to keep me off the hot seat, if you know what I mean. Honestly, he tends to get mad at me less. It's sort of worked out that I'm 'the good daughter', on one end of the spectrum, and Morgan is the 'bad daughter' on the other end, with the rest of the sisters sort of sprinkled between, back and forth as situations and Dad's moods dictate. But usually it's me on one end and Morgan on the other and maybe it's because of that or maybe because of our age difference, but we just don't see eye-to-eye on most things. It makes me sad. I want to understand her but I don't. I'm glad she has a job, though. We eat better.

***

Dear Miss J;

So here we are, another night, under the covers with a flashlight. Lots to report, though! My sisters and I put ads on bulletin boards in some of the shops in town today. Dad said we need to get more work, because he isn't getting the customers he used to get and he doesn't feel led to work for any of the mechanics in town. Dad's the best mechanic I know, but most of the mechanics in town are not Believers and Dad doesn't feel right submitting to their authority—he says it wouldn't be honoring to God. So we made up little three by five cards that said, *'No job too big, no job too small; no horse too short, no horse too tall, we shoe 'em all! Odd jobs and farrier work, good rates; we'll work early, we'll work late!'* Mom drove us around and I took mine to the IGA and then put one up on the corkboard inside the construction company office. The lady working there was nice. She had dark hair and dark eyes and was really pretty and spoke differently than most people I've heard, almost like she was from a foreign country. She asked us if we had any horses, and I was about to tell her about our little herd when Mom opened the door and gestured for me to come along, so I ran out right away. Mom said we shouldn't get too chatty with the people in town, they weren't Believers, and Dad would be upset, because Dad always said they were definitely not like-minded.

I hope we get calls, though. I put the house cell phone on the cards. It sure would be good to get some work. I like ground beef.

***

Dear Miss J;

I came up early because I just have to tell you! Megan and I are going to share a cell phone! Dad says that he can't be answering calls all hours of the day from people wanting us to work (there were only two calls all week), so he told Morgan to go get three cell phones. One for Morgan and Misty, one for Mia and Mandy, and one for Megan and I. He told Morgan to pay for them. Morgan has a steady job, which means we can all eat pretty regularly, which is a good thing, because if we're going to work, we'll need to be strong. Tonight is Sabbath, so I have to get ready now, but I'll be back and tell you more.

Okay, I'm back. Sabbath went okay. Things were a little tense tonight. Dad is bothered with Morgan because she wants to get a truck and Dad says that it doesn't make sense, that it won't be economical, and that Morgan will spend more money on gas than she will make from her new job, but Morgan is pretty firm about what she wants. She's sort of like Dad in that—I mean, they both are sure about what they want and it takes a kick from a mule to move them off an idea once they get it stuck in their heads. So Morgan isn't going to do what Dad wants, and as you know, Miss J, that makes things tense around the house. Dad read from the book of Joshua first, and he read where Aiken took some goods from their enemy—stuff that had been devoted to destruction—and hid it in his tent. Dad talked about how Aiken's disobedience caused a lot of problems in the camp. Morgan just sat there with her chin tucked into her hand, with her head down. Sometimes I feel so bad for her, but does she have to always head-butt Dad? He just wants what's best for us.

Morgan's birthday is next week—she will be 27. I know she wants to move out, but she won't. Dad has taught us all that the only way a biblical woman can live is either under the authority of her father, or under the authority of her husband. Women can't be on their own, without a 'head', and when he reads to us from Colossians or Ephesians, where it says for children to 'obey their parents in all things', and where it says that man is the head of the woman, I mean, why don't most Christians see this? Dad sees it, though, and I'm glad we have him as our covering protection.

Miss J, you know it's hard for Morgan. We all know she's the oldest, and we also all know she's sort of the 'black sheep' of the family. Dad will sometimes let slip that he doesn't even think she's a Believer. Sometimes I get so angry with her. Why does she have to argue with Dad all the time? But still, she must have some feelings for us, because she turns over almost all the money she makes teaching to the family.

I wonder why Morgan hasn't gotten married. There was a guy once, about five, no, seven years ago, who came from a like-minded family and he and Morgan got to know each other a little bit because they lived only eight miles away and whenever we had a holiday or celebration, their family would come over to our house or we would go to their house—remember how I would write you about those parties? They were fun. So anyway, the guy asked Dad if he could court Morgan and I was 15 at the time but I still remember Morgan blushing when Dad told her. I think Morgan kind of liked him—Jimmy, his name was. I could look it up in your pages, Miss J, but I trust my memory. Jimmy would come by—he was around 25 or so and he had his own car—and things were going along okay until one day he happened to mention to Dad that he was beginning to wonder about the doctrines associated with biblical patriarchy, and that was the last we ever saw of Jimmy. I don't know what Dad said to him, or to Morgan, but I remember Morgan sobbing under her blanket, night after night. I didn't think she would ever forget him. Eventually she did ... I think, anyway. I heard he got married and moved away, down somewhere in Wisconsin I think, to work on a dairy farm. We haven't heard from him since then. Ever since, no one else has come around the homestead to ask about Morgan, and Dad hasn't been working too hard to find her someone, I think partly because he isn't sure of her salvation and partly because if Morgan left, who would provide for the family? She is the main breadwinner and I would not want to go back to the days when we were wondering where our next meal would come from. You remember those days, don't you, Miss J? Lots of tears on those pages, but I don't have to remind you, do I? But hey, if we get odd jobs, maybe we can relieve Morgan of some of the load. At least we'll be able to get our horses some better feed!

***

Dear Miss J;

Answered prayer, answered prayer, answered prayer!!! We got a call yesterday on the phone Megan and I have, in response to one of the cards we left at the construction company's office. Some lady needs help with her horses—she has TEN! Yowies! And they're draft horses. We can't wait. Mom called them back—I was too nervous to talk on the phone, because I didn't want to mess up the deal and I was afraid I'd say something wrong and Dad would get angry. So Mom called and talked with them, and she said they have a small farm about sixteen miles from us and they're ready for us to start working right away. Mom is going to take us tomorrow to meet them and look at the horses and see what they want us to do. Dad thanked God tonight at the evening meal for answered prayer and that God led him to have us put up the cards. It speaks a lot to us about the need woman have for a covering.

***

Dear Miss J;

Lots to tell tonight. Dinner was strange; tense for some reason I can't explain. Dad was in a really bad mood and almost told Morgan to leave the table just because she asked about the horses we saw today. Dad said Morgan wasn't focused enough on her job and risked losing it and told her not to worry about what Megan and I are doing with this new job. Morgan didn't exactly answer back but she did say that she wasn't distracted, but just wanted to know what kind of horses we were going to deal with, and what we were going to do. I think there is something else behind Dad's bad mood but can't put my finger on it.

But the horses! Oh, they're beautiful, and so HUGE! I don't know them well yet, and the lady—a Miss Claire, and there was her daughter-in-law too, a Miss Zoe—wants us to care for their feet and then maybe train them to both drive and ride. Mom did most of the talking today, and Megan and I just sort of hung back and listened and took in the horses and the other animals on the farm. They have TONS of animals. There are the horses, and then they have a bunch of cows and, like, fifty sheep and they even have pigs. Oh, maybe THAT's the problem! Maybe Dad doesn't like us at a place that would have pigs, because the law says they're unclean, but we can't afford to turn down work now ... I don't know. But they raise pigs, and when I told everyone about that at dinner, Morgan looked up and asked if there were any piglets yet. I said I hadn't seen any but I did remember that Miss Claire said she wanted to breed them, so maybe there will be sometime later. So besides the horses, cows, sheep, and pigs, they have, I don't know, maybe forty or fifty chickens. Miss Claire has a husband, Mister Tack, but we didn't see him today. There's also another couple who live there, I think the guy is Miss Claire's son. His name is Mister Mace and his wife is Miss Zoe. I kind of liked her. She has red hair and she has so much energy and she seemed so happy the whole time we were there, she was always moving around and talking and sharing about what each horse was like. I don't know why four people have all those animals. Maybe Miss Claire just likes animals? That's got to be an awful lot of work for just four people, and from what we could figure out, Mister Mace and Miss Zoe milk all the cows and they run some kind of cheese business too.

The horses seem well cared for, and a couple of them are really well-trained, but there are a few young ones who haven't been ridden in a while and I'd bet keeping their feet trimmed would be a full-time job in itself.

More answer to prayer! They'll pay us a great rate (I'm not even going to put it down here because it might jinx the job) and boy, if we can get regular work there, it would really help things at home. Maybe Dad wouldn't be in such a bad mood all the time.

Another wonderful thing, and even more answer to prayer ... *they're Believers.* Mom says that Miss Claire and she talked a lot about God, and Miss Claire seems to really love the Lord. Mom was sort of reserved most of the time, because she has to check with Dad to see if Mr. Tack is of a like mind regarding how we look at the Bible, but Mom seemed to think it would be a good opportunity for us. Mom said that Dad probably won't be too bothered if Mr. Tack and Miss Claire aren't completely in line with our doctrine. Right now we need the income.

The coolest thing about the visit was that I got to spend some time just with Miss Zoe, us by ourselves. I don't know how it happened but I found myself in a stall, looking at one of the horse's feet and there she was and no one else was around. I was frightened. Mom or Dad wasn't around, but Miss Zoe and I talked about some stuff, and I can tell she loves God. It's like she really knows Him. It was ... different. The whole time we talked by ourselves I was always just a little anxious, but then the strangest thing happened: I became all at once calm and peaceful. It was weird; it was like someone threw a 'calm and peaceful' blanket over me. Then I looked up and there was Mister Mace, and he smiled at me but he didn't say anything—in fact, I don't think I heard him say anything to us the entire day. I hope he likes us. I know he and Zoe love each other a lot, because when Mr. Mace showed up in the stall, Zoe leapt up like someone put springs in her shoes and she just about jumped over the stall door and Mister Mace caught her and lifted her over the rest of the way and set her down outside the stall. Miss Zoe is a tiny little thing. I think we weigh the same.

So, Miss J, with all this great news I want to take some time and reflect on how good God has been to us. We could have waited for months for a response, or never gotten one. I mean, Granite Sky isn't the biggest city in Minnesota, and Mom says that we're really blessed to find these people. Not many people keep horses any more, because they're so expensive, and these people seem really nice. Miss Claire even gave Mom a huge beef roast from their freezer. She said they have more meat than they can eat. I was standing right there when she gave it to Mom, all wrapped up in white paper, and it was though she was happy to do it. Megan and I just stood there, holding our breath, wondering if Mom would even take it, but when she said we could put it in the back of the van, my heart (and my stomach) leapt with happiness. I think I started drooling right there! (Just kidding, Miss J).

It may be that they'll want us to do other odd jobs around the farm, too. Right now they're just getting to know us, and we them. Dad gave us a pretty stern talking-to at dinner, making sure we didn't screw things up and he wanted to make sure we did really good work while we were there so as to give a good report about the family. Megan and I said we would, for sure, and it might be that they'll want more than just Megan and I to work there. I know they've been having problems getting local people to work during hay season, and maybe we could all work there—we'll see, but that's, like, months away.

Anyway, Miss J, I'm really grateful God is working these things out. And Mom is defrosting the beef roast today so we can have it tomorrow. Hooray!

***

Dear Miss J;

It's been a while and I'm sorry but things have been crazy busy this last week. Mom has driven us over to the Ironbridge place (that's Miss Claire and Mr. Tack and Mr. Mace and Miss Zoe). They put Megan and I to work right away, trimming hooves. Megan knows all about how to do that and while I've been trying to learn, I usually get to do the odd jobs like cleaning the stalls and fixing some of the fencing around the place. I've told you before how curious Megan is, and how she's always so outgoing and asking a lot of questions, and it really doesn't take her much time to warm up to people. She's always been the extrovert in the family, and I've always been the shy, quiet one, so I don't talk much while I'm over there, but I just listen. Miss Claire listens to Megan, too, and Megan is beginning to ask a lot of questions. She can talk!

We met Mr. Tack for the first time a couple of days ago. He has a fake leg but he gets around okay. He got hurt in some kind of accident a while ago. He was building a stone wall with some guy from town—actually we learned later in the day that it was the owner of the construction company where we put our little paper advertisement on the corkboard, and Mr. Tack smiled at the coincidence. I'm nervous around him—Mr. Tack, that is. I don't exactly know what he's like, and I suppose I'm nervous around most men, because of Dad, I think. You just never know when they'll just 'go off' and get angry. It stops me in my tracks, and sometimes I get so nervous I just can't even eat. But Mr. Tack seems to recognize that and really doesn't interact with us much except to say hello and make sure we have enough to eat at lunch.

Oh my, did I tell you, they love to feed us lunch! We try to be polite and demure but they just keep plunking more food on our plates and we are NOT going to say no!

And another thing, Miss J; Mr. Tack talks to Miss Claire, well, sort of differently than Dad talks to Mom. I guess the best way I can describe it is that Mr. Tack talks *with* Miss Claire, where, most of the time, it seems Dad talks *to* Mom. I can't explain it, but it's definitely making Megan and I take notice more how Dad treats Mom at home. Maybe that's a good thing.

***

Dear Miss J;

Oh boy, the fat's in the fire now, thank you very much, Megan. Let me start at the beginning.

I told you Megan likes to talk and ask lots of questions, and so while she was trimming one of the horses this morning at the Ironbridge's, and I was standing there holding the horse's head, Mr. Tack walked by to get a hammer—I think he's still working on the stone wall. So Megan just pops up and comes right out with her question. "So Mr. Tack, what do you think of the Scripture about children obeying their parents in all things?"

A cold sense of dread overpowered me, knowing that Dad would not have wanted such things to be discussed with others, and certainly wouldn't have wanted Megan or any of us, to be asking such questions. I expected Mr. Tack to just sort of nod and say something cursory, like, "Uh, sure, why not," or "Well, what's to wonder about," or something, but he didn't. He stopped on his way to the tool room and looked at Megan—I mean, looked directly at her, like she was a real person, and said, "This is a scripture in the

Bible you're talking about, right?"

"Uh, yeah, that's right," Megan says, unbelievably comfortable with getting into a conversation with some guy who's not Dad. Trying to stifle my fear about what Dad would say when he found out, I was wondering why she would ask the question in the first place.

"Well, let me ask you ... if your parents asked you to help them rob a bank, would you do that?"

Megan hesitated for just a minute and then said, "Uh, well, I don't think our parents would ask us to do that."

"You're not talking about your parents, though, are you? You're asking about this Scripture, right?"

"Right."

"Okay then, so your interpretation has to apply to all cases. If you're telling me that you wouldn't help your parents rob a bank, then children should *not*, in some cases, obey their parents, right?" That brought both of us to a screeching mental halt.

Megan recovered first. "What if ... what if we trust our parents to do the right thing, though sometimes we might not understand what the right thing is. That's sort of how it is with God, too, isn't it? Sometimes God asks us to do things and we're not exactly sure why, but we have to just trust Him and do it, right?"

"God would never ask you to do anything which He has already declared to be a sin."

I surprised myself by saying, "Dad says that if he ever asks us to do anything which might look like sin to us, we're supposed to do it anyway, and if it turns out to be wrong, then he's accountable for it, not him." Megan looked over at me, surprised, but smiled. "Yeah," she said. "What Emma said!" as though I'd just solved the riddle of the ages. I gulped, shocked at myself for speaking up.

Mr. Tack set the hammer down on a saddle rack and sort of tilted his head at both of us. "So ... let me get this right ... and I want to make sure I understand what you two are telling me ... so ... if you do something you're told to do by your parents—"

"By Dad," Megan put it.

"Not by your Mom?" he asked.

Megan looked at me and I looked back at her, hoping she could interpret my look that was throwing daggers at her, meaning that she got us into this, she'd better get us out of it. "Um, well, Dad says that according to how he reads Scripture, women can't really ..."

"Can't really what?" he asked, plunking down on one of the small stools we used to trim the horses' feet.

"Uh ... since women need a head, they can't really interpret Scripture; they need a man to do that, and they don't have any kind of authority to direct someone else to do something, so ..."

"A 'head'?"

"Someone in authority over them, to sort of interpret what God says to them, and to represent them up to God."

"Oh." Mr. Tack just sort of shook his head at that, like he was digesting something he hadn't heard about. But both Megan and I were working in terra incognita and felt strange, because here was this adult man listening to the two of us—two girls, by the way—as though what we had to say actually had some merit. We wondered at it. But I don't think he noticed how surprised we were. He just hunched his shoulders a bit and I could see him digging his hands into the pockets of his farm coat. It was kind of cold in the barn, though Megan and I didn't mind it. We were used to much worse. We didn't even need gloves.

"So if your Mom told you to go rob a bank, you wouldn't do it, but if your Dad did, you would." It was terribly frustrating to hear him put it that way, but when I think about it now, he did sort of just boil it all down, though he was off just a bit. Megan was honest enough say so.

"Well, if Mom told us to rob a bank, we'd have to check with Dad. If he said to do it, we'd do it; if he said not to, we wouldn't."

He nodded his head and then stood up and picked up the hammer. He had sort of a faraway look on his face, like he was either confused or unsettled or wondering or worrying about something. "Thanks," he said. "That clears up some things."

"Glad to help," Megan said, hopeful that maybe she'd had some part in spreading the Gospel. Maybe that's what made her say what she said next. "So ... what *do* you think about that Scripture?"

Mr. Tack stopped and looked at both of us with eyes that frightened me a little—not in a bad way, but in the way you look at a storm on the horizon and know for sure that it will roll over you like a giant threshing wheel.

"I think ... I think that if you read a little further, you'll see that it instructs children to obey their parents *as unto the Lord*, which means that children—children, mind you—should obey their parents in all things that parents ask of them in the same way they would obey God, which means to obey their parents when what they are told to do is in accordance with the Lord's nature and character. I think that interpretation accords with the entire counsel of God, and not just one segmented chunk of Scripture out of context, and it's an interpretation you can apply to all cases. God would never ask us to sin; if parents ever did ask a child to sin, obeying such a request would not be 'as unto the Lord', and the child should not do what they were asked to do." He turned to go but then stopped. "And sorry to break it to you, ladies, but if your ... if your *Dad* asks you to do something that is clearly sinful, and you do it, then while he may be accountable to God for asking you to do that thing, *you* would be accountable to God, directly, for doing that thing." Then he left, carrying the hammer.

"Well now we're in for it," I said. "What's Dad gonna say when he hears about what Mr. Tack thinks?"

Megan looked at me sort of sideways. "Who's gonna tell Dad what Mr. Tack thinks?" she asked. Megan scares me sometimes.

***

Dear Miss J;

I don't know what to do. I've come up against something I can't handle and I don't know what to do. I can't talk to Megan or Mia or Misty or Mandy or Morgan and *no way* I can talk to Dad. I want to write it out for you, and maybe we can come up with something together. I know it's been a few days since I wrote to you last, so let me catch you up.

It's been almost a week since Megan popped that question of hers at Miss Claire's and Mr. Tack's, and we had to decide if we were going to tell Dad what Mr. Tack thinks of biblical patriarchy. I figured that since it was Megan who asked the question and who (mostly) carried the conversation, it was her responsibility to tell Dad what came of it. It would be almost as though I was snitching if I told Dad. But Megan didn't have anything to say to Dad that day when we came home, and she didn't say anything in the days after, so I am pretty sure she's not going to tell Dad. Dad won't read it here, that I know, because he considers it a matter of honor not to pry into our conversations. So we'll just have to go with it. I know Dad doesn't mind the money we're bringing home. Miss Claire pays us *at the end of every day*! That's never happened before, and it sure helps.

So after Mr. Tack didn't blow up or throw a hammer at us or get angry at Megan asking him questions, and since it seemed to both of us that he actually didn't mind discussing the questions we had, Megan really let loose. Oh, we all have so many questions about so many things about what is out there in the rest of the world. Morgan wants to know all about how to take care of animals. I don't think she deals very well with people but I think that's because ... well, I don't know why, but she seems more comfortable around animals. Misty and Mia just want to do what Mom tells them to do, and Mandy ... I can't figure Mandy out most of the time. She just sort of 'exists', and Mom doesn't seem to want to spend much time with her. Sometimes we're not sure she's 'firing on all thrusters', as Dad would say (he watches a lot of Star Trek and we've seen all the Star Wars movies ten times). But anyway, we all wonder about so many things and not one of us dares to ask Dad, and we know Dad wouldn't want us asking Mom anything, and Mom has never really seemed to want to answer our questions unless Dad was around—I don't know why that is, actually—so we live our lives with unanswered questions that we carry around like someone carries around a five-gallon bucket of water everywhere. Well, Megan started dumping that five-gallon bucket on Mr. Tack and Miss Claire and Miss Zoe and Mr. Mace, and they just started answering and didn't stop.

And the other thing—Mr. Tack and Miss Claire and Mr. Mace and Miss Zoe are way, *way* different than anyone we've ever seen before. Their Christianity is different. I mean, it seems like they really live what the Bible talks about. Miss Claire is constantly talking about God—about what He's like or what He likes or what He doesn't like, or about what things are happening in the world and how they match up with Scriptures that talk about how history is coming to an end and how Jesus will be returning soon, and I know Dad talks a lot about that, and I know that's why we live the way we do, with no power, no water, with all of us homeschooled—but how Dad deals with the end times and how Mr. Tack and Miss Claire deal with it are different.

Mr. Tack listens patiently to all our questions and then comes right back with questions of his own that shook the foundations of our world. And he always references Scripture. I'm beginning to think that he's reading a different Bible than the one we read. Megan and I are seeing some things we've never seen before. I hope God forgives me, Miss J, but Megan and I see fruit in their lives, where we don't really see any fruit at home. And another thing: Mr. Tack treats Miss Claire way different than how Dad treats Mom. Mr. Tack seems to actually *love* Miss Claire. He listens to her when she talks. I mean, seriously, she runs the farm and sometimes he lets her tell him what to do and then he just goes and does it. I can't figure this out, and this is just *one more* question I have.

And Mr. Mace: Whoa. I mean, the first time I saw that scar in his hand, I freaked. But then when one day when I saw Miss Zoe come home from town where she'd been doing something by herself, she pulled up in the driveway and I could tell she was upset, she was shaking and I thought I saw a tear in her eye, and Mace came out of the Carriage House (that's where Mr. Mace and Miss Zoe live) and it was as though he could tell she was upset. I saw her run from the car to where he was standing and she took his hand—the one with the scar in it-and pulled it to her face and then he wrapped his arms around her and she started crying on his chest and then I looked away because I couldn't see very clearly for a while either. But every time Mr. Mace comes near me, all my anxiety and fear just go away, and I am beginning to understand how Miss Zoe feels.

So with all these questions we have and seeing how Mr. Tack and Miss Claire and Mr. Mace and Miss Zoe are so different, and after we were confident that they didn't mind us asking us questions, Megan has let loose like a house on fire, and okay, so I'm too shy much to speak up but I listen too, and this is what finally got me. We were having lunch yesterday, sitting at the table, and the discussion came back to where it usually did—the thing about parents obeying their children. So Mr. Tack finally hits us with it.

"Okay, girls, so I want you ask you something." We'd been working there long enough and engaged them in enough discussions to know that we'd better watch out when he began the conversation like that. We both flicked up our shields ('Shields up, Scotty!') and got ready to fire photon torpedoes in return.

"You tell me that your Dad is basically responsible to God for you."

"Right," I said, jumping in. Whenever it came to defending Dad's doctrine of biblical patriarchy, it was me who did most of the talking, because I really believe it's truly biblical.

"Ah, the tree frog speaks," Mr. Tack said. I blushed a bit, because I didn't have much to say most of the time, and I was sort dependent on Megan to lead in conversations with others. So yeah, okay, I was sort of a tree frog and Megan was the tree in my life. I'm closer to her than to any of the others, maybe because we're closest in age. Mr. Tack went on.

"That's good," he said, smiling. "No worries. So let me ask you ... God says that we are to love Him with all our heart and soul and strength, right?"

"Right," Megan said. We both have memorized most of the New Testament and a lot of the Old Testament, and we could run rings around any of the people we ever met at any of the churches we went to—that is, before Dad had us stop going to churches. I think the last time I went to a church was when I was five. But I'm getting off topic, Miss J, sorry. We could run rings around anyone we'd met with Scripture, but not with Mr. Tack or Miss Claire, and definitely, whoa, definitely not Mr. Mace—they knew the Word as well as we did, but also, it seemed they knew it in a different way. It's almost like the difference between on one hand knowing *about* something, something you've read about, and on the other hand, knowing something because you've lived it.

So Mr. Tack presses on and says, "And how can we actually love Him? What are we supposed to do?"

I cast about in my mind for the answer, but it didn't come. Megan looked at me and I shook my head. You know, Miss J, that if it ever comes to a Scripture memory contest, everyone in the family looks at me for the answer, and yeah, so usually I have it, but this time I couldn't answer Mr. Tack.

"You remember that He said, 'If you love Me—"

"You'll obey my commandments!" I finished for him.

"Right ... we'll obey His commandments, and you know enough about Scripture to realize that when Jesus was talking about His commandments, He wasn't referring to just those ten things God chiseled in stone for Moses. He was talking about the things He would command us in each day, as we walked through the days in a relationship with Him. You know that from your reading, right?"

Megan and I nodded, wondering where Mr. Tack was going. So far it was clear.

"So in order for us to love God, we need to obey Him, you'd agree with that. Let me ask you then," he says, with Miss Claire sitting there beside him, "what if you don't *have* the choice to obey Him? What if all you had to do was just obey your Dad, or your husband when you get married, and you didn't have the responsibility to actually have a direct relationship with God. You just did whatever your 'head' told you to do. Would it be *you*, then, who was obeying God? Would it be *you* making the choice to do what God required? And if the answer is no—and that's what the answer is, by the way—then how could you say you loved God, then, if you weren't making any choices on your own, if you didn't exercise the choice to obey Him?"

I don't know what Megan did then, because I went into kind of a short-circuit overload. I couldn't immediately process what he was saying, because the implications were ... well, they were too enormous to consider. I remember working it through, sitting there with a half-eaten chicken breast on my plate, realizing that if what he was saying was true, then the concept that we'd grown up with all our lives, the idea that women needed a head between them and God, and that they didn't, or couldn't, have a direct relationship with God on their own, but only through their head—then that concept couldn't hold up any more.

What made this worse was that Mr. Tack and Miss Claire knew the Word as well or better than we did—I mean, they knew it like someone who's lived it knows it—and their lives were what we always thought lives would be if the Scriptures were really true. So we couldn't look at their lives and say they didn't know what they were talking about, because their lives looked more like what we thought biblical Christianity should look like than what our own parents' lives looked like. And Mr. Mace and Miss Zoe ... well, Megan and I both know we're looking at something really special when we think about their relationship. So we were stuck. Everything we'd been taught all our lives was called into question over a chicken lunch and we didn't have any answer for Mr. Tack's question. Well, to be honest, there *was* an answer; it was just that we didn't want to admit it. But Mr. Tack provided it nonetheless.

"The answer ladies, I am sorry to tell you, is that you *can't* love Him unless you have the choice to obey Him, which is why, now you see, He gave us the one thing He would never, ever take from us—our free will. Our free will was given to us by God and *cannot and should not* be taken away from us by anyone, ever," and here he paused and looked at me, "by parents ... fathers, specifically. And He gave free will to every one of us, not just to men. He gave it to women as well. You can't read through the Bible and come to any other conclusion. To think otherwise is to completely miss the heart of God." I remember him saying this so clearly; it's burned into my mind, because I remember he was holding Miss Claire's hand when he said it. He had such a heart for her. But he went on. "You each will need to decide if you are going to have a direct relationship with Jesus, or if you will let someone else interfere with that and keep you from obeying Him ... and loving Him."

Oh, Miss J, what do I do now? All I've ever wanted to do was to love God and obey Him. Something tells me that Mr. Tack and Miss Claire are right, and it means God wants to have a direct relationship with me—yes, me, directly, straight to me, between me and Him, He and I. I have no idea how to even *begin* that. I can understand God having a relationship with Dad, sure ... but with *me*?

But the problem with that is ... if I have a relationship with God directly, that's going to bring me into conflict with Dad. It will directly challenge the position he's had in my life since, well, forever. And that's plain terrifying ... I mean, I can't even imagine how this might end. To me, I don't think life could possibly exist after such a conflict.

What am I going to do, Miss J?

***

Dear Miss J;

I can't take it anymore. I have to know! So (big breath here) I started a study into Biblical patriarchy. I have to find Scriptures that will prove that Dad's view of Biblical patriarchy is correct doctrine. Megan and I are slamming questions at Miss Claire and Mr. Tack and Mr. Mace and Miss Zoe, and they just keep giving us answers back that tumble our whole world. So I have to just set everything aside—I started a fast today—and get to the bottom of what it really says in the Bible. Wish me luck!

***

Dear Miss J;

I read in Psalm 112 yesterday that '*Light arises in the darkness for the upright.*' I know what Dad would say about me thinking myself to be upright, but if we think of light being truth, then I so want to know the truth about this way we've lived all our lives—you know, having Dad as our head, our intermediary between us and God.

I decided to do a paper from the results of my study and when I'm finished I'll submit it to Mom and Dad. I'll fill you in on it when I'm finished!

***

Dear Miss J;

(Long deep breath) So I finished. I'm kind of weak, doing chores without any food for the last seven days, and staying up late to go through the Bible, but God has given me answers to my questions. I'm a different person now, Miss J, but I do not know what to do with the answers He's given me. I'm still very much afraid of what the results mean.

In my study, there are six parts: first, Part I—what the Bible says about the headship of men over women; Part II—the relationship of children to their parents; Part III—the equality of Believers under Christ; Part IV—about a personal relationship with God through Jesus alone; Part V—about idolatry; and Part VI—about personal responsibility before God for each individual's actions. Here's what I found.

In Part I, about the headship of men over women, the Bible clearly says that the husband is to be in a position of headship over the wife so as to represent how things are between Christ and the church. This means even that the husband must give up his life for the wife as Christ gave up His life for the church. The thing that I DID NOT find in my search of the Bible was that this headship of husbands over wives DOES NOT include headship of fathers over daughters. Nowhere did I see that concept—NOWHERE.

In Part II, about the relationship of children to their parents, the main question here was, 'If a daughter that is grown is not under her father's headship, what should her relationship with her father be?' You know, let me tell you about the Scripture that says to 'honor thy father and mother.' The Greek word translated 'honor' means to 'prize, fix a value on, revere.' This is the same Greek word used in 1 Peter 2:17, '*Honor all; love the brotherhood* ...' If honor meant obey, than God just commanded us to 'obey all' and by implication, that includes unbelievers! Not only is this a physical impossibility, it is also totally absurd and against God's character. Honor does not mean to 'blindly obey'; it means to value. We are to value and revere our parents, but if they make mistakes, or if they command us to do things we know are wrong, we are not to obey them in that.

I read 1 Corinthians 13:11, where it says, '*When I was a child, I spoke as a child, I understood as a child, I thought as a child; but when I became a man, I put away childish things.*' Well, Miss J, it seems to me clear that children should not always remain children. God expects children to grow up and become adults.

The verse in Ephesians—the 'big stick' my father used with all of us kids, says in Chapter 6, '*Children, obey your parents in the Lord, for this is right.*' The Greek word translated 'children' means 'a child as produced, that is, an offspring. This word '*teknon*' is not age-specific. It is used multiple times throughout the New Testament, usually in the sense of offspring. To interpret this verse, we must look at all the Scripture to determine the mind and heart of God. '*Children, obey your parents*' is not a blanket statement for all of humanity. If such were the case, parents would have absolute control over their sons and daughters for as long as the parents lived. Also, when you think about it, a daughter would never be able to marry while her parents lived because she would never be able to obey her parents *and* submit to her husband. And mindless obedience is against God's character—it was He who formed our brains, after all! He gives us choices. This is how He can tell we love Him, by *choosing* to love Him. If we didn't have true choice, then there would be no true love. We can choose to obey our parents or choose to disobey. Of course, God expects us to obey Him more than (or before) men (see Acts 5:29). If a father is a daughter's God-given authority, and God would never speak to her except through her father, how would God have a personal relationship with that daughter for whom He sent His Son to die? It goes against God's character. If a father is a daughter's God-given authority, and God would never tell the daughter to do something the father disapproved of or said 'no' to, then that would imply that the earthly father is perfect. That is not so; men are imperfect. All have sinned (Romans 3:23). Every one has to deal with his own fallen nature; no one is perfect. So why would God say '*Children obey your parents?*' It seems this verse (and also Colossians 3:20) is speaking of children who are unable to care for themselves physically or spiritually. They are unable to establish a foundation of their own, and must be 'trained up in the way they should go' (Proverbs 22:6) until they can establish their own relationship with Jesus.

There was another verse in Ephesians that spoke to me too, Miss J. Ephesians 6:4, where it says '*And ye fathers, provoke not your children to wrath; but bring them up in the nurture and admonition of the Lord.*' This passage seems to indicate the children referred to are younger because they need to be 'brought up.' The father is the figure of Christ to the children, so that they can learn how they ought to obey, to love, to be loved, and to relate to Christ. At some point, every human being ceases to be a 'child' and becomes an adult. I see it here in the phrase 'bring them up'. At some point in time, every human being ceases to need to be 'brought up.' When the children reach maturity, they are 'brought up.'

As the law was a 'schoolmaster to bring us to Christ' (Gal. 3:24 and 25), so our earthly fathers are a guide to show their children the way to Christ. At some point, children cease to need being 'brought up' or 'trained up', and they must establish a relationship with God themselves, through faith in God alone, laying a foundation of that faith in Jesus Christ. No one else can lay this foundation for them. They must lay it with God alone. No one, not even a father, can stand in the place of God. God alone must communicate with the grown child, because if a person follows God only because 'that's what Dad said', then that person actually does not have any relationship with God, but is simply living in the father's relationship with God—which is not what God wants. A person must be free to choose to obey Christ or disobey Him, to follow Him or reject Him. If the person is not free to do this, then it is not a relationship based on free will, and is therefore a relationship against the character of God. The relationship must be one of free will. If the earthly father inserts himself in the place of God, he sets himself as an idol in the hearts of his children. No one can come between God and His child. 1 Timothy 2:5: *'For there is one God, and one Mediator between God and men, the man Christ Jesus.'* If anyone tries to insert themselves between God and man, they place themselves in Jesus' position. They have crossed the line. And learning this, I wonder ... have I been an idolater? I'm scared, Miss J.

Part III talks about the equality of Believers under Jesus, and this is something I've struggled with, Miss J. All my life I've been taught that women are just 'second-class citizens', so I came to this part of the study knowing that I sort of have pre-existing filters on. Well, if what I read in Scripture is true, then I have some re-learning to do. My big question was, 'Are all Believers equal in their rights to a relationship with God?' The Scriptures say yes. Matthew 23:8 says *'But be not ye called 'Rabbi': for one is your Master, even Christ; and all ye are brethren.'* Jesus was speaking to His disciples and to the multitude here. He says Christ is our Master—no one else—and we are all brethren. Jesus puts all Believers as equal, with Him above all as Master. If a father were his daughter's God-given authority, wouldn't Jesus have instead said, 'but the daughters' master is her father'? I see from Luke 22:25-27 that God wants us to serve one another. He wants fathers to serve daughters as well as daughters to serve fathers. We all have a responsibility to *'put ye on the Lord Jesus Christ, and make no provision for the flesh to fulfill the lusts thereof* (Romans 13:14). If God had given authority to fathers over their daughters, why would He want fathers to serve daughters? It says in Acts that in the last days God will pour out His spirit upon all flesh, and that *'your sons and daughters shall prophesy, and your young men shall see visions and your old men shall dream dreams ...'* God speaks directly to all of His children, and gives them His Spirit—even daughters. Elsewhere in Acts we read of 'all being filled with the Holy Spirit—ALL. There are just too many other examples to write down, Miss J. All our lives, every day, we had Bible time with Dad and Mom and we know the New Testament pretty much by heart, and I've never seen what I've seen this week before, but I can't deny that it is there. I was just looking at it before with filters my Dad had put on the eyes of my heart.

Part IV answers the question I had: 'Does every Believer have the right to have a personal relationship directly with God through Jesus alone?' I can't write down all of what I learned here, Miss J, but I can tell you YES YES YES! I mean, look in Matthew 4 and 19, in Luke 14 and 16, in John 4 and 10 and 12 and 14 and 15, and, oh, so much more. It's EVERYWHERE, Miss J. It's so CLEAR! How could I have missed this? God wants a direct and personal relationship with each of us, with no one in between. It is a father's job to bring his children to understand this and to bring them to the point where they make their own choice, and if and when they do, to support them with wisdom and admonition and help and guidance, but NEVER to be God in the place of God. It is just beginning to dawn on me how much I have made my father an idol. Oh, Miss J, it terrifies me to think of how much that must hurt Jesus. Dad didn't die for us, but Jesus did.

That thought naturally brought me to Part V, about idolatry. It's not difficult to find what God thinks about idolatry, but when I read through what idolatry really was, it hit me...hard, especially knowing what Peter said to the Pharisees, telling them that *'we ought to obey God rather than men.'* Oh, Miss J, how can men obey God instead of men if they are not hearing from God directly? And THAT must mean that we CAN actually hear from God directly, not through some other person. And THAT is exciting, Miss J! If God says to do one thing, and any one, even a father or mother, says to do differently, we must obey God. Any other action would be idolatry. If you obeyed your father or mother instead of God, your father and mother will have turned into your gods. That is idolatry. Corinthians tells us that we are 'bought with a price,' therefore we should not be servants of men.' Jesus paid a high price for every one of His children's lives. The life Jesus died for belongs to no one but Jesus.

As I began to see how this doctrine clouded my mind and heart, Miss J, I began to see the truth about idols. What is an idol, really? An idol is anything that we value or set up or esteem above or put equal with God. God is a jealous God and He has said *'I will not give My glory to another.'* If a daughter goes to her earthly father instead of to God for permission or as her PRIMARY authority source, her father has become her idol. If a father compels or leads his daughter to obey him instead of God or tells her that she must go to God through him, he compels and leads his daughter into idolatry. And we are told that we must FLEE idolatry. Run away from it.

Part VI was about personal responsibility before God for each individual's actions, and my main question that I wanted to answer was, 'Is each individual responsible before God for their actions, or does a father have to be responsible for his daughter's actions?' Well, I got an answer to that question easily enough. Romans 2:6 tells us about God *'Who will render to every man according to his deeds.'* The Greek word here translated 'every man' means everyone, and it is not age or gender specific. If an earthly father tells the daughter to do one thing, and God tells her to do the opposite, and she submits to her earthly father, she alone will bear the consequences of not obeying God. In Hebrews 5:13-14, I read, *'For everyone that useth milk is unskillful in the word of righteousness; for he is a babe. But strong meat belongeth to them that are of full age, even those who by reason of use have their senses exercised to discern both good and evil.'* Miss J, if a person, ANY PERSON, cannot exercise their senses to 'discern both good and evil,' they will always be a spiritual babe. They will never grow. A person must exercise their senses, and to do that, they must be exposed to both good and evil, and made free to choose what is good and turn away from what is evil. I remember asking Dad if we girls had free choice, and he would always laugh and say, 'Sure, you're free to make a choice—as long as it's the right choice." If a person is controlled to the degree that they can only choose 'the right choice', then truly, they are not really free at all, and it is not their choice. Their senses haven't been exercised. Instead of the free-willed person that God made, they become a mindless robot, or worse ... a slave.

Miss J, there is so much more throughout the Bible that I never saw before until I cleared my mind and read it with only a desire to see the truth NO MATTER WHAT.

When I did that, oh, everything became so clear. BUT NOW WHAT? What do I do now?

I will tell you, Miss J. I am honor-bound to share with Dad and Mom what I've learned. What if they've never read the Scriptures like this? What if maybe they will see what I've seen in them?

So I am going to write them a letter, and I am going to put this letter at the end of the study. Do you mind, Miss J, if I use your pages to work up a draft? Thanks, so, okay, here goes:

'Dear Dad and Mom;

I've been studying the Bible now since I was able to read, but just in the last seven days, I've learned some new things that I wanted to share with you, and some pretty important news. I guess I should share with you the most important thing that came from the study up front.

I no longer believe that the father is the 'head' or God-given authority over a grown daughter. I know how this sounds, especially coming from someone raised the way I was. I realize the husband is the head of the wife—I can see that clearly in Scripture. And I still believe that the father is the head of the house, and the half-grown children need that figure. But my beliefs about my role as a grown daughter ... those have changed.

God made children to grow up. When they do they need to establish their relationship with God on their own. NO ONE can do it for them. I am sorry but I feel that for most of our lives—no, actually, for all of our lives, you have been the go-between (the 'mediator') between God and me. But every person—even daughters, even women, and yes, even Mom—must be free to worship and serve God and be free to obey Him directly, without any intermediary.

To even ask a father's permission to obey God is very dangerous because it makes the father as the final authority over God. You've told us we had to ask your permission before we could consider doing something we thought God was asking us to do, and it is my responsibility—it is on me, this sin—that I have obeyed you in doing so. I repent for that. But I can't keep asking you if it is okay for me to obey God any longer. God can and will speak in His children's lives. He has plans and purposes for every one—even daughters, even women. An infinite God would never confine women to one or two roles (daughter or wife). God would not make a woman a widow or an orphan before He used her to do something in the world; God is a God of love, not of cruelty.

I know this might be hard to read, but if after reading this study you still take the opposite point of view, I challenge you to study it in the Bible yourselves. Pray about it. Come to the Bible with open eyes and no pre-conceived conclusions. Please ... ask God to send His Holy Spirit to 'guide you into all truth'. Seek out the mind of Christ on this.

Remember the first and greatest commandment? 'Thou shalt love the Lord they God with all they heart, with all thy soul, and with all thy mind.' And the second that was 'like unto it.' 'Thou shalt love thy neighbor as thyself.' Jesus said that on these two commandments hang all the law and the prophets. And Jesus agreed when the scribe or lawyer said 'and to do these is more than whole burnt offerings and sacrifices.' This is the true nature of God. God wants our hearts. Structured 'religion' that becomes a list of do's and don't turns a vibrant, living, personal relationship with Him into nothing but a dead, works-based system in which men think they will attain salvation.

Dad, I love you very much, but you have been an idol in my life. The Lord helped me see that and warned me about it. I must follow Jesus.

Dad and Mom, I love you both very much. I don't want to hurt you. God showed me a wonderful truth in His Word and I just wanted to share it with you. Please, take it, read it, study it, pray about it, learn from it.

Because of what Jesus did for ALL of us;
Lots of love;
Emma

Well? What do you think, Miss J? I'll tell you what I think. I feel like I'm jumping off a cliff into the unknown, like I'm facing a firing squad almost. I KNOW the world I have lived in all my life is coming to an end, but ... but what's after that? I can't really believe what Mr. Tack and Miss Claire tell me, that God cares as much about women as He does men; sorry, that just doesn't compute, and so when I jump off the cliff here by going against my Dad, I mean, then what? Where will I go? What will happen? Yeah, I know I have to do this, because with what little working brain I have left, I can realize that it's the right thing to do, but, honestly Miss J, I feel like I'm going to my execution ... like a dead girl walkin'.

***

Miss J;

It's been, I don't know, almost ten days since I've been able to sit down and write to you. My heart has not been this painful ever in my life. I am grieving. I am an emotional puddle; I'm like Jello right now. I don't know what to do, so (like I always seem to do), I will tell you about what happened and maybe in your pages I can see what to do, even though in my own mind and heart, I can't.

I feel utter despair, Miss J. Life has no more meaning, and everything is tasteless. Yes, I've done the study, it's clear, but I still doubt God is there. Everything seems dark; my soul seems empty now, almost like I've ripped something out that will never be replaced, and I'm overcome with feelings of fear, darkness, and despondence. I know God says we're not to take our own lives, but honestly, I'm ready to go. I feel like just asking God to take me now. My soul is filled with darkness and a burden I cannot bear. Give me a minute, would you?

Okay ... so ...

I gave the paper to my Mom first. She knew something was up, because I'd been fasting for a week and that of course tipped her off, and ever since I've been wondering about this, I think she sensed it. So when I gave her the paper, she didn't seem too surprised. She just asked me what it was and I told her it was a study I'd done in the Bible on patriarchy. She sort of looked at me sideways but took it and promised to read it.

She read it two days later. I was going CRAZY waiting for her to get to it, and finally she did. The third afternoon from when I'd given it to her, she gave it back to me and said, "I don't think your Dad will like it."

"But what do you think of it, Mom?"

"Let your Dad look it over."

"But ... I mean, do you ... does it make sense to you?"

She looked at me and suddenly—I think the word people use is 'epiphany'—I realized that my Mom was the product of what happens when a woman completely surrenders her mind and soul and makes an idol of her husband, abdicating her personal responsibility before God and making her 'head'—the husband—her god. I saw clearly that she didn't have any opinion on what I'd said because all her life she'd been trained NOT to have any opinions, but just defer to her husband. She couldn't have anything to say about it, because it would have violated the doctrine of patriarchy. What would happen if her opinions differed from Dad's? Then what? Would she recant? Would she repent? Would she stand up to him? No, it was just easier, after 28 years of marriage, just not to have her own opinion.

Miss J, I truly for the first time felt sorry for my Mom.

And then my Dad read it.

I don't want to complain or sound harsh, but let me just say that things did not go well ... oh no, not at all. But God was with me the entire time, I have to tell you, Miss J. He was strong for me when I was just a trembling stalk in front of my Dad. I gave it to him while he was sitting down before we went out to do chores. I handed it to him saying, "Dad, would you read this please? It's a paper that describes the results of a study I think God led me to do."

"Sure," he said, flicking through the DVD collection. "I'll get to it." I went out to do afternoon chores.

When I came back in, I could tell he'd read at least some of it. His face was red and he was more angry than anyone had seen him in a long time. His anger always terrified me—or more accurately, petrified me, freezing me in place like a little rabbit in front of a wolf, or like a deer in the headlights of an oncoming car. But this time, BOY was he angry. I came through the door and he threw the paper at my feet.

"THAT," he yelled, "is from the pit of hell. I renounce it! What are you thinking, after all you've been taught, to write something like that?!"

I started trembling then, but I knew that if I didn't stand my ground, I'd never be able to again. And truthfully, Miss J, I honestly felt that God had intervened during the study and shown me things—personally reached into my heart and shown me things—and if I was to back away from what God showed me, those truths, because of my father's anger, then it would be almost like denying God. It would be 'obeying men instead of God.' Oh boy, was I ever learning now what that Scripture REALLY meant! It's one thing to read Scripture; it is another thing entirely to have to actually DO WHAT IT SAYS when the rubber meets the road.

"I believe God gave me those things, Dad. I believe they're—"

"They're from the pit, I'm telling you! I am not even going to discuss this with you. This is what comes from running out from under your authority head. You can stand there and tell me you were completely deranged when you wrote it, and maybe you can stay under this roof. But oh, won't we have some remedial Bible studies, let me tell you! This has nothing to do with God," he yelled again, kicking at the paper on the floor. "This is from a deceiving spirit. Those people you're working with have influenced you. I *never* should have let your mother take you over there." He stopped and then looked at me. He hadn't spanked me in years, but I'd never seen him this angry and I was very frightened.

Though my stomach was in knots and my legs were shaking, I answered him. It must have been God who gave me the strength to say what I said next. "I ... I can't recant, Dad. I believe in those things. I believe that's truth."

He looked at me and I got the strangest feeling then, Miss J, that—and I hope I am wrong—a sort of switch turned in him. It was almost instantaneous, but I felt like I could see how his mind was working, like it was almost on display, and I felt like the switch he turned was his relationship with me, the daughter who had spent most of the time with him, who out of all his daughters believed in him the most.

"You won't recant?" he asked, his voice like iron.

"No ... no, Dad, I can't. You taught us to be honest, and I'm being honest."

"I didn't teach you any of this ... this *filth!*" he said, again kicking at the paper on the floor. "So ... you don't want to recant, then you can leave. Put your house key on the table by the door. Be out by tomorrow afternoon. Get your animal off the property by then or I'll sell it." And he turned away, went back to his chair in front of the television, and turned on some movie or other. I was so rattled I had no idea what it was, but what I had heard was that he was kicking me out of the house.

You don't want to know all that happened between then and now, Miss J, but I can fill you in on the basics. I went up to my room. I could barely walk up the ladder, my legs where shaking so badly, but I made it up there and was grateful to see our phone on Megan's bed. I picked it up and texted Miss Zoe, letting her know what happened. I got a text back immediately.

"We'll come get you tomorrow morning. We'll bring the trailer for Rags."

Honestly, I was operating on autopilot then, because I realize now that I was in shock. So I made plans—I'm a planner, Miss J, you know that—and I sorted what few clothes I had and my tack and the little box I carry you around in, and then sat down on my bed and waited for Megan to come in so I could tell her what happened.

I wasn't permitted at the table that night, because Dad said I wasn't part of the family any longer. No one had much to say at dinner. I spent the night praying, asking God for strength not to deny Him. I should tell you, Miss J, that after I stood up to my Dad, my resolve became even stronger! It was as if God was waiting to see if I would really be willing to have a relationship with Him, even if my Dad told me I couldn't. But oh, He was so close to me that last night in my father's home.

The next day came and went in a blur. Mr. Mace and Miss Zoe were standing on the road that led to our property—Dad said they were not permitted to come on the property, so I had to carry my stuff the three-quarters of a mile down the access road to get to them. They brought their stock trailer and I loaded up Rags, my horse. I can't remember much. I know Megan came out to say goodbye, and I know Morgan stood at the door watching me go, but I didn't see any of my other sisters. Dad had made it clear that if any one of them even so much as spoke to me, he'd kick them out too. Megan just disregarded him, and I sensed that she wasn't long for the house either.

Once my stuff was loaded in the back of their truck, we drove to the Ironbridge farm. They said they had a cottage for me, in the back of their property, but for the first few weeks or so, Miss Zoe said that I could stay with them—with Mr. Mace and her, in the spare room in the Carriage House. Honestly, I would probably have gone nuts in the little cottage in the back of their property by myself. I've never been by myself—ever. When I walked into my room in the Carriage House I began to tremble and then broke down. Miss Zoe held me and I cried for a long time. I told her how I felt and what my Dad had said and she told me that she was proud of me for risking everything for Jesus. What she said surprised me at first, but later, as the both of them talked through what had happened, I realized she was right.

Mr. Tack didn't say much those first few days. Whenever he did say anything, it was to just encourage me, telling me that it was a brave thing I'd done. Honestly, I was in so much of an emotional meltdown then that I can't remember much. I'd had my parents and sisters around me all my life, and now, my family had been yanked out from under me—all because I wanted a relationship with Jesus. But ... I want a relationship with the real Jesus, not the Jesus I was taught about, the Jesus described in this patriarchy doctrine. All my life, my future was stretched out straight ahead, easy, comfortable, off into the horizon for as far as I could see, the same thing, day after day, *known*: but now ... now, I don't know what's going to happen from one day to the next. I don't know this different Jesus. They say that people only change when the fear of the known exceeds the fear of the unknown, and that's kind of where I am. I know the god of patriarchy now, and I just can't believe in that any longer; it's so wrong, I fear it. So I have to jump off into the unknown, off the cliff and into the arms of this Jesus I'm learning about. I've become a tree frog without a tree. But maybe God doesn't want me to be a tree frog any longer.

The only times of real clarity during those first days were when Mr. Mace would come in with Miss Zoe, and again there came that 'calm and peaceful' blanket down on top of me and I could breathe again. The pain was there but it was just ... different. I know there's something because Miss Zoe feels it too. I need to talk to her about it sometime when we're by ourselves.

Miss J, all those hymns we used to sing at family Bible time each Sabbath are becoming real to me now, especially the one that says, '*I'd Rather have Jesus.*' You can sing that for decades, but until you actually do give up everything for Him, you don't know what it really means.

I'd rather have Jesus than silver or gold;
I'd rather be His than have riches untold;
I'd rather have Jesus than houses or lands;
I'd rather be led by His nail-pierced hand

Than to be the king of a vast domain
Or be held in sin's dread sway;
I'd rather have Jesus than anything
This world affords today.

***

"Oh, Mace, what a horrible thing to do to a child."

"Is she asleep?"

"I think so. I left her in bed, trembling, crying, but I think she's drifted off. Oh, man, Mace, did I tell you what she said to me when she handed me her little bag of clothes? Which, oh by the way, were all the clothes she has in the entire world. She said, 'Hello, Miss Zoe. Thanks for picking me up.' I could tell she was crazy upset but she was also, I don't know, almost spitting mad, and she looked up at me and said, 'I'd rather live in a ditch with Jesus than anywhere else without Him.' That girl has some courage."

"Men will stop at nothing to be gods, Zoe; even making slaves of their children so they might rule in their own little kingdoms."

"What's going to happen to her, Mace? Her family has thrown her out, her sisters won't talk to her or they'll get the same treatment, her mother turned her back on her ... God, can you imagine having your mother turn her back on you?"

"It may be an experience she'll need in the future, love."

Zoe looked at Mace with surprise. "What do you mean? How can that possibly be something she'll need?"

"Well, imagine in the future someone comes to her, someone who's been thrown out of their own home, someone who's own mother turned her back to that person, someone who's feeling utterly and completely dejected and turned inside out and lost. When that happens—not if, but when—then she'll be able to speak comfort to that person because she'll have known what comfort is, because she'll have gotten it, here," he said, and then turned to his slim, red-haired wife, "from you, my love."

"What can I do for her? She's, like, I don't know, almost what, twenty-two, twenty-three? She's an adult."

"Not so much, when you think about it," Mace replied. "She's been kept isolated from the world, and worse, from learning anything of the Spirit. She's been fed one specific doctrine all her life. She's never interacted with other adults, except her parents. She's had no role models, no examples, no one to look to, no one to model behaviors after except her parents and her sisters who, if we can believe half of what she's told us, are all just slaves in the kingdom of her father. You've seen how she soaks up everything you talk about, especially when you speak about the things of God. I'd say emotionally, she's about 15 or so."

"But what do I *do*?" Zoe asked. She sat next to him, wondering. "What does she need? It's like having someone from another planet dropped into your house."

Mace looked across the small coffee table at the little pen, where now two rejected lambs were quietly sleeping, having been fed before Emma arrived. He nodded his head in their direction.

"Look there," he said. "Those are precious little lambs. You feed them, you protect them, you slowly introduce them back into the world God made for them in a way that keeps fear at bay, with love and a concern for what will be best for them. You're a mother to them. You hold them when they're frightened and you make sure they know where their sustenance comes from. God has just dropped another precious little lamb into our home, into your arms. She's left everything to have a relationship with the living God. She's your child now, my love. Care for her."

Chapter 9
Marcus

"Have I not commanded you? Be strong and courageous! Do not tremble or be dismayed, for the Lord your God is with you wherever you go."

Joshua 1:9

Captain Marcus Arminius Ironbridge, U.S.M.C. looked through the window of the CH-47 Chinook as the blades whipped the parched Afghan dust into an angry cloud that obscured the LZ. The helicopter vibrated intensely in the thin mountain air; understandable, as the helicopter was older than Ironbridge. He was bringing Kilo Company, 3rd Battalion, 5th Marines, to the fight in the Korengal Valley in the Kunar Province. It had been sporting its nickname—'The Valley of Death'—for some time. A while ago, 1st Battalion, 3rd Marines, had built the command outpost in the Korengal Valley on a spot that once had been a lumberyard, manhandling huge square-cut cedar timbers to make defensive bunkers and mortar-proof billets. Ownership shuffled back and forth between the Army and the Marines, and now it was the Marines' turn to occupy the command position and the few firebases and observation posts dotted in and on the ridges surrounding the valley.

The helicopter landed like a drunken water buffalo, first one wheel, then the other, and finally the nose wheel banging down. The crew chief stood up and hit a switch and the ramp wheezed downward. Ironbridge's Executive Officer, First Lieutenant Dag Wilson, slid goggles up over his eyes and stood up, gesturing at Ironbridge with a thumb, telling him it was time to go. Ironbridge's command element headed down the ramp first—the first sergeant, Tom Custer; the communications people; and finally the XO. Ironbridge came off last, the stink of aviation fuel mixing with swirling, powdery dust choking him. He carried his ruck, which had every article of clothing he'd live in for the next fifteen months; his M4, fifteen magazines, several boxes of ammunition, his personal 1911 .45 caliber sidearm; and some of the battalion's surveillance and target acquisition equipment. He had requested and been granted the battalion's SATA[2] detail—the scout snipers—and he was carrying in some of their optics gear.

Ironbridge was thirty-two years old the day he stepped off the helicopter in the Korengal Valley. He had the rangy build, toughness, and cunning of his father's Scottish ancestors, and from his mother's French heritage his passionate, sometimes impulsive approach to life. As a 180-pound sophomore at the U.S. Naval Academy, he had fought for and won a starting position on the football team when no major college squad had running backs weighing less than 220 pounds. He captained the team in his senior year. He was a good student, though he didn't win any academic honors—those were not his priority or interest at the time—and he graduated somewhere around the middle of his class. Ironbridge chose to serve in the Marines. After graduation and 30 days of leave at home, he had reported to The Basic School (TBS) at Quantico. After TBS and the Infantry Officer's Course, where he graduated first in his class—for his true passion was all things military, and TBS focused on just those things he had loved and read about and practiced and ached for all his life—he piled everything he owned into his used Toyota pick-up and drove like a bullet across country to Camp Pendleton for his assignment with the 3rd Battalion, 5th Marines as a platoon commander. After a year leading a platoon,

2 Surveillance, Acquisition, Targeting, and Assault

another year on the battalion operations staff, and a third year as an executive officer in India Company, Ironbridge completed the Army's Ranger School at Fort Benning and did a short tour as an Aide-de-Camp for the Commanding General of the 2nd Marine Division. He went back to The Basic School as an instructor, and after that three-year tour, he'd come back to the 5th Marines and been given command of Kilo Company a few months ago.

As he came off the ramp, the crew chief slammed the switch, the ramp heaved upwards again, and the Chinook pilot yanked back on the collective and pulled the straining aircraft back up and out of the LZ. In the time it had taken to offload ten Marines, the helicopter had taken three rounds in various places, none of which, fortunately, would keep it from functioning in the unnatural condition known as a helicopter in flight.

Out from under the artificial dust storm as the helo departed, Marcus could see the sun, high and bright in a blue, crisp, cloudless sky. Snow capped the mountain ridges in the distance, and there was an alkaline smell in the air, familiar to him from his time in the high desert in the American west. He heard snapping sounds now and again in the cold air. He saw soldiers from Zulu Company, a unit out of the Army's 10th Mountain Division, around the LZ, heads up now after the dust settled. They were armored up; the bad people on the hills were welcoming Kilo company with a few courtesy rounds.

He jogged heavily, the gear on his combat harness shuffled by the long flight in the helicopter. He followed the rest of the command element as they in turn followed someone from the 10th Mountain Division into the command bunker.

The Army soldiers were taking an aggressive delight in returning the incoming fire. Marcus could hear the sharp bark of the M4, the plunk of the M19 grenade launcher going off, and the deeper, guttural sound of the M240 echoing against the ridgelines that rose up above the command post. Men yelled possible targets to each other across the Hesco barriers. His adrenalin began to pump; this, finally, was combat. Finally someone was shooting at him. Finally.

He ducked down into the large timber-lined bunker. "Captain Ironbridge, this is Captain McNally." Wilson was introducing the CO for the 10th Mountain's unit at the Korengal Outpost, usually referred to as just the 'COP'. Marcus dropped his ruck and shook the officer's hand, nodding. There was no saluting; the enemy particularly liked to plink at officers.

"Glad to see you, Captain ... very, very glad. If my wife were here, she'd be glad to see you too." Marcus smiled silently, understanding. "Have your people dump their stuff, get settled, and then we can meet back here at, say, 1800, once the rest of your people get on the mountain, and we can talk about how we'll do the turnover." Marcus had had briefings with 10th Mountain Division personnel back in Jalalabad about the general procedures for assuming the responsibilities in the Korengal from the Army, but it was expected that once on the ground, he and the Army's people would work through the details. Captain McNally turned to Custer, reading the name on his desert fatigues.

"First Sergeant ... Custer," McNally paused, and they could see him working through the name, "... right ... the logistics hooch is that way. Corporal Withers will walk you over. Company First Sergeant Melendez is out at OP1 looking over a few things. He'll be back in a few hours; we've given him a shout so he knows you're here."

First Sergeant Custer nodded. Custer was short, thin, wiry man with fifteen years service in the Corps. He wore a salty-looking, heavily faded green utility cap with the globe and anchor barely visible on the brow, and was already chomping on the obligatory cigar. He too had a 1911 on his hip in a soft brown leather flap holster. He wasn't bald, but he had zero hair. He nodded tersely to acknowledge McNally's pointer to the chief enlisted soldier on the COP. He looked around for Withers. "Let's go, son," he growled—a strangely deep voice for such a short, thin man—and Withers picked up his M4 and walked out of the hooch with Custer on his heels.

"I wouldn't make any jokes about the First Sergeant's name," Wilson said quietly after the First Sergeant had ascended the log steps out of the hooch.

"Never crossed my mind," Captain McNally replied.

***

After more Chinooks had brought in his company, escorted all the while by the Army's Apache attack helicopters, and two more inconsequential firefights during which the 10th Mountain soldiers unloaded almost a metric ton of ammunition into the hillsides and took almost as much back at them in the form of 7.62 rounds, mortars, and a couple of RPGs, Marcus, Wilson, the platoon leaders, and First Sergeant Custer met with Captain McNally, his executive officer, a Lieutenant Swanson, the Army's First Sergeant, Sergeant Melendez, and the 10th Mountain platoon leaders in the command bunker.

"Okay," McNally started, "so what we do, like they hopefully told you in J-bad, is that we take your people out on patrols that we lead, then we go out with your people on patrols that they lead, and then we leave and you got the ball. That's the basic plan. Was that what they passed to you?"

Marcus nodded. "That's the basic plan. They said you'd fill us in on the local tribes, the Shura protocols, the patrol routes, the major TIC[3] events you've had, and any issues."

"Okay ... good." McNally rolled out a map on a table in the center of the room, and the men gathered round. "Here we are," he said, pointing out the hill where the COP was located. "We're south of the Pech river, west of Asadabad—that's the capital of the province at the moment, though I haven't see one damn sign of any Afghan government official anywhere near here or there—too afraid, I suppose, or too busy scarfing up the goods back in Kabul. No surprise to you; government, ours or theirs, isn't too popular around here. The valley basically lies along several routes the ACM[4]s are taking out of Pakistan into Afghanistan. Our job is to cut the flow of bad guys through this valley, and that means we make sure the villagers are happy. You've got about five or six different tribes in the Korengal. Zippy, what the hell are their names, I can never remember."

Zulu Company's Intel officer moved to the edge of the table. Lieutenant Zipkowski spoke rapidly with a Brooklyn accent. "You got the Baba, the Ghasu, the Langer, the Malik, the Mutiara, and the Kathee. Every one of 'em has their elders; every one of 'em has their own ways of doing business, but so far they've presented a fairly united front to us during the weekly meetings. We've had a couple come in and try to play one tribe off against the other—you know, promising to turn in some ACMs in return for us looking the other way when they try to pound some other tribe. We tell 'em that won't work; we don't give 'em any kind of grief, we just don't support that kind of activity. We

3 Troops in Contact

4 Anti-Coalition Militia—essentially the Taliban, Al Qaeda forces, and any other elements devoted to fighting the U.S. / Afghan coalition.

tell 'em we're here to make sure they can get on with their lives and that their people will have the freedom to earn a living and raise their families without being bothered by the ACMs. We respect their culture; we respect their religion. We try to keep their villages clear of the ACMs, but hey, there are guys up in the mountains shooting at us who've lived in those villages all their lives. Who do you think they're gonna support?"

McNally continued. "We put up a couple observation posts while we've been here. Guys basically humped the tools and materials up the mountain at night, dug in as fast as they could, and in a couple days had a functional OP up where the locals never thought we'd go. OP1 is here," he said, putting his finger about 1000 yards away from the COP, westward down the valley along the northern ridge. "OP2 is here, about the same distance, on the southern ridgeline. You've got a bunch of little mountainside villages all throughout this area here, up in the eastern portion of the valley ranging up the foot of the slopes. The COP used to be a pretty busy lumberyard, pushing black market timber out to Pakistan. The new government has tried to shut that down, but that's why most of the villages are up at this end of the valley. Doing the patrols, you'll see that most of the houses are stone and timber, and most of the timber came from this place before the Afghan Government shut it down.

"Don't be fooled; the bad guys are roaming pretty much all over this place—east, west, north, south. The villagers won't ever rat them out; they're all related, anyway. So don't expect too much cooperation. The best we can recommend is for you to make sure they know you won't be taking anything that isn't yours, that you'll respect their women, and that you respect their religion. The Army actually sent us a Muslim chaplain up here, and he's had some pretty good discussions with the elders. It helped."

"The Marines don't have chaplains," First Sergeant Custer pointed out. "Would the Army send the guy up here to support a Marine effort?"

"I think if you put in a request to get the guy up here, I'm pretty sure the Army will send him out. He didn't mind, I can tell you. What's his name again, Zippy?"

"Captain Al-Menarim. Tall, thin guy, the Army lets him have a beard and all, and when he's up here he does the whole 'Imam' thing. He made a pretty big impression on some of the elders. From what the terps tell me, some of 'em got in his face pretty hard for playin' on the infidel team, but he was all back in their face, and they went hard at it, waving the Koran back and forth. The terps say that he settled them down."

Marcus listened, stone-faced, his arms crossed over his body armor and then said quietly, "We'll get along without the Captain."

McNally looked over at him quickly. "Yeah, well, I can understand where you're coming from, him being an Army thumper and all. And the other thing I don't get is that he comes up here and three days later we get hit the hardest we've been hit our entire time before or since. We took ... how many did we lose, Zippy, eight, ten casualties on one patrol down the valley?"

"Four KIA, seven wounded, sir." Zipkowski replied.

"Right. Couldn't understand that. Elders told us we were good with them, they were patting Al-Menarim on the back and we thought they were gonna marry off their daughters to him. We thought the Captain had sort of won us some hearts and minds for a while, but I wasn't too impressed with the results. But hey, the Army says to keep trying, so we keep having him up here."

Zipkowski spoke up, turning to Marcus. "Captain, I know we got hit after he showed up, but we're pretty sure that was a coincidence, and it would make you some serious points up here if the locals knew you were okay with their religion. They're pretty serious about that stuff, and Al-Menarim can do that better than any of us grunts."

"He can take fifteen months off," Ironbridge said flatly. Custer rolled his cigar from one side of his mouth to the other.

"Right. Whatever you say," McNally said flatly, and went on. "It's your ball game. So ... well, these people up here, I mean, they're basically illiterate farmers, but they've been carving out a living for a few millennia, so they're good at surviving in this place. That's all we want to do, too."

"How often do you meet with them," Lieutenant Wilson asked.

"We have a Shura once a week, and we rotate it among the various villages. We go, we sit, we drink tea, they tell us what bothers them, they tell us what they want us to do, and we tell them how we want them to pony up info on the bad guys moving through the valley. Some days they shrug and say that it's impossible; other days they just shrug and don't say anything, and then tell us about some cow they think we whacked, or when then need some HA[5]."

"So where are you on interdicting fighters," Wilson pressed. "Anything definite?"

Zipkowski looked over at McNally, who nodded for him to pick up the question. "Well ... we don't really have any hard data. We know we've hit them pretty hard, but for some reason they still keep moving through the valley. Our casualty rate is the highest in the U.S. Army; it is not a pleasant place to be. They want this route and they're willing to fight for it, and so they keep coming through and we keep calling down crap on their heads and sometimes we get the bear and sometimes the bear gets us."

"Anything more definitive, sir?" Custer growled from the corner of the bunker.

"As far as body count, do you mean?"

"As far as intelligence on what kind of material, personnel, or equipment the enemy is moving through this geographic location," Custer replied, and then remembered to add "...sir."

"We don't have anything on that, First Sergeant. We think we're killin' 'em, but it's that Vietnam thing again ... they drag off the bodies and we really don't know if we're hittin' 'em or not."

"Okay, so what are the parameters you're using to determine if you're successful up here?" Wilson asked the question the others had been wondering about since Zipkowski began his rambling excuse for the unit's abysmal performance.

McNally stepped in again to defuse some of the heat from his intelligence officer. "We basically measure whether we're successful by the number of reports we get from villagers about the enemy; we measure how profitable the villagers are in their own little economies, and how many villages get whacked by the ACMs; we measure our casualty rates, and we try to get a feel for where we are on the 'hearts and minds' scale with the locals. We can tell if we're moving in the right direction if they start keeping the fighters out of their villages and stop supporting them. And we can tell that by how many times elders show up and rat them out."

"And how many times so far have the elders come up and given you any kind information like that?" Wilson asked.

Zipkowski looked at McNally who looked at the Zulu Company's First Sergeant,

5 Humanitarian Assistance, usually in the form of food.

and then McNally said, bluntly, "Hasn't happened yet; not on my tour. I think getting the Chaplain up here is making some headway toward that, and he's trying to work them around to seeing things our way, but we really haven't seen any progress."

"How are you fixed for terps?" Wilson asked.

McNally replied, "Yeah, that's a good question. We've got three, all from the ANA[6]. So far they've worked out pretty well. The Chaplain has been up here and he seems to think they're okay, too."

"What kind of casualty rates you guys seeing, sir?" Custer asked.

"Well, like I said, we took eleven on that one patrol; we've had ... Zippy, give me those figures." Zipkowski handed McNally a clipboard. "Right ... we've had a total of forty-three people killed or wounded in the last fifteen months."

Marcus remained stoic; Wilson looked over at Custer, who just looked down at the dirt floor and pulled his cigar out of his mouth. It wasn't considered professional to trash-talk the unit you're replacing, especially not having yet walked in their shoes, but forty-three people knocked out of a company was ... well, it was pretty significant.

"You people have had a tough time up here," Ironbridge said. "I hope we don't get hit as hard."

"Yeah, we hope so too. Did they tell you what kind of air support you'd have up here?" McNally asked, changing the subject.

"We'll have Cobras out of J-bad," Wilson replied. "Hornets out of Kabul, and the stuff you've had so far, too—Apaches, Hogs, the rest."

"That's good—I don't know anything about Hornets, but you'll like the Hogs. They're like blood sausage; either you like 'em or you hate 'em. You'll like 'em; the bad guys, they hate 'em."

"How about patrol routes?" Marcus asked. He was becoming less impressed by the minute with the Zulu Company commander, who was trying overly hard to seem macho and bloodthirsty.

Zipkowski pushed a pencil over the map, showing a route that led down the valley from north to south, up and around the north and south ridgelines. "We typically do a circuit from here down the valley, into one or two villages, and then sometimes we cut back behind the ridges to see if there are any new ratlines getting put in." Ratlines were the term used for paths made by the enemy moving through the mountains, carrying weapons, ammunition, and equipment back and forth to supply the fighters. Marcus and Wilson and Kilo's platoon leaders looked over the map carefully.

"Where do you get hit most of the time?" Wilson asked.

Zipkowski pointed to two places. "Mainly here and here," he said. "It seems like they're giving us this segment of the valley, from this gridline north, and they're keeping the territory from the gridline down south. But if we step down into their territory, it's gangland central, and almost a guaranteed TIC."

"What are they hitting you with?"

"Mostly small arms, but two weeks ago we think they moved in a Dishka, and there are always RPGs. They'll throw some mortar rounds at you too, if the harvest is good and they have money to pay for the ammo. Try and move along the roads out of Asadabad or J-bad, and they'll hit you with an IED for sure."

"They definitely got at least one and more like two or three Dishkas," Sergeant

6 Afghan National Army

Melendez put in. "We took a bunch of rounds last week, and we reported that mo'skosh. I'm pretty surprised you people choppered in without getting shot up."

"They probably didn't want to lose their guns," McNally said. "The Hogs would've been all over anything firing at the birds as they came in. And I'm not sure those were Dishka rounds anyway." Melendez didn't reply, but Marcus could tell there was some disagreement between the Zulu Company commander and the Company's First Sergeant. He was more surprised that the Army Captain would contradict his First Sergeant in a group setting.

"So ... that's pretty much the situation," McNally said. "The platoon leaders can break out and talk about what happens where they're stationed, and then let's set a patrol schedule. I'd like to push the first one out tomorrow."

McNally definitely wanted to get off this rock and get home. That suited Marcus just fine. "Sounds good," he said, and the meeting broke up.

Ironbridge and Wilson stepped out of the bunker while Captain McNally introduced his platoon leaders to Kilo Company's platoon commanders. Sergeant Melendez fell in alongside the two Marines as they were making their way to their bunker.

"Sergeant ... your people have been in a tough fight up here," Marcus observed.

"Yeah, Captain, thanks and all, but how about a quick word." Both Marines could tell the Army Sergeant was disconcerted—not nervous, but definitely angry. He pointed a stubby forefinger at them from chest level. "You keep that sonnuvabitch Menarim outta here. Three days after he comes up I lose an entire squad of troops, and there ain't no *way* they should've known where we were that day, 'cept that friggin' Haji ratted us out." Marcus and Lieutenant Wilson kept their own counsel, but they were not disagreeing with Melendez.

"Any proof of that?" Marcus asked.

"No way there's gonna be proof, Captain. None of us up here speak the language, and if you ain't a Muslim, you ain't gonna know what they don't want you to know."

Ironbridge nodded. Wilson and Custer stood there with their arms folded across their chest. Having a company First Sergeant cut across the Company Commander's fire lane like this wasn't something anyone liked to see—but what the guy was saying needed to be said. Apparently Melendez felt lives were more important than protocol.

"And another thing, sirs," Melendez said as he turned to go, "you keep three eyes on those terps. I don't like the way they look either." He walked off back toward one of the Zulu Company platoon areas. The Captain and the Lieutenant looked at each other and continued walking.

"What do you think?"

Wilson shrugged. "I think he may have a little issue with the indigenous," he replied. "But I wouldn't discount what he says."

"No," Marcus answered. "Not one little bit."

***

The patrol schedules were set. Typically units being relieved would walk the new units into the ground. The patrol routes went up and down the mountain trails at elevations at or above 2500 meters, and not having been acclimatized, the new men would finish their first patrols with their tongues hanging out. Not so Kilo's people. Ironbridge had asked, and his Battalion Commander had agreed, to train his people at Pickle Meadows, in the Sierra Nevada mountain range in California. Instead of taking just the winter warfare survival course, Kilo Company stayed an entire four months, with just two weeks off prior to deploying to visit home. Marcus had directed his XO to make sure the company would show up in shape, and Lieutenant Hughes, the XO at the time, pursued that order with a vengeance. Hughes had overseen a brutally rigorous hiking course, with Kilo's Marines sometimes putting in eight or ten miles a day over boot-cracking terrain. They hiked in snow, wind, rain, and heat. They carried packs that were between fifty and eighty pounds, along with their weapons. The officers in the company humped along with the men, and Ironbridge wouldn't put up with any officer who couldn't outhike or outshoot his men. So when Kilo Company showed up, and Zulu's troopers waited for them to barf and crawl their way up the trails, there was some initial surprise as most of the Kilo Company Marines basically out-walked their Army escorts. And while it was the cause of not a little chagrin to the 10th Mountain Division troops, it actually made Captain McNally happy, for it meant that he could pull Zulu off the mountain sooner than he thought. The patrol schedule was pushed up and five days later, the valley resounded with the noise of Apache helicopters escorting Blackhawk troop carriers, pulling Zulu Company back off the mountain, back to Jalalabad and then back home, to civilization and wives and girlfriends and Starbucks and Wal-Mart and a life where the odds of getting shot while you slept were much, much lower—except for the troops from Washington, D.C. or Detroit or Chicago.

Custer had come to Ironbridge and Wilson and expressed his dissatisfaction with the length of turnover. They were pretty sure that Melendez had had some frank discussions with Kilo's First Sergeant, and they were grateful, because they suspected that the information Custer had gotten was probably more substantial than the stuff they got from the Zulu's command elements. That Custer wasn't happy with the turnover time made Marcus a little nervous.

Marcus, Lieutenant Wilson, and the First Sergeant were alone in Marcus' small hole that served as his bunk, his office, and the company conference room. First Sergeant Custer still had the same cigar in his mouth.

"I know what you heard, Captain," Custer began, "but from what I'm getting on the E-net, there's a lot we haven't heard. I mean, every unit that's been up here has gotten seriously whacked. This is the meat grinder of the world right now. Not one unit has done their time without takin' at least twenty percent casualties."

Wilson's eyes bugged. "What do you think they're not telling us?" he asked.

"Well sir, how about four or five months ago, one of their platoons is down around Dakalbat when they get into some contact, and they lose two people in two minutes, and McNally gets seriously pissed. They scope a couple of runners heading into the ville, and he calls in some Hogs and they waste some big house, which turns out to be the home of one of the elders in the village. They kill about eight of the locals and there's a bunch of others wounded."

"Fair enough," Wilson responded. "They hide the bad guys, they pay the price."

"Roger that, sir, but then he goes to the Shura the next week, and when the elders rake him over the coals for what happened, he flat out apologizes to the villages, tells them he's gonna pay to make it right, and commits the United States Army to rebuilding the guy's house. I mean, when Melendez took a squad in there, they found like four or five RPGs, a bunch of mortar shells, and a few dozen Dishka rounds."

"Hence the Dishka denials," Wilson noted.

"That's the ticket," Custer replied, spitting out a piece of lose cigar. "I don't know what program the Army is on, but it seems that they're taking the 'hearts and minds' approach a little too far. They've also had locals inside the wire here, *inside the COP*. Now, I'm not one to get overly excited, Lieutenant, but bringing in the indigenous is just about as crazy as it gets."

That piece of information surprised both Wilson and Ironbridge, who looked at each other carefully. Wilson turned to Custer again. "Why would they do that?"

"Melendez says that 'they'—by whom I think he means McNally, but he wouldn't say—were trying to get some kind of discussion program going with the locals about some kind of 'interfaith dialogue' or some such happy horse hockey to kind of defuse the intensity of the opposition. Their intel weenies were thinking that maybe they'd get some of the indigs to open up if they felt all warm and fuzzy about the soldiers 'being on their side' in this religious thing, or maybe they thought the enemy would just lay off if they thought maybe we were leanin' toward Islam. Maybe they thought that if they could teach 'em the words to Kumbaya, they'd establish world peace right here in the valley. I have no friggin' idea, Lieutenant."

"Let me guess, First Sergeant ... most of the people they got in here were young men, not the older guys from the villages." Wilson looked over at Ironbridge.

"Right," Custer answered, disgusted, spitting out part of his cigar, "and if those guys were interested in interfaith harmony, I'm a Mennonite."

"So," Marcus interjected, "they know the layout here pretty well. That's a given. XO, that program ends as of now."

"Yes sir," Wilson replied.

Custer chomped hard on his cigar, smiling. "Glad to hear it, sir. 'Cause that's just askin' for another Ranch House." He was referring to a U.S. outpost called Ranch House that earlier in the campaign in Afghanistan had been almost completely overrun by Taliban fighters. It had been so bad that the defenders had to call in airstrikes on their own positions. It was the worst firefight for the U.S. since Vietnam.

"Since they fragged the locals, their Battalion CO tightened up the reins. McNally and his is people have been just sitting on their asses behind their Hescos, doin' nothing. The patrol routes they took us on? They haven't walked those routes for months. If I was the enemy, I'd be thinking about hitting us here, hard, real quick before we get the lay of the land and get ourselves squared away."

"Then we make sure that doesn't happen."

"How do we do that, sir?" Wilson asked.

Ironbridge thought for a moment. "We're going to change how things work around here," he said after a long pause. "A lot of things ..."

Custer bit further into his cigar and smiled uncertainly. "Our people gonna like that," he said, "I hope."

"I hope so, too" said Lieutenant Wilson.

Custer looked at Marcus, chewed on his cigar for a bit, and then asked tentatively, "So ... sir ... what's your plan for this Chaplain guy?" Custer knew what he was asking, and Wilson knew why he was asking it.

Ironbridge's reputation in the small tribe that was the Marine infantry community was unique. He was known to be extremely professional and highly competent, but he didn't have too many friends among the other officers and some of the whisperings were that he didn't have too many friends in higher places either. The reason was personal. While the Marine Corps, and most other services as well, tolerated those who were religious, and while Chaplains detached to them from the Navy supported just about every faith there was, the movers and shakers in the higher ranks always distrusted officers who took their religion seriously, or who let themselves make decisions in their professional lives that were guided by or based on their faith. Oh, the picture-window Christian that went to church on Sundays at the base chapel was okay—preferably if they were Episcopalian; definitely not something too radical in any case—but if an officer actually began to let his religion affect how he did his job or how he lived his life, it was a signal of the first order that he wasn't serious about his profession: too emotional ... too dependent on intangibles ... not enough 'sand' in their character. And there was still the prevailing attitude, common among most military officers, that if a man didn't drink hard, fast, and often, he wasn't a real man. This unofficial clique, which existed in every service, would usually see to it that real Christians were weeded out, which began in the lower ranks, somewhere around the Lieutenant Colonel level and below. It was rare for a true Believer to advance to the rank of Colonel, and rarer still to see one among General officers. There may be a 'monk' now and again—some one-off aesthetic or eccentric personality—but there was just too much compromise in that rarefied atmosphere for any real Believer to survive.

Custer and Wilson knew Ironbridge's reputation. Since he was new to the company, both Custer and Wilson had tapped their respective personal networks to get what information they could about the new CO. What they heard was confusing. On one hand they learned that he was tough, fair, that he didn't push religion at anyone but he didn't tolerate anything that he might think would be detrimental to the best interests of his unit—by his own reckoning. He didn't apply any discipline standard other than the Uniform Code of Military Justice—he couldn't by rights—but everyone knew that he held his people to an even higher standard. That rankled some—usually the ones who wanted to cheat on their wives the first time they deployed—but it settled unusually well with others, usually the ones whose opinion of doing a good job went above and beyond the norm, and the ones who had particular opinions about integrity.

On the other hand, they'd heard that he was sort of a loose cannon. Wilson had heard from a friend the story about the time when Ironbridge had first reported aboard at Pendleton as a young platoon commander and was attending the orientation briefing held at the base theater. "The Navy Chaplain does his dog and pony and talks about how all faiths were essentially welcome at the base religious center. Apparently Ironbridge stands up and starts asking him why the Marine Corps considered Islam a viable religion when Islam was directly opposed to every tenet the Corps fights for, and has fought for in its history. You coulda heard a pin drop," his friend told Wilson. "I mean, the Chaplain turned about three shades of red, and then started sputtering the typical crap they teach 'em at Chaplain school about everybody loving each other ... yadda yadda yadda. So Ironbridge says, 'We're not supposed to agree with people who hate the true God; God gives us specific direction not to associate with them. Islam is a cancer in this society, and in every other society they've been in. They turn prosperous countries into junkyards. They hate women; their holy book says it's okay to beat them, or kill them if they do something their husbands don't like. We're *supposed* to tell them they're wrong, and tell them that if they go on opposing God, they'll burn in hell. That's real love,' he says. 'And if they get militant about it, we're supposed to burn down their altars and burn down their mosques and kick them out of our society.' I mean, the rest of the place is just freakin' out, wonderin' why the hell this wet-behind-the-ears Lieutenant, who doesn't know his ass from a hole in the ground yet is gettin' up on his high horse. 'Who cares what lieutenants think, anyway,' they were sayin'. But let me tell you, Dag my man, not a month later that Muslim guy in the Army shoots those people on the base, down in Texas or someplace. I can tell ya, it got a bunch of us thinkin' that maybe the Lieutenant wasn't so stupid after all. Who'd a thought that could happen?" Wilson came away from the story with the understanding that his new CO wasn't afraid to take on the establishment. In some ways that was a good thing; in other ways, it could be dangerous.

Custer's information was from a different perspective. He'd checked with the enlisted people who had served under Ironbridge, and most of the reports he got were favorable. "Best officer I ever worked for," one of Custer's best friends told him over a beer at Custer's house one evening while they were burning steaks. "But I didn't think so at first. 'Oh Christ, here comes another holy roller,' I thought. Didn't turn out that way, Tom. Oh no, not at all." Master Sergeant Linnseckit chuckled. "There was this first day in the Close Quarters Defense course at Benning, I was taking a refresher and it was Ironbridge's first time on the mat. We had Gerry Buckshaw—you remember him, whacked about ten ragheads in Baghdad before they blew him full of holes, got the Silver Star and survived to make it back on active duty—anyway, Buck is the lead instructor for the CQD course and Buck knows Ironbridge is some kind of Holy Joe, and Buck just hates them types 'cause usually they ain't worth crap, and Buck is just about drooling to take this guy down on the mat and make him regret ever joining the Corps. So the first day Buck is standing up there and telling everyone about how this course is all about hand-to-hand combat and how this stuff might save your life one day, and how it can be pretty useful and all that. So he points at Ironbridge and says, 'Okay sir, why don't you step out here and we'll give everyone a little demonstration of what we're gonna learn these next two weeks.' 'Here we go,' I say to myself. 'Another Lieutenant bites the dust.' So Ironbridge steps out of the line—and you remember Buck, now, Tom, he was no slouch; guy could bench something like 340 or so, quicker than a snake, and he was just a little taller than Ironbridge—so Ironbridge steps out of the line and Buck turns to the rest of the class and says something like, 'Okay, so here's how you can disable a guy real quick.' So Buck squares off, you know, takes up the fighting stance, and says, 'Okay, Lieutenant, defend yourself.' The Lieutenant kind of just gets settled into a sort of relaxed kind of position and Buck just launches into the guy. He throws just about everything he's got at him and it takes about eight seconds and then the next thing you know Buck is on the mat with the Lieutenant's boot on his neck, Buck's hand turned around almost sideways, and blood comin' out of his nose. The kid leans over, cool as a cucumber, and looks at Buck and says, 'Did I do okay, Sergeant?' I mean, there were guys in tears, trying not to laugh, 'cause, I mean, well, no one wanted to get Buck angry. After that Buck didn't say boo to the kid for the rest of the class. I mean, I gotta tell ya, Tom, he may be a roller an' all that, but god help you if you try and tangle with him. He's a tough SOB."

Custer had a very different input from another old acquaintance he'd worked with in the past. "Guy's a damn Bible thumper," the man said, a Staff Sergeant. "Sonnavabitch thinks he has a direct line with God. Those people are friggin' dangerous, Tommy Boy."

"I hear ya," Custer had replied. "What made him so bad?"

The Staff Sergeant grimaced and rolled his eyes. "Okay, so first off, he doesn't let anyone get wet on the boat. I mean, every other cruise I go on, somebody's packed a stash of the good stuff—I mean, I ain't been on a float in twenty years in the Corps where you couldn't get a good malt whiskey when things were lookin' bleak, you know? This platoon? Nothin', man. He put a Corporal down two months' pay and busted him in grade for trying to carry a six-pack aboard one night in Cubi."

"The Officer of the Deck woulda caught him, guy woulda swung," Custer said.

"Well, yeah, but hey, Marines don't burn Marines." Custer didn't say anything about that opinion.

"Next thing: Ironbridge gets the platoon together on the hangar deck one afternoon just before we pull into the PI. He starts off giving everyone their training assignments while we'll be ashore, and then he gets all huffy and looks down his nose and says, 'I know we're coming into the PI and I know what happens there, and I know you people are adults, but let me tell you one thing. If your wife can't trust you, the Marine Corps can't trust you. That's all I'm gonna say.'"

"Have any affect?"

The Staff Sergeant laughed. "Hell no. We just thought he was trying to play Joe Straight Arrow or something; what an ass. Guys were laughing at him from the time they went over the brow until the time they dragged their asses back to the ship through four different whorehouses." Custer didn't think it the right time to ask about the Staff Sergeant's divorce after that cruise, or his getting busted for disorderly conduct in Seoul during another float.

"Takes all kinds," Custer said judiciously.

"You got that right," the Staff Sergeant replied.

Custer came away from his information-gathering expedition with the decision to just wait and see. Tom Custer had zero interest in religion, unless it had something to do with the Church of the Holy Globe and Anchor—the U.S. Marine Corps. Touch the Scarlet and Gold Temple and he'd declare war in a heartbeat. He didn't trust anyone who walked around with religion on his sleeve, because in his experience those kinds of people were happy to be mediocre, and they couldn't pour piss out of a boot if the instructions were written on the heel. But the information he was getting on Ironbridge was that he was different; he wasn't the typical Casper Milquetoast Christian. And that worried the First Sergeant; he didn't like different.

Marcus knew why his command team was asking him about this Army Chaplain. He looked at his XO. He hadn't wanted Dag Wilson. Five days before they were shipped out to Afghanistan, Lieutenant Ronnie Hughes, his original executive officer and a good friend, had broken his leg in a snowmobile accident coming down a mountain at Pickle Meadows. It had been a compound fracture of the femur, and the doctors told him it would be at least six months before he could think about walking on it. Lieutenant Wilson had just come off a tour leading a platoon in Hawaii, and the Marine Corps jerked him out of an assignment to his Battalion staff and made him the XO for Kilo Company. Dag Wilson was a well-built young man, also on the rangy side, moderately tall, with sort of reddish-blond hair, green eyes, and a sort of mocha-cream complexion that confused everyone who spent more than two seconds thinking about it. He could have been from Jamaica, Jersey, or the Bronx. All Marcus knew about him—and there hadn't been time to get to know much—was that his parents, both still alive, both still married to each other, lived on a farm in North Carolina and raised pigs, rabbits, and sheep. His father was a retired Special Operations guy, his mother a basic housewife. Wilson had graduated from the Citadel; Marcus respected that institution and knew of a number of outstanding Marine officers who'd come from that commissioning source. Wilson had done okay at The Basic School and at the Infantry Officer's Course. His first assignment was as a platoon leader in Alpha Company, with the 1st Battalion, 3rd Marine Division in Hawaii. Word was that Wilson was a quiet officer, as friendly as he needed to be, knew his business, and wasn't easily taken in by the enlisted marines, which was more than most first lieutenants could say. Word also was that he didn't drink. *Maybe that was why Headquarters slotted him to me*, Marcus thought. Wilson had been rated the top platoon commander in Alpha during his assignment, and he'd earned a spot on the Battalion operations staff before Ronnie Hughes slammed into a tree. Wilson was yanked out of the 1st Marine Division and found himself with the 3rd Battalion, 5th Marines as XO of Kilo Company.

So Marcus knew what was on the minds of his command team. They, like most everyone else he worked with initially, didn't know how to take him, and while that situation was uncomfortable in the States, it could be fatal in a shooting war. Men needed to depend on each other, and they didn't know if they could depend on him. They would have to learn.

"Look," he said. "You guys know what I think of Islam. I think it's pure dark; there isn't anything good about it. People talk about 'moderate' Muslims; I'm telling you, there isn't any such thing. A 'moderate' Muslim is like dry water. Either it's water or it's dry—can't be both. I'm not going to play their game out here, kissing up and making nice, telling them how wonderful their religion is, how we understand it's a good thing, how nice it is for them. It's poison for anyone, and any nation, it touches."

Custer's eyes were now seriously locked on to the Company Commander. Wilson's face was unreadable. "I said we're going to take the war to them. Well, that means we get out from behind the Hescos and start tracking them down and killing them." Marcus saw Custer's eyes widen a bit.

Marcus wanted to know what Custer's issue was. "What?" he asked.

"Nothing, sir. It's just ... well ... hey, I'm way locked on to that plan, sir, I mean ..."

"You mean, you're surprised that some religious guy is hot to take it to the enemy and go do some serious killing?"

Custer rolled his cigar round his mouth for a couple of turns and then looked Ironbridge straight in the eye. "Yes sir, now that you put it that way, that's exactly what I'm thinkin'."

"Right. Might as well get this out on the table now." Marcus put his hands together and rested them on his field vest. "I don't push my faith on anybody, and one of the downsides of that is that people just assume I'm like most of the 'religious' people they know. Nothing I'll *say* will change your mind about that. What I *do* might. Usually at the end of a tour they figure me out. So far I've had no complaints ... at least from anyone I respect. As to killing ... I can give you twenty reasons why the profession of arms fits just fine with Christianity, but the one main reason you need to know about why I am out here is this. These Taliban folks and the people behind them want to make the world into one giant Muslim-controlled empire—they call it a Caliphate. That means a lot of things, but to me it means that they're trying to kick the real God out and install their own. That pisses me off, number one. Number two, it means they'll stash your mothers and daughters and sisters and wives into some dark hole with an oven and no shoes and make them into breeding machines to make a whole lot more good little Muslim slaves." Marcus recognized he was working his way onto a soapbox. "Okay, look, you probably don't want to hear all this, but hey, just know one thing. Where we find these people, we're going to make them room temperature as quick and as hard and as often as possible. And we are not going to wait for them to come to us; we are going to go looking for them. Does that answer your concerns, First Sergeant?"

"Shack, sir. I get it."

"Good. XO, what about you?"

Wilson had been quiet throughout the discussion, but he replied quickly. "Yes sir, I understand. I may have some questions later, but I think I know what you're getting at, and I can support that." This approach squared with what both Custer and Wilson had heard; a religious fanatic, but different.

"Now about this Chaplain guy. We're not going to ask for him. But unless I miss my guess, I expect he'll be back here again to try and continue his 'interfaith dialogue.' Lieutenant, I want you to ride herd on our terps and make sure that they give a good rundown on any discussions that guy has with the locals. I want one of us present in those meetings at all times."

Wilson, reminded of something by Ironbridge's reference to meetings, asked, "What about the Shuras, sir? When will you want to start those?"

Ironbridge stood up. Apparently the meeting was over. "We'll set one up for ten days from now. We'll talk about how I want it set up a little closer to the time, but I want the first one to be held here, in the clearing down at the base of this hill. It'll be the first, and I suspect it'll be the last."

Custer and Wilson both looked at each other, wondering what that meant.

They would find out soon enough.

Chapter 10

Marcus

'The enemy said, 'I will pursue, I will overtake, I will divide the spoil; my desire shall be gratified against them; I will draw out my sword, my hand will destroy them.'

"You blew with Your wind, the sea covered them; they sank like lead in the mighty waters. Who is like You among the gods, O Lord? Who is like You, majestic in holiness, awesome in praises, working wonders? You stretched out Your right hand, the earth swallowed them."

Exodus 15:9-12

MAIronbridge <maironbridge7@arcmail.com>
To: Thackeray Ironbridge <tackiron45@arcmail.com>
Sent: October 14, 7:43:52 PM
Subj: Arrived Safe

Dad;

Wanted to let you know we arrived safely here last week. Things are pretty hectic, as you can imagine. My Marines are handling the shift into the place okay. It was good we spent all that time out in Pickle Meadows. They were cursing me then, but they're thanking me now. You always said the more we bleed in peace, the less we bleed in war. You were right.

My new XO seems to be working out okay. He knows the business, seems to have the respect of his Marines, and doesn't get too wrapped up about anything that I've been able to figure out so far. The morale in the company still is pretty high, so that's an indicator too. I mean, they liked Ronnie a lot and they were really bothered about his accident, but it seems that the Green Machine actually did something right this time and gave us someone who knows what they're doing.

My enlisted leadership is excellent. Like everywhere else I've been, they're still trying to figure me out. My 1st Sergeant has looked at me sideways a few times. You're right, in the times we're living, not many people know what real Christianity is. With apologies to Will Rogers, most of them would say, 'The only stuff I know about Christianity is what I see on TV." I guess for most of them, the only experience they have with real Christianity is someone they might work with who wouldn't say a thing to them if they sacrificed a goat on an altar under a pentagram on their front lawn. I know some of the other Christians I've seen roll through the military, and I sort of understand the confusion. Most of them think that because they've got their ticket to heaven, they really don't have to trouble themselves to do any hard work down here on earth. Don't they see that everything they do reflects on the One they represent? If they show a mediocre face to the world, the world just thinks of God as mediocre—and I think that explains why most men I know (real men) think that religion is just something for old women, young children, and weak guys who don't or can't or won't aspire to accomplishing anything truly worthwhile or excellent ... in their eyes, at least.

The young Marines ... well, they're doing okay, Pa. Every time I look at one of them I feel a combination of pride and frustration; pride because they are walking into the world's most dangerous piece of real estate with their heads held up, ready to fight. No one is complaining about why they're here or bitching or moaning about orders and duty schedules. If anything, they're probably ten times more bloodthirsty than the guys you served with. I mean, you kill a million guys in video games, sooner or later you're going to want to know what the real thing is like. But they're afraid, too. Dad, I can't tell you how much fear they have. Oh, they hide it well, behind tough talk and lots of physical violence (punching and wrestling and such) and talk about how they're going to wreak mayhem on the enemy—you know, the same stuff every war hears. I mean, up here, there was a guy who got shot just sleeping in his bunk. Single rounds come in all the time, and every Marine on this base lives with the fact that whatever they're doing at the time, that could be the last thing they do, and whatever else that does, it makes them fear death. Death to them is like the end of all things, an act that will obliterate consciousness, a thing that will end everything they are entitled to—long life, girlfriends, wife, kids, house, car, boat, big-screen TV, getting drunk or high or both whenever they feel like it—whatever they think of as 'life', death is something they feel will cut that short, that will cheat them out of what they're owed. And they look at it as though it's the very last thing that will happen to them. It's like the ultimate gyp. What a crushing, overpowering burden to bear, knowing that without any warning, without any notice, your life could come to an immediate and involuntary halt at any time, without you having any choice in the matter. Poof; everything you were or could have been is immediately snuffed out. At the very least it must seem monstrously unfair.

For most of them, serving who they do, they're right to be afraid. But this is why I'm frustrated, because, being in this place where you could die in the blink of an eye, wouldn't any normal sane person want to make sure that if that happens ... well, wouldn't they want to basically set themselves up to avoid worrying about death? By obeying God, they don't have to worry about that, and that kind of relief is something that just can't be bought, and up here, it's priceless. But not many have it. Christianity has been so hijacked by our culture that most times I can't blame them for not wanting anything to do with it. They don't see any power in it; they don't see any change that it makes in people's lives; they don't see how it can make you any more of a man—more courageous, more honest, more able to fight for what's right, more real. All they see is that it will cut into their time Sunday and Wednesday nights and it will really cut into their vocabulary. They'll have to walk around like they're sucking lemons or something, following dutifully behind some bossy woman who drags them to church and complains to her friends about how her husband doesn't do this or that. I mean really, why would any real man want something like that?

Sorry to go on like this, Pa. You'll probably have some good thoughts on the things I've shared. I always appreciate your wisdom. I cannot tell you how grateful I am to have a father who is wise in the ways of God. You've been a strong tower for me all my life, Pops.

Give my love to everyone home, and ask them to pray for me—not that I stay safe, but rather that I have the courage to do His will.

Love;
Marcus

Thackeray Ironbridge <tackiron45@arcmail.com>
To: MAIronbridge <maironbridge7@arcmail.com>
Sent: October 16, 4:43:52 AM
Subj: Re: Arrived Safe

Marcus;

Your mother and brother and Zoe say hello. We are all praying that God's will be done for you, as you ask, but give your mother some slack ... she's praying like a house afire that God will keep you safe, too. Things are well here, son, and I am glad to hear that Kilo Company is adjusting to combat conditions. You are in the devil's back yard, but we know that you are in God's hands.

You were mentioning that most of the young men don't really see any power in today's Christianity. I cannot tell you how much I agree with you, son. Have you ever wondered why? I've done a lot of thinking about that and come to the conclusion that most people walking around claiming His name really don't want to lay everything out on the line for Him—and by that I mean, they're not willing to obey Him in every aspect of their lives, totally and completely—and that's because they are afraid of how such unfettered obedience might make them look to people around them. Consider: as long as being a Christian requires simply an investment of time—one simply attends church; if it simply requires an adjustment of behavior (which you can make on your own), like, say, keeping your language controlled or adhering to a list that your local denomination generates ... no smoking, no drinking, no movies, no dancing, no cards, etc. etc.—anyway if that is all Christianity means, then hey, what's the problem? None of that really requires them to die. *But if you might have to do something that might make you look a little foolish or fanatical in their eyes, man oh man, stay away from that kind of stuff (as you know, dead men don't really care how they look). No one really wants to be fanatical these days, but to tell you the truth, son, those are the only ones He really can work through. Any exercise of power requires a faith that is based on rock-like obedience; saying it differently, 'real power requires real faith.' Milk-toast believers who won't risk their good name in the world (whatever good that will do them) or their fancy reputations by going out on a limb and just doing what they know is right in the face of overwhelming pressure ... well, you're right, there's just no power in that. It's like trying to make a long jump standing on a giant marshmallow.*

The one thing I think that might help your people see the power that comes from faith would be for someone to show it to them, Marcus. I think this is why our country is in the condition it's in—Christians have 'lost their salt' and we just have nothing to show people, nothing that might present an alternative to what they see elsewhere around them in the world. We aren't different *from everyone else, and being different is what we've always been called to be. Remember Elijah, when he went up against the 450 prophets of Baal? He stood up to the enemies of God and his prophets and in doing so showed the people of Israel Who the real God was and the power He had. Even Jesus—He showed the stone-hearted religious leaders of His day what real power was, so they might see what He was doing and believe in Him. Well, like Elijah, like Jesus, demonstrations of God's power may convince some, but it can also get you chased into the wilderness, or strung up on a cross. Don't let it dissuade you, son. You want your people out there to be free from fear? Show them Who can free them from that slavery.*

The hay is all in the barn, and it's clean, full of protein, not dusty at all. We've had the right amount of rain at the right time, and we haven't yet been caught with any hay on the ground. There's been enough people helping that I didn't have to be slinging too many bales as your Mom drives the truck. Those days were fun but this old man is getting older, and throwing hay bales with one leg doesn't work so well. Mace and Zoe corralled a few young boys to work and it's nice to see young men come along, full of youth and strength, enjoying the hot sun and the hard work. Remember those days, Marcus? We had some good times.

You come home now, my son, if it is God's will, and we'll have those times again. If it is not God's will that you return to us, we know we will see you a bit later, in a much better place.

All my love;
Dad

***

Marcus spent the days and nights before the Shura constantly begging God for wisdom and guidance. A plan of action had formed in his mind, and he asked God to confirm that it was God's and not his own. He didn't want to conduct operations based on something Marcus Ironbridge had worked up in his own imagination. The plan would definitely involve significant risk, to his Marines and to himself personally. It would probably result in his dismissal from the Marines, the service, and a way of life, a culture that he loved; a way of life that so thoroughly defined who he was. He felt he was called to be a warrior, to be a defender, a fighter, a protector. To do what he was thinking about would, sadly, result in the Marine Corps discharging him. But most fearfully he considered that if he failed, he would stain God's reputation, and that was a risk that made him tremble. He wasn't so much afraid for his life as he was afraid of what would happen to God's reputation should the plan fail. He did not want to discredit God's name, either to the Afghans in this valley, or to his Marines. And finally, he had to wrestle down and put to death the understandable concerns that rose in his human nature about his own reputation. This was the hardest thing, the darkest, deepest thing he struggled with, no matter what he would have liked to admit to anyone else. He fought hardest against the doubts that rose up against him, doubts which bored in upon the utter loss of his reputation.

The days moved forward in an agony of internal moral wrestling. Outwardly, he led the company through the transition into the valley's operational tempo. Inwardly, there was a constant series of questions and debates ... there were sometimes answers, and sometimes there was nothing but the wind whistling through the mountain valley in response to his soul's cry.

He kept at it, distracted yet fully focused, besieging God constantly with his desperate desire to know His will, many times not even knowing how to form his requests into words. And yet as he prayed, gradually, a sense of complete peace was established in his spirit whenever he thought about the course of action he'd asked about. Marcus took this as confirmation that what he had proposed to God was actually what God had put into his mind to do.

And so after a time of wrestling and questioning that resulted in a clearer picture of how attached he had been to his own reputation (which shamed him), and his decision to proceed no matter what would happen to that reputation (which freed him from that shame), a peace descended, and he went forward in confidence to do what he knew to be the right thing—no matter how crazy it sounded, no matter what the consequences might be. He knew what it would sound like to his people—especially to his command team. He knew he was considered a 'loose cannon', but he also knew that any real believer will be considered as such by those in the world, so that didn't bother him ... much.

The first Shura with Kilo Company in the Korengal was held on a gray day in December, with low, threatening clouds and a few snowflakes the size of salt grains dancing in the air, in a clearing at the base of the hill on which the COP was built. Surrounded by a few trees and green, scraggly shrubs and backed by a huge, 30-meter high flat-faced boulder that served almost as a giant wall, one could stand in the clearing with the flat rock face at one's back and see down almost the entire valley.

Elders from about a dozen villages scattered throughout the valley had made their way down from their villages terraced into the face of mountain ridges, along the valley's central, rock-strewn, boulder-potted pathways in the low ground, and into the little assembly area for the meeting. First Sergeant Custer had posted the first platoon in a semi-circle around the clearing, unobtrusive but obvious enough so the elders could see the command element wasn't out there on their own. Custer himself was standing there chewing on the ever-present cigar as each of the elders came into the clearing.

A Sergeant Mosul, one of three terps assigned by the Afghan National Army to support Kilo Company, was the one picked to work the meeting. Mosul was a thin man with a black beard under a young chin and shiny black hair. He wore the Afghan National Army uniform. He was making small talk with the elders as they arrived, while he sat on a rug in the dirt next to Lieutenant Wilson, who sat on an ammo can. Wilson sat still, arms folded, and stood as the old men began filing in.

The elders milled around, waiting for the meeting to start. They were all older men, some with beards dyed a reddish-orange from the local henna plants that proliferated in the valley. Some had the traditional brown or gray flattened Pashtu cap woven of sheep's wool; others just wore a piece of wrapped linen over their heads. They all wore the 'Perahan Tunban', or what some called the 'kamiz shalwar', or what the Americans had come to call 'man-jammies'—attire that was a composition of a shirt and a long dress that went down to the knees. The outfit was completed with a pair of baggy trousers. They all had an embroidered waistcoat over their man-jammies, and they wore either sandals or light leather shoes—in December, in the mountains.

Custer had been amazed at the endurance demonstrated by these mountain tribesmen as they humped up and down massive mountain ranges, sharp karst rocks, and up and over hardscrabble hills in what amounted to flip-flops. They may look scraggly, he thought, but there were some rough customers in the bunch ... hard men and no mistake. In the group of men before him, he thought, there were probably at least one or two who, from 1979 to 1989, had taken the best the Soviet military could throw at them and kicked their red asses back to Russia.

Custer could tell they seemed at little uneasy. Normally these meetings were held in some type of building or structure; there would be tea and some cookies or bread set out. Ironbridge had specifically not arranged for things to be that way this time, and it worried Custer—anything out of the ordinary worried the First Sergeant, which was why he was one of the best First Sergeants in the Marine Corps. This is why First Platoon was arranged the way they were, and why each of the squad leaders had gotten a very quick but pointed briefing prior to the meeting from First Sergeant Custer.

Captain Ironbridge was the last one into the clearing, and he did not sit down. He walked into the clearing with two 40-kilo sacks of grain, one over each shoulder. Custer watched the elders' eyes get a little wider. No two of them together could probably carry even one of those sacks. Ironbridge dropped one sack, then the other, and turned to Mosul. "You tell them exactly ... *exactly* ... what I say, do you understand, Sergeant Mosul?"

"Easily, Captain, yes, I understand." Mosul smiled like a Cheshire cat.

Ironbridge turned to the assembled group of elders. "Welcome," he began in a quiet, controlled voice, speaking slowly so Mosul's reedy, penetrating soprano echoing Ironbridge's deeper tenor, could translate his English into Pashto.

"My name is Captain Ironbridge. I am in command of Kilo Company, 3rd Battalion, 5th Marines. This seed grain is a gift from the United States Marine Corps to the people of this valley. You may take it when you leave." A few of the older men nodded. One or two smiled. They could use it to augment next summer's crop, or sell it to the Taliban. The Taliban were paying good prices for food lately. Ironbridge continued, with Sergeant Mosul translating.

"We have come to your valley to do what your government has asked us to do—to keep you safe, and to kill those who would kill you. This is my job for the next fifteen months. Do you understand?" Mosul translated this last. The elders, standing around, some with arms crossed, some squatting on their haunches, in their way nodded. Marcus went on.

"I know that some of you do not like American soldiers or Marines in your valley. I know that in the past, some Americans have made mistakes. Mistakes will happen in a war. This is not right, but my Marines did not do these things, and these things will not happen while my men are here. Do you understand?" More nods, head tilts, hands fluttering.

"I know that fighters live in or move through your villages. There is nothing I can do about that. I know that other Americans have told you that if they find fighters in your villages, they will drop bombs on the houses where those fighters are." Ironbridge paused to let the translator catch up, and then went on. "We will not do that." As the translation came, a few eyebrows were raised under hats, both Afghan and American. Marcus pressed on. "You are Muslims; the fighters are Muslims. If you are a Muslim, you must help another Muslim, especially when he is fighting unbelievers. And we," Marcus said slowly and deliberately, raising his arm and indicating his command element standing there, "are infidels." Mosul paused at this last comment and looked at the Captain, who nodded firmly and gestured to him to finish the translation. When he did, the elders shuffled uncomfortably. One or two looked angry; a few looked curious. Custer was getting worried.

"Now I will tell you something you should remember," Marcus spoke slowly, with ominous portent, and every elder saw the fire in his eyes. He looked at each of the elders as he moved slowly in front of them. "I did not come to this valley to fight against the Taliban. I did not come to fight against Al-Qaeda. I did not come here to fight against the enemies of the Afghan Government. No," he said, "I am a servant of the one true God—the God of Abraham, Isaac, and Jacob—and I have come to this valley to war against Allah."

Mosul got through the first sentences and then balked. Ironbridge looked at him, put his finger in the man's chest, and said, "You tell them *exactly* what I said. *Do it.*" Custer's stomach muscles tensed, and Wilson was now standing up, one hand on his sidearm, wondering what would happen. Mosul stuttered once, repeated the first part of the sentence, and then the last part, about going to war with Allah.

Tension skyrocketed. Some of the elders yelled; some were shaking their fists, some whipped off their hats, threw them on the ground, and there wasn't a need for an interpreter—it was obvious there was a lot of cursing and damning going on. Custer was suddenly very glad he'd had first platoon standing around the group with their weapons drawn. Two or three of the elders began to walk out of the clearing, but Ironbridge barked one word: "*Stop.*" The word, understood in any language, pierced all the yelling and cursing; the men walking away stopped and, as if against their will, turned back and rejoined the group, still furious. "Be quiet!" Ironbridge commanded; Mosul translated, and Custer couldn't believe it but the yelling and cursing quieted down. The Captain went on, looking at each one of the Afghans directly in the eye.

"I come to fight against Allah because Allah is a false god; Allah hates every living thing, and Allah ..." Marcus stopped because the translator had stopped translating. He looked once at him, and the translator began again; he wasn't looking very happy. "Allah hates every living thing on earth," Marcus said, "and he hates you ..." the Captain pointed at one of the elders who stood, spittle dribbling into his beard from his curses.

"Yes, you. Allah wants you to die ... and he wants your children to die, and their children, and their children's children ... he wants them all to die and burn with him in hell."

"You lie!" Sergeant Mosul yelled. "I will not speak your lies to these people any more."

The mountains around them held their breath. The elders were all quiet now; they watched the conflict between the American officer and the Afghan translator, who was from the southwest part of Afghanistan, they knew from his accent, and who therefore could not be trusted, but something must be happening to make him so upset. They watched as the other man, the short thin American Marine with the short-billed khaki cap, went up to the Afghan sergeant, pulled a pistol from his holster and put the barrel of the pistol under the Afghan sergeant's chin. There were words in English, and the Afghan sergeant spoke aloud, in Pashtu.

"My fathers, you see, they are holding a gun to my head. I must say exactly what this infidel wishes you to hear. Please, please, these are not my words."

"Just tell us what they are saying, brother," said one of the older elders in the same language. "We know these things do not come from you. Just let us hear what is in their minds before we kill them all. If you tell us what they say, it will help us kill them more easily. So do not fear to speak."

Wilson saw the translator relax slightly—as much as anyone can relax with a gun to their head. Sergeant Mosul translated what Ironbridge had said about Allah hating the people in the valley and wanting them in hell where they would burn forever ... along with Allah himself. Then the Captain continued.

"You will see that what I say is the truth. I know that what I am telling you, you will not believe. You will not believe my words—I know this. But maybe you will believe what you see with your own eyes. I will prove that my God is God and that Allah is the enemy of your souls and wants to send you all to hell."

As Mosul's translation of this last statement rolled out, a few of the elders advanced, shaking their fists, yelling and spitting curses, but the older man who had spoken to the translator held up one arm, and they halted. "Wait," he said. "Wait and let him spew out all his garbage. We would not want to bury him here in our valley with even one of these words in his mouth. Let all the filth come out of him and disappear into the wind." The older man nodded to Mosul, who was still nonetheless trembling with anger. "Go on; speak."

Marcus stopped pacing and looked at the older man, obviously the leading elder, but spoke loudly enough for all of them to hear. "You will see that my God is stronger than your god. I will not prove this with words. These are the last words you will hear from me until you ask to speak with me again, or until I return to my home. The God of Abraham, Isaac, and Jacob will prove what I say is true. Watch what happens in this valley while we are here. *Watch what happens.* You will see that my God has power over all things. My God loves you, and because he loves you, he will show you that He is more powerful than Allah. When you see this, you come to me and ask what you should do to escape from Allah. Most of you will not see this ... but some of you may. If you come, you will be welcome. These are all the words I have for you." Mosul finished translating, still shaking. Custer removed the gun from his head and holstered his pistol. As soon as he did so, the Afghan sergeant bolted up the path toward the small hooch where the Afghan soldiers lived.

The Captain turned his back on the elders and walked slowly up the hill toward the COP. The elders, spitting mad, could not leave fast enough. Custer pulled first platoon back wide, making sure no accidental conflicts could arise, and then had the squad leaders get their men back up to their positions on the double. Every member of the first platoon had heard the Captain's speech. They all wanted to know what was going to happen now. Custer had no idea, other than a whole lot of hell was gonna come down on their heads.

The two sacks of seed lay where they'd been dropped. The Afghans wanted none of the food Ironbridge was offering.

***

Next morning, Lieutenant Sauberg, second platoon commander, knocked on the upright cedar timber outside Marcus' small bunker.

"Come."

"Morning sir. Thought you'd want to know ... terps are gone."

"Which ones?" Marcus asked, not surprised.

Sauberg hesitated for a moment. "Uh ... all of 'em, sir. They must've cleared the wire and humped down the hill into one of the villages before it got light."

Ironbridge nodded absently; he'd expected it. "Right. Have Lieutenant Wilson give Battalion a call and see if they can send us out another batch." Sauberg nodded and went to find Lieutenant Wilson. *Should've made that call yesterday*, Marcus thought.

A few minutes later, Lieutenant Wilson approached, his boots crunching over a light layer of snow that had fallen in the night. Wilson and Custer had both studiously avoided Marcus after his speech at the Shura, and Marcus knew he'd have to take some serious heat from them for what he'd said to the elders. They probably thought that he'd needlessly ratcheted up the threat level by several orders of magnitude just to scratch his personal religious itch. Looking out for one's own interest above those of the Company was just about the only unforgiveable sin you could commit in combat, and he understood that they would think that what he'd done had been exactly that. He would have to tough this out; he knew he'd done what God asked him to do. Now it was God's turn to come through.

"Rudy says you want me to call Battalion and get more terps up. That right, sir?"

"That's right, Lieutenant."

Wilson still hesitated at the door of the bunker. "Well, okay sir ... what do I tell 'em about the others?"

Marcus realized that was a good question. "Tell them the truth; that they jumped the wire and abandoned their post because they didn't like how we plan to prosecute the war."

Wilson nodded as though he wasn't quite convinced that there wouldn't be a few more questions about the 'how we plan to prosecute the war' part of Marcus' instructions. After another few seconds standing there in the snow, uncertain, he headed over to the communications bunker. He was back in three minutes.

"They say fine, sir. They'll helo three guys out as soon as they can."

"Uh huh. And did they ask any hard questions?"

"No sir. Actually ... they didn't. They should have, but, well ... they, uh ... they didn't."

"Right. Get me the platoon leaders at 1300, Lieutenant. We'll plan the first night's patrols."

Thanks, God, Marcus said quietly, to an empty bunker.

***

Before he could talk to the platoon leaders, he knew he'd have to talk with the command team—Custer and Wilson. Wilson would be straightforward; dealing with Custer, he knew, would be like handling a mad hornet. They showed up in his bunker at his request in the middle of the morning, after the platoons were set up and started on the day's routine. Wilson came in, set his helmet down on a crate, and sat down on an ammo can. Custer came in, cigar stub screwed into a granite countenance. He came into the bunker, stood two inches inside the door, arms folded, with his faded khaki fatigue cap over his stubbled skull. He pegged his eyes on the opposite wall of the bunker.

"You guys think I did something stupid yesterday; something selfish; something personal, something not in the best interests of the Company. Am I right?"

Wilson looked over at Custer, who was too mature to pout. Custer looked directly at Ironbridge. "You put this entire Company's head in a noose ... *sir*. I don't know what kind of personal religious war you feel you owe your God, and frankly I don't give a goddam, but when you put the lives of my Marines at risk because you think you gotta be some self-righteous saint, we're gonna have a disagreement. Every friggin' human being in this valley, and the next and the next—and don't think they won't put out the friggin' word throughout this entire friggin' country—is gonna come gunning for the infidel that spit on Allah in public, and we are gonna have so much manure come down on us you won't believe. I mean, for krissakes, Captain, you're smack in the middle of the most dangerous Muslim country in the world, where, you know, Muslims carry around live weapons and rockets and grenades like people at home carry cell phones, and you tell them Allah is just a piece of…hell, I have no friggin' idea what you were thinking ... no friggin' idea at all ..." Custer spat out some of his cigar on the floor. "... *sir*."

If Marcus hadn't been so sure of his course of action, this would have caused a serious breach in his ability to work with the First Sergeant, but he'd expected this reaction; it was normal, and, Marcus knew, the more vociferous the reaction, the more serious, the more intense, and the more passionate the man was about his job. He could work with that. He turned to Wilson. "Lieutenant?"

Wilson shrugged his shoulders. "Pretty much what the First Sergeant said, sir. I guess I just don't see what good it did for us to make this into a religious war. I mean, why give the enemy all that motivation?"

Marcus nodded; thoughtful response by Wilson, too. But he also knew he couldn't explain himself to these men—yet. He couldn't ask them to trust him, but he needed their trust.

"Okay, fair enough. I hear what you're saying. All I can tell you is that this is part of a plan. I didn't just shoot my mouth off on my own."

Custer looked up sharply at him. "You mean someone *asked* you to put a stick in this hornet's nest?"

"That's right."

"Wait ... did they *ask* you, or did they *tell* you to do this incredibly stupid thing, sir?"

"They asked, but I had the choice. I could have just fallen into line with the standard posture units take out here, kissing up to Muslims and making like we're all one big happy family, or I could lay down the gauntlet. I chose to challenge Islam. I don't know what will happen, but whatever happens, they're going to see who the real God is. And you'll be front row center for the show."

The light came on for Wilson before it did for Custer, but after a couple of seconds, Custer realized what Marcus was talking about, and he shook his head.

"So ... okay, so, let me make sure I got this right ... *God* asked you to piss on Allah's picnic up here, right? Because as sure as He made little green apples the United States Marine Corps would not do something so incredibly stupid."

Wilson's eyebrows went up. "You sure about that, First Sergeant?" Wilson's light attempt at humor encouraged Marcus. Maybe Wilson saw more than he was giving him credit for.

Custer took the cigar out of his mouth and made a sort of figure eight with his head, a sort of head-shaking gesture of denial. "In all my time in the Green Machine I have never ... look, Captain, I checked you out with my network before you showed up here."

"And what did you find?" Marcus asked.

Custer paused for a moment. "Well to tell you the truth, sir, what I found out was exactly what's happening now. They said you were some kind of way different religious fanatic; some folks used the phrase 'loose cannon'. That worried me a bit, but hey, I said, let's give the man a chance to show what he's like before I stick a label on him. And so I guess I should not have been surprised yesterday."

"And did your sources fill you in on how things turned out after a few months or a year or two with the 'loose cannon'?"

Custer tilted his head back slightly and looked at Ironbridge through hooded eyes. "Well, now that you mention it, some of the people did say that things worked out okay."

"Uh huh ... well, things are going to work out here okay, too. I don't exactly know what 'okay' is going to mean, but ... and I know this will be hard for you guys ... but I am going to ask you ... no, I am going to *need* you to trust me that I know what I'm doing."

"You are asking us to trust you with the lives of every man in this Company," Lieutenant Wilson said.

"That's right," Marcus replied. "What's so different about this situation than one, say, where a commanding officer figures he'll take a hill using a strategy he's used before, successfully, but it's a strategy which his staff doesn't understand. Doesn't the staff trust him then?"

Custer replied in a gravel-edged voice. "I've been in the Corps for close on fifteen years. I've been in Iraq, the first and the second time, and I've been other places we won't talk about here. Begging the Captain's pardon, sir, but what experience have *you* had in this realm that I won't understand?"

Ah, thought Marcus, *now we come to it*. "You're absolutely right—good point, First Sergeant, because it is experience we're talking about—*exactly* that thing. So let me ask you ... what experience do *you* have fighting things in the spiritual realm? Do you have any experience calling in spiritual artillery? What experience do you have wrestling with demonic entities ... what you call 'evil spirits'? What experience do *you* have talking with the God who created the earth and the heavens and you and me and every living thing on this mountain, talking with Him and getting to know Him and learning what He wants and doesn't want or likes and doesn't like? What experience do *you* have obeying the God of all creation? And why would you think that when we're engaged in a war against a people who hold up the demon Allah on a banner and yell out to the world that this Allah is responsible for the power and success that they have everywhere they go, who spit on the real God—why would you think it *wouldn't* be a spiritual war? Because some guy walks into a boxing ring blindfolded doesn't mean he doesn't have an opponent ready to knock his head off. I can guarantee you *they* are fighting one! I mean, in all your extensive battle experience, did you ever know one person who saw the bullet that killed them?"

Marcus stood up from the cot and looked at both men. "I see the bullets that are coming at us, gentlemen, and you don't—that's the bottom line. Oh, you think you do, but you don't. You're going to have to trust me on this. And if I was you, I'd want someone running the show who can see the bullets coming." Marcus halted, waiting. The crux of his relationship with these two men rode on their response to this one key point. They were both warriors; hopefully they would at least understand.

Surprisingly, it was Custer who declared himself first. He cleared his throat, sounding like a dump truck dumping gravel, and hawked up and spit through the front door of the bunker. "Well I'll tell ya, sir. If I hadn't checked with some people before you showed up, I would've been on the horn last night, calling Battalion, telling them exactly what you said and that you had flipped your lid and you were not capable of commanding this Company. But these people I talked with, they said that somehow—and none of 'em really understood how—that somehow things always worked out right in the end ... actually better than just all right. So ... okay. I'll go along. But if we get hurt and it's clear that we got hurt because the enemy came after us with the fire in their belly that you stoked ... well, like you said to some folks a while ago, 'If the Company can't trust you, the Marine Corps can't trust you.' That's where I stand."

"Fair enough, First Sergeant." Marcus turned to Lieutenant Wilson.

Wilson turned to Custer. "Give us the hooch, would you please, First Sergeant?"

"Roger that, sir." Custer turned and ducked out of the bunker, but not before Wilson spoke again. "And keep the people away from the door for a while, First Sergeant." Custer paused and growled, "Roger that, Lieutenant," and closed the door behind him.

"I need to tell you a story, Captain, and it needs to stay between the two of us."

Marcus sat down again on the bunk. Something told him that Wilson was going to share something personal, and he composed himself to listen very carefully to Wilson's story.

"Clear; what you say here stays here," he replied.

"Okay. So ... you know about my father, right?" Wilson took up his ammo can again. Their heads were not four feet apart. Wilson spoke in a slow, quiet, determined voice.

"All I know is that he was in some sort of Special Ops."

"Well, yeah, that's right, he was in Delta actually, and he was one rock-hard operator. They formed Delta in the 70's after the U.S. took some hits from terrorists. When Russia invaded Afghanistan in '79, they dropped him and his team up into the northern part of the country and he messed about with the mujahedeen for about a year or so."

"He must have seen some hard things," Marcus observed quietly.

"Yeah ... yes sir, he did. So anyway, long story short, he and his team and a bunch of Mooj were moving down the Faizabad valley looking for Russians to ambush one day and they came up on a village about forty clicks out of the city of Faizabad, close up against the Faizabad River. Only the Russians had come up on it just before they did. Dad's team cased the place first, and the Mooj wanted to bypass it, but for some reason Dad wanted to see why the Russians had stopped in the village. I mean, the place was only ten or fifteen mud-walled compounds, and they could see three Russian trucks parked near one of them. No other Russians seemed to be around. So anyway, he and three other Deltas move in on foot and they get to the side of one of the houses where the Russian trucks are parked, and they see that the Russians had shot all the men in the village, dumped them in the street, and were busy raping the women. They had 'em all in a line, like, and after they raped one, they'd pass her on to the next, and the last guy would shoot her. Anyway, Dad and his team moved in, took out the Russians, and did the best they could for the survivors. The hard part was when the Mooj wanted to waste the surviving women. The surviving women hadn't ... ah, they hadn't been raped yet, but still, the Mooj felt that they'd been dishonored or whatever, so they were going to line them up against the wall and just shoot them all. Dad couldn't believe it. Well, he got into a serious argument with the Mooj and they were major-league pissed about him interfering with what they thought was some kind of holy mandate they had to kill the women. They told him they couldn't just take these women on patrol, and they couldn't leave them in the village. Any Russians come through again, they would rat out the Mooj for sure. That didn't make any sense to my Dad, but then, not much about the country made sense to anybody back then.

"So my Dad tells them that America will take custody of the women—remember, this was in, what, I think he said it was in 1982—and so he loads the rest of the women on two of the trucks and he and the other Delta guys drive something like 500 miles down to Kabul. Well, you want to talk about causing a stink; the team gets to Kabul with two trucks full of Afghan women, most of whom are beat up, shrieking or yelling or crying or doing all three at once; man, he said it was terrible.

"But the officials there in Kabul wouldn't let the women out of the country, and of course the U.S. government wasn't going to stick their noses in the situation. Now, along the drive down from Faizabad, there was this one particular girl that caught my Dad's eye. She was the only one who wasn't coming apart. She had this wicked bruise up on her face ... right here ..." Wilson moved his hand along the side of his own face to show Marcus, and he coughed once to clear his throat, and paused for a minute. He took a breath and continued. "They'd knocked her around pretty good. But she was one of the last in the line, you know, so they hadn't gotten around to her before my Dad's team showed up and smoked 'em all. My Dad said she was still, even banged up like she was, drop-dead stunning. She had green eyes." Wilson paused, waiting for Marcus to get what he was telling him. It took about fifteen seconds. Ironbridge's eyebrows shot up in a question, and Wilson nodded.

"He married her in Kabul, right there in the U.S. embassy, and he flew her home the next day. You wanna talk about pissing off the Delta command team—let me tell you, they sent those guys over there to defend Afghanistan, sure, but not to marry 'em and bring 'em home. I came along about three years later."

"So you're part...you're half Afghan?"

"My mother was part Afghan, part Tajik. I grew up speaking Pashto, Dari, and *zaboni forsi*—basically Farsi—at home. My father only knows a little Pashto and some Farsi. But Captain ... I really, really don't want to let anyone know I can speak this stuff."

Marcus' eyes widened. "Why not, Dag? I mean, it's a major asset."

"Yes sir, but if the Marines find out I can speak these languages, I'll get yanked out of a line Company and stuck behind some desk wearing a headset, plugged into some UAV feed for the rest of my life. I mean, that's what the guys at Prophet are. I don't want to go there." Wilson referred to the counter-intelligence assets intercepting enemy radio communications with their call sign, 'Prophet'. "I want to stay in combat."

Marcus nodded his head. "Okay, I understand. I'd want the same thing if I were you. So okay," he continued, thinking for a moment, "let's just keep what you know to ourselves for now. No one else in the Company knows this either, right?" Wilson nodded. "Good; so ... during the meeting yesterday, you really didn't need Mosul, did you?"

Wilson shook his head. "No sir. I mean, he translated everything you said, but you should know that the elders told him it was okay to let you speak, so that when they kill you, you won't have all those words about Allah in your body when they put you in the ground. They're kind of funny about certain things like that. You should know they're gonna try and waste us all. You really did harden their determination to kill us. There's no chance—I would say less than no chance at all—of making any allies in this valley for at least three or four years. I mean, I even picked up some new four-letter words in Pashto from those guys. And this is the part Custer didn't talk about; the speech yesterday not only fired them up for us, but for every other unit that comes in behind us; they're gonna get the same treatment."

Marcus was watching Wilson carefully. "Yeah, well, let's see how things work out. But what I want to know is, how are *you* with my 'War on Allah' speech?" Marcus was concerned; here was his own XO, whose mother had most definitively been raised as a Muslim, and he hadn't known a thing about it.

"Well, I'll tell you, sir ... the Russians, I mean, I don't agree with what they did but I understand them. Russians are Russians ... everywhere they go, their soldiers rape the local women. Probably today they'll rape the local men, too, I don't know. But when my Dad wanted to save the lives of those women, the local Mooj—all Muslims, by the way, and a couple of them were Imams—wanted to kill the women. That told me all I needed to know about Islam."

"And your Mom ... she's not a fan, then?"

Wilson looked slightly uncomfortable. "Well sir, actually, she's a little in your line, religious-wise. My Dad and I, we don't exactly follow what she's into, but she'd been in the U.S. for about ten years or so when she had some kind of religious experience—she said she actually saw Jesus one day, while she was doing the laundry, and he told her ... well, he told her a lot of things. After that she was different; 'born again' I guess is what people call it—and my Dad says she became a different woman. She seemed to get stronger, and quieter, and a whole lot more, well ... settled, and what had happened to her seemed to bother her less. I know she stopped having nightmares about that time, too, and if there was one thing that convinced my Dad to stand down and let her have her way with the religious stuff, that was it. Whatever it was she got, she got it solid, and it seemed to do her a world of good. She doesn't pester my Dad or me with it, but the more I remember what she's like, the more she reminds me of what I heard about ..." here Wilson paused.

"You mean, what you learned about me when you put out your own RFI[7]s?" Marcus asked, smiling slightly.

Wilson seemed a little embarrassed. "Well, yeah ... yes sir, exactly. Hey, I mean, everyone is curious, you know? New CO and all ... anyway, you remind me a little of how she thinks about things."

"So you think your mother would be okay with my war on Allah, then?"

Wilson looked at him and he suddenly appeared very much a harder, older man. "My mother spits on the memory of Islam every day of her life."

Marcus picked at a callous on his thumb and looked up again at Wilson. "Sounds like we'd get along fairly well."

"I suppose you would, sir. So ... you see, I have a little different perspective on things than First Sergeant Custer. But I also take his point that the bad people are gonna be way, *way* hopped up about your war against Allah. They take this stuff seriously."

"So do I, Lieutenant," Marcus said grimly, "so do I. And so does God."

***

Two days later, the Company briefed their first patrol. First platoon would take the lead; they would sweep through around one of the villages in the middle of the valley. They wouldn't be moving through the village; Ironbridge didn't feel the time was right. The terp was given a partial brief about the upcoming mission, telling him which villages they'd be moving through and the general set of objectives. The platoon was a little nervous headed out into the valley without an interpreter, but since they weren't technically moving through any villages, they decided to press on. First platoon led out of the wire just before 1700. They moved down the trail and along the western ridge of one of the smaller hills that lined the valley.

The night prior, Ironbridge and three men from the Battalion's Surveillance and Target Acquisition team had gone through the wire unannounced, unseen, with night vision goggles, ghillie suits, and silenced weapons; the weapons all had night sights. The team had set up an overwatch position overlooking what they estimated to be the most likely ambush spot on the patrol's route. Now, 24 hours later, the four of them were lying still as death, breathing quietly, tucked into the shrubbery. They had customized their own ghillie suits by hand back in the states, knowing the terrain they'd encounter. They used strips of burlap in various earth-toned colors and here and there, patches of dirty whitish-gray. They were hard to see from ten feet away, and impossible to see from thirty yards.

An hour before first platoon was scheduled to move past their overwatch position, Ironbridge picked up movement along a draw to the east. Men were moving silently along the wash that flowed down from a hill perpendicular to the patrol's route. Through the NVGs, the team could see men in the group carrying small arms; a few had RPGs. They moved furtively, and as they came to a ridge overlooking the patrol's line of movement, they began to set up the ambush. They took up positions about ten or fifteen yards apart from each other, hunkering down in the brush. Ironbridge counted fourteen. He tapped Corporal Raeche on the heel. Raeche slid backward an inch at a time until his ear was parallel with the Captain's mouth.

"Fourteen; AKs, RPGs."

---

7 "Request for Information'

Raeche's head nodded slightly. "Same," he whispered.

Ironbridge had at first been worried about the enemy setting up an L-shaped ambush, where one line was parallel to the route of the advancing ambush targets and another lay across that route, usually in front to block any forward movement after the ambush was sprung, but it seemed that the enemy wasn't that sophisticated—or they were in a serious hurry, or their command structure didn't have that kind of experience. He discounted the lack of experience option; the fighters in this valley had more combat experience than probably his entire team combined.

The wind began to spring up now and it was blowing the trees and shrubs; the leaves rustled noisily in the dark. He whispered to Raeche. "Looks like a basic one-side hit. Take 'em in left to right segments," the Captain made a vertical slicing motion with his gloved hand toward the enemy. Raeche nodded again and moved up to his firing position. The four Marines were now laying in a line parallel to the formation of Taliban fighters across the road, slightly higher up on the hill across that road, with eyes on all fourteen. During the mission brief, the rules of engagement were such that the team, when alerted, would fire on Marcus' first shot.

The wind now began to whip down the draw, building up almost to a howl. The Captain counted off eight men from the left end of the line of ambushers, sighted his night vision scope on the forehead of one fighter hiding in the brush, and slowly, slowly squeezed the trigger. Coming out of the suppressed weapon, there was nothing but a slight cough, whipped away by the wind in an instant.

***

Custer was in the middle of the line of men in second squad, which was the middle squad as First platoon moved along the ridgeline. He had accompanied the platoon because the platoon commander, Lieutenant Untermeigen, was five months out of Infantry Officer's School and hadn't seen much combat other than a high score on his Call of Duty shooter game. Custer didn't like this part of the route; it was an ideal position for an ambush and he had his SAW gunners and the M240 up and walking the line with their weapons up to their shoulders in the ready position, sighting down the barrels, ready to shoot immediately. The platoon had been briefed intensively on what to do if they got ambushed, and they'd practiced counter-ambush tactics endlessly, both at Pendleton and Pickle Meadows.

Suddenly the signal to halt came by hand down the line from the front squad. Custer squatted down automatically. Untermeigen looked a question at him. He nodded and then ran forward, hunched over, to find out what was happening. He ran about a fifty yards to where Corporal Raymone, the squad leader for First squad, was kneeling down, looking intensely to his front.

"Raymone, what's the holdup?" Custer whispered, face close to the Corporal's helmet, only inches off the ground.

"Gooly is on point; he's holding us up for some reason. Okay, he's waving us up."

"I'll go," Custer hissed. "You stick here." Custer moved forward slowly until he saw Private First Class Hector Gooly prone in the dirt, rifle pointed forward, locked on. Custer tapped the man on his boot as he came up from behind him. Gooly shuddered a bit, looked over his shoulder, and then nodded.

The point whispered hoarsely. "Hey Sarge ... whaddya make o' that to my front, twenty meters?"

Custer moved up to lie alongside of the private. He let his eyes adjust to the conditions and looked where Gooly had pointed. At first all he could see were what looked like small boulders in the path along the platoon's route. He couldn't make out what they were.

"Kee-rist," he swore, frustrated. "Gimme your mono." The point carried a thermal monocular. Even through the monocular, Custer still couldn't make out what they were, although now they looked more alike, more like boulders of the same size or shape—no, more like *logs*, laid out in the road. Was somebody trying to block their route? A sudden thought: *can they hide an IED in a log?*

A voice came out of the dark: "Samson ..." Custer knew the signal but even so, he jumped out of his skin and yanked his head toward the sound. There was the broken silhouette of something large right beside him on the ground.

"Jesus H. Christ ..." Custer hissed, adrenaline coursing.

"No, it's me," Ironbridge whispered. "They were gonna pull a one-side hit from the left on the platoon, First Sergeant. We changed their plans. They're laid out along the route ... there. I want every man in First platoon to walk by and see the results of Kilo Company's overwatch. When you go by, pick up their weapons and bring them back to the COP."

Custer whispered a question. "What the hell do you want us to do with the bodies?"

"Leave them exactly where they lay," Ironbridge replied out of the blackness, almost in his ear. Custer looked again at the forms in the path. Fourteen men; they would have hit the platoon hard for sure. He looked back at Ironbridge, but he was gone. Custer fumbled with the monocular, but even through that, he couldn't catch a glimpse of the Captain anywhere.

Custer was trembling slightly, but he looked back to his other side more relieved than he thought he could be on a night patrol. Gooly was still there; hadn't moved a muscle, and hadn't heard a thing. He slugged Gooly in the arm and stood up. "Let's move," he said. "I'll take point."

Every Marine in First Platoon walked through that dangerous segment of the patrol route, and each of them walked past fourteen dead men, stretched out on the road, laid neatly side by side, an AK-47 or RPG lined up next to each. Custer thought he recognized one of the village elders among the dead; the same henna-streaks in the beard, same long, proud face. He collected the enemy's weapons and distributed them across the squads, and they finished their patrol and moved back through the wire into the COP by 0300 the next morning.

***

Two nights later, another patrol went out; this time, it was Second Platoon, and in the most dangerous part of their route, they walked past eight dead Taliban fighters laid out like cordwood, each with their weapons laid down next to them. The platoon commander had each man walk by the line of dead men, and they regretted trash-talking First platoon when they spoke about this same experience.

Three nights later another patrol moved through the valley. This time they found no dead men, but 600 meters before they came to the base of the hill where they would start their climb to the COP, they suddenly began taking a small volume of fire from their left. Everyone hit the dirt and Sauberg immediately called for fire back toward the line of attack. He moved the front squad forward and had them bound up and left, trying to flank the attackers; the second squad laid down a base of fire that served to keep the incoming fire subdued. He had third squad follow up to support the second as they poured counter-ambush fire into the hillside. Four minutes later the M240 came up and tracer rounds began slicing into the enemy from their front right as the first squad hit them from the side. Sauberg got on the radio and called for illumination rounds, passing the coordinates calmly into the headset. In twenty seconds illumination rounds were thunking out of mortar tubes firing from the COP. The hill to the left of the platoon's route of march lit up with an eerie whitish glare, and on the hillside Sauberg and the rest of the platoon could see eight or ten enemy fighters now running, trying to get out from under the illumination umbrella like cockroaches fleeing light. They had no chance. Every rifle came up on line and the Taliban fighters were cut down before they could move twenty meters.

Sauberg had third squad bound up the hill, with first squad holding the right flank and second squad the left. Third squad searched the bodies but found nothing but one or two copies of the Koran and one bundle of round bread the Afghans typically ate, called Nan. They took the weapons and ammunition and left the bread. Out of habit, they arranged the dead bodies in a row and left them on the hillside and then moved back through the wire and into the COP. Not one Marine had a scratch.

Patrols went out almost every night for the next two weeks. Sometimes they were covered by Ironbridge and his three-man team; when that was the case, the platoons ended up finding dead enemy fighters either laid out or, if there were trees, hung from the lower branches. They began to wonder what was happening in the valley. To date the Company had suffered not one casualty; they weren't complaining, but it wasn't normal, and the whisperings started, the beginnings of wondering. They knew the patrolling was aggressive and doing a 12-click hump every other night wasn't good for their beauty sleep, but so far no one had taken even a hint of an incoming round ... and they knew *that* wouldn't last.

***

One morning Ironbridge pulled in the platoon leaders and told them the patrols would be suspended for a bit. "Something like a couple of weeks or so; give the men some down time. Give the enemy some time to chew on what's happening; let it sit in his gut for a while and fester." The platoon commanders all nodded; their men were dragging from the hard night patrols, but there was also a growing question mark in many minds—how was Ironbridge's small four-man team finding and killing so many of the enemy? And what were the villagers in the valley thinking when they woke up and moved into their fields and found dead Taliban or Al-Qaeda fighters—or worse, their own dead elders—strewn about like so much detritus?

Wilson finally brought the questions to Ironbridge one snappish cold afternoon as snow began to fall seriously. He and Sauberg and Untermeigen and Fowler, the Third platoon commander, trailed by First Sergeant Custer, showed up at his bunker. They filed in and ranged themselves around the small table in the center of the hole and sat down where they could find a spot.

"Things won't be going this way for long," Ironbridge answered, looking at their questioning faces. "In fact, that's why we're standing down for a while. I'm thinking we're going to get hit hard pretty shortly, and so everyone needs to stay sharp. But when we get hit, I want to be standing behind large Hescos instead of hanging out there in the bush, exposed."

"Has Battalion sent you any intel on what's comin', sir?" Custer asked. Marcus could hear just the beginning shades of trust and confidence in the First Sergeant's question.

Ironbridge shook his head. "No ... I haven't heard anything from them; nothing from Prophet either. I just get a sense that this is what they'll do." The assembled group in Ironbridge's hooch threw glances at each other; they were beginning to understand what it meant when Ironbridge had 'a sense' of things. Marcus went on. "We've strung up, I don't know, forty or fifty dead guys from one end of the valley to the other, and I'm thinking the word is buzzing through every one of the villages by now."

"So you think these villagers are taking these dead guys as sort of a 'first shot' in your ... in this ..."

"In my personal 'war with Allah'? Yeah, that's what I'm thinking. In fact I'm sure of it. Have any other U.S. units you know about come through here and hit this place this so hard so quickly?" Ironbridge looked around the room. "First Sergeant, you've got a pretty good network; any of your contacts hear about this kind of activity before?"

Custer took the cigar out of his mouth with two fingers. "Yeah, sir," he replied flatly, "I've checked, and no, sir, no one has seen anything like this."

"So what are you thinking, First Sergeant?"

Custer's jaw clenched slightly and he half-closed one eye. "I'm thinkin', sir, that probably they got so pissed at what you said that first day that they ran in a bunch of amateurs who wanted to get their Martyr Merit Badge, who didn't know the difference between a fire lane and a fire hose, handed up whatever weapons they had layin' around, and stuck 'em out there at night to whack us. Your team cleaned house on 'em because you and those bad-asses from SATA are top-drawer, and ... well, the patrols have been kickin' ass too." Some of the platoon commanders chuckled.

"So basically you're saying that there really hasn't been the level of opposition the other units have faced so far?"

Custer folded his arms slowly. "That's about it, sir. My point of view, anyway."

Ironbridge nodded slowly. "Okay, that's fair. Let's say that's the situation. Let's look down the road a bit, though. I'm thinking that it may be like the First Sergeant says—they really haven't run in the first team yet. These guys we've been plinking are just to keep us occupied until they can figure out what we're doing, how we're operating, and where our strengths and weaknesses are. So we're going to stand down for a while and let them come to us. But before they hit us, I'd like to draw down their ammo stocks a bit."

"How you gonna do that, sir?" Untermeigen asked, eyes wide behind black-framed combat glasses.

"Paint," Ironbridge said. "Red paint, and some rope."

***

Dawn struck the valley the next morning with clear bright shafts of sunlight streaming over the ridges. As the light shone upon the eastern-facing wall of rock behind the clearing, it revealed a message in red splashed across the rock face in two-meter tall letters. The rock face was the closest thing to a billboard that existed in the valley. Almost every village had a clear line of sight to the wall, and for those who couldn't see it directly, irate runners were sent to spread the word of the blasphemy. Others were sent elsewhere, out of the valley, into the surrounding regions, to communicate to the faithful about the evil growing in the Korengal. And three men, valued elders, were launched on the difficult trek to Kabul to personally tell the Afghan Government what was happening.

The letters glowed in the dawn's light, tall and bright and strident. "Allah the pretender will burn in hell," they proclaimed, with drips like blood streaking from each letter, "with all those who follow him." And the last line, below the others: "Thus says the God of Abraham, Isaac, and Jacob, Who hates Allah, and all other false gods."

***

The first mortar rounds began impacting two hours after sunrise. The men came out of their bunks, threw on armor and helmets, grabbed weapons, and ran to the Hesco walls, ready to dodge incoming blasts. There were none hitting the compound—but they could hear them nearby. It took them a while to realize that the rounds were hitting lower, down at the base of the hill. It took them just a little longer to realize that the enemy was shooting at the rock wall. Most of the men had no idea why that was happening until Marines from First Platoon, manning Outpost Restrepo, looked back at the wall in the growing light and saw words—giant words—painted in what looked like the native language. They rang the field phone to the COP.

"Base, OP1, they're trying to hit the backstage rock wall. Someone painted something that apparently is really pissing them off."

"Roger that, OP1 ... can you tell what it says?"

"Well, it looks like a giant chicken jumped in a can of red paint and then ran up and down the rock. Do I look like a friggin' raghead?"

A pause. "Uh ... roger, OP1, right, sorry man. We'll try and get a terp up and see if they can't read what it says."

"Roger, Base, but I wouldn't rush anything if I were you. Better they waste the shells on the rock than dropping 'em on us."

***

By mid-afternoon it was apparent that mortars weren't going to erase the blood-red blasphemy painted on the rock. They stopped firing, and there was a lull for about half an hour, and then suddenly Kilo's Marines manning the Hesco barriers at the top of the hill saw fighters rushing through the brush carrying RPGs, trying to get close enough to blast the letters off the rock face with the rocket-propelled grenades.

"Snipers up!" the cry went out, and the SATA team manned their prepared positions, their spotters set up their scopes, and the teams went into action. The enemy made it easy; berserk with rage, they were tossing caution to the winds and rushing as fast as they could toward the rock wall, running in the open, trying to get close enough for a clear shot at each letter. The snipers were killing them as fast as they could recycle their single-action M40 rifles and select another target in their scopes.

In twenty minutes, forty-eight bodies were strewn around the approach to the clearing. Another wave followed. The barrels on the snipers' rifles were beginning to heat up.

"Pace your shots," Custer yelled, moving between their positions, "pace your shots. Valencia, get your people up here with ammo!" A private ran off with three others and began hauling large cans of specialized .308 ammunition to each sniper's position.

OP Restrepo exploded with the sounds of machine-gun and small arms fire as the men manning that outcrop finally gained clear lines of sight to the advancing Muslims. A second wave was cut down. About this time some of the leadership began to wonder just how many fighters there were in the Korengal, and when Sauberg passed Untermeigen near one of the Hescos, they looked at each other, and their wide eyes asked the question without words, because while there were dozens of enemy, not one round was coming at the Marines.

The last fanatical fighter took three M240 rounds in the back and fell into the dirt 300 yards from the wall. There were no more targets; there were no more fighters. Silence descended; the smell of cordite reeked throughout the COP gun positions. The men were ankle-deep in expended brass. There wasn't the normal adrenaline high that accompanied the end of a firefight, though. This had been more like a slaughter. Still, no Marine had a complaint, but more than a few were now beginning to wonder at what was happening. This was an entirely new and different way to fight a war. They didn't know how long this kind of success would last.

***

"This isn't exactly the way to fight an insurgency, Captain. You're supposed to get the people on your side ... you know, 'hearts and minds' and all."

Ironbridge looked down at his hands and then back up at his second-in-command. He didn't know how far to go in explaining how he felt, but he tried to put it in terms the Marine lieutenant could understand. "We're not fighting an insurgency, though, Dag ... it's a war. Think about it; in an insurgency, you have two sides competing to win control of a third group, the people, in the middle. In a war, there are two sides trying to compel the other's political will with force. We've got Muslims fighting a global *war* to establish Islam throughout the world; they are trying to compel the will of nations by using force—in just the same way, Hitler wanted to establish National Socialism around the world. Lenin and Mao wanted to establish Communism around the world. There are two sides; Islam against non-Muslims. Pretty clear. The villagers out there, they're all Muslims. They're not up for being co-opted. Islam doesn't permit it."

Wilson threw up a hand. "Wait a minute, sir. The villagers have been content for the last few years to play one side against the other just to get what they want out of the deal. That sounds like an insurgency to me."

"I disagree, Dag. It sounds more like two groups of people, both on the same side—the villagers and the Muslim fighters—have agreed to play different roles in sapping the energy out of their common enemy—us. The fighters try and take our lives; the Muslim 'people' simply take our resources, and then pass on to the fighters information and anything else that will help them take our lives. Don't you understand yet? This is a global war coordinated by some very dark spiritual forces at the very highest levels. Islam is simply one of their tools. Do you think it's some kind of coincidence that the single main thing these people have in common is the desire to whack the Jews and the Christians? Hitler himself said that it would have been his preference for the German nation to have been rooted in Islam rather than Christianity, because it would have made what he came to do easier. The agenda, the objective, the spirit that drove the Nazis is driving Islam, only these guys are much, much more dangerous."

"Islam?" Wilson asked, surprised. "That's ridiculous ... sir. How can you compare Germany, with their industrial base and the incredible military power they had, to Muslims, most of whom don't even know how to read, who've been inbreeding with their cousins for so long that most of them have double-digit IQs?"

"Dag, look around. The lifeblood of industrial society is oil; most of the oil is in the hands of Muslims."

Wilson blinked; he'd never thought of that. "Or the Russians," he added.

"Or the Russians, right, and that's another part of the story. And consider ... how many Muslims are there in the world today? What, around a billion? There certainly weren't one billion screaming Germans fighting World War II; if there had been, things might have been different.

"There were two main things that stopped Hitler from dominating the world, Dag. The first was that there was a national structure back then—basically the world was made up of nations ... nations which each had their own leadership, their own cultures, their own histories and peoples and traditions and goals and objectives, and while Hitler overran a bunch of smaller nations, most of the others didn't take kindly to the thought of losing their sovereignty. The second thing was the influence in the world that Christianity still had then, especially in America. I'm not saying things were perfect in America, but we were still considered a Christian nation, even by the politicians we had at the time and while many of them were certainly not real Christians, at least they were disciplined enough to maintain the forms, and when a nation even just keeps the forms of Christianity in place, it carries an enormous amount of power. It was the concept of freedom, and justice, and opposition to tyranny—all concepts that spring from Christianity—which formed the foundation of opposition to Hitler's agenda. It was these same things that formed the foundation of opposition to Communism.

"But now, we're moving toward a time when most of what is left of the nations in the world have voluntarily chosen to submit to an emerging world leadership, and any influence Christianity had has basically disappeared. Christianity has lost what salt it ever had. I'd go so far as to say that Christianity is dead as a force that can compel behavior at the national level."

Wilson listened quietly to this assessment. "So ... here we sit, about 120 guys in the middle of an entire nation of Muslims, and you've decided to co-opt the Company into your personal war against Islam. Oh, yeah, and Christianity is dead. So ... what now?"

"You say it like you think I've lessened our chances of survival, Dag."

Wilson's eyes snapped and he threw up his hand, sweeping it up toward the valley. "Haven't you? Since when has this place seen so many fighters? And for my money, we haven't even begun to see the numbers they're gonna throw at us."

"True, but since when has a unit been in place in this valley without sustaining even one casualty? When has *that* ever happened?" Wilson looked down at the floor and pushed some dirt around with his boot. He couldn't argue with that. Ironbridge went on.

"Dag, our best and sole protection is in taking a stand with the real God. This is something Christians have forgotten; they think they have to 'work with the system' and 'go along to get along'. And I know you don't believe that we're under God's protection in stepping out like this, risking what we're risking, but if for some reason you didn't believe two plus two was four, truth wouldn't change ... two and two would still be four, whether you believed it or not. Because most people don't believe in God doesn't mean that He doesn't exist. So I'm telling you that if you're worried about the safety of the Company, actually my way of fighting this war is the best way. Can you argue with results so far?"

"No sir, but ... there are no guarantees this is going to continue."

Ironbridge shook his head. "I don't know what it will take to convince you, Dag, but God does."

"Convince me of what?" Wilson asked suspiciously.

"To convince you that there is a God, that He has power on earth to affect the lives of men, and that He wants each and every man and woman to realize who He is, obey Him, and in so doing find the answers to life."

"Sounds no different from Islam, if you ask me," Wilson shot back. "Islam means 'submission', right? Aren't you advocating simply a submission to your God, like the Muslims argue for submission to theirs?"

There were times when he wished Mace were with him. Mace had an uncanny ability to answer these hard questions, but then again, Marcus was a natural teacher—it was something one needed to be as a leader, and he thought about Wilson's question for long seconds. He asked God quickly for wisdom, and immediately something occurred to him. "You're right, Dag, but think of it this way. Once there were two shepherds, each with their own flock of sheep. One shepherd mistreated the sheep, starved them, kept them from good water, never protected them from predators, and butchered them whenever the fancy struck him; the other shepherd protected the sheep, fed and watered them well, and made sure their lives were safe and productive. Both shepherds required obedience from their flocks; because one shepherd was evil doesn't make the concept of obedience evil. You could say that the bad shepherd actually took advantage of the essential dynamic of obedience set up by the good shepherd and abused that idea of obedience so that it came to mean something very different from what the good shepherd had intended."

Wilson twisted his mouth in a sort of half-smile, half-grimace. "I guess," he replied, still unconvinced.

"No worries, Dag, I'm not trying to convert you. If a man can be talked into something, he can be talked out of it. You're going to have to come to this on your own."

"That may be, sir, but for now, we have a pretty difficult tactical situation on our hands. And there's another thing. How long do you think it will be before the Corps yanks your ass out of here for all this anti-Muslim stuff? If the media at home ever hears of what we're doing out here, they'll be screaming for your head."

Ironbridge nodded slowly. "I worry about that constantly," he answered, "but there is nothing I can do about, so I leave it in God's hands. If He wants me yanked, I'll get yanked. If He doesn't want me yanked, there's nothing anyone will be able to do to get me yanked out of here."

Wilson left the bunker after a few more minutes arranging the next day's schedule of events, and as he walked back to his own bunk, the thought kept nagging at him that he'd never heard of any combat unit come through this much contact unscathed; that he'd never seen an enemy force so disorganized, uncoordinated, and ineffective. It wasn't making sense; there was no explanation for it—except the one Ironbridge was suggesting, and Dag Wilson just wasn't ready to accept that.

***

"Get the Captain! Now!" Staff Sergeant Fuhlen yelled at Private Dobovich. Dobovich took off for the command bunker and slammed into the First Platoon's commander as he ran down the wooden steps into the hole.

" 'Scuse me, sir. Sarn't Fuhlen says he needs Captain Ironbridge up to the wall. Sir." Dobovich stood there with wide eyes, sweating in the cold; it had been a long run.

"What's wrong, Marine?"

Dobovich looked around the bunker. First Sergeant Custer was there, with Lieutenant Wilson and Lieutenant Sauberg.

"He didn't say, sir, but there's a buttload of people moving up the valley comin' our way."

"People? What do you mean? Fighters?"

"No sir, well, I don't think so." Ironbridge had picked up his helmet and armor and his weapon and followed Dobovich out the door, and they were talking as they went. "I ... well ... they looked like a bunch of non-combatants to me, sir. They had women and kids with 'em."

Ironbridge stopped, surprised, turned to face Dobovich for just a moment, and then broke into a run.

***

Staff Sergeant Fuhlen stood adjacent to one of the Hescos bordering the entrance to the COP. Three Marines backed him up; he was looking through a pair of binoculars when Ironbridge and his officers appeared.

"What've we got, Staff Sergeant?"

"Yessir ... looks like they turned out the whole village ... no, more like two or three villages. That guy in front is carrying a white flag."

"What?" Custer said, unbelieving.

"That's what it looks like to me, First Sergeant. What it is is a big ol' bedsheet stuck up on a large branch, but I'm pretty sure they mean for us to take it as some kind of flag of truce or something."

Ironbridge was looking through his own binoculars. "That's exactly what it looks like, Staff Sergeant. Now what do you suppose they want to talk about?"

Wilson's head yanked around, along with everyone else standing there. Ironbridge was smiling.

"They'd better have someone who speaks English, Captain. Our terps are long gone, and we haven't gotten any replacements from J-Bad." Untermeigen added this needless piece of information for the crowd at the Hesco.

"That is true, Lieutenant," Ironbridge said offhandedly. "I wonder what they're thinking."

What they were thinking soon became apparent. The man with the white flag detached from the rest of the group and moved forward, accompanied by two men—and one, the Marines saw, looked like one of their Afghan Army terps that had deserted. They were motioning for the Marines to come down the hill and parley.

"You think they're serious, sir?" Wilson asked.

"I do, Lieutenant. They wouldn't have emptied the villages if they had just wanted to ambush us."

"You can trust them as far as you can throw them, sir," Custer interjected. "If I were them, this is a perfect way to whack the guy causing all this trouble. They get you out of the way, the Marines will send someone in here that ..." Custer hesitated and then stopped.

"You mean, they'll send someone who won't have his hair on fire for Allah?"

Custer scratched the back of his head for a second or two. "All I mean, sir, is that this is a perfect setup. They know we're inclined to respect that flag thing; they know we're up here surrounded by God knows how many Muslims ..."

"He does, yes."

"... and it's a simple thing to just get your ass down there and waste you. Dollars to donuts one of 'em is wired up with a vest."

Ironbridge knew that was a very real possibility. "I'm going down," he said, "but I'm not stupid. I'll talk to them from a distance."

Custer looked around. "Fuhlen, get your people. Captain's not going down on his own."

Wilson spoke up. "Lieutenant Sauberg, get over to the command hooch and give Restrepo a call; tell 'em to lock on to the guys around the flag. Anything even looks funny, they cut loose with everything they have, you understand?"

Ironbridge moved down the hill with Staff Sergeant Fuhlen's squad, First Sergeant Custer, and Lieutenant Wilson. He'd left Lieutenant Sauberg in charge on the top of the hill in case anything happened.

"First Sergeant, it might be better if you stayed up here as well. Something happens down there, the Company will need you."

Custer stood there, folded his arms, pulled the cigar from his mouth, and motioned for the Captain to step away from the group for a private word. He lowered his voice. "Sir, if Lieutenant Wilson's coming, I'm comin', and that's that, and so let's not get into any disagreements. Someone has to keep your crazy bible-thumping ass from getting busted, and I'm the only one that can do that."

Ironbridge just lifted an eyebrow and moved back to the group. "Alright then ... let's get on. Party's waiting."

***

They halted about twenty meters away from the three Afghans. They could see men in their rough field clothes, women in brightly colored silk and wool burkhas, and children running to and fro at their feet; some of the younger ones hid behind the women; some of the adolescents seethed with palpable anger. The elders looked on with a mixture of fear and fire in their eyes. That the women were there in public was remarkable, and it struck Custer why.

"They got their women and kids down here to keep us from firin' 'em up, sir."

"Well," Ironbridge replied, "that's a piece of information we can tuck away to use later." Custer looked at the Captain sharply, not sure what he meant.

Ironbridge brought his group down the hill and then held up his hand; they halted. "This is close enough to speak," said Ironbridge to the translator. "What do they want, Sergeant Mosul?"

"I am Tarriq Muhammed Mosul," the man replied, "and the elders of all the villages in this valley wish you to know that you are damned to an eternal fire for the blasphemies that you are committing in our holy land—you and all your men with you, you are all damned."

Ironbridge stood there, rock-like, with his arms folded across his chest. He looked over at all the villagers and then back at Mosul. He made no reply, but turned his head to the side and, deliberately, still locking eyes with Mosul, spit on the ground. Mosul's eyes widened at the insult and, giving the appearance of great and holy indignation, yelled back, "Say what you wish to say, infidel, and I will tell them the words."

Marcus spoke directly at the leaders in the group, looking them in the eyes. "You tell them, then, that their god is nothing but a demon, and he has no power here."

Mosul looked as though he would choke, but then turned to the other two men and spoke in Pashto. The two elders became angry, but held their tempers. Mosul turned back to speak to the Americans.

"They say that you lie, like Satan. They say that they will test the power of your God. They want to know if you have the courage to permit this test."

"Jesus, Mary, and Joseph," Fuhlen whispered.

"Can it," Custer hissed. "Stand fast."

"What kind of test do they offer?" Ironbridge asked the terp.

"They will bring holy men to this place, here," Mosul said, pointing to the clearing. "They will bring twenty holy men, Imams, and the Imams will fast and then pray and curse your God, and will ask Allah to wipe off the filth that you have painted on his mountain, and you will see that you are serving Satan."

"That's not paint, Mosul," Ironbridge replied. "It is the blood of twenty pigs."

Mosul's eyes went wide; he took it for granted that Ironbridge was telling the truth, never stopping to think how impossible it would have been for the Americans to get a pig into a Moslem country. In his mind, Americans could do anything. He turned to the other elders with him, related what Marcus had said, and collectively they began to froth at the mouth.

Ironbridge spoke loudly enough for Mosul to hear clearly. "You tell them that the Imams can come to this clearing, here, at the base of our hill, and they can fast and pray all they want—they must carry no weapons, however. If we see them with a weapon, we will kill them, do you understand? They are not holy men but servants of Satan, and we will kill them if they carry weapons."

Mosul translated this to the group of elders, almost spitting the words, and they jerked their heads or waved their arms angrily, and one turned to the assembled mass of villagers and shouted something. They all broke into triumphant shouts and ululations. Their Imams would come; the infidels would burn in hell, and the offending writing on their mountain, the word about which was even now spreading to every corner of Islam and bringing unending shame and disgrace upon their heads, would be removed. The crowd turned as one and began to walk back to their villages. Their goats and dogs followed, barking and bleating, mimicking their masters.

Mosul turned again to Ironbridge, and his voice, high and clear, echoing off the sides of the hills around him, pierced the air, and they could even hear him up at the COP. "The Imams will be here in three days. They will gather here," he said, pointing to the clearing, "and they will fast for three days under your eyes—they will not eat or drink, but they will pray, and then on the seventh day from this day, you will all die." Mosul turned around with the other two men and they followed the crowd back down the valley.

"Everybody back up, now!" Custer barked. "We ain't gonna hang around waiting for them to drop a mortar on us. God knows they got this place zeroed. Let's git." The team walked back up the mountain, Custer's profanity bluing the air all the way up as he cursed about how stupid they'd been to even think about stepping into that mortared ground. Each man kept his own counsel on the walk back. It had become a very, very different war, and they were each wrestling with what it might mean to them, personally, if it was actually true that there was a God and He did care about whether someone was Christian or Muslim or Buddhist or whatever else. A contest between Gods wasn't something covered in the Marine Corps' field manual.

Three days later, to the hour, the men on watch in the COP saw the twenty Imams walk down the road and take up their positions in the clearing. Ironbridge watched through binoculars as they each spread their prayer rugs, pushed out their long white robes, and knelt down. They arrayed themselves in lines, ten in one line, another ten in a line behind the first, under the shadow of the rock upon which the offending words cried out to the valley. They knelt down and prostrated themselves toward the east, which put their backs to the wall, literally.

For three days the Imams knelt and prayed. Ironbridge had the watch on the wall doubled, and he pushed another squad into Restrepo and the other OP in case the enemy used the distraction to hit his smaller teams. But nothing happened; the only way they could tell the Imams were alive was that they would occasionally bob up and down on their rugs.

The second night Wilson and Ironbridge stood together behind one of the Hescos. The sky was clear and the stars were stunning in their clarity and brilliance, and Marcus could not get enough of just standing outside and soaking in their majesty.

"There's something I don't understand," Wilson said quietly, wanting to talk.

"What's that?" Marius replied.

"Well, here you have twenty guys down there, and you can still see 'em in the moonlight, not eating or drinking for three days. I mean, that's gotta take some kind of faith, doesn't it?"

"I'll tell you what, Dag. If one of our Marines decided to jump up on this Hesco and leap over the edge of the mountain because he truly, sincerely believed he could fly, what would you think?"

"That the guy's a nutcase," Wilson replied.

"But hey, he's got *faith* that he can do it."

Wilson hesitated for a moment. "Yes sir, I see your point. You can be sincere about something, but sincerely wrong."

"True, but it's worse than that, Dag. Those men down there have voluntarily chosen to serve a god that is directly opposed to the true God. The bad part about that is that they *enjoy* serving him, Dag. That evil spirit *does* give his servants power, and they *enjoy* having power in their society; they *enjoy* whipping up illiterate masses to go and slaughter and rape and pillage—in their eyes, that's real power. They *enjoy* beating or mutilating their women and killing their daughters when they're raped, as if it were the daughters' fault. Islam speaks to men and encourages them to seek power over others, and to love death; Christianity speaks to men and encourages them to treat others as more important than themselves, to die to their own selfish nature, and to love life. It's that simple. And those men down there love the power that comes from serving Allah—they thirst for it;

they *burn* for it. Make no mistake, Dag, Allah is real. There is an entity who has chosen to make itself known by that name, a very, very powerful evil spirit—a demon—who has enormous power and authority over massive numbers of people on earth. And he rewards those who serve him well."

"How ... I mean, okay, let's say you've got this demon Allah or whatever ... if your God is so powerful, why doesn't he just squash this upstart and let people live their own lives?"

Marcus leaned over the barrier and paused to watch a falling star shoot across the far horizon, then spoke into the darkness to answer Wilson. "Because for love to be true it must be chosen, not forced, and for men to truly love God they must have a choice—which is why free will is so important—and for there to be a choice, there must be different things from which to choose. God has permitted the existence of evil, of Islam, as well as every other man-generated religion, to present men choices. Will they serve God, or will they serve the enemy of their souls, who feeds them all sorts of power and possessions and suckers them away from God by filling them with pride in themselves, or their nations, or their people, or their accomplishments? There's no other choice available to men, Lieutenant; no one can avoid choosing sides in this war."

In an uncomfortable burst of clarity, Wilson finally put his finger on what it was that irritated him about this developing 'religious' war they'd started in the valley. It was because it was forcing him to choose; the demonstrations of power that were occurring before their eyes were forcing him—forcing them all—to acknowledge that there was a God who could assert His sovereignty and demand their obedience, and that meant that life under such sovereignty might be very, very different than the life he'd always known, always wanted, and always expected to have. And Dag Wilson was not sure he wanted to let go of who he was and his current way of life to live in such a way.

***

On the third day, as the sun rose, the villagers again appeared en masse a few hundred meters behind the Imams. Mosul and the two leading elders came forward and shouted up at the hill. "Be ready, infidels, today you die!"

"Hold your fire," Custer barked harshly, as one of the Marines propped his rifle in a firing position. "No one fires; stand down." Rifles came off the barriers, muzzles tipped up, and the men watched with curiosity to see what would happen next.

"Looks like the paint is still there," Private Dobovich said.

"It does, doesn't it," Staff Sergeant Fuhlen replied dryly. "Imagine that."

The Imams began to bob up and down fiercely, raising their hands in the air, and the men on the barriers could hear them wailing and crying out to Allah. Some began to cut themselves with small knives they had in their sleeves. Their blood began to drip down onto the rugs and stain their white robes.

"Oh shit," Dobovich said, "this is not good. This is *not* good."

As their blood began to spatter the ground in the clearing, there came a deep, tremulous BOOM, then a rumbling, like a freight train in the distance, and suddenly the ground began to shake. Branches snapped off trees, rocks were dislodged from the high hills, the men on the COP and at Restrepo held on as the ground shook beneath their feet, and the Imams, shocked but pleased at this wondrously supernatural response to their prayers, redoubled their prostrations. They waved their arms, their blood profusely splaying about with holy passion. They shouted curses at the infidels on the hill; they foamed at the mouth and spittle flecked their beards; their faces twisted in rage and anger and bitterness at the letters on the rock face at their backs; and upon their faces too there was triumph and joy at the thought of Allah coming to claim his vengeance. And across the face of every Imam and all those in the crowd, there flashed an expression of fierce satisfaction at the thought that they had such power at their command.

The ground near the clearing was now shaking violently, and suddenly a great wrenching crack was heard, and a deep, narrow chasm opened in the clearing, gaping like an open maw, growing. The Imams stopped their bowing and splattering, frozen in fear. The chasm widened and the ground fell away beneath the Imams, beneath Mosul and the two elders, and all the Imams fell, swallowed up, fists clenched, blood streaming down their arms, screaming and cursing the God of the Christians and Jews. The villagers pelted away in terror—people, goats, and dogs running for their lives.

When the last of the Imams had fallen into the pit, the ground shook again once more, terribly, the gaping crack snapped shut with a sharp, dreadful crash, and all was silent. Dust filled the air, and the men from Kilo Company, now more than ever, began to seriously think about what kind of war was being fought there in the Korengal—and who was fighting it.

The red letters remained on the rock face.

***

MAIronbridge <maironbridge7@arcmail.com>
To: Thackeray Ironbridge <tackiron45@arcmail.com>
Sent: February 23, 06:32:17 AM
Subj: Interesting Events

Dad;

Some interesting things have been happening here. I know I've told you about the patrols and stuff, and how so far none of my people have been hurt—and thanks, by the way, for all your prayers. Please remember to thank God for His mercies out here.

Thank you for your strong encouragement to walk in faith, Dad, and to trust in nothing but God. There has been some enormous opposition spiritually and physically out here, but God has so far kept everyone safe. I think he is trying to demonstrate to my people that He is still powerful, that He still can work, and, well, I suppose there are a lot of other things He's got in the works that I don't know about.

We had a tough time with some local religious leaders the other day, Pa. As you can guess, this direct opposition to Allah is riling up the powers and principalities, and they had twenty or so of their Imams at the foot of our mountain, praying and fasting and yelling out to Allah to have him come and kick our butts. Funny thing—and please don't go spreading this around—while they were screaming out their curses on the third day of their long prayer and fasting vigil, the ground just opened up and swallowed them.

That's right—you aren't reading it wrong. I've never seen anything like it in my life, and I probably never will again, but I can tell you that from that moment forward, I will always know that there is no power on earth like the power of the God of Abraham, Isaac, and Jacob, and I know what level of faith in Him He calls us to; I feel ashamed at my lack of faith in the past, and how I let so many things in the world 'go by' without standing up and opposing it and standing up for what I know Jesus would have opposed. But not any more, Dad, not after watching the ground literally open up and swallow those dark and evil men.

I can tell you it is causing some head-scratching among my Marines. I don't think they ever thought that God would or could actually just step into their lives in such a dramatic way, and for some of the more thoughtful, I suspect they are beginning to wonder why God is fighting on our side (that's how they would think of it). Hopefully they are beginning to see that He is God, there is no other God besides Him, and that He is owed all their dedication and devotion and obedience. But you know, wherever Jesus went, he demonstrated power in the things He did—He demonstrated His father's power to make the blind see, the deaf hear, the lame walk, and heal the sick and infirm. He healed lives and raised the dead. When He comes back, He'll demonstrate His power by whacking an enormous number of people. We don't see anything like that kind of power anymore in Christianity—at least, I would have said that until we saw what we saw yesterday. 127 U.S. servicemen know exactly what happened to those Muslim Imams, Dad, and nothing—no amount of media criticism or joking or ridiculing Christianity—will ever change what they know in their minds to be true, what they saw*—that God DOES have power in this world, and he WILL use it to defend His children and to uphold the glory of His name. I wish every Christian would declare war on Allah.*

Thackeray Ironbridge <tackiron45@arcmail.com>
To: MAIronbridge <maironbridge7@arcmail.com>
Sent: February 27, 4:14:25 AM
Subj: Re: Interesting Events

Marcus;

You have been allowed to see something few Believers ever get to see, my son—that God does truly respond in power to a trusting faith. But remember, regarding your people ... seeing power is one thing; falling on the rock that is the Son of Man, crucifying one's own flesh, and admitting that one is a sinner, is something else completely.

Have you thought about what the Marine Corps will say when they find out that you 'declared war' on Islam? From everything we are seeing on the net and in the media, it seems as if such a position might be contrary to U.S. policy. Not that I want to dissuade you, but it is always good to think about the implications or consequences.

Your mother and Mace and Zoe send their love, and yes, they are still praying that you get back safely.

Love;
Dad

Chapter 11

Marcus & Marie-Clémence

"Deliver those who are being taken away to death, and those who are staggering to slaughter, oh hold them back."

Proverbs 24:11

Fontainebleau was a beautiful city, even in the rain. Traffic on the Rue Grande was heavy, so Marcus had pedaled his bike from his rented room in the northern part of the city and up the Rue Des Bois. He took a table inside *L'Escapade*, a small restaurant with its own sidewalk café known in Fontainebleau for its salads, deciding to leave the patio tables for tourists who didn't know enough to come in out of the rain.

A tall, trim Malaysian man and a blonde woman came in, saw Marcus at his table, and joined him.

"So you biked all the way in this rain?" the man asked, setting down his backpack.

"It's only rain, Ramsay," Marcus replied. "You get enough of that where you're from, don't you?"

"Ah, yes, but we are wealthy enough not to ride around in it on a bicycle," Ramsay said good-naturedly.

"I'm surprised you haven't shown up to class yet in a rickshaw wearing a loincloth."

"Not afraid for your computer?" asked the blonde, arranging her own laptop on the small table, pushing aside a vase and a pot of whipped butter. Smells of fresh-baked bread wafted out of the café's kitchen. Their table was up close against the ubiquitous dark wooden bar found in every French café, and close to the door to the kitchen. The rain began to come down noticeably, pattering on the green awning that extended over the patio tables. It was a soothing sound.

"It is why God invented plastic, Christienne," Marcus said, holding up a two-gallon plastic Ziploc bag.

She adopted a faux mien of offended dignity. "You Americans ... so pedestrian."

"I biked here, Christienne, so it doesn't apply, and hey, if it works for the hoi polloi," Marcus answered, shrugging, "it's good enough for me." Turning to Ramsay, he asked, "So you wanted to talk about the thesis?"

The Malaysian, whose real name was Ramsay Amatporutu, grandson of one of the richest and most famous Malaysians in history, Tengku Raza Amatporutu, put his hands on the table. "Yes, we must," he said, suddenly all intensity. "Professor Gruniére assigned working groups this morning, and I think we need to settle on a topic quickly." Ramsay was a short, trim young man with black hair and smooth, olive skin, black eyes, and typical Malaysian features. He also was a world-class cricket player, a sport Marcus found infinitely amusing to watch, though completely incomprehensible.

"I knew we had a group thesis requirement, but didn't know about the working group assignments. Are we it?" Marcus asked, making a small circling gesture with his glass.

"No," Christienne replied loftily, "we are waiting on one other person." Christienne paused, ordered a coffee from the hovering waiter, gazed at the menu, and in flawless French asked for a salad with goat cheese and walnuts. She arranged her silverware coyly, moved her napkin just so. She leaned over and bussed Ramsay on the cheek. They had been an item since the term began.

"The other person?" Marcus asked, looking the question at her. She raised one eyebrow archly and said, "Oh, didn't I mention her name? Let me see ... let me call it up." She tapped her phone, opened up a file. "Ah, here it is. Marie-Clémence Saffron."

"You're kidding me," Marcus growled, sitting back in his chair.

"Sorry, Marcus," Ramsay said, smiling, not sorry at all.

***

INSEAD[8] was one of Europe's finest business schools, its campus situated in the historic town of Fontainebleau, about an hour southeast of Paris, home to a famous forest and an even more famous 12th century castle. After the Marine Corps had unceremoniously thrown him out, Marcus had chosen INSEAD because of its reputation, because he spoke French like a native and all the classes at INSEAD were conducted in French, and because he needed to get out of America for a while.

While Marcus felt very much like a fish out of water in a business environment, the term had been uneventful until one day in the second week of his Private Equity class, when he somehow found himself embroiled in a religious argument.

The professor was a middle-aged milksop of a man, a Spaniard, with no chin, a protruding belly, and a weakness for female students. The subject that day had been likely sources of private equity.

"Private equity is a source of investment capital from high net worth individuals or institutions," the professor was saying, in surprisingly bad French. "The investment is typically made to invest in or acquire equity ownership in companies. Partners at private equity firms will raise money and then manage the funds to generate favorable rates of return."

"What's the investment horizon?" someone had asked.

"About four to seven years, typically," the professor had answered.

"Do some private equity firms impose any constraints or limitations on the funding sources?" a young man from Greece asked.

"This is a developing situation," the professor said slowly. "Recently some firms have adopted a strategy called 'Focused Investor Reach', which just means that the private equity firm targets investors who may have common financial, political, social, or," he said, holding up a finger to note a particularly new development, "even religious goals."

"What kind of religious goals are finding a common investment pool?" Marcus had asked, seizing on the last point. He wondered if the professor would know anything about recent inclinations among a number of Islamic private equity firms to fund terrorist activities.

The professor paused for a long moment, thinking. Apparently no one had asked such a question in his class before. Before he could reply, a voice spoke from one of the back rows.

"They are most probably Islamic investors," said a thin, dark-haired female

8 Institut Européen d'Administration des Affaires

student whose nametag in front of her said that she came from Marseille. "And they would be investing in companies who are intending to advance the cause of Islam in the world."

"How does an investment company advance the cause of Islam?" Marcus shot back, turning around to face the speaker, without thinking where the discussion could lead.

The woman didn't hesitate. "Companies in many parts of the world consider involvement in the religion of their constituents to be a natural part of their activities," she replied in a professional tone, though laced with disparagement. "While they recognize they need to be profitable, they also recognize that profit is not their ultimate, or even their primary, motive for existence."

"But I still don't understand what things a company would do to advance the cause of a religion," Marcus said. He could think of several, but he wanted to know what this woman would say.

She leaned around in her chair slightly so as to look at him directly. "You are from America, Monsieur ... is it *Pont métallique*?" She used the literal French translation for 'metal bridge'.

"*Pont de Fer*—Ironbridge," Marcus corrected, in English, "and yes, I am from America."

"*Oui*, then are you not aware that your American anti-terrorism organizations constantly track funds to make sure companies do not spend money to help Muslims?"

"I'd heard something about that," Marcus replied. "But it was something along the line of not helping fund terrorist activities."

"Oh certainly, for example, when a construction company in, say, Saudi Arabia decides it wants to build low-income housing for Muslim immigrants fleeing central Africa, and it goes to a private equity firm that is interested in helping Muslims find a better life, then perhaps you also have heard that America tracks this activity as well, and pressures private equity firms away from the deal if there is even the slightest hint that it might be involved with terrorism—by which they mean that there is the slightest chance the deal might benefit Muslims. Or when an aviation company in Tunisia needs start-up capital to begin an airline servicing primarily Muslim countries in north and central Africa, that suddenly finds its ability to locate capital blocked unless it goes to an Islamic-friendly private equity firm. And even if they do get the money, they find themselves constantly hounded by American military and intelligence organizations terrified that they will be flying Osama bin Laden's family around. Or what about a group of Muslim doctors in Kazakhstan who want to start a practice designed to help the poor in Astana. They go out for private equity funding and suddenly they cannot travel because they are on some type of universal no-fly list."

Marcus sat and listened to the woman's growing irritation, wondering how far the professor would let her rant. He didn't want to get into any controversy; it would serve no useful purpose in such a public setting.

"I see what you mean," he said slowly. "Those are ... interesting ... examples of how private equity can advance a religion. Thank you."

"Those are the tip of the icebox," she replied testily in English, mixing her metaphor. "Private equity firms can advance anyone's religion. It is just that in today's world, Islam is the only religion that feels that it *should* advance, that it has something to offer the world, and whose adherents are not ashamed of their own religion."

The professor finally made a placating gesture, holding up his hand. "Thank you, Ms. Saffron, for that succinct but pointed summary of religiously-focused private equity."

That discussion opened Pandora's box, and throughout the next three months, Ms. Saffron would use any pretense to contradict Marcus's assertions or disparage his questions. It was all done professionally, but with a razor-sharp wit, and while it got so blatant that others in the class noted the tension, the professor would not curb her antagonism, partly because he shared her political inclinations and partly because he hoped for a romantic liaison.

Things went on in this vein until one cold, wet November afternoon, when Marcus had finished his classes for the day and was walking out of the Doriot Library, he heard a voice emanating from under an umbrella covering a bench, asking a question in English. "Why did you come here?"

He turned, surprised. Saffron was sitting on a bench along the walkway, under a black umbrella. She wore pale blue jeans, black Doc Marten boots, and a gray fleece pullover. Her hair was tucked into a headscarf, like she always wore in class. She had no gloves. Her backpack was next to her on the bench, and she was shivering slightly in the cold. He could smell salt on the wind for some reason.

"*Pardon moi?*" Marcus replied in French, caught by surprise.

"It was a simple question," she said, again in English. "What are you doing here?"

The rain, until then just a wet mist, now began to pick up. Marcus didn't relish getting drenched on the ride home.

"Hoping to get a very good education in the principles of business," he said, dropping his bag and hunching his shoulders to keep the rain from running down his back. He put his hands in the pockets of his Gore-Tex rain jacket.

"Are there no good business schools in America?"

"I'm not going to be checking up on any private equity firms you might engage, if that is what's worrying you," Marcus answered, shifting to English to match her.

"America seems to think she is the policeman of the world," she replied, snapping her hand flat in a gesture that conveyed disgust. "And she has her nose pushed into everyone else's business. It is not appropriate."

"I suspect there are some things you French have done in the past which have not been irreproachable, yet I do not hold them against you personally."

"I am French, and I am a Muslim, so I can hold things against anyone personally," she snapped, and then said, "So ... you know where I come from. I am surprised you even know of the country. And what is this word, 'irreproachable'?

"*Irréprochable*." He used the French word.

She shrugged off his helpful translation. "We French do not control most of the world's capital, and so we do not have your responsibilities." She hesitated, as though displeased. "But you ... you speak French like you were born here. Most Americans don't even speak their own language well, not to mention another."

"My mother was born and raised in Normandy," he replied.

"So that explains your French. But it does not explain what you are doing here. You are not suited for business, Monsieur Ironbridge."

"I am not suited for business?"

"No. You are not suited for it. You ask the most elementary questions, your understanding of finance is basic at best, and your principles are based upon some type of outdated concept that people must be fair and good to one another. You will get eaten down."

"That's eaten up, or beaten down, take your pick."

"Up, down, it doesn't matter. I don't like it. I could name ten friends of mine more qualified than you. You take up a seat; you take up space, and you do nothing with what you are getting."

Marcus looked at her, shivering on the bench. He didn't want to be impertinent but her approach was just too blunt to be believed. He shook his head and chuckled.

"You are a piece of work, Ms. Saffron."

"What does that mean?" she asked, unfamiliar with the expression.

"Nothing."

"Yes, it means something. If I was to guess, you feel you are too noble to engage me directly with how you really feel, so you cover it up with some type of expression that obscurely disparages me, but doesn't get to the issue."

Marcus was brought up short. With a whip-crack assessment she'd discerned exactly what he had meant. He decided not to underestimate her again. "Okay, Ms. Saffron. In America we have lots of issues, and there are times I don't identify myself as an American, but one thing my parents taught me was to be polite to people, to give them the benefit of the doubt, and not to pick fights where fights weren't required."

"That's strange."

"What is? That I was taught to be polite?"

"No ... that you do not identify yourself as an American. So what are you if you are not an American?"

Marcus stood in the rain and looked off into the distance, watching the people go by, wondering why this woman had taken an instant and intense dislike towards him. He didn't want to continue this conversation, but he was also aware that being liked wasn't a prerequisite for an opportunity to test for spiritual openness.

"I am a Christian," he said, looking directly at her. "I identify myself as a servant of the God of Abraham, Isaac, and Jacob." He threw in that last to tweak the Muslim in her.

Her eyes widened, and then she nodded, eyes half-closed. "That ... would ... explain things," she replied slowly.

"What things?"

"Why you have no head for business, for one," she shot back. "Christians have always had terrible business sense. Look to the Jews for that. And it explains why you will not be direct. Christians are always afraid they might offend someone. And why you—"

Marcus held up a hand. "Excuse me, Ms. Saffron—"

"And interrupting is also something Americans do, always and everywhere they go."

Marcus pushed on, undeterred. "One of the other things that marks a servant of God, Ms. Saffron, is that we speak truth, but truth seasoned with a concern to edify those with whom we speak. So permit me to share with you my ignorance ... my ignorance of any situation in which *any* Saudi Arabian company would embark on *any* project that would help Muslim immigrants when Saudi Arabia is the worst country *in the world* when it comes to enslaving those very same poor Muslim immigrants. And since when would any Saudi firm even *need* equity financing?" Marcus leaned forward to emphasize his disdain for the Saudi kingdom's hypocritical domestic policies. "Perhaps you're not aware of how many workers have their passports confiscated upon entry into Saudi Arabia—that paragon of Islamic virtues—and are trapped until their years of servitude are up. And that wonderful enterprising aviation company trying to start up an airline ... I wonder why they wanted cargo aircraft instead of passenger aircraft? Funny thing, do you know that I heard about a company very similar to the one you described, and I also heard that one of their aircraft, forced down by those pesky interrupting Americans, was found to have a load of surface-to-air missiles in it? Do you want to explain to me how surface-to-air missiles advance the cause of Islam? And those nice doctors in Kazakhstan, wanting to help those poor Muslims ... is there a reason they don't treat women who've been assaulted by their own parents in the name of Islam, and bury evidence of honor killings at their clinics?"

She sat silently, not responding to his information in the slightest. And then she said, "So back to my original question: why are you here, Mr. Ironbridge?"

"If you want an answer, permit me to take a seat on the bench."

She didn't say anything, but moved her backpack a few inches closer to her on the bench. Marcus sat down as far away from her as possible.

"I am thinking about starting my own company," he said.

She erupted with a barking, derisive laugh. "Congratulations, and please permit me to also extend my condolences in advance. It will never get off the ground. But you still have not said why you came to France, to INSEAD. There are plenty of good business schools in America. If you can get into INSEAD, you can get into any of them. Why here? And do not tell me it is because your mother is French. You can get a baguette in America."

"Not as good, though," Marcus interjected.

"No," she agreed reluctantly, "not as good. But get to the point."

Marcus didn't know how much to tell her, and he certainly didn't want to give this Muslim woman any details about why the United States Marine Corps court-martialed him just before they discharged him. But before he could frame an answer, she speculated.

"If I was to guess, I would say that something happened to you because of something you did which did not agree with your people in America—perhaps someone or some organization you worked for—and you decided to look for an education out of the country. You chose France, perhaps, because of your mother, and because you speak the *language du pays*."

"Why would you say that?" he asked, curious about her logic.

"Because you said that at times you don't identify yourself as an American. Do you know how few Americans would actually say such a thing? I will tell you who would say such a thing—someone who is incredibly disillusioned, and I suspect your disillusionment had something to do with a conflict over your Christianity."

"Why would you say that?" he asked again.

"For the same reason. How many Americans would identify themselves as Christians first, and Americans only second? Not many; so this tells me—and it isn't hard to see—that you are some sort of religious fanatic or nut case who disagreed with the authorities who were probably asking you to do something fairly reasonable, but you could not do so because of your *conscience*"—she spat the word out with disdain—"and you probably felt you were being 'persecuted' or some such stupid thing simply because you wouldn't do what you were asked to do."

Marcus sat there with his hands in his pockets. "Not exactly," he replied quietly.

"What did you do in America, anyway?" she asked.

Marcus could not tell her what he had done because the terms of his honorable discharge prevented him from relating any details about the incredible combat success of his 'War against Allah'. The USMC did not want the truth about those events to get out, nor did the U.S. media, nor did the international media, nor did any other world institution charged with maintaining the global anti-Christian narrative. So they made his future silence a condition for issuing him an honorable discharge. His lawyer during the court martial had told him that such a condition was a blatant infringement on his rights and violated the Universal Code of Military Justice. Marcus had replied to him that when it came to the ensuring the world's narrative was preeminent in the court of public opinion, truth is flung to the ground. The court martial hearing had gone on for almost a year, and Marcus didn't want to continue the fight. He just wanted things to be finished. He was extremely and bitterly disillusioned with the Marine Corps, an organization he had hoped to serve for at least the next twenty years. But God interfered with that plan.

"I was in the Marines," he said flatly. He had been permitted to say that much.

"The Marines," she said, turning fully on the bench to look at him directly. "You were a Marine, in the United States?"

"Yes. Why, does that surprise you?"

"Now that I think of it, not at all. It explains the obstinacy, the hard-headed inability to grasp simple concepts, and your awareness of what are, you should know, mere rumors about various Islamic funding activities. Where did you serve?"

Strange, that she would use that term. "Afghanistan," he answered.

"Afghanistan? Ah, and so they tossed you out. What have you been doing since then?" Marcus didn't offer any explanation, so she pressed. "What did you do in the Marine Corps?"

Marcus looked at her, trying to get a sense of how serious she was. "Why is that important?"

"Were you some kind of supply clerk or something? Did you risk your life to make three copies of the bedpan stock list instead of two?"

"Something like that," Marcus said woodenly. He saw in his mind's eye stacks of dead Afghan fighters who had tried to kill his own men, and remembered the ground cracking open and swallowing the crazed, blood-streaked mullahs, prophets of the same demonic entity that this woman, sitting next to him, worshipped. The connection disoriented him.

"So you really didn't do anything you would call 'noble' or 'heroic', right?"

"And why would you ask that?" Marcus replied, dodging her question again.

"Because it fits with the rest of the normal Christian profile." She waved her hand again with disgust, fingers splayed. "You Christians are always talking about your martyrs, always talking about 'risking your lives for God', when the most dangerous thing you do is to risk missing a table at the restaurant because you let someone out of the parking lot in front of you late some Sunday morning." She was unreasonably incensed, and Marcus could not understand her mixture of cynicism and anger.

"You don't know what Christianity is," Marcus replied.

She looked up at him, startled. "What do you mean? I have not lived in Marseille all my life. I was born in Uzbekistan, I lived in Chicago for three years, did you know, going to school, and then in Boston for five years, working at a brokerage firm. Don't tell me I don't know Christianity. I know Christianity up to here," she said, and lifted a flat hand up to her chin. She leaned toward him, angry, throwing her words at him. "It is a bankrupt religion, a religion for weak men and masculinized women sporting short butch haircuts who want to dominate men. It is a religion for a debased people, a people who revel in the filth of their culture like pigs revel in mud up to their faces. They have no conception of a life lived in devotion to God, of everything in one's life being submitted to God. Did you know that 'Islam' means submission? Did they teach you that in Marine school, before they taught you how to kill Muslim children?"

Marcus realized he shouldn't have been surprised by her animosity. The U.S. Marines were remorseless killers of Muslim fighters, and it was probably just religious loyalty behind her boiling hatred. But then again ... he almost felt as though she was lying to him, but no, that couldn't be. So he just sat there, listening, like a large, strong, intelligent horse being beaten in his traces by an irate passer-by.

She stopped her tirade and pushed the umbrella back so she could look directly at him. She had the most striking pale green eyes he had ever seen, and at the moment they were filled with ... with something he couldn't quite put his finger on. It was if she wanted him to think it was anger, but instead, he saw something that looked more like frustration.

"Why don't you people take your god more seriously?" she asked, pushing out her hand that held the umbrella, shaking it, causing water to fall onto the bench between them. Finally something came to Marcus.

"You don't have a 'people' sitting here on this bench with you. It's just me. I can only answer for myself. But you wouldn't want to hear my answer, Ms. Saffron. 'People' have never wanted to hear my answer. The answer I have for you is one that the God of Abraham, Isaac, and Jacob gives to each man, to each woman. Yes, He speaks to peoples and nations and kings and tribes, but first He speaks to men and women individually."

"Fine," she spat derisively. "So what is the answer from the great Marcus Metalbridge?"

"It is God's answer, and people don't want to hear God's answer because God requires people give up their sin. They don't want to truly hear from God because they suspect He'll demand everything from them, and people would rather have a set of rules that they can keep, so that when they keep their own invented set of rules, they can call themselves holy and righteous and convince themselves that they will all go to heaven."

She seemed taken aback at first by that, but then fought him. "Sin?! Bah! Says who? One man's sinner is another man's saint. You don't know what you are talking about. You are stuck in some corn-fed, Middle American bible belt do-loop. You are just repeating what you've been taught."

He ignored her cut, looked directly into her eyes, and said with deep sincerity, "I take God seriously, Ms. Saffron. He drives everything in my life. He tells me what to do and I do it."

"Ridiculous!" she yelled, incensed. "Don't give me that line of manure. That is the excuse used by every mass murderer in history, by every power-hungry man that dominates his wife and daughters, by every poufy-haired televangelist ripping off old women and corn-fed idiots like you. Everyone says it because no one can gainsay them."

She sat up straight, wagged her head, and said, "Oh, all you have to do is say, 'Oh, Oh, God told me to do this, or God told me to do that,' and 'pfffft', you have carte blanche to do what you want. Who can say that God did *not* talk to you?" She stood up and shook the umbrella at him. "That's a miserable way to live. You should be ashamed of yourself, and I should pity you, but I think you and your kind are *disgusting*." She vomited the word at him, yanked her bag up to her shoulder and strode away, but then suddenly stopped and turned back to him. She stretched out a long arm at him, curved her hand backward, and poked her finger into the front of her gray fleece pullover and shouted at him. "*I say it*," she yelled, standing up straight, throwing her shoulders back, her headscarf whipping in the wind. "*I* say that it is *not* God talking to you. *I* say that you are delusional—at best—but more probably a brutal, power-hungry scum who cannot generate in others the respect you crave, so you roam around saying God speaks to you. *There is no God!* Do you hear me? Is this making it through your Cro-Magnon skull?" She lowered the umbrella and lifted her free hand up to the sky and shook her fist at the gray clouds, the rain now spattering her face. "There is no God!" she shouted, then again: "There is no God!" She looked back at him. "And you ... you are a complete idiot," she said, and turned and walked away, her bag over her shoulder, her feet making small splashes in the uneven concrete of the walkway, the umbrella collapsed, dragging in the grass.

***

Sitting in *L'Escapade*, Marcus recalled that last conversation with Marie-Clémence Saffron, remembering her shouting at God that He didn't exist. He wondered why a Muslim woman would say such a thing, and then he wondered if she knew he'd been assigned to her thesis group. He brought himself back to the present, watching Ramsay and Christienne huddled with their heads close together.

"Why did Professor Gruniére assign you two to the same working group? How did that happen?"

Ramsay looked up and said, as though talking to a child, "Why, Marcus, for two reasons: one, because she is not blind, and two, because she is French," as though that explained everything. Christienne laughed gaily and Ramsay took her hand and kissed it gallantly. Two large men watched Ramsay carefully from across the restaurant, and Marcus remembered that they were Christienne's bodyguards. As the granddaughter of the ninth richest man in the world, they went everywhere with her.

"Well then, why would she put Saffron in with us? I mean, knowing I'm in the group as well." Marcus countered.

Christienne, giggling, controlled herself just long enough to say in her delightful Swiss-German accent, "Because she is not blind, and because she is French, my dear!" She and Ramsay both crumpled with laughter. As Christienne's jibe landed, Marie-Clémence arrived at the entrance to the restaurant.

She stopped in the doorway when she made out Marcus at the table, and hesitated, one thin, delicate hand poised on the shoulder strap of her stylish messenger bag. He could tell she was trying to decide whether to demand a reassignment or put up with him in her thesis group. Marcus had a flushing thought that after all that he'd been through, all the combat, the risk, the danger, the demonstration of what God could and did do, he really shouldn't be worried about the opinion of one rabid female Muslim. And with that thought came a relief, a letting go of anxiety. He would just take her as she was and not worry about her misconceptions. He said a quick prayer for her. The thought came to him that after facing down a raging group of mullahs thirsting for his blood, this woman wasn't all that much of a threat. The comparison gave him some perspective, and in so doing, disarmed her ability to bother him—he hoped.

After a long few moments, Saffron made her way to their table and took the last chair. Marcus stood as she approached, although Ramsay did not.

"Do they stand for royalty in America?" Marie-Clémence asked innocently to no one in particular. Marcus said nothing, distancing himself emotionally. She went on immediately. "See, I told you, you Christians, you can't even engage in witty, harmless banter. You have no conversation unless it has to do with sending money to a church or the latest fantasy football results. And that reminds me of something else—you Christians have the sense of humor of a five-year old. Why do you always have to be so juvenile?"

Christienne chipped in with a smile expressing droll humor. "Marie-Clémence dear, you must not start in so quickly on Marcus. What will you do later in the evening after we finish discussing our thesis topic?" She laughed softly at Marcus' discomfiture. Christienne, tall, blond, sparklingly beautiful, never worried about how she might make others feel. So far Ramsay hadn't figured that out.

"If I must, I must," Saffron replied, tossing her head. She had long black hair, and she'd worn it down for some reason, though braided. Normally it was always up, and always in a headscarf.

The waiter arrived, arrayed in a white shirt, black pants, and a white apron over his waist hanging down to his knees, dripping Gallic charm. "A latté," Saffron said, "and this." She pointed to an item on the menu. The waiter bent over to look. "*Oui, Madame*, superb, the foie gras, excellent. With toasts?"

"*Mais biên sur*," Marie-Clémence replied. "And bring a bottle of champagne. It is not every day one gets assigned to a very important project with ..." she pursed her lips with disdain and shot a dark look at Marcus, "such professional colleagues."

The sarcasm flew over the waiter's head and he bowed and said, "Very good, Madame," took up her menu, and disappeared.

"So what should the subject be?" Ramsay asked after the waiter had cleared the last of the dinner plates. They were left with smaller plates on which there were crusts of bread, a smear of Brie, a stranded pickle. A third bottle of champagne stood half empty. Large glass bottles of water stood on the table like stiff soldiers, some dead, some still charged.

"We could write about the resurgence of the Uzbek economy," Marie-Clémence put in, a little tipsy from too much champagne. She was the only one who'd been drinking steadily. Marcus sensed she was upset about something. Perhaps just being around him bothered her. She poured herself another glass, spilling some onto the table. Marcus watched as two customers sitting at another table glanced over at them, not able to ignore Marie-Clémence's rapidly deteriorating condition. They looked slightly offended.

"We could discuss how the reigning Prince of Liechtenstein has single-handedly saved his country economically, and in the process become one of the world's wealthiest heads of state," Christienne said.

"You're kidding," Ramsay replied, still holding her hand.

"I am not," Christienne answered with gravity, her nose slightly in the air. "I happen to have personal, first-hand knowledge of the entire story."

"What would the objective of the research be?" Marcus asked.

"Forget that," Marie-Clémence put in harshly. She slammed her champagne flute down onto the table. "What do you recommend, Mister not-suited-for-business American?" Her eyes, wandering around the room in an uncontrolled fashion just seconds ago, locked onto Marcus like lasers. The pale green eyes were wild and round, shot with redness. She's drunk, he thought.

"I think," he replied slowly, hoping to calm her down, "that we ought to study the affect private security companies are having on the world security situation, and how nations might integrate these private actors into the course of international events."

Marie-Clémence looked at him hard for a few seconds, which stretched into a minute. "I think," she said ... but they never did get to hear what she thought.

"Excuse me," said one of the customers who'd looked at them earlier with disdain, "but I see that the lady is a bit too much in her cups. May I be of assistance?" He had come over to their table and was standing close by, respectfully. He spoke with what seemed to Marcus to be almost a British accent, but yet it had the lilting cadence of a Pakistani or Indian.

This is strange, thought Marcus. Typically, French diners never interfered with one another, now matter how bad anyone's behavior was. There were two of them: the tall customer, a youngish man, broad in the shoulders and narrow at the waist, wore a white dress shirt under an overlarge brown corduroy sport jacket and black jeans. The shorter man, stocky, was dressed the same. Very fashionable, but strange, and Marcus couldn't recall seeing him in any of his classes. His friend also seemed to be in very good physical shape. Both had jet-black hair and the stylish male three-day old stubble.

Christienne's bodyguards stood, wondering why two strange men were approaching their charge, when Marie-Clémence did a strange thing. She turned, half stood, half-stumbled in her chair, and said something that sounded very much like Arabic, something Marcus couldn't understand but was undoubtedly laced with disdain. Marcus knew she was drunk but he didn't think she was so drunk as to insult a complete stranger ... in Arabic.

The shorter customer, standing there at first with his hands clasped respectfully in front of his thick waist, head bowed, suddenly looked up, snarled, and lashed out with a vicious backhand, striking Marie-Clémence forcefully across her forehead. Marcus was shocked by the look of hatred on the man's face. He hit her so hard she left her feet, flying backwards into another table, spilling chairs, bottles, and glasses everywhere, and collapsed on the floor. Marcus was on his feet in a flash, but as he stood he saw the tall customer reaching into his jacket. A pistol was in the man's hand, on its way out of a concealed shoulder holster. Ramsay and Christienne were still sitting, frozen, watching Marie-Clémence fall backwards. The pistol was up and Marcus had a quick impression that it was moving toward where Marie-Clémence was lying on the floor when Marcus' right hand, sweeping up toward the first assailant, snatched up the champagne bottle and in a fearfully quick move, smashed it down on the shooter's hand. The pistol dropped onto the table; the bottle shattered, with the neck and shards still in Marcus' hand.

From near the front of the restaurant, three loud cracks resounded, and Christienne's bodyguards fell, shot from someone behind them, just outside.

At the table, the shorter man drew back his fist to strike Marcus, but Marcus struck with snake-like quickness and backhanded the man across the face with the broken bottle, cutting him. The man yelled and his hands flew to his face, blood streaming. Marcus dropped the bottle and snatched up the pistol when out of the corner of his eye he saw two other men, similar in build, style, and attire, running from across the street toward the open door of the restaurant carrying automatic weapons. For some reason the fact that they both were wearing black jeans stuck in his mind. In a scintillating rush of intuition, he knew that he was in the middle of a planned assault and the two men running toward him were not his friends.

His attention was yanked back to the table when the first man, his gun hand disabled, pulled a knife from a pocket and slashed at Marcus. Christienne was screaming; Ramsay had bolted back from the table and was grabbing at his girlfriend, pulling her out of the line of danger. The knife was flowing toward him in a lethal arc; Marcus had no choice. He didn't need to move the barrel very far, and pulled the trigger. There was a blasting noise and a hole appeared in the attacker's chest, ruining the white dress shirt. Blood splattered against the bar. The man fell backward, choking, bellowing.

Patrons were screaming now, trying to get out of the restaurant. Three quick gunshots cut across his focus. Marcus recognized the distinctive sound of a G36 assault rifle on semi-automatic, and he saw Ramsay leap backwards and fall into the bar, then to the floor. Christienne was frozen, screaming, curled in a ball. Marcus saw one of the men coming into the restaurant standing under the awning at the door, holding an automatic weapon, pointing it at him. Marcus leveled the pistol and fired twice, hitting the man in the chest, then the head. The short man who had struck Marie-Clémence had wiped the blood from his face and, miraculously, even after being shot, was moving toward Christienne, a knife in his hand. Marcus shot him in the side of the chest again, and then finally in the head. The sound of the gunshots in the crowded little café was deafening. There was a stink of cordite and the fruity smell of splashed champagne everywhere. There were three dead men in the café when the fourth man, who had backed out of the doorway, leveled his weapon and sprayed rounds toward the back of the restaurant.

Marcus hit the floor, leaping to cover Marie-Clémence, who was still unconscious. The rain outside was now pelting down, splattering in the street like bullets. He looked at the gun in his hand for the first time. It was a Sig Sauer 9mm. He automatically ejected the magazine and counted the remaining rounds. He slammed the magazine back into the weapon. Something hit his left leg like a baseball bat, knocking it over against his right. He pushed Marie-Clémence's inert form behind him, interposing his body, shielding her from the incoming rounds. Something stuck him a glancing blow on the hip, stinging. It made him angry. He got up on his knees to sight more accurately at the shooter, but the man had ducked down behind the stone wall that made up the front of *L'Escapade*. He saw them trying to maneuver around to get to Christienne.

And then Marcus saw another car pull up just at the curb adjacent to the restaurant, and three more men got out. They all had automatic weapons, and they were not dressed like French policemen.

His leg hurt. He glanced over at Ramsay. The young Malaysian prince was splayed out on the floor, his head resting on the brass foot rail, a neat round red hole between his eyes, which were open and staring sightlessly at the slowly turning ceiling fan. Christienne was curled in a ball by his side, fortunately tucked behind the thick oak side of the bar, whimpering, shaking, terrified. Each time the shooter would fire rounds into the restaurant, she would scream.

There was an unopened bottle of anise on the floor in front of him. Some other customer must have left it as they dashed out of the place, trying to get away from the gunfire. He scrabbled around the floor, looking for one of the ashtrays that was on every table in every French restaurant, and found a book of matches. He found a cloth napkin, rolled it up, ripped open the bottle of Anise, and jammed the napkin down into the opening, struck a match, and lit the cloth napkin on fire. Rounds peppered the wall behind him. There was yelling in Arabic; the assailants were talking to each other. There was screaming out in the street. The shooter behind the stone wall, apparently goaded into action, stood up, stepped further into the restaurant, and put aimed fire at Marcus. Marcus, on one knee behind an upended table, fired back.

The shooter hit Marcus in the shoulder, knocking him backward. Marcus's round struck the shooter in the throat, the bullet going through soft flesh and then striking the base of the man's skull, killing him instantly. He dropped like a rag doll.

Marcus found himself up against the back wall of the restaurant. He wasn't feeling much pain; he knew he was in shock. The pain would come later. He was surprised to see that he was holding a bottle of Anise, in which someone had put a cloth napkin. The napkin was burning. He was confused.

The three men were getting ready to rush the restaurant. They were holding their fire; apparently they wanted to take Christienne alive. Marcus knew he couldn't hold off three of them. He was outnumbered and outgunned. The cloth napkin was smoking. The smoke stung his eyes.

"Throw it," he heard someone say. Time was compressing. He looked around casually, taking what seemed to him forever. No one was close by.

"Throw it now, toward the front door," he heard. There was no one nearby, but the voice was compelling. Marcus threw the bottle toward the door to the restaurant.

The bottle hit the ground, shattered, and flames leapt up. Before the Anise burned away, flames spread to the curtains on the door and by the doorway. Black smoke billowed out of the entrance. The smoke kept the three men from putting aimed fire onto Marcus' position. They were gathering to rush him through the smoke when Christienne screamed again.

Marcus was getting very angry but his body was not following his commands. He thought he heard the ridiculous wailing of a European police siren—"bee ooo, bee ooo." The killers outside the restaurant were yelling at each other. They were not happy. Marcus realized he had spoiled their plans. But they weren't giving up.

A hole parted in the wall of smoke, slit by a waft of rainy wind. A shooter stepped through it. He was massive. He had a huge chest, thick arms, with almost no neck. He had a ski mask on, black jeans, and a black leather jacket. His rifle was up. Marcus saw him look toward Ramsay, and as Christienne screamed again, the man's eyes, moving over Marcus' inert form, darted toward the sound. The muzzle of the G36 moved away from Marcus toward the screaming woman. The shooter must have thought Marcus was dead. Then the man saw Marie-Clémence, lying under Marcus' legs. She was trying to get up, groaning. The man turned back, lifted his rifle, aimed it directly at Marie-Clémence 's struggling form, and Marcus shot him in the chest. He staggered, went to his knees, tried to bring his rifle to bear. Marcus' eyes blurred from the smoke. The shooter, gurgling on his knees, aimed at Marcus and pulled the trigger. Missing Marcus, he hit Marie-Clémence. She jerked and lay still at Marcus' feet. A spray of blood spattered across Marcus' face.

He wiped it, cleared his eyes, and shot the dying assailant in the forehead. The man's head snapped back, his rifle flew out of his hands, and he fell backward.

The rifle hit Marcus' left foot. He tried to drag it closer using his left foot, but his left leg wasn't responding. He leaned forward. There was a fiery pain in his shoulder, but he reached the rifle—a very expensive assault weapon common to European law enforcement agencies. He checked the rifle's magazine. Lots of rounds ... good; he couldn't count very well, but he could see it still had lots of rounds. He jammed the magazine back into the weapon. The smoke was really beginning to sting his eyes. He shook his head to clear his vision and when he looked up, two men were coming through the smoky doorway, rifles up, pointing at Christienne cowering under the oak bar. They couldn't see Marcus, down on the floor up against the wall behind an upended table, but he could see them. He propped the rifle up on the table's edge with one hand, ignored the pain in his left shoulder, and squeezed the trigger.

The table exploded in front of him and something kicked him in the chest. He flew backward, struck his head on the wall, and then there was darkness.

Chapter 12

Marcus

"But for you who fear My name, the sun of righteousness will rise with healing in its wings; and you will go forth and skip about like calves from the stall."

Malachi 4:2

There was a voice. "*Merde*, Patrice, you idiot, this is a crime scene. Leave it lay, and don't touch anything else."

"Yes, Chief Inspector."

"Leave the cartridges alone. Don't step in the blood."

"Yes, Chief Inspector."

Darkness, silence again.

***

There was a light; bright, piercing, shining into his eyes.

"This one is alive, Chief Inspector."

Marcus opened his eyes. There was a face over him, with a male-model stubble over a dirty white shirt. Marcus remembered the men he fought, and his eyes widened.

"No, no, it's good, no problem," he heard—English, with a thick French accent. "We are the police." He must have seen Marcus' eyes relax. "*Merde*, you left us a mess, Monsieur," he replied. "What did they want?"

Marcus lifted his head and turned to look to his right. The younger policeman was bending over Marie-Clémence. He put a finger on her throat. "I cannot tell about this one, Chief Inspector."

Marcus heard the Chief Inspector curse under his breath, and he opened his mouth to say something, but the Chief Inspector put a pencil over his lips. "Do not exert yourself," he replied. "Sorry I asked."

Marcus lay back, staring at the ceiling fan, which, inexplicably, was still turning its lazy circles, blowing stuffy, humid French air into the blood-drenched café. It was still raining.

"Hey, hey, look at me, do not go to sleep," the Chief Inspector said. The pencil waved before Marcus' eyes and then was tapping him on the forehead. "Listen. We are going to take you to hospital, do you understand? You have some holes in you, and there is part of a table sticking out of your chest."

Marcus tilted his head toward Marie-Clémence. The Chief Inspector seemed to know what he was asking.

"Yes, she is coming also. She is not well; we are not sure she will make it. And I am sorry about your friend, the Malaysian. No one can do anything for him now. I am afraid his girlfriend is not in good shape. Not as bad as you—at least she doesn't have any bullet holes in her, and she is alive and still here—but she isn't thinking very clearly." He tapped the side of his head with his pencil. "She's coming with us to hospital." The Chief Inspector stood up, putting the pencil in a shirt pocket. "Patrice, get the video from the back room. Do it now."

"Yes, Chief Inspector."

The French policeman looked down at Marcus. "Do you want us to call anyone for you?"

But Marcus was already out.

***

The noise of the ambulance siren woke him. He jerked, but didn't move very far; straps held him down. "*Merde*, Monsieur, you must not move. You have a bullet very close to your liver. Do you understand? Stay still!" The paramedic pushed his head back down onto the gurney, the pain arrived, and Marcus went out again.

He was at home in Granite Sky, playing football with his father and younger brother. He heard his mother laughing, and then he was on the sidelines in a huge stadium with the crowd roaring and his teammates were running out onto the field, but he was trying to find his shoes ... he couldn't find his shoes, then he found his shoes but lost his helmet. He couldn't go out on the field without his helmet. He was desperate, and grieved, because he wasn't ready. "He's not prepped," the coach said. "You're not prepped," his teammates said. "You're not prepped," the referee said. They all turned away and faced the field, and he knew the game would go on without him. It was the worst fear of his life.

"You're prepped, Marcus, you are ready to play. Don't listen to those fools. But these people here, they must take you into surgery, do you understand? Here are your helmet and shoes." It was his mother, speaking to him in French, standing next to him on the sidelines, holding his helmet and shoes and pointing to a group of strangers dressed in sheets. He wondered what she was doing there, and why the strangers weren't in uniform.

"Can you hear me, Monsieur Ironbridge? Do you understand?" It was a feminine voice, French, soft, sibilant, soothing but urgent. His mother's voice, but not ... it was melding now, running together. "He's still out."

"Take him now; not much time. Start the IV."

The nurse told Marcus to count backward from ten, but he never heard a word she said.

***

He smelled flowers. His nose wrinkled, and then it itched. He tried to scratch it but he couldn't move his arms.

There was that feminine French voice again.

"Good evening, Monsieur Ironbridge. We are glad you are with us."

Marcus tried to turn his head and focus his eyes, but all he could see was a blue blurry form. It moved toward him, and he felt his head lifted slightly.

"You are going to be thirsty. Here, drink this." He felt a straw in his mouth and he sucked on it. The tepid water coursed into his throat, and he sucked harder. It took a monumental effort to just keep his head up.

"Lay back now, Monsieur Ironbridge."

"Hospital?" he said, or tried to. His voice was cracked, dry, brittle.

"Yes, yes, you are in hospital," the nurse replied. "And a very nice one it is, too. But you cannot stay, I am sorry to say. You must leave us soon."

Marcus raised his eyebrows. She caught the question mark in his eyes. "No, do not worry, there will be a man come in to explain it all. He will be in with you in in a few hours. You must get some rest now."

Marcus felt he could listen to this woman speak French for the rest of his life, and then realized he was probably heavily drugged, with zero ability to clearly discern anything. He was beginning to ... wonder where ... true ... place ... his ... was ...

***

There was a tapping sound. It sounded strangely familiar.

"Hey ... are you awake yet? Let's go, I don't have all day."

Marcus felt a tapping on his forehead. He opened his eyes, saw the yellow blur of a pencil in a man's hand. He looked out to see the same three-day male-model stubble, the same dirty white shirt: the Chief Inspector.

"Good, you are awake. Can you understand what I am saying to you? Do you speak French well enough? What am I saying, of course you do, you are halfway through INSEAD and they obviously have not thrown you out. Maybe they should have, you wouldn't have been in that café." The Chief Inspector stopped waving the pencil in front of Marcus' face. "But too bad, those bad men in black jeans have brought your INSEAD education to an abrupt termination," he said. "You will not be finishing your classes this semester."

"That bad?" Marcus asked weakly.

"Yes, that bad. Even though I saw on the video how part of the table ended up in your chest, it is still hard to believe. But you are young and strong and you will pull through. The bullet near your liver caused them the most difficulty."

"Saffron?" Marcus asked, wondering whether Marie-Clémence was still alive.

The Chief Inspector shook his head. "Tough woman, that. No one thought she would make it. Did you know the scum hit her in the head? Well, yes, I guess you did know, they wiped some of her blood off your face. From the video it looks like he was aiming at you and missed. Yes, they shot her in the head, and the bullet went right here," and the Chief Inspector reached a hand behind his head and indicated a line from the back of his head, upward, sort of coursing along just the outside of his skull. "Left quite a furrow, but the doctors tell me it never got into the brain." The Chief Inspector tapped his own skull with his pencil. "Tough thing, the human skull," he said, ruminating absently, "and too, she is a woman." The Chief Inspector leaned back, pushed the curtains aside, and stared out the window of Marcus' hotel room. "Ah, but she does have quite a furrow, did I tell you? And she still has not come out of her coma. The round may not have pierced the skull but it certainly did give her a few things to think about. She has, how do you Americans say, not jumped from the forest yet."

Marcus nodded. "Thanks."

"No need, no need," the Chief Inspector growled, turning back to the bed. Though he was a youngish-looking man, he had a deep, gravelly, smoker's voice. Marcus saw his fingers twitching, and looked up above the door to his room, saw the 'No Smoking' sign. It explained the twitch. "We didn't do anything except arrive too late, and clean up your mess." The Chief Inspector stopped playing with the pencil and grasped Marcus' forearm just below where the IV was taped. He lowered his voice. "We watched the video, Monsieur Ironbridge. What, you didn't know? Yes, the owner had several closed circuit television cameras up in the corners of the ceiling, you know. Every French restaurant has them, to catch the thieves who never tire of breaking in, like stupid rats who break into a trap that has already caught their brothers, sisters, fathers, and mothers. But ... yes, yes, we saw the whole thing. Like a wild west shooting film."

"Not like that at all," Marcus said, eyes full of pain ... for Ramsay, for Marie-Clémence, for Christienne. "What about Christienne?" he asked.

"She is ... she is *heavily* sedated," the Chief Inspector replied. "And yes, you are correct, it was nothing like a movie. I am sorry for the allusion."

"Not a problem," Marcus replied.

"I am not going to dance around things, Monsieur Ironbridge. What we saw on the film ... if the owner had not had that film, we would not have believed whatever story you would have told us, if you ever stayed awake long enough to give us a statement, and we would most certainly have arrested you after you finished your time in hospital for having a weapon on French soil. But, as I said, the video shows that the weapons—the pistol or any of the assault rifles—were not yours, but you did make very good use of them. On behalf of the French government, I have been directed to extend our formal thanks and appreciation for eliminating dangerous criminals and foiling a diabolical kidnapping plot."

"Thought as much," Marcus said, throat raw. "They put down her bodyguards?"

"Unfortunately yes," the Chief Inspector replied. "Both dead."

"I'm ... I'm sorry."

"Do not be ... you were quite effective. You killed six men in a café, men with automatic weapons. You started with nothing."

"A champagne bottle," Marcus corrected, staring now out of the open window. "There was a champagne bottle."

"Yes, I stand corrected, and now I remember from the video. Very quick," the Chief Inspector said slowly.

"What now?" Marcus asked.

"We are going to move you."

Marcus stared at him questioningly. "I cannot tell you why, but I can tell you that it will be explained to you when you get where you are going. I *can* tell you, though, that a very rich man has taken an interest in your case and he is transporting you, Marie-Clémence, and Christienne to his private medical facility. Trust me, Monsieur Ironbridge, there is no better facility in Europe, nor probably in the world. You are still not out of danger yet, and Ms. Saffron is still on the edge ... further out on the edge than you, unfortunately."

"Who ... who's the guy? And why is he so interested in three business school students?" Marcus asked.

"Why, it is Christienne's grandfather," the Chief Inspector replied.

"I don't know him."

"No, you don't know him, but you have *heard* of him," the Chief Inspector grumbled, holding up his pencil like a lecturing professor. "He is the current reigning Prince of Liechtenstein."

***

The French government arranged to have the three of them transported by TGV, the high-speed train that was the poster program for modern transportation in Europe. They modified a car to accept hospital beds. They brought Christienne up first, still sedated. They were careful with Marcus, rolling the hospital bed up on a special ramp, and they were extremely careful with Saffron, still in a coma.

The Chief Inspector was standing by the railway car ramp as Marcus was loaded. "*Bonne journée*," he said, one hand in a pocket of a tan overcoat, a cigarette jutting out of his mouth, the stubble even darker. It was very early in the morning and there were few passengers about. He held up a hand and the paramedics rolling the gurney stopped. "I want you to meet a Monsieur De Vette," he rasped. The Chief Inspector tilted his head, indicating a very tall, rangy, broad-shouldered man in blue jeans standing next to him, swimming in a huge faded olive green trench coat over a Springbok's rugby jersey, wearing wrap-around sunglasses, which Marcus recognized as ballistic eye protection. The man nodded wordlessly.

"Be nice to him. The men in the restaurant, guarding Christienne ... they were his friends. He is not a man you want to make angry."

Marcus nodded slowly, eyeing the big man, who was surveying the station platform like a hawk.

"The man who you will be ... visiting ... has engaged Monsieur De Vette and a number of his colleagues to see that you arrive safely. You may be at rest, Monsieur Ironbridge. They are quite capable. And they know what you did to the men who killed their friends. I was directed to tell you that they wish you to know that they are ... grateful."

Marcus reached up a hand to the Chief Inspector. "Want to thank you, Chief Inspector," he said, looking directly at the French policeman. "I never did get your name."

The Chief Inspector took the cigarette out of his mouth, crushed it into the ground with his foot, and casually extended his hand to Marcus. It was a firm grip with a strength that conveyed more feeling than it appeared he wanted others to see. The Chief Inspector bent over the gurney, put his head close to Marcus' ear, and said, in accented English, "Jean-Patrique, and I am not a Chief Inspector; the role is, how do you say in English, 'handy' at times. Ms. Levinson, or, my apologies, you know her as Ms. Saffron ... she works for us; 'worked' for us, I should say. I do not think she will be returning to service."

"Who is 'us'?" Marcus asked.

"Ah, well, she will tell you that in good time ... if she lives. If she does wake up, tell her Jean-Patrique said 'well done.' Now, off you go. *Bonne journée*."

They put the patients to sleep on the train and Marcus woke up when they were wheeling him out. De Vette saw him come around.

"We are in Zurich," he said, with a thick South African accent, a large brown hand on one side of the gurney. "We go to the airfield."

They were loaded into more ambulances. De Vette got into the front seat of the ambulance carrying Marcus; one more behind them carried Saffron, while Christienne was wheeled into what Marcus recognized as a B6 armored SUV. Other men who looked a lot like De Vette—large, determined, professional, brooking no interference—filed into each of the vehicles. Another B6 took up station in front of Marcus' ambulance and the motorcade headed off at a clipped pace toward Zurich airport.

After ten minutes or so there was a short cricket chirp emanating from De Vette's pocket, and he put a cell phone to his ear. There was a brief exchange in a language Marcus presumed was Afrikaans. De Vette finished the conversation and tilted his head slightly toward the back of the ambulance, keeping his eyes on the road in front of him.

"The woman ... she has come out of her coma," he said.

Marcus, overcome by the motion of the car and residuals from pain medication, was already asleep.

***

He woke up again, not knowing where he was. The walls were lined with what looked like a white ceramic material. He focused his eyes and saw an IV stand hanging to his right. He checked his arm and confirmed the IV was still there. Thirsty ... he was thirsty. Maybe that's why he woke up. The meds were leaving a bad taste in his mouth. The strange thought occurred to him that he couldn't recall the number of firefights and engagements he'd gone through in Afghanistan—at least two or three a week—without a scratch, and then here he ends up flat on his back after a bar fight. Didn't seem right.

The ceiling was white, with what looked like old wooden beams stained a dark brown. He smelled ... he didn't know what it was exactly, but it seemed to him something like old stones, or leaves in a forest.

"It is a very old room," a voice said. He looked to his left. There was a man sitting in a chair in the corner of the room. He looked to be in his mid-60's, maybe early 70's, very distinguished, with close-cropped gray hair and a handsome, fine-featured face, pale blue eyes, wearing a dark gray suit, white shirt, and a red tie. He seemed tired, or preoccupied, or somewhat sad. His hands were clasped in front of him, and in the midst of his preoccupation he looked serene, one leg crossed over the other, ankle on a knee. A very large man wearing clear ballistic protection was standing off to one side, hands clasped respectfully in front of him.

"Herr Ironbridge," the man said, and then gave a slight nod toward the larger man up against the wall. "Please meet Freddy."

Marcus took in the security guard. Out of the same mold as De Vette, he was wearing a similar oversized olive-green trench coat, a casual knit polo shirt, and what looked like tactical cargo pants with a crease in them. "Freddy," Marcus said, nodding to the guy—he was extremely large and very intimidating.

"Sir." Clipped accent, just like De Vette—also South African.

"How are you feeling?" the older man asked.

Marcus gazed around the room, trying to get his bearings, and then he remembered the trip. "Liechtenstein?" Marcus asked.

The man nodded slowly and spread out one hand in a panoramic gesture. "Welcome to Edelschloss," he replied. "This is my home. You happen to be ensconced in a guest bedroom once reserved for Kaiser Wilhelm, did you know? He was a distant relative."

"Thanks," Marcus replied, taking in the stone walls, the incredible view of mountains and valleys stretching into the distance. It was very different than Paris.

The Head of State of the Principality of Liechtenstein laughed slightly. "Well, I can understand your confusion." He spoke softly, and his English was tinged with a slight German accent.

"Why am I here, sir?" Marcus asked.

The Prince rose and walked closer to Marcus' hospital bed and put his hands on the railing. "My name is Rainer; Rainer Christian Zeck the Fourth, to be precise. I understand you would have questions about why you are here, Mr. Ironbridge. I have been authorized to tell you that you are here because the French Intelligence service is indebted to you. This is all I can say at the moment."

"Ah," Marcus said, comprehension dawning. "Ms. Saffron?"

"Yes, precisely. In the process of saving my granddaughter's life, you also secured the life of one of their younger agents, one operating undercover at Insead, looking for Muslim networks."

"The kidnappers?"

"Pakistani, actually, and yes, of course, Muslims. Interpol is tracking things down, but they were apparently very well-paid."

Marcus looked at the man, still hazy from medication. "Is Christienne okay?"

"Oh yes. She is not completely recovered, but she is in much better condition than you or your fellow combatant," he paused for dramatic effect, "the DGSI[9] agent."

"Saffron?"

"Correct, Mr. Ironbridge. Ms. Saffron is not from Uzbekistan, nor is she Muslim. Our mutual friend, the Chief Inspector, told me you would eventually come to this conclusion."

"Jean-Patrique?"

"He is not actually a Chief Inspector," Zeck answered.

"Yeah ... yes sir, he did tell me that. Is Saffron still alive?" Marcus asked.

"She is ... barely ... but the French do not want the world to know that she survived. They are humane about things like that, you know, unlike some of the other intelligence services with whom I have had dealings. Sad, actually," he said, and appeared to remember something that gave him pain. Then he came back to the present. "She will most certainly not be of any use to them after this," he said. "Your pictures were plastered over every French newspaper, and the restaurant owner, unfortunately, had backup copies of the video which Jean-Patrique seized, and the owner sold them to Le Monde, who of course put them all over the Internet for the world to see. While one cannot make out Ramsay or, thankfully, Christienne in the video, there was a full-face shot of Ms. Saffron, standing at the table just before she was struck, angrily confronting her two attackers. And you are there as well, clearly visible, hiding behind a table, pointing an automatic weapon at three assailants."

"She was insulting the two men who first came to the table, I think," Marcus said. "And I'm pretty sure she was speaking Arabic."

"She was. We've had the video analyzed. She must have been quite drunk, to give herself away like that," Zeck said quietly.

"Perhaps ... or perhaps she thought she wasn't going to survive and wanted to let them know exactly what she thought of them."

"Also a possibility," the Prince replied.

"Sir, is she ... is she conscious?"

"She is, but she is not yet cognizant. And please, do call me Rainer."

Marcus glanced at the distinguished older man, a Head of State, a Prince, and someone who was, apparently, footing his medical bills. "With all due respect, sir, that's not gonna happen."

His Serene Highness Rainer Christian Zeck the Fourth chuckled slightly, his eyes crinkling with amusement. "Ah well ... you did save my granddaughter's life, Mr.

9 *Direction générale de la sécurité intérieure,* the General Directorate for Internal Security.

Ironbridge, something for which I extend my deepest thanks. Her parents will be along shortly to also express their grateful appreciation." The reigning Prince of Liechtenstein extended his hand, and Marcus pushed himself up on one elbow and grasped it as firmly as he could.

"You are quite welcome, sir." Marcus leaned back and wondered out loud. "So Saffron is still alive? Jean-Patrique said they shot her in the head. And you say she works for the DGSI?" The Prince nodded.

"She did have a pretty hard head," Marcus mused, not entirely to himself.

"Apparently so," the Prince replied diplomatically. "Permit me to suggest that you take some rest now, Marcus ... if I may call you Marcus? I would ask that you permit my personal physician to give you a brief on a few further medical exigencies."

"Forgive me for asking, sir, but why would the DGSI think to involve you in this," Marcus asked directly.

The Prince was thoughtful for a few moments, and the tinge of preoccupation or sadness appeared again. "Ah, well, there may be things we might need to speak about at a later time. My suspicion is that this was just a coincidence. A happy coincidence, in some ways, for Christienne and the Zeck family, in that you were there to save her from God knows what. Unhappily, Ramsay lost his life. And Ms. Levinson— Marie-Clémence, as you know her—was also, unhappily, there by chance."

Zeck turned and was about to leave when he stopped and faced Marcus. "We have done some checking, Mr.— Marcus. The DGSI is not without its sources here and there. They have heard an interesting story about something that happened in the Korengal, in Afghanistan, many years ago, but they were unclear about the details." The Prince waited, clearly inviting Marcus to provide those details.

Marcus was silent for a long moment. "As you said, sir, we have some things to talk about."

The Prince of Liechtenstein nodded and withdrew. As he opened a door in one of the white ceramic walls, an older man came in wearing doctor's scrubs. "Your highness," he said, bowing slightly. He actually clicked his heels together.

"Herr Professor Doktor Kronzplatz. Good of you to look in on our patient."

"Thank you, your highness." Kronzplatz was a tall man, cadaverously thin, with leathery skin and eyes almost completely occluded by a profuse thatch of gray-haired eyebrows. The reigning Prince of Liechtenstein left the room, closing the door quietly.

The doctor approached a transparent touchscreen monitor suspended on a temporary frame and began to call up files. Turning to Marcus, said in slow, determined, meticulously annunciated words, in German-accented English, "May I give you a summary of your treatment to date, Herr Ironbridge?"

"I have no other appointments this morning," Marcus replied, attempting a smile.

"That is good," the doctor replied, devoid of any humor, "for you would not survive them. Now ... your artifacts." He pronounced each symbol of that last word as though they were critically important. A short woman in scrubs, whom Marcus presumed was a nurse, entered the room behind him with a sheaf of films and records. The doctor nodded wordlessly and removed a small gold-rimmed pair of reading glasses from the tweed vest pocket under his white smock; the nurse bobbed her head respectfully and handed Kronzplatz the materials with a deeply respectful, "Herr Professor Doktor."

Kronzplatz removed the first set, an array of x-rays, and waved them under the bottom edge of the monitor's frame. The x-rays showed up on the monitor. Marcus hadn't been in a hospital for more than a decade, but he didn't think American hospitals had this kind of technology.

"We have a Caucasian male, 40 years of age, approximately 1.9 meters in height, at this time approximately 88 kilos," the doctor began, reciting as if he was in front of a classroom. He turned to Marcus. "You would prefer English units, Herr Ironbridge? Yes, of course," he answered himself without waiting for Marcus to reply. "You are slightly over six feet and two inches, and at the moment you are weighing about 195 pounds. Further distinguishing marks, let me see." The doctor paused, swiped a file across the screen, looking obviously for Marcus' medical history. "Yes, here we are. Blue eyes, black hair, a scar above the left eye, another along the left cheek." The doctor paused, glanced at Marcus, and continued his recitation. "Note that these are barely noticeable."

"A German surgeon in the emergency room doing loco tenens put thirteen stitches in my face about twelve years ago," Marcus said. "Bitten by a dog. He was very good. The surgeon, I mean, not the dog."

The doctor appraised Marcus' face clinically, a finger pressing the skin of his cheek, trying to discern where the surgeon had stitched up Marcus from lip to just under his left eye, ignoring Marcus' attempt at humor. "Quite," the doctor replied drily. "We will do at least as well, however," he answered in a detached manner. He continued dictating for a recording of the visit. "There is above-average musculature for men of this demographic group. The patient appears in excellent physical condition, other than the current injuries. Upon arrival at emergency facilities in France, the patient presented with a portion of a table embedded in his person, a gunshot wound to the shoulder that shattered the scapula, a perforated liver, apparently from a bullet or a fragment of some type, and a gunshot wound to the left leg. Surgical treatment addressed the criticality of the liver. Further work is required for the other injuries. There are no other visible signs of additional trauma at this juncture. The patient appears to be awake, of a reasonable disposition, and, other than the normal dislocation occasioned by the trauma, not unduly concerned about his condition."

The doctor turned to him with a dispassionate stare. "Would you say this is an accurate summary of your condition at the moment, Herr Ironbridge?"

"It is, sir."

"Then let us proceed." He touched the screen again, swiping more files until he found the one he wanted. "Ah, yes, here we are. Very interesting; you should know, Herr Ironbridge, that the liver is one of the most commonly injured organs in cases of adult abdominal trauma." He was tilting his head slightly backward so as to look through his glasses. "Thus, we have made advancements in imaging studies, and these, coupled with enhanced critical care monitoring strategies, have shifted paradigms for the management of liver injuries. In many cases, non-operative management of both low- and high-grade injuries can be successful in hemodynamically stable patients."

"What is a ... a 'hemodynamically stable' patient?" Marcus asked.

Dr. Kronzplatz removed his glasses and looked down at him as though one of the chairs had spoken. The nurse looked reproachfully at Marcus for interrupting the doctor's recitation. The doctor cleared his throat and said, "Yes, well, your understanding would best be achieved by describing the antonym. The term 'hemodynamic *instability*' is most commonly associated with an abnormal or unstable blood pressure, especially hypotension. In such a case, hemodynamic instability is usually defined more broadly as global or regional perfusion that is not adequate to support normal organ function."

"Thank you, Doctor." The nurse darted another glance at Marcus, warning him not to even think about interrupting the esteemed Herr Professor Doktor Kronzplatz again, who pressed on with a distinguished swipe of the screen to call up what was apparently some type of technical depiction of his liver.

"Your hemodynamic presentation appeared to the initial treating physicians to be extremely *unstable*, you understand, hence their indications. Based on the initial description of the incident and my own analysis of bullet trajectories compared to a time-phased analysis of the sequence of events, I would tend to agree with their assessment. Your injury in this area," he continued, indicating a spot on the x-ray that to Marcus looked like every other white blurry spot on the x-ray, "was the most significant threat to continued organ viability. I was told the assailants used a Heckler and Koch G36 assault rifle, is this so?"

"That is correct, sir." No more humorous asides from Marcus.

"Yes, well, the G36 fires a 5.56 by 45 millimeter round via a gas-operated mechanism. The rifle holds 30 rounds, and can be fired semi-automatically, automatically, or on single shot. Its rate of fire is, let me see," he paused for a moment, stared away from the monitor into the distance, trying to remember, "ah, yes, approximately 750 rounds per minute. However, you, Herr Ironbridge, do not have a G36 round in your body at this point...at least in the proximity of your liver."

Marcus was a little surprised at that. He was pretty sure everyone was using G36 rifles. Maybe he'd missed something.

"No ... you have a *fragment* of a G36 round threatening your liver. One of the assailant's rounds struck something external to your corpus, shredded, and a fragment sliced into your body. Once through the musculature, it ripped a ten-centimeter gash in your liver. I would suspect the entry wound presented as a stinging sensation rather than the typical and more dynamic kinetic impact made by a solid round."

"I do recall that, sir," Marcus replied, surprised at the accuracy of the doctor's analysis. "You are exactly right."

The nurse shot Marcus another look, this time even more reproachful, even more distressed.

"Yes, quite," Dr. Kronzplatz replied drily. "In such cases, you should know that direct suture ligation of bleeding parenchymal vessels, total vascular isolation with repair of venous injuries, and the advent of damage control surgery have all improved outcomes in hemodynamically unstable patient populations. Therefore the French surgeons embarked upon this course of treatment since you, Herr Ironbridge, were, at the time of injury and definitely during your initial surgery, hemodynamically unstable."

"Yes sir," Marcus replied, checking the nurse in his peripheral vision.

"Anatomical resection of the liver and use of an atriocaval shunt are rarely indicated, and it appears the French surgeons rightly disdained this protocol. You should know, however," the doctor went on sonorously, "that at times operative intervention in high-grade injuries may result in high mortality rates. You were, at the time, not sufficiently conscious to make an informed decision regarding the advisability of surgical intervention, and therefore the surgeons did so for you."

Marcus decided not to reply, which was apparently the correct approach. "Introduction of computer tomography scan technology, the use of ultrasonography in trauma, and the availability of angiography, enhanced critical care monitoring, and damage control surgery have revolutionized the management of liver trauma, Herr Ironbridge." The doctor sounded as though he was giving a lecture in a classroom while analyzing the x-ray. "Numerous studies have shown better outcomes with conservative management. Though there is a broader consensus regarding the non-operative approach even in high-grade injuries, you should be aware that some controversies still exist." Kronzplatz removed his glasses, closed the file on the monitor, and turned to Marcus. "Even so, we shall apply conservative management protocols relative to your liver during your convalescence."

Marcus nodded. "Thank you," he said quietly.

"And now, the second issue," the doctor said, pulling another film from the sheaf and waving it under the monitor's frame. "This may not be perhaps quite the most interesting presentation I have observed in the past few years," Kronzplatz said, evincing the first shred of interest since he'd appeared. "Though I must say, Herr Ironbridge, how you managed to appear in my medical facility with the remains of ... of an *oaken table* embedded in your anatomy ... does certainly contend for that honor."

The nurse's eyebrows lifted under her surgical mask, and then contorted.

"Well, let us attend to this sinistro crure, shall we? Now then, you have endured a gunshot wound to the tibioperoneal trunk." The nurse looked warningly at Marcus, who remained silent. The doctor, however, caught her glance and, presuming Marcus had somehow interrupted again, looked over his gold-rims and pronounced with an excruciating display of tolerance, "The tibioperoneal trunk is a segment of artery below the knee, Herr Ironbridge, distal to the origin of the anterior tibial artery off the popliteal artery, and proximal to the branch point of the posterior tibial artery and the fibular artery. Though perhaps you are more accustomed to the term 'tibio-fibular trunk'. They are at times used interchangeably.'"

"Under here?" Marcus asked, pointing to where a spot behind his left knee which was still painful, throbbing, and swollen.

"Very good," the doctor said dryly, nodding with an exaggerated gesture, as if pronouncing a Mosaic blessing. The nurse tilted her head and made it vibrate slightly at Marcus behind the doctor's back, as if to warn Marcus about interacting with such a medical god.

"Your anatomical precision does you credit," Kronzplatz intoned slowly in precise English. Marcus couldn't tell if the gentleman was devoid of any sense of humor or was the world's driest wit.

"To continue," he went on, with a quick, disapproving glance over his gold rim spectacles at Marcus. Marcus smoothed the sheets over his legs. "You may have noticed that your leg is not returning to its normative functions with the same degree of rapidity as your other ... traumas," he said. "Would you consider this to be an accurate statement of the case?"

Marcus, not wanting to interrupt again, almost missed the question. "Yes sir," he said, quickly, as though answering an upper classman at the Naval Academy. It apparently mollified the doctor.

Kronzplatz rattled off a description of the medical condition of his left leg as though he was reading from printed notes, though Marcus could see that all he was looking at was the x-ray picture on the monitor of his leg. "As noted, an acute occlusion of the tibio-peroneal trunk due to gunshot wound injury is presented. Delineation of the injury was determined during wound exploration. The wounded vessel was resected and arterial reconstruction was achieved by contralateral non-reversed greater saphenous vein graft interposition pretreated with blind valvulotomy. A large venous tributary allowed a bifurcated graft to be constructed. This case describes the technique of bifurcated non-reversed venous grafting, which has not been reported in an acute trauma scenario." He finished and turned to Marcus. "Unfortunately, Herr Ironbridge, the French surgeons, being somewhat rushed due to their need to repair your liver and keep large slivers of a dining accouterment from entering your thoracic cavity, were not quite as attentive to this injury as I would have preferred. This is the reason it is not healing appropriately. Therefore, we shall embark upon a restorative surgical procedure that will more robustly repair the arterial structure behind your leg." He added as an afterthought. "With your consent, of course." The doctor paused and looked down at Marcus, waiting for Marcus to reply. The nurse looked around from behind the doctor, wondering what was taking Marcus so long. Suddenly Marcus discerned the reason for their looks.

Marcus wasn't going to be rushed about this, however. "How long will the recovery take?" he asked.

"An apropos question," Kronzplatz replied as generously as his manner would allow. "I expect it will be between four to six weeks before you will be capable of walking, and perhaps six months before you should consider any strenuous use of the leg. However," he went on, "after six months of proper post-operative care, I expect you will have full use of the appendage. Keep in mind that the arterial wall was apparently damaged perhaps to a degree beyond the point at which the procedure performed by the French would have had any chance of success. They did what they could, however," he said gracefully, "and here you are."

"Six weeks is a long time," he said.

"Your left scapula is shattered, Herr Ironbridge—a recitation to which I have not yet attended—and you will require at least that much time for it to be restored. Which, I should mention, is another surgery required here, for which we must obtain your permission." The nurse peeked around the doctor's gaunt form and looked reproachfully at Marcus, as though a requirement for permission to operate somehow impugned the great doctor's capabilities.

Marcus leaned back on the pillow. The recitation was sapping his strength, and talking about his leg made it hurt. Beads of perspiration appeared on his forehead, and he gritted his teeth against the onslaught of another wave of pain. He was refusing his pain meds now, frightened of coming anywhere close to an addiction. They'd told him that the French paramedics had popped him with several ampules of morphine at the scene, and the French doctors had put him on morphine during and after his first surgery. He was grateful at the time, but he wanted to be cautious. They'd told him that he had several punctures in his body, more than what would normally be considered acceptable if one wanted to remain healthy, and definitely enough such that pain medications were just not, at that point in the human condition, discretionary.

"The oaken table," the doctor pronounced, "was, truly, a first. Pictures of the initial presentation have been useful, however, in extending the body of knowledge regarding thoracic trauma."

"You could have gotten dozens of pictures like that from any emergency room in any American city. Typical bar fight injury," Marcus said, gasping slightly. He had to force the words out. The meds were definitely wearing off. He wasn't sure coming off them was such a good idea, especially with another surgery coming up.

"You are no doubt correct, Herr Ironbridge," the doctor replied, looking over his reading glasses, which gave the impression of looking down his nose at Marcus. "However, permit me to express a relatively high level of unfamiliarity with this type of injury. 'Bar fights', I believe you said, are somewhat uncommon in Liechtenstein. I believe we have no actual bars in Liechtenstein." He paused for a second, ruminating over this apparently amazing fact. "Is this not so, Frau Henzig?"

"You are quite correct, Herr Professor Doktor," Frau Henzig replied with awe.

Marcus could see Freddy, standing over against the wall with his hands still folded, try to suppress the tiniest crack in the stone edifice that was his impassive, granite countenance. Freddy had massive shoulders, barely-noticeable stubble on a head that looked like it was chiseled out of marble, and was wearing sunglasses. Inside. He was about the most intimidating guy Marcus had seen in a long while, and he'd seen some intimidating people.

South Africans, the DGSI, gunfights in cafés ... it was getting to be a little overwhelming, but then he remembered that nothing in his life had yet happened that did not have a specific purpose. While that thought calmed him, he still found himself wondering what God was doing, putting him in a castle in Liechtenstein, guarded by numerous South African security professionals, having saved the life of a hard-headed French intelligence agent.

Marcus put his head back on the pillow, wrestling with the pain. "Six months is a long time," he said tightly. "Not sure the clinic will put me up for that long."

"Oh, there is no fear of that, Mr. Ironbridge" the doctor replied. "No fear at all. His Highness has indicated that you can stay as long as you like—or as long as you need, whichever is longer."

Marcus was sweating freely now, panting quietly, one hand gripping the rail on his bed, the other bunching the blanket. "Okay ... right, okay ... I'll take your word for it, Doctor. Thanks."

The doctor nodded to Frau Henzig and then approached the hospital bed. "Herr Ironbridge, I am not unaware of your level of discomfort. If you consent to the surgical procedure to restore your sinistro crure—your left leg—we should begin at once."

Marcus turned his head; it was getting difficult to focus, the pain was blurring the edges of his vision. He grunted, shook his head, and his vision cleared. He sat up, pushing himself, wincing, trying to overcome the pain with physical effort. "You're saying what, the sooner the better?"

"Your leg will deteriorate rapidly. It will not repair itself on its own. I am a doctor, and I am very good at what I do. You do not wish to lose it, yes? You wish to walk again? And while I have not described the injury to your shoulder, I have indicated that it too will require extensive repair—surgical repair, and it too will not repair itself."

Things were happening too fast, and he wasn't able to think clearly.

"I see that I need to show you something," the doctor said. He stepped back from the bed and removed his white lab coat, handing it to Frau Henzig, whose eyes were large and dark and somewhat sad now. He then removed his tweed vest, laying it down at the foot of the bed, and then slowly unbuttoned his shirt. When it too was at the foot of Marcus' bed on top of the vest, the doctor turned around, showing Marcus his back.

"Look here," he said. Marcus saw thick, dark, reddish-colored lines crossing everywhere on the man's back, in a pattern Marcus could not make out. "Scars, yes. There was an incident at a school in Beslan, in North Ossetia. You may have heard of it. His Highness asked me to intervene, as a neutral. There were issues with a number of children, and there was a concern that perhaps field surgery might be needed." The doctor turned and began to put his shirt on. "The Chechens at first agreed to let me into the school. What, after all, does anyone have to fear from someone from Liechtenstein? We are neutrals, yes? And so they let me in. But somehow the Chechens discovered my real name—we had given them a false name, you realize—and so they let me in, but as I entered the large gymnasium, they laughed and crowded around and made sport of me for a time, and then shoved me into another room. There were men waiting there, men with whips made from barbed wire." The vest went on next, buttoned carefully. He saw Marcus' confused expression. "Kronzplatz," he said, pronouncing his name, "is a Jewish name. I am a Jew. The pattern you saw on my back is supposed to be the star of David ... at least, what one looks like when carved by drunken butchers wielding razor wire." He went on with the story. "When the first explosions happened, I was stretched out on a wire bed frame, and there were other injuries from the ceiling as it collapsed, which is perhaps why you could not make out the attempted decoration." Frau Henzig handed him the white lab coat, which he donned, smoothing it over the vest. Frau Henzig wiped her eyes. "So," he said, turning again to face Marcus, "I know a little of what you are afraid of ... the addiction, I mean. I know what you are concerned about, and you are right to worry." He approached the bed again and put his hand on Marcus' arm. "But we will be careful with these things," he said intently, "and we have developed a few interesting alternative pain medications here, the benefits of which are that they are much, much less addictive." The doctor stood to his full height and put both of his hands on the rail of the bed. "Come now, Herr Ironbridge, you must trust me, nothing is to be gained by waiting."

Marcus sensed that he was just a small chip of wood along for a ride in a turbulent river. He lay back again on the bed. Time to trust. Trust that God had put him here, trust that God had provided medical talent sufficient for his needs. He didn't have to know why, and he didn't have to know, at this point, what to do. Things, apparently, needed to follow their own course.

"Thank you, sir," he said, and held up a hand to the doctor, who clasped it firmly in his own. "I'm ready anytime."

"Good," the doctor said, nodding, slipping again into his professorial demeanor. "I believe the Americans have a saying, Frau Henzig," he began, looking at the nurse, who was standing next to the IV drip with a syringe. "No time like the present. Sleep well, Herr Ironbridge."

Chapter 13

Marie-Clémence

"Come to Me, all who are weary and heavy-laden, and I will give you rest."

Matthew 11:28

Light, small noises, hushed voice. "Miss, you should not be here, please you must rest."

"Not until he is awake."

"Oh, but Miss, the Herr Professor Doktor has ordered it. You must return to your room."

More voices, fluster, incoherence, conflict. Dark.

***

Smell: flowers, shampoo, clean, woman, perfume.

"Herr Ironbridge, good afternoon. Herr Professor Doktor wishes you to drink this now please, *Ja*?"

Straw in mouth, water, gel, fruit. Eyes open. Light, blurs. Tired. Sleep.

***

"Not until he is awake."

"You must sleep, Madam." More arguing, fussing, rebuttals, complaints of violating Herr Professor Doktor's orders.

"I'm awake." His voice, weak and scratchy though it was, caught the attention of the two women in the corner of his room. One was sitting on a couch, the other standing by its edge. The woman sitting down stood, leaning heavily on a walker. She made her way, awkwardly, toward Marcus' hospital bed. The other, Frau Henzig, was torn between hovering anxiously near the woman struggling to walk, and trying to find out how Marcus was feeling upon coming out of anesthesia.

"How are you feeling, Herr Ironbridge?" Frau Henzig asked, at the same time steadying the woman as she almost tipped over.

"I'll be fine, I can do this," the woman said, shrugging off Frau Henzig's support. Saffron's voice: Marcus tried to focus his vision. Tall, thinnish woman, dark hair; he couldn't see the eyes.

"I feel a little disoriented," Marcus replied deliberately, tentatively, "but hungry."

"*Ja*, that is normal, and that you are hungry, the Herr Professor Doktor will be pleased." The nurse addressed herself to Saffron. "You should not be up and about at this stage, Madam," Frau Henzig said in a tone of high umbrage at the woman violating the Herr Professor Doktor's orders as though she was violating one of the Ten Commandments.

"She has a very hard head, Frau Henzig," Marcus said. Frau Henzig said nothing, but Marcus thought he could hear her eyes rolling.

"Hard-headed is one thing, stupid is another," Marie-Clémence grumbled, struggling to make her legs work. "One guy with a champagne bottle against six guys with automatic weapons." This last she said, almost, to herself.

"Why all this trouble, Ms. Saffron?" Marcus asked, turning his head to watch her make her way to his bed.

"Because," she said, out of breath, working hard to sound dignified, "one cannot apologize properly from across a room." She finally pulled up next to Marcus' railing and grasped it first with one hand, then the other, and pulled herself up straighter. "Legs are not quite getting all the signals yet, but Kronzplatz says the wiring should uncross soon."

"Good to know. So ... now that you're here, what did you want me to apologize for?"

Marie-Clémence looked at him and frowned, hesitant. "Not you; me. I must apologize to you," she said, and then snapped, as though someone was compelling her behavior, "and remember this, because it won't happen often." There was a forced, almost artificial hardness. "No, that is not right," she said more softly, drawing back from that hard edge, her head tucking down into her chest. She looked up at him again. "I should not have said that. It was unkind. What I meant was ... I must apologize. I said some very ... very *hard* things when we spoke, in the quad, on the bench. Do you remember?" She looked up, hoping he hadn't, knowing he would, and he nodded, slowly, his head still unsteady. "Well, I said some very mean things. Untrue things. I watched the video, Mr. Ironbridge." She could not continue for some moments. A flash of anger, a tear, some long breaths, and then she was clearing her throat and staring up with some strength. "I see that I owe you my life, and I saw that the last thing you are is a coward."

"It's okay, Ms. Saffron."

"And I am sorry about the things that were said about your ... your faith."

"I understand; it's okay. You were playing a part. They explained to me about the DGSI."

She made a waving gesture with her hand, dismissing the role her handlers had played in her conduct. "I was playing at being a Muslim, that was part of my job, yes, I admit, but I must confess ... I must tell you that my feelings about your religion ... Christianity ... were not, I mean, I did not need to put on an act about that," she replied, somber but defiant. "I still believe it is an insipid religion for weak men and domineering women. You, perhaps, are an exception, but overall, it is what I believe, it is what I have seen; apologies must be honest, yes?"

"Yes, apologies are better when they're honest. I don't doubt that you've seen things to validate such an opinion." Marcus hesitated for a moment, not sure of what to say. "Look, Ms. Saffron, there are many different pictures and beliefs and opinions people have about Christianity. I'm sure that of the people who know you, each has a different opinion about who you are. Each has different perspectives about who you are, truly, and what you do, but there is only just one *you*. Your personality has many facets, but what if someone you cared about, someone you wanted to get to know better, heard you described by one of your worst enemies? Would they get an accurate picture of who you really were? Do you think they would want to get to know you after hearing your enemy describe your character and behavior from their perspectives?"

"Perhaps not," she replied, noncommittally.

"We can leave that for another time," Marcus said, not wanting to press. "But I hope you can see that some Christians might be more ready to face the lions than others." He was looking directly into her face, challenging the assertion she'd made, what seemed ages ago, about Christians and cowardice.

She would not look at him, staring down at her hands, trying to find her balance on legs that were still not working well. She had some kind of helmet on, and Marcus saw it was probably both to keep the bandages on her head wound fixed, and to protect her head from any impact. Walking around like she was, he understood the need for it.

"In my experience, Mr. Ironbridge, your actions were ... I don't know, let's just say they were not representative of what I have seen so far of Christianity. And I do not consider myself an enemy of God, either."

"I'm not surprised about what you've seen," he replied, "yet nonetheless, here you stand—more or less." She smiled, struggling to remain upright by his hospital bed.

"The jury remains uncommitted and admits to extreme prejudice toward a preconceived position," she said. "Yet counterarguments may be entertained," she went on, a grim smile on her face.

He could see her fingers were whitening with the strain of holding on to the bed rail. He shot a glance at Frau Henzig, who darted across the room and brought back a wheelchair. "Madam, please," she said, and Marie-Clémence gratefully released her grip on the bed and fell gracelessly into the chair. There was an electric whining sound, and then she was face-level with him.

"Thank you, Frau Henzig," she gasped. Marie-Clémence wiped a bead of perspiration from her forehead. "Don't know how much longer I could have held myself up there." Frau Henzig chose not to reproach the younger woman. "Amazing things they have here, you know?" she said, referring to the wheelchair, which, Marcus saw, was floating in the air on its own. "It conforms to me, and it goes where I tell it to go. I don't even have to wheel it about. Very advanced little principality, Liechtenstein." She maneuvered the chair around his bed as a demonstration.

"You could have come over in the chair and made your apology," he said.

"Wouldn't have meant as much."

"True," Marcus agreed. "In that way, apologies are like cancer surgery."

"How is that?" Marie-Clémence asked, whirring around, coming to a stable position off to his right.

Marcus lay back on the bed, the pain medications diminishing. He could feel the ache below his left knee. And there was some kind of sticking, putty-like substance on his left shoulder. He turned back to look at the woman sitting, or rather floating steadily, next to his bed.

"Both are painful, both require the removal of something that will not come out on its own, yet the removal of which is required to save your life. You felt instinctively that suffering was something that should be part of your apology, didn't you."

The woman didn't answer him right away. "What is removed with an apology?" Marie-Clémence asked, dodging his question, a drawn look on her face.

"Pride," Marcus replied softly. Her chair whirred slightly, compensating as she shifted her weight.

More silence, and then, grudgingly, "Well ... that may be. But this is not something one hears from business school students," she said, bantering again, though with less rancor than he remembered. "Is this another facet of Christianity—the emergence of an inscrutable sage persona?"

"The God of all creation is a wise God," Marcus said, shrugging slightly, "and one sign that His Son lives in us is that our lives reflect at least some of His wisdom."

Marie-Clémence sat in the chair and did not answer for a time. Frau Henzig had already left, trusting that Marie-Clémence would not get up out of the chair again. "As I said, Mr. Ironbridge, you are unique. But I have a rule not to form opinions about groups based upon experiences with singularities."

"One of the principles of Christianity is that the Spirit of God lives in us, guides us, directs us, and through us expresses Himself to others. You are not seeing a singularity. It should be the same in every real Christian."

"And yet, empirical evidence shouts the contrary," she stated baldly.

"Too true, sadly," Marcus answered.

"About this spirit thing living in a person ... I have never heard anything like that," she said, oddly, "and even if I had, I wouldn't have understood any of it." The hardness was creeping back into her voice, almost as if she was growing defensive. It made sense. People became defensive when confronted by things they couldn't understand.

Marcus, speaking gently, said, "Well, since I don't have anything else to do for the next six weeks or so, and, they tell me, you aren't going anywhere for a while either, permit me to spend some of that time helping you understand what that means, Ms. Saffron, and perhaps convincing the jury about the error of their preconceived position."

Her face twisted, and her features arranged themselves in a way Marcus could see reflected disgust. "Please, do not call me that."

"What?"

"That, that *name*. If we are going to speak about truth, then ... then do not use that name, please."

Saffron. Of course…it wasn't hers and she didn't like the tag following her from her previous assignment. "Ah, right, of course, I am sorry. It would not be yours, after all. Then what shall I call you, Miss?"

There was a long pause. "Marie-Clémence, I think." No last name ... yet. Not a surprise; the lady *did* work for the DGSI.

"Marie-Clémence. Okay, if you're good with Marcus."

She looked at him for a long second and then reached out from the chair and extended her hand. He awkwardly lifted his arm over the bed rail, trailing the IV line, and shook her hand. She wasn't smiling. "Marcus," she said. "I am not sure that it will be safe to know you."

"Good, but not safe," Marcus replied, smiling into her confusion. "Good, but not safe."

***

Ten days later, Marcus was able to sit up for hours at a stretch without too much fatigue. Herr Professor Doktor Kronzplatz had started him on physical therapy immediately, and his leg was healing 'acceptably' according to the Herr Professor Doktor. Marcus' left side was pretty much out of commission, the leg and shoulder both having taken rounds, and the liver damage, healing though it was, kept him constantly fighting low-grade pain. It was not a pleasant convalescence.

But there were bright spots. His parents had come, flown over by the reigning Prince, and his mother had fussed over him and his father's eyes misted with pride after he watched the video of Marcus fighting in *L'Escapade*. He shared with Marcus that he was having some 'interesting' discussions with the Prince; apparently the Prince's Catholicism was not as rock-solid as the Pope could wish it to be, and as the Prince aged, as the end of his life approached, he was beginning to face truths that no Catholic could ever successfully face, and fear was setting in. Tack encouraged Marcus to watch for an opening to share the truth. "A cat can look at a King," Tack quoted, "so then why can't a young warrior speak truth to a Prince?" Marcus promised he would remain alert.

What was truly surprising was the result of his mother's visit with Marie-Clémence. Apparently they had spent an entire afternoon together, Claire shooing Tack out of the room after Marie-Clémence had respectfully acknowledged her gratitude to Tack about Marcus' intervention. And after her talk with Marie-Clémence, her mother came and sat down with Marcus, asking Tack to leave them alone for a moment.

"Look, *Mon fils*, I must share something with you about this Marie-Clémence." His mother was uncharacteristically somber. Marcus sensed she was somewhat tentative, almost hesitant, pleading, beseeching. "What is it, *Maman*?" he asked in French, reaching out to hold her hand. "Do you think she is a danger? Honestly, there is nothing between us."

A tear formed in his mother's eye and slid slowly down her cheek, and she gave a small laugh, almost a derisive, despairing gasp. "No, *Mon fils*, no, for some reason, God forgive me, but no, I don't think she is a danger to you."

"Then what's the matter? Did she say something to upset you?"

Claire was openly weeping now, and couldn't respond. She reached into her purse and put a tissue to her eyes. Marcus waited, wondering. After a moment, Claire collected herself and looked up at her son.

"She is *me*," she said, almost in a whisper, tapping a hand to her heart, speaking in French. "I mean, what I was. I see so much of me in her, Marcus. She is tough, calculating, scheming, convinced she is in control of her life, not at all aware of what a horrible thing she will soon become."

This surprised Marcus, and he didn't interrupt. "She needs ... she needs something, something to break her. I ... I don't know what that could be, my son, but unless something happens in her life to ... to awaken her, I fear for her." Claire wiped her eyes again, lightly sobbed. "Oh, Marcus," she pleaded, looking up at him. "If you could do something ... anything ... to turn her from the path she is choosing ... it would mean a lot to me."

Marcus didn't know how to reply. He'd rarely seen his mother this upset. "I'll try, *Maman*," he said quietly, taking her hand, accompanying this statement with a prayer in his own heart to God, asking Him to show him where he might help this woman, because his mother had asked it.

His parents stayed but a few days, not wanting to burden the Prince's household, as the castle was also the Prince's family residence. His parents said that the Prince's family had been meticulously kind and generous, but they were worried about how Mace and Zoe would be getting on.

"Mace is beginning to blog, did we tell you?" his father said. "He's taking the church to task, and he's getting quite an underground following."

"It doesn't surprise me," Marcus replied. "And Mace is the one to do it. He sees things that most of us just can't see."

"Well, if that's true, times are going to get interesting, because Mace is making a convincing case that the world is in the midst of the great apostasy—the great 'falling away'—Paul talked of. Honestly, I can't argue with the kid; he makes a good case."

***

After Tack and Claire departed, Christienne had come in with her parents and visited for a brief time. She cried on Marcus' shoulder (the good one), both shared memories about Ramsay, and then her parents had led her away. Her father, though, had come in by himself a little later.

"Herr Ironbridge, on behalf of myself and my wife, permit me to again express our gratefulness for your bravery in saving our daughter."

Christienne's father, Prince Richter Wallich Zeck, named after one of his famous old great uncles, was the acting Head of State of the Principality of Liechtenstein.

Richter Wallich Zeck was a tall, trim man, with his father's distinctive, fine facial features, rich dark hair, and an eminently accomplished tailor. When he was five, his parents had sent him to a boarding school in Switzerland, where he immediately picked up French and Italian in addition to his native German. When he was fourteen, his father brought him home to work in one of the many native industries in Liechtenstein. Richter started in a robotics factory, at first sweeping the floors, and then learning to piece together small, articulated legs on small roverbots, or 'RBs', the development and production of which Liechtenstein had pioneered as a national export. Better than anything out of China, more reliable than anything out of Russia or Brazil, and definitely more resilient than anything with a chipset out of the U.S., every one of which was effectively contaminated with Chinese technology. At first Richter did the leg assemblies by hand, one at a time, and his supervisors would bin most of the RBs he touched for the first week or so, but hey, his Dad could afford them anyway, and then they taught him to use the computer to control the assembly, and after that he did quite well.

When Richter was sixteen, his father directed that he come off the assembly floor and into the upper offices, there to learn how the business was managed from the executive suite. Richter discovered in himself a unique affinity for managing finances—no surprise, since his father was perhaps the most successful financial manager in the world—and Richter helped improve the robotic company's financial picture somewhat during his twelve-week stint as an intern.

Richter was always a serious young man, taken frequently to be older than he was. He was conservative in habit and outlook, and in no way gave his father any of the trouble normal parents experienced with teenagers. His preference was to retire early with a book about financial histories of nations or biographies of some of the world's wealthiest men or thick tomes about European history. He was never drawn to the mindless preoccupations with alcohol or drugs that seemed to inevitably infect every pre-teen in Europe, preferred hot chocolate to coffee, and would have an obligatory beer once every month (he did, after all, speak German as his native tongue). Richter knew what life had in store for him from a very early age, and like a true German engineer, meticulously prepared for every possible contingency or exigency that might be required of him in that eventual responsibility. He was exceptionally self-disciplined. He kept himself chaste, his relations with women being the model of propriety and decorum. He loved and respected his mother and greatly respected and honored his father. His life was structured, straightforward, clean, and focused. He was, on the whole, quite happy with it.

Richter's preference for order, for plans, for structure, for tradition and the need for solemnity associated with things of gravity (which one cannot help but absorb, growing up as the son of a European Prince) all inclined him directly and with zeal into the arms of the Catholic church. Liechtenstein's ancient involvement and history with Catholicism could not be avoided. Unlike many men of his age and generation, most of whom were abandoning the church faster than lemmings can leap over a cliff, Richter embraced it. He loved the mystery, the ritual, the sense of solemn assembly, and, while he would not be able to elucidate this last, the rules in the Catholic church suited his temperament; rules which he found rather easy to keep; rules which in no way ever came close to crucifying his flesh and calling him away from his own deeply-ingrained sin nature. Absent the work of the cross in his life, his religious activity generated in him a deep, steadily growing, persistent, and pervasive idea that he was pleasing to God, that God was pleased with him, and that his life was an example to others. Which, he thought, is as things should be—Princes should be an example to their people.

In an interesting twist, his father, the Reigning Prince, had worked to reduce the hold the Catholic Church had in Liechtenstein. Though it was officially recognized in the Principality's Constitution as the State religion, Prince Rainer did not like the disparities he was observing in the Church, both as a whole and personally, in his own life, where, as he aged, he was beginning to get a bitter taste of Catholicism's inability to answer the deeper questions of life, or to provide any power in an individual's life to live truly holy, separate, Godly lives. It is the elders who come to this realization first, after they have spent their years fruitlessly working to produce their own righteousness. Sometimes they come to it late, on their deathbeds; sometimes, if they are thoughtful and honest, they see it sooner. Though inexpressible, this growing doubt about the Church was the cause of some tension between father and son.

When Richter was 26, he met a young, blond, very pretty Swiss accountant at mass one day who also happened to work in the national bank of Liechtenstein—which his father owned—and after a sedate, structured, and well-planned relationship, with her background duly investigated with a thorough due diligence process that would have done an investment banking firm proud, they married.

Apparently it was a tradition, started many generations ago, that the Reigning Prince and current Head of State train up the next Head of State *before* the current Head of State was no longer capable of performing his duties by essentially permitting the eldest son (so far in history it had always been a son) to take over the reins of the country as the *acting* Head of State while the current Head of State served as sort of a live-in mentor. Marcus thought this arrangement eminently reasonable, typifying the quality of servant leadership, in which the leader sought not to gain power but to share it, and in so doing offering the next Head of State an excellent opportunity to 'learn on the job', as it were.

"Sir," Marcus replied, "please, people keep describing what I did as something brave. I was only trying to keep myself and my friends alive."

The acting Head of State stared at Marcus for a few seconds, and then said, "Herr Ironbridge, forgive me, but I have seen the video of the event. I saw a man defend his friends, yes, but I also saw a man driven by ... by something most people do not have. It was almost as if you were fearless. Most people, when they are shot at, do not react that way."

Marcus realized the man was right, but not for the correct reason. "Sir, it wasn't fearlessness, it was anger. I was *angry*. Yes, at first there was the shock of violence, and I was angry that a man would strike a woman as he did. But then, as they fired their weapons in that crowded café, carelessly killing people, I was angry that they felt such a disdain for human life, caring nothing for the lives they might end, the tragedies they might cause, just to accomplish their one objective which was rooted only in hatred." Marcus was impassioned now, and looked directly at the young Zeck. "These people hate, sir. Hate is what drives them, it is what motivates them, it is what feeds the dark maw of the furnace they call their souls. So yes sir, I was angry. My father taught me, when you are faced with that kind of hatred, to go right back at it, to fight it in any way and every way you can." Marcus stopped, realized he'd probably offended one of the richest men in the world, and then realized he really didn't care. "No apologies, sir."

Zeck looked at him strangely for a bit, and then shook his head. "None required, Herr Ironbridge. It is as I said, fortunate for Christienne, and for us, that you were there." The Prince prepared to leave. "Again, thank you," he said, nodding his head slightly. "If you wouldn't mind, I would like to talk to you further during your convalescence," he asked.

"My pleasure, sir," Marcus replied.

Richter Zeck smiled grimly, shook Marcus' hand, and left. Marcus got a different sense about Richter than he had from Rainer, his father. He couldn't put his finger on it, but it was there nonetheless.

***

A tall brunette in a tailored business suit knocked on the door of the office and then stepped into the carpeted area. "Your Highness, we have the Swiss delegation this morning at ten o'clock," she said, in flawless German.

"Thank you, Marguerite. This will be in the main conference room, correct?"

"Yes, your Highness."

"Very good. Richter, let's talk a moment about this meeting. That will be all, Marguerite." Marguerite bowed slightly and left, closing the door.

"Her German is the best in this country, you know," Richter said. "She puts us all to shame."

"We speak a different German, my son," Rainer said, in Liechtenstein's Alemannic version of German. "I'm fine with what we know."

Richter smiled. "As it should be, Father. But to the Swiss ... you know what they will want."

"I know, Richter. Truthfully, I am wondering why it took them so long. What are your thoughts?"

Richter sat on the leather couch in his father's office, legs crossed, his iPad on his lap, wearing a bespoke suit tailored in Munich, with black leather loafers. His father sat behind a large oak desk, with a dark blue V-neck sweater over a casual white collared polo shirt. There was a fire in the fireplace, and snow was hitting up against the windowpanes, trying desperately to cling to the glass. Rainer sat back and worked the deep bowl of his pipe.

"You are worried about this meeting?" Richter asked.

"No ... well, perhaps. Why do you ask?"

"Because you never smoke unless you are concerned about something," his son said. Rainer pursed his lips, tilted his head to acknowledge his son's perceptive analysis, and went on stoking his pipe.

"So let me read over what they have sent," Richter began, and pressed buttons on the iPad. "Here ... so ... they say, 'It is our opinion that it would be in the best interest of the region if Liechtenstein were to reconsider its tradition of eschewing any military force, and begin to shoulder its commensurate burden regarding the defense of our shared geography, history, and culture.'"

"They want us to have a military."

"That's about the size of it, Father."

"So what are your thoughts on the matter?" Rainer asked. His pipe was up and away, smoke winding upward. The room filled with the redolent, aromatic smell of pipe tobacco. It was a smell Richter loved.

Richter laid his iPad aside on the couch and folded his hands together. He was thoughtful for a moment, considering his response. "I understand the reasons we haven't seen the need for a military, Father; our size, our geography, tucked away as we are, here in the mountains between Germany, Austria, and Switzerland. We've wanted to align ourselves internationally as a neutral, like Switzerland. We've seen the devastation that can come to a European nation that rushes into conflict, waving the flag of some ideology or cause. Britain lost more men at the Somme in one day than we have in our entire nation. I think our positioning has been wise; look at the results. If you don't adjust for purchasing power parity, we have the highest gross domestic product per person in the world. We have more registered companies than we do people. Our manufacturing capacity per capita was rated as number two in the world, second only to Japan. Our robotics industry is number three in the world. Our financial services sector is the second most active in Europe, and fourth in the world overall. All this with only, what, maybe 45,000 people all told? I am not sure we could have accomplished all of this if we had sent ten or twenty percent of our men off to war every generation or so, dying while embroiled in some global cause that our nation just wouldn't have much of concern about."

Rainer raised an eyebrow at this last comment.

"Yes, I know, but now we have a pointed interest in what is coming," Richter went on.

"Explain."

"Very well," Richter answered, knowing that his father simply wanted him to rehearse what he intended to tell the Swiss delegation. "Eight percent of our population is Muslim," Richter began. "And it is growing. Four years ago it was five percent. The birthrate among Muslims in our country is something like eight to ten times greater than our native population. In five years, they will be ten percent of our population. In Germany, the riots are becoming intense; they are destabilizing entire cities, and they will soon have the Chancellor out of office. The far right zealots are growing in power—very frightening there, but at this point no one seems to be standing up to the destabilizing activities of the Islamic immigrants. France is having its own problems." Both men paused, recalling that one of the problems in France had almost resulted in Richter losing his only daughter. "Switzerland has been the most proactive nation in Europe, with a number of ministers agitating that they cannot stand by and do nothing."

"Who was it, one of their former Defense Ministers, advocated that every citizen needs to be armed?"

"It was Blattman, their Army Chief. He warned of social unrest due to terrorism and unchecked immigration. He was concerned that the very foundation of prosperity the Swiss have built is being called into question."

Rainer nodded, puffing once on his pipe, and then said, "It seems logical that what would apply to them might apply to us."

"So far neither snow, mountains, nor cold weather has seemed to be an obstacle to Islam," Richter said. "I hesitate to sound Islamaphobic, but facts are facts."

"My advice, Richter, is to make decisions based upon facts and avoid those who might want to bludgeon us with rhetoric about being racist or Islamaphobic."

"Agreed, Father."

"And so the Swiss are seeing that this massive infusion of Islamic refugees does not portend anything but serious risk for our region, and they want us to shoulder our share of regional defense."

"That's correct. I've been in touch with their foreign ministry prior to this meeting, and they are going to press us to commit to bringing into being a force capable of defending our own borders. What I don't understand is why they would do this now."

"I think it is clear," Rainer replied, cradling his pipe in both his hands on the desk. "They are going to close their borders, and they will want us to agree to do the same. This is a dramatic departure from Germany's position, but I think the key here is that the Swiss have convinced Austria to do the same."

Richter sat up, surprised. "What makes you say that?"

"Because Forchtenblum met with Grau three days ago, and Switzerland and Austria have signed, in secret, a mutual regional defence agreement."

Richter was shocked. He leaned forward on the couch. "My God, Father, this is a huge departure for the Swiss. Their foreign minister meets with the Austrian President and no one hears about it? How did you find this out? I've heard nothing of it."

Rainer twisted his mouth slightly, an expression combining irony and acceptance. "The DGSI has been helpful," he replied.

After a moment, Richter asked, "So what do we tell the Swiss?"

"What do you want to tell them?"

Richter shot a fierce look out the window. "I can tell you, my decisions at this point, with my daughter still recovering from an attempted assassination by Muslims, are probably not well-balanced. And yet the Pope wants Christianity to coexist with Islam. I'm torn. My heart wants to strike back at those who attacked Christienne, but I need to think about what is best for the country, and what is best for our people. And I have to consider, as a Catholic, what the head of the Church directs."

Rainer sat back in his chair, steepling his fingers. These were deep waters, and he did not want to alienate Richter with his recently emerging opinions about the Catholic Church. "The older I get, son, the more I realize that some decisions must be made with the heart less than the mind. Your heart can sometimes get to the central issue more quickly than can all sorts of intellectual reasoning."

Richter processed what his father had said without evincing any reaction. "What are you inclined to do, Father? I am the acting Head of State, but you are the reigning Prince. It is your decision."

"I know, son, I know. I don't think we have any choice but to at least agree to consider the Swiss proposal. I would not immediately acquiesce, but let us try to get them to give us some time to consider how we might want to go about things."

Richter nodded slowly. "Understand. I think that would be prudent. I frankly do not know how I would answer them at the moment."

"Don't think the timing of their visit is a coincidence, Richter."

"What are you saying?"

"I am saying that they are not stupid. They know you are the acting Head of State. They also know your daughter was almost killed by Muslim terrorists. What answer do you think they will expect to get from you?"

Richter sat back against the plush leather cushion. "I hadn't thought of that," he replied. "Have I comported myself in such a way as they would think I could be so influenced?"

Rainer looked at his son and smiled sadly. "Any man with breath in his body would be so influenced, after what they did to your child," Rainer said. "It is nothing to be ashamed of."

"And your granddaughter, don't forget," Richter said.

"And my granddaughter too, yes, my son. I won't forget. The Swiss haven't."

"So what should we tell them?"

Rainer stood up and set his pipe in the glass holder next to Rodin's statue. "I think we tell them that we fully understand their request and that we are not without sympathies regarding their concept of regional defence. I would ask them for some time to consider how we might best respond to their request in a way that would meet both their need for a more distributed sharing of the load relative to regional defence, and our need to ensure our country and our people are not negatively affected by such a course of action. It is a momentous decision, my son, to build a sword. Sooner or later one will be tempted greatly to use it."

"How do you think they'll take that answer?" Richter asked.

"I am fairly sure it is the answer they expect. They certainly don't expect us to immediately acquiesce; it is not our style, nor would it be prudent, and the Swiss appreciate nothing more than prudence. So yes, I am content that they will hear what we are saying to them."

"How will such a decision be received in Rome?" Richter put the question out on the table tentatively, not wanting to irritate his father, but needing to know how far his father would go in opposing Rome.

"Who can say?" Rainer answered diplomatically. "I am sure they would counsel caution and restraint, advising against any precipitate action that might inflame anti-Islamic sentiments."

"What about our people, Father? You know most Liechtensteiners are Catholic. If the head of the Church encourages them to embrace Muslims, and we put up a border to keep them out, what will they think?"

Rainer looked at his son, wondering how the man could ask such a question while his daughter was still emotionally unbalanced from the attack by Muslim terrorists. He said nothing.

"You're going to do this, aren't you, Father?" Richter asked quietly, in a somber, serious tone.

Rainer looked at his son, strong and confident, yet on edge about this decision, for he knew that should they undertake to create their own national military, sooner or later Islam would put it to the test. Rainer was not sure Richter realized yet that Islam would no more respect a nation's neutrality than the young Islamic refugees were currently respecting the rights of the women they were raping across Europe at the moment.

"I am, son. But first, I want to have a talk with Mr. Ironbridge."

Richter looked confused for a moment. "Ironbridge? Who is ... oh ... the man who ... but why? What would he know about these things?"

"He is a former Marine, Richter. And he has done things in Afghanistan that may help us here."

"What things did he do in Afghanistan that would in any way help us with this issue, Father?"

"Things we can't talk about at the moment, my son. I promise, I'll share them with you when the time is right."

Richter was confused, and he was worried about the impact Rainer's decision might have on the nation's relations with Rome. "Well, when you can, share with me the substance of your discussions, Father, because the Swiss will not want us to take too much time to consider our course of action. They will want a decision soon."

"I am thinking something like a year," Rainer replied. "They will give us a year."

"To make a decision? That's generous, even for the Swiss."

"No, Richter, not a year to make a decision. The Swiss will be expecting us to have a military up and operating within a year from today."

"How do you know this?" Richter asked, surprised again.

"The DGSI is not as incompetent as they are made out to be," Rainer replied. "And now if you will excuse me, I must dress for our meeting with the Swiss."

***

"Mr. Ironbridge, thank you for taking the time this afternoon to talk." The Prince shook Marcus' hand as he opened the door to his office.

"Well sir, I'm not going anywhere very quickly, as you see," Marcus said, gesturing to his cane, "and this is your house. I appreciate the care you're providing."

Rainer waved his hand deprecatingly. It was late in the afternoon of a gray, threatening day, the Alps covered in white rippling blankets of snow. The Prince had his pipe with him, and was casually dressed in jeans and a wool pullover sweater. "Come in, come in. Really, it is nothing, seriously. As you can see, you and Miss ... you and Marie-Clémence and my granddaughter are the only patients we have had for quite some time, and between you and me and the four hundred year old stones in the wall, Herr Professor Doktor Kronzplatz is rather overjoyed to have three patients who present such medical challenges. The occasional cold or flu we get here does not serve to hold his interest."

"Glad I could be of service to the good Professor Doctor," Marcus quipped, but with a grimace as he moved through the room. Walking was difficult, and the pain was still present, although he was more on the downhill side, and was just beginning to see the benefits of Doctor Kronzplatz' non-addictive treatment strategy.

"Tell me about your convalescence," the Prince asked, sitting behind his desk. "Please, sit."

"Thank you, sir. The Professor Doctor tells me things are 'according to schedule.' I sense he doesn't want to appear too optimistic, but he hasn't expressed any major concerns."

"Yes, well, that is good. He is quite competent, you know. I would trust him with my life, and the lives of my family." Rainer's English was superb, with a touch of a German Swiss accent.

"Good to know, sir. I appreciate the care you and he are providing. You don't have to—"

"Yes, yes, I understand, Marcus, but actually I consider it an obligation. You did save my granddaughter's life. We cannot repay you enough." Marcus just nodded his head. He didn't know what to say to that.

The Prince leaned back in the tall black leather executive chair and rubbed his chin with one hand. "Would it be acceptable to you if we were to talk of some, ah ... some personal things?" the Prince ventured in a questioning tone.

Marcus wondered what the Head of State of one of the world's richest principalities wanted to talk to him about personally. "Of course, sir," he replied, yet with some small degree of reserve.

"Good, good," Rainer replied, rubbing his hands together. "So then we must be frank. Shall I assume that you know who Marie-Clémence worked for?"

"I was told she worked for the DGSI."

"Yes, you're correct. Marie-Clémence was the target of the action in the restaurant in France. But I think you know that."

"I watched one of them shoot her in the head," Marcus answered grimly. "They left Christienne alone. And when Marie-Clémence went off on the guy coming to the table in what sounded to me like fluent Arabic, I suspected something wasn't quite what it seemed to be. And it explains why the official story was that they wanted to kidnap your granddaughter."

"A story I permitted," Rainer went on. "So ... you are recovering well?" To Marcus he seemed somewhat ill at ease, as if he wanted to discuss something but couldn't work himself around to bringing it up.

"I'm fine, sir."

"Will you able to walk without the cane soon?"

"Herr Professor Doktor Kronzplatz tells me it should be another few weeks. I don't think he'll let me go until I can run five miles through the mountains there," Marcus said, pointing through the window at the line of snow-covered Alps. It was beginning to snow, the flakes large and flat hitting the windowpanes like tiny slaps.

"We hope you will stay with us long enough to do just that," the Prince replied. He arranged a pen on his desk blotter, and pushed scattered sheets of paper into a semblance of order.

"What is it that you wanted to talk about, sir?" Marcus said, hoping to help the Prince past his initial discomfort.

The Prince hesitated for a moment, but then asked, "Can you tell me about your time in the Marine Corps, Marcus?"

Marcus was slightly taken aback. It wasn't something he was expecting. "Why, I suppose so." It wasn't something he thought one of the world's richest men would be interested in, but he sensed the Prince was using the question to just break the ice. "I graduated from the Naval Academy and selected the Marines as my service choice. I went to the Basic School and did well enough to earn a spot as an infantry officer."

"Why infantry? Why not aviation, or armor?"

Marcus thought this was a strangely informed question, coming from the Head of a European principality. "Well sir, to be honest, I've always felt that I was supposed to be on the ground, on my feet, leading other men, fighting in the dirt, so to speak. There is something basic, something honest, about a man with a rifle, moving on his feet, carrying his supplies and equipment on his back, depending on other men doing the same thing, standing shoulder to shoulder to fight against the enemy." Marcus wasn't sure the Prince would understand where he was going with his explanation, but it was an honest answer. "You don't find that kind of thing—at least as intensely—flying in a cockpit by yourself, or riding around in 60 tons of armor with five other guys, shooting SABOT rounds at other tanks."

"It sounds almost as if technology creates a distance from the fight, like you are once removed from the feeling of battle," the Prince observed.

"Actually that's quite accurate, sir," Marcus said, nodding his head in acknowledgement. "And I would add that technology can also create a distance, a gap, almost a blurring if you will, of the bond that exists between warriors. No one is or ever will be closer to you than the men you stand side-by-side with in battle."

The Prince spoke in a measured cadence, as though reciting from a prepared speech. "We few, we happy few, we band of brothers—for whoever sheds his blood with me today shall be my brother. However humble his birth, this day shall grant him nobility."

"Shakespeare, the speech on St. Crispin's day, exactly," Marcus replied, smiling. "Very appropriate, and to the point as to why I wanted to be in the infantry."

The Prince nodded with appreciation. "It is something I applaud," he replied, "though it is something I am just beginning to understand of late," he said cryptically. "But tell me about your time in the Marines. Did you enjoy it? And if so, why did you leave? And what did you do afterward?"

Marcus felt awkward about the barrage of questions, but it came to him that the man, Head of State though he was, wealthy beyond imaging though he was, was still a man, and one who had something on his mind that he could not bring himself to raise. And so Marcus played along with the conversation, waiting perhaps for something he said to provide the man with an opening.

"I had the normal tours of duty, sir, and was fortunate enough to experience combat in Afghanistan."

"That must have been difficult," the Prince offered diplomatically.

"Like most of what you read, sir, combat is a defining moment in a man's life. It was for me. I left Afghanistan a different person."

The Prince folded his hands together and leaned forward on his desk. "I want to talk to you about what happened in Afghanistan," the Prince began, catching Marcus by surprise with the intensity of his tone.

Marcus stopped for a moment. "Forgive me, sir, but I guess I can't understand why you would be interested in what happened in Afghanistan. I commanded a company of Marines during my tour there. I finished the tour, returned home, left the Marines, and ..."

Rainer held up his hand, interrupting. "Marcus, forgive me, but I have access to information which leads me to believe that something rather remarkable occurred there. I understand you may be hesitant to speak about it, but I assure you, I am very interested in what happened. I am not asking casually."

Perhaps this is was the Prince was trying to get around to discussing. "What do you mean, sir?"

"If I may share this information with you in confidence?" the Prince asked, with raised eyebrows, looking at Marcus.

"Of course sir."

"Well, good. So ... the Swiss want Liechtenstein to establish a military force to provide defence for our borders. They are pointedly requesting that we establish a regional defence capability, specifically in response to the uncontrolled migration of Islamic immigrants that are flooding Europe. They are going to close their borders, prohibiting further Islamic immigration."

"So the Swiss are declaring war on Islam?" Marcus asked.

"Precisely," Rainer replied, thrusting a finger into the desk blotter. "You see this right away."

"Islam considers any attempt to forestall their attempt at world domination as opposition. Join them or die, I believe they say."

"Unfortunately not many others see this," the Prince replied. "The Swiss want us to do the same with our borders as a gesture, obviously, since our borders are nothing. The Austrians will also close their borders to Islamic immigrants."

"What will you do with the Muslims you have in your country now?" Marcus asked.

"It is not something we've thought about," the Prince replied. "But we are not helped by the fact that the Church is stridently working to unite the two houses of faith."

Marcus looked slightly uneasy, and the Prince saw it immediately. "Go ahead, Marcus. You have an opinion about this?"

"Well, sir, I realize you are a Catholic, and I realize Liechtenstein is mostly Catholic, but ..."

"Yes?" the Prince asked, seeming to be open to what Marcus might have to say.

"But I would consider that the Catholic Church and Islam are essentially two thrusts of the same campaign, sir. They're working for the same General."

Rainer was taken aback. "That's a rather bold comment, Marcus," he said.

"I can back it up with facts, sir. But really, I shouldn't need to. You can see for yourself the similarities between the two faiths, and really, doesn't the Pope's position make my point?" Marcus paused. "But this doesn't have anything to do with Afghanistan, does it?"

"Well, actually yes, and I want to talk about that now, but let us not forget to discuss these similarities between Catholicism and Islam, Marcus. You shock me ... but ... please understand ... and this is difficult to say ... I am at the time of my life where I am more interested in the truth than I am concerned about complying with a particular religious tradition."

"Good," Marcus replied, surprised and somewhat encouraged. The Holy Spirit tugged at him, alerting him to the possibility that he was sitting with a man who might have an open heart to hear truth. Marcus sat up on the edge of his spiritual seat.

"So ... Afghanistan?" the Prince asked.

"You want the truth?" Marcus asked.

"I need the truth."

"Okay then. So here's what happened."

***

It was six o'clock in the evening. Snow was beginning to build up on the windows of Rainer's study. Pipe smoke curled around the ceiling. The fire was low and banked, and two snifters of brandy sat on the desk. Rainer looked to be in deep thought, digesting what Marcus had shared for the past three hours. Finally he spoke.

"You realize that most people would immediately dismiss what you've told me as simply a very far-fetched story, most probably constructed—invented, some would say—to justify why you were summarily dismissed from your service."

"That's actually what most people think," Marcus replied. "Completely understand. But if you need confirmation, well, for one, here I am, dismissed from the U.S. Marine Corps, and for another, there are some people I could call."

The Prince shook his head, waving away Marcus' offer. "No need, Marcus. For some strange reason," the Prince said musingly, "I believe you; I do. And why is that?" he went on in a tone of wonderment. "I listen to what you tell me and something confirms in me that you're speaking truth. This is just not in accord with anything that has happened to me in my life before. I'm a banker, for God's sake! We don't believe in these things."

"What do you mean, sir?"

"Consider, Marcus. I am one of the world's wealthiest men. I am the head of a nation. I built our economy almost single-handedly, making decisions that have created one of the world's best standards of living in any nation on the planet. Liechtenstein has been the center of my life, the sum and substance of everything I've done and worked for my entire life. I have been a good Catholic, going to mass every week, dutifully attending to the obligations of the faith, and raising my children as good Catholics. I have believed what the Church has taught me since my youth, and yet here you come, thrust into my home with a story that truly beggars belief, yet one that I find myself hoping is true more than I care to admit. Now why *is* that?" Rainer looked at Marcus with confusion, wonder, and consternation, and continued, almost as though he was talking to himself. "I've been a reasonable man my entire life; a man grounded in the realities of the world, a man who in his past spurned any reference to the supernatural, considering references to such things at best misguided, at worst, intentionally deceptive. And here you come into my study with a story describing how God literally fought against your Islamic enemies in Afghanistan, interfering supernaturally to ensure your success." The Prince paused for a moment, overwrought. "Marcus, nothing in my entire life's experience has ever led me to believe that such a story as you've related could possibly be true. To do so would be so excessive, so dramatic, so emotional, so ... *unseemly*. And yet why do I believe you?"

Marcus could see Rainer was truly conflicted. He paused, waiting to hear what God wanted him to say to the reigning Prince of Liechtenstein. And then it came, and he spoke what he was given. "Perhaps, sir," he replied, "you believe this because you've always wanted such a thing to be true. Perhaps you've always, deep down, hoped that there would be a God who involves Himself in the affairs of men, that there would be more to life in the spirit than just mass once a week, and discharging a list of obligations. Maybe you've hoped all your life that there would be a way to really have a relationship with the living God, directly, without the intervention and interference of other men. And maybe it's because you are finally beginning to see the worthlessness of pretty much everything else in the world. And finally, perhaps, God knows that your heart is ready to hear truth."

Rainer sat back in his chair, struck to his heart. "Yes," he said quietly, with deep emotion, staring at his desktop, seeing his past life. "You're right. I've hoped for such a thing all my life."

"But you've never spoken of it to anyone, have you?" Marcus asked.

"No," Rainer said, shaking his head. "Never." He looked up at Marcus. "But why now?" he asked Marcus, and then, more so to himself, "Why now?"

The Prince shook himself like a dog coming out of a dream, and stood. "Let's get some coffee. Would you like some coffee?" He pressed a small buzzer next to the Rodin statue.

"Actually sir, I'm not a coffee drinker."

"Well then, perhaps some hot chocolate?"

"Now that would be great, thank you sir."

"Yes, your Highness?"

"Marguerite, would you please bring me an espresso, and for my friend here, a pot of chocolate, furiously whipped, with whipped cream."

"Of course sir. Would you like anything else?"

"No thank you, Marguerite." The woman departed, closing the door to the office.

The Prince walked over to the window and stared out at the snow still glistening under a darkening sky. "Could we talk more about this assertion you've made that Catholicism is similar to Islam ... that they are working for the same General, I believe you said."

"Yes sir."

"You see, it has a bearing on some decisions our country needs to make. I mentioned to you that the Swiss are asking for Liechtenstein to contribute to the defence of our region, and to the point, defence against encroaching Islamic immigration. The Church would paint such a position as opposed to their efforts to unite these religions." The Prince paused in his review, and Marcus tilted his head as if to make a point. "Yes, I see, to your point that the two are working for the same General ... I'd never thought about it that way, but when you consider it from such a perspective ... hmmm."

"Both religious systems are implacable regarding their objectives, sir. Both systems require their adherents to believe in their doctrines exclusively, demanding absolute, unthinking obedience, regardless of the nature of the one being obeyed. Both systems are works based."

"Works based ... what is that?" the Prince asked.

"Basically both systems teach that one can attain an acceptable level of righteousness in God's eyes by doing something—be that abstaining from meat on Friday, or from marriage, or by killing infidels, or by flogging oneself, or crawling on one's knees for miles, or by worshipping some image or rock or relic. Both systems have their own series of prayer beads, mindlessly repeating prayers as if God is obligated to answer based upon the shear volume of noise being sent His way. Both systems have a history of killing those who disagree with them. And finally, both systems are ultimately opposed to Jesus; opposed to the application of the cross of Christ in an individual's life, and opposed to the Holy Spirit. They both have the same origins, by the way—in Babylon—where the pagan Babylonian worship system migrated into many different parts of the world, mutating in one place into worship of a moon god, which in Arabic is 'illah'; in other places, mutating into worship of a Sun god. The names are different, but they all come from the same source—pagan Babylon. Isis, Ishtar, Ashtarte, Bel, Marduk, Ba'al ... they've all the same source. Catholicism and Islam are just two different large branches of the same tree, with its roots in pagan Babylonian worship. And that worship system worshipped demons, sir ... demonic entities which still today direct men and nations; a kingdom of darkness that is staffed with evil so dark, so bloody, so dangerous, and filled with a choking hatred for mankind. And this kingdom of darkness men have chosen over the kingdom of Light, because it is our nature to love darkness more than light."

"That's a lot to digest, Marcus."

"Just think back over your life, sir. Has not your own experience shown you that Catholicism generates a toxic level of self-righteousness?"

The Prince paused for a long moment, staring out through the window. There was a knock on the door, and Marguerite brought in a tray with coffee and chocolate, with some croissants and fruit.

"Thank you Marguerite, please, put it there on the desk."

"Will there be anything else, your Highness?"

"No, my dear, thank you." Marguerite left.

"To answer your question honestly, Marcus ... yes. It is difficult for me to say, and if you had asked me that question three years ago, I would have thrown you out of the house, but now ... now I cannot escape the truth of that assertion. In my position I haven't been able to blatantly let my disdain for people show externally, but if I was honest I would have to tell you that I have felt, for most of life, just slightly better than most of the people with whom I've come in contact. Yes, you could say it is because most of the people I come in contact with are not royalty, but honestly, our family dispensed with the concept that our right to rule comes out of some God-given mandate a long time ago, so no, it is not for that reason. If I were to be honest, I have always just felt slightly superior to others I've known in my life because, I think, I feel I've kept the rules better than most."

"And have always been careful to make sure they do not become aware of your feelings," Marcus added.

The Prince turned, a wry smile on his face. "Precisely. So you know. When you put it that way, my life has been one big construct, one large Potemkin village, showing people one thing on the outside while feeling and thinking something very different inwardly. I mean, seriously, the thought rises up in me right now, a wonderment that I am talking to someone like you ..."

"You mean, a commoner?"

"Well, something like that."

"You are going to experience a number of thoughts that will generate opposition to what I'm telling you, sir. You've decided to engage in a spiritual fight, and you have not had experience yet with what will come against you. Thoughts will just pop into your head that will try and convince you this is all foolishness. Old memories, old thought patterns, old habits will raise their ugly head and try to drag you back into old ways of living."

Rainer paused again, picked up his pipe, and began to pack it from tobacco in a brown leather pouch. "I can just begin to sense the truth of what you say, Marcus. I am experiencing a riot of internal emotions even now, and I must tell you, riotous internal emotions are not something I've experienced so far in my life."

"If you press on with this, sir, expect to encounter opposition from a lot of different sources. Riotous internal emotions will be the least of your problems."

"Oh, no doubt, Marcus, no doubt." Rainer chuckled with irony. "I can just see Richter's eyebrows arching upward, and wondering to himself if he has the family psychiatrist's number in his phone. And it goes without saying that most of the country will think their Prince has gone over the edge, embraced some sort of fanatical Protestant sect, or been brainwashed, or maybe just taken leave of his senses."

"All very real possibilities, sir," Marcus observed in a deadly serious tone of voice. "And when you think about it, you have to agree with them from a certain point of view."

"What do you mean?" the Prince asked, slightly confused.

"Jesus said that it would be easier for a camel to pass through the eye of a needle than for a rich man to enter the kingdom of heaven. What is happening to you—that you would even consider these things—is a miracle. People don't usually comprehend miracles; they dismiss them as some type of psychiatric aberration if you're lucky, or consider you demented, suitable for being committed ... or killed."

Rainer darted a glance at him, noting the gravity of his reply. "Yes ... well, perhaps as we proceed, I may learn how to deal with those reactions."

"You will sir ... if we proceed."

Rainer put his pipe to his mouth and drew long on the stem and then puffed out a cloud of smoke. He looked at Marcus, determination in his countenance. "Oh, we're going to proceed, Marcus. Have no doubt."

***

At nine o'clock, Marcus asked the Prince a question. "What will Richter do about the Swiss request?"

"Well, it is still my decision, but if I were to hazard a guess, I would say he is quite conflicted. He is a devout Catholic, he feels very strongly attached to his faith, and feels that direction from the Pope is direction from God. If the Pope indicates that the Catholic faithful should embrace Islam, he will find it difficult."

"With his daughter so damaged by Muslim terrorists?" Marcus put in.

"There is that, yes, and it pulls at him. He is not totally devoid of conscience ... but Marcus, I have to tell you, I am seeing something amazing, something I never thought I would see again. When I was young, during Hitler's war, I saw men follow after an abominable lie. Men became blind to the truth, even as the truth would stare them in the face. They were deaf to the truth, even as truth would shout louder and louder. Hitler came and deceived an entire nation, and let me tell you, there were others outside of Germany who were blinded as well, deaf to the voices of reason. And now again I am seeing men become blind to the truth in the face of this horrendous lie that we are fed, that Islam is just one of a number of peaceful religions. Does mankind never learn?"

"God said that in these times, He would send a deluding influence on men who do not love the truth, sir. It is God's nature to give men what they want. If they want a life without Him, this is what they get. If they want Him, however, they must give up everything for Him. But then, He is worth more than everything."

"Richter cannot see that Islam will never stop until the world is at its feet."

"Sin blinds us to its consequences, sir. Unless Richter puts away his sin—unless any of us put away the sin in our lives—we'll remain blind and deaf, unable to see the truth. As long as Richter remains devoted to a religious system instead of the true God, he'll remain blind."

"As you say it, I see the truth of it in my life, and in others lives. I have watched it play out here, now that you mention it, in the heart of Europe, among men of high and low degree ... among leaders of nations who were so debauched that they could not see beyond the borders of the corrupted walls of their gloriously degenerate palaces. Truth to be told," he said, bowing his head, "there are a few corrupt walls in this degenerate palace, walls I am ashamed to even speak of."

"No need to speak of them with me, sir. Confess them to God, in the quiet privacy of your own heart. He knows about them anyway. And we all, all of us, have numerous corrupt walls in our own gloriously degenerate palaces."

There was a time of silent reflection then, until the Prince cleared his throat. "So, to your question. I think Richter would support a decision to close our borders, but I am not sure how supportive he would be of Liechtenstein creating its own military. That we haven't had a military in much of our history is something of a point of pride with us, actually. It's an aspect of our culture." Rainer looked at Marcus. "I can only imagine that a former Marine would find that difficult to comprehend."

"No sir, actually. It would be great if we lived in a world where a military wasn't needed. It would be great if Liechtenstein could continue to be neutral. But notice, after all these centuries, the world wars, the conflicts around the world, the thing that calls the Swiss out of their neutrality is the threat from Islam. They know Islam won't respect any position of neutrality."

"Yes, I think Richter recognizes this; he is not blinded to what is happening around the world these last decades. I suppose he is just wondering how to react to it, and you must understand he has no cultural heritage of fighting for one's rights or freedoms, or engaging in violent confrontations to secure one's lands or property. His has always been, as I think about it, mine as well, a world where diplomacy and reasoned debate has always served to bring about compromise and solutions to the dilemmas we've faced. Our weapons have been the debating rostrum, the referendum, and the democratic process."

"Islam spits on all those means of social interactions, sir."

The Prince grimaced. "Too true, Marcus, too true. We can wish that it were not so, but it would be criminal to let our wishes blind us to the truth that they will require us to either submit to their religion, or die. This is something people in my circle cannot grasp. Richter cannot understand this yet."

"You'll forgive me, sir, but anyone so invested in the world's ways of living and acting and believing will never see this truth. They will remain deluded and deceived up until the point when either some Imam swipes their head off, or God comes and delivers them up to judgment."

Rainer looked at Marcus for a long moment. "The eye of a needle, you say?"

"Just so, sir ..."

There was another long period of silence in the room. Marcus finished his chocolate and devoured a croissant. The Prince held his cup of coffee retrospectively, staring off into the distance, lost in thought. Marcus would not hurry the conversation, letting it play out in its own time, as God worked things.

Rainer turned again to Marcus. "This military thing, Marcus. I might be able to convince our people that closing our borders is a good thing—Catholic or not, they are seeing the truth of Islam played out in the cities of Europe and Scandinavia now and they want no part of it in their own nation. But building a military ... that's a different kettle of fish. That will be a hard sell."

Marcus watched the Prince move back and forth. "How will you get around the need for a protective force, sir? Just enlarging the police force won't do it. Policing and warfighting are two different skill sets, and you're going to need a force that can fight a war."

Rainer was pacing back and forth, increasingly excited about something, and then he stopped. "Tell me, Marcus, have you read my book?"

"I ... I didn't know you'd written a book, sir. No, I haven't."

The Prince turned and went to a wall in the office covered in bookshelves, looked over the titles for a moment, found what he was looking for, and pulled out a thin volume with the Zeck coat of arms on the cover. "Do me a favor, Marcus," he said. "Take a day or two and read this—it's a quick read—and when you are through, come back and let's talk about it. I think there may be an idea or two in there that might help us with this dilemma."

***

Frau Henzig changed his dressing. There was still significant pain, but he was over the worst now and he knew he could get by without the medication they were giving him if he needed to.

Marie-Clémence came in, still in her chair, her hair growing fuller on her head, mostly white, with whisps here and there fighting back to their original shade of dark brunette. Frau Henzig nodded once to make sure Marie-Clémence would not upset herself in the chair, and then, picking up the old bandages, left.

"Are you comfortable?" Marie-Clémence asked. "There is something I need to talk to you about."

Marcus leaned back into the bed, head and shoulders raised up in a slight incline, and put his hands behind his head. "Okay," he said. "I'm comfortable."

She looked at the door to make sure Frau Henzig had gone, and then began to maneuver her chair behind his bed. "They told you I worked for the DGSI, right?"

"They did. I don't think I've ever met a spy before."

"You wouldn't know if you had, if the person was a good spy," she replied.

"Goes without saying," he answered. "Why did you become a spy?"

He couldn't see her reaction to his question, which is probably the reason she was hiding out behind his bed. "I feel very strongly about making sure my people can live in France and feel safe. If I can help build a France like that, then my life will have been spent on something worthwhile. Can you understand that?"

"From which perspective?" Marcus asked.

"What do you mean?"

"I mean, are you asking me if I understand the need for the Jews to be able to live in safety, where they're not constantly hunted and killed because they're Jews, or are you asking if I understand a person's need to spend their life on something more than just earning a living so they can watch movies and play video games and eat what they want until they die?"

"So tell me what you think about both of them," she replied, "if you want to get semantic."

"Sure, I understand the need a person would have to make some contribution in the world; it helps them feel as though they're a person, that they mean something to someone, that what they do matters at least to someone or some group of people. I can understand that. About the Jews, I understand their desire to have a place they can be safe, but that will never happen."

"And why do you think so?" she shot back, obviously irritated.

"What I mean is that the Jews will never have a place of safety on this earth *until Messiah returns*. He is the only one who can guarantee the safety of any Jew—of *every* Jew."

"So then what, we should just sit around like those pathetic scarecrows in *The Fiddler on the Roof*, scraping up a living in some ghetto, letting whatever brutal ruling power ride us down or blow us up, moving from one hovel to the next, just waiting for Messiah to return? What are we supposed to do until then?"

"Look, Marie-Clémence, I didn't say you shouldn't work to make the world a safer place. In fact I think that is probably the most important work anyone can do at this point in history."

"What? You mean, make a place for their people to be safe?"

"No, I mean make a place for Jews to be safe."

"But you just said you don't think it will happen. You're not making any sense."

Marcus put one hand on the rail. "Do you mind floating over here where I can see you? It's difficult talking with just a voice."

"People do it all the time; there is a recent invention called the telephone; perhaps you've heard of it. And no, I am fine where I am, thank you."

Marcus sat back. "Fine, maybe it will be easier for me to explain then. Here's what I think. I think—"

"I don't want any regurgitated Christian sermon about how the Jews are the 'chosen people,' do you understand? I've heard enough of that garbage. I meant what I said on the bench that day."

Marcus was thoughtful for a few seconds, and then said, "Okay then, would you listen to what I thought if my opinions agreed with some of the world's most famous Jewish scholarship?"

"I would still be suspicious, but opinions based upon Jewish thought would be ... acceptable. So ... you've formed your opinions based upon Jewish scholarship? You, a former Marine? This I have to hear."

"Unilaterally Jewish."

She was silent for a few seconds. "Fine."

"Fine," he replied. "So here is what some of the world's most prominent Jews think about why there won't be a safe place for your people in the world until the Messiah returns. It has to do with a job God has for the Jews to do."

"What, to convert all the goyim? You've got us mixed up with the Muslims."

"No, not to convert anyone. God chose the Jews to represent Him to the rest of the world, to demonstrate His righteousness and character and holiness and love to humanity."

"I've heard this before," she said disdainfully.

"Yeah, you probably have, because the Jews themselves have known this since

Abraham walked out of Ur in the Chaldees to follow Yahweh, this amazing God who came and talked with him and promised him descendants without number—if he would just obey Him."

"Right—so you can teach at a good Hebrew school. What's the point?"

"The point is that God did not pick the Jewish people because of their holiness, their marvelous character, or their natural inclination to submit themselves to His authority. No, He picked them because they were the most stubborn, stiff-necked, irascible, irritating, and rebellious people on the planet, immersed in a sewer of demonic influences, false religions, and a filthy, degenerate world."

Marie-Clémence 's eyes widened at that. "That's your opinion of who we were as a people?" she snapped.

"Do you want to disagree with me?"

He could hear the chair hum and whir; she was moving around behind the bed. Nothing ... and then, "No. But my question stands; why would this God you think exists do such a thing?"

"Imagine," Marcus replied slowly, "a people surrounded and influenced by everything history's greatest adversary could do to oppose Him, a stubborn, stiff-necked people ... and then imagine if God could get them to obey Him, to submit to His authority, to actually *love* him ... then it would be a statement to the world that He could get *anyone* to love and obey Him. It would say that He could rescue *anyone*. No one was beyond hope."

"You must not think much of us," she said.

"I think more highly of your people than I do of any other people on earth," Marcus replied, "but I think less of any people than I do of God. The Jews are humanity writ large, Marie-Clémence. What do you see in the Jew, really? Think about it. I dare you to disagree." Marcus was launched now, and it didn't matter that he couldn't see the woman he was talking to. "The Jews have, beyond all reasonable measurement compared to their relatively small proportions among humanity, made enormous contributions to the world—some that have been amazingly beneficial, some that have been horribly destructive. Think about it—Moses, Jesus, Marx, Lenin, Freud, Einstein, so many others. Does it make sense that such incredibly good things, and some incredibly bad things, would come from one people group, one race? God set the Jews on the planet so that man would see what mankind is capable of becoming—the best of what man can be, and the worst."

Long pause, chair moving around: "What does this all have to do with us not having a safe place until this Messiah of yours shows up?"

"The enemy of mankind is the Devil. I know you don't believe that, but you asked me what I believe. The enemy of man is this evil, hate-filled, intelligent, scheming entity that has hated mankind since he was thrown down from his prominence. He hates man because he hates what God loves."

"Maybe God should love something else for a while."

"Don't be flippant, Marie-Clémence," Marcus said, bringing her up sharply. "It's not worthy of you, and what we are talking about is too important to be deflected by foolishness."

Everything stopped behind him; no movement, no chair sounds, no breathing. He could tell she was bristling at his rebuke, but after a few moments, she said, "You're right. I apologize. It is an old habit I have; it is something I do when I am uncomfortable."

"Many people do, but you should not be among them. Okay?"

"Okay." Long pause. "So this devil you say hates all of mankind because God loves us. And he hates God because why?"

"Because he wants to take God's place, and he can't, because, well, because he isn't God."

"Your theory fails on the clear, logical premise that that this 'dark, powerful, highly intelligent though demonic being' you refer to would immediately realize the hopelessness of his goal and cease from any attempt to supplant or usurp the power of this God you talk about."

"You are wrong, Marie-Clémence, because when any being, either natural or supernatural, sins—when they directly oppose God, they begin to lose the ability to see or think clearly, and their picture of reality is distorted. Sin blinds us to reality. Basically they get to a point where they can't recognize truth or reality. Satan's sin was a pride so massive as to think he could replace God, and such a massive sin blinded him massively, immeasurably. Opposing God essentially and eventually darkens our minds; we just can't see the logical end of the road we're on. All we know is that we want what we want, and nothing, we think, will get in the way of us getting to the end of that road. But the problem is that since we can't see clearly, we don't see that the end of the road is just a sharp drop off into a deep, dark place."

***

She came in at three in the afternoon the next day, and once again began to meander around his room aimlessly. She was quite practiced getting around in her chair now, though she would occasionally try to walk. She'd graduated from a walker to just a cane, and when the Herr Professor Doktor cleared Marcus to begin putting weight on his leg, Marcus needed a cane as well, although using a cane for his left leg required he use his left arm, which required he use his left shoulder, which was problematic for a while. They would occasionally try walking around the room, but he had to be careful, and his preliminary physical therapy was at first painfully difficult.

She had made a habit of coming into his room just as Frau Henzig was finishing her rounds. Marie-Clémence would dawdle and fritter until Frau Henzig left his room, and then, after some predictable small talk at which neither was very accomplished, she would leave, but it was as if she was leaving something hanging in the air, some question unasked, some task undone. Marcus just waited. But that afternoon, he sensed it was time to ask.

"Marie-Clémence, what it is? What do you want to talk about? Something is bothering you."

The chair stopped whirring around; he could hear it humming though, behind his bed. He waited. When she was nervous, she would tend to stay out of his line of vision. It started up again and she appeared in front of the window.

"It's stupid," she said, more softly than normal. Marcus waited patiently. Marie-Clémence twisted her hands in her lap and then tugged at the blanket Frau Henzig had given her to keep her warm.

"It's not stupid if it is causing you this much concern."

She sighed heavily and glanced out of the window. Her hair was growing back, thin, but dark. At the moment it was nothing but an inch or two of spiky down. She was wearing a turquoise blouse with a high collar, something Frau Henzig had found in town for her—something local, and something different than the normal hospital gown.

"Look, it ... it is just that ... it is something about your mother."

"You two had some time together, yes?"

Marie-Clémence tugged at the blanket again. "We did. It was ... disturbing."

"My mother can be pretty intense."

"No, no, it was nothing like that; nothing she said, or, well, rather ..." Marcus could see she was struggling to come out with something. He decided to be patient and let it come in its own time.

Marie-Clémence dug and twisted and wore at the edge of the blanket and then turned to face him, apparently deciding to share her angst. "The things she said ... it was as if she could see right through me, right *into* me. It was as if she knew what I was thinking before I said a thing. How ... I mean, what did you tell her about me?"

Marcus looked down at his hands, gathered calmly together in his lap. "I actually didn't say a thing to her about you. I'm sorry, but, well, you never came up; at least, before she had her talk with you."

"*Merde.*"

"What's wrong?"

Marie-Clémence hesitated again, and he could see her eyes begin to fill. She looked up, not wanting to wipe at her eyes, trying to get the tears to fall by just shaking her head in frustration. She threw out an arm in frustration and she drove the chair behind his bed again, out of his line of sight. "If you didn't say anything to her, then how did she know?"

"How did she know what?"

"How did she know *everything*! What *didn't* she know? It was like she has been looking through my window my entire life. She told me what was in my mind when I was going to ENS; she told me what was in my head when I accepted the job with DGSI. She even told me how I felt about my own parents. It was damned scary, I can tell you. And she even knew what I was thinkng about *you*, for God's sake." She gave a despairing little laugh, and he heard a hand flop in the blanket. "That was rich! Can you imagine, a mother recalling to woman she's never met—a woman who's recently been shot in the head and is now recovering—every disparaging thought, every negative idea, every particle of disdain she has hidden in her heart concerning her son the religious fanatic?" Marie-Clémence paused, torn between laughing and crying. "How could she have known that? How is that *possible*? Are you *sure* you didn't speak to her about me?"

"I told her nothing ... but she had some things to say about you after your talk."

Marie-Clémence wiped at her face then in frustration. "God, you people are so damned frustrating!" she cried. "You get in my head too much. This is not right."

"Marie-Clémence ..."

"You people meet someone and do your tricks and somehow you know all about them ..."

"Marie-Clémence ..."

"And all we want is to just be left alone, but no, you have to interfere, to intervene, to push yourself into everything, everywhere you go, shoving your religion in people's faces, constantly ..."

"Marie-Clémence ..."

"What! *What!* What do you want *now*?"

Marcus reached up and put his hand on the bed rail and tried to turn to see her, but couldn't. He gently laid the words out into the room without being able to see her: "What are you afraid of?"

There was a gasp, and he pushed himself up and turned as hard as he could. He saw here sitting in the chair, tears flowing like a dam breaking, her face in her hands, shoulders shaking uncontrollably.

Marcus made a huge effort and slid out of bed, struggled to walk to where she was up against the wall behind his hospital bed, and put his arm around her. Pain shot up through his leg and back, up through his shoulder. He ignored it.

"Ah, god, no, please, no, I can't ... I can't endure it. No!" she cried, shaking him off. She looked at him with anguished but angry eyes. "I ... will ... not ... be ... *trapped*! *Comprenez vous?* I will never let someone do that to me!" She whipped the chair around and left the room, leaving Marcus stumbling for balance, wondering what had happened.

Though not for long ... remembering his mother's imprecation, he spent time that evening asking God for wisdom and discernment, and ... it was given.

***

She walked slowly into his room the next day using her cane, with Frau Henzig guiding her chair behind her. "Won't get any better sitting in that damn chair," she growled by way of explanation when he cast a questioning look at her. He could see it was a struggle for her to walk, but she was doing better with it, though he could see it was even more of a struggle for her to come back into his room.

"Rewiring still not 100% complete," she said, uncomfortable with her ungainly progress.

"You are doing better than I am," Marcus replied. "This natural course of pain alleviation may keep a person from getting addicted, but it leaves something to be desired when it comes to relieving pain."

"Quit complaining, Mr. Tough Guy, and suck it up. You're a Marine, right?"

"*Ex*-Marine," Marcus corrected.

"I thought there was no such thing as an 'ex-Marine'. I thought that once you were a Marine, you were always a Marine."

"Not this farm boy," Marcus replied with finality, and she could see there was something about the finality of his answer that carried the hint of something not quite right in his past, some hint of bitterness or betrayal. "And how would you know that?" he asked, looking up, surprised. "Not many people know that particular piece of Marine Corps trivia."

"I know a lot of things about the Marine Corps," she replied darkly. "I dated a Marine once, a long time ago."

"How did that work out?" Marcus asked.

"He owns a landscape business in Milwaukee," she said, "and has five children and two dogs."

She made it to the edge of Marcus' hospital bed, then grabbed the handrail. Frau Henzig set the chair in position, and Marie-Clémence eased herself back into the adjustable seat. She let out a long breath. The chair took her weight and rose to its normal height, about a meter or so from the polished marble floor.

"How are things coming?" he asked, by which he meant to ask how she was handling the fallout from yesterday's discussion.

"So, so," she replied, and pushed up a spike of hair that was leaning over her forehead. She chose not to reply to his unspoken question, but he noticed that she positioned her chair just next to the side of his bed. She ran her hand along the back of her head. "You know, I can still feel the track of the bullet. Good thing for me that Arab couldn't shoot straight. My father always said I had a hard head."

"Tell me about your father," Marcus began, as he had been instructed to do the evening prior, by God. Apparently there was an issue with Marie-Clémence and her father. "Does he know what happened to you—your father, I mean?" Marcus gently pressed. She looked at him in a strange way.

"I have no idea what he knows," she replied in a dead voice.

"Marie-Clémence," Marcus urged in a soft voice, tenderly, "tell me about him."

***

Zasha Levinson was an extremely successful businessman, selling catering services for restaurants throughout France. As food was in France one member of the Holy Trinity (the other members being wine and women), he became extremely wealthy, but had spent much of his life on the road when Marie-Clémence was growing up. She told Marcus first about the small things, the relocations, a favorite dog that died when she was three, the new positions as her father rose in the company, the holidays they'd had together, and then she just stalled and couldn't say any more. Marcus waited. She grunted derisively.

"You know the French word for caterer, right?" Marcus didn't answer. "*Traiteur*" she said. "Funny, that." Marcus remained quietly waiting, silent.

She opened her mouth and closed it again. She looked out of the window at the magnificent view overlooking the snow-covered Alps in the distance, the sky a brilliant blue, the sun bright and sparkling on white fields and housetops. Her hands began to twist in the blanket again. Marcus waited ... and then reached out over the bed railing and took one of her hands in his own. "It's okay," he said. "Tell me."

And so she did. Her tears dropped in a steady cadence, but she told him. "He was never home, you know? And when he was, well, for me it was just heaven, my father could do no wrong. I mean, if he even just said he was disappointed in me, why, it crushed me for three days. I would be inconsolable. But for my mother ... for her, it was hell. You see, he had another family ... yeah, a mistress in another town, for *ten years*. Can you imagine? For *ten years* he carried on with this woman, who I learned later was half his age, and there was my mother, at home, faithfully trying to raise his daughter, keeping the home, waiting like a good little wife for her husband to come home and maybe grace us with his presence for a few days each month, maybe to give her some affection, some love, some sense that she was a person who mattered to someone else. But no," she went on, and now it was more difficult for her to speak. "No, he just popped in and popped out and left her there ... *trapped*. Trapped ... with a child, with nothing else she could have done, with no one to talk to, no job skills, no one to help, with ... ah, god, with no one to *love* her." And here Marie-Clémence broke down and began to sob deeply, her heart overflowing with grief for her mother's wasted life of being unloved, rejected, forgotten, disdained. But this time she did not let go of Marcus' hand. After some minutes of grieving, she looked up at him with shattered eyes. "Don't you see?" she whispered, imploring him to understand. "Don't you *see?* I don't want that life. I don't want to spend my life invested in some man who will just leave me, dump me like yesterday's garbage, reject me for some younger model, rip my heart out, and then throw me to the curb like a piece of used tissue. I'd be trapped and I'll have had nothing! No life, no career, no accomplishment, no ..." and she couldn't go on any longer. She sat there, grief and tears pouring from her eyes as she stared through the window, seeing nothing.

"No love," Marcus said softly.

"No love," she whispered, looking at him. "I can't. Do you understand this?"

"This is why you chose to work for the government ... to do the work you do ... the espionage."

"Yes, partly, but more accurately, it was a career, a way out of being trapped with nothing at the end of my life."

Marcus looked down, not wanting to look directly at her, not wanting to be confrontational at this point. "I understand your fear," he replied, "but you don't have to live with this fear any longer. There is One who will never leave you or forsake you and who will always, always love you."

"You are talking about your God now, right?"

"Right. Jesus. He said specifically that He would never leave us or forsake us."

"My father said the same thing to my mother the day he married her," Marie-Clémence answered with a tinge of bitterness.

"Did your father give up his life for her? Did he sacrifice everything that was precious to him so that she could feel loved and cherished and cared for and prized? Did your father die for your mother?"

Marie-Clémence looked away, out toward the far horizon. "No," she whispered, and coughed once. "No, he did none of those things."

"Marie-Clémence, God is not some impersonal embodiment of doctrine or rules sitting in the sky or in men's minds. God is not some old man in a long beard sitting on a throne far above us, looking down on the world that he wound up and not caring a bit about the little peons running around on the rock he made. He is love and truth and beauty and everything, even your desire for love, exists because He exists, because He *is* love. You desire love because He made you to desire Him. You wanted love and truth from your father, you want love and truth from others, because He *is* love and truth, and He wants us to want Him. Your heart sings whenever it encounters beauty because He is beauty, and He wants our hearts to learn how to sing whenever we see Him in whatever beauty our eyes behold."

She looked down at her hands in the blanket, now twisted around her fingers. "Pleasant words," she said. "But what do they mean, really? Seriously, Mr. Ironbridge, what do they mean?"

Marcus was quiet for a long moment, for he did not know how to answer her, so he formed a quick prayer in his mind. *'God, what do I tell this woman?'* The answer came unbidden, unexpected.

"Yes, they're just words, Marie-Clémence, you're right. It is in the *doing* that His truth and love and beauty are seen and believed, not in hearing words. This is why He has a people of His own here on earth, so people will see Him doing things in their lives, not just so they might hear about Him. He said that He would live in us if we would be willing to let Him. Many years ago I opened my life to Him and submitted to His authority in my life, and my relationship with Him began then. His nature has been growing in me, and, I hope, my own human nature has over the years been diminishing. And what He is telling me now is that you need to *see* His truth and love and beauty, Marie-Clémence, not just hear about it. You need to be shown who and what He is and what He can be to you. Words will not do it for you. You must see it lived before you."

She looked at him sadly and laughed softly, derisively, almost in despair, eyes still full of tears. "And how, Mr. *ex*-Marine, do you suggest that happens? Shall I undertake to join a convent? Or no, maybe I should sign up to be a missionary in Haiti? Or no, wait, maybe I should donate half my life savings to the next televangelist I see on the cable show in my room? How *exactly* do you recommend I see such things lived before me, as you say?"

Marcus looked at her and said to her what he'd been told to say. "You come back with me to America; to Minnesota, to my home, and you stay with my parents and my brother and his wife, and me, so you can see what real love looks like, what life looks like—so you can see and then come to believe in Love and Truth and Righteousness and Beauty."

Historian's Commentary: How and Why the Church in America was Deceived

[***Note:*** *Daniel Steiner contributes this historical commentary. I asked Daniel to write this segment because he had direct personal experience with the events that fall naturally here in the sequence of this history. Readers are referred to his more expansive and detailed discussion of these times in his own work:* How the American Church was Deceived.]

> *"Then that lawless one will be revealed whom the Lord will slay with the breath of His mouth and bring to an end by the appearance of His coming; that is, the one whose coming is in accord with the activity of Satan, with all power and signs and false wonders, and with all the deception of wickedness for those who perish, because they did not receive the love of the truth so as to be saved. For this reason God will send upon them a deluding influence so that they will believe what is false, in order that they all may be judged who did not believe the truth, but took pleasure in wickedness."*
>
> *2 Thessalonians 2:8-12*

Daniel Steiner writes: There have been so many theories and explanations about what happened to the Church, when really, it's simple. Christians stopped loving the truth. Instead they loved themselves, or their stuff, or their children, or their money, or 'the ministry', or their jobs—anything but God. When men stopped receiving the love of the truth, they began to believe what was false. It wasn't because they were overcome and taken by surprise by some all-powerful spiritual force. Jesus made more than sufficient provision for the church's defense. No, it was simply that Christians just started taking more pleasure in wicked stuff than they did in stuff that was Godly. It was God Himself who sent them a deluding influence.

I once had someone in my church who came to me and said that a local pastor down the way was promising him that he wouldn't have any more money problems if he just started giving away his money—to that pastor. I told him that wasn't exactly how things worked in the Word. He left anyway. He wanted a solution that didn't require self-control. Someone else came into my office one day and told me that they were tired of being a doormat for everyone in their office 'because I have to be a Christian', and that they'd heard a sermon by this guy talking about 'taking the world for Christ' or whatever, and he was sorry, but he didn't want to hear any more about all this namby-pamby stuff about sin and forgiveness and the cross and loving one's neighbor and turning the other cheek. 'God gave us all dominion over the earth," he said, obviously repeating what he'd heard in a ten-minute

Dominionist sermon, "and that's what me and the family are gonna do." So off he went. A woman came to me with a health issue; she said she heard that the church down the way would heal her, and wondered if I could. I told her that God could definitely heal her, and that I would pray for her to be healed. She didn't want to hear that, so off she went, down the way to the church where they were falling down in the aisles, where every Sunday some new person would stand up at the front and knock the same people down, week after week. I never found out if she ever was healed.

All these and more I saw in my time during the last age, and they simply confirmed the truth of God's Word. Every one of those people, and tons more, in one area or another, stopped wanting to hear the truth and started to want something more than they wanted God's truth. I could never quite get this across to people who would come and ask me about one thing or another, because usually by the time they came to me, the weed of desire for that thing they really wanted had grown its roots down into their soul so far that nothing I could tell them would dislodge it. The lethal thing was that that root didn't go into their guts, or their feet, or their minds. No ... first it struck their ears, to clog them up, and then it climbed up into their eyes to blind them to the truth that was easily seen by others, and then finally it snuck directly into their hearts, to insulate it from the truth. It was lethal, let me tell you.

So let's summarize some of the things that combined to really choke the Church to death. None of these doctrines were new—they were all simply old lies in new packaging, presented in different ways to more successfully deceive those whose hearts were not seeking truth, but instead seeking—well, anything else.

First let's talk about the Dominionists. In the early part of this time we're writing about, they were pretty tame, but as things began to ramp up, and especially after the destabilization happened in the West, they became downright violent. I can speak from personal experience about that.

The Dominionists believed that the Church would grow in power and influence until Jesus returned (boy were they mistaken, we know now, but back then ... wow!). They knew they couldn't take complete dominion over everything, but they were looking for what they called a 'preparatory' dominion, or in other words, they wanted the world to be under the control of Christians such that it was actively being prepared for the return of Jesus. They held that God's purpose was for mankind to possess and bless the earth. They stressed that this theme of dominion was included in every covenant (or 'agreement') God made with mankind—the Noahic Covenant, the Abrahamic Covenant, the Old Testament, the New Testament, and a bunch of others they came up with. They say that because we humans are blessed by God, we blessed humans are given a mandate to take dominion over the earth so we can bless it. Not sure I follow their logic there, but that's what they were saying. They would use Genesis 1:28:

> *"Then God blessed them, and God said to them, 'Be fruitful and multiply; fill the earth and subdue it; have dominion over the fish of the sea, over the birds of the air, and over every living thing that moves on the earth.'"*

They would say that under man's authority, the earth was supposed to be blessed because man is blessed. They linked the condition of the earth to the condition of mankind by the fact that when Adam and Eve sinned, man and the earth were both cursed. They used the phrase, "As man goeth, so goeth the earth." They said that the verse meant that man needed to take dominion over all of man's society, cultures, and governments, when traditional, biblical Christianity interpreted the verse in its plain and literal sense—that God meant mankind to be over all other creatures made by God. But there was enough in the verse for those who wanted to control others to use as leverage, no doubt.

One of the big prophets of Dominionism was a guy named C. Peter Wagner—I don't know what the 'C' stood for, but he was the big engine in what came to be known as the New Apostolic Reformation, and truthfully, a lot of the false doctrines and teachings we saw in those last days flowed out of that movement—it was sort of a mix of Pentecostal and Charismatic thought processes and forms of worship, and it drew from a lot of heresy in earlier times and movements, and it did the Church no end of harm. Anyway, Wagner once said the following at some conference someplace:

> "Dominion has to do with control. Dominion has to do with rulership. Dominion has to do with authority and subduing and it relates to society. In other words, what the values are in Heaven need to be made manifest here on earth. Dominion means being the head and not the tail. Dominion means ruling as kings. It says in Revelation Chapter 1:6 that He has made us kings and priests - and check the rest of that verse; it says for dominion. So we are kings for dominion."[10]

Besides Wagner there were lots of other folks jumping on the bandwagon, weaving a bunch of additional teachings or threads into the doctrine. The poison of the New Apostolic Reformation came directly out of the Latter Rain movement, which had its roots in occultic, demonic forces influencing neo-Pentecostal theologies. Disciples would advocate that while Jesus *began* the work of conquering death on an individual basis, the *Church* would complete the task, and alleged that the Church had the same power over life and death on heaven and earth that Jesus had (insert forehead smack here). All that was required for that to happen was for the Church to just stand up and proclaim, "We have DOMINION over the earth." Yes, they were

---

10 This a transcription of a recording of C. Peter Wagner delivering a speech to the 2008 "Starting The Year Off Right" conference. Readers may consult this recording if they have access to the media once known as YouTube. The recording may be located here: http://www.youtube.com/watch?v=ecszOPc95s8. SCV.

big into the power of words, just like the ancient sorcerers were—they were coming from the same source, unfortunately.

As the Latter Rain morphed into the New Apostolic Reformation, all kinds of strange and devious theological serpents sprung out from this demonic ball of snakes. The 'Five-Fold Ministries' concept alleged that in the 'last days', apostles and prophets needed to take their places as leaders among man's social infrastructure systems in order for the kingdom of God to be established on earth. And as usual, there was always the poison introduced by the enemy. Men who stood at the head of these movements would cry out that God would guide the movement using 'fresh angelic visitations' as well as visitations from dead saints communicating 'new strategic direction'.

Always they took words or some current fad phrase or a Scripture and used it from a wrong heart position, striving for something unbiblical, unchristian, unworthy of the Great King, but instead with their own devious desires, their own love of wickedness, corrupting the words or phrases or scriptures into a wrong teaching—and so many, many people, also harboring those same desires in the depths of their own hearts, would follow them off the path and down to destruction. This massive following by so many people opened up the opportunity for the enemy to come in openly and manifest in church meetings, during worship services, and whenever these people got together. All kinds of what they called 'signs and wonders' would emerge during their meetings—people barking like dogs, acting like animals, climbing the walls, literally; feathers would manifest out of thin air, sparkly 'gold dust' would suddenly appear, drifting down on the assembled crowds—and those with little or no discernment were swept away and convinced that a 'great move of God' was happening, all the while, tragically, their Bibles sat unread, undigested, on their shelves, covered in all that gold dust falling from the heavens.

Later in the movement there were calls for 'a corporate mature man' that could exercise dominion. They would allege that Jesus chose to bring about the will of God on earth by divinely ordaining various apostles, prophets, evangelists, shepherds, and teachers (hence the 'five-fold' phrase).

This Dominionist poison filtered into other false teachings, like the global prayer movement, the mission movement, the cultural renewal movement, the leadership training movement, the emergent church movement, and of course heavily supported that noxious bucket of poison, the New Apostolic Reformation (NAR). As a critic of the movement, Rachel Tabachnick, wrote:

> "Wagner has a gift for making the NAR's agenda of elimination of all other belief systems sound benign, as he speaks glowingly of a future without poverty, disease, and corruption ... Wagner does not specify how this utopian vision is to be achieved or the role that the demonization and scapegoating of others plays in bringing it about. The movement has developed a blueprint for justification of the demonization of

others and markets it as love, charity, and social justice."

And of course, as soon as what Tabachnick wrote got into the mainstream, all the little rats started jumping off the NAR ship. Always a sign of demonic infestation, we began to see a huge amount of internecine warfare. Other groups came up with a new doctrine a little more palatable to modern Americans beaten down by governmental leanings toward socialism, rising taxes, massive increases in public and private perversion, a society increasingly at odds with Christian values, and the legalizing of homosexual marriage everywhere—this new doctrine was the 'Seven Mountains Mandate', in which they picked out seven different areas that they could creatively market. They picked business (always the biggest, because hey, that's where the money is, right?), government, religion, the family, the media, arts and entertainment, and education. Funny thing ... just after the leading market guru came up with the 'Seven Mountains of Culture' thing, two prominent Christian leaders 'suddenly remembered' that they each had had a vision about these seven areas of culture, individually, a long time ago. Hmmm. So they marketed this new thrust and coerced Christians ignorant of the Scriptures to work to 'take dominion' in these various areas—and it was no coincidence that these teachers always called for attacking the business mountain first, to get businessmen into their camp—because hey, where else would they get the money they needed to fund the rest of their efforts?

So anyway, off they went down this path, and no one was too worried, because they were just sort of a splinter faction in the larger Pentecostal movement, weren't they? Well, not for long.

The basic thought underlying all this had to do with undermining how Christians understood the return of the King. The Word clearly taught that Jesus would return bodily to judge and rule the earth. These Dominion people, though, taught that Jesus would not return bodily, but instead, He would rule and reign through His body on earth, spiritually. Christians would 'Christianize' the world through some force called 'Joel's Army', and His elect would be victorious here on earth. Nothing could have been better designed to fall into the Antichrist's agenda than to convince Christians that they would themselves bring 'heaven on earth'—just the thing the Antichrist trumpeted, and the very reason so many of them fell, deceived, into the pit, with the Antichrist's mark burned into their wrists.

Men would advocate 'conquering the culture for Christ', or that it was the 'moral obligation of Christians to recapture every institution for Jesus Christ.' A man, predicting what did in fact come upon the earth—only in a way he never imagined—said this: *"What is about to come upon the earth is not just a revival, or another awakening, it is a veritable revolution. The vision was given in order to begin to awaken those who are destined to radically change the course, and even the very definition of Christianity."* Men said things like the following: *"The Church has been foreordained of God to become that people who will become so glorified that we can bring Christ back to the earth. This glorified church must make the earth God's footstool before Jesus can come again."*

I fought and fought against this until one group in Sacramento, acting on orders from a higher headquarters in Colorado, sent three men to my home in Grass Valley. They knocked on the door one night, and my wife answered. They were polite; two men stood close to the door, one stood behind them, obscured. They asked if I was at home. I came to the door and in one quick movement, the one man standing behind the other two pointed a gun at me, pulled the trigger, and killed me instantly. He then shot and killed my wife as she leaned over my body. They came into the house, turned over some furniture to make it look like a robbery, threw down a few bags of cocaine to make it look as though I was some sort of druggie, and then left.

I can tell you *why* I was killed. I was killed because through the Spirit of God I shed the light of His truth on the darkness of Dominionist poison, and this so enraged their demonic masters that they had the men whom they controlled, alleged Christians, do away with me. Yet that isn't *how* I was killed. Three men, at close range, killed me with a gun: that is *how* I was killed.

Why was the Church deceived? Simple—they refused to love the truth. They would not just sit down and read the Word of God and depend on the Holy Spirit to interpret it for them; no, they needed someone 'famous' or a 'personality' to tell them what it meant. They needed a famous book or a commentary or some Internet video full of dramatic music, with flashy images and preferably, exploding cars, shooting stars, and lots of sparkly things to scratch their itching ears. One person at a time chose to love the world and its passing pleasures of sin instead of loving the cross, reveling in the glory to which such pain and suffering would lead. That is *why* the Church was deceived—but *how* was the Church was deceived? Here is my explanation of 'the smoking gun' that was used to kill faith in the Church, and I record it for posterity so that mankind may know just *how* the Church was deceived and where in the Bible they could have seen the deception.

Dominion theology was one of the bullets in that smoking gun. The doctrines of Dominionism were rooted in the earth, not heaven. Their main point was that man needed to take dominion over the earth and change it for the better before Jesus could spiritually reign on the planet. Oh how wonderfully noble all that sounded. But it never matched Scripture. Why?

Dominionists dredged up their poisonous doctrine out of the pit of hell, and in a shiny rocket fueled with man's desire for power launched it into the minds and hearts of unsuspecting Christian sheep who were completely ignorant of what was plainly written in their Bibles. Dominionists spoke of a universal kingdom of God on earth. For such a thing to emerge, society would need to be drastically altered (from the perspective of the time in which they spoke these things, the latter portion of the twentieth century, and the early part of the twenty-first century, there was massive apostasy). Obviously, if one took their teaching to its logical conclusion, it required a world government headed and policed by Christians. Such a world government would naturally require obedience to a specific Law or set of Laws, enforced and governed by rules and regulations. The Dominionists actually proposed a type of government most closely resembling Old Testament Law. But they apparently did not read the part in their Bibles where it mentioned that Law cannot save mankind, and that the only way for man to be saved, to be acceptable before God, is through faith, not through the works of the Law. The Law, admittedly, failed to transform mankind, as Paul points out in Romans. But Dominionist's false teachers, calling for this dependence upon man instead of God, calling upon the Law instead of grace through faith to establish righteousness, opened themselves up to massive deception, and thus it happened.

Most of the Dominionists succumbed to the man of sin when he made his appearance because this man appealed to the world on the basis of a Law that would establish what they, in their deceived state, perceived to be one that would bring peace. Having its roots in the Latter Rain, neo-Pentecostal threads of Christianity, when the man of sin began to do all manner of miracles, they fell over themselves in wonder, proclaiming him first as a 'true apostle.' When he proclaimed himself to be god, they saw this man as the validation or fulfillment of their prophesied 'fully mature corporate man'—one who fully demonstrated the principles of godhood and, should all men emulate him, would be the advent of Christ on earth. It matched what the evil man said perfectly.

When this evil man proposed himself as the great arbiter of peace for all of humanity, they eagerly lined up as his supporters, quietly saying to each other that only through the good graces of this man would they ever be able to come to realize their final vision of 'conquering the world through Christ'. And then when this man walked into the temple and declared himself to be god, these same Dominionists all as one shouted with a great shout in triumphant glory, believing that finally their work had brought about the advent of 'Christ on earth'. Most of them died believing this, and now burn for it.

Another unmistakable sign that Dominionism was from the pit was its attempt to rob the Jews of their inheritance. The Replacement Theologians, who trumpeted their teaching that God had replaced Israel with the Church, broke this ground, saying that all the promises to Israel were now only valid for, and would be fulfilled only by, the Church. This corrupt teaching fell quite well in line with Dominionism's holding that only Christians would be able to establish law and order and righteousness on the earth, flying in the face of so many Old Testament prophecies and proclamations that promised one day the redeemed remnant of Israel would return to their own land in grief at their shocking apostasy, and in those days and only then, would the 'law go forth from Zion', and 'the word of the Lord from Jerusalem'—literally when Jesus sat on the throne in Jerusalem. And so thus did the Dominion teachers proclaim loudly, with great reception by many in the Church who hated the Jews, that Israel no longer had a place in God's plan, and that God would now be blessing the nations through Christians, not through the Jews, who had denied their Messiah and thus forfeited their birthright and promises.

As more and more Christians fell into this honey trap of false teaching that so catered to the flesh, it took their eyes away from waiting for the return of the King, and so, like the five virgins that did not have enough oil, they were not ready when He did return. They saw the door closed to them because He did not know them—they had not taken the path of the cross, to put to death their own human nature, but instead tried to save their lives by holding on to what was comfortable, what was palatable, what was, to their human minds and perspectives, understandable, instead of trusting in what Jesus told them. They eventually just had to throw out most of the Scriptures that clearly spoke about what would happen during the end times. They spiritualized them away; they crafted convoluted doctrinal explanations that shunted the truth into some dark 'past' that had already happened.

These false teachers denied the sovereignty of God—another reason He would on Judgment Day say that He did not know them. They taught that Jesus could not return until all His enemies had been put under subjection to the Church. They taught that Jesus would need to wait until the Church got around to subjecting all things under their dominion. The world would be completely evangelized, all the denominations would be united, the Church utterly without sin, no spot or wrinkle, before He comes. They ignored Jesus' own words, indicating that there would be a paucity of faith upon His return. They also failed to read in the Word that the purification of the Church was a work of the Holy Spirit, not man. This teaching also led to men being deceived by the Man of Sin, in that this man's last drive to unite all the world religions dovetailed precisely with Dominionist teaching that 'all religions would become one.' The Dominionists actually taught that Christianity would be united with Roman Catholicism; with Mormons; with Jehovah's Witnesses, with the Buddhists, the Hindus, and with all other religions so as to be unified—exactly the plan executed by the Man of Sin, uniting all the world's religions under his own stench of death.

The main reason they had me killed was that Dominionism depends upon human leadership, with a structured Church system of law, instead of the leadership of the Holy Spirit. Dominionists, as well as most neo-Pentecostals, those deceived by the Toronto Blessing, the Prosperity movement, the Faith Healing movement, and the other lumps of dough leavened by the poison of man controlling his own destiny, believed that Christians needed to fully obey their doctrines. A system to control Christians therefore needed to be put in place to make sure every Christian would be under some sort of authority chain, held in line so as not to deviate from their truth. They did so using this man Wagner as their head 'apostle' (no surprise there). They began to use the phrase a 'one world kingdom'—dangerous, as we can see now, but too many Christians, wanting power and authority, desperately eager to avoid the cross in their own lives, lunged for it, like they went after so many other shiny, flashy things, and held on to it in what became, literally, a death grip. Dominionist churches began to exclude all those who disagreed with this 'one world kingdom' teaching and disinherited all other Christians from the Body of Christ—very similar to what other bodies of men did before they killed them in mass numbers; they had to somehow dehumanize them. Just so did these Dominionists convince themselves that all Christians who disagreed with their teaching were not true Christians at all, and could be killed with abandon—they were, after all, just unbelievers. To strengthen their doctrines, to emphasize that the Church was now God's regent on earth—not Jesus—Dominionism essentially replaced the Lord Jesus with His body. Everything conferred to Jesus was appropriated by the Church, they taught, and so it then became the responsibility of the Church to destroy the wicked, to establish the Kingdom of God on earth, and to rule and reign until such time as Jesus decided to show up. The false teachers from the Word of Faith movement, the Latter Rain, and all the New Apostolic Reformation garbage had been teaching this before Dominionism raised its ugly head. Again, this aspect, like so many others of its doctrine, would lead to an immense degree of human arrogance, interpersonal rivalries, obsessive degrees of control by Church leaders of their fellowships, and the replacement of obedience to God with submission to Church leaders. I fought against it with everything I had.

I read once where a man named Sandy Simpson summarized the error of this poison. Uncannily prophetic, he wrote, before the Man of Sin made his appearance:

> "Dominionism is heresy and the Bible is clear that we are to reject heresy and heretics (Titus 3:10), mark and avoid false teachers (Rom. 16:17), and prove that we love the Lord by obeying His commands (John 5:10). Our mandate is the same as when Christ ascended until He returns: preach the gospel (Mark 16:15) and disciple believers from all the nations (Matt. 28:19). We are NOT to overthrow the governments of the world, take over businesses, or throw our collective Christian weight around in a bid to take over everything. We are to be light and salt (Matt. 5:13-15) to a dying world (1 Cor. 7:31) and abide till He comes (1 John 2:28). Christians need to get busy witnessing for Christ and drop this Dominionist, Kingdom building rhetoric and planning because if they do not they will be playing right into the hands of the coming antichrist."

Sadly, few Christians heeded Simpson's message. They certainly did not heed the plain message in the Word of God. Shame ... shame upon them all; shame upon them, for they forfeited the truth of God for the passing pleasures of a corrupt, poisonous, depraved world, and chose to serve those which by nature were not gods, and defrauded the true God of His rightfully deserved worship.

Chapter 14
Tony

"Woe to the shepherds who are destroying and scattering the sheep of My pasture!" declares the Lord. Therefore thus says the Lord God of Israel concerning the shepherds who are tending My people: 'You have scattered My flock and driven them away, and have not attended to them; behold, I am about to attend to you for the evil of your deeds,' declares the Lord."

Jeremiah 23:1-2

I was out for bear when my cell phone buzzed, and it was God's mercy it was in my inside pocket. I would never have felt the vibration if I'd have stuck the thing in one of the outside pockets on my parka. I'd been baiting for this one particular bear for almost a month, and finally felt like the odds were good he'd be coming around for his breakfast today.

I pulled the phone out and read the text. "Need you home. Now." It was from Penny. The bear gets another free day in the woods. I climb down out of the stand, extra vigilant, my .44 Colt revolver out and in my hand. Though he dodged being my breakfast, I don't want to be his. I stomp through the snow until I get to my snowmobile, about a quarter mile from the stand, and it starts right away. The revolver goes in its holster, the .308 in the scabbard on the back of the snowmobile, and I turn on the hand warmers. Man is it cold, and it will be colder at 35 miles per hour. But Penny usually has a good reason to pull me out of the woods. Something was up, probably to do with the church. So goes a pastor's life.

After a quick ten-minute ride I pull the snowmobile into its shed, collect the guns and my lunch, uneaten, and move into the house. It was a nice house. We'd lived in it for twenty-some years; technically it was the parsonage for Living Waters Church, a non-denominational church in Granite Sky, of which I have been the Pastor for the past twenty-some years. It had four bedrooms, three bathrooms, a huge living room, a nice kitchen, and plenty of garage space. My boys had grown up in this house, and my wife and I had cemented our lives here. It was tucked up against the forest, and it was just a quick jump to the Gunflint Trail and then on into the complete wilderness. And God knows how much I loved to hunt.

I shake the snow off my boots, put my parka and goggles on the hooks in the snow room, and step into the warmth of the kitchen.

"Message on the machine," Penny says, sitting at the table. She is reading the morning news on her computer, drinking some coffee. Penny is a tall woman, slightly taller than I am, though I never admit that. She has long black hair going gray, but with the complexion of a high school girl still. I'd known her since I was fifteen. "There's coffee in the carafe if you want it."

"What's the issue?" I ask, moving to get a mug from the cupboard.

"Alicia said she and Todd need to talk to you. Today."

"Must be something important. Any idea what?" The coffee was strong and hot, the way I liked it.

"She didn't say." Penny scrolled down, clicking a couple of times. "She asked if you could meet them at the church at seven."

I look at my watch. "That's in ten minutes," I say.

"Then it's a good thing you got my text, and it's a good thing we live two minutes away from the church," she replies, still reading the news, sipping her coffee.

"And a good thing I didn't get all this gear off," I mumble to myself, because I would have just needed to put it all back on to take the snowmobile to the church.

"She didn't want to come here?" I asked as I went back to the snow room to put on my boots.

"She didn't," Penny replied. "Hey, you should read about what's happening with the Fed," she says. Penny is an executive in the town's largest bank, and sometimes I think she dreams about rising interest rates, loan percentages, and fiduciary bond yields. I have a tough time just balancing the checkbook.

"What's happening with the Fed?" I ask, knowing that I will in no way comprehend what she will tell me.

"The President is thinking about dumping the central bank and using a computer program to manage interest rates and monetary policy."

"And would that be a bad thing?" I ask, trying to cloak my ignorance with curiosity, jamming on one of my boots.

"Depends on whom you talk to," she answered, always grammatically correct, still staring at the screen. I wonder at times like this why she married some dumb Italian off the streets of St. Louis who was and still is financially and grammatically challenged.

"Some say the Fed causes more problems than it fixes. I think they need to focus on controlling inflation and stop worrying about short-term growth. The advantage of the Fed is that they're insulated from short-term political pressure—or at least, they should be." If I knew how inflation related to short-term economic growth, I might have had something substantial to contribute to the conversation, but I was way, way out of my league.

"The Fed is driving asset prices to levels that aren't sustainable," she says, going on, "and we're going to find ourselves in a big fat bubble that will pop any moment."

"Well, as long as it doesn't pop before I get over to the church, we'll be okay. Gotta go."

"Stay warm," she says, hoisting her mug to say goodbye.

"Thanks. I'll say hello to Alicia and Todd for you."

She nods and doesn't say anything, and I trudge out to the snowmobile. It starts right up.

***

Two and a half hours later I park the snowmobile in the shed again and go back into the house. Penny is sitting where I left her, still reading. "What's up?" she asks, seeing my face.

"Todd has cancer," I say dully, leaning against the door into the kitchen. She puts her mug down.

"Todd is what, thirty-five? They have three kids. Is it bad? What's Alicia going to do?"

I sit down. She gets up and pours me another cup of coffee. It smells of dark, rich brown earth, and life, and it strikes me that my friend Todd might not have too much longer to live.

"What are the doctors telling him?" Penny asks.

"They don't exactly know yet. They have to go down to Minneapolis this weekend to do some tests."

"Will their insurance cover it?" Penny asks.

"Alicia is DHS[11], and I'm pretty sure her insurance will cover the expenses."

"Do they need us to watch the kids?" Penny says.

"They set it up with Eva already."

"Right. The Zees would be more comfortable with Allison anyway." She was referring to the three Watson kids—Zach, Zana, and Zebra—all of whom, for some reason, had names beginning with the last letter in the alphabet. Allison was Eva Gunderson's youngest daughter, in her late teens somewhere. "Zach is what, five?"

"Six," I say. "Zana is four, and Zebra is two."

"Have they told them yet?" Penny asks.

"Don't think so," I say, suddenly tired and feeling the weight of fifty-six years on my shoulders. "She didn't say. We need to pray for them."

"Right," Penny says. "When will they get the test results?"

"I think Alicia said they'll know just afterward, before they leave the hospital, but I'm not sure she knows much more." I was feeling a desire to get alone and pray for Todd, and maybe ask God what He was doing. It didn't make any sense to me that God would take a young father and leave his children fatherless. It was one of the things that made my job difficult, trying to explain to my sheep why sometimes it seemed as though the Big Shepherd took time off.

***

I didn't see Todd until the following Saturday, when I decide to drive over to their house that morning. Penny was working on a presentation for the bank she was giving in Duluth the following week; she couldn't come. So Bailey and I decide to go—Bailey is my dog, an Irish wolfhound. He sits in the front with me when I drive around by myself, which is a lot of the time, since Penny works a full-time job. Bailey and I jump in our beat up Volkswagen and get ourselves to Todd and Alicia's house.

They lived in a very nice new house they had built when Alicia was transferred to run the border station north of Granite Sky. People say that if you work for the government, you don't make much money. At least, that's what they used to say. Now, when around 25% of the country's workforce works for the federal government, a government salary usually tops whatever people in the commercial sector can pull down. I take in their two-story red brick colonial that sits on about twenty acres, fronted by a massive manicured lawn. A fence lines the long asphalt driveway, which is a luxury up here where most roads not maintained by the county are mud twelve months a year. Alicia is doing quite well.

Bailey jumps out and immediately heads to the back yard, barking. He knows the three Zees and loves to play with them. He clears the backyard fence in a single bound and starts sniffing around. The front door opens. Alicia is waiting. She is not in uniform; probably her day off.

"Morning, Alicia. How you feeling?"

"Good, Tony, pretty good."

11 Department of Homeland Security.

"How's Todd?" I ask. I step into the entryway, a finely-paneled room with tiled floors bordering a railed stairway leading upstairs. The room is a far cry from my plywood-floored snow room. I start to take my boots off.

"Todd is in the back yard with the kids," Alicia says. Alicia is a medium-sized, very thin woman with an air of natural authority that, I figured, must come from being in charge of government operations for fifteen years or so. She signed on with the Department of Homeland Security after five years in the Army as a military policewoman. She's tough but I can see she's stressed. It's not every day you find out your husband may die and leave you with three kids to raise.

"You not working today, Alicia?" I ask.

"No, I took the week off."

"Understand." I follow Alicia to the kitchen. Todd comes into the kitchen through the sliding door.

"Hey, Tony. Good to see you," he says to me. Todd is only slightly taller than his wife, and a little heavier, though not by much. He looks a little drawn around the eyes, but I can't see much of a difference. We shake hands and take seats around the kitchen table. Alicia puts a kettle on for some tea.

It's always awkward for me, visiting people in a crisis. I want to give them strong assurances, but sometimes I don't have the words to say. Sometimes I can dig around and come up with Scripture that might fit the situation, but a lot of times the situations just don't make any sense and try as I might, I can't piece together verses that bring any comfort.

"How was the big city?" I ask, trying to start light. Todd tilts his head, as though to say it was no big deal. Alicia waits for him to say something, but he stays silent.

"It was an easy trip," she says, jumping in awkwardly. "The hospital was—"

"Why is God doing this?" Todd asks, to no one in particular, although I assume he's talking to me. My mouth gets dry.

"Did you find out the ... the extent of things?" I ask.

"Liver, one lung, both kidneys, and the spleen," he says, like he is reciting items on a grocery list. "I wonder what He's doing." Alicia blinks hard, as though her husband had just wondered out loud why God was killing him.

"God knows what he's doing," I say weakly. The words sound hollow and banal as they hang in the air over the table. To me their effect is like some malodorous, souring piece of fish suspended just under the hanging table light. But Todd surprises me.

"I know that," he says, with surprising confidence. "I mean, I know that, seriously. I really do have confidence that He knows what He's doing. It's just that, well, I'd like to sort of know what that is. I mean, it's my life, right? I know this is supposed to happen but I don't know why, and I kind of would like to. I don't want to go out not knowing." Alicia's eyes are tearing up, but Todd sits there, dry-eyed, not emotional at all.

"Well, it's good to keep a positive attitude," I reply diffidently. Alicia nods to back me up.

"Positive attitude ... I dunno," Todd says hesitantly. "I'm not sure how much our attitude affects what happens to us. I think God has His way no matter what. I mean, yeah, how we feel about things is important, don't get me wrong, but what I mean is that, like, if I have cancer and I have a 'positive attitude', that doesn't make the cancer go away. Right?" He looks at me like they all do, like since I'm the pastor I have all the answers, like

I'm some fount of wisdom or something.

"No, you're right, Todd, but keeping a positive attitude will help the others around you deal with things." He doesn't look convinced.

"The doctors say I have to go back down to Minneapolis next month to begin treatments," he says, his voice dry.

"That's good," I reply. "Alicia, will ... how's the insurance handling things? Are you guys okay?"

"Yeah, yeah, we're good with that, Pastor, thanks," she says, sort of eager to let me know they're covered financially. That's a relief.

I stay for a few more minutes, killing the time with small talk about the Harvest party and what the church will be doing for the Christmas holidays, and, duty discharged, I say goodbye. I am dissatisfied with myself; I never get these things right. I go outside, call Bailey, who jumps the fence, leaving in his wake happy yells from the Zees. We drive home, the dog sticking his face out the window. I split the previous night's leftovers with man's best friend while we watch a football game. Neither of us uses utensils.

***

The next Sunday I'm standing in the door of the church at my station when an older couple comes in, visitors. The man is, I guess, slightly older than I am, with solid silver hair and a close-cropped beard and an old black drover coat. He's limping. The woman, just about as tall as he is, with dark hair, is dressed a little more stylishly in a long blue coat with black lapels. They're about my age, maybe a little older, but their bearing is somewhat different, almost straighter, like life hasn't beaten them down. We get some farmers up here that would make Methuselah look like a spring chicken. These folks look reserved but ... I don't know, almost confident. Most visitors resemble someone walking into a dentist's office for their drilling appointment, but these two, they walk in almost as if they own the place. Well, maybe not like that, but you can tell they're comfortable in a church. I shake hands and introduce myself, smiling. They smile back, both of them holding their bulletins and the other assorted paper we give out at every service, and both of them looking at me with a strange intensity, like they are trying to see through me and get to what's inside, but it wasn't unpleasant. They take a seat just in front of Todd and Alicia, just behind the first row. Another interesting surprise; most visitors jump in the back row, somewhere close to the door in case the pews start to heat up or something.

I stood at the entrance, greeting everyone as they came in, but I sneak a glance now and again at the older couple. They seem to be in conversation with Todd and Alicia. Around eight minutes past ten, Sharon goes up to the podium and looks around, trying to gather everyone's attention. Everyone quiets down and she begins to read the announcements. I glance over and Todd is leaning forward, still talking with the older guy, and they seem to still be having an intense conversation. Then Todd sits back and I see Alicia dart a questioning look at him, almost fearful, and then I turn back to listen as Sharon finishes the announcements.

Announcements come first at our church. Talking about what is happening in the church is how we connect with the church family. And when I say 'family', I really mean family. We do care for each other. I know that's sort of my doing, so let me explain.

***

I was raised in an extremely dysfunctional Catholic family. I like to tell people that when I was eight, my family moved ... but I found them again. Seriously, religion generated more fights in my house than the U.S. Boxing Commission. My father was a rabid Catholic who also happened to be an alcoholic. My mother, I would say looking back, was probably some sort of lapsed Protestant, of what particular denomination was never clear. If I had to guess, though, I'd say she was probably a Stubbornist: God, was she stubborn. Unfortunately, so was my father, and he outweighed her by around 100 lbs. It made for a lot of screaming, yelling, cussing, and then slaps, and then the inevitable punches and once, a knife brandished with killing intent. I don't know how that would have turned out. Maybe my mother would have killed him in his sleep, but when I was eleven a drunk driver hit my Dad when he was walking home one night from his shift at the refinery, so I never had that to worry about. My mother reacted as though she'd won the lottery. She sued the guy that killed my Dad and the settlement put her in a house without the need to ever work again. She saw what the drink had done to my father, so she never touched a drop. When I was thirteen, though, she decided cocaine was the answer to all of life's ills, and up her nose went all the settlement money, then her house, then what savings she had left, and finally her soul. She became an empty, soulless creature that lived for the next hit. When she died, she died screaming at me, my brothers, my absent father, and, finally, God, because we wouldn't give her another hit.

It was in my high school years, I think, that I began to hate. I hated the kids in my school that had functional families, with real parents. I hated the people in the neighborhood where I grew up. I began to hate my brothers, and finally began to hate my mother, and my father in absentia. And then one day some kid challenged me on a dare to go into a church. It was a joke among the crowd of kids I ran with, to try and pull some kind of stunt near churches or on what we called "church people". I mean, looking back, it had sort of a diabolical logic. The worse you can hurt the things of God, the worse you can hurt God, and when you think about it, the guys I ran with at the time, we all pretty much hated God, if we ever even gave Him a thought, blaming Him for our crappy lives.

My plan was to actually go into a church during a service and do something. I didn't know exactly what—maybe blow out candles or draw a moustache on a statue. But not having enough courage to go into a Catholic church, I picked the Baptist church on the outskirts of town. Growing up in Little Italy, the only real church was the Catholic Church. Miscreants and delinquents we were, but even we feared what we thought was holy, and while we would cross to the other side of the street if we saw one of the parish priests walking down the road, it was a matter of certainty to us that the Protestants were all doomed, outside the true church as they were, all of them going to hell—and never once thinking that we too were in just such a condition. But there you have the power of sin and self-righteousness ... it blinds you to your own condition.

The church I picked must have been the only non-denominational church within a hundred miles of Little Italy. I wanted to be as offensive as possible right from the start, so I decided I'd go dressed in some dirty jeans and a t-shirt. Low as my family was, my mother had forced us to keep a jacket and tie clean and ready for mass on Sundays. I'd blown off going to mass for years, but even though the jacket and tie were still hanging in my closet, I needed to let those church hypocrites know I wasn't one of them.

I was thirteen and a half when I pushed open the door of that non-denominational church on a Sunday in October, so many years ago, with the crowd of ne'er-do-wells I ran with outside, at the same time laughing up their sleeves and egging me on. The first person I met was, it turned out, the Pastor, though I wouldn't have known it. He was wearing jeans and a clean blue polo shirt, and my first thought was, 'Hey, is there some other guy here planning on making a scene too? Did I miss the boat?' But no, he came up to me, smiled, shook my hand, welcomed me to the church, and asked me my name. I was too surprised and shocked to lie. I tell him 'Tony', and he says, "Welcome, Tony. We're glad you're in God's house today." I wasn't too shocked to react to that, though, getting back on my plan, and I gave him a cynical sneer, like I was too much a tough guy to believe there was a God, or that He had a house.

I looked around the place. No candles, no statues—my first plan went out the window. As I was trying to come up with some kind of offensive activity to perform off the cuff, some lady about forty came up and smiled and took my hand, shook it, welcomed me to the church, and asked me my name. She had some guy standing next to her, and two little kids. They looked ... happy. It was a look I didn't know was associated with families. This threw me for a loop. I told her my name. She asked if "I was just visiting." I mumbled something and jumped into the first seat I could find. Another shock: no pews, just folding chairs with little cushions on them. For a moment I thought that maybe I'd wandered into some sort of community bingo parlor or something. There was no altar up front, no cross hanging down from the ceiling, no statues of dead guys in robes, no racks of candles, and the head guy was dressed like everyone else. I sat there trying to process the strange new environment.

But it was the people that threw me the most, and more specifically, it was the families. Yeah, I could tell they were families. A guy would come in with a lady who was obviously his wife, and there would be one or two or four or, in one case, seven kids trailing after them. The guy would be smiling and usually he'd migrate to talk with the other husbands. All the men were dressed in clean clothes, and no one had puke on his shirt or was unshaved or had rips in his pants where his wife had tried to knife him. The wife would be smiling and then she would go over and talk with the other wives, and to my thirteen-year old eyes, all the women looked like they came out of the pages of some glamor magazine. None of the wives had bruises or black eyes or missing teeth. The kids would be laughing or talking or punching each other good-naturedly, and I could tell that just before they came no one had threatened to beat the living hell out of any of them because their tie was crooked or because they'd mouthed off at their mother or because they complained about no food for breakfast or because they'd been out late and come back drunk or stoned the night before. It was like someone had dropped me onto a different planet populated by different beings. I had no idea such people, such a world, existed. I remember thinking that the best thing in the world would be if I could just stay there forever. And so I did.

***

Sharon is finishing up the announcements and that's my cue. I move up to the podium and give Sharon a smile as we pass. A shadow of a smile appears for a moment and then she goes back to sit with her husband, Gary. Gary is the town's police chief and as I turn I see him sitting in the back of the far right section. He once told me he likes to keep an eye on everyone who comes in. Gary was a former Marine, and you can tell by the close-cropped haircut and the broad shoulders. He's still incredibly fit and he's been a deacon in the church since I've been the Pastor, and we're good friends. He and I hunt together most of the time, when he can get time from work, and fortunately Granite Sky isn't like Minneapolis or Chicago, so we go hunting together a lot. Sharon teaches the kids at Children's Church, and she's a lifesaver, always ready to volunteer if the church needs something done. They're one of the few couples in the church family that don't have kids. I know that bothers Gary, because he and I have talked about it some, but I've never talked with Sharon about it and it really doesn't seem like it bothers her. Penny tried to talk to her once a while ago but it didn't seem to her like Sharon wanted to talk about it.

Penny is in the back row and I see her lean forward to talk with Eva Gunderson, who is sitting there with her husband and kids. Sharon had read during one of the announcements that Allison Gunderson had been elected as the girls' basketball team captain for the next year, and as we all clapped, I could see that Eva was proud of her youngest daughter. Eva was the mainstay of our church, always busy helping out with one program or another. Johnny Gunderson, their younger son, was next to his sister. He was just entering his freshman year and looking forward to high school. They were both good-looking kids, like a lot of kids up here in Minnesota with Nordic ancestry. Tall, blond, muscular, with clear blue eyes ... not like their Italian pastor—pudgy, short, a little darker than most of the folks in Minnesota, with dark brown eyes and a thatch of brown hair that sticks out amidst all the blond heads like a sore thumb. Every time I thought about how different I was from the people God has me looking after I marvel at God's goodness and mercy—and His sense of humor.

After the announcements, I call the church family to pray for those on our prayer list. We keep a running list of church family members who need prayer for various things—illnesses mostly, along with operations that were becoming more frequent as many of our members were getting along in years. We pray for Todd, that he would get a good report from the doctors when he went to Minneapolis for treatment. We pray for others diagnosed with various ills. We pray for church family members whose relatives were having difficult times; that they would come to know the Lord and come to church. We pray for the kids in the church—kids who were sick or having problems or going to college or joining the service or getting married or just leaving home to start their lives in a new job somewhere. We pray for the older members of our church family, that they would stay healthy. We pray that the church family overall would be a blessing to the community during the upcoming Christmas season. Praying together as a church family brings us closer together. Talking about our problems with God helps people understand that God is concerned with their issues and difficulties and wants to help them.

Don't get the wrong idea here, though. It's not like I call people up to the front of the church and babble incoherently while I lay hands on them and they leap out of their wheelchairs or something. That doesn't happen here and the way I see things, it shouldn't be happening anywhere. The days when miracles like that occurred are over; the 'gifts' of the Holy Spirit were for a time when the early church needed to be firmly established, and now that it is, we have God's perfect Word in the form of the Bible to keep it established and strong. I'm no theology professor but I did pretty well in my theology classes at seminary and believe I can hold my own with anyone who might argue that the gifts of the Holy Spirit are working today. My experience in thirty years of ministry has been that most of the time, the people who are always prating on about the Holy Spirit are the ones whose relationship with God is based primarily on emotion and not God's written Word.

These folks blow in the wind. Some days when they're up, they're in love with God and all is right with the world; on days when they're down emotionally, God is some far-off distant concept and they are constantly doubting their faith and the truth in general. I hate that kind of emotional rollercoaster; I grew up in a house like that, where you never knew what you would find when you came home, and I determined not to let that that kind of emotionally-based faith near my people.

After the prayer for those on the prayer list, I turn it over to Agnes Baker, who leads the worship. Jenny is in the back, working the computer projector, projecting the words of the songs via PowerPoint slides on the overhead projector. Rollie Magnusson is on the piano—the guy is amazing, he could play professionally, but fortunately for us he just likes to play for the church. His wife Estelle leads the singing. I stand there, belting out the words of one of our contemporary songs, not in any way bothered by my lousy singing voice, but just rejoicing in having my church family around me as we sing. I can hear people talking together as we go on to the next song, chatting, interacting, sharing their lives, enjoying, *reveling* in the time we have together. This is the best part of the week for me.

After the worship, we have special music, which is just a phrase for when some member of the church family gets up and either sings a selected song or plays an instrument while someone sings. It's a time to highlight the talents of individual church family members and to give them a chance to get up in front of the entire church and demonstrate their devotion to the Lord. No matter the skill or quality of the performance, the church family always gives them a rousing applause, which makes me proud of them. Today the three Zees are signing 'Silent Night', getting ready for Christmas, and I see Gary and Sharon watching them raptly, Sharon wiping her eyes. Estelle is looking pleased as punch, because she worked with them for a couple of weeks on the song, and then I see Todd looking at his kids with, I don't know, a strange look, as though he was confused or questioning something, and then I realize that he's probably just thinking about what will happen to his kids if he passes away. I find myself praying that he would stay positive and be optimistic about his visit to the doctor. I find myself praying that he would be healed.

After the special music I take the church family into Luke, interrupting our normal study in Galatians, where I talk about the events leading up to the birth of our Savior, in preparation for the Christmas season. Before I do, though, Allison and Johnny Gunderson come up the main aisle with one large white candle each, walking slowly so as not to extinguish the flame. I had them turn down the lights in the sanctuary for this little procession, just to make things a little more solemn. They come up the center aisle and Allison hands me my Bible, and then they break off, one to each side of the stage, where they place the still-lit candles in special holders set in place there. They then turn and go back down the side aisles to their seats. I watch the faces of the congregation while this happens and see a mixture of pleasure, peace, contentment, some even the beginnings of awakening awe. I get a shock, though, when I see the old couple looking almost stunned, like they were watching someone walking across the stage naked. Maybe they just can't abide rituals that have their origins in Catholicism—which is where I got the idea to dim the lights and have the candle procession, by the way, from the local parish priest, Father Jourdain. I've seen it before, Protestants in every denomination, where they have this issue with Catholicism, and the spirit they bring is always divisive.

Every first Monday of the month, all the pastors and ministers in Granite Sky and, lately, the parish priests from the three Catholic churches in town, get together at the Bluefish Grill to meet and talk about life as shepherds of God's flocks. I didn't get much from Catholicism growing up, but lately I'm beginning to see how the ritual and reverence they maintain in the mass appeals to a growing number of people, especially younger people who are hungry for spiritual things. It's probably why most of the Protestant churches in the area are moving more toward a focus on the more reverential aspects of the upcoming Christmas season and it's why I'm integrating some of their rituals into our services. For me, the ritual kind of made me feel like things were being restored—both between me and the memories I had of my dysfunctional Catholic upbringing, but also between Protestants and Catholics in general. I'm beginning to realize that while there were many good things about the Reformation, one of the things the Protestant community as a whole has lost is the sense of awe and reverence for God. It's one way I can help drive the body of Christ closer together and maybe one day eliminate the divisiveness and separateness that today marks Christianity in a negative way throughout the world. We've been too long separated. I make a mental note to be wary of the older couple.

After the sermon Rollie and Estelle come up and we sing a hymn that Father Jourdain mentioned to me during our recent Monday meeting. It was a hymn he particularly likes, calling the people to worship the sacred heart of God; there's sort of a solemnity to it that our Protestant hymns are missing. I kind of like it.

When we finish, I dismiss the congregation with a blessing and the mass of people dissolves into numerous little knots of diverse fellowships. I delight to see the church family interacting together as family members ought to—no fighting, no discord, no anger or irritation or broken homes or, worse, broken bones. Hey, I'm not walking around with rose-colored glasses on. I've been a Pastor for close to thirty years and I know people have problems in their life, even people in the church, and I'm here to tell you that my church family has its share. But we get through them—together, leaning on each other, turning to each other and supporting each other in times of difficulty and stress and heartbreak.

I take my stand at the back of the church, near the doors to the parking lot, and try to say goodbye to each person as they leave. I look over the heads of the people to see Todd and the old guy shaking hands. Todd looks serious and contemplative. The old guy looks like something I've never seen before. He's looking at Todd with a mixture of intensity and grief and hope. I can't describe it any better than that.

The old couple moves to the door and I shake their hands and thank them for coming and ask if they'd like me to come by and visit. Most visitors just sort of blow me off there, thanking me, but saying politely that no, that's not necessary and they really enjoyed the sermon and we won't come back even if someone puts razor-sharp bamboo under our fingernails, thank you very much. But the old guy looks at me like a laser beam and says, "If you're up to it, have at it." If I didn't know better it sounded like a challenge, and there's not much this street-smart tough guy from Little Italy likes more than a challenge. We exchange phone numbers and I promise to call them in the next week.

After most everyone leaves, Todd and Alicia come up. The Zees race on through the doors and head out to the now empty parking lot. Todd shakes my hand. Alicia thanks me for the sermon. Todd is still holding my hand.

"New friends?" I ask, referring to the old couple Todd had spoken with.

"Yeah, it was ... it was an interesting discussion."

"How'd it go?"

"Zana said hello first, actually," Alicia put in, pulling on her coat, "and she doesn't normally do that, so it kind of surprised us. And then, oh my God, after saying hello, she pipes up and says, 'My Dad has cancer!' like he won the lottery or something. I was so embarrassed! But you know, they didn't bat an eye, they just—"

Todd interrupts: "They looked at each other for a quick moment and then the old guy turns to me and says, 'So why has God given you cancer?'"

I laughed, nervously. "That's not something you usually hear, starting off a conversation."

"It's not."

"What did you tell him?"

"I told him I had no idea, but I was pretty sure God wanted me to get something from it."

"It's what he told you at our house, remember?" Alicia asks me.

"And then the old guy says to me, 'God wants you to have a deeper relationship with Him, which is why you have cancer. This is the ultimate ... objective—" Todd was working hard to remember what the old guy had said.

"*Purpose*, he said, didn't he?" Alicia interrupts.

Todd hesitates. "No," he replies, "I'm sure he said 'objective'. He said 'This is the ultimate *objective* of suffering. To make us more like God.' I'd never heard that before, but it's beginning to make sense to me."

"Why is that?" I ask, wondering where the old guy was coming from, getting a nervous feeling in my stomach. Talking about suffering around my flock made me nervous.

"Because lately I've been looking at things a little differently," Todd says. "I want to know more about ... about what a relationship with God would be like. I want to learn about ... about stuff. All the stuff I used to do, you know, watching sports, working out, going to work, all the normal stuff in life ... it's like none of that holds any interest for me any more. I want to know *why* we're living. I want to know why we're here on earth. What are we supposed to do? What does God want us to do? It can't be that the whole sum and substance of Christian life consists of just going to church and doing this event or that event or having Bible studies Wednesday nights. I mean, if I look in the Bible, the people we read about, they were talking to God all the time. He *talked* to them. Sometimes they were even in His presence." He lifted up a hand in a gesture of futility. "There has to be more."

I'd never heard any of my people talk like this before, and I wondered if it had more to do with his talking with the old guy or if the cancer was making him fatalistic.

"You have a church family," I said, in partial answer to his question. "We're there for you all the time. That's something."

Penny had come up and she was standing next to me and heard my last encouragement to Todd. She smiled and took my arm. "He's right here," she said, patting my shoulder. "Good ol' Dad." Alicia laughed nervously. I could tell she didn't know where Todd was going with all these new questions, and for some reason Penny made Alicia nervous.

Todd looked at me directly. "You know, Tony, maybe I'm not thinking right, but I just have this weird sense that we're missing something important here, you know? More important than anything else we're doing." Todd was still standing there, now holding little Zebra, whose arms were wrapped around her favorite stuffed animal—right, a little black and white zebra.

"What do you mean?" I asked, reaching out to take little Zebra, who stretched out her arms. I love kids, and the Zees think I'm their grandfather anyway.

"Like, I dunno, think about Halloween. It's, like, some kind of satanic holiday, isn't it? I was reading about it the other night, and I was wondering if Christians should be celebrating it."

"Good question, Todd," I reply, handing little Zebra a tootsie roll, "and the answer is no, we shouldn't ... which is why we have 'Harvest Parties' instead of Halloween parties."

Todd looks down at his feet and sort of shuffles them around a bit. "Yeah, I suppose," he says, definitely unconvinced and definitely still bothered by something.

"Sweetie, we have to go. My shift starts in a bit." Alicia pulls him along out the door and we say goodbye and they gather up all the Zees and Todd drives them out of the driveway, and I stand there, after Penny takes the car home leaving me to clean up after the service, wondering just what it was the old guy said to Todd.

Part 2
Soil

"When a large crowd was coming together, and those from the various cities were journeying to Him, He spoke by way of a parable: 'The sower went out to sow his seed; and as he sowed, some fell beside the road, and it was trampled under foot and the birds of the air ate it up. Other seed fell on rocky soil, and as soon as it grew up, it withered away, because it had no moisture. Other seed fell among the thorns; and the thorns grew up with it and choked it out. Other seed fell into the good soil, and grew up, and produced a crop a hundred times as great.' As He said these things, He would call out, 'He who has ears to hear, let him hear.'"

Luke 8:4-8

Chapter 15
Bryant

"And working together with Him, we also urge you not to receive the grace of God in vain—for He says, 'At the acceptable time I listened to you, and on the day of salvation I helped you.' Behold, now is "the acceptable time," behold, now is "the day of salvation ..."

2 Corinthians 6:1-2

"No, Marcy, I'm not sure I'll be back by then."

"Yes sir, but, um, we've got the PKG account briefing slated for Friday of next week. Mr. Grantham is expecting you to spearhead the MITRE team as well, and ..."

"And I'm not sure I'll be back by then, okay?" My administrative assistant was quiet for a moment and I knew she was trying to figure out what I was up to. She'd graduated top of her class at Yale law, she is dangerously close to being almost as smart as I am, and she isn't letting any moss grow under her feet as she plows toward the upper levels of the international management consulting corporate pyramid.

Silence for a moment, and then, "Okay, well, where are you now?"

"I'm driving the Gunflint trail, up here near the border."

"What border?"

"The border between Minnesota and Canada, hey?" She didn't get it.

"Oh. What's the traffic like?" she asked, like any city denizen.

I chuckled. "Traffic? What's that? I haven't seen another car for half an hour."

"Okay," she says, completely unimpressed by my manly courage in braving such a wilderness, "well, Mr. Grantham mentioned that the White Paper you delivered about the Russia-China Agreement has generated a lot of interest. He said he wanted to talk to you about it before it gets briefed in the public sector."

"Understandable," I replied.

"And then he said that he fully expects it to get briefed to UN officials soon as well."

"That's a surprise. Why did he think that?"

"He didn't tell me that, sir, sorry." Of course one of the Managing Directors wouldn't convey that kind of information to an administrative assistant to a Senior Partner. I could probably guess.

"Well, okay Marcy, so I'll be up here for probably the next week, but tell Grantham I'll catch a flight back into San Francisco probably Saturday or Sunday, and ask him where he wants to meet."

"Yes sir. Do you want me to make flight reservations?"

"Yeah, that would be good, Marcy. Yeah, so, do me a favor, if you could, get me a flight out of Duluth let's say Sunday afternoon. Schedule the service to pick me up at the airport."

"The whole package, right sir, got it."

"Thanks, Marcy."

"You're welcome, sir. Call if you need anything else."

***

I'd rented the white Toyota pickup in Duluth. I'd wanted to see what the Gunflint Trail looked like for a while, actually since my parents passed away. They'd lived up near the trail many years ago, after they retired, and they always talked about how nice it was. I never visited them at their home up here—I was always too busy. But something had happened at work that bothered me, and I needed some time to clear my head, and so here I found myself, driving through gorgeous countryside and endless forests, rationalizing to myself that I was fulfilling my filial duties by at least visiting where my parents used to live.

I didn't see how people could live up here. I think I passed maybe two gas stations in forty miles. I thought there would have been at least a motel or something where I could stop for the night, but apparently people don't sleep up here, so I just kept driving.

The phone rang again. I checked the number. It was from Zander, one of my team leaders.

"Gillenkamp."

"Bryant, it's Zander. How's things?"

"Good, Zander. What's up?"

"Hey, I talked to Marcy and she told me you were up in Minnesota."

"I am. What's up?"

"Well, nothing, except I thought we were going to prep to kick off the MITRE team later this week."

"Yeah, well, let's put that on hold, okay? We can push it to the right for a week or so."

The line was silent for a moment. I pulled the phone down to check the signal—yeah, good signal.

"Zander, you there?"

"Yeah, yeah, Bryant, I'm here."

"What's the problem?"

Another brief delay, and then, "Hey, Bryant, I'm not trying to pry or anything, but are you up there because of the State Department's ruling on the Senegal thing? I know that was a sewer of a situation, Bryant, but those things happen in our business."

"Senegal's President was running a massive human trafficking ring, Zander, and I'm not exactly sure Grantham didn't know about it. The President, you know? Not the President of the company, or the President of the Stock Exchange, but the friggin' President of Senegal, for God's sake."

He was silent for a moment. My outburst, especially the indiscretion about one of the company's managing directors, Grantham, took him by surprise, but he recovered quickly. "We can't be totally responsible for what our clients do, Bryant. We're just advising them. You know that; you've only been an international management consultant for, what, the past twelve years? You're a Senior Partner, for God's sake."

"And how would you feel if one of those girls Senegal was pushing into Chicago had been your little sister, Zander? Would you have been okay with knowing we'd been doing our best to support and improve and streamline Adoulam Sahi's operations so his profit margin would increase, so he could put his hands on even more victims?"

Quiet on his end now. I gave him some space, but he snapped right back.

"Nobody has proven anything yet, Bryant. Sure, State is trying to make a case, but you know those people, they're as corrupt as the people they're investigating. The most State will do is make some kind of 'advisory ruling' or maybe publish some kind of exploratory findings based on 'preliminary research'. You were just doing your job. When the UN bought off on your argument, it was a huge win for the firm; you know that. Grantham was pleased as hell."

I didn't reply, because I knew he was right ... as if the State Department was going to find the President of some other country guilty ... yeah, right. For all I knew, Sahi was probably providing underage kids to half their senior diplomats. I'd had my suspicions about the Senegal regime for months, but I didn't let them interfere with the efforts my team was providing. We advised Senegal's Chief Executive about a range of things, especially how to transport perishable goods—that paper and the effort and expertise we put into that one really made me sick. We thought he was transporting vegetables into Burkina Faso. Now I was spending a lot of time looking at dark asphalt and wondering where the kids were who Sahi had trafficked, and what was happening to them, and what me or my team had done or said that had helped that bastard improve his human trafficking operations.

"Are you going to call your sister?" he asked accusingly, yanking me back into my own sewer of thoughts. Zander had been working with me for so long, sometimes he can read my mind.

"She wouldn't take my calls," I replied, feeling morose, but not even bothering to argue. "I might try texting her, though."

"Don't text and drive, Bryant. You might hit a moose."

"Yeah, well, I rented a pickup, so I'll be fine. And for your information, my folks lived up here for, like ten years about a century ago and they never saw one moose, ever, period, end of story."

"Don't call your sister, Bryant. She'll just rake you over the coals, *again*. She's unbalanced."

That rankled. "She's a religious nutcase, Zander, yeah, but that doesn't make her unbalanced."

"She calls gays 'sodomites'; *sodomites*, Bryant. I mean, really ... *sodomites*?" I could hear his barking laugh—understandable, since Zander was what my sister would call a sodomite, and I suspected her term rankled. "She thinks Muslims are trying to take over the country. She thinks there is some shadow government getting ready to take over the world. She thinks cities are, like, satanic dens of iniquity, she doesn't even vote *Republican*, for God's sake, and she thinks Jesus is coming back on a white horse to clean house. Yeah, she's out there, Bryant, sorry."

I was quiet again for a few hundred feet. "I won't text her," I mumbled, and was disappointed with myself for saying it.

"Seriously, don't call her, for God's sake, she'll rip you a new one. The Sahi issue has been all over the tinfoil hat blogger circuit. She'll know exactly what happened."

"Look, Zander, I said I won't call her, okay? But she's entitled to her opinions." I tossed this out to defend my older sister, who was married and living in some off-grid log cabin and growing her own food with her husband and some other people she knew somewhere in North Dakota. I never had gotten around to visiting her. I didn't know what bothered Zander more; that my sister was way, way out of the narrative mainstream, or that she'd been married to the same guy for twenty years and they were still crazy in love with each other. In the eight years Zander had been a team leader working for me, he'd had something like, I don't know, at least thirty different relationships with all sorts of men.

"She's not entitled to her opinions if they're contrary to the public good will and are generally considered to be encouraging wrong civic virtues," Zander replied. "Ali-Bahzi vs. Taylor, 2016."

"Landmark case, I remember it," I replied, not wanting to get into an argument. "Let's talk about it when I get back."

Zander took the hint. "Right, Bryant, sure, okay. Marcy says you're coming in on Sunday afternoon?"

"Yeah, she'll have the details. See you at the office."

"Sure. Hey, don't hit a moose or anything up there," he said, laughing lightly, "and don't use your phone to get on the Internet. Not while you're driving."

I barked a laugh. "I'm lucky to get a voice connection up here at all, forget about the Internet." Out of habit I held up my phone and checked to see how strong the signal was.

"I'm not sure they even have the Internet up there, Bryant. I think Sarah Palin outlawed it ... no, wait, that was in Alaska, right, yeah, one of those places that has the white stuff. Ugh, gross, I don't see how people put up with it."

"They do, nonetheless," I answered. Sometimes Zander was a bit much.

"I mean, really, how can anyone live up there? I know I wouldn't want to, and anyone worth knowing wouldn't want to either."

"I'll take your word for it," I replied dryly. When he was comfortable or feeling too casual with our relationship, he would start to lisp, which I really detested.

"Yeah, and you could hit a moose," he said.

I was angry all at once at Zander's familiarity, his sense of entitlement because our company was headquartered in San Francisco, which pretty much made him and his kind unassailable when it came to infractions in the workplace, and the effeminate part of his nature. I'd been a management consultant for twelve years and eaten my share of crow at a client's table, but there were still shades of the alpha male I'd once been, lurking around inside me somewhere, someplace. "There aren't any moose left up here," I snapped, trying to sound convincing.

Zander took that hint even more strongly. "Right, okay Bryant, see you Sunday," and disconnected as my white Toyota Tundra cruised around a curve in the dark road. I threw the phone down on the passenger seat and put my eyes back on the dark asphalt just in time to behold a very large, shaggy, long-faced, long-legged creature with antlers the size of cricket bats, eyes staring at me blankly in my headlights, snow streaking the scene like little white meteors. I jammed the wheel to the right.

***

Snow ... cold, wet, sticky. I wiped my face. It was dark and I realized it was the cold that woke me. I felt groggy, like I'd been sleeping. Why was that? Right ... now I remember ... moose in the road, swerving, snow spray all over the windshield, tree, tree, *really big tree.* My vision cleared. Snow was blowing through the windshield, which didn't seem to be there any longer. There seemed to be a large branch in the passenger seat, tinged with snow. Yeah, there it was ... prickly, hard, real ... nature intruding into my little metal and leather safe space. That didn't seem right. And it was cold—really cold—in the truck. That didn't seem right either.

I wiped my face again. Evidently the truck wasn't going anywhere anytime soon.

Without the windshield, staying in the truck for the night wasn't an option. I tried to push open the driver's door; but the door was buried to the middle of the window in snow; too heavy. Nothing for it but to crawl out through what had been the windshield, which I did, grinding glass into my expensive chinos. The moon was out, broad and round and full and bright white. I could see that the truck had come to rest in the ditch along the road, deeply buried, tilted slightly up on its left side with snow halfway up the hood, smack up against the base of a huge evergreen, part of which was parked in the cab of the truck. I slid down off the hood through thick branches and found myself buried up to my hips in snow. At least I was out of the wind. There was no sign of any moose.

Phone; I needed my phone. Powered by desperation, I pushed and swam through hip-deep snow to get to the passenger door. I scraped and swam back up onto the hood again and peered through where the windshield had been into the cab and saw my phone in two pieces on the center console, utterly smashed by the intruding branch, useless. I realized my only hope was to get picked up by some traveler driving down the road, and that, I began to understand, was chancy at best. Things were getting sporty. I climbed back down off the hood in disgust and pushed through the snow toward the road.

I got to the shoulder of the road on my hands and knees after making swimming motions through hip-deep snow for ten minutes. It was a deep ditch. The moonlight showed my pants stained dark, soaking wet from the snow. I wasn't any kind of outdoorsman but I knew by immediate personal experience that wet coupled with cold and wind wasn't good. Standing up on the shoulder of the road, the wind hit me and my pants began to freeze, like, right away. My vision was blurry and I wiped my eyes, my hands coming away bloody. I touched my forehead; there was a stinging sensation. Head cut, great. I'd heard they bled a lot but weren't fatal. I couldn't feel the blood very well, though, and I realized it was because my fingers were getting numb. I didn't have any gloves.

I looked up and down the road: no headlights. I debated staying with the truck or trying to walk out. Drawing upon some inexplicable logic, I determined that if I moved I would be more likely to encounter someone who could help. Powered by a combination of ignorance and optimistic thoughts of swirly blue and red lights from some Minnesota State Police car coming along—which was about as likely as a sled with eight flying reindeer—I stuck my hands into the pockets of my thin, high-dollar, high-tech fleece jacket and started walking.

After what seemed like an hour I realized that things were not working out well. An elementary and unforgiving mother nature in the form of a bitterly freezing wind was defeating my high-tech fleece jacket. My legs were trembling and my feet didn't feel comfortable. I wondered what I'd been thinking, driving around northern Minnesota in spring hiking shoes, even if they did cost me $450. I began to seriously wonder how this was going to work out. The thought that I could die on this frozen road hadn't begun to dawn on me; it wasn't a possibility I was even considering. My life was my life, as permanent as the sun coming up in the morning; it had always been and would always be. I'd never considered my own mortality. I just expected that I'd get out of this situation. I never thought of it as potentially fatal. Ignorance, they say, is bliss. My life to this point had been quite blissful.

About the time I lost feeling in my feet, I saw a small wooden sign hanging from a tall signpost, neatly hand-painted, partially covered in snow: "Eagles Wings' Creamery," with a golden arrow pointing down what I saw to be a side road branching off from the main highway. I stumbled over and swiped away at the snow, uncovering the rest of the sign. "Eight Miles," it said. I stood there debating whether to head eight miles toward the dairy, or press on along what was sure to be a more populated roadway, keeping in mind that I hadn't seen anyone on the road for at least an hour. I wondered which way to go, as if I had a choice, with my feet now completely numb. Eight miles would kill me.

Headlights. O joy, headlights, coming along down the small side road from the dairy. They were yellow and as they approached they blurred the snow blown up from the road by the wind. I realized that this person might just drive right on by without even seeing me, and that thought suddenly terrified me. I stumbled clumsily into the center of the road and started waving my arms like a man possessed, completely ignorant of the possibility that the driver might not see me in time to stop.

He did. Driving around with his high beams on, he saw me in time. The truck slowed and pulled up next to me as I stood to one side of the road, and I could see the driver's window go down. It was a man about my own age with a strong face wearing a tan farm jacket and some kind of fur hat that looked, at least to me, incredibly warm.

"Hey, thanks for stopping. My truck ..."

He waved me in without a word, jerking his head to the other side of the truck. I didn't argue. I stumbled around to the other side of the truck and tried to open the door, but after fumbling with the handle, I realized my hands wouldn't work. He leaned across the cab and pushed the door open and I climbed in. I pulled the door shut and blessed whatever person had invented car heaters. A light hit me in the face.

The driver pointed to a tablet mounted on the dash, pulled of one of his gloves and then began to type on it. I read *Cut your head* and then he pulled up the center console box and yanked out something that looked like a thick rag—it was a thick rag—and handed it to me while he held a small tactical flashlight. I put my hand up to my forehead and was surprised to see it was bleeding ... still. I looked down and saw blood all over my pants, mixed with the wetness from the snow. The driver shone the flashlight over my pants, showing me the dark patches were blood, not water. I took the rag and slapped it over my cut. The truck pulled away from the side of the road. When he'd been typing, I'd noticed the man had a huge thick red knot of scar tissue in the middle of his right hand.

He was typing again. *Accident?* The guy must be some kind of mute.

"Ran off the road about ... about ... I don't know, a ways back," I replied.

He pointed in both directions with both hands, asking me which direction to go. We'd come to the intersection, and I pointed back to where I'd come from.

"Back there, I think." He nodded and turned the truck onto the Gunflint Trail road. We came to my truck in less time than I'd expected. I felt like I'd been walking for an hour; the truck must have been something like fifty yards from the intersection. The man pulled to the side of the road, put the hazard lights on, and gestured for me to just sit in the truck. I was fine with that. I still wasn't feeling my feet. The Good Samaritan got out of the truck. I noticed he was wearing heavy, fleece-lined winter boots and he pulled even thicker gloves out of his pockets. He stepped carefully across the road and stood on the opposite shoulder, shining his tactical flashlight down towards the forest into the ditch.

He climbed back into the truck, took off his glove slowly, and then typed on the tablet. *You're truck isn't going anywhere soon.* And then: *Name?* He stared at me hard for a long moment.

"Bryant," I replied, still shivering. "Bryant Gillenkamp."

He punched a shortcut key and the tablet showed his name: *Mace Ironbridge* He stuck out his right hand. I shook it, feeling that hard knot of knurled flesh, but his grip was thin, tough, strong, and much warmer than mine.

"Thanks for picking me up," I said.

Ironbridge waved a hand deprecatingly, smiled grimly, and drew a finger across his throat, which I took to mean I would have been dead if he hadn't. I wasn't going to disagree with him.

"Hey, seriously, uhm, if you could, like, I dunno, just drop me off at the closest gas station, I'd really appreciate it. Don't want to put you to any trouble."

Ironbridge did the strangest thing then. He had both hands on the wheel and he looked over and just stared at me, like someone had told him to look for something and he wasn't exactly sure why. He must have stared at me for a full five seconds or so, and then punched more keys on the tablet. *Came out here to get U. No station 4 20mi. Home w/me. UB okay.*

***

The big pickup pulled into a circular driveway in front of a stone house with an honest-to-god turreted stone tower on the side. Ironbridge popped the locks and hopped out. It was pelting snow, hard, driving, with a fierce wind, and I realized with a shot to my gut that I probably wouldn't have lasted much longer out there on the road. But I wasn't sure I was any safer. I mean, seriously, was he some kind of dumb serial killer, trolling the road for victims? He'd said as much on that weird type pad he used—*came out to get me.* Seriously? When he indicated I should follow him, I started to get a little nervous.

Out of the corner of my eye I saw a shape moving in our direction from another stone building, sort of like a garage off to the side of the main house. It was a person wearing a large white parka, and the person was running ... towards us.

"Hey Mace, you're back!" The running shape took the form of a woman and she was running toward Ironbridge. She didn't stop until she ran right into him. He caught her and they held each other closely for a moment. That was a little helpful, ratcheting my anxiety down a notch. I mean, how many serial killers get such a reception when they come home?

"Man, we thought you were stuck! And what made you just up and leave like that?" She smacked a gloved hand on his chest. "I mean, I just took a short nap and then I wake up and find you gone and ... oh. Hi."

"Hi," I said. I unwrapped myself and held out a shivering hand. "Bryant Gillenkamp," I said, introducing myself. She had long red hair that was rapidly disappearing under the hard-falling snow, bright eyes, was shorter than Ironbridge, and I could tell she was sort of petite.

"Zoe, yeah, nice to meet you. Husband," she said, indicating the guy who'd picked me up and smacking him on the chest. "So you're the one he had to go pick up? Man, you look cold, you'd better get inside."

Ironbridge held out a hand toward the turret-shaped entryway, and the woman—Zoe—went ahead of me.

"Come on, you have to meet Tack and Claire and man, Tack is gonna *freak* when he hears about you. There's something happening, that's for sure."

I had no idea what she was talking about, and my concern notched up to consider the possibility that perhaps I'd fallen into a den of serial killers or maybe a family of cannibals who preyed on unsuspecting travelers in the middle of the northern Minnesota wilderness.

Zoe stepped in and announced my arrival before she threw off her parka. "Hey Mom, hey Dad, Mace picked up another city-sickle!"

Cannibals, maybe? "City-sickle?" I asked, perhaps not wanting to hear the answer.

I followed the young woman into a kitchen and an older man was sitting on a couch in the kitchen. He had one leg and was in the process of fitting a prosthetic limb to the bottom of his left. I began to seriously get nervous. They have movies about places, families like this.

He smiled slowly. "That's just a word we have up here for city slickers who've watched too many episodes of the Nature Show on their big-screen televisions and think that nature is just this warm, smiley-faced Mommy that'll embrace them if they just think nice thoughts about it." He looked at me standing there, shivering. "So they come up here in fancy clothes and expensive hiking boots and every year in the spring we find one or two of them in the woods, dead, frozen stiff, because they didn't want to face reality."

He looked down at my lightweight hiking boots, now almost frozen to my feet. "You can leave those in the mudroom," he said. I smiled because I didn't know what else to do.

Ironbridge walked in and showed the tablet to the older man.

"Bryant ... Gillenkamp. That your name?"

"Yes sir, nice to meet you."

"Tack Ironbridge." He held out a hand, and I shook it. "Mace's father. Seriously, Bryant, you dodged a bullet out there tonight, you know?"

"Yeah, I uh ... I guess I did," I replied, knowing I'd leapt out of the frying pan, wondering what fire I'd jumped into. "I'm sorry about interrupting whatever it was you had planned. If you could just drop me off at a gas station or somewhere ..."

"You didn't interrupt anything," he replied, fiddling with something on his prosthetic, "and there's nothing within twenty miles of here. We're going to get hit with another storm in about two hours. We don't want to be driving in that, so unless you want Mace to take you back to your truck, it looks like you're gonna have to hole up with us."

"I smashed into a tree and there isn't anything left of my windshield," I explained.

"Well, then you really don't want to go back to your truck. But hey, we can put you up here until you get yourself sorted."

My evening was not turning out as I'd planned, and that has always bothered me, not knowing what will happen, not being in control. But I didn't have much of a choice. "Hey, uh, Mr. Ironbridge, that's fine, I appreciate it. Sorry for being a bother."

He nodded. "It's Tack; and how'd you run off the road, anyway?" he asked.

"I almost hit a moose, and I swerved to miss it, I guess," I replied, waiting for him to tell me there weren't any moose up here any longer.

"Yeah, there are moose all over up here," he said, with a finality I found galling.

"Thanks," I said. "I, uh ... I thought all the moose had disappeared."

He looked over at me. "Who told you that?" he asked, shaking his head. I saw Mace standing in the mudroom, having taken off his tan coat, his mouth open in silent laughter. He was about my age, maybe a little younger, but in much better shape, with broad shoulders, a narrow waist, and a strong jaw. I could see the resemblance to his father. His hands were strong and ropy, with forearms that had probably gotten to be like iron milking cows—or whatever else people like this did out here in the middle of nowhere.

"So, uh, when do you think we'll be able to get my truck out of the ditch?"

Tack thought for a moment. "Well, it's Saturday night. Booker won't be open tomorrow. You have triple-A?"

"No, I don't think so," I replied. "But it's a rental. The company should be able to come and get it."

"Right. Where'd you rent it from?" he asked.

"In Duluth," I replied, "at the airport."

"Hmmm ... what they'll probably do is just call a local company to pick it up, and since Booker is the only local company up here, he might be able to get up here Monday if the storm isn't too bad. If it dumps a bunch of snow, though, it might be Tuesday or Wednesday before they can get to it. Or you. You figure they'll bring another rental?"

"I'm thinkin'," I said. "At least I hope they do. They probably don't have taxis out here, do they?" I asked, staring through a beautiful kitchen window out into what looked to be an endless snow-covered forest under snow darting down in angry white streaks.

"Nope. Don't have Uber, either," he said, his voice deep and rich and he wasn't smiling.

A tall slim woman with rich dark hair wound up in a French braid came into the kitchen and moved toward a large black iron appliance I hadn't noticed. She was holding what looked like a piece of firewood in her hand, and she was wearing a dark green fleece.

"Hey, love, we've got a visitor."

"Great," she replied in some sort of accent—French, I guessed, since we were so close to the French-speaking part of Canada. "Hold on." She used some sort of spiral-handled metal thing to lift up a round metal plate from the top of the large black appliance and dropped the wood into it. Curiosity overcame good manners.

"What is *that*?" I asked, nodding toward the large black item which, I then noticed, had some sort of pipe leading up from behind it up and through the wall.

"It's a wood cook stove," the woman replied, as though I'd just asked her a really dumb question. She brushed her hands on her jeans and held out her hand. "Claire Ironbridge, Tack's wife; nice to meet you. And you?"

I was staring at the wood stove. I'd heard that such things existed but had never seen one. "I didn't know those things still existed," I said, and then remembered my manners. "Bryant," I said. "Sorry ... Bryant Gillenkamp. Thanks for, well ..." I shook her hand, not exactly knowing how to describe getting rescued from a very bad situation and probably having my life saved. My concern about falling into a nest of cannibals was diminishing.

"Sure, no problem." She was smiling at my curiosity over the stove. "We thought there might be some reason Mace had a crazy notion to cruise the road at this hour." I must have looked like I didn't know what she was talking about, so she went on. "He didn't tell you?"

"Well, he said he had gone out to pick me up, but, uh ... I mean ..."

She smiled then and said, "*Certainement*, but of course, you are probably wondering how Mace knew you would be in trouble. Well ... join the club. All of us are wondering how it is so, too. Don't we, *Mon fils*?" She touched her son's face and kissed him on both cheeks, like the French do in the movies. "You are safe, yes?" Mace nodded and kissed his mother in the same way.

"So," she went on, with a tone of deliberate direction, "now you will sit, we will get some soup into you, and you will tell us everything, about why you drove off the road, about why you came to be on the road in the first place, and most importantly you can tell us all about why God brought you all the way up to northern Minnesota, to this little farm."

If the cannibal idea made me uncomfortable, it didn't come close to the unease that came when the tall lady mentioned God. I was rescued from the need to reply when Zoe came in from the smaller front entrance room. "You can hang your fleece up in there when you get warm, Bryant. Go stand over by the stove. It heats the whole house, by the way, and it'll dry out your fleece by tomorrow. You want some hot chocolate?" she asked me, and then, to her husband, "Hey, babe, you want some hot chocolate?"

I heard a quiet "Sure ..." from the other room. My savior speaks.

"Sure," the woman replied, and waved at me. "Chocolate for everyone. Bryant, sit down and tell everyone what got you out on the road at this crazy hour. Mace, in the spare closet you should find some dry things for Bryant."

Tack and Claire were maybe in their early 60's. It was hard to tell; they were both in excellent shape. Both were tall; Tack was around six one or so, and his wife looked as though she was just less than six feet. They had an easy air about them; I could tell they were comfortable with each other and with where they were in the world. They exuded a strong sense of confidence, as though they'd been places and done things that made hacking out a life in the wilderness a walk in the park.

Zoe, who looked younger than her husband, was just a ball of energy, like some kind of energizer bunny, zipping around, first over to Mace, and then over to help Claire make the drinks, and then over to Tack to help him maneuver around a chair, all the time talking and smiling and just ... I don't know, just being happy.

"I feel bad for imposing on everyone like this. I hope I didn't interfere with something important."

"You're the most important thing happening here tonight," Tack said, which made me slightly more uncomfortable.

Claire took a glass bottle of milk—the kind they used to deliver from milk wagons pulled by horses, if I remember the commercials right—and began to whisk cocoa and sugar and hot water together in what looked like a French copper saucepan, plunking it down on the top of the cast iron wood cook stove. She saw me staring. "Heats the house *and* doubles as a stove," she said in a delightful French accent. She leaned down and opened a door on the front of the appliance and showed me a large oven. "It's an oven, too, yes? Pretty handy if there isn't any electricity, which happens now and again up here," she said.

Mace came back into the kitchen with a pile of clothes and a towel. "Here," Claire said, taking them from Mace and handing them to me. "Let me know if they don't fit. You can change in the bathroom there." She pointed toward a small room off a narrow hallway out of the kitchen.

"Thanks." In the bathroom I shed my frozen jeans and shirt, dried off with the towel, and changed into a fleece pullover and a pair of soft cotton jeans. They were loose but workable. I came back out to the kitchen.

"They seem to fit you fine," she said. "We don't have much need for jeans in that size with two legs," and she looked over at her husband, who chuckled easily.

"Did you call anyone yet, let them know where you are?" Tack asked.

I shook my head. "Cell got smashed somehow in the truck, so no."

"Is there someone we can call for you?" he offered, standing by the stove, stirring the chocolate.

"I, uh ... well, yes, actually. I should check in with my company."

"You work around here?"

"No, actually, I work for ... for a consulting company based out of San Francisco. I'm just up here looking around."

"You thinking about moving up here?" Zoe asked pleasantly.

"Oh, no, no, nothing like that," I laughed automatically, the thought ludicrous. "My parents lived in western Minnesota a long time ago, and they mentioned how nice the Gunflint Trail was, so I had some time off and thought I'd see what things were like. They had lots of interesting things to say about the area. And, well, I just wanted to take some time to get my head together."

Tack looked at me for a long moment—and Mace was staring at me like he knew exactly what I wasn't saying. But Tack, catching the dynamic and, I suspect, realizing his son knew I was holding back on something, said, "Well, sure, go ahead, use our phone to call your people. Will they be open on a Saturday?"

I thought for a moment. "You know, I think the call will probably go directly to the message service, so I might as well let them know where I am. They might be worried."

Claire put down five mugs and poured the steaming chocolate. "Hey, Claire," Tack said, eyes watching the mugs carefully, "grab the Kahlua and give this kid a shot. He'll want it."

"Hey, that sounds great, thanks," I said. "You did say you thought we might be able to get out by around Monday or Tuesday?" I asked.

"That's the best estimate," Tack replied, topping off the mugs. He nodded his head. "The phone's over there on the table," he said, and Mace looked at me as if to say, '*We know better than you why you're up here.*'

The storm hit just about the time we were finishing our hot chocolate that first night and it was a good thing I called into the office because everything went hard down—power, phone lines, everything. With no cell coverage, I was well and truly out for the count, not connected to anything. I went into withdrawal. Tack and Claire commiserated with me, but Zoe just laughed at my consternation.

***

The next morning I came down around 7:30 or so and found Claire standing in front of the wood stove and the smell of bacon wafting in the air. There was a large stack of pancakes on a little sideboard. Through the windows in the dawning light I could see snow blowing almost sideways in a fierce wind.

"Breakfast is up, Mr. Gillenkamp. Do they eat pancakes and bacon where you're from?"

I smiled slightly. "They do, ma'am, though not very often."

"Yes, well, they probably aren't out pushing through two feet of snow in a blizzard for a couple of hours before breakfast, are they?"

I laughed out loud at that. "No ma'am, they most certainly are not doing that." I couldn't picture Grantham or Marcy or Zander or any of my other fellow employees even living in a flyover state, much less being out and about in snow without skis, expensive ski outfits, and a rented chalet with cooperative *femmes de chamber* with whom they would retire afterward, though on second thought, maybe not for Zander.

"Well, pull up a chair, Tack and Mace and Zoe will be in shortly."

Tack came in just about then, threw a black drover on a peg, and washed his hands in the sink. I was astounded at how well the man moved around with the prosthetic leg. Tack noticed me sitting at the table. "Hey, Bryant, good morning. Sleep well?"

"Yes sir, I did, actually. Something about sleeping with snow all around ... it sort of makes things quiet I suppose."

"Yeah, you could say that. With the wind coming up now, well, it won't be quiet for much longer." Tack looked out the window and then moved to a cupboard and started pulling plates out to set the table. "What kind of work do you do, Bryant?"

"I'm a management consultant."

"A management consultant ... that's got to be interesting work."

I was pretty sure these old folks, sitting out here in the middle of the northern Minnesota forests, had no idea how interesting it could be. "Yeah, you could say that. Not as peaceful as this place, though," I said.

The old man ignored my attempt to patronize him. "I had a friend that worked for the Worldwide Business Network once—I think he told me they were bought by the Monitor Group, and then I thought I read that Deloitte bought the Monitor Group."

I was amazed. "I ... I work for Monitor Deloitte. You're right, Deloitte bought out Monitor a few years ago."

"Reminds me of that picture of the little fish getting eaten by the bigger fish getting eaten by the bigger fish getting eaten by the bigger fish, and so on." He was smiling thinly at some dim memory. He put the plates on the table.

"Who did you know at WBN?" I asked.

"Some guy named Simonsen Lehrner. You probably don't—"

"You knew ... you *know* Simonsen Lehrner?" I couldn't believe I was sitting here in some off-planet hole in the woods with an old man who walked around in a farm coat out of 'Green Acres' who happened to know one of the most legendary figures in the management consulting industry. Lehrner was something of a personal hero.

Ironbridge turned and looked at me in a piercing, unsettling way. "Simonson something of a notable these days, is he?"

"Notable? Well, yeah, I guess you could say that. He's been advising the last four U.S. Presidents and I can't keep track of the number of heads of state he talks to on a regular basis. He's written a couple of extremely prescient books about international relations as well, and—"

"Yeah, we've got 'em in the other room," he said nonchalantly, pointing down a small hallway into what looked to be a living room, where I could just see one wall covered in bookshelves. "They were good, though I think he's missing some of the most important things."

"How do you know him?" I asked again, not wanting to pry into why this old guy stuck on some flyover farm in the middle of nowhere would think Simonsen Lehrner's books weren't exactly getting the main points of today's international political relationships right, seeing that Mr. Lehrner was advising presidents and heads of state and all.

The old man folded his arms across his chest and didn't answer right away. "We did some business together, a while ago," he finally answered. "But what are you into now?" he asked, changing the subject.

I grinned. "Should I get you to sign an non-disclosure agreement?"

He didn't laugh, which surprised me, but instead just said, "Yeah, well, we should make it mutual."

I chose to disregard that attempt to imply that there was anything he would know that would be important in my life—or anybody else's life—and thought it more polite to just answer his question. I saw Mace come into the mudroom and peel off his tan chore coat. The guy looked like some advertisement for Woodsman of the Year, with his plaid shirt rolled up to his forearms, roughed-out pants, and dark good looks. Zander would've gone absolutely nuts if he'd have been here. I turned to answer Tack.

"Actually I'm working on an initiative right now to provide management consulting support to a couple of large governments that are working on drafting what we think could be a major diplomatic agreement that would change the face of international relations in the world." I could see Mace listening closely and stop on the last word. He picked up the tablet lying on the kitchen table and typed on it, then showed it to his father, who looked up at me again.

"What brought you up here?" Tack asked. He had a direct way of getting right to the point in his conversation, as though he wanted to cut away any type of small talk or side banter or extraneous subject matter that was not to the main topic of conversation. And when he looked at you, it felt like he was boring into your soul. It was uncomfortable, but then I remembered that he was just some old guy living in a stone-built house in some fly-over state and I was making, oh, probably a gazillion times more money than he'd ever seen in his life, so that helped me get back to some semblance of normalcy in our discourse.

"My parents used to live up here and I just wanted to look around."

"In the dark?" his wife put in.

"Yeah, well, that was an accident. I thought there would be someplace to stop, some motel or something, but I didn't see anything, so I had to keep driving."

I could tell the old man wasn't buying it. Somehow, I *knew* Mace wasn't buying it. That guy seriously bothered me.

"Yeah, nice, but what's the real reason you're up here? You're not looking for property to buy, are you?"

I laughed out loud—again. "Oh no, no, not me. I don't think ... I mean, I've got ... no, I've got a nice place in Palo Alto, and my work and all ..."

"So you aren't looking for property and you really aren't looking around in the dark, so if you don't mind me asking again, what brings you up here?"

I felt almost uncomfortable with this old guy pressing into my business—it wasn't polite or socially correct, and being around people who didn't adhere to accepted social norms always made me uncomfortable. But I did sort of owe them for picking me up and letting me stay in their house while I got myself sorted. So if these old birds wanted to know why I was here, then hell, why not tell them? Why was I worried about that? Who were *they* going to tell?

"Okay, well, since you asked, my last engagement was with the head of a foreign state and it didn't turn out so well."

"You talking about Senegal?"

I just sat there, and I have to admit, my mouth was probably at least partially open. I know that sounds stupid, but hey, as Forest Gump says, 'stupid is as stupid does' and right then I was doing stupid.

"Do you mind if I ask how you knew about that?"

He looked at me and just folded his hands. "Not at all. You just told me you worked for Monitor Deloitte. You said you were up here, partially, to 'get your head together', if my memory serves. Anyone can read about the hot water Monitor Deloitte's been in about Senegal on the net. If one follows what's been happening in West Africa and if one knows people in the consulting industry, one can put two and two together. How were you involved?"

Claire, chuckling quietly, put down a plate of perfectly crisped, thickly sliced bacon and a measuring cup filled with hot maple syrup, followed by a plate stacked with pancakes. *"L'eau profonde, mon ami, soyez prudent,"* she said, which went over my head, since I don't speak French. And then, in English, she said "Go ahead, they won't bite. Made 'em with the buttermilk we get from making butter, which we did yesterday."

She pushed a plate at me and I took a slice of bacon and a pancake. My usual breakfast was a cup of yoghurt and a few slices of organic fruit, with some organic whole-wheat toast and organic strawberry jelly, but I thought I'd humor them.

"Tack does the bacon himself," she said, sitting down, putting a napkin on her lap. "Does the slaughtering and butchering himself, then cures the pork belly. Mace does our hams," she went on. "You haven't had ham until you've had one of his cured hams." Mace was busy with something in the other room and just waved a hand in acknowledgement. I got the eerie sense that Mace really wasn't buying my act. As a consultant, success depended on my ability to read people and situations, and in this little home, it seemed to me like Mace was the strength and Tack was the wisdom—which is why Mace's almost preternatural awareness of what I was thinking bothered me. Something wasn't fitting my paradigm.

After she sat down they actually said grace. I was kind of caught by surprise but didn't do anything embarrassing.

I turned to the old man. "To answer your question, sir, yes, I was the Senior Partner in charge of Monitor Deloitte's consulting team supporting Senegal's president."

"Ow ... and you got blindsided when someone dimed out his human trafficking ring, right?"

"How do you *know* that?" I said, calmly enough, but inside I was almost shouting.

The old man looked down at his own plate, now with four pancakes and a few strips of bacon on it ... and these people were in way better shape than I was. Something wasn't adding up.

"Just because we live out here in the middle of nowhere, Bryant, doesn't mean we don't follow what's going on." He took a bite of his pancakes and then pointed his fork at me. "Everything that happened was in the news, if you know where to look. And if I recall, Monitor Deloitte's team appealed to the UN after State said they were going to look into things. How did that go?"

I sat back from the table and put my fork down. "You know an awful lot about where things are."

"I can send you to the links where I read about it on the Internet, son, don't get worried. Stuff is all on the open source intelligence market."

That surprised me, but it probably shouldn't have. I realized that I had by coincidence fallen into an association with someone who at least knew something about how the world works and what was happening in it—unlikely as that might have been in the middle of a frigid, blasted wilderness.

"Yeah, well, okay, State said they haven't found anything yet but will be 'continuing their research', whatever that means, and the UN came back and said that their team didn't find anything at all and that Monitor Deloitte was in the clear—so much so that they've engaged us to work another issue."

"This is the deal with two governments that will change international relations so dramatically?"

I realized I had assumed I was dealing with a couple of old farmers. This guy was tracking. "Yes sir, though I shouldn't say which ones."

He looked down at his plate and cut another chunk of pancake. "Don't need to, it's fairly obvious."

I was stretched about as far as I would stretch. "So ... okay, I'll bet you a twenty you can't guess," I challenged.

The old guy looked at me and then at his wife, put down his fork, and turned Mace's tablet so I could read what he'd typed oh, about five minutes or so ago.

'Russia and China'.

***

I stayed at the Ironbridge farm for four days. We never talked more about how they knew there was something working with Russia or China. I couldn't go into what I was doing, and they didn't seem interested in expounding on how they knew something was up. I met some young woman named Emma, who was staying with the Ironbridges. Apparently she'd been kicked out of her house over some religious disagreement she'd had with her parents, which I couldn't figure out ... something about having a direct relationship with Jesus instead of doing what her father told her to do. I couldn't really follow it.

However, something happened to me on the third day I was there that was seriously weird. Each day I helped bring in wood for the stove from the woodshed, which was about thirty yards away from the house. I cleared the walkway to the shed, shoveling snow for the first time in my life. I liked it. So on the third day, in the morning, I dumped the last load of wood into the box in the mudroom and something hit me. It was like a waft of wind, stronger than a breeze but nothing that was *physical*, nothing tangible. I can't explain it, but it was like a combination of something stripping off, something sliding away coupled with an infusion of, I don't know, *reality* almost, as though reality was *outside* of myself and just blew in for the moment. I stood there for what must have been 30 seconds or so, just staring into the wood box but not seeing anything. It was totally overwashing me and I was totally disoriented. I felt as though I'd never really lived, or, like that guy in the Matrix movies who'd been shown that everything he thought was reality was just an illusion, and someone had pulled back the curtain—like I'd taken the red pill.

Claire opened the kitchen door and when I didn't move, she looked at me ... and looked at me, and kept looking at me. I just stood there, trying to figure out what I felt like. There had been a first overpowering sense of reality, of, I don't know, almost *cleanness*, like a breath of summer, of warmth and life, in the middle of a frigid, cold death-like place. There was this overpowering sense or draw toward *truth.* I can't forget that; it was this crushing pull to tell the truth, hear the truth, to almost *swim* in it, if that makes any sense. Distressingly, along with that sense, because of the comparison with my own life, I also got a powerful sense of how full of artifice I'd been all my life and I felt an overwashing sense of disgust, recoiling at who I was and what I was like. It was as if I was standing there watching a movie replay of my life and I saw all the years of insincerity and falseness and ... and it wasn't very pleasant ... but there was also this huge thirst that came along for something real, something right, something *true.*

Claire was still standing there in the door to the kitchen and I turned around after I don't know how long and said, in the grip of this new aura of reality, something I would never have said if I'd been in my right mind.

"Who *are* you people?"

Claire opened the kitchen door wider and said softly, "Come in, Bryant. I'll get Tack and Mace ... and *oui*, there must be Zoe, too."

***

The five of us sat at the kitchen table. I'd been there three days and knew there was something different about them. Yeah, there was the confidence and all, but they also seemed to be just more settled with things, easier, more peaceful, and happier. And I hadn't been there three hours the first day before it was obvious they were like my sister ... religious, I mean. They had Bibles sitting around on tables, more Bibles in bookshelves, and titles that were obviously religious stuffed everywhere. My sister was the same way. And yet they hadn't said a thing to me about religion for three days, whereas my sister would have been down around my ears in about fifteen minutes about my lifestyle.

So for the first couple of days I was like a cat in a room full of rocking chairs. They prayed at every meal, holding hands, and Tack would kiss Claire after each prayer. Zoe and Mace were inseparable. I'd never seen anything like those two; it was almost as if Zoe was drawing life and energy just being around Mace, and Mace was never impatient, always there, always willing to give her a hand or strengthen her or caress her or just look at her, and it always seemed to, I don't know, thrill her, I guess. I thought it was…quaint at best, though my cynicism at first suspected it was all for my benefit. But they didn't push anything at me—nothing, not a word. For three days I helped them with chores, and wondered how they kept the place going. They milked cows morning and evening—and I'm talking, like six in the morning and six at night. I hadn't gotten out of bed before seven in the morning since college. They had to feed the cows, two bulls; twenty sheep or so, along with the two breeder sows and the twelve little piglets they were carrying through the winter, not to mention about fifty chickens. They had ten very large horses—'draft horses', they called them, and they were the hugest horses I'd ever seen, but incredibly gentle, and each horse ate a bale of hay a day. I didn't think that was possible. Tack and Claire had to trudge out on paths buried in snow and use a sledgehammer to break up the ice in the water troughs, then carry buckets of water from the one hydrant they had in the barn. They gave me some warm clothes to work in, with some heavy boots and thick work gloves, but even so I was half-frozen before the end of each chore cycle. I don't know how those old folks did it. And throughout all of it they never tried to push their religion on me. I found that ... weird. I was on my guard the entire time.

And then, dropping off the last load of wood that morning into the wood box, I was hit with that overwhelming combination of clarity and reality, and an overpowering desire to just be rid of behavior patterns I knew characterized my entire life up to that moment. And that little taste of reality wasn't very pleasant.

***

"What's up, Bryant?" Tack started, pulling up a kitchen stool. "You look like you've seen a ghost. You okay?" He didn't sound like he was too worried though. I could've sworn he wasn't surprised at all ... but that didn't make any sense. Mace and Zoe sat on the couch in the kitchen, he with his arm around her, she snuggled into his chest. Tack went on. "You asked Claire who we were. Why was that?"

I felt myself backing away a little from my recent swell of courage and desire for reality. It was almost as though I had been filled up and now this furiously intense clarity was receding like a wave on a beach—or being forcibly pushed back. That really threw me. I decided to try and hang on to it, if I could, to push back by honestly describing what I thought had happened to me.

"I ... I can't really say," I said, "but I was just dumping an armful of wood into the box there and I just felt ... almost like a wind, like some breath of air hit me and it was as if I could see things clearly for the first time, that everything I've considered to be real in my life isn't, and I got the sense that—and I know this is weird—but I got the sense that I'm playing at life, not really living it at all, but sort of like I'm playing on some kind of stage and I've been carrying around this expectation my entire life that I have to play my part the way people expect me to play it." I'd said enough, and I looked up from my clenched hands to see how the two of them were reacting. They were looking at each other like they knew something I didn't. What I didn't see was any signs of surprise. It was almost as if they knew something like this would happen ... which really shook me.

"So in the spirit of this new-found clarity, where I feel like just saying what I think without trying to calculate what people will think about it, I have to say, neither of you two seems surprised ... and if I'm being honest, I'm *really* sure Mace isn't surprised." I looked over at the man sitting on the couch with his wife and he sort of just nodded slightly.

"Of course," Zoe put in, smiling, placing her hand on Mace's chest.

I pushed on. "Is this something that happens to all your visitors after three days of farm life? Maybe it has to do with working in the cold, right? Do all farmers have this sudden clarity accompanied by a feeling that they've been living a lie all their lives when their brains are half-frozen? Is that why they have to get back to the land, whatever that means?"

"Nope. Not even close," Tack said, firmly but quietly.

"So you *know* what this is?" I said, somewhat taken aback.

"We know *Who* it is, yeah," he replied.

"And that makes absolutely no sense to me," I shot back. This inclination I had to just say what I felt was sort of liberating. I liked it. I went with it. And something about the word '*Who*' stirred an intense distaste in me.

"Of course it doesn't," Tack said, right back at me. "But if you want truth, you've come to the right bar, Counselor."

"Maybe you'd better explain it to me, then," I replied.

"Hearing the truth and accepting it as truth are two different things," Tack replied.

I would have snapped off a quick retort right back at him if he'd said that kind of corny platitude just a couple of hours ago ... but after feeling truth blow around inside my head like I had, I was beginning to think that maybe I didn't have a handle on everything that happens in the world.

"Yeah, I've seen the same thing in some of my clients," I shot back.

"Not the same thing," Tack replied, sternly.

"Look, Tack, maybe I just got chilled and a little disoriented."

"Is that what you think happened?"

In the clutches of this newfound inclination to be truthful, I honestly didn't. "No," I said, surprising myself, "not if I'm being truthful."

"You're just trying to rationalize something you don't understand."

I thought about that statement for a moment and realized that he was right on the money. "Yeah," I answered, "I guess you're right. Hey, I'm a 21st century guy—if I can't see it, it ain't there."

"That particular brand of skepticism isn't inimical to the 21st century, unfortunately, Bryant," Claire pitched in, sounding like some college anthropology professor.

"So if you know, just tell me," I said, sort of sounding desperate ... which was true, since I was.

Tack squared up and said, "So we never told you why Mace was out driving around just an hour or so before one of the biggest storms of the year, did we?"

"Actually no, you didn't," I replied, curious now.

"Do you believe in God, Bryant?" Tack asked.

Here it was. "Not really," I said slowly, not wanting to offend them, but also still breathing the fumes of this new clarity I had experienced, and I was less inclined to offend against that ... against that imperative, almost as if it was some*one*, not some thing, that I'd encountered near the wood box. "Does this thing that happened to me have to do with religion?"

"Nope," answered Tack. "Relationship, not religion."

"I don't—"

"Yeah, I know you don't understand, so we're gonna tell you, and remember, it was you that asked, we didn't push this at you, got it?"

"Right," I said, settling down. "Right ... I'm askin' what the—"

"So we'll tell you. We'll tell you the truth. If you don't like what we tell you, or if you don't understand what it is we're going to tell you, that doesn't make it any less the truth than if I tried to explain calculus to a first-grader who couldn't understand it. Doesn't make calculus some kind of thing I made up in my head because the first-grader doesn't understand it. Got it?"

"Got it," I said, thinking to myself that I didn't like being compared to a first-grader. I heard keys being punched, and turned. Mace handed the tablet to Zoe, who got up off the couch and handed it to me. I read what it said. *Pay close attention; important 4U.* Like I said, Mace was sort of scary.

Tack paused for a moment to gather himself and then began. "So about an hour or so before Mace picked you up that night, we were sitting here in the kitchen. We'd finished up dinner, and I was just about to pour us all a glass of wine when Mace had the oddest but most compelling feeling that he needed to drive out to the main road. Zoe was taking a nap and so he asked me to let her know where he was if he wasn't back in time. We talked about it, and he said that God had told him to head out—"

I turned to face Mace, who was still sitting there comfortably with his arm around Zoe. "Wait a minute. You say God told you to go out and pick me up?" Mace slowly nodded. I turned back to address Tack. "Sorry, but that's just religious-speak to me. Seriously, what exactly does that mean?"

Tack looked me in the eye. "If I was telling someone else a story and you were part of it, and in part of the story I mentioned that I had asked you something, what would you think it meant?"

"It ... it would have meant that you asked me something—but with words, that you would speak and which I would hear, and then I would be talking back to you with words you could hear, like two people having a conversation. Not the same thing at all."

"Actually it *is* the same thing. God talks to us in ways we can hear. You may not be able to hear them if you were in the same room with me at the time, but we can."

"Kind of like some people hearing voices in their heads?" Whenever I found myself involved in a discussion about religion I tended to get defensive or abusive, or both. Tack seemed to take it in stride.

"Not the same thing at all. Since I know God, I know what His voice sounds like. He said that His sheep would know His voice. I'm one of His sheep. If you pay attention tomorrow, watch what happens when Claire goes out to the barn. She'll call the sheep and they know her voice, because they're her sheep. Usually every time they hear her voice and respond to it, nice things come along, like food and water or treats or something. Then you try to call them. See what happens. They'll ignore you."

"Yeah, I get it," I replied.

"So anyway ... God tells Mace that he needed to get in the truck and head out to the main road."

This was sort of freaking me out. I turned around again to address Mace, since he was the operative agent in this fiction. "Wait, just wait. Just because you think you heard some voice you think is God doesn't prove God exists. It isn't something someone can validate or prove. You could just be making this up; you could be delusional."

Tack looked at me and I could see his eyes get sort of hard and intense. He shook his head slightly, as though I was just some sort of first-grader really not getting it. "You can argue all you want about voices or whatever, but let me ask you one question, and your own answer will prove that what I'm telling you is true. Are you sitting here this morning, warm, breathing, and alive, or are you some frozen city-sickle laying dead on the side of the main road under about five feet of snow, wearing fancy hiking boots you paid too much money for? Take your time, don't rush; see if you can get it right."

"I'm not in the first grade, Tack."

Tack bored into me. "In this realm, Counselor, you haven't even made it to first grade yet. You're still what is known in our vernacular as dead—you're not even born yet.

You're not alive to real life."

Zoe handed Tack Mace's tablet. That tablet was starting to freak me out. "What?" I asked.

Tack read it out loud. "Mace writes, *When you were standing in the woodshed and truth and reality blew through, you smelled something rotten, something like death, didn't you?*" Tack looked at me, and I didn't have the guts to come back at him. Instead I turned to Mace.

"How did you *know* that?" I asked.

But Tack picked up where he'd left off. "You haven't even graduated to becoming a baby, so let's get that understood. We're talking about things that you won't be able to comprehend because you're still dead. You've probably never thought about it before, but dead people actually don't know they're dead. You can't grasp what I'm telling you."

"You just said I'm sitting here alive," I replied, confused, but trying to fight back by using my opponent's words against him.

"He means you're dead, spiritually," Claire put in, assuming I needed an explanation, which of course I did.

"You're physically alive, yes, but people can be physically alive and spiritually dead. In fact, most are."

"Are what?"

"Physically alive, but spiritually dead. Dead to the realm of the spirit, dead to reality, dead to what is really true. Man is born dead, and before he can understand the things of the Spirit and before he can have a relationship with God, he has to come alive."

"I don't understand any of this ... but ... but when you say that most people are dead to reality, I'm telling you, out there in the woodpile, that is exactly what I felt ... like something, like reality itself tapped me on the shoulder and I felt clearly that I'd never met him before. This is ... this is stuff I don't understand."

Suddenly, surprising all of us, Mace spoke in a clear, normal cadence. He had a deep, calming voice that for some reason banished all my trepidation about how weird he'd appeared to me. He looked at me directly.

"We don't expect you to understand it," he started out. "The things of the Spirit are not apprehended by the mind, by the intellect. It was the Spirit of God you felt. Make no mistake. Yes, God calls for us to develop and cultivate wisdom and intelligence and understanding, but God can't be grasped or understood with our intelligence. One comes to a relationship with Him through another sense altogether. It is this other sense that you encountered out there in the wood box."

Everyone was so surprised that they sat there, silent, until Zoe piped up. "He does that sometimes." Mace opened his mouth in silent laughter and put his arm around Zoe.

"And keep this in mind when your cynicism springs up, Bryant," Tack continued. "No one here manufactured what you felt out there in the mudroom. It wasn't us; it couldn't have been, and you know that to be a fact."

Now he had my attention. "That ... I mean, what happened out there ... I felt, it was like, something outside of me, something not internal. And yeah, nobody had anything to do with it. I know that."

"Good. Keep that in mind when you're tempted to think we just engineered this entire discussion. What you had out there was an experience with the Spirit of the living God, what most Christians call the Holy Spirit. Mace is right; God is tapping you gently on the shoulder to let you know that you're dead at the moment, that you've never truly apprehended either reality or truth, and you've been living in a make-believe world all your life. And there was one other thing," Tack said, lowering his voice slightly. "He told you there wasn't much time, didn't He?"

I sat back and felt a chill run down my back. I had been told exactly that, but hadn't told any of them that part of the experience, because it scared me too much. "How ... how did you know?" I asked, not wanting to hear the answer.

"God tells him things," Claire answered.

"He told me what He said to you out there, just to prove to you that you're not imagining all this," Tack went on. "What we're telling you is truth; this is reality, Bryant. The realm of the supernatural is reality, and there are opposing forces working in this realm, many which want to convince you that the supernatural doesn't even exist. You've been given an amazing gift here."

"My sister tells me about this ... this *stuff* all the time."

"And you haven't paid much attention to her, have you?" Claire said, more like a statement than a question.

"Nope. Like water off a duck's back, if you want to know the truth. She just keeps banging away, trying to pound this stuff at me and it has never made any sense."

Tack paused for a moment, but I could tell he wanted to say something. "It's like this," he began. "We humans are born dead, and we have to become alive to the things of the Spirit, to the things in the realm of the supernatural, but we can't be forced into it. We have to *want* to know, we have to reach out for Him. But typically, we don't reach out for Him until we first become aware that we need a relationship with Him."

"People don't go to a doctor unless they realize they're sick," Zoe kicked in.

"And let me add to that," Tack said. "Many won't go to a doctor even if they do realize they're sick. What it takes for them to go to the doctor is first, they realize they're sick, and second, they want to get better."

"So what, you're telling me I'm sick?"

"I'm telling you that you're dead spiritually, and unless you respond to the One who is calling you to develop a relationship with Him, you're gonna stay dead for the rest of eternity. You may not believe in hell but it's real nonetheless, and if you think just the whiff of rot and death you got in the mudroom there was bad, wait until you're surrounded by that smell, all while there is the hottest fire you can imagine, burning you."

I thought to myself that this guy was off the reservation for sure, but didn't say anything. There were typing sounds, and then Zoe came over to the table and handed me Mace's tablet.

Tack is not 'off the reservation'. He is telling U truth U need to hear.

That more than anything knocked me down. I began to tremble, honestly. This was just too weird. Something was happening in this place, and either there was a God or these people were the most accomplished tricksters I'd ever encountered.

But Tack was going on, and what he was saying snapped my attention back to him. "God knows that just hearing about Him isn't sufficient, so He came and sort of intruded in your life to let you know He's real and that He wants to have a relationship with you ... because, as He told you, there isn't much time."

I remember thinking just then that all of this was getting to be too much to process, and then Tack said, "Seems like too much to process, right?"

"How did you *know*?" I asked, shocked. "What is *with* you people?" I looked at Tack, and then looked over at Mace.

"It's not a processing problem," Tack said, "but most people think it is."

That confused me. "So what's the issue?" I asked.

"It's a problem of the will. You can understand the words I'm telling you," he replied. "You understand the logic and the concepts and the relative juxtaposition of cause and effect I've described, but what is interfering with your ability to accept what I'm telling you as truth is first, your will *not* to believe, and that is driven by your own nature, which is intensely and violently opposed to giving up control of your life to someone else."

I was about to come flat out and tell him he was full of crap, when the last words about 'giving up control' struck home like a spear, and I knew he was right. Control was my thing, and I prided myself on my ability to control every situation in every aspect of my life.

"So what's so wrong with controlling my own life?" I asked, somewhat boldly, I thought.

"If you want a relationship with God, there has to be truth. And that means that God has to be God, and you have to be you. God is perfect, omniscient, all-powerful, omnipresent, doesn't sin, and also, don't forget, loves you more than you love yourself and therefore wants the best for you. You, on the other hand, are not omniscient, you can only be in one place at a time, don't have much power at all, and you have a nature that inclines you toward sin constantly, and if left to yourself you would make choices that will end up killing you and sending you to hell for eternity. So you tell me ... who do you think should be in charge of your own life ... that is, presuming you want things to turn out well for you after you go from this world to the next?"

"So you're saying that unless I let this God person you talk about control my life, I'm going to hell?"

"That's exactly right. God said something just like that. He said that if you want to save your life, you'll lose it—that is, if you want to live eternally in fellowship with God, you'd give up control of your life. He said that if you try to keep your life—that is, if you keep trying to control it yourself—you'll lose it."

"Sounds damned harsh to me," I replied, angrily. When something or someone threatened my control, I got aggressive.

"Actually it's incredibly loving," Tack replied quietly, nonplussed. "Think about it. You have this all-knowing, all-powerful God who loves you and who wants to care for you and wants what is best for you, willing to take you into His care and relieve you of the burdens of controlling and administering your life. Or you can muddle through, being the boss of your own life, screwing things up left and right, hurting people left and right, and end up with nothing but eternal fire to look forward to because of how you approached things."

"Sounds nice," I replied cynically. "What's the catch?"

"The catch is," Tack shot back immediately, "that you have to *obey* Him. You have to do what He says, and what He tells you to do will be against your human nature. Your nature will be to fight Him, and it will be impossible to obey Him."

I threw up my hands. "Then what's the point?" I said. "If you're telling me I have to obey this God, but it's impossible to obey Him, then, I mean, seriously, what's the point? You see, this is what is so damn *frustrating* about you people. You talk about these lofty, pie-in-the-sky holy-Joe concepts but it turns out that your formula to actually get there is impossible."

"It's not impossible," Tack answered softly, but then gave me a hard stare. "It's not impossible because God says that it is possible, and He offers the way to do it to every man, woman, and child that has ever lived. You can obey Him, but you have to put this human nature of yours to death and get a new nature."

"So what are you telling me, that I have to jump off a cliff or shoot myself in the head, and then what? He'll raise me from the dead and I'll become like you all?"

"We're talking about your nature that needs to be dead, not your physical life, Bryant," Claire put in, trying to dampen my irritation.

"You have a human nature, Bryant," Tack began. "We all do. This human nature of ours is opposed to God because, well, because it's just who we are. Think about it. You don't have to teach children to lie when they're young. They do it naturally, to get out of trouble. It's just our human nature. You have to teach children to tell the truth. Doing what's right does not come naturally to the human species. We have to learn what is right and work to do it. Doing what's wrong comes naturally."

His point hit home. I didn't have any kids but I'd been around too many lawyers to doubt what he was saying.

"How can you switch natures, then?" I asked. "That's, like, impossible."

"It's not impossible. I can tell you exactly how to do it. It's simple to describe, but it's hard to do."

"Sounds dangerous," I answered.

"You could say that. So let me start by asking you what you know about crucifixion."

I couldn't stop myself; I was on a roll with this 'truth' thing. "You people are really out there, you know? Now I know why there are initiatives about putting you people in camps. You're dangerous. What does cruci-whatever you call it have to do with what we're talking about?"

"The word is *crucifixion*, and it was a way the Romans put people to death. It's how ISIS puts Christians to death, when they can catch them. And try to keep a lid on your fear for a moment while we answer your question, okay?"

"Fear? What fear?" Like most people of my generation, I didn't like having my weaknesses called out.

"People get aggressive and defensive when they're afraid, it's natural," Claire said with a bit of fire in her eye. I could see she didn't think much of me attacking her husband. Tack, on the other hand, didn't seem bothered a bit.

"So when a person gets crucified, they get hung up or nailed to a cross, okay?" Tack began again.

"Right," I said. "Got it. Two pieces of wood put up crossways. Arms stretched out, legs down. Nails in the wrist, nails in the feet…got that part; saw the movie."

Tack went on patiently. "So good, you know. When a person's arms get stretched out like that and the weight of their body pulls the torso down, it dislocates the shoulders and, unable to lift themselves up, the weight of the body compresses the diaphragm, and unless you push up with your legs, you can't breathe."

"Yeah? I didn't know that," I said, doubtfully, willing to give him the benefit of the doubt. "So how does this bear on me changing my nature."

"We'll get there. So the person being crucified essentially has to push up with their legs to keep breathing. When their legs get tired, they suffocate. It happens very, very slowly, and it is very painful. It is like being choked to death over a period of hours or days."

"Yeah, well ... that seems pretty brutal."

"When you think about it, it seems strange," Tack said. "Why go to all the trouble of putting up a cross? You want to kill someone, just run them through with a sword, or shoot them in the head with your AK47, right? But the Romans did this primarily to criminals and rebels because they wanted to send a very clear message. They were saying, 'Look, all you criminals and all you rebels who want to damage or overthrow our Roman society, we are going to choke you out, no matter how long it takes. We won't get all of you at once, but eventually we are going to cut off your air and your movement will die slowly, painfully, until there aren't any of you left.' ISIS is saying something different. Putting Christians to death on a cross is a way they mock the death of Jesus. They're saying, 'See, your fake God died, no matter what you say, and if you want to worship him, then you can die the same way.'"

I hadn't thought about these things. "I didn't know ISIS was killing people on crosses," I said.

"All the time. Now they're doing it in Detroit," Tack replied.

"Yeah, I heard about that. But I thought that was some kind of Sharia law thing. I know the Michigan State Supreme court made it legal a few years ago."

"The Muslims only kill Christians that way," Tack replied. "And you'll take note of the fact that the same court made beheading legal too."

"Yeah, what's up with that?" I asked. "That seems way too inhumane."

"Muslims who obey the Koran are not concerned with being humane," Zoe said, darkly.

"They cut off peoples' heads because it is symbolic, again," Tack said. "In Christian theology, God is the 'head' of His people, and His people are His 'body'. When someone cuts of the head, they are symbolically saying that they are severing God from His people."

A thought struck me. "So ... so this is why they cut off people's heads in the French revolution? They essentially were throwing God out of their society."

"Right," Tack replied. "You're beginning to get it."

"But what does this have to do with a new nature."

"Jesus said that if we wanted to follow Him—that is, if we wanted to obey Him—we would need to pick up our cross *every day*. What he meant was that we would need to put our human nature on a cross, figuratively, *every day*. We would need to choke out or deprive our human nature of the things that it needs to live, and what it needs most, the 'air' for our human nature is to *have its own way*. He said we needed to therefore deny ourselves—stop giving our human nature what it naturally wants—daily, because our human nature won't die easily. Our human nature rebels against God's rule. There are some things in our human nature that die quickly, and other things take a long time to die, sometimes weeks or months or years. But He promised that if we would do that, if we would choke out the things that feed our human nature, He would give us a new nature. His Spirit—that very same Person you felt in the woodshed—would come to live in us and we would have His nature."

"God would come to live in us?" I asked, clearly in a way that indicated I thought Tack was around the bend.

He looked at me with hard eyes. "Pay attention," he said, his voice like gravel. "What happened to you in the mud room, dumping off the wood?"

The reminder caught me by surprise. "I'd ... I'd forgotten about that," I replied.

"Yeah, well, keep it in mind, because the enemy will try to remove any remembrance of it."

"And what's up with this 'enemy' thing," I asked with obvious curiosity. "My sister keeps talking about the 'enemy this' or 'the enemy that'. Who or what is she talking about?"

Zoe answered, and I sensed she had as much gravitas as energy. "She's referring to the fact that we are all in a spiritual war. The enemy is Satan, the devil, who wants you dead. God wants you alive, living with Him in heaven. Satan wants you burning in hell."

"What did I ever do to him?" I asked, trying to be funny.

"Satan hates you because God loves you, and Satan hates anything God loves." Tack wasn't amused. "We can't conceive of the level of hate Satan has for us. And he has a vast kingdom of minions—demons—that are tasked with making sure God does not succeed in keeping human beings from hell. Hell was made for the angels that rebelled against God, and don't think for a minute Satan—the head angel who led the rebellion—cares a whit for any human being. He'd rather see us all dead and burning. Satan has a supernatural organization that is arranged hierarchically and its sole objective is to have all the people in the world worship him instead of God, and he uses our human nature as leverage to get us to do that."

Things were beginning to dawn on me. "This is ... this doesn't ... I mean, why don't more people know about this?" I asked.

"Everyone who wants to know about it can read about it in this book here," Tack said, gesturing to the Bible on the side table. "It's been the best-selling book in the world until recently. But few actually take the time to read it, because it tells us that if we want to win in this war against the devil, we will have to voluntarily choke out our human nature, and very few people are willing to do that."

"Wait, wait, okay, so tell me in words I can understand, how exactly do we choke out our human nature?" I asked.

"You deprive it of what it wants," Tack said directly. "And that's different for each of us, although there are some things that are the same. There are three main things common to human nature that the enemy uses as leverage to keep our human natures fed and strong, so let's start there. First, there is the physical—whatever it is you crave: sex, food, alcohol, tobacco, or whatever else unnaturally stimulates your body to the point at which the body becomes dependent upon that substance. If the enemy can create in your life a dependence on those things, he can keep you from obeying God. Second, there is the desire to get what you don't have—a constant irritation that makes you dissatisfied with what you have and constantly draws your eyes and your mind to the thought that you need something else, which creates a life of always wanting something more, something different, something better, no matter what it is you have already, and you're never satisfied, which means, oh by the way, that you can never be satisfied with what God gives you—or God Himself. And last is pride—being proud of who or what you are or what you've done or what you have. Pride always sets you above and against others who may not have done what you've done or have what you have. Satan uses these three main things to feed your human nature and it keeps us from hearing God, seeing God, and obeying God."

"If I want a relationship with God then, what, I can't have sex, can't eat, can't drink, can't smoke, can't want stuff, and can't be proud of anything. Do I have that right?"

"No; not at all. God invented sex; it's something within marriage that is designed to teach us a little more about the nature of God's love for us. Our bodies need nourishment. God Himself turned 300 gallons of water into wine, and wine is suggested in God's word as something to help with indigestion, and it brings joy to life. There are no injunctions against tobacco anywhere in the Word. But ... you can't let any of those things get to a point where they control what you do or where they might interfere with your ability to obey God. Every one of the things you mentioned was created by God, but Satan perverts them, and our human nature encourages the perversion—or, at least, it doesn't fight against it. Sex is good in marriage, but outside marriage it's a powerfully destructive force. Food is good, but when men's stomachs become their God, they become either gluttons or overly obsessed with food to the point where food becomes their god, and they eventually dig their grave with their teeth. Alcohol is something to be used in moderation; when it is used in excess, it too becomes a destructive force that interferes with or destroys our ability to obey God. Tobacco, same thing ... back in the day when tobacco was just tobacco, people would smoke and not get addicted. Now you have commercially-marketed cigarettes that not only get people addicted, but kill them at the same time. Drugs, alcohol, cigarettes, whatever it is that destroys the body when used in excess tends also to kill the soul, because if our bodies are not under control, then the enemy will always find a way to use that lack of control as a lever to keep us from obeying God. All these things—the physical, the desire for stuff, pride—they all feed our human nature, and if you say to God that you want a relationship with Him and are willing to obey Him, then you will need to choke out those things which feed your human nature. You will have to stop indulging yourself in those things. You cannot say that you want a relationship with God and yet feed your human nature; doesn't work."

This was a lot for me to absorb, and I thought about what Tack was saying. On one hand it seemed more nuanced than what my sister would tell me, but on the other hand, it seemed to make so much more sense; it seemed to 'fit' together better.

"Look, Bryant, the reason people don't want to choke out their human nature is because they like it. Our human nature feeds on stuff in the world like our animals feed on green grass—they take to it naturally, and they like the stuff the world has to offer—unlimited gratification of whatever senses they choose to feed, an environment that constantly pushes the latest car or gadget or fashion or health fad in front of them and feeds their desire to consume, to be better than someone else, or to be rich or be healthy, and an environment that constantly drives them to be proud of who they are or what they've done. Sure, it's *natural* to want to feel good about yourself. Bottom line, people just don't want to deprive themselves of these things."

"I can see that," I replied. "I mean, right now, I don't want to give up any of that stuff. Why should I? So I can live in the middle of nowhere, like this, throwing wood in a stove so the house stays warm, milking cows twice a day? I mean, really, who would want this lifestyle?"

"It's not about lifestyle, Bryant," Claire replied. "We're doing these things because

God has asked us to. He asks others to do other things."

"The answer to your question," Tack put in, "can be found in what you experienced in the mud room a while ago. Remember what you felt—that you weren't living in reality, and that you've been artificial all your life? You felt just for a moment the breath of true reality, of life, of truth itself. You saw, you *felt*, how dead you were. The lifestyle people live outside of a relationship with God ends up creating an artificial life, a dead life, no matter what lifestyle it is they're living. People can live in luxury in the city, or live in poverty on some farm in the middle of nowhere, and if they are living outside of a relationship with God, it doesn't matter what kind of lifestyle they have. Lifestyle isn't a substitute for a relationship with God."

"A lifestyle doesn't determine one's relationship with God," Claire said quietly, "rather, one's relationship with God determines one's lifestyle."

***

The storm blew through, the roads were plowed, the local Goober picked up my smashed rental truck and the rental agency delivered another vehicle—I asked for a BMW for my return to Duluth. I was a little subdued when I said goodbye to the Ironbridge clan, but I promised to keep in touch.

It was a strange experience, those four days at their farm. As I drove south, the power and impression the experience had made on me began to dim, but unlike encounters with my sister, I sensed that these people had something real, something true, and I knew it deserved a closer look. That nagging coincidence—that Tack had known that I'd gotten the sense that there wasn't much time, and the incredible sense Mace had of knowing what I was thinking—that really bothered me. I could shrug off my sister's constant harpings about reading the Bible and going to church and her clumsy attempts to set me up with some single woman from her church—all that rolled off me like water off a duck's back. But these people, this *experience*, were beyond the natural—I'd seen true *power*—and it shook my preconceived notions about the world to their foundations. I couldn't deny it was anything other than something supernatural that I'd dealt with unloading wood that day, and then in our discussions, all of them presented such a strikingly different picture of religion than I'd ever heard or seen before. Added to all this was the frustrating fact that they just seemed so happy together. I'd never seen people more connected. In my circle, I didn't know *any* married people that had such a close relationship. Both couples attributed their closeness to the fact that they had the Spirit of Jesus living in them and smiling, I remembered Zoe smacking her forehead in jest at my amazement when I told them how different they were. While I had no idea how what they had came about, I couldn't deny what I saw with my own eyes. I know people—it's my job to read them, and I am very good at my job. They weren't trying to pull the wool over my eyes, nor did they have any kind of spiritual scalp-hunting agenda like my sister and her friends. They were just real. They seemed to actually live what they believed. The more I thought about it, the more it bothered me.

Approaching the outskirts of Duluth, after all my internal debates and arguing with myself for 200 miles, I resolved to look into the subject a little further ... maybe consider taking in a local church service or something. But I also resolved not to mention it to Zander—he *would* crucify me.

***

I was due to brief Grantham at Renissande and was running late. When I'd returned from Minnesota, Marcy met me at the airport. I tried to talk to her about this weird spiritual experience I'd had out there, and how I almost froze to death on the Gunflint Trail, and about my interest in maybe getting to a local church, but after about thirty minutes I realized she wasn't interested in any of that. Somehow one thing led to another and we ended up at her apartment and didn't come up for air until around, I don't know, maybe ten in the morning. I had no idea Marcy was so ... *motivated* to succeed, but hey, I'm not complaining.

I had a raging headache—we'd been chasing that crazy Mexican, Jose Cuervo, with ol' redneck Jack Daniels most of the night and into the early morning—and was hoping Grantham just wanted to talk about the upcoming meeting we were going to have with representatives from the Administration.

I pulled into valet parking at Grantham's exclusive club about three minutes before my scheduled meeting. The Renissande was modeled after an old English-style country house, with natural stone facing, steeply-sloping rooflines, stone walls all around the grounds, and attendants looking very much like the staff at Downton Abbey. I think the parking attendant was even affecting some kind of English accent.

Some guy that looked like a butler pulled open the main door.

"Bryant Gillenkamp for Giles Grantham."

"Very *good* sir," he said, as if I'd just swished a shot from mid-court. "If you would be so kind as to follow me?"

I walked into the entryway, a gorgeous, arching hallway lined with richly paneled dark walnut sections. The floor was white marble. I smelled cigar smoke and lemon wax and the indefinable, indescribable smell of wealth and affluence.

This smell rises redolently everywhere, from the upholstery in the cars we own, the fabric on the furniture we buy, the woolens and tweeds and fine silk or cashmere fabrics we wear, even from the gazillion-thread count sheets we sleep on. Such things defined our lives and made them worthwhile, and as the soles of my tailored Italian loafers clicked along on the marble walkway, my mind was suddenly recast back in time, where I recalled standing in a small mudroom entryway, throwing wood in a box and being overwhelmed by a feeling that my life up until that point had consisted of nothing more than artifice. It was the strangest sense, and it threatened to interfere with my settled, determined pursuit of this life of wealth I'd wanted for, oh, as long as I could remember. I was not sure I wanted anything to interrupt that. I began to wonder if perhaps the Ironbridges hadn't engineered that little experience after all.

The butler led me to a meeting room lined with books, literally up to the twelve-foot ceiling, in dark wood-trimmed bookshelves.

"Bryant, welcome." Giles Grantham was middle-aged, a former Olympic athlete (sculls, Princeton), though he possessed one of the smartest business minds in the world. He was also one of the most connected individuals in the country—definitely one of the people who belonged to that group Deplorables referred to as 'Elites'. His hair was stylishly cut and appropriately grayed at the temples. He had a square face and fine, aquiline features. From what I was able to find in the research I did before joining the firm, he hadn't put a foot wrong since he came out of Princeton straight into the investment banking industry.

"Giles, thanks for the invitation."

"First time at Renissande?"

"Actually it is, yes; very impressive."

"We like to keep it comfortable," he said, tugging at the creases of his woolen slacks before sitting down. "Can we get you a drink?"

I had to decide which way to go—cold turkey, or hair of the dog. I looked at the little coffee table between us and saw amber liquid in a tumbler in front of him. I pointed at it. "How about a whiskey on the rocks?"

Giles made a quick, subtle gesture and a barman in livery came to our little alcove and took my drink order, bowed slightly, and left. I sat down in the firm leather-covered wing chair. Our alcove was private, tucked into a small niche out of the way of the main part of the room. Even the little niche was lined with books, though. My mind darted back to Marcy and last night—no, this morning—and I mentally kicked myself under the table and scolded myself to keep focused.

"Trip went well?" he asked, beginning, as was customary, with polite chitchat.

"Very well, thanks."

"Marcy tells me you had a bit of a dust-up with your rental car."

"I did, yeah, actually I almost hit a moose and ran off the road into a ditch. A branch came through the windshield and, well, there wasn't much I could do to get out of the ditch. One of the locals happened by, and I was lucky he did, because it was a bit nippy." By the way I framed it, I conveyed without words that I'd have been okay, it was no big deal, that I would have easily survived a night in the freezing Minnesota wilderness because, after all, my land survival skills were unparalleled and, besides that, I was thirty-six and an international political consulting genius, rich and, oh yeah, invincible.

Grantham made the appropriate noises and gestures to express the appropriate level of surprise, amazement, and relief that I had survived the ordeal. My mind snapped back to the 'local' who had just 'happened by'. I still couldn't get my mind around Ironbridge's explanation about why he was out there, and sort of settled on believing that he'd just been going for some groceries or something and came upon me unexpectedly, but then used the coincidence to manipulate me into believing that some sort of higher power had arranged the meeting. Some sort of little thing in my head jabbed at me over that story, though, but I couldn't come up with anything else, and Ironbridge's explanation—well, I just couldn't even process that. I began to get a visceral appreciation for why some of my kind of people wanted to put those kinds of people in camps.

"Well, we're glad you survived the wilds of Minnesota, because we have a very interesting challenge in front of us, and the Directors have determined that there is only one man in the firm capable of addressing that challenge." He said this with his hands clasped together in his lap, his legs crossed at the knee—it seems old guys can do that better than young guys can, I've never figured out why. I'll have to wait until I'm an old guy.

"Me," I said, more of a statement than a question. I was sitting here with him at his top-of-the-line, elite, god-level club after all, wasn't I?

"Precisely." I knew Grantham was a politician at heart, which meant he was always angling for something, but hey, *quid pro quo* is my modus operandi, and I wouldn't mind anything this set would offer by way of exchange. They had a fairly well-stocked larder.

"Well, let's get at it. What's the issue?"

Grantham made a small gesture indicating his discomfiture with my directness, but decided to overlook it. "We've had a request from some people that are incredibly well-placed in ... well, let's just say in highly-placed circles, who would appreciate the benefit of the firm's analyses regarding a particular question."

"You talking about the current Administration? They're gonna be out on their collective progressive asses in a few weeks. I mean, don't get me wrong, I'm sure the firm wouldn't mind taking their money, but—"

"Not the Administration," Grantham interrupted, with a little bit of the steely 'Managing Director' edge to his voice.

"Not the Administration?" I asked, surprised.

"Higher."

I sat there for a bit, waiting, wondering what he was talking about. I didn't think there *was* anything higher than the U.S. Presidential Administration. Sometimes Grantham's imagination would run riot, planning and scheming at amazing levels. I'd heard in the past that one particular machination of his had resulted in massive oppression in some two-bit African country somewhere in the middle of that continent, but had made the firm millions. I knew of at least two former U.S. Presidents who'd consulted with him, and whenever he wrote anything, it was immediately pushed out to a very high-level clientele around the world. From what I'd been able to discover, he'd always been wealthy, and his wealth just kept increasing.

The EU had crapped out after Brexit and massive Muslim migration had killed the centralizing, socialistic movement that founded the European Union, transforming what was left of the EU into just some proxy force arguing for Islamic justice around the world. Which answered another question I'd stashed in my head ever since I'd come to work for perhaps the most exclusive international management consulting firm on the planet. I wasn't stupid—the company I worked for didn't hire stupid people—and I'd been suspecting for a long time the firm had been working for some entity, some 'guiding organization' that was not associated with the U.S. Government or, for that matter, any other foreign government. The decisions they made, the analyses we produced, our objectives, our client lists, and the projects we took on all seemed to point to an effort to create a different international structure than the current, nationalistic-based structure we were working with. And that, boys and girls, really gets my interest.

"So ... are you interested?" Grantham queried.

"You had me at 'higher'," I quipped, and he chuckled graciously. Grantham did everything graciously.

"As we thought. So I want to describe to you the particular question our clients would like addressed, and then we could perhaps discuss the team you'd like to put together to attack it. I should mention that you'll have carte blanche on this."

When he said this, I got a little tingle all the way down to the silk socks in my Italian loafers. Getting carte blanche on a project in this firm was one step removed from an invitation to a seat as a Managing Director. I was speechless for a moment. For some reason—again, damn it—my mind snapped back to the Ironbridge's kitchen and the old guy telling me that there wasn't much time left before things in our country would be completely disrupted, and that this issue of my relationship to God would be important to my future ... as if he knew anything about my future. But that little thought excursion also tripped up the name of Simonsen Lehrner, and I knew right then that I wanted Lehrner on this team.

"Giles, that's an incredibly generous offer, and I would really like to thank you."

"Not at all. So ... the question we've been asked to analyze is this: 'What would the reaction in America be to having one or two major powers act in an assisting role in the event of a major disruption to our current way of life?'"

My mind had already leapt out of the starting block and was beginning to parse out the areas of investigation required for this new and exhilarating professional challenge when what Grantham actually said hit me—that is, the similarity to what the old farmer in northern Minnesota had said. But it only threw me for a minute. Hell, I rationalized, any blind man can see what's coming down the pipe for this country. You can't click twice away from Google's home page without coming on some tinfoil hat blog that screamed about the end of the world and the end of America and the need to 'hole up' in some flyover state and tuck in two years' worth of salt, sugar, canned goods, and, oh yeah, don't forget the ammunition, for the good God's sake. So get a grip, Gillenkamp.

"Fascinating line of enquiry," I responded. "Are we expecting anything like that to happen?"

Grantham explored the creases of his impeccably tailored trousers for specks of lint. "Who knows? The world is not as stable as it once was, I think we can all agree on that." From Grantham, I took that as a resounding, 'Hell yes' answer to my question, which just added more emphasis to my enthusiasm.

"Can I assume that the two major powers are those I discussed in my paper?"

Grantham tilted his head—graciously—and said, "Yes, I think that's a fair assumption. The document you produced generated quite a bit of interest in those ... *higher* levels ... and you've been specifically requested."

I nodded in acknowledgement of Grantham's sideways compliment. "What's their timetable?"

"Six months," he replied, holding up a hand as if to forestall what he knew would be my immediate objection, "and we realize it's incredibly abbreviated."

I stuffed my irritation at the short timeline back into my sock when I realized what he was actually telling me. "There must be some urgency then," I speculated.

Grantham just raised his eyebrows and shivered his shoulders to resemble a shrug; noncommittal as usual, but it was sufficient enough to serve as an answer for me. And again my mind was almost involuntarily yanked back to Ironbridge's observation that I didn't have much time. These mental interruptions were becoming tiresome.

"Well then," I said, "we'd better get to it."

"Well said," Grantham replied, seasoned mentor encouraging Young Turk.

"You said carte blanche. So okay—then I'd like to begin with getting Simonsen Lehrner on board. He's got the breadth of experience, unsurpassed knowledge, the ability to work with intangibles and he's probably the world's best scenario planner—and, of course, he's got one world class network."

I sensed Grantham hesitate for an imperceptible minute, as though some shade had passed across his eyes, but it was only for a moment and then he answered me. "Lehrner it is," he said. "Carte blanche means just that. But permit me to inject a minor note of caution here," Grantham said, and I waited for what would explain the hesitation, that shadow I'd seen. "One possible outcome of such potential future disruptions, one possible thread in one or two possible scenarios ... might be that certain ethnicities are, shall we say, offered less options relative to survivability than others."

I sat very still, translating what one of the Managing Directors of my firm was actually telling me. I knew exactly what he was saying, but needed him to actually say it.

"Giles, I'm not sure what you're trying to say."

He put his palms flat on the tops of his trousers, a gesture that conveyed he was trying to be subtle without being explicit. "In the event we have ... external governments ... supporting a recovery period in the U.S., there may be a need for those governments to apply or impose certain ... shall we say, *restrictions* on the freedoms enjoyed by certain specific groups of people."

"You mean, like the 'guns and bible' crowd?"

"Those, definitely, oh my yes. Actually those may be ... I should say *would be* among the first groups of people whose freedoms should be restricted. There may be others as well ... others who might be considered, oh, let's say *destabilizing* ... or maybe even threatening."

"Sure, I can understand that. That's just logical."

"And in the scenarios you may consider, keep in mind that while we in the U.S. may deplore such courses of action, we may not be in positions where we can exert sufficient leverage or authority to prevent these external governments from imposing such ... restrictions ... upon the people group ... upon, let's say, specific ethnicities ... they may consider threatening. It will, after all, be their task to re-establish law and order and peace and harmony—again, should such disruptions occur, hypothetically speaking."

Giles always talked this way, so I had to interpret what he was saying. Basically, as best I could discern, it seemed as though he was telling me there might be certain groups of people who these two 'supporting' governments might just run roughshod over, and we—that is, we Americans—may just have to throw those people groups under the bus.

"Well, Giles, I suppose we would have to wait and see what develops, right? One of the keys to good scenario planning is to keep an open mind."

Grantham nodded sagely. "Well said," he replied. He liked that expression, because he liked to say things well and because it was sufficiently vague as not to require admitting that he'd passed on to me any kind of firm instructions. Dealing with Grantham was at times painful.

"Once Lehrner is aboard, I'd like to tap his network and populate the rest of the team."

"That would be fine," Grantham replied, tossing off the rest of the drink. "So now that you're onboard, I've been instructed to bring you to the next meeting." He stood up, surprising me.

"We've another meeting?"

"We do, yes ... with the client."

"The client?"

"Clients, to be precise. It's about a ten-minute drive. And do please remember what I said about specific people groups now, won't you?"

Chapter 16
Stan

"I permitted Myself to be sought by those who did not ask for Me; I permitted Myself to be found by those who did not seek Me. I said, 'Here am I, here am I,' to a nation which did not call on My name."

Isaiah 65:1

I cannot believe sometimes how stupid young engineers are these days. Where do they get their diplomas, at Wal-Mart? Seriously, I have to remind them constantly about the smallest things.

"Did you pack the chain?" I asked, putting on thick gloves against the morning's cold.

"Uh, yeah, Stan, we did."

"How many did you pack?"

"Um, just one. How many did you want?"

"At least three. How many times have I told you? Three makes two; two makes one; one makes none. How about the transit and the theodolite?"

"You want 'em both?"

"How many times do I have to tell you?"

"Yeah, I know, two makes one." The kid sneered, thinking I couldn't see him through the truck windows.

"Yes I want them both."

"What's the difference?" he asked. He was a recent graduate from the University of Michigan, who was maybe twenty-five and had not yet discovered the recent invention called a razor.

"The difference, genius, is that the transits we pack have an accuracy down to a minute of angle, and the theodolites measure down to a tenth of a second of angle."

"Oh," he says, remarkably erudite, even for a Michigan graduate.

"So let's think about that. A minute of angle at a mile would be what?"

I could see the wheels turning in his head, doing the math, but apparently the participation ribbons he got in math class weren't for anything related to math skills. I didn't have the time to wait.

"Approximately a foot and a half," I said. "And you wanna try figuring what a tenth of a second of angle would be at a mile? No? I'll tell you ... it's about three thousandths of a foot. So we pack them both, got it?"

"Yes sir," the mathematical genius from Michigan said, and went back to the trailer to get what I'd asked for.

Another member of the team came out of the hotel and approached the Land Cruiser, holding a can of beer in one hand and a bag of little chocolate donuts in the other. "Breakfast of champions, Stan," he said, smiling, holding them both up.

"Yeah," I growled. I didn't want to get friendly with this other idiot either. The only reason he was on the crew was that his father was special friends with one of the executives in the accounting department at Grayson International Construction, and in San Francisco, when you say two guys are 'special friends', that's shorthand for the fact that they're nestled up tight in a homosexual relationship. Made me sick but there wasn't anything I could do about it, since the gays had enormous power in the upper corporate echelons. This kid had graduated from the University of Southern California, and looked it, all tanned and fit and strong and as dumb as a surfboard. The kid's name was 'Tug', for God's sake. Who names a kid 'Tug'?

"What electronics are we packing?" I asked.

He wandered around to the back of the Land Cruiser, set a donut on the bumper, and opened the hatchback. "Well, looks like we got us a green thing, then a gray thing with some long yellow sticks next to it, and a big yellow thing there, and then another orange thing."

"Funny," I said. "Is there a rack on the top for a big white plastic thing?"

"Yeah, that would be cool," he answered. "We could, like, go surf in Lake Superior."

"Or just go dunk your head in it if you can't tell me what electronics we have."

"Whoa, dude, easy. So, like, we got here one optical theodolite, and—"

"I thought Jason said he didn't pack the theodolite?"

"Yeah, well, I packed it."

"Right. What else?"

"What else? Let's see," he replied, taking another pull on the beer, "we got us one robotic total station, one GPS base station, and the optical level."

"What about the tripods?"

"Yeah, we got those, they're the long yellow sticks I mentioned."

I turned away, satisfied that at least we had the right equipment for the day's job. I wasn't happy with the crew they'd given me, but I was accustomed to getting the younger ones, the dregs, the ones without any experience. As Grayson's leadership came to resemble a convention of lettuce, grape, bacon, and tomato sandwich eaters instead of a group of qualified, seasoned, international construction company executives, my reputation in the company just kept getting lower and lower, until I was finally consigned to jobs with new kids wet behind the ears, tasked with training them in the basics of field surveying on marginalized tasking not critical to our main contracts. You'd think these kids would have learned the basics when they got their degree in civil engineering, but no, I think they were all too busy protesting or sitting drinking their lattes somewhere besides their classrooms—maybe they just spent too much time eating milk and cookies in their safe place. I was disgusted with the whole racket and knew it was time for me to leave soon.

As I was ruminating on that chunk of disappointment in my life, I got a call on my cell from, speak of the devil, Grayson Corporate. Specifically, one Mackinder Sellers, the Chief Engineer for Grayson's U.S. operations. He was one of the few men at corporate who still had a female wife, but he didn't seem fazed by the sexual shenanigans. He's a few years younger than I am, and, if I had to admit it, I'd say he was a half-decent civil engineer. And least he knew the difference between a theodolite and a transit.

"Morning, Stan," he began cheerfully.

"You're up early," I growled. We had an easy relationship, by which I mean that I wasn't going to call him 'Sir' and he knew it and wasn't bothered by it.

"No, actually I'm in Paris, talking with the Levalie-Cheval team."

"What do those frogs want?" I asked.

"Tactful as always," he shoots back. "We do not say 'frogs', Stan. They are very important corporate partners on this massive international contract who happen to speak French."

"They're frogs."

"Did I happen to mention that they are helping pay your salary?"

"What do you want, Mackinder?"

"Tact, Stan, tact; this is why you are freezing your ass off leading a survey team of 'nubies' in some flyover state and I am sitting here very comfortably in the City of Lights, having a cappuccino and a *pain au chocolat* with senior company executives."

"And I could give a flyover leap," I replied. "What do you want? Me and my 'nubies' need to get going, doing the scut work that will keep your 'massive international contract' from falling down around your ears while you drink frog coffee and eat frog food."

Sellers finally figured out that I wasn't going to be humored, so he got down to business. "Levalie-Cheval engineers are considering bringing cement in over the lake and through Granite Sky instead of packing it overland."

"Why is that?"

"Because they happen to have just purchased a cement plant in Ontario, almost on the shores of Superior, and they know that shipping cement by boat is cheaper than putting it on trucks. They can ship more—"

"Yeah, I know, they can ship more, faster, at less cost than if they push it out on wheels. Got it. So what do you want from me?"

I could hear him clearing his throat. Sellers didn't like to be interrupted, but he put up with it because he needed me. They all did, which is why they all put up with me. "We want to know what size ship we can get into Granite Sky."

"Why don't you just run them into Thunder Bay?" I asked, referring to the Canadian port north along the western shore of Lake Superior.

"Because we want the cement to move through the U.S.," he answered.

"Why is that? That doesn't make any sense. If you want the cement to go by boat for the longest distance, then unload the boats at Duluth. That's as far east as Superior goes, anyway."

I could hear the silence on the other end of the line, all the way from Paris. I'm a jerk but I'm not a stupid jerk, and I knew there was something he wasn't telling me.

"Just go survey the entry areas at Granite Sky," he said crisply, in his corporate 'just go do it because I said so' voice. "Consider dredging the bay if you discover it's too shallow."

"What size ships are you thinking about bringing in?" I asked.

"Basically they can't exceed a draft of 26.5 feet."

"The Seawaymax standard, then," I said.

He seemed surprised that I knew that. "Uh, yeah, actually, that's what it is. It limits—"

"I know the source. It's the standard for ships that need to get through the St. Lawrence Seaway. So you want to see how we can get ships in that class into Granite Sky?"

"Yeah, Stan, that's what we want," he said with a detectable air of frustration.

"Can't do it," I said baldly, with a tinge of satisfaction.

"What do you mean, you can't do it?"

"Do you need me to say it in French?" I was walking the line of insubordination but I really didn't care. "I can't do it with the tools I have. I have, what, a GPS station, a robotic total station, a couple of theodolites, a transit, some levels, and rods. And you want—"

"I want you to figure out how to get the cement off the ships, Stan. Stop being such a damn obstructionist and do your job. Yes, I know, you don't have a side-scanning sonar and you don't have Lidar—no problem. We've dispatched a vessel out of Duluth to do the side-scan and we've got a Lidar flight scheduled next week out of Minneapolis. You're not the only damn engineer in the company."

I let him blow off steam for a moment, and he continued. "What's the best way to get the cement off the ships? Do they pull up to docks? Do we build a transfer system between an artificial island we build and the mainland? Do we pipe it underground from a floating dock off the coast? Do we bring it ashore in lighters? Lots of questions, Stan; we need information to make the best decision. Get some engineering eyes on the ground out there. Do what we pay you to do."

"And you want me to do that with just Laurel and Hardy?" I asked, frustrated because corporate wouldn't give me the tools to do what I needed to do.

"I don't give a flying leap, Stan, if you use the three stooges or your pet dog. Just get the damn job done, got it?"

"Don't I always?" I asked. He hung up.

I was enjoying the taste of that last little shot, getting the last word with Sellers, when another call came through, this time from my wife.

"Hello, Janet."

"Where are you today, Stan?"

"Still here in Minnesota. We were going to go out west, but we just got a call—"

"Don't really care, Stan. Tell me, did you talk to accounting to make sure they'll deposit our paycheck in the bill pay account?"

I was confused for a second. "Um, oh, yeah, now I remember, and no, I haven't done that yet."

"Well, when are you going to do it? You're more absent-minded than your son, who is only ten and can't remember to put his toys away unless I tell him ten times. I've got the mortgage and the insurance to pay, the kids' tuition is due, we've got your credit card and mine to pay down, and we've got, what, $8000 in the account? That's not enough."

"So just move what you need out of the savings account. That's what it's for. When I change where the money goes, you can replenish the saving account."

"So that's just more work for me."

"You don't have any other job," I snapped, stating what was only true, tired of being bullied.

"You watch your tone, Stan. You don't want to be flying off the handle again, do you? Taking care of your children is enough work for any two people, while you're off with your friends, living in hotels, eating out every night, and you don't have a thing to worry about, except figuring out where to get your next beer."

"I don't drink," I mumbled into the phone, cowed but not wanting to back down.

"I don't give a tinker's damn if you drink or not, and you know it. Just get the damn paycheck going into the right account so I can live the way a normal person should live, you understand?"

I paused for a moment, not wanting to appear too submissive, but it didn't help, and I just couldn't risk getting her too angry. The most important thing in my life was hanging on to my family, so I choked down my response. "Yeah, sure, I'll get it done."

"Good," she snapped, and hung up.

I put the phone away and went back into the hotel lobby to wait for Jason and Tug to finish whatever it was millennials did in the morning. It certainly didn't have anything to do with a razor.

Things were not going well on the home front, but then, they hadn't been going well for a long time. Last summer Janet and I really got into it. I was tired of her bullying and disrespecting me. She was actively turning the kids against me. I finally got so fed up that I went out into the backyard and stood near the grill I was building. I was so angry that I picked up a sledgehammer and started smashing the built-up brick walls that made up the sides of the grill. I just went on smashing and smashing, brick chips flying. I heard Janet yelling from the kitchen, but I didn't pay her any mind, and just went on hitting the thing until it was just a pile of crumbled red brick fragments and a lot of dust. So for some crazy reason Janet decides to lock the doors and call the police, and she ends up getting a restraining order against me because she felt 'unsafe', and she said the kids were frightened, which was a line of crock, since they weren't even home then. But the court agreed with her and I found myself going to 'anger management counseling' for 90 days to get the restraining order lifted. I sat through it and parroted all the stuff they wanted me to say and got the hell out of there as soon as possible, but now she's got the whip hand, and if I don't tow the line in the house, I'll find myself unable to see the kids—in my own home, in a stable marriage. It drives me up the wall. She's always worn the pants in the family—I know that—but now she wears them openly, and she lets the kids know she's wearing them.

My son is ten and he's just like me. I don't interact easily with people and neither does he. He's got some significant behavioral issues at school, and we've had a hard time getting him from one grade to another. My daughter, thirteen, on the other hand, is very smart, but she's becoming her mother, which means she thinks I have to do what she says, no matter what. There are times when I really don't even like my family, and I know they don't like me.

***

We spend the day looking over what little maritime capabilities Granite Sky offered. There is a tiny marina fit for pleasure boats, a couple of private homes have wooden piers out into the bay for their little fishing rowboats or whatever, and a little bay encased by a couple of fragile breakwaters. That was about it. Granite Sky was a fairly big town but they'd sort of grown away from the coast, not along it. I see no reason why the company would consider pulling in tons and tons of cement through here.

"Yo, Stan, so what are you gonna tell Corporate?" Tug asks, still nursing a beer. I can't tell if it's the same one from this morning, or a new one. He is sitting in the passenger seat of the truck the company rented for us.

I consider biting his head off again but that game is getting old. "I can't say ... Tug." I have to work to get the name right. "There's obviously nothing along the mainland coast they can use to build on; it's mostly shallow sand and loose gravel. It would cost them a fortune to dredge out some kind of harbor deep enough ... which is probably why it's not here already. And whatever it is they want, they'll have to build it from scratch."

"What about that island out there?" the kid from Michigan, Jason, asks.

"That's Black Dog Island, and it's a possibility," I say, "but we'd need to look at the depth readings and see what the floor is like out there. If it's a long shallow run to its coastline all around, then it won't be cost-effective to get the freighters in there, but if the side-scans they do show maybe something like a deep drop-off close to one of the island's edges, maybe they could build a pier there."

"And then, like, how would they get the cement off the island?" Tug asks.

"We'd pipe it off," I say, enthusiastic in spite of myself. "We dig an underground pipeline from the island out there to some receiving point on the mainland here, and that would actually be the fastest way. They just run a large hose into the cargo bay and pump the stuff into the pipe and then across the bay and into the trucks at the receiving station."

"They'd need to build a receiving station, right?" Jason asks, a little slow.

"Um, yeah, they would, Jason."

"And a pipeline under the bay, right?"

"In the bay, actually, but yeah."

"Cool."

"Yeah," I reply, "cool."

"Hey, dude, like, I'd come up here in the summer and work, ya know?" Tug contributes, waving his hand to cover the entire bay 'out there'. "It'd be cool, man. Imagine digging a pipeline under the water."

"The Indians'll take all the money you earn, Tug," Jason says derisively, smiling at Tug. Tug only wags his head.

"Yeah, well, can't argue with you there, dude. Can't resist the tables, man."

I look at my watch and decide it is time to knock off for the day. "Look, you two, we're done for the day. Tomorrow I do a recon of the local construction capabilities. There," I said, pointing to a moderately-sized warehouse-looking building on the edge of the bay.

"The Northern Minnesota Construction Company?" Jason says, reading the sign at the front of the parking lot.

"That would be them, yes," I reply dryly. "That's the first place I'll try. I'm thinking they'll be the only place in this dump of a town that has any kind of marine construction capability, but we'll see."

"What will you want us to do?" Jason asks.

"You two are going to get me some measurements," I tell them. "I want readings on a multitude of bearings out to the island. Tomorrow I'll give you a map of the area where I will have marked potential locations for a receiving facility and I want you to survey those areas."

"You thinkin' they'll go for puttin' a pier on the island out there?" Tug asks.

"I'm not sure but if the floor of the bay out there is the way I think it is, the odds are good that they'll go that way. Can't say for sure, but let's at least have the information if it turns out they need it. So ... you guys know what you have to do tomorrow?"

"We're good, man," Tug replies, looking out the window toward the Indian casino on the shore of the bay, taking a hit from his beer. "We be good."

The next morning I pull into the parking lot of the Northern Minnesota Construction Company and get out of the truck. Jason slides into the driver's seat. "You two got the map?" I ask.

"Dude," Tug says, holding up the well-marked map I made for them last night in the hotel room. "We be clear, no worries, man."

"With two college graduates who can't speak in complete sentences, there are always worries," I rumble, and Jason and Tug drive off while I walk toward the office. Tug waves his beer out the window in farewell; what a confidence builder.

I had called ahead last night, and fortunately got the owner, who happened to be working late. That was a good sign, one I didn't expect in this two-bit town. I set up a meeting in the office for this morning, early, and he said it was not a problem. I didn't think it would be; they didn't look all that busy.

When I open the door, I walk into a small area with a bunch of chairs and a window that looks through to what is obviously the main office. There are two doors off to my right—restrooms, one for men, one for women, obviously, by the gender-specific signs. A young kid about thirty-five looks up from behind a desk. He was wearing some kind of plaid flannel shirt and heavy work pants.

"You Stan Pankowicz?" he asks, pronouncing my name dead on.

"That's me," I say. "Grayson International. "You guys not get the memo?"

"Uh, I'm sorry, sir. A memo?"

I nodded my head toward the restroom signs. "Didn't they tell you people that those signs are illegal now?"

"Signs?"

"Yeah ... what's so hard? You know, 'man', 'woman' ... the law says places of business can't differentiate genders by any type of visual, auditory, or sensory symbols, signage, or sound."

"Oh, oh, yeah, I see ... yeah, well, we heard about that, but we're still going with the old standard." He smiled slightly. "Besides, I think Daria would kill anyone who walked in on her."

I looked at him and just shrugged my shoulders, as if to say, 'Hey, it's your lawsuit, Mister.' I looked around the office and asked, "Is Mr. Riesling in?"

"That's me," he says. "Come on in, please. Josh Riesling ... my Dad owned the company. I took it over a while ago. Don't worry, I get that all the time."

"Not worried," I said, worried that I would have to deal with some young kid who probably knew next to nothing about engineering or, God save us, marine construction. "Thanks for taking the meeting so early in the morning."

"Sure, yeah, hey, have a seat, I'll get us some coffee."

I shake his hand—it's like grabbing leather wrapped around steel rods—and sit down at a small round table they have and he pours me a cup of coffee from the carafe he has on the side. The office isn't fancy, just a desk, a small round table for meetings, some bookshelves holding manuals and codes, most likely, and a coffee pot on the side—pretty much what I expected. Except for the cross on the wall above the guy's desk. That wasn't what I expected in a professional setting. It irritated me—more than normal.

I take the coffee—in a Styrofoam cup—and open right up, forgetting polite chitchat, which I'm not good at anyway. "Grayson is thinking about moving some cement through here," I begin, "freighting it in. We were looking at dredging the bay up close to the island out there," I point to the scrub-covered rock we could see through his window, "and maybe putting a pier out there, then piping the cement to a receiving station on the mainland and then trucking it out."

Riesling nods as I talk, watching me. I feel strange; the kid seems older than he looks. He bothers me, right away, right from the start. Yeah, yeah, most people bother me, but not like this kid. It was like he was getting inside my head and I didn't like it.

"So you're with the guys orchestrating the sonar surveys?" he asks quickly.

"Uh, yeah, actually that's us."

"Have you thought about Wamegasset Bay?" he asks.

"Wamegasset what?"

"The bay just north of here."

"No, I haven't looked at that, and the company just told me to look at Granite Sky Bay, or whatever it is you call it ... the bay where the town is."

He smiles easily. "Yeah, no worries, but I can tell you they won't find good bottom conditions here, and you probably won't like the floor conditions they find around Black Dog Island, either. You'll spend a mint of money trying to dredge a harbor and probably not get a good result, otherwise, of course, they'd have done it already."

I pursed my lips, recognizing my own logic. "So what's in ... in the bay north of here? Why would that be good?"

"Because of the bottom contour," he replies. It's deep, deep enough for deep drafts to come right up almost to the coast, and the rock bed is solid. They put Route 61 along the coast there and didn't have any problems." He was referring to the main road artery that came up from Duluth to Granite Sky.

"Hmmm, okay, maybe I can get crew up there to look at that." Just as I conceded his point, the door opened and an older man walked in. He was tall—taller than I was—and sort of thin, with silver hair, in an old ragged farm coat that had seen better days. He was limping. I did a quick side-scan and noticed he had some kind of prosthetic leg.

"Can I help you?" Riesling asks, standing up from our table.

"I see the sign out there, says you guys do stonemasonry."

"Yes sir, we do, actually. We're just now starting to do that kind of work."

"Hey, sounds good, but I don't want to interrupt your meeting. I can wait outside."

"Sure, thanks, I'll be right with you." The old guy takes a seat in one of the three chairs in the little anteroom and I could tell the Riesling kid was eager to get to his new customer, which kind of brought out my naturally ornery nature, of which I was inordinately proud. I needed more information, and I wasn't ready for the meeting to end.

"So what are things like around here?" I ask, intentionally delaying the kid.

"Uh, what do you mean sir?"

"I mean, like, jobs and such. Are things okay, or are folks kind of short on employment?"

"Oh ... well, I guess you could say things are not booming, but no one is starving. Up here, we tend not to benefit much when the economy booms, but we also don't get hit as hard when things are thin. The Ojibwe tribe is getting sustenance from the Government, and most of the people in town work at the casino or the schools or the fast food restaurants that serve what tourists come through."

I nodded, as though I was digesting his assessment, but it wasn't helping me much. "In your opinion do you think Grayson would need to import our labor if we went ahead with the project, or would we be able to find local workers from here?"

This got his attention. "Oh, you could get what you need from around here, sir. Obviously we—I mean, Northern Minnesota Construction—could help. We know the ground, we know how to get the permits and licenses, we know where the potholes are, I guess you could say. And we know where to get the labor—and where not to get the labor, if you know what I mean." I did know what he meant; one of the biggest problems construction companies had when they did remote work was unreliable local labor, but we had to constantly use local labor because it was inordinately expensive to truck around our own indigenous labor pool. And I could see the kid was realizing I was offering him something probably larger than a stonewall project at some deadbeat's farm. Knowing that establishing good relations with local construction companies was always important to the company, I thought I'd diverge a bit from business and maybe establish good relations. I looked up at the cross over his desk.

"You guys religious here?" I said.

"Well, not exactly," he replied, "if by 'religious' you mean being into a bunch of rules. We do take our faith seriously, though," he went on. I could sense he was going to launch into more detail, but I cut him off. I'd heard that story before.

"I'm an atheist," I said, looking out the window. "Have been for fifty-six years. Don't have much time for religion. Haven't seen anything that would change my mind, either." The guy didn't say anything, just sat there, nodding. Typical…when you come right out and get in their faces, these people don't really know how to handle confrontation.

"So ... would you like maybe some survey maps of Wamegasset Bay?" he asked, adroitly changing the subject.

"Yeah, actually, those would be helpful." I stood up. I was done. I had a potential construction spot to survey. The kid had been helpful, I had to admit; I'd never thought about the bay just north of the town, probably because Sellers hadn't included it in my instructions. And I'd established good relations with the local company by engaging in some personal dialogue ... so far, a good day's work. As I left, he walked me out through the anteroom where the old guy was sitting, reading a book. I couldn't resist dragging the conversation out, just to put a spoke in the kid's wheel.

"I'm coming up on retirement," I said. "What's it like, living around here?"

The kid looked kind of surprised, but seemed to take it in stride. "Well, okay I guess. What were you thinking about doing after you retire?"

"My specialty is building roads," I replied. "I might go on the mission field—they have a mission up here to the Indians, right? Or maybe I'll help build roads for disadvantaged people in different parts of the world."

"That would be a disaster."

I turned around. The kid hadn't said that. It was the old man, sitting there with the book in his lap, closed now.

"Pardon me?" I asked.

"I said that would be a disaster. I did hear you say you were an atheist in there, right?"

"Uh, yeah, that's right."

"Well then, why would you go out to the mission field? You'd do more harm than good. People who go on the mission field need to at least believe in God. That's kind of basic."

"But ... what about ... I'm pretty sure they need roads," I said condescendingly, sure that this guy didn't know a thing about what made a good road.

"They don't need roads, they need truth, which is something you can't give them, because you don't have it."

I couldn't believe what this guy was saying to me. I began to get seriously irritated. And I was even more surprised to see the young Riesling kid sort of smiling, even though an opportunity of a lifetime had just come through his door, and now some worn-out, run-down farmer was going to ruin it. I sort of enjoyed waiting for the kid to figure out the moral dilemma he was in and start squirming. But that didn't happen.

"I kind of would have to agree with Mister ... with the gentlemen here, sir," Riesling said. "Wouldn't make much sense to become a missionary. I mean, what gospel would you be preaching?" I was too surprised to say anything in reply. Didn't this kid know how important my recommendation about the construction work would be?

"You can be a hypocrite in the world all by yourself without joining a mission and confirming it," the old guy said, arms folded, staring straight at me.

"Excuse me, have we been introduced?" I asked, angry and irritated. "And how do you get off, calling me a hypocrite?"

"What's so hard to figure out? You said you were an atheist. Then you said you wanted to go join a missionary organization. Missionary organizations have as their primary focus the spreading of the gospel, which oh by the way is simply a Greek word for 'Good News', which for centuries men have understood to refer to the fact that because God became man and then died for man, man now has access to a relationship with God. This is good news, and it is what missionaries communicate to others. So explain to me why you joining a missionary organization as an atheist isn't hypocritical."

It was obvious the Riesling kid had never met the old man before, but if I didn't know better I'd swear he was actually enjoying the showdown.

"I'm not a hypocrite," I said, and it was true. I prided myself on telling anyone what was on my mind, no matter how it made them feel. I didn't really care about how people felt about me, I just told them the truth.

"Yeah, well prove it," the old man said, still sitting there, as sure as death and twice as obnoxious.

"How?" I asked, not really interested, but not wanting to make a scene, and not wanting to back down in front of the Riesling kid.

"Get by yourself and ask God if He really exists. Ask Him to prove that He's real by making Himself evident to you in a way you can't mistake."

"You're kidding me, right?"

"Are you afraid you might get an answer?"

I didn't know what to say to that, since I didn't believe in God in the first place. "I'm headed out," I said, turning to the young Riesling kid. "If I find any potential on the north shore of that bay, whatever it's called, I'll let you know." And I turned and walked out the office door, slamming it just a little for emphasis. There was nothing I hated more than self-righteous religious people.

***

The next morning I took Laurel and Hardy out to the north bay, the name of which I refused to remember. I dropped them off at the southern tip with one set of equipment and I took the other set in the truck to the northern end of the area to do my surveying on my own. I was steaming over a phone call I'd had with Janet the night before.

"You're never home," she'd complained.

"If you can find a job around home that pays as well as what we're making now, let me know, I'll be all over it. This isn't any picnic for me either, you know."

"And you're totally not involved in the kids' lives, Stan. They need a father. I'm the one that takes them to church. I'm the one that runs them to school and to wherever else they need to go. I spend my life in the car."

"I spend my life in hotels and airplanes," I replied, growing angrier by the minute. "It's no fun on the road."

"You know, you keep saying that but that's not what I see. As soon as you're home, you're angling with Corporate to get sent out on another job. It's like you're intentionally avoiding responsibilities here."

"That's not true," I said, knowing it was. And she knew I knew.

"And it's embarrassing, every time I go to our Ladies' Bible study, for me to have to admit that my husband isn't home, or if you are, you're 'busy with a project at home' to explain why you never come to church."

"You knew that about me when we got married," I said. "Nothing's changed. Why don't you just tell them the truth—that your husband is an atheist, and proud of it. Those hypocrites in church make me sick."

"We didn't have two kids when we got married," she shot back. "These kids need some kind of spiritual guidance, and you're not providing it. And you have no idea how embarrassing it is to be the only woman at church with a husband who's an atheist."

"I told you when we got married, that if we ever had kids, I wanted them to make up their own mind about that stuff. And don't tell me you're the only woman whose husband isn't a saint. I know some of those guys and I could tell you stories." And then I had an inspired thought. "I tell you what, though," I began. "How about I quit this job and I'll come home and maybe get a job as a substitute teacher there at the high school. They make around $80 a day, but hey, I'd get off the road and I'd be around for the kids more."

Silence on the other end of the line ... and then, "That's stupid; completely, utterly stupid. How are we going to live on $80 a day?"

"We could move. We don't have to live in that palace. We could get an apartment. We could sell the BMW and get, I don't know, maybe a used minivan or a pickup truck." I was having fun now, pulling her chain. She hadn't caught on.

"I will not live in an apartment, and I will not drive a junk car. I want the kids to have private schooling; they deserve it, and I refuse to live in a dump."

"So you're okay with me staying on the road, earning the money I do, so you can live in the manner to which you've become accustomed?"

She caught on then. "Listen you son-of-a-bitch, everything isn't black and white. It's not an engineering world, and you don't have all the answers. If you can't hear what I'm trying to tell you, then you can go to hell. Enjoy your life by yourself!" The phone clicked—once again, she'd hung up on me. I smiled, reveling in the fact that I'd gotten her riled *and* kept the moral high ground. It didn't happen often.

But as the evening wore on, the taste of the conversation soured and it began to eat at me. I grew angry, wondering what it was she wanted. She wanted me home, but she wasn't willing for us to take a cut in pay for me to be there, which made me wonder what it was she really wanted—did she want *me*, or just my money? She wanted me to be some kind of 'Holy Joe' church guy, when she's known since we dated that I wanted nothing to do with church or God or any of that hypocrisy. Now we have kids, what, all that has to change? Sorry, but it doesn't work that way. My parents spent most of their lives in Malaysia with a missionary organization, and I was raised there. My parents weren't Christians—far from it, but the missionary team needed their expertise in teaching the locals about better agricultural techniques, and my father had a degree in agricultural chemistry, and my mother and he didn't mind living in grass huts or snakes or detouring around herds of water buffalo occasionally. It was an interesting life, growing up as an atheist with other kids whose parents were Christians. I saw the hypocrisy up close and personal, and I swore I didn't want anything to do with it. Religion to me has always been just lip service and a bunch of people with fake smiles trying to convince others how wonderful they were by jumping through a set of specific hoops set up by the owners of whatever denomination they belonged to. As the night wore on I drilled myself deeper and deeper into a depression, realizing my life wasn't working out the way I'd planned.

***

The northern segment of the bay looked very promising. I could tell the ground was solid, and from the way the water moved, it seemed the bottom dropped off significantly, and close to the shoreline. I began to set up the transit and other tools to take the necessary measurements at the first potential pier location. There was absolutely no wind, with a thick, low, gray overcast. The water looked cold and forbidding. Thinking about last night's conversation, I had a fleeting thought of just walking into the water and swimming out into the lake as far as I could go, until the cold just put me to sleep and I would be done with all this turbulence and stress and angst and anger and anxiety. I hated my life. I absolutely hated it but, I reflected, not enough to take it—yet. But if things went on, well ... that option wasn't off the table.

Laurel and Hardy were miles away at the southern tip of the bay, and I was standing there alone on the rocky shoreline, maybe all of a hundred yards of crushed rock from the edge of the road shoulder to the water's edge. The transit was up and I remember I was just getting ready to take the first bearing when out of the blue the thought came, recalling the challenge the old man had thrown at me yesterday. *"Ask God if He exists."* I could hear the guy's voice, clear as a bell. I stepped back from the transit and put my arm on the tube and just thought, 'Well, what *are* you afraid of, seriously? All your life you've been convinced there's no God. But what if there is?' And so I did what the old guy had challenged me to do. I said, out loud, there on the shore of Lake Superior in the freezing cold morning, with no one around, "Okay God, if you exist, show me. Prove you're there." The words floated out and hung portentously over the dark gray water, and I began to realize how desperate I was, talking to myself in the middle of nowhere.

Feeling stupid, I was about to turn back to the transit and take my bearing when I saw a light appear out over the water, on the horizon. There was a solid overcast, so it definitely couldn't have been the sun shining through and also, the light was more of a pinpoint, like someone was shining a flashlight at me from just above the horizon. I watched as it grew brighter and closer and larger until it was about the size of ... well, my thought at the time was that it was about the size of the round conference table I'd seen at the construction office the day before. This bright shining light was coming straight at me, moving over the water at incredible speed, and as it came closer I saw something like a bird highlighted in the middle of the disc. And then, I swear, this round light stopped about fifty yards out over the water and the bird—it was a white bird, a dove, carrying something in its mouth—kept on coming, flying in my direction. The bird flew straight at me and perched on the transit. It looked at me and somehow I knew it wanted me to extend my hand, which I did, and it deposited an eight-inch long piece of what looked like a twig or branch with small leaves on it in my hand. And then I heard, as clear as day, a voice that seemed to come from behind me, or above me, or from all around me, I couldn't be sure. It said, "Be at peace ... through me." And then the bird flew off back into the disc of light and the light just ... I don't know, seemed to fade away, and there was no bird, no light, just the dark gray water under a dark gray sky. I was thinking I'd just had some kind of weird reaction to the pizza we'd had for dinner last night, until I looked down in my hand and I found myself still holding a branch with leaves on it.

***

I left the transit on the rocks, stumbled back to the truck, and drove back to the Northern Minnesota Construction office. This was something I didn't understand and it was something well outside my base of experience and those two things frightened me. But I couldn't deny the fact that I'd asked a question and I'd gotten an answer. I had to be honest, and I wasn't stupid. Was it possible, seriously? Did God really exist? Was He really ... there? It seemed I'd gotten an answer, but I now had more questions than ever and there was only one guy I wanted to talk to—that old guy in the ragged farm coat I'd met at the construction office. He knew something. The only thing that steered me to the construction office instead of the hospital was the fact that there was an eight-inch long piece of tree or branch sitting on the console of the truck.

The truck screamed into the Northern Minnesota Construction Company parking lot and I picked up the branch and jumped out, crossed the lot in three seconds, knocked on the door, and just went in. It was unlocked, but I didn't see anyone in the main office. Then a lady of about thirty came through a side door and I asked her if the Riesling kid was around.

"Sure is, sir. What did you say your name was?" She had sort of a casual, laid-back, but foreign accent. She didn't seem to be local, but she was dressed in jeans and a plaid shirt and she obviously worked for the construction company.

"Pankowicz," I answered.

"Did you have an appointment?"

"Uh, well, no, actually, but it's kind of important. Is he busy?"

"Ah, no, not really. Mr. Riesling's out on the back loading dock. I can get him if you like."

"No, hey, um, I wonder if I could just go out there?"

She looked at me a little strangely, her eyes glanced down at what I had in my hand, but then said, "Sure thing, sir. Follow me." I went through the side door behind her and we went through the warehouse and back through a huge door that opened out to a dock that extended into the lake. There was a small barge tied up to the dock with a group of men unloading supplies.

"He's right out there, Mr. Pankowicz." She pointed to the group of men carrying sacks off the barge.

"Thanks," I replied, and walked out to where the men were dropping the sacks onto a flatbed truck.

Riesling saw me after he'd just dropped a sack onto the flatbed and smiled. "Hey, Mr. Pankowicz. You find anything of interest out on the north cut?"

I came a little closer and, lowering my voice, asked, "I wonder if I could ask you to put me in touch with that old guy you had in the office the other morning."

Riesling kind of tilted his head a little and then I could see a sort of comprehension dawn, almost as though he knew what had happened but didn't want to blow my secret. "So, uh, yeah, actually, he did leave his phone number."

"He won't mind you giving it out, will he?"

"Well, I'm not sure. Hang on." The kid pulled his cell out of a pocket and dialed a number. "Mr. Ironbridge? Yeah, good morning, I hope it's not too early." ... "Yes sir, I suppose the livestock do get up early." ... "So I was wondering, uh, I'm actually standing out here on our dock with Mr. Pankowicz, and Mr. Pankowicz wanted to know ..." ... "Oh, uh, he's the guy that was in the office yesterday when you came in." ... "Yes sir, that's the guy ... yeah, the missionary. Right." Riesling chuckled a little and then looked up at me. "He, uh, wants to talk to you." Riesling handed me the phone.

"Mr., uh, Ironbridge, right?"

"Morning. What's up?"

I thought it best to just dive right in. "I don't exactly know how to say this, but I tried what you suggested."

"Yeah? And what happened?"

"I'd kind of like to talk about what happened."

"But something happened, didn't it?" he said, with a strange confidence I found additionally unnerving.

"It did, yes."

"Well, okay, then we'd better talk. I can be into the office there in about, oh, say an hour. And make sure Josh Riesling is there, too. You ask him, okay?"

"Uh, do you think he would ...?"

"Yeah, he'll be okay with it. He and I had a little chat yesterday and it will benefit him to hear about what's happened."

"Uh ... I don't mean to be rude but how do you know what we're gonna be talking about?"

"We're gonna be talking about God speaking directly to you, I'm thinking," he answered. "Just make sure Josh is there. I'll see you in about an hour." And the guy hung up. I handed the phone back to Riesling with a quizzical look on my face. "He said that he wants you with me when I ... when I tell him what happened."

Riesling smiled a slow smile and rubbed his face over his stubble. "Yeah," he said, "I'd kind of like to be a fly on the wall for that conversation. Let me get this grain off the barge with the guys and I'll see you in the office in an hour."

He took his phone and went back to unloading bags of grain with his crew while I walked back to the truck. I went out to pick up my equipment, then I got the crew and had them drive me to one of the small fast food restaurants across from the construction office for a coffee and some time to think by myself while they went back to work. They gave me some strange looks but I let them think I needed more consultation with the local construction people about where the pier might go.

***

Ironbridge limped in wearing the same ragged old brown coat, which he hung up on the peg because the office was warming up. He didn't shake hands; I would learn there wasn't much small talk with the guy. We sat down around that same round conference table—Ironbridge, Riesling, and me. The table gave me a start, and I found my hands trembling a little. This was new ground for me. My whole world had been shaken up and it was a little disconcerting. I felt like a newborn babe in the woods—raw, tender, and not knowing what might happen next.

"So He spoke to you," he began, like it was a statement instead of a question, even before I'd sat down to the coffee.

"Uh, I think so," I replied hesitantly.

"Why don't you tell us what happened?" He folded rough hands together and looked right at me.

So I did. I told them about my state of mind that morning, which meant I had to tell them about the phone call with Janet the night before, and then about our marriage in general, which took me back to what happened on the rocks that morning. I told them about this disc of light and the bird and the voice I'd heard.

"Be at peace ... through me," Ironbridge repeated softly. "You realize that you are extremely fortunate, don't you? Not many people have God speak directly to them."

"You sure you weren't, like, imagining it?" Riesling asked.

"Absolutely not," I said firmly, convinced about what I'd seen and heard. "I know what happened. I can't *explain* what happened, but I *know* it happened."

"Yeah, that's good that you're convinced," Ironbridge put it, "because in the days to come you're gonna have a lot of doubts about it—from you and from others." I didn't understand what he meant at the time, but he did turn out to be right.

"And then there's this," I said, and held out the twig thing.

"That's what the bird put in your hand?" Ironbridge asked, looking at it.

"It is. I'm wondering ... do you think the bird ... do you think it was just one of the birds out there from one of the lake islands or something?"

Riesling took the twig out of my hand and looked at it, turning it over and examining it. "I'm not sure," he said, drawing it out slowly, "but I think I know what this is. Hang on, I need to check. Wait a minute." He stood up and went to the door. "Daria," he said, and the same woman I'd seen earlier came into the office. Riesling held up the twig thing. "You recognize this?" he asked.

The woman took it and looked at it for only a moment. "Of course I do, but where did you get this? They don't grow anywhere around here." She looked amazed but somehow pleased.

"What?" I asked, standing up from the table. "What doesn't grow around here? Are you saying it didn't come from one of the lake islands?"

"Of course not," she said, and again I could discern that English wasn't her native language. "These are olive leaves. It's a branch from an olive tree. I grew up in Israel,

I don't know what an olive branch looks like?"

I sat down again, now more at a loss than ever. Something had happened to me, something supernatural, something that shattered every concept I'd treasured my entire life. There *was* a God; He *did* exist. He spoke to me. I sat there at the table, stunned, not able to move along with what was happening in my life.

"What He said to you," Ironbridge added, "is important. Look at where you are in your life. There is one thing you want, one thing you need—peace. He is telling you that the only way you are going to have that is through Him."

"Okay, sooo, what does that mean? I mean, 'through Him'? What's that supposed to mean?" Riesling and the woman were standing there, staring at me, waiting for Ironbridge to answer.

"Imagine he'd said, 'Surveying expertise ... through study, diligence, and hard work.' It means you get one by applying the other. Basically, it means you learn about Him," he said quietly. "You learn about who He is, what He's like, what He wants or doesn't want, and how to obey Him. You develop a relationship with Him. It means He becomes your King—or in modern-day parlance, He becomes the one in charge of what happens in your life. You become His servant. You give up directing the course of your life and you let Him order your days and direct what you do, from now on. It means, bottom line, that you start obeying Him and stop doing what you think is right, which usually isn't. It means that you let Him change your nature from the one you have to the one He wants you to have ... to His."

"This is kind of too much for me to process," I replied, holding up my hands. "I have no idea what you're talking about ... but ... but I have to say ... I want to try. No one can make me forget what happened this morning. God is real, and you're right, I want peace in my life more than anything."

Ironbridge nodded his head slowly. "That's good. It's a good way to start. Just make sure you remember what you just said."

"What? What did I say?"

"That you want this peace more than anything. Because you're going to get a lot of opposition." As he said that, I truly didn't believe Him. I was just beginning to revel in the fact that God had spoken to me—to *me*—and really, what could go wrong from here on out? But there was one question I had.

"But how do I start? I mean, seriously, until about two hours ago I didn't even think there was a God. Now He's talked to me and told me I can have peace through Him, but I have no idea how to go about finding that."

"Well, he's put a few people here that can help you," Ironbridge said. "Our meeting certainly wasn't a coincidence. You can ask me for help, and you can ask Josh here, I expect?" Ironbridge glanced at the younger man, who nodded quickly. "Absolutely," he replied.

"Good. So the first thing to do," Ironbridge went on, pulling something out of a bag by his foot, "is begin to read. Here," he said, plunking a large Bible down on the table in front of me. "I thought you might need this, and they won't let you take the one you have in the hotel room."

"There is no Bible in my hotel room. They don't do that anymore. It's actually illegal."

He ignored my comment and put his finger on the book. "This is a magic book,

Pankowicz. You'll learn that as you grow."

"Grow?"

Ironbridge saw my look of confusion, and that seemed to remind him of something, and he stared at me, hard. "What you have to understand is that just having God talk to you doesn't guarantee that you're completely okay with Him and that you've got a wired ticket to Heaven. What God requires of us first, before there can be any kind of forgiveness from Him, is that we first *repent* of what we've done in our lives up to the point at which we tell Him we want a relationship with Him, and that we are willing to let Him be God ... at least, in our own lives. Repent first; without repentance, one can't be forgiven, and one can't truly believe and obey."

"Repentance ... what's that?" I asked.

I saw Riesling sort of shrink a little, apparently taken aback by Ironbridge's hard approach. But I could tell the kid wasn't questioning the old man; no, it was more like he was watching and learning.

"It's where we acknowledge to God—and to others, where it's necessary—that we have sinned; we admit that we've come short of what we should have been or done, that we've hurt others, that we've basically screwed up our lives. You have to agree with God, deep in your soul, that you are flawed and it is your fault that you do bad things. And that's just one half of the job; the next half is to resolve not to keep screwing up. To repent means, literally, to turn and move in the opposite direction. To repent of your past life means that you make a decision to move in a completely opposite direction than the one you've been following so far. And beyond making the decision, you actually have to do the work. And you have to do it every day."

This was hard news. "This will be hard," I said.

"Of course it's hard," he replied.

"No, you don't understand. I can tell you, it's just not in my nature to ... to apologize, or even admit I've ever done anything wrong. I just don't do it. I can't." I sat there, despondent, my hands flat out on the table, wondering how things were going to work out. I knew I couldn't do what this old man was telling me I had to do.

"Well," he said in a low, gravelly voice, "this is why they have this thing called 'the cross'. You know what the cross was, right? That thing they hung Jesus on?"

"Yeah, I know about that part."

"Well, the cross was a thing that they used to kill people, slowly. It basically chokes the life out of you. Jesus told us that if we ever decide to follow Him, we will need to pick up our cross every day and choke the life out of whatever it is that keeps us from doing what He tells us to do, which is, as you've probably already figured out, your human nature. You have to choke that nature down every day because if you don't, it just grows back, like weeds. You'll learn pretty quickly that the thing that most gets in the way of following Jesus is our own human nature."

"So I have to choke the life out of my own human nature?" I asked, again completely lost.

"Yeah, basically, that's exactly what you do." I could see Riesling and the girl, Daria was her name I think, standing there by the door, listening carefully. Her arms were folded.

"What does that look like? I mean, how exactly do you do that?"

"To be blunt, if I'm hearing what you're telling me, expect circumstances to come along that will give you the chance to screw up, and then you'll have to admit you were wrong or made a mistake. God will give you plenty of opportunities to deal with your issues."

"That's not gonna be fun."

"We're talking about eternal issues here, Stan. Fun isn't in the equation. The first thing you need to realize is that you can't do it by yourself. You need God to come and help you do it. All you have to do is be willing for the work to be done, and He will do the actual killing part.

"What does it look like?" He looked around the room, as though he was looking for something. "I'll tell you," he said. "It looks just the same as any close relationship you've had. First you start out by getting to know the person, and you do that mostly by talking with them, and reading the things they've written, and the things people have written about that person, and talking with them again, and, in this particular case, doing what He asks you to do. Most of your early days in this relationship will be spent just trying to hear what He's saying to you. And you can get to know Him quickly and effectively by reading this," he said, tapping the Bible. "It tells you about who He is, what He's done, what His character is like, what makes Him happy or sad or angry or jealous or passionate."

"God has all those feelings? He ... He feels stuff?"

"More than any of us can possibly imagine," Ironbridge said somberly.

"I don't know," I replied. "I've heard about people reading the Bible and I've read some stuff out of it before, and none of it ever made any kind of sense to me."

"It wouldn't have," Ironbridge said. "You need your eyes to be opened before you can understand it. You haven't ever repented before. You can tell a person who's repented of their past life by how much they want to take in this Word here. With true repentance comes a desire to live the way He wants us to live. He puts His Spirit in us as we make ourselves available to Him, and with our willingness to obey, combined with His Spirit, and our willingness to let Him kill the things in our nature that keep us from Him, He'll do the work in us. We have to kind of work with Him, but He does the hard parts."

"So all I have to do is be willing," I asked.

"That's it ... and do what He tells you to do, no matter what."

"That sounds easy."

Ironbridge looked over at Riesling, who looked down at his feet. "What do you think, Josh?" Ironbridge asked him.

"I think it won't be as easy as he makes it out to be, sir," Riesling replied.

"He's right," Ironbridge said, turning to me. "Your flesh—what we call your human nature—doesn't go down easy. It'll be a fight, and the enemy—that's the devil, in case you were wondering—will work with your flesh to keep you from obeying God, and to keep you from building a relationship with Him."

"The devil. So ..." I began slowly, thinking, and Ironbridge picked up my train of thought.

"Yeah, now you're getting it. If there really is a God, then yes, there really is a devil opposing Him. And make no mistake, the devil wants you in hell with him."

"Hell is real too?" My world was being reshaped by the minute.

"Yup. Welcome to the real world."

"So ... what did I ever do to the devil?" I asked.

"He hates you because God loves you, and he hates anything God loves. When you choose to serve God, when you agree with God about how you've sinned and when you repent and decide to make Him King in your life, you make one huge friend and one dangerous enemy. Fortunately God can keep you from the enemy ... but you have to stay close to God."

I sat back in the chair, sort of overwhelmed.

"Look, it's not that hard," Ironbridge said. "Jesus said that we need to become like little children. Just believe what He said, do what He says to do, and you'll be okay." Before I could get my next question out, he continued. "Yeah, so, the first thing you want to do is begin to read here, and I'd recommend you start in the New Testament. Read about who Jesus is, what He did when He walked on the earth, and what He asks of those who choose to follow Him. But don't ignore the Old Testament either. There is no difference in the message in either one. There's a ton of stuff about Jesus in the Old Testament—He's called 'the Holy One of Israel', by the way, in that part—and it's a rich source to discover who God is. It's all in here," he said, nudging the Bible toward me.

"And you say that ... that I'll be able to understand it?"

"If you've repented of who you were and what you've done in your past, and if you're willing to obey Him going forward, then yes, you will. Stuff will actually jump out at you. You'll be shocked at what you understand; at the stuff you'll see."

I shook my head. "Okay," I said tentatively. I looked up at them all. "No one can tell me that what happened this morning by the shore didn't happen. I know He told me that I can have peace, and I'm beginning to understand that meeting you," I looked at Ironbridge, "wasn't a coincidence. You didn't just happen to be here yesterday morning."

"Nope. I thought I was coming here to find someone to build a stone wall on my farm. God had something different in mind. He wanted me to put a finger in your chest and challenge your belief system."

"Could've knocked me over with a feather," Riesling put in, which kicked up chuckles from everyone except the old man.

I looked hard at Ironbridge. I stood, and my hands found their way into my pockets and my shoulders rounded. "We need to stay in touch," I said, with just a tinge of desperation.

"Don't worry," he replied. "God has things planned. Trust Him."

Chapter 17
Jedburgh

"Consider it all joy, my brethren, when you encounter various trials, knowing that the testing of your faith produces endurance. And let endurance have its perfect result, so that you may be perfect and complete, lacking in nothing."

James 1:2-4

"Hey, could I get some help here?"

"Yes ma'am, how can I help you?"

"Where might the plumbing supplies be, young man?"

"Aisle fourteen, ma'am."

"Aisle fourteen—well, that's helpful, except, as you probably know since you work here, there are more than three hundred aisles in this store and for some reason, they've decided to paint the aisle numbers in little tiny numbers and put those little tiny numbers 18 feet high, so they are impossible to find and so, therefore, young man, customers are required to ask a sales person—oh, sorry, 'associate'—if by some minor miracle we can actually find someone who works here." She paused to take a breath and then rushed on, pointing a wizened finger at me. "I've got it! It's so you can have a job, right? That's why they make you memorize where everything is and then force you to give people directions about how to find what they need, but they *also* require you to give the directions in code so they can't find it on their own. Right? That's how it works?"

I couldn't tell if she was being serious or sarcastic—I wasn't born with the sarcastic bone like everyone else seems to have. I've never been able to understand sarcasm unless someone explains it, and it always ends up burning me. The lady seemed nice. She was about sixty or so, kind of short, neat, trim, wearing jeans and a short-sleeved blue-checked blouse, with yellow rain boots. It was raining outside, just another Minnesota spring day.

"You know, you look like an intelligent young man. You're tall—what, six one, six two?"

"Six three, actually, Ma'am."

"Six three, I should have guessed, my neck is already killing me; typical tall dark and handsome. If I were twenty years younger you'd have your hands full. But right now," she paused to read my name on the tag, head back, looking through spectacles, "tall dark and handsome Jed Sloan, I have my hands full with an overflowing toilet and all I want is a plunger and do you think that maybe you could point me to where 'plumbing supplies' would be?"

"Uhm ... four aisles down that way, Ma'am." I pointed to the west end of the store. I hunched my shoulders a bit, trying my best not to be physically intimidating, although this didn't seem like it was an issue for her.

"Great. Thank you. Four aisles that way ... plumbing supplies; thank you." She patted my elbow, which was about as high as she could reach. She smacked her forehead, making fun (I think). "Of course," she says, kind of loudly, "The plungers would naturally be next to the portraits of our presidential candidates." She peppered off toward the plumbing supplies. I thought she was what Mary Poppins might be like when she got old—in this century, I mean.

***

I did the closeouts at each register at nine-thirty. Bob closed the gates, checked the doors, set the alarm system, and handed me the keys before he headed home at ten, and by ten-thirty, I was the last one out of the store, as usual. I stared up at the big yellow letters that proclaimed the name of the famous home hardware store chain I worked for. I managed their biggest store in Minneapolis. It was a job. It wasn't what I'd dreamed about when I was a little kid. I recalled those old commercials where some little kid is standing there, saying in some southern accent, '*When ah grow up, ah wanna claw mah way up ta middle management*', or '*When I grow up, I wanna file stuff all day long.*' I saw some ten-year old Jed Sloan standing out in the middle of some field saying, '*When I grow up, I want to manage a hardware store and work crushing hours for peanuts.*' When I was that age, actually, I wanted to be a football coach. Now, being a farmer looks good. But as I look up at those dominating yellow letters I see every day in and every night out, I realize this is what my life has come to.

Jean had asked me to stop by Wal-Mart to pick up some things, which I did, and then drove home. The kids were asleep, but Jean was still awake when I walked through the door.

"Did you get what I asked you to get?"

"I did," I replied. "Here in the bag." I set the bag and the car keys down on the kitchen table and sat down heavily.

She ruffled through the bag. "This isn't blue icing, Jed. It's purple."

"Really?" Besides not getting sarcasm, I'm slightly colorblind as well.

"We want blue icing, remember? The school colors are blue and white, not purple and white."

I looked over at her. She was normally high-strung, but tonight she seemed exceptionally wired. "You're gonna just have to go back and get the right kind."

"It's 11:30. It's been a long day."

"I gave you the list, right? On the list, didn't it say 'blue icing'?"

I pulled the crumpled list out of my pocket. I looked at it. There, amidst the wrinkles, in Jean's meticulous handwriting, were the words 'blue icing.' "Yeah, it's right here. 'Blue icing.'"

"I wanted blue icing. Does this look like blue icing?" She held up the little tube of squirtable icing. I looked at it. I couldn't tell what color it was, only that it was dark. She reached over, turned the tube around in my hand, and showed me the little letters at the bottom. "See? P-u-r-p-l-e; pretty simple. Says so on the bottom." She handed me the keys. "I'm going back to bed." I went back to Wal-Mart.

***

My life wasn't turning out exactly the way I thought it would when I graduated from the University of Minnesota. I was an all-state tight end in high school and Minnesota brought me aboard on a scholarship. I started all four years and was on my way to a career in the pros when some strong-side safety dislocated my knee the third game of my senior year. That finished my football career, and for some reason the coaches decided not to red-shirt me ... something about too many players on the roster. I completed my degree with mediocre grades but had no idea what to do, so I looked into joining the Navy. My great-grandfather, who I was named for, was one of the original Jedburghs dropped into France on D-Day, so the military was always in the back of my mind. The recruiter seemed happy with a college graduate and former football player, and put me in their officer's program.

After I was commissioned I ended up driving ships for about ten years. I loved it. I qualified as Officer of the Deck on the U.S.S. Forrestal, something not every junior officer could do, and the Captain was impressed. He was from Minneapolis, and he became a mentor. When I was thinking about getting out, he put me in touch with some of his associates in the Twin Cities business world. One of them, a former Admiral, helped me get a job in an investment banking firm. He had a niece, a pretty girl: short, petite, long brown hair, with a lot of energy. He thought we'd make a good match and who was I to argue? I'm not sure but I think Jean's thoughts going in were that if she took this guy's advice, he might help her with her career. There wasn't anything related to romance or love or passion on either side in our relationship—for me, it was because someone I respected recommended it, and one of my life-long problems has been an inability to say no to people—still is, actually. For Jean, I'm pretty sure it was about career advantage.

So shortly after I left the Navy after ten years' of service, I found myself married, working in a field where, to be honest, I really didn't know what I was doing. Connections can take you only so far, and pretty soon it became apparent that investment banking wasn't my strength. Actually I hated it. And I learned that if you hate something, it's really hard to do well at it. I lasted about three years and then the company Vice President called me into the office and suggested that perhaps I find another line of work, because it was apparent I just didn't have the personality one needed in the investment-banking world. Jean didn't take the news so well, and things got fairly cold between us for a time. To be honest, things were never so hot between us in the first place, but after I lost my job at the banking firm, they got positively arctic, and they've stayed that way ever since. I think she'd leave me if it wasn't for Jeanine, our daughter, who was born a year after we married. She's twelve now, and it's pretty clear to me my marriage is just one of convenience. Jean was a financial consultant before we married, and she still tries to get some consulting gigs when she can, but she's complained for years that taking care of Jeanine takes up whatever 'creative energy' she has, and so she doesn't have a full-time job, but spends a lot of her time doing lunch with her sorority sisters and visiting old friends and just trying to stay up with the financial markets. She convinced me to put an addition on to the house three years ago, and then do a renovation of the kitchen a year ago, and combined with the Lexus in the driveway and Jeanine's private school tuition, we're pretty much buried in debt. When I made manager here, the salary picked up but that just encouraged Jean to spend more. I never said anything; I just let her do it. We're in deeper than ever.

***

I was driving to work the next day when my old college roommate called my cell. Josh had been Minnesota's quarterback, and we'd been friends since our sophomore year. Whenever the team traveled, we roomed together, and during our senior year, we worked it out to stay in the same dorm. For some reason he's always just understood me. So he calls and sure enough we end up talking about God. I'd always been a Catholic—so is Jean—but Josh sort of 'got religion' after he graduated. I didn't understand how that happened at the time, because Josh was sort of a hell-raiser in college. He moved to Seattle to take a job with some computer start-up firm and met some hot babe and got married and had two kids right away and he seemed like his life was on the fast track. Then he got involved in a church out there for some reason, and he suddenly gets 'born again'. Then things went south. His wife left him and took his kids when he became a Christian. She said something about not wanting to be married to a 'religious terrorist' or something, and she didn't want the kids to be stigmatized by having a Dad that was mentally unbalanced. Funny thing, the courts in Washington bought her argument and Josh found himself out on the sidewalk without his family. His Dad, apparently, didn't think much of Josh's life choice either, but his Dad's construction company was desperate at the time and Josh was willing to work for peanuts. So Josh moved to some dink town in Minnesota to work for his Dad. When his Dad passed away, Josh took over running the company and he seems to be doing okay.

Josh never pushes religion on me, but today's phone call went a little differently. Maybe it was because I've been so down lately, or maybe because I'm just beginning to see what my life is really looking like and don't like what I see.

He always starts the call the same way, with something one of our old coaches always used to say. "Hey Jed, you're *lousy*!" he begins. I know he doesn't mean this, and it makes us both laugh, remembering the coach moving around the practice field, berating the players, telling everyone they were lousy. I think that was just his coaching style. It might have worked for a lot of guys but it never worked for me. I just wanted to do the best I could and I don't think the coach ever learned that you don't need to whip thoroughbreds; they'll run harder with just a little encouragement. But I don't think our coach knew how to spell the 'e' word.

"Hey, what's up Josh?"

"My hands look like Mount Rushmore," he says. "We're getting into stonemasonry and I'm the guinea pig. I'm telling you, working stone is murder on your hands. Mine are turning to stone."

I paused for a moment, thinking. "I always thought you had rock hands anyway, you never could catch anything. It's amazing you could even take the snap from center. It's a good thing you were the quarterback and all you had to do was throw the ball." We took shots at each other whenever we could.

He throws one back. "Yeah, well, that reminds me, you were so slow, people thought you poured your cleats out of a mixer."

"Yeah, yeah."

He laughs and I laugh and this part of the conversation ends. Our conversations have certain defined parts to them, based on how I'm doing, basically. If I'm doing okay, we tease each other for a while. If I'm not, it ends pretty quickly. Today it ended pretty quickly. He can tell today is not one of my good days.

"What's up, Jedburgh?" He always calls me that. Josh knows a bunch about World War II history. He was the only guy I've ever met who knew right away what my name meant. First time we met, he asked me if I was named after the Jedburghs in World War II. No one else ever figured that out unless I told them. Most people think I'm named after that guy who shot the ground and struck oil, from the television show. I think even today Jean still doesn't know.

"Oh, nothing," I reply, and he knows right away that that's not true and that I'm in one of my down times, and I know he knows, and it doesn't bother me.

"Jean giving you a hard time?" he asks. "Or did someone steal the store while you were gone?"

I paused for a moment, letting some jerk in a black mustang blow past me on the freeway. I blurt out a commentary on the guy's parentage. And suddenly, for some weird reason, I get fed up with everything—my job, my wife, my life, everything. It feels like the mainspring in my life just snaps, and I am really glad Josh called. "I'll tell you, Josh, things just don't make sense. It's like I can never do anything right, or nothing ever works out. Nothing I ever do is good enough for Jean; the more I give, the more she wants. And the Regional Manager wants more revenue out of the store. We hit our numbers three months ago and the month before that, we broke records on how much we made, but do you think he's happy with that? No, he waits a month and then he starts up again, pushing." I go on for the next eighteen miles, telling Josh about everything that's wrong with my life. He listens; he's good at that. Finally I wind down, and when I review what I said I realize that I can't remember being this down. I make a decision then and there not to tell my therapist about this conversation with Josh, or for sure she'll put me on more meds. Josh and I have these conversations occasionally, and it's been more frequent lately, and they're usually all about the crappy life I have. But he's the only one I can talk to.

"Jedburgh," Josh begins, his voice serious and intense, and I can tell he's been listening to what I've been saying, "there's a solution to where you are, man. You don't have to feel this way. You're my best friend and I want you to have some peace."

"Don't even know how to spell that word," I reply bitterly. "It's been nothing but 'do, do, do' or 'give me this, or give me that' since I can remember. And you know what it is? I just can't say no to people. Some recruiter says, 'Hey, join the Navy,' and I sign up. Some guy with admiral's stripes says, 'Hey, marry this girl,' so I say, 'Sure, okay.' Some really important guy in the community says, 'Hey, why don't you be an investment banker?' and I say, 'Sure, okay.' Doesn't matter if I can't swim, or don't particularly like the girl, or if I can't even balance my checkbook, I just do it. It's like I don't have any mind of my own."

"That's not it," Josh says quietly.

"My whole life is a wreck. This isn't what I thought it would be, and do you know how crushing that is, how that destroys hope for the future? Sometimes I just want to curl up and disappear. I'm sick of myself, but I can't change. Do you know what that feels like?"

"Uh ... yeah," he replies, but I ride over him.

"And, I'm ashamed to admit it, but there are times when I think Jean and Jeanine would just be better off with the insurance money they'd get if I kicked the bucket. I mean, seriously, Josh, I've thought about it. I got so close one night ... and you know, that's weird, but it was just before that time you called me at night, remember?"

"I do.'"

"You never call at night but for some reason you did that night. Jean was out and I'd just bought her that .357 for home protection and I had it out and was staring at the barrel when you called. You didn't know that, did you?"

Silence for a bit, then, "No, but I was worried about it. That's why I called."

"So ... Josh, I don't know what to do. My wife runs me around like some dog she owns, my boss thinks I'm some kind of robot, my kid is already starting to ignore me. Life sucks, man and it's all because I'm just trying to do what people want."

"That's not the problem," he says softly, but I sense a vein of confidence, like he knows what the problem is but also knows I won't like it.

"So what is it?" I ask.

"You won't like it," he says.

"I don't care. I can't keep living like this."

"You do all these things because, bottom line, you are thinking about yourself first. The root problem is selfishness."

I almost drive off the road I'm so surprised, but I don't get mad because I trust my friend. "What do you mean?" I ask, hesitantly, almost fearfully.

"Look at it this way. Why is it that you don't say no to people? I think the main reason is, you want them to like you. You'll do whatever it is someone tells you to do, or even just suggests that you do, because basically *you want them to like you*. Or, you just don't want them to yell at you if you cross them. So you end up in one sticky situation after another, and your life basically isn't your own, because you want everyone to like you. And that's just not going to be possible."

As he talked, I wanted to argue with him, but something was nagging at me, something hinting that what he was saying might be the truth.

"Look, Jedburgh, it's easy for you to rationalize this as you just being nice to everyone, but when you think about it, you're actually hurting people. What about the people you could have helped if you worked in a different job, one that you liked, one you were good at? What about the girl out there who was made for you—what's happening to her? What about all the situations where someone might have needed to hear the word 'no' for their own good, but you said yes instead, and they continued on with abusive or damaging behavior? What will you do when your twelve-year old daughter decides she wants to start dressing like some prostitute, with short skirts and tight tops? Will you say okay because you want her to like you or will you wait till she comes home pregnant? Because that's where this will end up."

"Yeah, I see what you mean." I was never one who could argue for myself. "But I don't know how else to be. I don't know what else to do. It's my nature."

"Then get a new nature."

"How do I do that?" I asked, throwing both my hands in the air out of frustration, half thinking he was being silly, and half hoping that there was an antidote for my problem. I was at the end of myself. For some reason, Jean handing me the keys and pushing me out of the house at 11:30 last night just pushed me over the edge.

"Glad you asked," he said. We talked for another hour.

***

Two days later I was still wrestling with what Josh had said to me, rehashing the things he'd talked about. He had talked about dying to self, which he had spoken about before, but I never really heard or understood him until he made it clear to me about what my 'self' was doing, trying to make everyone like me. He was right, the root of that was just selfishness, and when I realized that, and when I realized that there was no way I could myself change who I was, and when, on the heels of *that* realization I realized that I was condemned to a life of slavery, probably a short life because I would probably run myself into an early grave—well, after all that, it boiled down to me crying out to God for help. I'd never done that before and I didn't even know you could do that, but I did anyway. I knew there was no way I was going to be able to succeed in life, or worse, stop hurting people, without some kind of miracle, and one of the things Josh told me was that God was in the miracle business. So I just asked. I said something like, "God, I need help; I mean, I *really* need help. I don't understand all the complicated religious stuff or what the big religious words mean, but I do understand that the way I've been living has been hurting a lot of people and I'm sorry for that and I need your help to stop. I can't. So please, like Josh said you would, come and live inside me. Take over my life. You can have it. I've made a big mess of it. Whatever I have in my life now is yours. You take it and do with it what you want. I'm yours. Do with me whatever you want. And please, help me to obey you." Basically, I surrendered to God. I would learn later that this is just what God wants. He has everything except one thing. He can speak anything into existence, but the one thing He doesn't have, the one thing He won't take for Himself, is our own freely-given love that springs from a will that is freely our own, our free will. This, I would learn later, is why we actually have free will, because love that is not freely given isn't really love and when I learned that what God wants most is for us to love Him because He first loved us, that sort of floored me, and it changed me drastically. But that was later.

So I called Josh back and told him what I had said to God, and he congratulated me and welcomed me to the family. That made me feel kind of good, actually. And then he had some advice. "Start reading," he said. "Open the Bible and just start reading."

"The Bible?" I asked, surprised. "I've never been able to make head or tails out of that book."

"You will now," he shoots back. "The Bible is a spiritual book, almost a magical book. People who are dead spiritually can't understand it, they don't get anything out of it—certainly nothing of spiritual value. Only the people who are alive spiritually can get spiritual 'food' from it. That's what it is. It is one form of God's Word and He said that we should feed on His Word—that is, take it in, digest it, think about it, study it, and come to learn the many facets of its meanings. Feed on it like sheep feed on grass."

"So ... since I'm just starting out, should I get some other books to help me understand the Bible? Like, I don't know, what do they call those books that—"

"They call them 'commentaries', and while they can sometimes be helpful, I would stay away from them. They will just tell you what other men have to say about God's Word. What you want is for the Holy Spirit to tell you what the Word means. You want to develop the habit as a Believer of letting the Holy Spirit interpret the Word for you. If you let men do your interpreting, you'll just get confused and you'll never stand on solid ground. If you learn to let the Holy Spirit interpret what God's Word is saying, you'll never go wrong and you'll always stand on a solid foundation. Only then should you consider looking into the commentaries."

So I took his advice and went out and got a Bible and started reading. Josh had suggested I start reading in the New Testament about Jesus, but also read in the Old Testament, because he said God doesn't change and the story about Him and His Son doesn't change, it goes straight on from the beginning to the—well, not to any end, he said, but for eternity. He told me that the Old and the New Testaments are consistent and they reveal the same heart of God. Later I would take some flack from other Christians about this point, but I believe Josh was spot on.

Speaking of taking flack ... it started from the very first day I brought the Bible home. Jean's jaw dropped when I came home from the Christian bookstore with this big old Bible. She couldn't believe it. "What the hell has gotten into *you*?" she exclaimed.

Looking back I can see how me coming home with a Bible would have shaken her a bit, but at the time, I was still enjoying the realization that someone else was taking care of my problems and my backpack had gotten, like, a ton lighter. It wasn't really until a little later in my growth did I realize that Christians should rejoice not because our load gets lighter in this world (it usually doesn't, by the way), but because the Creator of the Universe loves us and we get to be in His family. But back then, all I knew was that I'd decided to give up controlling my life. So when Jean got in my face that first night, it was sort of a shock, because I thought that once I turned my life over to God, everything would be all unicorns and rainbows. But I suddenly remembered something Josh had said. "You're going to be opposed, Jedburgh, so get ready for it. The enemy will come at you hard, and usually it will come from the people closest to you. They know best where to throw the spears." I didn't have a clue about what he was talking about then. I was beginning to understand now.

"You've been talking to your friend from college, right?" she said, laughing in a strange way. "He finally convinced you to start reading the Bible?"

"It was his idea, yeah," I said, "but I want to as well. I ... I've given my life to God and if He has something to say to me, I want to know what it is." I felt sheepish telling her this, but I told her anyway.

She started laughing ... laughing *at* me, I could tell, but her face was pale. "You're doing that just because your friend from college, what's his name, just told you to, like everything else you do."

"We talked, yeah, but this is my decision," I said timorously, defending my action.

"And were you even thinking about *us*?" she shot back. "What about Jeanine and I? What are *we* supposed to do? Just follow along like good little disciples? What, should we get some headscarves maybe, or maybe some long dresses, and oh, I forgot, maybe a lobotomy to go along with the Bibles you get us, too? Maybe we should start driving around in buggies? You've done a lot of stupid things since we've been married, Jed, but this tops 'em all." She shook her head and stood up from the couch and went to the kitchen. "What are you thinking about?" she asked.

"I didn't ... I mean, I don't like my *life*, Jean." There ... I'd said it out loud. "It's not ... it's not working out the way I thought it would."

"You mean I'm not what you want, right? That's what you mean?"

"No, that's not ... well, that's not what I'm trying to say ... at least—"

"Yeah, that's what you're trying to say, only you don't have the guts to say it. Typical," she said, dismissively, with a level of disgust I'd never seen before. "What a sham," she spat. "Big tall football player and you wouldn't stick up for your own mother, your own wife, your own daughter, if someone threatened us."

"No one is threatening you," I said, surprised that she would feel threatened.

"Yeah, right," she said with real anger. "You wait and see. People start toting around some big black Bible and the next thing you know, it's 'What would Jesus do', and 'Oh, oh, we shouldn't be harming things,' or 'Oh, there should just be peace and love and everyone should love each other,' or 'stop doing this, stop doing that.'" As I said, I don't process sarcasm so what she was saying just confused me.

"Jean, all I want to do is have a relationship with God," I replied dully, feeling a little overwhelmed and out of my depth. "It's something I should do. It's something everyone should do, actually. My life isn't going so well, you know." I wished Josh was there to carry the argument. I didn't know what was causing her anger. "What's wrong with that?"

"Fine," she said, in a tone that told me the discussion was over. "Fine, go ahead. But when your friends start laughing at you, when your boss fires you, when the neighbor kids stop playing with Jeanine because her Daddy is 'one of them', then don't blame me. When this destroys you, don't blame me. Call up your loser friend, who, oh by the way has such a wonderful marriage and ... oh, wait, that's right, his wife and kids left him, didn't they? That's right, they *did*, how about that? Isn't that just so *sad*! Hmmm, I wonder why ... no, wait, we *know* why, don't we? He actually called you up and told you why, didn't he? What did he say?"

"You know what he said."

"Yeah, remind me."

I was getting angry now too. "Yeah, okay, so they left because he'd become a Christian."

"They left because they didn't want to be trapped with some mentally deficient, probably emotionally dangerous religious nutcase, that's why!"

I was stuck. I never developed the ability to defend myself in arguments or disagreements, which is why I avoided them like the plague, and now I found myself at a complete loss about what to say to my wife. Her reaction to this wonderful thing I'd found was throwing me for a loop, and I was terribly confused. And then I remembered again what Josh had said about being opposed and suddenly it was like the clouds parted and the fog lifted and I could clearly see that my wife was opposing me—not just now, but she had been opposing me throughout the entire marriage, either by disagreeing with my choices in life, or trying a lot of times to run the family which, I would learn, was not in God's plan for how families should be. And she *was* the boss most of the time, if I was honest. What she decided was what usually happened, whether I agreed or not.

"One of the things I'm learning, Jean, is that I can't just keep being a pushover. I have to start standing up for what's right."

"What the *hell* are you talking about?" she barked, laughing out loud. "You've been a damn tyrant the entire time I've been married to you! You've always got to be in control, always telling us what we can or can't do. Yeah, so I guess it makes sense, you getting religion. Now you have a valid reason to be the boss in the house, snapping your fingers, ordering us around. Sure, and cover it up, make it look acceptable, with your Bible and your religion. Well, let me tell you, Buster, I'm not putting up with it, not for one minute. So you'd better decide real quick what you want." She stopped short of giving me an ultimatum, but I could see it lurking in the background, like someone hanging around behind the curtains, waiting to come on stage.

"Jean," I said, trying to pacify things, "I don't want to—"

"Just talk to the hand," she said, holding up her hand, flattened out, in my face. "I don't want to hear it." She stalked off to the bedroom. "Sleep on the couch tonight," she said over her shoulder. "You certainly wouldn't want to have any wicked thoughts now, would you? I mean, what would Jesus think? You'll be nice and safe from this wicked woman on the couch there, Boy-o, just you and your Bible. Hope you're nice and cozy."

***

In the days after that fight, I realized what Josh had meant when he said things would probably get worse before they got better. Jean started making snide comments about religion every now and then, either making fun of it or acting surprised when I did something she thought wasn't what Jesus would do. The worst thing was that she would make fun of me in front of Jeanine, and I could see the impact it was having on my daughter, even though she was so young. I usually didn't say anything because I didn't want to start a fight, and I suspected that wasn't right, either. Those were not good days.

At work things went along for a while as they had been, but soon I learned what Josh was talking about when he said God would test my level of commitment. "He's going to put something in the flow of your life that will show you where your heart is," he said. We were talking pretty much on a daily basis, now, as I drove to work. I couldn't call him from home because Jean would freak out. She had told me I couldn't talk to him from the house. I kept quiet because I didn't want to start another fight, never thinking about how that might make Josh feel. "It's not like God doesn't know," he said, talking about God testing me, "but He wants *you* to see where you are. And remember, faith isn't faith unless it is proclaimed publicly. We can have all the faith in the world, hiding away from the world in our little closets or whatever, but when we have to get out and let people see what we believe in and Whom we believe in and Whom we are choosing to obey in our lives, then it gets difficult. Then we become accountable for what we say we believe and Whom it is we're worshipping. Jesus said that if we acknowledge Him before men, He would acknowledge us before His Father in heaven. And another thing; if I know God, He'll go right after your gods."

"What gods?" I asked, confused.

"The things that you tend to give priority to instead of Him and His way. So expect a situation to pop up where you're going to have to tell someone 'no', because all your life you've wanted to people to like you, and that's just the god of self, man. He's gonna kill that little god of self in your life. So stand by."

At the time I remember I wanted to just blow him off, because if that 'test' didn't come along it would prove that I actually wasn't all that selfish and I was really just trying to be a good servant to everyone by doing what they asked. I was still in the 'lying to myself' mode, in heavy denial. This, I have learned, is why God has to bring hard events into our life to shake us out of that denial and kill that habit of lying to ourselves.

The next week my Regional Manager calls me and tells me to meet him for lunch at the Fireside Grill, a fancy local restaurant. I think to myself, '*Hey, this is a good sign. God must be blessing me.*' I'd been steadily reading in the Bible and things were making sense, which completely shocked me, in a pleasant way, though, because, like I said, I'd never been able to make sense out of it before. So, using my old frame of reference, my old way of Catholic transactional thinking, my thought process was that since I was spending some of my time reading the Bible, which I translated as 'doing something for God,' God was going to do something good for me. Well, I was sort of right and sort of not.

Don Chenerith was the Southeastern Regional Manager for my company and we had lunch at the Fireside Grill on a Thursday afternoon. He was a short little guy, a little overweight—actually, a lot overweight, with not much hair left. He always wore an expensive suit and he pulled up in a slick Mercedes. I supposed they paid their regional managers pretty well; makes sense, I guess, since they spend a lot of time on the road. The lunch started well, with Don congratulating me on exceeding my numbers a couple of months ago and giving me some good-natured ribbing about missing our numbers this month. I tried to explain that it was after hurricane season and the volume always went down around this time of year, but he just sort of smiled and waved that off, telling me it was no big deal. Then he started telling me about how things were actually going pretty well for him and that I had a strong future in the company.

"You see that Mercedes out there, right?" he asked. He had kind of a low, gravelly kind of voice, and I could tell he was from New York originally, because he'd never lost the accent.

"Yeah, it's nice," I replied, not really caring about cars one way or another. To me, a car is just a means to get from one place to another but I know some people attach a lot of status to the car they have. I tried to be polite and feign interest.

"You could have one like it in three months," he said, "and I happen to know that you're almost upside down on your mortgage. You could flip that and be debt-free in, like, six months."

Now he had my attention. From where I sat there was no way I could get out from under the giant rock of debt on my shoulders.

"Oh, do me a favor, put your phone on the table, would you?" he asked. I must have looked surprised, because he said, "Hey, it's just a professional thing, okay? This is an important conversation we're having and I don't want it to be interrupted." He put his phone on the table, flipping the tiny switch to kill the ringer. I did the same.

"So here's how you can get to where I said," he began. "You close up the store at night, right?"

"Yeah, every night," I replied, wondering what this had to do with my promotion.

"Good. What I want you to do is some nights, when I call you, leave one of the warehouse doors unlocked."

I paused for a moment, wondering why he would want to ask me to do that.

"Look," he said, and then pulled out a large leather portfolio. He opens it and shows me page after page of what look like drivers' licenses. "Let's just say all these people are my friends, okay? What I want you to do is leave the warehouse door open on certain nights. I have some other friends who'll come in, pick up some of the merchandise, and then later, some of these friends I have here," and he brushed a hand against the portfolio, "will just take it to another store and exchange the merchandise for a refund."

I sat back in my chair and realized this lunch wasn't about discussing a promotion for me. The guy was asking me to do something illegal. I was about to get on my high horse and flatly refuse the guy, but then I remembered that he was my boss and something in me wouldn't let me stand up, tell him what to do with his scheme, and leave the restaurant. I looked out the window and saw his Mercedes in the lot. I saw his cufflinks and silk tie, aware of the contrast his attire made with my own cotton polo shirt and worn khaki chinos. Truthfully, the stuff wasn't any kind of attraction or temptation to me, but I recognized that I was having a hard time saying no to this guy, especially since he was my boss. I started trying to think about ways to rationalize leaving the warehouse door open to avoid telling my boss no. To give myself some time, because I knew this was something I shouldn't do, but also, because I just couldn't say no, I asked, "What about the receipts?"

"Don't worry about the receipts. I can get those made, easy." Apparently he took my question as an indication that I was wanted to go along with the plan. "You get twenty percent of the proceeds," he explained. "Some days are good. Other days," he said, smiling like a predator, "are just huge."

Now I was stuck. I would make him mad by not going along with the plan, and if I just flat out turned him down here, after making him think I was going along with things, he'd be even angrier. I didn't say anything. But then something came into my mind like a white-hot bolt of electricity. *'Here's your test: will you do what I ask you to do?'* I suddenly realized that I had a choice to make, and that I had a higher boss.

"No," I said ... barely getting out just the one word.

"No what?" he asked, confused.

"No, I won't do it," I explained. Emboldened, I said, "It's not right."

"What do you mean, it's not right?" he replied, slightly angry, and with the onset of his anger I felt my gut tighten with stress and anxiety. I was making someone mad; this wasn't something I was comfortable with. "Do you think the chain cares if they loose a few thousand dollars here and there? They'll fire you in a heartbeat if you don't make your numbers but do you think they care if the accounts aren't squaring at the end of the month? Absolutely not; for krissakes, Sloan, I'm telling you, they write this stuff off on their taxes. It doesn't hurt them a bit."

"Mr. Chenerith, I ... I'm a Christian, I mean, I just became one, and this isn't right." There; I'd laid it out on the table, letting him know the source of my objection. I was supposed to acknowledge God before men, right?

"Hey, so am I, Sloan. What are you trying to say?" Now he was really angry and I was beginning to get sick. "I'm in church every Sunday, and just because we see things differently about this, don't go insulting my faith, you got it?"

"Uh, yeah ... yessir," I said, backing down.

"Look, I like you, so I'll tell you what. I'll give you until Sunday to make up your mind about this. Don't make any hasty decisions." He looked up and raised a hand for the waiter to bring the check. "You think about what some extra cash could do to help you and your wife and kid out. I'm thinkin' they're probably tired of living in that trash heap you're living in now, and I don't think they would mind driving around in a better car." He leaned to his right to look out into the parking lot, where I am sure he was contemplating my very old minivan. I was sure because I saw the outline of a contemptuous smile on his face.

He stood up to go, and I said, "Mr. Chenerith, I'm pretty sure the answer is no."

"Yeah, yeah, let's see how it goes," he said. "Give it some thought. You call me Sunday and let me know what your answer is."

I didn't have the courage to just tell him no there on the spot, to his face, and as he walked out of the restaurant, I realized it was a failure on my part to stand up for what was right. I felt as though I'd failed the test, and if there was one thing I was frightened of more than saying no to someone, it was failing at something. I really believed that God was testing me. I shook myself out of my stupor and chased after him, catching him as he was getting into his car.

"Mr. Chenerith," I said, a little more loudly than I wanted to, but he didn't seem to mind. It almost seemed as though he was expecting me. He smiled.

"Come to your senses?" he asked.

"No sir," I said, "but, well, yeah, yes, I guess you could say that," I stammered, unsure of words but dead certain that I was doing the right thing. "Answer is no. No is no."

He looked up at me from the seat of his Mercedes and I could sense wheels turning in his head. "Till Sunday," he replied in an ugly voice, then shut the door. I stood there as he drove out of the lot. It started to rain.

My mind was moving a hundred miles an hour, churning like crazy on the ride home. I had no idea what I was going to tell Jean about this conversation. She was expecting me to come home with some big promotion. They don't fire people by taking them to an expensive lunch on Thursday; they do it after the workday on Monday. But about the test, I was sure I'd passed. Yeah, I'd felt uncomfortable about the whole experience but after I told him no in the parking lot, I had a peace that I had done what God wanted me to do. When my cell rang and I picked it up and saw it was Mr. Chenerith, I defaulted to my old way of thinking again, and my first thought was that he was going to tell me that I'd been promoted and our conversation in the restaurant was a sort of company test that he put to all potential executives to see where their integrity was, and that I'd passed with flying colors.

"Yes sir," I said.

"Sloan?"

"Yes sir?"

"I've been thinking about our conversation this afternoon," he began, and I could sense that I was right about things. *'See Jedburgh,'* I told myself, *'just do what God requires and He'll take care of everything.'* "I know I told you to call me Sunday," he said, "but ... uh, I'll be a little busy Sunday—there's a baptism at our church, and then a social afterwards, so let's have this conversation now."

"Yes sir," I said, more convinced than ever that I'd made the right decision. He doesn't want to wait to give me the promotion. Makes sense if you pass the test.

"You're terminated, effective immediately, Sloan. Don't even go back to the store. I've already called security. They won't let you through the door. They're cleaning out your desk and they'll mail your personal effects to your home. A guy from Regional Security will be coming by your house to collect your keys to the store. We're having all the passwords changed. Are you there? Can you hear me?"

My hands were shaking on the wheel. Fired. Up to my eyeballs in debt. This wasn't computing. I was supposed to ... things were supposed to get better when I got right with God ... things weren't making any sense, and I began to hyperventilate, the first symptom of a panic attack, which I would get frequently when I got super-stressed.

"Yes sir, I'm here."

"And if you try and get a lawyer or are thinking about any kind of legal action regarding this termination, you should know that I have a tape recording of a conversation you had with me in which you proposed a refund fraud scheme with the intention of defrauding the company. This is the reason you are being fired, and you should be glad that, because I'm a Christian, I'm not pursuing criminal charges against you."

"Yes sir," I said, still stunned.

He was about to hang up when he remembered something. "Oh, and when my security people show up at your house, don't forget to give them your phone, too."

He hung up before I could say 'Yes sir' again, which is a good thing because he didn't hear the onset of my panic attack. All I could think of was that Jean had been right, what she'd said during our first fight after I became a Christian. It would destroy me. It would destroy me.

Chapter 18
Daria

"Because I know that you are obstinate, and your neck is an iron sinew and your forehead bronze, therefore I declared them to you long ago, before they took place I proclaimed them to you, so that you would not say, 'My idol has done them, and my graven image and my molten image have commanded them.'"

Isaiah 48:4-5

"They live off the beaten path?"

"They do, yeah. They're out on Red Rock Peninsula."

"Where's that?"

Josh took one hand off the wheel and adjusted the GPS screen on the dash so Daria could see. "It's uncontrolled territory, up here," he said, pointing to a finger of forested land that pushed up into Saganaga Lake. "We just keep on the Gunflint Trail, and when that ends at the circuit ... see it, here, the road does sort of a circle ... we take a side road across Red Rock Bay, cross the bridge they made, and then we'll be on their peninsula."

"'Their' peninsula? They own it?"

"From the land survey I checked in the town office yesterday, it looks like they pretty much own most of it."

"That's a lot of land for, what, some guy that retired from the Navy?"

"The Marines, actually. And yeah, it is, but on the other hand, it's not the most desirable land around. There's a lot of wetland; not much good land to grow things. Who knows, maybe his wife's folks are rich. Maybe his folks are rich. You never know."

"Why are they living way out here? Are they in some kind of survivalist cult?"

Josh didn't answer right away, thinking. "Fair question, I guess, and honestly, I don't know him or any of his family well enough to give you a good answer."

"He was pretty tough on that Pankowicz guy yesterday. I don't think I've ever seen an American bite that hard."

Josh smiled over at her. "I thought you Israelis prided yourself on being blunt?"

"I said I've never seen an *American* be that brutal. He's tame by our standards. He kind of reminded me of being at one of my family reunions, when everyone's being nice. Most of you mealy-mouthed Christian goyim wouldn't last ten seconds."

Josh chuckled wryly. "Can't disagree with you there, though Ironbridge didn't strike me as being all that mealy-mouthed. He gave it to Pankowicz straight."

"I wouldn't know, being Jewish and ignorant of your mixed-up goy denominations and religious arguments. Although I can tell you, if he ever talked like that about Jesus in public in Israel, they'd kick his stumpy old ass out faster than a Muslim immigrant applies for welfare."

Josh looked over at her. "What is it that you all have against Jesus? Seriously, it's like he's Jewish kryptonite. Bring up his name and suddenly any relationship with a Jewish friend goes weak; keep talking and pretty soon the relationship is dead."

Daria looked out her window as the white Northern Minnesota Construction truck moved through the thick forest wilderness. She wondered at the answer to Josh's question; unfortunately her personal life lately was beginning to cloud her understanding of what had once been clear to her. She had stock answers, the regurgitated historical accounts of centuries of Christian persecution, the history of Jews being hunted down and forced to convert to Catholicism, Jews being put to death during the Inquisition, and the old standby throw-out line that Hitler was a Christian, and look how that turned out for the children of Abraham. In the past she also liked to throw out the line about how Christians in their churches would sing louder to drown out the sound of Jews crying out for help, for just a crust of bread or a cup of water as they were being driven by the trainloads through towns in Europe on the way to the ovens. In her past, especially during her years in Israel, she absorbed the tribal sense of solidarity, and more; a feeling that 'everyone was out to get us, and if we don't stick together, we'll all go down.' She thought personally that this last sentiment was the underlying driver that caused most Jews to immediately turn their back on Christianity. Most Jews saw the proclamation of Jesus as a direct assault on Judaism, because every religious Jew she knew stated without a doubt that no Jew could be a Jew and extend any allegiance whatsoever toward the Gentile pretender. And, they said, that was because the pretender alleged that God was 'three-in-one', which directly and blasphemously contradicted Judaism's most sacred tenant: *Hear, O Israel, the Lord is our God, the Lord is One.*

She wondered what she was doing here, driving through the northern Minnesota wilderness in a pickup truck with some goy religious fanatic. But that part of her she'd tried to bury most of her life popped up with the most inconvenient answer: *'Because if he were some Israeli hotshot he'd have already been pestering you to answer his question. For that matter, if he were some Israeli guy, he'd have already slept with and then dumped you. If he were someone your father would have picked, he'd have laughed at both Ironbridge and Pankowicz and been all over your case for even associating with them, and probably would be complaining about your clothes, too. And last but not least, Caroline Lehrner, you find the man irritatingly, frustratingly, unpredictably attractive. He's probably the first man you've met who's as smart or smarter than you are.'*

"Shut *up*," she said, murmuring into the closed window, and when Josh turned to face her, she realized she'd spoken out loud. "No, sorry, no, hey, I was thinking of something else, sorry." She patted his arm as an apology.

"No worries," he said, looking back at the road, once again giving that other voice leverage to tug at her. 'The guy is so damn *understanding*' the voice said again. *'Shut up!'* she argued, this time, for certain, to herself.

"Look, Josh, you know I'm not religious."

"Yeah."

"But ... my people are my people, you know? We've taken a lot of misery and pain and destruction dished out over the centuries by Christians, people who lift up this Jesus you talk about. You sitting there asking me that question would be like me driving you through New York after the twin towers came down and asking you, 'Hey, Josh, what's up with you Christians and Mohammed? What is it that whenever someone mentions Mohammed, you guys start foaming at the mouth and looking around for suicide bombers?'"

Josh drove for a few moments in silence and then said, "Do you think that's a fair analogy, or is that just your Jewish intellect dredging up a handy conversational spear to throw?"

"No, seriously, that's a fair question."

"Okay, here's a fair answer. There is absolutely no comparison between Jesus and Mohammed, or between Jesus' followers and Mohammed's followers."

"What about the Crusades and all the slaughter that followed in their wake?

What about the Inquisition, where Jews were slaughtered if they didn't convert to believe in Jesus?"

"None of those events had anything to do with followers of Jesus. You're mixing up Catholicism with Christianity. That's like saying Jews and Arabs are the same because they live in the same part of the world."

"We're absolutely nothing like them."

"Yeah, well, don't get confused, thinking Catholicism is some form of Christianity. Catholicism comes from a very ancient pagan, Babylonian religious system that started with Satan."

"I ... I've never heard any of that."

"Yeah, well, neither have most of the evangelicals today who are trying to merge with Rome. Don't get me started with that."

"But do you see what I'm talking about, this comparison? You'd say that one was a good and loving teacher, and the other some half-crazed desert madman."

"Not exactly. If you really listened to what Jesus said about Himself, you'd have to logically conclude that either He *was* a half-crazed desert madman, or He was Who He said he was. That crap about Him being just a 'good and loving teacher' comes from people who haven't read what He said about Himself. You can't come to the conclusion that He was just some good and loving teacher. No 'good and loving teacher' would ever say the things He said about Himself. He said He was the Son of God. So He was either the worst kind of liar or He was Who He said He was ... the Son of God."

"Yeah, well, okay, so we Jews have concluded that he's a liar. He can't be the Son of God. God doesn't have 'children'."

"Says who?"

"Says ... I don't know ... Jews, I suppose."

"Not if you look in that big old book you like to call the Torah, which unfortunately was written by Jews; or the rest of the Tanakh, which was also written by Jews, or the Book of Proverbs— '*What is His name, or the name of His son?*' Your own Hebrew prophets—even David, the best King your people ever produced—talked about the Son of God a lot. '*Kiss the Son, lest He be angry*'. Read what your own people said about God's Son."

Daria threw up a hand. "Look, I told you I'm not religious. I can get any Rabbi in a hundred-mile radius that you want to pick and he'll run rings around your arguments, but that's not me, okay?"

Josh looked at her. "So ... you're letting the Rabbis now figure out how you should relate to God?"

Daria turned in her seat, angry now. "*There is no God,* Josh, don't you get it? Okay? Just because I'm Jewish don't think I'm some sort of Old Testament scholar. For God's sake, like, I don't know, almost fifty percent of Israelis don't even *believe* in the God in that damn book, and yet for some reason the entire world thinks we're constantly bobbing up and down, wearing black, reading that damn book all the time since, hey, after all, we live in the *Holy Land*." She spit these last words out with derision. "Holy land my ass! You Christians are pumping that up because you make a gazillion dollars a year trucking Ma and Pa and the congregation from some dump town in the middle of Red America over to see where Jesus walked. Woooo ..." She waved both hands in the air, imitating some televangelist. "'*Cain't ya'll just see 'im, struggling there with that big ol' wooden cross, that big ol' load o' yer sins on his poor flayed back! Now come on and give just a little more to th' ministry, won't y'all just pony up now, c'mon, how 'bout it y'all?* Oh give me a break! Can't you see it for the racket it is? '*People of the Book'*—what a load of crap. We put that behind us when most of the oldsters who crawled out of Christian Europe's gas chambers decided to make a place where a Jew could be a Jew without having to worry about getting killed just because they're a Jew!"

Josh was quiet for a long moment, and then said, "How's that working out for you so far?"

"Well don't look at us!" she snapped back. "All *we* want to do is to be left alone, but can the world do that? *No!*" She smacked the dash with her hand. "Either it's the damn Muslims who want us dead because, hell, I don't know why, just because, or its you damn Christians who can't let us alone, pestering us to give up this chunk of land, or that chunk of land." She put on a whiny voice and mimicked, "Oh please, just let the Muslims have this last teensy weensy little piece of real estate they're asking for and then they've *promised* to stop blowing us all up in our shopping malls here in Dubuque or Memphis or St. Paul or wherever else." She pushed out a hand and tapped forcefully on the center console with a hardened index finger. "These are the same Christians who oh by the way are constantly harping about how the Jews are God's chosen people and then they try and turn us into Christians—why the hell is that, Mister Christian? So we can't be God's chosen people any more? Yeah, I guess so, who wouldn't want to be the chosen people of this God of yours, and have every idiot in the world try and kill you wherever you go? *That's* how it's friggin' working out for us so far, nice of you to ask, thank you very much." She tossed a lock of hair back from her face in a furious gesture and thrust herself as far away from the driver's side as she could get, but then she thought of something else. "Hey, here's one last thing for you. What about this movement in Christianity that says that Christians are now God's chosen people—how friggin' convenient is *that*?—and God isn't going to have anything to do any more with us shit-for-brains Hebrews because we didn't think that some freaking carpenter who went around doing magic tricks two thousand years ago and got stuck up on a stick for his trouble by the ruling government of the time was actually the Holy, Glorious, Almighty, Most High friggin' God of the Universe!"

Josh didn't answer right away. After a mile or two of trees had gone by, he lifted the center console, reached in and pulled out a Kleenex and held it out to her. She threw him a burning stare for a full five seconds and then snatched it from his hand, put it to her face, and shot a stream of Hebrew at him in return which, strangely, needed no translation.

***

They arrived at the Ironbridge farm just before nine in the morning. Tack had asked Josh to come out and talk about where he wanted a stone wall built so Josh could work up some sort of solid estimate. Daria was subdued but polite. She'd never been out this far north in Minnesota before, and Josh had mentioned to her that he'd never been to the Ironbridge farm. She was especially curious to see if these people were off-the-wall survivalist nutcases or just your plain, run-of-the-mill religious fanatics. She wasn't too sure about Tack Ironbridge, though. He struck her as someone who really believed, and in her experience, and in the Mossad classrooms, she'd learned that such people were the most dangerous. She made a mental note to make mention of him in her next report to her handlers. Her job was to gather intelligence, so she'd gather intelligence. Her handler trusted her instincts.

They stepped out of the car and were met with a cold, hard, biting wind. While she stood there looking around with her arms wrapped around herself, Josh opened the back driver's door and reached in, pulled something out, and handed it to her. It was a large insulated parka; she had come out that morning wearing just a thin fleece pullover. He'd remembered to carry something extra for her before they left. She looked at him hard, said something again in the same vein of Hebrew she'd used in the truck earlier, and snatched the parka. Josh looked at her questioningly.

She saw Ironbridge limping toward them, coming out of a large barn. The main house door opened and a very pretty woman, who, she presumed, was Ironbridge's wife, came out to meet them as well.

"I'm Claire," the pretty woman said, in a very strong French accent.

"*Enchanté*," Daria replied, and the woman smiled.

"*Je ne peux pas vous dire combien de temps il a été depuis que j'ai entendu le français parlé avec un accent hébreu. Le plus beau!*"

Josh glanced at Daria, who lifted one eyebrow and turned her shoulder to him.

With a gesture of Gallic intimacy, Claire took Daria's arm and spoke to Josh. "Oh, forgive me, Mr. Riesling, but it is just that it's been so long since I've heard French spoken with a Hebrew accent. It reminds me ... reminds of some very pleasant days gone by." Daria saw Claire give Tack Ironbridge a long, significant look, and with a strange bolt of both pleasure and jealously, Daria realized this woman was deeply in love with her husband.

"Welcome to Eagles Wings' Creamery," Ironbridge said, and stuck out a hand. Josh shook it. "Do you want to check out the site now or do you need to hit the head? I know it's a long drive out here."

"*Bah, Mon chéri*," Claire said, having none of it. "They will come in, get themselves around something warm, and take the wind out of their hair, and then you can drag them wherever you wish." Still holding her arm, Claire led Daria into the small stone structure that served as the farm's main house. On the way in, Josh, sotto voce, said, "And you speak French? When were you going to tell me about *that*?" She ignored him, fighting with that little voice that was increasingly beginning to bother her. The last thing she needed—the very *last* thing—was some romantic entanglement on a mission. It had felt good to blow off steam at him in the car, but then he'd thrown her right back to living life upside down with his incredibly understanding, incomprehensibly compassionate response of saying nothing and just handing her a tissue, acknowledging her need to cry without imposing on her some no doubt monstrously clever riposte to her emotional outburst. If he'd been an Israeli, he'd have laughed her to scorn.

As Daria entered the kitchen a young man stood, wearing the lean, longish, square jaw from Tack Ironbridge and the dark eyes, high prominent cheekbones, and long straight nose from Claire Ironbridge. She was surprised when the young man stood when she came ... old world manners in the middle of the northern Minnesota wilderness? Americans ... you just never knew what you'd find in this freakin' country. He looked to be in his mid-twenties, and was beside a young woman, somewhat thin, with gorgeous long flowing red hair. Daria was immediately struck with her bright and sparkling eyes radiating life and happiness. She wondered if she was pregnant ... or maybe just out there walking some kind of religious emotional high wire.

She turned her attention back to the young man and she suddenly felt twisted inside; conflicted, as if some deep, dark hidden force was struggling mightily against an equally secretive hope or desire. This internal tension stunned her for a moment—it hit her like a physical blow, the sense of such turmoil within her. *Where did that come from?* The sensation literally knocked her backward, and she bumped into Josh, behind her.

"Excuse me," she murmured, completely at a lost, disoriented,

"*Puis-je présenter Mon fils, Mace, et sa femme Zoe?*" Claire remarked from behind her somewhere in fluid French, like a silken *velouté*.

"*Pardon*?" she replied, confused, her French not up to overcoming the storm inside her. She was shocked to realize she couldn't focus her eyes easily.

"Mace," the young man said, very slowly, nodding, "she ... said ... I'm ... her ... son," and Mace held out a hand toward the red-haired woman. "Wife ... Zoe." Obviously the young man had some sort of speech defect, but Daria got no sense of any mental impairment. And then the red-haired woman leapt up and held out her hand and when Zoe touched her hand Daria felt a slight settling—only very slight, though.

"I'm Zoe. Glad to meet you. Here, sit down, you look ... whoa, hey, Dad, how long is the drive from Granite Sky, anyway? Hey, come on, come with me." Zoe took Daria, stumbling slightly, by the arm and led her out of the kitchen into a hallway and back into the restroom. "Here," she said, opening the door into a bright stone-lined washroom that doubled as a laundry. "Take a deep breath and freshen up. There's a clean towel there to the side of the sink. Throw some water on your face or something. You feel alright?" Zoe put her hand on Daria's, a touch of kindness.

Daria put her hand out to steady herself against the wall and, still disoriented, mumbled in rapid Hebrew: "What the *hell* just happened?"

And adding more surprise to her confusion, Zoe smiled and shot back an answer in absolutely flawless Hebrew. "You just met Mace, that's all. You should pay attention to what happened, to whatever it was you felt. It's important." And Zoe closed the door while Daria wondered what planet she was on.

***

Josh and Tack went outside and walked the ground where Tack was thinking about putting in a stone wall. Tack envisioned a perimeter encircling the main house and what he called the 'Carriage House', where most of the horse-drawn equipment was stored on the ground floor, where also Mace and Zoe lived in a second-story apartment. It was a much, much larger job than Josh had anticipated, and he realized right away he was going to need to bring on more labor than his standard crew, and he'd need someone to manage the project on site here since he was fairly sure he couldn't be spending his time out on the peninsula.

After they talked about footings and plastic sheeting and gravel and the best place to get stone, Josh gave Tack a very rough estimate of how long he thought it would take. Mace joined them, acknowledging Josh with a nod. Josh noticed Mace was carrying a small tablet. Josh said hello again, and as he looked at Mace he noticed the younger man had what looked like a vicious scar in the center of his right hand. The moment Josh saw that scar, something hit him like adrenalin, and he felt a pulse of power and strength and some strange, soaring sense of great deeds to be done on the horizon. He took a deep breath and the air tasted like the very fuel of life.

"What did you think about that little interaction with Stan Pankowicz yesterday?" Tack asked, bringing him back to reality.

Josh shook himself and glanced at Mace—what's *up* with that guy?—and then replied, "Honestly? I thought it was the hardest-hitting piece of evangelism I'd ever seen. It was ... well, sir ... he needed to hear what you had to say."

"Sharing the Spirit of God should be real, because He's real," Tack replied.

"Yes sir. It was about the most energizing thing I've seen around here in, well, in a long time." Josh stood there, hands in the pockets of his parka, and all three of them turned their backs against a strong gust of wind.

Mace typed something on the tablet he had with him and then held it up so Josh could read it. "*Your story*?" it read.

"My story?" Josh asked.

Mace tapped his heart in a spare but powerfully clear gesture.

"Ah, yeah, right. Well, here I am, thirty-three, single now."

"Married before?" Tack asked.

Josh, sensitive to religious types ever ready to disdain him for being divorced, nodded, antennae out.

"Yeah, well, tell us about it." The son put a hand on his upper arm, and Josh felt a sudden rush of support and peace. The guy is way strange, Josh thought.

"Yeah, so, I graduated from the University of Minnesota and the very last thing I wanted to do was follow my father's footsteps into the construction world. I majored in software engineering and I was lucky enough to get a job in Seattle, with a small company you might have heard of—Microsoft?—and things were looking rosy."

"I get the sense they didn't continue that way," Tack said quietly.

"You could say that. After about a year there I get promoted, they like what I'm doing, and I meet a girl, drop-dead gorgeous, and one thing leads to another and after three years out in Seattle, I'm living the dream, pulling down six figures with Microsoft, driving a Lexus, married to a seriously hot babe, and, well, life couldn't get any better."

"And then?"

Josh looked at Tack, a serious look from one man to another, and Mace sensed that Josh was wondering how to broach the next part of his history.

"And then one night I was driving home and there was an accident on the freeway, it was bumper to bumper and not getting any better, so I got off and took a detour through one of the uglier parts of Seattle to get back to my condo. I'm driving along—it was, I guess, around eight in the evening—and I've got the windows up and the doors locked, if you know what I mean. This was a particularly nasty part of Seattle. So I'm stopped at a light and I look over across the intersection and it happens to be just under a streetlight. I see a scarecrow of a woman, dressed in rags, lifting something up, trying to throw it into a dumpster. It was wrapped up in some sort of large blanket or box or something, but just before she dumped it over the edge, I saw a little arm pop out of the edge of the blanket, and I could see the little fingers clench into a fist. Her baby was still alive. She threw it into the dumpster and then just walked away.

"So the light turns green and I drive on through the intersection. I said to myself at the time, 'Hey, this stuff probably happens all the time down here,' and 'She's just strung out on drugs and the kid would have probably had a terrible life anyway,'—just to rationalize not stopping. But I get home and I can't sleep, because what I had seen reminded me of something ... something that had happened the summer before I went to college."

Here Josh paused and Tack and Mace could see him gathering himself to tell the crux of his story. Mace typed something and held the pad up. *God redeems.*

Josh took a breath and nodded, agreeing with Mace, but he couldn't speak. Tack could tell he wasn't accustomed to sharing his story. The Ironbridges waited.

"Yeah, they say He does. Well, I was seventeen, getting ready to head down to the University of Minnesota after I graduated from high school, here in town—I grew up here—and there was a girl I'd been going with through my senior year." Josh's shoulders stayed hunched against the cold, though the wind wasn't gusting. "Life with Dad wasn't the easiest thing in the world, and I was a hellion, no argument, so things weren't the best at home. It really wrecked my Mom, I can tell you, as I think back on it." Josh coughed once and then went on. "So anyway, this girl and I, we get pretty serious over the summer before I left and one thing leads to another and the next thing you know, she's telling me she's pregnant. There I am, about ready to finally get out of the hell that was my house, and suddenly find that this girl—"

Mace put his hand out, touching Josh's arm, interrupting. More tapping, then the tablet: *Name?*

"Yeah ... Mindy," Josh replied, and took a long breath. "Mindy ... so I tell Mindy one night that the kid thing just wasn't gonna work for me. I threw a bunch of other things at her too, like, 'how do you know it's mine,' and stuff that guys who do that kind of thing always say. I ... I ran her into the ground, Mr. Ironbridge." Josh turned and was looking directly at Tack. Mace moved closer, as if to shelter Josh from the gusts. "I remember watching her crumble in front of me. She was ... invested pretty heavily, and she just sort of came apart when I told her it wasn't going to work."

Tack and Mace waited.

Josh looked out into the forest that seemed to surround the farm like some legion of sentinels. The trees were blurred for a while, and then he coughed again, and said, "They found her a couple of days later, a crew running one of the lake ferries. Her body, I mean. She'd just walked out into the lake and started swimming until she couldn't anymore. There were...there was some publicity, you know, stories in the paper, and I think a few of the folks in town had some idea why she did what she did, but ... she said she hadn't told anyone, and I believe that. But, the strangest thing, Mr. Ironbridge," and here Josh paused and Tack and Mace could see the tears begin then in earnest. "My mother knew. Somehow, she knew. I remember the morning she saw the article in the paper, she gasped, and she looked up at me and I said, 'What? What's wrong?' and she just held out the article for me to read, and ... like I said, she just knew, and I couldn't say anything. 'Did you?' she asked, and I still didn't say anything.

"I could see her start to cry, and she ... she put her hand up to her mouth and then stood up and I could see she that knew, and she went into her bedroom and she laid down, and I swear, sir, it must have broken her heart or done something because she laid down and that was the day she died, around ten o'clock that morning, one hour and twelve minutes after she realized her son had caused the death of a girl he'd gotten with child. I ... I tell people it was my Dad's hard ways that put her in the ground, but I know, it was that ... it was Mindy; what I did to Mindy."

Mace and Tack stood in the wind, shielding Josh as the man stared grimly out at the horizon, letting the tears fall. He ducked his head, swiped a sleeve across his face, cleared his throat and said, "So ... as I said, it's not a pretty story. When my mother died, it hit me ... I'd caused the deaths of two people, maybe three; one who loved me but couldn't stand what I'd become, another who loved me but who would never know who I was, and maybe one I never knew." He turned to face the Ironbridges, father and son. "So what does a guy do with that, seriously? What does someone do when they realize what they're capable of, that because of who they are, they've killed others? How do you overcome that?"

Tack looked down for a moment, remembering how another person he knew had caused the deaths of others, and how God used death to restore life. Josh continued.

"I tried the only way I knew how. I buried myself in the world. I hit the books hard at school, did well, got a great job, started out on a great life, but then ... then I'm driving home and I see that woman dump her baby into the dumpster and everything came to a screeching halt, and God spoke directly to me saying, 'This is what you did. This is what you are guilty of.' He showed me what I'd done finally, after years of me trying to bury it.

"Something hit me that night. I knew it was God. The next day I root around the city and find a church, and so I tell my wife that I'd like to visit the place, and she looks at me kind of sideways—we had two kids by then, by the way, I think they were around, oh, maybe one and two, two girls—and I'd never expressed any interest at all in religion. But the wife was okay with visiting the church, so off we went, and it was, well, I guess the only word would be 'dead'. I got no sense of anything at that church, or the others we tried for the next, probably six months. Finally I gave up.

"But seeing that woman throw the baby in the dumpster was bothering me, eating at me, because I knew I was carrying that same guilt around. It was as if someone or something had turned a light on in me and I'd seen what trash was in my own closet, but I didn't know how to get rid of it, to make the closet clean. Honestly, I remember feeling at times back then that I'd been happier with not knowing the trash was there in the first place."

Mace tapped on the tablet again and held it up. *Weight of conviction from the Spirit.*

"It was definitely that," Josh replied, "and it was driving me into the dirt. I was trying to find out how to get my closet clean and none of the churches I had been going to had any answers—they were all just big fake smiles and glad hands and songs and entertainment and—"

"A waste of time," Tack finished.

"Yeah, exactly that. Then one day the company decides to hire a consultant to help with a particularly difficult portion of a specialized software development effort my department was tasked to do. I had to work with this guy for like, ten hours a day for a month, so we got to know each other pretty well. He was an older guy, and he'd been in the military—the Navy, I think—and he was different, I mean, very different from any of the other consultants we had come in to support us. He was extremely professional, he knew what he was doing, and in about half the time we thought it would take, he had the development effort just about completed.

"About the fifth week in on a ten week contract, I ask him if he wanted to get a beer. I don't know what possessed me to do that, because every other night we finished work, he'd head back to the hotel on his own, but this time he said 'Sure' and we went to a local restaurant close to work.

"So I'm sitting there with this guy and after the small talk, the guy looks at me and says that I'm carrying a burden that will eventually kill me if I don't figure out how to get free from it.

"I didn't know what he was talking about at first. I thought he was referring to something in the project, but then I realized he was talking about this thing with Mindy, and what I'd seen that night driving home through the city ... my guilt.

"'What do you know about that?' I ask the guy, and he says that, and I'm quoting him here, 'God told him that I was carrying around a load of guilt for something I'd done a long time ago, and he was supposed to tell me how to be relieved from it.'

"This was the first time I'd ever had any kind of supernatural experience, okay? I'm not the kind of guy that swings around on chandeliers and my relationship with God isn't based on emotion in any way—I'm generally not an emotional guy in the first place—but this was beyond natural, that this guy would know what had been bothering me.

"So I get right in his face in a good way. 'This is awesome,' I tell him. 'So how am I gonna get rid of this guilt?' And he says that I needed to die and be raised again 'in the newness of life', or something like that, and then he basically gave me the truth, right there in the bar not two blocks from one of Microsoft's biggest offices in the city. And I don't mean that he just spit out the four spiritual laws ... no, he told me ... he told me what I needed to hear. He explained the reason why I was feeling this compulsion to get rid of my guilt." And here Josh turned to Mace. "He said what you said; that it was the conviction from God's Spirit that was pressing me to admit my guilt and my sin and to admit who I was and agree with God that there was nothing good in me at all, and that I needed to have God live in me if there would ever be any kind of hope for true, real, honest, peaceful, joyful life.

"If he'd told me that before I'd seen the woman throw her baby away, I'd have told him, 'Hey, I've got an honest, peaceful, joyful life. Take a look at my job, my condo, my car, my wife, my kids! Hey, I've *got* this!' I would have told him all that, but then I saw that woman do in front of my eyes what I had done in secret so many years ago, and I couldn't do anything except agree with him. And then the strangest thing, there I am, Microsoft software engineer big shot sitting at dinner in some swank bar and I start to cry. Yeah, seriously, I've cried, I don't know, maybe three times in my life, and that was the second time. Something happened there at the table with that guy, an overwhelming sense of my own sin and how much it had cost a number of people, and how much in the end it had cost God, because He had loved them far more than I could have ever loved them. I was pierced with my own sin there, having a beer with that old guy, and I just balled my eyes out.

"So after I get things under control, he tells me I need to pick up a Bible and start reading about Jesus—about Who He was and what He did and everything else.

"I tell the guy that I'd tried to read the Bible before and got absolutely zero out of it. He told me that it wouldn't be the case any longer; I'd be able to understand what I would read from here on out. I was so emotionally wrung-out at that point that I just believed what he said and told him I would try it.

"So I did, and man, the old guy was right. The book came alive and started smacking me left and right with insights and convictions and things I needed to clean out of my life, and it explained the dynamic of God coming to live in us, and the life we're supposed to live isn't ours any longer but His, living through us.

"So after that night in the bar with the old guy, I go home and actually start doing what God tells me to do, and oh my, didn't that cause difficulties. My wife didn't like the new direction one bit. Yeah, absolutely I had shared with her what had happened to me and how God brought me to repentance. I told her about seeing the scraggly woman kill her baby in the dumpster and I told her about Mindy—I told her everything—and she just sort of sat there looking at me like some slowly rotting piece of fruit. She thought I was some high-powered Microsoft up-and-coming prodigy that would be pulling down seven figures in a couple of years, and she was looking forward to hitting the cocktail circuit and drinking Mai-Tais with Bill Gates, and as I sit there and describe to her who I really am and what I am now thinking about how I need to live, she starts to get nervous.

"I didn't realize how nervous until about five months later, when I'm at work and I get buzzed from the main desk downstairs. There's a messenger for me with a package at the front desk. So I go down and there's this middle-aged guy who hands me a thick manila envelope and I go back upstairs to my office and open it and read about how my wife has taken out a restraining order against me because of 'Mental instability brought on by excessive religious-based delusion.' I can't go home, can't see my kids, can't go anywhere near them until some Judge makes a decision in forty-five days.

Josh looked down and kicked at some loose stones and then looked back up at Tack and Mace. "So anyway, long story short ... before we come to the court case on the restraining order, she files for divorce, and I find myself completely cut off from my kids. The Judge ruled at the divorce hearing that my symptoms were, how did she put it, 'regrettably familiar' to her, and based on her familiarity with how such unbalanced individuals usually functioned in society, 'infected' as they were with Christianity—yeah, the judge actually used that word—she had no choice but to grant my new ex-wife full custody of the children, with no visitation and no contact whatsoever permitted until they reached eighteen years of age."

"And your relationship ... with God? What happened to that?" Tack asked.

Josh looked up at him. "You'd think it would've been wrecked, wouldn't you? Actually it got stronger. I read where Jesus said that those who lose families—mothers, fathers, brothers, sisters, husbands, wives, for His sake—well, they would be recompensed. I think He wanted to let us know that for some of us, if we make a choice for Him, it will cost us dearly. I have two daughters I haven't seen in ... well, a lot of years. They don't even know who I am."

The pain was evident on Josh's face, and Mace grabbed him by the upper arm in a masculine gesture of support and solidarity. Josh seemed to strengthen.

"So that's my story, gentlemen. About the time the courts tore my two children out of my life, my dad died of a heart attack and left the business to me. That was, I'm guessing, about five years ago or so. We've done okay."

"Dad a Believer?" Tack asked.

"Dad? No, no, he wasn't," Josh said, with a grim, regretful tone. "He was a hard-drinking, hard-fighting, construction worker who grew up '*walkin' the red arn*' out on the Pacific coast, mostly in Oregon and Washington, in the early years when they were building the tall ones out there. He met my mom, who was going to college at Oregon State, but she was from around here and she convinced him to move back, so he did. He started Northern Minnesota Construction and built it up to a pretty good operation, but he was a hard man who'd had a hard life and ... and, well, so things went."

Mace tapped again on the tablet and held it up. *Dad alcoholic?*

"Born and bred," Josh replied grimly. Mace nodded and looked at him, and Josh felt a sense of compassion almost overwhelm him.

Tack spoke up. "So let me guess ... you get your intuition and ability to read people from that ... experience."

Josh looked at Tack sideways for a minute. "How'd you know that?"

"What? That kids who grow up with an alcoholic parent develop hypersensitive human antennae just to stay alive? How do you think?"

Mace held the tablet for his father to read and Tack looked at Josh. "Josh ... we're wondering ... why don't you guys stay for dinner? I think it would be important. If you stay for dinner, you'll need to stay the night, because you don't want to be driving back down through the peninsula this time of year that late."

"Well, uh, yeah, sir, I mean, it's okay with me. I'd have to check with Daria, though."

"Good," Tack replied, "because you need to sit down with my wife. She has a story to tell you."

As the three of them walked back around the barn and through the center of the farm, before they approached the main house, Mace held the tablet out for Josh. *Caroline?*

"Caroline who?" Josh asked, wondering.

Mace made a quick hand sign to his father, too quick for Josh to catch, but Tack asked Mace, "The lady here? Working for him ... her name is Caroline?"

Before Mace could type a reply, Josh said, "Uh, no, her name is Daria. Sorry, I thought I introduced you. Daria's worked for me now for, I guess around seven months or so. She got her full-time work visa just about three months ago. She's from Israel."

Mace just looked at Josh and didn't say anything.

***

When they walked into the kitchen, Claire and Zoe were talking to Daria, three heads together, and they immediately stopped when the men trooped in, bringing the clear cold air in with them. Tack and Mace both sensed they'd been discussing something serious; Josh wasn't aware at all.

"Ca ... Daria, we were wondering. Would it be possible for you to stay the night and head back in the morning? We'd like to invite you both to stay for dinner, and Claire has some things she needs to share with Josh."

Claire's eyes widened, looking inquiringly at Tack, and Daria sat back in her chair, a look of wide-eyed wonder on her face, but Zoe clapped her hands and spoke up.

"Hah. See! God's doing *something*, I'm telling you. We were just sitting here convincing Daria she needed to stay for dinner and in you three come."

"*You people are scary*," she said, whispering, slipping once more into Hebrew.

"*You don't know the half of it, sister*," Zoe replied, in the same language.

Tack spoke up. "Forgot to tell you, Daria, Zoe speaks, well, a few languages."

"Yeah, she already knows all that, Dad, and she hasn't even heard half of my life story." Zoe looked at Mace. "Though I haven't explained about us," she said, and as Mace came close, Zoe took his hand, kissed his palm, and then turned it over and held it up, the dark, red knot of twisted flesh so different from the skin around it. "See here, Daria? See this? Tonight I'm gonna tell you all about *this*!"

***

So it was that Daria, purportedly the administrative assistant to the owner of Northern Minnesota Construction company, in reality a Mossad agent assigned to gather intelligence on Muslim movement particularly, and religious extremism in general throughout the American Midwest, found herself sitting with a young lady named Emma Devereaux, whose story she did not know yet, both listening, riveted, to the story of how young Mace Ironbridge had rescued a young twelve-year old Zoe, a precocious well-traveled Jewish girl attacked in the northern Minnesota wilderness by a vicious, Jew-hating Arab. As it dawned on Daria that Zoe was, truly, a Jewess, that her parents were Russian Jews and that young Mace Ironbridge had risked his life for her ... and knowing that this same Zoe was what some would call a 'Messianic Jew', it disoriented her. She wasn't familiar with the literature that told about how often Christians risked their lives for Jews; such legends and heroism were omitted from the narrative put out by the Israeli Left. What she was seeing here at the Ironbridge farm was beyond her comprehension—especially the semi-supernatural stuff.

Yet, the one thing that caused her the greatest amount of consternation was that sense of inner twisting, of gut-wrenching conflict she'd experienced when she met Mace for the first time and whenever he was near her thereafter. The tangible, physical experience was having an impact on her, an impact she couldn't deny. That experience more than anything awoke her to the possibility that maybe there was something real about these people, something she needed to know about, something that maybe, just maybe, would help make sense of who she was, who her people were, and what was happening to her, and them. What kept her riveted during Zoe's story was the whispering hidden sense that something here, something at this geographic location, with these people—something she absolutely sensed but could not comprehend what it was—would be able to finally, *finally* answer her questions. She sensed it like someone smells salt on the wind and knows (or, perhaps, hopes) the ocean may not be far away, aware of it while it is yet still at the very edges of realization—a great, living mass of swelling, enormous power that both sustains and sweeps away small and great. What she was looking for, and did not yet know she was looking for, was the main element in Zoe's story, which is why she was riveted—love. Daria desperately wanted to love and be loved.

***

And so it was also that Josh Riesling, thirty-three that year, heard how the Great Redeemer rescued a beautiful but arrogant former French professor of comparative religion from hell after she too had been responsible for the deaths of others, how she had come to realize her own fault in the affairs, how she had come to the end of herself and learned the true meaning of the cross and how it was applied to one's life. She told Josh her story, all the while holding Tack's hand. She even brought out Tack's old letter and read it to him, verbatim, crying while she did so. When she finished, she looked at Josh with wet eyes, and said, "So, my dear boy, you see, only He can give you the forgiveness you seek."

Tack leaned forward over the kitchen table, a powerfully intense look in his eyes, and locked a strong grip on Josh's forearm. "You're a young man, with all the strength and power and courage God gives young men. *Take* those things and use them to become like Him! You've lost your family for His sake. Be perfect like He was and is perfect. I've seen your courage; I saw it yesterday with Pankowicz. You had a big contract riding on that guy and yet you spoke the truth to him. That's courage—God-given courage. I see Him making you into what He wants you to be, Josh. The deaths of your mother and Mindy and that other precious little life—they haven't been meaningless. Far from it, He's used death to bring forth life, and so, our question to you tonight is this. What does He want from you?"

"What do you mean, sir?"

"I mean, did God go through all the trouble to bring you to repentance, to send some old man in Seattle to share with you how to find Him, to take you through that crushing refinement of losing your precious daughters as you stood for Him, all of that for what? So you could just go knock on doors or throw some tracts around?"

Josh sat still for a moment. "I don't think I've ever asked myself that question."

"Look Josh, you've been given a priceless gift. God took you through a furnace few choose to undergo, but you have. Your faith in Him, your relationship with Him, is so much stronger than most other Christians because of what you've suffered. So if I were you, I'd start asking myself what He wants from you. Why did He put you through all that?"

Josh still looked as though he didn't understand what Tack was asking him, so he continued. "Have you bought any equipment or tooling for your business since you took it over from your Dad?"

Josh, confused at the change in direction, said, "Well, yes sir, we have. Standard stuff ... some mechanized scaffolding, a lot of tools, and, yeah, an excavator and a used bulldozer."

"And did you buy any tools that you just sort of put in the back room or parked in the lot and didn't use?"

Josh chuckled slightly. "We're not that flush, sir. Can't afford to spend money buying something or repairing something and then not use it."

Tack and Claire looked at Josh for a long minute before Josh finally understood what Tack was driving at. "Yeah, okay, I see."

"Why did God pay the blood price for your sin, take the time to make you aware of it, send one of His own to tell you what to do about it, refine you through the loss of your family, and then put you here, now, in this time, owning and operating a construction company? He doesn't refine men and then not put them to use. What does He want from you? What are you supposed to do?"

***

The next morning came early. Tack, Claire, Mace, Zoe, and Emma arose at 4:45AM, bustled about the kitchen, revived the fire in the wood stove, put on coffee and hot chocolate, and prepared for their Bible study. Josh joined them. Josh had slept on the couch in the main house, while Daria took the couch in Mace and Zoe's little apartment. Emma had her own room in the Carriage House—a little single bed tucked into a room that had originally been planned as a nursery.

They spent about an hour and a half in the Scriptures, the four Ironbridges discussing freely what it was the Word was speaking to them about or what they'd noticed.

Emma, newcomer that she was, terrified still to even think about having an independent thought about anything in the Bible, sat quiet as a mouse. Josh listened and just let the discussion wash over him, soaking him, as he ruminated on the question Tack had put to him last night. *What does God want me to do?*

Daria stayed in the Carriage House that morning. She'd been invited to come listen to the family study the book of Job—it was where they were that day, reading through three chapters every morning from Genesis to Revelation—but she honestly wanted some time to try and re-orient herself. Her emotional and intellectual dislocation yesterday was causing her distress, and every time Mace would come into the same room she felt that same internal twisting, a tumultuous conflict and tension, a physically tangible expression of something she suspected was emotional ... or something spiritual, Zoe would probably say.

***

Everyone met for breakfast after morning chores. Josh had consulted with Daria and they both agreed they should probably leave for the office soon.

"There is one thing I want to talk about with you, Mr. Ironbridge, but it should probably wait until we can come back again," Daria said tentatively.

"What is that, young lady?"

"The Holocaust."

Tack looked surprised, but said "Well, you're right, I don't think we could do that justice in the next ten minutes. But," he went on, "before you come back—and we want you to come back if you're willing—I want you to spend some time thinking about a question."

Josh, drying a breakfast plate, paused to hear what Tack would say.

"Ask yourself this: to what extent was the Holocaust the fulfillment of the prophecies made in the Torah?"

Daria paused only a moment and held up both hands in a gesture of surrender. "Well, sir, you've got me there. I wouldn't know where to look. Don't know anything about that—any of it."

"Okay, then, Josh, do us a favor, would you? When you get some time back in town, open up Deuteronomy 28 and read through it with Daria, would you?"

"Sure, sir; my pleasure." Josh wasn't sure what Tack was getting at, since he couldn't exactly call to mind what that particular scripture had to say either.

***

As they stood outside, ready to leave, Tack and Claire came around to Daria. Claire hugged her and Daria got up in the truck and Tack closed the door after her.

Daria looked at Tack and sensed a white-hot intensity flowing out of the man. She felt somehow more comfortable with him than with anyone, because he was always so direct, and because of that she just couldn't be shallow around him. So she decided to be blunt and see how he handled it.

"You know I don't believe in this God of yours," she said.

"If God was like what you've heard about all your life, I wouldn't believe in Him either, to tell you the truth. But the reality is that you don't know Him well enough to believe or disbelieve Him."

His reply took her aback slightly; again, with this man, always the unexpected. But she wouldn't give. "Nothing you say is going to change my mind, either," she said, pushing.

He wasn't bothered a bit. "I'm not going to say anything at all to you. Either God will talk to you directly, or He won't. You won't be convinced that He's real by words, by sermons, by some fancy talk. Either you'll experience the living God, like those of your fathers who knew Him because they met Him, talked to Him, worked with Him, bled with Him, and died for Him ... or you won't. Up to Him, not me."

Daria bridled at the reference to her Jewish ancestry, but she couldn't deny any of it. But she did anyway. "I'd love to have that argument with you sometime," she answered.

"You'd lose. Out of the mouths of your own people, your own Torah, your own Tanakh, comes the truths we Gentiles trust in. Isaiah, a nice Jewish boy, predicted that the Messiah would come and the Jews themselves would kill him, but 'in His name the Gentiles would trust.' So you can argue with Isaiah if you like."

"Sounds like your Gentile God could be a lot of trouble."

"Hear, O Daria, the Lord is our God, the Lord is One. We have the same God. You Jews just haven't recognized Him yet. And about the trouble, yes, you're right. A very wise man once wrote that God is good, but He's not safe."

Daria looked at him and finally laughed out loud. "This you tell to a daughter of Israel, that being the chosen people of God isn't so safe?" she asked, waving one hand in the air.

Zoe came up, Emma trailing behind, and she reached through the window and gave Daria a hug. In Hebrew, she said, "*You come back now, and don't let anything keep you away!*"

Daria, overwhelmed by then, couldn't respond.

Josh started the truck and they drove out of the yard, down the winding driveway, and began the long drive back to Granite Sky and normal life back on planet Earth.

***

It was a very quiet drive on the way back into town. They were about halfway when Josh turned to her and in a questioning voice asked, "Hey, who's Caroline?"

Daria, startled beyond all measure, said, "Caroline? I don't know; is she a customer or something?"

Josh shook his head. "Ah, no, it's just ... I don't know, it's pretty weird. Mace ... you know—"

"Yeah, what about him?"

"Well, it's just that he came up to me in the yard yesterday, when I was outside with Tack, and basically he thought your name was Caroline."

Daria shrugged her shoulders and looked out the passenger window, barely suppressing the cold shudder of dread that coursed through her. The Mace guy was flat dangerous. "And what did you tell him?"

"I told him your real name and apologized; I probably forgot to introduce you in the house."

"And what did he say?"

"He just kind of stood there; didn't say anything."

"He didn't talk much the entire time we were there, did you notice? I slept on their couch and even when he came in after milking the cows in the evening, with Emma and I and Zoe there talking, he didn't say much at all."

"Tack was telling me that Mace has some kind of speech issue. He's had it since he was born. Tack says he's as smart as a whip, but he just doesn't talk much, or very quickly. Except—"

"Except when?"

"When he's with Zoe, by themselves. Tack and Claire can't figure it out, but ever since they met, he's been able to talk normally when he's with her."

"Yeah, Zoe told me about what happened to her in high school. That was a story! It explained the scar in his hand."

"Guy's got some guts, gotta admit," Josh said.

"Yeah, well, I'm not sure he's firing on all thrusters."

"I don't know," Josh replied. "Of anyone we've met in the last two days—or the last two years, if you want the truth—I'd say that guy is burning some seriously different fuel that neither you nor I know anything about."

Daria wanted to get off the subject of Mace and his freaky shot-in-the-dark identification trick that threatened to blow her cover. But the dangerous thought struck her ... what if this was what Tack had meant when he'd told her that God would make Himself known to her? That was one *hell* of shot in the dark.

"What did you and Tack and Claire talk about last night?"

A mile or two of silence went by and then Josh spoke up. "I want to tell you a story," he said.

"That bad?"

Josh looked over at her. "Yeah."

Daria turned in her seat toward Josh and looked at him. She could see he was distressed, but also that he wanted to tell her what he'd shared the previous night. "Well, hit me with your best shot. If it's that bad, I can always quit and go find a serial killer or ax murderer to work for, right?"

So Josh unraveled his very long story to the younger woman who worked for him, recognizing that the sharing of this personal history marked a watershed in their relationship, a turning point. It couldn't just be 'employer-employee' any longer, not after she heard what he'd done. He was making himself vulnerable to a woman he didn't know very well, but somehow trusted. She struck him as supremely competent. It was the first word he thought of when he thought of her.

Daria sat for a while after he finished, processing what he'd shared. "What did ... what did the Ironbridges have to say about that? I note they didn't kick us out last night. Actually it might explain why they invited us back so readily. You're now on their religious radar, a sinner to save, a spiritual scalp to put up on their lodge pole."

Josh looked at her. "Did anyone ever tell you you're too cynical for your own good? You don't have to be that way. It's unfair, unkind, presumptuous, unattractive ... and it's inaccurate. If you want to know what they said, I'll tell you. Claire shared with me her story, about ... well, it's her story to tell, but suffice it to say that she knew how I felt and she had some extremely helpful advice. They've both been through the wringer, Daria. They're not after anyone's spiritual scalp, just the opposite. They want to help me—and you too, if you'll let them. I haven't felt such ... such *relief*, such *optimism* about the future, for ... I guess ... I guess since I found out Mindy killed herself because of me, and since I lost my two daughters. These people are real Christians. You've seen people playing at being Christians since you've been here, I know. But you haven't seen people like this. They're real, and they have the Spirit of the Living God in them. You don't know what you're talking about, and I'm not gonna sit here and listen to you disparage them, Daria."

Josh had never spoken to her like this before, and her human nature bridled at being brought up short—*'How dare he speak to me that way!'*—but then another inner voice struggled, pressing her, pushing her, reminding her that she had always wanted to be an honest woman, and warning her that her pride would one day kill her if she didn't take it in hand. She knew *that* was the truth.

"I apologize, Josh. You're right, I'm too damn cynical sometimes. The Ironbridges treated me with every kindness and they bent over backward to make me feel welcome and I never got the feeling they were trying to sell me anything."

She could see Josh visibly relax.

"But I *will* tell you that there are some pretty weird things going on in that house."

"You noticed."

"Seriously, I mean, what's *up* with them? They didn't strike me as your garden-variety survivalists, and you're right that they *definitely* didn't remind me of any Christians I've ever met in this country—or any other country, come to think of it ... except ... well ..."

"Except what?"

"I don't want to say."

"You have to say, that's the rule."

She looked at him strangely.

"Fine. What I was going to say was that they reminded me of you, only weirder, of course. You all have something ... I don't know, I can't define it, but while you're all different, there's this weird, indefinable thing you all have in common."

"We all make you uncomfortable?"

"No! Well, yeah, actually, you do, but that's not what I meant. I don't know."

"I'll tell you what it is. It's the Spirit of God in us that makes you uncomfortable, that unsettles you, that makes you aware of your own emptiness. You don't like to hear that, but it's the truth. He makes you aware of the fact that you need Him and at the same time are trying to push Him away."

It shook her that Josh would put his finger on the internal dynamic that she hadn't shared with him, that internal conflict she'd experienced at the Ironbridges, and it also reminded her of something which she tossed up to distract Josh from digging any deeper in that part of her emotional yard.

"And the Mace and Zoe show! What's up with that? I mean, I have to tell you, we're in their apartment last night, and Emma was making some tea and Zoe and I were talking and I could visibly see Zoe start to, I don't know, just sort of wind down in front of me, like a computer screen that does the auto-dimming thing before it goes to sleep. I mean, she didn't get weird or anything but it was just that she was getting progressively more nervous, more uncomfortable, more anxious about something."

"You sure it wasn't something—"

"No, actually, like, two hours before then, she told me part of the story about her and Mace and how she just always felt better when he was around, but man, I didn't think I'd get a front-row seat to a demonstration. But absolutely, you should have seen what happened when Mace came in from evening chores. Boom! Anxiety went out the window and Zoe looked like someone had just plugged in the computer again and set the screen back to full brightness. Her eyes lit up, she smiled, her face colored ... I mean, it was smack-down amazing."

"Smack-down?"

"Hey, I learned it from American TV, so shut up. No, it was the most amazing thing you've ever seen."

"Maybe it's just because she's in love with him."

Daria's features took on a cynical cast and said, in a tone tinged with acid, "She's been married to the guy for, what, almost five years or so?"

"Yeah, well, didn't you see Tack and Claire? When Claire was telling me her story, she held Tack's hand the entire time. No doubt in my mind those two love each other like ..." and here Josh couldn't speak clearly for a moment, and Daria was stunned to see his eyes moisten. He wiped his hand across his face and made a sound like a low grunt. "No doubt in my mind those two love each other. Why wouldn't it be the same for Mace and Zoe?"

Daria didn't have an answer to that.

***

As she thought about it during the rest of the drive, she recognized that the source of her instinctive distaste toward the Ironbridge clan was jealousy ... she felt jealous of the peace they had, the joy they had ... the love they shared. When Claire had looked at Tack yesterday as they'd arrived, it was like a spear had been thrust into her chest. Just the memory of it now brought tears to her eyes, and she turned to face the window and wipe them away. Her irritation, her impatience, her snapping cynicism were all from jealousy. She'd never had anything like peace or joy or love, and *definitely* not anything springing from a root of relationship with God they all seemed to have. And as she admitted that hard fact to herself, she suddenly realized what was causing that weird feeling of internal conflict, that wrestling, that tumult inside her heart that Mace Ironbridge set off. She realized that there was in her own heart a pull toward those things, toward peace and joy and love and contentment with whatever life would bring ... ah, god, what a price she'd pay to have such things!

But something, something inside her, was working *against* that pull towards truth and beauty and love, something—amazingly, *also* within her own heart—fighting *against* her own deepest desire. As they pulled into NMC's parking lot, the realization that something of her own nature was viciously fighting to keep her miserable and lonely and frightened for the rest of her life hit her hard. She stumbled out of the truck, more uncomfortable and unstable than she'd ever been before in her life.

Chapter 19
Abrielle

"I heard about you with the hearing of my ears, but now I see you with my eyes, and I abhor myself, and repent in dust and ashes."

Job 42:5-6

Abrielle Dumont, you are an idiot.

I say this to myself, what, maybe ten or twenty times a day? This time it is because when I forgot to bring the milk can from the house as I go to milk the cow, and I go back to the house to get the milk can, on my way back to the barn, I am forgetting my over-bonnet. But I just say to myself, *'you are an idiot, but going back once in this freezing cold is enough. Just go milk the cow and get it over with.'* So I just milk the cow in my white head covering. I am not accustomed to wearing this larger black bonnet over our normal white head covering, but while we are staying with the community here, we are asked to fall in with their ways. Walking outside without it, I suppose, is a violation of the rules.

"*Webishtew*, Abrielle," Abigail says as I come into the large kitchen in the house where we are living. Abigail is a nice young woman of 15 who has been very kind to my sister and her sons and me since we've come to stay with the community.

"Good morning, Abigail," I reply. "I'm good, *danke*."

"It looks like the cow gave you quite a bit," she says, peering over my shoulder at the full milk can.

"*Oui*, yes," I say, still mixing my French with English and the community's mélange of Dutch and German and ... and some polyglot tongue I haven't been able to figure out yet. "She is a good creature, and kind. Not like our last, oh my no, not at all."

Abigail smiles pleasantly, letting me know that the direction and type of this conversation is approved. "Oh yes, she is that. What was your other one like?" Abigail began to lay the fire in the large wood cook stove.

"Oh, she was a feisty one. You never knew when she would kick, and then, bang, there went the day's milk."

"Oh my," Abigail responded, suitably shocked at the behavior of our erstwhile cow, who I fervently hoped was now contentedly strung peacefully from lines as plain, unseasoned jerky somewhere.

"Yes, well, we made do," I said, not wanting to appear too negative.

Abigail struck a match and heat and light leapt up from the fire and swept into the dark kitchen. I worked the pump handle near the sink to fill a pot of water to put on the stove to make it hot, so as to wash the milk can, when Abigail noticed what I was doing.

"Oh, Abrielle, there is no need for the water to be hot," she said sweetly, so as not to appear to be correcting me. "The cold water will be enough good," she said. With English still strange to my ears after growing up speaking French, the sentence structure derived from the mixture of Old German and Dutch would give me pause. Abigail began emptying the cream collected from the large milk can into a butter churn. Today was the day she made butter.

As she put the cream she'd skimmed from the milk into the churn, she began to emote signs of being uncomfortable, which in Mennonite emotional shorthand means that they wish to speak about something that might be controversial or painful to talk about, but something which nonetheless was for them something significant.

"What is it, Abigail? You can with me ask what you want, please, with no problems."

She looked relieved. "Can you tell me what took you away from your previous community?" she asked.

Though I berate myself many times a day for being a foolish woman, I can put together a few things, and I noted that Abigail was asking me this question during a time when we would normally have at least an hour together before the other members of the family would be around. Her younger sisters were out feeding the pigs and chickens; her younger brothers were hauling water from the pond, which, she knew, would take them some time since they first had to cut a hole in the ice, and since the two brothers assigned to this task were five and six, respectively, it would take them a long time to haul eighteen five-gallon buckets of water from the pond to the kitchen tank. I also knew that my sister Brigitte, with her four sons, would not be in for another hour. I set down the milk can and turned to the young woman.

"I will tell you, Abigail, but may I ask why it is you wish to know?"

She blushed slightly, not accustomed to engaging in an interactive discussion. All her life she'd been spoken to, or spoken about, but no one, it seemed, ever took the time to speak *with* her. She stumbled when she sought words to express herself, although maybe what I perceived as stumbling was simply a language barrier. Abigail had stopped her education when she was thirteen, generally what we would know in British Columbia as the first year of secondary school, or in France, the *quatrième*. Therefore I supposed that an ability to express herself or communicate complex thoughts had not yet been developed. Yet I saw in her a hunger for, how shall I say, 'newer things', 'different things', things outside the closed environment of her Mennonite community.

"It ... it helps me understand better things here," she began, and I understood what she meant.

I have always been slightly rebellious; my sister tells me it is one of my greater faults. I discover part of that rebellious nature rising up now as a slow, glimmering resentment begins to form against the rules of the community in which she has lived all her life, rules that would keep a woman—or a man, for that matter—from knowing what was happening in the world outside of their sheltered sanctuary. So I pushed at the rules a little.

"I will tell you, Abigail. But some things may be hard for you to hear. If you do not want me to continue, just tell me to stop, okay?" Her eyes widened at this warning, seemingly full of portent, but her courage and curiosity overcame her caution.

"Yah, sure, but it will be okay," she replied, not knowing enough about the world to know what she was saying.

I hung up the towel I was using to dry the milk can and we together sat at the small kitchen table in the breakfast nook the family used for when only two or three wanted a quiet cup of tea or coffee or maybe just a piece of toast.

"My sister married a Muslim man when she was sixteen," I began, and then brought myself up short. "Do you know what a Muslim is?"

Her eyes were still large and open and full of curiosity. "Are these the Mennonites near Great Forks?" she asked.

"No, dear. Muslims are what we call people who follow the religion of Islam. This is the major religion in most of the eastern parts of the world—the Middle East and Far East."

"What is this religion? Are they like us? I know many communities have different rules. Are they plain?" she wanted to know.

"No, Abigail, they are nothing like the plain people. We worship the God of Abraham, Isaac, and Jacob, and His Son, Jesus. Muslims believe that a being named 'Allah' is God, and that his most important representative was Mohammed, who lived in the sixth century. This person, they say, wrote a book called the Koran, which is what Muslims consider to be the same thing as what we consider the Bible to be—a holy book that holds God's instructions for living a life pleasing to Him."

"So they have a different set of rules?" she asked.

"They do," I replied, and then said, "Their rules are very different than ours, though."

"How?" she pressed, curiosity blazing in her eyes.

"Well, I will tell you another time, but right now, all you need know is that Muslim men have very strict rules about how women should behave."

"But so do we," she answered straightaway, making a point that was obvious but which I'd never seen before.

I smiled, realizing that while she may not be aware of much beyond the borders of her little community in Teal Lake, Minnesota, she nonetheless had a sharp mind. "Well, Abigail, now that you mention it, that's true. One thing you should know is that Muslim men are told in their holy book to beat their wives if they misbehave." I expected this to generate some surprise, but a look of pained cynicism appeared.

"There are many ways wives can be beaten," she whispered, with her head down, seemingly ashamed, "not just with hands or sticks."

I was surprised at her perceptiveness, but did not want to dwell on what it was she was thinking about. "Well, so it may be, but one rule the Muslims have that we do not have is if the father believes a daughter is not behaving in a way that will honor his family, he can cut off her head with no penalty."

She did look up at this, but instead of shocked surprise, again there was a look of bitter cynicism and pain. "There are many ways to kill daughters," she said, almost too softly to be heard, but I heard her. It seemed as though this untraveled young woman, who had not read a book since she was thirteen, sensed that every Muslim rule had a parallel in today's practical outworking of Anabaptist theology. Or maybe she was just bitter, or unhappy, or naturally dissatisfied. Or ... maybe she was right. I couldn't tell.

"Yes, well, Abigail, there are many other Muslim rules, but we've not time to go into them now if I am to answer your question."

"Yes, yes, right, I'm sorry, go on." She was struggling to contain any evidence of eagerness, since that was considered unseemly in the community—especially in a woman—but she was not succeeding.

"Well, Brigitte did not know about such rules when she married Ahmad. And I believe Ahmad, her husband, did not fully ... *apply* ... Islamic rules in their early years. But as time went by and Ahmad became older, he became more affected by his religion, and he began to take it more seriously. By then, Brigitte and he had three boys, and Ahmad began to press more intensely for them to learn about Islam and become devout Muslims."

"So he married her under false pretenses?"

I thought about her observation for a moment. "I am not sure," I replied. "When people are young, they tend not to think so much about their religion, or faith, or God. But as they get older, as they realize that they will not live forever, many times they begin to search for God, and many times they turn to the faith they were raised with. I think this is what happened to Ahmad."

"Wasn't Brigitte a Christian when she married?"

"Not when she was married, no," I replied. "She was very bright for her age and she began college at 16. That was where she met Ahmad. By the time she'd had her second child, she'd finished college and was beginning her internship for her medical degree. By the time she'd had her third, she'd gotten her degree and was practicing medicine in a little town in British Columbia."

"So she wasn't raised plain then?" asked Abigail, eyebrows raised in surprise. She would work the butter churn a bit, then stop to ask a question, and then churn while I answered her.

"No, no, not at all," I replied. "None of us were. Our father ran a shipping business in Vancouver, and we were very well off. My mother ... my mother died in childbirth, giving birth to my younger brother, but he died too, and so it was just Brigitte and I with our father. Our father raised us very strictly. My mother had been born and raised in France, you know, so my father wanted us to speak French in the home, to remind us of her, and so we grew up speaking French, which was not at all a problem in British Columbia in those days, no, not at all. So," I continued, "Brigitte was the smart daughter, and my father was very proud of her, especially when she was accepted into college at such an early age."

"Were you ... were you married too?" Abigail asked tentatively.

"I was," I said, choosing to be direct. Again, with my rebellious nature, I chose to oppose the natural disinclination plain people have of saying anything controversial in an open way. I wanted to be open about my past, even though I was very well aware of the Anabaptist doctrine related to divorce, which required that once divorced, one was not permitted to remarry unless the previous spouse had died. "I was very young, and I was not a very good daughter, and when I was fifteen, just a little older than you, I ran away from home with a young man."

"Was he a Christian?" she asked, unable to hide her look of shocked surprise, only able to draw water from her own well as yet.

"No," I replied, pushing on through the story. "Not at all. We didn't even know about such things, for my father hated religion. You see, my mother died in a Catholic hospital and I think my father held them responsible for her death. It wasn't fair and it wasn't true, but, well, there it is."

"That's sad," she said softly.

"Yes ... and so after my sister left home for college, things were not ... not so pleasant there, and when this young man promised me a new life, I didn't think about the consequences, I just left with him. My father was very angry. It is not something I am very proud of."

"Was it ... was it very difficult?" she asked. "I mean, leaving your family and everything?"

The memories, kept buried for so many years, suddenly began to sting again, surprising me, because I thought I'd buried them deeply. But no, here they were again. I found it difficult to speak. "It was, yes. At first ... at first, things were very good, but then ... well, let us just say that when life became difficult, we chose to go in different directions."

"I *see*," she said, with an uptick on the last word in the way the plain people have of filling the conversational gap with something non-confrontational so as not to appear condemning, all the while making it apparent that they completely disapprove of what you've told them.

I pressed on through her disapproval, granting that perhaps it was just her inability to comprehend such a course of action. "It was a difficult time for me. And this is when I met some plain people, Mennonites actually, who were kind enough to take me in. They helped me very much."

Her eyes widened slightly at this part of the story. "Is this when you became a Christian?"

"It was," I answered, blending the action of joining the Mennonites with the automatic procurement of salvation. "They explained to me the way of salvation, and the things God requires of one who wishes to live a holy life."

Her face remained impassive. Anabaptists—the women, particularly—develop an amazing ability to don a look of complete blankness, rendering them opaque to others, making it impossible to get to know them. Yet it did not seem that her expression was so just then.

"So were you with the Mennonites before you came here?" she asked, twisting her apron absentmindedly.

"We were," I went on.

"And what made you leave?"

And here I came to the question we had been asked at so many other communities. I was tempted to just tell her what I had been told to share—about the Muslim religious rule that directed that the child of a Muslim must be brought up as a Muslim, and that a Muslim man's greatest obligation, over law or truth or compassion or love, was that his children become Muslim as well, and if they would ever stray from the faith or marry an infidel, they could be, by Muslim law, put to death. And I was to say that we feared that Brigitte's husband was getting too close to us, and therefore we left to move to another community essentially to hide. And so this is what I told Abigail. I could have stopped there, but some strange feeling compelled me to add more to the story—information that I could easily have omitted without abusing truth.

"And," I went on, seeing her eyes glazed at the story, not really understanding Islamic law, and probably not caring, "there was something else."

"Yes?" she asked, slightly more curious.

"It is a hard thing to talk about," I said, twisting my cup in the saucer. She replied by putting her hand on mine. "You see," I went on, "in some communities ... certain things happen; bad things. People—men, boys—sometimes do not behave as they should, do you understand." I saw her looking at me darkly, almost with a cynical anger, and definitely with more comprehension that I expected, which somehow strengthened my resolve to continue. "Sometimes people ... men, mostly ... do things which are ... they are hard to talk about."

"You do not need to talk about such things," she whispered again, and I knew that she was aware of the things I was alluding to.

My heart sank. I had hoped things were different in this community, partially because I did not want to move again, and partially because I am an idiot, as I have said, and hoped that things might be different here. But I swallowed and went on with the story.

"You know Brigitte, that she is a doctor, yes? And you know I am a nurse? So it has been natural for the women sometimes to come for ... to come and, well, to get things, medicine, from us to help them in their pain, and sometimes they tell us things that have happened. Most times, though, they do not. In our previous community, Brigitte and I would help the women who were ... hurt this way. You know that they could not go to the outside for help, of course."

"Of course," she replied, "it is against the *Ordnung*." Her bald comment, rendered in such a matter-of-fact fashion, chilled me, but I continued.

"And so we helped them. What else were we to do? So you can guess ... our last community had this kind of problem. One day the daughter of one of the elders came to me and I thought she was coming just to deliver some peach butter she'd made, but she came into the kitchen—Brigitte was away, at work—and she began to talk, and to talk, and then things just spilled out, and she told me everything. She was crushed and so ashamed—"

"I can imagine," she said in a dull voice. I was beginning to sense that we were going to encounter the same things in this community. Abigail was altogether too familiar with what I was describing. But I hoped that it was perhaps just something she'd heard about from other communities, idle gossip among the women.

"Well, there I was, stuck. You don't know but it is a law among the English that if someone tells you about ... about such things, you have an obligation to report it to local authorities."

"Did you report it to the *Bishop*?" she asked, wide-eyed.

It pained me to answer her. "No, we ... we didn't ... we couldn't do that. It would have just caused more problems for her. No, dear, what I meant was that there is a law which requires a person who hears such things to go to the English authorities—the outsiders, their police—and tell them what they've heard."

Abigail's eyes widened at that. "That ... that would be difficult."

"No, we didn't report it to anyone but soon enough the elder discovered that we knew and then the next thing was that the elder complained to the Bishop that we were 'interfering' in his home life and claimed that we were not sufficiently in support of the church ... no, how do you say it, not agreeing so much with the community's doctrines."

"You were not *grundsatzen*," she supplied.

"Yes, thank you, we were not *grundsatzen* enough. It wasn't long after that that we were asked to leave by the leadership, and so we came here."

I was about to continue when I heard someone coming down the steps, and we both communicated in an unspoken way that the conversation was, for now, over. My sister appeared at the foot of the stairs wearing her brown dress with a black apron with a white head covering, dressed and ready to begin the day. She was heavier than I, with rounder features, but her hair was still jet black, thick, lustrous, and perfectly arranged. Mine, for reasons not shared, was utterly white, with strands like stragglers flowing out from my head covering like passengers trying to escape from a sinking ship. Brigitte smiled and bid us good morning.

"Do you want some coffee, Brigitte?" I asked, getting up from the table.

"Oh, why yes, Abrielle, thank you. I've got to get my records ready before Jacob takes me in to the clinic this morning. How are you, Abigail?"

"*Gut*, Ma'am."

"So you're going in today?" I asked, setting a saucepan with water on the wood stove for her coffee.

"*Ach yah*," she answered, using Pennsylvania Dutch. She liked to do that frequently, thinking it would help us fit in. "I know the weather might be *baremlich*, but there can be no *rutsching* around today. There are some important appointments that must be kept."

"I am sure the sick people will appreciate it," Abigail replied timidly.

Brigitte looked at me and then at Abigail, who was still churning away on the butter, and in a flash I knew that she intuited we'd been talking. Brigitte always was able to know things with just a little bit of information. Sometimes it was scary.

"Abigail, would you please make sure Jacob includes some extra blankets in the buggy?" she asked.

"*Ach yah*," Abigail said, jumping up and moving quickly through the corridor that led from the kitchen through into the covered area where the family kept the buggies. Brigitte turned to me. I turned to watch the water boil in the saucepan.

"Having a talk with the young lady?" Brigitte asked.

"We were," I said, trying to keep the nervousness from my voice.

"You know why we're here," she said.

"I know," I replied, defensively.

"If he finds us, he'll come after us, do you understand?" she said. "I don't want to lose the boys."

"I *understand*," I said, now slightly angry. "She just wanted to know a little bit about where we came from before here, that's all. Who is she going to tell?" The water was boiling now and I poured it over the ground beans.

"You never know who she'll tell, and that's the problem."

"She's stuck away in a Mennonite community in the middle of the wilderness, Brigitte. I don't really think there's anything to worry about."

She was silent for a moment. "Perhaps," she said. "Just make sure you don't tell her anything that could link us to him. Remember, if anyone asks, I was married to 'Ahmad'—use that name."

"I did," I said. "I did that very thing. I told her your story, or at least the one you want me to tell. I can do that much, you know." For some reason I did not tell her what I had added to the story. Sometimes my courage fails me.

"Good. Make sure you do, please, Abrielle. You know sometimes how you get carried away."

I looked down at the floor with a humility that wasn't feigned. "I ... I know," I said. "I won't ... get carried away, that is."

"Please. Moving again wouldn't be easy, especially now the boys are getting older. They need a steady place, a community where they can put down roots, where they can find girls to marry and start families. I don't want to move again."

I turned and handed her the coffee and debated telling her my suspicions that abuse was occurring here in this community as well, but almost immediately realized I had no hard evidence other than the frightened looks of a cynical young woman, which, strangely, made me angry.

"How long is this going to go on, Brigitte?" I hissed quietly. "There has to be some time where we quit being afraid, quit running. Surely he knows the boys will get too old for him to just take by force, doesn't he?"

Brigitte took the mug from my hand, nodded her thanks perfunctorily, but then gave me a dark, intense look. "Look, Abrielle, you don't understand. Time has no meaning for these people. They don't care how old their children are; they'll always be their *property*. Their father will feel he can do whatever they want with them, whenever he wants. And you know how much those boys need a father. It may be that he won't need to force them; they might just up and go with him on their own. Only God knows what he might promise them." I looked around hastily to see if anyone else was in the kitchen. Brigitte sometimes forgot that the community very much frowned on using God's name in vain.

"So what will we do?" I asked, twisting my fingers together.

"We just keep doing what we're doing," she replied with a confidence I've never known or felt. "I earn us a living as a doctor. You keep working as a nurse at the local hospital. We stay in the community. Here we're just two women with a past no one wants to talk about, about whom no one is interested. They won't come near the plain people, and if they did, everyone is so close-mouthed and wary of outsiders that they won't say a thing. It's a natural place to hide. But if we start advertising our life story," she said, "or if we do something to make these people kick us out," and here she looked hard at me, with words unspoken directing me not to be offering our help to any abuse victims if I could possibly avoid doing so, "sooner or later someone from outside these communities will begin to talk, and he may find us."

We were both standing and leaning against the counter with our arms folded against the chill. "I understand," I said meekly.

She patted my arm. "Good. And thanks for the coffee."

"*De rien.*"

We heard Jacob making his way through the corridor from the buggy barn, Abigail trailing after her younger brother, and as he came into the kitchen, he said politely that the buggy was ready whenever Brigitte was. My sister gave me a quick hug and picked up her records and her black medical bag and went out with Jacob. Abigail stayed in the kitchen. When we heard Jacob snap the reins and the clip-clop of the horses moving down the driveway, Abigail turned to me.

"She frightens me sometimes," she whispered, head down in typical 'shamefaced' posture, trusting in our newfound confidence.

I wanted to dismiss her concerns out of hand, to lay them aside with some trite meaningless confectionary platitude, but instead, the truth slipped out. "*Moi aussi*," I whispered. Eyes still down, she turned her head slightly toward me—she did not speak French—and I explained. "Me too."

***

"What do you do with *that*?" a voice asked me. I just about jumped out of my skin. I wasn't used to talking with strangers and this woman just came right up and asked me a question out of the blue, bold as sin.

"Why ... it's ... it's a potato masher, actually," I stammered.

"You can mash quite a lot of potatoes with that—or you could beat your husband with it, if you didn't have any potatoes." I put what I felt was an appropriate mien of amazed shock at such a suggestion, but she was smiling. She had bright, warm eyes that I liked right away ... but my, wasn't she bold! We meet the strangest people at the Mennonite community's store, I must say. We plain people frequented the store because it was part of our community, but others, from outside—'the English', some call them, even tucked away here in the northern part of America—would also shop there too, because the prices were low and, perhaps, because they thought us 'quaint' and it was some sort of cultural adventure.

"Well, I suppose you could," I answered, automatically agreeing as was my habit, being trained in the plain communities for so long.

"*Alors, battez-vous souvent votre mari, alors?*" she asked in French, surprising me, but pleasing me as well.

"I ... I don't have a husband, and if I did I certainly wouldn't beat him!" I replied, in English, laughing a little. She was quite younger than I by many years. She had long red hair, plaited beautifully, and a little part of me stung with the memory of how my own hair had glistened and flowed down my back, oh, so many years ago—before it was shorn off, sacrificed at the altar of modesty and the plain communities' habit of avoiding any kind of overt beauty or adornment, and certainly to avoid attention being drawn to oneself.

"Oh, my, no," I replied, again not thinking, out of habit conforming to the conversational leading of someone else.

"Beating him once in a while is okay, I suppose," she said, still smiling, nodding her head as though she considered infrequently beating a husband to be something she should think about. She took another large potato masher up in her hand and rotated it as though she was considering purchasing it.

"I ... I actually don't have a husband," I said, still a little unsure of myself.

"You did mention that."

She had a very striking presence, especially as she was wearing what looked like a man's farm coverall and waterproof field boots. In my defense I should say that it was not often one saw such a petite woman with strikingly beautiful hair wearing men's clothes—even at the community store.

"Well," the young woman replied, hefting the masher and whispering softly, "if you get one, these look pretty handy!" It was almost like sharing a secret with someone. Something in her reached out to me, and I could not resist the sense of friendliness I felt from her—and toward her.

I stuck out my hand. "I'm Abrielle," I said. I was never very cautious. I chanced a quick smile.

"Zoe," she answered, clasping my hand in her own. "Zoe Ironbridge."

A man approached and he spoke very slowly to the woman. "Love ... you ... ready?" He was taller than she was, with broad shoulders and a clean-shaven, well-shaped face, a thin waist, wearing a tan-colored chore coat. He wore a ragged brown woolen cap and the same waterproof field boots. He had the most impactful eyes, and as he approached I felt the strangest thing, almost as though I was a spring that had been compressed and was suddenly being freed, a sensation of springing up and out, flying up and out and away ... oh, my the strangest feeling it was. He had his hands full with what looked like bolts and springs and hinges, plus a roll of electric fence wire and two, no three bags of plastic insulators.

"Oh, wait, husband, I just found something else I need." She picked up one of the large potato mashers and winked at me as she joined him.

***

When I got home I put the potato masher in one of the long drawers. I couldn't resist buying it, not after the ... *interesting* exchange it had generated with that very bold, strange, but friendly woman.

As I closed the drawer, smiling, I looked up to see Brigitte coming into the kitchen from the garage, and the look on her face cleaned the smile from my own.

"What it is?" I asked, seeing clearly that she was upset.

"I am not going to be pushed out of another community because a straw-brained woman can't keep her mouth shut," she said.

I gasped. "What do you mean? What happened?"

Brigitte stopped and turned to me. She looked toward the garage and then back toward the other kitchen door. No one was around. She shook her head angrily. "Sit," she said, and pulled out a kitchen chair. I did so.

"Naomi has a broken arm," she said.

"How did it happen? Did she fall? Naomi is, remind me?" I cast about in my memory, trying to recall who Naomi was. I didn't have the mind my sister had for such things.

"Derek Yoder's wife," she said brusquely, but I could tell she wasn't angry with me—yet.

"Right, right, of course. She has, what, five, no, six children?"

"Six."

"What was she doing, chasing one of them up a tree?" I asked, trying to be humorous, not wanting to face what probably did in fact happen.

"He broke her arm, that's what happened," she snapped grimly. "It doesn't happen often but it happens sometimes, you know it does."

"What happened though, I mean, how—"

"Derek was taking a strap to one of the horses, like he always does, and the animal was screaming its guts out, like it always does, and when Naomi saw him draw blood, she came out of the house like a bullet—or so Luke says—and came at him screaming and yelling."

"That doesn't sound ... quite right."

"No it doesn't, but we don't really see what goes on inside most families, do we?" she replied.

"Luke is their oldest?"

"Yeah, he's fifteen, and Luke got to watch his father turn the strap on his mother, but unfortunately the buckle was still on the strap—the big metal buckle—and it snapped her left humerus like a dry twig."

"Oh, oh no," I cried, my hands flying to my face. "Not ... not again, not here too?"

Brigitte looked at me, ducking her head to appear even more secretive than we had to, with anger in her face. "Where *isn't* it?" she hissed furiously. "Tell me, where is there a place in the world where men don't think they can beat their women like their horses?"

I was distraught, and then caught myself. "But ... but where is she?" I stood up. "I'll get my bag, and—"

"You sit right down again," Brigitte said. "You're not going anywhere. Neither am I."

"But ... but what about Naomi?"

"Naomi can learn to keep her mouth shut when her husband has a whip in his hand," she said with a bitterness I hadn't heard in a long, long time.

"Brigitte," I said in a shocked whisper, "you can't leave her where she is. How did you ... how did you find out?"

Brigitte ground her hands together on the table. "Luke was just here; you missed him by five minutes."

"What ... what did you tell him?"

She looked down again at her hands. "I told him that I couldn't help him, and that he needed to call the hospital in town."

I sat back, stunned. "Brigitte ... you know they won't do that."

"I don't know what they'll do," Brigitte said, "but I do know this, little sister. If we get in the habit of fixing every woman's issues in this community, sooner or later we'll end up in another black buggy with our bags and baggage trailing behind us, looking for just another plain community that might be willing to take in a couple of trouble-making *schnickelfritz* women with boys who need wives."

"Brigitte, you *can't* do this."

She looked hard at me, and she spoke words at me like gunshots. "My children need their own lives, a place where they can grow up around other people, *sane* people, where they are not afraid of being kidnapped, where they can have some expectation of a real future with wives and children of their own. So yes, Abrielle, I *can* do this."

I stood then. "You call this sane? Sane people don't beat their women like horses. If you can't help Naomi, I can. I have my bag, and I—"

"You won't go anywhere, little sister. *Sit down.*"

"Brigitte, I have to—"

"You don't have to do anything. You *won't* do anything; now, I'm telling you, sit *down*. If you interfere, they'll toss us both out, you know that. It happened in Ohio, and it happened twice in Illinois. What needs to happen before you learn? Do they need to maybe take us out back and strip us and whip us against a post? Yeah, we saw that in Pennsylvania, didn't we, at the same place that nice old man spent a lot of time visiting with the little girls in the community, no matter what their parents said. No place is perfect, Abrielle, and we've chosen to live in the plain communities, and we chose to live by their rules. And these are *my* children, Abrielle, not yours."

I was distraught, and I knew she was right about her children needing a steady, solid place to grow up; they couldn't be tumbleweeds all their lives. "But we can't let this be, Brigitte," I said meekly. "What about Naomi?"

"She should have thought of things like this before she started yelling at her husband in front of his oldest son," she replied. "Listen," she said, with a cutting edge to her voice, "you leave it, do you understand me? You *will* let it lie ... just leave it. If they take her to the emergency room, she'll get the help she needs. The pain will do her good."

God forgive me ... but I sat down. My sister always knew what was right and she had protected us so far. But it was the strangest thing ... as I sat down, I had the oddest impression that the young woman with the long red hair was looking at me with sad, disappointed eyes.

***

I went to sleep that night and had the most frightening dream I can remember, besides the one I had after my husband tried to kill me—but that is another story. The dream I had that night was so strange, I couldn't understand it, but I couldn't forget it either. It wasn't frightening in itself, but I woke up terrified, shouting, but not knowing what had frightened me. I sat up against my small headboard, sweat on my brow under the sleeping bonnet, and I recalled the dream in every detail. I couldn't forget it, it was so clear. I couldn't get back to sleep. I didn't know what else to do, so I began to pray. I always pray when I wake up in the middle of the night. I struggle to sleep well; it's a problem for me, ever since ... well, again, another story. And so I prayed, and the thought came into my mind to ask God to interpret the dream for me, but everything I'd been taught in the Anabaptist communities told me that such dreams were nothing, and that God did not speak to men in such ways. It bothered me; I felt the dream was from God, but I had to fight against so many years of teaching to the contrary, and besides, I had no idea what it meant.

The next morning I woke early and was out of the house before Brigitte began her day. She had taken the late night shift the night before at the hospital, and my Emergency Room shift was, thankfully, early this morning. I don't think I could have faced her after last night's confrontation about Naomi. I walked the mile in the dark to the bus stop and took the bus to the clinic, arriving just in time to begin my shift. I was a nurse, and fortunately the clinic's Director didn't mind me working in my plainclothes garb, even though I wore a lab coat over my dress. He said it seemed to calm some of the patients. I suppose that was nice. For sanitary reasons, I didn't wear my apron or my bonnet, though I usually did keep a headscarf on.

I checked the emergency room log to see if a Naomi Yoder had checked in as a patient, and as I had feared, there was no entry at all for anyone named either Naomi or Yoder. I thought for a moment of checking via the Granite Sky hospital intranet with the other hospitals in town, but I knew that if she hadn't come here, she wouldn't have gone anywhere else. I grieved for the woman who was most certainly in a great amount of pain, and I couldn't understand what my sister was thinking about, to be so callous. But again, I didn't have children of my own, so maybe there were things hidden from me, things I didn't understand. Yet it was still upsetting to think about the poor woman, and the shift wore on like ground glass in my heart. And my dream sat like a stone in my memory as well, because even though I didn't understand it, I had a sense that there was some sort of dark portent associated with it. Or, maybe I was just acting like a scared rabbit, which happened to be my sister's pet name for me. "*Lapin peur*" she would call me, in French.

I came out to the administration desk to file some medical records when I looked up to see the same tall, red-haired woman I'd seen in the store with the potato masher, staring me in the face, holding one hand in another with a large towel wrapped around everything. It gave me a start, for the first thing I thought of, seeing her eyes, was the sense of disappointment I'd sensed in them last night. The same man was standing next to her.

It couldn't be that she was here to see me. "You're not ..."

"No, I'm not here to see you, but I *am* glad you're here," she said. I could see she was in some pain. "Cow," she said, in reply to my raised eyebrow, holding up her arm. "Husband," she said, tilting her head in the man's direction.

The man did the strangest thing. He held up one of those electronic tablets for me to read. *Mace Ironbridge; Zoe's husband; left potato masher at home.* I laughed involuntarily, and my hand flew to cover my mouth. And there again came that strange feeling of being a spring unleashed, flying out ... somewhere.

"Is there some place we can sit down?" the woman asked. I could see she was in pain.

"Oh, oh, yes, I'm sorry, please, come this way." She was in luck; there were no other patients in the Emergency Room that morning—understandable, as it was only around six or so—6:17, to be precise, as I noted on her admissions chart—and one of the assistants soon had Zoe in a wheelchair. I wheeled her into one of the examining rooms myself and took her vital signs. I could see she was in pain, and coming from my experience the night prior, I looked askance at Mr. Ironbridge.

"Unwrap the towel, Mace," she said, and her husband gingerly unwrapped the pale green bath towel. "We use it in the barn for necessities," she explained, as the husband handed me the towel. As the towel came off I saw the clear imprint of a hoof on the arm of her coverall—the same coverall I'd seen her in at the community's store, actually. For some reason it released a weight I hadn't known was on my heart, and I barely stifled a sob. The husband glanced at me piercingly, but Zoe met my eye and had the understanding not to mention it.

"We'll need to get that coverall off and then I can wash that arm," I said, trying to shake the overwashing memory of Naomi Yoder with a broken arm ... and here was this strange woman I'd just met the other day, in my clinic with, possibly, the same problem, though clearly not for the same reason.

I was cleaning her arm as gently as I could—from what I could tell, it didn't look broken, though we were going to x-ray it to be sure—when she smiled over at me and said, "I shouldn't have picked up that potato masher, hey?" She couldn't have known how those words would have affected me, and she surely didn't know what had happened to Naomi Yoder yesterday, and even though she meant to lighten the atmosphere, I couldn't restrain the tears. I kept swabbing the same spot on her arm as tears fell on the sleeves of my lab coat.

"That's pretty good there, I'm thinking."

"Oh ... oh, right, yes, I'm sorry. Here, let's turn your arm over, and—"

"Abrielle, what's wrong?" She put her other hand on mine. The touch, a human touch, something I hadn't had in, oh so many years, crushed what restraint I had left.

I dropped my head from aching grief over so many lost years and sobbed for a moment, but then lifted it up, remembering my responsibilities, trying to drain the tears without using my hands, as both of them were cleaning her arm.

"I'm ... I'm very sorry, but, really ... it's nothing, it's ..."

"Thou shalt not bear false witness," said the man in his soft voice, no hesitation, no pausing, strangely. He was by his wife's side as she sat on the treatment table. He said it softly, though, understanding where my emotions were, and, I sensed, he understood the conventions that constrained those of us in the plain communities.

I took a deep breath. "I ... I can't ... I mean, I'm not at liberty to share ... to say anything about it," I said, between short gasps for air.

"Well, okay then, we won't pry," Zoe answered quietly. She and her husband remained silent as I prepped her for the x-ray. The duty physician came in, a very competent doctor from Sri Lanka, and took Zoe into the x-ray lab. Minutes went by while her husband waited outside the lab door and I began to fill out the paperwork we'd need to complete for her visit.

The emergency room physician finished with Zoe, and it turned out that she did have a hairline fracture of her radius. The doctor and I took her into the casting room and we wrapped her arm first with an ace bandage and then put a plaster cast on, from her wrist to her elbow.

The doctor left while she waited in the casting room for the plaster to dry, and her husband went outside to complete some of the insurance paperwork. I was left alone with her for a moment, and she looked up and I could tell she wanted to help me, and it had been so, so long since I'd confided in anyone. I couldn't stand it.

"There was something," I began, frightened but desperate to talk to someone. She looked calm and peaceful and ready to listen, and so I said, "There was a dream I had last night, and it has upset me for some reason. I don't know what it means, and, oh, my, wait, I'm sorry, I don't even know if you believe in such things."

"Abrielle, we read the same Bible, and from what we read, God still speaks to His children in dreams occasionally. He said He would do so more frequently in the last days, as you remember."

I didn't recall that part of the Scripture—honestly, one of the great secrets about the plain communities was that most of us really don't know much about the Bible. We have our standard memory verses, true, and we know the verses that our various sects and divisions use to hammer home the community's particular *Ordnung*—the rules that govern the community—but wherever I'd been, I've noticed that not many could call much else of the Word to mind. But I was glad to hear this woman was at least open to what I had to say.

"Can you remember it?" she asked.

"Oh yes," I replied, "I can remember every detail like, like it just happened a few minutes ago. I have no idea what it means but ... but after I awoke, it just gave me a bad feeling, like something, I can't explain it, it just ... I don't know ... it was strange. Maybe that's why I'm so," I fluttered my hands toward my face, "so emotional."

"Do you want an interpretation?" she asked. Of all things, that wasn't what I was expecting to hear.

"What? What do you mean?"

"Would you like to know what the dream means?"

"Well, yes, but I ... I didn't think such things were ... well, you know—"

"You mean you aren't sure such things happen today."

"Yes, to put it bluntly. That is what I mean." Outsiders sometimes had a way of conversing that left much to be desired—but they did get their point across.

She looked at me and smiled, almost sadly. "Well, Abrielle, I've been sitting here wondering why God let that sweet old cow we have up and break my arm this morning. She's never done anything like that before, and we've had her for eight years. But now I know why that happened."

I looked at her, completely confused. She went on.

"I'm here for *you.* I'm not too familiar with Anabaptist doctrine, Abrielle, but I know that most Anabaptists don't believe that the Holy Spirit is still active in the body of believers today. Yet from what we read in the Bible, there is nothing that indicates that the gifts and activities of the Holy Spirit have stopped. Jesus said, *'I will send you the Comforter, and He will be with you forever.'* I sort of think Jesus meant 'forever' when He said 'forever'."

"Oh," I said, not ever having thought about before. Sitting there, I was overwhelmed with the striking thought that there was quite a bit of Scripture I hadn't really given much thought to before. I'd simply let the community I was in at the time dictate my spiritual walk—the rules I obeyed, the clothes I wore, the people I spoke with, the parts of the Bible I became familiar with, how I worshipped—everything.

"So, one of the things about the gifts of the Holy Spirit is that they're given so that His body can be strengthened, edified ... you know ... built up."

"Yes, that would make sense."

"Mace tells me that too many people have made a circus out of the Holy Spirit and the gifts He provides, but truthfully, they do still exist and operate and God still uses them to strengthen His children. And the funny thing is," she said, "Mace, my husband—he's the guy who happens to be sitting outside at the moment—also happens to have the gift of interpreting dreams. So I'll ask you again, would you like an interpretation of your dream?"

I blinked at her, amazed at the coincidence that she would come into the ER this morning with the same injury Naomi Yoder had—at least similar enough to call it to my mind and to have my emotions triggered, and now she was telling me her husband could interpret my dream.

She seemed to be able to read my mind. "There are no coincidences in the life of Believers, Abrielle."

"Oh," I said, taking a deep breath; I was the *lapin peur*, after all. "Well, okay," I said timidly.

"You sure? This isn't something you should feel pressured about."

Actually I felt just the opposite. I *wanted* to know, if it was possible to know, what that dream meant. I know God talked to people, no matter what the Anabaptists said, because it said so in the Bible, but ... but He just had never talked to *me* before. And if it was possible that He *was* talking to me, then I certainly wanted to know what He was saying.

"No, no, please, absolutely, yes, I mean, if you think he—"

"Mace; his name is Mace."

"Right, if you think Mace could make anything of it."

"Why don't you call him in here?" She held up her casted arm. "This thing is still a bit sticky."

"Oh, right, just ... just wait here, I'll get him." I lifted both hands, gesturing for her to say put, which she was going to do anyway, and I darted out the door, more desperate than I had thought myself to be, hoping her husband hadn't decided to wait in the car.

I looked at the registration desk, and he wasn't there, and I was about to run out to the parking lot when I remembered I wouldn't know what kind of car to look for, so I turned back to the casting room, and there he was, sitting in a chair just outside the door.

I'd run right past him. I was in a bad way.

"Sir, I wonder, could you, I mean, Mace, right, Mace ... could you come in for a few moments?"

I could tell Mace knew I was flustered but he was kind enough not to mention anything about it, and he just stood and followed me into the small room. There was just enough space for the three of us, plus a long table and some chairs, plus the machinery that made the casts and molds.

Zoe spoke up right away. "Mace, this woman has had a dream and she would like to know if you could provide an interpretation for it."

"Can't," he said flatly. I surprised myself at how disappointed I was. "God can," he went on.

"Very funny," Zoe said, "the first twenty-five times I heard it. Sorry, Abrielle. He tends to be pretty serious about that."

I looked from one to the other. I wasn't sure what they were saying.

"He's trying to tell you that the interpretation, if it comes, comes from God, not from him. Now, Abrielle, here, just sit down," Zoe said, pointing to the only empty chair in the room. "Now, Mace, please."

Mace's voice was softer than I recalled from the store, as though he knew I'd be nervous. And again, his words weren't hesitant or stumbling; he was speaking normally. "Abrielle, the way it works is that if God wants the interpretation given, He'll give it to me as I hear the dream. The meaning just sort of unfolds in my mind. If it happens that way as you tell me your dream, I'll give you the interpretation. If God does not reveal anything to me, I'll tell you that too. Okay?"

"Okay," I said, a little nervous but more eager than I thought I would be in such circumstances. This was very definitely far, far outside the norm for anyone living their lives by Anabaptist doctrine. I sat, twisting the edge of my lab coat in my hands.

"So ... tell Mace your dream, Abrielle," Zoe prompted, after a few seconds.

"Oh, right, sorry. So," I began, composing myself, remembering. "In my dream, there was a cart pulled by two horses, much like what many of the communities have; these two were large draft horses. The horses pulling the cart were dappled white with pale gray manes, and it was like I was watching the cart move from a distance, but I was also on the cart. I don't know if that makes any sense."

"You're fine, go on," Mace said. As I began to describe the dream to him, that feeling of being 'unleashed', of flying out, of launching away from something, became more intense.

"So the cart was moving along a small road and then one of the horses pulled away from the other, or tried to, and then the other horse pulled that horse back, but then it was like another horse, almost a shadow horse, came out of the one that had tried to pull away, and suddenly there were two carts, each pulled by one horse, but the horse that pulled away changed from being a shadow horse to almost pure white, I mean, *really* white, almost too bright to look at. Then I looked back at the first cart and there were two horses again, the same colors as before, only the cart was coming to a cliff and I yelled and yelled but they just kept going along and they went over the cliff. Then I woke up."

Zoe's husband sat there with a strange look on his face for just a moment, and then said, "Okay, so, yeah, I think I can tell you what your dream means, although you have to keep in mind, Abrielle, that I don't know anything about your life, so I don't know what God is trying to tell you with it. You will have to figure that out."

"I understand," I said, very nervous, feeling more like a compressed spring now than ever.

"You said that you felt you were both watching the cart and on it at the same time," he began.

"That's right."

"The cart is your life. You are watching your life and you are living it at the same time."

"Oh, oh ... of course. That's obvious; I should have known that."

Zoe spoke up. "See, man oh man, I say that all the time, don't let it bother you. Dreams I get are like that, and whenever Mace give me the interpretation, I usually smack my forehead and say, 'Well duh, that's so obvious,' but until the Spirit gives the interpretation, it isn't."

I sat and listened and wondered how these two people had learned such things.

"The rest of your dream is the important part." Mace continued. "So ... your life is moving along, and if I am getting the interpretation correctly, you or your life is tethered or harnessed to someone or something else. You are coming up to a point where a decision will need to be made. You will either separate from this other person or thing that you are harnessed to, or you won't. It will be up to you."

I sat there, stunned, knowing beyond a shadow of a doubt that I was hearing from the Spirit of God directly, through the gift of the Holy Spirit given to this man. I began to understand what Zoe had meant when she said that the gifts were given to build up the body of Christ. I felt so ... so encouraged, so amazed, that God was actually talking directly to me, that He was actually directly involving Himself in my life. Oh, it was so overwhelming, I can't tell you.

"The colors of the horses are important," Mace said, with more. "If you don't break away from whatever it is you're tethered to, or whoever it is you're tethered to, you will continue in the same path you are currently on, but ... remember that the horses on the first cart were dappled, with pale gray manes. These are the colors of death, Abrielle. If you continue on the path, tethered as you are, it will lead to death. This is why, when you looked back at the first cart, it was two horses again, going over the cliff."

I was completely unaware that my eyes were filling with tears—I was so confused. I didn't know if they were tears of joy, that God was talking to me, or tears of fear, because I *knew* what—or rather *who*—I was tethered to, and I was terrified, because I wasn't sure I had the power to pull away from her, as this man sitting here speaking God's words to me said I must, if the dream was true.

Mace continued. "If you do break way from whatever it is you're tied to, then the dream seems to indicate that you'll be healthy, spiritually, as those in Revelation were clothed in white, well. Going in that different direction is probably what God is trying to tell you to do. I don't know what that means where you are in your life right now, though."

"Abrielle, when you get a correct interpretation, God's Spirit will testify to your spirit, and you'll just know." Zoe somehow knew that I needed that confirmation, because I sensed strongly that the interpretation I'd been given was from God. It frightened me, but I *knew* it was from Him. Besides this strong conviction I had, there was no way Mace or Zoe could have known such details about my life, about how I had been harnessed to my sister for years, going where she goes, doing what she tells me to do no matter what.

She'd always been the strong one, the courageous one, the one making the decisions for the two of us, and me, the little *lapin peur*, just went along. There wasn't any way the Ironbridges could have known this. It was from God, no question, no doubt.

"A very wise man once wrote that God is good but not safe," Mace said, as though he could read my mind, aware of my fears. "There are times when God will ask us to do hard things, but He will be with us when we need to do them. And for Him to give you this dream—well, He's telling you that you can trust that He'll be with you, in whatever decision it is you have to make. I sense too that the decision point is coming upon you shortly. The only thing we can say to you is that we hope you'll make that decision to break away from whatever it is you're tied to. It will be death for you if you don't." He said it with grim seriousness, solid and sure, but caring.

"I understand, Mace," I said, "and I thank you, and I thank God for what He's told me." I was unabashedly crying, not worried about what Zoe or Mace thought of my display of emotion. This would never have happened in the community, I can tell you. No one wants to show emotion. I suppose because no one wants to be vulnerable, and I suppose that's because there is so little trust; I don't know, maybe I'm mistaken.

The time in the casting room that morning, with those two people, almost total strangers, was the most spiritually therapeutic time I'd had in, well, forever. Finally, for the first time in my life, I *knew* without question that God was involving Himself in my life. It was an experience with the Living God, resulting in *experiential* knowledge of the Most High, and suddenly what Job said came to mind, after God finished setting His case before him: *"I heard about you with the hearing of my ears, but now I see you with my eyes, and I abhor myself, and repent in dust and ashes."* Everything changes when we actually *see* God, or experience His hand in our lives. Everything changed for me in that room—*everything*. My faith, my awareness of God's presence, my appreciation for Him, my conviction that He exists and that He is involved in His children's lives, everything became *real*—it wasn't any longer just something I read about, or listened to someone read about or talk about, but now I *knew* the Great King of all Creation was actively touching my life in a way that left me no doubt that I'd had a definable experience with Him. And I found myself wanting more—more of Him.

As I thought about it, my Anabaptist training kicked in and I cautioned myself against any over-emotional reactions. I sought to call to mind others in the Bible who might have had such an experiential knowledge of God, testing things by measuring them against Scripture, and as I called to mind one person, then another, then another, the realization broke upon me that most of the people we revered in Scripture, most of the people who were central actors in the Bible stories we knew and loved and loved to tell to the children—oh my goodness, *all* of them had experiences with God; they had an experiential knowledge of Him. They knew about Him through the 'seeing of their eyes', not only with the hearing of their ears. From Adam, to Moses, to Samuel and David, Isaiah, Jeremiah, the prophets, through to the apostles, to John the Revelator, all of them had interacted in some real way with God, had heard from Him or spoken to Him in some way, clearly, in some cases face to face, the way a man speaks with his friend. They *knew* Him, they didn't just know *about* Him. Oh, oh, this was so *different*; this was so much richer, so much *more* than what I ever thought the Christian life could be.

All of this washed over me in less time than it takes to tell, and as I sat there in the casting room with those two people, God gave me such a love for them that I couldn't bear it. I turned to Zoe and embraced her. She did the best she could to hug me with one arm, but it was enough. I don't think I've hugged a person in, oh, almost ten years or so. I was trembling with emotion and the overwhelming awareness of God's involvement in my life. Zoe just held me. I think she knew what I was feeling.

"Your life will change now, if you let it," she said quietly.

I looked up at her. "Oh, Zoe, I want it to change. I don't ever want to lose what I feel now. Never." I said the words with as much ferocity and intensity as I could muster.

"That's good," Mace said, putting his hand on my shoulder. "But you will need to be strong, because now is when the enemy will really begin to oppose your walk with God."

I turned to face Zoe's husband. "Enemy?" I said. "What enemy?"

***

I met Mace and Zoe later that day for lunch at one of the smaller restaurants in town after my shift ended. Zoe, mostly, explained to me about the spiritual warfare that swirled throughout the unseen realms around us, every day, everywhere. Along with a disdain for the workings of the Holy Spirit, Anabaptist doctrine also failed to discuss or teach how the enemy of mankind works, and our first discussion at Walter's, over a chicken pot pie and a hot chocolate, was eye-opening. And I began to recall, oh, so many times when I would form a conviction in my heart about something I just knew God wanted me to do, but then Brigitte would make a comment or even just her proximity would, in the strangest way, wipe that conviction from my mind, as though I had some form of temporary memory loss.

"I have to ask you something," I said, interrupting. "This is important, I have to know."

They both waited patiently for me. The man, Mace, was unlike any I'd encountered in the plain communities. He would speak to me as though he thought I was his equal, as though my opinions about what he was sharing would matter. And of course there was that strange sense I would get whenever he was around of being like a spring, compressed, ready to uncoil into ... I didn't know what.

"There was a time," I started, "about eight years ago. Things were very tense between Brigitte and I. You see, I was essentially raising her children while she carried on with her practice, but oh, things were difficult. Finally I'd had enough and I was in my room packing, deaf to Brigitte's strident remonstrations with me. Oh, she pleaded and then counseled and then threatened and then yelled, and nothing worked. So I went on packing.

"As my bags and things were finally secured in two bags and a trunk, I was about ready to get on the phone and call a cab when a line of black buggies from the community came trotting up our driveway. As I looked through the window, there was this horribly dark sense of being pressed down, of fear, and pure terror, and I began to tremble. You see, Brigitte had called the elders in the community. I don't know what she told them but they must have started a call tree or rung the bell or did whatever it was they do to gather the leadership, because they all appeared at our door that day, dressed meticulously as though they were going to church. The women came, shamefaced, following behind the men, but with eyes darting, searching for me, piercing, questioning, accusing. I felt so condemned. I felt trapped as the elders sat in our tiny living room and talked in their roundabout way about how I was being selfish, leaving my sister, wanting a life of my own centered on wanton pleasure and selfishness—so they assumed. This desire to leave was most certainly not from God, they said. And throughout this entire time, I sat on my little chair in the corner, face turned to the floor, bonnet covering my flaming ears, feeling an unbearably dark, heavy presence suffusing the room. Oh, it was ... it was terrible. Is this what you're talking about?

Mace looked at Zoe and then back at me. "You've already seen what it can do," he said quietly. "You've felt their power. You stayed, didn't you?"

I looked down at my hands. "I did. I'm not proud of staying, but I wish you could believe me when I tell you that I was utterly convinced that if I'd left that day, I would have been killed in some horrible way."

"Yeah, that's oppression," Zoe said. She put out her hand and took mine. "But that doesn't have to continue. You can be free of that evil. You can be free of it."

As I listened to them both, a glowing flame of confidence was growing in my heart. Nothing could dissuade me now. Every time they mentioned something about how Satan or his minions worked, or how they were arrayed in the world, or some of their methods, I would think back, like falling back into a peaceful room, to the fact that God was involving Himself in my life. Oh, I cannot tell you, when you experience God working in your life—I mean *experience* Him, not just read about Him or hear about Him or be told about Him, no—you move beyond intellectual discussions and into the realm of *knowing*. Such a calm peace He gives! The little *lapin peur* sat there at Walter's, listening to all manner of Satan's machinations, and just rested quietly in the knowledge that if God was working in my life, everything would be okay. Soon Mace and Zoe could see where I was, and they looked at each other knowingly.

"So, Abrielle, along with knowing now that God does exist, and that He is actively and directly involved in your life, one of the first things you specifically want to make sure you do is to commit to obeying Him. He said, 'If you love me, you'll obey me,' remember?"

"Yes, I know that Scripture," I replied. "But how do you know what, or when, He is asking you to do something?"

"This is the sum and substance of the Christian life," Zoe said, "just learning how to talk with Him and hear Him when He speaks with us, and then building the trust and courage to go do what He has told us to do."

I sat there for a moment, casting about in my mind for any memory of God ever talking to me before, wondering how I would ever learn to hear the supernatural voice of God. I looked at Zoe and saw her newly casted arm, and suddenly was struck with a very clear answer.

"Can you drive me someplace?" I asked.

They looked at each other and nodded. "Sure. Do you need us to drive you home?"

"No," I answered, standing up. "And we have to go now."

***

Naomi Yoder's home was a large, square, unattractive farmhouse sided with tan vinyl and a dark maroon tin roof surrounded by a porch. When we drove up into the yard, one of the buggies was tied to the post, and I could see another large horse tied to a rail behind their barn, with their flock of sheep nosing up into the shelter for the afternoon feeding. A thin cow was standing among the sheep, but no one was in sight.

On the way over, I explained what had happened to Naomi, and why my sister didn't want to intervene. Mace and Zoe listened, Mace looking grim. We got out of the car and I went up to the door and knocked, hard. One of Naomi's daughters came to the door.

"Hello, sweetie. Is your Momma home?" I could tell the young girl was confused. Maybe five or six years old, she was looking at one woman dressed like the people in her community, and two outsiders. I didn't know if she remembered me or not, and here I was, speaking English instead of her own language.

"My Daddy is home. Mommy is sleeping. *Wilkommen* ... would you like to come in?" she said, in a mixture of passable English and Deutsch, with precise manners. The children were all raised to have meticulous manners. She opened the door wider and the three of us went into the Yoder's kitchen.

"Can I help you?"

Derek Yoder came out of a hallway from the back of the house. He was a short, stocky man with broad shoulders and a growing belly.

"We're here to see Naomi, if that is acceptable," I said. I knew the scene we presented. I wanted to be as non-confrontational as possible.

"Well, she's sleeping now, like Sarah has said." His English was tinged with the typical Deutsch accent, with flat, drawn-out vowels one gets with the mixture of German and English. He was wiping his hands on a towel.

"Mr. Yoder, you can let us see her or you can let the local Sheriff examine her." Mace spoke from over my shoulder, and it gave me strength. I risked a glance at him and he seemed composed and sure of himself, but somehow coiled and ominous.

Yoder suddenly looked torn, as though he was debating something within himself. He ground his hands in the towel and looked down at the planked floor. I could see him trembling. "Sarah, I want you to go upstairs now, and keep the other little ones in their rooms."

The little girl said "Yes Poppa," and raced up the wide staircase. Yoder extended a hand toward the kitchen table, a large wooden rectangle with two long benches on each side. "Sit down, please." When Ironbridge didn't move, Yoder said, in almost a tone of surrender, "I'll get her." He turned to go back down the hallway and then stopped. "I didn't mean to hurt her," he said, not meeting our eyes.

"Many times that's true," Mace growled, not conceding any moral ground, and nodded his head in the direction of the hallway. In place of that strange springing sensation, there was instead inside me a feeling of a gathering storm, of something boiling up in fierce but controlled anger. It disoriented me for a moment.

Yoder was gone for just a few minutes and then returned with Naomi on his arm. She was a pencil-thin woman with a long, drawn, pale face under a white sleeping bonnet and a nightgown. Her left arm was wrapped in a feed sack. They had tried a poultice for the pain. From the look on her face, it wasn't working.

"The nurse is here," Yoder said in Deutsch to his wife.

"*Wilkommen*," she said weakly, looking up at me. She saw the Ironbridges, two people she did not know, and clutched the neck of her high-necked nightgown with her good hand.

"We're here to look at your arm," I said, transitioning to Deutsch. "These people gave me a ride." Her eyes widened in fear, and she looked at her husband, who would not, or could not, meet her eyes; it was impossible to tell.

"Come, now, sit in the chair there and let me look at it. We know all about what happened and I am just here to see to your arm, Naomi." I tried to speak as reassuringly as I could, but the fear in which women lived in the community—in most communities I'd lived in, actually—was palpable. She was beginning to shake, and I was not sure if it was from her injury or her fear of what her husband would do to her once we left. And then I too felt that tangible fear that crept over me every time Brigitte was nearby and upset with me for something. Yoder sat there like a statue, but I sensed there a smoldering darkness.

This community of Mennonites, like every other Anabaptist community we'd lived in, strongly emphasized non-resistance and pacifism, as it was a central Anabaptist doctrine, and so there was no fear Yoder would get violent—at least towards us—but they had their ways. After Mace and Zoe's discussion with me about spiritual warfare and the power of darkness and that power had made itself evident, I wondered at what was happening here, in this very kitchen, so soon after that discussion.

"So are you a representative of the law?" he asked Mace directly after he helped Naomi to sit in one of the two rocking chairs. This was his way of challenging Ironbridge's presence in his house.

"I'm providing this health professional transportation so she can examine a reported injury to your wife's arm," Ironbridge said, nodding toward me as I was gingerly attempting to unwrap the feed sack. As the sack came off I could see the distension under the skin. The bone was out of place and if it wasn't set, she would lose the use of her arm permanently. I had feared this. The longer they went without treatment, the harder it would be to set the arm. This was almost impossible to do correctly at home, even though Brigitte and I have done many things in a home setting that one wouldn't think possible. The problem wasn't extending the arm—we could do that with carefully placed straps, and I know the Yoders would have those. It was the pain caused by pulling the bones into alignment, and ... and I was nervous about putting Naomi through that. At the Emergency Room, they would give her something to dull the pain. I looked up at Derek Yoder and carefully scanned his face.

"Her bone is broken, Mr. Yoder. If we don't reset it, she'll lose the use of her arm permanently."

"Yah, I understand," he replied in Deutsch, nodding and asking, "What must we do?"

"We need to take her in to the hospital," I said, watching his reaction.

He nodded and pulled on his beard. "Yah, so ... and what will they do there that you can't do here?"

"Your wife is in quite a bit of pain," I replied. "When we pull on her arm to reset the bone, we're going to be moving it around to make sure it resets properly. This will be very, very painful."

"Waaaeeell," he answered, drawing out the word in the way the plain people do to indicate they are not quite in agreement with what you are suggesting, "she's had six children, you know. She is okay with pain."

I felt a tap on my shoulder, and Zoe leaned close to my ear and whispered, "Could it be that we should be asking Naomi what she wants?"

"Yes, waaeell, maybe," I said, hearing myself drawing out the words in the same way, "but that isn't how they live. The wife doesn't have much say when it comes to dealing with outside things. At the least I'm thinking they will have to ask the Bishop."

"And how long will that take?"

"Too long," I replied. I turned to Mr. Yoder. "Sir, we need to take your wife into the hospital immediately, or she'll lose the use of her arm without major corrective surgery, and I know you don't want that."

I could see Yoder hesitating between wanting to minimize his wife's pain and measuring the consequences he would suffer for letting this situation get so out of hand that outside authorities might have occasion to look into the community's affairs. Such an event was almost the worst sin one could commit in the plain communities. They wanted to remain accountable only to themselves, and while that was a laudable goal, I saw where it left those who found themselves at the mercy of those in authority within each community.

"Tell me, Mr. Yoder, is your wife worth more than one of those sheep you have outside?"

Mr. Yoder's head snapped around to look directly at Mace. "Well of course she is," he replied.

"Then if Jesus tells us that we should pull one of our sheep out of a well on the Sabbath, shouldn't you extend at least the same courtesy to helping your wife here?"

"Well, it's not the Sabbath today, and I don't think that really—"

"The point isn't what day it is, but that Jesus expected compassion to override man-made religious rules," Ironbridge replied, with no little asperity. I think I would have just punched the man, but Mace went on with grim determination. "And if Jesus expected the people of his day to have compassion for an animal sufficient to break their man-made ordnung about the Sabbath, don't you think He would expect you to have at least as much compassion for you to transcend your community rule about using outside help?"

Yoder pulled on his beard at this, deliberating about what Mace had said. I began to worry that he would launch into a long Scriptural debate about the doctrinal applications of the example Ironbridge had used. We would be here most of the day.

"Yah, well, okay, I can see that," he said, in a way that the plain communities use to indicate that they found what was proposed to be acceptable. I was astounded, but didn't waste any time.

"Mr. Yoder, I need a clean towel please, and let's get your wife's coat. We need to leave right away."

"Oh, oh, I need to get dressed," Naomi said.

"Nonsense," I replied. "We'll just take it all off again at the hospital and give you a robe that isn't half as nice as what you have on now. You just need a coat; it's quite cold. Now, Mr. Yoder, about that towel?"

***

We got Naomi Yoder to the hospital in the next hour, and I don't know what Naomi told the staff about how she'd been injured, and I didn't ask. We brought her in in a wheelchair and the duty physician—the same one that had treated Zoe's arm earlier that morning—did the x-ray and saw the displaced radius and expressed some curiosity about the amount of swelling around the fracture. It had been almost 24 hours since the injury, but it seemed that he could tell that. It also seemed that he didn't ask as many questions as he normally would about such an injury. I've seen this before, where outsiders tend to accept the idea that the plain communities can live the way they want to live and leave them be more than they would 'normal' folk. In many ways the plain people appreciate that extra level of forbearance, but it can wreak havoc on the innocent community victims of physical and sexual abuse, of which there were too many in places allegedly based upon God's Word.

The physician gave Naomi sufficient medication to keep her oblivious to the pain before he manipulated the fracture. As the meds took effect we could see her features finally relax, the lines across her forehead ease, and her trembling stopped. The doctor was very gentle and respectful and gave her husband directions on how he wanted the arm positioned. She laid back on the hospital bed and the doctor put a steel-mesh netting over each of the fingers on her left hand.

"Pretty glove," Naomi said, completely out of it, as she looked at the wire meshing that would seize her hand and help the doctor apply the amount of pressure needed to realign the bone.

"Hold her shoulder down, now," the doctor said to Mr. Yoder, and he proceeded to pull on her hand and, finally, turning and twisting gently, all the time feeling her arm, set the bone. They wheeled her back into x-ray to confirm that it was set properly, which it was, and after another hour of paperwork and casting and instructions about post-injury care, which I saw go in one Yoder ear and out the other, the Ironbridges drove us back to the Yoder home. Mr. Yoder got out of the truck and walked toward the house. I helped Naomi walk to the porch and up the stairs. He opened the door, took her arm, and nodded to me brusquely, extending a hand to indicate that I was not to come into the house, and shut the door. No expression of thanks, no acknowledgement that I was even a person who had involved herself in their life—nothing.

I stood there for a moment, shaking my head, wondering why my sister had decided to pick these people as a hiding place. I turned and walked back to the Ironbridge's truck. Mace got out and silently opened the back passenger door for me and handed me up to the seat and shut the door. I began to cry. They took me home.

***

If I thought that was the end of the day's drama, I was mistaken. Little did I know that Mace's prediction about how things would get difficult would prove to be prescient. I didn't even make it into the house before my sister yanked the front door open with a look on her face that told me she'd already heard about what I'd done with Naomi Yoder.

"You just can't leave things, can you?" she began, in a controlled but angry tone. I could tell someone else was in the kitchen from the way she was standing and the level of her voice. She stepped outside and shut the door. "We need to talk," she said. "We're going to the barn." I looked over her shoulder and saw Abigail in the kitchen, ostensibly making biscuits, but looking surreptitiously toward the front door.

I obediently turned to follow Brigitte as she slipped on her coat, and she just then noticed the Ironbridge's truck, idling, waiting. "Who are those people?" she asked, nodding her head to the driveway while she walked toward the barn.

"I ... they ... I mean, I treated the woman this morning for a fractured arm—the same as Naomi, funny that—and then they drove me to the Yoder's, and then they drove me here." I could immediately feel my conviction draining away like water down a sink, my awareness of God's presence that was just so short a time ago so real now seemed to be ... something I couldn't quite recall. And the light outside seemed darker to me, dimmed somehow.

"What would they do that for?" she asked, looking daggers at me, stunning my rapidly numbing senses. Mace and Zoe had said something about this ... what *was* it they'd talked about? "What do they know about this?" she pressed.

I looked at my sister's angry, anxious face and wondered what lay behind her fear. "Everything," I said, forcing a boldness against whatever it was that was choking me and stealing my confidence; boldness that my sister wasn't accustomed to hearing from me, for she looked at me sharply.

We got to the barn and she went through the smaller man door on the side of the barn and turned on me. "I don't know how I'm going to fix this," she began, turning on me. "Do you realize that we will never be able to find another community if they kick us out of this one? Their world isn't that big. I may just tell them that it was you, and I didn't have anything to do with it."

And then I felt the darkness 'stumble' almost, as though a curtain was ripped in two, and things cleared for a moment, and I took a breath and struck out.

"Good, because you didn't. And ... and you should be ashamed that you didn't!" I said, amazing myself. I stood there with my hands at my sides, fists clenched.

She looked at me then—really looked at me as though seeing me for the first time in a long time. "What's up with you, *lapin peur*? Did they take you out for a drink before coming here? A shot of whiskey to stiffen your spine ... something's gotten into you. What is it?"

"Nothing ... I mean, well, no, really, Brigitte, we should have seen Naomi last night. It was a dislocation fracture."

"And they took her in and got it fixed, right?"

"They wouldn't have if we ... I mean, if I hadn't taken her. They had a poultice on it, for God's sake!"

Brigitte stood there in the cold, her breath a cloud in front of the bonnet like some steam locomotive. "Well, I'll tell you, little sister. This is the last time you're going to do anything like this, do you understand me? From now on you'll do what I tell you, when I tell you, the way I tell you." She was pointing her finger at me now, really angry, and all I could think of was how strange it was that the Ironbridge's truck was still idling in the driveway.

I thought about my dream, and the interpretation Mace had given, and I saw suddenly that here was my decision point. My sister, the other horse to whom I'd been tied most of my life, was yanking on my harness, trying to keep me pulling the cart in her direction, in harness with her. Everything became so clear.

"No."

Her eyes blinked once and then narrowed. "What did you say?"

"I said *no*. If ... if I think I should do something, or ... or if God asks me to do something, then I'm going to do it, no matter what you say." I was drawing breath as fast as I could, trying to get the words out as quickly as possible.

"If you do this ... wait, you're serious, aren't you, little sister?" She looked at me differently then, with what seemed to me to be derision. "So if you do this, we're done, you understand? Don't expect me to help you, and don't expect me to take the fall for this thing with Naomi, either. If you want to go this way, you're going on your own, and you might as well start packing now."

That hit me hard. I hadn't thought that far in advance about what the ramifications might be to this new course of action. Yet something kept me on that path. "Fine," I said, not wanting her to see how much I was trembling inside.

"In fact," she said, "I'm not moving again; I've told you that. So what I think you ought to do is just pack up now and get out."

"Out?"

"Yes, out, like, out of the house, now. *Now.* You have a job, you can get an apartment in town. When the Bishop starts asking questions—and notice I said 'when', not 'if'—and I can tell him tell him exactly what happened—that you went off on your own after I directly warned you not to, and if I can tell him that I told you to leave, then maybe, just maybe, they'll let me and the boys stay. And I will do whatever it takes to make sure I don't have to move again, do you understand me?"

I stood there in the barn, wondering who this person was standing in front of me, kicking me out of her life and, more to the point, kicking me out of the house I lived in. But I didn't stand there for long, because the awareness of what God had spoken to me burst again through all the confusion and angst caused by this choking, black anxiety I always seemed to feel around my sister. God had spoken to me, telling me I had to break away from the one I was harnessed to, and here it was, the decision. 'Well,' I thought, 'if I'm going to make a decision, then I'd better make it.' I turned on my heel and walked out of the barn, leaving my sister standing there, unanswered. I walked up to the driver's side of the Ironbridge's truck, and Mace powered the window down.

Before I could say a word, Zoe leaned over the console and said, "If you like, come and stay with us for a while."

To tell the truth, I felt that I took this in stride well, as it was just one more surprise in an already amazingly supernatural day. I wiped the tears from my eyes with what I thought was a brave gesture, held my head up and said, "Why, yes, thank you Zoe, I'd like that very much. Could you wait until I get my things together?"

"We'll be right here, Abrielle," Zoe said, smiling kindly, and her voice together with the sound of the idling diesel was to me a rock of comfort and assurance just then.

Chapter 20
Jedburgh

"Do not think that I came to bring peace on the earth; I did not come to bring peace, but a sword. For I came to set a man against his father, and a daughter against her mother, and a daughter-in-law against her mother-in-law, and a man's enemies will be members of his own household."

Matthew 10:34-36

Getting fired isn't all it's cracked up to be. I mean, why do they make it seem so cool in the movies? You know, the hero thumbs his nose at the corporation or 'the Man', and some corrupt office flunky delivers the pink slip and the hero gets tossed off the job and walks off the site, usually after performing some kind of defiant gesture that cements his status as a rebellious champion of the masses. Well, I'm here to tell you, that's not how it works. How it really works is that you are not even allowed back anywhere near your place of employment—they change the locks, they change your password, they confiscate your computer—the one they gave you, anyway—and they take away your company phone. You never hear again from the friends you spoke to every day ... it's as if you've moved to a different planet. The daily routine that ordered your entire life for ten years is, just ... gone. It's as if someone detonates a massive bomb and 75% of your life just disappears into some kind of hole in the ground. But that's not the worst part. The worst part is how people look at you, strangers even; people you see on the street or at the store or at the gas station and you wonder about how they even knew you've been fired. Is there some kind of underground *"This guy's been fired"* social media site that I don't know about, like Facebook and Twitter, or 'DumpedOut.Com', the opposite of Linked In?

No, I'm wrong. The really worst part is when you go home after six weeks of looking for a job, after an entire day of being told you aren't qualified, or you're too qualified, and you sit down in your chair at the end of a day like that and your wife comes in after just another lunch with her friends that lasted for three hours and complains about why you're not working and why you're hanging around the house all the time.

It was funny, looking back, but that is exactly what was being said that night my cell phone rang. My wife was ripping into me again about me not getting any work, as had been her habit, and the phone interrupted her railing. I grabbed for it, not knowing who it was, just grateful for any interruption to the tirade.

"Jed Sloan."

"Mr. Sloan, I'm Daria Avidora. I'm with the HR department at Northern Minnesota Construction, and we've received your résumé. We'd be interested in talking with you about a position."

I was so surprised I held the cell phone away from my face and just stared at it.

"What? Who is it?" my wife snapped, angry at being interrupted in mid-rant.

In a flash I realized what Josh was trying to do and, as to why, the reason was standing in my living room in front of me, waiting for the phone call to end so she could continue raking me over the coals. So I decided to go with it.

"It's a job offer," I said, with my hand over the phone. My wife seemed taken aback and then a bit conflicted—she wanted to continue the rant, but with a job offer tendered in front of me, her case was weakening ... but she couldn't disparage the new opportunity, as it would scrape across the logic of her argument, even though she would regret not being able to continue. She compromised by just making an impatient gesture at me to get on with the call, and stood there with her hands on her hips, letting me know with body language that I'd better not screw it up.

I really didn't want to screw this up by laughing, and I almost blew it, but I choked it down just in time.

"Uh, yeah, I mean, yes, sure, uh, what kind of position were you thinking of?" My wife's eyes got wider with interest, still tinged with an eager desire to bite into me if things didn't go well on this call.

The woman on the other end of the line sounded foreign to me, almost Hispanic or, I don't know, maybe Middle Eastern, I couldn't tell. "We need a supervisor up here at one of our job sites, as we've just received a new contract, and we're short of supervisory labor. It says here that you have a lot of experience supervising construction crews."

I knew my résumé didn't say any such thing, but I suspected what Josh was trying to do and I was just grateful about how he was going about it.

"Well, sure, sure, I mean, I could do that. I'd really like the opportunity, actually." My wife looked at me with impatience, waiting for me to expound on what this opportunity was, but I let the HR person from NMC drive the conversation because I suspected this was going according to Josh's script.

"So, Mr. Sloan, could you talk to us about your availability?"

"My availability?" I echoed, for the benefit of the audience in front of me, with impatient claws on hips. I looked at her and raised my eyebrows, asking an unspoken question. She stuck both her hands out, palms up, as though she was pushing, to indicate that I should tell them I was available immediately.

"Uh, sure, I'm, uh, available right away, actually. When does your contract start?"

"In about a week or two, sir, but we would really like it if you could get up here in the next couple of days to begin our onboarding and orientation processes. There are a lot of classes you'll need to take on Minnesota construction codes, getting familiar with Minnesota labor laws, and host of other items."

"In a couple of days?" I said. "That's pretty short notice," I said out loud into the phone, again so my wife could follow the conversation. She made another impatient gesture, which I understood clearly to mean that I was an idiot for even questioning what they wanted, and I was to get my keister out of the chair and on a plane if that's what they needed.

"But hey, sure, I can get up there ... well, tomorrow if you need me that quickly."

"Actually that would be quite helpful, Mr. Sloan. With your concurrence we'll make the booking and email your itinerary. Oh, and could you tell us what airport you'd like to fly out of?"

"Minneapolis is good," I answered.

"Okay, sir, we'll email your itinerary to the email on your résumé. Is that still a good address?"

"That will work," I replied. I looked up to see my wife making another gesture, which I understood to mean that I should ask them what the salary would be.

"Oh, hey, uh, I'm wondering, uh ... could you tell me what the salary will be?"

"We'll start you at a base of $48K per year and based on overtime and additional contract work, it could turn out to be quite a bit more, sir." I realized that for someone at my stage of life and where I was in my professional career, $48K was like, worse than what most college graduates were getting, but at the moment I was in no position to be picky. "Sounds fine," I replied, with my wife's eyebrows moving up and down like they were electrified, wondering what the number was. I held up my hand. "And I'd like to thank you for the opportunity you're offering," I said, as it was obvious the conversation was coming to an end. My wife's face took on a look of disdain at what she presumed was my pro forma courtesy, although it wasn't, from my perspective. I really was grateful.

"Yes, of course, Mr. Sloan. Oh, there is one more thing ... there is a message I am supposed to pass on from the owner."

"Yes?"

"Uh, let's see, here it is. It says here that I am to say, 'You're *lousy*.'"

***

Before I hung up the phone I realized Josh had given me a golden opportunity. I went with it.

"Well? Well? Who was it?" My wife jumped on as soon as I pressed the 'end' button.

"Uh, it was a construction firm up north, actually."

"A construction firm? That's good, I suppose."

"Yeah, they just got a huge contract and they need supervisors."

"Wait ... I didn't know you knew anything about construction."

"Well, apparently the contract will require areas that I have expertise in ... I think they'll be needing people with retail management experience ... I don't know, maybe because they'll be ordering a ton of hardware, I'm not sure. I didn't argue with them when they told me I had the experience they were looking for."

She thought for a moment. "I suppose," she agreed, grudgingly. Then she looked at me sharply. "So what are they going to pay you?"

I mentally put on my imaginary helmet. "They start me at forty-eight a year," I said quietly.

She blinked, hard, and then I saw the color drain her face. "You said forty-eight, right? Not one forty-eight?"

"You heard me—forty-eight to start, though they did say that didn't count what I could make on overtime and on any additional contract requirements that might come up."

"Forty-eight?" she said, baldly, in unbelief, obviously stunned and very disappointed. "We ... we can't live on that."

"Yeah, I've been thinking about that, and you're probably right," I said. I sat there for a moment, seeming to deliberate thoughtfully, and then said, "You know, you're right. I'll call them back and just tell them thanks, but no thanks. I'll just keep looking." I reached for the phone ... slowly.

"Wait," she said, and I made a mental note to compliment Josh on his sense of the strategic. "Forty-eight isn't so bad, and it's the only job offer you've gotten in what, six weeks? We need *something*."

I sat back, my hand retreating from the phone on the table. "If you think so," I said. "I guess we could get an apartment up there to start, and—"

She shook her head like someone coming out of a dream. "Wait, wait ... you don't think we're going to *move* there, do you?" She was looking at me with a stunned expression, her hand on her chest to indicate she was referring to her and Jeanine. "*That's* not gonna happen."

"Well, we sure as God made little green apples can't maintain two houses on that kind of salary. We can get an apartment up there, sell a car—we can get along on one car, Jeanine goes to public school ... or better, you could homeschool her."

She looked at me then as though I was a complete stranger. "What is happening to you?" she said, with a mixture of wonder and disdain. "Is all that Bible reading turning your brain to mush? Don't you care that your kid gets the best education possible?"

"I do," I replied, "as long as we can pay for it."

"You can damn well get the kind of job that'll pay for it!" she shouted.

"So you think I shouldn't take this one?"

She threw up her hands. I was on the edge of enjoying myself. "For God's sake, of *course* you have to take it, it's the only thing you're gonna get in this job market."

Snap went the trap. Now she was stuck—she had told me to take the job, even though she knew the salary wouldn't be enough to keep her in the style to which she'd become accustomed. If my situation wasn't so pathetic—if *I* wasn't so pathetic—it would have been hilarious, like something out of a sitcom.

"So we're supposed to what, just uproot our whole lives here, Jeanine is supposed to leave school and all her friends, and I just leave my friends, and we pack off to ... to where? Where is this job, anyway? You said up north somewhere. Where, exactly?"

"In a place called Granite Sky," I said, waiting for her to make the connection.

"That place is almost all the way up the coast."

"Yup."

"And what kind of schools are up there?" she asked.

"No idea."

"Granite Sky ..."

"Yup."

I could see the wheels turning in her head, and she finally put it together. "Up in the northeast ... that's where your friend from college works, somewhere up there, doesn't he?"

"Yup." I was practicing my Minnesota vocabulary.

"What's the name of the company you'll be working for?" She sat down in front of her laptop and pulled up a search engine.

I didn't have any reason to draw this out. "Uh, I think the lady on the phone said 'Northern Minnesota Construction'."

"Northern ... Minnesota ... Construction," she said slowly, Googling it. I watched her watch the site loading. I watched her eyes move across the website—the website that had Josh Riesling's picture and name prominently plastered across the home page—and in just a few seconds she looked up at me.

"You son of a bitch."

***

I was through my third week working for Josh when I finally realized how much stress I'd been under at home. I realized this because, basically, the stress wasn't there working at Northern Minnesota Construction. I had a job; it might not have been the job my wife would have preferred, but it was something. I was sending my entire paycheck home to her and Jeanine while I roomed with Josh. He was a bachelor, and though he only had a one-bedroom apartment, I slept on the couch and he paid for the meals. His apartment was in the center of Granite Sky, which meant it was maybe a two-block walk from his apartment to the company's main office, so I didn't need a car.

So there wasn't any more stress about finding a job. And there wasn't any stress when I would come back to Josh's apartment in the evenings after work, because no one was there waiting to remind me about how much of a failure in life I was. It was strange, not getting in a fight every day. I sort of felt at times like I was suffering from PTSD[12].

Josh was a pretty solid guy. He didn't hit the bars after work, like some of the guys on the crew. I got to see into his life as I lived with him and he was the same at home as he was at work—a steady guy who took his Christianity seriously.

Josh treated Daria like a respected colleague. Daria was the 'girl Friday' at work—secretary, accountant, human resource specialist—we had a good laugh about that when I got there—caterer, and building code expert. She had been born and raised in Israel—in Haifa, I think Josh said—and she'd come to this country a few months ago. Apparently she'd gotten some construction experience when she was in the Israeli Defense Force; that's how she got this job. She could be pushy, Josh warned me—while she was standing right next to him. Her brother was still in the IDF[13], in the Special Forces. Josh was always meticulously courteous with her, and he didn't put up with anyone disrespecting her. It didn't matter if she was around or not, Josh controlled the language on the job sites and at the office. He wouldn't put up with any profanity, and guys who couldn't control their mouths found themselves out of a job. A couple of the guys told me about once when some temp worker tried to put the moves on Daria at a job site a while ago, and she didn't want any of it, and the guy started getting physical ... well, they tell me the guy woke up in the hospital after Josh kicked him all over the site. Apparently we have a pretty good relationship with the paramedics in town.

Josh and I got into the habit right away of having a Bible study early in the morning before work. He was doing this by himself before I moved in, and it was natural for me to fall in with him. Boy, it was an education. He saw things in the book that I'd never imagined were there, and I learned a lot about Christianity, and about what God wanted for my relationships, both with my family and my coworkers and others. We talked a lot about what my role should be as a father and husband, and how I should be relating to my wife and daughter. We talked about what God wants to build in our characters, about how He wants to make us more like Jesus; and about the spiritual opposition we'll face as Christians. Every day I learned something new. I felt like God had strapped a fire hose onto my face, but funny thing, though it was exhilarating and intense and surprising and challenging and fascinating, it was never stressful. I felt like I was learning more about who God was. Josh says that God comes close to new converts and helps them walk through their early days, and I believe him, because I felt like I was on cloud nine my first three weeks there on the new job in Minnesota. Josh said this wouldn't last forever, just like a parent will hold a child's hand for a while until they're ready to take their first steps and they take their hand away. To tell the truth, I didn't believe him about that, because I thought that things would just go on as they were. I was happy, not stressed, doing solid work on the job, learning about God—what could go wrong? Yeah, seriously, what could go wrong?

12 Post-Traumatic Stress Disorder

13 Israeli Defense Force

Three weeks and one day after I left home, I got a letter in the mail from someone I didn't know, with the letters 'Esq.' after the name. I sat down at the desk Josh had put in for me, which was right next to his, after we'd come in that morning from arranging some of the metal framing we were going to need for an upcoming job.

"You get mail already?" Josh asked. It was around eleven in the morning and the mail didn't usually come until around two or so. We were sitting there, me with a coffee, he with a hot chocolate.

"Must've come in yesterday," I speculated. It was large white special delivery envelope.

"It came in late yesterday by FEDEX," Daria said, leaning against the doorway that led to her own office. "Jonnie dropped it off." Jonnie was the local FEDEX delivery guy. Josh stood up and poured Daria a cup of coffee, for which she thanked him.

"So Daria, what do you think, Jonnie's kind of cute, hey?" Josh asked.

Daria gave him a sideways look. "Not my type," she said, and it sounded to me like she was stressing her accent.

"Yeah, well, okay, so ... what's next on the docket?" Josh asked, nodding, smiling slightly, moving into the day's work as I slid open the envelope.

"We have to do the Grayson cost proposal," she said, looking at me, since it had sort of fallen to me to do cost proposals. I'd had some experience costing in a number of former jobs and it just sort of came easy to me, though I needed Josh and Daria's expertise to help with the materials estimates.

I looked at the contents of the envelope.

"So when do you want to get to that, Jed?" Josh asked.

I didn't reply. I just sat there looking at the papers that had fallen out of the envelope.

"Jedburgh, you okay?"

Daria put her coffee cup down on the desk. "What is it, Jed?"

I just stared at the papers. Josh came round behind me.

"What's up, man? Can I see?" I slid the papers sideways, inviting him to see what new direction my life was taking, and he bent over to read them.

"Carolyn Perlmutter, Esq.," he said, reading the top of the address line. "Who's that?"

I pointed my finger to the subject line in the letter.

"Oh," he said dully. He stood up. "Your wife wants a divorce?"

"We've been married ten years and she wants a divorce." I couldn't say much else. I was too stunned to think clearly.

Daria strode over to the desk. "Let me see," she said, snatching the papers from my hand. She riffed through them expertly for a moment and then said, "She's claiming you abandoned them. Here it is, in line 148, third page." She pointed her finger to the line that had the reason Jean was filing for divorce. "And she says on line 243 that there are 'Significant concerns stemming from husband's unstable mental condition." Daria looked up at me. "What is she talking about with this?"

"I have no idea," I said. "Maybe it's because I decided to move to Granite Sky to find work?"

"No, Jedburgh, that's not it," Josh said. "It's because of your relationship with God."

"Oh, you Gentiles cause more trouble for yourselves over religion," Daria said, throwing the papers down on the desk and striding back into her office.

"What do you mean?" I asked Josh after she'd gone.

"Jed, a lot of people say they believe in God. Sure, that's nice, so do the demons in hell. But you've had the courage to actually obey Him, to let Him intrude in how you live your life—and that's why your wife is accusing you of being mentally unstable."

I looked over at him as he sat at his desk. "You went through this, didn't you? This is what happened to you." I held up the papers in my hand.

"It did," Josh replied, after a quick glance at Daria's closed door.

"So ... you know," I said.

"Not a coincidence, Jedburgh," he replied. "God comforts us with the comforts we will extend to others."

Daria came back into the office and stood there with her arms folded. I knew Josh had shared with Daria what happened to his past marriage, and I caught a passing glance that made me think she might be interested in hearing what he would say to me. He went on anyway.

"So you have a choice now, Jedburgh. You can back away from this relationship you're building with the God of Abraham, Isaac, and Jacob—" here he threw a look at Daria, "or you can press on and let God arrange things."

"But if I don't go back, I'll never be able to defend myself from the charge of abandoning them."

"He has a point," Daria said, standing there, obviously fuming over something I couldn't discern. I thought her eyes looked red.

"That's not the point at all," Josh countered. "Your marriage isn't the main thing in question here, Jed. Get that through your head."

"Wait, are you saying God doesn't think my marriage is important?"

"Not what I'm saying. Yes, God thinks your marriage is important, but in the same way you would think a house or a building is important, but it needs a foundation if it will be survivable and safe. A marriage without a foundation in God is unsafe at best." He looked over at Daria again. *Something* was going on with those two. Josh continued. "And He would also tell you that if you ever have to make a choice between God and anything else, you should choose God."

Daria rolled her eyes and lifted a hand in the air. "You sound like a Rabbi!" she said, sounding exasperated.

I thought about what Josh had said. "Yeah, okay, yeah, I realize that, sorry. My relationship with God needs to come before anything." I knew Daria wasn't a Christian—she was Jewish, I thought, and not a religious Jew, either—but just then I didn't care what she heard or how my words would affect her. "And you're right too, Daria."

"About what?" she asked.

"He sounds like a Rabbi—a Jewish Rabbi I'm getting to know." Daria looked confused for a moment until she figured out Who I was talking about, and then made a rude noise. "Goyim."

Josh reminded me of something. "You remember you were telling me a couple of days ago that you thought things were just going to go on all nice and steady, the same way they've been for the past three weeks, easy. Remember?"

"Yeah, don't remind me."

"Well, God knows what He's doing. He's going to take His hand away and see if you want to walk with Him, or walk back home to your wife and family."

"I have to make that choice?"

"You do."

"Why is God forcing that on me?" It didn't seem fair to me.

"God isn't forcing this on you; your wife is, but make no mistake, whenever you give any indication that you're interested in having a relationship with God, stand by, because the world is going to intrude and make you choose between it and Him. She's saying that it's either God or her and your daughter. You can renounce this newfound faith you have, claim it was just some momentary aberration, that you were overly influenced by your college roommate, that you didn't know what you were doing, and go back. God is waiting to see what you're going to do, Jedburgh."

I sat there for a long minute and then looked up at both of them. I knew that learning about God was what I was *supposed* to do, and I'd definitely seen that it made for a better life—at least, a life with a lot less stress—until now, that is. But I also didn't want to lose my marriage, and my daughter meant the world to me. If I was honest, I would have also said that I didn't want to be just another divorce statistic. It would have been a bald, embarrassingly public statement that I'd failed in the most important decision a man makes in his life. I'd been a failure in everything else I'd handled in my life—my sports life, my career—and now this. I didn't know if I could let this go.

"There is one thing you might try," Josh said slowly, as though not sure if he should mention it.

"What?"

"Have you talked to her about just coming along with you in this relationship with God you're developing? Have you shared with her how you came to trust Him and how you made a commitment to obey Him?"

I sat there for a minute, thinking. I remember talking to Jeanine a little about what I was getting out of reading the Bible, and I remember all the abuse and scorn I got in return for just that little bit of effort. I wasn't sure I wanted to. I could see Daria staring hard at me, wondering what I would do, waiting.

"It's ... it's something I could try, I suppose," I replied.

Josh raised an eyebrow. "Couldn't hurt."

"Good luck with that," Daria said, and went back to her office.

***

"Couldn't hurt," he said. Wrong. Here's how that played out.

So they left for lunch and Josh let me use the conference room phone to make the call to Jean.

"Hey Jean."

"Jed ... it's you." I could tell right away she hadn't been expecting my call.

"Yeah. How's Jeanine?"

"She's fine ... what's this number?"

"The conference room number at the company's office."

"Oh," she said dully, by which I realized that if she'd known it was me she wouldn't have picked up the phone.

"I got your request for a divorce," I said.

"Yeah, well, I'm sorry about that Jed, but I have a life and a daughter to think about, and you going mental on me with your Christian crap, not to mention you pulling down a whopping forty-eight thousand dollars a year isn't going to hack it."

"Jean, we could make it work, I know we could. If I could just talk to you a little about the relationship I'm building with God, I think we could—"

"Don't *even* go there, buddy. Ever since you started talking to that idiot friend of yours, you've become mentally unstable. You're not safe for us to be around."

"Not *safe*!" I almost yelled into the phone.

"That's right, so don't get any ideas about coming back here, because when I told my lawyer you were reading the Bible regularly, she said that I could get a restraining order on you automatically, based on the Pelisor-Hadad Act."

"What ... what the heck is that?"

"You don't know? Jesus, you're like some idiot bird that's had its head stuck in the sand for the last few years. Where have you been? Google it, for God's sake."

I sat there, stunned, not realizing how far off the beaten track I'd taken myself with my decision to develop a relationship with God. Since I'd never considered a life of obedience to God before, I'd never noticed the laws the country had against such a life.

But I was always sort of slow on the uptake in a lot of things. "So ... so how do we ... how do we make this better, Jean. I really don't want to get a divorce."

She laughed then, a scornful, derisive, and, if I were honest, I'd say a hateful laugh. "Look, you son of a bitch, you want to run off and play Sunday school with your old friend, that's your business. You want to start thumping the Bible at people, hey, that's your business. But don't think I'm going to have anything to do with anyone who's going in that direction. And seriously, Jed, I mean, *seriously*, what direction have you *ever* gone in your life? I mean, what have you ever done that was *your* idea? Has there been *anything*? You know, maybe there's enough time for me to find someone that has at least a semblance of initiative, of get-up-and-go, of, God, I don't know—*something*!" I could tell she was frustrated, but I didn't realize how frustrated she was.

"Jed, I've lived with you for ten years, and you still amaze me, how stupid you can be sometimes. I'm done, okay? Enough! I don't want to learn about your God or read your Bible with you. I don't want to turn into some mindless bimbo that just smiles and does whatever her husband or the Pastor says, in between making cookies and cakes for the church bake sale. If it was up to me, I'd have your ass thrown in jail. It's people like you that are causing most of the terrorism in the world. We can't lock you people up yet, but the day is coming, count on it. You people make me *sick*. You come near me or Jeanine and the *least* I'll do is have your ass thrown in jail, you understand me?"

I didn't know what to say to her. Slowpoke that I am, I did realize that it probably wasn't the time to press her to confess her sins and ask God for forgiveness. Something about not throwing pearls before swine came to mind as well. Funny, though, talking to this women I'd lived with for the last ten years, listening to her spew her hatred at me, made me more determined, not less, to follow wherever it was God would lead. I'm stubborn like that ... some would say stupid.

"Okay, Jean. Sure, if that's what you want. I'm sorry you feel that way, but—"

"Don't give me that 'Sorry you feel that way' line, like you're all better than I am. You're a loser, Jed, and you owe me for the last ten years. So just sign the papers and like it says in the document, send me fifty percent of what you make for the next five years and we'll be good." Then she hung up.

I sat there for a few minutes, trying to imagine how my life was going to change, worrying about my failure to evangelize my wife, wondering what my daughter was thinking about what was happening, aching for her. I turned to the laptop on the table and Googled the Pelisor-Hadad act. Apparently Congress passed the Pelisor-Hadad Act three years ago. It stipulated that any spouse who had concerns about another spouse or partner reading the Bible or in any way being inclined toward a non-approved Christian environment could immediately get protection with a restraining order. They don't need to go through a judge to get one. I wondered what a 'non-approved Christian environment' was. I closed the screen, and then I got up and walked out of the conference room. Josh and Daria were in the office, going over the Grayson bid. They both looked up.

"How'd it go?" Daria asked, with a look of concern as she saw my face.

I looked at her and Josh and realized that he was about the only friend I had at the moment, and then ... then an amazing thing happened. A peace came over me ... a peace even in he midst of the deepest agony of my life as I considered the impact it would have on my daughter. It was the strangest thing.; my heart was at the same time grieving, in unimaginable pain, yet also quiet, peaceful, content in the knowledge that I was going where I needed to go, and more so, a path that was the best for my wife and daughter, whether they chose to acknowledge that or not. It was a peace that translated to a pure, complete confidence that things were going the way they should, that things would work out, despite what I was seeing.

I looked at them both with an enormous pain in my heart, the pain of loss and grief, but also a strange sense of freedom that comes from obedience, and said, "I think ... I think I'll be okay."

***

A couple of days later, I had gotten into the office before we opened to get grounded in the Grayson cost proposal when an older gentleman knocked on the door. He was a tall guy—not as tall as I am, but not many are—and seemed friendly, standing there in the entryway, though he hadn't said anything.

"Good morning sir, can I help you?"

"Good morning. Yeah, I'm wondering if Josh is here."

I looked at my watch. "Well, he should be here in about five minutes or so, sir. You're welcome to wait."

"Thanks, if you don't mind, I will. It's a bit parky outside." 'Parky'—I hadn't heard that word in a while. He came in—he was limping slightly—and took one of the chairs in the outer room and removed his took, uncovering a head of short-cropped gray hair that matched a closely-trimmed beard.

"Would you like some coffee?" I asked. "We've got some ready to go."

He held up a hand. "No, thanks, I'm good."

I went back to sit down at my desk and when I looked up he was standing there in the doorway to the main office.

"You're Josh's friend from down south ... Jedburgh, right? The guy named after the commando teams?"

"Yeah, sir, that's me."

"Tack ... Tack Ironbridge." He stuck out a hand.

"Nice to meet you sir."

"Josh tells me you've become a Christian."

I was a little surprised to hear this from some guy I'd never met, but his words seemed respectful and encouraging.

"Yes sir. I'm still new at it."

"We're all new at it, son, when you consider God is working on an eternal time scale."

I didn't get that, exactly. "What do you mean, sir?"

"When two Christians are together talking about their relative degree of progress in getting to know God, it's like two ants, standing on the sidewalk at the foot of one of those giant skyscrapers, talking about which ant is taller."

I laughed at that. "Yeah, okay, sir, I understand."

"So what has your decision cost you so far?"

This question sort of knocked me back on my heels. It was fairly personal, coming from some guy I'd just met.

"You don't beat around the bush much, do you?" I said, trying to be tactful.

"Neither did Jesus, and if you've decided to let God make you into the image of His Son, then you might want to consider the habit."

I couldn't argue with that. "You're right, I guess. But how do you know ... I mean, why do you ask about what it cost me?"

He sat down in Josh's chair and swiveled around to face me. "Because it helps me get an understanding about your level of commitment. Most people, the commitment doesn't cost them much, which, if you ask me, isn't much of a commitment."

"You get what you pay for, hey?"

"More like, if something costs you a lot, you value it more."

"Right." I looked down at the papers on my desk and was thinking about how to answer the old man when Josh came in.

"Good morning, sir," he said. I could see Josh knew the old guy.

"Josh, how are you?" Ironbridge stood up and shook Josh's hand.

"Good sir. I see you've met Jedburgh."

Mr. Ironbridge turned to look at me. "I think he hasn't figured me out yet. I make him nervous."

Josh laughed a little. "Yes sir, well, most new people make Jedburgh a little nervous. He's actually kind of shy."

"Big guy like him, shy?" Ironbridge looked at me—I mean, really looked at me, hard—and I felt like he was seeing more of me than was comfortable. He made me want to tell the truth, no matter what.

"My family," I said.

"Say again?" Josh asked.

"Mr. Ironbridge asked me what my decision to follow God cost me, and I was telling him that it cost me my family."

The old man smiled at me then, and I liked him a lot more. "Doesn't seem shy to me," he said. "Why don't you tell me about it?"

So I did.

***

Two hours later, I had finished a long tale of woe about my entire life, beginning from when I met Josh in college, our football days, the bitter ending to that effort, and then my life since I'd married Jean, up until the phone call a couple of days ago. Ironbridge just sat there and listened intently, focusing, once in a while asking me questions so he could better understand what I had been thinking or feeling at certain points, or asking for further details about why I made certain decisions. It almost felt as though he was looking for something.

Just about the time I finished, Daria came in. She looked at us with bright, intelligent eyes, all of us sitting around the conference table, obviously just having finished some kind of intense meeting. Her eyes darted over to the sideboard and noted the empty coffee carafe. Josh stood up and the old man stood up, and I looked from one to the other and then figured I didn't want to be the odd non-gentleman out, so I stood up.

"Good to see you again, Daria. When are we going to have that talk about the Holocaust?"

"We need to do that, you're right," Daria replied, not committing to anything.

"Zoe misses you. She's driving us all nuts, throwing Hebrew words around, waiting for you to come back."

Daria laughed but I could see the tension in her at the thought of visiting whoever the Zoe person was.

We stood around the table like three guys who'd just finished talking about the meaning of life. She looked at each of us and said, "I don't know if I want to know what you all have been talking about," and turned to leave, but Ironbridge stopped her.

"We've been talking about that Jewish Rabbi, and what He's been telling this young man lately," Ironbridge said, yanking a friendly thumb in my direction.

Daria was a polite and courteous woman, and she knew Ironbridge was a client, so she didn't go full burner on him. "That's nice," she said, and turned to leave.

Ironbridge said something obviously in Hebrew, with absolutely no English accent. Josh and I whipped our heads around in surprise to hear this completely foreign language, spoken like a native, coming out of the old guy.

Apparently Daria understood, because she responded in the same language, and they talked foreign to beat the band for a few minutes. I could tell her attitude toward him was still wary, as though she considered him more like a worthy adversary. Josh and I just sat there, looking from one to the other, until Ironbridge changed back to English.

Daria came over and sat down at the table, and we all took our seats again. "Zoe I can understand," she said, and turned to me. "Zoe is his daughter-in-law, married to his son Mace. You'll probably end up meeting them sometime."

"But you, sir," she said, turning back to Ironbridge. "Where did you get your Hebrew? I mean, seriously, it's excellent. Where did you learn it? And you didn't say you knew Hebrew when I was out at your farm."

Ironbridge didn't answer right away. "It was ... it was a long time ago. There were some good friends. We did some things together ... in parts of the world you probably know." We got the sense there was a story behind that, though we also sensed it was a story he didn't want to relate at the moment.

"Christians!" she exclaimed, exasperated, throwing up her hands. "The minute you think you have them figured out, they throw you a curve." She looked at Josh when she said this. Ironbridge said something to her in Hebrew, and she laughed, and then asked him a long question in rapid-fire Hebrew. When she stopped, Ironbridge turned to look at Josh and became reflective, then gave her a long response in the same language. When they stopped, I could tell both of them were thinking about some important things.

"So okay," she said, back in English, "let me ask you, Mr. Ironbridge. You make a good point but there is one thing that completely eliminates any possibility I could consider what you say." She stood, obviously to leave, and we stood. "When we have our talk, I'd like you to try and explain to me where your precious God was during the Holocaust, okay?" She left the conference room and we heard the door to the back lot open and shut.

Josh looked at Ironbridge. "What did she say to you, and what did you say to her?"

"Let's take a walk," he replied. "Jedburgh, do us a favor and wait here, would you? Thanks." They left through the front door and walked into the parking lot, and I went back to the Grayson file.

***

They came back in a couple of hours, and Josh looked a little subdued. Ironbridge shook Josh's hand at the door, gave a quick nod to me, and then left. Josh came back to his desk.

"Jed, let's get another load of rocks out to Tack's place today, you and me, okay? I need you to get some time on the Peterbilt."

"Sounds good."

"He's liking the work we're doing so far, and he wants to press on with it before things start to freeze."

"Okay." I waited for him to open up about the discussion he'd had with Ironbridge. Nothing ... so I just sat and stared at him.

"What? What are you looking at?"

"Nothing ... just waiting."

"For what?"

"Well, let's see, in the last three weeks or so I've told you and a complete stranger, oh by the way," I said, indicating Daria, "my entire life story, and every morning we seem to come across some key lesson in the Bible that uncovers some issue in my life that needs talking about, and so when some old Obi-wan sort of guy comes blowing through here and starts talking foreign to Daria and then calls you out for a two-hour discussion, I mean, hmmm, let's see here, I'm thinking, 'where's the quid pro quo'?"

Josh sat down and looked at his desk for a minute before he responded. "Tack is ... I don't know, he's a mature Christian, you understand? You won't find many of them these days. He's got some serious wisdom. And you haven't met his son, Mace. That's gonna be interesting too."

I wondered at Josh saying that about Ironbridge's son, but agreed with him about the father. "I got that sense too ... like he's been around the block a few times."

"Yeah ... okay, so I'll tell you what he told me. First, he started telling me about how critical it was, absolutely critical, to make sure that Believers marry other Believers. He seemed to think that this is especially critical in the near future. He thinks we're in for some hard times."

"Check on that," I replied dryly.

"No, no, what he's talking about is, like, way more than that. He's talking about the country going down, about the economy crashing, about all kinds of stuff. Foreign troops, invasions, the whole enchilada. He seems to think America is Babylon and we're in for some serious crushing. He doesn't expect our society to function normally for much longer."

"And ... where are you on that?"

Josh hesitated for a moment. "Let's come back to that question. So he tells me that it's really important for Believers to be equally yoked, especially now, and I ask him why he's telling me this. He knows what happened to my first wife and he knows why she divorced me—"

"He okay with that?"

"Yeah, yeah, he isn't an Anabaptist—he recognizes there can be an innocent party in a divorce. No, the reason he's telling me this is because he thinks—no, he *knows*—Daria has designs."

"Designs?"

Josh stared at me until I got it. I told you, I'm not quick on the uptake.

"Oh ... like, designs on *you*."

"Duh."

"How does *he* know?"

"Apparently she told him."

My eyebrows went up. "She told him? You mean, like, just before, when she was here? With us sitting here?"

"In Hebrew, I guess. That must have been what they were talking about."

"She's got guts," I said.

"No argument," he replied.

"So what are you going to do?"

"I don't know."

"That's no answer. Better question is, why do you think Ironbridge gave you that warning?"

Josh looked at me, half-smiled and tilted his head. "It wasn't that he was warning me off, though ... it's kind of weird, but I have the strangest feeling that it was almost as if he were trying to explain or justify something he was going to do."

"That's weird."

"Yeah, I know, but that's the sense I get."

We sat quietly for a few moments and then I went back to my previous question. "You can't make four clicks with a mouse on the internet without coming across some moonbat.com site that is talking about the end of the world. What are your thoughts on that? I know something like that is in the Bible."

"To tell you the truth, I haven't really looked into it, Jed, but I also know it's something we need to think about. Things just can't keep going on like they're going."

"Do you think this guy Ironbridge would know anything about it? Why not ask him."

Josh looked around at me. "You know, Jedburgh, that's not a bad idea. We'll be out at his place this afternoon. Let's see what he says about it."

"Deal."

***

Driving the Peterbilt was awesome. Lots of power, good sense of control, and a complete lack of concern for anything else on the road, because in a war of lug nuts, the Peterbilt won against anything else out there, hands down. I had fourteen tons of small rock in the back, and Josh ran pilot for me in the small company pickup. It was a serious haul out to Ironbridge's farm, out on the Gunflint Trail, then onto a small access road, and we arrived in the early afternoon.

They had a nice spread. There was a small stone cottage that looked like their main house, and then a larger barn with more outbuildings, and there was a side building that looked like it housed a bunch of horse-drawn farm equipment, with something over it on a second level. I could see the half-completed stone wall that ran around the front of the main house, and it looked like they were planning to make the wall go all around his barn and outbuildings.

Josh got out and said hello to Ironbridge, and quickly got the instructions on where to dump the rock load. He and Ironbridge were working the project sort of in a combined way—Ironbridge paid for the materials, and Josh—and now me, too—would work on the project with him to get the stone working experience. I learned on the drive up that Josh had hired me specifically to supervise this job. Josh had told me it was an ashlar masonry project, which meant it was just roughly dressed fieldstone laid up with mortar. And that was about as far as Josh's masonry vocabulary went—which was more than mine, at any rate.

I maneuvered the Peterbilt dump truck to where they needed the load and then activated the bed and dumped the load where they'd asked for it. After the dust settled, I parked the truck out of the way and went to where we'd begin to sort the rocks.

"Afternoon, sir," I said, greeting Mr. Ironbridge.

"Afternoon, Jedburgh."

"You've got a nice farm here, sir."

"Thanks. So what is God doing in your life since we talked last, like, what, about four hours ago?"

"Oh." This guy didn't have much small talk at all. "Well, actually, I had a question about that."

"Good. We can talk while we sort the rocks. Large fill in this pile, small facers here, flat capstones here, and small fillers here." He pointed to the various piles and described what kind of rocks he wanted in each. We got the idea quickly and set about the massive rock pile I'd just unloaded.

"So what was your question, Jedburgh?"

"Oh, yeah, well sir, Josh told me what you'd warned him about—Daria, I mean. You said it was important for Believers to be married to other Believers. Why is that?"

Ironbridge's eyes scanned the rock pile and rapidly sorted each rock according to his form of classification, and didn't stop while he answered me. "If you want the scriptural answer, it's because light can't exist with or have any kind of fellowship with darkness. Practically speaking, when a Believer tries to live with an unbeliever, they are always pulling in two directions, even when it seems they're getting along. What happens most of the time is that the Believer just stops growing, because whenever God calls them to some activity that will require obedience, which oh by the way is how the Believer grows, the unbelieving partner either directly opposes the activity, or makes such a fuss that the Believer eventually gets tired of the friction in the home and gives up—and stops growing."

"Why exactly does that happen?"

"Because," he replied, "the way God grows us into the image of His Son, which is the same thing as growing in the realm of the Spirit, is by calling us to do things that require us to die to ourselves and be filled with His Spirit. Since an unbeliever is by definition spiritually dead, but not dead to their own natures, nor filled with the Spirit, there's this mismatch. Let's say there could be a task in front of a husband and wife, and if one is a Believer and the other isn't, they're going to want to approach that same task very differently. And that will cause friction."

"So you're worried about that with Josh? Him getting into a relationship with Daria, I mean?"

Ironbridge stopped sorting the rocks and looked at me. He was a tough old bird. "Jedburgh, how much do you know about eschatology?"

"I don't even know how to spell it ... what's that?"

"Basically it's the study of End Times, what's going to happen at the end of man's history, when God comes back, sets up His kingdom, and history moves forward from there."

"Well, funny you mention it, but Josh and I were kind of wanting to ask you about that stuff, too. That's kind of what my question was about."

"Good. We have lots to talk about then, don't we?" He bent over again and his rough hands started moving over the pile again.

"But what does that have to do with Daria?"

"She's Jewish, you knew that, right?"

"Yes sir."

"Times are coming that will make the Holocaust look like a picnic," he replied, wiping his forehead, "and one of the key litmus tests God will apply to those who call themselves Believers will be how they treat the Jews in those coming times."

Half of my mind was on sorting the rocks while the other was trying to process what he was saying.

"What does that have to do with me and Daria, sir?" Josh asked.

"Did you two ever get around to looking at Deuteronomy 28?"

Josh paused in mid-toss. "Actually, no, we haven't gotten around to that yet. You know, strange now that I think about it, but ever since we came back from our first visit here, she's been ... different."

"Let me guess—upset, distracted, irritable, and emotional?"

Josh looked at Ironbridge sharply for a moment. "Smack on, sir. That's exactly what it's been like. What's up with that?"

"Good news," the old man said, picking up another rock. "God's working on her, addressing the inconsistencies in her life, and that will make anyone upset, distracted, irritable, and emotional."

"Yeah, that's what she's been going through, then, for sure."

Ironbridge looked hard at Josh. "She and I are going to have a discussion about the Holocaust soon—we were going to do that the weekend you guys were going to come out to stay, but that got cancelled for something she had on, remember? I wanted you to know about this talk I want to have with her, because I may need to say some things that might be hard for her to hear. I wanted you to know that I'm saying those things because I hope she'll hear those hard things and accept the truth about her people and what they've thought about the Holy One of Israel so far—another name for Jesus, by the way. If she can see and understand and repent of her part in that, then maybe she'll have a chance of seeing the truth and surrendering her life to her Messiah."

"Um ... why would you want that, sir?" Josh asked. I could tell he was a little nervous.

"Because, young man, I think God has plans for you and the young lady."

***

We met Mrs. Ironbridge when she rode up into the yard on a huge black horse, just before lunch. She was almost as tall as her husband, looked to be about the same age, with long dark hair tucked up under a riding helmet and what looked like some kind of thick black leather vest on.

She dismounted and Ironbridge introduced me. "My wife, Claire. Claire, this is Jed Sloan; he's an old friend of Josh's and he's working at Northern Minnesota Construction."

"We have you to thank for all this beautiful stone?" she asked.

"Actually no, Ma'am, I just drove the delivery truck."

She looked up at me. "Tall bottle of wine, aren't you?" She turned to Ironbridge. "Tack, have you fed 'em yet?"

"Not yet, Babe."

"Well, give me twenty minutes and we'll get something presentable for them. You guys keep on with the rocks." She turned toward the barn, leading the huge horse.

After we'd come into the house, just as we'd sat down at the table, there was a knock on the door and a woman dressed like one of the local Mennonites came in. Josh stood up—I can never remember to do that—and then I did. Tack was already standing at the head of the table, ready to say a blessing.

Claire made the introductions. "Gentlemen, Abrielle Dumont. She's staying with us for a while. This is Josh Riesling, and the tall bottle of wine at the end of the table is a friend of his, Jed Sloan."

We said hello. Abrielle seemed extremely shy, almost as if she was afraid of us. She didn't look us in the eyes when she said hello, and there was no hand shaking.

Lunch was pulled pork from one of the farm's pigs, with a huge pile of mashed potatoes they'd grown on the property, with croissants Claire had made that morning, and green beans from their garden. For a couple of bachelors it was pure heaven.

I thought the conversation would be light, since that Mennonite lady was there, but I didn't know the Ironbridges very well. It started right after everyone had food on plates.

"Jed, you were asking about what our views were on how things might be developing in the country."

"We get a sense that things can't keep going on this vector," Josh replied, jumping in "but we're not sure, from Scripture, how things will be playing out."

"What is this vector you talk about?" Every head turned. The Mennonite lady had spoken.

"Basically, the direction the country is going in now. The drastic divisions that we have politically and socially ... the economic division as well ... it's all getting worse. More people are working harder, longer hours, for less pay, while a few people seem to just get wealthier. Socially, I mean, the younger generation—the kids in their twenties and early thirties—are completely convinced that sodomy is a normal thing, just a different lifestyle, and any opposition to it is reprehensible. Most people today don't think twice about the immorality of abortion—they've been convinced after several decades of lies that the baby has no voice, and the mother has the right to kill it. Both political parties are okay with it. The nation is teetering on the economic brink with our horrendous debt, but no one is worried about the moral cesspool we've made of our country."

"There are other things as bad, too, as these you speak of," the Mennonite woman said. "There are serious problems in the Amish and Mennonite communities ... problems that make me think that they have nothing to do with real Christianity."

"They're a cult," Tack said, in a low grumble from the head of the table. "Whenever a group of people put anything above God, His Son, and His Spirit, then they're in a cult. They worship a god of their own making."

"What does that mean, sir?" I asked. I felt like a broken record, constantly asking him to explain things, but I knew less than nothing about Mennonites or Amish.

"It means that they have picked through the Bible, selected things that fit their lifestyle, or fit the lifestyle they think they ought to have, and they use those things as rules which they say people must follow to be acceptable to God. So in place of the real God, the group now has a set of rules that they've set up as god in His place. They don't look like a golden calf, but it's the same thing."

"So where is all this going to go?" Josh asked.

"I believe this country is Babylon," Claire spoke up. She saw my look of confusion and went on. "Babylon is talked about in different places in the Bible, Jed. It is a massively powerful nation—the most powerful nation on the earth during the End Times, one that exports its culture to the world, and one that uses its military power wherever it pleases—I think it was Jeremiah who refers to Babylon as the 'hammer of the whole earth'."

"Why is that important ... I mean, that this country might be Babylon?" I asked.

"Because Babylon is utterly destroyed as a nation in the time leading up to Jesus' return," Tack answered. "Right after Israel is just about completely wiped out." I saw the Mennonite lady taking all this in with wide eyes, as though it was the first she'd ever heard of it.

"If we are where I think we are in time," Tack said, "time is running out for America."

Josh was leaning forward over the table. "So what do we do?" he asked. "I mean, Believers? How should we prepare?"

Tack and Claire looked at each other and Tack said, "It's important you realize something," he began. "A lot of people are seeing that times will be getting hard. This is why there's been such a huge increase in prepping. You combine the massive amount of distrust today most people have of our government with the huge political and social splits we're seeing, the world economy, and the U.S. debt, and it's no surprise that a huge cottage industry has shot up to convince people they need to 'get prepared' for the end of the world as we know it.

"Getting ready to face the times to come is important, but the crucial thing is the *objective*—that is, what you're hoping to achieve with your preparations." Tack paused and looked at Josh. "Remember the question I asked you the last time we sat at this table—what does God want you to do?" Then he went on, talking to everyone. "Most preppers are getting ready for some horrendous societal collapse, and based on who you talk to, it will come either through some terrorists setting off a bunch of nuclear weapons in our cities, or a giant economic failure, or some electromagnetic pulse that shuts down our country's electrical grid, or some horrible virus that kills most of the people in the country. Regardless of what scenario they're thinking about, all of them think that history will continue on as it has in the past. After the preppers survive the big bang, in whatever form it comes, their plan, their *hope*, is to rebuild America in one way or another, based on the group—but most would say they want to rebuild the country after the pattern laid down by the Founding Fathers."

"I get the sense you think that isn't going to happen," Josh said quietly.

"America is a stench in God's nostrils," Tack said vehemently. He got everyone's attention. "We have taken the enormous blessings He has poured out on us and spit in his face. We have shaken our fist at Him, rebelled against His sovereignty and rejected His love. We murder millions of babies a year in this country. Do we think God will just overlook this if a few churches decide to have a little prayer vigil over a weekend, praying that God will 'turn and heal our land'?

"Would God turn and heal our land? Sure He would ... if the leadership changed the laws about sodomy and abortion and the thousands of other evils and injustices that are codified into our laws now. Sure He would ... if the U.S. Government started a program to burn down every Mosque, every Catholic church, every Jehovah's Witness temple, every Mormon temple, and any other house of worship that isn't focused on the God of Abraham, Isaac, and Jacob.

"But those things won't happen. We have imported the world's culture into our churches, and Christians have turned to worshipping gods they make themselves, and Christianity was the only thing preserving this country. We were the salt that preserved the nation, and now we've lost our ability to preserve anything. We've lost our savor, as the Scripture says, and now we're going to discover what God does with salt that has lost its ability to preserve. God is saying the same thing to America as He said to Israel, through Micah. 'O that one of you would shut the gates of the place where you worship!' He's tired of it! The time for all the handwringing and praying for revival has passed, and now comes the judgment. So no, I don't think America getting rebuilt is in His plan, since I don't see Babylon getting rebuilt in Scripture ... not in the cards. When this country ends, it won't stand up again."

When Tack spoke about this, he seemed to swell, or become, I don't know, almost brighter, larger somehow. It wasn't just me who noticed it; Josh mentioned it to me later that evening. And I could see the Mennonite woman's eyes get rounder as he described the state of America.

"That perspective wouldn't sit too well with a lot of the prepper communities I'm familiar with," Josh said. "And I read a lot of their stuff."

"There are some out there who realize what's coming, and they feel it's their duty to God to stand up for the freedoms He gave us here, to fight, if necessary, to the death. I can't disagree with them, as far as that goes," Tack answered. "But I think there is a huge gap in understanding where we are in the End Times scenario. Not many think He's coming back soon—at least, in their lifetime. So most of them end up thinking that if they can just hang on and survive, if they get the right combination of resources or assets or networks or food or bug-out bag components or the right bug out place, then hey, they'll make it out to the other end of all the chaos and help build a new America. From what I read in Scripture, that won't happen."

"So back to my question, sir. How should we be preparing if the 'prepper' model won't work?"

"The first thing, the most important thing, is to make sure, make sure, make sure you *know* Him." Tack was pointing his fork at Josh. "Make sure you have a relationship with Him. I don't know how many times in Scripture He says that He will keep those who know Him through the difficult times we're talking about. He says that the ones who know His voice, who are in the habit of obeying Him, will find Him to be a rock and a fortress and a safe place. He says to those who are His people to 'enter into your rooms and close your doors behind you and hide for a little while, until indignation runs its course'. He's talking about when the Lord returns to judge the earth because they've forsaken Him. Proverbs says that riches or wealth won't profit a man in the day of wrath, but righteousness will deliver him from death—there's one clear piece of advice about how to prepare—and I can promise you, His day of wrath is coming on this country very shortly.

"A relationship with God is the most essential thing any time in a person's life, but in these days to come, it's more critical than ever to actually know Him. I don't mean know *about* Him, but really *know* Him. To answer your question, Josh, the best way to prepare is to begin aggressively pursuing a relationship with God ... and that's what I see you three trying to do." Tack lifted a hand and pointed toward Josh and I and the Mennonite woman.

I didn't know too much about the Mennonites, but I had always thought they were extra-devout Christians. Tack's opinion that they were just another cult really threw me.

"Jedburgh, you've lost your family to follow God, yeah?"

"I suppose that's true, sir," I replied.

"Josh, your wife left you because you were His disciple, true?"

"Yes sir."

"And Abrielle's story is hers to tell, but everyone at this table needs to know that she has also 'jumped off the cliff' and abandoned every support structure or relationship she had just to get to know Him, and been kicked out of her home for it."

Tack looked around the table at all of us. "This is what it takes. You have to set every other thing that was most important in your life as second priority, and you have to make Him the most important thing. Like the parable says, you find a treasure in a field and you sell everything else if you have to just to get that treasure. And there will always be pushback from the world; from those other things that at one time were a priority. The world will fight you on this, which is why Jesus talked of this causing a sword to come down and divide families. All of you are seeing how painful that can truly be. And a lot of times, when you put those other things as second priority, they choose to just leave, or they force you out of their lives."

"They take a big bite before they go, though," I said.

After the laughter died away, the Mennonite woman began to talk.

"I'm just beginning this ... this relationship, like you say, Mr. Ironbridge. I don't consider myself Mennonite now. Claire and I have talked a lot these past few days about what that means and I can't in good conscience be part of that group any longer. I just want to learn about Him and try to hear when He speaks to me so I can do what He tells me to do."

Claire put her hand on Abrielle's arm. "And He'll take care of you in the bargain, dear. He won't leave His lambs to be slaughtered by the wolves."

***

After we finished sorting the entire pile of rocks I'd dumped, Josh went into the house for a moment to square up the bill with Claire. She had a habit of paying us at the end of each day for the day's work—she said there was something in the Bible about making sure not to withhold a worker's wages ... something like that. While Josh was in the house, Mr. Ironbridge called me over.

"Jed, let's you and me jump in the truck and take a ride."

I thought there were more rocks he wanted to pick up, so I hopped into the passenger side of his pickup and he took me down a dirt road that led away from their collection of buildings, further into the forest. We drove for maybe a minute or so when a clearing suddenly opened up to the right of the road. It was a long, oval-shaped area about 400 yards long and a hundred yards wide, covered with close-cut grass. A thick line of trees surrounded the area, and just inside the edge of the trees were maybe ten or fifteen small cabins, spaced evenly around the perimeter. I saw a small trail in the grass connecting the cabins with a small footpath.

"Claire and I bought this place when it was an old bed and breakfast, and when the new laws came through, we just stopped having customers. We didn't feel like being forced to put up sodomites on the property. But we've kept the cabins up. Each has a small solar-powered generator for electricity and there's gravity-fed running water and flush toilets. I don't know, there must be two or three septic tanks back here, but we've never had 'em pumped out. The previous owners pumped 'em out before we left and we've really never used the cabins since, so ... they should be good for a few more years."

"Looks nice, sir," I said. "What are you and Claire going to do with these? I mean, it must be a lot to keep up, just the two of you."

"Maybe so, Jed, but it's what God has called us to do. Now, one of the reasons we think God has called us to keep up these cabins is to provide a place for His people who might need a sanctuary in the coming days. And you, young man, sort of fit that category at the moment."

He startled me. I wasn't expecting this had anything to do with me. "What do you mean, sir?"

"I know where you are with your family, Jed. I know how Josh is situated too, and while I know he doesn't mind putting you up, you can't keep sleeping on the guy's couch. You should have a place of your own, get on with your life."

"So ... so you're proposing that I stay in one of these?"

"That's the idea."

I paused and then asked, "How much would it be to stay here ... I mean, per month? If you know my situation, you know I probably can't afford something like, well, any one of these places."

"Price is right, Jed. Help around the place with chores when you're not working at NMC and we'll call it square."

I turned to him. "Uh, which one did you have in mind?"

He pointed to one cottage off by itself. "You see the one there, the one a little closer to the road and a little bit set apart from the rest? That's for a reason. We had in mind that someone staying there might serve as sort of a Watchman on the place. It was the only one we've built ourselves. We put it there to sort of protect the place. You go inside and you'll see all the windows have clear lanes of ... of visibility to the cabins and the entranceway. There is only one way in or out, and the woods are fairly thick all around. Once we get more folks in, we can put up some kind of gate, but for now, I'd like you to consider taking that one, the Watchman's house.

"And there's another reason I'd like to see you move in, Jed. That young lady you met at lunch, Abrielle, has been tossed out of her community and if you asked me, it doesn't look like she wants to go back. She's staying in our spare room right now, but it's kind of a small house, and we'd really like to relocate her into one of these cabins."

"But if I'm back here, I can sort of keep an eye out for her," I filled in.

"That's the idea. And there may be others, as the days go by. You didn't meet Mace or Zoe today, they were out ... on an errand, and they had a young lady with them, Emma Devereaux, who was also just recently kicked out of her house because she wanted a relationship with Jesus. We haven't moved the ladies back here yet because, well, as you can see, this is sort of out in the middle of nowhere."

I looked at him, and said, half-jokingly, "Expensive entry fee."

"Yeah, well, keep in mind, it's not yet been as expensive as the one His Son paid to open the opportunity."

"Right," I replied, getting his point. I looked around the clearing, at the cabins, and then at the Watchman's cabin, wondering what my days there would see.

"Okay, sir," I said, shaking his hand. "I appreciate the offer, and I'd be glad to help."

Chapter 21
Stan

"I am the Lord your God, who brought you out of the land of Egypt, out of the house of slavery. You shall have no other gods before Me."

Exodus 20:2-4

I knocked on the main office door at NMC that morning and opened it, still not used to the informality up here. A tallish, younger man was sitting near Riesling's desk, someone I didn't know. He looked up when I came in, and then stood.

"Morning sir, I'm Jed Sloan."

I shook his hand. "Stan Pankowicz ... Riesling told me to expect you here. He said I'd be working with you."

"Yes sir, and Josh told me to tell you that we really appreciate the help."

"My pleasure." The tall kid rustled up some coffee and we sat down. I had offered to help NMC price some of the work they were proposing on Grayson's dock and unloading facilities.

"If you don't mind, sir, can I ask why you—why you volunteered to help us with this?"

The old me would have grumbled and fussed about the 'intrusion of privacy these days', or just told him to shut up and get to work. I was finding myself not doing that much anymore.

"I retired from Grayson recently. The wife wasn't too happy; she wasn't sure the pension I would pull down would be enough. She was constantly pushing me to get a new job with another large firm, 'something at corporate', she would say."

The kid nodded in a way that seemed to indicate he knew what I was talking about. I went on. "But my taste for that just isn't there anymore. I was out here a while ago, you know. Something happened to me."

"Josh told me about it, sir, I hope you don't mind. That must have been pretty amazing."

"Yeah, so, you can see why this corporate stuff just doesn't do it for me anymore. Something more is at stake. I've been hanging out with Tack Ironbridge, visiting him from time to time."

"Where do you stay when you come up? I haven't seen you before."

"At the Lodge there," I answered, pointing pretty much across the parking lot to the motel I would put up at when I was in town.

"You should consider asking Tack if you can bunk in one of the cabins he's got," the kid said.

"Yeah? What cabins are those?"

"He's got eight cabins that he rents out at times," Sloan replied.

"You don't think he'd mind?"

"I'm pretty sure he wouldn't mind. He's told me to make the offer if I encounter another Believer who might need a place to stay."

"Good idea," I said, "and thanks. I'll ask him about it when I see him." If I haven't mentioned it before, one of my redeeming characteristics is that I do like to rub nickels together until the buffalo screams. I like to get my money's worth. "The wife wouldn't mind that either."

"Sounds good, sir."

"So ... what's on the docket? How far have you gotten?"

We took the next couple of hours and the kid showed me what he'd done so far on the cost proposal for the facilities, and it was looking good. They had the right cost categories, though I wasn't sure I agreed with their manpower estimations or materials requirement descriptions. Those I needed to go over with Riesling directly. And their graphics needed work.

"Josh is out at Tack's, working on that stone wall," Sloan said, when I asked him where we might find Riesling.

"Well, hey, maybe I'll just drive out there and catch both of them."

"Let me give him a call," Sloan said, and picked up his cell.

***

This was my third visit out to Granite Sky since God extended His olive branch to me that day on the shore of the inlet. I'd found myself liking this place and these people more and more. Each time I came, I would visit with Tack and we would talk about God and His Son and so many things about life that I could never talk about with anyone else before. I was coming alive here, I could feel it, and my desire to learn more about God was growing. And I was experiencing a contentment I'd never known before.

The Sloan kid had to stay back at the NMC office, but Josh said it would be okay for me to come out and talk to him about the estimations and materials requirement descriptions. I took a copy of their draft proposal and headed out the door.

After a long drive through some pretty intense wilderness, I pulled up into Tack's driveway, never having been there before. We'd always met either at the NMC office or in the coffee shop at the Lodge. I was impressed with his homestead. I hadn't met his wife, either, but she came out as I pulled up into the driveway and she seemed very nice. Seeing her generated a quick stab of guilt, wishing my wife were up here as well, pursuing this newfound thing I'd found with God. It wasn't working out that way. The more I felt attracted to this new life, the more my wife seemed to oppose it. That just didn't make sense to me. She'd been after me our entire marriage to be more active in religious things. And now, when I have this experience and can't get enough of wanting to learn about Him, she doesn't want anything to do with it. It's a head-shaker.

My talks with Tack were the most refreshing encounters I've ever had. We talked a lot about the Bible, but mostly about what God was doing in my life, and why. Tack would explain about the nature of God and what God was requiring of me and my relationships. It was fulfilling.

"Hey Stan, welcome to the homestead." Tack came stumping up from around the back of the house, where I could see a large mound of rocks.

"Hey Tack, Josh. Good to see you guys again."

Before I went too far with the small talk, Tack asked, "What's God up to, Stan? What are you learning?"

"You get right to it, don't you?" I asked.

"Is there something else more important?" he said.

"Yeah, well ... you remember when you said I'd get some opposition? Well, it's coming like crazy now."

Tack stood there and took off his work gloves. "Yeah? Maybe you ought to tell us about it." He seemed to want to include Josh, and I didn't mind. Josh knew my whole story.

"Okay, sure."

"Come on in. Claire and Abrielle probably have something ready for lunch. Perfect timing, by the way."

"My specialty," I said. "Who's Abrielle?" I asked, walking up the porch steps.

"A lady who got tossed out of her home a while ago; she wants to have a relationship with God and her family didn't think that was such a good idea, so she's staying with us for a while."

I thought of Jed Sloan. "Lot of that going around, it seems."

"Stand by," Tack replied ominously, wiping his hands on his pants.

***

After lunch Tack took care of a few things on the farm while Josh and I went through NMC's Grayson proposal draft. I made some suggestions and he took a lot of notes and seemed to appreciate my help. Claire and the Abrielle lady had set out a large pot of soup, but then had to run out to the Mennonite store. I did see, though, as Claire left, that Tack stood up and pulled Claire to him and kissed her. It struck me, that act of married affection. Nothing like that happened in my house. Seeing it was like having someone unintentionally stick a hot iron poker in my side.

Tack came in as we finished up, and he took us both into their living room. It was a big room, lined with bookshelves. Apparently the Ironbridges were avid readers. They even had texts on engineering. I pulled one book on the physics of light off the shelf and paged through it.

"What's up, Stan?"

"Oh, nothing much. Retirement is going well, and—"

"Not what I'm talking about, Stan. What's the opposition you were talking about?"

Still not adjusted to Tack's direct 'out of the chute' style, I hemmed and hawed about things at home in general, talking about the wife and kids and their schools and the wife's job until Tack cut me off—again.

"Not having any of it, Stan. Get to the issue."

I could only squirm so long. "Okay, so, here's the problem. You remember I told you my wife constantly complained about me being an atheist before, right? You know, before God talked to me? So when I got home from my first time here, when I *knew* God spoke to me and I *knew* He was real, you sent me home and told me to read the Bible, remember?"

"I do."

"So I did. It was, like, opening up a gold mine. I started understanding things I'd never understood before. Things—and not just things I was reading, but other things, stuff in my life that always drove me nuts, I started seeing more clearly."

"That's good. It's a sign God is working in you."

"And then after one of my visits up here you encouraged me to have Bible studies with my wife, remember?"

"I do; the Word says that we're to 'wash our wives with the water of the Word', which just means we're to lead our wives through the Word, explaining it, teaching it, drawing her out, encouraging her to develop her understanding of it and in so doing, improving her own relationship with God."

"Yeah, well, that's becoming a problem. My wife resents me leading these studies. She says that she's been a Christian all her life, and who am I to suddenly show up and start leading her in a Bible study." I threw up my hands. "She told me that she leads other Bible studies at the church—a couple of ladies' Bible studies."

"Basically she doesn't like you taking a position of spiritual leadership in the home."

I thought about what he said. "Now that you say it, that's exactly it. She either won't join me, or if I insist, she'll just sit there and either ignore what I say until the time is done, or argue with me that what I think the passage says is wrong, and tells me what the 'right' interpretation is."

"And you say that she says she's a Christian?" Tack asked ... strange question.

"Well, yeah, she's been one, like, all her life."

"Then hasn't she read all the parts in Scripture about how the husband is to represent Christ, and the wife to represent the Church? How the husband is to lead in the home?"

I grimaced at that. "Uh, well, I've tried to point those out, but she says I'm misinterpreting all that stuff."

"How else can you interpret it?" Tack asked.

"She actually doesn't give me any other interpretation. When I go through the different Scriptures with her, she just gets upset and complains that 'I'm just a better debater' than she is, but she knows what she knows, which is what she's learned over lots and lots of years—years I don't have under my belt, she keeps emphasizing."

"So here's your first opposition, hey?" he asked.

"Looks like it. It's really splitting things up at home. She'll slander me to the kids, it's terrible."

"Why is she doing that?"

"Because, as you've said, I think she wants to have the lead in the family. That's really what it comes down to. And it's not just in this ... in spiritual things, it's in everything. Where the kids go to school, where we spend our money, how we spend our money, who are friends are—I mean, I hate her friends. We have nothing in common."

"You're supposed to have the Spirit of God in common."

"Yeah, you'd think that would be obvious, but that's not the way it's working out."

Tack sat quietly for a moment and then looked at me hard. "Stan, there are always two sides to marital issues, and I'm pretty sure you guys have those kinds of issues, but this ... this doesn't sound like that. Tell me, has your wife ever died?"

I knew what he was talking about; he'd explained it to me often enough. "I can't say."

"How did she become a Christian?"

"I asked her that, like you suggested the last time, and she just said she's been a Christian ever since she can remember. She's always gone to church and she's always believed in God. That's what she tells me."

"I guess what I'm asking is if she's ever come to a point in her life where she realized she's a sinner, culpable for the sins in her past, sought God's forgiveness for those sins, and then turned from them?"

I shook my head slowly. "How would I know?"

"Actually it's fairly easy. People who've died and then been raised to spiritual life have a few things in common. They have a thirst for the Word; they have an increasing desire to obey Him, and an increasing desire to hear from Him, to be closer to Him, to get to know Him better. These things drive a person to do things that are easy to see, and they also shape a person's character. If she's denigrating you to your children, she's not upholding several of God's commands to respect her husband. If she isn't taking your leadership, she's not respecting the clear mandate in Scripture that requires husbands to provide the spiritual leadership in the home, I don't care how many female Christian personalities and teachers say otherwise. And if she can't pick a point in her life where she knowingly died to herself—that is, when she recognized in the depths of her soul that she's a sinner by nature, and that she can't make herself better, when she gave up controlling her own life and let the Spirit of God fill her—then she isn't really a Believer, I don't care what she says."

As Tack talked my heart grew heavier. Everything he was describing fit the profile of where my wife was spiritually. Even I as a young Believer could see that she really had no ability to understand even the most elementary stuff I was reading in the Word. When I would sit down and try and draw her out about what it meant, she would just sit there, or get angry with me, as though I was trying to test her, or compete with her. I began to see what was really happening.

"So what do I do, Tack? I just read that part where it says the husband and wife are supposed to be equally yoked, which I presume means they should both be Christians."

"You do what God has told you to do—what He's told every husband to do—and let Him work in your wife's life," he replied. "You lead. You step up and do what the Word requires husbands to do. You discipline your children, you show by example what Jesus would do in their home. Remember—when you comport yourself in your home as a Christian father, you're representing God. Your wife is to represent the church. If you let your wife lead in the home, you are doing damage to your children's perception of who and what God is. You must *not* misrepresent Him, Stan. That's crucial, both for you, your wife, and your children."

I shook my head. "You don't know my wife, Tack. She won't go for that, and if I try to push back and take the lead in the home ... I mean, I've been on the road for the last twenty years, in and out of the house, and she's had to direct things there by default. And now, what, I show up and tell her God spoke to me on some rocky beach in Minnesota and now all of a sudden she has to do what I say?"

"Look at the Scripture again, Stan. Does it say, 'Wives, respect your husbands *unless his job has kept him away from home for a time*?' or does it say, 'Wives, submit yourselves to your own husbands *unless his job has kept him out of the home for a long period of time*?' or maybe where it says, 'Wives, respect and obey your husbands *unless you disagree with what they say*?' No. In all these things, wives are to respect and obey their husbands even if they might disagree with their husband's opinion or approach to something. Obviously if a husband asks her to sin, then certainly the wife is not required to obey her husband—it would not be, in that case, as unto the Lord. There aren't any caveats in the Scripture, Stan.

She has no room to insist on leading in the home—unless she wants to admit she's not a Christian."

"She'd never admit that," I shot back, and then we sat for a few moments in silence while I digested what Tack had said. I couldn't argue with him, but I couldn't face what I knew would happen if I started doing what he was recommending. Josh was sitting quietly, listening to the exchange, not saying anything.

"Tack, if I try and assert any leadership at home, it's going to cost me my family."

"Then, my friend, you will have to decide what you want more—your family, or obeying the God who said that you can be at peace with Him. But don't put your family as a higher priority than God and then expect Him to remain in a relationship with you. '*You shall have no other Gods before Me,*' it says somewhere in that big black book.

"Remember what I told you? Very early in a Believer's walk with Him, He will present them a situation in which they will have to choose between their old god and Him. He will give them a chance to kill that old god—kill it by putting it lower in priority than our relationship with Him, and a lot of times the way that works out is that He creates a situation where we have to choose between the two."

I didn't want to hear that. I *really* didn't want to hear that. I'd already gone through one divorce, and that just about killed me. I had two daughters with my first wife over twenty years ago, and when they were two and three, my ex decided she didn't want to be my wife any longer. She had a very good lawyer and I had a fierce temper in those days, and to make a long story short, she disappeared from my life. I got no custody and no visitation. It was as if my children had been wiped off the planet and out of my life forever. I don't know if I could go through that again. But I didn't know how much of that story I could tell Tack, and I certainly didn't want to say anything like that in front of Riesling.

I wanted to change the subject. I always changed the subject whenever something made me uncomfortable—it was a habit. "Hey, Tack, Jed Sloan mentioned that you might want to rent me a cabin for a while."

"Sure," he replied, accepting my change of direction—for the moment. "How long are you thinking you'll need it?"

"I'm actually thinking about retiring up here, so I might want to stay for a couple of weeks and look around, do some house-hunting."

Tack looked at me with half-closed eyes. "Now what would possess you to move out of your nice little townhouse in Chicago and out into this howling, freezing wilderness with a wife who wants absolutely no part in what's going on here with your friends?"

I went over to one of the couches in the living room and before I took a seat I looked out through the window. The view was beautiful—a field surrounded by trees on a slight mountain just behind the house. Off in the distance we could see a beautiful lake. "I've always wanted something like this," I said, waving my hand at the window. "I've always wanted to live out somewhere on a farm, work with a tractor, get my hands dirty, maybe have a few chickens. I'll tell you, Tack, after spending most of my life as an engineer, working for corporations, I'd really like to just spend some time doing what I want to do."

Tack didn't say anything and I turned to look at him. "What?" I asked.

"So you know what *you* want to do," he answered. "What does *God* want of you at this stage in your life?"

I shrugged my shoulders. "I have no idea. How am I supposed to know that?"

"Maybe you should ask Him. You can know for sure that He wants you to get to know Him and become adept at hearing Him when He talks to you. He's talked to you once before, to get your attention, but now He wants a continual dialogue with you, through His Spirit. He's going to work on building your relationship with Him."

"How will He do that?"

"By asking you to obey Him. Remember what He said? *'If you love me, you'll obey Me.'* So He's going to see if you were serious about what you committed to, after He spoke to you that day. He'll put you to the test."

"I ... I know what you're talking about, Tack. I mean, every time I'm here, I feel like I grow. I can understand the Scripture better, and I feel like this is truth, this is reality here. I go back to Chicago and it just seems, I don't know, like I'm choking."

"Is that why you're considering moving up here?"

I hesitated a bit. "Well, yeah, that."

"What else?"

"It's like I see the lifestyle that you and Claire have. Out here, pretty much self-sustaining, nobody bothering you. That's what I want, Tack. You guys seem like you have a good relationship. That's what I want too."

"I understand, but you want to be careful about wanting something—anything, actually—that comes from your own desires. Sure, it might seem to be wonderful. I mean, who wouldn't want to live on a nice farm in the wilderness? God may or may not have that planned for you, Stan. Don't let your desires shape what you think God is asking of you, and most definitely don't think that God requires you to live in a certain place or a certain way to be acceptable to Him."

"Then how do you know what He's asking?"

Tack thought for a moment. "Think of a father who has complete control over a child's world, and who wants to steer his child in the right direction. He puts things into the child's life designed to move the child along the path the father wants him to take. People, circumstances, events—all of those things the father will create or structure or plan to use to try and get the child to move in the direction the father knows is best. Typically, when the child is moving along the right path, certain things happen; when the child moves down the wrong path, other things happen."

"What things? Okay, okay, so now you're getting to practicalities. I'm an engineer, I need tangible things I can see, touch, and understand. What things should be happening, like what you said?"

"So if the child is moving along the path the father wants, you'll see the child get healthier and grow stronger," Tack replied. "As the child moves along the path the father wants, the child will find himself able to understand the father's directions more easily, and, as the child sees the benefits come from moving along that path, the child's trust in the father grows, and then the father can ask the child to move along sometimes difficult or dangerous paths, and the child will because the child trusts the father. You'll see fruit in the child's life, and if a Believer is moving in the direction God wants for them, you'll see that Believer bear fruit in their spirit: love, joy, peace, forbearance, kindness, goodness, faithfulness, gentleness and self-control. And all these things happening will add up to an increasing love of the father growing in the heart of the child. When you see these qualities grow in your character, Stan, you will know you're walking where your Father wants you to go. But two things need to happen, two conditions need to exist, for the child to successfully go where the father wants him to go, Stan. First, the child has to *trust* that the father knows what's best for him—which in day-to-day living means that the child truly believes that the father knows better than the child—and second, the child needs to be *willing* to go wherever the father tells him to go. These two conditions are inseparable, okay?

"But if the child decides to take their own path, then other things happen. They may find a short period where they're satisfied, because they've maybe obtained what it is they wanted to get, or gone where they wanted to go, but as the child continues to disregard the father's direction, soon the child finds it harder to hear him. The child can't understand the father's direction as clearly as they once did, and the father may let the child wander into dark or dangerous places so that the child might get frightened enough to run back to the father again. If the child's heart remains hard, though, and the child continues to walk down their own path, eventually God will let them go, and what does that look like? Gradually the child becomes someone who has no desire at all to do what the father wants; the child actually grows to disdain everything the father stands for, and eventually the child begins to hate the father or worse, becomes indifferent to him. And in the child's character you'll see the absence of love, the lack of joy, no peace, a decreasing amount of patience, and an increasing degree of meanness, evil, treachery, cruelty, and a lack of personal control.

"Truthfully, Stan, it's not hard to determine if a child is walking where the father wants him to walk, and just so, it's not hard to figure out if you're making the right choices in life. Are you understanding Him better? Are you hearing Him more clearly? Is your love for Him growing?"

I listened as Tack made things clearer, and it frightened me. I was seeing the things he was talking about. I was finding a growing ability to understand what was written in Scripture. I was finding more peace in life, and I was finding myself more patient with my kids at home, even though their behavior was becoming worse as I tried to live my faith at home, and that was something I couldn't really figure out yet. I could see that I still had miles and miles to go to work on patience and kindness and goodness and gentleness and (alas) self-control, but all the things Tack said made sense. As I spent more time with him, in the Word, talking to other Believers, there was a growing hope that I could find in me the things he was talking about. I didn't want to be the way I was.

But I didn't want to lose my family. That happened to me once before and I vowed it would never happen again, no matter what. And if I had to take the leadership at home, I knew I risked losing them.

"Tack, I don't think I even know *how* to assume leadership at home. I've never done it, and I never saw my father do it. My mother ran the home when I grew up. I have no idea what it looks like for the man to lead in the home."

"You just do what He says, each day, okay? One day at a time. He promised to make you into the likeness of His Son, and I guarantee you, Jesus knows how to lead in your family. Let Him change your character and your nature into what He wants you to be, and He has already said in His Word that He wants husbands to be the spiritual leaders in the home. This is clear; this is what you can consider a 'commandment'—one of the things Jesus wants you to do. You don't have to be a tyrant, you don't have to yell or scream or threaten anyone with physical violence to get your way. Just let His Spirit guide and direct what you do at home and let what happens happen. There is no guarantee that your wife or your kids will ever submit to God's authority and become Believers, Stan, and don't think that just because you now have a relationship with God that they're all 'grandfathered in'. Christianity can't be inherited. Each of them will need to make their own decisions, to offer Him their own surrender. But you can give them the best chance to do that if you model God correctly in your home."

"What if they don't do what I ask of them?" I said, knowing that's what would happen if I went home and tried to lead.

"You explain to them clearly and with love that God requires fathers to be the spiritual head of the home because in the great symbology that God made which we call the world, fathers represent Him in the home; men represent Him in the world. You explain to them that if they are going to call themselves Christians, they must submit to your leadership. And you have to live as an example to them, in a way that would make them want to also surrender to God. You have to die to yourself, like Christ died for the church. You have to give yourself up for them."

"What does that look like, Tack? You're talking about stuff I've never heard about. I just started on this path, remember?"

"I understand, Stan. What does it look like? It's different everywhere, which is why I can't give you a 'one-size-fits-all' description. In some cases, giving yourself up for your family might mean that you quit your job and stay home; in another case, it might mean you take a job you hate, a job that takes you away from them a lot, so you can provide for them, or because God has something for you to specifically accomplish in that work. In some other cases though, Stan, you may have to make some hard decisions for their good that they might not like, and which might cause them to dislike you—maybe for a long time. In all cases, though, it means that you live your life in a way where *you* decrease—that is, your nature, your desires, your personality and character all become less, and God's nature, character, personality, and character all begin to grow and eventually there is more of God than there is of you—or, more of God and less of who you once were. The Christian life is just a process of letting Him be more in you, and who you once were become less."

"Does it ever stop? I mean, do you ever 'arrive'?"

"I don't think so, at least not in these bodies we have, with the human nature we have. I think that's why He's asked us to pick up our crosses daily—every day we need to be choking out our human nature and letting His nature be predominant. We have to wait for our new bodies before we're done with the flesh and its nature."

"New bodies?" I asked, completely mystified.

"You haven't gotten to that part yet."

***

I got myself settled into one of the cabins that afternoon. Tack wasn't charging me rent, he just asked that I help out around the farm when I wasn't out on the road, looking for properties. I learned that Jed Sloan was staying in the cabin that was separate, closer to the road, and the lady that had been Mennonite at one time was living in another. Apparently she wasn't calling herself Mennonite any longer, although she still was wearing the same period clothing.

Before I went out house hunting, I went through all the cabins and fixed some minor plumbing problems and some not-so-minor electrical problems. I had to chase a raccoon out of one closet, and had to face down a moose in the back yard of another when I was dumping some ashes out of the small pot-bellied stove in still another. I adjusted the alternator on Tack's John Deere tractor, and it took a while to get his snow-blower working. I felt needed; I felt useful. I felt productive—more productive than I'd felt in a long time.

Another thing; I found myself grousing and grumbling less. Maybe it was because I was just happy, maybe it was because I was finding myself useful. Part of me, afraid to admit it, realized that one reason I was less stressed and grumpy was because I wasn't around my family all the time. I feel terrible for saying this, but ... I just didn't like them. I was constantly derided or berated or laughed at while I was home. After being on the road most of my career, I would have thought that they would have liked me home more often, but since I'd been retired, that wasn't the situation at all. It seemed to me that their true feelings were just now coming out, and they were just hiding them during my relatively short periods of time at home. That was hard to face. I mean, I wasn't the easiest guy in the world to live with, but I thought I'd changed after ... after the olive branch. I wanted to be better, I really did.

Each night I would call home and tell Janet about the properties I'd seen. She listened, didn't have anything to say one way or the other, and when I asked her about what she thought, I just got monosyllabic replies. She was making it clear that she had no interest in moving to a farm in the freezing northern wasteland of Minnesota.

But what disturbed me most was her reaction to the friends I was making here. She developed an instant dislike for Tack, probably because I'd told her that Tack was giving me advice to take leadership in the home. She became irrationally jealous over Claire, and began to insinuate that I was getting too emotionally involved with her—*that* accusation came out of left field and rocked me backward. We argued about that for a few days, but she really floored me when one night she told me she'd gone to her ladies' Bible study the night prior and told them that she suspected her husband was having an affair. I admit, I lost my temper and there were some hot words, and things were not getting better on the home front.

One afternoon I'd just returned from helping Josh work on NMC's Grayson proposal—I wasn't charging him for that, after all the folks out here were doing for me—and I found Tack in the kitchen, making dinner. Tack would cook as often as Claire would. He said it relaxed him.

"Tack, I need to talk."

"Fire away, as long as you don't mind me chopping these mushrooms."

"Janet accused me of having an affair the other night."

Tack stopped chopping mushrooms. "Seriously? I mean, where? With who?"

I struggled to answer him. I hadn't thought this conversation through, I'd just come back into the house and there he was and this was the biggest thing on my mind, but I was in too far to back away.

"With Claire."

Tack stood there for just a second before he started laughing. "You're serious?" he asked incredulously.

"Don't laugh. I think Janet's gone off the deep end, but she actually made this accusation at our church, in a ladies' Bible study. I mean, seriously, the pastor emailed me on my phone and wants to set up a counseling appointment."

Tack stopped laughing after a while and then just smiled. "Yeah, well, I see what's happening, Stan. This is more opposition."

"Opposition? To what? Do you know what this is doing to my reputation back home?

"Okay, so let's lay it out. You ask God to prove He's real if He exists, and He does. And what happens? You respond; you change your life. You start reading *and understanding* His Word. You start getting fed at the Bible studies we have here. You start *growing*. You go home and take what you've learned in the Word and try to apply it in your home and your wife is getting uncomfortable. Sooner or later she'll need to confront the fact that she isn't walking in accordance with what the Bible calls her to. She probably doesn't think much of me, since I'm the guy giving you the heavy advice about making sure you carry the burden of leadership at home. No, I can't imagine she'd like that, or me, one bit. So she's going to throw something at you that you can't defend against, and the only way you're going to be able to prove her wrong is to do what she wants."

"Drop the idea of moving out here and just go home."

"Right."

"So what do I do?"

"What's God telling you to do?"

"I ... I haven't been able to figure that out."

"Remember what we talked about? Where are you growing most toward Him?"

"Here, no question."

"Haven't people been telling you that they see some massive changes in you?"

"They have, yeah. Even Janet, in her saner moments, has said she's seen a huge difference. And the kids say the same thing."

"Most of the time, Stan, when God wants a person to take a certain direction, He makes it clear to them by illuminating the Word to a greater degree, by filling them with His Spirit, and the result is that the person feels a contentment, a peace, a sense of 'this is where I belong'. I'm not saying we should be guided by our emotions, and there are times that He puts us in very difficult, even dangerous places, but when all we want to do is what God wants us to do, we find a contentment that passes all understanding when we're in the center of His will, no matter where we are."

"I've been more content out here than I've ever been, anywhere, in my life. I feel this is where He wants me."

"Then it may be that He's calling you out here, and if He's calling you out here, then you can be certain—and this is important, Stan—that it is the best thing in the world for your family. So now you're faced with a real decision."

I looked at him. "Which one is that?"

"If you're sure God wants you out here—"

"I'm sure, by all the benchmarks you've described and besides that, I know I'm supposed to be here. I've never been more at peace, and that's what He said he would give me."

"Then since you're sure God wants you out here, then you need to find a place to buy and tell Janet to load up the kids and the dogs and the bags and get on up here. She may not like it, but if you believe this is where God wants you, I can tell you for sure it's the best thing for your family, too."

I was shaking my head. "I have to be honest, Tack, I don't know if I even want them out here. I mean, I know it's hard to say, but most of the time I really don't like my family."

"You wouldn't be the first, Stan. But God can work amazing things in people's lives. He *is* in the redemption business, remember?"

"Fixing my family would be a miracle."

Tack gave me a close look and said, "Fixing you has been a miracle, wouldn't you say? God's in the miracle business, but you have to do what He tells you to do. If He's telling you to move up here, then you've got to do it."

"Tack, if we move up here, what am I going to do? I'll want to come over here, I'll want to work with Josh at NMC, I'll want Janet and the kids to come to the Bible studies you're having here, and that's the *last* thing she's going to want to do. She *hates* you guys."

Tack threw the mushrooms into a pan with a block of hard yellow butter. "You're trying to figure out all the answers before you take the step, Stan. God doesn't tell us what will happen at each step in our lives in the future. He just says, 'do step 1', and then, when we do step 1, He says, 'Okay, do step 2', and usually what happens is that when we get to step 17 or 78 somewhere, we finally just begin to see what the entire tapestry looks like. But if you're going to require Him to give you some kind of assurance that 'everything will be just fine', or worse, if you wait for everyone to agree with the decision God is asking you to make, well, I can tell you He doesn't work that way, because what that really is is you obeying everyone else and not God. No man can serve two masters—you've read that far? Good. And the last thing you want to do is try to work things out on your own."

"What would that look like, I mean, me working things out on my own?"

"Okay, so, let's say God tells you that you need to move up here. You know your wife and kids won't want to, so what you do is start a big program of trying to change their mind, jumping through hoops, bending over backwards to make them like the idea of coming up here."

"What's wrong with that?"

"You'd be trying to bring about a work that only God can do, and you'll be tempted to say to yourself, 'Self, I'll move up there, sure—God told me to—but only after I have all the details worked out.' With that, well, suddenly it's now you in the driver's seat. Sorry to break it to you but when God tells you to do something, you go do it. You don't try and work out all the surrounding details yourself. Leave those to Him."

This conversation was making my physically ill, because I knew what would happen if I told Janet we were moving up to Minnesota without any background preparation and some honest-to-Injun manipulation on my part. And here Tack was, telling me I shouldn't be trying to make arrangements on my own to try to get her and the kids to buy into the idea.

"Either you lead, or you don't, Stan," Tack was saying. "You can talk to them about it, and they can bring up issues and problems and you should try and work through those issues and problems with them, yeah, no problem, but none of those should in any way put you off from what God has told you to go do."

"Tack, it comes down to this. What do I do if they won't come?"

There it was—the main question and my greatest fear, because I knew that if I pressed the issue of moving up here, Janet would just put her foot down and flat refuse to come. I dreaded Tack's answer, but it came nonetheless.

"You move up here anyway. You do what God tells you to do and let Him work out the issues and problems and details."

I was afraid that was what he was going to say. "I'm not sure my trust is up to that level yet."

"You have to decide what you want, Stan ... your family or your God. If your family tells you it's one or the other, who will you choose?"

Chapter 22
Samantha

"When you sit down to dine with a ruler, consider carefully what is before you, and put a knife to your throat if you are a man of great appetite. Do not desire his delicacies, for it is deceptive food.

Proverbs 23:1-3

The Guilder, Atchison, and Steckam building, all steel, opaque blue glass, and polished Italian marble, arched upward into a sparkling blue Minneapolis sky, proudly holding its own in the city's skyline. The building was known as 'the Gashouse' to its detractors, due to the acronym formed by the names of the company's three founders. Most of the people in Minneapolis just called it the Guilder building. Unarguably, they were the world's largest Christian communications firm, specializing in publishing, Internet communications, and marketing. They informed, and formed opinions for, millions of Christians around the world.

Samantha Gunderson got out of a cab, paid the driver, slung her brown leather messenger bag over the shoulder of her tailored business suit and looked up at what she hoped would be her future. Three days from her thirtieth birthday, she was going to her second interview with the company, this time with senior executives. She was applying for the job of New Acquisitions editor.

Samantha was tall, blonde, with pale green eyes, a straight nose turned up slightly, remnants of freckles on a complexion burnished by working in open, sun-washed fields, shoulders broader than most women would have preferred, and a striking, fulsome, athletic figure. From good Scandinavian stock, her family had settled in rural Minnesota generations ago—her father's lineage from Sweden, her mother's from Denmark. She'd been raised in America's heartland, on a dairy farm in Severson, a tiny town in northeast Minnesota just outside of Granite Sky, with all that meant—milking cows before the sun was up, learning to push through the burning pain in her forearms and building up surprising strength in her hands; helping her father and brothers hay in the summers by driving the truck; skiing through groomed pathways in the deep Minnesota woods on crisp winter days. Sundays meant sitting with her brothers and sisters in the family pew at Living Waters, their non-denominational church. When she was five, her parents had gotten cable and the Internet; when she was ten, a big-screen TV; when she was fifteen, she had her first cell phone, and suddenly discovered that boys could be somewhat interesting.

She'd breezed through the local public high school, not bothered by most of its atheistic doctrines. Her family wanted her in public school to be a witness, and she did well. She'd been captain of the girl's basketball team, had more dates than a palm tree, and graduated second in her class, but if she was honest, she would also have said that her relationship with God wasn't in any way advanced or improved during those years.

Samantha was physically tough, and growing up on the farm, wrestling cows and working in conditions that required physical endurance, she developed an inner courage as well. One day when she was a junior in high school, after a basketball game against an Minneapolis inner-city team that had bussed up to play the County's varsity and junior-varsity teams, she went into the girl's room and saw a stocky inner-city girl holding one of her friends, Juliette Flannery, up against the pink tiled wall. The girl had Juliette's throat in one hand and was brandishing a wicked, gleaming straight razor in the other, surrounded by a crowd of friends, yelling, cursing, and threatening. Two local girls cowered in one of the stalls while three of the inner-city girls took turns reaching in and slapping them in the face. Tears ran down their cheeks; they were both trembling. Samantha took in the situation at a glance, and without thinking, moved up behind the girl holding Juliette, yanked the arm holding the razor, and twisted.

The girl, shorter than Samantha but rabid with rage, swung around, following Samantha's motion, let go of Juliette's throat, but held on to the razor. She ducked her hand under Samantha's arm and in a fearfully quick gesture, whipped the razor back toward Samantha. It opened a gash in her left side, across her ribs, and suddenly all the screaming in the lavatory stopped in the presence of blood. The inner-city girl looked at the blood splashed against the stall door and stepped back instinctively. Her friends stood still, shocked. Juliette's eyes widened, she wilted, and then fainted, sliding down the wall slowly.

Pain leapt up Samantha's side as though someone had branded her with a hot iron. Instead of daunting her, it ignited a fierce, boiling anger, and she felt a welling, irresistible rage. Her pupils dilated, her blood pressure lowered, her vision tunneled, and adrenaline shot through her body. She turned, and with a wrench from her powerful arms and strong hands, yanked the hand towel dispenser from the wall in one massive pull. The inner-city girl was staring at Samantha's blood-stained blouse and as she raised her eyes, Samantha swung the metal cabinet with every ounce of strength she possessed. She hit the girl squarely on the side of her head. She collapsed like someone had let go the strings on a marionette, still clutching her razor. One of the other inner-city girls screamed and launched at her, hands up, nails out, and Samantha, as though simply completing a graceful turn, swung the metal case through its arc and struck the rushing girl. She staggered back, forehead split, bleeding badly, into the arms of her friends.

And then Samantha roared; it wasn't any kind of feminine, high-pitched scream—no, it was a bellow, an angry, deep, resounding, blood-lustful roar that struck fear into her assailants. They bolted from the room as fast as they could, carrying their bleeding friend, leaving the owner of the razor lying on the floor.

The school hushed things up. Samantha was quickly taken to the hospital, where a wide-eyed young male intern delicately put fourteen stitches along the skin outside her fifth rib under the stern, watchful eyes of Samantha's mother, Eva. The assailant turned out to be eighteen years old with a minor criminal record. She'd suffered a minor concussion. Juliette's mother didn't bring charges because there were no witnesses. The local police dropped the matter entirely. But after that day, Samantha and Juliette were inseparable—and, needless to say, no one ever threatened Samantha again. The event left her with a thin scar high up across her ribcage, a visceral understanding that defending a good cause might result in pain, and shaken confidence in the workings of justice in her society—for nothing happened to the girl who'd assaulted her friend with a deadly weapon.

Samantha was close to her mother, brother, and sister—her mother had divorced her father a long time ago, and her brother was, well, different—and she was generally an obedient, compliant child. She was a studious girl—her grades were very good, though not scintillating—but she loved to read. When she wasn't working on the farm, she was reading, and often her mother would find her settled in the barn between bales of hay, or in the attic, or in an old rocking chair, oblivious to wind or weather, transported to some other world by whatever book lay to hand.

Most of the boys in Severson weren't interested in spending their evenings with a statuesque young blonde reading, tucked away in a corner recliner with Dickens, Wouk, or—horrors—C.S. Lewis. As snakes' eggs hatch little snakes, so the local boys—eggs dropped by American culture—hatched into little snakes and took their predatory behaviors elsewhere. She watched her girlfriends—many of whom went to the same church—one after another, succumb to a pregnancy, a disastrous early marriage, or worse, one or more abortions—all pitfalls she avoided. As she successfully stepped around these American cultural land mines, some seed of an idea began to unconsciously grow in her heart and mind ... the merest wisp, the gentlest impression, just the breath of a belief, that she was maybe just slightly of better stock than some of her peers there in Granite Sky. She looked at the quality of her upbringing, her still-strong ties to her family, and her Christianity—she was a youth Bible study group leader—and compared her life so far, as so many, many young adults do, to those around her. She was not displeased with the results.

Samantha launched off to Patrick Henry College in Virginia with a bursting heart and great optimism, eager to tackle greater challenges and influence the world for Christ. Though it was far from home, she'd chosen Patrick Henry because of the chance to major in classical liberal arts. She'd developed an early love for classic literature and, as they advertised, she wanted to 'shape the culture through good literature'. With her love for literature, she knew the only field for her would be publishing. She was heartily disappointed in the quality of what was passing for Christian literature in her time, and felt it a noble life's calling to seek to improve that genre.

And so, as Samantha stood there on the slick concrete plaza outside the Guilder building, she looked up at the steel and glass and marble and saw her future like a bright brass ring. She burned with a determination to let *nothing* stop her from reaching out and grabbing it.

***

Samantha walked through the tall glass doors and into the lobby. A flowing liquid wall of water cascading down from a dramatic eight-story tall fountain immediately caught her eye as she moved toward the reception desk. A glittering sign in three-foot high metal letters near the fountain proclaimed, "*I will give to the one who thirsts from the spring of the water of life without cost ...*" The lobby was expansive, opening up almost twenty stories, and Samantha stopped and just stared upward for a moment. Everything was so beautiful! She could see people moving about hundreds of feet above her, walking purposely along terraces lined in glass, engaged in casting forth the Word of God to every corner of the world from this bright and sparkling modern temple. Her heart pounded; she so wanted to be one of those people!

She inhaled slowly for a few seconds and then moved to the reception desk, where a bright and professional-looking young woman smiled up at her. Samantha pulled the invitation from her messenger bag, handing it to the receptionist with a warm look of gratefulness.

"Yes, of course, Ms. Gunderson, Ms. Witherspoon is expecting you. She's on the fourth floor, suite 475. The elevators are just there," she said, all smiles, leaning over the desk and stretching out a long, delicate arm toward the bank of six elevators, "and the facilities are just off to the right as you exit the elevators on that floor."

"Thank you," Samantha replied, took her invitation back, and tucked it away in her case. Her high heels clicked purposefully as she stepped across the marble-floored lobby and took the elevator to the fourth floor.

Sally Witherspoon was the company's Senior Director for Human Resources. Sally was forty-five, with two decades of experience handling personnel for large corporations. After a strong start at Smith, she'd garnered a personnel position with Microsoft, and then moved to Hewlett-Packard after marrying her high school sweetheart, who also happened to be a rising executive at HP. After five years there, she moved to take an opening with John Deere when her husband lost his job. They'd needed the extra income the move would provide, even though she'd been happy at HP. Jack wanted to get out of the high tech industry anyway and focus on returning to the simple life; he wanted to try carpentry. She didn't think much of that shift, and she thought even less of it every day she found herself still at her desk at six in the evening, working through a stack of new résumés or handling the latest personnel complaint. But Sally was a dutiful wife and since Jack was good with the two kids, she was on the whole satisfied with her life. She was a reserved woman—meticulously polite, circumspect, and proper—and found that a healthy application of professional reserve kept her from all kinds of difficulties in the personnel field.

One of Sally's junior personnel directors had already handled the preliminary interviews with the larger crop of candidates, and it was Sally's turn to take the finalists through a second round of interviews. She had a Samantha Gunderson at nine, a Gillian Nelson at eleven, and a Bill Fortescue at one. She looked up at the wall clock—eight forty-five. As her eyes left the clock, her office door opened and in walked a very tall blonde in a tailored business suit and a brown leather messenger bag.

She stood. "Ms. Gunderson? Hi, I'm Sally Witherspoon, and welcome to Guilder, Atchison, and Steckam." Sally shook Samantha's hand, grasping it firmly.

"Thank you so much, Ms. Witherspoon. I'm extremely grateful for the opportunity to talk with your staff today." Samantha conveyed a warm though professional demeanor. She'd dressed carefully for the interview in a gray silk suit with a high-necked ruffled white blouse, a mid-calf skirt, and a single strand of pearls at her throat. It was the most expensive ensemble she owned, and she probably would have thought twice about wearing it if she knew it cost about what Sally Witherspoon made in a month.

"Well, great. Let's get started." Sally took Samantha to a table and chairs set off in an alcove. One of her assistants came by and set a sheaf of papers down. "We'll need to you to fill these in ... won't take a moment ... and I'll see what they have for coffee this morning." Sally headed off for the coffee and Samantha addressed herself to the forms, which only took a moment or two to complete.

"The first interaction today is with our Executive Vice President for Sales, Manston Lewis—he goes by Manny. He'll explain in detail what we have in mind for the position and you two can talk about how you might fit in that role."

"That would be great," Samantha replied.

"So ... let's start. I'll take you over to see Manny. After Manny we want you to talk with our Senior Marketing Manager, Jason Cruz, and after that discussion, we'll wrap up with a few minutes in with Ms. Moehlen."

"The President?" Samantha exclaimed. "She interviews candidates?"

"Oh yah," Sally replied in a low, certain tone with an unmistakable northern Minnesota accent. "Dominique Moehlen is *extremely* particular about who we hire; she considers our people to be the main factor in the company' success, and her policy is to sit with every candidate we're considering. But don't worry, she's quite pleasant to talk with and ... trust me ... nothing you can prepare for." Sally smiled at this last, hoping it wouldn't put this Gunderson girl too much on edge. She glanced at her quickly, and it seemed that the tall young women took it in stride.

"Well, I think that's smart," Samantha answered after a moment. "If I was ultimately responsible for how well my car worked, I sure would want to have a look at the engine now and again."

Sally smiled to herself at the analogy. *Not bad*, she thought.

"There is one thing we should probably talk about before your series of interviews begins, though," Sally said, "and it's just this. In typical corporate interviews, religion isn't discussed—and that's by law. But state and federal law *does* permit a company to discuss matters of faith when it can be proven that such faith-based issues are central to the company's main product, mission, or service, and we're pretty sure Guilder, Atchison, and Steckam can make that case. So we hope you won't find it difficult to discuss matters of faith during your talks here."

"Oh, goodness no," Samantha said, almost gushing, "I mean, this is a Christian publishing house, right? Why would anyone come to work here not wanting to discuss their faith?"

"Well, that's the logic, true ... but you'd be surprised with some of the reactions I get to that little spiel." Sally paused, as though she was going to add something, but thought better of it. "So ... let's get on up and talk with Manny. Celine," Sally said over her shoulder to her assistant, "give Manny a call and let him know we're on the way."

***

Manny Lewis was a balding man in a wrinkled gray suit and a patterned blue tie over a gray shirt. He was short—shorter than Samantha—with a small round face, and brown eyes crinkled above fat cheeks. The shirt strained against a fairly sizable paunch as he stood to shake Samantha's hand.

"Sit down, sit down, very nice to have you ..." he looked down at a paper on his desk, "... Samantha. Would you like some coffee? How about a doughnut?" There was a box of doughnuts on the side table.

"Oh, thank you, no sir, I've got coffee here, thanks to Ms. Witherspoon, and I've eaten already, but thanks."

"Well good, good ... let me just take care of one item. Please, have a seat." Samantha took a seat at the round table in Lewis' office by Sally Witherspoon, and Manny punched a button on his phone. "Marcie, hold the calls for an hour, would you please?"

"Yes, Mr. Lewis," the secretary replied.

"Okay, now, good, good. Hey, Sally, thanks for bringing Samantha up." He turned to Samantha. "I'm sure you've got lots of questions, but I did want to discuss first with you the position we're looking to fill. You've read the job description, I'm thinking?"

"I have, yes." Samantha pulled it out of her bag and smoothed it out before her on the table.

"Good. Now, let's talk about this for a minute. See here where it says, that we want you to be aware of the firm's editorial needs of the end consumer 'by reviewing current publications and other content sources'. By that we mean you'd be working with other divisions in the company to gather and analyze their market research, and we'd expect you to attend whatever conferences or conventions that might be appropriate to our market areas."

"Yes sir; actually when I worked for Mackenzie and Wiles, I was traveling quite a bit, attending a conference or a convention maybe two or three times a month."

"Forgive me, Samantha ... what does Mackenzie and Wiles do?"

"Oh, I'm sorry—they're a political lobbying firm, based in Washington. That was my previous position—as a political researcher."

Lewis' eyebrows shot up. "Seriously? I mean, you spent time in a lobbying firm researching—wait, what exactly does a political researcher do?"

"Mainly we would conduct opinion polls around the country, gathering information on, oh, quite a range of different topics: politics, the environment, the economy, the war—"

"Religion?" Lewis asked, interrupting.

"Well ... Mackenzie and Wiles *was* a Republican firm, but they really didn't have us go after religious information," Samantha paused, and then said, "I suppose that was kind of strange, but nonetheless it wasn't something they were interested in."

"Well, forgive me for interrupting, but this is fortuitous. We were hoping for someone with experience in canvassing opinions, with an ability to go out there and dig up what people are thinking about the key issues of the day—and here, we're pretty curious about what people are thinking about faith-related topics. Will that be a difficulty for you?"

Samantha recognized the tactful opening Lewis was offering to speak of her faith, and she did just that. "Oh no, sir, not at all. I've been a Christian all my life; a Lutheran, though since I've been five my parents and I have attended a non-denominational church in Granite Sky, where I grew up. My folks took me to church all my life, and I still go. In fact, it's one of the reasons I've applied here—it's much closer to home, and I can tell you that the lack of faith in the nation's capital, among the 'movers and shakers' as they call themselves, can be pretty draining."

"I'm sure, I'm sure," Lewis replied absently. "This is good, very good. So here's our problem. Christianity is rapidly expanding, changing, and how the world defines Christianity is changing just as fast. I've been going to Snowfield Community for years now and since they've been following Rick Warren's teachings, the place has exploded."

"What's the membership now?" Samantha asked brightly.

"Well, I think we're up around thirty or forty thousand. But anyway, there are dozens of different new trends we're looking into, from just our one church. But there are quite a few other denominations, new trends, and philosophies that are coming into the Christian fold, and the ecumenical movement in the Catholic church is perhaps one of the most exciting things happening in Christianity since, well, maybe since the Reformation. Our new acquisitions editor will need to be out there in the field most of the time, getting a feel for the pulse of how Christianity is moving in the new century. He or she will not, as we see it, be tucked behind a desk, looking at manuscripts."

Samantha took just a minute to recalibrate her expectations and analyzed what Lewis was saying. "Okay, I can understand that," she replied. "You want someone who is tactful, energetic, maybe a tiny bit aggressive in going after substantial issues without being scared off, with some strong analytical skills to be your eyes and ears out in the field, discovering not just what people think, but also what new forms or shapes Christianity might be taking as we move into the future, and how the firm might design or market its products and services to meet emerging expectations."

Lewis sat back, a surprised, pleased smile on his face. He lifted both hands in the air, palms up, fingers spread apart. "Well there it is, Samantha, I don't think anyone in our Sales department could have said it better." He lowered his hands and pointed at her. "What you said is *exactly* what we want, and the characteristics you mentioned are just what we'll need." Lewis put his hands down flat on the table and smiled over at Witherspoon. "Man, Sally, where did you dig up this gem?"

Witherspoon looked down at her hands, folded demurely over Samantha's résumé, and with a noticeable tinge of professional reserve, so as not to make it seem as though Guilder, Atchison, and Steckam was, with unseemly haste, committing to Samantha, said "This is what Personnel does, Manny. All the candidates you'll see today will be very well qualified."

"Oh, right, right, no question. No doubt."

The interview wound on, Samantha talking about where she was from, what her life was like, why she wanted to change from her current position, and what she hoped to accomplish as an employee of Guilder, Atchison, and Steckam.

"I want to make a difference," she said. "I've worked in the past for companies that had clear missions and objectives, but ... you know, some missions and objectives are better than others. I mean, if a company's mission is to, say, share the Word of God to the whole world, wouldn't that be better than working in a company whose mission is to, I don't know ... to make the best refrigerators in the world? There's a difference there ... at least to me, anyway. And I believe I can help you here," she went on. "I have some pretty solid experience getting out there and identifying what people are thinking and feeling—people talk to me. Anyway," she said, pausing, not wanting to go on too much about her talents, "I think I'd do well here, and make a difference for Christ in the world. Not that I have anything against refrigerators, though."

Lewis laughed at that with an honest chuckle.

"Well, good, I'm glad, and thank you for coming in to talk with us, Samantha." Lewis stood up; the interview was over. Samantha shook his hand and followed Sally out of his office and on to the next interview.

***

The Senior Marketing Manager was a trim, dark young Hispanic man named Jason Cruz. Jason was youngish—younger than Samantha expected—and, she could see right away, definitely a high-energy executive. He wore a trim, body-hugging fashionable black suit with thin lapels, a thin fluorescent green tie, a diamond cross stud in one ear, square-toed, elongated black leather shoes, and a starched white silk shirt. He was very handsome, with dark eyes, short dark curly hair frosted with a few blonde streaks, and he sported what was for fashionable younger men the almost obligatory three-day old movie star stubble on his face. He stood up quickly as she and Sally entered his office.

"Hey, Samantha Gunderson, welcome to the big house!" he said, full of energy and enthusiasm. "Sit down, sit down. Sally, hey, how are you?"

"Very well, Jason, thanks," Sally replied calmly.

"Good, good." He looked at his watch. There was no round table in Cruz' office; he sat behind his normal large working desk and the two women took chairs across from him. "Good timing, good timing ... so hey, let's get down to business." Cruz took off his jacket and draped it over the back of his chair. "So tell me about what you want to do here," he asked, rubbing his hands together and launching the question like a bull explodes from a rodeo chute.

Samantha took her cue from Witherspoon, and, sitting straight in her chair, hands folded quietly in her lap over her résumé, at a slightly lower energy level went through with Cruz the type of activities she'd laid out to Manny Lewis, and was pleased to see that apparently internal communications at Guilder, Atchison, and Steckam were good, because it appeared that Lewis and Cruz were on the same page regarding what they wanted from the New Acquisitions editor.

"*Exactly* what we want," Cruz cut in as she was describing the position. "We want you out there, digging around, seeing what people are thinking and feeling and expecting." He paused. "Let me show you something." Cruz pulled a single piece of paper from his desk and handed it to her. She saw a list of names on one side, and what looked like names of denominations or movements on the other.

"You think you could give a try at matching the names on the left to the movements on the right?" he asked, smiling. "There might be more than one name to a movement." Through all his high energy and outgoing mannerisms, Samantha sensed that the young Cruz was ambitious and intensely competitive. She'd dealt with the type before. Washington was littered with them.

"Sure," she replied pleasantly, trying to diminish any sense of challenge in her reply. "I'll give it a try. So let's see ..." She read names on the left: "Doug Pagitt, Brian McLaren, Sally Morgenthaler, Alice Bailey, Willis Harman, Peter Senge, George Barna, Jim Van Yperen, Nancy Beach, Dan Limber, John Wimber. C. Peter Wagner, and Leonard Sweet. And then you've got what looks like topics down the right side of the paper." Samantha read them off in order. "Vintage Christianity, ageless wisdom, worship and evangelism, Church polling, Willow Creek Community Church, Vineyard Church, church conflict, the Emergent Church, New Apostolic Reformation, The New Man, The Jesus Manifesto, and Building Networks. Well, that's a long list. Let me see…I know Dan Limber, I've read his book and I seem to remember him mentioning Vintage Christianity."

"Correct ... that's one," Cruz said. "Good. What else?"

"Okay ... now, everyone pretty much knows Brian McLaren is with the Emergent Church, but I don't know this Sally Morgenthaler, so I'll pass on her. Let's see ..." She ran her eyes down the names, looking for someone familiar. "I know Peter Senge; I actually went to a seminar he gave in DC. So that one is easy—I'd match him with building networks."

"Smack on," Cruz exulted, though his eyes were sharpened. "A lot of people consider Senge and others, like Margaret Wheatley, as having something significant to contribute to a twenty-first century church."

Samantha nodded, impressed with Cruz's broad knowledge. She went on. "So okay, and here's John Wimber, who I'm pretty sure started Vineyard Fellowship, coming out of Calvary Chapel?"

"Right, right. Any more?" Witherspoon looked over at Cruz with veiled eyes, wondering why he had chosen to put this rather unorthodox test to the candidate; she wasn't sure these kinds of high-stress assessments really proved anything, although she had to admit that Gunderson seemed to be rolling with it quite well.

"You've got Leonard Sweet; I am pretty sure he and Frank Viola wrote *The Jesus Manifesto*. And of course you've got George Barna here, who would match with 'Church polling', no question. Jim Van Yperen ... I know him, I read one of his books, and, yes, right here, his specialty is on church conflict. Sally Morgenthaler ... yup, I remember now; I read her book on Worship and Evangelism, so I'd match her to that line ... and Nancy Beach ... I know about her, she pretty much built the arts ministry at Willow Creek, so I'd match her to that. C. Peter Wagner, I'd probably link him with the New Apostolic Reformation. But these last two, Alice Bailey and Willis Harman ... I've never heard of them before."

"Wow, that's excellent." Cruz was truly surprised; he'd worked up this little test just the day prior, and while he had jotted them down and could make the matches out of hand, he didn't think he'd find a candidate so up to speed on recent church events, able to match more than one or two.

"That's quite good," Sally spoke up, encouragingly. "I don't think I would have gotten half that many."

"Well, I feel I should have gotten them all, actually. I do enough reading; I should have known the rest."

"Oh, seriously, that's no problem," Cruz put in. "Really. Alice Bailey would match with 'ageless wisdom'; her writings are being reviewed by a number of folks in the Emergent Church movement as having a lot to contribute to the new spirituality we're seeing. And Willis, well, Willis is pretty out there, and I'm not surprised you'd not make that connection. He'd connect to 'the New Man'—Harman had this idea that sooner or later mankind is going to sort of press through our current physiological, psychological, and emotional structures and sort of emerge or evolve into new ones."

Samantha put on an expression of polite interest. "I'll have to look into that. Has he written anything I could read about?"

"Well, he wrote *Global Mind Change: The New Revolution in the Way We Think*, and it is really out on the cutting edge."

"I'll pull it down from Amazon right away," Samantha said eagerly. She pulled her phone from the messenger bag, swiped a finger across the screen, tapped twice, and typed in the title. "Thanks, Mr. Cruz, that sounds interesting."

"No, thank *you*, and Sally, thanks, this actually has been a treat. I'm way impressed. Samantha, seriously, I'm very grateful. I worked this little test up just last night—I guess I'd better make it a little more difficult."

"Oh, no, no, that was hard enough. Remember I didn't get them all," Samantha said modestly.

Witherspoon looked down as her phone vibrated, and she flipped it out of the case and read the message. "Jason, if that's all, we should move on. Dominique will be ready for her in about five minutes."

Cruz stood up quickly. "Right. Good to meet you, Samantha, and best of luck." They shook hands and Samantha followed Sally back out of the office, into the elevator. She pressed the button for the top floor.

"Executive suite," she quipped, and Samantha nodded, smiling wanly.

"Oh, don't worry. You'll do fine. Dominique's probably one of the best Chief Executive Officers in this or any other business. Are you familiar with her background?"

"A little," Samantha replied. "I know she spent most of her time in the high tech industries, around computers I think, mostly in the financial aspects of leadership, until she headed up, what was it, the Forman Corporation, about eight years ago. I know she's been on the cover of *Business Leadership*; I know she's written a few books, one of which I just finished reading last week on female executives."

"My, you do read a bit, don't you?" Sally turned to face Samantha, smiling, impressed.

"Well, it's pretty much my favorite thing to do," she replied.

Sally looked at the tall women frankly. "Well that's a good hobby for an editor, I'll admit. Do you have any family, that sort of thing?" Sally asked.

"No, not really. I mean, there were a few low-level things in DC, and there's this one situation that might develop into something serious, but I've just moved out here, and though my mother lives up in Granite Sky, I don't expect to get up there that often."

"No, I wouldn't think so. It's a bit of a drive. Okay, here we are."

They stepped out of the elevator and Sally spoke to the executive secretary. "Right, Samantha Gunderson, candidate for New Acquisitions. Good. Okay." Sally turned back to Samantha. "Okay, Samantha, why don't you go right in? I'll wait out here." Samantha nodded, gathered herself, squared her broad shoulders, and moved to the President's door.

As Samantha entered, Dominique Moehlen stood up and came around a massive steel and glass-topped desk to welcome her. Moehlen wore a sedate, soft blue suit and a skirt just exactly, Samantha was relieved to see, as long as her own. She had short brown hair that curled at her neckline, and wore small gold earrings and a single gold wedding band. Her fingers were long and thin, and her handshake was firm, her skin smooth and cool.

"Samantha, welcome to Guilder, Atchison, and Steckam. You're probably tired of hearing that long, drawn out name all day."

"No ma'am, actually, it's nice to hear. I hope to hear it more often, actually."

Moehlen laughed, a lilting, quick enjoyment of Samantha's eagerness mixed with humor. "Please, let's sit down and we can chat for a while. Tell me a little bit about yourself."

Samantha went through the story of her life, edited to fit what she hoped a modern CEO would want to hear. When she was finished, Moehlen nodded.

"That sounds like a good solid life, Samantha. And so tell me ... what is it that you want to do with your life from this point forward?"

Samantha had practiced the answer to that question, and for her, it was easy, since she'd known the answer since her first years in high school. "Ma'am, ever since I was in high school, aching to find good Christian literature, and pretty much failing, I promised myself that if I got the chance, I'd try and improve the quality of what is put out as Christian literature. I guess you could say that's sort of what I've devoted my life to."

"That's impressive," Moehlen responded. "So tell me how we might help you do that here?"

"Oh, there's no question about that, Ma'am," Samantha replied quickly. "I mean, in just the few interviews I've had today I've learned how broad the field is out there and there are so *many* areas I haven't even touched on about what is happening in Christianity ... there is *so much* out there I don't know about, well, I think that as your New Acquisitions editor, I could really get a better picture of what Christianity is becoming, and maybe help to shape that just a little."

"And that," Moehlen said, leaning forward with just a tinge of authority, indicating she was pleased with Samantha's answer, "is what we're about here. Christianity is changing so rapidly, and our mission is to make the Word understandable to the emerging generations of people around the world who might not otherwise be able to make any sense of what in the past might have been a little confusing. Our job is to blend what might appear to many to be disparate or diverse doctrines, different threads or interpretations of the faith, so that perhaps common ground might emerge; maybe a degree of commonality might be perceived in the dialectic, a level of harmony that hasn't ever been achieved before. There are so many threads to faith in the next century, as you say, and so many exciting new things, and the nature of that faith is changing in so many ways that I think anyone would be thrilled simply to be a part of this market space and that mission—and I can tell you, that's *my* mission in life."

"Yes ma'am. It would be an honor and a pleasure for me to have the opportunity to help you do that."

"Well, Samantha, it sounds sort of like we've something similar as far as life missions go, now doesn't it?" Moehlen smiled openly and stood; Samantha did as well, and they walked to the door.

"Thanks for coming, and I wish you the best in the process here, and wherever your life takes you."

"Thank you, Ms. Moehlen, and I really do appreciate what your company is trying to do in the faith."

Moehlen shook her hand, and Samantha left the office, short of breath but hoping that she'd performed adequately. She had the funny feeling as she stepped out of the CEO's office that her life seemed to have been nothing but a string of small performances, one after the other, always striving to impress or please, working to hit the right note, or put the correct face on things, and wondered if that was all there was to life ... it was just a brief, flashing, discordant thought, especially standing there in the anteroom of one of the world's most powerful and successful CEOs, and probably was a result of enduring three high-stress interviews in the space of an hour—but it wasn't something she easily forgot.

***

Eight days passed, during which Samantha visited with her family. She hadn't made any permanent living arrangements in Minneapolis since she wasn't sure she'd get the job, but she had other applications in and wanted to take some time to visit her parents. On the eighth day, she plugged her MacBook Pro into the wall in her old bedroom—all pink and white frills, with the same wallpaper that she had stared at night after night growing up, dreaming first of horses, then of one boy or another. She waited for the machine to power up and was brushing her hair at the nightstand when the computer notified her that she had email. She opened her email application and saw that one of messages was from the Human Resources department at Guilder, Atchison, and Steckam.

She didn't know if she should open it or not. What if it was a polite rejection?

She wanted this job so *badly*. Where would she go if she didn't get this? The chance to get out of Washington, the chance to be near her parents, the opportunity to work with a world-class company doing something Christian ... it was too much to hope for, but hope she did. She said a quick prayer, mouthing simply, *God, oh please, I want this so badly, please make this happen*, and clicked to open the email.

The word '*Congratulations*' jumped out, and she jumped off the night table stool, let out a gloriously loud whoop, and then read the rest of the email. Yes, they were definitely offering her the job, she'd scored at the top of a very competitive field, and the offer letter, with other necessary documents, was attached to the email. They were asking her to start in two weeks. Samantha bolted down the stairs to tell her Mom the good news.

Historian's Note: ENEMY DOCUMENTS

Thousands of enemy documents were captured when the usurper's kingdom was crushed, although the word 'document' may be somewhat misleading. In truth they were ephemeral spheres of spiritual substance which angelic warriors secured. Translatable only in the realm of the spirit, many spent much time trying to transpose the threads of emotion and spiritual energy in these spheres. It was truly hard work, since to be translated they needed to be broken, and when broken, the stench was truly monstrous.

While many of these spheres contained high-level strategic plans and directives—such as the Protocols contained in this and other volumes of this series—thousands more were writings, directions, and plans from a lower level, showing how demonic influence struck at human beings to keep them from the Truth. I include one of the lower-level reports at this juncture in the story to show the enemy's tactics. I include the report verbatim to display the variation in expression, tone, and intensity that ranged through the enemy's ranks. These reports were not filed in words but in emotions, which were only afterward translated by our translators, hence the crapulous grammatical structure. We have found it best to try only and follow the emotional vectors instead of attaching any specific meaning to words. Only the barest rudiments of punctuation have been inserted to provide a semblance of readability. Consider it simply a flood of emotion with some nebulous intention.

I attach the translator's 'Archive label' at the head of these captured eruptions of hate simply to provide context.

***

[Archive label:
Marduk Principality
Layer 14 Power
Interdiction Report]

Pankowicz hated / burning wind strong bad too close aagghh bad we send CONFUSE CONFUSE STAY GO bad stay bad stay RUN RUN / we brave we use mate / mate close control / [name occluded] wields great power in mate since squirming[14] / we sting with pride / we send message keep family, keep family, keep family ... shower down shame second divorce, shame; second divorce, shame / we send Ironbridge bad use Pankowicz no care about Pankowicz Ironbridge bad / we send burning wind bad, Pankowicz burning wind listen not / we send burning wind bad; burning wind bad scream hate hate hate

Hate Pankowicz we / he listen Ironbridge / bad / kill / consume / destroy / hate

Fear great fear run flee leave Ironbridge pit fear / we send children need father mother needs father wife needs husband / attack strike pierce circle kill / we send RUN RUN get home get

14 A term that apparently refers to a young age, or youth.

home / send Ironbridge fake understand not Hateful One bad bad use Pankowicz for own lust RUN RUN get home get home / we use mate use mate twist stab pierce pride hate hate so much filled / [name occluded] fills mate with hate pride puff puff / send to mate WISE WISE, CAREFUL CAREFUL Minnesota bad bad, husband not wise, hate, hurtful, bad, not care of squirming things, burn burn mate be food for us yes food for us to kill eat soon to come yet mate knows not [here some sort of jubilant cry or some type of expression of gleeful anticipation]

Kill mate kill Pankowicz kill squirmings kill Ironbridge death all grind chop blood splatter eat kill destroy hate hate ahh burn burn we do.

***

A very rough translation of the above would indicate that apparently the demonic entity or entities assigned to assault or interfere with Stan Pankowicz were complaining about the presence of the Holy Spirit during Pankowicz' association with the Ironbridge family. The enemy used Pankowicz' wife, who they had been influencing since she was just a child, to interfere with the Holy Spirit's communications with Pankowicz. The enemy leveraged Pankowicz' fear of a second divorce to move him away from obedience to the Great King's direction for his life. The enemy tried to communicate to Pankowicz that listening to the things Ironbridge was telling him was bad, and would result in the loss of everything he held dear. The enemy could not help but disclose their true feelings for Pankowicz--they hated him intensely, they wanted to see him destroyed, burning in hell, consigned to eternal misery ... just as they were. The enemy closes with ruminations upon how in the future they will consume the souls of both Pankowicz and his wife and children if they can but lure Pankowicz away from Ironbridge and the hated influence of the 'Burning Wind'—the Holy Spirit.

Chapter 23
Stan

"For they exchanged the truth of God for a lie, and worshiped and served the creature rather than the Creator, who is blessed forever. Amen."

Romans 1:25

I was at a complete loss as to how I should do what I needed to do. I had decided after thinking about things long and hard that if I was going to hold on to at least a shred of who I was as a man, I just couldn't lose another family. I was pretty sure God would understand. I needed to get back home, put Janet's mind at ease that we wouldn't be relocating—at least right away, and try and bring her and the kids around to understanding a little bit about real Christianity.

The only thing I'd ever wanted since I had been a kid was a solid family. I was sure God wouldn't want me to leave them, and if I decided to move to Minnesota, well, they were certainly not going to come along and there I'd be again, another family down the drain. But I didn't know how to explain this to Tack.

Things were coming to a head. I had been staying in his cabin for the last three weeks and I was able to find at least one or two things that just wouldn't suit in every place I'd looked. What brought me to the point of just telling him straight out about my decision was when I ran across his son, Mace.

I hadn't actually met Mace to that point. The cabin where I stayed was out of the way of the main farm, and each time I would come to visit Tack, Mace and his wife Zoe happened to be out on some errand or another. I think Tack may have mentioned that they were working out in the pastures, getting them ready for summer, which, he said, meant that they would stay out there for days or weeks at a time. There was a small satellite milking operation closer to the pastures and though it was portable it wasn't as automated nor as easy to use as the main system in the barn, so, Tack said, it took them quite some time to get all the systems working.

So I was a little surprised when I pulled up to talk just one more time to Tack, to see if he had any ideas on how I might work out a compromise to keep on learning about God and building a relationship with Him but keep my family, to see a strapping young man in a tan chore coat and a woman with long red hair in overalls, both standing next to Tack just outside the barn.

As I parked and walked toward them, the young man, Mace, looked at me from a distance and suddenly I felt like I was walking in mud, my feet as heavy as lead, and I began to feel nauseous. And then I smelled the strangest odor ... actually not strange, but foul, like something had died in or near the barn and was rotting, the stench wafting in thick waves of ordure all around me as I approached them. I couldn't believe the three of them didn't smell it. But then I thought, maybe that's what they're discussing.

"Morning, Tack," I said, and Tack looked at me with what I could only describe as a saddened countenance. I approached, wondering what it was that had put him out of humor.

"Stan," he said. "Meet my son, Mace, and his wife Zoe."

I shook Mace's hand and the smell of rotten flesh overwhelmed me. I couldn't help myself. "Ughh," I exclaimed. "Are you all smelling that?"

The woman looked strangely at me. "Smelling what? And hi, I'm Zoe." She stood with her hands stuffed in the pockets of her overalls.

"You guys don't smell that?"

Tack looked at me with a hard eye. "Stan, we don't smell anything. What is it that you smell?"

"Something's died around here, no doubt about it," I said, looking around the edge of the barn, maybe to see some dead rodent or something.

But instead of hounding down that line of curiosity with me, Tack said, "Stan, you look like you've got something to say."

That kind of took me up short. How did he know that? I hadn't planned on telling Tack what my decision was, but something pushed me, something I can't define, something that rose up and compelled me to tell Tack about my decision.

"Yeah, actually, Tack, I was wondering if we could step inside for a moment."

"Sure, hold on." Tack turned to Mace and gave him some kind of instruction about something or other, but truthfully I couldn't follow what he was saying because I was in such fierce passion to get away from Mace that I couldn't focus on anything. And that smell! I was astounded that they didn't smell it! It must have been a dead cow or something, it was so powerful, and it must have been dead for a week. I'd never smelled anything so overpoweringly awful in my life.

"Okay, Stan, come on in." He led the way into the house and he took of his muck boot and his prosthetic leg he used around the farm, doing chores. I took off my own boots and we both went into the living room.

"Claire's out with Emma this morning, riding. Emma is a superb horse trainer and as you can see we need horses trained."

"Yeah, I can see that," I said, somewhat distractedly, because as I came into the house the awful smell diminished. It *must* have been something near the barn. "And you didn't smell anything out near the barn?" I asked Tack again. "I can't believe you guys couldn't smell it. It was disgusting."

Tack didn't say anything, but I could see him sigh once, and then we moved into the living room, or library, or whatever it was they called it.

Tack turned and got to the point right away, like always. "What's up?"

I moved through the room, my hands in my pockets, circling one of the chairs like a dog looking for a place to sleep. Now that I was there, I had a hard time starting.

"You want to leave, don't you?" Tack said, helping.

I looked up at him, hoping to find a kind, compassionate, understanding look on his face. Nothing of the sort stared back at me, but simply a hard, flat, expressionless face, though perhaps tinged with sadness.

"Tack, there's nothing I can do. Janet just won't move out here, and if she won't come out here, the kids won't either."

Tack nodded slightly. "Yeah, I hear you, but you were telling me not last week that you were convinced God wanted you to come out here."

"I won't lose my family again, Tack."

"Are you sure you have one, Stan? From everything you've said, everything we've heard, it seems you're simply a meal ticket. None of them seem to have any regard for your position as a father, any love for you as a husband, any respect for your position as head of the home as appointed by God. So tell me, what exactly are you referring to when you talk about your family?"

I really didn't have any answer to that, putting it the way he did. He was right, unfortunately.

"So you're determined to go?" he asked.

"I have to. Janet won't follow me."

"Stan, let me read you something." Tack pulled a Bible off a shelf—there must have been twenty of them lying around—and then said, "this is from Colossians. It says, *'Therefore, if you have been raised up with Christ, keep seeking the things above, where Christ is, seated at the right hand of God. Set your mind on the things above, not on the things that are on earth.'"* He put the Bible down and looked at me. "Do you understand this? Do you understand the counsel here?"

"Look, Tack, if I come out here, I'll lose my family."

"So you're going to let your wife take the leadership in your home. This is the example you're going to show to your kids?"

"My plan is to go back and maybe be some sort of influence in her life and the lives of my kids, maybe show them the light of Christ."

Tack held up a hand. "Don't even think that such a thing will happen, Stan. Let me read you something else, from Hebrews. Have you gotten that far yet? No, well, you'll want to hear this too." He picked up the Bible again and read, "*For in the case of those who have once been enlightened and have tasted of the heavenly gift and have been made partakers of the Holy Spirit, and have tasted the good word of God and the powers of the age to come, and then have fallen away, it is impossible to renew them again to repentance, since they again crucify to themselves the Son of God and put Him to open shame.*" He closed the book and looked at me. "What does that mean in practical terms for you? Let me give you a better idea of what might happen, if the Bible and my knowledge of God is any guide. What happens when we know what God wants us to do and we do the opposite? I'll tell you, in your situation.

"If you go back there, don't expect them to welcome you with open arms. In fact, expect them to be even more disdainful, because they'll have broken you to their will and they'll be convinced that from now on they can make you do anything they want you to do. And they'll be right. But that won't be the worst of it. No, the worst part will be that shortly after you get back, your desire to get into the Word will diminish and then disappear. You'll find that you won't really be able to understand as much of the Word as you have been while you've been here, obeying Him. You'll find actually that you won't really want to read the Word any longer. Things like studying the Bible, being in fellowship with other Believers, and, most important, your relationship with the living God will all just fade away like some fuzzy dream, and you'll look back on the weeks you spent here as some kind of weird aberration, some transitory phase or fad you were going through, and eventually you'll come to the place where you really won't even want to admit that you knew us. And," he said, and I felt this would be the hardest thing he would tell me, "you will forget that the Creator of the Universe ever spoke to you directly; you'll forget His gift of that olive branch. You'll forget that He offered you peace, and as you go off to find peace on your own, in your own strength, abandoning what He's told you very clearly what to do, such a peace will become even more elusive. Your family will hate you, and you'll end up hating yourself and your situation, and one day you'll wake up and look up and shake your fist at the heavens and curse God for your situation."

***

I packed out of the cabin that afternoon, leaving Jed Sloan my key. I didn't stop at the main farm as I drove out, but simply drove on down the lane past their house. As I drove by, I saw Mace standing in front of the Carriage House, standing there in his tan chore coat watching me, and I felt he was looking straight into my soul. It was not a pleasant experience.

The last thing I remember about the Ironbridge farm was that as I drove past the young kid, that stench of death rose up in my nostrils again, and I almost gagged. It lasted until he disappeared from sight, fading away in the rearview mirror. A sense of relief washed over me as I left. I would keep my family; I would. Everything would work out.

PART 3
Instruments

A sound of tumult on the mountains, like that of many people! A sound of the uproar of kingdoms, of nations gathered together! The Lord of hosts is mustering the army for battle. They are coming from a far country, from the farthest horizons, the Lord and His instruments of indignation, to destroy the whole land.

Isaiah 13:4-6

Chapter 24

PROTOCOLS OF THE ZHONGGUO PRINCIPALITY

Historian's Preface: The Mandarin word Zhōngdōng wángguó, or 'Zhongguo' means, simply, 'Middle Kingdom'. The Power in authority over this Principality chose the name with a great and consuming arrogance, attempting, as was its nature, to set itself above all other extant principalities by alleging that it ruled all that was not the Higher Kingdom—i.e. Heaven, nor the Lower Kingdom—that is, hell. Throughout the history of the nation over which it ruled one can clearly see the fingerprint of this particular Principality suffused throughout China's leaders, philosophy, politics, culture, and national behaviors—specifically, an all-consuming conviction that they were destined to rule the entire world.

This Protocol excerpt was generated during what was apparently a planning conference convened within the Zhongguo Principality to chart out the strategy to invade America.

Sartorius Crux Vita
Diamond Gate, Jerusalem
AR 40

***

Philosophical Basis for Action

From the time of the Great Ascent[15], mankind has desired to be as God. This desire was used as leverage within the Principality by installing the legend of an Emperor descended from Heaven, reinforcing the belief of those under the authority of this Principality that men could be Gods; that there were human individuals endowed with a supernatural dictum to rule—in effect, a mandate from heaven. Accompanying this worship of man, the worship of dead men was also injected as a means to keep the stones'[16] focus on man instead of anything higher in nature. This system of worship came with the normal accoutrements applied in other principalities, although the particulars originated here—the worship of human or animal bones or other artifacts belonging to ancestors, attribution of failed crops or local victories in battle to the whims of the dead having influence over the living. This initiative had the beneficial ancillary effect of generating in the stone a desire to sacrifice to these dead ancestors, and so myriads of convicts, slaves, or others more precious to them were slaughtered en masse, producing a rich, varied, and delectable bouquet of suffering, misery, and despair, which greatly served our purpose. As a unique and very effective corollary application of these fundamental philosophies,

15 The adversary's vernacular includes reference to the Fall of Mankind in the Garden as his 'Great Ascent'.

16 'Stones' was the term used by the Zhongguo Principality to refer to those humans living in its territories.

this Principality established a cultural value which dictated that the stones could depose the Emperor should he be judged as insufficiently serving their best interests, thereby cementing in their minds with ineluctable authority the idea that men could call into question the decisions and actions of their gods, and that these so-called gods were in fact subject to man's judgment. The Principality obscured this blatantly illogical idea by, with equal firmness, establishing the cultural ethic of blind, mindless obedience to authority; instilling in every fabric of the stones' history and culture the idea that to oppose authority was deeply and unquestionably wrong. This was made more palatable to the stones by establishing in the national consciousness an idea that authority was paternal; that its role was as that of a father in a family—to provide for and look after every member. In so doing, the concept of obedience to a true God was effectively and efficiently deflected, and instead the people were easily led to confer their obedience instead on, at first, a line of Emperors whom, they were convinced, had a direct connection to a supernatural power. In consonance with this obedience to man-gods, the idea of obedience to dead ancestors was overlaid, further confounding reality. Only later, when history, technology, and political philosophies made it expedient to debunk the concept of the supernatural, did the Principality subtly displace their obeisance from the Emperor to the State. This was easily and effectively achieved through the utilization of a particularly powerful version of the political philosophy known as Communism. In a truly ironic and elegant twist, however, obedience and dedication to dead ancestors was retained as a cultural value highly esteemed, thereby enslaving stones to the past, discouraging new paths and effectively occluding their understanding of the enemy's vicious concept of righteousness.

It need not be mentioned that any sign of allegiance to the Higher Kingdom, or any instance where stones are adhering to the tenets of that realm, is to be immediately and brutally repressed or eliminated. The Principality has been so successful with this effort that in no aspect have the cultures, philosophies, foundational ideas, values, ethics, mores, or behaviors present in the Middle Kingdom been in any way influenced by that malignant spirit from the Higher Kingdom.

Cultural Background for Action

The Principality has established four main culturally-based methodologies to ensure the ruling stones make decisions supporting our cause regarding military action contemplated against the Pathetic Land[17]. The stones thus ruled are convinced that it is through the interplay of these various cultures that decisions emerge; they are completely unaware that the Principality has structured the composition and nature of each of these cultural decision-making tools and therefore maintains comprehensive and complete control of all decisions made throughout every level of Zhongguo society—especially in regards to the use of military force. Subjugation

17 'The Pathetic Land' is a shortened translation of the term used within the Zhongguo Principality to refer to America. The Adversary's language is mangled, full of contradictions and innuendo, but when they can use a disparaging term in place of an accurate one, they will. A literal translation from that language reads, "The land that strangled itself, that was light but will now be dark, that is being judged by the High Kingdom due to its own weak and pathetic ennui." I have shortened this to 'the Pathetic Land'—a term the Adversary's adherents also used, which, I believe reflects to some degree their irritation about the fact that America had once been a pinnacle of Light to the nations. America at the time was ruled by perhaps the most powerful Principality under the Prince of Darkness. America was more accurately known as the Marduk Principality—under the same Principality that ruled ancient Babylon.

of awareness[18] has been comprehensively and completely achieved.

The four cultures within this Principality applicable to the exertion of military force against the Pathetic Land are the Political Culture, the Strategic Culture, the Civil-Military Culture, and the Organizational Culture. The stones believe that these have miraculously 'evolved' throughout their long and glorious history. They have remained unaware that each step of their historical evolution has been carefully influenced and guided. The efficacy of how each of these cultures has been formed will now be expounded upon so as to more fully inform planners regarding coming operations.

Political culture has been, within this Principality, a means whereby extensive degrees of control have been established, keeping the stones off-balance, disconcerted, and unconnected to their original design functionality by changing it so often. Historically, political culture has been defined as those value systems, ethics, mores, and patterns of behaviors or beliefs associated with the political activities of a nation. This definition served its purpose for the time period in which it was applied, but in preparation for this new operation, a new definition was needed so as to adequately compel stone leadership to adopt the required policies and decisions. This new definition incorporated an alleged concern for individuals as much more than passive recipients of political dictates; now, rather, the culture of politics is considered the realm of both state and societal entities. This alteration allowed us room to then begin a campaign of influence in which various symbols, rituals, and languages could be included—elements which we had, of course, already prepared and had standing by, ready to play their parts. Fueling social unrest because of perceived global economic injustices fostered by the Pathetic Land simply contributed to political leadership's agenda toward undertaking the planned operations, though without this shift in definition of political culture, such dissatisfaction would have been most likely ignored. With the mass of stones in this Principality, with their usual levels of energy and intelligence, such a storm of discontent needed to be harnessed.

Chinese foreign and military policy also needed impetus, and so recently we have influenced stone leadership in those areas to adopt the concept or application of strategic culture in their decision-making processes. So as to validate offensive operations of such a magnitude, there was a need to awaken the stones to the necessity of moving from a defensive-minded national strategic mindset toward a more offensive outlook. This was accomplished by influencing various historians and scholars to 'discover' that in 'truth', China has throughout its history not been averse to offensive operations. Archeological evidence was planted or fabricated; scholars were influenced or compelled; emotional and mental leverages were applied so as to obtain the desired results. The final accomplishment produced a mentality in stone decision-makers in this Principality that China has always had two aspects to its strategic culture—one a peace-loving defensive-minded stance, but the other a Realpolitik position favoring offensive operations when 'justified'. With this historical obstacle removed, the Principality's stone leadership could with validity and justification consider offensive operations. The manipulation of these opinions, discoveries, and results was simplistic, achieved via normal methodologies.

Civil-military culture was the third aspect necessary to adjust. This cultural aspect deals simply with how those stones not assigned to military organizations view those who are, and what is or is not permissible (in their minds, of course) regarding the application of violence in a society. This aspect of culture is responsible for setting policies and constraints upon the

18 The Principality's term, 'Subjugation of Awareness' refers to one of its most central strategies—the effort to subjugate any awareness in those it rules regarding the existence of those Powers and Principalities.

nation's military force, and as such needed to be adjusted so as to prepare the stones in this Principality for our desired operations against the Pathetic Land. Whereas in the past the civil segment in this Principality viewed the military as significantly intertwined with civil leadership—thanks primarily to our arrangement of what the stones term 'the Long March'—of late this connection has been allowed to fall into disrepair because the current stone leadership essential to our purposes were not permitted to obtain experience in the military. With the operations contemplated, an increase to more robust levels of interaction has been required, where civil sectors fully embrace and support military actions and philosophies. Fortunately, current leadership has been easily influenced to more fully embrace military-style solutions to national difficulties.

Finally, to ensure successful military operations once deployed, the particular organizational culture of the military used by this Principality must be addressed. This is simply the doctrines, employment methodologies, policies, and structures within the military organization as a whole. Stones applied to military duties develop different perspectives, philosophies, and biases than those possessed by stones in civil leadership positions. Strangely, military stones tend to be more conservative and cautious than their civil counterparts, although this has its own logic—the civil counterparts are not as closely associated with the savory affects of military violence and therefore have less motivation to avoid it. The stones have a regrettable tendency toward self-preservation which, unfortunately, is difficult to remove. When the stone Deng became food for our Master's table, we took steps to ensure the military retained its position of high influence in civil sectors, and this has been accomplished. As well, current military leadership has been selected specifically for their inclinations toward offensive operations. Internal organizational structures, doctrines, policies, and tactics are being reconstructed so as to favor the offensive, and philosophically, steps are being taken to inject key leadership stones with expertise in commercial business and economic development, civil infrastructure, social destabilization efforts, and military operations, into the Pathetic Land (under jurisdiction of that Principality) so as to conduct suitable reconnaissance. Where these injections occur, care must be taken such that the stones dispatched are not unduly influenced by elements from the Higher Kingdom. Weak though that influence has become, yet it remains in much greater force within that jurisdiction than in any form the stones here have experienced, and it can tend to be disconcerting unless their associations are carefully controlled and their influences forcefully handled.

The upshot of these cultural adjustments has been to shift China's traditional 'Cult of the Defense' to something which, as a policy, would with reasonable consideration undertake offensive operations against the Pathetic Land while rationalizing those operations as necessary for China's national security, as being purely defensive, and seeing such operations as a 'last resort' before the China's inevitable collapse. This fear has its grounds in the intense national pride this Principality has fostered within Chinese stones regarding their history and their 'past accomplishments'. Offensive operations against the Pathetic Land will be conducted based upon two main national security policy memes we have taken pains to instill: (1) the unquestionable requirement that the nation remain united, and (2) that the Pathetic Land actually threatens China's survival in the way a millstone around a stone's neck, thrown into the water, would threaten the stone's life. In this analogy, we have coerced Chinese stone leadership to perceive the Pathetic Land as the millstone, and in seeing things thusly, they feel fully confident that leaping out with a knife to cut the rope is a purely defensive action. The ease with which such concepts have been sequentially arranged within the stone's minds has been, as always, laughable. There has been a significant degree of satisfaction in seeing just how far this Principality's constituents can go in compelling these stones to adopt ever-wilder discontinuities in their philosophies and keeping them from seeing the illogical and blatantly contradictory positions these adoptions force them to assume.

As a consequence, at this juncture, we are confident in recording that the stones in this Principality possess the requisite social, civil, political, and military cultural inclinations so as to extrude decisions necessary to undertake offensive operations against the Pathetic Land.

Diplomatic Initiatives

The major diplomatic initiative pursuant to these operations has obviously been the Cooperation Agreement forged by this Principality with the Pryp'yat[19] Principality, known in stone reality as the *Sino-Russian Economic Cooperation and Non-Aggression Treaty*, signed secretly several years prior to this convocation. During the signing of this treaty, the stone President was easily induced to collaborate with the mud[20] Chairman in clandestinely partitioning the Pathetic Land. It was also agreed that the Scissors strategy[21] would be applied in accordance with traditional doctrines during critical segments of the military phase of the operation. This agreement comprehensively prescribed intended diplomatic initiatives designed to prepare the object of operations; preliminary economic development activities, designed to entrench stone businesses within the target's economy; subsequent oppositional economic coercion strategies, designed to compel behaviors and shape the target's political landscape; and eventual military operations designed to complete the conquest.

During the Principality Congress, the Stain[22] Principality was compelled to assume an appropriately subjugated position vis-à-vis the two more prominent Principalities in contravention of established geographic guidelines marking territories. Due to Stain's decrepit record, regardless of recent reversals, no confidence existed such that the Power ruling the Stain Principality would be capable of sufficiently addressing the heavy opposition anticipated when operations against the Pathetic Land commence. This opinion, stridently forwarded by this Principality, was eagerly seconded by the Aryan delegation; Stain had no recourse, in its weakened condition, to pose any substantial objections.

An agreement was reached as well with the Xipe Totec[23] Principality, compelling them to coerce their slaves[24] to commence operations against the southern border of the Pathetic

19 That Principality which ruled most of Eastern Europe, Scandinavia, and Russia.

20 The term 'mud' referred to an individual human being living under the rule of the Pryp'yat Principality, ruling in the geographic area know at the time as Russia. It was allegedly a complimentary term used among the enemy's leadership.

21 The 'Scissors Strategy' was a Russian term used to describe a deception technique wherein one nation would pretend to befriend and defend another nation—the 'object of operations'—against a third belligerent, but in reality, when the befriended nation was at its weakest point, the first nation, secretly in congress with the belligerent, would turn against the befriended nation and together the two antagonists would easily defeat the object of their operations.

22 The 'Stain' Principality referred to that entity which ruled most of America; it was a derogatory term used by the Adversary, since for much of its history, American had been a beacon of light to the world for Christianity. It was later replaced by the Marduk Principality.

23 That Principality which ruled most of South America; literally translated, this meant 'the Flayed One'.

24 The term used by the Xipe Totec Power to refer to those humans living within its Principality.

Land. This agreement was known among the stones as the *Economic Cooperation Agreement with Mexico*. In return for enormous sums of money, Mexico would launch an incursion into the southern states of the Pathetic Land so as to destabilize the economy, social structures, and political establishments.

Another diplomatic initiative of primary importance involved the New Moon[25] Principality. Throughout its history, it has been unruly, unconstrained, wild, and antagonistic, never willing to cooperate, and therefore its rise to power during this period of our history was unexpected. Yet the Lower Kingdom orders things correctly; the New Moon Principality began to achieve enormous success globally. Its irritating influence was even felt in this Principality, where its particularly effective ordure spread into our periphery. Little objection was made, but their efforts were tightly controlled and subjugated by our constituency. The intended use of this fierce, ignorant, untamed entity was to distract the object of operations such that they would consider Islam to be a major threat. The beauty of this approach was that there was a large degree of truth to this; the worship of any god other than that which rules from the Higher Kingdom significantly enhances the effectivity and power of every Principality. It was this benefit the convened Principalities most desired from the New Moon. Though never useful to require this entity to follow any kind of plan, the assembled Powers and Principalities were able to compel its agreement to conduct internal irritations within the Pathetic Land sufficient to cause the desired effects. Ignorance, too, has its utility.

The final agreement germane to the diplomatic phase of this operation was that concluded with the White Deceiver[26], who agreed to compel those it ruled to sign an *Economic Cooperation Agreement with China*, which dictated a range of Sino-Canadian economic initiatives and laid the groundwork for greater control by the stones of this Principality over Canada's national activities. Never a significant power in the machinations arranged by the Lower Kingdom, nonetheless this entity was in certain points useful, and for operations in the Pathetic Land, would be essential.

At the end of the Congress, the Lower Kingdom expressed, with undisclosed reservations, its qualified satisfaction that the necessary Principalities were appropriately aligned and prepared for further operations. The Lower Kingdom's representative warned the assembly that failure at this juncture, after the necessary and successful trial runs performed in that time known by the stones as the Second World War, was not an option. After appropriate sacrifices—five stone children procured by agents highly placed in political leadership positions in the Pathetic Land and killed, struggling to the last, exuding the delectable fragrance of unreasoning terror and fear, all suffused in a background aroma of hundreds of slaughtered unborn stones—the Congress concluded.

25 That Principality which ruled over most of the Middle East and Southwest and Southeast Asia—wherever the religion once known as 'Islam' flourished.

26 'The White Deceiver' was that term used to denote the Principality administering most of Canada and the Northern Territories in North America. Apparently quite respected among the Adversary for its ability to silently, lethally deceive those under its control, this entity's reach extended into the Arctic regions, where its boundary conflicted frequently with the Pryp'yat Principality.

Chapter 25
Wei Bolin

"Therefore, behold, I will bring strangers upon you, the most ruthless of the nations. and they will draw their swords against the beauty of your wisdom and defile your splendor."

Ezekiel 28:7

Captain Wei Bolin walked slowly down the stairs and out of the Central Military Commission headquarters building in Beijing, a massive, domineering gray stone edifice that housed the bureaucrats and functionaries who administered the world's largest military organization—the People's Liberation Army. The sky was dark, the air somewhat foul that evening, as it was most evenings, and the sounds of traffic on the streets ebbed and rose like the sound of some temperamental sea. He tucked himself into his dark green overcoat, ducked his head down, and merged with the swirling mass of humanity that was Beijing emptying at the end of the working day.

Bolin worked in an obscure office in the Second Department under the General Staff. For much of its history, the Second Department only collected military intelligence, but as the world rapidly became more complex, Chinese military leadership identified a need to collect and analyze scientific and technological intelligence as well. Bolin was a Captain in the People's Liberation Army—known more commonly as the PLA. Somewhat short, which was strange for a Chinese with ancestors from the Heilongjiang province far in the northern part of China, he had the wiry build of a gymnast, which he had been in his youth, and worked hard to keep himself in shape as he approached his thirtieth birthday. He had dark hair, hard black eyes, a broad, smooth forehead, finely-shaped facial features, and strong, calloused hands. Bolin worked as an analyst in the research section of the Second Department, known publicly as the Institute for International Strategic Studies, evaluating published information about foreign civil infrastructures, architectures, and systems. As a lieutenant he had published two articles about these topics in the Institute's classified publication, *Foreign Military Trends*, but it was the most recent article, published just a month ago, after he'd been promoted to Captain, on how to rapidly create ad hoc civil infrastructures in areas ravaged by combat damage, disease, or environmental disasters, that was causing him concern as he walked toward the Beijing Subway, one hand holding his briefcase, the other tucked in a pocket, oblivious to the crowds around him.

His immediate senior officer, Comrade Colonel Cheng Lin Tao, had called him into his office late that afternoon to discuss the article. Smoke rose from Cheng's cigarette, sitting placidly in the ashtray while Cheng's fat fingers held the newest *Foreign Military Trends* magazine, rolled open to Wei's article.

"You have made some insightful assessments in this piece, Bolin," the Colonel remarked, picking up his cigarette and drawing in a great lungful of smoke. The windows in the office were closed, black and grimy with soot. Bolin coughed once, slightly. He felt his eyes watering. He said nothing in reply. The Colonel went on.

"This phase sequence you discuss is most interesting; how did you determine this?"

"Logic, Comrade Colonel, and historical precedent," Bolin replied. "Using what we are currently doing, I simply moved from those points forward to elements which would naturally occur afterward."

Cheng nodded, smiling sardonically, and said, almost to himself, "Perhaps to you, my friend; not so naturally to others." The Colonel set the magazine down on the desk and looked at Bolin. "You live with your Uncle, yes?"

Bolin covered his surprise. "I do, Comrade Colonel, yes. Wei Liwei."

"You have no wife?"

Bolin looked down and picked at a callous in his palm. "No wife, Comrade Colonel—at least, not yet."

The Colonel nodded, smiling again slightly, "There is time enough, Bolin, time enough for such things. But you are young still, and strong, and you have a future ahead of you. Have you considered what such a future might look like?"

Bolin thought for a moment. "I truthfully have not, Comrade Colonel. I am content here; I believe my work is valued, that it benefits the Party, that it helps the PLA move China toward a stronger position in the world, and I am content in being part of that movement."

"Very proper, very proper Bolin, yes," the Colonel answered, nodding with honest approval. "Your work is valued. This assessment here," he said, tapping the magazine on the desk with a single sausage-like finger, "has gathered the attention of some interesting eyes. I wanted to just congratulate you, and ask that you think slightly more often about your future."

Bolin nodded gratefully. "Thank you, Comrade Colonel, for speaking to me as an Uncle about this. I will certainly do as you advise."

Bolin replayed the conversation in his head repeatedly while he rode the subway toward his Uncle's home. He wondered who it was that had found his article so interesting. He was still wondering as he walked through the door of his Uncle's home and found himself pleasurably plunged into the familiar cacophony that was Liwei's home—a home with three daughters, Bolin's cherished cousins, all close to his age, and none, amazingly, as yet married. Two of the girls were holding a conversation about the disparate qualities of their bosses at work—while each stood at opposite ends of the house. A third cousin was laughing with his Aunt about something or other in the kitchen. There was the smell of frying vegetables, steamed rice, and he caught the sound of something sizzling.

"You are home, my boy, welcome, welcome, come, sit down, it is almost time to eat. Have you had your rice today? Grandfather is in the back house, we'll call him before we eat." Bolin's Uncle Liwei came out from his office, a small room tucked in off the central hallway. Liwei was slightly taller than Bolin, with a growing paunch, a receding hairline, and a face seamed with creases. His blue eyes, most especially, were surrounded by dozens of age lines. His wife said they were lines caused by worrying about his company. He said they were simply lines caused by smiling too much at his good fortune in having three beautiful daughters. If people in the West could see how much Liwei delighted in his daughters, Bolin thought, it would change that pernicious impression that Chinese parents only valued sons.

"I am well, Uncle; how goes the business?" Liwei owned a very profitable software business that produced a number of unique but powerful applications used in the control systems of large industrial plants and factories. He had a staff of fifteen, most of whom were programmers.

"Ah, business is business, Bolin ... when is it ever anything else? No new thing arose in your life today, we hope?"

Bolin set his briefcase down and shook his head slowly. "Ah, well ... perhaps,

perhaps not," he said slowly.

"Ah, yes, yes, something is causing the honored cousin some concern," shouted Daiyu from across the room as she set the table. "I can see it in his shoulders." Daiyu was a tall, raven-haired beauty with a heart-shaped face, Liwei's blue eyes, and a thin figure. She was the youngest of the three cousins, with an impish sense of humor, who loved to plague Bolin with all manners of jabs about his work, his love life—or the lack thereof—and his obsession with physical fitness. For his part he played along, a willing foil to her constant teasing. They were very close. Only he could console her when, three years ago, her heart was broken from a failed romance.

Liwei took Bolin's arm. "Come." He turned slightly and spoke toward the kitchen, "Beloved, is there some time before we eat?"

"We can eat when you wish, husband," replied the beloved wife from the kitchen.

"Ah, good, good," Liwei murmured to himself. "Come, let's sit in my office and we can talk." Bolin picked up his briefcase.

"He has probably been ordered by the Comrade Colonel to marry and is trying to figure out how to disobey that order without being denounced!" shouted Daiyu, smiling broadly while her sisters laughed.

The Uncle waved a hand in the air dismissively and grumbled over his shoulder at the daughters. "Women," he growled. "They think they are the center of the universe."

"Are they not, Uncle?" Bolin asked—and then smiled as his Uncle's eyebrows flew up and shot him a quick look. Liwei chuckled and closed the door to the office.

"Now ... what is it?"

Bolin sat in the chair across from Liwei, set his briefcase down, and steepled his fingers together. "I was called to the Colonel's office this afternoon," he began. "He wanted to tell me that an article I've had published in one of our classified publications has gathered some interest in 'interesting places'."

"Interesting places?" Liwei asked. "He was not more specific?"

Bolin shook his head. "No ... no, and I do not think he wanted to be. But he encouraged me to think about my future. Now what would such a comment mean?"

Liwei paused and thought for a moment. "It could mean one of two things, Bolin. That he is warning you about sticking your neck out in what you write—and remember, I do not know what it is you wrote about—or he is telling you that what you have written may open doors for you in the future."

Bolin nodded slowly, digesting his Uncle's assessment. "It could be," he replied. "Those are two logical options."

"Did he say anything else?"

Bolin thought for a few seconds, and then said, "He did congratulate me on the quality of analysis and logic the paper demonstrated. He said my work was valued."

Liwei screwed up one eye and one side of his mouth rose. His head bobbed forward, and he pointed one smooth forefinger at Bolin. "Ah, there, there, you see, that is the key. This is good, this is good ... the Colonel is pleased with your work and he is telling you that it may open doors for you in the future, nephew. And when he asks you to consider your future, he is telling you that something will be coming soon, a strong opportunity for you, something you should consider carefully. If he was warning you about your writings, he would have found something to complain about, something to denigrate. But if he was complimentary, then he is aware of someone or others above his level that see in your work something of value. This is good!"

Bolin pursed his lips and shrugged. "Could be, Uncle," he said. "That would be nice."

"Of course it would be nice, and how can you doubt such a thing? You are very, very smart, my boy. Soon they will understand how much they need you ... how much China needs you."

"Right now all of China needs you two to come and eat!" yelled Daiyu. Liwei yanked the door open; Daiyu giggled and ran.

"There is no respect in this house, wife!" Liwei shouted good-naturedly, shaking a fist in the air.

"This is your fault, honored husband," replied his wife placidly, carrying in the pot of vegetables, "do not complain to me. I was happy with two; you were the one who wanted a third. Daiyu, now go, call Grandfather, and we can eat."

***

Liwei was extraordinarily fortunate; many years ago he had taken the proceeds of one particularly successful application he'd invented and purchased a relatively large home. Four bedrooms enclosed a living room, off of which was a blue and white checkerboard-tiled kitchen. Outside, there was a garden, and just beyond the garden Liwei had built a small apartment for his father, Wei Jin. A concrete wall surrounded the home. The furniture was teak, from Malaysia; the kitchen appliances from South Korea or Germany; the food from the local Beijing markets.

The dinner finished, Bolin helped the girls clear the table and wash the dishes while Liwei and An, his wife, settled in the main room with Wei Jin, Liwei's father, Bolin's grandfather. The cousins enjoyed this time, when they caught up with each other on what was happening in their lives.

Cuifen was the oldest. She had her mother's features—a heart-shaped face, deep-set brown eyes, and was somewhat thick-waisted. She was firm with the younger two daughters, like oldest daughters tend to be, and felt herself to be a stand-in for her mother at times. She was sternest with Daiyu, who tended to be flighty and aberrant in her attention to the things Cuifen thought important in life. Mature, sometimes blunt, and highly intelligent, Cuifen was a senior accountant with China's third largest oil company: China National Offshore Oil Company. She had attended Tsinghua University and then earned her advanced degree in England, at the Manchester Business School. She ran a department of many dozens of accountants, handling dossiers for numerous initiatives around the world, and she was very well-informed about the financial perspectives associated with China's growing energy needs.

Mingzhu, the middle daughter, was the family's literary jewel. Intense, passionate and quiet, she had learned to read at a very early age and she'd kept her nose in a book since. Short like her older sister, but thin, she had her father's face, his sharper features, blue eyes, and a willowy figure. She had been afflicted with emphysema since the age of 10, and it caused her difficulties now and again. She had been embroiled in a passionate affair for several months with a journalist from Shanghai. Liwei and An did not approve, and Mingzhu was in the midst of just beginning to understand why, as the young man's less-desirable traits became more evident by the day. She, more than her other sisters, though, tended to keep her own counsel. Mingzhu had attended Beijing University, and a friendly rivalry with her older sister over which school was best was a continual thread throughout their relationship. Mingzhu worked as an assistant director at the National Museum of China; her specialty was in literature from the Qing Dynasty and the Analects of Confucius. She had been consulted by anthropologists and social scientists, many times by Party members seeking to identify historical trends or patterns in the literature of that time, and once by an American film producer from Los Angeles who was thinking of making a movie about that period of Chinese history. She loved her work and was very good at it.

Daiyu was the tallest of the three sisters, and the most athletic, with a willowy feminine frame, her father's sharp features and height, and her mother's heart-shaped face and flawless skin. She was finishing her last year of a Master's program at the Beijing Institute of Technology, studying to be, of all things, an aerospace engineer at the School of Aerospace Engineering. Since she was three years old she had been entranced with anything that flew; birds and butterflies, or rockets and jets. She had spent the first decade of her life convincing anyone who would listen that she would become the first female fighter pilot in the PLA Air Force. She had a remarkable degree of hand-eye coordination—so remarkable that her parents had once thought seriously of taking her to audition with Beijing's most exclusive acrobatics club. When they were children, she would relentlessly pester Bolin into juggling contests, or games of darts, or 'catch seven pieces' or 'cat catching mice'—and though three years younger than Bolin, invariably she would best him unmercifully. As they grew older they become the closest of friends. Daiyu would occasionally exercise with Bolin when the fancy struck her. And remarkably, of the entire family, only Daiyu could come close to holding her own against Bolin when they played Weiqi. She was viciously aggressive on the board, and played with a wily contempt for traditional strategies, which, Bolin said, made her all the more unpredictable.

***

Bolin had come to live with Wei Liwei when he was three years old. Bolin's parents and younger brother died tragically in a house fire while he had been visiting his grandfather, Wei Jin. Wei Liwei took his nephew in without a second thought, glad to be able to help a member of the family after the tragedy. Bolin was younger than Cuifen and Mingzhu, and two years older than Daiyu when he came into their family, and the girls were delighted to have a brother to pester, or coddle, or mother, as the case might be. An's heart flew to the young orphan and she raised him as her own son. Bolin thought of An as his true mother.

Though Liwei's family each in their way demonstrated marked intelligence, Bolin outshone them all. Identified early in confidential testing as possessing a remarkably high IQ, Bolin proved to be a true genius in the disciplines of complexity, chaos theory, social systems, and the new science of emergence. He raced through Beijing University's undergraduate curriculum at the age of 15, earned a Master's degree in social sciences by his eighteenth birthday, and then took his Doctorate in Complexity theory at the age of twenty-one. His doctoral thesis directly opposed Friedrich Hayek's work regarding emergence relative to political systems and markets. Hayek had delineated two main types of societies—those built on principles of 'cosmos'—that is, a society whose principles, features, and dynamics 'emerged' or were 'grown' from a multiplicity of individual, simplistic behaviors— and societies that were 'made' or consciously created by a specific agent, be that a 'God' or any political agency, theory, state, or sovereign. Hayek's thesis was that for a society to be valid it must inculcate the principles of emergence; he contended that most of a society's laws and the dynamics governing interactions and relations between people come about spontaneously, through random interactions. He dismissed the idea that a society and its internal dynamics might be intentionally built by rational agents. Hayek based his theories on research conducted in Western societies. Hayek's work was almost purely based on Western structures of politics, social interactions, societies, and thought patterns. Bolin, well aware of Chinese history and its political philosophies, and knowing that Hayek was asserting that Emergentism rejects the state on grounds that it violates the concept that societies' rules emerge spontaneously, wondered if perhaps Hayek's assertion was flawed when applied to Eastern thought and Eastern history. His thesis made a strong case that Hayek's work simply did not apply in Eastern societies, and especially when confronting the very successful society created by the Communist Chinese party—most assuredly a definable political theory.

Bolin had two unique hobbies in his life. The first was Weiqi, a game with simple rules, yet rich in strategy—the Japanese called it *Go*. No one in his family could come close to beating him by the time he was twelve. Even spotting Liwei four to six stones, he would defeat him handily. Only Daiyu could even give him anything one might consider a match, and to do so he would spot her three stones.

Liwei and An had once taken the family to one of the street markets in downtown Beijing one weekend when Bolin had been 14. While they shopped, he sat down with some of the greybeards playing on the benches that lined the boulevard. By the time Liwei and An returned, the girls carrying boxes of shoes or clothes, Bolin had scoured through eight opponents and was playing against a middle-aged man in glasses and an open-necked white shirt and sport jacket while dozens of others stood round the two, silent and hushed, watching every move breathlessly. The smell of peppermint lozenges mixed with the scent from flowers that lined the street and filled the florist stalls.

Cuifen and Mingzhu complained about the wait, but Liwei did not want to call the boy until the game was over. One older man, with a wispy beard and bad teeth, saw that Liwei was related to Bolin.

"He is yours?" he asked.

"My nephew," Liwei replied, with a tinge of pride.

The older man shook his head. "Do you see who he is playing?"

Liwei looked over a number of heads, took in the man with the sport jacket, and shrugged his shoulders. "I don't know him."

"You should; he is Nie Weiping."

Liwei's eyes widened. "No!"

"Yes, your nephew is ..." he hesitated and looked down at the board to watch Bolin place a stone, snapping it down with a quick flicking thumbnail, "Your nephew is playing the world's first amateur *Go* champion almost to a draw. And Nie Weiping is a professional now, do you understand?" The old man looked at him again and pushed a finger in his chest. "Who is this nephew of yours?"

Amazingly, Bolin won the game with Weiping by two stones, and the champion, with good grace, queried the young boy about who he was and if he had ever thought about a career as a professional player. Bolin stood, thanked the man, replied that no, it wasn't something he was considering, bowed to the assembled group, and then took some of Daiyu's packages under one arm, her hand with the other, and walked to the car obediently with Liwei and his family.

A second hobby Bolin undertook was myrmecology—the study of ants. When he'd been five, Liwei brought home a small toy ant farm. Bolin had been riveted for months. When not studying, he would sit before the small glass frame for hours, watching the little ants move about, making tunnels and pathways. When he was fourteen he made his own larger ant farm of two three-meter square plates of Plexiglas, erected vertically, filled with sand and almost ten thousand ants. This preoccupation with ants helped him discover the principles of emergence, for he soon learned that while each individual ant had very limited intelligence, the combination of each ant's activities, all driven by simplistic rules, produced results which, amazingly, modeled strikingly intelligent behavior. These intelligent results, which seemed to 'emerge' from a massive number of individuals performing simplistic actions fascinated Bolin, and led him to consider further studies in complexity, chaos theory, and social science, looking for the mathematical and scientific principles that might undergird such phenomena. He devoured Wolfram's work on how computer algorithms produce emergent behaviors; he raced through Johnson's work, intended for a lay audience, which introduced the science of Emergence to the general public—notably by referencing how ants modeled the new theories. He taught himself differential geometry and tensor calculus so as to master the tools needed to work in the Emergent sciences and address the related disciplines of complexity and chaos theory.

***

The cousins shared the events of their day with each other, and while they all stood in the small kitchen, Bolin told them of his interview by the Comrade Colonel.

"What is this article you wrote?" Cuifen asked, drying a plate.

"It had something to do with how one might build a civil infrastructure rapidly, in ... in difficult environments."

"And was he positive about what you'd written?" Cuifen always bored straight into the heart of things.

"He said that the logic was very strong, and that it had garnered interest in higher places."

Mingzhu coughed softly, and Daiyu handed her a tissue.

"He said also that I should be thinking of my future more often," Bolin added. "And he asked me if I had a wife."

Cuifen looked at Daiyu; they both raised eyebrows. "What?" Bolin asked. "What is that supposed to mean?"

"I think," Cuifen said, "that you will be getting a promotion shortly, and that it will require that you adjust your lifestyle. Why else would he ask about a wife? They are going to offer you something and they wish to know if there might be obstacles to you accepting what they offer."

Mingzhu nodded. "Cuifen's analysis makes sense, Cousin. That's what I think, too. So ... hold yourself in readiness, and put no foot wrong."

"What do you think, Daiyu?" Bolin asked.

Daiyu stood with her arms folded and looked solemn for a moment. "I agree," she replied. "The whole conversation would make no sense otherwise. But will you wish to change your life if it is required?"

Bolin thought for a few seconds. "If the state asks, can we say no? Of course I will. But how will I know what they're asking?"

Daiyu pressed her lips together firmly. "You'll know," she rapped out. "They'll leave no questions. So you have nothing to worry about, except that you may have to leave us, and if that happens, you will have no one to guide you in your daily life. Who will talk to you about what happens in your day? Who will give you sage and wise advice? You will be in great danger, Bolin, without your three guardian angels." She spread her arm out to indicate the three girls there in the small kitchen. "You should pay our phone bills so that we can counsel you on a daily basis."

"If I pay your phone bills you'd be talking to every guy from here to Los Angeles," he replied.

"She cannot help it if she is desired by the entire world," Mingzhu put in. "It is only logical."

"Ah, yes, Bolin, this may be a terrible risk," Cuifen said, shaking her head, looking seriously at him, her dark eyebrows contorted. "Alone, on your own, wherever they send you ... a babe in the woods. Forget phone calls; you should definitely pay for us to come visit."

"And to fly first class, no doubt," Bolin said sarcastically.

"But ... of course," Mingzhu replied. "Is there another way to fly?"

***

Two days later, Bolin still had heard nothing from the Colonel, and he resolved to simply go about his routine and not worry further about the perplexing discussion. He came home that day again to the same warm conviviality of family and raucous laughter and teasing, ate dinner, and cleaned up, talking to the girls about their day. He was about to retire to his room when his grandfather asked him to come and talk in the small apartment behind the house.

Wei Jin's apartment had a small sitting room with a straight-backed teak couch, a matching coffee table, two hard wooden rocking chairs, and a wonderfully intricate carpet that covered only a small part of the polished wooden floor. An had brought tea, which sat steaming on the coffee table. A brazier sat in a corner, empty now, but it would be used often later in the year, as Wei Jin chilled easily. One small bedroom led off from the sitting room, and there was a tiny room at the other end that served as a kitchen. The most prominent feature of the apartment was the number of books—there were books everywhere; on the walls in bookshelves, on the chairs, on the floor, on tables. Wei Jin was very well read; he'd been a professor of political philosophy before he'd retired, and his mind was still sharp and active.

Liwei joined them; Liwei took one of the rocking chairs, Bolin the other, and his grandfather sat on the couch.

"Bolin, I hear that Cheng Lin Tao spoke with you the other day."

"This is true, Grandfather. He said that—"

"Yes, I know what he said. He intimated that you might have something different in your future. Is this true?"

Bolin nodded. "Yes ... well, sort of. He suggested I give some greater thought to my future."

"Yes, so ..." Wei Jin went on, "I have something for you that conforms to that event." Wei Jin handed Bolin a thick, cream-colored envelope. It was addressed to Wei Jin, with no return address on the envelope. "Go ahead, pull it out. It is a message from my brother."

Bolin looked up quickly. Wei Jin's brother, Wei Feng, was the family's most prominent member. Wei Feng had once been a very highly placed member of the Party. For decades he had held the chair of Senior Strategic Advisor to the Central Military Commission's General Secretary. "It concerns you," Wei Jin said crisply. "Open it and read it aloud. Liwei has not seen it yet."

Bolin pulled the thick stationary out of the envelope. There was Wei Feng's bold, choppy handwriting, in black ink. Bolin read, "My brother; a quick note. Please advise young Wei Bolin to be prepared for a series of interviews. These may, if addressed successfully, lead to a significant posting for our favored progeny to perform a critical mission for China. Tell him to do well, to be strong, and that he has my best wishes. Wei Feng." Bolin looked up.

"What does it mean, Grandfather?"

Wei Jin did not reply at once, but pulled a book from a side table. "My brother breathes high air, you know, Bolin, and he has a great heart for China. I suspect that many of the things you have written, starting with this," he held up the book, which turned out to be Wei Bolin's doctoral thesis, "are showing a number of important people that you have the capability to make even greater contributions in areas other than those in which you are now engaged. I think Feng is giving you notice that your life is about to change; that before you are offered this opportunity, you will need to go through a series of interviews."

"Surely such interviews occur only for very responsible positions, do they not?" asked Liwei from the chair in the corner.

"You are exactly right, my son," Wei Jin replied, turning to face Bolin again. "Feng would never have written to me, Bolin, unless what you face will result in something very significant, both for you and for China. I want you to be ready and do well at what is asked of you."

Bolin looked at the two men and opened his hands. "I will do my best, Grandfather, but unless I know what it is I must do, how can I prepare for it?"

"I do not think Feng refers to an activity like studying for a test, Bolin; no, he is instead referring to this, in here," and Wei Jin tapped his chest, "and up here," he said, tapping his forehead. "You need to be mentally and emotionally ready to undergo these interviews—I think Wei Feng is very confident in your ability to give satisfactory answers."

"Why do you say that, Father?" Liwei asked.

"Because of the note," Jin replied. "He would not have shared the knowledge he has about these interviews with us if he felt there was some lack in Bolin's ability to actually satisfy the interviewers. And it would not surprise me if Wei Feng himself had brought this sequence of events to pass, by recommending Bolin's writings to key people, in specific circumstances."

"Can Wei Feng do such things?" Bolin asked in a hushed tone.

Liwei cringed inwardly, for he knew his father's opinions regarding his brother's capabilities. Bolin would now learn them as well. Wei Jin took the envelope back from Bolin and, looking at it for several seconds, tapped the thick cream stationary with one wrinkled finger and looked up at the PLA Captain. "I have not yet come to see the end of what my brother can do," he answered, "when he works for China."

***

Five days passed, and then Cheng Lin Tao stepped into Bolin's small cube, tapped him on the shoulder, and crooked a finger, indicating that he should follow him. They wound through the massive cubicles, each housing a brilliant, eager, aggressive, devoted PLA officer, and, still with Bolin on his heels, took the stairwell to the fourteenth floor. Bolin had never been there before. Cheng opened a heavy door and they both walked into a long, gray-carpeted corridor. The Colonel walked down almost the entire length, pushed open a gray metal door, and motioned for Bolin to walk in.

Bolin moved into a typical bureaucrat's sparsely furnished office—a gray-green metal desk, cluttered with papers, staplers, a hole punch, a calculator, and a keyboard, with the monitor off to one side. There were three four-drawer filing cabinets along one wall, and a glass cabinet along the other. A picture of Mao hung over the back wall, and a number of faded yellow spots on otherwise pale eggshell walls showed where pictures had been removed. There was a white enamel dry-erase board on the wall opposite the desk, where a man sat, smoking a cigarette. There was a window behind him, overlooking the gray Beijing skyline. The man stood, shook Bolin's hand—"Comrade Shien," he said in precise, formal Mandarin, brusquely introducing himself, and nodded toward the chair, indicating that Bolin should take a seat in the single metal chair placed in front of the desk. Colonel Cheng said something quickly to Shien, which Bolin didn't catch, and left, closing the door quietly.

Shien was dressed in the uniform of a PLA Major. He was a short man, stocky, with a leathery face, black eyes, and thinning gray hair. He exuded the faint smell of soap. Bolin noticed Shien's nails were manicured, and the cuffs of his shirt were crisp and starched. The man had a settled, confident presence.

"So ... Wei Bolin. Would you like some tea?"

"I ... I think not at this time, thank you, Comrade Major." Shien picked up a pen, unfolded a dossier, and began the conversation in a pleasant tone.

"Your work has been noted by certain people, and there is thought that you may have potential to help China in a number of future initiatives, Wei. It is my task to ask you a number of questions to determine if you are suited to participate in the support of these initiatives. We will begin by talking about you and your family. Do you have any questions before we start."

"Whatever I can do to help, Comrade Shien, I am at your service."

"Good. So ... let's begin."

***

Shien went on for several hours, asking Bolin about his parents, about the fire in which they met their end—Bolin knew very little about it, and could only relate what his Uncle had told him later, that it had been caused by a faulty electrical circuit, and that his parents and brother had died of smoke inhalation. Shien evinced no obvious sympathy, but just nodded and made notes as he talked. He spoke of his Uncle and Aunt, his cousins, and his grandfather. Shien asked about each in turn, probing into what they did for a living, where they worked, what their opinions were on politics, on the Party, their working environment, and China's future. He asked particularly about Liwei's software business and the types of applications he developed, and Bolin gave him a comprehensive technical summary of each. Bolin was curious about the interview but not disturbed. He had, with his mother's milk, taken in the concept that the State had every right to this information and more. He freely shared his impressions about each of his relatives.

"You're grandfather's brother ..." Shien began.

"Wei Feng, yes," replied Bolin.

"What occupies Wei Feng?" Shien asked.

"I would not begin to know, Comrade Shien. My grandfather very rarely speaks of him, though when he does it is with the greatest respect. I only know that he once had a position supporting the Central Military Commission. I have no idea what occupies his time now."

"Yes ... well, you should know, Comrade Wei, that Wei Feng has served China well and faithfully for over fifty years, and he is known and revered at the highest levels in the Party. The *highest* levels ..." Shien emphasized this last with a piercing look at Bolin, and the young captain dared hope that the discussions might turn out well.

"Yes, Comrade Shien. I am proud to know this."

Shien grunted quietly. "Do keep it in mind," he said, and went on with the interview.

"What do you know of religion?" Shien asked.

Bolin was surprised, and showed it. "Well ... well, Comrade Shien, I ... I know very little actually. This is not an area in which I've specialized."

"I do not require a doctrinal treatise on the topic, Comrade Wei, simply share with me what you know of religion."

Bolin processed this question and, like a student regurgitating a set of boring facts, recited back to Shien, "I know there is no God, if God is defined as a supreme, separate entity. I know that there are many in this country that do believe, though, in a concept of a supernatural being. I have heard that Islam has a growing presence in Xianjiang; I know that the Catholic Church has some presence in many regions, but that this presence is not supported by Rome. I know that Protestants have a growing presence in our country, and that they have many different sects."

"Let us dwell here for a moment," Shien said, holding up one manicured finger. "Tell me what you know of these different Protestant sects."

"I truly could not differentiate, Comrade," Bolin replied. "Apparently they differ in their belief structures from Catholics, although I do not understand the grounds for their differences. And within Protestantism, I understand that there are a wide number of different groups, none of which agrees fully with the other. To me this seems illogical; it is not conducive to a successful movement, at any rate, to have such disparate opinions on what I would think would be something quite fundamental."

Shien pursed his lips and tucked his head to the right slightly. "Yes, their shadings are complex and hard to comprehend. But, from what you understand, do you think you could, if asked, undertake to try and comprehend those differences?"

Bolin sat up straight in his chair and thought for a moment. "Comrade, if asked by the State to undertake such a thing, I would not foresee too much difficulty. It simply requires an apprehension of each specific doctrinal position, which, I am told, are not at all complex, but simply matters of opinions."

"What do you know of their Evangelical sects?"

"Nothing much, Comrade. Only the definition of the word leads me to suppose that they tend to be more externally oriented. I am also aware that the philosophies which motivate this external focus are considered by the Party to be ... to be ... well, not approved ... discouraged, actually."

"True, Comrade Wei. Most of these sects are not approved, but unfortunately reports are that they are growing, especially throughout many rural areas. And what do you know of such sects in other nations ... say, in England ... in Saudi Arabia ... in America?"

Bolin shook his head slowly. "I can tell you nothing of such things, Comrade Shien, truly. Other than recognizing the various demographic proportions in these countries you've mentioned, which I've studied for purposes of civil infrastructure planning, I could not speak to any of their particular doctrinal positions or belief systems. I know there are few if any Christian sects in Saudi Arabia; I know that, demographically speaking, there is little or no Christian presence in England or anywhere in Europe. I am aware that Islam has a tendency toward radicalism, and that the doctrine appears to be more politically oriented than possessing any relation to religion. I am aware that American Protestantism has trends toward divisiveness and hypocrisy, but other than these basic impressions, I could not be more specific."

"And what of Buddhism?"

Bolin recognized the need to tread carefully here. "There are Buddhists in China, yes. Most of those are in Tibet, I understand, but I do not know any personally, and I am not aware of the central tenets of Buddhism beyond those which any layman possesses."

"Does any member of your family have tendencies toward religious belief?" Shien asked quietly.

Bolin shook his head. "No, Comrade, not that any have shared with me, and I see them every day. I would know if they were even thinking about considering such opinions, and I have seen no evidence of anything like such consideration."

"Your cousins? They are women, and can be easily drawn out or influenced."

"Absolutely not, Comrade ... I speak with them every day; we are very close, and not one has expressed a hint of interest in such things." Bolin chuckled slightly. "I am imagining my cousin Cuifen entertaining a religious discussion," he said, explaining his levity, "and it is laughable. She would ask to see their proofs, numerically and mathematically, and then kick them through the door."

Shien smiled agreeably at the picture Bolin described, scribbled notes on his paper, and took a sip of tea.

"What do you know of the Qigong?" Shien asked.

"I know that our revered Chairman Mao had once thought it important to reclaim our lost ancient treasures, and that the exercises taught in Qigong were thought to be part of those treasures. I know that there was some data indicating that they were truly helpful. I also know that as the re-discovery of the discipline evolved, unscrupulous men took great advantage of the people's general low level of knowledge of these techniques and claimed for themselves titles they had not earned, attesting to knowledge and powers they did not have. This corruption was unacceptable, and it caused the system as a whole to fall into disrepute, but I personally am not yet convinced that it should be discarded. If the ancients revered such things—and I am told that there may be merit in some of the elements associated with Daoism as well—then there may yet be something in it to benefit the people of China in this period of history."

Shien made more notes and then looked up. "And tell me about your thoughts regarding the writings of Lu Xun." Lu was perhaps the most influential writer in China's modern history.

Bolin handled the shift in topics smoothly. "I have read his work, of course," Bolin replied easily, "but take issue with much of his cynicism."

"Explain," Shien directed.

"So, consider his *Diary of a Madman*."

"And what issues do you have with this work?"

"Ah yes, then, to be brief, the work portrays traditional Chinese value systems—"

"By which you mean Confucianism?"

"Yes, Comrade, particularly those ... I am familiar with much of what Master Kong has written and tend to favor much of his philosophy. Anyway, Lu alleges that such value systems like those taught by Master Kong destroy the heart and soul of the Chinese people. I confess to being more of a traditionalist than Lu; I believe there were and still are significant benefits to be found in the wisdom of our ancestors, and that such things should not be discarded lightly—nor should they be treated with contempt or scorn. Those who developed these philosophies and thought systems were men, like you and I, trying to do their best for the China in which they lived, and I do not believe it is right for those who live in one time to judge the actions or philosophies of those who lived in another."

"Hmm. You seem quite opinionated about this," Shien observed passively.

"I am, Comrade. I ... I have a great love for my grandfather and I have seen how, even though he is of a different generation, his wisdom can apply to me and the problems I face in my time. I would be a fool to discard it, and dishonorable to disdain it."

Shien made more notes on his pad, his pen scratching in the quietness of the office. Bolin heard a door shut further down the corridor. He wiped his palms on his thighs and stretched his leg to ease a cramp.

Shien looked up. "Would you like tea now?" he asked.

Bolin cleared his throat, parched after the long discussions. "Why yes, Comrade Major, that would be very kind, thank you."

Shien picked up a phone, spoke softly but imperiously, and in a moment the door opened and a short woman brought in a tray with a steaming pot of tea and two cups. There were cookies and mints. She poured for Bolin and refreshed Shien's cup and left, closing the door softly. Bolin could hear the sound of traffic on the streets below.

"This should be enough for today," Shien said after they had spoken of inconsequential matters while Bolin enjoyed the tea—a brisk leaf from Thailand. "Tomorrow you will speak with others on political and technical matters." Shien stood up, dismissing Bolin. Wei stood, bowed, shook the man's proffered hand, and left the office. He hesitated outside the door. Shien came out of the office and directed him down the corridor to the stairwell, where he descended to his more familiar level, reported the end of the interview to Colonel Cheng, and then returned to his cubicle. He had several reports to finish to complete his self-assigned quota of work for the day.

***

The next day Bolin reported to the same office, where another man sat with Major Shien. A tea service waited on the desk, Shien invited him with a gesture to partake, and he gratefully settled in for another long interview with a cup in his lap.

"This is Colonel Wang," Shien explained. Wang was a tall man, thin, with a paunch, with the shoulder tabs indicating experience as a political officer. Shien asked, "Oh, Comrade Bolin, do you have any Xiang?"

"I am partially fluent, Comrade Major," Bolin replied.

"Good. There may be portions of our discussion this morning that might benefit from excursions into that language. Now, please, would you explain to us your understanding of the main underpinning tenets of the Party's philosophies?"

"Yes, of course, Comrade Major." Bolin coughed slightly and began. "Of first and fundamental importance it must be recognized that Marxism-Leninism comprises a set of fundamental principles, principles which alone provide the basis for the scientific analysis one must perform to understand the nature of objective reality. On the basis of such an analysis," Bolin declaimed, "Marxism-Leninism guides the revolutionary struggles of the proletariat, providing signposts and specific programs for action."

"And how is one to determine an individual's understanding of objective reality?" Colonel Wang interjected, speaking for the first time.

"One determines this, Comrade Colonel, by the individual's expressed styles or actions. One may determine an individual's correct assessment of true objective reality only by their defined actions on behalf of society as a whole, especially on behalf of society's most advanced integrative segment, the working class."

"And what must precede this apprehension or understanding, Comrade Captain?" Wang persisted.

"According to the revered Chairman Mao's definition of 'theory and practice', Comrade Colonel, a true understanding and perception of the working class can come only through experience as a worker; therefore it follows that before an individual can truly comprehend the true meanings or purpose of their actions, they must work on behalf of the proletariat. This dynamic requires an advanced intelligence to direct practice toward a rational, appropriate, and accurate comprehension of objective reality. Therefore the individual must follow the direction and guidance of that segment of society that will best ensure correct thought. As the individual does so, he is rewarded with a greater awareness of that objective reality."

"And can you encapsulate your understanding of objective reality, Comrade Captain?"

"Yes, Comrade Colonel. All reality is comprised of *contradiction*—the essential result of an eternal, ongoing dialectic, which, with correct guidance, one might extract truth. Contradictions form the foundation for all perception and comprehension. Only by observing and analyzing the contradictions inherent in an issue can the individual come to a true understanding or perception of that issue. Man and woman, life and death, earth and sky, night and day, water and stone—these and every other issue associated with life can be comprehended only by examining it as a contradiction, pressing it through an ongoing dialectic, and extruding a third, different perspective."

"Tell me, Comrade Wei, how you handle contradictions in your own life," Shien asked.

"Yes, Comrade Major. Of critical importance is the resolution of each contradiction."

"And how do you accomplish such resolution?"

"By modeling my behaviors, insights, and methodologies upon Party leadership, Comrade—upon those higher in the Party who have clearly demonstrated advanced modes of thought and demonstrated action. It is only thus that one might resolve contradictions that arise. There is truth only in the Party, Comrade."

"Well said, Comrade Wei ... well said. Now tell us, what role do you see in society for the intellectual?"

Bolin thought for a moment before framing his response, and took a sip of tea. "We have established that practice underlies and informs thought. Therefore it might be reasoned that those who have attained advanced or higher levels of thought should guide the practice of those who have less advanced thought. We could also expect practice to change as changes occur in objective reality. I would also expect those operating at higher levels of thought to be able to anticipate changes in objective reality prior to those changes, and structure new methods of practice to conform to and leverage benefits occasioned by impending changes in reality. Therefore intellectuals, operating at those higher, advanced levels of thought, should be seizing every opportunity to retain their excellence. And because of this, one should expect that those intellectuals operating at these advanced levels of thought should themselves be guiding or shaping the emerging objective reality by reasoned application of new practice, and experimentation with new forms."

"You would therefore commend the principle of flexibility?" asked Wang.

"One must be cautious in such a commendation, Comrade Colonel," Bolin replied hesitantly. "One must adhere to policies based on principles, and in so doing exercise flexibility. One *must* adjust to changing circumstances, and seek alternative ways or methods to achieve one's objectives—no question. But to carry out actions which might be initially perceived to be 'flexible' without any basis in principled policies would be opportunist, revisionist, and an incorrect application of right Marxist-Leninist thought."

"You describe the essential differences between the Soviet and Chinese modes of thought well, Comrade." Wang stood, and Bolin put his cup on the desk and stood also. "I am pleased," Wang said to Shien. "Your candidate demonstrates acceptable understanding of the basics of Marxist-Leninist thought, Comrade Major. You will have my assessment before the end of the day, though I will say before I leave that I am impressed. But," he said quietly to Shien, "I expected no less from your department." The Colonel bowed to Shien and walked out. Shien motioned for Bolin to be seated.

"You are fortunate," Shien said, "that the Colonel seems to be of an amenable disposition this morning. You prepared well for the discourse."

"It is only what I have been privileged to learn from those who are more advanced than I," Bolin replied.

"Undoubtedly, Comrade Captain. Now ... let us depart from politics for the moment, Bolin. For this portion of the discussion, we must wait for another colleague." Bolin sipped at his tea and took a mint while Shien picked up the phone, spoke quickly, and hung up. Soon the door opened and a woman entered, carrying a briefcase and wearing a PLA Major's uniform. She was tall—as tall as Bolin, with longish black hair pulled back severely from an oval-shaped face, and a thin, spare figure. She had a fierce, aggressive expression, as though she was angry. Her black almond-shaped eyes looked out at him proudly; her lips were compressed, and a muscle in her cheek pulsed. She seemed to be in a hurry just standing there—or, he thought, ready to explode.

When Tuan saw Bolin, rising to greet her, he struck her as just another PLA officer, though perhaps slightly more intense than most. She had read his thesis confuting Hayek and posing a differing foundation for Emergence based on Eastern principles, and she regarded it as very good, perhaps outstanding scholarship. She had quite a bit of experience with academics; she had earned her doctorate in social and political theory at Moscow State University in Russia, and so she was slightly surprised to see the author of what she'd spent the last three days reading possessing a pair of broad shoulders, a flat belly, and looking like an intense, highly-focused, somewhat short-sighted athlete. She had also read his recent article in *Foreign Military Trends*, and it was this article that had caused her supervisor to have her attend Bolin's initial briefing here on the fourteenth floor. Tuan was a member of a highly placed, carefully selected team of PLA officers and Party officials working on one of the most daring projects in Chinese history, and they were very, very careful about who participated. Bolin looked like a shy, well-formed intellectual with good genes. She had a very pressing engagement not two hours from the time she walked through the door, and had no more interest in Bolin than she would have if her task had been to identify a particularly interesting form of animal life which might be needed to supplement the project's team.

"Comrade Major Tuan Meifeng, this is Comrade Captain Wei Bolin. Bolin, Comrade Major Tuan has a doctorate in Sociology, and is one of the PLA's experts on both religion and human reactions during times of stress. She will be helping us assess your technical competence as we continue our discussion."

"It is a pleasure to meet you, Comrade Major," Bolin bowed and shook the woman's hand. She simply made a quick head nod in reply and sat, saying nothing. She crossed her uniformed legs and pulled a pen from her pocket and a clipboard from the briefcase.

"So," Shien went on, "to continue, Comrade Captain ... we will ask that you explain to us your perception of the major challenges that stand before China today."

Bolin cleared his throat, nodded once to Major Tuan, and shifted in his seat somewhat. "Yes, Comrade Shien. There are four very clear, very obvious problems that face our people." Bolin began ticking them off, one by one, his arms held placidly across his chest. "The first is the economy; the second, our environment; the third, providing sufficient energy sources for the future, and fourth, arresting the corruption we find as a remnant of insidious Western influences upon past generations."

"You mention the economy," Tuan questioned, holding up her pen. "Explain in detail, please." She had a deeper voice than Bolin had expected, and a harsh, almost grating manner, although he was in no position to respond unfavorably.

"Yes, Comrade Major. From my perspective, the Chinese civilization-state is poised at a great crossroads in its history," Bolin explained, "and the single most important factor that will ensure we maintain suitable national and international options in the future will be the strength of our economy." Tuan thought he spoke like a propaganda recording from Central Party Headquarters, though she kept silent while he continued. "We have recorded amazing growth rates in the last two decades, yes, but because of this very fact, we must continue to do so, for as it grows rapidly, our economy, as we know, is creating many winners—but also many losers ... those who have not adjusted as well to the rapidly changing economic environment ... and therefore the Party should ensure that these many millions of less fortunate people are 'caught up', so to speak, in a further growth spurt. For the economy to leave these people behind without any chance themselves to experience the benefits of our booming prosperity—well, such a situation might foster a sense of injustice or unfairness in their minds, which would be counterproductive to national harmony."

Tuan asked sharply, "Do you dispute the Party's move recently to reduce health care, educational benefits, and government-sponsored agricultural subsidies?"

"Not at all, Comrade Major," Bolin replied serenely, "yet, and this is to my point, the Party has wisely noticed the impact of these policies and is making adjustments already, to ensure those in the areas most impacted by these policies are to some degree remunerated."

"Are there any other negatives associated with the scenario in which our economy does not continue its growth?" she asked. She made notes on a clipboard as he spoke.

"I believe that we as a people have become almost addicted to the current rate of growth, and therefore we have come to expect it—and this is a dangerous thing."

"Dangerous? In what way?" she asked, now slightly curious.

"If we look at America, Comrade Major, we can see the effects of what happens when a people come to expect high growth rates and the luxuries which come from a booming economy over a long period of time. Soon they develop a mentality described most accurately as one of entitlement; they *expect* that the government will give them everything they desire; they *expect* that they will live in luxury; and they *expect* to live in luxury for a very, very long time. When, for example, there were more than 3000 deaths during the Muslim attacks in New York, the survivors sued the Government—as though the Government had some responsibility for ensuring their lives continued on pain-free, untouched by trauma—and remarkably, the U.S. Government actually paid their claims."

"Do you anticipate such a thing could happen in China?" she asked, seemingly disagreeing with Wei's intimation.

Bolin narrowed his eyes and tilted his head slightly, screwing up his forehead in thought. "There are many factors to your question," he replied slowly, "and it needs to be, how is it said ... 'unpacked' ..."

"It is not a—"

"Forgive me for interrupting, Comrade Major, but it is, though," Bolin said quickly, anticipating her objection. "It *is* a complicated question. Consider ... on one hand, we Chinese are human beings. Any human being might fall into the trap of developing this mentality of entitlement—it is simply human nature, and such caution is, in my opinion, prudent, and there is always room in the Party for prudence. But such a mentality is just that—a mode of thought, and if the Chinese maintain their strong attachment to the Party, and if the Party anticipates that the development of such a deleterious mentality of entitlement might emerge, they can take steps in advance to avoid such a development by—"

"—By directing the thoughts of the proletariat appropriately," she said, completing his thought. "Yes, I see." She noted on her pad that the candidate—she almost had thought of him as 'the subject'—had no qualms about presenting his ideas forcefully, and that he held firm opinions based on solid analysis.

Shien spoke up. "Bolin, your specialty is the creation of civil infrastructures in hostile environments—is this correct?"

"Yes, Comrade Shien. I've spent most of the past few years on this work."

"What are some of the main elements you find to be critical when you first begin crafting an infrastructure?" Tuan asked, looking up from her clipboard.

Bolin hesitated. "Ah, Comrade Major, much depends upon the environment into which the infrastructure will be placed."

"What do you mean?" Tuan pressed. "Expand, please."

Bolin paused for a moment to frame his reply. He felt uncomfortable around Tuan, but could not explain why. He pulled slightly at his uniform collar, took another sip of tea, and answered the question. "Consider ... consider that the environment may be contaminated by some type of biological dispersion; or perhaps the area has been struck by some natural disaster, such as a typhoon; there may be extensive combat trauma among the population, as was the case when the Germans invaded Russia."

"Then consider," said Tuan, speaking pedantically, clipping her words, "that the environment is comprised of a population—a somewhat decadent but robust mass of people—existing in a modern, developed nation undergoing significant social upheaval, but still with a rigorous economy. The land area is expansive—for our purposes, consider a space about half the size of China itself, with a mixture of terrains, both plains and mountains, and a range of climatic conditions. There is internal political turmoil, with uncertainty and tension levels very high. National cohesiveness among the people is extremely low. So ... how would you proceed?"

Bolin sat unblinking, not wanting to make any expression or give any indication that he suspected the region Tuan was posing as a fictional basis for the question. He kept his face impassive, ran a finger over a callous in his palm, and looked over at Major Shien, whose face reflected nothing. "Okay," he began, the response forming in his mind as the words flowed, "consider this framework—one would establish major strategic objectives, and within each strategic objective, one would outline specific operational programs, or campaigns, and for each of these campaigns, a suite of tactical objectives necessary to succeed. Are we clear? Yes, good," he went on, not waiting for them to respond. "Let me put this up on the board." He stood up and went to the white board on the wall without waiting for permission, took up a marker and drew three columns, giving each a heading: 'Major Strategic Objectives', 'Operational / Campaign', and 'Tactical'. "The first major strategic objective," he said, turning to the others in the room, "would be first development, then infiltration and then control of major sectors of the economy in the area in question." He turned back to the board and wrote 'Major Industries' under the 'Major Strategic Objectives' column. "The specific areas would be dependent upon the nation under consideration, but typically one would embark upon initiatives in industrial areas where China has a robust advantage—I would recommend areas such as the transportation, aviation, energy, and food industries, and of course manufacturing. I would put new companies in place—controlled by Chinese, of course—inside the nation in question. I would initiate economic partnerships with various global corporations in the industries I mentioned, working to appropriate the key technologies from each, and, if possible, start projects designed to further develop a Chinese presence in the environment." He wrote another entry under the 'Major Strategic Objectives' column. "One would then leverage the positioning, influence, and access provided by a robust economic presence to conduct a reconnaissance on the existing civil infrastructure—the emergency response systems, the medical support, the power and water supply systems, the food distribution systems, and the systems, software, and dynamics associated with port or transportation nodes." Bolin paused and turned to Major Tuan.

"The next logical strategic objective would have to do with the population. Tell me, Major, what would a Party objective be in such a ... a scenario ... for the indigenous population?"

"What would you recommend, Comrade Captain?" She was growing more impressed by the minute with the paradox of Comrade Wei.

"It again depends on the Party's ultimate objective for the environment. Do they wish to appropriate only the land, or do they wish to leverage the utility and resources offered by the people living there as well?"

Tuan hesitated, chewed the end of her pen, and thought for a moment. "Let us say," she began hesitatingly, " ... let us say that the Party wishes to simply have the land and implement a colonization program."

Bolin was hard-pressed to keep an impassive countenance; Tuan was suggesting a massive ethnic cleansing program. Yet Bolin was surprised not by the idea of mass murder—such a course of action, if commanded by the state, would not be a problem for him— but rather impressed with the scope of the proposed effort. He pursed his lips, folded his arms across his chest, and began slowly pacing before the board, like a professor contemplating a particularly thorny question posed by a student.

"I see," he said. "So ... okay then. The next major strategic objective would obviously be to address the security issues—"

"Why security?" Shien interposed quietly.

"Ah, Comrade Major, because if I understand Major Tuan correctly, we must somehow eliminate the indigenous population before installing our own, and I am assuming that there is some type of extant military or civil defense force in place. Such a force would need to be dealt with before we would proceed with colonization."

Shien nodded his understanding and lifted one manicured hand. "Very good," he replied, "please continue. Oh, wait ... Comrade Captain, for demonstration purposes, please outline what the operational or campaign steps would be for the Security objective."

"Of course, Comrade Shien." Bolin snapped back to the board. "First of course one will need to establish clear and secure lines of communication and supply. Second..." he paused and turned to Tuan with a question. "May I suppose, Comrade Tuan, that there is a coastline involved in our fictional scenario?"

Tuan touched a hand to her hair to cover her surprise. This Bolin was too perceptive by half. "You may suppose so, Comrade Captain, though it is not necessary for the exercise."

"Of course, of course. So," he went on, turning back to the board, absorbed in the intellectual challenge of the problem, "after establishing the lines of supply and communication, one would establish a naval quarantine, especially if the subject nation possesses any kind of naval force that might threaten our lines." He penned this up in a rapid scribble under the 'Operational / Campaign' column. "Thirdly, we would step to questions of internal security, and—"

"Excuse me, Comrade Captain, but define this term, 'internal security'," Shien directed, interrupting once again.

"Yes, of course, my apologies, Comrade Shien. By this I mean—and these elements would, by the way, comprise the *tactical* constituents of the hypothetical plan we are discussing—the efforts to pacify the local populations, and of course the need to neutralize or defeat existing civil militias, or more formidable state military forces that might oppose the initiative."

"So you would target these forces specifically?"

"Target them, or permit them to expose themselves as they undertake offensive action and then eliminate them from a stronger defensive posture," Bolin replied. "Of course the specifics of the tactical engagements are dependent upon the tactical situation, the geography, the weapons involved, and the degree to which the indigenous population is armed—or not. Such considerations must of course be subordinate to a broader, more comprehensive analysis of the political situation and direction from Party leadership."

"Thank you, Comrade. Continue where you left off ..." Shien looked down at his notes. "You were discussing the operational campaigns associated with the Security objective."

"Of course, Comrade. So ... after establishing internal security, we would look to the border and commence border security operations. Actually, if the internal security campaign is conducted with forethought, pushing from inside outward to the nation's borders—"

"Or whichever borders the Party chooses to establish," Tuan added.

"Yes, yes, thank you, Major Tuan ... very good, yes, thank you," Bolin, unthinkingly blurted like a professor praising a quick student, and went on. "As you say, outward to the nation's borders, however they are defined, then establishing border security for the new environment would be a natural step flowing from the previous effort."

"Jot that down, please, Comrade Captain," Tuan directed, pointing to the board with her pen. "This is intriguing, and we may wish to capture your thoughts for a later discussion."

"Of course, Comrade Tuan." Bolin dutifully turned and penned up the words 'Border Security' under the 'Operational / Campaign' column. He also wrote 'Defensive Operations' under the Border Security heading. "And finally," he said, turning back to face the two majors, "we must consider a Defensive Operations campaign."

"Define this as well, please, Comrade Wei," Shien asked.

"Of course this is dependent upon the status of force extant within the environment in question," he answered, "but it is logical to expect, with a robust indigenous population, that military initiatives will be undertaken to oppose the creation of Chinese infrastructures, and in return, or in response, or better, in anticipation of, those military initiatives, Chinese forces should move to preemptively strike key military targets in the subsumed environment."

In a burst of intellectual fervor for the next hour, Bolin went on to complete the matrix, filling in the major strategic objectives and, for each, a set of operational campaigns. Shien's eyes blazed with interest. After a brief pause of maybe five or ten seconds, he then went on to fill in the tactical column for each of the operational campaigns he'd suggested, and then outlined where and how each of the tactical initiatives would link to infrastructure elements. It was a fluid, scintillating, masterful ad hoc demonstration of operational genius.

Tuan's mind was racing as she struggled to keep up with Bolin's logic. She felt she was back in school, listening to a strikingly brilliant but eccentric genius, trying to intellectually grasp key tangential points in the substance of the argument so as to comprehend Bolin's thought process. She recognized a few of these steps, but her effort to understand was undermined by the shock of realizing that a relatively obscure PLA Captain could, prodded by a simple hypothetical question, capture on a white board in front of her eyes the essence of her project's initiative, add a few items her team had overlooked—and, most probably, guess the intended target. She dared not look at Shien lest she reveal her suspicion.

Instead, she brushed away a lock of hair and said demurely, "Comrade Captain, ah ... yes ... well, this has been helpful in one or two points, but other duties require my attention." She turned to Shien. "May I ask, if it is possible, for Comrade Bolin to excuse us? I'd like a private word before I go."

"Yes, yes," Shien replied, pushing himself up from the desk with both hands. "Bolin, actually, we are at the end of our time, and you are dismissed. You know the way back down to your office? Good, and thank you for your time."

Bolin blinked once, yanked his mind out of the track in which it was racing, working up details for a massive invasion of the hypothetical nation, contemplating further strategic objectives, campaigns, and tactics. He looked just then to Tuan like some befuddled but very well-built absent-minded professor. "Why ... why yes, of course, Comrade Major. Right away. Yes, of course." Bolin strode to the door, stopped, returned to his chair, picked up his cap from a side table, nodded once to Major Tuan, and distractedly left the room.

Tuan turned to Shien and stridently, eyes wide, said, "Where did you get this asset, Comrade Major? Have you checked his security? I mean, there is so much he knows about what we are doing already! Are you sure there has not been some sort of compromise?"

"Calmness and serenity, Major ... calmness and serenity," said Shien reassuringly, smiling, making a small gesture with his hand. "He has this effect on everyone. He is truly a national asset—though he is unaware of the fact, and," he went on, changing demeanor suddenly and casting a stern glance toward Tuan, "it is critical that he remains unaware of that fact. Do you understand?"

"Of course, and I fully agree, Comrade Shien. But I can tell you right now that the Director will want this man on the team immediately; he'll want a full briefing protocol executed as quickly as possible—visits to all sites, full disclosure of program objectives, everything. Seriously, Comrade Shien, he could easily step into a position of leadership in this effort."

"Slowly, slowly, Comrade Tuan. Yes, he is impressive, but we will take things at a reasonable pace. First, as you say, he will be put through the familiarization protocols, and we will see how he interacts with the team, for this is my main concern."

"Sir?"

"The man's level of intelligence is remarkable, Comrade Tuan, but nothing moves forward on the back of only one man—this is a typical Western heresy. So we must ensure that he can work with your team. Actually, forgive me, I have misspoken. *You* must make sure he can work with your team. That is, or will be, the main aspect of your future assignment."

Tuan sat back, taken completely by surprise. "There is ... that is, I have quite a significant amount of work already planned, Comrade Shien. The Director would have to approve such an adjustment in—"

"The Director has already done so, Comrade Tuan," Shien replied, pushing a single page across the desk. She looked down: it read, in part, that Comrade Tuan "was to consider herself assigned as the main integrating officer charged with ensuring the successful integration of Captain Bolin into the project's team." She looked up at Shien.

"They knew this would happen?" she asked.

"The suspected it might," he answered. "And so they made provisions. But one of the other provisions, which you have already confirmed to me, is your approval."

"Yes, Comrade Shien, true, I ... well, yes, I approve of his participation in the program in principle, most assuredly, but—"

"So then, Comrade Tuan, you have your new assignment."

Tuan paused to look out the window and wondered about this sudden wrench in her career, and what it might do. Accompanying an eccentric genius might be perceived as beneficial to her plans, but then remembered that her path through the PLA was not hers to chart—she, and whatever career she extruded during her short life, belonged to the Party. With this thought she looked back at Shien.

"Very well, Comrade Major, then I will make sure he is seamlessly—" She stopped in mid-sentence, suddenly remembering something.

"Yes, Comrade Tuan? What is it?"

"Comrade Shien, as you know, one of the key phases of the preparation protocols is for the subject ... I mean, for Captain Bolin, to undertake exposure to the objective environment."

Shien was nodding. "We are aware of this, Comrade Major." He looked at her and read the question in her face. "Yes, therefore you will need to accompany him, so ... it appears that you must prepare yourself once again to descend into the bowels of Western decadence, Comrade Tuan."

"Yes, Comrade Major, to return to ... that is ... in ... "

"Yes, it is harsh duty, Comrade Tuan, but we expect you will undertake the sacrifice for the greater good of China." Shien clasped his hands together at his waist in a gesture meant to convey approval coupled with a quietly expressed desire that Tuan would quickly resign herself to this new direction in her life.

"It really is quite an opportunity, Comrade Tuan ... and you have not yet heard the best part," he said. Unwrapping a peppermint lozenge, he could not quite contain the smile.

Chapter 26
Sasha

"For a nation has come up against her out of the north; it will make her land an object of horror, and there will be no inhabitant in it. Both man and beast have wandered off, they have gone away!"

Jeremiah 50:3

Captain Sasha Sokolov looked at the Russian sergeant. Ice crystals had formed on the man's short-cropped moustache and the fur of his hat. His face was ruddy from the wind, and prominent, alcohol-infused veins crawled across both cheeks. There were wrinkles about the man's eyes.

"Sergeant, are you comfortable driving this icebox?"

The sergeant blinked twice against the blowing snow, wiped his nose with his sleeve, and said, slowly, "I am, Captain. It has the latest steering improvements and they put in a better heating system to keep ice from forming on the bubble."

"Good. We push in a few hours; I want nothing to go wrong."

"Yes, Captain. The skids are fully lubricated, the heating system is clear, and the blades are new. There should be no problems."

Sokolov grunted, as though unconvinced, let the steel hatch fall, and descended the crude ladder along the side of the shipping container that had the numbers '77265' painted in tall white letters on its side—what he'd referred to as an 'icebox'. He moved along the pier, boots crunching thin ice along the planks. His breath steamed before his face as he looked over the pier area. Several dozen ice transport vehicles were lined up on the ice that choked the port. Men loaded supplies and equipment; maintenance workers hammered or chipped or pounded at the steel containers, the front steering skids, or the rear runners. There was the smell of burning solder, diesel fumes, and roasting sausages. He saw the Division's Logistics Officer outside a nondescript wooden building that served as the port's main office. He jogged down the pier and caught up to the major before he made it into the building.

"Major Vlasovich, a moment, please."

Vlasovich paused, his hand on the door. "Come inside, Sokolov, we'll talk there." The major pushed the door open and the captain followed the major into the office. They took off hats, gloves, goggles, and their large outer parkas. Vlasovich moved to a shelf, pulled two cigars from a box and handed one to Sokolov. Sokolov declined, and Vlasovich bit off the end of one, spat it onto the floor, pulled a thin silver lighter from his pocket and puffed his cigar to life. Vlasovich pulled a chair out, turned it around, and sat down with his chest against its back and looked at the captain.

"So ... your company is ready to embark, Sasha?"

"We are, Dmitri. We have the timetables and I have spoken with all the unit commanders. Their people are ready."

"Good. And you are happy with the ITV[27] program?"

Sokolov didn't answer right away. Sokolov was responsible for managing the operational employment of the Ice Transport Vehicle program—a highly secret research and development effort. He had been assigned this duty because he had originated the concept. Two years ago, after one particularly bitter night following another failed winter exercise due to inefficient troop transportation, he mentioned to his uncle, who happened

27 Ice Transport Vehicle

to be a member of the Red Army's acquisition system, an idea of putting a ducted turbofan engine on the back of a standard shipping container mounted on skis, essentially making a huge snowmobile that could transport soldiers and their gear over large distances in arctic terrain at very little cost. Solar panels on the top of the container provided power for batteries and communications. The front and rear skids were turned via controls from inside the container. His uncle laughed, told him he had been drinking too much vodka, and the conversation moved elsewhere. But the uncle knew people; he quietly made a few phone calls, and suddenly Sasha found himself yanked from his motorized rifle division and on a plane to Moscow, where he overcame his initial reluctance and more fully described the concept to a group of very interested technical bureaucrats.

Money and resources were allocated. Unknown to Sokolov, his concept appeared just in time to solve a problem presented to the Red Army's Transportation Development division. Higher command had demanded they develop a way to transport men and equipment across vast seas of ice. Essentially the Russian leadership wanted to begin a crash development program for landing craft that would operate on ice, not water. Sokolov's idea was deemed worthy of investigation. He had recommended taking a standard 12 by 2.5 meter steel shipping container used throughout the world, of which Russia had millions, and mount it on four two-meter long steel I-beams with a fat ducted turbofan engine fixed to one end, similar to those that powered modern hydrofoils. He sketched out a compartment for eight 200-liter drums for fuel in the back end, a space for rations for three days, shelves to store weapons, lockers to store ammunition, and a rudimentary but functional heating system that ported hot air directly from the early stages of the turbofan's compressor into the crew compartment. The internal temperature was regulated by simply opening sliding steel panels to let in outside air. The Bureau's designers added a recommendation that the containers be covered with a painted insulation the Americans invented, to reduce heat loss, and included a portable toilet (the designers were, on average, older men). And now, two years later, Sasha found himself in the temporary headquarters of a battalion from the 77th Motorized Rifle Division, shuttled to Dikson Island, about ready to lead eight hundred Russian infantrymen and a platoon of Spetsnaz on an exercise to assault Yuzhny Island in the Novaya Zemlya archipelago. A force of Finnish infantry would oppose the exercise during the wargame. The Finns were included to help establish closer military and political ties between Russia and Finland. No one trusted them to do anything but cause difficulties, interfere with the flow of the tactical problem, and most likely ruin a career or two.

Vlasovich drew on the cigar, and puffed for a moment. "You are quiet. What is the problem?"

Sokolov paused for a moment, looking around the shed. Windows were crusted with frost. A small iron coal-burning stove in the corner was losing its struggle to heat the room, and the ceiling was coated in a thin film of coal dust.

"Major ... I have been looking over the maps ... and the radiation data. That was a huge bomb they set off near Rogachevo. I think—"

Vlasovich nodded, holding up a hand and interrupting the younger officer. "No, Sasha, you should not worry. The Tsar Bomba went off in 1961. We have been over this before; dozens of operations have been conducted there since it was declared safe. I went myself four months ago with the science team and personally inspected their instruments. My teeth are not falling out, are they? Do I look like a walking night-light to you? Your people will be okay."

"Major, it was the largest nuclear detonation in the world."

"Of course it was, Sasha. This is Russia; is there anything we do that is not the largest in the world?"

Sokolov wasn't satisfied. He said, "What are we doing, crawling all over that terrain anyway? Is there not enough empty space elsewhere on the island where we can run this exercise that we have to trundle through a poisoned swamp?"

Vlasovich said nothing but just shook his head back and forth slowly and shrugged his shoulders. "First, Sasha, there is no poison. This I can promise you on my own; I have investigated things personally. Second, it is no longer a swamp, it is a solidly frozen sheet of ice about five meters thick. And lastly, while it is true that I am the Division's Logistics Officer, the Central Committee has not asked my opinion on where we should conduct our exercises for quite some time."

One side of Sokolov's mouth turned up in a half smile and he looked away slightly, almost laughing. Vlasovich too was smiling, and continued. "Sasha, you are not worried about the ITVs, are you? As you know better than I, they are made in a factory in Siberia by the world's most industrious and reliable engineers who volunteered to work in that garden spot of the world. They are shipped to Murmansk on the world's most efficient rail system. They are offloaded by the world's most careful longshoremen who, when they are not offloading material for the glorious Red Army, offload boatloads of china from Dresden on a regular basis, and they have yet to break even one teacup. So what is bothering you, Sasha? Ah! I have come to it." Vlasovich took the cigar out of his mouth, tapped the side of his nose with his finger, and picked up a cold pickle from the plate on the table and pointed it at the captain. "You are worried about spending twenty hours in a large steel box with your soldiers, eh? Are you afraid they will discover that you do needlepoint in your spare time?" The pickle crunched.

Sokolov, the last man on earth to take up needlepoint, turned to face the major again and smiled. "Dmitri, you may be right, there is really nothing to worry about. Only ... I wonder what will happen if there is no fuel at the resupply point; I wonder what kind of radar signature the large front faces of these iceboxes present; I wonder what will happen if we hit a crevice in the ice field or if the front skids catch a floe, or ..."

Vlasovich waved his hand, the smoke from the cigar tracing elegant lines in the air. "Sasha, you worry too much. This worrying is my job. I am the Logistics Officer, remember? Your job is to take your invention six hundred or so kilometers over the ice, overrun Rogachevo and make the motherless Finns defending the place look like the sardine-sucking incompetents that they are, and then we can all go back home and get off this god-forsaken frozen hell of an island. What is so hard to understand?"

Sokolov smiled slowly; he had been accused before now of worrying too much, and others before Vlasovich had implied that it might be a professional weakness—but it had kept him alive in the past.

"Nothing, Major ... I understand. Sometimes I worry too much."

"Sometimes it is good to worry, Sasha. Good. So," he puffed on the cigar for a moment, changing the subject, "will you be at the club this evening? Colonel Semyonatsk is throwing a party. It will be the last chance for revelry for a while."

"No sir, we push off very early tomorrow. I don't want anything to interfere with the exercise, and I want to get in a few kilometers while there is still some light."

"You still train?"

"Every day, Comrade Major."

"When are the trials?"

"In three months. They will be in Spitsbergen this year."

Vlasovich nodded. "Commendable ... very commendable, Sasha ... you realize that if you win a medal in the Biathlon, you are going to attract the attention of a more serious group of people." The major bit into the last of the pickle and picked up a slice of black bread.

Sokolov nodded and smiled grimly. "Bring it," he said.

Vlasovich laughed out loud. "Be careful what you wish for, Sasha." He slapped a rank-smelling cheese from a small brown can onto the bread. "You young bucks from the north always try to be as tough as the ice you live on."

Sokolov stood up, pushed the chair back, and winked slowly. "No, Dmitri," he said, picking up Vlasovich's cigar and extinguishing it on the back of his hand without blinking an eye, "we are tougher ... much tougher."

Vlasovich was still laughing as Sasha pushed through the door and stepped out into the blowing, bitter wind. He went back to his unit, changed out of his arctic combat boots into cross-country ski boots, picked up skis, goggles, and weapons, and climbed back out of the container. When he got off the pier, he stepped into the skis, shouldered his rifle—a Dragunov for the day—slid a P6 pistol into a chest rig, lowered his snow goggles, and poled off into the bleak, blowing whiteness. He would ski the perimeter of Dikson Island—about 25 kilometers—as he had every day since his unit deployed to the barren rock.

***

ITV 77265, along with seventy-two other improved Ice Transport Vehicles, hammered across the ice that was for much of the year known as the Kara Sea. Sokolov was huddled over a map that rested on the small shelf that folded down from the steel walls with Lieutenant Lohniverisk, the Spetsnaz officer assigned to the exercise. The lieutenant's nickname was 'Kong'; he was over two meters tall, with a barrel chest and arms that seemed to be just a little longer than normal, and hands covered in a thick mat of hair. His mottled gray-white camouflage jacket made him appear even more massive.

"We are averaging about 42 kilometers per hour," Lohniverisk said, his fingers punching a calculator, looking at the GPS readout. "This is much better than what we estimated. This should put us at the coast in ... about eight hours. We should hit the fueling point in about...about two."

Sokolov followed the course on the map that would take them into the Matochkin Strait and then up and over the beach onto the landing positions.

"When we get to the landing site, I want to run up onto the tundra. I am going to try and see if these iceboxes can negotiate frozen terrain. We can save some time and maybe outrun the Finns to the airfield."

Lohniverisk nodded slowly. "That wasn't in the plan, but it might work." Kong lifted a finger to scratch at ice forming on the inside of the container wall. "But no one has scouted the terrain from the landing zone on into the objective."

"I realize that, Kong. It's a risk we will take. I have to see what these things can do. I'll take three or four units as an advance scouting party; the rest will wait to see how we progress before they disembark the battalion. If the terrain is unworkable, we'll let them know and they'll disembark and move up on foot."

"Right; okay, sir. That may work. The Finns are supposed to defend on a line from here ... to here." Lohniverisk drew a line across the map, showing where the Finns were expected to dig in.

"If we can get three or four platoons up to this point," Sokolov said, pointing to high ground that sat astride the Finns' anticipated defensive line, "we could hold the door open for the rest of the battalion and push a larger force into the airfield before the Finns could fall back and set up another defensive line."

"That could be. The exercise rules indicate the Finns can't move to their first line before we hit the beach ... here. It will be a race."

"I don't expect the Finns to obey the rules any more than we will." Kong smiled with grim menace.

Sokolov grabbed for the map as the ITV struck a large chunk of ice.

"The ride has been ... has been ... interesting so far," Kong said, watching his breath form clouds in the air. "The heating system is keeping the interior to around three degrees Celsius[28]."

"That's warm enough." They bounced again from another chunk of ice. "We worked hard to get the shocks just right."

"What are they made of?" The lieutenant stood up and grabbed one of the shelf supports.

"They're very simple. The front skids and the rear runners are just I-beams, as you know, and they have a solid piece of pipe welded on them, vertically. A massive metal spring is mounted around the pipe. A sleeve is welded onto the container and the pipe goes through the sleeve. The sleeve rests on the spring. We drill a hole through the top of the pipe and weld a peg through it to stop the container from maybe slipping off the top of the pipe if we hit something too big."

"Seems to work well. We can even keep things on the shelves."

Sokolov nodded. "That's good ... though some of the men seem not to like it."

Lohniverisk looked in the direction Sokolov indicated. "Oh, don't worry about him. Pig Dog gets sick driving to work every day in his wife's car." Other men around the table laughed.

"No, Lieutenant," another man said, "it is his wife that makes him sick, not the car." More laughter.

"Whoever thought of the buckets, we should give him a medal," Pig Dog said, weakly. Men shouted at him to shut up and toss his detritus out the window. He got up and emptied it through one of the sliding panels. There were more shouts to shut the window. Hand gestures were exchanged; comments on female relatives were shared.

"Combat soldiers are combat soldiers," Kong said, smiling. "It is the nature of the beast."

"I think I'll drive for a while," Sokolov said, standing slowly.

"Good idea. Maybe you can hit less potholes than Stain." He moved forward through the container. Men moved their rifles, with the laser simulation system on the end of each barrel, out of the way. Lohniverisk stumbled as the ITV pounded over the ice, and Sokolov made a mental note to mention adding overhead handholds, like those on subway

28 About 38 degrees Fahrenheit

trains, to the Design bureau.

Lohniverisk tapped the driver on the thigh, yelled something upward, and the driver slotted a lever and came down out of the driver's chair. Sokolov rapidly moved up and sat down.

The operator's position was simply a leather pad suspended from the ceiling of the container with nylon strapping beneath a circular cut in the ceiling of the container over which a Plexiglas bubble was installed. It looked just like the top turret of an old bomber from the Great Patriotic War. The driver shifted the two front skids by pressing foot levers that activated a simple cold-weather hydraulic system. When the operator pressed down on, say, the left pedal, fins behind the turbofan engine directed the exhaust air appropriately, and with the front skids, was sufficient to turn the 12-meter long steel shipping container easily. The turning control rods ran along the inside ceiling of the ITV, easily accessible by the crew if maintenance was required. Engine controls were like those in a fighter aircraft. The throttle was on the left, and was simply a mechanical lever that controlled how much fuel was fed into the engine. There were gauges for engine temperature and pressures in the various stages of the compressor and turbine, and for the current speed. A simple compass rose was adjacent to the speedometer. The designers had needed to do some tricky arrangements there, trying to get a compass to work inside a large steel box, but they succeeded by just using a standard compass designed to be used in aircraft. There was a fuel gauge, which at the moment indicated they had less than 30 liters left. The refueling point should be coming up soon.

Sokolov donned the operator's helmet and looked out through the Plexiglas bubble. The field of view was striking; he could see in every direction. He saw the ice clouds off to his right and left, slightly behind him. One advantage of this vehicle they hadn't anticipated was the cloud of ice particles the front skis threw up, which served almost as natural chaff, deceiving most surface to surface radar systems, as well as obscuring most of the vehicle itself. When seen from the surface, an ITV under full power looked like a cloud moving over the ice with a small Plexiglas canopy just visible in the top froth. Ice clouds near the surface were not uncommon in arctic terrain. Another benefit they'd discovered was that the ice crystals tossed up by the skids handily defeated thermal sights and weaponry. No matter how hard they tried, they couldn't get their thermal systems to lock on to the vehicle. During tests Sasha had modified the back runners to throw up clouds of ice crystals over the engine to cool it and conceal it from more sophisticated thermal targeting systems. It worked superbly.

One of the disadvantages was the noise. The engine's vibrations traveled throughout the container's steel frame, and very early on they realized that ear protection was essential. They finally devolved to equipping every passenger with small ear-bud microphones fitted under thick soundproof ear cups to ensure adequate communications, which they purchased off the web from a firm in China.

Another innovation Sokolov had insisted on was the communication system used between units. It was 'voice over light'—a simple but elegant technology pioneered in Russia that pushed sound waves over low-power laser light. Set to specific coherent light frequencies and used only via line of sight, communications between the ITVs were impossible to intercept. To talk, Sokolov simply turned in the direction of the unit he wanted to communicate with and spoke. Early in the tests they discovered that the ice crystals thrown up by the ITV tended to scatter the laser light and interfere with communications. They fixed this by simply bolting on a two-meter steel pipe through which the laser was funneled, and on which was fixed a rotating transmitter/receiver, because some genius had the idea that if you rotated the transmitter/receiver, it didn't matter where you looked, the transmission would be a 360 degree broadcast, and, rotating at around 300 revolutions per second, the system would receive transmissions from any direction. The two-meter pipe put the transmission and reception apparatus out of the ice cloud. In future versions, Sokolov wanted to put the communications tool on something like a periscope, able to be raised at will and then lowered back down into the container, so as to maintain the appearance of an ice cloud. Not many ice clouds had steel pipes sticking up out of them.

Sokolov looked off to his right, from instinct, where the officer commanding the western landing teams should be.

"Icebox 891, Icebox 265, how copy, over?"

"265, 891, have you loud and clear."

"Roger, 891. How is the ride?"

There was a pause. "265, the ride is okay. We are getting some small vibration from one of the rear runners, but other than that, things are solid."

"Roger, 891. Make a note of it in your report."

"891, copy. Be advised that I have reports from three units—they have each speared a runner and are making repairs."

"Copy, 891. Any additional damage?"

"Nothing reported, sir."

"Keep me informed if you lose contact with those units."

"Roger, 265. 891 out."

Three units had been disabled. 'Spearing a runner' was the term for one of the forward skids impaling itself into a chunk of ice or snowdrift so thick or deep that it snapped off the container mount. He made a note to recommend the leading edges of the I-beam runners be shaped down to points, to better cut through the ice. But three among so many was acceptable ... so far.

Sasha turned to face forward again. He could barely make out the high mountains on the Novaya Zemlya archipelago in the dim light. They would only have about three hours of sunlight at this time of year. He looked at his watch: less than eight hours to go. It was a good test for the ITV, he thought ... a fair test. He saw the refueling tower ahead; they were right on course. He felt the runners hit small chunks of ice and plow through drifts with little impact and no damage to the skids. He smiled grimly, climbed down out of the bubble, and let the sergeant back up into the driver's seat.

***

Sokolov banged the hatch open and pulled himself up to the top of the container. They had slowed to a mere 10 kilometers per hour to keep the wind chill survivable. It was minus fifteen degrees Celsius, the wind about five knots off the island. Sokolov had his night vision goggles up, scanning the eastern entrance to the Matochkin Strait. Solid ice as far as he could see, with very little vertical development. No large chunks or mountains or bergs—this was good. He looked beyond the mouth of the Strait and could see nothing but a blurred greenish haze. He contracted his stomach muscles, willing the ITV to make it into the Strait proper and out of the entrance, where the placid waters of the Strait emptied into the waters of the fierce Kara Sea, whipped by an ever-present arctic wind, and formed what they called a 'cauldron' that sculpted jutting bergs of ice into unnatural shapes, every one of which with edges sharp enough to slice into a steel-walled container or yank off a skid or runner like a dry twig.

Sasha turned his back to the wind and scanned the ice behind him. The ice crystals flowed up and around him so fiercely that he couldn't see. He knelt down and banged on the roof of the container. Kong poked his head through the hatch, and Sokolov waved him up. He grabbed Kong by the front of his parka, guided him firmly between his spot and the front of the container to break the wind, and then turned again to look aft.

He saw the lines of ice clouds, slightly blurred greenish in his goggles, as the other ITVs followed his unit through the cauldron. He saw three bright lights in the distance, then another flare appeared, and another. Disabled units; that would be five, total. If they could get into the Strait and out of the cauldron without losing more, it would be acceptable. He would send other units, specially equipped for towing, to get the disabled ITVs. He wiped the goggles with his gloves and turned back to Kong. He pointed down with his thumb; Kong nodded, lifted the steel hatch as though lifting a pillow, and made a motion with his hand. 'After you,' it said. Kong waved his arm, as though inviting royalty. Sokolov punched him in the chest and climbed down the ladder, smiling ... only five units broken down ... he had expected far more: so far, so good.

***

Sixty-eight ITVs ranged on half-moon shaped shoreline, sitting in the dark like squat, one-eyed, ice-crusted snow beetles.

"Seventy-three degrees, fourteen point five minutes north; fifty-five degrees, fifty-nine point nine minutes east," Kong sang out. "We're generally where we should be. I don't see any shoreline, though, Comrade." The wind was increasing; the dimness had faded into utter blackness. Standing on the top of 77265, they could hear the sounds of other engines winding down. Their own was idling.

"There goes the heat," Kong said, disdainfully. "I wonder if the girls from the infantry will call for permission to make fires." Sokolov didn't bother to answer. Anyone making a fire would be arrested at best; if an officer shot the person responsible, not many questions would be asked. Russians trained as they fought.

"891, 265, how copy?"

"265, 891, go."

"891, I am going to move up over the shoreline and test the capability of the unit to move over the tundra." Sokolov turned and looked directly at the units adjacent to his as he spoke to each. "775, 802, and 455, you will fall in behind 265. Follow me. 891, if the vehicles are successful, we'll call for the others. If not, disembark where you are and follow the original route on foot." Then to the driver: "Stain, ahead slow. Keep us at 10 clicks."

"891 copies."

Stain keyed his microphone a little too early; a belch came across the internal platoon circuit, and then a pause. "Yes, Comrade Captain."

"Stain, if you are filching the vodka without sharing with the rest of us, we will use your guts to grease the skids." Kong looked over at Sokolov and nodded in the darkness. Sokolov leaned over and yelled into his ears over the wind.

"How did he get the name 'Stain'?"

Kong shook his head and cupped his hands over his mouth and yelled back. "You don't want to know."

"Better to use them for anti-freeze," Pig Dog said over the platoon net. Sokolov couldn't suppress a chuckle. There was a solid bang from something metallic hitting the container's wall, and more laughter could be heard over the platoon net. The ITV's engine whined and spun up and the giant cargo container that had become a snowmobile jerked forward, Kong and Sokolov lurched, grabbed for the edge of the open hatch, and 265 moved up over the beach and onto the frozen tundra that covered most of Yuzhny Island. Sokolov looked astern to make sure the other units followed. One by one, they each lurched over the breakwater formed by the contour made by the curling edges of ice-covered rocks and frozen foam at the water's edge and fell into single file behind his ITV.

***

Sokolov took the column almost directly south from their landing coordinates into an alluvial valley. Standing in the open top like the commander of a tank, he steered by giving Stain compass headings. To the east and west, the ground sloped upward sliced by glaciers, covered in ice and snow. In his goggles it looked like a fluorescent jungle. The ITV banged harder now as the frozen ground rose up through the snow patches and slammed the skid and runner pipes up into the springs and jacked them against the pegs holding the container down. The ride was getting worse. He could hear equipment banging around inside the container, and the men were shouting instructions over the platoon net, trying to keep things from sliding around inside, trying to keep their small arms secure. He made a mental note to have weapon holders, and maybe cages, installed. Disregarding the rough ride, he radioed back to the commanding officers of the remaining units and advised them to come ahead with the ITVs over the tundra, but advised them to stay on the hard snow pack as much as possible.

Eight minutes later, a message came over the laser communication system. "265, this is 802, we've lost the rear starboard peg."

Sokolov snarled a curse, looked back over his shoulder, and switched his radio frequency. He couldn't make out which of the three ice clouds behind him was 802. As the wind blew and the ITV hit a hidden rock, the jolt almost bounced him over the side. Kong grabbed him just in time.

"802, copy. Is the spring still on the pipe?"

There was a pause; the wind howled louder, and there was blowing snow across the field of view in his NVGs. He looked at Kong, who just shrugged his shoulders and made a hand gesture to convey an impression of fatalism.

"265, roger, the spring is up over the pipe. Half the spring has snapped; the other half is bent. No way the pipe is going back over that piece of—"

"Copy, 802." Sokolov switched back to the platoon net. "Stain, hold up." The turbine on 265 wound down and the ITV slowly coasted over the rough ice to a halt.

"802, get your people out of the box and distribute them into the other units. Take as much equipment as you can carry. And I want you to execute the self-destruct protocols. You copy?"

More wind for a long, slow minute. "Uh, 265, 802 ... copy you want us to blow this pig?"

"Affirmative, 802."

Kong leaned over and yelled in his ear, over the wind, off the channel. "You are asking them to destroy a piece of the people's property, Captain."

Sokolov snapped a look at Kong, but all he could see was the checked scarf Kong wore, snapping in the wind, crystal-caked goggles under a Kevlar helmet, foggy goggles, and Kong's massive shoulders. Kong had said the scarf was a war souvenir from his father's time in Afghanistan.

"The people will need to be confident that the demolition charges we carry—to destroy these units if they are disabled—will work. The people would not want these valuable pieces of their priceless property to fall into the hands of the capitalist enemy, now, would they? So yes, I am going to destroy a piece of the people's property during this exercise, Kong."

Sokolov looked over at Kong. The man stood still, like a mountain of ice, but he thought he caught Kong's shouted reply out of the wind. "The People would be most concerned that the capitalist enemy would take the ITV concept and make a ton of money with it before they can."

"265, this is 802, copy, we'll set the charges."

Sokolov laughed at Kong's wry observation, and keyed the mike again. "Roger, 802...push your people to the other units, make sure you load the fuel into ... into whatever containers you can, take whatever else you can carry out of that thing, set the charges for 30 minutes, and let's get moving."

They were twelve kilometers away when the charges went off, a dull crump that reverberated against the unseen mountains in the darkness. In his NVGs, he could barely see a trickle of darker colored green against the pale green mountains.

"Sounds like the thunder god, walking through the mountain passes," Kong said.

"I don't have Wagner on my iPod," Sokolov replied. Kong's shoulders shook slightly.

***

The three remaining ITVs moved along the valley paralleling the coast. Snow and ice covered most of the ground near the rising mountains; razor-edged rocks occasionally poked above the surface of the snow throughout the valley plain. It was one of these that had taken 802's peg and ruined the ITV. Sokolov got the column up and out of the low valley and into the rising ground, which meant he could push up the speed to 30 clicks per hour. They had no more incidents.

He halted the column after a six-hour run south, every minute a strain as he willed the vehicles to push over the ice, to hold together. He spent most of the run on the roof, braced against the top hatch. Kong, like an imperturbable mountain, stayed with him.

As 265 bounced to a halt, they stiffly climbed down the ladder and put their feet, finally, on the island's surface. The wind still howled. The platoon piled out of the box, eager to put their feet on any non-moving surface. The side door opened on the windward side; soon the inside was as cold as the outside. The men had to move round to the lee side of the container to get out of the wind. Pig Dog ripped off his parka and ran in circles, beating his chest and grunting. Borg immediately ripped the top from a bottle of water and guzzled, then set out his weapon on three ammunition crates he'd carried from inside the box and began cleaning it, using graphite power instead of the normal oils or grease, which would freeze in the climate. Once the groups were sorted, they fired up the engines again and maneuvered the ITVs to make a triangle, with the container doors all facing to the inside.

"Comrade Lieutenant, can I go for bear?" asked Snake, a frighteningly thin Russian from Siberia, rocking the slide back on his Kalashnikov.

"If he doesn't kill you first, Snake."

"No, Comrade Lieutenant," yelled Rhino, a thick young man from Moscow with a strikingly long nose, "we should take a picture of the bear eating Snake, and send it to the SPCA in Dallas, America, and we could get dates with their cheering women. We could tell them we saved a polar bear. For this they will have love with us." Rhino was practicing his English.

"Feed Snake to a polar bear and it will die of indigestion," Borg said, in Russian.

"Can the crap and get your defensive positions up and ready," growled Sergeant Kishkit, or 'Guts' as he was known in the platoon. He was the platoon sergeant. No one argued with Guts. The men, well-trained, began to place weapons, ammunition, and supplies around the lager.

Sokolov, Kong, and the other unit commanders huddled in a corner of 265. Sokolov flattened a map on the floor. "We are about here," he said, pointing to a spot about 50 kilometers east by northeast of the Rogachevo airfield. "Rogachevo's runway is 2400 meters. We think the Finns may have helicopters to serve as close air support for the defense. Those need to be taken out first. Two kilometers west is this large inlet that spikes up into the tundra from the south and runs 12 to 15 kilometers north of the airfield. About a kilometer wide, it is a natural defensive barrier, and the Finns will most likely be arrayed along its length on the far side. They will have ground radar to cover anything coming across the inlet. If we can put our mortars here," he said, pointing to the only high ground within thirty kilometers of the airfield, the southern island's only waterfall, "we can see every defensive position they'll have."

"They won't be expecting us for another two days," said Lieutenant Racowicz, the commander of 775. "We busted our asses getting here." Racowicz was a slightly overweight young man from Leningrad with dark hair that swept lazily across a broad forehead. His family had close Party connections and it was said that he lived well above the level of the people.

"More than just our asses," Lieutenant Andreij Bushkin commented. Bushkin had been the commander of 802 before it broke.

"Yeah, but the time we save here we'll need for kidney surgery later."

There was a fearfully quick *zzzllllttt* sound, and a knife appeared in Kong's hand. "I could remove one now, Racowicz, and cut your problem in half." The others laughed tentatively. Racowicz, though, wasn't sure about Kong—none of the regulars from the 77th Motorized Rifle Division were. Kong was Spetsnaz, and it was a known fact that Spetsnaz people were crazy.

"Stand down, Kong," Sokolov cautioned quietly.

"I'm kidding, I'm kidding," Racowicz said, hands up.

"Of course you were," Kong grumbled, sliding the weapon back into its sheath. He put a monster hand on Racowicz' shoulder. "So was I."

"What I don't see," said Lieutenant Pasha Fedoroskva, who commanded 455, "is how we are going to get the mortars up on to the waterfall. I don't think the ITVs will climb those hills. From the satellite photos, it looks like there are too many ravines, too many rocks."

Sokolov took out his own folder with the photos and looked them over. "You may be right," he said, grudgingly. "We'll have to see what it looks like when we get there."

Fedoroskva only nodded. Sokolov studied the map for a while longer.

"We need to eliminate the helicopters first," Sokolov announced finally. "265 will take care of those. I want 775 to push to the waterfall and emplace the mortars. Make sure you have a working radio, too."

"That means we load the mortars and the ammunition from the other units into 775, right?" Kong asked.

"Correct. The plan is for 265 to light up the ground radar and pull the Finn defenses down toward the southern portion of the inlet. The rest of the battalion will be pushing down directly from the north, so the more defenders we can attract our way, the easier the main force will have it. 775 will push as far as they can up the slope until they either break the ITV or get to the waterfall. If you break down before you get there, abandon the ITV, leave it in place, and move to the waterfall on foot with all your equipment. Take half of 802's platoon. When you arrive on location, you'll transmit the phrase '775 rests in the water'."

"'775 rests in the water'" Racowicz repeated. He jotted it down in a small reddish brown notebook. "Right. Is there a deadline?"

Sokolov looked at his watch. "It's 2000 now. 455 and 775 will leave in three hours. 265 will leave immediately. From the time you depart here, let's estimate four hours to cover this distance ... about 20 clicks. Your team needs to cover about the same distance, so let's say the attack kicks off at 0330. That is four hours to get your men into position and 30 minutes to gear up and prepare for the attack. Make sure everyone has the laser simulation systems on their weapons. I will personally crucify any officer who forgets to check his men's weapons to ensure there is no live ammunition loaded. If one of your men pulls the trigger on a live round, you will not live to regret the ruin of your career. Do you understand me?"

Racowicz, Kong, Bushkin, and Fedoroskva all nodded their assent.

"You make sure your people, especially, heed this," Sokolov said, looking at Kong.

"They will pay attention," Kong said grimly. The others in the room had no doubt.

Sokolov continued. "265 commences out of the hills east of the inlet and moves west over the ice—probably on foot, to cause as much distraction as possible—at 0330. We'll shoot off a green flare just to make things interesting. You should see some kind of reaction from the Finns from your position on the waterfall. When you see them moving into the open to intercept 265, start hitting them with the airburst shells." Each platoon carried three PODNOS 82mm mortars and several boxes of exercise ammunition—essentially mortar shells rigged to explode approximately 30 meters above ground level, with a cellulose casing and a colored liquid instead of a fragmenting metal casing and high explosive. Anything under an umbrella of about 50 meters in circumference would be covered under a slick, oily mist of red.

"I expect the Novaya Zemlya effect to help us here," Sokolov said. "Sunrise is geologically going to be at 0543; the effect will bring up the sun on the horizon about an hour earlier." A number of eyebrows raised; few had heard of this phenomenon. "I want 455 and the other half of 802 to fill in the gaps across the inlet. Where you see the Finns leaving any holes, you make for those holes, understand?"

Fedoroskva nodded quickly. "Do we push through on foot or with the ITV?"

Sokolov thought for a moment. "I tell you what, Pasha. *If* you can get 455 to the edge of the inlet in one piece, and *if* you can see a reasonably-sized hole, then try to push through with the icebox."

Fedoroskva smiled. "We'll give it a good try."

"I'd give a few kopeks to see the Finns' faces when they watch that beast blowing across the ice," said Racowicz.

"Let's just hope it gets their attention." Sokolov replied. "I've spoken with Lieutenant Vlastaya; the rest of the battalion will be on a line that runs from the northern tip of the inlet eastward on the 52, 32 grid line by 0400, ready to push off directly for the airfield. So ... is everyone clear? We hit the Finns, try to garner as much attention as possible and then slam them as hard as you can. If you can push through to the airfield to link up with the rest of the battalion, good; if not, no worries, your job is to pull the Finns onto the ice and get them off their northern defensive line."

"Where is the rendezvous at the wrap?" Kong asked.

"Right; once the three white flares go up, the exercise is over. Bring your people to the airfield. We'll regroup in the Base Operations building. From this point, if one of the ITVs break down, leave it; we'll try to recover it later."

"We already know the demolition charges work as advertised," Lieutenant Bushkin noted dryly.

"There is not much time," Sokolov pointed out, packing his map away inside his parka. "Get the men moving."

Most of the enlisted Spetsnaz were gathered around 265's turbine, trying to suck the last of the heat from the metal. Rasputin, the oldest enlisted man in the group, held his hands close to the metal casing.

The Persian, a thin Russian from Tajikistan, spoke up, rubbing his hands. "This is a frozen hell. Nothing lives out here."

"Just like Tajikistan," Borg replied.

The Persian spat. "In my village there was a fire every night, there was plenty to eat, plenty to drink, elk and gazelle on the spit, and women wherever you look."

"I *thought* the women in Tajikistan looked like elk and gazelles," Snake said, "and I did hear that they spit."

"You should talk," the Persian replied. "The women in Siberia look like bulldogs in scarves."

Snake threw an unopened can of hash and hit the Persian in the helmet. The Persian launched at Snake and they were on the frozen ground in a second, punching, wrestling, and flat-hand smacking until Rasputin snapped his fingers, once. The men stopped immediately, pushed themselves from the ground and brushed the snow off their uniforms. They were both laughing.

"Barentsz died here, you know ... in 1597." Rasputin had spoken; no one knew what he was talking about, but they held still. He had a low, sibilant voice; hypnotizing, some said.

"His body was buried in the ice. They thought it was over land, but it turned out to be over the ocean, and now his remains are out there somewhere." Rasputin made a graceful gesture out toward the ocean. "You know who Barentsz was, Snake?"

Snake kicked at the snow. "He won Siberian kick-boxing championship last year, yes?" The Persian smacked Snake on the helmet.

"No, Snake. Willem Barentsz ... as in the Barents Sea. They named an entire ocean after the man. He was an explorer. He came here with a party of Dutch explorers. There were 16 men and a boy. They discovered Novaya Zemlya, but couldn't get off the island because of the ice, so they broke up some boats and built a shelter to make it through the winter. They were so cold that their socks would burn before their feet felt any heat, so they began to sleep with warmed cannonballs."

"Like Siberian woman," the Persian hissed.

Rasputin went on. "Only twelve survived that winter. They had no parkas, no batteries, nothing like what we have now. Yet twelve of them lived. They crossed the Kara Sea in two small boats, and they were rescued by a Russian ship from the Kola." The other men listened respectfully. "In 1992, an anthropologist decided to explore the site where Barentsz and some of his crew died, and he spent the winter in this place. In his research, do you know what he found? Do you know what he said about why those twelve men survived?" Rasputin looked around; the others leaned against the casing or stood quietly in the dark, watching the older man. "It was said that those who survived were religious. It was said that faith brings confidence and supplies hope for the future."

The others kept their faces impassive, though talking about religion in the Spetsnaz was like praising capitalism in a Politburo meeting. Only the Mad Monk would do such a thing. They called him 'the Mad Monk' behind his back; no one would dare do so to his face. In the barracks they told stories about Rasputin; about how he had gotten his name. No one knew his real name, nor did they want to know. Once, before Rasputin had gotten this name, he was just a junior sergeant, a *salagi*—a 'small-fry'—in the Spetsnaz units. Rasputin had made some reference to faith or religion and an older sergeant—a *stariki*, or 'older man'—laughed him to scorn, and then made him crawl through a field of rotten sheep guts for three hours, taunting him all the time about the 'joys of blood and faith and sacrifice' that he could find in religion. The *stariki* then had him hang from a steel bar for another hour, while he dripped pig's blood over his head. He then ordered Rasputin to clean the platoon's toilets with his toothbrush. All this Rasputin bore without a word, but that night in the *stariki* barracks, they say that the older sergeant sat up suddenly, yelling, terrified, and began choking ... on his own blood. He died spitting blood, watched by the platoon's senior sergeants and the medic, before anyone could do a thing. There were no marks, no cuts, nothing. And they said that the man they would call Rasputin was laying in the *salagi* barracks, a hundred meters away, wide awake, smiling.

The door to 265 slammed open, and Kong filled the doorway after the other officers had piled out.

"Mount up, slime," he growled. "The easy part of the trip is over."

***

265 departed company five minutes later and powered over the snow toward their southern point. Stain drove; Borg would stand on the front edge of the ITV and make a signal left or right if they were approaching a particularly dangerous looking

obstruction in the snow pack. Sokolov directed them to push the speed up to 40 clicks per hour, and to their surprise they discovered the ride smoothed out slightly. As the speed picked up, the men in the box whooped and yelled. Borg stolidly hung on to a rope they'd rigged from the top hatch to keep him from falling overboard. The rig still took bumps reluctantly. They arrived at their jump-off point two hours later.

"Okay," Sokolov said, mostly to himself. "Kong, your people brought the Barrett, right?" Kong looked at him questioningly.

"We did, Captain. Usually either Borg or I carry the beast. It weighs 14 kilos."

Sokolov was stepping into his cross-country boots and pulling down his skis and poles. "Right; I'll take it and move around to the south, where the inlet is the widest, and swing around under the airfield. I'm going to start now; you wait until 0330 and kick off the attack as ordered with the rest of the platoon."

Kong didn't say anything for a moment. He went to the chart table and leaned over the map. "Where ... exactly ... will you go?"

Sokolov moved to the map and picked up a pencil. "We're here; I'll move from here to here ... then here ... then across the mouth of the inlet ... then up to here. I want to try to climb on top of the Base Operations building and set up the Barrett. From there I can take out every one of their helicopters before sunrise."

Kong looked at the points Sokolov had made on the map and did some quick figuring. "That's ... that's about 25 kilometers," he said, "with 14, no, more like 30 kilos, because you will need to carry ammunition for it, or the umpires will ignore you."

Sokolov was lacing his boots. "Yes, that is about what I calculated."

"You can do 25 kilometers carrying 30 kilos in ... what ... how much time?"

"I am thinking it will take about an hour ... maybe a little less."

Kong knelt down and put his face close to Sokolov's. "You are not wearing tight spandex here, Captain, with pretty colors and a tight little cap, racing on a groomed course. You are moving across 25 kilometers of rough terrain in full combat rig carrying a very heavy rifle and lots of ammunition."

Sokolov yanked the last laces up tight and smiled. "Yes, Lieutenant, I know." He stood up and began to cinch the Barrett to the shoulder rig.

"You'll take a radio, yes?" Kong asked.

"I am not so foolish as to do this without a radio, Lieutenant."

Kong nodded. "No, no, I didn't think so, Comrade Captain. So," Kong smiled slyly and leaned against the steel wall of the container, "I bet you a thousand rubles and a bottle of American Jack Daniels that you will call for someone to rescue you before you make it to the Base Operations building."

The rest of the men in the box stopped what they were doing. This kind of confrontation was nothing like any kind of challenge in the Spetsnaz, but the Captain was not in the Spetsnaz and all they knew about him was that he was some kind of engineer sent by higher headquarters, responsible for observing how the vehicles worked and for executing the exercise. But he was still a Captain and Kong was still a Lieutenant. A few smiles appeared while the men loaded their packs. They wouldn't mind seeing some smart, bandbox headquarters soldier be made to look foolish.

Sokolov looked up at Kong, who was at least 12 centimeters taller than he was. "I tell you what, Lieutenant," he said, "let's make it a hundred thousand rubles and a case of Jack Daniels."

The room hushed. That was more than what a Russian Spetsnaz officer made in month, but Kong only smiled. "Sure, Captain, sure. Let's make it that, what you said."

Sokolov nodded, looked hard at Kong, yanked the straps for the Barrett tightly across his chest, and picked up the ammunition bandoleer.

"Where did you people get this gun, anyway?" he asked. "It's American, right?"

"Of course it is," Borg said.

"We bought it in the interspace," Snake put in.

"We had it shipped from Dallas America," Rhino finished, "where the cheering women are, who will love us when we come to visit."

Sokolov picked up his skis and poles, shoved the door to the ITV open, lowered his goggles, and stepped down onto the tundra. He stepped into his skis, shuffled his shoulders to settle the load, looked at his wrist compass, took a bearing, and poled off into the dark, barren, windswept tundra.

***

A Norwegian had posted a recent record for a 12.5-kilometer biathlon; it took him approximately 31 minutes to run the course, including the stops to shoot. Sokolov had proposed to match that speed, going twice as far, carrying about 30 kilos more than the Norwegian. He didn't have to stop and plink any targets, however. Kong felt it was a safe bet. So did Sokolov.

One hour and six minutes later, Sokolov approached the Finnish sentry at base of the Operations building. As a green flare shot up into the darkness from beyond the inlet, he came at the guard from behind, threw his forearm across the man's carotid artery and tightened. The man crumpled eight seconds later. Sokolov lowered him into the snow behind a dumpster and donned the man's cap and parka. He shouldered the Barrett and climbed the ladder that was bolted to the side of the building leading to the tower on the roof. He pulled his Sig Sauer P6 from its holster and climbed with the pistol in one hand. He crested the roof, saw two female Finnish scouts, binoculars to their eyes, looking in the direction of where the flare had gone up. As he came through the doorway, one turned, saw the hat and parka, and was about to turn back when Sokolov's Simunition round took her in the back. The other turned at the sound of the shot and Sokolov put a shot into her solar plexus. After the shock of being surprised, they smiled grudgingly, set their weapons in the corner of the tower observation post, sat down, opened a ration box, and began to eat what looked to Sokolov like small, oily fish on large, dark brown crackers. They smiled shyly at him, offering him some of their food. He smiled back and declined.

Sokolov set the Barrett up on the sill overlooking the ramp while the two Finnish ladies watched him, eating their rations, laughing at one thing, then another. The sun was just cresting the hills in the east, and the light cascaded across the tarmac onto four mottled gray NH90 helicopters. Sokolov slammed a blank .50 caliber round into the chamber, yanked back the bolt, aimed the weapon well above the helicopters, and pulled the trigger. The weapon boomed across the bleak landscape.

The crews near the helicopters jumped. Sokolov ratcheted the bolt back, pushed another round into the chamber, elevated the barrel, and pulled the trigger again. By this time the Finn defenders were reacting, and Simunition rounds were splattering against the walls of the tower platform. Sokolov threw another round in the rifle, stood up, aimed the weapon high, and pulled the trigger again. A paint pellet smacked into the roof of the tower. The two Finns, dead soldiers that they were, cursed and scrambled to cover their fish with their ration boxes. As Sokolov fired the last round, a paint pellet smacked into the Barrett's barrel, constructively putting it out of commission. The Finnish defenders stormed up the ladder. Sokolov emptied his pistol, taking out four until a paint pellet smacked him directly in the forehead. His head snapped backward. He took off his helmet to see a blue stain, and then glowered at the Finns as they clambered up into the observation tower. He sat down, and one of the female Finnish tower guards handed him sardines on a cracker and bottle of Sahti.

***

Exercise Novaya Zemlya 97781
After Action Report

This report summarizes the events of Exercise Novaya Zemlya 97781, held during [date redacted].

1. *Units Participating:*
    a. *[Unit redacted] Battalion / 77th Motorized Rifle Division*
    b. *[Unit redacted] Spetsnaz platoon / 33rd Spetsnaz Brigade*
2. *Exercise Objectives:*
    a. *Assault the Rogachevo airfield, rendering it inoperable for enemy air operations.*
    b. *Field test the ITV401 Ice Transport Vehicle, assessing its operational effectiveness and tactical suitability for frozen ocean operations.*
3. *Operational Events:*

Seventy-three of 75 ITV units launched from Dikson pier at 0400 on the 24th. Two ITV engines were inoperable and would not start. The platoons in the inoperable units were distributed into others, along with their equipment and fuel cans. The passage of approximately 750 kilometers over the fully frozen ice of the Kara Sea was in the main uneventful. During the crossing, two ITV units were disabled by striking a forward skid against either a rock or ice shelf. Another lost its aft starboard runner, also by striking either a rock or an ice formation. Crews and equipment were distributed into other units. The disabled units have been recovered and are undergoing repairs.

Seventy units entered the opening to the Matochkin Strait. Landing was made at the planned coordinates. Unit 265, along with units 775, 802, and 455, commanded by Lieutenants Racowicz, Bushkin, and Fedoroskva, conducted an ad hoc tactical field experiment to determine if the ITV would successfully negotiate tundra. This detachment, under the command of Captain S. Sokolov, moved south ahead of the main body. The main body, under the command of Lieutenant A. Vlastaya, waited for the report from the forward detachment as to whether they would disembark and continue on foot or press ahead in the ITVs. Conditions were assessed as favorable for ITV transport as long as the vehicles remained as much as possible on the snow pack. Direction was given to the main body to proceed to the pre-established jump off point for the attack. Speed over viable snow pack on tundra terrain can be, with modifications noted in the Recommendations section, up to 40 kilometers per hour.

Unit 802 was disabled during the run south by the forward detachment. As a test of unit destruction systems, the commanding officer for 802 was directed to destroy the unit in place with the destruct system. The unit commander complied with this direction after all crew, equipment, and fuel was removed from the unit. Upon inspection by maintenance personnel after the exercise, it was determined that the charges would probably not have rendered the unit fully unusable for other forces. See the Recommendations section of this report for further details.

Upon reaching [location redacted], units 265, 775, 455, and elements from 802 established a lager for rest and equipment checks. A hasty battle conference was held, at which final plans for attacking the airfield were made and transmitted to the main body via encrypted radio communications. Lieutenant Vlastaya concurred with all elements of the attack order.

After the battle conference, unit 265 pushed ahead of the remaining two units of the forward detachment and positioned itself at [location redacted]. Units 775 and 455 moved to take up their positions: 775 was positioned at [location redacted]; its task was to provide covering mortar fire and fire support for simulated artillery and close air support. 455 found itself at [location redacted] when the attack commenced. 455's task was to penetrate any perceived holes in the Finn's line of defense.

The attack commenced at 0330 on the 26th. Signal for the attack was the firing of a green flare. Lieutenant Vlastaya brought the main body of the battalion to the jump-off line, performed the necessary equipment and weapon checks, and commenced the attack on time. Three ITVs were disabled in the main body as they moved from the landing site to the jump-off line. These units have been recovered. Like the others, they struck either ice or rock with a skid or runner. Men, equipment, and fuel were distributed into following units and the movement pressed toward the jump-off line.

When the green flare was launched, unit 265 began a ground assault across the inlet on foot, widely distributed so at to cause as much distraction as possible. This served to pull two companies of Finns from the defensive line they had established, which ran parallel to the jump-off line extending from [points redacted]. As these companies tried to move south, unit 755's mortar team attacked with three of the unit's 82mm mortars. Umpires report Finnish casualties among the two companies at 70%, and the mortar attack halted the Finns before they could regroup. Unit 455 noticed a gap in the Finns' line caused by the mortar attack and, using its ITV, rapidly pushed through this gap. Lieutenant Fedoroskva reports speeds across the inlet of up to 55 kilometers per hour, and his data record confirms this claim. Most likely the higher speed was due to the fact that the ice over an inland body of water was much smoother, allowing for more rapid transit.

Unit 455 pushed through the thin Finn line and turned south immediately to assault the airfield. The main body pushed through the lines vacated by the two Finnish companies, and it then became a race to the airfield. The crews in the ITVs in the main body, recognizing they were intermixed with Finnish troops racing to the airfield, climbed to the roof on the containers and began firing at the Finns. Several simulated casualties on the fleeing Finns were inflicted via this method. Extreme care was taken by ITV drivers to avoid running down Finnish troops on the ground. It is the considered estimation of several ITV commanders that many Finnish troops, facing the ITVs for the first time, experienced shock and fear not unlike that experienced by infantry when facing tanks.

Unit 455, realizing it was ahead of the main body and watching the battle unfolding, decided to halt in place. Lieutenant Fedoroskva deployed his platoon, setting up heavy machine guns and mortars behind a line of ammunition crates behind a slight rise in terrain. The fleeing Finnish troops hit this ad hoc 'anvil'. Umpires ruled over 80% casualties among the remaining Finnish defenders, confirmed by the laser and Simunition hit recorders. Lieutenants Fedoroskva and Vlastaya are to be commended for their quick-thinking adjustment to battlefield conditions in a rapidly changing situation.

The commanding officer of unit 265 detached from the unit and, carrying the platoon's long-range sniper weapon, moved to a position on top of Base Operations where he eliminated the four NH90 helicopters that were being prepared for attack operations against our forces. The remainder of unit 265 continued its assault across the inlet and met remains of the two companies the Finns had detached to stop them. Unit 265 quickly dispatched these forces and moved to overrun the runway, meeting the main body ITVs almost in the middle of the airfield.

The umpires fired three white flares at approximately 0835. Personnel, equipment, and vehicles were accounted for and the men fed. Russian units rendezvoused with elements of the Finnish forces for an After Action conference at the Base Operations building at 1200. During the conference, Finnish leadership was unstinting in their praise of the 77th Motorized Rifle Division's performance (note: the Finns were and remain unaware that unit 265 carried a Spetsnaz platoon). No disagreements as to casualty rates or mission objective accomplishments were experienced; the Finns acknowledged that the 77th Division had accomplished all its objectives. They expressed strong surprise and intense curiosity regarding the ITVs; apparently they had never seen or imagined such a vehicle, and several Russian officers noted many Finnish officers taking detailed notes and observations regarding the vehicles.

Sasha finished his Exercise Report, slid the hard copy into a manila envelope, and addressed it to the Head of the Transportation Development Division at Central Red

Army Headquarters. He would not trust this report to be delivered via email. He made a copy and sent it to his uncle as well. Lastly he copied it to a memory stick, then turned off the computer and the printer, closed the desk, turned off the lights in the office, and made his way to his quarters, where he drank a quart of water, ate some black bread and sausage, and fell instantly asleep.

***

Three weeks later, Sasha found himself walking along the streets of Moscow, headed toward what had once been the Leningrad Military District Headquarters, but which had been merged with several other headquarters regions to become the Western Operational Strategic Command, and moved to Moscow. He was there, he supposed, to complete his report on the exercise in Novaya Zemlya. He presented his papers at the front security checkpoint and was escorted through corridor after endless corridor until he came to a first door and began an unexpected ordeal.

Four different people interviewed him that day, each asking about something different. The first asked him about his experiences during the exercise on Novaya Zemlya, raising questions about almost every command decision he'd made as well as his opinions regarding the suitability and effectiveness of the ITV. He explained himself fully, covering all the recommendations he'd made, with no apologies. Another asked about his youth and what it had been like growing up in his family. He asked what his parents were like and what they did and what they were doing and why his mother had been an American. The man who put these personal questions did so while smoking a foul-smelling cigarette, drinking cup after cup of coffee, and apparently thinking nothing of prying into Sokolov's personal family life. Sasha thought nothing of it either; in Russia, in Communism, there was no such thing as personal privacy. He felt no angst; it was, in the very fiber of his being, completely acceptable for the State to have the right to know everything about a person they sheltered and cared for. At a third interview they spoke only of biathlon—what Sasha was training for presently, what he thought his chances were at the upcoming Olympic trials, and his training methods. He could tell the interviewer was, if not a professional, at least highly knowledgeable about the sport, and athletes in general. The fourth interview was political, grilling him to assess his level of political reliability and queried him regarding the languages he possessed. Sasha handled all of these interviews, especially the last, easily. He responded to his questioners during the last interview easily in Russian, German, and English—all flawless, without accents in any language. He could tell the interrogators were impressed, though they did their best to hide it. A Major General conducted most of this last interview, and at the end, he looked at Sasha with a firm eye. "I do not have to tell you, Comrade Captain, that you are not to mention anything about the sessions conducted here."

"I understand, Comrade General."

"Should it be deemed necessary to speak with you further about these sessions, someone will contact you. So that you know the subject of the discussion, they will give you a series of five numbers." The General pushed a piece of paper across the table. Sasha picked it up, memorized the numbers, and set the paper down again.

"You are dismissed, Comrade Captain."

"Thank you, Comrade General." Sasha stood up, saluted, and left the room, followed by a silent major of airborne troops, who escorted him wordlessly to the main exit and brusquely dismissed him after mentioning that 'he would be contacted if it was determined to be in the best interests of the State'. Sasha clicked his heels, saluted, and left not knowing exactly what had happened, or who he had spoken with—or why.

***

In the late spring Sasha traveled to Longyearbyen in Spitsbergen to compete in the Olympic biathlon trials. He walked the streets the first day, and his Spartan soul approved of the Scandinavian architecture and the neat, clean streets, but gazed disinterestedly at the colored houses, wondering what would possess a people to paint their houses yellow, green, blue, or orange. He stayed in the Longyearbyen House, a massive, monolithic white structure overlooking a bleak, snow-covered valley. He was surprised the Party had booked him into one of the more expensive hotels in Spitsbergen until he walked into the restaurant Kroa and saw a huge white marble bust of Lenin behind the bar. Smiling, he supposed that even Party tourist agents had a soft spot in their Communist hearts. His first evening he ate a grilled whale steak with soy sauce, and supported it with a robust German lager; the fare was superb. Tourists filled the hotel and clambered over the bleak mountainous pathways with the sun bright in the sky at midnight, eagerly waiting to watch some of the world's best biathletes compete for Olympic positions. Norway, Sweden, Finland, and Russia had agreed to conduct joint Scandinavian national trials at the same location, which explained the large numbers of tourists. Norwegian and Swedish competitors would be vying for two spots on their respective national Olympic teams; Finland and Russia each had three spots vacant. There were twenty-eight other Russians competing. The trials, run separately for each national team, consisted of three 7.5-kilometer time-trial sprint races, scored using a 'percent-back'—a formula wherein a competitor's three best times are averaged together to get a base score. Sasha felt confident he would earn a spot. He wouldn't be carrying thirty kilograms of weapons and ammunition, nor would he be required to simulate killing people or destroying helicopters just prior to the finish line.

***

Two days later, Sasha was sitting alone at a table in the Kroa, waiting for his dinner, wondering still why a bust of Lenin was featured prominently in a Norwegian restaurant, and perusing the more attractive women as they moved through the hotel. He would be flying out the next day, and he was celebrating his success with another whale steak and a large stein of Belgian ale. He was fixedly occupied with considering which of the two women he would invite for the evening's further celebration, both of whom had been giving him the eye since he walked into the restaurant, when two men approached his table.

"Captain Sokolov," one began. The man was dressed in well-tailored camel hair coat over soft gray slacks. At first Sasha looked up rather sharply; he very definitely did not appreciate being addressed by his military rank in public, and definitely not while he was attempting to pose as an amateur athlete from Russia. His eye must have conveyed some of the steel in his attitude at the imposition, for the other man, wearing a long dark green overcoat, said, quietly but firmly, "You met with some of our friends in Moscow recently; four times, to be precise."

Sasha's attitude rapidly adjusted itself as he realized who the men were and where they were from. He nodded without saying anything, and the two men slid into his booth with an easy, athletic grace.

"So ... have you enjoyed the trials?" Sasha asked, wanting to appear friendly.

"We have, very much, Sasha. Yes, and congratulations ... we see that you were quite successful," said Camel Hair.

"He placed first among the Russians and was second overall," said Green Overcoat quietly, but with some pride.

"Yes, yes, we noted this," said Camel Hair. "You have done well for the State, Captain." The man stopped talking and loosened his coat, getting comfortable. Sasha pegged Camel Hair as a Party political officer; the second was from ... well, he wasn't sure, but he would have bet a month's pay that Green Overcoat was Army—and probably not regular Army, but something ... special.

Camel Hair shot his cuffs and asked a question. "We would like to know your thoughts, Captain, on how you would feel about joining a very special unit that occasionally performs some rather particular services for the State."

The waiter came, bringing a loaf of bread, a pot of butter, bottled water, ashtrays, a dish of nuts, and napkins, and asked if the men at the table would care for a drink. Camel Hair ordered a white wine; Green Overcoat asked for a glass of tea. The waiter left.

"The results of your visit with our people in Moscow were ... satisfactory. We think you would add to the effectiveness of a unit we are putting together."

Sasha paused. "Visit to Moscow? I am not sure to what visit you refer, Comrade."

Green Overcoat smiled up at Camel Hair. He pulled a pen from a pocket and wrote quickly on a napkin and pushed it to Sasha. There were five numbers on it—numbers he'd last seen in front of a General in Moscow.

Sasha smiled to himself, but to Camel Hair he said, "May I ask, Comrade, what type of unit? I mean, what types of things would such a unit do? Because if it involves sitting behind a desk, or filling out reports, or counting how many copies the fourth secretary from the third directorate filed in the previous six months ... I do not think I would be your best choice."

Sasha perceived a small gleam in Green Overcoat's eye; Camel's Hair sat somewhat more stiffly and cleared his throat. "No," he said, "there would be nothing so ... tedious as you describe." Sasha suspected that what he had described was just what Camel Hair spent most of his days doing. Before he could speak, the waiter returned with the drinks. No one spoke.

Green Overcoat took the same napkin and wrote the words '*spetsialnoye nazhacheniye*', turned the napkin so Sasha could read it again, waited for two seconds, pulled a lighter from his pocket, and lit the napkin on fire in the ashtray. He looked Sasha in the eye, waiting for an answer.

Sasha's jaw was firmly set, and his eyes were hard. He had hoped for just this turn of events. *Spetsnaz!* He had taken particular pains to impress Lieutenant Lohniverisk and the other members of the Spetsnaz platoon during the exercise in Novaya Zemlya. It was why he had detailed himself as the commanding officer of Unit 265, and directed the Spetsnaz platoon to ride in his ITV. He made a tight bar of fist and forearm and pushed them forward slightly, the very male gesture of strong affirmation. Under the normal volume of sound in the restaurant, he leaned forward and said, '*Da*'. Green Overcoat had his answer. The three of them adjourned to Sokolov's hotel room.

***

"Okay," Green Overcoat said, reverting to English as they stepped into the room. He pulled a manila folder from his under his overcoat. Camel Hair closed the door, took his coat off, draped it over a chair carefully, and took a seat in one of the lounge chairs in the corner. Green Overcoat sat on the hard IKEA desk chair; Sasha sat on the bed. Green Overcoat handed him the folder.

"You will go to America," he said. "You will pose as a marine construction engineer on holiday. You will do a cross-country ski reconnaissance of the northern border throughout the American Midwest—the states of North Dakota and Minnesota, to be precise. You will observe as much detail as possible on the ground."

"What should I be looking for, specifically?" Sasha asked, holding his beer in both hands.

Green Overcoat looked at Camel Hair, who shook his head slightly. "We want you to observe as much as possible about the terrain, especially transportation routes, fueling locations, industrial areas, and the location of local food distribution centers."

"Food distribution centers?" Sasha asked, surprised.

"Yes, food distribution centers ... and the people as well. Do not forget to take special note of the people you encounter. We want your opinions about their ..." Green Overcoat looked to Camel Hair for guidance.

Camel Hair interjected quietly from the corner: "About their character; their fortitude, if you will. And your mother's heritage will be especially helpful, Comrade Captain."

"My mother detested America," Sasha replied testily.

"We know all about your mother's political inclinations," Camel Hair replied, in a voice tinged with iron, "and they are appropriate. Otherwise we would not be having this conversation."

Green Overcoat continued. "You will be taking a holiday from your job as an maritime industrial design engineer from Murmansk."

"I see," Sasha replied. "Will there be ... other duties?"

"Perhaps," Camel Hair interjected emphatically, while gracefully smoothing lint from his meticulously creased gray slacks. Sasha noticed the manicured nails, the gold watch, the cufflinks. "You may be tasked to interact with members of the diplomatic service we have working in America; members of my staff, actually. You may even be required to file three or four copies of your reports for the fourth secretary of the Third Directorate."

After a drawn-out moment, Sasha said, "Touché." Camel Hair nodded his acceptance of Sasha's tacit apology and went on. "You will report to me; my staff and I work in the Russian embassy in the American capitol. Part of your responsibilities will be to delve into as much of American society as possible while you reconnoiter the terrain. During your selection process our people discerned that this will not be too much of a difficulty for you." Sasha smiled. "Good," Camel Hair went on, "we understand each other then." Sasha realized he had misjudged Camel Hair—apparently an iron fist in a velvet glove—and the narrow brush with potential disaster gave him his first lesson in diplomacy. Green Overcoat continued with the briefing, pulling out a map of the northern United States.

"You will fly into Boston," he said, "and begin your reconnaissance route by heading west across the top of the country until you reach North Dakota, where you will then turn north toward the Canadian border, then turn east to traverse the country into and across Minnesota to here, on Lake Superior." Green Overcoat pointed to a town on the map. "Granite Sky; it is a medium-sized American town, out of the way, very active right now with oil exploration activity, close to the coast of this large body of water, here. We want you to settle there. We will take care of your visa and travel documents. Your story will be that you are considering opening a factory there, to build ships. The Americans will salivate at the opportunity for new jobs, no matter who owns the factory. Our information is that this location is particularly depressed, economically." Green Overcoat paused and looked over at Camel Hair, who shrugged and nodded. Sasha got the sense that this was a final nod of acceptance from the real authority in the meeting. "You will be given instructions on how to stay in touch with our people in America once you get there," Camel Hair said, looking at his watch. Green Overcoat turned back to Sasha. "Do you have any questions?"

"Only one," Sasha said, leaning forward. "Where is Lieutenant Lohniverisk? He owes me a case of Jack Daniels."

Chapter 27

Marcus

"What is desirable in a man is his kindness, and it is better to be a poor man than a liar."

Proverbs 19:22

When USOCO decided to make a move to Minnesota, Billy Rob, in public, played the dumb old country boy. In reality, he was a snake-shrewd businessman who, it was rumored, could 'scheme like an Ay-rab.' Billy Rob demonstrated a singular genius for buying and selling companies, and took his father's nascent empire and expanded and solidified its foundation, acquiring companies working in numerous oil and gas support industries such as technology firms creating new drilling systems for use specifically in cold weather environments, in lakes, and under ice. He went after new software applications designed specifically for the oil and gas industry and bought training companies who trained oil rig workers, and purchased companies that were developing systems, processes, procedures, and technologies for the burgeoning oil and gas safety industry, which at the time was roundly and unanimously ignored by every other company in the industry as being an impediment to progress. But Billy Rob was a shrewd and intuitive observer and he'd spent his time out on the rigs. He cared for his people, too, the way he had cared for his Marines. He knew that it was simply a matter of time before a major oilrig accident would happen—he'd seen dozens of smaller accidents occur on his family's rigs and on other companies platforms, and he knew a bigger accident was just waiting in the wings. As the rigs and offshore oil platforms got bigger, he realized that an oil spill would create a massive environmental hazard, and as trends moved toward a greater concern about the environment in the US and other parts of the world, he put the pieces together. He got in early in two main market segments: one, the oil and gas safety industry, purchasing companies such that soon, USOCO became known as the leader in oil and gas safety training, safety technologies, and safety processes and procedures. And second, USOCO became known as the world leader in drilling under inland lakes for oil. He built drilling platforms that were extremely low profile, much smaller, more efficient, and with a ton of redundant safety features. Billy Rob didn't want to go near any kind of inland environmental disaster. He knew that an oil spill on a rig in an inland lake would pretty much kill the lake, the marine life, the wildlife that depended on the lake, and every ounce of political support he had spent years building.

USOCO pioneered technologies designed to make working on oil rigs safer, and as the years unfolded, USOCO had the industry's best safety record. If you were an oil worker concerned for your safety, you wanted to work on a USOCO rig. With his background flying the Super Cobra, it was an easy transition for Billy Rob to qualify in the corporation helicopters. He bought helicopter companies to make sure their safety procedures were up to snuff when they flew the crews out to the rigs. Where the most dangerous part of working on other companies' oilrigs was actually the helicopter flights out and back, USOCO's pilots and aircraft always had the best safety record in the industry. And it helped that most of the USOCO rigs weren't offshore in some horrendous weather, but tucked inland, floating in some placid northern Minnesota lake. It meant that the rig workers could get off the rig and spend their off-shift time in towns instead of some isolated floating barracks on the rigs.

One day Billy Rob took the right seat of the Sikorsky S76 helicopter and, with a senior check pilot in the left seat, launched out of a small municipal airport outside of Minneapolis as pilot-in-command and landed out on one of USOCO's drilling rigs in Sea Gull Lake, a fairly large inland lake up in north central Minnesota. It was late in a gloomy afternoon, with low ceilings and storm winds, a driving rain, and the lake was stirring itself up like something out of a Beethoven symphony. The bad part of having rigs on lakes was that when the weather got bad, the water conditions got really bad, because there just wasn't that much place for the water to go. He'd heard tell of storm conditions in the Great Lakes being so much worse than the stuff out on open ocean rigs that it would just turn ships completely over, capsize 'em in a heartbeat. This is why he put so much time and attention and engineering work and extra funds into making his inland lake rigs safer.

Waves pounded the oil platform's huge concrete support pillars and the helicopter landing zone was shifting back and forth. But Billy Rob piloted the aircraft directly in on a flawless instrument approach, hovering just over the helipad's designated landing zone, chewing on a big black cigar while the check pilot sat, white-faced, hands hovering scant millimeters over the stick and collective, feet just a centimeter from the rudder pedals. He knew that if he let the President of the company crash on one of his own oilrigs, he'd never hear the end of it. But Billy set the big helicopter down with no problems, the aircraft rocking gently as the lift vector came off the rotors.

"Not bad, Billy Rob," Ol' Digger Jack yelled from the back seat. A consulting engineer and his team of three support engineers were the only other passengers. They were all terrified.

"Like a sick butterfly with sore feet," Billy Rob yelled back, the cigar back in his mouth again after being tucked away, unlit, in a pocket of his flight suit.

The linemen rushed out to chain the aircraft to the landing platform, slipping on the greasy non-skid, and watching through the rain-spattered windscreen, Billy Rob made a mental note to check the last time the non-skid had been replaced. This was one of the company's older platforms, and he didn't want his line crews slipping off into the lake while trying to chain down a 10,000-pound helicopter. They clambered out of the aircraft, ducking in the driving rain and spray, watching the shortened, choppy waves form and come smashing into the platform's concrete support pillars driven by a fierce wind.

When Billy Rob stepped into the operations shack to fill out the paperwork on the flight, with water streaming from his flight jacket, he said, "Jimmy, when's the last time we put down new non-skid on the helipad?"

"I'll find out, boss," the Rig Manager, Jimmy Fields answered. He was waiting in the operations shack to greet the President of the company.

"Well, let's just get some put down anyway. It's looking a mite slippery out there. Is the staff ready?"

"All set, BR, we're in the conference room."

They made their way through the rabbit warren of passageways amidst the sound of pumps, clanking machinery, and engines, accompanied by the smell of burning metal and the ever-present odor of fresh, hot, black oil. They came to a small conference room. Seven others waited there for Billy Rob and his team, and without any ceremony he took the head chair and started the meeting. In the field, BR was all business.

"Hey y'all. Thanks for coming." The consulting engineers ranged themselves around the sides of the room and Billy Rob began the briefing. "We're gonna talk about this safety report you sent in." He pulled a sheaf of papers from a leather portfolio. Jimmy Fields, the General Manager on the rig, shifted uncomfortably in his seat. "Okay. From what I read here, seems like we almost had a blowout on the B condensate pipe. The rig shift supervisor caught the issue. Seems, if I read this right, that one of the pressure safety valves on the B condensate injection pump had been yanked for maintenance. The maintenance crew sealed the pipe with some blind flange covers. I'm guessing the maintenance people couldn't finish the job before the shift change, so they left the covers on the pipe, right?"

Jimmy Fields piped up. "Right, boss. That's what happened. Standard procedure."

"So," Billy Rob continued, "during the next shift, when the A condensate pump tripped for some reason, someone could have just started the B condensate pump. But," he said, pausing, "that didn't happen. And why? Because Simon Abernathy, the rig shift supervisor, had the B condensate pump switch flagged off, and when someone—I won't ask who—tried to light off that pump, Abernathy caught it and stopped him. Is Simon here? Right, there you are. Simon, as of now you're making twice what you were making, got it?"

Simon Abernathy, one of the rig shift supervisors with four kids at home and a wife with lupus, sat there stunned. "Th, thanks, BR," he said.

"And that ain't countin' the one-time performance bonus yer gittin fer this."

The others in the room broke into loud applause, sincerely happy for Simon, one of the most popular men on the rig. And they knew it would help at home.

"Now listen," Billy Rob went on. "We could've had one hell of a major explosion with that. Ol' Digger Jack, run it down for us."

Ol' Digger Jack sat in a chair on the side of the room, his arms folded, wearing an old dungaree jacket, a red plaid work shirt, patched jeans, and a faded orange hard hat. "Ah'm thinkin' you'd a had an uncontrolled gas explosion, and that woulda started a fire that probably would have disabled the fire-fighting systems. You had divers in the water that night, right?"

"Yeah, actually, we did," Fields said, his voice low.

"Well, so, the fire-fighting system would have been under manual control then, right?" Fields nodded. Divers were in the water constantly, at least 12 hours out of the day, in the summer weather around the rig. "So maybe that's something we need to think about too. Them skinny dippin' divers don't go anywhere near those pump intakes, and even if they did, those intakes are covered with solid screens that would keep anything larger than a needlefish from being ingested. So let's make that procedure change, okay?"

"Right, boss," Fields said, jotting notes on a pad. "Automatic systems on while the divers are in the water."

"Right. Now, the temporary covers on the valve would've blown out from the overpressure, and probably started a fire. The explosion would've probably blown through the firewall—it ain't made to contain a blowout like that—and that's something else we've learned, lookin' into your report. This platform was originally designed for oil; the walls were designed to resist fire, not explosions. An explosion like what we avoided would have probably blown out a whole mess o' panels, and any one o' them could've cut into a bunch of other condensate pipes, and that woulda started more fires."

"So that means," Billy Rob interrupted, "that as of now, we're gittin' a complete facility redesign. That's what these four people are here for." Billy Rob gestured toward the four engineers. "They're gonna spend the next month on this rig, lookin' over every inch, and they're gonna produce a redesign that can withstand an explosion as well as a fire." The engineers, still pale from the bumpy flight, looked like condemned prisoners, but they bravely smiled and nodded at the rig crew around the table.

"Next thing ah'm thinkin'," Ol' Digger Jack continued, "is that once a fire around that pump valve started, it woulda spread until your control room was cut off. Now, Jimmy, tell me, what if somethin' happened and y'all couldn't use the control room?"

Fields turned to face the company's Chief Operating Officer. "I'm thinking, sir, that, well ... we'd be pretty much outta luck."

"Right answer," Billy Rob jumped in from the head of the room. "And that's something else we're gonna fix. I'm gonna install backup control capabilities on every company rig, separate, off and away from the main control rooms, with enough communications links and systems to make sure the leadership on the rig can still function of the main control room goes down. We'll make up drills to run the rig from those backup locations, got it?"

Fields flipped over another page in his notebook. "Got it, boss."

"So, Jimmy, let's say this explosion happened and you couldn't get back into the control room, and things are goin' to hell in a hand basket. What would you have done then?"

"I'd have ordered an evacuation, Boss."

"Right answer. Nothin' on this rig is more valuable than the people on it, you got that?" Billy Rob looked around the room, making sure everyone there understood what he was saying, because it was a different cultural expectation than any other oil company on the planet at the time. "I can build a hundred rigs, but no one can replace any of you people." He turned back to Jimmy Fields. "And how would that have gone?"

"Everyone is trained to make their way to the lifeboat stations, and—"

"Yeah, but let's say the fire cuts them off, and some of 'em can't get to the boats," Billy Rob interrupted. "Then what?"

"Then the procedure is to move into the fireproofed accommodation blocks under the helicopter deck."

"Uh huh," Ol' Digger Jack cut in, and said, "Now, Jimmy, we don't want you ta git th' idea we're pickin' on ya, 'cause we ain't. But we had one o' them accommodation blocks built back in Houston, at the test facility. We lit a bunch of fires all around the thing, and don't ya know, pretty soon it started leakin' smoke. So it might be fireproof, but that ain't gonna matter, 'cause everyone inside'll be smoked like a Kansas City brisket."

"So," Billy Rob went on, "let's say our folks, at least the ones who could get to 'em, are down in the blocks, waitin' on evac, but the weather is such that the birds just can't get in. The smoke starts fillin' up those accommodation blocks. Then what?"

"We'd just have to go down the ladders or jump for it," Angela Cordova said. Angela was the rig's personnel manager. The others in the room laughed loudly; the consulting engineers looked around nervously.

"Yeah, Angela, that's about the only thing left to do. But we noticed that there ain't that many lifejackets in the accommodation blocks."

"That's somethin' else we're gonna change," Ol' Digger Jack piped up from the side of the room.

"And we're gonna put some automatically-deployable life rafts that will be attached to the support pillars," Billy Rob said. "Sort of like the things they have in airplanes. They'll open once they hit the water, and ya'll can just climb aboard. We'll make it so anyone can deploy 'em with their cell phone."

"Yeah, but God help any one of you if you git drunk in some bar ashore and punch in the code and set 'em off." The group laughed as Ol' Digger Jack growled his warning.

"So we jump in and make our way to the rafts?" Angela asked. She was a hardy woman, short, stocky, with shoulders broader than most men, and she'd been living and working around wildcatters her whole life. No one wanted to get on the wrong side of Angela.

"If'n you can fight off the fresh-water sharks and them poisonous screechin' eels," Ol' Digger Jack said, with one eye on the consulting engineers.

"Sounds like my ex," Angela growled, "bring 'em!" The room broke up.

Billy Rob had one more thing. "Look, Jimmy," he said, while the room got quiet, "we don't want you to get the idea we were pickin' on ya, you know?"

"I know, Boss." There was a rustling of light laughter as the group was amused at Jimmy's discomfort.

"No, now, seriously, here's what I mean. You run a tight ship out here." Billy Rob was interrupted with numerous exclamations of strong agreement among the crowd. "Now pipe down, ya'll. Jimmy, you're the one responsible for the safety report that started all of our research—it was a good report—and you're the one responsible for pickin' Simon A, aren't you?"

"Yes sir. I ... I hired him two years ago, and tagged him to be a shift supervisor four months ago."

"Yeah, well, so what ah'm tryin' to say is that you're just as responsible for keepin' us from having that potential accident as anyone, and so you're gonna see a goodly pay hike as well, along with a performance bonus. Here." Billy Rob pulled an envelope out of his pocket and beckoned for Fields to come up to the head of the table. The room again erupted in spontaneous applause, because while he was tough, Jimmy Fields was fair, and everyone in the room knew that the tougher Jimmy Fields was on them, the more likely they were to get home safe to their families. Jimmy got out of his seat, flustered, not accustomed to this much personal, focused attention, and shook hands with Billy Rob. Ol' Digger Jack came up and shook his hand as well. Billy Rob wanted a company where the people who worked there felt like the people they worked with were their friends, and according to Billy Rob, friends looked out for their friends. And he always knew, sort of by instinct, that old leadership paradigm that says you praise in public and punish in private. He kept to that religiously.

After the meeting on the Sea Gull Lake rig, Billy Rob, Ol' Digger Jack, and the check pilot flew off the rig that afternoon in weather that had changed dramatically, the sky blown clear of clouds, and not even a breeze to ruffle the waters.

"Where we goin' next, boss?" Ol' Digger Jack asked as they walked out to the helicopter.

"Place called 'Granite Sky'. Got me a line on a possible Security Director candidate for our operations up here."

Ol' Digger Jack climbed into the back seat while the check pilot took the left seat and Billy Rob sat in the right seat as the command pilot. He put his headset on, clicked the button, and spoke. "Since when do we need a Security Director? What's the threat up here?"

Billy Rob didn't say anything right away, but rooted around in his flight publications case and pulled out an iPad, flicked his fingers across it for a couple of moments, and then handed it back to Ol' Digger Jack while he went on with the pre-Takeoff checklist with the check pilot. "Open up the 'Security' folder and you'll see what the issues are," Billy Rob said over the intercom.

Ol' Digger Jack opened the folder and looked at the files Billy Rob had compiled. There were articles about terrorists, insurgents, pirates, criminal syndicates, environmentalist whacko-nutjobs, anti-oil activists, and a bunch of other ne'er-do-wells. Ol' Digger Jack was familiar with all of these threats, because they'd had to fend them off to conduct USOCO operations around different parts of the world ... but in Minnesota? He couldn't figure it, but Billy Rob had a reason for everything he did—just like his Daddy.

After reading through the files, he clicked the internal intercom again. By then they'd lifted off the rig and were just about to go feet dry over the southern edge of the lake.

"Ah'm confused, Billy Rob. I git there's a threat o' pirates for our rigs off the coast of Somalia, and I can see the threat of syndicates on our pipeline operations across Siberia, but on an inland lake in Minnesota?"

The intercom clicked back on, but just then the helicopter jerked to the left and Billy Rob's head snapped to the right as a huge bald eagle whipped by the aircraft, barely missing them. "Open up the 'News Clips' folder," Billy Rob said a moment later.

Ol' Digger Jack's finger swiped over his pad to open the News Clips folder and there was only one file in it from a source Ol' Digger Jack recognized as someone they had on their 'double-secret-probation, really deep, really black' payroll, developing open-source and some not-so-open-source intelligence. The file described the growing potential of foreign oil companies turning to sabotage and utilizing special operations-type military actions against U.S. domestic oil company facilities and operations to try and eliminate their advantage in the U.S. oil extraction industry. What bothered Ol' Digger Jack was that their source had never been wrong before on the intelligence he'd turned up, and so he began to wonder what might be developing up here in the 'land o' lakes.'

Ol' Digger Jack thought about that all the way to the Granite Sky airport. He waited until the helicopter had landed, the pilots removed their headsets, and then climbed out under the still-turning rotors. Billy Rob did his post-flight walk-around and then they both got into the car waiting for them.

"So who's this guy you're thinkin' about?" Ol' Digger Jack asked. "Where's he worked before? And what self-respectin' Security Director is gonna want to relocate all the way up into this god-fersakin' wilderness?"

Billy Rob looked at him, took out the big black cigar from his flight suit, and just smiled. "Now Ol' Digger Jack, what makes you think this place up here is fersakin' by the Lord Hisself? Why, it's pristine lakes, majestic forests, wide-open blue sky—"

"It's a whole lotta mud and a giant toothpick factory, Billy Rob, that's what it is up here."

"Ah, but Ol' Digger Jack, yer fergittin' all that oil underneath that mud and all them toothpicks. If that ain't evidence of th' Almighty's favor, well then, call me an Ay-rab."

"Yeah, okay, but who's this guy we're gonna interview? I didn't hear anything about it from HR."

"So I got a hit from my own personal network on this one, Ol' Digger Jack. He did some ... well, if'n you can believe it, some pretty amazing stuff over in the sandbox back in the day, and then there was something he just pulled off in France, which I can tell you about later, or show you about, since I got the surveillance video on it."

"What's his background?" Ol' Digger Jack asked, hands tucked into his jacket as he watched the city of Granite Sky slide by the window.

"He's a former Marine, of all things," Billy Rob said, chewing on the end of the black cigar. "And I am gonna seriously wanna know if half of what I heard is th' actual truth."

"He know you're comin'?"

"Yeah. We're set up for a three o'clock meeting."

"Well, hell, Billy Rob, it's like, what, five minutes before three now. Where we gonna meet this ol' boy?"

"Right here," Billy Rob said, pointing out the window as the car pulled up into a parking lot. A sign proclaimed they had arrived at the Northern Minnesota Construction Company.

***

About two weeks before Billy Rob and Ol' Digger Jack pulled into the NMC parking lot, Marcus and Marie-Clémence had arrived from Liechtenstein. Tack and Claire met them at the airport in Minneapolis. When Marcus, leaning on a cane, slowly walked into the baggage claim area where they'd agreed to meet, Claire was shocked at how much weight her oldest son had lost. He seemed pale to her, but somehow, different ... more at peace, she thought, as though he'd solved some particularly intractable internal problem he hadn't even known he was working on. Behind Marcus she saw Marie-Clémence, the woman with whom she'd visited in the hospital in Liechtenstein. Though Marcus had made it very clear that they were in no way romantically involved, that he only wanted the woman to have a chance to see what a normal home life looked like and what true Christianity could be, when she saw them together, Claire knew instantly in her French soul what problem had been solved for her son.

Tack's eyes watered when he saw Marcus. God, he was so proud of his sons, and he'd been praying constantly that Marcus would find some reason to return home after the attack in France and his stay in hospital in Liechtenstein. When Marcus had emailed them about his desire to come home and just make a life there with them on the farm, Tack and Claire had gone into their bedroom and dropped to their knees and tearfully thanked God for His mercy, keeping their son alive through war and then a terrorist attack and then turning his heart to come home. For them, it was a miracle.

Mace was overjoyed to learn Marcus was coming home. Mace had always exalted his brother, looked up to him, and always pointed people to Marcus if they needed help or protection. When Mace heard the news he went into the barn, up into the top loft, knelt down, and thanked God for returning His brother home.

In that short time of prayer and thankfulness, God gave Mace a vision about the future that stunned and shocked him. Coming down from the barn, he immediately sought out Zoe and shared it with her. Mace sensed that God did not want him to share what he'd seen with anyone else yet, and so both he and Zoe kept the knowledge to themselves.

Meeting Marcus's parents had been difficult for Marie-Clémence. She was still traveling in a wheelchair, and Marcus still needed a cane to get around, and she joked about the situation to ease the tension, but Claire could easily see the woman was uneasy, unsure of how to act, and uncertain about how she would be regarded.

Tack gathered their few bags onto a wheeled luggage cart, Marcus carried a backpack over his shoulder and walked with a cane, and Claire, waving away Marie-Clémence 's objections, pushed Marie-Clémence in the wheelchair. "Not another word," Claire said in rapid French, and as they made their way out to the parking lot, Claire regaled Marie-Clémence with a summary of what Minnesota was like, all in humorous, slightly disparaging French, getting Marie-Clémence to chuckle once or twice.

Yet during the drive up to Granite Sky and then through the city and up toward Red Rock Peninsula and the Ironbridge farm, Marie-Clémence grew increasingly tense. Her head began to ache again from a combination of the time-zone change, lack of sleep, and stress. The Herr Professor Doktor had said such would be the case for a very long time, but nonetheless it made her life unpleasant. She reached up and unconsciously touched the still-noticeable furrow along the back of her skull. Marcus watched her carefully.

Tack filled Marcus in on the spiritual progress being made in the battleground that was their life in Minnesota. They told him about Abrielle Dumont and what had happened to her, and how God had used Mace and Zoe to pull her out of the cult she was trapped in and bring her to the farm. She was staying in one of the cabins in the back pasture along the lake's edge.

"Ah, but that dear Emma, oh, Marcus, you should see, she's such a timid little creature! She too was booted out of her family and, oh, she was like a frightened bird when she first came to us. She still cannot be away from Zoe more than ten minutes before she begins to tremble. They didn't have the heart to put her out in one of the cabins, she was just too terrified to be by herself—and overnight, at that! Oh, *Mon Dieu*, so they told her to just settle into the spare room in the Carriage House until she was more comfortable."

"How old is she?" Marie-Clémence asked.

"She is twenty-four, but she is like sometimes a fourteen-year old, you know. She was never allowed to see other people, she never went to a church, and the only people she really knew were her sisters and her parents."

"Did she not attend school?" Marie-Clémence pursued.

"Ah, no, it was not allowed. She was taught at home."

"Is that legal?"

"It's actually quite legal, and if it's done correctly, I'd say it's the best way to teach one's children," Tack observed from the front of the truck. Marie-Clémence said nothing in reply.

"Ah," Claire said, going on, "but the poor *colombe* knows nothing of other people, nothing of how the world works, what normal social conventions are, how people normally react to things ... *Mon Dieu*, it is like having someone live with you from another planet sometimes. But she shows sometimes such flashes of wisdom! She said the sweetest thing yesterday. I was talking with Zoe about things, you know, and I make reference to the Girl Manual—"

"The Girl Manual?" Marie-Clémence asked.

"Oh, you know, that secret book of instructions that tells women how to be; the book no man can ever understand."

"Ah, *that* book!" Marie-Clémence said, smiling, rolling a finger at Marcus as if to say, 'pay attention!'.

"Yes, so I am talking with Zoe and Emma is there and Tack comes in and begins to say something about how men know all about the Girl Manual, even though they are men, and Emma pipes up and says, 'the knowledge itself would slay you.' The car dissolved in laughter.

"I laughed for an hour," Tack said, smiling still. "So you can see a little bit why Mace and Zoe don't mind her living with them."

"Of course not, *Mon chéri*, and why not?" Claire exclaimed. "Zoe is a woman, and every woman needs to be a mother, one way or the other, and here God has closed one door for her, but opened another, dropping a frightened young woman, all trembling and aquiver, into her very arms. *Of course* she is going to mother the precious child ... *certainement*."

Marcus had told Marie-Clémence of the living arrangements at the farm, and a little of the history of how the Ironbridges had come to settle in Minnesota, but whether because of some premonition or perhaps a leading by God, he had intentionally not expounded too much about Mace and his effect on people, and he certainly didn't tell Marie-Clémence about Mace and Zoe's relationship, and the strange bond Zoe had with his brother.

Tack shared with them a little about Jed Sloan's adventures and how he had ended up staying in the Watchkeeper's cabin, doing light maintenance on his off days in exchange for rent. "You'll like him, Marcus. He's not your typical Type A personality, and he's shy—more shy than I would expect from most guys in their mid-thirties or so, but he's got a dry wit and he's hungry to learn more about God, and totally committed." Tack described briefly about how Jed's family had disintegrated because of his pursuit of a real relationship with God.

Marie-Clémence's curiosity got the better of her stress-induced reserve. "*Pardon moi s'il vous plaît,*" she said, speaking French since she was more comfortable in that language and had gathered during the drive that everyone in the truck understood French, "but it seems ... it seems as though everyone you have staying with you has been, I don't know, how do you say, ejected or 'put out' from their families because of a religious disagreement."

There was silence for half a moment, and then Marcus spoke. "Remember what we talked about in the hospital, Marie-Clémence? The people they're taking in at the farm have been kicked out or ejected, and you're right, they've been 'put out', not because of religion, but rather because of their desire to have a *relationship* directly with God."

"You will have to excuse me but at this point I don't see the difference."

"You will," Tack said with a confidence that somewhat frightened Marie-Clémence.

Claire said gently, "Ah, *ma petite colombe*, don't be worried, you will see. There is such a world of difference between the two, I cannot tell you the half of it."

"Let me ask you," Tack went on, "does Marcus seem to you like every other Christian you've ever met?"

Marie-Clémence shot a glance at Marcus, then turned to look out the window and in a low voice, said "He is like no one else, Christian or otherwise," as though she didn't want to admit it.

This somewhat forcefully wrung admission elicited unexpected gales of laughter from the three Ironbridge family members, surprising Marie-Clémence. She hadn't meant it to be humorous.

"I'm sorry, Marie-Clémence, it's sort of a family joke."

"What, that you are different from everyone else?"

"Actually no, what's funny is that everyone has always said that about Mace, not me."

"Mace ... your brother?"

"Yeah, you haven't met him yet."

Claire turned around in her seat and looked at Marie-Clémence, seated behind Tack. "You will see, my dear. Just wait for a little. We're almost home."

"There's another one at home stranger than you?" Marie-Clémence asked, turning to Marcus.

"Well, it depends on what you mean by strange," he replied, smiling but somber as well.

"This I will have to see to believe," Marie-Clémence remarked under her breath.

"He's not like anyone you've met before, Marie-Clémence," Tack said with an authority that Marie-Clémence found strangely comforting. Her own father had never provided her any confidence or assurance about anything in life, and here, seeing Marcus' father so sure about the character of both of his sons spoke to her volumes about the man's involvement in his sons' lives. Claire went on to tell her about Mace's particular speech defect, and how it would disappear only when he was alone with Zoe. Marie-Clémence thought this too farfetched to believe, and so resolved not to believe it.

Before Claire could continue on too much about Mace, Marcus asked his father about the dairy, and how business was coming, and what the economy was like around the area. Marie-Clémence retreated into a shell of silence, wondering what type of weird family she'd agreed to put up with for the season. She briefly thought about making up some excuse to flee back to France and stay with ... with someone, *anyone*, over the summer until she could get back on her feet, but as she thought about the wheelchair tucked away in the back of the truck, 'fleeing' anywhere didn't seem to be a viable option at the moment. Her tension rose by degrees, intensifying as they passed from metropolitan Minneapolis through the city of Granite Sky and then on through the suburbs, then the outskirts of the city, farther and further on, deeper and deeper into wilderness, where there was nothing but trees mile after mile—interrupted here and there by vast stretches of mud, or little muddy lakes—and then more trees. She began to despair.

***

They pulled up the long driveway and Mace and Zoe and Emma and Abrielle and Jed Sloan were there, waiting to greet them. Marie-Clémence, her stomach clutching with tension, her head pounding, the ache in her skull piercing downward to her lower back, wondered what new strange behavior these Americans would confront her with next.

Tack stopped the truck and as soon as Marcus stepped out his brother pulled him close and held him in a strong, masculine embrace. Zoe stepped close and kissed him, and while Mace hung on his shoulder, saying absolutely nothing but exuding a great sense of joy. Zoe introduced Marcus to Emma, who, struck dumb with shyness, just nodded hello. Abrielle welcomed him home with a smile and shook his hand, and Marcus thanked her for the care she'd provided to Zoe when she'd broken her arm. Abrielle waved the thanks away, blushing slightly. Zoe introduced Jed Sloan, and Marcus smiled at him, man-to-man, shaking his hand and giving him a man-hug, making him feel like a brother.

Claire and Marie-Clémence waited until the introductions were complete and Tack had pulled the wheelchair from the bed of the truck. But before he could help Marie-Clémence out, Mace held up his hand in a quick gesture. Tack stopped, alert to something, and waited while Mace himself went round to the driver's side and opened the back door.

Marie-Clémence Genevieve Gabrielle Levinson had had many strange experiences in her short life, but none in any way matched what happened to her when Mace Ironbridge opened the door to the truck, extended his hand, and invited her to step out. When she touched his hand, all her anxiety, stress, tension, and concerns suddenly disappeared like a wisp of smoke in a strong, clean wind. She gasped with the pure shock of it and the first breath of air she drew at the Ironbridge farm was taken in without a shred of pain, anxiety, or tension, in a bouquet of pure peace. As she tightened her grip on Mace's hand to step out of the truck, she suddenly realized that her head no longer hurt; in fact, there was no longer any sense of the injury whatsoever, anywhere in her head or down her back. And as she looked at Marcus' brother, holding her hand, inviting her to step out and stand on her feet, she took courage and did so, and found she could walk, free from pain and, strangely, free from fear.

***

Billy Rob and Ol' Digger Jack walked into the office of Northern Maine Construction Company and were greeted by a very attractive woman with dark hair, dark eyes, and a foreign accent.

"Mr. Brewster, Mr. Riker, welcome to NMC."

"It's Ol' Digger Jack, young lady, that's all. I ain't been called 'Mr. Riker' since, well, hell, how long's it been, Billy Rob?"

"Probably around the time you met your first wife, Ol' Digger Jack. Thanks, Ma'am. I'm supposed to meet—"

"Yes sir, right here." A tall man appeared in the door to what looked like a conference room. "Marcus Ironbridge. Nice to meet you," Marcus said. "We can talk in here if you'd like."

"Sounds good."

The woman spoke up. "Coffee Mr. Brewster? Mr ... uh, Digger Jack?'"

"Sounds good," Ol' Digger Jack replied, and Billy Rob took sharp notice that it was Marcus Ironbridge who went over to the sideboard and poured Ol' Digger Jack a cup of coffee, even with the cane he needed to get around. The woman nodded once and closed the door, leaving them alone. The sounds of a busy construction outfit would occasionally intrude, but otherwise it was quiet.

Ol' Digger Jack started in on the approach they'd decided on in the parking lot.

"So Marcus ... you mind if I call you Marcus?"

"No sir."

"Good, so tell me, why would we wanna hire a Security Director that needs a cane to git around?"

Marcus looked at Ol' Digger Jack for just a minute and then smiled easily. "You don't have to, Ol' Digger Jack. And do you mind if I call you Ol' Digger Jack?"

"Hell, son, that's what my momma used to call me, I dug so many goddamn holes in the backyard afore I was breeched." Billy Rob punched Ol' Digger Jack in the arm and gave a head nod toward the large cross on the wall.

"Yeah, yeah," Ol' Digger Jack said, and turning to Marcus, said "apologies for my language. Ah'm an old cuss what's never learnt better."

"I'm not the One you need to worry about offending," Marcus said.

Ol' Digger Jack, taken aback for a moment, nodded slowly at that, sizing Marcus up. "You ain't afraid of us, are you, son?"

"Should I be?"

"Well, hell, son, some folks might git jist a touchy bit nervous, some billionaire comes strolling in ta offer'm a job."

Marcus turned to Billy Rob. "You got out as a Captain, right?"

"I did," Billy Rob replied.

"You get out to take over your father's business?"

"He died, yeah, so I kinda had to."

"Understand. You flew Cobras?

"Best machine known to God or man," Billy Rob answered.

Marcus nodded his head, agreeing, and then turned to Ol' Digger Jack. "Ol' Digger Jack, I don't know about any billionaire, but I'll tell you what. How about former Captain Ironbridge, a one-time officer of infantry, and former Captain Brewster, a one-time Marine aviator, talk about how the former Infantry Officer might help the former Marine aviator with security for his business. That sound okay to you?"

Ol' Digger Jack sat there for a few seconds and then a smile stretched across his leathery face slowly. "Billy Rob, ah'm tellin' ya, I like this kid."

Marcus and Billy Rob and Ol' Digger Jack talked for three hours. Billy Rob explained the security concerns he had, and Marcus explained that he'd just returned from Europe, so he wasn't as familiar with the area as Billy Rob's operations might require.

"No worries there, Marcus," Ol' Digger Jack interrupted. "You'll git up to speed fast, especially when we plug ya into th' intelligence network we have."

"Do you really think the foreign oil companies will be coming after your operations with military-style tactics?" Marcus asked.

Billy Rob nodded slowly. "Based on the information we have, it seems likely. I don't want some guy who's been spending most of his career checking ID cards at some gate, or some guy who's been jacking around at the Government trough, trying to drum up security business. I need a warfighter here."

Marcus didn't say anything for a moment, but then replied. "I don't have that much combat experience," he said.

"Sometimes it ain't how much, but maybe how *intense* that might matter more," Ol' Digger Jack said softly.

"I got your name from an old friend," Billy Rob said. "Actually, his kid was the original source. He told his Dad what happened to him in Afghanistan and his Dad told me, though frankly his Dad didn't believe it. Not sure I do."

"But here you are," Marcus said blandly.

"That I am," Billy Rob replied. And then he leaned over the table and looked at Marcus directly. "And I would sorely love to hear you tell me what exactly the hell happened in the Korengal back then."

Marcus nodded slowly, unsure about telling this man he'd just met what had cost him his treasured career in the Marine Corps.

"Do you mind if I ask you where you got the ... the story?"

"Jamie Wilson."

Marcus shook his head. "I don't think I know any—"

"You might know his boy, Dag. Dag Wilson."

Marcus smiled then. "Lieutenant Dag Wilson? Well, sure, he was our XO. Of course I know Dag. How is he?"

"Can't say. I think he's tryin' to scrape a living as a security guard at a Wal-Mart somewhere. Jamie wasn't too happy about what's happened to him."

"He got out?"

"The Corps tossed him out," Billy Rob replied. "You didn't know? Yeah, I guess you wouldn't. Well, I got this from Jamie, so I'm pretty sure it's accurate, but it turns out that after your little escapade in Afghanistan—"

"Which we note you ain't tolt us a thing about yet," Ol' Digger Jack said, interrupting.

Billy Rob looked at Marcus for a second, and as there was nothing forthcoming, went on. "Yeah, so after your little thing over there, I guess they tossed you out, but what you might not know is that they put the rest of your command group through some kind of hell. They interviewed 'em a bunch of times and tried to get them to change their story."

Marcus, not knowing any of this, began to get angry, but listened intently. Billy Rob went on.

"So yeah, they pressed Jamie's boy, and there was a First Sergeant Custer—"

"Tom Custer; solid man."

"Yeah, well, it might surprise you to know that the Green Machine tried everything they could to try and get those boys to change their story about what happened—whatever that was—and then when they didn't, well, hell, they court-martialed Jamie's boy and they actually put that Custer fella in the slammer for, I think it was ... wait, lemme check." Billy Rob swiped a finger across the iPad he had in front of him on the table, looked up a file, and then said, "Yeah, here it is. Tom Custer, incarcerated at the military prison in Le Jeune, North Carolina, for eight months and six days, and then they gave him a Big Chicken Dinner on the way out."

"They gave Tom Custer a Bad Conduct Discharge?" Marcus said, stunned.

"Well, hell, son, they stuck it to your XO worse'n that. They court-martialed his ass as well and then when he *still* wouldn't change his story, they gave him a dishonorable discharge—somethin' about treason or mutiny or some such-like, and so that is why your former illustrious XO is out and about with a felony conviction on his record, trying to find a job at Wal-Mart, and, oh by the way, not having too much success at it if I can gage his Daddy's opinions about things."

Marcus sat back, digesting what Brewster had just disclosed. He hadn't thought to reach out to his old company command team because he'd always assumed that they'd gone on with their careers in the Corps—he'd been told as much by the Marine Corps lawyers who were prosecuting him, liars all, apparently—and he didn't want any kind of disparagement or opprobrium to stain them by association. He was sick, though, at hearing what had happened to those two men, fine warriors both. What a loss.

"Marcus, you know what we're looking for. I wanna offer you the job, I do, but I really need to hear what happened in Afghanistan." Billy Rob looked at him, straight in the eye. "And some friends of mine have suggested that I ask you to tell me a little bit about what happened in Fontainebleau as well. They said something about getting a copy of a surveillance video if I needed confirmation."

Marcus, still downcast about what had happened to those two men who'd trusted him, who were put in positions where, truthfully, they could have done nothing to change what happened, looked up at Billy Rob and Ol' Digger Jack.

"You guys want to know what happened in Afghanistan? Fine, I'll tell you, sure, but that's no guarantee you'll believe it." And so Marcus told the Texas oil billionaire and his Chief Operating Officer exactly what God had done in the Korengal those many years ago. He left nothing out, using the story to deliver a piercing message of God's power. He told them about his deliberations with God about how to proceed against the evil religion of Islam, his convictions from God about what he was to do, about how God delivered the Taliban fighters into the hands of his SATA unit, and then how God caused every other platoon in Kilo company to succeed beyond what had ever been experienced in that theater before. He told them directly that his company had had zero casualties—information the Marine Corps had classified as Top Secret, though Marcus didn't care—and which had never happened before in, well, ever ... at least since the U.S. or any other military organization had tried fighting in that degraded country. And finally he told them about the seven days when the twenty mullahs fasted and prayed and tried to bring the power of Allah against his Marines, and how on the seventh day the ground shook and trembled and then cracked and opened up and swallowed the screaming, bleeding satanic priests of a satanic demonic god, and then slammed shut, and how the villagers all ran screaming. He told them how they didn't see one villager for the next week—and certainly no fighters. They'd had zero contact with any human being that wasn't a Marine that next week. Apparently what had happened had so terrified the local nationals that they'd fled the valley for parts unknown. The story took an hour to tell.

"And then somehow the Corps found out what happened and a JAG[29] lawyer showed up in a CH-47 with a squad of Air Force military police, and they arrested me and put me in handcuffs and loaded me on the helo and flew me back to J-bad. They kept me in isolation there until they could arrange transportation directly back to the States; they didn't want me flying through Frankfurt or Dubai or anywhere else in case I talked to anyone about what had happened, how the Muslims got their butts kicked by the God of Abraham, Isaac, and Jacob. So finally they put me on the next C-17 that was headed

29 Judge Advocate General ... essentially a military lawyer

back, and they locked me to the seat with two military policemen sitting next to me. They unlocked me to let me use the head, but other than that, there I sat for twenty hours, chained to a seat, until we landed at Andrews."

"What was the deal they made?" Billy Rob asked, looking at his hands. He was strangely ashamed for his Corps and what it had done. For some reason he didn't doubt Marcus' version of events.

"They said that if I kept my mouth shut, they'd let me out without a dishonorable discharge. Apparently they were afraid that the word about Kilo Company not having any casualties would get out, which might lead to investigations as to why that happened, and all the talk there about our war being against Allah, and how the Christian and Jewish God came and demonstrated in a powerful way that their demon god Allah is nothing but just some noxious demonic entity, and then why other companies were losing a ton of their people, and it was a can of worms the secular military just didn't want to open. I mean, they were shouting in my face, accusing me of trying to start a world religious war."

"What'd you have to say to them?" Ol' Digger Jack interjected.

Marcus shrugged and looked at his hands. "As best I can recall, I think it was something like, 'Bring it'."

Both Billy Rob and Ol' Digger Jack sat there, a little shocked. They'd never expected to hear a story like that, although Jamie Wilson had warned Billy Rob that Marcus was some sort of 'holy roller' who was constantly on about 'God this' or 'God that'. But Jamie had said that his boy, Dag, thought the world of the guy, which is why neither Dag nor the company's First Sergeant would lie for the Corps against him. It cost Dag something big not to toe the Corps' line, but, his father had said, shaking his head, 'the boy was like iron; wouldn't budge. I respect 'im for that. And you don't even wanna ask what my wife thinks. She thinks that kid Ironbridge hung the moon.' Billy Rob didn't quite get why Jamie had mentioned that, but he let it go.

Neither Billy Rob nor Ol' Digger Jack had a religious bone in their body, but they were from Texas, so they didn't openly disparage the story. More than that, though, especially with Billy Rob, something was sticking in him. He was more affected by Marcus' tale than he'd been by anything he could remember since the death of his mother. Something about that story resonated in him, as though it triggered a deep longing he'd had his entire life, but one he couldn't quite identify. A thought of his mother crossed his mind for some reason. Marcus' story both pulled at him and seeped into him like salt enters into a person and makes them thirsty. Billy Rob realized that he'd do anything to keep Marcus Ironbridge around until he found out what it was that would slake this weird thirst the guy's story had ignited.

Finally Billy Rob took a breath and said, "Well, okay, Marcus, we thought it would be something like that, and while we don't pretend to understand the parts about God and Allah and all that, you've described some seriously intense combat—intense enough for us, I can tell you. We think ... we think some of the companies we're competing against wouldn't hesitate to start bringing stuff against us—I'm talkin' hard, military-grade action. And, well," and here Billy Rob looked down at his hands, "I'm thinking it wouldn't be so bad to have a little help from the Lord, either." He looked up again at Marcus. "Would you consider taking the job?"

Marcus had prayed about the interview before coming, and he'd talked it over with Tack and Mace, seeking their counsel. He'd expected some ambivalence, but strangely, both of them seemed extremely supportive, and Mace went so far as to tell him that the job would be very important to everyone's future.

"Hey," Marcus had replied, "I don't have it yet."

You will, Mace had typed.

That had been enough for Marcus to settle any concerns he might have had. And although he trusted Mace completely, he still had put it to God that if the job was something God wanted for him, the interview would wind up with them offering him the position. If it wasn't what God wanted, well then, it would turn out that he wouldn't be a fit and they'd say thank you and head off back to wherever it was they came from without offering him the job. Armed with the trust that his Father in heaven would direct all things, and completely at ease with whatever the decision might be, he went off to the interview.

So here now they were offering him the position. Prayer answered. As he sat there thinking about how to answer them, a thought came into his head and he smiled inwardly.

"Okay, gentlemen, on two conditions."

Billy Rob's eyebrow raised just a bit. "What would they be?" he asked.

"You bring me on, sure, but bring on Dag Wilson as my Deputy, and bring on Tom Custer—wherever he is, if they're willing—and we'll figure out a position for him, too. If things are going like you think they're going, we're gonna need a few good men."

Ol' Digger Jack couldn't hide a smile, and he smacked Billy Rob in the arm. "There now, what'd I tell ya, Billy Rob? The kid's got style. We shoulda thought o' that."

Billy Rob smiled as well and reached a hand across the table. "It would be an honor to work with a man who cares for his people like ... well, like we're seeing here," Billy Rob said. "Absolutely, condition agreed with my wholehearted approval. Ol' Digger Jack'll get on the horn today and see about getting those gentlemen a job working with you here—they may or may not accept, but I'm assuming you'll be okay with whatever they decide?"

"I will, Billy Rob," Marcus replied, shaking Billy Rob's hand. "They may have things in their respective lives that would make this inconvenient, but I feel at least obligated to include them, and I appreciate your generosity in including them. They paid a high price for what happened over there. They stayed true; they're honest men and we should do everything we can for them."

"Totally agree," Billy Rob said.

"Hot damn!" said Ol' Digger Jack.

Just then the door to the conference room opened and Zoe, long red hair hanging down in braids, looked in. "There you are, Marcus." She turned to the two men sitting across the table from Marcus. "Hey," she said, smiling, hesitant, and then decided to just come in and shake hands. "Zoe Ironbridge," she said, introducing herself and reaching out for Billy Rob's hand. She was too friendly and energized to resist. Marcus could tell immediately that Mace was nearby, probably waiting in the truck.

Billy Rob Brewster, billionaire, leapt up from his chair and took Zoe's hand, and Zoe pumped it up and down. "Billy Rob Brewster, ma'am, nice to meet you."

"You're the guy Marcus is here to talk to?"

"I am ma'am."

"Well, good. If you're lucky, he'll agree to come work with you."

"Ol' Digger Jack," the oilman said, introducing himself, smiling from ear to ear.

"Well, now *that's* a cool name," Zoe exclaimed happily, beaming.

"Well, ah'm right glad ya think so, little lady."

"Ahha, 'little lady'! I mean, how COOL is that! Never been called a 'little lady' before." And Zoe reached up and kissed Ol' Digger Jack on a grizzled cheek. Marcus watched Ol' Digger Jack just about melt down to a puddle right there in the Northern Minnesota Construction Company conference room.

Marcus caught Zoe's eye. "Marie-Clémence?"

"Oh, yeah, she's with your Mom ... *shopping. Yechhh.*"

"Thanks, Zoe."

"Sure. Hey, gotta go; Mace is outside waiting. Take your time, Marcus. 'Bye," she said to everyone generally, waved, and launched out of the room.

Billy Rob and Ol' Digger Jack turned from the door and faced Marcus, and he could see immediately that Zoe had made a big impact on both of them, especially Ol' Digger Jack.

"That little filly just flat warms ma heart," he said softly, to no one in particular. "Imagine that."

"Your wife?" Billy Rob asked respectfully.

"Sister-in-law; she's married to my brother."

"If that's yer sister-in-law, young fella, I would surely be struck dead o' happiness were I ta meet the rest o' yer clan." Billy Rob looked at the old man and smiled.

"Ol' Digger Jack—and you too, Billy Rob—you should come by next week if you're in the area. My folks are throwing a welcome-home party for me," Marcus said, "and you two gentlemen are officially invited."

Chapter 28
Marie-Clémence

"A bruised reed He will not break and a dimly burning wick He will not extinguish; He will faithfully bring forth justice."

Isaiah 42:3

The party was a unique event in the Ironbridge family history. Tack and Claire had invited a broad variety of guests, one objective being to welcome Marcus back to Granite Sky and introduce him to those who didn't know him or those who knew him when he was a famous high school quarterback, playing for Granite Sky High. The Spirit as well had His own agenda—to introduce hearts in the area that might be open to responding to God, so as to find a new life. Thus were Tack and Claire led to visit a number of the churches in the area, explaining the situation to pastors about Marcus returning home from his adventures abroad, and offering an opportunity for the community to welcome him back. They put up flyers in the various fellowship halls, churches, and meeting places, hoping to attract those who, though perhaps not yet Believers, might be ready to become so.

Thinking it unwise to ask people to drive so far out into the wilderness, they asked Josh Riesling if he would open the large warehouse at Northern Minnesota Construction for the party, and Josh enthusiastically offered the use of the facility gratis.

Tack and Claire delighted in the requirement for two chefs, and they divided up the cooking responsibilities. Tack slaughtered and butchered a pig and a several lambs, and his job was to prepare the meat. He and Josh built a rotating barbecue spit over 50-gallon steel containers sliced in half lengthwise for the pig and the lambs. Claire worked for five days to prepare salads, appetizers, vegetables, and the *coup de grâce*, desserts.

Guests started arriving around two in the afternoon. The weather was cooperating, grudgingly, clouds seeming to gather but then holding off, the sun valiant in its efforts to shed light and warmth in northern Minnesota.

Tack, Claire, Mace, Zoe, Jed, Abrielle, and Emma were the designated cooks, greeters, servers, and dishwashers. Josh and Daria were gracious hosts, making sure the facility was spic-and-span. Tack and Claire insisted Marcus stay free to move and talk among the guests, and though Marie-Clémence was remarkably ambulatory, walking now easily and with no pain, Claire's ulterior motive was to keep her as close to Marcus as possible, and so Claire, in rapid French, convinced Marie-Clémence to accompany Marcus as he made his rounds among the guests.

***

Marie-Clémence had been subdued since she arrived at the farm, but in a way that reflected an introspective contemplation, a sense of increasing contentment, combined with a deeply internalized amazement at what had happened when Mace first touched her hand. She was disoriented, but not dismayingly so. She had spoken to Marcus about it afterward.

"I don't know how to tell you this, but something happened when Mace helped me out of the truck."

Marcus listed patiently. He'd clearly seen something make an impact on her as she walked out of the truck and into the house without the aid of the wheelchair. It was the first time he'd seen her walk unaided since she strolled into *L'Escapade* in Fontainebleau, eons ago.

"I saw."

"What is ... what is *up* with your brother?"

"What do you mean?"

"He's different."

"We told you that."

"Yes, I remember, but—"

"But you didn't believe us."

"No, that's not it." They were on the porch alone, the others remaining around the kitchen table. She turned to face him. He was leaning on his cane, face was drawn at the end of a very long travel day.

"I ... I just don't have any frame of reference for such things," she went on, then paused. "Do you remember what I said to you on that bench in the park at Fontainebleau?"

Marcus was silent for a moment, then said, gently, "I do."

"You have to understand that throughout my entire life religion—the Judaism I came to hate in my own home, and Christianity, which I came to despise for its weakness and hypocrisy, and Buddhism, and whatever else—has always, *always* been something that someone else is talking about, or forcing on someone, or preaching, or insisting upon, or using to lay down a guilt trip. Religion in France, and in every other country I've been, has been an utter farce, and no one I've ever respected has ever had the slightest involvement with it. And then *you* come along," she said, throwing up her hands. "You show up and for some inexplicable reason almost get killed saving my life. I mean, I *despised* you at school, do you know that? I despised you because you labeled yourself as a Christian. The only Christians I ever knew were ... they weren't *men*; they were hypocrites, preaching one thing, doing another. And then along you come! You talk me into coming out here to the middle of God knows where, and then that brother of yours ... just touches my hand," she sobs slightly but continued in a tone of wonder. "That's all, he just took my hand to help me out of a car, and suddenly I'm not in pain anymore and I can walk!" She spread out her hands as if to say, '*See?*' "This isn't something I can process in an hour."

"No one is asking you to."

"But everything is so damned ... I don't know, *foreign*; *out-of-whack*; I'm feel like that song, living upside down."

Marcus moved to the porch railing and looked out into the forest, smelling the fragrance of God's creation, wondering what God was doing in this woman's life. He had risked his life for her when he had not a shred of feeling toward her, unless one counted the frustrating irritation and general dislike he felt whenever he encountered her at business school.

He turned to look at her. "Something you need to understand, Marie-Clémence. We won't make any apologies for how we live here and we certainly won't hide our relationship with God. He's everything to us. You *will* see Him here—I submit that you've already seen Him, through what happened to you, because it wasn't Mace that did that, but God working through Mace. Whenever a person encounters the living God, they *are* going to feel out-of-whack, upside down, and disoriented—and definitely uncomfortable. Expect it."

She nodded. "Nice to know."

"Let's talk about religion for a minute. You've just told me what religion has been to you. That's not anything strange. Religion everywhere is dead. God never meant for man to create 'religion'. Religion is man's creation; it is man's attempt to reach God, to bring God down to them, to have God on man's terms. That's why you've hated it all your life. *God* hates it! It's a stench to Him."

"Everything is so confusing!" She pushed out a hand at him. "I mean, there you stand, or rather, lean, on your cane! I saw you hug your brother. Where is your miraculous healing?"

Marcus looked at her. "I know who God is and I have a relationship with Him already, and for His own reasons I find myself a little ... immobilized. But when *you* put foot on this property, when you first drew breath on this land, God did something miraculous for you so you would know that He exists, so you'd know that He is a compassionate and caring God, that He loves you, and He wants a relationship with you. He has nothing to do with religion, Marie-Clémence, so I suggest you let your concepts about religion disappear into the past." Marcus made a dismissive gesture with his hand. "And, you might ask yourself, why did He choose to make this demonstration at the precise moment when you first came to this farm, when you drew your first breath on this property?"

Marie-Clémence stood, both arms wrapped around herself, not looking at him. "I've no earthly idea."

"I can't say I have the answer either, but knowing how God works, I'd say that he wants you to identify freedom from fear and anxiety and pain with this land, this farm ..." Marcus hesitated, waiting, and then said, "with these people here," and then, hesitatingly, "with this family." She darted a frightened glance at him, fearing what he might be implying, but he wasn't looking at her. He made a wide, sweeping gesture back toward the house, where the others were still inside. "There is freedom here, and love, and peace, and He wanted you to know that. It is why He told me to invite you here. He wants you to not just see these things, but live them; to *experience* them in the very depths of your soul."

She was quiet for a long time. He saw her shaking, cold in a brisk afternoon wind. After a time she said, not looking at him, "Look, I am an honest woman. I cannot gainsay what happened. I will not deny it by trying to explain it away or dismiss it as something from my imagination. Something happened. You say it was God—"

"Working through my brother."

"Working through your brother, okay, fine. So now you have to let me come to grips with this ... this *thing*, this incomprehensible idea you keep talking about."

Marcus knew what she meant. The 'incomprehensible idea' was the existence of a living, loving God. He looked out toward the forest and saw a flock of about twenty wild turkeys poking and pecking out of the woods, in a loose line, all headed toward the back of the barn.

She saw him looking in that direction and followed his gaze. "What are those things?" asked the city girl.

"Wild turkeys. They can't fly very well, they're slower than molasses compared to everything else on four legs in the forest, and if Insead had an admissions choice to make between a turkey and a rock, they'd pick the rock. They don't plant, they don't harvest, they don't store nuts like squirrels, they don't hibernate. And yet ... and yet there they are, having survived the winter, dumber than the dirt they're walking on, still alive, and they know exactly where to go to get food." He turned back to face her.

"God takes care of them—He knows where every one of them nests, how many eggs they hatch, how many each flock has, where they go; He feeds them and moves them and knows the day they're hatched and the day they die or get eaten. He cares for them. If God can take care of such creatures, Marie-Clémence, He can take care of you."

She stood there, watching the birds slowly move to the back of the barn where the manure piles where, in which they would hunt and peck for grains of oats the cows ate and then passed. She was shaking slightly; it had been colder than she expected.

"As I say, such things are incomprehensible to me."

Marcus was quiet for a few seconds, and then said, "Well, I know you can comprehend the fact that your head no longer causes you pain, and I know you can comprehend the fact that you are walking unaided, again, without pain. He cares for you and He is trying to get your attention."

"He has that, make no mistake."

"Good," he replied quietly. "That's enough for now. I'll leave you two alone so you can talk about it." He set his cane against the railing, took off his black fleece pullover he'd been traveling in, draped it over Marie-Clémence's shoulders, took up his cane again, and then quietly opened the front door and went back into the house, leaving the woman standing there, no longer shivering, looking out toward the forest, watching the turkeys stroll across the pasture.

***

At the party they ran across Tony Ponti, the pastor of the largest church in Granite Sky, after Marcus and Marie-Clémence had welcomed and talked to a number of guests. Pleasant, gregarious, obviously a people-person, Ponti shook Marcus' hand, welcomed him back home, thanked him for his service to the country, and invited him to come to his church—Living Waters.

"I've been the Pastor there, what, almost twenty-three years, Marcus, and the hallmark of the place is family. It's a church family. We take care of each other, you know? Everybody knows everyone else's kids, and if anyone ever needs anything, we're right there for 'em."

Marcus listened patiently as Ponti went on about his fellowship. Marie-Clémence stood beside him, a large glass of red wine in her hand.

"We're basically Baptist, for all intents and purposes," the Pastor described. "But we like to say we're non-denominational because we really don't discriminate."

"What *is* a Baptist?" Marie-Clémence interjected, curious, almost, Marcus sensed, a bit playful. "The denomination, I mean. I know a Baptist is someone who dunks others in water, yes, but what do you mean when you say you are a 'Baptist'? Do Baptists teach something unique?"

After their talk on the porch that first day, he'd expected Marie-Clémence to retreat into herself, descending perhaps into a morose brown study, preoccupied with contemplating the ground shifting under her spiritual and moral feet. But ... that hadn't happened. Rather, it seemed almost as each day went by that she grew ... lighter, somehow, easier in her own mind, a tad more outgoing, as though she had resolved to enjoy herself here until she made up her mind about this strange God swirling around. She was still reserved, still uncomfortable, but he sensed a slight thaw.

The Pastor was energized by her interest. "We focus on telling people about Jesus," he replied. "We tell them about how to get saved."

"I see," Marie-Clémence replied noncommittally.

"Have you accepted Jesus as your personal Lord and Savior?"

"Accepted? What do you mean by this word?" Her French accent was strong, and Marcus knew she leaned on it heavily if there was something in English she didn't understand.

"It means to ask Him into your heart."

"And how does one 'ask Him into one's heart'?"

"You just tell God that you're sorry for the sins you've committed and that you want to invite Him into your life."

"And what does 'invite him into your life' mean?"

Marcus found Ponti's inability to describe conversion in plain language and his dependence on stock Christian phrases that made no sense to an unbeliever sad, but also irritating.

"Well, it means that we invite him to help us live our lives."

"Live our lives?"

Marcus watched Ponti flounder, and just as his irritation was about to increase he sensed that Ponti's frustrating and futile attempts to make himself understood were actually contributing to what Marcus hoped Marie-Clémence would see and understand about dead religion.

"It means that as we walk through life, we try our best, with God's help, to do what it says in the Bible."

"I see," Marie-Clémence, though she appeared more confused than she'd been at the start of the conversation. "That's it?"

Ponti was smiling broadly, enthusiastic at the possibility that he would make a convert here, of all places. "That's it!"

"It seems ... it seems so ... *cheap*. No, what you say can't be right. I can't believe such a thing. You are telling me that all one has to do is to just say some words and suddenly one is, how do you say, 'saved'?"

"It's really very simple. Jesus said that even a child could understand it."

Marie-Clémence seemed unconvinced, but she did not want to argue with the man and possibly embarrass him in front of Marcus or his other friends. She took a sip of wine, held up the wine glass, and looked at the wine, sparkling in the cup.

"Someone once told me Christians aren't allowed to drink wine."

"It's, yeah, it's something a lot of Christians have talked about and disagreed about over the centuries, that's true."

"But ... but I thought Jesus ... didn't he turn water into, like, a lot of wine?" She turned to Marcus. "It was at a wedding, wasn't it?"

Ponti smiled, but Marcus could see he was a little uncomfortable. Marcus had no urge to bail him out, either, since he couldn't think of any true answer that would, and because he'd had too much experience with Christians who alleged that keeping some law would make them holy. Marcus felt about them as Jesus felt about the Pharisees.

Ponti answered her. "You know, you're right, it was at a wedding in Cana, in Galilee. But some people would argue that it was really grape juice, not alcoholic at all. But we kind of think of it more along the lines of staying away from alcohol so we don't cause others to stumble."

"Stumble, you mean like a drunk stumbles?"

Ponti chuckled. "Sorry, what I meant was that if we hold to the doctrine of absolutely no alcohol, then maybe that might help others who shouldn't have any at all. I mean, if one of the people who went to my church saw me drinking a glass of wine, they might say to themselves, 'Hey, the Pastor's okay with it, so it must be okay for me.' It might temp them to indulge when they shouldn't. So out of concern for them, we don't drink."

"But you don't mind if I drink?"

Ponti's glib ship of man-made doctrine was grounding on the rocks of unavoidable scriptural truth. Ponti laughed again to cover his growing unease at the French woman's direct questions. He wasn't accustomed to such hard questions. When Ponti went out into the highways and byways to talk to the lost, none of them knew enough about what Jesus did or didn't do to put any kind of question like this to him. He wondered how she knew about Jesus and what He'd done.

"No, well, I mean, we believe that Christians shouldn't drink alcohol, I have to say that."

"It is a sin?"

Ponti waffled but then pressed up to the bar. "We think so, yes, again, because it might cause someone else to suffer."

"But it is okay for non-Christians to drink?"

"People can argue that there would be a lot less problems in the world if people didn't drink so much."

"Ah, well, I am French, and we drink more wine that water, Mr. Ponti. To tell you the truth, I think it is not the wine that is the problem, it is the lack of self-control on the person's part—this is the problem."

"Agree, agree, and we believe Jesus can help a person with that," Ponti said.

"I read somewhere else, too, that gluttony was a sin."

"Yeah, that's true," Ponti said, a little less glibly, as he was carrying around probably an extra 50 or 60 pounds.

"So ... do people in your church ... do they not eat, either? I mean, in case a fat person sees you eating and might think it is okay for them?"

"No, well, really, that's sort of a different thing."

"I see," Marie-Clémence replied, not seeing at all. "Interesting. Thank you, Mr. Ponti." She turned to Marcus. "Excuse me, but I need to find your mother." She nodded again to the Pastor. "Nice speaking with you, Tony."

Ponti sipped his Coke, Marcus his water. "She seemed curious," Ponti said to Marcus.

"Are you saying she seems strange, or she seems interested?"

"Both, I suppose. Have you known her long?" Ponti shifted his weight and looked around the large warehouse.

"About six months. We met at business school, in France."

Ponti grabbed Marcus' arm lightly and smiled at him. "You know, someone from our fellowship—Samantha Gunderson—got a job recently with a big global company. They may send her to France; at least that's what her mother says. She grew up here, went to church here, and we're happy to see her succeed."

"What's the job?" Marcus asked.

"She's an editor I think, or a writer, not sure. I talked to her mother and she'll be here at the party, actually. I'll bring her over so you can meet her."

Marcus nodded. "That would be nice, thanks. Let's hope she keeps her feet on the ground."

"Oh, she's solid," Ponti replied. "She taught Sunday School classes for, like, years, from when she was a freshman in high school. Her mother's pretty active in the church too."

Marcus refrained from sharing what he thought of equating vigorous church activity with a strong faith. Ponti saw a member of his church family from across the room and excused himself. A slow distaste swirled in his wake.

"Do you know," a low, feminine voice said in French, coming up to him from behind, "what you said about your brother?"

Marcus half-turned to find Marie-Clémence, lurking. "What was that?"

"That he was so different?"

"Yeah, I remember."

"Well, and so are you, I see ... I mean, I knew this, but here, among these people, it makes it clearer. And that man," she said, tilting her half-full wine glass in his direction, "is not."

"Is not what?"

"Is not *different*. He reminds me of so many of the religious people I knew."

"Hmmm, yeah, well, one of the things we haven't talked about yet is the state of Christianity in this country. Most of the churches, most of the 'Christian environments' you may see in town here are dead."

"Dead?"

"Sorry; spiritually dead, no life, no power."

"What do you mean?"

"Basically, not *different*, as you use the term."

They began walking toward an open area near the waterfront where the construction company's pier stretched out into the lake, and he stopped and turned toward her, one hand in a pocket of his pullover, the other holding his cane.

"Mace touched you and suddenly your headache disappeared and you could walk. Do you remember that?"

"Of course."

"*That's* power, Marie-Clémence. That's the *difference* you sense; that's the power of God working through a Believer who has a living relationship with the living God—Mace didn't do that on his own."

"Ah, I can understand that."

"You know the little analogy of the seed, yes?"

"No, actually I don't."

"When you put a seed into the ground, what is the first thing that happens?"

Marie-Clémence folded her arms across her chest and stared back at him "I am—I was—an intelligence officer, not a biologist."

"Okay, so what happens is, the seed dies. It's put into the ground, buried under dirt, and then it dies. If the seed sits in the box, or in the bag, or even in your hand, it doesn't die. It has to go into the ground. From the dead seed comes a plant—tiny at first, but soon it grows up enough to poke up out of the soil and look for sun and air and it begins to push its roots through the soil to find water. God designed this elemental biological principle to teach us what coming alive in the Spirit is like. We are seeds, Marie-Clémence; each one of us, and before we can become what God wants us to become, we need our old husks, the thing the Bible calls the 'natural man'—our human nature—to die. There's a principle, see, in both nature and in the Spirit: *without death, there is no life*." He waved his hands back toward the crowd. "Most of the people you see who call themselves Christians, they've never died, so they are not really alive, so they have no power, and so they don't look any different to you. What you are seeing, this difference you see in Mace and Zoe and my parents, and in me, is because we've died and a new nature is growing in us. It's this new nature, God's nature, you see that's different—the 'alive' part. But if a person won't undergo that death, they'll never really come alive. They'll never be truly *different*."

Marie-Clémence turned without comment, though Marcus could see she was processing what he'd shared with her. She turned, deep in thought, to walk toward the pier again, and Marcus, limping slightly, followed her.

She paused and looked back at him. "It is okay for you to walk? You should sit down, no?"

"I'm fine," he replied.

"Maybe we should call Mace and ask him to heal you."

"Funny woman."

She smiled at his comment. "But seriously, maybe you should go back and visit with the guests."

"I will," Marcus said, but made no move to turn around.

They walked a little further in silence and then she said, "All this talk of seeds and death and human natures and dying ... you realize that it doesn't make any sense to me. No, wait," she said quickly, "I don't really mean that. I mean, I can follow your logic, yes, and I understand what it is you are trying to convey, but ..."

"But you have no experiential knowledge of it; you don't understand it because nothing like that has happened to you."

"Yes, *exactement*," she exclaimed, and grasped his arm in her enthusiasm.

Marcus turned to look back at the crowd back in the warehouse, and then faced her again. There was a smell of diesel oil in the air, and he saw a small workboat chugging along the coastline, headed north.

"But here you are, walking, with no pain in your head."

"So, well, but what does that mean? What I am supposed to understand from that?"

"God sometimes intrudes in a person's life supernaturally, like your healing, to 'wake them up' to their need for Him; to get their attention, so to speak. He would do it with nations; He does it with people. He's trying to get your attention."

She nodded, looking out over the water, and didn't reply.

"Marie-Clémence, everyone has something which is *the most important thing* in their life to them. That thing, whatever it is, is their god. You have one, I have one, we all have one. People will do anything, say anything, sacrifice anything, give up everything they have, for that one most important thing, for their god. For some it's drugs; for others it's alcohol, or sex, or their job, or their spouse, or their children, but most often, overwhelmingly, it's themselves. They are their own little gods. They will do anything, say anything, sacrifice anything, and give up everything they have as long as they themselves can stay in control of their own lives, as long as they can keep steering their ship, as long as they can stay on the throne of their own lives, dictating what happens. No matter that invariably they make their own lives—and the lives around them—into a living hell, they would rather rule in hell than serve in heaven. And what do you see when a person is their own little god? They want comfortable lives, a life of ease, pleasantness, so they either compromise, or they become tyrants in their own homes, forcing their wives or husbands or children in effect to become slaves. There are as many different ways people live out their lives as their own god as there are people, but the one thing they all have in common is that they absolutely do *not* want to be confronted with the possibility of having their own selves tossed off their self-made thrones."

"So you are saying that these people, they are their own gods?" She waved a hand deprecatingly back toward the crowds at the party.

"I'm saying that in their minds most of them think they're following God, but the God they have in their minds is a god they made up, not the true God."

Marie-Clémence thought about what Marcus had said. A shadow crossed her face. She recognized Marcus was describing her own state of being. She had directed the course of her own life since she'd been old enough to walk. Certainly no one else had 'been on the throne', as he put it, and she would never have had it any other way. Hearing that such a path in life wasn't advisable disturbed her deeply, for she was coming to believe the things Marcus was telling her.

She stumbled over a loose board on the pier, and Marcus reached out and caught her, steadying her by the arm. When he touched her, instantly there came a fleeting vision pressing into her conscious awareness—a montage, a clear picture of an amalgamation of billions of lives, each pursuing their own interests. It looked like a massive anthill observed from a vast distance above, tiny beings striving, thrusting, fighting, grinding one another down, climbing up a million tiny hills that all sooner or later collapsed down upon themselves. This went on for a few seconds until suddenly a blazing flame swept through and burned everything to cinders.

"Marie-Clémence, are you okay?" She was gasping for breath, eyes unfocused, mouth open, staring at nothing.

She found herself dizzy, disoriented by what she'd seen, and Marcus quickly but gently steadied her, putting both hands on her shoulders. She looked up at him.

"What is happening to me?" she cried softly.

"What's the matter?"

"I saw ... I saw a *mélange*," she used the French word, "a massive, swirling rush of, I don't know, things, *living* things, they were so small but I knew they were people, millions and millions, all crawling and climbing over each other and crushing each other, and there was so much *hate* everywhere, and then a massive fire burned everything away."

Marcus was moved, and wondered with no small amazement at what God was doing in this woman's life. She had not been there a week and God had supernaturally intervened in her life twice.

"What *was* that?" she asked.

"I think God showed you what the world looks like from one of His perspectives, Marie-Clémence."

She was still wide-eyed, flushed with emotion, and disoriented. She looked up at him with frightened eyes. "This is not good," she whispered.

"Oh, no, Marie-Clémence, no, this is a very good thing. The God of All Creation is speaking to you, showing you what the future will bring. That He showed you what you just saw is a good thing, Marie-Clémence. *What* He showed you, though, is not good, you're right in that way—and it is coming soon."

He took her hand and gently led her back to the party.

***

Billy Rob Brewster and Ol' Digger Jack joined the party just about the time the sun went down. They'd flown into the Granite Sky airport in one of the company's private jets, a little Gulfstream, and Jed Sloan had picked them up.

"Nice o' y'all ta invite us," Ol' Digger Jack said upon meeting Claire Ironbridge as the walked into the party.

"You are more than welcome," Claire replied. "Marcus told us about your interview."

Ol' Digger Jack was smiling, apparently enchanted with Claire's French accent. "Yer from France, then, would ya be?" he asked.

"*Oui*, but of course. I grew up in Paris. But please, come in, join the party." Billy Rob and Ol' Digger Jack melded into the ebb and flow of people milling around the large warehouse, Billy Rob picking up a small cream-filled pastry from a silver tray on one of the tables.

"Hey, there's Ol' Digger Jack!" They both turned at once to see Zoe coming toward them, carrying a cooler full of ice and soda. Ol' Digger Jack's face lit up—again—and he leaned over to Billy Rob and said, "I tol' ya that ah'd purely die o' happiness if'n I met the rest o' this clan, didn't I? That is sure one fine filly."

Billy Rob looked at him sideways, but Ol' Digger Jack was just as happy as could be.

"Hey, Miss Zoe, it's good ta' see ya agin'."

She put the cooler down on the table and bussed Ol' Digger Jack on the cheek and shook hands with Billy Rob. "You gentlemen are surely welcome. We appreciate you coming, especially since after you left we read up on how big your company is, and you must both be busier than a ... well, pretty busy."

"We are that, Zoe, but we didn't want to miss this. And we'd like to talk a little more to Marcus."

"Sure, sure, he's wandering around here somewhere. And you need to meet Mace."

"Mace?"

"Yeah ... Mace, my husband, Marcus' brother."

"Right," Billy Rob said.

"What's he do fer a livin'?" asked Ol' Digger Jack, looking around at all the people, sizing up the warehouse facility, and picking up a soda, all at once.

Zoe stopped setting out the cans of soda and looked at Ol' Digger Jack for a second. "Well, I'll tell you, Ol' Digger Jack, the main thing he does is take care of me. And in his spare time he and I run the Eagles Wings' Creamery and we make all kinds of cheese, which you can taste over there on that table." She pointed to another table laden with wheels of all kinds of cheeses.

"Got it," Ol' Digger Jack replied.

"Hey, do me a favor, would you? Here," and Zoe handed Billy Rob the empty cooler. "Would you take this back there, through that corridor there to the back room and fill it up with more ice and soda? I've got to get more of those wheels sliced up." She patted Billy Rob on the arm and headed off to the cheese table, leaving the eccentric Texas billionaire holding an empty blue Coleman cooler, smiling slightly.

"In fer a penny, in fer a pound, they say, Billy Rob," quoted Ol' Digger Jack, laughing heartily.

"Well hell, I guess. Where'd she say to go?"

"You never could follow directions, boy, did ah ever tell you that? Back that way yonder." Ol' Digger Jack, who hadn't forgotten a thing anyone had ever told him since he was five, pointed the way, and Billy Rob went where he was told.

He got to the back room, saw the area they were using as a stock room, and walked in with the cooler.

"*Ah, Zoe, mets-le là-bas, s'il vous plaît.*"

Billy Rob stood there for maybe five seconds and then the woman who'd spoken turned around and saw him. She was wearing an over-sized blue and red flannel work shirt, jeans, and a well-worn tan apron. Her hair, a kind of dirty blonde, spiked out here and there from a headscarf, and she was leaning over a sink washing dishes.

"Uh, sorry ma'am, but I, uh, don't speak ... French, is it?"

"*Oui*, no, sorry, of course not. And who are you?"

"Name's Billy Rob, ma'am."

"Well, nice to meet you Billy Rob. I'm Abrielle. Just put that over there, would you?" she asked, pointing to a table.

"Uh, the lady, Zoe, told me to fill it up with ice and more soda."

"Right. The ice is just through that door there, and you'll see the freezer. The pop is here, under this table."

Billy Rob filled the cooler with ice from the freezer and then went back to the table where the pop was and started stabbing cans into the ice. The woman looked at him, pulling a wisp of hair away from her face with a wet hand.

"Thank you," she said. "There are so many more people here than we expected and I have to get these dishes washed and out again or people will be eating from their hands."

"Uh huh." Billy Rob stood up and hefted the now-full cooler. "Out to the main floor I'm supposin'?"

"Oh, yes, please, thanks." She turned back to attack the dishes in the sink again, and Billy Rob saw a growing stack of plates, glasses, and silverware by the side.

"Right," he said, and took the cooler back to where Zoe had asked for it.

By then Ol' Digger Jack had disappeared into the crowd. The Texas billionaire found himself standing alone, not knowing another soul at the party, when a young man came up to him. He was slightly taller than Billy Rob, with a lean, square face, dark hair, an old tan chore coat, and eyes that sort of came right at him, but in a good way. Billy Rob held out his hand.

"Billy Rob Brewster," he said.

The man just shook his hand and nodded, smiled slightly, and didn't say a word.

As the young man took his hand, Billy Rob was flooded with feelings of exuberance and exhilaration, and yet too a sense of danger, challenge, and the feeling that he was at the edge of a cliff, facing a decision whether to leap off or not ... and then the strangest sense that he should go back and wash dishes ... all from one handshake. Billy Rob looked down at his hand for several seconds, shaken and disoriented, and then looked back up at the young man, but he'd gone, melted into the crowd.

So ... Billy Rob Brewster turned his back on the crowd and went and helped the woman wash dishes.

***

Washing the one hundred and fifty-third plate, Abrielle asked, "So what do you do, Billy Rob?"

"Well, Abrielle, me and my friend—Ol' Digger Jack, he came with me tonight, but he kind of got away from me—we sort of have a little company in the energy business."

"That's nice," Abrielle replied. "Do you enjoy it?"

Billy Rob, hands immersed completely in hot water, thought about that for a minute. "You know, I haven't really thought about that for, I dunno, quite a long time. But now that I do think about it, yeah, I do. I do enjoy it."

"And what do you enjoy about it most?" she asked, drying the plate Billy Rob handed her with a towel. She had a pleasant, easy manner and there was something else besides the French accent that he couldn't quite put his finger on.

Billy Rob smiled and stopped washing for just a minute. "Now that's rich, because no one's ever really asked me that before, but I can tell you right off the bat exactly what I like best. Hands down, it's the leadership, and by that I mean it's taking care of my people."

"So you have other people working for you besides your friend, Mr. Jack? Here, let me have that." She took a particularly delicate long-stemmed wine glass, dried it carefully, and put it into a special box with cardboard-sectioned compartments.

"Well, yeah, we've got a few fellers scattered here and there."

"And you like taking care of them?"

"Yeah, that I do," he said, scrubbing at one stubborn plate. "I like makin' sure they have jobs and their families are taken care of and they get home safe at night at the end of each day." He picked up a knife crusted with cheese and began scrubbing. "I never really thought about it before, but now that you asked, I mean, the answer was right there in my mind. Strangest thing."

"No, actually, it isn't strange at all. Sometimes I have that experience. I wonder and wander and fuss and fret and get lost and then discover the answer was right in front of me all the time."

"And speakin' of strange things," he said, looking up at her, "I met a guy out there, he came up, shook my hand, and I had the weirdest impressions."

Abrielle continued to dry and stack the plates as Billy Rob washed them and handed them to her. "What did you feel?"

"You'll think it's stupid," he said.

"Oh no," she replied quickly, with just a tinge of sadness, or regret, or remembrance ... he couldn't discern exactly what it was in her eyes. "No, I wouldn't think that."

"Okay, so ... I felt ... at the same time full of energy and life and also like there was some danger or challenge in front of me, and the weirdest thing was that I felt like I was standing on the edge of a cliff, and the choice to jump off the cliff was coming up. I mean, talk about off-the-wall! It must have been something I ate. I had one of those little cream pastries when I came in. Are you sure those things haven't gone south?"

"Was the young man wearing sort of a tan farm coat?" She waved her hand down her front.

Billy Rob snapped his head around and looked at Abrielle. "Now ... how did ... yeah, he did."

Abrielle shook her head knowingly and finished drying a glass. "You met Mace."

"Mace ... Mace Ironbridge, right, Zoe's husband. I didn't know."

She looked at him. "You know now, don't you?" She dabbed him on the arm with the wet towel.

"He didn't say hello or anything."

"He has a defect of speech. He *can* speak, only he speaks very slowly, so most of the time he chooses either not to say anything, or he will type on a tablet he carries around."

"I didn't know."

"Ah, yes, well, Mace and Zoe are ... they're very special, Billy Rob. You should get to know them."

Billy Rob stuck his hands back in the sink and pulled the plug to drain the water and refill it again to wash the next batch of plates coming in from the party. "I think I will," he said. "He's Marcus' brother, right?"

"Do you know Marcus?"

"Yeah, we've met. Nice guy."

"He's just come home from Europe, you know. He was in a bad accident over there."

"What happened?"

"I don't really know," Abrielle replied, looking off into the distance for a moment. "But he was in hospital for quite some time. And have you met Marie-Clémence?"

"Not yet, no."

"Yes, well, she came back from Europe with him. I haven't heard the entire story yet but I did hear that somehow he saved her life over there, I don't know how."

Billy Rob picked up a stack of plates and put them into the deep sink. "The Ironbridges sound like a unique family."

"They are; they've been a godsend," she said in a firm but somber tone.

"How do you know them?"

Abrielle looked at this man who had literally wandered in off the street and started washing dishes with her out of kindness and perhaps because he didn't know anyone else at the party. She wondered how much she should tell him. She'd come out of the plain community but there was still a lot of the plain community in her, and the habit of being closemouthed was yet redolant in the cache of her soul.

"They ... Zoe helped me with an issue recently. She and Mace were very kind."

Billy Rob's success in business was due largely to his personal intuition and he could tell Abrielle didn't want to talk about that particular slice of her life at the moment.

"So ... yeah, hey, do you have any family around here?"

Abrielle let a plate slip out of her hands, and it cracked against the counter. "Oh, sorry."

"No harm done."

"I ... I have a sister."

"You get to visit much?"

She turned away to stack the dried plates in a laundry basket they'd used to bring them to the warehouse, and in which they'd take them back to the Ironbridge's farm. "No, actually, we ... we don't see much of each other."

Billy Rob's intuition kicked in again, and he realized Abrielle's family was terra no-go either. Abrielle turned, looked down at the floor for a moment and lifted a hand to her face, brushing back a strand of hair and as she stood there, framed just in front of one of the windows that looked out over the lake, the picture suddenly reminded him of his mother so poignantly that it took his breath away. He hadn't thought of his mother in, well, years, and then along comes this woman and sweeps a bit of hair off her face and he's back with his mother again. He coughed and wiped the back of his hand across his eyes. Just thinking of his mother hurt; he and his father had loved her so much.

"What's wrong, Billy Rob?"

"Oh, hey, nothin', just some soap in my eyes, that's all."

"Here," she said and handed him a dry towel.

Jed Sloan came in with Emma and they relieved Abrielle and Billy Rob from dish detail.

"Tack is gonna give his speech soon. Don't wanna miss that," Jed said. "We can finish up here. Why don't you two go get something to eat?"

Billy Rob and Abrielle wandered out to the warehouse and were amazed at the number of people at the party. "There must be half the town here," she said.

"Any of your friends here?" Billy Rob asked, his head on a swivel, wondering where Ol' Digger Jack had gone.

"Oh, probably not," she said, a look of wistful sadness passing across her face.

Billy Rob caught the expression, fleeting as it was. "You're not gonna tell me you don't have friends, Abrielle. That's just not believable."

"I ... I did have. I mean, I have some now, sure ... the Ironbridges, you know, Zoe and Mace, and Marcus, and Tack and Claire for sure, and there is young Emma, you saw her with Jed there, she's very sweet."

Billy Rob didn't need a neon sign. "Well, so ... do you wanna get something to eat?"

"Sure," she said, relieved. "We should try the cheese."

***

About the time Billy Rob and Abrielle finished a sandwich each with some wine and cheese, which Billy Rob said was fantastic, there was a small commotion up near one wall of the warehouse, and they saw Tack Ironbridge clamber up somewhat clumsily onto a table. People began gathering around and Billy Rob and Abrielle wandered easily together toward that part of the warehouse. Billy Rob was still thinking about his mother, though, and there was still that strange fresh wound under his heart.

***

"Ladies, gentlemen, can I have your attention for just a moment? Thank you." Tack let people gather around and waited for the room to settle down. "I would like to begin by thanking you all for coming out tonight to welcome my son home." He turned to Marcus and extended an arm and Marcus came up—slowly—onto the table with him. The crowd applauded lightly.

"As you know, Marcus spent some time in Afghanistan, and by God's mercy he survived that hell-hole. He decided to change course in life and pursue a business degree, but apparently that didn't work out so well either." Tack looked at his son, standing on the table leaning on his cane, and laughter rippled through the crowd. "So ... he decided to come home. I'd tell you that I feel like the father of the prodigal, but Marcus has never given me one minute's worth of trouble, and he's never 'squandered his inheritance' on loose living. He and Mace both are sons any father would be proud to have." The crowd clapped again.

"Now we discover that Marcus will be going to work right here in northern Minnesota for a little energy company owned by Mr. Billy Rob Brewster. Are you out there, Mr. Brewster?"

Billy Rob shrunk back against the wall he was leaning against and tucked his head into his shoulders.

"Oh, don't be such a silly," Abrielle said, and she pushed up a hand. "He's right here, Tack. If he's as good at running his little company as he is at washing dishes, Marcus will do alright!" The crowd laughed again, watching Billy Rob stand a little taller and wave.

"Marcus has a guest with him tonight, a young lady named Marie-Clémence Levinson, and I would appreciate it if you all made her feel welcome. I'm sure you have so far, and thank you." Tack paused.

"So okay, that's where we are with welcoming Marcus home. I wanted to share something else with you tonight, something not so pleasant, but since we've got quite a few folks here who claim to be followers of Jesus, and, too, some who aren't, I wanted to say a few things." Tack shifted his weight. It was clear his prosthetic was causing some pain. Mace swiftly took a folding chair and set it up and pushed it behind him on the table, and Tack sat down and thanked Mace quietly.

"We all know the world we're living in," Tack began. "And most of us are to a greater or lesser degree watching what's happening—at least I hope you are. I won't go into all the signs and symptoms; we've all seen them. I wanted to tell you all tonight ... I want to issue a warning." The crowd grew silent, not expecting this. Claire looked up at Tack and wondered where he was going. He leaned forward in the chair and clasped his hands together. "Things are going to become very difficult soon in the world, and yes, most especially in this country. I know, we Americans find it hard to conceive of the fact that life could be any different than the way it's always been, but I feel compelled to tell you that things will change, very soon, and not for the better.

"I'm not saying anything that many other Spirit-filled believers haven't already said. God is warning those who have ears to hear. The proverb about the five wise and five foolish virgins comes to mind."

Billy Rob leaned over and whispered to Abrielle. "Virgins? What's he talkin' about?"

"I'll tell you later," she replied, whispering.

Tack continued. "But the main thing I wanted to share tonight are my opinions about how to prepare." Marcus looked around and saw almost everyone's eyes riveted on Tack. Tack continued. "There are people out there who are stocking up food, and guns, and fuel, and ammunition, and all kinds of survival equipment and supplies, and if God has told you to do that, then great, but the most important thing we all need to do is to build a relationship with the living God so that you can hear Him in these coming times. There will come a flood—actually, it's already here—a flood of deception, and unless you have a solid, established, working relationship with the God of Abraham, Isaac, and Jacob, you'll get caught in it.

"There are people here from a lot of different churches in town tonight. My guess is that a lot of the deception I'm talking about has made its way into your fellowships. What am I talking about? Well, let's consider ..." Tack began counting on his fingers. "The New Age has pushed into churches in a big way. Anyone been to a fellowship where they talk about 'spiritual formation'? How about 'centering prayer' or 'contemplative prayer'? How about 'holy laughter'? How about the Emerging Church or the Latter Rain movement? How about Dominionism—anyone here ready to take over the world for Jesus? Has anyone's church been moved to draw closer to Catholicism? Those are just the most obvious. And I don't have to ask how many people who claim to follow Jesus are standing here tonight expecting God to bring down a major, world-shaking revival in the world, because I've heard it from many of you, this very night." A grim cast of fierce determination froze on his face. "There is only one revival promised in the times of the end, and that's a revival of deception. Let no one deceive you, there won't be any 'great revival' coming." He spat out the last words with disdain. "You buy into that theory and you'll be following the coming man of sin. Stay away from it."

Abrielle noted a ripple of discontent flash through the crowd. Ironbridge went on.

"There are movements today that will convince you that whatever comes out of your mouth will come to pass as long as you believe strongly enough. That's just another name for sorcery. But the worst thing, the thing that will catch so many if they're not ready for it, is this diabolical drive to unite all the religions of the world." He looked around, trying to meet everyone's eyes. "Stay away from it. It will sound nice, it will look great, it'll appear oh so holy and 'Christian', but its end is death, for no man can serve two masters, and light will have no fellowship with darkness."

Tack took a long breath. He could tell many of the people in the crowd had been pricked with his list of what he termed 'deceptions'. Many of them were too far gone into the delusion to understand what he was saying, but if he could reach just one, it would be worth it.

"So what do we do? How does one defend against such things, things Jesus said would, if it were possible—and it will be—deceive even the elect? People think they can come to God pretty much in any way they want, but I'm here to tell you, the relationship you build with Him needs to be on His terms, not on your terms, not your parents' terms, not your denomination's terms. It needs to be on God's terms, and it can only be brought to pass through acknowledging and then bowing down in obedience to His Son, Jesus." Zoe, standing with Claire near a large crate, saw Tony Ponti shift uncomfortably.

"God's terms for the relationship He wants with us are simply laid out in the Bible." Tack said. "Find one. Read it. Obey it. Time is short. I'll offer up anyone in my family to help you with understanding what it says to you: my wife Claire, Marcus, Mace, or Zoe his wife—any of us will help you understand what God is trying to say to you, but you have to want to hear from Him.

"Now I know this sounds sort of like a standard evangelistic spiel, and maybe it is, but here's something you don't hear much. For those who don't build a relationship with God—the true God—you'll either be deceived and wander off into some spiritual pit, or you'll not be ready when the time comes, but either way, eventually everyone who isn't living in a real relationship with God will end up dead, in hell.

"One more thing before I let you go. The times to come will be so hard, so deceptive, that many—many in this room—will turn against family members, and everyone who truly loves God will find their lives in danger from those family members, from friends, from relatives. So I'm here tonight to tell you—to warn you—don't let that happen. Don't get in the way of what God wants to do, both in your life and in the lives of others. Jesus is coming back and His robes will be dipped in the blood of all those He'll slaughter when He returns—those who will be fighting against Him as He comes back. Please," he said, standing then, and pausing, looking out over the assembled group, all of whom were stock still, "please, don't any of you here tonight be among those whose blood will splatter His robes. Come out of the world, come out of the lies and pretense and hypocrisy, come out and away from it. Turn away from your sin, live in truth, learn to love truth. Learn what He wants from you *now*, tonight, as soon as possible." He was holding out a hand clenched into a fist, imploring, beseeching, and then paused and looked around the crowd, trying to see into each heart. "There isn't much time," he said finally. "I stand here tonight to tell you that as for me and my family, we will serve the God of Abraham, Isaac, and Jacob. Let no man here tonight forget that." He stared out at them, almost defiantly, because he sensed that there would be some out there one day who would betray him and his family for a day's wage. He nodded once and then Mace helped him down from the table.

There was a smattering of half-hearted applause, and then the noise of the party picked up again, though Billy Rob could tell things were subdued. "That was probably the strangest after-dinner speech I've ever heard."

Abrielle looked at him. "You ... you aren't a Christian then?" she asked.

"No ma'am. Never had time for it. My father, I don't think he ever even thought about church, and my mother ..." Billy Rob stopped and cleared his throat for a moment. He took a sip of wine. "Well, my mother was, though, toward the end."

"Was what?"

"Religious, I mean. I can remember her, lying there on her bed, trying to read through the Bible. She'd struggle to try and make something of it, but, well, she'd spent her whole life in England, living in some castle, and I'm pretty sure they threw the last Bible out of England about the same time they tossed out ol' Winston Churchill, so she never really learned any of it when she was young and she just couldn't figure out how to make heads or tails of it when she ... when she was older."

Abrielle lightly laid a hand on Billy Rob's arm. "I'm so sorry, Billy Rob."

Billy Rob nodded but didn't speak. It was the strangest thing, getting these feelings about his mother, now of all times and places. First that Mace guy and that sense of exhilaration and danger, a sense of needing to jump from a cliff, and then this spear in his chest from out of the past ... there was something weird about this place and these people.

"I need to get back to the kitchen, Billy Rob. No, you stay here. Find your friend or something, or go talk to Marcus. You wanted to talk to Marcus, right? Well, he should be over there someplace." She lifted a hand in the general direction of where Tack had been standing up on a table.

"Abrielle, hey ..." Billy Rob said, almost without thinking. He didn't want her to just disappear. He'd felt so ... so comfortable with her. He said the first thing that popped into his mind. "Hey, how are you getting home?"

Her eyes widened slightly; she hadn't been expecting this, and it frightened her. "Oh, Tack and Claire or Mace and Zoe will take me home. If not with them, I'll get a ride with Jed and Emma. I live out at the Ironbridge farm and that's quite a drive from town."

"Yeah, that's right, you did mention that. Well, look, can I give you a hand in the kitchen?"

Abrielle folded her arms across her chest and looked down at the floor and then ventured a quick glance at him. "Billy Rob, you go find Marcus and tell him what it is you need to tell him. And then you go on back to that little group of men in your little energy company and take good care of them, now, okay? It was nice talking with you." And she turned and moved off through the crowd.

Billy Rob was standing there watching her go when he heard a familiar voice at his shoulder. "Now who is that tall stalk o' prairie grass?" Billy Rob turned to find Ol' Digger Jack by his elbow, drink in one hand, a pastry in the other.

"Ol' Digger Jack, you wouldn't know a stalk of prairie grass from a rose bush."

Ol' Digger Jack chuckled, but he was still staring at Abrielle. "Now ain't that the strangest thing," he said in a voice threaded with wonder.

"What?"

"That yonder lady, the one you were talkin' with ..."

"What about her?"

Ol' Digger Jack popped the pastry into his mouth, ate it, then put a hand on Billy Rob's shoulder. "Son, I ain't never showed you pictures of your Momma back when she married your Daddy, have I? Well, that there filly is the spittin' image of your Momma. Exceptin' the poofy hair, o' course."

It took Billy Rob a moment to recover from that, but then he shook his head slightly and took Ol' Digger Jack's drink from his hand. "What're you drinking?"

Ol' Digger Jack looked at Billy Rob. "Just tonic water, son, just tonic water. And that lady," he said, snatching his drink back, "didn't appear outta no glass o' tonic water. I'm serious. She looks a lot like your Momma. You tellin' me you ain't noticed? Who is she?"

"Name's Abrielle."

"Yeah? Abrielle what?"

Billy Rob shook his head. "You know, I have absolutely no clue."

"Well, what did she want?"

"She didn't want anything. We spent most of the party washing dishes."

Ol' Digger Jack looked at Billy Rob in surprise and smiled slowly. "You? Washin' dishes?"

"We talked for most of the night."

"Where'd she run off to?"

"Well, and keep in mind I'm a bit rusty at this, I think she just told me to pound sand."

"Not too many times some filly tells Texas billionaire most eligible bachelor of the year Billy Rob Brewster to go pound sand."

"Yeah, well, I'm pretty sure she doesn't know about the Texas billionaire part."

"Really? So the fact that you own, like, half o' Texas and have maybe just slightly less money than God didn't come up while you and her was washin' dishes?"

Billy Rob turned and smiled at Ol' Digger Jack. "In point of fact it did not, old friend. It surely did not. How about that?"

"Well, hell, are ya just gonna stand there and pound sand or are you gonna git on yer horse and trot on after her?"

Billy Rob stood there with his hands in his pockets, with a mixture of confusion, satisfaction, and a shade of eagerness on his face. "Did I tell you, Ol' Digger Jack, that earlier this evening I had the strangest sense that I was gonna come upon some sort of a cliff that needed jumpin' off from."

"You're startin' ta worry me, boy."

Billy Rob smiled slowly and then slapped his friend on the shoulder. "Nah, nothing to worry about here, Ol' Digger Jack. Now let's get on and find Marcus and then get over to the airport."

"Boy howdy," Ol' Digger Jack replied. "We got a meeting with them Statoil fellas tomorrow afternoon in Oslo, and I can never get any sleep in that damn Gulfstream."

They found Marcus standing with a very attractive woman with dark hair that looked like it had been cut short recently. She wore a headband around most of her head. Billy Rob wondered if that was the style for women around these parts.

"Marcus, I wonder if we could talk for a just a few minutes?"

The woman turned to leave, making her apologies in what sounded to Billy Rob like a heavy French accent, but Marcus put his hand on her arm. "Stay," he said. She stopped, and Marcus introduced her to Billy Rob and Ol' Digger Jack.

"Anything particularly private?" Marcus asked, looking at Billy Rob.

"Actually not at all," Billy Rob replied. "But it would be easier if we could go someplace quieter."

"Let's try the conference room," Marcus said. "Through there." He pointed toward the hall that led out of the warehouse area back into the main offices of NMC, and directly into the conference room. Marcus led, walking somewhat unsteadily, and he could see the dark-haired woman keep a hand under his arm.

They sat down at the conference room table where they'd had their first interview—there was the same big cross up on the wall—and Billy Rob nodded to Ol' Digger Jack, who began. "Marcus, we just wanted you ta know that we got in touch with Dag Wilson."

"And?"

"And he said ... wait, I got it here, he said I was supposed ta read it exactly ... hang on." Ol' Digger Jack pulled out a small green notebook from a pocket and flipped it open. "Here 'tis. He says to tell you, 'He's been having some conversations with his mother lately,' and he said to say, 'she would never forgive him if he didn't take this opportunity.' So he said he's in. What's he talkin' about, by the way, about his mother?"

"Private issue," Marcus replied. Marie-Clémence could tell he was pleased, though she didn't know who Dag Wilson was.

"He wondered when we wanted him to start, and we asked if two weeks was too soon, and he said two days would be better, so we got him all set up and he'll be flyin' in to Granite Sky here, not tomorrow but the next day."

"That's great, sir, thank you. It means a lot."

Ol' Digger Jack waved off Marcus' thanks. "Hell, boy, if you hadn'a put us up to it, that young kid woulda still been rollin' carts at Wal-Mart."

"He's a solid man," Marcus said, turning to Billy Rob. "He'll do a good job."

"Yeah, well, okay," Ol' Digger Jack continued, "and then we also wanted to tell you that we *finally* found Tom Custer after, what, I dunno, musta been, like twenty-three phone calls, a couple of major favors called in, and hirin' not one but two, count 'em, *two* private investigators. We finally tracked him down—get this—one of the PIs we hired eventually found him on the side of some road in Wyoming, workin' for the WYDOT—that's the Wyomin' Dee-partment o' Transportation, in case you didn't know—diggin' ditches for ten dollars an hour."

Marcus' jaw clenched in anger and grief at what the Marines had done to that fine man. He lowered his head and looked at his hands on the table. "What did he say?"

Ol' Digger Jack flipped through the pages of the small green notebook. "Hold on ... hold on, it's in here somewhere ... yeah, here it is." Ol' Digger Jack started to chuckle. "So it says here that for a few minutes ol' Tom didn't actually believe our trusty PI, and that good ol' boy thought he was gonna be on the wrong side of shovel for a few moments there. So the PI—apparently he's pretty quick on his feet—he says he can have you give ol' Tom a call directly if he wanted confirmation. So," Ol' Digger Jack said, reaching in and pulling his cell phone out of his jacket pocket, "here ya go. Ah got the number right here, and it is exactly, let's see ... 6:08 in the evening there." Ol' Digger Jack handed Marcus the phone.

"He said he wanted me to call him?"

"Not 'zactly. He was about to brain our trusty PI until the PI told him you'd call and make the offer yerself. Apparently ol' Tom's been carryin' around a bucketload of suspicious since the Green Machine done 'im wrong."

"You still want him aboard?" Billy Rob asked Marcus.

"Absolutely," Marcus replied with zero hesitation. "Let's call him."

Marcus took the phone and dialed the number. A gravelly, raspy voice answered on the fourth ring.

"Custer."

"First Sergeant Tom Custer?"

There was a moment of silence on the line, then, "Who's askin'?"

"Marcus Ironbridge. I'm on a speaker phone with ... with a couple of others in the room here. I'm in Minnesota."

Silence on the other end of the line ... then, "Yeah, I don't give two hoots in hell about who's in the room with you. You say you're Marcus Ironbridge?"

"I am."

"Yeah, okay, so then, think back now ... Afghanistan, Korengal province, and it's the company's first night out of the wire. Captain Ironbridge led the SATA team—but then you'd know that, right, I forgot, you're him—and there was a password we rigged up to make sure we didn't whack each other when one of the platoons went out early the next day. What was the password that night?"

Marcus thought, God, that was so long ago, what was—and suddenly the word popped into his mind. "Samson."

Silence on the phone, and then, "Yeah, okay, so if you're Marcus Ironbridge, you remember that you came up out of nowhere and scared the crap out of me and I said, 'Jesus Christ.' So if you *are* Captain Marcus Ironbridge, tell me what you said then."

Marcus smiled slowly to himself, remembering. "Actually, First Sergeant, you said 'Jesus *H.* Christ,' and I said, 'No, it's me.'

Another long silence; "It *is* you, then."

"Yeah, First Sergeant, it is."

More silence ... then, "I put up with a world of smackdown for you, do you know that?"

"I recently learned about that, Sergeant, and I'm sorry for what happened."

"Every time one of those prosecutors would be tearin' me a new one up or down, I would think back to when I gave you so much grief for pissin' on Allah's picnic out there and wonder just why the hell I didn't tell them sumbitches what they wanted to hear."

"I'm told you didn't do that, First Sergeant."

"No I did not, Captain, because ... because of all the things I have seen in my illustrious career, including a bunch of crap out here on the line crew digging ditches in Wyoming, thank you very much, I have never, *ever* seen anything like what I saw there in that valley, and nothing—certainly no piss-ant JAG lawyer what ain't even shaved yet would ever get me to say otherwise. I will go to my grave thinkin' about what happened out there, and why, and how." Billy Rob and Ol' Digger Jack's eyes got a little rounder at that. Marie-Clémence looked at Marcus questioningly.

"I appreciate your integrity, First Sergeant."

"And hell, why, look at things now! The entire U.S. military is kissin' Muslim ass over every little thing faster'n you can say 'Moo-hammed'. God forbid we should offend a Muslim somewhere. It makes me plain sick to see my beloved Corps fold up into nothing but another politically correct collection of kool-aid drinkin' ass kissers."

"Things have gotten pretty bad," Marcus put in.

"So ... this guy comes out and finds me on the road and tells me you have a job offer."

"I do. I've been hired as the Security Director for a U.S. oil company, and they told me I could have a couple of people to help me stand up a complete team, and I told them I wanted you."

Silence again. "What's the work?"

Marcus began to reply, but Custer interrupted. "Hell, listen to me, I'm asking about a security job while I'm out here digging ditches. Hell yes I'll take the job, Captain, but it's not for the reason you think."

"Glad to hear it, but ... if you don't mind me asking, why *are* you taking the job?"

There was a moment or two of silence, and then, "Take me off speakerphone," and Marcus complied, putting the phone to his ear.

"Alright First Sergeant, you're off the speaker, it's just you and I."

"Captain, I'm taking this job because I will not go down into the ground until

I find out exactly what happened out there in Afghanistan with Kilo Company, and why we never lost a man while you were out there, and what kind of war it was we fought. If it was some kind of 'God against Allah' thing, well ... I've got to find out just exactly how that works."

Marcus nodded as the others in the room watched. "Sergeant, I think I can promise you we can help with that."

"Good. Put me back on the speaker now, Captain, would you?" Marcus pressed the button. "Back on speaker again, First Sergeant."

"Good, now tell those Texas panty-wastes to get me on a flight out of this hell-hole. You tell 'em I'll be ready to deploy at zero five hundred tomorrow morning. You think that fly-by-night outfit of theirs can make that happen?" Marcus looked up at Billy Rob and Ol' Digger Jack.

"Uh, Mr. Custer, this is Billy Rob Brewster. What's the closest airport to you?"

"We're working a stretch of Interstate 90 up near Sheridan, and they've put us up in a motel nearby. I'm good with the line boss out here and just in case the man you sent was on the level, I made arrangements with him for a quick extract. Your LZ[30] should be the Sheridan County airport."

"We'll have an aircraft at Sheridan County airport tomorrow at 0500, First Sergeant." Billy Rob looked at Ol' Digger Jack, who gave him a thumbs up and then held out his hand for Billy Rob's mobile. Ol' Digger Jack stood up and went to a quiet corner of the conference room and began making a call.

"Good. We'll see what kind of outfit you're running, Mr. Brewster." Custer paused and then said, "You have any more wars planned, Captain?" Marie-Clémence eyes widened at that comment, and Billy Rob wondered exactly what she was thinking about just then.

"You never know what might come along in the days to come, First Sergeant," Marcus replied.

"Okay, well, I will see you shortly, Captain. And oh, one more thing ..."

"Yes?"

"Thank you," Custer growled, and hung up.

***

Samantha Gunderson had the most uncomfortable feelings as Tack made his speech. She'd come to the party after driving most of the day from Minneapolis. She would be staying with her parents for a few days and her mother had told her about the big event the Ironbridges were putting on, and everyone who claimed to be in any way religious had been invited, and most of those who weren't were coming anyway. Samantha's mother, Eva Gunderson, suggested she stop by. Eva had gotten a quick glimpse of Marcus Ironbridge, and thoughts of matchmaking stirred in her head.

Every thing Tack Ironbridge had labeled heresy in his little after-dinner diatribe was something Samantha's company was actively promoting, or researching, or pitching, or steering people to read about or discover.

And here Samantha Gunderson came to a fork in the road of her life, a choice, where her very eternal future turned upon the knife-edge of a single decision, a cast of the heart. What worked for her was what little exposure she'd had to the Bible in

30 Landing Zone.

her youth, and that she'd been raised in some semblance of normalcy. What worked against her was the fact that her parents—her mother, particularly—interpreted 'faith' as simply 'involvement in church', and had no concept of true conversion or salvation. As damaging was the working environment at Guilder, Atchison, and Steckam, where she was surrounded by a growing circle of acquaintances and associates actively opposed to the kingdom of God and to God Himself. There was also a lifetime of church teaching which, every Sunday, just told her over and over and over again that she needed to be saved, never feeding her the meat of true Christianity. There was too her love of reading, which was leading her into many dangerous pastures. But what tipped the scales, the deciding factor, the thing that pushed Samantha one way and not the other, was what she herself wanted most in life. She wanted to *accomplish something great*; she wanted to *do* something important, something remarkable, something epic—a desire that is sadly and so often a very short walk round the block to wanting to *be* someone important. This was the true fire in her belly; it was what at the bottom of things directed her life, that *most important thing* which drove the decisions she made.

And the decision she made that night? Helped by the many evil influences she'd allowed to become part of her life, helped in part by a small flurry of demonic spirits that had recently been assigned to affect her life and stave off encroaching influences from the Kingdom of Light, and helped by a fleeting perception of her surroundings that cast the people, and especially the Ironbridges, as small-town hacks; unsophisticated, unintelligent, uninformed people—all these things together pushed her to disbelieve Tack Ironbridge, to take umbrage with his assertions that the things she and her very prominent, very successful, very powerful company were supporting were heresy. It was just a tiny seed then, just the smallest shade of offense, of distaste, of being insulted, of having one's foundations checked and shaken. She didn't like it, and the thought arose unbidden that perhaps her dislike was due to the fact that Tack Ironbridge—and those who might agree with him—were at best uninformed and at worst, ignorant, insular, and probably associated with some cult. Like a tasty, dainty morsel, it was sweet to the taste but then lodged down in her heart, there to grow bitter. Truth is a powerful force in life. It prevents comfort from becoming fuel for self-pity, and it prevents power from feeding the lust for glory, and it stays the flood of pride. Yet if in our pride we lust for glory and power, truth is choked and dies.

This decision, this resolve, this impression—whatever it was, it was only in its infancy, something she herself would not in any way have been able to fully describe. It was only a loose sense of something disagreeable having passed across her spirit. If she had been looking in a mirror at that moment, she would have seen the very tiniest of lines of concern, worry, anxiety, pride, and anger—all etched with hell's iron stylus—imperceptibly making their tracks ever so slightly upon her countenance and pushing down the tiniest little tendrils of roots into her soul, all designed to suck up the bitter waters of hate, ambition, jealousy, pride, and the fear of man.

And as Samantha made this critical knife-edge decision in an instantaeneous, flashing celestial second, she came upon Pastor Tony.

"There she is!" he said, a broad smile welcoming her, and she felt a rush of affection for him. She'd never known Pastor Tony to ever be either dismissive or judgmental.

"Hello, Pastor Tony! It's *wonderful* to see you!" Samantha was wearing a classic 'little black dress' that she filled with quite impressive female charm. Long blonde hair cascaded down behind her; she'd let it down during the drive up to Granite Sky and decided to just come to the party with it down. Woman that she was, she knew the effect she was having on some of the men. It pleased her; it fed her ego, and having just had her newly-built foundations shaken, she needed the affirmation. She was glad she'd dressed to kill.

"You look great!" the pastor cried, holding both her hands out, standing back and looking her over. "The big city girl comes to visit the country cousins. The city must agree with you." She twirled around, dress swirling in a silky, alluring trace.

"I ... I really love it. And the things we're doing, Pastor, oh, I cannot tell you how exciting things are. It feels like we're on the crest of something, oh, I don't know, like, *amazing*."

Tony's face took on a look of focused intensity. "I'm telling you, Samantha, that's just the sense I get, and a lot of others too. I was talking with Father Jourdain and he tells me that there is the same sense of, like you said, something exciting just over the horizon, about to break."

Sensing an ally, she asked tentatively, "So ... so what do you make of Mr. Ironbridge's talk tonight?"

The Pastor took her arm and they moved to a more secluded spot on the large warehouse floor. "I understand it. It's basically fear. Some people have a fixed way of looking at God and their relationship with Him and to consider that there might be other ways, or that their own ways might need to grow or evolve or change, well, for some folks—and they might be the smartest people in the world, and some of them are the best people you'll ever meet—for some folks the things to come are just plain too scary to think about. It's like the ground is moving under their feet, or its like they wake up one day and find the sky is green and the grass is blue."

"Do you think that's all it is ... fear?"

He looked at her. "Why ... is there something else you're thinking?"

"I don't know ... I mean, it's almost as if there's some kind of 'desire to control' going on, some effort to put himself up as a teacher. For him to make that kind of speech was sort of over-the-top presumption, wouldn't you say? Especially when there must be, what, at least four or five pastors here tonight? Seriously, why would he feel obligated to tell everyone how wrong they are?"

Pastor Tony thought for a moment as they walked toward one of the tables laden with food. "I've seen it before. A lot of people find the presence of a pastor or a minister or a priest almost irresistible, and they feel compelled to trot out their pet doctrine. I can't tell you how many times I get buttonholed at some social event by some lay person who's got some kind of theological bone to pick. It's his party, so I guess he felt entitled."

"Not very considerate."

"Perhaps not," Tony agreed. "But really, he's a nice guy, and he's got a great family. You should meet them."

"If you think so, I guess, sure," she replied uncertainly. Coming face to face with the person who had just shaken the foundations of her world wasn't something she particularly wanted to do, but doing what she was told was more a part of her nature than she cared to admit, so she let Pastor Tony lead her through the crowds, thinning now that the evening was getting on, to where Tack and Claire were sitting at a table talking with

Marcus and Marie-Clémence, Josh, Daria, Jed, Emma, and Abrielle, Mace, and Zoe. Most of the tables had been bussed and folded; most of the chairs folded up again and stacked in their rolling carts, ready to be returned to the caterers.

"Hey, folks, I want to introduce you to Samantha Gunderson." Tony's voice was bright and upbeat, and the group at the table turned to say hello. The men stood, which Daria still wasn't accustomed to. Tony introduced Samantha to Tack and then Claire, and Tack made the rest of the introductions. Josh pulled another folding chair over to the table and slid over to make room for Samantha.

"You in town long?" Jed asked.

"Just for about a week. I'm taking some time off to visit with my parents."

"Tony tells me you're working for a fairly large company out of Minneapolis."

"I am; at Guilder, Atchison, and Steckam, actually."

"The publishing company?" Josh asked.

"That's right, but they're much more than just a publishing company. They've become the largest Christian communications company in the world. Publishing, yes, but also television, radio, and we own the largest Christian film studio in existence right now."

"How long have you been working with them?" Josh asked again.

"A couple of years, actually, and it's still thrilling."

Marcus was across the table from her, taking her in, trying to get a sense of who she was beyond the surface glitz.

"What kinds of things do you do?" Daria asked.

Samantha didn't exactly know how to share with this group what Guilder, Atchison, and Steckam was all about, but then she decided to just throw caution to the winds. "I'm one of their senior editors, and my job is to track trends in Christianity to see what kind of books we should be publishing. Essentially my job is to make sure we're publishing books people want to read."

Tack turned to Samantha. "So ... and keep in mind I know nothing about the publishing business ... are you saying that you let what people think is the truth drive what you print?"

"Yes, because people tend to buy what they believe is true."

"So your goal is to sell books, not truth," Marcus said, getting a better picture of the type of woman who would work in such an environment.

"I know how that sounds, sure, but it's really not like that. What we publish influences a lot of people—I mean, a *lot* of people."

"I would think, then, that it would be even more important for your company to make sure that what you sell, what you push out to the public, would be truth."

"Yes, but really, what is truth? For you, it's one thing. You're very clear about what it is you believe to be the truth, but I've met people who are just as convinced that the things they believe are true."

The Ironbridge clan held their collective breath, since they'd all heard in Samantha's response the echo of Pontius Pilate's query from centuries ago, asking *'What is truth'* when Pilate was in fact standing before Truth Himself. They turned to Tack, as a group waiting for him to respond.

"Do you believe truth is relative?" Tack asked. Everyone around the table was quiet.

Tony Ponti jumped into the discussion. "I believe, and I think this is what

Samantha is saying, that we all perceive truth differently, sort of like the blind men touching different parts of the elephant. It was the same elephant, but they couldn't see all of it, just the part they could touch."

"That's it, that's what I mean!" Samantha exclaimed. "In fact I interviewed some people who were instrumental in helping the Emergent Church movement develop, and they said exactly the same thing."

"To compare those searching for truth to blind men ignores quite a bit of teaching in Scripture which tells us that while we are blind in the world, Jesus came to open our eyes so that we might see truth. 'We were blind, but now we see.'"

Samantha's inner spirit grimaced at Tack's bald assertion that he could see—that anyone, for that matter, could see truth in its fullness. It seemed to grate on her, and the comment from one of the Emergent Church leaders flashed into her consciousness: *'Anyone who says they can see is actually blind, and those who realize they're blind are the ones who truly see.'* But she didn't want to make such a confrontational statement, even though it was what she thought, for she was rapidly becoming a woman operating in the spirit of the world, in the spirit of lies. "Well," she said, compromising, "I understand what you're saying, but there are a lot of people who are not as convinced as you about where the truth really is, or what it is, and so we have to reach those people with the message of the gospel as well."

"But what gospel will you reach them with?" Claire asked. "Because someone is hungry does not mean one feeds them rancid milk."

Samantha didn't know how to react to Claire's blunt, confrontational statement, but it stirred her soul to anger. "I ... I really don't think we're feeding them rancid milk, Mrs. Ironbridge. I think we're doing the Lord's work in the world. People need to understand God, I think you'd agree with that, and I believe God is merciful enough to make himself known in different ways."

Marcus leaned over the table and said, "Samantha, I think what you're doing is misinterpreting how God applies His compassion and His mercy. Yes, God is merciful; He doesn't want anyone to go to hell. He wants every person to have a relationship with Him. He wants this so much that He let His own Son—the One who was a complete reflection of His own nature and personality—be degraded, shamed, spat upon, beaten, and then killed, because it was the only way ... the *only* way ... anyone would be able to stand in His presence. Only Jesus could pay the price for sin, the price required before God would accept us."

"Don't you think that's a little too black and white?" Tony Ponti asked.

Tack, taken aback that he would hear such a statement from a Baptist pastor, looked at him for a second, thinking perhaps he didn't understand. "What do you mean?"

"Well, Jesus died for our sins, I understand that, I get that, I've been preaching that for almost half my life. Yet sometimes I wonder if we've focused on that so much that we lose sight of how really merciful God can be, and that maybe we limit him when we say it just has to be through one path, or one person."

Tack was too stunned for a moment to reply, but Zoe pitched in from across the table. "Tack's not the one saying there's just one path to God; Jesus said that. He said *'No man comes to the Father but through Me.'* Pretty clear; and what Peter said through the Holy Spirit, about salvation coming only from Jesus, backs that up. I mean, if all these people you're interviewing can't read and believe what's in the Bible, then their argument is with

God, not with us."

"Honestly," Samantha said, frustrated at having Scripture constantly thrown at her, "I guess what I'm trying to say is that a lot of people are coming to a new understanding of what sin is and what we have to do to have a relationship with God. There are a lot of smart people out there who've done a lot of thinking about this—"

"And this isn't new," Ponti put in. "I talk to Father Jourdain a lot; we've gotten very close lately, and my understanding of how the Catholic church has looked at salvation—how they've always looked at salvation, going back to when the church first started, with the early church fathers—they were involved in a lot of things, a lot of things related to the deeper life that I think you're talking about when you refer to the Spirit."

"Not the same thing at all," Tack said with finality.

"Maybe, maybe not," Ponti demurred, "but what we're saying is that at least be open to the possibility that maybe some other folks want God just as much as you do. Maybe some other folks have an ability to hear from God, just like you do. Maybe," and here he paused, "maybe your truth isn't the only truth. Just, you know, have an open mind, that's all we're asking."

Tack sat without speaking for a moment, and those in his family waited to hear what he would say in reply. Somehow they knew it had to be Tack to answer this. Finally he looked up at Ponti and said, "Tony, I'm tempted to just nod my head and make some polite conversational extension that indicates we'll agree to disagree on this, but you know ... that wouldn't be true. I've been reading lately about how important it is for us to be true men, true souls, who not only recognize and speak factual truth, but also men whose lives themselves are true, who *walk* in the truth. So let me tell you, on this, we won't be able to 'agree to disagree'. And I'll tell you why. Because where you're going with this will end up either killing you or deceiving you so badly that you'll try and kill me and every one of my family here." Tack gestured around the table with an arm. "Because this ... this heresy you and your young lady friend are pushing isn't like some difference of opinion." He turned to face Samantha. "That's where you're mistaken, Samantha. You think these people you're interviewing just have different opinions about what truth is and where it is. But the problem is, truth is absolute. It isn't dependent on someone's opinion, and someone's opinion doesn't constitute truth. If I believe truly, sincerely and with all my being that a block of rat poison isn't harmful, because either I'm uninformed or because someone I respect has told me it's harmless, and I eat it, I'll die. If I believe truly, sincerely, and with all my being that I can fly because my friends all 'support me in whatever I want to do or be', or because someone I work with tells me I can, and I jump off a building, I'll get hurt ... or die. If you believe truly, sincerely, and with all your heart that Islam is a religion of peace and then you as a woman try and walk in Mecca or Baghdad or Mosul or Kabul or, for that matter, in Dearborn, Michigan, without a head covering, you'll learn very quickly that your sincerity of belief doesn't matter. Truth matters, don't you see? Truth isn't subjective; it isn't relative. You've chosen to agree with people who either don't know better," and here he threw a stern look at Tony Ponti, "or with people who actively know what they're doing and are intentionally deceiving you, or who themselves are utterly deceived and are just feeding you the Kool-Aid. Come out of it, Samantha ... come away from them, come stay with us for a while, learn what truth and righteousness and life and light and love really look like."

Samantha felt the pull of the Holy Spirit then, oh so strongly, and Tack's words were like hammer blows to her soul, waking her, working against the poison that had been leeching into her soul at Guilder, Atchison, and Steckam. And then, looking directly at her, taking her hand, Claire said, "Come out of that place, quit your job, Samantha. It's killing you."

When she heard the words *'quit your job'*, her heart suddenly froze and hardened. She pulled her hand back in a reflexive action that mirrored her soul's recoil from the spirit of Claire's words, for she loved her job. She loved the money and power and prestige it afforded. Those who want the world will, sadly, in the end, get it.

Marie-Clémence, not understanding the eternal import of what was transpiring between Tack and Samantha, let her eyes stray around the warehouse, wondering if any guests were still at the party. She was surprised to see that everyone not sitting around the table had gone, but then she saw Zoe standing next to Mace, leaning against his arm with one hand on his chest while Mace stared at the young woman in the black dress, tears running down his face.

Chapter 29
Daria

"As I live," declares the Lord God, "surely with a mighty hand and with an outstretched arm and with wrath poured out, I shall be king over you."

Ezekiel 20:33

Four days after the Ironbridge party, Marcus sat with Dag Wilson and Tom Custer in a tiny office in a rented hangar at the Granite Sky airport. Marcus thought it would be efficient to have his working space at the busiest transportation nexus in the area, so he'd rented one of the older hangars tucked away on the back part of the airport grounds.

Tom Custer had been the first one to arrive in Granite Sky, the day after the party, grudgingly impressed that USOCO's jet had in fact been there at the Sheridan County airport waiting for him at 0500 in the morning after Marcus' phone call. Marcus met him at the Granite Sky airport, outside of the baggage pickup area in an old white NMC pickup truck he'd borrowed from Josh Riesling.

Marcus got out of the truck and went around to greet Custer, who looked just as slim, fit, and strong as he'd remembered the last time he'd seen him, standing near the COP while Marcus was sitting in handcuffs looking through the window of a helicopter as the Marine Corps had relieved him of his command and flown him out of the Korengal after they'd learned about his war on Allah.

"It's good to see you again, Tom."

Custer stopped and held up a hand, which happened to be holding a thick black cigar. "Excuse me, Captain, and I know we're not working for the Green Machine any more, but if you don't mind, why don't I call you Captain and you call me First Sergeant?"

At first Marcus wondered about the propriety; they weren't, after all, in the military. But then a thought struck him: *'you will be; go with it.'* And then a follow-on thought came, and he said, "Well ... I'm not sure I can go along with that."

Custer looked at him with flinty eyes.

"See, for us to use military ranks with each other might imply to others that we're in some sort of military organization." Marcus held up a hand before Custer could interrupt. "But I'm okay with that. What I'm not okay with is the 'First Sergeant' part. We're starting something new here, and I've got a feeling that what we're starting will grow. You're here as the first man on the ground in this new unit, so from my point of view, if you don't mind, how about you call me Captain and I'll call you Sergeant Major?"

Custer looked at Ironbridge for just a second and then nodded slowly. "One of the things I've been thinking about since we last met was that if we ever got together again, I'd damn sure make certain to pay attention to any more hunches of yours. Sergeant Major it is." And 'Sergeant Major' Custer shook 'Captain' Ironbridge's hand.

"Let's get the most important thing up front," Marcus said. "Thank you for standing on your integrity and not denying what happened."

Custer chuckled then, which sounded like a small cement mixer turning a mix of dry gravel. "Hell, Captain, a whole lot o' good that did either you or me."

Marcus shook his head. "Actually, Sergeant Major, it does everyone a whole lot of good when we do the right thing, and you did the right thing. And if you want a practical proof of that ... here you stand."

"Hell, can't argue with that." Custer threw his bags in the back of Marcus' pickup and while they drove back into town, the Sergeant Major regaled the Captain with the story about how they'd interrogated him before his prosecution and dishonorable discharge. It wasn't a pleasant story.

Marcus first stopped off at a local hotel and had Custer check in to the room he'd reserved, drop off his bags, and then they moved on to the NMC office.

"Josh, meet Tom Custer."

Custer stuck the cigar in his mouth and stuck out a hand. "Call me Sergeant Major." Josh shook Custer's hand and looked sideways at Marcus, who just said, "He's been promoted."

***

Dag Wilson came in two days later. Sergeant Major Custer and Marcus were waiting for him at the same spot, this time in an old pickup truck Custer had found and purchased as the first vehicle in USOCO's northern Minnesota fleet. It wasn't pretty and it sounded more like a tank than a truck, and it had a habit of kicking up rocks, but it had a solid engine, no rust, and wasn't cluttered up with a mess of computer-controlled circuitry—all characteristics, the Sergeant Major commented, that reminded him of himself.

"Lieutenant, welcome to the outfit," Custer said, welcoming Wilson as he came through the door. It was raining, with a low ceiling of clouds, and the air smelled like a storm.

"First Sergeant, it's good to see you again."

"Yeah, well, actually," Custer said, throwing a glance over his shoulder toward Marcus, picking up Wilson's only bag, "it's Sergeant Major."

Dag looked at Marcus.

Custer hefted Wilson's bag like it was nothing and headed toward the truck "Rapid promotion in this outfit," he growled. "Let's go, we're burnin' daylight."

"Everyone's in on the ground floor," Marcus said, smiling, and shook Dag's hand. "Glad to have you here."

"Yeah, well, don't I know it," Wilson replied, with such a sense of blatant relief that both Custer and Ironbridge laughed.

"Been there, Lieutenant. Now let's see if we can make sure the Captain here stays out of trouble this time, okay?"

They all laughed, but then Wilson said, "You know, Fir—Sergeant Major, I'm pretty sure the Captain kept all of *us* out of trouble the last time."

"That may be, but one of the first things they teach you at Sergeant Major school is to not let your senior officers get too high up on their horse; gotta keep 'em honest."

Marcus smiled. "No worries about that, Sergeant Major, because I'm here to tell you both that it wasn't Captain Marcus Ironbridge that kept us all out of trouble in the Korengal. It was the God of Abraham, Isaac, and Jacob."

Boy howdy, Custer said to himself.

On the drive back, Custer, at the wheel, turned to Marcus and said, "I'm thinking the Lieutenant and I coulda' used a little of that protection afterwards, if you know what I mean."

"Not exactly. What do you mean?"

"You wanna tell 'em or should I, Lieutenant?"

Dag, sitting in the back, began in a dull monotone to tell the story. "Literally the day they lifted you out under lock and key ... uh, Captain ... one of our patrols was decimated. We lost eight guys in like, two minutes, and had another four wounded. The medevac helo that came in took an RPG in the tail rotor and crashed and everyone onboard was killed. Three days after that they hit us with a mortar attack, killed another ten and wounded fifteen. Eighteen days after that the position was overrun and we lost ... how many did we lose, Fir—Sergeant Major?"

"Forty-three. Worst casualty count the Green Machine's seen since they blew up the barracks in Beirut."

"That must have put the company down, like, to how many effectives?"

"Don't recall, because things got a little confused there for a few days," Custer replied. "Things were so bad that the Lieutenant here had to call in rounds on top of the position."

Marcus turned around to look at Dag, who was staring out the window, tears coming down his face. Custer went on. "We told everyone to get as low down and deep in their bunkers as they could and then the Lieutenant put in the call. It was the only thing that kept any of us alive." Custer looked up in the rear view mirror. "Believe it, Lieutenant. You had to do what you had to do."

Wilson coughed once in the back, cleared his throat, wiped the back of his arm across his face. "Yeah, well, I wonder about that."

Marcus turned around again, facing front, and pointed down toward the airport's main offices. "We need to go there," he said, and didn't say anything else.

They'd stopped off at the airport management office, and since Granite Sky's airport was so small, it didn't take them more than an hour to arrange to rent the old hangar with its surrounding concrete apron. They filled out the forms that would provide them the badges they'd need to get access to the airport grounds, and then they drove over to the old hangar with the keys to look over their new digs.

***

So it was that the three members of Kilo Company's old command team found themselves sitting in another tiny space in another country, together, wondering what would come about in the future.

Marcus was visibly upset at hearing about what had happened to his company. Custer carried on with the explanation. "Captain, the main reason we're here—the Lieutenant and I—is because we didn't tell the Corps what they wanted to hear. And the main reason we didn't do that was because we both believed you when you said it was God fighting our war out there."

"And the reason we believe that," Wilson said, "is because of what happened after you left. It was so tangible; it was like some kind of weird protective blanket had been taken away. You know, I talked to some of the survivors about the days right after you left, Captain, and every one of them told me they couldn't sleep at night after they yanked you because they had such terrible nightmares."

"Don't remind me," Custer growled in a low voice.

"And there was a story about one of the guys up on Restrepo that saw something moving across the position, something, I don't know, he said later that it didn't look human."

Marcus listened carefully, knowing that they were telling these things for a reason—or better, God was having them tell him at this time for a reason.

"So ... so you realized that there was something we were fighting against that wasn't in the natural realm."

"And both of us," Wilson said, nodding at the Sergeant Major, "just couldn't deny what we'd seen, both when you were there, but more importantly, after you'd left. Black and white; no question ... your God was there, fighting for us, keeping every one of us alive because—well, hell, I have no idea why, but it's something I want to ask you about. And then when you left, *bang*, it was like a light switch, and it was as if someone had unbarred the gates of hell."

"I didn't see what we were fighting, Captain," the Sergeant Major said, as seriously as Marcus had ever seen him. "And the reason I came back—I can't speak for the Lieutenant—but the reason *I* came back was to learn about just what this thing is you have with ... with God. You told me before things heated up over there, we were in your hooch one afternoon, and you said you could see the bullets that were coming at us, and I couldn't. Well, I didn't believe you then but I believe you now. So ... tell us what we gotta do to make sure we're on the winning side in whatever fight you got planned now."

Marcus gave Custer a blank look. "What fight is that, Sergeant Major? We're supposed to provide security for an oil company, that's all."

Dag Wilson stood up and walked over to the window that looked out over one of the runways and rubbed his hands against the grimy windowpane. "Captain, we know that's why you hired us but it's not why we're here. We know as well as you do that something is coming. My mother told me as much when she found out you'd called, before I left home to come out here. We just don't know what. But what the Sergeant Major and I saw in Afghanistan convinced us that we need to know who you know in this next fight, because we're not so sure who the good guys will be."

"What the Lieutenant is trying to say, I think, Captain, is that we're here to sign up to whatever fight your God of ... of Abraham, Isaac, and Jacob ... has planned."

***

With the realization that both men were actively seeking to know more about God, Marcus suggested that they both check out of their hotel rooms and put up in one of the cabins on the back of the property at the Ironbridge farm. The environment there was much better when it came to learning about the God of Abraham, Isaac, and Jacob.

"We can keep this office, use it when Billy Rob or someone else from corporate shows up, or when we need to talk to others ..."

"Like others we're going to be recruiting, I'm hoping," Custer opined.

"Right, like those others, but that comes a little later, Sergeant Major. As far as operational planning, and then determining how we'll set up the organization, Brewster's left that pretty much up to us, so the first order of business is for the three of us to figure out what we think we need to do—the mission—and then who we'll need on board, what resources we'll need, and how and where we'll need to do that mission."

"What's Brewster's biggest concern?" Dag asked.

"He has intel that a number of the foreign oil companies are bothered about the relative advantage U.S. companies have over the development of oil here. They may try to actively sabotage U.S. oil extraction or distribution operations, or they may try some other things, like terrorizing employees, low-grade cyber hacking to interrupt the distribution systems, or maybe something worse, attacking the extraction software itself."

"Can we stop those kinds of things?" Wilson asked.

"That's our job, Lieutenant," the Sergeant Major answered.

"I'm not so sure," Marcus said. "I've seen his intel. I want you both to look at the material as well. My analysis indicates something very different than the conclusions his people have drawn."

"So what's your take, sir?" Wilson asked.

"I'd rather you both look at the material before I give you my assessment. Give it a fresh look. Take a couple of days, chew on it, and tell me what you think. Then we can go from there."

***

From the day she'd visited the Ironbridge farm and returned with Josh, from the time she stepped out of the truck in the NMC parking lot on her return, Daria wasn't the same person. Had she been familiar with the poem, she would have recognized that the Hound of Heaven had been set upon her trail and she would find no rest for her soul until she confronted the Source of her disquiet.

That week she'd been irritable, short with Josh for no reason, and out of sorts, unable to focus. Her handler took her to task for the paucity of detail in her summary report on local conditions. She kept returning in her mind to that undeniable experience she'd had when she met Mace Ironbridge, that internal conflict, the sense of a twisting, a convulsing, a fight going on within her. Tack's speech at the party hadn't helped, but had only added to her confusion and sense of being displaced, the feeling that her world was shifting under her feet. She desperately tried to avoid Mace Ironbridge at the party, but there was one instance during which she'd been carrying on an intense conversation with Josh about Sharia law being imposed in four U.S. cities when she wasn't paying attention to who was around, and suddenly that feeling of intense internal conflict arose—the tugging, twisting, and pulling that felt as though her heart was almost being torn in two. She turned to see Mace behind her, smiling slightly at Josh, holding up his typing pad. *Welcome*, it said. Daria stood there, smiling weakly and trembling, until Mace moved off. Her palms were wet, and a line of perspiration formed across her brow in the cold evening air.

"You okay?" Josh asked.

"Fine, fine. What were we talking about?"

"You were saying it's the end of the U.S. Constitution as we know it, letting Sharia stand in U.S. jurisdiction." And off she went, picking up her argument, as Mace moved through the crowds, away from where she stood trembling like a leaf.

And now she found herself in the same truck with Josh again, heading out Friday afternoon for a weekend at the Ironbridge's farm. She was at her wit's end. She didn't know how she would survive the disorientation and internal conflict she was experiencing, but part of her also knew she couldn't stay away—she *had* to find out what was happening to her. She wasn't sure she would report this situation to her handler. How would she explain what she was beginning to believe were supernatural events? If she couldn't explain it to herself, how could she explain it to anyone else, much less to some cynical, hard-bitten, died-in-the-wool Israeli atheist with an uncle and two cousins who'd perished in the camps, who'd been controlling undercover agents for longer than she'd been alive?

Josh, sensing she was nervous, didn't say much on the drive out, another small consideration for which she wanted to scream at him, yelling for him not to be so damned sensitive and understanding and considerate. It drove her to further distraction.

They arrived at the farm in the late afternoon and again Claire greeted Daria with traditional French warmth, but also with a sense of tenderness, as though she sensed Daria was unsettled, wary, and tense. Zoe was there too, but Mace was in the barn, milking. Daria was relieved Mace wasn't there to greet them.

"Let's get you in and settled," Claire said, tucking Daria's arm in her own. "My, you must be freezing! We need to get something hot into you. Mace and Jed should be finished up soon. Emma and Abrielle are cooking tonight. Dinner should be in about an hour. Josh, Tack's in the barn if you want to talk with him."

Daria followed Claire into the main house while Josh, taking the broad hint, headed for the barn to find Tack.

***

There were quite a few around the table that Friday evening. The Ironbridges—Tack and Claire, Mace and Zoe, and Marcus; Marie-Clémence was there, as was Emma and Abrielle and Jed and Daria and Josh, and then too Dag Wilson and Tom Custer were there, accepting the invitation to eat with the family instead of downing something cold in their cabins.

Dinner that night was ... comfortable; that is to say, non-confrontational. Listening to the Spirit, both Tack and Marcus sensed that it wasn't quite the time to begin the discussion about the Holocaust with Daria. They could see she was wound as tight as a coiled spring and ready to snap.

As dinner ended, Claire stood up from the table. "Gentlemen, I wonder if you would do me a kindness and see to the dishes. I would like some time with a few of the ladies here. Emma, Abrielle, would you help the men? Marie-Clémence, Zoe, Daria, could you come with me over to the Carriage House?"

Surprised yet trusting that his wife knew what she was about, Tack led the men into the kitchen, where they all made short work of cleaning up the dinner dishes, wiping the table, sweeping the kitchen floor, and otherwise squaring the kitchen away.

***

Settled on one of the couches in Mace and Zoe's small apartment in the upper floor of the Carriage House, Claire looked at the women seated before her. "Ladies," she began, "I want you to tell me the one thing we all have in common."

Marie-Clémence looked confused. Daria sat, feeling somewhat hunted and tremulous, unsure of herself in the Ironbridge 'environment', but Zoe leaned back with her arms crossed, a look of assurance pasted on her face like a student who already knows the answer before the question is asked.

"We're all Jews," Zoe said finally, after a few uncomfortable seconds while Marie-Clémence and Daria pecked around for the answer to Claire's question.

"Jewish women," Claire added. "Right, Zoe. We are all Jewish women. Now I want to tell you something that Zoe knows, but which perhaps still eludes the two of you." Claire looked at Marie-Clémence and Daria. "Like most Jews in the world, you seem to have an allergic reaction to Jesus." Claire held up her hand, forestalling any inputs or disputation from either woman. "Yes, yes, don't deny it. Marie-Clémence, though Marcus has told me very little about the things you've talked about with him, I can tell that you and he are ... *être en désaccord* ... you are in opposition, *vous pas partager le point de vue*. What are the words in English, Zoe?"

"Not seeing eye-to-eye."

"Thank you."

"We're Jews, Claire. We're not supposed to see eye-to-eye with Christians," Daria said.

"And who says this?" Claire exclaimed suddenly with passion, slapping a hand down on her thigh, sitting up straight. "Upon what stone tablet is this written? You don't answer me? Of course you don't answer me, because there *is* no answer. Both of you, intelligent women, women of the world, women who have done many difficult or perhaps dangerous things, both so strong and brave, so able to move around in so many countries, and here, regarding one of the most important questions you will ever face in your life, you have decided to let some old tradition-bound haters form your opinions for you. *Bah!* Don't you have enough courage to form your own opinions? Don't you have enough nobility of character, or truth, or integrity, or discernment to face the facts on your own and then assess those facts and make up your own mind?" Marie-Clémence and Daria sat quietly, neither being inclined to interrupt.

"I will tell you both something," she went on in a thick rush of feeling, switching to French because she could best express herself in that language and because all three of the women there were fluent. She stood and began to pace the small room. "I have one son who is married to a Jewess. This was ordered by God—the God of Abraham, Isaac, and Jacob, mind you—and it was clear to anyone with eyes in their head from the moment those two met that God had ordained them to be husband and wife. Did Zoe complain when Mace spoke to her about Jesus? Did she immediately jump up, throw a fit, complain about centuries of mistreatment, or complain that Hitler was a Christian, or vomit up some other such foolishness? No. She listened to Mace and based upon what she heard—"

"And what I saw, and what he did for me," Zoe put in.

"Yes, thank you, Zoe, based on all that, this Jewish woman—who if you didn't know was accepted to Yale when she was just fifteen, so don't think she doesn't have a brain in her head—made a reasoned decision to commit her life to the Jewish Messiah." Claire held up her hand. "Argue with me later about whether Jesus is the Messiah or not, we will have time for that, I promise you. This is not what I am speaking to you about now. I am trying now to tell you that you do our people and our God a disservice when you willy-nilly follow rote tradition when you should be applying your mind and your heart to such questions, when you should be considering what you see and what is put before you, instead of instinctively reacting like some frightened, silly, unthinking animal that runs off at the first sign of something they've been taught all their lives was dangerous. You are *not* unthinking creatures," she said, pointing at both Marie-Clémence and Daria, "or at least you should not be. And I will tell you something else.

"You, Daria, you work with Josh. This is a fine young man; a finer young man you will be hard-pressed to find, and if you do not see that he thinks very highly of you, then you are blinder than you are appearing to be. And yet, there you sit, flinching away at the very mention of the name of Jesus only because this is something you've been taught. You can't even give a reasoned, valid explanation for why you do so. I do not know but I suspect you have raked him over the coals because of all the horrible things so-called Christians have done to Jews over the centuries. *Bah!* The people that would do such things to Jews are no more true Christians than the couch you're sitting on. I will tell you this: anyone who hates a Jew only because he is a Jew has nothing of the Spirit of God in them. But no, you and centuries and generations and millions of Jews would rather believe such utter foolishness than actually confront what that Jewish carpenter did and said in Jerusalem and throughout Israel so long ago. You won't even listen to our own prophets! They *told* us our Messiah would come; they *told* us we wouldn't recognize Him; they *told* us that those who did not recognize Him would kill him. Don't you see? You are falling into the trap that all our people have fallen into over the centuries. Our fathers were not open to what God said to them; they never have been.

"And it is not just Jesus our people are allergic to; our people have reacted with instinctive hatred toward anyone who comes with a message from the God of Abraham, Isaac, and Jacob, telling them that they are in sin, that they do not in fact know Him, and that they must turn away from their stiff-necked, stubborn, prideful lives—yes, lives full of, *choked* with pride—and turn to Him and obey and trust in and depend on and rely on Him. But no, what happened? Our fathers stoned or killed the prophets." She threw up her hands in frustration and intensity.

"But let me tell you this, ladies. We think very highly of Josh, and it would pain me to think that he would entertain a life-long relationship with a woman without courage. Yes, yes, don't look so shocked or offended, yes, that's you, Daria, instantly, instinctively rejecting Jesus just because you're Jewish. Such idiocy! Such…such *cowardice*!" Claire did not wait to see Daria's reaction, but turned to Marie-Clémence.

"And to you, Marie-Clémence, I say the same thing, only with even more of my heart. I know my oldest son, sometimes better than he knows himself, and he would *never* in a million years consider welding himself to a woman who would be so unthinking and cowardly as to dismiss any important issue without hearing the facts, without weighing the evidence; a woman so shallow, so cowardly as to make a decision because someone else told her it was the right thing to do.

"And make no mistake, ladies, at the bottom of your skittish reaction to Jesus, which you think is just because you're Jewish, is in fact a repugnance—yes, I use that word, it is an ugly word but it reflects an ugly truth—a repugnance to face your own sins, your own immorality, your own flawed human nature. At the bottom of things, it is not tradition or any type of reasoned intellectual arguments from centuries of Jewish scholarship that keeps you from confronting this ... no, all that is hogwash. It is purely and only the same thing that keeps every human being from facing God ... a desire not to put away our sin and to keep a death grip on control of own lives. Such mindless flight away from anything remotely connected with Jesus simply covers a hatred of actually considering the facts of the matter, and your reactions are an excuse that lets you evade the potential consequences that might come about if you actually had the courage to delve into the matter. You lack courage, so you hide behind centuries of tradition so as to disregard what you might discover."

Claire stopped pacing back and forth and looked at Marie-Clémence and Daria. She was flushed and intense and they could see she was on in the midst of a Gallic passion. "I am telling you both that each of you stands before a man who may one day love you and care for you and cherish you, perhaps give his life for you, and *neither* of you yet has shown the degree of courage such men deserve from their women, the courage this one here had," and she pointed to Zoe, "when she was *fifteen.* Yes, at fifteen she faced this question with an open mind and more importantly an open heart, and she made her decision ... not the decision her parents would have liked her to make, not the decision her tribe would have compelled her to make, not the decision centuries of Jewish tradition would have driven her to make, no ... she made her own decision., from her own heart!" Claire held a fist out in front of her, clenched, and then pulled it to her chest. "Such a gift stares you in the face! Do you realize how rare such love is these days? Do you realize what you may turn away from, simply because you react according to something your fathers taught you? Fathers who, you must not forget, hated God and wanted nothing to do with him? How long will you willfully choose not to see?"

Claire took a deep breath and then said, "Listen to me. I am not telling you that you should consider believing in Jesus as Messiah because it might get you a husband. That is not what I am saying. I am just saying that two men I know, one I know well and love, deserve at least women of courage, and I called you in here this evening to speak sternly to both of you, to chastise you for your foolishness, but also to encourage you both to be women of courage and integrity, to make your own decisions, to stand and walk forward into life without depending on something someone else may have told you."

Claire finished then, and after a few moments collected herself, turned to them, and said, "I am going to join my husband. I will let you three talk about what I've said. Tomorrow, I think Tack wants to talk about the Holocaust, Daria, as I think he mentioned to you a while ago. You would both do me a kindness if you would have the courage to listen to him. You should know by now that none of us here are about arm-twisting anyone to convert. This was not the way of the God of Abraham, Isaac, and Jacob; it is not Jesus' way; it will not be our way. But we have ... I suppose you could say some *particular* points of view relative to this horrible, horrible thing that happened to the Jews, so perhaps if you both have the moral strength to face this perspective and consider the information and then make your own conclusions, well, that would be nice." Claire turned and walked down the stairs, but paused on the top step, looked over her shoulder and said, "It would be ... courageous," and then walked downstairs and out into the darkening night.

***

After the morning milking, after the chores, after breakfast, after the kitchen was policed, Tack, Claire, Marcus, Mace, and Zoe sat down with Marie-Clémence, Daria, Josh, Jed, Emma, and Abrielle. Dag Wilson and Tom Custer were hunkered down, each in their own cabin, poring over the information Marcus had gathered from USOCO and supplemented with some of his own material.

Tack began right away, looking directly at Daria. "You remember you asked me about the Holocaust when you were here last, and I asked you to look into Deuteronomy 28?" He looked up and from Josh's reaction saw that they hadn't exactly gotten around to that. "Well, no matter, I've got the text right here." Tack opened the Bible by his hand and flipped it open to the 28th chapter of the Book of Deuteronomy. "It starts with

Moses talking to the children of Israel in the desert. The chapter gives a promise of either blessings or curses, based upon the degree to which the children of Israel would obey God. The description of the blessings and the curses are what I wanted to talk about. The blessings are plain, and you can read them another time. The curses are also very clear, and I want to read some of them to you as background to explain my answer to your question about the Holocaust.

"The curses Moses pronounces on Israel in the event they disobeyed God applied to both the city and the country, upon their vegetables and their bread, upon the health of their children, on their crops, and on their livestock. Basically the curse would affect their homes and hearths, their ability to generate a productive living, and upon their children—their future. But there was more. There is a promise that God would send curses, confusion, and rebuke upon everything the children of Israel would put their hand to, until they would be destroyed and come to sudden ruin. There would be a plague of diseases until they could no longer live in the land God gave to them. There would be wasting diseases, fever, inflammation, scorching heat, drought, blight, and mildew, all of which He said would plague them until they perished. He would withhold the rain from them, and the ground would become iron, the rain becoming instead dust and powder. But there was more. There was a promise that Israel would be defeated before her enemies; when they would attack enemies in unity, they would end up running away in seven different directions, their cohesion shattered. Jews would become a thing of horror to all the kingdoms on earth, and their carcasses would become food for all the birds and wild animals, and there would be no one to frighten them away. There is a promise that the Lord will drive them and the king they picked into exile, to a nation unknown to them or their ancestors. In that place Jews would worship other gods, gods of wood and stone. They would become a thing of horror, a byword and an object of ridicule among all the peoples where the Lord would drive them. It says that the foreigners who reside among them will rise above them higher and higher, but they will sink lower and lower. There is the promise that the Jews would become slaves. The nations over them will be the head, but the Jews will be the tail. It goes on with many more promised curses; it says that though Israel would be as numerous as the stars in the sky, they would instead be left but few in number, because they did not obey the Lord their God. Moses said that just as it pleased the Lord to make your people prosper and increase in number, so it will please him to ruin and destroy them. They would be uprooted from the land they were entering to possess.

"Moses pronounced these blessings and these curses upon the children of Israel just before they entered the land He had promised to give them." Tack looked at Marie-Clémence and Daria. "Read this chapter; look at the curses, and then tell me that such things haven't been a part of the history of the Jews if you can. I don't think you can. You'll see that almost every curse pronounced by Moses—not Jesus, but Moses—has come upon your people, and remains upon your people—and worse is coming.

"And so you ask me about the Holocaust. My answer? Consider that the Holocaust was a judgment, harsh, yes, but not as harsh as what will come ... a judgment upon the children of Israel because they rejected the Messiah that was sent to call them to repentance, to shake them out of their religious pride, to proclaim to them the favorable year of the Lord."

Had Claire not spoken to Marie-Clémence and Daria as she had the evening prior, Daria for sure, and perhaps Marie-Clémence as well, would have stood up and walked out and put their foot on the road back to Granite Sky, resolving never to come anywhere near the Ironbridge farm or speak to an Ironbridge again. But that didn't happen. Claire's words had made a piercing impact, and while they wrestled with Tack's supposition, considering it the height of insult to Judaism and Jews, they held their peace. Tack went on.

"A man once came up to Elie Wiesel—you know who he was, the famous author who wrote about the Holocaust—after Wiesel had given a speech. This man posed to Wiesel this very question I'm posing to you: *'To what degree would you consider the Holocaust to be simply a fulfillment of the prophecy made by Moses in Deuteronomy 28?'* Wiesel knew the text. But he turned to the man and dismissively, but also in a tone that showed he was disturbed, said, 'I ... I won't allow myself to even consider such a thing.' The noted scholar, the Nobel prize-winning author, the esteemed and honored professor *wouldn't even consider it.* He wouldn't let it into his calculus. He wouldn't even consider that perhaps God meant what He had said. He would not even consider that perhaps there was some sort of collective national or ethnic guilt lying so heavily upon the Jewish people and the Jewish nation, a guilt so damning, that the verdict, the judgment for that guilt would be so horrific. No, he wouldn't consider it, and neither would most Jews, because it would call into question too many things, it would shake too many prized, cherished Jewish traditions; it would shake too many Jewish habits and modes of thought ingrained over centuries."

"It would mean the Jews have been wrong about the most central thing that holds us together as a people," Daria said, with perceptive clarity.

Tack pointed a finger at her. "Exactly. You've put your finger on exactly what it would mean, and you've also identified why so few Jews would ever consider such a thing. It explains why any Jew that turns to Jesus in faith is considered a traitor to the Jewish people, because in effect such a decision, such a commitment, asserts what you described—that the Jews have been wrong about Jesus from the day He began His ministry until today. What Jew has the courage to tell the tribe they've been wrong for centuries? For really, what holds Jews together as a people is your traditions—an adherence to specific historic events, activities, a sequence of ceremonies and rituals, and a tribal agreement to interpret those historic events a certain way ... in ways that elevate themselves *even above God.*

"But we're not here to talk about whether Jesus is the Messiah or not. I am going to pointedly avoid talking to either of you about that. Marcus will not, nor will Josh either, I expect. We talked, and the four of us—Mace as well—have agreed that there is too much at stake to muddy up the water with talk. If a person can be talked into something, a person can be talked out of that same thing. So no, none of us will be talking to you about Jesus and whether He is the Messiah. Either He will speak to you directly, at which time you will know, and no one will ever convince you otherwise, or He won't, and you will continue on as you are."

"Then why this ... this background, as you said, about Jewish responsibility for the Holocaust?" Marie-Clémence asked.

"Because of what's to come," Tack replied. "It would take a number of weeks to go into all the Scriptures which make it clear, but what I want to tell you both is that there is another Holocaust coming upon the Jews, only this time it will not be localized to just one part of the world. No, it will be worldwide, and it will be so comprehensive and brutal that it will make the Holocaust that occurred during World War II look like a picnic."

"You can't be serious," Daria said, agitated now. "We've made a promise as a nation that nothing like the Holocaust will ever happen again. I can't see Israel letting such a thing happen, such a thing that you talk about."

"It will not be up to Israel. The first Holocaust wasn't Israel's choice either, yet it happened. This coming destruction will happen as well, and you should be aware that in your own Tanakh, in the writings of your own Jewish prophets in the Old Testament, there is a warning to the children of Israel to be careful about claiming in pride that such a thing would 'never again' occur." Tack picked up his Bible and began to thumb through it, but then Mace put his tablet in front of him. *Amos 9:10.* "Right," Tack said, and read from the text. "God is talking to Israel about a time of horrendous coming calamity, a time that hasn't happened yet, and Amos says that *'All the sinners of My people will die by the sword, Those who say, 'The calamity will not overtake or confront us.'* If this isn't a direct prophecy regarding the phrase 'Never Again', I don't know what is."

The two ladies sat unmoving, unnerved at hearing words from an old shepherd-prophet, an old *Jewish* shepherd-prophet, speaking to the times in which they were living with such accuracy. It bothered them.

"So I wouldn't put too much hope in Israel's ability to prevent what God has ordained will happen."

"Then okay," Marie-Clémence said, with rising emotion, "if what you say is going to come upon the Jews, and if what you say about the Jews rejecting this claimed Messiah is what you believe, then why would your son marry a Jewess, and why would your other son risk his own idiot neck to save another Jewess? For God's sake, *you* married one as well. And why are you entertaining two Jewesses here?" She turned a thumb to Daria. "Why don't you all just shoot us and fulfill these curses God made?"

The room grew silent as a tomb, and Tack looked up at Marie-Clémence with patient eyes. "Because God loves you," he said into the storm of silence. "The Jewish people are the very apple of His eye, and—yes, wait, I know that doesn't make sense to you, but just wait a minute. He loves them—He loves *you*—so He's done these things to wake you up, to get you to pay attention so that something worse doesn't befall you."

"Something worse than centuries of persecution, shame, murder, pogroms ... something worse than having six million of your relatives killed?" Daria asked.

"Yes," Tack said, on the heels of Daria's question. "Yes, exactly. What could be worse than losing your life here on earth? I'll tell you; spending eternity in hell, and worse, the *entire tribe* spending their lives in hell." Tack held up a hand to forestall another interruption from Marie-Clémence. "Yes, yes, I know you don't believe in an afterlife, but just because you don't believe in it doesn't mean that it doesn't exist, and if God exists, and if an afterlife exists, if *hell* exists, and if a people God loves for some reason choose to live in willful, intentional, foolish ignorance of the fact that hell is real, wouldn't it be the most merciful thing in the world for that God to take steps to try and get their attention?"

"You'd think the God of the Universe could think of a better way to get the attention of a people you say he loves than to let them be murdered," Daria said disdainfully.

Mace held up his hand and typed on his pad, then pushed it in front of Tack, who read out what Mace had written. *Psalm 78: When He killed them, then they sought Him, and returned and searched diligently for God, and they remembered that God was their rock, and the Most High God their Redeemer.*

Tack looked at Daria. "He tried all sorts of ways, Daria, but unfortunately, by the admission of your own prophets and poets and kings, the *only* way your people ever pay attention to Him is after you've been crushed, decimated, exiled, destroyed, burned like lime in a kiln, or in some other way brutalized by enemies. Only *then* do Jews cry out to Him in humility and lose their pride and consider that perhaps He knew what was best for them, and only *then* would they resolve to put away their sin—sin that was killing them, by the way, sins like cheating widows, afflicting the poor and needy, burning their children in fire as a sacrifice to false gods; sacrificing them to evil, demonic spirits, which today's society does medically, in the womb; people call it abortion.

"'Thou art a stiff-necked people,' the Lord said, but don't you see? He loves you. He is trying to speak to you, but unfortunately you yourselves are forcing Him to speak in a language of such painful historical events. The Holocaust wasn't the first time He tried to get your attention, nor was it the first time Israel as a nation and the Jews as a people were held accountable for their collective national sin. You know enough about your history to know that; you don't have to know anything about the Bible to know about the Diasporas, the deportations to Babylon, the crushing Roman occupation and then expulsion from the land Israel inherited from God. The Holocaust was just one event among so many others in your history."

"And each time we somehow come back as a nation," Marie-Clémence asserted stubbornly. "I know little about Christianity but I do know that most Christians consider the restoration of Israel to the land we'd been promised was a miracle of God."

"It was brought about by God, sure," Tack replied, "but for what purpose?"

"If most of you Christians are to be believed, it's because the Jews have to be back in the land before your Messiah returns."

"Most of what you might see as mainstream Christianity today is dead, Marie-Clémence. I wouldn't depend on what 'most of Christianity today' has to say. You can read clearly from another old Jewish prophet exactly why the Jews were permitted to come back to Israel in 1948 after being scattered all over the world."

Mace, running ahead of the discussion, foreseeing where it would go, again held up the tablet. *Ezekiel 22:20.* Tack turned to the passage and began to read. *"'As they gather silver and bronze and iron and lead and tin into the furnace to blow fire on it in order to melt it, so I will gather you in My anger and in My wrath and I will lay you there and melt you.'* This isn't talking about some horrific event in ancient history. He's referring to Israel in the last days. He's talking about something that hasn't happened yet."

Tack looked up at the two ladies. "This is God, speaking through Ezekiel, telling the Jews that in the end times, He himself will gather them together to burn them, to refine them. He says in other places that the sinners among His people will die. God brought your people back to the land in 1948 because He will bring a destruction on them there that will finally, *finally*, bring them to their knees. Your own prophet Zechariah said that after this coming destruction, some of your people will 'look on Him Whom they pierced'—referring to the Messiah—and then they will lament and be ashamed and mourn for Him as one would mourn for an only son.

"There is coming such a time for the Jews that one can only think about and shudder," Tack went on. "But God has specifically asked Gentiles who've put their trust in Him to care for the Jews in these times, to risk their very lives for the Jews. Jesus Himself asks this of us, do you understand? Do you want to know why Mace risked his life to save

Zoe? Do you want to know why Marcus risked his life to save Marie-Clémence?"

"He didn't even know I was Jewish!" Marie-Clémence exclaimed.

"More proof then. The Spirit of God knew, and drove Marcus to risk his life for one rebellious, God-hating Jewess. And why? Why are you sitting here now? Because God wants you to know that in the times to come, only those Jews who turn to Him will survive."

"And by 'turning to Him', you mean acceding to the fact that Jesus was, is, the Messiah."

"Not just acceding to a collection of facts, no, and we are not talking about intellectual assent here. I promise you, because I know the nature of God, that He would not have put you here if He wasn't going to make Himself manifest to you, and when that happens, in each one of your lives, in the way He chooses for each one of you, then you will have a choice to make. Will you fall down on that rock and be broken, or will you resist Him, and one day have that rock fall on you and crush you to dust? When He makes Himself known to you—and only you will know when that is—then you will either acknowledge that He is Who He said He is, or you will continue on in your rejection of Him. You will each bear the consequences of your decision.

"But I am here to tell you that the reason my sons, my wife, and I are here on this farm is for one purpose, and one purpose only. For those Jews who God brings to our doorstep, we will risk our lives to keep them alive."

Daria threw up her hands at that. "And for God's sake, why on earth would you do such a thing after all the things you've told us that we horrible, sinful Jews have done?"

"*Precisely* for God's sake," Tack shot back. "And make no mistake. All those charges I laid at the feet of the Jews can be laid at the foot of every human being—the Jews are basically humanity writ large. They are the distillation of the best and the worst in human nature. But why we would risk our lives for the Jews? Because first, God has promised that the Jews as a people would not perish from the earth. If Satan kills every Jew, he proves God a liar. Jesus said those who put their trust in Him and obey Him would be His body on earth, so as His body, we work to uphold God's promises made to your people by striving to keep alive those Jews God has commended to our care. There won't be many, by the way. And second, God has said that those Jews who *do* repent, who *do* acknowledge Jesus as the Messiah, will be for the world such a blessing as no one can at this point imagine.

"We are here on this farm to provide a place where Jews will be able to survive the times to come. We—we Ironbridges—are willing to give up our lives to save even one Jew. Jesus, the Holy One of Israel, is coming to rule and reign on David's throne, and He will be the Keeper of Israel. We will give up our lives if He requires it of us to make sure the remnant of His people are alive to see Him when He returns."

***

The rest of the weekend was spent in quiet personal discussions. Marcus took Marie-Clémence on a long walk Saturday afternoon, talking about what Tack had discussed. Josh and Daria did the same, walking into the forest by themselves. For Josh it was a major shift in perspective. He'd been steeped in the standard Christian teaching that taught nothing bad would ever happen to Israel again, that they would be victorious over the armies of Gog and Magog, and that Christians would be gone before anything difficult would come upon them.

Daria was disturbed. Had it been a month ago, she would have dismissed Tack's premise out-of-hand, but she had experienced some strange things lately, things that were throwing her preconceived notions—and her most cherished hopes for the future—out of whack.

Before both couples had stepped off into the wilderness trails, Tack had given them a list of Scriptures to review. Surprising as it was, neither Marie-Clémence nor Daria resisted the effort Marcus and Josh made to read through and try and grasp what Tack had described about Israel's future. There were no miraculous conversions; the veil was still there and their resistance strong, but they had taken Claire's admonition to listen and process and react based on the facts presented, for both wanted to be courageous women. And for Marie-Clémence at least, in whom God had already begun to make Himself evident through her physical healing, such things were beginning to come to a point where she could no longer dismiss them as mere 'differences of religious opinion'.

While the two couples were gone, Tack sat with Jed, Emma, and Abrielle, and walked them through the Scriptures that showed clearly what was going to happen. For Emma, who'd been raised in a home where her father was the fount of all knowledge and wisdom and who unfortunately had an undercurrent of distaste for Jews in general, it wasn't anything she'd ever heard about. For Abrielle, coming from an agnostic home and then tucked away in a community of Anabaptists where nothing is really spoken of regarding eschatology, this was a surprise as well. And for Jed, he also, like Josh, had just gone along with conventional Christian teaching about what would happen to the Jews in the end times. To realize that there was a coming devastation upon the Jewish people that would eclipse what happened in the Holocaust and that there was a clearly-expressed duty for Christians to protect the Jew in these end times, perhaps to risk their own lives ... such things were a revelation.

***

The Monday after what Daria facetiously called the 'Come to Jesus' weekend at the Ironbridges, when Tack had shared with them his assessment of what would happen to Israel in the future, Marcus, Dag Wilson, and Tom Custer sat around the kitchen table in Dag Wilson's cabin with the USOCO intelligence materials spread about.

"Look," Marcus began. "I'm not convinced the Intel adds up *just* to a threat against USOCO operations. There are some other things we need to look at."

"Such as?" Wilson asked.

"Such as the fact that you've got the major oil companies from Russia and China here, in northern Minnesota, working together; the fact that Russia and China have a non-aggression treaty and a mutual defense treaty, which means one won't attack the other, and if anyone attacks either, the other party must come to the attacked party's defense. There have been a number of meetings between Chinese and Russian diplomats, engineers, military leaders, and senior political leadership for the last several years. China is working with Russia to wean the world away from the petrodollar and make the Yuan the world's reserve currency, which would completely tank the American economy."

The Sergeant Major rolled his cigar around his mouth and then said, "Yeah, sir, but what does all that have to do with this little piece of northern Minnesota and us protecting USOCO oil operations?"

"If the threat was just foreign oil companies trying to sabotage our operations, okay, sure, we would work out strategies to try and prevent those activities. But I think it's worse than that."

Wilson looked at Custer, and they both looked at Marcus. "We obviously didn't pick up what you picked up when we looked through this stuff, Captain. What is it we're missing?"

Marcus opened his computer and pulled up Google Earth. He turned the screen so they both could see. "I think China is going to invade the U.S.," he said. "They'll hit us on the west coast. When that happens, Russia will come in as a sort of 'defender', a 'peace-keeping force' if you will, because I am not sure how much of the U.S. military will be left, nor I am sure how much of the U.S. as a whole will be functional."

"Now, Captain," the Sergeant Major said, "if I hadn't seen what I saw in Afghanistan, with your war on Allah ... well, I'd say you're a few bricks shy of a load. But I'm not gonna say that anymore. At least this old dog can learn some new tricks. What makes you say so?"

"A lot of things," Marcus said, and then, tentatively, "but mainly it's the Spirit. For some reason I keep recalling World War II, when the Germans and Russians were, for a time, allies. They carved up Poland between them, which both Germany and Russia thought might be troublesome to them in the future, because both had future plans and having a large functional nation with a huge, well-trained Polish military on their borders made them uncomfortable. So they both conspired to make Poland go away. They made a non-aggression treaty and then when Germany hit Poland from the west, Russia hit Poland from the east in the guise of 'stabilizing' things.

"I think China will hit us on the west coast and if they intend to split up the country, then I think China will get the western half, to about here," Marcus pointed to the middle of the country, a line down from Minnesota to Louisiana, "and Russia will take the eastern half. China wants land."

"What do the Russians want?" Dag asked.

"Well, the first thing they want is a free hand operating in the Middle East, and they'll never have that while the U.S. has a functional military. But more importantly, Russia wants people."

"Well hell, why will they start a war then?" Custer exclaimed.

"I don't think Russia will start it," Marcus said. "China will start it. We'll go to war with China over something minor over in the Pacific and that conflict will roar back toward us and China will come screaming in and take pretty much most of the western half of the country. I mean, they own quite a bit of our debt already, and they may simply consider that they're coming to collect on that debt. You buy a car and don't pay the loan, pretty soon the collection agency will send some big bruiser, maybe beat you up, and take your car back.

"No, China will start it, and Russia will come in, probably over through the Arctic, here," Marcus pointed out the likely route over the Arctic circle, down through Canada, "and then, through probably North Dakota or here." He pointed to the state of Minnesota.

Wilson looked at the screen. "Why would they want to come through Minnesota when North Dakota is so much flatter, there are no trees, and it's pretty much an open route all the way south?"

"They may," Marcus said. "Those are all good reasons. But what I suspect is that somehow the Russians and the Chinese have already parceled up the country and the dividing line will be something like what's between North and South Korea now, some kind of 'fake demilitarized zone' where it's like a buffer area. It doesn't belong to either one of them, and it's there to separate the two halves of the country."

"Sounds like a waste of land to me," Dag put in. "Why do that?"

"I'm not sure they'll do that," Marcus replied, "but if they do, then the only thing I can think of that they might use that buffer zone area for would be for ... for the 'disposal' of U.S. citizens who they won't find useful in the new arrangement."

Custer rolled his cigar animatedly. "I still don't see what information USOCO gave us led you to come up with that scenario."

"It wasn't so much what they gave us, Sergeant Major. It was a combination of things. First, I know this country is under judgment. We've thumbed our noses at God for so long, in so many ways, that He won't be long in administering what this nation has coming. Second, I know that God said in the Bible that judgment would come upon the church first, and as I see the massive amount of deception and delusion that is happening within the mainstream church today, I can't come to any other conclusion than that this is judgment; that God Himself has sent them a deluding influence, because, as the Scripture says, 'they refused to love the truth.' Third, a number of people I trust have seen visions about what is coming to this country. But most importantly, the thing that most convinces me that something like this is going to happen, is what our President is doing now"

"What's that?" Dag asked.

"He's carving up Israel," Marcus replied. "America is forcing Israel to accept the famous 'two-state' solution, to in effect split their country in half. Well, I think that's what's going to happen to us. We don't have long, and when things happen here, America will no longer be a functional nation.

"And then I see USOCO's Intel that says they have Chinese agents moving throughout most of the west coast cities where there are refineries; that they've seen Russians scouting most of our nuclear power plant locations. This report here," Marcus said, holding up a file, "describes how the Russians are strengthening both their logistics bases and their military forces in the Arctic. I mean, seriously, why the Arctic? Are there a lot of people up there?"

"Is there oil up there?" Custer asked.

"If there is, no one's found it yet," Marcus replied. "At least, that's what this ... where did it go ... yeah, here it is. That's what this report says." Marcus pulled out a couple of sheets of paper stapled together. "This is from a guy USOCO has in Norway, and they're up around there with the Russians, like, all the time. If there was oil up there, you can bet that Norway, Sweden, and yeah, the U.S., would be all over that."

"Well then, what's our mission? I mean, we're three mean hombres and all, but I don't think the three of us and whoever else that crazy Texan can rustle up will do much to hold off, hell, I dunno, a hundred million screamin' Chinamen and God knows how many Russians."

"Sergeant Major, you put your finger on how we need to approach things. I think our first phase is to ensure that USOCO's current operations are safe. That's something we're obligated to do, no matter what scenario we see coming in the future. We keep them safely working for as long as we can—at least, before China and Russia do what I think they'll do."

"Check; understand that. But what do we do when what you say will happen happens?" Wilson asked.

"We stand up an insurgency," the Sergeant Major said, "until the U.S. gets back up on its feet and the cavalry comes over the hill."

Marcus looked at Wilson and Custer and then closed his computer and sat back in his chair. "Sergeant Major, it would be nice if what you said was an option, but I'm pretty sure there won't be any cavalry coming over the hill, and I'm also pretty sure America won't ever be a nation again."

Custer looked pensive, struggling to accept Marcus's assertion.

"Well, sir," Wilson said quietly, "if this country is on the way out, and what you say is going to happen happens, what exactly should we be doing?"

"Have I told you about what God requires of Christians in the last days ... I mean, relative to protecting people?"

"This more of what your God is talking to you about?" Custer put in.

"It is, Sergeant Major. God is very specific about what He wants His people to be doing."

Sergeant Major Custer pulled the cigar out of his mouth and looked at the two other men. "Before you answer the Lieutenant's question, Captain, when do you think this will happen? Anything in that material tell you that?"

"No," Marcus said. "Nothing in here says that, but I did get from one Believer, someone I trust, that when the U.S. turns our back on Israel and either permits or forces that nation to be divided, like what we're doing right now—very, very soon after that—we're going to see the same thing happen to America."

"Well hell, I didn't believe you the last time you told me something like that, but I ain't gonna make the same mistake twice. So what exactly are we supposed to be doing when the excrement impacts the rotating aerator?"

Chapter 30

Cold Water Parables
A Blog from the Lakes of Minnesota
by Mace Ironbridge

The Wisdom Shop
- The Blind Shall See -

A smallish, mousy woman with stooped shoulders, straggling dishwater-blonde hair tucked under a nondescript hat, and a tentative, hesitant step pushed open the door to the Wisdom Shop. She stepped across the threshold and looked in.

"Excuse me," she said, "but are you open?"

"We are, Madam," came the reply. "Please do come in."

"Oh, yes, thank you. Very kind. What a nice little shop! Oh, my," she exclaimed as she looked around, "perhaps not so little after all. Goodness," she said, craning her head round here and there, "why, I don't think I can see all the way to the back of your shop, actually. Though perhaps it's the light?"

"You've come to find something to help you see," the Proprietor, Mr. Invia, stated.

"What? No, I just mentioned that I couldn't really see to the end of ... your ... the end of your aisle there ... actually," she said, apologetically pointing into the back of the shop, her sentence drifting off into uncertainty.

"You've heard my daughter then," Mr. Invia said.

"Your daughter? Why, I'm sure I don't know to whom you refer."

"Tall girl, dark hair done simply with a strand of pearls, sapphire blue dress, good voice."

"Oh! Oh, yes, *that* woman! Why yes, she gave me this, actually," and the mousy woman pulled out one of the shimmering silken flyers for the Wisdom Shop, with the logo of golden apples set in silver.

"The very one," the Proprietor said.

"I suppose you want this back? It looks to be quite valuable."

"No, no, please do keep it, we have an abundance."

"Oh, well then, thank you."

"You would like to see more clearly."

"Pardon?"

"I believe you've come to the shop for something to help you see more clearly ... see people more clearly, to be precise."

"Oh! But I can't recall mentioning ... but, now that you mention it ...

I suppose it would be nice to be able to see a little more clearly these days. Can't see how anyone would object to that, the city getting so big, and so many new and different types of people rambling about."

"Precisely," Mr. Invia replied. "Mr. Verum, if you would please?"

A tall man came down one of the long aisles, materializing almost out of nowhere. "Of course, sir. Madam, if you would be so kind, please follow me?"

"Certainly, I suppose, then, you want me to ... to go back *there*?"

"All perfectly safe," Mr. Verum said, extending his arm, which the young woman seized.

"Marjorie," she said briskly, almost in a gasp, "Marjorie Wellbrin."

"A pleasure, Ms. Wellbrin. Mind the stack there."

They walked down a very long aisle until Mr. Verum stopped and bent down, looking at one of the lower shelves. "Ah, here it is." He pulled a small box from the shelf, blew the dust from its top, and showed it to Marjorie. "Here you have one of two components to what you are seeking, Ms. Wellbrin. The other, I believe, is just along this way."

"Oh, thank you, I suppose ..."

"And we'll come along down this way for a small bit," Mr. Verum said conversationally. "Tell us a little about yourself."

"Oh, there's nothing to tell." Mr. Verum looked at her then, and she suddenly felt as though perhaps there was, so she went on. "Though perhaps you wouldn't know it to look at me now, I once had a rather promising career."

"A career?" Mr. Verum said, encouraging her to continue.

"Yes, I was a ... a writer. I've published a few books actually, and then one very popular book, all about Christianity." She looked around as she walked down the long aisle and she saw books on shelves. "Perhaps you have it in stock?"

"We do, actually, yes, although perhaps you wouldn't recognize it."

"That's strange. Why wouldn't I recognize my own book?"

"Because, you see, everything that comes into the shop and goes onto the shelves for sale is re-packaged. As you see," he said, and pointed to the small box he was carrying, the one part of two that Ms. Wellbrin was seeking.

"Yes, I see," she said, looking around, and as she moved along she saw that each item, though of vastly different sizes, were all wrapped in the same silky golden fabric the flyers were made from, with silver ribbons around the boxes, and three small golden apples where normally a bow would be.

"And so you would see simply something rectangular in shape, wrapped thusly, " Mr. Verum said, indicating the items on the shelves.

"Ah, I see, yes, well," she said.

"And so, you're a writer," Mr. Verum prompted.

"Yes, of course, my apologies, so yes, there I was, having just sold a remarkably popular book on some of the newer emerging truths of Christianity, and then along comes, well, I suppose one might say a rather handsome, dashing young man who quite admired my work. And wouldn't you know it, he works for my publishing house and he's been assigned as my personal agent."

"Dashing," Mr. Verum repeated.

"Yes, oh, my, quite so. He has a wonderful job and lives in the best part of the city and he thinks so much of my work."

"Are things ... progressing?"

Marjorie blushed slightly and coughed slightly once. "Ah, well, yes they are, actually. He's expressed himself quite ardently."

"Ah," Mr. Verum said. "And if I may ask, what type of work is your most recent publication?"

Marjorie brightened, like all authors do when they discuss their work. "An exploration into how each of us is becoming like unto God," Ms. Wellbrin replied with a faraway voice she adopted when she wanted to sound religious. "Oh, the raptures I enjoyed, writing that work! The insights, the spirit guides I met on days when I found myself struggling to get the words down, I cannot express to you." Mr. Verum made no comment.

"You see, in Christianity today, Mr ... Mr. Verum, isn't it? Yes, in Christianity today, Mr. Verum, why, you cannot imagine how things are changing. Basic, fundamental truths are being reworked, their real essences recovered by the ancient mystics that, if we can believe what we are being shown in the spirit realms, once worked with the Early Church Fathers themselves! The very concept and practice of prayer is returning to its ancient roots. We can center ourselves, cleanse and empty our minds so that they can be filled with the glory and brightness of a perfect understanding of God!"

"An understanding of the Infinite?" Mr. Verum queried, but Ms. Wellbrin did not hear him. She was in full throat.

"And as society changes, as mankind evolves, that which was once truth is now evolving into some amazingly deep areas."

"And the old truths?" Mr. Verum asked.

"Oh, those! I've been convinced by the people I've spoken with that those are quite passé, and best left to the past. Emily especially has given me quite a convincing summary that puts paid to those, I can assure you."

"Emily?"

"Oh, yes, my apologies, Emily ... Emily is my, well, how shall I describe her? She's been a friend since college days, you know, and she's become a very famous professor of Women's Studies at one of the leading universities here in the city."

"Is her husband of the same opinion about the ... the 'old' truths?"

Marjorie turned and looked at Mr. Verum while they were walking, she still holding his arm. "Why, strange that you should ask, Mr. Verum, but truth be told, she doesn't exactly have what most people would term a 'husband.' She's actually the husband, if you know what I mean, and her companion, a very fine and gentle woman named Elizabeth, is her wife. They both care very much for each other, and Emily has been one of my most ardent supporters through the years. Elizabeth must not have a jealous bone in her body!"

"I see," Mr. Verum replied dryly. "Ah, here we are. If you'd be so kind as to wait here, I need to ascend into the upper reaches, as you see." He pointed at the ladder that leaned against the shelf and seemed to go impossibly high and upward out of sight. Ms. Wellbrin looked up and up and still couldn't see the topmost shelf.

"Oh, yes, if you must, of course, I'll wait here," she replied meekly.

Mr. Verum climbed up and up and then seemed to disappear from her sight until not thirty seconds later he appeared at her elbow. She gave a little start.

"There is only one way up, Ms. Wellbrin, but there are many ways down. Here you are." Mr. Verum handed her a small box about the size of a glass case—in fact, that is exactly what it was, wrapped in golden silk and with the logo of golden apples in settings of silver on the top of the box.

"This seems a bit ... a bit small," she said tentatively.

"They're glasses; that's the case, and the glasses are inside the case."

"Glasses?"

"Yes. They will help you see."

"Oh, Mr. Verum, I do apologize, and I don't know what I've said to make you think that my eyesight is less than perfect, but I really can see quite well. There, now, take that book-sized thing about, what, ten yards away? I can read out the letters on the cover for you, just hold on now, it says—"

"Excuse me, Ms. Wellbrin, but these glasses are not intended to accommodate for a lack of visual acuity. They will help you see *people* more clearly."

"I ... I'm not sure I understand."

"Permit me to explain. To obtain the benefit of the product you are considering purchasing, you must take from the first box and eat a portion of what you find in it."

"It *does* remind one of a box of candy," she said.

"Just so. After eating what you are told to eat from it in the morning, you then proceed into your day, and at any time during that day you put on these glasses, you will see the people around you more clearly."

"But ... but Mr. Verum, I *do* see them clearly. I mean, I *never* bump into people—I'm really not that clumsy, you know. I'm quite confused."

Mr. Verum paused for a moment and then took Marjorie's hand. "The products we sell here in this shop work in ways that sometimes our customers do not understand at first. Those customers who choose to follow the instructions we send home with them, however, find that their products provide exactly what they need. Sometimes, my dear Ms. Wellbrin, I must confess, our customers themselves are not quite so sure about what they need.

"And would you believe, there are as well other customers who exchange significant value for our products and yet, when they take them home, do not follow the instructions at all, and therefore get no benefit from the products. They end up quite disillusioned with both the product they purchased and the shop and, I fear, Mr. Invia, Mr. Vita, and myself."

"Oh dear," Marjorie exclaimed.

"Even though through it all, through the entire lifecycle of the product, we are always here to immediately answer any questions they might have. We have a 24/7/365 support hotline, constantly open." He proffered a beautifully embossed business card.

Marjorie did not hear this last bit of wisdom, as she was attempting to process what Mr. Verum had shared with her about people paying for things but not following the instructions. This was anathema to Marjorie, for of all things, Marjorie Wellbrin wanted to please. She wanted to do well. She wanted to be well thought of also, but most importantly wanted to make sure that she was doing things right, and most certainly, most adamantly, wanted to make sure she was in no way offending anyone.

So as not to offend Mr. Verum, she accepted the small glass case wrapped in golden silk, placed it with the other box, took his business car, and smiled up at him. "Thank you very much."

***

Three days later, Ms. Wellbrin appeared again at the door of the shop just as the shop opened, the very first customer. Trembling, she pushed the door open and entered, looking about for the Proprietor.

"Welcome back, Ms. Wellbrin." Mr. Invia stood at her elbow.

Marjorie turned with alacrity. "Mr. Invia, yes ... nice to see you again." She nodded her head and found it hard to look him in the eyes. "I'm terribly sorry if I'm early, and I can come back if you like, but ... I mean ... I *am* glad you're here, and ... well, might I have a moment?"

"But of course," Mr. Invia replied gently. "You are more than welcome. If you'll come this way, we've a small niche tucked away. We can have a cup of tea if you like."

"Of all things," she replied. "I'm parched."

Marjorie sat while Mr. Invia adjusted a number of old copper implements and he soon set out two cups with their saucers, a pot of tea, smaller pots of cream and honey, and a plate of small cakes, fruit, and mints. The china all had that interesting little logo of the golden apples with silver threads wound round about.

"Oh, please, don't go to any much trouble on my account, please, Mr. Invia!"

"No trouble at all," he answered, smiling slightly. "It is not often we get customers coming back to the shop so soon. Something unique has arrested your attention." Again, a statement instead of a question: Mr. Invia poured Marjorie a cup, then one for himself, and sat down. "So now then, tell me all about it."

Marjorie took up one of the small cakes, nibbled at the edge, and then, eyes widening with amazement and delight, took a larger bite. "Ummm," she said, mouth full, "this is amazingly delightful! I'm suddenly famished!"

"Home recipe," Mr. Invia replied. "Very old; been in the family for, well, quite a long time."

"Well it's angelic, I can tell you."

"We think so."

Marjorie devoured the rest of her little cake, took another sip of the tea and plucked a small piece of fruit from the plate. She began to pick at the fabric of her sleeve.

"You needn't be nervous, Ms. Wellbrin."

"Oh, Mr. Invia, it's not nervousness, it's ... it's an almost crushing realization about what a *fool* I've been! An absolute *fool*!"

"Perhaps you'd better explain."

"So Mr. Verum sold me ... do you know, I'm not exactly sure what one would call what he sold me, but—"

"We put down 'Perception and Discernment' on the invoice."

Marjorie took a start at that, but then smiled slowly. "Yes, yes, I see, yes, that's *exactly* what you sold me. Strange name for a box and a pair of glasses, but now that you mention it, I couldn't think of one better."

Mr. Invia nodded and made a gesture for her to continue.

"Well, I took ... 'Perception and Discernment' home and the next morning opened the box and followed the instructions. As you probably know there were all sorts of delicacies there, and so I just picked one, as the instructions said—they were quite clear that one could pick any selection from the box—and popped it into my mouth."

"And how did it taste?" Mr. Invia asked.

"The strangest thing," she began, "is that it was rather sweet in my mouth but very shortly thereafter I'm sorry to say, it became bitter in my stomach."

"Precisely how it should taste ... very good so far."

Marjorie looked somewhat surprised but pleased. "Ah, well then ... so, as Mr. Verum had instructed, I went on into my day. That day," she said, "I was scheduled to meet with Geoffrey, my agent and, well, I'm ashamed to say it now ..."

"Your paramour," Mr. Invia finished for her.

"Just so, but at the time, mind you," she said, "most assuredly not now." She took a bite of a small purple fruit. "We began our meeting that morning and the subject was my next book. It's been, oh, maybe, what, ten months since my first book came out and the sales have been just smashing but the House has been on about when I'll be starting on my next book, you see, and so this is what the meeting was all about."

"I understand, yes," Mr. Invia replied, and refreshed her cup with a blend that smelled of honey and wildflowers.

"And so Geoffrey began to get on about the need for a first-time author to hit the next book very hard and very quick, you know, but, well, I just haven't had the motivation I had for the first, do you see? And Geoffrey was going on in such a fashion and I really couldn't understand what he was so bothered about when the thought suddenly popped into my head that perhaps I might just try on Mr. Verum's glasses, as a distraction, you understand, something to keep me occupied while Geoffrey was ranting, and, well, maybe to see what might be behind his concerns." She paused and then looked at Mr. Invia with large eyes. "And you cannot imagine what happened next!"

"Perhaps ... perhaps not, but please, go on."

"Well perhaps you can, this is such a strange place. But anyway, so on the glasses come and I turn to face Geoffrey, since he'd just been about to discuss another first-time writer that had come to grief because he'd delayed his second book when I just gasped out loud, I was so startled!"

"Yes? From what?"

"Why, from what Geoffrey looked like! I mean, when we'd started the meeting he'd had on a very dashing gray herringbone blazer, a maroon shirt, and dark gray trousers. I notice these things, you know, Mr. Invia, it's something I do."

"Yes, quite natural."

"But when I looked at him with the glasses on, oh, the change!"

"What did he look like through the glasses?"

"I was utterly shocked, and to tell you the truth, not a little bit frightened. You see, Geoffrey was—is—was, I don' know, always quite a handsome man, but the face I saw looking at me at that table was horrible; lean, cadaverous, pinched, ravenous, and ... and *rapacious*. Yes, rapacious! I could see him slavering, and there was drool, and when I looked at his mouth, oh, there were such teeth, like a wolf or some sort of deranged beast! His complexion had become dusky, flushed ... a dark, blood red color. When he held up one of his hands, I saw not flesh but hair, with claws. I can tell you I had the dickens of a time not to scream."

"Perhaps you have not come to the place in the manual that says the product tends to protect first-time users from the reactions that ensue upon their first viewings."

"Oh, well, yes, you're quite right, I haven't gotten to that part yet, but I am so glad you've installed that feature because it would have been quite impossible to try and explain to Geoffrey why I was gaping at him.

"And there was another thing; as he began to talk I began to actually feel his words. They were like bludgeons hitting me; it's hard to explain, I know. I felt his words like blows, but they were doing me no harm. Some words I felt as stabs, almost, and whenever he looked at me I felt a piercing, a ravening, a sense of being grasped at, of being devoured, as though bites of me were flying off here and there."

"It must have been dreadful."

"I haven't told you the half of it. Well, it began to dawn on me that... and please don't think this strange, but it began to dawn on me that I was beginning to see what Geoffrey actually was, underneath, if you know what I mean."

"You mean his inner man, his soul?"

"Yes, quite exactly that. You don't think it strange?"

"It is one of the benefits of the product."

"Well it's a benefit, I can tell you, because at that very moment I stood up, told the entire staff there at the House that I would not be publishing my next book with them, and walked out."

"Quite a decision," Mr. Invia remarked quietly.

"But understandable, you see, because as I'd been listening to Geoffrey rant, I'd been looking around the conference table at the gathered staff, and oh my, what I saw! There was the Chief Financial Officer at the end of the table, and he was covered in, I can only describe it as 'slime'; he looked like a human slug. There were three senior editors there and one looked like a snake, actually; I actually saw a forked tongue dart from his mouth. The other two looked horrid—they looked like they'd been dead for a year, rotting in their graves. I could smell them, and it was revolting, they stank of death. And then I looked at the Managing Director and was stunned! He looked as though he must have weighed four hundred pounds, layers of fat covered him, and there was encrusted filth and a horrible green substance oozing from, well, from not very nice places. He was disgusting! I couldn't stand it any longer, so I left."

"A wise decision, if I may say so," Mr. Invia answered. "It sounds quite traumatic."

"I'm not finished, sadly," she said. "Because I immediately called my friend, Emily. I don't know if I've mentioned Emily to you—"

"We know Emily," Mr. Invia replied in a somewhat darkened tone.

"And so I called and said I needed to see her immediately, and so I went right to her house from the meeting."

"She was home?"

"She was."

"And did you still have your glasses on?"

"No, it was such a shock to see the staff that I took them off as I ran from the room."

"I see."

"So I went to Emily's apartment and I talked to her about what had happened and initially she was ever so understanding. She began to hint that perhaps my spirit guides were 'working overtime' or some such thing, allowing me to see the truth about people.

"I told her that I didn't think that was the case—you see, I hadn't told her about the glasses—and just before I was going to tell her, another thought popped into my head suddenly, much like that morning, and it compelled me to don those glasses once again to look at Emily."

"Propitious, such thoughts."

"Oh my yes. And so I put them on and was stunned and sickened to see Emily as ... as she apparently is."

"And what did she look like?"

"Why, she looked like some sinuous, death-like black and green wormy thing. It ... she was disgusting! Teeth like fangs, hair that was truly like tiny writhing snakes, and where her breath emanated from what looked like a maw, everything withered before it. She too was slavering, like Geoffrey, and her saliva would hit the floor and I would see it bubble and burn through the carpet like acid. But the strangest thing was that I saw several other, oh, much more horrible creatures all around her and everywhere in the apartment, sitting on things like tables, lamps, and chairs. Some were perched on the wall itself. They were horrid, scaled, winged things, chattering, ranting, scrabbling at themselves or each other, and I was shocked to see one or another of them constantly fly off the wall or the lamp or table where they were perched and land on Emily's shoulder, claws digging into the black and green scales. Apparently Emily never noticed, not even when there were two or three of them on her back at once. She went into the other room to make tea, I suppose, but by then I was too horrified to consider staying. I think I did scream, actually. That's when the horrible winged things saw me and recognized that I could see them. Oh, that was a moment, I can tell you. I was so frightened that I began to remove the glasses, I suppose wondering if I could see those things with my own eyes, and also wondering if perhaps I removed them and couldn't see those things any longer, perhaps they wouldn't really be there."

"I can assure you, Marjorie, that removing the glasses would have been one of the most dangerous things you could have done at that point. Did you not read that part of the manual?"

"No, but I will tell you that you're absolutely correct, for when I reached up to the frames and was about to pull them off I suddenly heard Mr. Verum's voice in my head, saying that should I remove the glasses, I would be quite defenseless."

"Mr. Verum has always been quite faithful in providing constant product support."

"Well I can tell you I will be eternally grateful, and if he is in today, I would like to express my gratitude personally."

"I can call him now if you like."

"No, no, actually, there's more to tell. The worst parts, actually, but I'm compelled to share them with you."

"Go on then."

"Well, I literally ran screaming out of Emily's apartment and when I got home I was a nervous wreck. I put the glasses back in their case and set the case on top of the box by my bedside and spent the rest of the day in bed, trembling."

"I see."

"And then I woke up the next morning and, I confess, I was tempted not to take another bite from the box, but I must tell you, as I was lying in bed the previous day I'd called Mr. Verum and had a talk with him and he referred me to the place in the instruction manual that mentioned that the glasses combined with what was in the box would show one the true natures, the inner souls, of the people one looked at. Well, I couldn't deny it. I'd seen what Geoffrey looked like and I'd seen what Emily truly was, and those horrid things with her in her apartment, but there was something nagging at me that morning, and so I took another selection from the box and then...then I took up my first book, the one I'm so famous for, and began to read."

"Ah," said Mr. Invia.

"Yes, well, the truth leaped off the pages at me in ways that struck me with such a loathing that words cannot express—a loathing of *myself*, Mr.

Invia, do you understand? For I saw what those words were! They were like dainty morsels, almost a replica of the tiny little things that were in my box, but I could tell they were counterfeit, and as I watched, I saw little moving pictures of events that were happening as people would read my book, and the words would go into them and twist their hearts and cut out their eyes—yes, my words would blind people to the truth, I now understand—and I saw pictures of men and women, young and old, eating up the words of my book like they were candy and then it was as if time was rolled rapidly forward and they would begin dying from the inside, poisoned, their hearts turning to stone, and then they would begin to choke and then they would die, spewing their insides out, foaming at the mouth in anger, shaking their fist at ... at someone, I couldn't see who.

"Oh Mr. Invia, one look at my book through those glasses made me so horrified at what I'd done, I'm desperate! What can I do to undo this? I don't know any other word for what my book is than 'evil'. What can I do to take back those words?"

"Before we talk about that, dear woman, was this the worst thing you saw?"

Marjorie hung her head then, but after a moment shook it slowly, slightly. Mr. Invia waited.

"No," came the whisper. "That was not ... that was not the worst."

"Tell me the worst."

She began to tremble again, and Mr. Invia watched as great tears began to drop down onto her hands clutched together in her lap. She reached for a napkin—of golden silk, oddly enough—and touched it to her eyes, but the tears would not stop.

"You can tell me the worst," Invia encouraged.

She took another deep breath and through the sobs, said, "When I looked in the mirror with the glasses on ... that ... that was the worst ... the *worst.*"

Mr. Invia waited patiently.

"I saw a woman staring back at me. This woman ... she had several different faces at once; I can't describe it any better than that. One face was like a hardened, debauched slut; another had the face of a timid, fearful child; another face looked for all the world like the face of greed—hungry, ravenously hungry, yet fat, but never satisfied; another face, oh, Mr. Invia, it was horrible... this other face was someone who looked so disgustingly pleased with herself while at the same time her features were covered in the blood of those she'd killed and devoured. Oh, Mr. Invia, I don't know what to do. I was—I *am*—so horrid!" And she put her face in her hands and sobbed, groaning, keening in pain at the realization of her own true nature.

"And now, dear woman, let us talk about what you can do now that you have seen what you needed to see."

PART 4
Delusions

Then that lawless one will be revealed whom the Lord will slay with the breath of His mouth and bring to an end by the appearance of His coming; that is, the one whose coming is in accord with the activity of Satan, with all power and signs and false wonders, and with all the deception of wickedness for those who perish, because they did not receive the love of the truth so as to be saved. For this reason God will send upon them a deluding influence so that they will believe what is false, in order that they all may be judged who did not believe the truth, but took pleasure in wickedness.

2 Thessalonians 2:8-12

Chapter 31
Tony

"They will make you outcasts from the synagogue, but an hour is coming for everyone who kills you to think that he is offering service to God. These things they will do because they have not known the Father or Me."

John 16:2-3

I was thinking about the Ironbridge's soiree they'd put on for the town to welcome their oldest son back to the community when Penny called and asked when I was coming home.

"I'm on my way."

"Okay, well dinner's in the freezer. I've got a meeting tonight at the bank; we're implementing a new accounting system, and it's turning out to be a mess."

"Right, okay, I'll see you when you get home."

I hung up the phone and stood up and put on my coat, and as I was cleaning up my desk, I saw a picture of the church family we'd had taken, oh, it must have been fifteen years ago. I looked at the picture and was struck with the blessings God had provided for the church in these people. Certain individuals stood out, though.

Eva Gunderson was there in the picture, looking tall and thin. This was right about the time she'd gone through her divorce. She had divorced Sven Gunderson, her husband, about the time the picture was taken. She told me back then that he just wasn't sitting right with her, and she'd tried getting him into church, but there just wasn't any life left in the marriage and so they decided to just wrap it up. Eva carried on like a trooper, though, and the whole church family had been there to support her when things were tough early on, especially for the kids.

Samantha, the oldest, had left Granite Sky some years ago to make her fortune in the Christian publishing world, and she'd made her mother proud by landing an amazing job with the world's largest Christian communications company, working out of Minneapolis. She was back in town at the moment, visiting with her parents before traveling off to who knows where. I'd seen her at the Ironbridge's party; she looked great, and her job was working out great for her as well.

Johnny was next, Johnny Gunderson, named after Eva's brother who'd died in a logging accident when he was twenty-three. Johnny was now sixteen, very intelligent and obedient and tall and strong like his father had been, and he was developing a real interest in the church. We were having him teach the young kids' bible study.

Allison was Eva's youngest; she was fifteen, just coming into high school. She was different somehow, more shy and reserved, almost fearful, although she was developing into a beautiful girl.

Eva was the mainstay of the church. She was everywhere, heading up the bake sales or fund raisers, scheduling who would teach what class, who would be giving the announcements, even bringing in the occasional worship singers who might be traveling through. She was always upbeat, always happy, and her kids were a superb example to the other families in the church. She was a blessing.

I saw Gary and Sharon Fielding in the picture, Gary looking young and thin, with massively broad shoulders and a narrow waist, and Sharon with the long blonde hair she'd had back then. Gary was the police chief in town then; still is. They'd never been able to have children, but that didn't stop them from participating in the church's activities. Sharon especially liked teaching the younger kids, and Gary would faithfully attend each of the men's bible studies we had before the formal church service would begin. He'd been a Marine in his younger days, though I don't think he saw any combat, and when he got out he went into law enforcement. He was a strong guy, and whenever we had any building projects or lawn work or some other type of activity that required heavy lifting, he was the first guy I called.

I sometimes wondered if Sharon was ill with some kind of recurring disease, because there were times over the years, Sundays I mean, when only Gary would show up at church. It seemed Sharon wasn't all that healthy, and she'd get these 'spells' he called them, where she just had to lie down in a dark room. Gary was thinking it was something hereditary, because Sharon's mother had had severe migraine headaches, and Sharon had them as well when she'd been young, but they thought she would grow out of them. It isn't turning out that way, and it was getting worse as the years went on. Back when this picture was taken she might have missed, I don't know, maybe one Sunday in twenty; lately she was missing something like one Sunday in eight, and then if Penny or I called to say we'd be over to visit, to see how she was, she or Gary would be polite but firm and say that she'd get better faster if she could just lie still in a dark room without any talk or visitors. So ... anyway, thinking about it, I jotted her name down on the prayer list I kept at my elbow, hoping that maybe God would do something for her.

I remembered the first time I'd met them. They came to one of our outreach events, I think it was like the second Christmas I'd been here, and we were having a Christmas Eve party at the church. Come to think of it that was the first time I'd met Father Jourdain, too. So Gary came in and Sharon came walking in behind him. He looked around, sort of scoping the place out, and I came up and shook his hand and welcomed him to the church and asked if they were worshipping anywhere in town at the moment.

"We've been going to—"

Gary's head snapped around at Sharon, who'd started to answer me, and she sort of shrunk back slightly, but he just smiled and said no, they weren't going anywhere special, and they were actually kind of looking for a church home. They were such a good-looking couple, and with Gary's experience in the Marines, and then in law enforcement, he provided some real stability to our church family. There were times when I'd send some of the younger husbands over to Gary for marriage counseling when things weren't going so well. Sharon sort of fell into the role of reading the announcements each week, and she seemed to like that, and everyone was praying that she would get over those intermittent spells she was having.

And then there were the Magnusson's, Rollie and Estelle. In the picture they were the ones at the end, the tallest couple in the church. Rollie was young and thin in the picture, and Estelle was young and not so thin in the picture. Nothing had changed. They were in their mid-forties, I guess, their kids all grown up and gone, and Rollie was about the best piano player in northern Minnesota. We felt blessed to have him, because occasionally he'd cut loose with some of his talent and we'd all just sit there, rockin' out—it was amazing. Estelle, though, she was, of all the women in the church, probably the most spiritual, and the one I turned to the most whenever I had questions about things.

Rollie sold tractors at the John Deere dealership downtown, and Estelle ran a personal health and massage business. She'd had, oh, it must have been dozens of members from the church come in for one reason or another over the years—a sore back, torn muscles, spines out of alignment, and she would really do them all some good. For the last twenty years she's been practicing a particular massage technique called Reiki, and it was just amazing. I threw out my back two years ago and she eased the pain to the point where I could function again. She was one of just a few Reiki 'masters'—apparently that was some sort of certification they issued—in northern Minnesota. So she was helpful there with the church family for our physical ailments, but her real blessing to the church was how she looked at the realm of the spirit.

She started teaching a class in *Lectio Divina*, which was a prayer technique I'd never heard of, but when I mentioned it at the monthly pastor's meeting we had in town, several of the pastors had heard about it, and Father Jourdain gave me some fascinating books to read, which is where I learned how powerful and beneficial the technique can be. I saw some of the folks in her class make amazing spiritual progress, and soon they were the ones that began to branch out and start their own little classes for the church family on contemplative and centering prayer. We've got, I don't know, something like twenty or thirty people in the Contemplative Prayer class, and maybe fifty or so studying Centering Prayer. The classes are amazing, and it's really focusing everyone on spiritual things a lot more. If it didn't sound so hokey, I'd say the church overall is coming into a new level of awareness about the realm of the spirit—which is, I suppose, what should be happening in a church, right?

I looked again at the picture, all those people there from so long ago, most of us still in the church family, still plowing on, doing God's work. I considered all these people I have in this church family a blessing. I sort of stand back and let them run and make sure I support them, and it's amazing to see how God is blessing them and us.

***

Three days later I called Father Jourdain, and we arranged to meet in town. There was something bothering me, something that wasn't sitting quite right about the Ironbridge party.

We sat down at Walter's the next day and I started right in, sharing about some of the things that were bothering me.

"Father, you were there so I don't need to tell you about Tack's speech. I don't know how you held it together. He didn't have very much good to say about Catholicism."

"We've both heard it before," Jourdain replied dismissively. I admired his restraint. Aloysius Jourdain was a tall, thin, athletic man, young to be a parish priest, but I could tell he was also scintillatingly intelligent. He was a Jesuit, so I suppose that would make sense. I read somewhere that Jesuits were sort of the brainy bunch when it came to priests. He had short sandy hair and blue eyes, and (Penny tells me) if he had not been a priest he would have been number one on a very short list kept by mothers looking for eligible potential husbands for their eligible daughters.

"Yeah, true, but what is it that bothers me so much?"

"Was it his way of implying only his truth was valid?" Jourdain asked.

I pressed my lips together in thought. "No, I don't think that was it, although that was irritating."

"How about the threats regarding how things might get bad in the country?"

"Nah, he's just talking through his tinfoil hat on that. Lots of people are thinking that now, over at the 'church of the moonbat.com'." Jourdain chuckled. "No, I think it was sort of the way he tried to brainwash Samantha. Yeah, that was it. The kid's just been hired by that big firm down in Minneapolis, she's ready to eat up the world, and what do the Ironbridges do but try and convince her to quit her job and hole up with them at their compound."

"Sounds sort of radical," Jourdain opined.

"Yeah, but also, I think ... sort of mean."

"In what way?"

"Small of them, actually; mean-spirited, as though the poor kid shouldn't have an opinion unless it came from them."

Jourdain sat with his hands folded together on the tabletop and was lost in thought for a long few moments. I sipped my coffee. Walter serves great coffee.

"I think ... I think it might benefit you to visit a friend of mine," he said.

"Yeah, who would that be?"

"I want you to come with me the next time I go to Chicago, to visit my Provincial."

I looked at Aloysius; he wasn't smiling. "You're serious."

"I am, very much. There are things he could share with you that would, I don't know, set your mind at ease, help you understand a little better about the dynamic you're seeing with people like the Ironbridges."

"There aren't many like the Ironbridges," I replied.

"Fortunately, yes—"

"But what would your Provincial ... it's the Very Reverend Father Provincial Thomas R. Grummond, isn't it? Why would he want to talk with me? Seriously, your Provincial is pretty high up in your organization, isn't he?"

"He is, yes. He actually reports to the curia in Rome."

"Whoa, Rome! What would he want to talk to *me* about?"

Jourdain leaned forward in the booth. "Tony, you've been a pastor up here for more than twenty years. You know just about everyone in northern Minnesota, and more importantly, you know where they stand spiritually. You've got your finger on the spiritual pulse of this area, and if anything, your opinions about what is happening spiritually up here would be of great interest to the Provincial. But also," he continued, "he can share things with you that I can't—things I think you'll want to know.

***

I'd been back from my visit with the Provincial for three days, and I desperately needed to talk to someone. I couldn't talk to Penny. She wasn't around much, what with the new position she'd taken with the bank, and she never seemed interested in church things anyway. I was going back and forth and then the thought struck me—probably from God—that maybe Samantha Gunderson might be interested in the discussion I'd had with the Jesuits. And maybe she might be able to shed some light on the things I'd learned.

So I called and fortunately she was visiting her folks for the weekend, home with her parents. It was a Saturday, and she normally spent the weekends in the city, but I suspect God wanted us to have this discussion. We agreed to meet at the church.

She came into the church office about an hour after I called, wearing a great-looking fleece pullover and jeans, and while on the surface she seemed upbeat and enthusiastic, I sensed an undercurrent of disquiet, almost a sadness or a wondering, almost as if she was lost, or looking for something, or had lost something. I wondered what was bothering her.

She settled into one of the chairs in my office and we sat down each with a cup of coffee. "So Samantha, let me start right in by telling you that my weekend in Chicago with the Provincial was probably the most influential, motivating event that's happened to me in my entire Christian life."

"Whoa! That's fantastic!" she exclaimed. "You've *got* to tell me everything!"

"So first of all, they flew me into Chicago and put me up in the Renaissance, on the river in downtown Chicago."

"Oh yeah, I know that place, it's *gorgeous.* Dominique—our CEO—she stays there occasionally and we put up our principals, board members, and important guests there whenever we have meetings in Chicago."

"I can tell you, I was blown away. Here's some dinky pastor from the backwoods in Minnesota being treated almost like royalty. I mean, the suite they put me in was bigger than the bottom floor of my entire house!"

Samantha laughed, and I could tell she was impressed. I'd been impressed as well.

"And then it turns out that the Provincial, a Father Grummond, had just returned from a meeting of the Joint Working Group between the Roman Catholic Church and the World Council of Churches."

Samantha's eyes grew wide. "You're *joking*!" she said, amazed. "That's like, the main group working on the ecumenical movement in the world!"

"No, seriously, and that's what he wanted to talk to me about."

"Was Father Jourdain there with you?"

"He was, and there was another guy, a Father Petasch, from the Czech Republic. He was the guy Grummond reports to; he works in the Curia in Rome."

"Whoa," she exclaimed. "You were talking with some pretty amazing company."

I shook my head. "I was as amazed as you are," I replied. "But I was even more amazed by what they shared with me." Samantha sat, enlivened now, looked eager, happy, and interested. There wasn't a shred of that shadow I'd seen when she first came into the office. "So ... so what did they have to say?" she asked, laughing.

"So yeah, like, you probably know more about this than I do, working where you do. What do you know about the ecumenical movement?"

She sat back in her chair. "Yeah, okay, we've dealt with a lot of the players from that, and we've put out a lot of articles lately about where it's going, what it's objectives are, that kind of thing. Basically it's a movement that started, formally, back in 1910, out of Edinburgh if you can believe that. The Episcopal Church was involved heavily in starting it, and it was sort of under the radar for a long time, but when the Second Vatican Council came along, things began to heat up. Pope John XXIII established something called the 'Secretariat for Promoting Christian Unity' as a sort of preparatory document or commission for the Council, and one of its first responsibilities was to advise the Pope on how to move forward and integrate other churches and those from other religious communities."

I looked at her with surprise. "How do you know all this?"

She laughed again; I liked her laugh. "Ah, it's nothing. I had to edit an article we did on the movement, like, two weeks ago, and it's all still in my memory. It's pretty amazing, how the Catholic Church and the World Council of Churches have been steadily over the years just plugging away, trying to quietly bring about unity among the world's religions. I think that is one of the most noble causes anyone can work toward."

Sitting there with the very attractive young lady whose interests mirrored my own, I couldn't help but agree with her, and it made me want to be part of that noble cause.

"We might be able to work together to bring that about," I said.

"No way!" she cried, surprised.

"Seriously; they wanted to set up communications between me—my church, here—and the Provincial's headquarters in Chicago, and they want Father Jourdain and I to work closely together to further the objectives of the Joint Working Group." I was sort of hoping this would impress her, and it did.

"That's amazing!" she exclaimed. "What do they want you to do?"

"Actually, nothing more than what I'm doing now—just keeping an eye on the spiritual pulse of things in this area. And this is where I think you can help. You're in touch with a lot of the new things happening in the world spiritually, and if we could work together on this, we could provide the Provincial with a lot of solid information and maybe help bring about the unity we're all looking for."

She looked thoughtful for a moment. "I can do that," she said, after a few quiet moments. "Yeah, I mean, why not? But what exactly are they looking for? What kind of information will help them?"

"Here," I said, and I handed her a brochure they'd given me in Chicago. "It's sort of a summary of the last working group's notes, and I think we can help them with this part right here." I pointed to a passage in the brochure. "Here are notes from their assessment of the status of the ecumenical movement in 2005. It says that in general things are going well, but it points out where one of the key hindrances are." I showed her the passage, which said:

> "On the one hand, we gratefully acknowledge the good fruits of the ecumenical dialogue, particularly the rediscovery of Christian brotherhood among the members of the different Christian communities, which no longer consider each other as enemies or competitors but as brothers and sisters in Christ on the common pilgrimage towards full communion. On the other hand, we cannot overlook the theological, political and institutional critique of the ecumenical movement, which comes not only from so-called fundamentalist groups but from some venerable old churches and serious theologians as well. For some of them ecumenism has become a negative term, equivalent to syncretism, doctrinal relativism and indifferentism."[31]

31 This is text taken from a presentation at the event marking the 40th anniversary of the Joint Working Group between the Roman Catholic Church and the World Council of Churches, which, if readers are interested and have access to the ancient Internet archives, may be found here: https://www.oikoumene.org/en/resources/documents/commissions/jwg-rcc-wcc/the-ecumenical-movement-in-the-21st-century.

"And here," I said, pulling out another brochure, "are the most recent notes from the Joint Working Group. I'll summarize for you and just tell you that they've very strongly established a solid theological basis for spiritual ecumenism in their work, and it's something I'm going to be reading over in the next few days. But what they say also is that the main obstacle left to real unity is still so-called 'fundamentalists'."

Samantha seemed to identify with that. "Based on what I'm seeing around the world and the inputs and mail we get at work, I'd have to agree with them. The fundamentalists just can't move forward," she said. "They're stuck on blind support for Israel, they're stuck on opposing most of what we're seeing are new, powerful movements of God, and they just can't get past the whole homosexual thing."

"They're stuck on an ancient way of looking at truth," I replied. "They're not getting the fact that God loves everyone, that God wants to reach everyone, and that God will do whatever he needs to do to reach even the strangest, most out-of-the-way, unconventional 'sinner'. They just don't get that."

"And that's probably why they identify those folks as obstacles, wouldn't you say?" she asked?

"Absolutely. They—I mean, the Roman Catholic Church—have been fighting this battle for, well, since the Reformation, and the more I study things out, the more I'm beginning to see that while Martin Luther may have had a few original thoughts, the upshot of the Reformation has been nothing but disunity, factionalism, and hatred. Look, Samantha," I said, "remember I told you that this meeting was the most important thing to happen in my ministry? It's because for the first time I feel like I can be part of something, a part of a movement that will do something that really matters in the world, in people's lives. They want me—me, Tony Ponti, backwoods pastor—to be part of the great call to 'Come home to Mother Church.' I sometimes can't believe it."

"So … what do they want you to do?"

"Just to keep in eye out for where fundamentalism might be growing," I answered, "or where there might be particularly troublesome fundamentalists that would work in the spiritual realm against the move toward unity. To share with them who those people might be, what they're doing, and what kind of a threat I think they might be to the greater ecumenical movement."

She sat there, nodding her head, and I could tell she understood just what I was feeling. "That would be … yeah, I can see where that would be helpful," she said, and with that, I saw the shadow reappear on her face.

"Hey, Samantha, what's wrong? I know something's bothering you. What is it?"

She hesitated; "I don't want to burden you with silly stuff," she replied.

"No way, Samantha, now, seriously, tell me what it is. Maybe I can help."

She shuffled in her seat and then came out with it. "Well, you're talking about fundamentalists, and it's just that, ever since that party, the speech Ironbridge made, and then the discussion we had afterwards … I mean, I stand by what I believe, and I truly think those people are sort of, I don't know, 'off the wall' I guess you could say, but it … it bothers me."

I suddenly felt vindicated, as though my initial sense of how Ironbridge was off had been confirmed by Samantha's disquiet, and it made me angry that Ironbridge's arrogant theology would throw this poor kid into a spiritual tailspin.

I stood up out of my chair and walked around the desk and sat on the desk's edge, closer to Samantha. "Look, Samantha, you can't let those kind of people get to you."

"I know, I know, but if you want to know the truth, the reason I'm home this weekend was, well, I just felt like I had to get away from the city. Can't say why; I just wanted to be near home."

I looked into her eyes and said, as seriously as I could, "Maybe it was because God knew I needed to talk to you, and He also wanted you to talk to me."

She looked up at me and I was surprised to see tears in her eyes. "Oh, I hope that's why. It's the only thing that makes sense to me."

"Samantha, these kind of people—like the Ironbridges, I mean—they will hammer at you and throw all kinds of Bible verses around, but what they don't have is love. They don't get it. They're missing everything about what God wants for his people; he wants us to love and support and care for each other." I reached out a hand and put it reassuringly on her shoulder, and she covered my hand with hers.

"I cannot tell you how much I needed to hear that," she said, a little breathlessly.

I reached up and wiped a tear from her cheek.

Historian's Note: America and Israel

There have been throughout history many ways the King sought to garner man's attention and arrest his headlong flight toward folly. Few were as obvious or so hard to ignore as the incredible series of direct cause-and-effect events that occurred when a nation opposed Israel in some way. America pressured Israel to divide her God-given land prior to and during the years covered by this history. Wherever America reached out its political hand to interfere with Israel's freedom, it was struck with natural disasters. When American presidents hosted international conferences to adjust Israel's borders, America itself was struck with record storms, causing enormous economic damage, leaving hundreds of thousands of Americans homeless. On the very day America committed some grievous national sin by entertaining political initiatives to rip land from Israel, earthquakes would strike America. When a renowned Palestinian terrorist set foot on American soil at the invitation of an American president, record-breaking tornadoes devastated large sections of the American Midwest. When this terrorist departed America, the storms immediately ceased. When America reached out its political hand to adjust Israel's borders, its own southern border was adjusted by a massive hurricane, devastating its coastline. When America pressured Israel to evacuate the Gaza Strip, after which Palestinians entered and desecrated the Jewish burial grounds; just so did a massive storm flood America's cemeteries, floating hundreds of caskets out of the ground, floating the dead back into the streets. When both American presidential candidates during an election year advocated giving away Israel's land to the Palestinians in a mythical 'two-state' solution, and when America's UN Ambassador issued a statement that declared the United States did not accept the legitimacy of Israel's settlements in the West Bank, another storm struck America's eastern seaboard, devastating the same city in which the United Nations had its headquarters, flooding major segments, derailing political activities. This major storm devastated the same states that had, just days prior, legalized homosexual marriage.

Whenever America attempted to pressure Israel to divide its land, America was struck with horrendous, record-setting natural disasters, and the greater the pressure exerted, the greater the disaster. As David recorded in his book of Psalms, even the stormy winds do God's bidding:

> *"Praise the Lord from the earth, sea monsters and all deeps; fire and hail, snow and clouds; stormy wind, fulfilling His word ..."*
>
> *Psalm 148:7-8*

But America and Americans ignored these blatant, obvious warnings that could only have come from God. President after President, from both parties, continued to pressure Israel to divide its land, to broker 'land for peace', even when the glaring facts of Palestinian terrorism, lies, and betrayals mounted. When I spoke with a number of angels and prophets about this issue, they were of the unanimous opinion that, just as during another period of human history when six million Jews were slaughtered and evidence was presented to the nations of the world and those nations failed to act, so too was America failing to act—not because of a lack of evidence, but because of the *will not to believe.* As the King's Son once said, a man could be raised from the dead and people still would not believe: no amount of facts will ever overcome the *will* not to believe. And so America pressed on to her doom.

Sliding precipitously down the greasy slope of socialism and onward, unknowingly, into totalitarianism, Americans were still of the opinion that they controlled their own destinies through the democratic process. And in some ways this was true; just as every man gets what he wants, just so does every nation obtain the leadership, and move in the direction, that its people desire. America during this time was almost completely perverted. The church, meant to be salt and light, had lost its savor and was in the process of being trampled down underfoot, although the actualization of that prophetic warning was yet to come. Its people, full of luxuries, surfeited with all manner of entertainments, had no time for God, no time for morality, no patience for anything that might require their sensual gratifications to be delayed. They rushed headlong into sin; they crowed over every 'victory' they obtained, in their vain imaginings, thinking they were throwing off the yoke of God. They shook their fists at God, and even what passed for the Church held up the slaughter of the unborn as a 'moral act' by 'good women'. So-called church members went into voting booths and on record set forth their opinion that men should marry men, or women marry women, disdaining God's dire warnings about such blasphemies. They began to work against the little light that was left, crushing church after church with edicts prohibiting the teaching of God's Word as though it were 'hate speech'—using unrighteous edicts to spread unrighteousness and to choke the truth.

America's Presidents, with the connivance and support of most of the elected representatives of the people and the massively growing false church, wrought a major shift in America's level of support to Israel. American political leadership, unknown to the vast majority of Americans, made common cause with Russia, offering the Russians military weaponry, support, and a free hand in the Middle East, all the while maintaining a façade of support to Israel. During a joint U.S.-Russian military exercise in the city of Denver, high in the Colorado Rocky Mountains, a U.S. President allegedly took a few days off to play golf. The President of Russia—secreted into America by the Russian military while he was ostensibly in Russia, recovering from a sports injury—met with the American President. The American President committed American support for Russia's objectives in the Middle East. There were numerous reasons given shortly thereafter as to why America joined in support of Russia during this time in history, but with the access we have now, it can be clearly explained. The American President, influenced by the enemy from his youth, was at the time of his Presidency a fully-committed disciple of the adversary, wholly devoted to every initiative, every policy, every diabolical premise and procedure that would eradicate truth, justice, and beauty from the world. Unbeknown to Americans, deceived and blinded as they were by their own disobedience and perversity and refusal to love the truth, becoming a nation that loved deceit and treachery, they found themselves at this time in history led by one of the enemy's most successful deceivers—God's judgments are so fitting. We Romans had an expression for this state of affairs; we would say that the wolf had been elected as shepherd by the very sheep it would devour. Just so, the American President, agent of the enemy of all mankind, aligned the full might of America's power behind Russia at this time in their histories.

When considering the application of military power, there are different levels of military activity that must be planned. There is the *strategic*—the level at which major decisions are made, the level dealing with the allocation and deployment of national resources and national priorities, the level that provides the foundation for, and drives, activities at every other level. When America, in its second global conflict, made the strategic decision to defeat Germany first, before Japan, that decision drove the allocation of national assets and resources toward Europe first, and secondarily to Japan. Then there is the operational—what we Romans knew as the 'campaign' level, where military operations are actually conducted, where various combat and logistics forces are marshaled and deployed so as to obtain strategic objectives. Expertise in this level of warfare was particularly a Russian specialty, having learned in the hard school of experience when Germany invaded Russia in 1941 and 1942. And finally there is the tactical—this is the level at which men actually fight; they take a hill, they conduct a patrol, they close with and fight hand-to-hand with the enemy. One might view things thusly: strategy determines upon which continent or in which region forces are placed; the operational level of decisions determines what battles are fought and where those battles are fought—these decisions are made so as to obtain the strategic objectives; and finally, the tactical level of decision-making determines how those battles are fought.

The enemy's efforts to bring down America also had these same three levels of activity. The main strategic thrust against America was the decision to ignore its vast economic and military power and instead assault its morality, for its morality was the kingpin with which America had its wagon hitched to God. If the enemy could dislodge this main connection, it would have a free hand in anything else it attempted. America's prosperity depended upon their alignment with and obedience to God's principles. If the enemy could disrupt that alignment and shatter that obedience, America would, like other nations before it, find itself at the mercy of the enemy. This strategic decision to assault America's morality involved operational decisions, or choices of which battles to fight, and where—the decision to undermine and discredit the Christian church; the decision to eviscerate morality and righteousness using the power of entertainment and the media; and the decision to reward supporters of the enemy's agenda with wealth and power. The American President during this time was the beneficiary of one of the operational decisions made by the enemy—to reward his disciples with power.

Once these operational objectives were obtained, they opened other operational opportunities—the decision to erode America's economic power and eliminate their military power. They were mutually supportive. For example, several American Presidents from both parties played a large part in destroying America's economic vitality as well as disarming the American military.

The American economy was eviscerated in much the same way as most others—by loading it with debt. The strategic decision to undermine America's morality had created an American public that disdained savings, that greedily sought the latest luxury items, that felt any type of delayed gratification was anathema, and, departing from an obedience to God, elevated Baal, the god of material wealth, in His place. America's blessed productivity soon became poisonous profligacy, like manna gathered and stored in disobedience turned to worms.

The operational campaign against the American military was also enabled by the main strategic decision eviscerating America's morality. America elected political leaders that soon bowed to pressure from social lobbying groups, integrating homosexuals into their ranks, blatantly ignoring God's warnings about this practice. America elected political leaders who shunted funds elsewhere, denuding the military of necessary assets. Corporations necessary to advance the technologies required for parity in the modern age were demonized in the media; the essential activity of making a profit was ridiculed; investigations were convened. Laws were passed requiring such onerous corporate policies that these large corporations simply dismissed thousands of their employees to maintain solvency.

Every success flowed from the successful strategic campaign against America's morality. The media kept Americans from perceiving what was happening to their country until it was far too late to recover any semblance of freedom. This wasn't difficult; choosing sin, they had intentionally blinded themselves to the truth, so the media's task wasn't difficult—they were in effect tasked with deceiving slaves willing to be deceived and enslaved as long as they were kept entertained.

In its relations with other nations, America's foreign policy had also undergone a dramatic shift. Its traditional support for Israel, a remnant of America's once-vibrant morality, was disdainfully shredded and discarded when a Muslim President was re-elected for a second term. Now with comprehensive flexibility to act according to his diabolical mandate without regard to concerns for re-election or any opposing party philosophies, he would more fully execute the tasks assigned by his master. One of the first items of foreign policy he addressed was to provide support for a drastic realignment of national power in the Middle East. Dictators not fully supportive of a radical Islamist agenda were removed by what the media termed 'populist' demonstrations. One by one, these dictators—scoundrels, but American allies nonetheless—were hunted down, brutalized on national television, and killed. Libya, Egypt, Tunisia ... these Islamic nations felt the brunt of Satan's assault fostered by surreptitious support from American arms shipments, intelligence, or special military operations. This rapid, tumultuous period in history was labeled, 'the Arab Spring', referencing the movement toward freedom and democracy—the desire for 'a new start'—that allegedly motivated those deposing the dictatorships. It was also a time when it became quite dangerous to be a Middle Eastern government allied with the United States, and most of all this applied to Israel.

Shipments of American missiles were shunted through Libya to support Arab terrorists who would fire them from Gaza at Israeli farmers. American intelligence was provided to Arab terrorists to help them adjust their tactics. American money was secretly funneled to support the evisceration of the Israeli economy by terrorists in secret, or by boycott movements in the open.

America's leadership—most of whom were devoted to Israel's destruction, in accordance with the enemy's agenda—conducted these activities in secret while openly advocating support for Israel. This was for a specific reason—to keep Israel blindly believing that America was still her main source of international support. Buttressed by the extremely deceived and deceiving media in Israel itself, this fiction was maintained, and served to convince the majority of Israelis that they could always turn to America if things became too difficult. When the right moment came, however, the American President removed this support, effectively pulling the rug from under Israel's feet and leaving her utterly defenseless.

With the long-term strategic initiative a proven success, and each carefully selected operational plan developed and brought to fruition, the enemy then implemented the tactical activities enabled by the success of its operational campaigns.

Sartorius Crux Vita
Diamond Gate, Jerusalem
AR 40

Chapter 32
Samantha

"Justice is turned back, and righteousness stands far away; for truth has stumbled in the street, and uprightness cannot enter. Yes, truth is lacking; and he who turns aside from evil makes himself a prey."

Isaiah 59:14-15

Samantha Gunderson strode confidently into the lobby of the Guilder, Atchison, and Steckam building on a cold winter morning, full of energy, enthusiasm, and excitement. She wore a light brown cashmere blazer and matching skirt with a white silk scarf under a stylish and athletic fleece parka. Life was going well; since joining the firm, she'd gotten two promotions and was now the Senior Editor for New Theological Lines—a fancy title that meant she was responsible for researching information about the dozens of new branches of Christianity that were developing in America.

She'd been preparing a week for this morning's meeting. As the new Senior Editor, and more importantly as one of the more photogenic females on the staff, she'd been asked to facilitate a critical corporate meeting that would explore how Guilder, Atchison, and Steckam would position themselves relative to emerging political, economic, and religious perspectives swirling around Israel. There were innumerous key issues and theological threads winding through America's relationship with their oldest Middle Eastern ally, not the least of which was the opinion held by some evangelicals that Israel still had something to do with God's prophetic timetable. Yet Samantha would not ignore the massive numbers of newer Christians and Christian trends coming to terms with different perspectives, and she'd been tasked with researching and then introducing those perspectives to the staff at the meeting this morning.

Her latest promotion had come with an executive assistant—Wendy—a college intern who'd decided to take the winter school term off to work at the publishing firm. She and Wendy were good friends and worked well together, though there was about ten years difference in age between them. Wendy met her at the door to Samantha's office with a tall mug of designer coffee and a smile. Wendy, like Samantha, was slim and athletic, though shorter, with a striking figure. She wore a slimming black jacket and gray slacks, with three-inch black heels to make her look taller.

"All set for the meeting?" she asked.

"Ready," Samantha replied. "Did you get the files I sent last night?"

"All printed out, ported to your iPad, and there are hard copies in your portfolio. Copies are in the folders you'll be distributing as well."

"Excellent." Samantha took a sip of her latte, thanked Wendy with a nod, and sat down to review her materials before the meeting.

"Everyone will be there," Wendy said, taking a seat in front of Samantha's desk. "Every guest has shown up; I checked with transportation and Denny said that they got them all in from the airport yesterday and settled in the Wyndham downtown." Wendy pointed at Samantha's desk. "I downloaded the surveys on Israel that you asked for, too. They're in the 'Surveys' folder in your iPad."

Samantha pursed her lips and nodded. She opened her iPad, swiped the screen, popped open the Surveys folder, and perused the contents.

"Good ... good. You've got State's position paper, speculations from the

Department of Defense, and some wide-ranging market surveys. Did Braunhausen's market survey come in on time?"

"It did—and it's a good thing, for the amount of money we paid them," Wendy answered, swinging a lock of hair from her face with a pen. "They're expensive but they're good."

Samantha was speed-reading the results of the market survey on what the Christian demographic was polling on Israel topics. Braunhausen was one of the country's leading polling and survey firms, and Guilder, Atchison, and Steckam made use of them frequently to support key business decisions. She'd been personally coordinating with the Braunhausen representative for the last two weeks, so the results weren't a surprise. She looked up, satisfied. "Wendy, this is solid material. Thanks. It will help a lot."

Wendy smiled, flushed, and looked pleased. "Glad it will help, Samantha." Wendy went back to her own desk and Samantha looked over the folders she'd be distributing to the attendees. Each folder had copies of position papers issued by key social opinion drivers in the Administration, in academia, in the economic and business realms, and, with a touch of her own, she'd included popular bloggers who were carrying large readerships. She wanted each of the participants to have a permanent record of the materials she'd collected. Many of those opinion leaders had been invited to the meeting—several identified and invited by Samantha—and Samantha wanted to make sure the company's leadership had copies of the articles and opinion pieces these guest speakers had written.

Guilder, Atchison, and Steckam's conference room was styled after the catacombs, following its Christian theme, and the room had a soft, golden glow from recessed lighting that made it look like candles were everywhere, flickering. The central table was round polished oak, modeled after Arthur's fictional round table, striving for a classic, diplomatic, inclusive atmosphere as opposed to a long, straight table with defined hierarchical leadership at its head. Samantha arrived early and positioned her materials on a side table. She went back out to the foyer to welcome the guests.

Sally Witherspoon was orchestrating the introductions. Manny Lewis was there, with Jason Cruz, several other vice presidents, and the CEO, Dominique Moehlen. They gathered around several of the guests.

Samantha recognized Adiba Fakhoury, one of the more prominent members of America's new pan-Arab constituency that had grown out of what had once been CAIR—the Council on American-Islamic Relations. She was a short woman, thin, with a pretty face, a sharp nose, coffee-colored skin, unmistakable in a shimmering silver hijab and a well-tailored black, swirling, floor-length embroidered abaya. Dark eyes flashing, graceful and composed, she conveyed a sense of confidence and modernity with just a tinge of unapologetic boldness as she strolled into the hallowed halls of the Christian publishing world in traditional Islamic garb.

A well-received writer, Fakhoury had published several books explaining in clear terms the Palestinian position. There was talk that one might be made into a movie. She had an enormously popular blog and was a frequent guest on many different local and regional television shows, helping to explain what was happening in the Middle East from the American Muslim perspective. Directed to invite Fakhoury by Jason Cruz, Samantha had included a number of her opinion pieces, especially those pointedly advocating a major shift in the U.S. Administration's policies in the Middle East, and titles of her books as well, in the materials she would distribute to the participants.

Many of the employees gathered around Fakhoury as she arrived, and Moehlen herself greeted the Arab woman with warmth and open friendliness. Cruz, Lewis, and Witherspoon were clustered around as well, making an effort to ensure Fakhoury felt comfortable.

A large man strode into the foyer and Samantha immediately recognized Walter Ray Fritsch, the representative from Braunhausen with whom she'd been working for the previous two weeks. Fritsch was a stocky man, well over three hundred pounds, who would take Samantha to lunches that included amazing quantities of knockwurst, beer, and all manner of pies. He was a jovial sort, very effusive, highly extroverted, and possessed of a sharp and insightful talent to analyze trends in public opinion based on the thinnest threads of media reports, research papers, or just conversations with people on the street. At one lunch, he'd engaged the waitress for fifteen minutes about what she thought of the new president, and he had a talent for getting people to talk about the strangest things. And he left a huge tip. Samantha smiled at the memory.

"Walter Ray, you're late." He insisted on being called Walter Ray; she had no idea why.

"Why, Miz Gunderson, I'm not late. I meant to arrive this very moment." They laughed together politely, and she extended her hand, which disappeared in his massive paw. "It's good to be back at Guilder, Atchison, and Steckam, my dear. Just the smell of old leather and paste makes my bones scintillate with the pleasures attendant to the traditional publishing trade."

"Contain yourself, Walter Ray. You and I know we're as far from some old leather-and-paste-up shop as you can get."

"Of course," he said quietly, and, looking around at the woman in the abaya, "and about as far from Christian traditionalism as you can get as well."

Samantha could think of no retort that wouldn't tread on the current corporate environment of inclusiveness toward all faiths, so she said, "Walter Ray, do me a favor now, would you? After the meeting, let's get together and talk about your thoughts on the dynamics. You've got an eye for these things."

Walter Ray's eyes twinkled in his fat face and he bent over her hand. "It will be my pleasure, young lady." He moved off toward a side table upon which rested pastries from a local boutique bakery.

Turning to watch him depart, Samantha bumped into a small, diminutive woman standing off to the side, alone, and quickly apologized. The woman didn't seem to know anyone, so Samantha asked her if she needed help.

"I'm here for a meeting," she replied. "I was invited by a Samantha Gunderson, and—"

"Why, I'm Samantha, and you are ... let me guess. You must be Ramona Jäger."

The woman smiled shyly. "That's me. Stranger in a strange land." Jäger looked up at the huge mural on the wall depicting all the world's religions intertwined together in a modernistic, stylish depiction of harmony and peace.

"Welcome, Ramona, I'm glad you could come." Samantha had invited Jäger because she was a noted columnist who wrote for the Jerusalem Post, who also had a very popular blog that Samantha had been reading for the past year as part of her research. Jäger looked over at crowd gathered around Fakhoury, and then up at the end of the room where a very stylized cross hung on the wall.

"I feel a little like Daniel at the moment," she said, not without a trace of dismay.

Finding herself again with nothing to say that wouldn't step on the corporate narrative, Samantha smiled once more and gave a quick, firm nod of her head as an encouragement. "You're over there," she said, placing one hand gently on Ramona's shoulder, pointing to one of the chairs around the main table. "I've included a number of your pieces in the handouts, and I'll be asking you to speak."

"Yes, thanks, you mentioned that. So they haven't blackballed me yet?"

Samantha simply smiled and moved off toward the front of the room to take her seat.

Other guests included Edson Merrill and Rowan Sorenson, both representing the Emergent Church movement. Merrill had obviously brought along Sorenson as his business guru, and no one would know the business benefits and disadvantages of various positions relative to Israel better than Sorenson.

Arthur Gene Swallow, Doctor of Divinity, was there representing most of America's traditional evangelicals. Swallow, a youngish forty, was overweight, wore glasses, and his trademark balding pate reflected the soft golden faux candlelight as he moved about, working the room, giving him an aura of contentedness, Samantha thought. Swallow's church was the largest in America and when he spoke, it was a given that he spoke for a huge constituency of American Christians. His philosophies, touted in dozens of books, videos, internet blogs, and other media forms—courtesy of Guilder, Atchison, and Steckam—had grown rapidly into a massively profitable enterprise, and Arthur was definitely 'seated at the right hand of the throne', to use Manny Lewis' somewhat tongue-in-cheek phrase. Moehlen would unquestionably cater to the company's golden-egg laying goose, for it seemed that no one had their pulse on today's Christian scene like Swallow, and no one in Christianity today commanded a greater following. He was a powerful speaker, a compelling teacher, with a raft of interpersonal skills Samantha could see easily on display as he worked the crowd. Swallow made sure to greet Fakhoury, unabashedly fawning, complimenting her courage in coming into one of the largest bastions of Christian publishing in America.

"Not at all, Dr. Swallow, not at all," she replied brightly to his compliment. "In my conversations with Ms. Moehlen, and in what I see this house putting out lately, it is clear that her move toward a greater inclusiveness in matters of faith is quite compatible with Islam and its desire for a fuller embracing of every religion. I welcome the chance to come and explain our perspectives."

"Isa will be glad that you have," Swallow replied, using the Islamic reference to Jesus. Fakhoury nodded sagely in reply, smiling.

A delicate, tasteful bell rang over the room's speaker system, and the CEO arose.

Moehlen, in a soft gray and maroon tailored business suit with a matching skirt, addressed the room. "Ladies and Gentlemen, my name is Dominique Moehlen, and as the Chief Executive Officer at Guilder, Atchison, and Steckam, I'd like to welcome you and thank you for attending this conference designed to explore the company's position vis-à-vis the current State of Israel. Each possesses valuable opinions and perspectives, and we are eager to glean your opinions and perspectives over the course of the next day or so. If anyone has any questions about logistics or administrative issues, please see Sally Witherspoon, who coordinates those for us." Moehlen made a gesture, and Sally Witherspoon, in a toned green dress, stood and nodded to the group. Moehlen went on. "We've made provisions to record your inputs so we might avail ourselves of your expertise in later meetings, and we intend to distribute the minutes of the conference to everyone attending shortly afterward. Sally will be your point of contact for that information as well, should you have any questions, or don't receive it.

"So ... " Moehlen looked down at her program with a practiced motion, "permit me to introduce Ms. Samantha Gunderson, our Senior Editor for New Theologies, who will serve as our facilitator. Samantha will start by summarizing the conference's objectives. She'll also present a distillation of current positions on the topic from organizations we feel will be pertinent to Guilder, Atchison, and Steckam's stance in the future regarding the State of Israel." Moehlen smiled, nodded to Samantha, and sat.

Across the table, Samantha stood and took up the remote unit that controlled the holographic projection screen that appeared in the middle of the round table. Every participant seated at the table would see the same view, from the same perspective, directly in front of their respective chairs. Participants sitting along the wall, supporting the principal attendees, would view the material on screens at either end of the room.

"Ladies, Gentlemen, thank you for coming. Let me start by outlining the company's objectives for this meeting." Samantha read from a prepared document crafted by several vice presidents and finally approved by Moehlen. "Our desire is to more fully understand *all* the perspectives surrounding the political entity currently in that geographical location the world knows as Palestine so that we might better position the firm to correctly align with today's religiously-oriented literature, satisfy today's faith-based constituency with our range of published media, ensure our work is in consonance with an all-inclusive comprehension of what Israel has come to mean in today's world, and finally, to understand how we as a major international corporation should position ourselves relative to that entity." Samantha looked around the room for a moment after reading the statement and saw Ramona Jäger sitting stiffly. The statement could not have been constructed to be more detrimental to Israel's interests, but Samantha had no choice in its recital.

"I've been asked to summarize current positions relative to Israel which Guilder, Atchison, and Steckam feels may be pertinent to our purposes here today. The first is, obviously, the current Administration's position, as expressed by the State Department. In your handouts, you each have a copy of the Secretary of State's document relative to the topic. Permit me to read an excerpt." Samantha moved a sheaf of papers and began to read:

> *"This Administration, in concurrence with the recent mandate received from the majority of Americans, recognizes its need to review traditional relationships with the major nations comprising the Middle East region. America remains committed to the support and survival of every Middle Eastern nation, especially those who, with us, are aggressively dedicated to the pursuit of peace. We will not, however, support any nation that may, contrary to international law, seek to overthrow or evict any other national entity or people from their homeland, and will not support any type of occupation force, wherever it may appear."*

There were a number of raised eyebrows at this last comment, since it so obviously referred to what many assumed to be Israel's occupation of their traditional geographic homeland. Samantha continued reading.

> *'This Administration stands with those who wish to see peace in the Middle East, and yet we are humble enough to recognize that those who live closest to the problems may have clearer, more refined perspectives about what may constitute national privilege, legitimacy, or racism."*

This statement leapt out at the attendees, who recognized in it the veiled admission from the U.S. administration that they would align with those Middle Eastern nations who alleged that Zionism was equivalent to racism. Samantha continued:

> *"As a consequence of this realization, this Administration will support the upcoming United Nations resolution to declare a Palestinian state in the Middle East, with its capital as East Jerusalem."*

This last inclusion was no surprise, since the American Secretary of State, three months ago, had shocked most of the world by trumpeting this radical policy decision in complete contravention of the historical American position. In fact, this turnabout was a major precipitating cause of Guilder, Atchison, and Steckam's conference. Stripping away the politically correct parlance, everyone recognized that the Administration was clearly stating its support of the idea that Zionism was racism, and that the United States would no longer be an unquestioning supporter of the State of Israel.

Samantha finished reading the Administration's statement. She could not bring herself to glance at Jäger, even though she knew the Israeli correspondent would have known about the Administration's position. Jäger had recently posted an extensive article on her blog, which Samantha had read.

She picked up another sheaf of papers. "I've another statement, this one from the Wall Street Journal, in one of their recent editorials. I'll read an excerpt."

> *"As readers of this paper are well aware, we have been and continue to be strong supporters of Israel. They have consistently been the only trustworthy democracy in the Middle East and have historically stood with the United States since their inception as a nation. Yet as we observe the direction of the American economy and the poor condition of the world's economies overall, we face the undeniable fact that most of the world's wealth seems to be gravitating toward those areas controlled or significantly influenced by Islam. We see the undeniable spread of Islam in demographic figures throughout Europe and in many cities in the United States, and we recognize that it is people who create a business environment, and those people also create business environments which best match their own culture. It is therefore with the hard eye of pragmatism that this newspaper will come to recognize the shift in world demographics and world opinions toward a fuller inclusion of the Arab world's business perspectives, and in the future consider our counsel to business leadership in that light."*

Samantha, for some reason suddenly realizing how powerfully these statements of support for the Arab cause must sound, marshaled together, was in no position to extricate herself. As a key employee on the company's leadership team, she found herself now tied in and committed personally to the company's overall direction. She still could not bring herself to meet Jäger's eyes.

She cleared her throat and went on. "Permit me now to read something from one of the nation's most representative Christian leaders, Dr. Arthur Gene Swallow, published in a recent issue of *Christianity for Today*." She looked up at the crowd, a professional smile pasted on her face. "We're privileged to have Dr. Swallow with us today, and on behalf of Guilder, Atchison, and Steckam, Dr. Swallow, we appreciate your coming." Swallow gave a dignified nod, raising a hand in gratefulness at his recognition. "So," she went on, "to quote from Dr. Swallow's article ..."

> *'As today's Christians, recognizing that Jesus, or 'Isa' as He is also known in billions of homes around the world, embraces all peoples, we too in America must recognize that our theology has perhaps in the past been deficient, or, let us say not as inclusive as it could have been, when we come to realizing what God wants from us. In his final prayer, the Son prayed that we would be united, even as He and His Father were. It is time we in America took this prayer to heart and approached our brothers and sisters of other faiths to find where we might worship God together in unity and love. I know the Holy Father, leader of the world's millions of Catholics, would agree with me in this direction.*
>
> *'What this may mean for millions of American Christians tied to traditional interpretations of scripture and the attendant support for the nation of Israel which comes with those interpretation, is that we all might need to understand how the past, largely incorrect assessment of scripture led to monolithic support extended almost exclusively to one ethnicity to the great detriment of those other children of Abraham—the Arabs, sons of Ishmael, whom Abraham also loved dearly. Yet Christianity is not called to exclude some to the detriment of others; we are not called to disdain those who may not look, act, or think like we do. We are not called to turn away from one because we embrace another. We are living in times, and may God be praised for it, when we can realize that this all-embracing approach can be accomplished successfully; that we can love one without hating the other. 'Come now, let us reason together,' said the Lord, and so I too enjoin us all ... can we not reason together with those from Islam? Can we not see where our faiths commingle? Can we not realize that we worship the one true God together, regardless of whether we speak of Him as Jehovah or Allah? Now is the time, good people; now is the time for those whose hearts were designed by God to love, to love our neighbors as ourselves, to balance our perceptions regarding unabashed, exclusive support to one nation when it causes irreparable harm to others for whom the Son also died.*
>
> *'In line with these thoughts, then, be it known that from this point forward, Swallow Ministries will be working to increase the understanding and position of various Arab and Palestinian situations; we will soon issue a statement supporting the establishment of a Palestinian state, with its capital in East Jerusalem. We can think of no more demonstrable way to underline and emphasize our newfound understanding of what God asks us to do in these days, when His new clarity is breaking forth, when it will be required of everyone within the sound*

of His voice to stand with Him and embrace everyone for whom He died."

Samantha finished reading and looked up at the group. There were smiles and nods, and not a few congratulated Swallow from across the table. Samantha noticed Ms. Jäger sitting stone-faced, isolated in the middle of dozens of people.

Samantha found herself confused. She had *thought* she knew what the Bible had said about Israel, about how Israel was the apple of God's eye, about how God would discipline Israel when they ignored Him, but would chastise or crush any nation that would attempt to come against Israel. She *thought* she remembered such things in scripture, but listening to Dr. Swallow expound on his interpretation of the Bible, her memories dimmed, her certainty clouded. The man taught *millions*, for God's sake. Heads of state hung on his every word. How could she even think to question his position or the position of her nation's leadership? It didn't make sense, and it *certainly* wouldn't make sense in the current environment within Guilder, Atchison, and Steckam—such questioning might even cost her the job she'd worked so hard to get.

So, all things considered, Samantha stepped down without speaking up. She released her grip on the podium, put one hand on the microphone, and said, "Please now welcome Ms. Adiba Fakhoury."

The group applauded Ms. Fakhoury as she approached the podium, as though applauding for someone spearheading what had recently been declared to be a successful campaign against overwhelming odds. Ramona Jäger sat, unmoving, hands in her lap.

The Arab spoke in a clear, mellifluous English with almost no accent. "Thank you all for your kind invitation. I feel gratified to take up these issues, and appreciate the openness displayed by Guilder, Atchison, and Steckam in considering a newer, wider perspective on these issues.

"We do have so very much in common," Fakhoury began. "And to emphasize the truth of Dr. Swallow's statement, permit me to simply list a few key facts relevant to the decision your company needs to make in the next few days." Fakhoury had a deep, almost velvet voice, smooth in cadence and tone, almost caressing in its timbre.

"We all realize that Israel's occupation of Palestine is the cause of uncounted decades of destruction, damage, and death. Civilized people everywhere must come together to break this cycle of violence, and their efforts must be based upon a new and vibrant understanding of what rights are possessed by nations in this region. We must ask, what rights does Israel have—to occupy land, to build homes and institutions on what has forever been Palestinian territory, or ... and I say this most forthrightly as a student of history ... what rights to even exist as a people? Such questions *must* be asked today, and until America's communities of faith break out of their previously straightjacketed, blinkered view of theology, the peoples of the world cannot expect any help from America in moving toward a more global perspective of world peace.

"And beyond questions that must be asked, there are actions that must be taken by the world before almost two billion Muslims can believe they are taken seriously; these are unequivocal conditions for peace. I ask Guilder, Atchison, and Steckam to seriously consider how you will portray these potential but necessary actions as you seek to restructure your position relative to that political entity which now occupies Palestine. One of the most important actions that must occur before peace can emerge is that over five million Palestinians must—I say *must*—be allowed to settle in their ancestral homeland, an indivisible and historic Arab nation, a declared Palestinian state. That they have been kept out of their ancestral territory until now by the powers occupying the land is an unquestionable fact, and this condition has been made non-negotiable by the current President of the Palestinian Authority ... and rightfully so. I call on your company to make this perspective clear to those Americans of faith whom you touch.

"A second necessary action or condition for peace is the cessation of all Israeli action in or near Gaza, which is causing untold destruction among our future generations of children. Air strikes, tanks, and barbaric soldiers with automatic weapons routinely use Gaza as some sort of 'military training exercise area', and they do not care who they kill. Jews have subjugated our people in this area for dozens of years—ever since they first occupied the land in 1948. These activities must cease immediately. I call on your company to make this perspective clear to those Americans of faith whom you touch.

"A third critical action is the appropriate division of Al Quds—the city Americans know as Jerusalem. This has always been the capital of Arab Palestine and it is a Holy City to our people, and therefore at least half of the city should be remanded to the Palestinian state as its capital. Again, I call on your company to make this very important point clear to those Americans of faith whom you touch."

Fakhoury looked down at her notes, pausing for effect. "I realize that I am discussing very controversial issues. But I stress them because they are things that almost two billion people agree must be obtained if the world will be made whole; if those of faith in today's world will ever come together so as to fully understand the true depths of knowledge and power of Allah, blessed be his name. So I put these things to you all, knowing that you have heard them so many times before, knowing that in this country, such information has been painted in so many different ways. But I tell you this now ... the time has come for America to understand these facts in new ways. Two *billion* Muslims are opening their hands in friendship. Please do not mistake this time, or these days. So please, in your future publications, in those books and films and other media outlets you support, please, tell these stories in a fair and balanced way. Explain this truth to them—for them, and for their children." The woman finished with a short flourishing bow. "Thank you," she said, quietly but with strong feeling.

For a moment the group sat, silent, open-eyed, moved, and then with one spontaneous eruption, stood to their feet in loud, sustained applause. Some, noticing Jäger sitting like a stone, unmoving and patently unmoved, glared at her. Samantha, however, could not bring herself to look up, and busied herself with arranging a pile of folders so as to avoid using her hands to clap. She felt torn, duplicitous, and soiled in a way that was strange and uncomfortable. Moehlen was gazing at her curiously, wondering, and Samantha remembered her obligations.

She rose and moved to the podium, nodding and smiling politely to Fakhoury as the woman stepped down and walked past Samantha to her seat. As she passed, Samantha felt the strangest waft of darkness, a black, malodorous stench in her spirit. It struck her physically as well, so much so that she stumbled slightly, her hands reaching out to catch herself on the podium. She felt nauseous; she was disoriented, and for a moment Samantha could not focus. She looked down at her papers on the podium, trying to steady herself. The feeling passed. Samantha looked up as Fakhoury moved to her seat. Fakhoury smiled at her, and Samantha felt something like a dagger pierce her soul.

"We ... we are also privileged ... we are privileged to have with us, also, uh, yes,

Ms. Ramona Jäger, a noted columnist from the Jerusalem Post, and a reputable blogger with a wide international readership. Ms. Jäger." Samantha nodded once, quickly, and then moved down from the podium.

Jäger took the steps up to the podium slowly, a diminutive woman in a dull gray suit, feeling very much as Daniel did, descending into the lion's den.

"I address you," she began tremulously, "with humility, but ... but also with a deep sense of indignity." Jäger's voice was plain, clear, accustomed to public speaking, and she began unemotionally. "So I say to you: consider what you are about. You are contemplating departing from many hundreds of years of traditional support—based upon sound, solid, unquestioned biblical exegesis—for the nation and people of Israel."

"Forgive me, Ms. Jäger, but we have made no decisions at this point." Dominique Moehlen spoke softly but firmly.

Jäger laughed quickly, a despairing gasp, so obviously a statement that indicated she thought Moehlen incredibly disingenuous. Jäger made a gesture with her hand that expressed in a motion a world of futility and hopelessness. She collected herself and then continued. "Well then ... permit me to address just a few of the items Ms. Fakhoury discussed which so poignantly concern two billion Muslims.

"The word 'occupation' seems to command quite a lot of attention today. Okay, let's talk about occupation. Funny, but when the Egyptians owned the Gaza Strip for almost twenty years and wouldn't permit the Palestinians back, because they were a bunch of terrorists, no one talked about occupation. When the Jordanians owned Judea and Samaria—what you call the West Bank—and wouldn't let the Palestinians in because they were known by the Jordanians to be terrorists, no one complained about these lands being occupied. But yet, when Israel, attacked by her neighbors rampaging on a war of extermination, overcame their assaults and took possession of these territories, like every other nation that has prevailed in warfare, Israel has been called an occupying power. Okay then. Where is the movement to return the Alsace-Lorraine to Germany? Where is the media outcry against the Czech Republic, or against Poland, to return the German lands awarded to those countries after Germany's defeat in the Second World War? And those countries, by the way, evicted most of the people then living in those lands, or forced them to flee." Jäger pointed a finger at the audience to make her point. "But Israel has *never* evicted a single Arab from the Gaza Strip or the West Bank. If you checked your facts, you would see that tens of thousands of Arabs from neighboring Syria, or Jordan, or other parts of the Arab world, have come to live in these territories because of the prosperity and opportunity created by the Jews.

"We hear talk about Israel abandoning these territories as a 'condition of peace.'" Jäger laughed derisively, causing some in the crowd to bristle, but she disregarded their discomfort and plowed on. "When we abandoned the northern security zone of southern Lebanon, did we get peace? No, we got unending barrages of Katyusha rockets into our towns and villages. To appease world opinion and get the leftist media off our backs, we unilaterally vacated Gaza and evicted thousands of Israeli families from their homes. We ripped out Jewish families, we left richly productive farms, institutions, and infrastructure. We all just picked up and left ... to get peace, we thought. This is what we were told by the Arab nations; this is what we were told by the U.N.; this is what we were told by the American Administrations—so many different Administrations. Yet what happened? Did the 'Palestinian people'"—and here Jäger spoke the phrase with bald derision—"keep their word? No. They invited numerous terrorist organizations into their territory and these terrorists, along with the help of the Palestinians, built an infrastructure of death—tunnels, ammunition dumps, explosive factories, rocket launching positions—all woven into the fabric of their society—under or in their schools, their mosques, and the homes of private people.

"We hear the phrase, 'cycle of violence', as if it was something inevitable, as if it was something which could, with reasonable participants, be interrupted and then abolished. Many governments refer to this mythical 'cycle of violence', but I tell you the truth, there is no such thing. Israel selectively targets specific terrorists when it exerts force; the Arabs very specifically target Israeli civilians. Do you know how many Palestinian civilians have been intentionally killed by Israel? None—yes, that's right. We don't target civilians. In fact, we put our own soldiers at risk so as to ensure we don't in any way risk harming Palestinian civilians. But the Palestinians, however, go after Israelis at shopping malls, or bar mitzvahs, or weddings, or Passover celebrations, or in a bus. Had the 'Palestinian people' accepted the peace we have offered time and time again—five times as of this date, all rejected by the *alleged* Palestinian leadership—this *alleged* cycle of violence would be a thing of the past. But they cannot accept this, because it is a tenet of their religion—a religion you all here are considering embracing, if you even think of 'restructuring your support for Israel'—that they must hate Jews, that they must *kill* every Jew."

Jäger's eyes filmed, and she became somewhat more emotional. "My God, don't you people sitting here realize that it is perfectly acceptable for Muslims to lie to achieve their ends? How would *that* sit with the Jewish Rabbi for whom most of the Christian world has such great esteem? Don't you realize that Islam does not want to trade land for peace? Muslims want our land, true, but only after the death of every Jew will they agree to peace; *the death of every last Jew.* Can't you see this? This is what they teach every school child in every mosque throughout the Muslim world. Every uneducated Arab woman, most treated abominably by western standards, hope their children grow up to be martyrs, killing Jews. Don't you understand that no matter what lies are spewed by polished, prepared, tailored spokespeople they send into the world, there will never be any kind of peace until the Arabs learn to love their children more than they love death?"

It appeared that Jäger was finished speaking. Moehlen made as if to step up to the podium, but Ramona put up a hand, eyes flashing brightly. "I'm not through yet, Ms. Moehlen, and as you say, you haven't made any decisions. So permit me to address a few more of these poignant, heartfelt concerns shared by two billion Muslims." The edge of sarcasm in her voice was unmistakable.

"Let's talk about the great, heart-rending plight of the poor Arab 'refugee'. Let's talk about these refugees. Where did they come from? The world today says that the Jews threw them out of the 'ancestral lands of Palestine.' But what's the truth? I'll tell you. Jews have lived in the land of Israel since Biblical times. I mean, for God's sake, you of all people, immersed in your bible culture, ought to have at least read the damn thing once or twice!" Samantha could see Jäger was incensed. "Maybe I should refresh your memory. Israel, Judah ... the southern Kingdom, the northern Kingdom, Samuel, Saul, David, all the other kings of Israel and Judah? Remember Sunday school? Go back to Abraham; Jews have been on the land since then. And when did Mohammed show up? Something like the sixth or seventh century, after Israel had been a nation for something like two thousand years. And now the world wants to tell us that the Arabs have 'always owned the land of Palestine' and the Jews are simply usurping traditional Arab homelands.

"The League of Nations—remember them? They were a valid international organization whose deliberations were approved by the nations of the world, and they formed the nation of Israel via the Balfour Declaration, when the British put forth the concept of a nation in Palestine for the Jews, a Jewish homeland *once again where the Jews had always lived.* During World War Two, the British sided with the Arabs because they felt that's where their bread was buttered. Do you remember how well that worked out for them? They lost their vaunted empire. In 1947, they just got up and left Palestine, but made sure every door was open to any Arab who wanted to slaughter a Jew, while closing every door to Jews who wanted to defend themselves. But it didn't work out that way. The British left and immediately five Arab nations decided to try and wipe the Jews off the face of the earth. They tried; the Arab generals told the Arabs then living in Palestine to get out, to step aside and wait until all the Jews were killed, then they could come back and take whatever spoil they wanted. So these Arabs left; they walked out, they turned their backs on their own property, their own homeland, and left, walking into Jordan, or Syria, or Egypt, or wherever else, all hoping that it would just be a short wait before they could come back and steal the Jews blind.

"But it didn't work out that way. Those five Arab armies were defeated, and suddenly, all those Arabs who'd left had nowhere to come back to. But wait! Did the losing nations take in the poor Palestinians? Did those poor Palestinians who'd collaborated with the other Arab armies to try and plunder the Jews find homes in Syria, or Jordan, or Egypt? Well, no. It was in the interests of every other Arab nation to keep those people homeless, stateless, without any place to settle, so as to put pressure on the nascent Jewish state, using useless idiots in the leftist media to trumpet the plight of 'the poor Palestinian people.' And this is not some type of spin on a position—this is fact, people. Do you think the Arab nations couldn't afford to literally build a million homes in their own lands for their Arab brothers with their oil money? Hah. Their kings and princes could afford billions of dollars of luxuries, but would they spend one dime to bring some sort of help to their greedy relatives? No. It looked better in the eyes of the liberal world media to have a huge group of displaced refugees scrabbling at the borders of Israel than to have a prosperous, happy, flourishing population settled and living in peace. Oh, but wait, tell me again, what other Arab nation in the Middle East holds up democracy as a viable political system? What Muslim nation has a high regard for peace? What Middle Eastern Muslim nation highly esteems the education and protection of its children? How many Muslim nations hold to the rule of law? How many Muslim nations uphold the U.N.'s Declaration of Human Rights? How many Muslim nations offer freedom of religion in their countries? My God," she almost shouted, her hands pounding onto the podium in her anger, "every Muslim nation in the Middle East is simply a dictatorship, run by a select few, keeping millions enslaved to a diabolical, barbaric social system! Can't you see this? *How can you be so blind?*"

Jäger took a deep breath and paused, composing herself. Samantha could see she was trying to regain some semblance of decorous professionalism, but was losing the struggle. The Israeli woman pressed on. "Right now you are considering shifting your support—and let's not bandy words, that's what you're considering—from a peace-loving liberal democracy that has always and only sought to defend its people, to a genocidal jihadist culture that has always and only sponsored terrorism, which has constantly had only one objective—to eliminate the State of Israel and to kill every Jew on the face of the earth.

"You sit here ... you sit here and debate reassessing your position relative to the *only* nation in the Middle East that has shown a shred of compassion in its public and private policies. You debate whether you should 'realign' with nations that would as soon lie to your face than tell you the truth, which is that they intend to see you either convert to their faith or burn in hell, and they will bring the fire."

Jäger took a deep breath, put both hands on the sides of the podium, and looked directly at her audience. "I'll tell you this. I'm a Jew. All my life I've heard the stories about Christians killing Jews, Christians abandoning Jews to their fate. Yet I always found something different in the evangelical community in America. I always, heretofore, found support for Israel. Yet now, I ask myself, why would this Christian company even consider having a seminar like this, with such a topic? And the answer, unfortunately, comes raging at me out of history.

"Did you know, in the fourteenth century, when the Black Plague struck Europe and killed almost fifty percent of the people then living, that the first ones blamed for the calamity were the Jews? That's right; the lie spread that Jews were poisoning wells to kill off all the Christians in the world. The only reason this rumor didn't wipe out the Jews entirely was that Jews were dying right along with everyone else, and they eventually saw it was patently false. Did you know that some allege the plagues struck Europe because of Christianity's persecution of the Jews? Yes, it's true. Does it not say in your Book of Revelation that God gave the woman Jezebel time to repent, but she didn't, and she went on teaching and leading God's bond-servants astray, so that eventually God would cast Jezebel's children upon a bed of sickness; He would kill them with pestilence. Did you know, jumping forward, that in the eighteenth century, Russia felt that its backward position in the world was due to God's displeasure over the fact that the Jews in the Czar's kingdom were not converted? They blamed the Jews for their backward country. We get the word 'pogrom' from this time in history. Did you know, on the walls of an air raid shelter in London during World War Two that they found graffiti saying, "This is a Jew War"? Did you know that many Americans felt that they shouldn't get into the conflict against Hitler because they felt the war was all the fault of the Jews, and they just didn't want to send their corn-fed boys to die for a bunch of 'dirty Jews'?

"I could go on, but suffice it to say we Jews have been blamed for almost every calamity suffered by mankind since we've become a people. So what is the answer that comes to me from history? Why are you even thinking about this subject? Because like every other group throughout history, you are nothing but a bunch of anti-Semitic hypocrites." Jäger looked around the room. "You don't even have the courage to take a stand one way or the other. You'll 'explore options' or 'debate alignments' until the last Jew is hanged or gassed. What unmitigated horseshit." Jäger looked directly at Moehlen. "You are Jezebel, teaching and leading astray countless millions of American Christians." She looked around the room at all of them and spoke with a stinging disdain. "You are the children of your fathers, who killed Jews wherever they could find them. Your grandmothers just sang louder in church as trainloads of Jews went by, screaming for help. You tell yourselves it's for your religion, for your God, for your Messiah, for peace. But don't fool yourself. History knows better. You will kill us because ... because you *hate* and because you don't love truth. And if you represent that Jewish Rabbi that the Romans stuck up on a cross, well then, you can take him and your religion and stick them up your collective, well-tailored, dignified, executive asses."

The room was stiflingly silent. Jäger dropped her hands to her sides, tugged down at the edges of her jacket, stepped down from the podium, and strode out of the room, not looking back. The thought flashed across Samantha's mind that she ought to get up and somehow ease Ms. Jäger's agitation, but Samantha saw the look on Dominique Moehlen's face and froze in her chair. Jäger pushed out of the back door of the conference room, leaving behind a wide range of expressions. Some of the attendees were shocked; most had looks of condescending disdain; a few were downright angry. Adiba Fakhoury, however, sat with a look of silent triumph on her face.

After Jäger had left the room, Edson Merrill pushed his folder forward and stood up and cleared his throat, commanding the group's attention.

"Look ... I don't want to be negative, and yeah, admittedly, we've had a little negativity going here the last few minutes, no question. But let's consider the positives here. We saw two different perspectives presented just now, from these first two speakers. And I'd say that one of them sort of underlined the validity of the other. I'd say that's a plus and it should move Guilder, Atchison, and Steckam in a clear direction. I may be stepping out on a limb, but I get a sense that most of us are coming to a consensus that what we just heard isn't where we want to go. I mean, everyone has their own story, no mistake, and truth is something we are all working toward, and as for me and my people, we'll be praying for Ms. Jäger, that she comes to work more diligently to find her truth, 'cause to tell you *my* truth, I don't think she's there yet—not by a long shot. But that isn't your problem today. Your problem—our problem, actually, as we work together with you—is to understand who in the world will be partners on a path that will integrate real truth and search for peace, and who won't. You as a company need to understand what perspectives are beneficial to that work, and what perspectives are not. And I think we've been fortunate to have just seen a perspective which, frankly, isn't that helpful. Anyway," he said, diffidently, sitting down again, "those are my thoughts."

Dominique Moehlen stood, focusing the attention of everyone in the room, steadying their disquiet. "Well," she said, the composed professional, "we should have expected this topic to have engendered some emotion. It has for the last few centuries; why would it be any different now?" Moehlen looked directly at Adiba Fakhoury. "I certainly do appreciate your professional forbearance in the face of what was obviously severe provocation, Ms. Fakhoury. If your conduct here is any representation at all of the patience and forbearance of the Palestinian people in the face of such blatant intimidation, well, I can only say that the position this company takes will most definitely ensure that such a perspective is more accurately reflected in the future." Moehlen looked around to the assembly, and said, "We have the rest of the agenda to complete, and with God's help, we'll do that." She sat down. Samantha stood and facilitated the rest of the meeting. They finished at six that evening, and most of the participants adjourned back to the Wyndham hotel.

***

The Thai restaurant was almost empty at eight o'clock that evening, for which Samantha was grateful. She sat across from Walter Ray Fritsch, toying with a scallop while he scooped up what seemed to her buckets of fried rice and shrimp. He pointed his pair of chopsticks at her.

"See ... I told you this would be an issue, Samantha. Jäger is just too undisciplined to consider putting in front of a serious group like Guilder, Atchison, and Steckam. I mean, GAS is an international company that does more than fifteen *billion* dollars in sales a year. I mean seriously, read her blogs—she's always been a loose cannon. She's just not in this league."

"But what about what she had to say," Samantha asked weakly. And then more strongly, "Let's not be juvenile. She made key points; historical, biblical points which just can't be ignored."

"You aren't understanding how people think today," Walter Ray replied. "Facts and truth don't matter. Impressions matter. Feelings matter. The *narrative* matters. Get it through your head. Speaking the truth isn't as important as speaking correctly."

"In other words, what you say isn't as important as who you're agreeing with."

"Hasn't it always been so?" he replied stingingly. "She made the company's decision easy." He paused to swallow an entire eggroll. "She validated, right in front of the most influential evangelicals in America, everything that Fakhoury had alleged about Israeli intolerance and intimidation. She tried to browbeat and intimidate Moehlen, and you just don't browbeat the CEO of one of the world's major media corporations. I mean, what was she thinking? Moehlen wasn't having any of it. If you're looking for a reason as to why GAS will be coming out with their new position, I'd say look no further than Ramona Jäger."

Samantha leaned forward. "Walter Ray, come off it. Jäger exploded because she felt like Daniel in the lion's den, and the pure, unadulterated ... *crap* that was coming from the other statements was just too much to take, especially for someone who knows the facts."

Walter Ray paused with his chopsticks in the air. "I'm not saying she got her facts wrong, sweetie," he said. He looked at her intently. "In fact, you need to realize that one of the things she said was pretty much on point exactly, and that was the reason she gave for this shift in the corporation's position. And that's something you will have to deal with on a personal level, too, if I'm not mistaken."

"What reason?" Samantha asked, not able to call to mind immediately what Jäger had said.

"Why, the reason is, sweetie, that Guilder, Atchison, and Steckam has decided, in this day and age, that it will be more acceptable to the stockholders for the company to become haters of Jews. Frankly, that alignment is much more conducive to staying in the black. And you'd have to agree to that, dear, because that, too, is a hard, cold fact. And executives deal in facts, not feelings."

Samantha sat shocked, hearing the truth so baldly expressed, but she couldn't argue with Fritsch. She was about to try, though, when her iPhone buzzed. It was a text from Jason Cruz. "Just a sec," she said to Walter Ray, who smiled and began a delightful interlude with a stick of chicken satay.

Cruz's text, in terse language, explained that the company wanted her to cover a Dominion Theology conference in Seattle and on her way out, cover a speech scheduled at a Patriot's Convention in Boise by some guy named Beaujolais, apparently an up-and-coming red-hot pastor in the Patriot movement. The Patriot Convention would be starting in two weeks, and the Dominion conference two days afterward. Corporate travel had already made her reservations, and it was a tight schedule. In a short line in his text, Cruz also directed her to take Wendy as her assistant. He wanted to talk to Samantha in the morning, early, at eight o'clock.

Samantha wondered about the impact her invitation to Jäger would have on her future with Guilder, Atchison, and Steckam. She wondered what Cruz was playing at, requiring her to take Wendy; she'd never needed an assistant on a trip before. And she wondered what her personal responsibility was in response to Jäger's facts. She had on one hand wanted to comfort Jäger, to communicate that she, *and* Israel, had at least one friend in the company, but she'd been too frightened to buck the company's very clear position of growing support to Islam, and so she'd made no move to express her personal opinions or provide Jäger any solace. She was beginning to feel bad about that, and Walter Ray wasn't making her feel any better. She wished Pastor Tony was here. Their last interlude was ... well, it was something she wanted to tuck away and pull out and look at when she had more time.

All her life she'd prided herself on being a friend of Israel—it was what she'd been taught in every Sunday school, in every sermon she'd heard her entire fundamentalist Christian life. She'd been taught to 'pray for the peace of Jerusalem'. And now the esteemed Walter Ray Fritsch was making it unavoidably clear to her in no uncertain terms that the company for whom she worked—the company she supported with her effort, creativity, and energies, and to which she was utterly devoted—was deliberately, intentionally seeking to harm what she had always considered the apple of God's eye. She was beginning to feel the first pangs of conviction that perhaps she should re-evaluate her terms of employment, and her employer. The memories of Ironbridge's blunt assertions during that party came back to sting her. But in opposition to these thoughts, she told herself that she could do so much *good* at Guilder, Atchison, and Steckam. In her position she could influence the company's direction in so many positive ways, ways that might actually benefit Israel and the Jews. This argument in her mind militated against the facts shoved in her face by Fritsch, and it was beginning to generate conflict ... but not enough to keep her from playing the role of a determined professional.

She looked up at Fritsch and held up her phone, "Just one more minute," she said, and began texting a reply to Jason. "*On it*," she replied, conveying a hard, on-top-of-things professionalism, fingers flying over the glass. "*Will coordinate w/ Wendy*," she sent, to convey cooperation and her willingness to be an inclusive team player. She looked up at Fritsch.

"So how will this play out vis-à-vis my future with the company," she asked. The question just popped into her head and out of her mouth before she thought how it would sound—like any other self-seeking careerist.

Fritsch stopped eating to contemplate that. "To be blunt, not well," he answered after some thought. "But, hold on a minute, let me ask ... you were the one who invited her, right?"

"Right." Samantha looked out the window at traffic flowing by. "It was my job to get folks from differing viewpoints to the meeting, to provide a range of perspectives."

"Oh, well then, that's a different story. You told me that before ... I'd forgotten. That said, I don't see a problem. You did your job. You definitely put people in the room with a bunch of different perspectives, sweetie. Mission accomplished." He saluted her with an empty skewer. "In fact, if you're desperate, you can spin it such that you *knew* Jäger was a loose cannon because you'd been following her for years, and you wanted the group to see just exactly what those poor Palestinians have been up against all this time. You can frame it as though you stacked the deck."

Samantha wasn't comforted; she had an instinct that Moehlen and others had somehow sensed her affinity for Jäger regardless of how Fritsch suggested she spin things. It was that gut instinct warning that froze her in place instead of stepping out to soothe Jäger after she left the conference room. Frightened at her own grasping reaction to Fritsch's bald, greedy, selfish attempt at spinning the situation, Samantha found she needed to think about these things more, and all of a sudden discovered that she didn't want to talk about them with Walter Ray.

"Well ... it must not be too bad. They're sending me to Seattle to cover the Seven Mountains Conference." Walter Ray's eyebrows rose and he waited quietly for an explanation.

"It refers to a current trend in the Christian right where the feeling is that Christians need to dominate and control the seven main areas of today's culture."

"Uh huh. And what would those be?" Walter Ray asked, lifting a cup of hot tea.

"Let me think," Samantha replied, remembering. "I think they're talking about business, government, religion, entertainment, the media definitely ... what else ... oh, and education. How many is that?"

"Six by my count."

"I can't remember the other ... oh, no, wait, the family. That's the last one."

"Sounds like an ambitious agenda," Walter Ray opined neutrally.

"Well, we'll see. I'll be headed out with Wendy in a couple of weeks. It should be interesting."

Walter Ray narrowed his eyes at the mention of Wendy's name. "She'll be headed out with you?"

"Yeah ... Cruz mentioned it in his text."

"That normal?"

"Well, no, actually, this is the first time. I'm thinking they want to expose her to some of the work people are doing throughout the firm. It's sort of a minor mentoring program that they work all the interns into."

Walter Ray nodded his head slowly, acknowledging her explanation.

"What? You look like you don't believe me."

"Oh no, no, that's fine, perfectly fine. Makes all the sense in the world. Just ... "

"Just what?" Samantha pressed, now edgy, worried that the company might be prepping Wendy to take her job.

"Hmmm ... just don't worry about her being a threat to your position, okay? In her emails to me, let me just say that her writing skills leave something to be desired, so ... you've nothing to worry about there. And the company wouldn't be stupid or vindictive enough to put her in your position. She doesn't have the maturity or experience. That would be just cutting off their nose to spite their face, and companies with shareholders don't do that kind of thing."

"Hmmm," Samantha grunted. "I hope you're right. I like my job ... a lot."

"That, my dear, is evident. But as I say, she's no threat to you ... in that regard." Walter Ray left it at that, and Samantha, thinking about what she needed to do to prepare for the trip, completely missed his subtle innuendo.

***

The next morning Samantha met with Jason Cruz in his office at exactly eight o'clock. Cruz' office was now on the top floor of the building, with a dignified crimson, tight-pile carpet, a wide ranging collection of modern Christian, Hindu, and Moslem art on the walls or on the discreet but heavy coffee tables, and a large, burled wood desk. She was tired, not having slept well, under a lot of stress about the fallout from meeting, but Jason, as always, looked bright and fresh, full of energy and enthusiasm. He looked her over hard once, up and down, wondering why she seemed to be out of sorts.

"So we want you out in Seattle, Samantha. They're having something called a 'Patriot' convention. It seems the leadership from the Dominion movement wants more publicity than they can get on their own, and they want their message to get a broader platform. They've heard about what we arranged with the Emergent Church folks, and they want to talk to you with a view of going the same route."

Samantha listened, her head somewhat thick from lack of sleep. "Well, I guess that's good," she said slowly.

"Of course it's good," Cruz shot back. "And hey, Wendy talked with me during one of the breaks yesterday. She mentioned that she could be more help to you if she was with you on travel, and when this request came in from the Dominion people, I thought I'd kill two birds with one stone. We've got the budget for it, so take her along. Let's see how she works out."

"Sure, Jason. No problem. I'm sure she'll be a great help," she replied dully.

"You okay?" Cruz was looking at her sideways, a question mark across his features. Samantha had the strangest sensation that she was swimming with a very nice, very polite shark.

"Fine, fine," she answered, waving a hand in a deprecating gesture, trying to make light of things. "Didn't get much sleep last night."

"Okay ... and oh by the way, Ms. Moehlen asked me to pass to you that she was particularly impressed with the strategy you employed in selecting the speakers at the meeting yesterday. You made some points."

Samantha was caught by surprise. "Honestly? I mean, Jäger sort of went over the top, didn't she?"

Cruz smiled slowly, twirling in his Aeron chair to look out over the city. "Waal, yeah," he drawled, sliding back into a faux northern Minnesota accent, "she put her foot in it, to be honest. But Samantha, you told me you'd been following her for years. You knew that's how she'd come across, and Moehlen counted on it. Jäger came through; so did you."

Samantha simply nodded an acknowledgement. There would be time later, she said to herself, to flagellate herself for not having the courage to speak the truth to Cruz—that she hadn't at all planned such a thing to happen. But she didn't acknowledge that fact to Cruz; she let his assumption pass for the truth, to her own benefit. She just nodded, turned around, and walked out the door to continue doing research on Dominion theology before her meeting in Seattle, keeping her job but leaving her self-respect in a puddle on Cruz's rich, tightly-woven scarlet carpet.

***

A week later, Guilder, Atchison, and Steckam hit the publishing world with a prepared statement that left no room for doubt—the world's largest Christian religious communications corporation was solidly backing the Palestinian cause, and would henceforth question the previous unequivocal support extended to Israel in everything they published, in every media format. The announcement made it clear that this re-evaluation was a result of a reasoned assessment of emerging trends in Christianity, economics, culture, and politics, and the firm's desire was to both stay ahead of these trends and be fully and completely inclusive of all peoples, wherever they might be found, whatever their faith might be, making new truths and new revelations about the Christ relevant to all peoples everywhere.

Chapter 33
Simonsen

"For My people are foolish, they know Me not; they are stupid children and have no understanding. They are shrewd to do evil, but to do good they do not know."

Jeremiah 4:22

There are those upon whom the world confers privilege, propriety, and prosperity; those who wear such gifts like a mink wears its coat—but the price is always and only a life lived in consonance with the world's system of exchanges and transactions, philosophies, and values. Simonsen Lehrner, gazing at the Golden Gate Bridge rising up out of the fog one early evening, looking through a broad expanse of window in his study, was a member of this group of privileged conferees.

He was hosting a small dinner party that night, and the atmosphere was quickly becoming warm and convivial, with a unique and eclectic mixture of guests, drinks in hand, circulating throughout the sprawling, expansive home tucked high in the hills overlooking San Francisco bay. Yet he wanted this time alone in his study to reflect before going out to join the guests.

He felt contented, excited, energized, and confident with his lot in life. Simonsen was fifty-three that evening, of medium height with a spare frame, and sharp, intelligent brown eyes in an open, usually smiling face. He was Jewish; his father, Shim'on Lehrenstein, and his mother Tess, both Russian Jews, had emigrated to America literally days before Hitler scythed through western Russia in the summer of 1941, slaughtering Jews as he went. Serendipitous timing was a family trait.

His parents had put every child—three boys, two girls—through college. His father, a brilliant engineer, got on early in Southern California with Lockheed, building the sturdy propeller aircraft that would first support Russia via Lend Lease during WWII, and then sleek, fast, unutterably complex jets that would duel with his native land during the Cold War. Simonsen, the oldest son, had begun studying aeronautical engineering at Stanford, but in his second year, the bright thread of a scintillating business skill could not be suppressed. He graduated cum laude instead with a degree in business, and, recognizing that the future of the world lay primarily in the energy sector, launched into that industry with a deep passion and an intense work ethic. He was hired by the Anglo-Persian Oil Company, which later became British Petroleum, or BP for short.

In his salad days, Simonsen worked hard to ground himself in the foundations of the international oil business. Incisive, perceptive, energetic, and tireless, with a remarkable facility to work with a wide range of difficult personalities and egos, he rose rapidly. He learned about the research, science, and plain hard work involved in exploration and appraisals, and the commercial aspects associated with oil reserves around the world. He learned the basics of crude oil and gas production, and became somewhat of an expert in the emerging global market for liquid natural gas. He learned how companies evaluate and price the various grades of crude, how they refine it, and how they trade the commodity on international markets. He learned the oil and gas industry from a market perspective, and, since he worked for an international firm that produced and sold their products globally, could not avoid learning about the key geopolitical issues involved in the world energy markets.

In all this work and effort, Simonsen, always introspective and highly self-aware, realized that the activity of learning itself was critical, and he tucked that nugget of knowledge away for future use. But Simonsen did not discover his real love, the calling in his life, the specific niche which, once mastered, would launch him into global prominence, until BP assigned him to work for the strategic planning division. The geopolitical aspects of the energy industry particularly demanded an ability for companies in that market space to have clear ideas about how the future might develop. When Simonsen began working with the strategic planning cell in BP, strategic planning was simply an activity whereby a group of rather seasoned graybeards in the company gathered round a conference table and for about three days tossed their opinions on the table. Eventually someone would be tasked with the job of roping these various opinions into a corral of recommendations that made some degree of business sense. There was no rigor, no system, and no real process to the activity.

Again, the fortuitous family timing intervened. Lehrner was transferred into this high-level business unit just as it took on new leadership—a strong-willed but wily Norwegian, Lars Stiegkrom, possessing an unparelled skill in the care and handling of senior corporate leadership. Stiegkrom had an idea to tell *stories* about the future—scenarios, he called them, in which a company's directors might have the experience, not of trying to predict the future, but instead thinking about how various futures might emerge and what the firm might do in each of those futures. At first he was dismissed as a crank, but the success of the method was dramatically proven when one of his stories about potential oil and gas futures began to come about. BP's leadership, primed by Stiegkrom's methods regarding the signs to look for in the emerging future, leapt ahead of their competitors with the speed of their reactions—for they'd already spent the time strategizing about what they'd do if such a world came about—and suddenly Stiegkrom's method of long-range strategic planning became the de facto industry standard for the world's largest corporations. And there was Lehrner, a key member of the young team. With his natural intelligence, sparkling enthusiasm so obviously inclined toward looking forward, his unique ability to see things from different perspectives, and his inclination to soak up everything around him, he thrived in this new practice. Soon branching out on his own, he became the world's recognized leader in future planning, consultant to heads of State, Kings, Ministers, and countless corporate executives.

Lehrner had met, courted, and won his wife while in college; a stunning American-born Jewess whose parents had also, coincidentally, emigrated from Russia. Dania had wide-set almond-shaped eyes and skin like cream, she'd been studying law, and after graduating, began a successful career as a lawyer for one of the country's most prestigious technology firms. She kept her career and successfully juggled the legal profession with her husband's globetrotting activities and the delightful responsibilities of two daughters, Caroline and Naomi. Dania had recently been appointed as a judge on the U.S. Court of International Trade, headquartered in New York. They had quite a remarkable marriage, all in all, for a couple with such varied professional responsibilities. Yet they were very similar; they were Jews, and while certainly not practicing, nor in any way religious, they maintained a cultural pride that bonded them together. And they both had the same driving motivations in life—the drive to succeed, to contribute, to be excellent, to learn, to make the world a better place ... to do good deeds. Their natures were such that they both respected each other, which always bodes well as a foundation for any relationship.

They both doted on their daughters, yet were with equal diligence hard taskmasters when it came to insisting upon academic excellence.

Caroline, the oldest, had her father's scintillating curiosity for everything around her, his quick intellect, and a desire to absorb whatever she could from anyone she met. She was a woman with strong character, and she carried herself with confidence. She had dark hair, dark brown eyes, and a lithe, modest frame. And while she could be engaging and personable, she was an introvert, like her mother, happiest and most energized when tucked away by herself, reading, thinking, philosophizing, ruminating on the events that swirled beyond her horizons. Yet where her parents were utterly agnostic, completely assimilated Jews, Caroline had, somewhere in her upbringing, become a passionate Zionist—so passionate that after graduating from Brown, she made Aliyah to Israel, became an Israeli citizen, and joined the Israeli Defense Force. After two years working in administrative units improving her Hebrew, the IDF put her into an intelligence unit, where she demonstrated a flair for geopolitical analysis, especially when it came to Israel's relations with the U.S. While her parents knew she'd gone to Israel, they were under the impression that she worked with one of the local news agencies that specialized in international news, and Caroline did, in fact, work for one of Israel's conservative policy journals as a strategic analyst—her degree was in international relations—yet her real work was done for the IDF's intelligence branch. At the moment she was taking a short vacation from her undercover assignment as a secretary and administrative assistant to a small construction company in northern Minnesota. There she was known as Daria Avidora. Her parents knew nothing of her intelligence work, and she was determined to keep it that way. They thought she was on leave from her job in Israel.

Her job in Minnesota was to identify various political and economic trends in the midwest that Israel was watching closely, trends about which her handlers in Israel were greatly concerned. Eschewing the hotbeds of liberalism on both coasts, Israel wanted to keep a finger on what they thought was America's true pulse; the heartland in the Midwest. They'd directed Caroline to immerse herself in 'the American experience'. Her case officer had rushed this mission; there was a growing sense of urgency about the times in which they were living, and needed good intelligence about what people in America were thinking about Israel.

Naomi, the Lehrner's younger daughter, was taller than Caroline, with silky black hair, arrestingly large blue eyes, and the classical mixture of European and Semitic features that had throughout the centuries made Jewish women renowned for their beauty. Of the two, Naomi had always had more suitors—though Caroline did not lack in that area—but Naomi's striking figure and dark, classically European face mowed men down like Samson struck down Philistines. Naomi was an artist—and as passionate, outgoing, and impulsive as Caroline was reserved, introspective, and deliberate. Naomi was at the moment being hotly pursued by a smitten Connor Welling, perhaps the world's ablest writer on new technologies for the American technology magazine *Contek*. One of the reasons Simonsen had asked the technology guru to dinner was simply to please Naomi. Simonsen and Welling had an on-going collaboration founded in mutual respect, both men at the top of their respective disciplines, and it was actually during a story Connor was doing on Simonsen for *Contek* that he met Naomi. For her part, Naomi found Connor fascinating—he was an exciting combination of rakish intelligence and wild, unorthodox, but intellectually sound insights that she found both frustrating and compelling, and which served to constantly throw her off-balance, making her question the perspectives through which she perceived almost everything around her. Being on the other side of the initiative in a relationship wasn't something to which she was accustomed, and it gave her pause.

For most of his professional life, Lehrner specialized in gathering around him some of the world's most unique and interesting people—and the people Lehrner considered unique and interesting soon became so to the rest of the world. This had the rebounding effect of causing Lehrner to be perceived as a sort of 'reputation generator'—a human echo chamber for a person's splash they made in the world—someone with whom people definitely wanted to associate, and this in turn improved his capability to attract the global cream of the crop. If Lehrner didn't know a person, they were probably not closely involved in making the world work. A global news magazine had coined the term *global elite* in an article specifically describing Simonsen Lehrner and his impact on the world. Lehrner, with calm confidence, unaffected dignity and a truly world-class intellect, with a sense of humility but a clear awareness of his abilities, had attained that place in his profession where he frequently counseled the world's greatest men about the world's most important issues.

Tonight's affair was to welcome a minor Chinese diplomat and her husband, a key executive in one of China's national companies. Lehrner was closely involved with a number of critical diplomatic and economic initiatives at the highest levels between the Chinese and American governments, and as a gesture of friendship, felt it wise to host this small personal reception. He moved out of his study and, pausing at the entrance to the larger living room and looking around the room, sought to get a sense of how the evening was emerging.

James Huo, the producer of a recent epic film about the Han Dynasty, the first Chinese-produced film ever to gross over $85 million at U.S. box offices, stood in a corner dressed in a comfortable white linen suit conversing intensely with Anna Hoenkstrom, an actress famous for her portrayal of a young female hacker who played a key role in solving a murder in a film based on a best-selling novel. There was a young scientist just on the verge of a major breakthrough in three-dimensional holographic projectors for the business market; three key executives from Sany, the Chinese national machinery corporation making a bid on several U.S. federal and state contracts to improve America's port infrastructure; a sweating, overweight novelist who'd just finished a well-received piece of historical fiction on the Jews in Belorussia, and who found himself in town on a book tour when Lehrner's email invitation pulled him out of his hotel; a rotund little Chinese-American economics professor from Stanford with a moon face and razor-cuts for eyes whose area of expertise was integrating China's markets into the global economy, who had just published a popular scholarly work on the subject; a young, very shy man out of England, somewhat pear-shaped, in a brown suit and a sort of muddled expression, who'd just published a wildly successful fictional novel about two Chinese peasants whose marriage is arranged in the traditional way, and who go on to suffer a heartbreaking series of events as their lives follow in the turbulent wake of China's history from the time of the Japanese occupation to the advent of the PRC; and finally, there was Caroline, arguing as always in her quietly passionate way with Connor. Naomi stood behind Connor, drink in hand, staring at them both, then leaping into the argument with equally determined passion. He moved across the room as unobtrusively as possible to join them.

"You can believe what you like, but there really isn't room to argue," Caroline was saying, "and the facts are just the facts. I mean, seriously, Americans today have zero idea—*zero* idea—of what is happening in the world. They get their opinions fed to them from USA Today or Drudge or whatever nutcase tinfoil hat blog they happen to be reading that week. The next time you're in a hotel, look around outside the rooms on the floor some morning, in almost every hotel in the country. USA Today is the damn newspaper for the proletariat, for God's sake! And invariably it has a picture of some blonde bimbo or some demented male movie star topping out the right corner. Your media follows who they're told to follow, reports what they're told to report, puffs who they're told to puff, and pans who they're told to pan."

"That's not how it seems to us," Connor put in, "and I work in the media."

"So does she," Naomi put in, referring to her sister, unbiased at this point in the argument.

"You may work in the media, Connor, but seriously, who makes the decisions regarding what news you report on?"

"I do, absolutely! If you're trying to convince me there's some sort of secret 'cabal' of leftist world conspirators behind the scenes plotting to take over the world by controlling the media, you're selling old goods, sweetie."

"It doesn't have to be any kind of secret, Connor. You say you're the one who decides what to put out in *Contek*. Are you on the editorial board?"

Connor took a sip of his scotch and soda and looked at Caroline over the rim of his glass. "You know I'm not."

"And can you decide on your own to spend the money to go research a story on, say, a new Internet technology that some genius in Switzerland might have invented?" Caroline bored in.

"Any company has processes to approve the expenditure of funds, you know that," Naomi interjected.

"And those processes are there just so those with the money control where it's spent," Caroline shot back, "we all know that too. But my point is that Connor couldn't take a taxi on *Contek* business without someone approving the expenditure, and that means that Connor *isn't* really the one who decides what gets reported. He may *suggest* a story, but it's the editors who balance the revenues such a story might bring with a bunch of other factors, which I just don't think you're considering, before they approve what he undertakes."

"What factors?" Connor asked darkly; he didn't like being challenged intellectually on his home turf—by a woman who lived in another country. And though he wouldn't admit it, the media's narrative against Israel has fashioned in his own crusted soul a slight distaste and disdain for this woman who'd decided to make Israel her country.

"Things like how the information might impact the almighty narrative; how the information might impact the public's opinions regarding the current political regime..."

"In this country, sweetie, Americans call their political leadership an 'administration'."

Caroline leaned forward from the waist, irritated at his condescening use of the term 'sweetie' and said, "Whether I'm in Buffalo or Botswana, an elephant turd is an elephant turd, Connor. What you have now in America is not any kind of 'administration', it is purely and simply a regime, moving toward totalitarianism."

"That's ridiculous!" Naomi blurted. "How can you say that? You come from a part of the world where strong men ruling are the de facto standard—"

"Not in Israel," Caroline interrupted, but got no further.

"—so you see totalitarianism anywhere someone doesn't agree with you. We have unlimited freedom in this country. The political leadership we have is a viable representation of the American public, and the leadership is faithfully representing our wishes."

Caroline looked at her sister with hard eyes. "Oh come off it, Sis. Do you think the majority of Americans, who by the way have over twenty grand in credit card debt if they have a credit card, where 25% of the households in this country couldn't cover a payment for some emergency because they just don't have any savings—and we won't even talk about their mortgage debt—are being represented by the current re—sorry, the current administration? Most Americans are pounding out their five-day-a-week jobs just so they can eat that month, and rent some videos or pull down a few songs from the iTunes store. Do you *really* think they have any kind of freedom? My God, do they have the freedom to switch jobs? Good luck. They're indentured servants. What do you think would happen to their thin-iced life if they lost their jobs? Do they have the freedom to try and improve their lot in life, maybe get a better education, when they can't pay the debt they owe now?"

"This is what we're working for, don't you get it?" Connor exclaimed with passion. "We want people to have the freedom to not work if they choose to, to have access to free education to improve their lot in life."

"Oh please," Caroline replied scathingly. "How would you do that? By redistributing the wealth? Who pays for all that free education? Do you expect the professors and instructors and lab technicians all to work for free? And who pays for your food and rent if you choose not to work?" She turned to her sister. "Let's make a bet, Naomi ... I'll bet that if your particular opinions somehow moved to the right of the political spectrum, suddenly you'd find your political leadership a whole lot less representative. And if you ever came out publicly in support of Israel, you'd find yourself out of work, blacklisted, and all the friends you think you have wouldn't be returning your calls." Caroline looked pointedly at Connor and went on. "Someone moves to the right in this country and suddenly there is some sort of reaction as though that person has a deadly virus."

Connor rolled his eyes very slightly frustrated. "You may be right, Caroline, but think about why. The right *had* its shot; the capitalists had their shot, and look where they've left us ... an economy in shambles, an almost uncontrollable military that has enormous control over most of the country's wealth, and a tiny percentage of the country's wealthy living off the backs of most of the rest of the population. Do you *realize* what the data show on wealth disparity in this country alone? Now we have a President who's trying to re-align the country's domestic and foreign policy with reality. He's trying to establish at least some semblance of parity regarding who has enough money to live on; he's trying to get us off the bulls-eye regarding Muslim hatred, trying to convince the world that America has no argument with Islam, and he's doing a damn fine job of it."

Naomi's eyes widened; 'Muslim hatred' wasn't a topic to bring up in front of Caroline, who would rip Connor to shreds intellectually, and the evening would be a disaster. But her father stepped in before she could react.

"Hello, ladies; Connor, nice to see you again. Can I ask you all to join me as we greet the guests of honor? They're downstairs. This way, if you please." Simonsen held out his arm in an urbane gesture intended to quell the impending discord, but Caroline, swallowing a blistering retort to Connor about Muslim hatred in America, spun on her heels and moved off toward her father's study. Connor tossed off the rest of his scotch, threw a significant glance at Naomi, as if questioning what kind of family he was associating with, and followed Simonsen down the stairs to greet the Chinese guests.

***

Earlier that afternoon, Meifeng and her 'husband,' Wei Bolin, had spent several grueling hours in a private residence near San Francisco frequently used by the Chinese government as an informal extension of the Chinese Embassy. The property was acknowledged as such by the U.S. Government and accorded the appropriate diplomatic protections. Meifeng and Bolin had spent the time in briefings by different diplomats, intelligence agents, economic agents, and representatives of the PLA, on the current status of 'the Plan'.

Before they were briefed, they spent three hours briefing the assembled officials on the progress to date of the effort made to familiarize Bolin with the various elements of the Plan. They described their journeys out of China down through the participating southeast Asian ports—Saigon, Da Nang, and Hai Phong in Vietnam, Tanjung Pelapas in Malaysia, and Laem Chabong in Thailand—where they saw the massive new cargo vessels being constructed. At each location, Bolin asked and was asked in return about numerous details involving storage capacity, shipboard systems requirements for anticipated cargo, and, most importantly, loading plans for infrastructure support items. The naval architects at the firms needed to know which material would be offloaded first; which equipment was necessary to support immediate operations ashore, and which could be stowed farther back, offloaded at a later time. They discussed everything from construction equipment to medical supplies capable of supporting a full biological warfare scenario to portable housing materials.

One event occurred during this orientation trip that confirmed Meifeng's opinion that Bolin's towering intellect, though awe-inspiring, did not seem in any way connected to an awareness of human emotions or a need for sustainable human relationships. As it turned out, the Vietnamese ports were frustratingly deficient in their own infrastructure. Second only to China in its growth in the new century, Vietnam had made sure to cater diligently to foreign investors, and the attractiveness of low labor costs and a large, well-educated new generation made Vietnam a prime location for foreign investment. However, the government forgot to invest in its own infrastructure. Bolin tactlessly hammered Vietnamese officials for this oversight, and in one brilliant but scathingly caustic two-hour session, outlined a remarkably prescient plan for the country to quickly bring their port facilities up to scratch. Port officials, mayors, and the cleared officials from the Vietnamese government scrambled to capture every aspect of Bolin's plan. Enormous capital was flowing from China in return for Vietnamese support of this massive effort, and they would rather have cut off their arms than risk endangering that endless flow of wealth. Out of a professional instinct to ease ruffled feathers, Meifeng presented the Vietnamese with transcripts of Bolin's entire two-hour rant, transcribed word-for-word into Vietnamese, barely an hour after the meeting, using the Group's rapid translation technology.

During another incident on the trip, in one of China's 'ghost cities', now filled with hundreds of thousands of Japanese workers, refugees from the destruction of the Japanese main islands wrought during the massive earthquakes, they visited with a Japanese nuclear expert. The island nation of Japan had been destroyed not so much by the earthquakes but rather the subsequent flood of radioactivity that spilled from the wrecked nuclear reactors as nine of them eventually melted down, spewing Cesium 137 and poisoning all of what had been known as Japan and lofting that poison, almost as an afterthought, into the air and sea to eventually wreak havoc on the agricultural economy of the United States. A people no longer possessing a nation, most of the Japanese emigrated en masse to other lands, other countries, forced by the hand of God to make new lives as immigrants—a bitter but just judgment against a people who epitomized the exclusionary characteristics of a quintessentially racist society.

Millions of Japanese had been invited to come and live in what were known as China's 'ghost cities'—cities constructed in the wilderness of China's northern provinces, complete with roads, massive apartment complexes, art and sculpture, concert halls, municipal headquarters buildings, factories, bridges, road signs ... everything except people. When Japan melted down, China's leadership immediately recognized with a cold, predatory gleam in their collective eyes the deep richness of the saying, 'Revenge is a dish best served cold'. Ostensibly offering sanctuary, they imported millions of Japanese, offering them a set of ready-made cities, with only the utilities needing to be connected—water, power, sewage, and the importing of food. What could the Japanese do? They could not eat their bread or drink their water; nothing could be imported to Japan, because the world thought the Japanese, unlike the Haitians, too rich to need much support, and what was sent couldn't be distributed because the nation's infrastructure—its roads and ports and trains and fuel storage areas—had been destroyed. And so they migrated, the bitter gall of history kept jammed behind clenched teeth as they accepted the apparent largesse from their greatest enemy. They need not have been despondent about that, at least, for largesse, mercy, succor, and support was the last thing Chinese leadership had in mind.

Millions of Japanese were efficiently transported into these ghost cities, and the PLA had, in a dramatic display of industry, ensured that the cities' utilities were fully functional when the new immigrants arrived. In the midst of their stunned surprise and shock that the Chinese would be so magnanimous, no one at first realized that the infrastructure systems that would keep them alive in these cities which were, truly, in the middle of massively remote areas, were all controlled by the PLA—the water sources, the power, the sewage removal ... and, most importantly, the food. After a month, most of the Japanese refugees were getting over the shock of dislocation and it was then that the Chinese introduced their real terms and conditions. The Japanese were to become Chinese citizens—of the lower class, they were to note—and they would be responsible for invigorating China's economy with the skills and energy they had at one time applied to their own country. They would start up new electronics factories, new computer fabrication plants, new automobile manufacturing companies, and they would produce Japanese-quality products that would be sold on the world market as Chinese goods. The Chinese saved the best for last: with admirable restraint but deep satisfaction in their revenge-soaked souls, they announced to the Japanese that they would do all this work and thereby enrich the Middle Kingdom for wages that would be refused by the meanest pedicab coolie; wages that would barely sustain life, not to mention any attempts to abandon their new 'sanctuary'.

There were the obvious reactions. Some of the younger Japanese rebelled and tried to escape. They either died in the desolate wilderness surrounding the cities or were killed by the PLA, who ringed every city with sophisticated sensors, tracking devices, dogs, and thousands of soldiers. Some of the others simply refused to work; they were starved, slowly, as testimonies to the others about the futility of resistance. But most complied; the Japanese were a compliant people, and they had, in their history, suffered similar crushing events, though none that were so comprehensive, and never had such a defeat literally thrust them from their land.

And so one day the military VSTOL[32] jet carrying Meifeng and Bolin and their armed escort slammed down on the landing pad atop one of the skyscrapers reaching to the heavens in one of the ghost cities in the desert of Inner Mongolia. There, the PLA was keeping most of the Japanese nuclear experts—at least those who survived initial attempts to arrest the reactor meltdowns in Japan, who hadn't waded through water suffused with radioactivity a million times more powerful than was safe for the human body, who hadn't chosen to make heroic but fatally futile efforts to try and cool their scramming reactors, standing in frothing radioactive clouds of steam, pouring water on the reactors with fire hoses.

Five Japanese nuclear experts, speaking rudimentary Mandarin, had briefed Bolin on the effects of nuclear radiation—on people, buildings, water supplies, food supplies, the land, the air—on everything. For five hours they filled his photographic mind with pictures of what had happened in Japan—at Hiroshima, Nagasaki, Fukushima, Onagawa, and Tokai Daini, Kashwazald-Kariwa, Shika, Ohi, Hamaoka, and Takahama. Two of the five scientists who gave the briefings were themselves slowly dying—one from liver cancer, the other from skin cancer. It gave the material added significance, though it did not stir an ounce of pity in Bolin or Meifeng, and certainly not in the group of armed PLA commandos that accompanied them. The memory of the Japanese occupation during what had been called 'World War II' was still too fresh in Chinese memory, yet since that time, the Japanese had never apologized for their excess. Apology was not part of the culture which made 'saving face' so crucial. 'Saving face' was simply the eastern way of referring to the habit ingraned in our human, fleshly nature of never admitting error, of avoiding refinement at all costs—basically, the sin of pride. Men—eastern or western—are alike in this circumvention of the cross.

Meifeng had accompanied Bolin as they traveled to Qindao, headquarters for China's North Sea Fleet, to be briefed by Chinese naval leadership. There, an ancient-looking, flat-faced, flat-bellied, leathery-skinned executive stood before a map and spoke to them for two hours, off the cuff, about the maritime challenges facing China in the plan they were undertaking.

"You must realize we have done things very differently than most nations who have embarked upon maritime policies," the man began, dressed in a suit, standing before them with one hand on his hip, the other holding a pointer, which he would occasionally jab in their direction.

"Excuse me, Comrade, but are you ... are you in the Navy?" Bolin asked.

32 Vertical Short Takeoff and Landing

"The Navy? What gave you that idea?" The man waved his arms and the tip of the pointer described wild arcs around the room as he spoke. "This is what I am trying to tell you. In Soviet Russia, Germany, in Meiji Japan, it was the state that built a navy, a huge fleet of warships, and then they followed with building a merchant fleet, as though someone in the department suddenly remembered the country needed food and oil. Not so here. I am Fu San Ho; I am the president of Jiangnan Shipyard. We are the largest shipbuilding firm in China, young man. Now you sit and listen and I will tell you about how China will conquer the oceans of the world."

Uncharacteristically, Bolin demurred, even offering an apology to 'the honored Uncle.' Meifeng stole a sideways glance to see if he was being sarcastic, but Bolin's eyes were cast down. She filed that incident away for future reference.

"China comes into her own in the midst of a period of history when the world economies are integrated; there is global economic development, do you understand? Because of this, and because we are first a peace-loving people, it is our commercial interests that have led the way to us becoming masters of the oceans. It is not those gray wolves," he said, waving a pointer disdainfully toward the window, out of which could be seen, just beyond the new massive 500,000 deadweight ton dry docks, dozens of sleek warships at anchor in the harbor, all bristling with radars, missiles, helicopters, and antennas. "It is our economy that pulls us to the sea, not war," he went on. "China's businessmen have always led the world in the realization and awareness of the importance of the ocean to trade. And so the State recognizes this, and look where we are now. We are the world's leader in commercial shipbuilding. Yes, you did not know this, did you," he said, stating what he assumed was fact. "In 2006 we produced 13 million deadweight tons; by 2010 we exceeded 22 million tons. Today, we are on track to produce close to 45 million deadweight tons; no country in the world does this, not even the Koreans, productive sons of the seven hells that they are. This is almost 40% of the total world's production of shipping ... do you understand this?"

"So ... our businesses sell, other nations buy, and in buying, procure their ultimate demise." Bolin made the flat statement in a respectful tone of voice.

The old man blinked once, opened his mouth, then closed it and nodded his head slowly and pushed the pointer toward Bolin. "You ... you learn quickly. You will do well. Yes, you are right, it is their greed that will in the end earn them their demise. What is more open, more peaceful, more pacifying, then to simply build large, slow, merchants ships to carry radios and televisions and dolls and clothes to the nations of the world? Why, who could argue with such things?"

Bolin turned to look out the window, as though anticipating the older man's next words. "And you are right, young man, for that is what comes from the ability to build ships well. Yes, look all you want, there they are, and those wolves have a purpose, too. So let us talk about how those wolves might help you in yours."

The old man gave them some background first. "You do not know this but in the 1950's, we were doing quite well; we were making good progress. Then we split with the Soviets due to their faulty interpretation of correct socialistic doctrines. Unfortunately they took with them much of the knowledge and equipment we needed to succeed, and it was revealed to many sharper minds that in truth, China had little in the way of true shipbuilding knowledge. We reorganized, creating a central repository of knowledge to invigorate our efforts, and we brought in most of the technical and engineering expertise needed to move our initiatives forward." The old man paused, his eyes looked up and over their heads for a moment, unfocused, and then he shook his head sharply. "But the Cultural Revolution did away with those efforts; we will not speak of those times." He coughed once. "But then Deng Xiaoping began the great opening up and reforms, and converted the defense resources to commercial interests to revitalize our economy. This is when we began to make real progress. In 1982 the China State Shipbuilding Corporation was brought into being, and we were unleashed to compete in the market space with greatly increased autonomy." The old man leaned forward, smiling a grim smile, and pointed the stick at Bolin. "And we ate them up, I can tell you, like a coolie eats rice. We had control of everything in the country—the shipyards, design universities, suppliers, third-party vendors, training firms, repair firms, even control over building military vessels. We had the power to create joint ventures with the barbarian companies, and we did all our trading through the China Shipbuilding Trading Company."

"I know this firm," Bolin contributed. "My grandfather bought many things that were brought to our home by this company."

"Of course he did," the old man replied, pleased. "The State was wise; they knew that shipbuilding could serve as a foundation for its economy, and to launch other heavy industries, like steel, heavy equipment manufacture, and others. We succeeded where others, like the aerospace industry, failed."

The old man went on for another hour, educating Bolin on the history of how China's shipbuilding industry successfully navigated the conversion from a previous focus totally on defense to one almost exclusively focusing on the commercial sector, all while operating in the midst of a centrally-controlled communist economic structure.

"But now," he said, at the end of his history lesson, "you will want to know specifically how our maritime power will support the Plan. For this, you get someone in the Navy." The old man looked over their heads as the door in the back of the room opened. Another man, old but not as old as Fu San Ho, wearing the uniform of a PLAN admiral, strode forward, bowed low to Fu San Ho, and took the pointer. Fu San Ho snapped a few words to the admiral, which neither Meifeng nor Bolin could catch, and then walked briskly up to each, shook their hands, wished them good luck, and left the room.

"You have heard Comrade Fu describe our shipbuilding industry," the admiral began, holding the pointer in both hands. "Now I will tell you what we intend to do with it."

***

Bolin drove north on I5 after the reception at the Lehrner residence. Meifeng sat in the passenger seat. Bolin was a good driver, with strikingly quick reflexes, holding the wheel with strong hands. She noticed the whipcord muscles in his forearms.

"What did you think of the man?" Meifeng asked, referring to Lehrner. She had not noticed Bolin's forearms before.

Bolin thought for several moments before responding. "I am not sure," he replied. "He is most hospitable, no question, but then, so are most people who want something."

"Do you think he has any idea of the coming time?"

"You know, I really don't, and I think that strange, since he is in the business of looking into the future." Bolin looked over at her quickly, snatching a glance to convey a point before returning his eyes to the road. It was raining from low clouds and the road was slippery. "No, truthfully, if I can believe what I am reading and sensing elsewhere, I would say he is one of Lenin's 'useful idiots', and the more useful since he is so highly placed relative to international business and political leadership."

"Why would you classify him so?" Meifeng asked, taken aback. She had thoroughly enjoyed herself at the reception, and thought Lehrner and his family consummate hosts.

"It is obvious. He's a Jew, and they have no future. I mean, it is actually ironic, don't you think, that this Jew is a renowned expert on the future and yet cannot see his own? He cannot see that huge, looming black swan event coming for him. 'Never again', they always say. They make me laugh. He can see everyone's future but his own. This is always the way it has been with them."

"You are being too class-conscious," Meifeng argued. "When the time comes we will need intelligent people to satisfy a number of key integration tasks."

Bolin thought for a few more seconds. "Perhaps you are right," he said, "but I don't think the plan will utilize Jews. Maybe others, but not those like him. Not the Jews. No ... wherever they go, they rise to prominence. They are destabilizing in a socialistic environment."

"What are you talking about? They were the founders of socialism. Marx, Lenin, Trotsky ... these were all Jews."

"Yes, and what happened to them?" Bolin replied. "Stalin put them down or out, one way or the other. And do you see any Jews in major positions in any socialist country in the world, besides Israel?"

"You are saying that they have been killed because people are jealous of them?"

"No ... no, I don't mean that, though that is how it might appear. No, there is something else, something different that stalks them."

She snapped her head around and looked at him, her eyes widen, senses alert. "You are talking about something having to do with religion," she replied briskly.

"And that is another thing," Bolin continued, pounding the steering wheel smartly with one hand, quickly jumping onto the end of her thought before she could continue, not noticing her reaction to his earlier supposition. "You bring up an interesting hypothesis, for when you look through history, there are instances where truthfully I cannot explain either their rise or their fall other than to refer to some external entity, some external agency that operates outside of and independent from what the normal flow of history would commend as logical."

Meifeng's stomach clenched; did he know? Had he somehow discovered?

"What do you mean," she asked in a weak voice.

"I mean that historians have not yet plumbed sufficiently to identify the rational reasons why at times Jews rose to great prominence in nations, and at other times they were brought low, even murdered en masse. Why? What did you think I meant? You did not think I was referring to an actual supernatural entity, did you?"

"No, of course not ... yet," she said, in a thin voice, for she was unsure of the ground in this discussion and desperately wanted to hold on to position of superiority vis-à-vis Bolin, "you must keep in mind that religion in this country strays into such areas. These people believe in such an entity—in several, actually. At least they did at one period in their history."

"And they no longer believe in this entity, or entities?" Bolin asked, still focused on driving safely.

"It is part of what we are here to discover, but data indicates that the firm belief systems they had are being diluted, negated, brought to no effect."

"We should discover how this is happening and leverage the dynamic," he replied, smiling grimly.

She nodded, relieved he had not noticed her concern, and looked out of her window at the rain splattering down on the farm fields. "It is happening from within," she murmured.

"What did you say?"

She looked back at him. "I said, they are apparently doing it to themselves. There is an enormous amount of divisiveness in what Americans term 'Christianity.' And it is good that you are curious about such things, because part of our tasking is to research this phenomena of religion in America."

"What do you mean, 'research the phenomena'?"

"I mean we will go into various religious environments to try and discover what it is that communicates moral force or power, and then identify how we will deal with that social factor during our operations in the future."

"You don't mean going into their churches?" This was so surprising that Bolin stared at her for too long a period; a horn snapped his eyes back to the road.

"I do, yes."

Bolin frowned. "Whatever for? I don't understand this vector. The time could be much more effectively spent elsewhere. And we were discussing Jews, not Christians."

"You are new to the Plan, Comrade Wei, and you have not yet been introduced to the sociological research which indicates that one of the key pillars in many areas of our intended operations turns out to be religion. And you should know, if you don't already, that the Jewish religion is closely tied to Christianity. The latter came from the former."

He paused, reflecting. "I didn't know that. I thought Christians had been killing Jews for centuries."

"They have. It is complicated, but you must trust that I am working from strong sources of validated data. The Directors have authorized the research; they have actually directed it. It is part of the Plan. We will need to touch at various religious points of interest on this trip. May I suggest during these visits, you simply remain quiet. We can discuss your opinions afterward."

Bolin, whose only experience with religion was a passing familiarity with Buddhism, thought this research initiative somewhat odd. "What could religion have to do with anything meaningful? And what could it have to do with anything associated with our operations?"

Meifeng simply shook her head and stared out her window again. "You have a lot to learn, Comrade."

"No, I am serious. I am curious to find out what impact religion could make on our planned operations here."

Meifeng was now becoming uncomfortable, for there was not sufficient trust established between them for her to discuss in detail the fundamental points of the sociological research about how religion in America had in its past provided its people the same unifying motivation and moral force that the idea of a world-conquering Middle

Kingdom did for the Chinese. And she would certainly not speak of her own burgeoning hypothesis—that something beyond the natural *was* at work in this country, and in other parts of the world ... something, to be sure, that seemed to be cooperating in concert with their planned operations, but since it could not be classified in her mind as natural or scientific, it was something she did not trust and, therefore, something she feared. And nothing would get her to share that fear with this arrogant young man in the driver's seat.

"We can speak about it after you have read the data on the subject," she said, and lapsed into silence, broken only by the slap of the wipers across the rain-streaked glass.

***

The Plan called for the team to investigate the eastern boundary of the anticipated Western Protectorate and, specifically, the control facilities they would establish on the border between China's segment of the conquered territory and Russia's segment. This meant a trip for Bolin and Meifeng to the Canadian city of Thunder Bay, on the shores of Lake Superior, halfway across the continent.

Bolin and Meifeng and their entourage crossed north again into Canada from Seattle, and from Vancouver headed east on Route 1, one of the main east-west arteries across southern Canada. Their escorts—one car in front with four Chinese security guards, and one in the rear, also with four guards—followed. Since the guards were not cleared for the discussions Meifeng and Bolin would have, Bolin drove with Meifeng alone in their own car in the center of the three-car convoy. Along the way, Meifeng pointed out that the road was one of the main invasion routes.

"It is well-constructed," she said. "Reports from people we have here said as much."

"Very thorough," he said. "But if the invasion will be successfully repelled, it will be in these mountain ranges. It is the riskiest segment of the transit." Meifeng made no reply, as she was not part of the military operational-level planning group. Apparently the Group had briefed Bolin on some of the military's plans—but then, given his clearance and his role, they would have had to.

They left the alluvial plan in the Lower Mainland of British Columbia and made their way through the small town of Hope, gazing in amazement at the Coastal Mountains. They drove up and up, and further up, on narrow, winding roads, and Bolin's countenance became fixed and grim as he saw the terrain their forces would need to traverse. He suspected he knew why the route had been selected.

"Do you know why the planners selected this route?" he asked Meifeng as they drove through Princeton in British Colombia on the Crows Nest highway.

"I have no idea," she replied, staring at a branch of the rushing Thompson River.

"I think it is because it is not the United States," Bolin replied, "and the Canadian military is not considered to be a significant threat."

"That would be logical," she replied dismissively. They had not talked much as they came out of the Coastal Mountain range; the scenery was too striking to ignore, and it in some way unsettled Meifeng, who had been born in Shanghai, and then moved to Beijing when just a young girl. She had no idea such things—mountains, rivers, lakes, and endless, endless forests—would be so ... so emotionally moving. She did not trust herself to speak; she did not trust that she could control her emotions, and she did not trust Bolin enough to let him in any way see what effect the land was having on her.

"Such an environment will require adjustments for our people, will it not?" he asked, seeming to discern her thoughts.

"There are mountains in China; stunningly beautiful ones, I am told. And you forget, the Plan has us returning what land we capture in Canada in exchange for peaceful border relations with Canada after we have taken the Eastern Protectorate," she answered.

"I am not forgetting," he said solemnly, staring up at mountains.

They stayed in Kamloops that night. Their cover required they stay in a single room, with their security staff taking up four other rooms. Neither Bolin nor Meifeng had any thought that their cover would extend beyond just a surface appearance, and neither one entertained any thoughts of an intimate relationship. Meifeng had not yet built trust with Bolin, and there were times when his intellect frightened her. To Bolin, Meifeng seemed superior and condescending.

Bolin called his cousins at least once a week, just to say hello and stay in touch. They each harassed him in their own way, and he enjoyed the calls. He told them he was enjoying his trip and said that he was looking for husbands for each of them. This elicited the expected shrieks of outrage, and then, in the case of Cuifen, a wistful cynicism. Mingzhu threatened to bury him in some forgotten archeological dig in western China, and Daiyu challenged him to find someone with characteristics she went on to specify in detail, making Bolin blush.

"Hah, serves you right, little cousin, you ferret," she said. "Visiting America without me ... my spirit will haunt your dreams for the rest of your life."

"What if I find you an American husband? You can live here," Bolin offered.

"*Aiyee!* An American husband? Are you kidding? Do you hate me so much? Would you want your most precious cousin, your most favorite of cousins, to be tied forever to some barbarian man who sleeps with a gun under his pillow, who will beat me if I burn his rice? Would you want your little second cousins to be half-breeds, not understanding the true ways? Oh, Bolin, you wiry-haired son of a rat, how can you be so cruel?"

He enjoyed his cousins, and on the drive he told Meifeng about each one—how he had grown up with them, how their family had taken him in after his parents died, how good Liwei and An had been to him—and still were, to this day.

"They were kind to you, then?" she asked.

"Most kind. They loved me like their own son." Meifeng nodded, noting how Bolin changed when he talked of his family. He seemed softer somehow, more human, less like a machine.

"They must be very proud," she said.

Bolin smiled, and it struck Meifeng that she had not seen him smile before. It changed his face, she thought. *And why should I notice it now?* she asked herself introspectively. How strange.

Chapter 34

Bolin & Meifeng

"A lion has gone up from his thicket, and a destroyer of nations has set out; he has gone out from his place to make your land a waste. Your cities will be ruins without inhabitant."

Jeremiah 4:7

On the drive out of Vancouver through the mountains of British Columbia, things he saw along the route disturbed Bolin. He would stare intensely at certain terrain as he drove, or stop in other places and get out of the car to take longer looks. The security team accommodated his delays without comment. Finally, one day he asked Meifeng to contact representatives from the military operational planning cell in the Group. She did so using standard communication protocols over the Internet from a roadside Starbucks coffee shop when next they stopped. When they arrived in Calgary, a team of five men and one woman met them at the Four Points Sheraton hotel and resort in Calgary West.

The team, dressed casually as tourists enjoying the slopes at the resort, met in Bolin and Meifeng's suite. Their flight had been delayed by a sleet storm, and with great respect and deference, they apologized for the delay. Meifeng was astounded at the degree of esteem and honor everyone from the Group was extending to Bolin. She had asked the Group's Director about this during one of her longer communications, and he explained.

"Your 'husband' is perhaps one of the most brilliant mathematicians we have in the country," the Director answered, using their agreed-upon code that had Bolin referred to as her husband. A 'mathematician' was their term for a military strategist or planner. "His ability to create combinations from previously established formulas is, shall we say, unique. We found him at just the right time. As always, China produces the sons and daughters she most requires just when she is most in need." She found it daunting to have been selected as an escort for one of China's rising stars, and she held her emotions even more in check when interacting with Bolin after that conversation.

The team lead that came at their request was a Colonel Xian Sho Ping, Director of the Group's military operational planning cell. He was an older man, maybe in his mid-fifties, with a courtly demeanor, a weathered but handsome face, and a trim, healthy build, obviously still in excellent shape. The Colonel had been an infantry soldier who developed his reputation by ensuring his men were in the finest condition possible, and the State appreciated the care he exhibited toward their property. He had been rewarded with a post on the Group's operational planning staff. Bolin knew from his initial program briefings that Xian had worked many years ago with Colonels Qiao Lian and Wang Ziangsui, two very prominent members of the PLA who were responsible for compiling and publishing one of China's most far-reaching and widest-read military strategy analyses, and which many were purporting to be China's overarching operational plan for unrestricted warfare against America. Bolin remembered Qiao's quote about unrestricted warfare: *"The first rule of unrestricted warfare is that there are no rules, with nothing forbidden."* It was something he identified with deeply, for it was his own method of conflict, whenever he would apply his talents in building or taking down a societal infrastructure or against an opponent on the game board.

The second member of the team was a Gao Bong Gam, Vice President for Design and Engineering at China North Industries Corporation (NORINCO), the main state-run company responsible for most of the Chinese military's armored combat vehicles. He was a short, somewhat rotund man with very neatly trimmed hair, and his casual tourist clothes, Bolin observed, were of the highest quality. He was renowned in Chinese business circles for the success NORINCO enjoyed in the nation and around the world.

A third member of the team was Qi Ling Pao, a brilliant biochemist. Combined with a medical degree, Qi had provided the Group with an amazing breadth of expertise relative to biological warfare and its affects on the human organism. He was a tall, thin man from Beijing, younger than the others, who seemed to be somewhat ill at ease among the older team members. He was overly courteous whenever anyone addressed him.

A fourth team member was Zhiang Wei Bin. Zhiang was one of China's most astute financial warfare strategists. After three decades working in the West's investment banking and financial investment sectors, he returned to China and in a flash of stunning strategic brilliance submitted a massive document that outlined how China could conduct both broad and precise financial warfare against its enemies. The Group's leadership recognized the benefit such a strategist would be to its application of unrestricted warfare against its greatest enemy, and so brought Zhiang into the Group as well.

The fifth man on the team was somewhat of a different mold. Deng Sen was not as educated as the others, nor did he appear to conduct himself with the refinement or gentility the others did, though he was by no means disrespectful. He was short, squat, with massive shoulders, a thick neck, almost no waist, and legs the size of tree trunks. Bolin watched him from across the room before the first meeting began as he drained a can of Canadian beer and crushed the can end to end, pinching it with two fingers. Bolin at first did not understand why he had been included in the meeting, but when Meifeng handed him a short paper describing the qualifications of the members, he understood. Deng Sen was perhaps China's most accomplished emergency services coordinator. Deng had been sent to so many disaster sites in China that his name was synonymous with what Westerners would think of as 'the cavalry'. When Deng appeared on the scene of an emergency, suddenly things improved—communications improved, teams worked better together, objectives were attained, casualties were minimized, incidences of lost or damaged equipment didn't occur as often, and, after his reputation began to grow, affected populations would invariably give the State high marks for their response to the disaster. Up until he had been asked to participate in the Group, Deng was the senior instructor in China's most prestigious academy for training emergency services workers. His inclusion raised the opinion Bolin had of the Group's leadership.

The only woman in the team was Hsang Wei Lei. She also was short—shorter than Deng—and petite, thinner than the biochemist, Qi. She had a pleasant expression and was quite pretty. It seemed to Bolin that those in the media and public relations fields tended to be so, since, he noted, people tended to relate more easily with those they considered to be more physically attractive. He would have to devote some time to exploring why this was so. Hsang was an expert in the formulation of public opinions. She had studied journalism in Europe and psychology in the United States, and had worked for several different multi-national public relations firms. At the moment she was on a short leave from Griggs, Hanson, and Miller, the firm handling public relations for several U.S. congressmen. She had unparalleled access to some of the most critical American politicians' agendas and personal schedules, which the Group found too valuable to resist, and during a meeting one evening four years ago, invited her to participate in the Group. She accepted with grace and respect—of course she had no choice, but nonetheless, her acceptance in service to the State was something still talked about by Group leadership.

Before the meeting began, a member of the security team swept the room for listening devices and external security was surreptitiously ranged in key areas outside the hotel and in the hallway just outside the suite. Small devices consisting of suction cups with joining wires and a number of black boxes were placed on windows to deter laser listening devices.

"I am concerned that the timetable could encounter delays due to the terrain in the western Canadian mountains," Bolin began with no formalities or introductions. He was strange that way. "I am concerned about channeling and the ability of the enemy to oppose our progress. I need the team to review with me the application of combinations that have been selected for the various phases of the operation." The combinations he referred to were combinations of different methods of warfare—military, economic, social, financial, ecological, or biological—that the Group had planned to occur in each of the operation's phases. "I am concerned that the terrain may alter the affect we expect to emerge from the combinations we have selected."

Meifeng lifted a white board brought in for the occasion upon which was written the following in Chinese:

Preparations Phase
- Preliminary Preparations
- Advanced Preparations
- Initial Implementations – initiating the crises
- Checking Combination Coordination

Operational Phase
- Seizing land entry points
- Deep penetrations:links with partner (Russia)
- Checking Combination Coordination
- Securing land entry points
- Closing encirclements
- Filling gaps

Adjustment Phase
- Establishing communications
- Establishing government
- Removing conquered personnel

"Let us begin with the combinations selected for application during the Initial Implementations phase, as we have completed both the preliminary and advanced preparations segments. Comrade Colonel Xian, could you please describe what combinations you have decided to employ for this segment in the area of Vancouver."

"Certainly, Comrade Major," Xian replied, standing and bowing slightly, which

Bolin returned respectfully. "The Vancouver planning map, please." One of the security team members projected a meticulous map of the entire Vancouver city and port area onto the suite's cream-colored wall using a laptop and a portable projector. "Thank you. We will begin with a social media campaign to arouse domestic disharmony."

"How will this be done, please, Comrade Colonel?"

The Colonel looked to Hsang, who spoke up. "Some of our people will arrange the murder of a number of Asians by white gang members in the inner city, and then selected news outlets will frame the event as indicative of a wider split in the city's racial populace. We have been doing this for the past few years in Vancouver, and we have positioned the populace to be explosively reactive in the event another drastic incident occurs. The upshot of this is intended to make the Asian population in and around Vancouver sympathetic to our cause."

"I see. Essentially China will be coming to Vancouver in force to 'alleviate the sufferings of all Asians' and rescue them from white tyranny. Well-played," Bolin complimented. "And the next?" he asked, turning to Xian again.

"Doctor Qi, if you would?" Xian turned to the tall thin doctor, who stood and moved to the wall. "Here is where we intend to initiate an especially virulent form of influenza that we have been preparing for several years." He pointed to the map at Vancouver's airport. "We'll introduce what we term a 'trigger virus' at the airport in Vancouver, and simultaneously in local gathering places—supermarkets and shopping malls and such. We have even arranged to have some of our people employed as toll collectors in the 'cash only' lanes, and they will spread the trigger virus to every traveler on implementation day. He then pointed to a spot on the edge of Vancouver, in a small suburb called Pemberton Heights. "We have people working in the hospitals in this area. We also have control over the facilities where their antibiotics are produced."

"How has this control been achieved?" Bolin asked.

"Our people own the companies that produce the medicines," Xian interposed, to support the doctor. "Please, proceed."

"So yes, the antibiotics we have been issuing have been—'designed' to affect only a specific genetic composition. Caucasians, primarily ... so whenever in the past ten years a Caucasian has received a flu shot or any type of antibiotic produced by our firms, the solution works to build up certain chemicals in their body. These chemicals will react drastically to the specific virus we'll introduce. We call these chemicals 'amplifiers'."

"And its affect on Asians?" Bolin asked.

"None. The chemical does not build up in Asians, nor will the virus we introduce be particularly harmful to them. Oh, they may come down with a cold, maybe a moderate fever, but nothing greater."

"And the effect on Caucasians?"

"Initially, it will exhibit with a slow, gradual onset of malaise—aches, indiscriminate joint pain, fever, and some low-level dizziness that will last for two to three weeks, sometimes as long as a month. Of course, we expect affected individuals to seek medical assistance, and, we hope, be administered even more doses of our antibiotics. As the virus begins to take hold in the subject, however, the affects become more pronounced; we call this the 'hammer' period. The key symptom of this second period onset is a rapidly rising high fever—it will kill the aged and the young—and then there will be, well, shall we say some indelicate yet powerful and bloody effusions that will most probably require the affected person to seek medical attention at a hospital. It will be sudden and violent and very noticeable. We will be able to track its progress by observing the number of emergency room visits, I am sure," the doctor said. "The third stage is dementia, then delirium, then expiration of the host from, usually, heart failure, or sometimes by dehydration."

"Can you clarify the timeline regarding the second and third phases please?"

"Yes, of course, my apologies. While the first phase should exhibit within two to three days from exposure and last perhaps a month, the second phase onset will be within hours, and from the second to the third phase should be no more than three to five days."

"Do you expect this to be long enough to overtax the city's emergency response systems," Bolin asked, turning to Deng.

"It *is* a short time frame," Deng replied. "There are only so many emergency responders, and if they only get to, say, one third of the victims over the course of five days, that will leave maybe two thirds of the population that will remain ... unaddressed. These may get themselves to a hospital, or have their relatives or friends take them. But if they are not serviced by the responders after the responders service the first group, there may not be many left to generate service calls. And there is to be factored in the effect the virus has on non-Asian first responders; many will be going down themselves."

"My concern is that the second phase time period may not be long enough to infect sufficient numbers of emergency responders," Bolin said.

Deng nodded. "I see, yes." Deng turned to Qi. "Tell me again how many people you expect to be affected?".

Qi tapped his iPad. "Vancouver's population is projected to be more than 600,000 people currently, and that is just Vancouver proper."

"Oh, that shouldn't be a concern," Deng answered quickly. "You'll have the entire city's responders taxed to their maximum, and sooner or later, if Qi is to be believed, around 80% to 90% of them will contract the virus and go down."

"80% to 90% would be acceptable," Bolin said, and motioned to Qi to continue.

"With the projections we are making with the virus we intend to insert into the population, and calculating its vector through the projected target areas, we expect an infection rate of 67% within one month, and then up to 78% after three months. As well, we expect to initiate the same virus at the other land entry points, as it would be logical for port officials, cargo handlers, members of port workers' unions, and others associated with port cities to travel between the various ports."

"What is the name of the company making the antibiotics in Vancouver?" Bolin asked.

"Swanson Pharmaceuticals," Qi answered. "They are one of the largest Canadian producers of antibiotics but they do not distribute antibiotics into the U.S."

"How will you ensure the trigger virus has something against which to act if you do not have the foundation built up in American hosts from your treated antibiotics?"

"This is an astute question," Qi replied, almost rubbing his hands together in eagerness. "We do not control antibiotic production in the U.S., it is true," he said, "but we have interposed chemical compounds into the main product lines of four of America's largest food companies. Let me see, they are ... " he tapped his iPad again and read, "yes, they are Kraft, ConAgra, Nestle, and Pepsi."

"And how has this been done?" Bolin asked.

"Most of their products utilize common basic ingredients, Comrade Major. We have affected the suppliers for those ingredients and have already begun adjusting their chemical compounds to serve as amplifiers to the trigger virus we insert in the United States."

"An example please, Doctor." Bolin wanted to cover every detail.

"Yes, of course." More tapping on the iPad, "Yes, here, we have artificial sweeteners. They would include aspartame, which to date appears to have the most pronounced effect, but also acesulfame potassium, sucralose, and saccharin. Our suppliers have adjusted these chemicals that will serve as the amplifier for the trigger virus we initiate. Also, I should mention monosodium glutamate, or as is it is known more commonly, 'MSG'. This is an excitotoxin, and over the years we have encouraged food companies to add this chemical to countless processed food products, from frozen dinners and salad dressing to snack chips and meats. The term "monosodium glutamate" or its acronym MSG might not even appear in the ingredient list. Our efforts in the industry have been successful to the point that dozens of other names may be used, such as glutamic acid, hydrolyzed protein, yeast extract, and dozens of others. Yet it is our product, our tailored excitotoxin that we make and which will act as an amplifier for the virus."

"How will this MSG particularly affect the host, Doctor?" Meifeng asked from a chair near the wall. She knew Bolin would want to know.

"MSG is approximately 78% free glutamic acid, which is the same neurotransmitter that our brain, nervous system, eyes, pancreas, and other organs use to initiate certain various bodily processes. We began altering this chemical years ago with the collusion of selected officials in the U.S. Food and Drug Administration. Our testing indicates that the majority of effects will be centered around interruptions to the nervous system and pancreas."

"Excuse me, Doctor, but would your 'adjustments' to this chemical perhaps explain the significant rise in diabetes in the U.S.?"

"Precisely, colleague," the doctor replied. "Our adjusted compound attacks the insulin-producing beta cells in the pancreas."

"Permit me to interrupt here," Xian said, holding up a hand, "but it is an excellent point at which to introduce another element of our combination that is particularly relevant."

Bolin nodded, and Qi went on. "Yes, thank you, and thank you, Comrade Colonel Xian. Yes, so, we have inserted three biochemists into this organization," he said, and nodded to the projectionist. "Please bring up the frame showing the Novo Nordisk A/S headquarters." A picture of a huge factory appeared on the wall.

"This is Novo Nordisk A/S. They are the world's largest insulin producer, and the picture you are looking at is their plant in Denmark, the largest in the world. Several years ago, Novo Nordisk A/S built an even larger plant in the United States, in Kansas. It is centrally located in America to facilitate distribution. Novo Nordisk has begun production of oral semaglutide, a pill one administers to type 2 diabetics. Two of our three biochemists are on the production team, and the other is in quality control. With these individuals placed as they are, we can affect certain batches of the drug—enough to cause widespread panic and cast doubt on the medicine's efficacy."

"So," Bolin interrupted, turning to Xian, "you have affected the American's food supply through altering chemicals in their processed food that has caused a diabetes epidemic, and then inserted influence into the country's largest insulin production facility to destroy that at the right time."

"More or less, yes, Comrade Major," Xiam replied.

Bolin bowed deeply to the Colonel. "You have my extreme admiration, Comrade Colonel. Your efforts exemplify those advocated by your mentors, Comrades Qiao and Wang."

Xian bowed even more deeply to Bolin and maintained his composure, but Meifeng saw that he was significantly affected by Bolin's compliment. Bolin is wise, she thought, welding this team together with praise and encouragement. It was rare. She wondered where he had learned to do so. He turned to Qi.

"The collusion you mention with the U.S. FDA. How was this collusion brought about, Doctor?"

The doctor turned to Colonel Xian to answer Bolin's question. "Yes, Comrade Major, it is a fair question. Several years ago we reached the Chief of Staff in the Office of the Commissioner. We also successfully influenced the Director for Food Safety and Applied Nutrition—"

"Excuse me, Comrade Colonel," Bolin interrupted, "but could you please tell me exactly how you 'influenced' this person?"

Xian cleared his throat and answered Bolin directly. "We paid the Chief of Staff—he was pathetically easy to influence. He received a nominal sum of $500,000 U.S. dollars—what Americans call a 'signing bonus' in return for his cooperation, plus a retainer of $100,000 per year. We were surprised at how easy he sold his influence," the doctor said with a tinge of disdain. "The Director for Food Safety was, or I should say still is, a lesbian. We had her lover executed, and then communicated to her that her mother and two sisters would meet the same fate if she did not cooperate."

"And she has sufficient influence in such a bureaucratic organization that you are confident she will permit this line of operation to continue?"

"We do, Comrade Major, especially with the cover provided by the Chief of Staff. She has a very substantial offshore private account, her subsequent liaisons—with underage girls, I might add, arranged by our people through the local U.S. Congressional representative—have been quite thoroughly recorded, and occasionally we provide her with personal updates on her mother and sisters via a fictitious Facebook account. She seems quite happy to cooperate."

"Well played, Colonel, thank you," Bolin replied. "Please, Doctor, continue."

"To summarize, Comrade Major, we can introduce our trigger virus very selectively in designated geographic locations and we expect it to react to the amplifier that has been ingested by most of America's population and react in the expected fashion. It has been tested exhaustively in different parts of the world."

"And you say Asians will not be affected," Bolin asked.

"I have tested it on myself, actually, Comrade Major, as well as my family." Bolin could ask for no stronger vote of confidence. He nodded his approval and turned to Xiang. "What is the next element of the combination during the Implementation segment, Comrade Colonel?"

"We want to interdict air travel, which will very drastically affect America's economy. This will be accomplished through another virus—a computer virus this time—

introduced via a small component in a specific range of products. Gao, if you would please?"

Gao arose and went to the wall and spoke to the security guard operating the laptop. "The engine diagram." A cutaway diagram of a modern jet engine juxtaposed next to a circuit diagram appeared. This," he pointed to a small item on the diagram, "is a FADEC; a 'full authority digital engine or electronics control.' A FADEC works by receiving multiple input variables of the current flight condition, including external air conditions, engine control positions and temperatures and pressures, and other parameters. The inputs are analyzed up to 70 times per second. The engine operating parameters are computed in this unit and applied. The FADEC's basic purpose, Comrade Major, is to provide optimum engine efficiency for a given flight condition. We have affected the internal code used by the FADECs produced by all main engine manufacturers utilized by the world's carriers. We can, remotely, cause a single engine to fail, or all engines to fail at a selected time or in a designated order on one aircraft, or on all aircraft."

"I would think that the criticality of this component would require redundancies," Bolin interposed.

"Yes, actually, there are always two separate digital channels per engine, with one FADEC per channel, such that if one fails, the other will continue to provide its signals and keep the engine operating."

"And you have countered this by?"

"Our code essentially runs on all the FADECs, Comrade Major, so even if they have five or ten digital channels running to five or ten FADECs, they will all do what we tell them to do."

"What is the overall implementation protocol, Comrade Gao?"

Ms. Hsang answered instead. "We have another element that we want to implement in conjunction with this capability. We have scheduled a slate of stories that describe how a domestic terrorist group located in Houston and Louisiana has somehow polluted the fuel supply in a way that interferes with the fuel-air combustion cycle at altitudes above ten thousand feet," she replied.

"Will this be believable?" Bolin asked.

"It will be when the first aircraft's engines fail at altitude, and the Federal Aviation Administration's safety inspectors discover fuel contamination as the cause," Xian replied. "We have arranged, or I should say *aligned* lines of influence, with the main individuals responsible for producing safety reports and conducting safety inspections in the FAA."

"There must be hundreds of these people," Bolin countered.

"Yes, my apologies Comrade Major, but while there are many who conduct the inspections and write the reports, there are only three individuals who must approve what is written and who can confirm analyses. One is the Director for the FAA's safety investigations, another is the Deputy Administrator, and the other is the Director of Accident Investigations and Prevention. We believe these individuals are in positions offering sufficient leverage to communicate our specific narrative regarding fuel contamination, at least for a timespan short enough to generate sufficient confusion and disharmony in their transportation and economic sectors."

"And how has this alignment been achieved?"

"One, the Deputy Administrator, is a pedophile and a member of a very secretive group of highly-placed senior U.S. and foreign government officials who attend functions devoted to sexual engagements with minor children. We have videos of his ... encounters. The individual overseeing safety investigations has three daughters. We have put one on heroin, and we have promised him that the other two will meet a similar fate if he does not cooperate. The third ... the third is somewhat distasteful to discuss."

Bolin was surprised. He had rarely heard anyone in the group shy away from discussing any means of coercion when the objective was to further the Plan. Bolin just stared at the man. To save Gao some difficulties, Xian intervened and spoke up.

"This woman, the individual in charge of accident investigations, is part of a splinter religious group—a Satanist. As part of this group, she deals in human organs ... specifically, the organs of small babies. They conduct human sacrifices and remove the organs. Apparently the trade is quite lucrative. We have videos of both the sacrifices, the ... the removals ... and the woman arranging a sale to one of our operatives."

Bolin raised an eyebrow. "I apologize, Comrade Gao. I did not think it possible, but this has surprised me. The depths of depravity these people undertake to satisfy their urges surpasses comprehension."

Meifeng was listening with horror. "It makes what we are working on even more imperative," she said with what she hoped was an acceptable degree of passion.

Bolin looked over at her. "Yes, I could not agree more." He turned to Gao again. "Sir, this method of interfering with the FADEC ... is it viable from an engineering standpoint? By this I mean, will a FADEC failure above ten thousand feet be seen as something that could happen in the aircraft?"

"We are not so concerned about that, Comrade Major, as any determination of cause will take time. Our plan is to ensure that no engine fails until it gets above ten thousand feet."

"What will happen when it goes below ten thousand feet, which it invariably must if what we want to happen will happen? Will the pilots not simply restart the engines?"

"The failure mode will ensure the engines cannot be restarted regardless of altitude. The result of going above ten thousand feet will invariably be an irreversible engine failure—but only on selected engines, at selected times, that would match a pattern of fuel contamination, spotty incidents occurring only at intervals in selected locations, as though all stemming from a singular batch of contaminated fuel at a particular airport. We believe the number of occurrences will be sufficient for the FAA to eventually ground all commercial jet travel above ten thousand feet."

"That would cause extreme airspace congestion below ten thousand feet, which is what you wish to occur, I presume?"

"Yes, Comrade Major. If the FAA simply grounds all air travel—which they may do, and it is a contingency we have plans for—then their people will be put to work identifying the problem, and they will eventually discover the faulty code in the FADECs. However, if they are kept busy with a reduced amount of air travel in an increasingly congested, smaller national airspace, it will continue to be a drain on their manpower and increase the time it will take them to discover the root cause."

Bolin nodded. "Effective, yes, I see. Thank you. You say the FADEC code is ours. May I ask how it has been integrated into these components so ... so thoroughly?"

"Price, Comrade Major," Gao replied with authority. "Our commercial networks of software subcontractors in the U.S. have coordinated their efforts to provide the lowest priced FADEC code to the engine manufacturers. It has almost bankrupted our subcontractors, but subsidies from home have kept them afloat."

"According to the plan," Xian contributed.

"Yes, Comrade Colonel, precisely," Bolin added. "Are there other elements in our combinations?"

"There are," Xian replied. "Zhayzha Zhiang, please, if you would convey your elements to the Comrade Major?" Meifeng noted that Xian used a very old honorific toward Zhiang, which literally meant, 'under your pavilion' and which was used in modern parlance to confer respect.

Zhiang walked to the front of the room. He was perhaps the oldest member of the team, with gray hair, a dignified mien, and Meifeng noticed that he wore his very expensive casual tourist clothes with flair and style. Rumor had it that he was one of the wealthiest men in the State, and had as well contributed rivers of gold to the personal coffers of those in the Central Committee.

"As opposed to conducting surgical strikes at selected financial targets, we are going to conduct a 'carpet bombing' approach and attack their overall economic system in hopes of causing massive failure. Permit me to share with you how we intend to do this." The dignified elder nodded to the person manning the laptop, who put up a slide showing various graphs and charts.

"It has been somewhat problematic to attack America financially," he began. "We have arranged the purchase of a number of major stock exchanges—the one in Chicago and the one in Dallas come to mind. We have purchased significant interests in the U.S. manufacturing sector. We have key positions in the U.S. aerospace, shipbuilding, and oil production industries. These inroads you already know about. You know of the massive trade deficit that has built up between China and America. I think it must be, now, let me think…yes, almost $875 billion now. For years we have simply put this back into U.S. treasury bonds, which the U.S. was comfortable with, since it permitted them to simply maintain greater deficits. But we cannot continue to do this—we lose enormous sums of money by holding U.S. treasury bonds, especially when the Americans print new money and lower interest rates. It is extremely frustrating when they do this. So we have been working with the Russians and other nations to create a new world reserve currency—our own, the Yuan. Our economy officially exceeded the U.S. economy a few years ago, and when your Group initiates the implementation phase of this project, we will essentially terminate use of the U.S. dollar as our reserve currency and switch to the Yuan, in partnership with our Russian friends. Many other nations will follow suit. And the UN has endorsed the plan as well. They are eager for the world to break away from American domination."

Bolin raised a hand. "Zhayzha Zhiang, may I ask what the immediate ramifications will be—I mean, in America?"

"Certainly," Zhiang replied. "Several effects will emerge, and the combination will be severely debilitating to the U.S. economy and any efforts they might try and extend to interrupt our operations. Consider ... there will be in America massive inflation, very high interest rates on large purchases such as mortgages and vehicles, substantial increases in the cost of most consumables, to include food, clothing, gasoline, and medicines," he said this last with a nod to Doctor Qi. "We also expect there to be, at the same time, a significant degree of deflation: wages will decrease, while prices for goods and services will increase. It will be crushing. And very importantly, American financial sources will have a very difficult time financing the nation's debt. As you know, at the present time there is a large demand for U.S. dollars. Countries keep large reserves of U.S. currency on hand for the sake of international trade, but when we implement this initiative we will see the world's nations suddenly begin to hoard the Yuan and dispense with U.S. debt. It will ruin them. It will make the American financial crisis of 2008 look like a small wind compared to a hurricane."

"May I ask what the timeline would be for these effects to be felt?" Bolin continued with another question.

"This is hard to predict," Zhiang answered, "but we expect the immediate effects to be felt almost overnight when the announcement is made. There is a joint announcement planned by China, Russia, India, most of the Islamic nations in the Middle East, and several South American countries, stating that they will move immediately to the Yuan as their reserve currency and no longer consider the U.S. dollar as the currency they will use to do business. As I say, this announcement will have shattering and immediate effect on U.S. banking and lending institutions, their industries and markets, and their people's savings. Expect many banks to close or fail. Expect hoarding to begin immediately, with its concomitant social instability. Expect martial law to be declared as societal functions began to break down. Food prices will skyrocket, and I would then expect heating oil and gasoline to rapidly and dramatically increase in price. Expect this to occur within a period of one to three weeks, based upon the specific location and population density. In a month it will be a different country."

"Thank you, Zhayzha Zhiang." Bolin bowed to the older man, who acknowledged his bow with a nod, and Zhiang returned to his seat.

"May I turn now to my specific concerns about moving through the British Columbian mountain range during the northern spear's initial run inland. Comrade Colonel, there are numerous places in the route where the road is only two lanes wide, where curves prohibit rapid speed, or where strategically-placed demolition charges could bring down half a hill onto the only road route we must use to drive inland. What are the plans during the implementation phase to prevent this?"

Xian rose and again walked to the front of the room. "The VT6 please, Tien," he said to the security guard operating the projector, and the picture of a modern armored vehicle appeared, placed on a flatbed transport vehicle. "This is our new VT6," Xian began. "It is a lightweight main battle tank, and an improved version of the VT5. The VT6 was developed by our esteemed colleague Gao's team. It is designed to operate in mountainous terrain. It has a combat weight of between 33 to 36 tons, compared to our heavy tank that operates with a combat weight of around 45 tons. It has a 105mm gun with a thermal sleeve and fume extractor. Now, you see this picture here, yes? But this is not what anyone on the road will see. We are not going to transport this combat vehicle as you see it. The Leopard please, Tien." A picture of a Leopard 2A6M main battle tank appeared on the wall. "This is Canada's main battle tank they purchased from Germany—the Leopard 2A6M main battle tank. With some very easy fabrication of sheet metal parts and paint, we can transform this," and he nodded to Tien, who showed a picture of the VT6, "into this," and a picture of the Leopard appeared, now juxtaposed on the wall next to the picture of the VT6. "It will pass a cursory visual inspection. The plan is to transport the main force of tanks on the southern route as though Canada is responding to an incursion. There are parts of the Plan that have not been revealed to this group. Suffice it to say that we expect no resistance whatsoever during the run through the mountain range."

"Surely there will not be Chinese crews transporting the tanks?" Bolin said, curious.

"No, Comrade Major. We have arranged for a private Canadian security firm that specializes in transporting heavy equipment to provide drivers for the convoys.

"But there *will* be Chinese personnel accompanying the tanks during transport, yes?" Bolin asked.

"Yes, most definitely, all dressed in the livery of a vehicle maintenance subcontractor. Our crews will ride along in convoy trucks as maintenance technicians until we no longer need the transportation crews. This is why we do not anticipate any delay through the mountains. In fact, we expect the way to be cleared for us when our partner's 'incursion' occurs in the center of the country."

"As well, we will have public statements made by our clients, calling for Canada to support them during the ... during the incursion crisis that will develop. It will be the most natural thing in the world for Canadians to see massive military vehicle convoys moving toward the center of the country."

"How will you prevent the Canadian military from spoiling this plan? They will know it is not their tanks being sent through the mountains from Vancouver."

"You ask a good question," Xian replied. "Our planners have made the following assumptions. First, there will be significant chaos in Vancouver. These vehicles will be offloaded from our ships at night, already in Canadian livery, as though we are just making a delivery of armored vehicles to support the Canadian military. We will also be interfering with communications throughout Canada, at all levels. We do not expect much difficulty doing this. Second, we have plans for the Canadian military's central headquarters, as well as their regional command location for British Columbia."

"Plans?" Bolin asked.

"Islamic terrorists are going to assassinate the leadership and then blow up the headquarters and command facilities for both organizations," Xian replied.

"If their plans fail?" Bolin pressed. "Islam has no stellar record of success against point targets."

"Then we have our own people, two PLA special operations teams, in place to do the same thing. They will not fail."

"Of this I am certain," Bolin said, nodding. "You are wise to be redundant."

"There are also plans from other Group sections to disrupt communications throughout the southern portion of Canada to support ... other operations."

"I have been briefed on these other operations, Comrade Colonel, and I understand how what you describe will integrate with your approach."

"Thank you, Comrade Major, so yes, our approach to transit the difficult terrain is first to utilize deception, enlisting the aid of our enemy to help us; should such things fail, we will depend upon confusion caused by the loss of internal communications. Finally, should these two fail and the enemy muster enough combat power to offer resistance, we intend to employ a number of remotely operated air vehicles to destroy them. I am told you have been briefed on these units?"

"We have, yes, Comrade Colonel. We have in fact visited the factory where they were made, and were provided very convincing demonstrations."

Colonel Xian stood and addressed Bolin. "Have we answered your concerns, then, Comrade Major?"

"You have," Bolin answered, looking around the room. He nodded to Meifeng. "Comrade Major Tuan will address the group now." Meifeng stood up and made a closing statement.

"We are indebted to you all for a professional and thorough planning effort. Your exertions have been noticed by the highest levels of our leadership, who I am sure will not hesitate to express their appreciation more tangibly in the years to come in this new land we will conquer, where there will be enough room for generations upon generations of our people, where the Middle Kingdom will with a great shout take a most important step in its history to ensure its future, whatever fate brings upon us."

***

It is 2038 kilometers from Calgary to Thunder Bay, and Bolin, Meifeng, and their security escort made the trip in two days, driving hard.

On the first day out of Calgary, Bolin spoke to Meifeng. "So far we have not made any stops in religious locations. I recall that you mentioned we would be doing so. Why have these stops not been scheduled?"

"We are traveling through Canada," Meifeng replied. "Canada has no religion of note; it does not affect their politics or their culture much, if at all. It is America we are concerned about. Only in America will we need to be concerned about how religion affects the people and our plans."

"I see," Bolin said. "And when will we make visits to American religious locations?"

Meifeng tapped her iPad and pulled up a map of their itinerary. She swiped across the screen, magnified it, and then showed it to Bolin. "Here," she said, a finger pointing to a location on the screen. "In a city called Granite Sky at first. We must meet there with representatives from our partner in this grand enterprise, and we can take advantage of the time we spend there to investigate local religious rituals."

Chapter 35

Protocols of the Pryp'yat Principality

Historian's Preface: The Pryp'yat Principality took its name from the marshy area through which, it was reputed, demonic elements infiltrated into the region once known as Russia. It was throughout history one of the world's largest swamps, almost impassable to men, beasts, and later, machines. To make it more of a stench in the world's eyes, and for reasons of impenetrability and secrecy, agents of the enemy caused the Chernobyl nuclear accident there, poisoning much of the land around the Pryp'yat River. The accident at Chernobyl—a Russian word which, in English, is translated 'Wormwood'—caused the area to be severely depopulated, leaving it open for demonic entities. This principality was responsible for the area encompassed by the human nations of Russia and Eastern Europe. It was known for its brutality, cunning, and brazen disdain for human life.

This segment of the Pryp'yat Protocols has to do specifically with the agreement made with the Zhongguo Principality and their joint plans to conduct the assault on America. The reader's attention is drawn to the fact that since this Protocol segment involved two separate but equally powerful Principalities, we have concluded that it must have been authored by a higher entity ... and the only entity higher than these Principalities was Lucifer, the prince of darkness.

And so America, now weakened as to be almost completely devoid of common sense, strength, or discernment, was ready to be fully deceived and, like a ripe piece of fruit, sliced from the tree of nations with little or no effort to fall into the enemy's basket.

Sartorius Crux Vita
Diamond Gate, Jerusalem
AR 40

Opening

This document records the joint action agreed to by the Zhongguo and Pryp'yat Principalities against that human area known as the Pathetic Land. It is agreed that the Zhongguo Principality will incite its stones to assault the western portion of this geographical region. The Zhongguo stones will be given land, food, and females. Upon the incursion precipitated by Zhongguo stones, Pryp'yat mud[33] will be positioned as a 'peace-keeping force', to be invited into the Pathetic Land by the Marduk[34] Principality and the dung[35] under their control. Pryp'yat mud will

33 This was the Pryp'yat Principality's term for humans.

34 This was the Principality that controlled the area once known as the United States, replacing the Stain Principality.

35 The ruling Marduk Principality, when referring to the humans it controlled, used the derisive term 'Dung'.

be given land, resources, and dung will become their slaves.

Philosophies Guiding This Action

The basic philosophy undergirding this action is that the dung, under the control of the Marduk Principality, are sufficiently immersed in self-pleasures, self-gratification, and have been adequately detached from the Hateful One's[36] control that they can be threatened with one hand and offered security with the other. Like sheep, they will run to the opposite side of the pasture when threatened; like wolves, we will be at both sides of their pasture. Marduk's efforts over the past two centuries have now borne fruit, all thanks to only He Who is Most Powerful.[37]

Expectations are that dung will at first be confused, then frightened, then angry that their lives have been disrupted to such a degree. They will remain disturbed emotionally, mentally, and spiritually as they have no means of support in any of these realms, due to the work of He Who is Most Powerful in their society. They will not present any significant resistance to the stones flooding their land. They will instead tremble in their own hearts, and then strike out at each other in their anger and fear, stealing from each other, murdering each other. Feed and encourage these activities, as they will increase the level of darkness and despair that infects the land, and will be a glory to He Who is Most Powerful. After what little strength they have is exhausted by their thefts and murders, they will beg to be slaves. The stones at this point must not weaken. They must harden their own hearts. Zhongguo will be directed to ensure adequate motivation is provided to the stones so that the dung appointed to feed the pride of the stones are killed; that the dung appointed to feed the desire for material possessions are made slaves; that female dung appointed to feed the lusts of the male stones are degraded and debased until those dung either die of despair or are killed by abuse. It is imperative that the dung under Marduk's control be fully and utterly degraded; this is essential. Stones that demonstrate any pity whatsoever must be singled out for special action, their souls abrogated and set apart to be food for the Master's table.

Dealing with Spots of Filth[38]

History indicates that spots of filth present the main obstacle to the reign of He Who is Most Powerful. They must be dealt with aggressively. Two strategies must be applied because there are two groups of filth that must be handled, and this land under Marduk's control is particularly infested with this filth. The first group is comprised of true spots of filth—human creatures who have resolved to fully obey the Hateful One; these are protected by the Burning Wind[39] and strongly resist any attempts at detachment. The second group consists of those who think they are attached to the Hateful One, but their connection is only through their culture, or their upbringing, or through some other means other than through the required death of their pathetic human nature. We refer to these as Pretenders, for so they are. We can break and detach them and they have, historically, been most useful until, in the end, they have been quite tasty.

36 The blasphemous term 'Hateful One' was used by the enemy throughout their communications to refer to the Most High God of Abraham, Isaac, and Jacob.

37 This phrase, only identified as an acronym in the original document and which is unable to be replicated in written language, is expanded here in its full meaning for the benefit of the reader. As one may surmise, it is the Usurper's term by which he refers to himself.

38 As the reader may have surmised, the enemy and his minions refer to Christians as 'spots of filth'. While this is not the exact term, that term is untranslatable into written or spoken language, and so the closest (printable) expression must suffice.

39 The enemy's term for the Holy Spirit.

Dealing with True Spots of Filth: Care must be taken to quickly identify true spots of filth that may present obstacles. Stones will be of little or no help here; they are not equipped to operate in our realm and will be blind to the light surrounding the filth. Therefore the Zhongguo Principality will detail several legions to accompany and forcefully direct stones who have opened themselves up to the greatest possible degree for control, and the Principality will use these stones to find the true spots of filth. Once found, such spots of filth must be immediately seized and dispatched. This must be done quietly. These types have a disturbing tendency, in their deaths, to inspire other dung, and may in fact infect even stones with that nefarious virus of faith in the Hateful One. This cannot be allowed to happen. Throughout the history of our struggle we have seen that when we slash and burn and destroy, when our horns are most powerfully lifted up, when the blood flows freely from our fangs, when our claws rip flesh and we richly devour souls, lifting our voices in the victorious, exultant roar to He Who is Most Powerful, the deaths of these spots of filth who stray to the light always seem to inspire a greater spread of their deplorable sickness. And so the stones must be directed to immediately detect and then isolate these spots of filth, but they must do so with no outward prejudice or antipathy. The spots of filth must be treated with an outward show of detached disinterest. There must be no indication that they comprise some special category. They must, on one pretext or another, be separated from other dung. They must then be taken to special areas where their attachment to the Hateful One is broken, which results in a particularly exquisite delight to He Who is Most Powerful—or killed if they refuse to turn.

Detaching true spots of filth from the Hateful One gives He Who is Most Powerful the greatest pleasure, and therefore this activity must take special priority among stones administering this incursion. True spots of filth with an attachment to the Hateful One must be first broken of this attachment, and then shown the truth of their betrayal, and then killed, preferably in slow fashion, so that they might ruminate upon their betrayal. The agony derived from a true spot of filth betraying the Hateful One is exceedingly more than getting a Pretender to detach, but regardless, when they detach, you will see and taste the reward. Use whatever can be used: promises of death, promises of life, promises made masquerading as LightStains[40] or terrify them as Dark Knights[41]; make them promises from the past or promises of the future, by any Principality, by any power high or low, or by anything else you may use, make every effort to separate the spots of filth from the attachment extended to them from the Hateful One.

A most effective method utilized by the Marduk Principality has been to slowly infuse our own celebratory events into the flow of those ordained by the Hateful One. Move spots of filth to celebrate the Dark Days and disdain the feasts directed in the Blasphemous Rag[42]. Lift up the celebration of the Winter Solstice, surround them with visions of apple-cheeked children and sugar plums and trees bedecked with silver and gold, a holy man delivering presents to one and all, and drape all of it with a veneer of things that refer obliquely to the Hateful One. They will never know until it is too late that celebrating our holidays using their names is the same as worshipping us, no matter what veneer they apply to soothe their conscience.

40 The term used by this Principality to refer to angels.
41 The term used to refer to demons.
42 The term used by all Principalities to refer to the Bible.

Let it be known among stone inquisitors that if they do not break these true spots of filth and get them to freely detach from the Hateful One, they will suffer a worse fate.

There may be opposition by the Burning Wind. This must be fought and overcome at all costs. Stones will be useful here; they cannot detect its presence and may be immune to its influence. Dark Knights that do not press the attack to the fullest extent will be assured of a place on the Master's table.

Dealing with Pretenders: Pretenders are those who have no real connection to the Hateful One. The Hateful One does not know them. They pretend—for their own reasons—that they have an attachment to the Hateful One, but they obey only a god of their own making. You can identify Pretenders in this way; watch their lives, see what they do, and identify them by their disobedience. There will be no sense of the Burning Wind near these Pretenders. Upon the invasion, use stones to observe and act. One of the most important uses of Pretenders is that they can be tools to identify and betray true spots of filth. When threatened with confiscation of goods, loss of property, or death, these Pretenders will immediately rush to assure their stone captors that they were never truly attached to the Hateful One in the first place, and will be ever more likely to deliver the true spots of filth. Stones will most likely obtain names and locations of true spots of filth from threatened Pretenders. This will be preferable to coming upon true spots of filth unawares, for then stones can isolate and sequester true spots of filth before they demonstrate their deplorable 'faith' and infect other dung or stones. Therefore control the stones such that they do not immediately kill Pretenders, but make use of them.

Detachment methods must be tailored to the specific subject. Some may be successfully tempted to detach with promises of wealth, power, or position in the new order instituted by stone authority—this should be the first item offered. The approach, where suitable, might be one that makes the point that in the current regime, under Marduk's authority, no spot of filth was permitted to attain to any position of power, regardless of what media personalities may claim. Yet stones conducting these detachment interrogations can promise the spots of filth that they will truly attain to positions of authority, perhaps suggesting that the stones, not understanding religion per se as it does not exist within the Zhongguo Principality's geographic areas of control, will need these 'special individuals' to administer the others. This approach has been used successfully before in history, when the spots of filth first began to appear on earth after He Who is Most Powerful attained our great victory in Jerusalem against the son of the Hateful One. Another method will be to leverage the power of the lie, put in place by Marduk minions, that spots of filth would not encounter persecution or hardships. As they face the invasion and destruction of their land, as they see their fellow spots of filth being killed, they will more easily be convinced that their filth leadership[43] has lied to them about the future. Convince stone interrogators to press home one of our most powerful weapons—leverage their own filth teaching that they would be exempt from trouble and persecution. Leverage this, feed on the despair of souls that will arise when they are cast into the camps, when their loved ones are massacred, when their precious Protector abandons them to their horrible fate. See that stone interrogators remind these spots of filth about what their teachers said, that they would not undergo pain or suffering, and then extend the first thrust: *"What else has the filth leadership lied about?"* and after that, press home the killing blow: *"Your*

43 'Filth leadership' was a term used to apply to ministers, pastors, and leading Christian teachers during this time.

precious God has forgotten you." Then they should press them to detach.

Others may be detached with the simple promise of survival—tell them they will be killed unless they detach. And it must be stressed that the word 'betray' not be used by stone interrogators until such time as the spot of filth makes its declaration of allegiance to He Who is Most Powerful. Only *after* a spot of filth turns its back on the Hateful One and declares its allegiance to our Master should the stone interrogators make pointedly clear that he or she has in fact betrayed their precious Hateful One. Let that salt sit in their wound—for these creatures are made such that the act of betrayal generates a special, painful festering in their spirit which is highly attractive when devouring their souls. This is why the stone executioners must take care when dispatching spots of filth that have betrayed the Hateful One. We are not concerned about convincing other dung about the rightness of our cause—their convictions matter little to us. It is this exquisite agony that motivates and inspires us, this spiritual torture that we hope to exact in each of the betrayers, which will fuel our armies like water and wine fuels the human creatures. Stone interrogators who are particularly successful at extracting these betrayals should be rewarded. Those who fail will be set as examples for others.

We know from history that some will not detach. This is to be expected. So be it. Kill them as slowly and as painfully as possible. But it should not come to such extremes. Dung, it has been shown, will believe almost anything if they are promised some personal benefit. Leverage this.

Note on Killing

When killing spots of filth, make liberal use of that method of death to which they constantly refer, as a statement of disdain and irony. Spike them up on crosses. They ignored this in their rituals of worship while they were free—let them ruminate upon the quality of such a death while they hang there, at leisure. There should be sufficient spots of filth spiked up to line roads, places where other dung gather, or other key locations. Encourage stones to be creative in their application of this method. Do not let the lack of these spots of filth slow down the slaughter; if stones cannot find enough spots of filth—which may well be the case after the effectiveness of Marduk's efforts—then spike up any dung at hand. When fear spreads, all eat well.

Operational Plan of Action

The Zhongguo Principality will direct its stones to assault only when He Who is Most Powerful indicates the time is ripe. Preparations in the New Moon[44] Principality must be well along; its flag must first fly over Al Quds. The White Deceiver will cooperate and dull its flakes[45] appropriately. Dung leadership must be conditioned. Upon the stone assault, Marduk will compel dung leadership to request military assistance from Pryp'yat mud. Mud will travel through flake lands. The Aryan Principality will offer no resistance by the command of He Who is Most Powerful. Mud will be invited into dung territory and at first will make a show of halting stones and defending what remains of dung land. This will rapidly transition to a situation in which Pryp'yat mud will seize control of what remains of dung lands. Expect no resistance from dung against mud seizures. Expect there to be feasting on the souls of men as masses of millions starve. There will be oceans of blood, great swaths of fear and despair scything down the dung vermin, and everywhere, as music to our ears, will be the dung cursing the Hateful One.

---

44 The 'New Moon' Principality ruled over what was known as the Middle East.

45 'Flakes' was the term used to describe Canadians.

If any Principality needs additional information, reference the archives regarding the actions of He Who is Most Powerful in Poland during the last global feast, when our executive agents made common cause and sliced Poland into halves, easily devouring each.[46] Use this as a template if such is required.

When this scissors action occurs, there must be no discord displayed between any Principality and any other, or between stones and mud—disobedience here will result in offenders being served as food on the Master's table. Dung, while conditioned to be weak, self-gratifying, spineless creatures with predominately feminine characteristics, still have pockets where resistance may cause stones or mud difficulties, and this action must be accomplished quickly. He Who is Most Powerful will brook no delays in the execution of this plan.

46 Reference is made here to the Molotov-Ribbentrop pact in which Russia and Germany signed a non-aggression pact just prior to Germany invading Poland from the south and west in AD 1939; Russia quickly thereafter invaded Poland from the east. Known as a 'scissors' strategy in communist military doctrine, in which two supposed mortal enemies cooperate to eliminate a third, it was originally conceived by the Pryp'yat Principality during a minor skirmish in the Teutonic Forests between rival Germanic tribes.

Chapter 36

Sasha & Kong

'Were they ashamed because of the abomination they have done? They were not even ashamed at all; they did not even know how to blush. Therefore they shall fall among those who fall; at the time that I punish them, they shall be cast down," says the Lord.

Jeremiah 6:15

Newly-promoted Major Sokolov and newly-promoted Captain Lohniverisk flew into Boston from Prague on an Air France Airbus 388 in business class, since that fit their cover as senior executives for CDB ME Rubin, one of the largest marine engineering design firms in Russia. The firm was owned by the Joint Stock Company 'United Shipbuilding Corporation' and the Federal Agency for State Property Management and, while it wasn't in their briefing, they suspected that they knew the oligarchs who pulled the strings in those organizations. They were booked into the Mandarin Oriental, because it had what Sokolov thought was the best fitness center of the hotels on the list their handlers had given them to choose from.

Coming into the city, they'd been amazed at the widespread riots, civil disturbances, and destruction of property. Their Uber ride was a modified Toyota SUV with armor on the side panels and bulletproof glass. The driver took them on the main route from the airport, but still they saw countless incidents that told them the city was boiling with anger, division, and hatred. Prominently posted both on the back seat and the windshield of the car they took from the airport was a certificate testifying that the driver had passed a Tactical Assault Defensive Driving class. They made mental notes to record what they saw on the trip from the airport to the hotel in their reports. They occasionally recorded videos with their phones on the drive.

Their plan was to visit Boston as businessmen for about a week, and then begin an overland drive from Boston to Bismarck, North Dakota. When they checked into the Mandarin, the Concierge assigned a bellboy to take their luggage. He accompanied them up to their floor on the elevator, constantly chattering in a broad east Boston accent about the relative qualities of various tourist destinations, restaurants, and nightspots in the city. When they arrived in the room, the bellboy wheeled their bags into the room—they both had clothes and gear for over a month's stay in the country, along with long ski bags for their skiing equipment—and when Sasha handed him a ten-dollar tip, he took it and transferred a small note to Sasha in return. It was done smoothly, while the bellboy thanked them, again, in a thick Boston accent, and wished them a good stay. Sokolov made a mental note that Russia's foreign military intelligence arm was very much alive and well and working to great efficiency in America, and reminded himself not to underestimate old Camel Hair again.

They both changed out of their business travel clothes and into workout gear and hit the gym for two hours. Lohniverisk was massive, with little or no body fat, and Sasha knew from working with him previously that the big man's emotional, mental, and psychological condition was negatively affected if he didn't get in a daily workout. Sasha himself needed to stay in good condition. Their mission would require significant physical exertion, and he wanted to be fully functional. So while Kong hit the weights, Sasha worked on the cardio machines.

They had reserved a suite with two rooms adjoining a main salon. Sasha unpacked his small business case in the main suite area to set up a small workspace and set out the books he was carrying for the trip.

"What are these?" Kong asked, coming in from his room with a towel wrapped around his massive neck.

"These are books, Kong. They are a recent invention."

"Yeah, yeah, I have heard about them. Russians invented them, by the way. But why are you carrying them around? You could put them all into your iPad."

Sasha picked up one—Gibbon's *Decline and Fall of the Roman Empire*—and ran his hand over it. "Books are like people, Kong. Here you have a book in print, on paper, between two hard covers. You cannot know what's in the book just by the cover, but the cover protects the work. You cannot enter some search term and go immediately to where it is in the book, just as you cannot immediately know everything that is inside a person's character. You have to spend time with this book, reading through it, going back, reading the hard parts again, handling it, gleaning insights in the same way that one's association with a good friend works. Ah, but then you take your electronic marvel, this thing," Sasha said, lifting his iPad. "Yes, we can put books on it and you can carry so many more—but do you really get to know the work? Can you get a feel for it ... I mean a real, physical feel that combines tactile sense with the message in the words? No, you can't. And what happens when the battery dies?"

Kong nodded slowly and then put up a hand. "Enough," he said. "Rant off." He looked down on the table. "What else did you bring?"

Sokolov pulled out his other books: Spengler's *Decline of the West*; Kennedy's *Rise and Fall of the Great Powers*, and a last small volume, Martin van Creveld's *Pussycats*. Kong picked up van Creveld's work. "What's this about?"

"Its main assertion is similar to these other works."

"Which is?"

"That the relative power of nations isn't permanent; it is not guaranteed to last forever. A nation's power is affected by its internal social, political, economic, and cultural factors and processes. Over time, these factors and processes will generate weakness or strength, commitment or ennui, entropy or sudden periods of intense motivation and accomplishment. Van Creveld's assertion is that the West has lost influence in the world because these factors and processes are not sustaining the necessary motivation and accomplishment needed to ensure their power, and he says that military success is an outcome or a symptom of a nation's internal factors and processes. If they're arranged in one way, they produce a people and a nation of power and success in the world; if they're arranged in another way, they result in the dissolution and eventual decline and then death of the nation and the people."

Kong nodded his head slowly and set the book down next to the others. "Groundwork, then," he said.

"Precisely."

***

The week they spent in Boston was a stark introduction to America. It so happened that the day after they arrived coincided with the city's scheduled Boston Pride parade. They'd seen it advertised and so to get an idea of what Boston was so proud of that they would parade it on the streets, they had lunch at a restaurant on the parade route. They had visions of some type of patriotic procession, with military and law enforcement representatives marching to cheering crowds waving American flags.

They were sitting at the restaurant when Kong noticed something awry. "Sasha, there is something wrong here."

"What?" Sasha asked, eyeing a particularly attractive, long-legged blonde woman chatting with a red-headed female friend, also very attractive.

"Look at all the people."

"What? What are you talking about?"

"The people—the men are all with men, the women are with women."

Sasha couldn't make any sense of what Kong was saying. Then he looked around and noticed that Kong was right—where there were couples, they were all of the same sex. And as he began to look around—to really look around — he saw people in the strangest costumes, and when he looked closer, he couldn't believe his eyes.

"Give me that flyer," he said, snatching the promotional brochure off the table. Sasha opened it, something they hadn't done in the hotel, when one of the desk agents—a man—had handed it to them. With a sickening sensation he realized the 'Boston Pride' parade was an event celebrating homosexual and other perverted lifestyles. He almost gagged on his sandwich. He looked up at Kong, and suddenly realized that others in the crowd might take them for ...

"Let's get out of here," he said in Russian, disgusted, feeling as if the agent at the hotel had subtly tricked them into coming. They were everywhere! He threw the flyer on the table with a hundred-dollar bill to cover the lunch and tip and they almost leapt out of their chairs and hurried to the exit. As they moved through the restaurant they saw couples—men with men, women with women—and Sasha mentally berated himself for not noticing it when they came in. There was tangible disgust, and he felt his lunch rising in his gorge.

They were four blocks away, walking down an alley headed back to their hotel, heads down, faces burning in shame, still too shocked to even laugh about it when they were accosted by eight men in leathers. Most were thin and effeminate, but there were three men, larger, muscled, with chains looping over their shoulders, and they all had clearly had too much to drink. They were more than slightly aggressive.

"Hey boys," the leader cried out in a lisp that almost made Sasha sick on the spot, "looks like you're gonna get lucky today." The threat in the leader's voice was palpable, and Sasha had no question about what the eight men were going to do—or try to do. The other men began to range themselves around Sasha and Kong. Either they were too drunk to be frightened, or too filled with lust to care.

Sasha and Kong were both well trained in protocols requiring excessive degrees of restraint, control, and de-escalation to ensure Spetsnaz operatives remained undiscovered in their area of operations, and they'd been trained exhaustively to blend in with the indigenous population at their target areas. As the drunken sodomites prepared to rape them in the alley, that training went out the window.

Sasha tapped Kong slightly on the forearm and gave a quick body signal that meant, 'follow my lead, combat soon'. Sasha slowed. Kong hung back on his shoulder.

Sasha looked directly at the leading sodomite. Hoping to avoid a confrontation, he gave them a warning. "You people really do not want to do this; not today."

A few laughed, and a couple of the larger ones slid the chains from their shoulders and began swinging them back and forth threateningly.

"Oh, some kind of foreigner!" the leader exclaimed, picking up Sasha's accent. "You think you can come into our country and tell us what we're gonna do? I don't think so. Oh my, you boys look in AWFULLY good shape. You're going to be DELICIOUS!" The leading sodomite made a hand motion, and the eight closed in on Sasha and Kong.

***

The encounter was over in twenty-three seconds. The eight sodomites lay dead in the garbage-strewn alley. Sasha's small stiletto was covered in blood. Kong had used the lid of a trashcan and his belt. The two Spetznaz operatives threw the rapists into the dumpster.

"Ughh," Kong exclaimed in disgust, wiping his hands on the last. "They disgust me."

Sasha looked up and down the alley; no one had seen what happened. "Let's get out of this filthy city."

***

They did not leave Boston that day, or the next, or the one after that. Once back in their hotel suite, the priority of the mission rose up even above their disgust, and they stayed in Boston and dutifully accomplished their reconnaissance. The incident actually served to increase their motivation to discover everything they could to destroy American society—a society that would actually parade such filth in public, lifting up perversion as virtue, while gangs of perverts roamed the streets uncumbered, raping as they went.

Boston was America's main urban hub in the northeast, and would be a crucial focal point for any type of organized resistance should Americans choose to oppose what was to come. At least, that was the analysis Sasha and Kong were working with from their GRU[47] handlers. From what Sasha and Kong were seeing, they were convinced there would be little or no resistance.

At night they stayed off the streets, not out of fear of harm, but to avoid instances where they might disturb their cover. Neither trusted himself not to just kill any sodomite that might approach them again, and they didn't need trouble with the city's law enforcement. Fortunately, they discovered that they could get an enormous amount of intelligence about America and Americans from the Internet in the comfort of their rooms. As they watched the progress of the American presidential election, they were astounded at the success of GRU initiatives they'd known about. It was almost as if American politicians were on the GRU's payroll, advancing the GRU's own agenda, stirring passions and hatreds—crying up a war against women, or a war against blacks, or a war against whites, or Hispanics, or whatever other social divisions the politicians thought might get them votes. They had experienced first hand the effectiveness of the GRU's clandestine encouragement of the homosexual agenda and the confusions over gender issues. Even so, they were amazed that America had enacted laws to permit men who might feel like women on a particular day to use women's restrooms.

47 Glavnoye Razvedyvatelnoye Upravleniye - essentially Russia's Military Intelligence department

Sasha was particularly interested in the apocalyptic and survivalist genre of fiction he found on the web, and devoured at least a novel every evening. He stayed away from the zombie stories and focused on those fictional accounts that spoke of how frustrated Americans felt about an over-controlling, centralized government that was trampling on their freedoms.

"They sent the wrong men," Kong said one evening in disgust, looking at one lesbian, gay, bisexual, transgender site. "I do not think I can control myself; I just want to kill them all on sight."

Sasha looked at Kong and said grimly, "The time will come."

***

They made their first report to their East coast in-country controller six days after they'd arrived in Boston. Their controller was around fifty, female, shapeless, not overly attractive, who (Kong mentioned later) looked somewhat like someone's grandmother from the steppes. She was ostensibly Kong's aunt, and they were having dinner at her home since Kong happened to be passing through the city. She had been in America almost twenty-eight years—a deep cover plant that had recently been activated. She had been a secretary for Boston's City Council for the past eight years. She had a husband, a graying, pot-bellied professor at a local community college who was also an agent, doing very good work—and not needing to make much of an effort at it—convincing America's youth about the decadence and bankruptcy of America's systems, culture, and political structures, more often than not succeeding in his constant attempts to inject cynicism and disdain into the character of every student who, coming into his sphere of influence, gave any indication of promise. He was a staunch advocate of the progressive agenda and advocated the platforms advancing the very things that had disgusted Sasha and Kong during their short time in America. They were working together as a couple over the long term to bring down American society.

The Spetsnaz' officers' report included professional summaries of transportation hubs—airports, ports, bus, and rail stations, as well as major highways and road arteries in and out of the city. They had visited the office of CDB ME Rubin on the waterfront to cement their cover and improve their knowledge of marine engineering principles and vernacular. If there had been any surveillance, their visit to Rubin's offices would have reduced the likelihood that Sasha and Kong would be taken as anything other than Rubin employees. The executives there had no idea they weren't entertaining someone from the Russian corporate home office.

Sokolov and Lohniverisk covered Boston's main industrial capabilities and districts, showing where the power and water sources were, and where their key vulnerabilities appeared to be. The controller was most interested, however, in their assessment of how Americans would react to the fall of their government. Sasha then verbally debriefed her on the incident in the alley.

"From what we see, Americans have no backbone," Sasha said, holding a wine glass in his hand, speaking softly. "When a nation permits what they are permitting—their internal processes, cultures, and the things they are teaching their children," he shook his head, lips pursed derisively, but then tipped his glass to the woman's husband, "No offense, and I say this in all seriousness, you are doing a superb work, but to actually see the results! Aaauugghhh," he growled. "It's disgusting." He nodded his head, smiling. "My hat's off to you." Such plaudits from a field operative were the stuff of legend to deep cover agents, and the pot-bellied professor would cherish the comment for the rest of his life.

Sasha continued. "I mean, seriously, look who they put forth to promote critical health care legislation."

"Who?" the older woman asked; her husband began to smile.

Sasha waved a hand deprecatingly at Kong. "You tell her. It makes me too sick to even think of it."

Kong leaned forward, his huge frame overshadowing the modest suburban home's table setting. He opened his eyes wide, as though ready to deliver some horrible pronouncement. In a deep, portentous tone, he said "Pajama boy." Everyone chuckled and around the table there settled a sense of coming victory. The husband laughed out loud and tossed off the rest of his wine in one gulp.

***

Their trip out of Boston in a rented Toyota Highlander took them into Vernon, New Hampshire, then via back roads west across New Hampshire into Scriba, New York, and then Ontario, New York. Wherever there was any semblance of an urban population, they saw burned buildings, graffiti testifying to some type of 'Anti-Fascist' campaign, and, in more than one large city, they were delayed due to rioting in the streets. It was clear that law and order were breaking down across the country.

After a short sprint through Pennsylvania, they visited the small towns of North Perry and Oak Harbor, in Ohio. In Michigan they drove through Monroe, in the east, and South Haven, in the west. Moving through Illinois, they stopped in Seneca, then drove on to Cordova, in the western part of the State. Driving north through Wisconsin along the coast of Lake Michigan, they stopped at the town of Two Creeks, which was near Two Rivers. After driving through Green Bay they headed west, through Eau Claire. Diverting south a bit, they drove through Red Wing, Minnesota, and then on into Minneapolis. In Minneapolis, where the civil disturbance had the unmistakable flavor of Islam, they saw gangs of Muslim men roaming the streets, burning cars and breaking windows. They had to stay the night there, and as they parked in front of a chain hotel to check in, a gang of about seven Muslim men came strolling through the driveway where cars would temporarily park to check into the hotel. Kong had gone inside, leaving Sasha in the car, waiting.

Sitting there preoccupied, thinking about the next day's itinerary, Sasha heard a loud crack and, looking in the rear-view mirror, saw a crowd of young men around the Highlander. One of them had struck the bumper with a bat. Just then one of the larger youths pounded his fist on the driver's window. Sasha stared at him, not wanting any trouble. He pulled the car forward and parked it in in the back of the parking lot, as far away from the entrance as he could find, but the little knot of angry men followed him, sensing an easy target for their rage.

Sasha got out of the car and four of the young toughs immediately surrounded him while the others fanned out around the car. Sasha had intentionally parked away from any overhead light; it was dark and getting darker.

"You boys don't want any trouble now," Sasha said, trying as best he could to put on an American accent.

"You're dead, infidel."

"Wait, Yussef, wait ... what if he's a brother?"

This caused the leader to pause and ratchet back his arrogance a notch or two. It was something he should have thought of. "What of it?" he asked, looking at Sasha. "Are you a Muslim?"

It had been a long day and Sasha was very tired, but he could not help himself. "A Muslim? Me? Ah, thank you for letting me share my beliefs! Let me tell you what I believe, young friend. I believe Mohammed was a child rapist and possessed by the devil. I think Muslims in general are degenerate idiots who are the result of moronic in-breeding. I spit on Allah."

The men screamed at him and all of them pressed in to punch or kick or hit him somehow—but that didn't happen. Moving like flowing quicksilver, a knife appeared in Sasha's hand and the leader fell back slowly, clutching his throat, gurgling. Another's hand went to his chest, an artery severed, blood flowing through his fingers. A third felt a quick pain in his thigh and looked down to see the femoral artery severed and blood pouring out. He collapsed.

The others became even more enraged as they saw their friends fall to the ground, blood spattering everywhere. They failed to see a large man appearing out of the darkness behind them. Kong's combat knife skewered one man in the liver from behind and then in one stroke punched into another man's larynx. Kong ripped the knife from that man's throat and punched it into a third man's chest. Kneeling down as the victim fell forward, Kong turned and with a vicious uppercut, drove his now-bloodied knife into the last man's crotch just as he was lifting a baseball bat over his head. The man dropped the bat and before he could scream, Sasha cut his throat from behind.

Forty-eight seconds had elapsed since Sasha had stepped out of the car. Seven young Muslim hoodlums lay stretched out on the asphalt.

"It's dark; won't be able to see the blood," Sasha remarked.

"It's okay," Kong replied, holding up a small manila envelope. "I've got the keys and we can get in through the back door, there," Kong said, pointing to the back entrance to the hotel.

Sasha looked at the dead bodies. "Things in this country are worse than even we thought."

"We need to be careful to make sure who does the dying here, okay, Major?" Kong said, breathing hard from the quick adrenalin rush of hand-to-hand combat.

Sasha nodded. "Well said, Captain. Now what do we do with this filth?"

"If it wouldn't attract so much unwanted attention, I'd say just leave them here, but that would not be wise. I say we put them in those." Kong pointed to two dumpsters not far away, also placed as far from the hotel as possible, probably for the smell.

So they took the bodies one by one and threw them into the dumpster, which was almost completely empty.

"Do you think this will interfere with what we have to do?" Kong asked.

Sasha shook his head. "Not sure." He pulled out a flashlight and walked around the dumpster. "Ah, here it is. The collection schedule ... wait, let me read ... it says that the next pickup will be ... Saturday. What day is it today?"

"Tuesday."

"Good. And I haven't seen a single law enforcement vehicle in this part of town since we arrived. I'm not too worried."

"We're out of here in the morning, correct?" Kong asked, wiping the blood on the last dead man's shirt before they heaved him into the metal trash container.

"As early as possible," Sasha said.

"Right. Then let's get some sleep."

The two Russian Spetsnaz soldiers went into the hotel through the back door, took the stairway to their adjacent rooms, showered, and went to bed and slept the sleep of the just.

***

After the one night in Minneapolis they drove through Monticello and, getting on Interstate 94, took it all the way into Fargo, North Dakota and then on into Bismarck. They took pictures of the one common feature in every location where they either stopped or drove through—a nuclear power plant or generating station—but they also filmed civil disturbances, riots, gangs of youths decked out in black clothes with matching backpacks, or black gangs, or Muslim gangs. They took pictures of graffiti that was sprayed everywhere in the cities, proclaiming that the masses would soon be bringing down the 'Fascist' government.

After passing one long diatribe sprayed on the underside of a concrete overpass, Kong turned to Sasha. "They should see what it is like to live in a real Fascist country."

"They will," Sasha said. "They are actively making this country into a Fascist country."

"Ah," Kong said, nodding. "They have learned from the masters."

Sasha smiled. "Quite right," he said, and then declaimed in a pedantic tone, "always publicly fight against that which you privately work to accomplish."

Along the route they noted critical bridges and major airports, weather patterns, fueling facilities, and the terrain. They would engage Americans in conversation wherever they could—at truck stops, in small town cafes, and even at churches, where, on Sundays while they were on the road, they would attend as 'visitors'.

Without fail, at every church they attended, they were met at the door by some smiling attendee who shook their hand, told them he was especially pleased to see them, handed them some pamphlets related to the service schedule, and, in the larger churches, were directed to the coffee station. They noted that the smile and handshake was about as far as the interaction went. No one ever confronted them about what level of faith they had, or whether they were interested in growing in their faith, or even learning about the specific theology or doctrines being taught in the particular church they were attending. At each of the churches they visited, they were astounded that the protocols were so similar. First there would be singing, usually for about thirty minutes, followed by some individual ascending the stage to provide some form of 'special music'; then an event referred to as 'announcements', which covered various social obligations or events, after which came a sermon—the same sermon at each church, they noted—about the need to 'be saved', as though the people attending had not already signed up to the church's basic assertion and needed to hear this information over and over again. After what invariably to Sasha and Kong appeared to be pabulum, there followed two upbeat songs, then one slower song, then a dismissal, then the people would rush out of building as though they couldn't find the exits fast enough. The true gospel message never penetrated into Sokolov or

Lohniverisk because it was never delivered via the Spirit of Truth.

After five Sundays in five different churches, Sasha and Kong had the strong impression that American Christians were superficial, insincere, and bordering on the effeminate. Nowhere did the two Spetsnaz operatives encounter Americans outside of a church who discussed or even referred to their faith, which caused them both to conclude that the religious aspect in America they had been warned about was vastly overrated. Knowing little of the Bible and less of the Spirit, they nonetheless saw nothing of the impact made by Biblical doctrines they had been directed to look for in American society. It was as if their handlers back in Russia were operating on the assumption that religion in America was alive and well, vibrant and active, infusing American citizens with some type of supernatural motivation to persevere, to handle privation, to endure. But such did not at all accord with what Sasha and Kong were actually seeing in American society, government, and the legal system. They began to wonder if American Christianity was in reality just some type of social or cultural movement that was, strangely, restricted by the government to be exercised only within specially-designated buildings—usually buildings that had things called 'steeples'. They knew of the state-run churches in China and while they didn't think they were seeing outright government control of American churches, their opinion was that such control wasn't necessary. The churches themselves were devoid of anything that would threaten a godless government. They also began to form the opinion that the American government was permitting the existence of these churches for the specific reason that the churches were simply 'opiates to the masses'. The Spetsnaz operatives saw nothing of religion in America that might threaten Communist rule.

They spent the last night of their overland road trip in Bismarck, at a motel close to the Missouri Valley Millennium Legacy cross-country ski trail. They wanted to explore skiing conditions, but Bismarck that year hadn't had much snow, so instead they walked the trail and decided to wait to ski until they drove further north, hoping for snow. Compared to where both of them had operated, the late fall weather in North Dakota was almost balmy. There was no Muslim presence in Bismarck.

They left Bismarck with the taste of buffalo steaks from the previous evening's dinner—they'd never eaten bison, and both of them enjoyed it. The operatives were amazed at the profusion of wealth in America amidst a growing sense of poverty and urban decay. In some places there was a veritable bounty of food, drink, incredibly ornate houses, everyone with their own car, supermarkets full of food, but in others, mostly in the cities and suburbs, were burnt-out buildings, whole blocks abandoned, broken-down homes, and poverty, which they recognized from their own country, for if one went just thirty miles outside of Moscow, the rest of Russia looked like the third world. Sokolov and Lohniverisk knew what poverty looked like.

Yet there was plenty of affluence here still, and they wondered at the success the Russian intelligence organizations were having in convincing Americans to hate each other and tear down their own country. Why tear down what was obviously working so well? But they couldn't deny what they saw—an increasing disregard for rule of law; rising racial and ethnic tensions; a weak, morally decadent people where men were disparaged and women elevated. It was amazing. It was a country with its people split by political and cultural factors so intensely that the level of tension in the land would make even a meeting of Russian oligarchs nervous. While it encouraged them about the success of their overall mission, they wondered at the utter idiocy most American political leaders demonstrated by actually participating in the divisiveness. Did they not understand what would happen? Did they not see their own country tottering on the brink of disaster?

They drove through Minot and observed the commercial airport, and then drove a further 18 kilometers to view Minot Air Force Base.

"What we could do with such a place," Kong observed, staring at the tower, hangars, and runways through binoculars.

"Patience, my friend, patience. We will do those things. All things come to he who waits."

From Minot, they took back roads and small highways eastward to cover the almost 900 kilometers to Granite Sky in Minnesota, staying as close to the Canadian border as the road network would permit. On the last stretch into Granite Sky they drove along the Gunflint trail, paying particular attention to the quality of the road and the roadbed, wondering if it would support tanks.

***

When they stopped to check into the Granite Sky Lodge and Casino in the grim darkness early on a late fall morning, both were tired. "I need a workout," Kong said grimly, unpacking his huge frame from the car and stretching, eyeing the cars in the casino parking lot.

"No question about it," Sasha replied, eyeing the surrounding terrain and thinking about skiing the Gunflint trail later. There was a fine base of snow all around after a snowstorm two days earlier.

"Do they have legalized gambling here?" Kong asked, looking at the casino.

"It says they do," Sasha replied. "Apparently they permit the indigenous Indian tribes to control the gambling in various parts of the country."

"Hmmm ... what better way to keep them dependent on something that at the same time sucks the very marrow from the character of their people?"

"The capitalistic system is dangerously attractive," Sokolov answered. "I hope gambling doesn't interest you, my friend."

Kong rolled his arms backward and popped his shoulders. "Gambling? Bah. I need weights," Kong growled. "Weights interest me. I need to move large heavy things. This is what I am addicted to, Sasha." They used their first names with each other, as would any traveling pair of business executives.

"We shall see what we can find," Sasha replied.

They checked in and got adjoining rooms on the second floor with a stunning view overlooking Lake Superior, and after stowing their gear, they met in Sasha's room.

"Our first task is to meet with the owner of the local construction company," Sasha began, but Kong held up a hand.

"Our first task must be to get in a workout, comrade. We have been cooped up in a car for almost a month. I am going crazy."

Sasha nodded. "Right, right, first things first, very correct. But I want to meet with this company first thing today—it is a Friday, and they will be closed for the weekend—and then let us see what we can do about working out; what do you say?"

Kong looked unconvinced, but agreed, growling. "I reserve the right to rip someone's head off if they displease me."

***

Sasha and Kong parked in the lot at the Northern Minnesota Construction Company and locked their doors, the habit from rural Russia being handy in this new America they were discovering.

Kong knocked on the door and waited ... and waited.

"I called them not fifteen minutes ago," Kong said. "They said they'd be here."

As he spoke, the door opened and a slim, fit young man with broad shoulders, short dark brown hair, in worn jeans stared back at them. He was holding a large manila file and a mug. "Good morning, gentlemen. Are you from Rubin?"

Sasha stepped forward and shook the man's hand. "We are, yes. I'm Doctor Sasha Sakharin; this is my colleague, Dr. Karin Olyutsk. Thank you for meeting with us."

"I'd heard Rubin was teamed with Grayson. Good to know. I'm Josh Riesling, by the way. Hey, next time, just come in, no need to knock. We're pretty informal around here." Riesling led them through the small entry space and into what was obviously a conference room, plain, with utilitarian chairs and a laminated oblong table. On the way in, Sasha caught Kong's eyes and surreptitiously looked to a large cross hanging from the wall in the main office.

"*Do you want coffee, gentlemen?*" a woman asked, in Russian, surprising them. She was waiting in the conference room. She was slim but with wide shoulders, dark hair; olive skin; dark, almost Asian eyes; very attractive. Sasha noticed she had very strong hands, with callouses.

"*Da*, uh, yes, thank you," Sasha replied.

"*I'm Daria Avidora*," she said, still in Russian.

"*Where did you get your Russian?*" Sasha asked.

"*My grandfather lived with us for many years*," she replied, filling two Styrofoam cups and handing them to Sasha and Kong. "*He was from a very isolated part of northwest Russia. He moved there after they closed the Pale of Settlement.*"

"*He was ... he was a Jew, then?*"

"*He was. He moved the family to Israel before the '67 war. He died in '98.*"

"*What part of northwest Russia?*" asked Kong. Sasha was surprised to hear him ask the question, but said nothing.

"*You would not know of it, probably. It was a small town in the Yamalo-Nenets Autonomous Okrug*," Daria replied.

Kong's eyes narrowed. "*I have heard of this region. What town?*"

"*Nadym*," Daria replied, looking at Kong. "*Do you know it?*"

Kong took a sip of coffee and cleared his throat. "*I have heard of it, yes. It is a very small town, inconsequential.*"

"*Oh yes*," she replied pleasantly, still in excellent formal Russian. "*It would have to be if they let Jews live there.*"

"*What was his name, if I may ask?*" Kong said. "*Your grandfather.*"

"*Gregor ... Gregor Avidora.*"

Kong nodded and lifted his Styrofoam cup and in English, said with some emotion, "*Gregor Avidora.*"

Sasha lifted his cup and added, "*Dariovna Gregorevich Avidora.*"

Daria smiled and bowed her head slightly. "*You are too kind, gentlemen. Please, come,*

Mr. Riesling has the materials you've been asking about." She led them back to the conference table where Josh was sitting, open-mouthed, having just learned that his secretary spoke fluent Russian.

"There are some things we should talk about," Josh said, sotto voce, as Daria took her seat next to him.

"There certainly are," she replied in the same way, without even giving him a look.

***

The meeting stretched into two hours. Josh and Daria went over the initial projections Grayson had sent for building a receiving and unloading facility in the inlet just to the north of Granite Sky, on the coastline. Sasha and Kong spent most of the time listening to the proposal Josh and Daria were making for the integration of NMC as a subcontractor to Grayson. Where there were particularly technical points in the proposal, Daria switched to Russian and then explained what she'd said to Josh.

At the end of the meeting, Sasha said, "We are very impressed. It is not our decision to bring you into the team as a subcontractor, but if it were up to us, we would do so. I can tell you Rubin will be giving you a strong recommendation. And," he said, looking at Daria, "we didn't expect such excellent Russian, and such professionalism so far away from—"

"From civilization?" Josh finished for him.

"Yes, I apologize, but you must admit you are a bit off the beaten track."

"We kind of like it that way," Josh replied.

"Nonetheless, we're confident your firm can handle the work."

"Kind of you to say so."

"Would it be possible to see your facilities?" Sasha asked.

Daria stood, followed by Josh. "Of course, Doctor," she said, "if you'll follow me?" She led them out through the back door into the warehouse. She handed them each a hard hat and a yellow safety vest and they walked around the warehouse and dock—the undercover Mossad agent unknowingly showing two visiting Russian Spetsnaz operatives everything there was to see about NMC's equipment, supplies, storage, and construction capabilities.

At one point in the tour, they passed a small space in which were several white plastic five-gallon buckets filled to various levels with concrete, each with a thick manila rope sticking out of it by about a foot, knotted at the end. The pails had numbers painted on the outside, followed by the letters 'lbs'.

"What are those?" Kong asked, curious.

Josh stopped and explained. "Sorry, I know they probably don't belong here, but this little space is where I work out."

"You use these?"

Josh nodded. "Sure. They're cheaper than buying weights—we always have spare concrete around, and they're actually pretty easy to use."

"Is there a weight store ... a place to buy weights, as you said?" Kong asked. Josh could tell he was talking to another avid weightlifter.

"Well, you could, I suppose. There's a fine sports store at the mall." Josh saw the look of interest pass quickly over the large Russian's face, and then said, "But hey, why don't you let us make you a set of these?"

Kong darted a glance at Sasha before looking back at Riesling. "What do you mean?"

Josh laughed softly. "It'll take us about twenty minutes to make you up a set. We happen to be doing a pour this morning, actually, and making a set won't be a problem. Where are you staying in town?"

"You would make me a set of these?"

"Easy. Tell us what combinations and how much weight you'd like and it won't be a problem. But where are you staying? If you're staying in the Lodge, they may have an issue with you carting in buckets of concrete."

Kong looked disappointed. Josh could see the guy was desperate to move weight.

"*I tell you what, I know the owner of the Lodge,*" Daria put in, switching again to Russian, "*and I am sure she won't mind. I'll make it happen.*"

Kong looked at Josh and Daria and nodded. "*Thank you,*" he said, first in Russian to Daria, and then in English to Josh.

"Our pleasure," Josh replied. "I know how I feel when I don't get a workout in, and it would drive me crazy. I don't see how you do it, traveling all over the world like you do. And you still look like you stay in great shape."

"Russian donuts," Kong said darkly, patting his flat, firm belly, and they all chuckled. They spent the next few minutes with Kong testing the various buckets, and listing the amount of weight he wanted. They settled on a set of eight different plastic pails set at different weights—much more weight than Josh would have selected.

At the end of the tour, they handed their hard hats and vests back to Daria and Sasha thanked them both for the time they'd spent that morning. As they walked back through the offices, Sasha turned to Daria and, in Russian, said, "*Tell me, sister, what is a dazzling Russian Jewess doing in a place like this?*" As he asked the question, he tilted his head subtly toward the cross on the wall without Josh noticing.

Just as subtly, she tilted her head toward Josh and replied in Russian, "*Waiting for this potato-head to open his eyes,*" she said, with a completely straight face.

Sasha looked down, passed a hand over his mouth to cover his smile, and nodded. "*Yes, okay, I understand. Thanks for explaining,*" he answered in Russian. He turned to Josh and in English said, "Thank you again for the briefing and the tour. It was ... instructive," he said, looking toward Daria as he said the last word.

Josh looked sideways at Daria but didn't say anything. Instead, he extended his hand to Sasha and Kong. "We'll have your set finished in about an hour and get it over to the Lodge. Ms. White Hawk won't have a problem if Daria explains things."

"Thank you, you are very kind," Kong said, the words sounding strange, emanating from such a large man. He turned to Daria, took her hand, and in Russian said, "*You are right, little sister. He is a potato-head.*"

Daria laughed with delight as the two Spetsnaz operators left the office as Josh stood there, wondering.

***

The NMC pickup pulled into the parking area of the Granite Sky Lodge and Casino, and Josh and Daria got out and walked into the office. They talked to Anita White Hawk, the owner, who was just fine with making sure her Russian guests had everything they needed to stay happy. There was intense competition among the hotels in Granite Sky owing to the boom in oil exploration, and she would do her part to keep the Lodge solvent.

They hauled the first set of pails up to the room on the second floor. "How much is this, by the way?" Daria asked.

"Twenty-five kilos," he said. "And these are the lightest."

"The guy *is* ... in pretty good ... shape," Daria said, huffing up the stairs, but lacing the comment with a tinge of interest.

"Yeah, and hey, I didn't know you spoke Russian, by the way. That's pretty impressive."

"Lots of things you don't know about me."

Josh set the 55lb pail down and looked at Daria. "What does *kartofel'naya golova* mean," he asked.

"I have no idea what you're saying; your pronunciation is horrible. No one could understand that." She pushed past him toward the Rubin executives' rooms.

"Google has a translate capability, you know."

"Good luck with that."

She knocked on the door and Kong pulled it open at once. "Ah, weights! Thank you," he said in English, standing there in a t-shirt and sweat pants. He was massive. He had to bend down to pass through the door, and he stepped out onto the landing and took up the pails, one in each hand, and swung them through into the room like they were teacups.

Switching to Russian, he said over his shoulder, "*Little sister, come in, have a drink. Potato-head and I will get the others.*" Kong motioned to Josh and, while he didn't understand any Russian, he did recognize the *kartofel'naya golova* phrase again. He followed the large man out the door and back to the pickup. Josh hauled one of the 30-kilo pails while Kong took two 50-kilo pails. After a couple of trips they had moved the makeshift weights up to Kong's room while Daria talked with Sasha about their requirements to inspect the northern shoreline. Fortunately the drink they offered was grapefruit juice. She was glad it wasn't vodka this early in the day.

"They'll be here for at least a month, Josh," she said as Sasha and Kong rearranged the weights in another part of the room. "You should ask them if they want to come to the Harvest Festival."

He looked at her and said quietly, "You realize who's sponsoring that, right."

"Harvest Festival? This is local custom, yes?" Kong asked, filling the doorway between his and Sasha's room.

Josh turned to face the Rubin executive. "It is, and if you're interested in the local community, especially as it might give you an insight into the local labor market, you might consider it."

Kong looked at Sasha and as they both knew that mingling with local Americans was part of their mission, there was no question. "We would be pleased to accept," Sasha replied.

***

Josh and Daria walked down the steps of the hotel to the parking lot. "They're probably Russian orthodox," he said.

"Doesn't matter. They'll have a good time."

"I thought you weren't going within ten miles of that party."

Daria tossed her head and got in the truck. "It might be fun," she answered. "And what do you know about what I'm going to do or not?"

"Sorry," Josh said. "I just thought ... "

"Yeah, it's put on by the local churches. I know, but hey, Christianity was invented in Israel, right? Your Jesus was just a Jewish Rabbi, don't forget. And besides, it's just a Halloween party with a different name."

Josh was quiet for a moment while he started the truck and pulled out of the lot. It was a short drive to the NMC office, and as they arrived at the lot, he said, smiling, "I just thought you wanted to hang out with the big Russian."

Thereupon issued a flow of Hebrew he had no chance of understanding, but the meaning did not escape him.

***

Sokolov and Lohniverisk walked the shoreline of the northern inlet the next day, studying the ground composition, observing the terrain, noting where Grayson was planning on building the dock and unloading facilities. They spoke in Russian, unafraid of being overheard in the whipping wind blowing off the lake.

"Will it be sufficient?" Kong asked, all business now that he'd gotten in a solid workout.

"Probably," Sasha replied. "The presumption is that the landings and unloading operations will be unopposed. If that holds, we should be okay."

"Will they truck the supplies overland?"

"That's the initial plan, although if there is an available rail system, that would work much better."

"The closest rail lines are south. There was a line supporting a steel mine near Schroeder, but it has gone out of service. I think we will need to go down too far south to get to the closest functioning rail service." Kong kicked at a small mound of sand, bent down, and picked up a fistful to test its consistency.

"Do you think we could truck the cement to Two Harbors?" Sasha asked.

"We would have to supply drivers."

"Not necessarily," Sasha countered. "From what we've seen, I wouldn't be surprised if Americans volunteered to drive the trucks that will help cement the destruction of their country. Most will do anything for a job."

Kong stood up, completely missing the pun, and said, "What a collection of pathetic people." He looked out at the blue-gray horizon line of Lake Superior. "What of the meeting?"

"I pulled down a communication last night," Sasha replied. "They should be here in a week or so."

"Our objectives?"

"Apparently there are plans to put a joint command center nearby. For some reason they like this location as the northern anchor inside U.S. borders for the line extending south that will mark the western border of our protectorate. Our task is to work with the visitors and jointly determine appropriate facilities for the command center."

"Somewhat isolated for such a facility, wouldn't you say?"

"I think they are anticipating more resistance than we—you and I—are expecting. At the moment they are afraid of cities."

"Do you know who it is we're meeting?"

"They haven't told me that yet." Sasha looked north, toward Canada. "But our objectives are to determine the best location for a continental command center they would agree with. We are specifically instructed not to be controversial or argumentative."

"So you are telling me I should not kill them with one of our little spades?" Kong asked.

"Yes, that would be counterproductive to the mission. Maybe later, perhaps, if things don't work out."

"Good. I will keep the edges sharp. Have you considered the Border Stations?" Kong asked, referring to possible locations for a command center.

Sasha grunted. "I've looked at them and it's possible, but I think they'll want the facility on U.S. ground. The Canadians might get problematic. They are not sure at this point. So I think they would probably want something constructed specifically for the purpose."

Kong nodded. "I think you are right," he replied. "Sounds like more work for NMC."

Sasha turned and headed back down south along the shoreline. "Do you think Riesling would work for a occupation government?"

Kong thought for a moment. "You saw the cross on the wall, right? The Christians we've seen in this country have no backbone. They're handwringers. They won't say a word, and they'll probably thank their God and consider it 'Providence' that they have work when most of their country is a glowing night light. And besides, who is planning on giving him a choice?"

Sasha looked pensive. Both hands were in the pocket of his parka as he looked south toward Granite Sky. "I hope you are right, Kong, but I have my doubts."

"Why is that?"

"Two reasons: first, how many Christians have we seen who work out with pails of cement and rough manila rope?"

"None, granted, that we know of. And the second?"

"The Israeli woman. I do not get the sense that she would be waiting around for a wet chicken. That worries me. She seems to me to be neither stupid nor cowardly."

"That reminds me," Kong interrupted. "What is this 'Pale of Settlement' she spoke of yesterday?"

"You should read our history. The Pale of Settlement was the name given to areas in Russia where Jews were permitted to live. Outside of this, they could not go."

"She is Jewish," Kong rumbled. "The Jews ... just another thorn in the paw."

"Not for long. I see on CNN that our forces are in Syria, and the Iranians are there with us. Won't be long now."

"We're all one big happy family, I thought, fighting the ISIS hordes, right?"

Sasha looked at him and said nothing.

Kong walked along with his boss for a few more meters and then said, "Well, this explains why you are the mission commander and I am just the muscle."

Sasha looked at Kong. "Remember, the people we meet here may be pleasant, they may do us favors, they may invite us to their parties, but don't forget that we may have to cut their throats one day."

Kong nodded and smiled grimly. "My little spade can wait."

Chapter 37
Tony

"Why should I pardon you? Your sons have forsaken Me and sworn by those who are not gods. When I had fed them to the full, they committed adultery and trooped to the harlot's house."

Jeremiah 5:7

"Alicia and Todd need to go down to Minneapolis again," I said, depressed. Todd's cancer wasn't getting any better.

"You're not planning on going down there with them this weekend, are you?" Penny asked. "The Harvest Party is Saturday, and I don't want to handle trick-or-treaters Friday by myself, either."

"Yeah, I understand, and no, they'll go down by themselves. Alicia will drive. And I'll be here this weekend, no worries. We're carving pumpkins Wednesday night at youth group, and bagging candy for Halloween Thursday night."

"You'd probably just get in the way down there anyway," Penny says.

"You're probably right," I reply.

***

We carved pumpkins on Wednesday night at youth group. We set up tables covered with newspapers, and a farmer, one of the church family members, brought in a small load of pumpkins. The kids drew their designs on the pumpkins and I cut them out with a knife. We didn't let the kids use knives. There were all kinds of designs, but mostly just some kind of riff on the basic toothless smiley face. We didn't let any of the kids draw anything scary. Then we put candles in them and put them out by the road in front of the church.

Friday night the trick-or-treaters came by, and Penny and I took turns handing out candy and tracts to the kids who came to the door. That one freak snowstorm we'd had about a month ago had dropped several feet of snow.

We told all the kids who came to the door that Jesus loves them, although I think they just wanted the candy. There was one little girl though, no more than ten, dressed as a witch, who looked up at me as I told her that Jesus loves her and she said, "Why?"

"Well, just because, sweetie. He died for you so your sins could be forgiven."

"What are sins?" she asked, looking through what I'd dropped into her bag.

"That's when we do bad stuff," I replied.

"My mommies say that I don't really do any bad stuff," she said, looking back up at me.

"Everyone has sins," I said, not really expecting to have a theological discussion with a ten-year old while handing out Halloween candy.

"So how come sins need to be forgiven?" she pressed, and I thought I could see two women on the walk, standing close together in the dark just out of the glare of our porch light, probably wondering what I was talking about with their kid. "My mommies say that if I do bad stuff I just have to go to time-out."

"Well, if our sins aren't forgiven, we can't go to heaven."

"Is that a good place to go? My mommies are taking me to Disney World in the spring. That should be nice. Do my sins need to be forgiven to go there?"

Mommies, plural ... light bulb flashes on ... got it. The two women standing there arm in arm on the sidewalk in front of my house now made sense.

I smiled at the little girl in the witch costume. "No, not if you just go to Disney World. But heaven is a lot nicer than that."

"Can my mommies come to heaven if I go?" she asked.

"God loves everyone," I said, wishing that the church was more inclusive that it had been throughout its early history.

The little girl turned to look over her shoulder. "Hey, Jan, hey Daniela, do you want to go to heaven with me?"

Jan and Daniela unlocked arms and rushed up to escort their little pride and joy away from the nasty, judgmental pastor's door. They must have been new in town.

So the evening went on. Lots of the younger ones had their parents with them, but they just waved from the sidewalk, with the exception of Jan and Daniela, and no one wanted to come up to the pastor's door and risk having a tract shoved into their pocket or maybe endure the mention of Jesus. But we had a lot of kids from the church family come by too, and their parents would visit briefly with Penny and I while the kids munched on a candy bar or ran around the yard, chasing each other in their costumes. Man, they had so much energy. Youth is wasted on the young.

All in all, it was a great night and lots of kids got to hear the gospel message, if only in its briefest form, that Jesus loves them. Sometimes you just do what you can do.

***

A long time ago the pastors and ministers and priests in our area decided that the churches needed an alternative to Halloween, so as a group we decided to put on a Harvest Party. There were a range of different names proposed for the 'counter-Halloween event', like 'Jesus Jamboree' or 'Harvest Celebration' or the one from the Pentecostal church on the outskirts of town that everyone got a kick out of—'Harvest Hoedown'. I think the vote was something like ten to one in favor of 'Harvest Party'.

We rented the football field from the high school and had all kinds of booths and rides—there were carnival games where the kids could win prizes, and some of the farmers with teams of horses brought them in to give hay rides. There was a small portable corral set up for pony rides. We had a couple of booths that would continuously run Christian movies on large-screen televisions we set up, and this year we even had two booths where kids could compete against each other with some first-person shooter games projected on a large screen TV. Although there was still a bit of snow on the ground, the weather was warm enough for people to be outside comfortably, walking around in the early evening.

There was one booth in the center of the field, inside the rings of booths ranged throughout the field, that we called 'the Life Booth', where anyone could come and hear the gospel. We would get two or three kids wander in there a year, wondering what the booth was, and we would rush to get a tract in their hand before they figured out that it was something having to do with church and religion. We had a couple of kids a few years back who'd stayed and actually wanted to hear what the gospel message was about, and I think they invited Jesus into their hearts and were attending one of the other churches in town. Although the harvest wasn't plentiful, we were always hopeful. The fields were definitely white. We all told ourselves that the prophesied revival was just around the corner.

When we'd first begun having the Harvest Party alternative celebration, we didn't let any scary costumes onto the field because we didn't want to have the event be seen as mixing with the Halloween holiday. To tell you the truth, that generated more questions than anything else we would do each year. Kids and even some of the parents wanted to know about the origins of Halloween, and that gave us the opportunity to introduce the truth about the realms of the spirit. However, we began to see that we were excluding a lot of kids, and so the pastors and ministers and priests all decided to just quietly do away with the ban on scary costumes. I mean, really, when you think about it, it's just a kid in a costume, right? We didn't think that what they wore should keep some kid from hearing the gospel.

This year, something happened that was a little hard to explain, but I'll give it a try. The local parish priest, Father Jourdain, and I were manning the Life Booth after I had finished a stint in the pony ride corral and then helped serve cotton candy in another booth. It was around 8:00 pm when this very large guy came in to the booth, looking it over, clearly wondering what game or food was involved.

"Can I help you?" I asked in my most pleasant greeter's voice.

"Yes, you can," he said, with obvious gusto. "What tent is this?" I could tell right away that he wasn't from around here. He had some kind of foreign accent, although his English was understandable.

"We call it the Life Booth."

"Ah, this is emergency medical services?" he asked.

"Uh, no, not really. We're from the Living Waters church, and all the churches in the town put this party on every year. This booth is where people can come to hear about Jesus."

The big man looked around and then put two huge hands on the counter and leaned over to look inside the tent. "What do you tell people in this ... this Life Booth?" As he asked this question, another man joined him, somewhat smaller, but still in excellent shape, with intelligent eyes, wearing a white hooded parka that looked like something a skier would wear. The larger one turned and said something to White Hood in a foreign language. White Hood turned to me.

"So you tell people about Jesus?" he asked with a tinge of curiosity in excellent English. "What do you tell them?"

I couldn't believe how good God was, to give me a chance to evangelize two strangers who were obviously passing through Granite Sky. Who knew if they would ever have a chance to hear the gospel again? And, praise God, the local Catholic priest would get to see how the Protestant team pitches.

"We tell them that God loves them, and that God created each person to have a personal relationship with them. But man is sinful and separated from God, so he can't know God personally or experience his love. We tell them that Jesus is the only provision for man's sin and they must accept Jesus in their heart. Once they do, they can know God personally and receive His love."

Both of them were looking directly at me with expressions I couldn't fathom—sort of like amazement, distrust, and wonder all mixed together.

"This sounds like it would be something very important," White Hood said.

"Oh yeah, it is, it's like the most important thing there is."

"I see," he said, and then looked over at the big guy, who shook his head in a mournful way. Then, surprisingly, they turned to go.

"Wait!" I exclaimed, probably a little too loudly. "I'm curious. I mean, like, what do you think about what I've just told you?" I couldn't let them go without pressing to see if I could get at least one of them to make a commitment to accept Jesus in their heart.

"You would not want to know," White Hood said quietly.

"Yeah, actually, I would. It's important."

White Hood turned back to me and was about to open his mouth and tell me what he thought when the big man put a huge hand on White Hood's chest, preempting him. The big man stepped up to the counter and leaned toward me. He had a deep, rumbling voice that was, to tell the truth, a little intimidating.

"You know, what you just said? It makes no sense to anyone who is not already an initiate into your little social club. Where we come from, there are also social groups that have their own buzzwords that only those in the club can understand. But the rest of this," and here he waved one of those huge hands back toward the booths and rides, "it all makes sense now; the games, the rides, the *show*." He was waving his hands around at the entire party field. "You are *selling* something, and you need these things to draw in potential customers, like a spider draws in a fly. You have even arranged your party like a spider's web—all the things to catch the fly on the outside while the spider waits in the middle to catch the unwary bug."

I was a little taken aback by what the guy was saying. I smiled a little to try and take the intensity down a notch. "I guess you could look at it that way," I replied.

But he wasn't half finished.

"Handwringers, all of you," he spat. "Why should people believe what you say? You say you deal in truth. *Bah!* If what you are saying is truth, if what you speak of was real, why do you feel the need to structure all these things to attract people and to trick them into listening?"

I didn't have any answer to that. "We ... we're really not trying to trick anyone, sir."

He said something dismissive in his native language and waved his hand in the air like he was brushing away some pesky fly. "An honest person can only conclude that what you have to offer is not attractive enough in its essence. Do you know this English word, *essence*? It means the core, the foundation, what something is truly made of." He held up a closed fist in front of his chest like there was some secret, precious thing held in it. "The essence of your so-called message is obviously not attractive enough, not true enough, so you need other things to 'trap' people to get them close enough to hear your message. Even *you* do not believe it is attractive enough on its own, otherwise you would not have set up such an elaborate trap." He waved his hand around in the air again to indicate all the games and rides and booths nearby. He was a little scary. He turned and spoke into the night air. "This is ... this is the worst, the lowest form of trickery, of chicanery, of ... " the big man turned to White Hood and said something in their language, got an answer, then turned back to me. "Hucksterism, I think you call it in English. You are salesmen. You disgust me. Your message disgusts me. And the worst thing is, *the worst thing*, is that you pass off what you say as truth when even *you yourselves* do not believe it. *Bah!*"

Father Jourdain and I just sort of stood there, not knowing how to respond to this guy, not exactly sure if he was angry and wondering if he was going to decide to tear the booth down, stick by stick—he looked like he could do it. I thought maybe I should try and de-escalate the situation.

"May I ask where you're from, sir?"

The big guy was about to respond when White Hood lifted just a finger, very slightly, which stopped the big man in his tracks. I got the sense that the big man either worked for White Hood, or respected him a lot.

"We are from a country where truth and honesty are at least respected," he said in a quiet, almost sibilant voice laced with disdain, "and we know a trap when we see one." He turned to go.

"Excuse me, sir, but we really aren't wanting to trap anyone. We don't force this on people." This stopped him.

"You say you don't want to trap anyone. You say that this, this *message* of yours is the most important thing ever?"

"Yes sir, I did say that, and I believe it."

"And yet you have this party on the same High Holy Day that belongs to your enemy, is this not true? Today is the 31st of October, it is not? We do not know much about your country, but we know that today is Halloween, which is some kind of satanic day, correct?"

"Well, yes, but we have this party today to give people an alternative."

White Hood laughed with what I could only think was derision. "Look around you," he said, stretching out his arm. "Look—there is a witch; there is a skeleton costume. There is some small boy with a rubber hatchet sticking out of his head. There is someone else with a skull attached to the top of his head. Everywhere I see costumes of death and what you people say are darkness and evil. What alternative are you talking about?"

I looked around and saw the kids he was pointing out. I tried to explain. "Sir, if we kept those kids from coming to the party, they might miss a chance to hear about how much God loves them." I spread out my hands in a pleading gesture. "We're just trying to work out a compromise so we can get the message to them."

The big man in the back shook his head slowly and turned to face away from the booth, obviously disgusted. White Hood looked at me. "You asked us where we come from. We come from a country where we know a lie when we hear it. You say you let these people in who wear costumes that represent things your God is supposedly opposed to, and you say it is a compromise, so that they might hear about your God. Tell me, *why* would anyone want to hear about a God whose servants are nothing but compromisers? What benefit could such a God possibly offer anyone?"

The big man looked over his shoulder, standing off by himself a bit away, and said something in their language. When White Hood didn't turn, the big man said in English, "There is no power in what they are selling; there never is. Come, let's kick the dirt of this place of our shoes."

White Hood and the big guy left. I didn't have any answer to their last question, and it disturbed me until Father Jourdain came up next to me and put his hand on my shoulder.

"Philistines," he said, and we both laughed. My reservations drained away. It was good to have another Believer to stand with you when times got tough.

"Some people just don't get it," I replied, shaking my head, grateful for the Father's support.

Chapter 38
Bolin & Meifeng

"Woe to you, scribes and Pharisees, hypocrites, because you travel around on sea and land to make one proselyte; and when he becomes one, you make him twice as much a son of hell as yourselves."

Matthew 23:15

Bolin and Meifeng moved through the crowds at the Harvest Festival slowly, not wanting to lose their security escort. Meifeng felt they could not adequately gather the requisite amount and quality of information if their security team was hovering nearby, so they were given instructions to mingle with the crowds while keeping an appropriate distance.

They had arrived in Thunder Bay two weeks ago and while staying in a hotel, conducted initial discussions with the two Russian representatives from the Rubin Company. Bolin took one look at them and knew they were not really marine engineers, but made no comment. He and Meifeng were not really Chinese diplomats, nor were they married.

The discussions went well. The lead, a 'Dr. Sakharin', explained what their intentions were regarding the border station facilities, and as Bolin studied their plans and the satellite pictures of the Granite Sky area, he assessed that their reconnaissance of the location was accurate, and the teams agreed to utilize the border control station facilities as their headquarters in the coming operation. Dr. Sakharin also indicated that there would be construction necessary, and proposed the use of a local Granite Sky construction firm to provide the work. Bolin questioned whether they would be willing to do the work once the operation had begun. This started a productive discussion among the team members at the meeting about what the operational environment would be in the vicinity of the border and in the general area of Granite Sky.

"As you know, one of the main routes for our equipment will be through a docking facility we hope to build just north of Granite Sky, on the coast," Sakharin said. "That should be completed within the next three months. You bring up a good question about the potential level of permissiveness in the area. My colleague has information on this." Sakharin turned to his companion, who had not given them any name, and they hadn't asked.

"We do not expect serious resistance," the large Russian explained. "We have analyzed the population and their culture, and throughout our travels in the United States we have seen no serious sign of any strong national character, social habits, or tendencies that would make us think our operations will be seriously opposed. Oh, they like to quote their rugged individual heroes and they watch them on television or in their videos, but we have seen no real situations where the people are willing to put their obligations to duty above their own gratification or sense of entitlement. There is an incomprehensible focus on individual rights in this country, and the people are so convinced that they have a divine right to lead a happy, fulfilled, and wealthy existence that should it be cut short by some accident or mischance, they feel cheated."

"You are correct," Bolin put in. "When the two towers fell in New York on 9/11, families of those who died sued the U.S. Government and won, as though it was the government's fault the terrorists attacked and lives were cut short. The sense of entitlement in this country is astounding."

"So yes," the large Russian continued, nodding, "no one chooses hardship, self-sacrifice, duty, or privation. Their greatest expenditure of effort is to make sure they live lives of luxury and ease. So to be brief, Comrade Majors, no, we do not think there will be much resistance. If we offer them food, shelter, security, electricity, and an opportunity to continue doing what they were doing, they will go along like sheep."

They spent the remainder of the week in meetings with the two Russians, coordinating timelines, milestones, and specific operational objectives for the area the partners had agreed would be considered the final settled border between the Western Protectorate, controlled by China, and the Eastern Protectorate, controlled by Russia.

On the last day, Bolin began their meeting with a summary of the overall project timeline.

"After certain initial implementations commence, we will begin active military operations against certain U.S. ports on the west coast and their southern border with what we have termed our central and southern spearheads. The objective of the central spearhead will be to create both a land beachhead and a sea-based foothold around those beachheads. The main risks during this phase will be our ability to defeat the U.S. Navy at sea, safeguarding our landing forces, and to defeat their land forces. Unfortunately there are a number of U.S. Marine bases located near our intended beachheads. We consider these forces to be our main threat in the central area of operations.

"On the southern border, our southern spearhead will pass through Mexico easily and push from southern Arizona and drive for the center of the target.

"Once we have captured the focus of their attention and penetrated inland, calls for international assistance will go out, issued by U.S. politicians we have influenced. This call will be answered by your forces."

"We will be positioned and waiting," Sakharin replied, coldly assessing the monumental task in front of them—invading the United States.

"Once your forces begin their intervention down from the north through central Canada, there will come a cry for support against Russia, this time made by Canadian politicians who will also be under our influence. Other U.S. politicians will oppose this request for U.S. assistance against Russian incursions into Canadian territory, as they will seek to maintain the fiction that you will be simply coming to the aid of the United States. The main objective of this public request from Canadian politicians for support will be to cover the move of our northern spearhead along the southern border of Canada, driving toward the eventual 'turn-south' point near the North Dakota/Minnesota border."

"For this to work, your central and southern spearheads must achieve a certain degree of penetration," Sakharin pointed out. "Otherwise the threat will not be seen as sufficiently dire to necessitate a call for Russian support."

"We recognize this," Bolin said. "And while we will make every effort to ensure our operational units exert themselves to the greatest degree, keep in mind that none of these calls for assistance made by either American or Canadian politicians will be grounded in anything related to accurate or valid facts. The media today is sufficiently under our control such that we can manufacture any story we wish to promulgate and it will be accepted as fact by millions of Americans. No, these stories are simply to condition the American and Canadian proletariats and confuse the various military units that might be offering resistance. After calls from various governing officials are made, we intend to sever communication capabilities as broadly as possible, leaving units on the ground with the impression that their political leadership has called for Russians to come into the United States, or that the Canadian armed forces are moving armored units to the central part of their country to oppose a Russian interdiction from the north."

Bolin looked at Sakharin. "The northern spearhead, in a pincer movement with the southern spearhead, will form an anvil, and our central spearhead, driving from the west coast through the center of the country, will be the hammer, crushing what forces might remain. We anticipate the final line of our progress to be the western borders of Minnesota, Iowa, Missouri, Arkansas, and Louisiana."

"I believe there is a caveat relative to joint use of the port facilities in New Orleans," Sakharin mentioned.

"Very true, to support your southern operations. This is not disputed," Bolin replied. Sakharin nodded in agreement.

The four-day meeting closed with all objectives attained. As they broke up, Meifeng asked about the details of their planned meeting in Granite Sky to discuss the Grayson project, and Dr. Sakharin and his colleague explained the basics of the project, the personnel involved, and how they recommended introducing the two Chinese diplomats to the Americans in Granite Sky.

"You are two Chinese diplomats, correct?" Sakharin asked.

"As you say," Meifeng answered, noncommittally.

"Then let us introduce you as two Chinese diplomats—you are posing as husband and wife, correct?"

Meifeng nodded, and Sakharin went on. "You are a husband and wife team on vacation in the States and in Canada, and you have been asked by your government to detour and make a quick inspection of the Russian company's efforts integrating with the Grayson project. Your government is considering engaging Grayson and teaming with a Russian subcontractor to build a port facility in Africa, and your government is curious about Grayson's opinions regarding how well their Russian subcontractor is performing."

"Will there be any Grayson executives present in Granite Sky?" Bolin asked, joining the conversation.

"No, but you will be able to have a conference call with Grayson executives using the offices at Northern Minnesota Construction; and you can also use the time to speak to the leadership at this construction company and ask them about their experiences working with us."

Bolin looked at Meifeng and they nodded. "We think this would be acceptable. Do you think there will be any potential for suspicion on their part?"

Sakharin looked at Kong and smiled. "You should have no concerns in this, Comrade Major. The Americans are particularly naïve when it comes to thinking ill of others. They will take you and your 'wife' at face value.

Meifeng looked at the Russian engineer and asked, "Tell me, while in this American town, part of our mission is to observe and evaluate indigenous religious rituals. Have you gathered any information about these?"

"We have," Sakharin replied. "We made visits to their churches throughout our tour of the northeast and, while we have been here, we have been invited to what they term a 'Harvest Party'. Apparently it is a social gathering of Christians, scheduled on the same day as a pagan festival called 'Halloween'. From what we have been able to discover, the objective is to oppose this pagan ritual with one of their own."

Meifeng listened closely. "It sounds interesting. Is there some type of protocol or requirement to obtain an invitation?"

Kong's chuckle rumbled deeply but respectfully, and Sakharin again smiled. "No, Comrade Major, this is an event open to the public. There is no requirement for an invitation; simply appear."

Bolin and Meifeng knew enough about America to know that such things open to the public did not require any type of papers or documentation or permits, nor would there likely be checkpoints where documentation would be examined, with the natural exception of crossing the border into the country.

But entering the U.S. was a non-event. The U.S. border agent looked cursorily at their passports and then just waved them through, throwing a perfunctory 'Welcome to the United States' at the back of their car as they pulled beyond the window. While they had been told what to expect and had spent many months in America, nonetheless it still generated some degree of cognitive dissonance. How easily people moved around in this part of the world!

***

And so Bolin and Meifeng found themselves strolling like tourists through the booths and corrals and haystacks of the Harvest Party. Dozens of people milled around, and most, they saw, had their faces down, looking at or typing on their phones. Many younger visitors had earplugs in, with a cord leading to their phones.

Meifeng leaned in toward Bolin as they walked and in precise Mandarin asked quietly, "We were told this was a religious gathering, were we not?" Bolin nodded. "Then I am confused. We have been to how many booths so far?"

"Five," Bolin answered, looking around at the crowd with an eye out for potential secret police.

"In not one of these places have we been engaged in any discussion about spiritual matters," she replied.

"Perhaps the custom here is that visitors to the booths should initiate such conversations," Bolin observed.

She considered this. "It is possible; yes. I realize we are not in China but that would be the expected protocol there."

"Most definitely," Bolin replied. "It is a dangerous thing to begin a discussion of spiritual things in China unless it is in a State-approved church facility. Perhaps these people are somewhat afraid as well."

"I cannot see why. The church is not underground here. I was told that the free exercise of religion was something permitted."

"Well, try bringing up the subject at the next booth."

"I shall do that very thing," she replied.

The next booth offered some type of shooting contest. She nudged Bolin, who took her meaning and stepped up to volunteer to try shooting tin metal outlines of ducks placed on shelves against the back wall of the booth. Meanwhile, Meifeng stepped up to the board and approached one of the young men manning the booth.

"Excuse me, is this a Christian activity?"

The young man removed one of the earplugs in his ear. "What?"

"Is this a Christian activity?" She felt odd asking such a blatantly obtuse question.

The young man looked strangely at her. "You mean, like, is shooting ducks Christian?"

Meifeng did not immediately follow what he was referring to, but then she realized he had misunderstood her. "No, I am sorry, I meant, here, this place, this event tonight, is it a Christian function?"

Another participant dressed in a macabre costume of a man with a ski mask, carrying a chainsaw, his clothes spattered red with what was obviously supposed to be blood, came alongside Bolin while he was aiming at the ducks, set down the chainsaw, and picked up a water pistol.

The young man operating the booth answered Meifeng. "Well, uh, like, yeah, I guess."

"So people talk about things of religion here?"

The young man scowled. "Nah, not here, that's over there somewhere, the booth with the pastors in it." He waved his hand in a direction toward the middle of the large field and reinserted his earplug.

"Thank you," Meifeng said, thinking that she had never met a more indecorous, disrespectful young person. She was mildly appalled. She tugged at Bolin, who immediately put his water pistol down on the counter and followed her away from the booth.

"Apparently there is—"

She was suddenly interrupted by a raucously loud, grating noise coming from somewhere behind them. They turned to see four young adults standing on a makeshift stage, three with guitars that were obviously electric. They could hear the screeching noise made by their amplifiers, and one sat before a set of drums. This ensemble began to play a loud tune with a strong bass and a rhythmic beat. Then the lead guitarist began to sing about a lost love, or something Meifeng could barely make out. She only knew it had something to do with romanticism and teen love—or so she thought.

She leaned over, pulled Bolin to her and had to almost yell in very formal Mandarin to be heard over the blaring noise. "Those idiot Russians were duped. This isn't any kind of religious ritual."

Bolin, intentionally not shaking her hand from his arm, put his mouth close to her ear and said, "Let us move away from this noise." They walked slowly away from the stage and the blaring music until they could hear each other again.

"Slowly, slowly, Meifeng," Bolin countered, replying as well in the same type of formal Mandarin. "Maybe their rituals are not what you would expect."

His response, cautious and open-minded as it was, surprised her. "You think like a social scientist," she said.

"I am just a lowly, itinerant Weiqi player, abandoned in a strange country, with nothing but my wits and my board to make my fortune." He bowed slightly to her.

She smiled at his attempt at humor. "Very well, itinerant Weiqi master, let us see if we cannot uncover what religious schemes may be on this board."

"Of course, O wisest of Social Scientists," he said, with a mock bow. "Lead on."

***

They found their way to another booth, this one offering hot dogs.

"I am hungry, Weiqi master. Would you perhaps consider exchanging an American dollar for one of those things encased in what looks like bread?"

"My pleasure," Bolin replied. He fished an American dollar bill from his pocket and handed it to the vendor, who handed him a six-inch roll with what looked like some sort of processed meat within. He in turn handed it to Meifeng. He pulled her away from the booth and said, "You realize that this is an example of processed American food, do you not?"

"One will not kill me, I think." She went back to the booth, took a stick and slathered a yellow substance over the processed meat object, and picked up a handful of napkins. She turned to the vendor.

"Tell me, is this a Christian activity?"

"You can eat a hot dog whether you're a Christian or not," came the reply, this time from an older man with an enormously distended stomach. She made a mental note to stop framing her initial request as she just had, and also noted that their preliminary research indicating that many Americans were obese was accurate. Even the children she saw at this event were disgustingly overweight, and many were obese. It was no surprise that many of them were wandering around the field with large cups of soda or candy bars in their hands.

"I am sorry, no, what I meant was, does this ... this *party* ... have anything to do with religion?"

The obese vendor laughed then. "Hell if I know. I'm just here to sell hot dogs, lady, okay?"

"Many thanks," she replied, and moved away.

"Gross man," she said in Xiang.

"He probably consumes too much of his product," Bolin answered, also in that dialect.

"This cannot be a religious ritual," she said.

"Didn't that younger person, at the shooting booth, indicate that there was someone of a religious inclination toward the center of the field?" Bolin reminded her.

"Yes, of course, let us move that way."

They stopped at three more booths, and at each, the attendants either could not answer her question about the event being a religious ritual, or did not choose to. At one booth, they came across a young woman who was scantily, almost scandalously clad in an extremely short skirt, a sweater that appeared to consist mostly of paint, and a jacket with a blatantly suggestive, lurid message written in English across the back.

"Excuse me, miss," Meifeng asked, "but does this event have something to do with religion? We are not from around here."

The young woman was chewing gum and did not remove it when she addressed them. "Well duh, I guess not. Where you guys from, seriously?"

"We are from China," Meifeng answered.

"Cool. Yeah, this is, like, the Harvest Party, so I guess you could call it religious or something. It's, like, you know, Christian Halloween. I mean, seriously, why do all the non-Christians get to have a good time and we don't?"

"So this *is* a religious event?"

"Well, I don't know if you want to call it a 'religious event'—whoa, heavy—but I know it's put on by a bunch of the churches in town."

"How do you know this?" Meifeng asked.

"Hey, like, I sing in the choir at our church and I play guitar on our worship team, so I should know, right? Hey, do you guys have worship teams in China? At your churches, I mean?"

"I am sorry," Bolin asked, interrupting, "but I am curious. Your attire—"

"You calling me fat?" she asked, appearing to be offended, still smacking her gum.

"I am sorry ... your clothes ... they leave very little to the imagination. Is it part of your religious practice in this country to display one's sexual attributes so ... ah, so openly?"

They could see that this line of questioning caused immediate and indignant offense. "What's wrong with the way I dress?" she shouted. "Are you judging me? Who the hell are you to judge how I dress? We're not supposed to judge, haven't you heard?" She turned her back on them and walked out of the booth. They heard her talking to herself as she left. "Damn! I *told* my mother I didn't want to do this."

"Perhaps she was in costume as a prostitute," Bolin mused in the Xian dialect. They were still standing there with a shocked look on their face when another young woman approached with what looked like a stack of papers in her hand. This young woman was dressed in a pair of very short shorts over fishnet stockings. The shorts were half red, half blue. She had a blond ponytail wig with one ponytail dyed red, the other blue. She had a tight-fitting leather jacket on, again with one red sleeve and one blue sleeve. Her form-fitting shirt, again leaving very little to the imagination, had spangled, sparkly silver lettering across the front that indicated that the young lady was, apparently, '*Daddy's lil' Monster*.'

"Are you guys visiting?" she asked in a pleasant, bouncy tone.

Bolin was still gazing in amazement after the departing prostitute, wondering what he had said that was so offensive. Also distracted, Meifeng said to the bouncy woman, "Why, yes, yes we are. Do you know," she said, turning her attention to this new apparition in front of her, "you will probably think this is funny, but we were told that this party was some sort of religious festival. I think we have visited into the wrong place."

"Oh no, you're right, this is the annual Harvest Party." She smiled and shifted from weight, thrusting one hip to the side. Meifeng saw that she was wearing what must have been eight-inch platform heels.

"So ... so this *is* a religious event?"

"Sure is. And here," she said brightly, leaning forward from the waist, jabbing a brochure into Meifeng's hands, and then, as Bolin turned to take her in, pushed a brochure into his hands as well. "Take this. Jesus loves you! Bye!" And the perky young woman trounced off, apparently to find other hapless visitors and advise them of this person Jesus who, presumably, also loved them.

Bolin looked down at the brochure. On the cover it had a picture of a tall, definitely European white man, with long flowing brown hair, a soft golden brown beard and kind eyes, with some sort of glowing circlet around his head, standing in front of what looked to be a large, thick wooden door with vertical slats. He appeared to be in the process of knocking on the door, at pains in the hope that someone would open it. The title of the brochure was 'The Four Spiritual Laws'.

He looked at Meifeng. "This does not appear to be a likeness of Buddha."

"Not funny, *husband*."

Bolin smiled. "Well, here is the religious discussion you were looking for. Do we know this person Jesus, who apparently loves us? Was he in one of the booths we have already visited?"

Meifeng looked at the pamphlet and dared not reveal the depth of her disappointment. She had so hoped for an opportunity to learn more about American religion. It had such an amazing history for a social scientist, it had been so powerful, with the hint even of something supernatural behind it, something not of this world, something capable of driving men to be burned or beheaded or drowned or used as candles, all without recanting their faith ... something she in her heart of hearts was hoping to learn more about. In all her years as a social scientist she had never encountered any other social force that contained even a fraction of such motivational power. And here she stood, with loud, dissonant music washing over her, with some small pamphlet in her hand. She could not reconcile what she had read of Christianity's history with what she was seeing.

Bolin, not aware of the source generating the emotional earthquake occurring in his colleague but noting her disquiet, simply took her by the elbow and began to maneuver her toward their car. On the way he saw a booth with a sign over it that proclaimed it to be a 'Life Booth'. Taking a chance, he steered Meifeng in that direction.

There was a tall, heavy-set middle-aged woman standing with another man, slightly shorter than she was, with a thick mop of brown hair, a sizeable paunch, and pleasant eyes.

"Tell me," he said, addressing them both, "is this a religious event?"

The woman looked at the shorter man, who said, "It is, yeah. I'm Tony Ponti, the pastor at Living Waters church here in town, and this is Eva Gunderson. Welcome." He stuck out his hand, and Bolin, having learned of this custom in the early days of his visit, barely stopped himself from bowing and instead grasped the man's hand. "Are you two visiting?"

Bolin had heard this word 'visiting' several times that evening and began to wonder if it had a hidden cultural meaning.

"I ... uh, yes, I suppose you could say we are visiting. Tell me, though," Bolin asked, true to his scientific, almost Asperger-like opacity regarding human emotional intelligence or intuition, "this word 'visiting'; what does it mean?"

He saw the taller woman smile slightly and the man said, "Well, it's just a thing we ask to see if someone isn't from around here."

"I see," Bolin replied. "Have you seen me in this town before?"

"Actually no, I haven't," Ponti answered. "Have you, Eva?"

"Not at all," the women said. "Welcome."

"I ask because in our walk through this tent space, we have been accosted numerous times by people asking us if we are visitors."

"Well, it's just a way we have of being friendly," the man explained.

Bolin nodded. "Ah, yes, a pro forma question. I see, thank you." He tilted his head slightly in acknowledgement of the man's effort to be friendly, though such efforts might exceed the bounds of sincerity. Americans were so blatantly blunt in a naïve, incautious, sometimes impolite way.

Meifeng approached the booth from behind Bolin. "We were handed these papers," she began, holding up the brochure that Daddy's lil' Monster had given them. "We were wondering what they contain."

Bolin could see the man's eyes widen with what he perceived to be increased interest. "Eva, could take this young lady over to the table there and maybe go over it with her while I talk to her husband here." Bolin and Meifeng both noticed this immediate move to separate them, reminiscent of the standard methods Communists used when attempting to indoctrinate groups, and they wondered at it, but complied.

"Certainly, Tony." The tall blond woman turned to Meifeng. "Come on in, dear," she said, opening the little tilting door in the counter through which people entered the booth, and the two women sat down at a little round table.

"Now," Eva began, "let me ask you straight out: are you right with God?"

"Right?"

"Yes, what I mean is, have you accepted Jesus in your heart as your Savior?"

"I have not heard about this ... this person you speak of, and no, there has been nothing about a 'heart', or whatever it was you said. No, wait, actually yes, I *have* heard of this person though. A woman, the woman who gave me this paper, actually, she mentioned this person. He is your God, is he not?"

"He's *everybody's* God, sweetie." The woman put her hand out and patted Meifeng on the forearm, which made her somewhat uncomfortable, not knowing what the appropriate social conventions were. "He's the only God around, and what you have here," she said, tapping the brochure Meifeng had set on the table, "is a little story that tells you how you can get to heaven."

"It is that easy?" Meifeng asked, wondering to herself why so many people had died over religion.

"Easy as pie, dear. Now let me tell you a little about our church and maybe you can consider coming and visiting with your husband. And oh, is your husband saved?"

Meifeng, peerless social scientist that she was, had in no way been prepared to encounter such a brutally personal interview. "I ... I do not think so," she stammered, wondering frantically to herself, 'saved from what?'. "Is that ... is that appropriate?"

"To be saved? Why, you can't get to heaven without being saved, dear, but once you're saved, well, you're safe and secure and you'll be fine."

"And how should I get ... how did you say ... get 'right' with this ... with your God?"

"Why, we can say a little prayer right now that'll guarantee you'll be accepted by God. And then you just come to church, dear, and the pastor there, he'll make everything else as clear as crystal."

Meifeng ignored the part about the prayer, because she could not comprehend any relationship with an infinite supernatural entity so shallow as to be entered into with a simple, cursory mouthing of stock phrases. So she changed the subject. "Church? Is this also another religious event?"

The woman laughed slightly, her face opening up, giving her the appearance of a pleasant, younger woman. "Well, I suppose you could call it that."

Meifeng sensed that the woman was finishing her conversation, but she hadn't learned a thing.

"Tell me," she asked, "why do you worship this ... this Jesus person you speak of? And how do you worship him? What exactly do you do?"

"Oh my, you're full of questions, aren't you? Well, everyone knows Jesus, dear. He's the Son of God; says so in the Bible. Do you have a Bible?"

Meifeng shook her head, not wanting to tell this tall blond apparition that possession of a Bible in China was punishable by years of imprisonment at hard labor.

"Well, we'll have to get you one, you wait right here." She stood up and rummaged through a small cardboard box in the back of the booth for a moment and came back with a small paperback book. "Here's the New Testament and the Book of Psalms. You don't need to bother with the Old Testament, it's just a bunch of stories. You take this and read it, and you'll learn all about who Jesus is."

"Thank you ... Eva. But can you tell me, how do you worship this person?"

"Why, we go to church, dear. We've got just the most wonderful church family you can imagine, and there are all sorts of activities God has us do, like, well, this one right here, as you can see." She swept her arm around to take in the booths on the large field. "And we have ladies' Bible studies, some of the men meet to pray in the middle of the week, and whenever someone in the church needs something, we help them out."

Meifeng was carefully digesting this, and wanted to make sure she understood. "So ... so in effect you are a very closely bonded social group?"

Eva had to chew on that for just a moment, but then answered, "Well, I guess you could call us that, sure. We take care of each other, pray for each other, and we try real hard to get along with each other."

"What ... what bonds you?" Meifeng asked, trying to get the answer to what had motivated so many Christians in the past to choose death instead of recanting their faith.

Eva spent more time thinking about that. "I suppose it's each other," she said, finally. "We care for each other, mostly. We think of ourselves as sort of family."

Meifeng nodded, listening closely. She wasn't hearing anything that was in any way related to this God Eva had described, or any information about a relationship with a supernatural, spiritual being. It appeared to her to be simply another type of social club or group.

Eva stood. "Now I've got to go, dear. My youngest daughter, she's got a game tonight—she's the captain of the girl's basketball team, and my oldest is up from Minneapolis visiting. She's got, like, the world's dream job, don't ya know—and on top of all that, the church is having a bake sale at the gym to raise money for the team's trip to the State Championship, if they're lucky enough to get through the semi-finals."

Meifeng smiled, bowed slightly out of habit, and thanked the woman for the Bible. Eva pulled her purse from under another chair and shook her hand. "I'll be praying for you, dear."

"Tony, gotta go," she said to the other man. "Allie's game starts in fifteen minutes and I've got the bake sale table."

Tony turned from his discussion with Bolin. "Sure, hey, thanks, Eva. God bless."

"God bless," Eva said over her shoulder as she pushed up the tilting counter door and moved off toward the high school, which Meifeng could see in the distance.

***

Meifeng and Bolin walked away from the Life Booth, each with their little paperback New Testament, more flyers, and what the pastor called a 'bulletin', which was just another brochure that described his church's location, their phone number, the various church activities, the schedule for these activities, and a large picture of the building which was, apparently, where the church family met.

They saw the security escort pick them up after leaving the Life Booth, still keeping their distance.

"So what did the woman have to say?" Bolin asked.

"I think she believes that since English is not my native language, my level of intelligence was low."

"Why would you say that?"

"Because her answers to my questions were puerile, like those one would give a child. They made no sense." She looked over at him to gage his reaction to what was obviously disappointment on her part. "And what about you? What did you learn from the pastor?"

Bolin thought about her question for a few steps. The raucous noise was still blaring from the band. The crowds, however, were thinning out, and they could tell the evening was drawing to its end. "He basically read the brochure back to me, as though I could not read English. He provided additional discourse to amplify each of the points. He began," and Bolin lifted one hand and began to tick off his fingers the points Ponti had spoken on, "by saying first that God loved me—you too, apparently, men *and* women, their God is in no way misogynistic—and that this God has created all persons to have a relationship with him."

Meifeng pasted a look of faint disdain and disbelief on her face as Bolin rehashed the foreigner's doctrine. "Typically American, so inclusive."

"So it appears. Then," Bolin continued, "he alleged that men—and yes, women too—were sinful creatures. Apparently our nature is flawed, and therefore we cannot have any type of relationship with this God."

"You mean, the perfect, all-knowing, supreme, perfect God who they allege created us to have a relationship with him, created human beings in such a way that they could *not* have this relationship??"

"My question exactly, it makes no sense, but I could not get in a word. It was like trying to interrupt a Shanghai noodle seller on the street."

"*Aiyee*," Meifeng exclaimed, almost laughing out loud.

"But wait, it continues," Bolin added. He held up his hand, pointing at his third finger. "Apparently there is some sort of provision or loophole this God has arranged. This person Jesus, the pastor says, is the only means whereby men or women may enter heaven."

"How does one enter this heaven through a person? Does he function as some sort of door or gate?"

"Again, my question precisely—tell me, have you ever played Weiqi? But again, there was no chance to get in a word with the noodle seller. The last point he made," Bolin said, pointing to his fourth finger, "was that all men must 'accept Jesus as their personal Lord and Savior,' and then one may enter heaven."

"Forgive me, Weiqi master, but I have another question."

"I can guess your question, esteemed Social Scientist. You will ask, 'what exactly does 'accept' mean, and how does one accept this Jesus, and what is the difference between a Lord and Savior and a personal Lord and Savior, correct?"

"You are correct. Did you get to ask these questions?"

"I did not. He asked if I had a Bible. I told him that I did not, and he handed me this and told me to read the Gospel of John."

"Is that—?"

"It is apparently a chapter in this book," Bolin answered, holding up the Bible.

"Tell me, did he ask *you* any questions?"

"Oh, yes, he asked me where I was from and if you were my wife, and what I thought of America, and where I had traveled. Truthfully, the entire experience seemed ... I would say... *formulaic.* It was as though he was reading from a printed agenda," and here Bolin held up the flyer they had been given by Daddy's lil' Monster, "and was simply proceeding along the points listed."

"Did he ask you if you were saved?"

"You know, he did ask me that. I had no idea what he was talking about. Saved from what?"

"She asked me the same thing; I had no understanding of this either."

They walked a little further and then he asked, "Tell me, what does the esteemed Social Scientist make of this segment of our religious research?"

Meifeng answered him honestly. "My analysis tells me that something is not quite aligned."

"What do you mean?"

"Consider," she replied, "from a social science perspective, and considering what the *foreign devils*"—she used the particularly derogatory Mandarin term for anyone not Chinese—"have written in their social history records, it appears that religion has been a force for social change since its adoption in this country."

"I am not sure these records are accurate."

"Most definitely," she hastened to agree, "yet this deception—it must have been a *powerful* deception, because many have willingly gone to their deaths for this thing they call faith."

"Muslims do it every day, and with pleasure take as many people along with them as they can." Bolin said quietly.

"I understand, yes, this is true. Yet there is something that does not sit exactly right with me here."

They walked for a few more meters together. "They told me that you are an astute observer of patterns," he said. "Therefore, it must be either that you have seen here something which does not fit a pattern, something that did not match what you expected to see, or that you have seen something which *does* fit a pattern you've seen before, but cannot immediately recall."

Meifeng narrowed her eyes in confusion. "That ... that *could* be it, but I am not exactly sure. But I get a sense it is more like, like someone has tried to represent something to us, something which they themselves either do not believe and are either intentionally maintaining as a fiction ... or are fooling themselves."

"True; there is nothing so powerful as self-deceit," Bolin admitted. "What brings you to such a suspicion?"

"You yourself said the man reminded you of a Shanghai noodle seller, yes?"

"More than anything I can think of."

"Well, in your experience, does your Shanghai noodle seller truly believe his noodles are the best, or is he just a very persistent salesman?"

"You have a point," Bolin replied. "Every noodle seller I ever knew was just a salesman."

"But at least the noodle seller knows what he is selling. These people, it is as if they feel it almost a social or cultural requirement to talk about these things, to go to this church they go to, or even their conversation—did you hear how they each would say, 'God bless' to each other, as though the words were some sort of code, or some kind of magic talisman?"

"I noted it, yes."

"And then we come to the most important things," she continued. "I am not informed about the details of their doctrines or beliefs, but I know from my readings and research that there is a certain type of moral behavior required of those who allege to be part of this cult, yet we did not see anything like that here this evening."

"No, actually, we saw the opposite." Bolin nodded and was quiet for a moment, and then queried her. "What does this tell you, esteemed Social Scientist?"

She rolled over in her mind what had happened that night, trying to piece together the segments of the pattern she'd seen, trying to match it with what she had either seen or read about elsewhere, and suddenly it hit her. She snapped her fingers. "I will tell you, Weiqi master." She stopped, having solved the problem, and turned to face him with dark, flashing eyes. "My analysis is that *they do not believe what they proclaim*," she said. "I have seen this before, oh yes. It's clear. I should have immediately recognized it. They are under some sort of compulsion to carry on as though they believe what is in this doctrine," she held out the Bible as her object, lifting it with two fingers as though it were something foul, "but they do not. For them it is simply a way of life, like something they do according to specific cultural mandates. They have all the marks of ones who do not believe what they say they believe."

Bolin looked at her, noting her certainty. "Impressive," he said. "And what does this mean for our ... for our plans?"

"It is a very positive analysis," she replied quickly. "It means we are dealing with a people that have no backbone, no character, a people who can be cowed and manipulated by fear or untruth or any other tool we may bring to bear. When one spends one's time affirming lies, one cannot stand for any kind of truth."

Bolin nodded, seemingly pleased. "Have you ever read Dostoevsky?" he asked. She looked at him blankly, and Bolin continued. "He was a Russian author who once said, wait, let me see if I can remember it. Ah, yes," he went on, in Mandarin, "'the man who lies to himself and listens to his own lie comes to a point that he cannot distinguish the truth within him, or around him, and so loses all respect for himself and for others. And having no respect he ceases to love.' Yes, I think that was it."

"Well, it is clear they have no respect, either for themselves or others. Did you see how so many of the young women are dressed? And how the young people addressed their elders? Shameful!"

"This is good news, esteemed Social Scientist. Perhaps we should celebrate with a beer?"

She glanced at him briefly. He was smiling. "I think that is a good idea," she said.

"Come, esteemed Social Scientist, escort the humble, itinerant Weiqi master to his libation." He held out his arm, and she took it.

It was not until she was almost asleep that night that she realized that she had not offered Bolin an explanation of *how* she knew these people did not believe what they said they believed. She did not tell him how she had identified the behavioral patterns of that mode of behavior. In truth, she had seen the behavior almost every day of her life, watching everyone around her in Communist China act in a way that was strikingly similar to how she had seen these supposed Christians act today. Both groups had a doctrine that they alleged to be that which ordered and directed their lives, a doctrine and a set of teachings that they said publicly they worshipped and revered—but which, by the actual testimony of their lives, made clear that they did not in fact believe. Both groups walked through life living a lie. But she couldn't tell Bolin that—and then she had a two-edged thought that struck her with both hope and fear: *he hadn't even asked how she'd recognized that pattern of behavior.* Either he himself recognized it, or he suspected what she thought of the Communist Party and was considering reporting her.

She slept poorly that evening.

Chapter 39

Sasha & Kong

"But to each one is given the manifestation of the Spirit for the common good. For to one is given the word of wisdom through the Spirit, and to another the word of knowledge according to the same Spirit…"

1 Corinthians 12:7-8

"We will leave the day after tomorrow," Sasha said as they walked across the field toward their truck, leaving the Harvest Party. "We have accomplished what we needed to accomplish here. There are other preparations in other places that need to be made."

Kong looked over at Sasha. "Will we ... will we be seeing each other again?"

Sasha knew what he was asking. "No one tells me anything, you realize, but from what I am able to gather, I suspect yes, we will be seeing a lot of each other." In other words, Sasha expected them to be deployed again soon.

They walked in silence until they got to their truck and Kong drove them out of the high school parking lot.

"Do you think this Riesling is of the same ilk as that snake oil salesman in the Life Booth?" Kong asked in Russian. "It will make working with him truly distasteful."

Sasha looked out the window into the darkness. "I cannot say. It's depressing, though. These Christians ... their fake smiles, their fake happiness—everything about them is fake; it lacks integrity, as if ... as if—"

"As if there is no truth in them," Kong said, finishing Sasha's thought.

"Yes, exactly, but it is worse. They say they represent 'truth', and yet they are not truthful. Can't they see they are fooling themselves, compromising just to get more asses plunked into pews and more coins in their coffers, to get just one more spiritual scalp on their belts? But to answer your question, I have no idea if this Riesling knows anything about such a sales approach. If this is his way, you're right, it will be awkward, working with him. I detest such men. Has he tried anything like that with you?" Sasha asked, turning to face Kong.

"No actually, and now that I remember, it was not Riesling's idea to invite us to this, this elaborate religious sales trap. It was actually the Israeli woman's idea."

"She's Jewish, what does she know of it?"

"Exactly—if she's Jewish, she probably has no idea that the entire event was just a web of trickery and deceit."

"Yeah, but she knows about these people. Seriously, no wonder the Jews mope around all their lives. They turn one way and the Muslims want to kill them, and then they turn the other way and they have these people who constantly try and shove some obviously poisonous claptrap down their throats, claptrap that even they themselves do not believe, all the time with fake smiles on their faces. Religion—what a wretched hive of scum and villainy."

"Well said, Obi-Wan," Kong joked under his breath. "Consider the Jews," Kong began, assuming a portentous tone, "stuck between a rock and a hard place; either death by the sword, or death by excrement. I don't know what is worse." Sasha looked at him and after two seconds they both burst out laughing.

But as Kong drove back toward the Lodge, Sasha found himself wondering, staring out again into the darkness. Why was he so affected? Why had he exploded in frustration at the religious snake oil salesman? Why should he care what one demented American was selling to another?

Kong's thoughts ran along similar veins. Why had he reacted so vehemently to those men in that tent, ludicrously labeled the 'Life Booth'? What had pushed him over the edge like that? He had stood in other places, in other dark holes in the world while men did unspeakable things to other men—sometimes he was the one doing those things—and such things had in no way affected his composure. But yesterday he'd gotten angry. He could not remember the last time he had gotten angry. Something was very, very strange about that encounter. He thought of asking Major Sokolov, but at the moment the major seemed to be keeping his own counsel. And now that Kong thought about it, the good major himself had seemed to be a little tweaked when he'd spoken with that charlatan. Strange ... very strange.

***

The next day, their last in Granite Sky before driving down to Minneapolis and flying back to Russia, Sasha and Kong had a meeting with Riesling at his office in the morning. When they got there, they saw an older man at the conference table in conversation with Riesling. Daria welcomed them in Russian, poured them each a coffee, and, making conversation, asked them if they enjoyed the Harvest Party.

Sasha looked at her. "*We found it ... interesting. Tell me, little sister, how did you find it?*" he asked in Russian.

Daria laughed. "*Oh, older brother, you would not catch me within a hundred kilometers of that place.*"

"*Why is that?*" Kong asked.

"*Maybe I shouldn't say.*"

"*So who will know? Does your boss speak Russian?*" Kong pressed.

"*No, but, well ... okay, I'll tell you. The religious community in this town puts it on. They think because they call it a 'Harvest Party', they're giving people an alternative to Halloween, which apparently is some kind of evil holiday in this country. But I cannot stand their hypocrisy, if you want to know the truth. They say it is not a Halloween party yet there are all the evil costumes—honestly, what are parents in this country thinking, letting their children dress up like that? They smile and offer games and rides and candy to the kids just so that can maybe catch one or two with their tracts and their doctrines and talk of Messiah. I am not buying it.*" By then Daria was fully incensed; her eyes were flashing.

Sasha sat and carefully controlled his countenance. "*No problems, little sister, we understand. Tell me, does your boss go to this party?*"

"*Potato-head?*" she said, eyes rolling toward the conference room where Josh was still talking with the old man. Sasha knew enough about women to see she was at the moment irritated with potato-head. "*No way. He hates it more than I do, and now that I think of it, that confuses me.*" She looked down into her coffee cup. "*He wouldn't have mentioned it to you except that I suggested it to him. I thought, well ... I just thought you might want to see what community life was like here in town.*"

"*Sure, we understand, no problems, little sister, we thank you for the thought.*"

"*So what did you think of it?*"

Kong looked at Sasha, who answered for them. "*Interesting,*" he said. "*From what little we know about this country, it was a very typical picture of small town community life in America."*

"Yeah ... depressing, isn't it," she replied. They laughed, but she wasn't trying to be funny.

***

Riesling came out of the conference room with the old man in tow. "Gentlemen, sorry for keeping you waiting, I was just visiting with Mr. Ironbridge here. Tack, please meet Doctor Sasha Sakharin; this is his colleague, Doctor Karin Olyutsk. Gentlemen, Mr. Tack Ironbridge."

Daria looked at Josh. "You, sir, have been practicing your pronunciation."

Josh waved her compliment off.

Sasha saw the old man was wearing an old brown farm coat and carrying a Bible—apparently he and Riesling had been talking about something to do with the Bible in the conference room. Religion was everywhere in this country—it was appalling. It galled him enough to take a poke at the old man.

"Nice to meet you, sir," Sasha said, as respectfully as he could. The old man shook their hands and nodded.

"Daria was kind enough to suggest we attend the Harvest Party last night," Sasha said to Ironbridge. "We were wondering, were you there? I ask because, well, I see that you have a Bible." He nodded toward the Bible in Tack's hands.

The old man looked down at the Bible and then back up at Sasha and Sasha felt an almost physical blow in his chest. The old man, Ironbridge they had called him, then turned to Riesling.

"Friends of yours?"

"Uh, yes sir, we're going to do some business together I think," Riesling replied.

"Not that it makes any difference," the old man muttered in a low voice, but Sasha heard him. The old man turned again and looked Sasha in the eye. "So, Doctor Sakharin, was it? No, I wasn't at that party. I wouldn't go within a hundred leagues of that place." The old man said this with such vehemence that Sasha was taken aback.

"Nice to meet you gentlemen," Ironbridge said, and stepped toward the door.

"Excuse me, sir," Sasha said, and moved to follow him, "but my colleague and I are here to conduct surveys to consider future construction in this area, and one of the things we are tasked to investigate is the stability of the local community. We went to this party last night. We were told that the local Christian community put it on. We see you have a Bible; you are a Christian, yes?"

"That's right," Ironbridge answered. Kong was getting the impression that Ironbridge was a tough old bird.

"So we are, I guess you would say, somewhat confused. You would not go near such an event and yet—"

"You're wondering why this Christian wouldn't go near the Christian party, right?"

Sasha nodded. "To put it bluntly, yes. Is there some sort of division or schism here that we don't know about?" Sasha looked from Ironbridge to Riesling, as if to express some type of official curiosity. If Kong didn't know better, he would have thought the question originated out of a concern for the best interests of the construction project. Sokolov had framed it that well.

"Not to be unkind, Doctor, but how much do you really want to know about Christianity?"

"I confess I'm intrigued about this. Let me be honest," Sasha replied sincerely, holding up a hand, and Kong was impressed at Sasha's ability to dissemble. "I just spoke with Miss Avidora here, who expressed, shall we say, *concern* about such a party." Sasha turned to Riesling.

"Mr. Riesling, may we ask, were you there? What were your thoughts?"

"No, I wouldn't go to a party like that either, Doctor."

"Why not?"

They saw Riesling look at the old man. "Do you want to tell them or should I?" he asked.

The old man sighed. "If you're really interested, Doctor, let's have a seat. It's not a short answer. And remember, you asked the question."

Kong could not understand where Sasha was going with his apparent interest in a foolish party the handwringers had put on, but he played along and followed everyone into the conference room.

"I'll get to the point," Ironbridge began. "In America, most of Christianity is dead."

"How can a religion be ... what word did you use ... *dead*, Mr. Ironbridge?" Sasha asked.

"Let's clarify terms, Doctor. I said 'Christianity', not 'religion'. I'm not talking about *religion*. A religion is just a set of rules that outline an approved set of behaviors; religion is a collection of doctrines that men have put together to define how they believe man should approach God, okay? The doctrines drive the rules. For example, if one religion has a doctrine that says men should never trim their beards, then one of the rules that define those who wish to adhere to that religion would be that men never trim their beards; follow?"

"So you are saying that religion is just a grouping of rules driven by a selected set of doctrines."

"Yeah, that's about right, but the key thing there is that the rules and doctrines are selected by men."

"Then what is the difference between a Muslim and a Jew or, for that matter, a Christian?" Sasha asked. Kong began to sense that something more than just establishing their cover was happening with Sasha, but did not want to interfere.

"Christianity—*true* Christianity—is about relationship with the Living God. It was never built on a set of rules," Ironbridge replied. "*Men* have made it into a religion, but the Founder never intended it to be so. When Jesus came, He came to the Jews first, because God has made a special arrangement with that people. But they were stubborn and wouldn't listen to the prophets He sent, so He sent His Son. But they didn't listen to Him either, because God's Son had an issue with the Jewish religious leadership. You see, religion—no matter what kind—is always opposed to the true God. The Jewish religious leadership, like every other religious leadership in the world, by the way, were convincing men that a relationship with God consisted of rules that they—those religious leaders—would make. Nothing makes God angrier. His Son came and told this group of religious leaders exactly what they were doing and how angry it made God, and they killed Him for it. Again, true Christianity is a *relationship* with God; Islam and rabbinic Judaism are religions or religious *systems*.

"But the problem is, most Christians won't pay the price to have that relationship, Doctor. They would rather just make up certain rules of their own which they can keep, which will then make them feel as though they're making God happy and God is happy with them. When this happens, there is no power in their life. They have no power to live the truth ... to live true, honest, Godly lives of integrity. Such an absence of power is what we mean when we say someone's Christianity is dead."

Kong saw that Daria was paying close attention to Ironbridge's words, while Josh stood behind her, leaning against the conference room wall.

Sasha spoke again, this time with a sense of gravity that made Kong nervous. "You speak of truth. I saw no truth yesterday at that party."

"Of course not. The people sponsoring that party have all decided to make their own rules; they worship a god of their own making. They've chosen to define God in their way, not in the way He has revealed Himself. We call that idolatry, Doctor—idolatry, someone once said, is the power of a culture to get the people of that culture to conform to a particular lifestyle. Yesterday, you saw a particular lifestyle not in conformance with the true God. Those people have let today's culture shape the kind of god they worship, and so you came away with this horrible taste in your mouth, the bitter taste of insincerity, of falsity, of having had something to do with tricksters."

"Hucksters," Kong interjected, unintentionally. Both Sasha and Ironbridge looked at him in surprise.

"Yeah, I'll go along with that—probably the best word so far, Doctor Olyutsk."

"Sorry to interrupt," Kong said, holding up a hand, surprised that he had let himself be drawn into the discussion.

Ironbridge turned back to Sasha. "So this is why you felt that way. People like this are followers of a religion; they're religious people, but they have no *power*. They're compromisers—they have no power to stand against what they know to be evil because they refuse to stand for truth. They're just like every other religious person—they live by their own set of rules, not God's. They probably reminded you of a salesman. They'll use all kinds of tricks to try and get their 'product' in front of a 'customer'. They've made their own god, and so the power of the real God isn't there. And since they allege that they have 'the truth', and you obviously see that they don't, when they try to convince you to accept their insincere belief system, it generates in you an intense distaste and distrust."

Sasha sat back, alert, somewhat amazed, and not a little bothered. This old man had identified exactly what had bothered him.

"Is that how you felt, Doctor?" Ironbridge was asking him.

Sasha couldn't help his answer. "That is exactly what I felt."

"So then ... you have to ask yourself, Doctor, *why* you felt that way."

Sasha had to know, and he sensed this old man knew. "I have no idea, but I think you'll tell me."

"Sure I'll tell you, Doctor. Easy answer. First, let me tell you a short story. Once upon a time in the West, we had people who went all around the frontier, selling miracle cures in little bottles. It's where we get the term 'snake oil salesman'. People would buy their stuff because these snake oil salesmen promised them it would cure just about anything. But of course it didn't, and when it didn't, people got angry. Not a few of those snake oil salesmen found themselves dancing at the end of a rope. And why were those people angry? For the same reason you're angry ... *because of the hope, the desire, for the real thing*. They knew they needed something. They were looking for truth, Doctor, and they were sold a bill of goods. You were looking for truth yesterday, whether you want to admit it or not, and when you recognized you were being sold snake oil, it left a bad taste in your mouth, and probably made you angry."

Sasha was disturbed that the man had alleged he was interested in spiritual matters, but ... but he couldn't deny the dynamic that had occurred at the party. He remembered how irate he'd been when it became evident the Life Booth was anything but. But this Ironbridge bothered Sasha. He was too insightful. "You may be right, Mr. Ironbridge. It is an interesting theory."

Ironbridge looked hard at him. "It's more than a theory, Doctor. Jesus talked about Christians being salt in the world. Salt's a preservative, you know, designed to give things taste but mainly to preserve them, to hold off rot and decay. The body can't do without it, actually. But God said that whenever salt loses its savor, when it loses its power to preserve, it's no longer good for anything but to be thrown out and trampled under the foot of men. And that," Ironbridge said, standing up and getting ready to leave, "is where Christianity in the West is at the moment. How else do you explain the laws constantly chipping away at what many remember to have been fundamental Christian truths and liberties? How else do you explain the utter failure of Christians in this country to have any impact on American life? How do you explain Sharia law in most of our cities now? Christianity is being judged, Doctor, and soon, Christians themselves—those who've compromised with the world, who've refused to love the truth, the ones you saw yesterday ... God will be judging them soon as well."

Sasha knew Ironbridge was leaving, but his warning senses were alerted. "What is this power you speak of, Mr. Ironbridge? Power to do what?"

"The power to preserve righteousness, to live a holy life, a good life, to be true, to be honest ... and to endure persecution and trials when they come."

"Do not all good men have this power in them?"

"They do not," Ironbridge said flatly. "That's the big lie—that people can be good enough to be accepted by God; doesn't work, I'm telling you. Only when God lives in a person does He confer power in them to obey Him ... essentially to become like His Son. Men can't do so without that power."

"Again ... an interesting theory."

Ironbridge looked at the Doctor and his colleague and then turned his head slightly and shook it once, very gently. He took a moment to gather himself, and looked at them strangely, as though seeing them for the first time. He stood there for what seemed like long seconds, and then said, "Well, I can tell you, *Doctor*, God sometimes provides demonstrations of power to those He wants to convince. Can't explain it, can't justify it, but sometimes people need to see evidence that He exists; just hearing about Him doesn't work. I don't know, maybe it's because of how they grew up or something, or where they grew up, but just having someone speak truth to them doesn't seem to get through—something more dramatic is required. So permit me to maybe show you that God is real, that He wants truth from men, and that He still works in the lives of men today."

"How would you do that?" Sasha asked, smiling with just the smallest tinge of derision.

Ironbridge hesitated for a moment, and then said, "Let's us three step outside."

Turning to Riesling, "Josh, I'll see you a little later this week, okay?"

"Sure thing, sir. Thanks for coming by this morning."

"Daria, nice to see you again." The Israeli woman smiled thinly but couldn't say anything. Kong saw that she was struggling with something, some kind of emotional turmoil.

Ironbridge limped through the door and stopping, turned to Sasha and Kong. "Coming? Let's go," and he stumped briskly into the parking lot.

About twenty yards from the entrance to NMC, he squared up his shoulders to Sasha and Kong.

"You wanted to know what power is? I'll tell you," Track said. "One example of God's power is that He sometimes tells His children things only He can know."

The two Russians stood in the gravel lot, wondering what the old one-legged man was on about.

"God has shared something with me about you both."

"What would that be?" Sasha asked, trying to sound dismissive.

"That you both have a job to do in this country, and He wants you to know that He is the one who has set things in motion so that what you and your countrymen are planning will come about. This job you must do is one He has directed."

"God wants a receiving facility built here in Granite Sky?" Kong asked sarcastically.

Ironbridge looked hard at Kong. "You know what I'm talking about, gentlemen. God is judging this country—America—and he will use you, your nation, your military power, and the military power of your friends the Chinese to do it. So let's put away the pretense, okay?"

"Mr. Ironbridge, we're just construction engineers, and—"

Ironbridge poked his finger toward Sasha's chest. "You two are Russian military; you're Spetsnaz."

There was just the briefest moment of silence, and then Sasha recovered. "I can assure you, Mr. Ironbridge, we're just—"

Ironbridge waved a hand and Sasha was silent. "Look. What's going to happen is going to happen. What do you think, I'm going to call the FBI or the Army and tell them I've got two little green men in Granite Sky running around pretending to be legitimate marine construction engineers and, oh yeah, the Russians are going to invade because God told me they would? Seriously, do you think I'd do that?"

"Why are you telling us this?" Kong asked, struggling to maintain his composure by smiling derisively.

"Good question. Two reasons: one, so that you know God is real. This is true power. Could I have known this on my own? I'm some dairy farmer in northern Minnesota, what do I know? I just met you this morning. God made this known to me, and I'm telling you because He wants you to know He exists. *Why* He wants you to know is something to explore later. You asked what kind of power God gives men? Sometimes the power He gives comes in this form, which we call a 'word of knowledge'. And the second reason is because I was told to give you a warning."

Ironbridge looked at both men with a piercing intensity. and pointed at both them, emphasizing his words with a pointed finger.

"*Stay away from the Jews in this country.* Stay away from them, and anyone protecting them. That's God warning to you both. Not to your senior officers, not to the commands that will give orders ... those aren't of concern here, today, now, in this parking lot, and you won't be able to affect those anyway. They're going to do what they're going to do. But you two ... you both need to know that the God who made the universe, who made all creation, is telling you and you," and Ironbridge pointed first to Sasha, then to Kong, "not to interfere with what He will do with the Jews in this country. *Leave them alone.*"

Sasha, struggling for composure, put on a mein of disbelief. "Why would your God give us such a warning?" he asked with a tinge of disdain.

"I asked Him that very same question," Ironbridge replied. "Do you want to know what He said?"

Sasha shook his head cynically. "Again, I suspect you'll tell us."

"Not this time; this time you have to ask."

There was a long silence. The wind whipped around them in the parking lot, and Sasha stared hard at Ironbridge, who would not look away.

"Okay, so tell us," Sasha replied.

Ironbridge looked at Kong. "Do you want to know as well?"

"Like it matters?" Kong asked derisively.

"Is that a yes or a no?"

"Fine. Tell me."

"God asked me to warn you about this because He has things for both of you to do, and since anyone who lifts their hands against the Jews will have done to them what they do to the Jews, apparently ... apparently He wants you spared."

Sasha and Kong were slowly realizing that this old man, just one old man in northern Minnesota, was aware of their mission. Sasha ran through in his mind where in the long train of events the mission might have been compromised, and wasn't uncovering anything. Kong was trembling with a combination of anger and fear—anger that their mission had been compromised, yet fear of the unknown, fear of the supernatural, and the clear demonstration of the numinous. That this man would know such things wasn't natural. And lastly, with a burning question: why would this God Ironbridge speaks of be concerned about a Captain in the Russian Special Forces? A thought began a slow burn in his mind: *What am I to this God?*

"So ... I've shared with you what God told me. You know it's true and I know it's true. I've told you this so you can know God is real, and that He wants to involve Himself in your lives. Seriously, you can answer the question of whether God is real right now, come on. Look," he said, pointing first to Sasha. "You can tell me, right here, if God is real or not."

"How would I do that, sir?" Sasha replied.

"If I'm right about what you are here to do, and what will happen soon, then you can know God is real. How would I have known about it otherwise? If, on the other hand, you are in fact two extremely well-conditioned, physically fit marine construction engineers here simply to build some facility on the coast, then, well, I suppose we can all agree that there really is no God who can speak to men, and that I'm a deluded old man. So, what is it? Is He real or not?"

Sasha stood there in the NMC parking lot, stunned by what Ironbridge had disclosed, amazed, and after a long moment made a decision, one that in the days to come he would wonder about. It would have been so easy to put Ironbridge down, to deny his assertion, to say Ironbridge was really just a deluded, pathetic handwringer trying to conjure up some weird plot so he could seem relevant. He could have just conformed to ironclad mission security protocols, and watched the man's face fall—but he couldn't do it.

"Your God is real, Mr. Ironbridge."

Kong snapped a shocked glance once at Sasha, realizing that a serving Spetsnaz officer had just admitted he was conducting a reconnaissance prior to an invasion—admitted it to an American—but then turned back to face Ironbridge. He found himself compelled as well by a strange feeling of abandonment, of fury, anger, yes, but also some strange awareness of light, of reality, of truth that he'd never experienced before. He drew himself up to his full height, pushed his shoulders back, and said in a tone of aggressiveness but with a touch of fierce commitment: "I also say that your God is real." He could not have said anything else.

The three of them stood there on the same ground, in the same context, the same frame of reference—a space in time wherein three men acknowledged that God was real and that He had miraculously made known to Tack Ironbridge the fact that the two of them were working for the Russian military, a force which was about to invade America. There was a tension in the air, crackling, as though something, someone would spring into action. Nothing happened for a long moment.

"But," Kong finally asked, "what is to keep us—either one of us—from just killing you here and keeping this little secret to ourselves?"

Ironbridge did the strangest thing then. He smiled. "Gentlemen, you can do nothing unless God permits it, and I'm pretty sure He didn't have me come out here this morning to prove to you that He's real and to give you a warning that has the possibility of keeping you alive ... just so you can do away with me." Ironbridge paused and then spoke to both men, his words conveying a sense of gravity. "Listen, you have a job to do, something God has ordained. I can't stop it. I'm not sure I would if I could. This country is a stench in God's nostrils, and it is only through the refining fire of judgment and persecution that anyone in it will be restored to any kind of true life. So pay attention to what's happened here this morning, the important thing." He reached over and tapped each one of them in the chest. "The God of all creation has directly and supernaturally involved Himself in your life. He is talking to you, passing a message of extreme importance that will keep you alive if you heed it. He has said that He wants something of you. So you both now must decide what you're going to do with the information. Sure, you could kill me, but where does that leave you? You kill me and that will just prove my point even more so, and you'd still need to deal with the fact that God is real and that He's warned you of something you need to be careful about in the future."

Sasha and Kong were silent, each wrestling with this new development, this encounter with the numinous, trying to understand something that exceeded the boundaries of their comprehension.

Ironbridge looked at both men for a long moment."Gentlemen, it's time for me to go. Here; take these." He gave each one of them a small business card. "You have any questions about ... well, about anything, you give me a call." The two Spetsnaz operators each took Ironbridge's card like men moving in slow motion, as though they couldn't believe what they were doing. "Before I go, though, you should know I'll be praying that you make the right decisions in the future. Help me out with that; God knows your real names, but I don't." Ironbridge let the question hang. It was more than a request for just their names; it was a request for them to acknowledge that they believed what they'd been told and that they would consider how they would respond to God's warning.

The two Russians stood for a long few seconds in the parking lot, until, oddly, Kong stuck out a hand. "Captain Maximus Lohniverisk." Ironbridge shook his hand.

Sasha hesitated for a moment, torn between the lifelong habit of hatred for America and all things American—especially Americans—and the strange, growing, grudging respect he was beginning to feel for this one-legged man standing before him, who somehow had some type of connection to ... to something numinous, something supernatural.

"You will not stop us from doing what we must," he said, almost in a whisper.

"Not my job," Ironbridge replied forthrightly. Then he held up a cautionary finger, pointing upward. "But remember, if you raise your hand against even one Jew, God will bring upon you what you bring upon that Jew."

Sasha nodded slowly and thought for several moments. He stared off into the distance, at the water now churning up in the lake, as snowflakes began to fall. He looked at Ironbridge.

"Major Sasha Sokolov," he said. Sasha shook Ironbridge's hand.

Ironbridge nodded, acknowledging the decision they'd both made, acknowledging that God had done something miraculous with the three of them that morning. "Gentlemen, for some reason God wants you both to know He's real. This is because He wants something of you. When you go back to wherever it is you've come from and you begin to do whatever it is you're supposed to do, keep that in mind. My strong recommendation is that you both get alone with Him and ask Him, directly, what exactly He wants of you. He *will* speak to you."

Ironbridge nodded to them both and then limped over to his truck and drove away, leaving Sasha and Kong standing in the parking lot.

Kong scuffed a foot in the gravel. Sasha stood with his hands in his parka, staring at nothing. Clouds of condensation swirled before their faces in the drifting snow.

"I can't believe we let him go," Kong said, shaking his head, staring at the receding truck.

Chapter 40
The Russians

"Then the Lord said to me, 'Out of the north the evil will break forth on all the inhabitants of the land.'"

Jeremiah 1:14

Major Sokolov stood in the waiting area looking through thick glass windows, slapping his arms against his chest, watching the ground crew do their preflight walk-around on the Antonov 72 aircraft sitting on the ramp at the Murmansk airport. The plane glinted in the grey arctic dawn, the lights on the control tower reflecting against millions of misty raindrops over its dulled flat white paint scheme. Fuel trucks and baggage trolleys clustered as men in thick blue parkas with yellow reflective vests moved like colorful frozen caterpillars around the aircraft, getting it ready to fly. Twenty-eight meters long, with a wingspan of almost thirty-two meters, the chunky aircraft looked remarkably like the old Soviet cartoon character, *Cheburashka*, a Russian imitation of Mickey Mouse. The fat jet engine intakes sat high over the wings and close to the fuselage, looking, when seen from the front, like large mouse ears. A crewman kicked at one of the tires and ran his hand over the skin of the wing's underside. *Cheburashka* would be their main source of transportation for the next three weeks, taking a team of Russian military and political officers, social scientists, and construction engineers on a sweeping tour of Russian arctic facilities. They had just come from visiting the first stop on the tour, a camp in Lovozero in the Russian Lapland, just north of Murmansk.

One of the original camps in the former Soviet Union's Corrective Labor system, Lovozero seemed to consist of nothing but endless kilometers of stark wooden barracks. It still retained a gray, heavy, foreboding prison atmosphere. The team had flown there from Murmansk in three Mi-10 cargo helicopters, taken dozens of photographs, hundreds of measurements, examined the barracks until Sasha wondered what they were looking at, and then finally got back into the helicopters for the short trip back to the airport in Murmansk.

The temperature at the field was exactly zero degrees Celsius, and the wind was like a knife, blowing across the flat, frozen tundra and sweeping up and over the airport's boundaries. Sasha thought about what the snow conditions were in the winter, and where he might find a good course for a long telemark workout.

"Are you able to make it out to the aircraft, Comrade Major? Do you need me to order you a heated car? Maybe some hot tea to keep you warm while the chauffer prepares the vehicle? Perhaps your promotion has convinced you that you must be treated gently in the new Russian military, yes?" General Fyodor Bugyachev smacked Sasha on the shoulder, in a massive and manly way pounding home blunt Russian humor.

"I think I can struggle out to the plane, Comrade General," Sasha replied, smiling respectfully.

The service agents came in from out on the tarmac preparing the aircraft and, blowing in their hands, stomping their feet, indicated that the flight was ready. The team picked up their hand baggage and walked down the ice-slick steps to the tarmac and out to the aircraft. The AN-72 typically seated around fifty passengers with a crew of five, but this was a Russian military version, modified to take high-ranking officers on trips such as this one. There were only forty decadent, American-style business class seats, and as the team found their seats on the plane, stewards served hot tea. The General turned to Sokolov, taking off his gloves and brushing the snow from the shoulders of his thick green greatcoat.

"Seriously, Sokolov, tell us, what was it like in America? You've been different since you returned. We thought you would be there for a long time. Did the CIA throw you out?" Other members of the team seated nearby paused and looked to Sokolov; they too were interested in his time in America.

Sasha smiled, a dart of anxiety registering at the general's comment about seeing a difference in him. Was it that obvious? What was happening to him?

"My assignment was to learn about how the Americans might react to our little planned 'incursion', and to reconnoiter specific geographical areas while posing as an executive with a Russian engineering company. I completed that assignment, Comrade General, and when I left, I told them I had other professional duties that required I work 'remotely'. And no, the CIA did not throw me out, sir. Regrettably, several fathers chased me out of the country with shotguns." Immediately there came the strangest feeling almost akin to regret, chagrin, or distaste at his crude jest ... *another* strange feeling!

Bugyachev roared at this, slapping Sokolov on the shoulder again. "Hah! So you made a few good little Russians in your spare time while you prepared to invade their country! Ah, Major, if this is not the stuff of a Russian novel! I don't know what could be more ironic." The general settled back in his seat, chuckling still. "What did you tell them your 'other professional duties' were? What are you supposed to be doing, then, while you are 'working remotely'?"

"I told them I was a Russian Spetsnaz officer reconnoitering their country prior to an invasion."

Bugyachev's smile froze for just a moment, and then he threw his head back and laughed even louder and punched him in the arm. "You're all right, Sokolov, I don't care what Comrade General Makarovitch has said about you."

"What ... what did he say about me?" Sokolov asked, suddenly on edge.

Bugyachev laughed again—it sounded more like a bear growling. "Ahahah, Sokolov, you're a typical Spetsnaz idiot. General Makarovitch thinks the world of you and those Spetsnaz panty-wastes you hang around with, though I have no idea why. Now get on your knees and pray to the God who doesn't exist that this piece of flying junk won't crash before we get where we're going."

***

After a two-hour flight, in which the piece of flying junk performed admirably, the delegation landed at a remote airstrip on the island of Novaya Zemlya, the aircraft shouldering its way through the harsh arctic wind and lumbering down onto the hard, crushed volcanic rock that served as a runway. The Antonov was designed as a short-takeoff-and-landing aircraft, so they would be able to land at every runway they would encounter on the trip, many of which were too short for conventional aircraft.

Many decades ago Novaya Zemlya had been used to test the Soviet Union's nuclear weapons, experiencing a total of 224 nuclear detonations, below and above ground, comprising slightly more than 260 megatons of explosives. When all the explosives from World War II, including the two nuclear bombs over Hiroshima and Nagasaki, are totaled, they equate to something like two megatons. With 260 megatons of nuclear detonations on the ground, it was said for many years that the frozen rocks of Novaya Zemlya would glow green in the arctic night. The world's largest nuclear weapon ever used—the *'Tsar Bomba'*, a hydrogen bomb originally designed as a 100 kiloton device, but reduced to 50 kilotons to safeguard the crew dropping it—was detonated at Novaya Zemlya on 30 October, 1961. After many decades and a massive environmental cleaning effort, the Russian authorities declared the island to be safe and free from any radioactivity. Uncharacteristically, they were correct. Scientists continually checked radiation levels and to date they'd remained well within safe ranges. Still, the men joked about double-headed penguins, five-legged arctic foxes, and, after any time spent on the island, of having mutant children with three heads, three arms, or six fingers. And now Russia had begun again testing underground nuclear weapons. A 12-kiloton weapon had been detonated underground on Novaya Zemlya a scant month before the team arrived.

"So, Sokolov, have you sired any three-eyed bastards since you were here last?" Bugyachev asked. He had read Sokolov's report on his Ice Transport Vehicle tests Sasha had conducted, right here on this island. "You may have to go back to America to find out."

"Unfortunately an occasion has not arisen, Comrade General," Sasha replied soberly. "We Spetsnaz officers are kept very busy with our official duties."

"Right, of course, how could I forget?" Bugyachev smiled grimly, and then in a more serious tone, said, "It was a good report, Major. We learned much from those tests."

"Thank you, Comrade General."

Bugyachev tapped his forearm with two fingers. "We're going to give you the same unit you worked with then, Sokolov. For this next operation, you will have the same men, but with very much graver responsibilities. Make sure you take care of them."

Sasha looked quickly at the General, seeing that he was serious. "I'm very grateful, General. They were ... they *are* a good team; they're good men."

"The best," Bugyachev said in a low voice, and tapped Sokolov on his arm. "But tell no one I said so." Sokolov simply ducked his head in acknowledgement, smiling, as they moved toward the exit.

The passengers stepped warily out of the aircraft and down the moveable stairway, careful not to slip on the ice while fighting a fierce wind, and made their way toward a low white building topped with large antennas and a satellite dish.

The team assembled in a sparsely furnished rectangular room that served as the airfield's operations center. Sokolov could see that operations were rudimentary, but signs of future growth were everywhere, inside and out. On approach, he'd seen huge earthmovers and graders extending the runway and gouging out great chunks of volcanic rock to serve, he presumed, as foundations for new structures. Manic clusters of jabbering technicians were installing computer terminals inside the operations building while unpacked status boards lined the floor waiting to be mounted on the walls. The ceiling was an unfinished tangle of wires, heating ducts, and panels in massive disarray. The room swirled with technicians and engineers moving about, supervisors yelling at each other, shouting directions or requests back and forth, eating sandwiches or drinking coffee while they worked, and no one minded or noticed the team coming into the operations center, their breath forming clouds in the frosty air, stomping snow from their boots in the entry way. Someone shouted at them to shut the door, and the cacophony continued.

"Engineers," grunted the intelligence officer, a colonel, shaking his head in disdain. "No interest in anything that doesn't revolve around either code or metal. The same everywhere." He turned to Sokolov. "Did you meet any American engineers during your stay there, Sasha?"

"My duties focused more on marine survey exploration and geographical surveying. I met some construction people, but no real engineers."

The aviator, a Major General, leaned over as he removed his gloves, and said, "I hear that the Americans are not turning out as many engineers in the States as they have been, Comrade Major."

"You're right about this, Comrade General, no question. I did ask enough questions to determine that engineering skills are just not an emphasis any longer in most of the colleges and universities in their country."

"Bodes well for us," the intelligence colonel said. "Actually the level of engineering skills in their military is declining, and it is showing up operationally. We've spent about four months putting up these facilities, and so far there are no signs they've detected what we're doing."

Sokolov lifted his eyebrows at this, doubtful, but the aviator nodded his head. "If anyone would know, Sokolov, Anatoly would," he said, referring to Anatoly Periotkin, the colonel from intelligence. "The big bad Americans are no longer as big or as bad as they were." The aviator smiled grimly. "They're still tough, no question, but we've closed the gap and, maybe ... just maybe ... we've pulled ahead a bit."

"We will see, Mikhail," General Bugyachev growled to the aviator, Major General Arenskiya, shaking his finger. "We will see."

"The most surprising thing I did notice," Sasha said, as a group of officers gathered around a steaming samovar on a makeshift table, "was the overwhelming weakness of the men." Eyebrows went up. "No, it's true. You wouldn't believe it. It's as if all the males have become emasculated. The men put up with things that no self-respecting Russian male would consider—from women, from ... well, from others in their society. The things you read about their homosexuals, well, it is worse than even what you read about, and their men—the *straight* men—obsess over clothes; they regale each other with the qualities of their internal decorating skills; they compete with each other to procure the finest kitchen appliances. They all watch sports, but none of them actually get out from behind their televisions to participate in anything physically strenuous."

Major General Arenskiya laughed derisively, along with the others. "This thing about homosexuals in America," he put in with conviction, "is that they cannot admit that it is anything but enlightened progress when it is in fact a decadent rot, eating away at the vitality of their society."

"My God," Bugyachev said, shaking his head, now serious, "if they only knew how much the rest of the world laughs at them."

Sasha replied, "Truthfully, Comrade General, I am not sure it would matter. They seem to exist in a completely isolated world of their own, and they look around at other nations in Europe and think that such a social policy is acceptable. To even question such a policy ... if one did so, one would get arrested in Boston."

Several eyebrows rose. "Sounds like they're getting a good dose," the colonel replied, with a subtle double entendre.

"The Europeans are past masters at putting lice in someone else's mattress,"

Arenskiya said cynically.

"That may be, Mikhail, but I am telling you," Bugyachev said, leaning forward and ladling sugar into his glass of tea, "no military unit can for any length of time maintain combat efficiency when men are screwing each other in the barracks. It doesn't work with women, why would it work with men? My God, it's gross. I don't care what crap they spew about Alexander and his queer Greek armies, it won't work. It *doesn't* work. It defies human nature."

"I tell you, and this is the truth," Sokolov said, looking around at each one of them, "there were queer men everywhere on the streets in downtown Boston. You couldn't believe it. You would be in great peril if you even questioned their right to parade around like fairies. There was a parade while I was there ... a *gay pride* parade, they called it, and there were men and women doing unspeakable things *in the streets*. I almost threw up. And they've got the media wrapped around their fingers."

"I should visit Boston sometime," the colonel said, mostly to himself.

"This manipulation of the media is not uncommon, Captain," Major General Arenskiya, said, *sotto voce*.

"Yes sir, you are correct, in a corrupt capitalistic country like America, it is easy, as you say, but to see the effects ... it was striking. I would find myself wondering, in a restaurant, or even at my work, if a man with whom I would be speaking was straight or queer."

"This was with *everyone*, Sasha?" Colonel Periotkin asked, with a cynical look.

Sokolov paused for a moment, thinking. "Well, no sir, not everyone. I would say in the social circles in which I moved—and please remember, it was mainly among the proletariat—that the only people who opposed this social convention were those who had fundamental religious objections, and those were only Americans. Those from other countries I met with found nothing wrong with this blatant filth."

"No religious fanatics left in Europe, anyway," the colonel said, deprecatingly.

"We've nothing to worry about from America's religious fairies," said the naval officer, Admiral Karentin Valyutczech, speaking for the first time. He was a former commander of an *Akula*-class fast attack submarine, a former submarine squadron commander, and had served as the director for all Russian naval personnel. He was at the time the commander of all Russian forces in the Arctic region. He was known as one of the most astute organizational geniuses the Russian military had ever produced.

"I don't know, Karentin," General Bugyachev replied, shaking his head. "You have to admit that they have at least some courage in their convictions, and if so, such might prove difficult for us."

"I agree with both of you," Sasha put in. "General Bugyachev is correct; these men—and there were not that many that I met—were the strongest men I saw while I was in America—yes, some had once been in their military—and they were nothing like what we have been led to believe evangelicals are supposed to be, with apologies to Comrade Admiral Valyutczech. They were definitely *not* effeminate. Yet the Admiral *is* correct in that we have little to fear from them, because they are so rare, and the U.S. military is apparently weeding out men with these proclivities. I overheard them in one discussion saying that many of their kind were leaving the service."

"Why would they get rid of them?" Periotkin pressed, curious. "If they truly have courage, as you say, I would expect them to be rising in the ranks."

"Well, Comrade Colonel, I would say—"

Bugyachev interrupted Sokolov, and answered Periotkin. "What you are seeing, Pyotr, is the result of Comrade Putin's wise policies relative to religious philosophies. He planted seeds with the American administration many, many years ago—"

"While he was snaking around East Germany, just after he killed James Bond, right?" Periotkin put in, and the group shared muted laughter.

"No, but seriously," Bugyachev went on, "American society has been denigrating Christianity in America for so long—and you know who started to kick *that* can of rubles down the cart path." They all laughed heartily, and Bugyachev continued. "If any American officer even *hints* that he has such leanings, they cull him out faster than a Russian noblewoman would kick a Spetsnaz dirt bag out of her bed." Bugyachev elbowed Sokolov.

The group laughed heartily at this, looking at Sokolov, waiting for him to reply. Bugyachev's incessant needling of any Spetsnaz officer was famous throughout the Red Army. Sasha looked down at his glass of tea and said, "The General's wisdom about what Russian noblewomen find in their beds obviously far surpasses my limited knowledge on the subject," and the men laughed freely. Bugyachev banged him on the shoulder again, spilling his tea.

"You're okay for a Spetsnaz troll," the General growled.

"So who and what are you supposed to be in America?" Admiral Valyutkin asked. Sasha darted a glance at the intelligence colonel, who just as surreptitiously nodded his approval. Apparently everyone on this reconnaissance expedition was fully cleared.

"I'm an executive for Rubin, Comrade Admiral, assisting that company in developing marine facilities in Minnesota," he replied.

"Did Rubin pay you while you worked for them?" the aviator asked, thick eyebrows raised.

"They did, yes," Sasha replied. "It was part of the cover."

"They paid him something like three times what he is making now," Bugyachev interjected, laughing in a gravelly voice. "Part of his cover; had to have it."

"Did they let you keep what they paid you, Major?"

"Well sir," Sasha replied, "actually they did, but I gave it all away to charity—a home for old retired Army veterans."

"Hah," Bugyachev exclaimed, "don't believe him. He spent it all on women and new skis."

"We're supposed to ... *visit* ... Minnesota, are we not?" asked the aviator again, darting a questioning look at Bugyachev.

"Perhaps," replied General Bugyachev, "and speaking of this visit, let's get to reviewing the plans." A tall, pretty female engineer wearing glasses, holding an electronic pad appeared at his elbow and nodded, indicating that they should follow her.

The group moved to a separate room, full of maps, charts, computers, and engineers still frantically scrambling around, dodging the officers as they gathered around a large planning map on a rectangular electronic map table.

"We're getting international," Major General Arenskiya said, pointing at the electronic map table. "That is made in America in a factory in Tallman, New York owned by a Frenchman, who sold it to one of our contacts in Lebanon. Amazing technology. What we could have done with this in Afghanistan."

The map set into the table was a computer screen that showed a view of the planet from directly above the North Pole. At the bottom of the map sat the island of Novaya Zemlya, where the men themselves were located at the moment; to the left of center sat the white mass of Greenland; just to its right were the tundra islands that choked the Northwest Passage between the Russian mainland and Canada. At the top of the map they saw the northern border of Canada. They saw lights that showed the locations of Russian air bases along the Arctic Circle—many more than there had been three years ago. The lights formed a line pointing directly into North America; they were disguised as research stations, civil airfields, or investments by private firms, mostly from the oil and gas industry. Bugyachev was speaking, using an electronic mouse as a pointer. They followed his spot of light over the map.

"You can see that if we go around the eastern tip of Greenland and back into the Hudson Bay to our potential landing area in James Bay, we're looking at a distance of around 7500 kilometers before we get on solid ground. If we come in directly through the Beaufort Sea, here, we're looking at something like 4300 kilometers, just slightly more than half the distance. The issue is the time over land. If we put ashore at James Bay, we'll be much closer to penetrating the American border."

"About 800 kilometers closer to your crop of American children, Sasha," Colonel Periotkin said wryly.

"Right," Bugyachev answered, "and if we put ashore here," and he indicated a spot on the barren Canadian coastline, "we've got, what, almost 2000 kilometers to cross, not to mention the terrain." The General highlighted the rugged Yukon, with its mountainous ridges and vast stretches of frozen, jagged tundra.

"I am assuming you are expecting light resistance from the Canadians?" Major General Arenskiya asked.

"Correct," Bugyachev replied, growling. "That is, if they want any semblance of their country to remain. So what we need to do here, Comrades, is to identify the advantages and disadvantages of the two possible routes and provide our recommendations to General Makarovitch. That's what will be keeping us busy from this point forward."

***

For the next three days the planning team worked through the variables and details associated with each of the invasion options. They argued about vehicles, men, equipment, power, food and water caches, distances, times, ammunition, potential threats, and objectives. At times, one or the other would step back from the table, shaking their head in wonder, or consternation, or concern. Bugyachev noticed this and finally spoke to the issue.

"Gentlemen, I know what you are thinking, so let me share something with you." They all looked at him with curiosity. "Yes, you are wondering just what we could possibly be doing, attacking the world's greatest superpower, putting our boots on land which has not been invaded for two hundred years." The old General reached for a piece of paper in a stack by his hand. "Here is a report written to me by our comrade, Major Sokolov, sent oh, maybe five weeks ago while he was 'suffering' in the land of desserts and perverts." The group dutifully laughed at the General's joke. Bugyachev donned a small pair of reading glasses and began to read:

"...These people are like wraiths, insipid shadows of what were once men. They are empty, vacuous, enervated, with no concern other than what luxuries or entertainments they will undertake in their next moment of leisure, and how they might cause that moment of leisure to come about sooner and last longer. They thirst for all manner of perversions in their entertainments, and there is discussion now in the mainstream media, as there was years ago regarding homosexuality, of the rightness of permitting adults to have sex with children. These people are deserving of everything that happens to them, and when we come into this place, we must of all things keep our hands clean of their perversions and pestilence."

The General put down the paper and looked over the lenses of his glasses, nodding once to Sasha in acknowledgement. "Gentlemen, you must understand that we are not attacking the America we knew as our opponent over the last twenty or thirty years. This is a different America; this is a country ripped in two by political disagreements, and we have many of our own to thank for that 'gray terror'. In their country they have disgusting perversions that have been bandied about to the public as acceptable to such a degree that it appears Americans no longer can discern right from wrong—and this is important to us not because of those perversions," the General put in this qualification because he knew that one or two of the men around the table indulged in perversions similar to those he was speaking about, "but because when we propose the rationale for our presence, too many of them will hesitate; they will not know what to do, and we will be there to tell them what to do, and they will listen, like the sheep that they are. These are people who will roll over and hand you everything they own if you simply promise them a comfortable living room with heat or air conditioning, access to fast food, the Internet, and a television with ninety-five channels. They are mindless slaves to their own habits, and let me tell you all now—and you must believe me—you have *nothing* to fear from them, do you understand? *Nothing!*"

Heartened by Bugyachev's talk, especially when they could directly question a source of the information Bugyachev had by frequently pulling Sokolov aside and buttonholing him about numerous issues relative to American morale, the planning team worked out the strategic and operational details, coming up with what Bugyachev called a remarkably brilliant solution—they would invade from both directions. Sasha was tasked with drafting the team's recommendations. He left the last meeting and commandeered a laptop from one of the scurrying engineers in the building, found a cold meat sandwich and a glass of tea, and sat down to write. The main element of his report ran as follows:

"The advantages sought for the invasion through James Bay produce a short ground run to the American border, a quicker timeline for ground forces, and a shorter logistics support schedule until such time as our ground units can appropriate localized American resources. The disadvantages are numerous: the first, obviously, is the passage through so much water—around Greenland, through the Hudson Bay, and on into James Bay. American submarines are the greatest threat, as is early detection and subsequent American and Canadian military assaults on our troop convoys. Weather will affect the transit for so many ships, and the time selected for the action will be a crucial factor. And finally, although we may expect assistance from our Muslim brethren in Michigan, we must keep in mind that our

other ally will be a distance away, westward along the northern U.S. border.

Advantages to landing in the Northwest Territories on the barren Canadian tundra from the Beaufort Sea and making the long trek down through the Canadian wilderness to cut the U.S. in two: (1) transit time over water is drastically shortened, (2) reduces risk of detection and delays caused by weather, interception, and interdiction by enemy forces both over water and on land. However, once on the ground, transiting the terrain will be difficult. There are few roads, and those that exist can easily be interdicted by opposing elements. The tundra in this region is filled with uncharted marsh, ice fields, and mountains in which entire divisions might be swallowed. The terrain resembles Afghanistan; there is also the heightened degree of uncertainty regarding the solidity of ground everywhere a Russian trooper will put his boot. As well, there is the threat of American interdiction from their forces relatively close by in Alaska.

The team recommends, therefore, that we leverage the advantages of both options while attempting to reduce risks. With a fast-striking ground force, we recommend the long maritime transit down through the Hudson Bay, disguised in some degree as merchant shipping, and once securing a beachhead near Nunavut Island, funnel our ground forces directly south to intercept the TransCanada highway near Kenogami Lake (see attached chart) and then, based upon the intensity and disposition of the threat, turn either west, to seize the border crossing point into America on the northern tip of the upper peninsula in Michigan, or turn east to head south of Montreal and on into New York by crossing the St. Laurence river. Theater and operational commanders will make this decision prior to the arrival at Kenogami Lake.

"A second, much larger ground force will embark on large maritime transports and make the assault into the Northwest Territories. Advance Spetsnaz elements will assault and capture Paulatuk Airport and use it as a staging base to secure our landings in that area. Troops will be offloaded in Ice Transport Vehicles (ITVs) to make the long tundra crossing. It is estimated that at least 85% of the vehicles will successfully make the transit, and pickups for troops whose vehicles fail will be scheduled. At an average of 100 kilometers per hour, lead elements of the force will arrive at the American border at Sweet Grass, Montana, in 30 days, factoring logistics and weather delays, maintenance issues, and opposition. Advance paratroop and Spetsnaz elements will assault and hold key route strongpoints, and the force should cross into the U.S. in the vicinity of the Coutts / Sweet Grass transit junction on the border."

Sokolov delivered the draft to General Bugyachev on a clean memory stick two hours later, and the General, distracted with other responsibilities, dismissed him with a wave of his hand. Sokolov found a corner of the operations building, asked a passing engineer where most people were bunking, found a bedroll, and grabbed some sleep.

Three hours and a sandwich later, Sokolov was standing in the corner of the operations room near the samovar when Colonel Periotkin called him over. "We're convening again," he said, as Sasha followed him into the planning room.

Bugyachev was standing at one end of the electronic map table; the others on the planning team were there. Sasha could see that the others had taken the opportunity to grab some sleep as well, except for General Bugyachev, who looked as though he hadn't slept in three days—which was the literal truth.

"Gentlemen, I have had some ... some interesting news from General Makarovitch. I have sent him our recommendations—thank you all for your contributions—and the General wishes to communicate that he is grateful for your excellent staff work. He also wishes to indicate that you have, by this excellent work, earned for yourselves permanent positions at the head of your respective service branches when the time comes to make our 'visits'." The planning members received this with hard, flat, emotionless stares; they were familiar with the longevity of promises made to Russian military officers. The General went on. "But there appears to be one option that we as a planning team have overlooked—an option which General Makarovitch has told me will be the one for which we should plan." The room hushed; they couldn't think of any option they might have overlooked, even though, truthfully, three days was a short time to put together almost three years of preliminary staff work.

"No, no, there are no deficiencies in the plans you have generated," the General said, loud enough for all to hear. "No ... but the option General Makarovitch wishes to be employed is one which is, I think, the best for all of us." Bugyachev hesitated for a moment, and the three days of no sleep began to tell; his attention wandered, until Colonel Periotkin touched him on the sleeve, leaned over, and asked him quietly, "General, what is General Makarovitch's option?""

"Right, of course, my apologies. Gentlemen, General Makarovitch wishes to inform you that we will exercise *both* of the options you have recommended ... but he predicts that there will be no opposition. Therefore, I find it necessary to ask you to rework and submit amended timetables for the operation."

The team members looked at each other, wondering how such a thing could be possible. The Americans had become decadent, it was true, but certainly not *that* decadent. The General let them wonder for a long minute, and then said into the growing silence, "The Americans will not oppose our forces; they will not fire on our ships, and they will not shoot down our airplanes. They will not decimate our ground forces with their artillery. No, comrades, they will invite us into their country—the Canadians will open the doors as quickly as they can—and the Americans will thank us for coming."

No one questioned the General's assertion. It was obvious that wheels were moving within wheels, and in the Red Army—like every other military organization in the world—when the wheels move, everyone just gets out of the way and then falls in line, otherwise one ends up with one's guts greasing those wheels. After twenty-four hours of downtime, insisted upon by General Bugyachev, in which most of the team caught up with their sleep, they again mounted the AN-72 for the next leg of their inspection tour.

***

From Novaya Zemlya they flew to the island of Severnaya Zemlya. Three years ago, this barren island had been nothing but a desolate collection of ice mountains with one small plateau of tundra at its southern tip. Yet as they approached the island from the Russian coast, Bugyachev leaned across Sokolov and pointed out the window.

"Look, Sasha, down there, just beyond the collection of three large rock clusters." Sasha gazed where Bugyachev was indicating and was surprised to see long, thin, obviously man-made lines extending from these rocks, all the way to the shoreline of the island. "What are they, Comrade General? Fueling lines?"

"Well, yes and no. Good guess, but there is more. They're also forming lines for piers. Within about twenty-four hours, those lines can be turned into a fully-functional deep water port."

"And the ice?" he asked.

"We have solved that problem," the General replied, but said nothing more.

They landed on a 4300-meter runway, large enough, Sasha realized, for the highest-speed fighter or the heaviest cargo aircraft. The Antonov, engines screaming, pulled up well short of the far end of the runway, the pilot showing off the aircraft's short-field landing capabilities. The aviator colonel on the team grumbled and complained when he spilled his tea.

Severnaya's operations center was nothing but a square white cement structure. The team came off the aircraft, wondering, looking out at the horizon that seemed thousands of miles away, wondering why they were stopping at this god-forsaken rock; there was no other structure in sight. It reminded Sasha of the steppes where he took part of his Spetsnaz training. Bugyachev wore a self-satisfied expression as he strode determinedly toward the small white building, trailing officers, scientists, and construction experts that looked like small black and green dots on a sea of white. The wind howled and whipped up stinging snow particles, and men bent into the wind, covering their faces. They mobbed the only door and filed in, one at a time. Bugyachev was nowhere to be seen, but they followed the breadcrumbs of men as each went through the single door, through the only small room, and then down a stairwell—still, one at a time. A few mumbled to each other, wondering, but most were silent, recognizing finally that most of what they were here to inspect was going to be underground. A construction expert ran a hand along the concrete wall as they descended ever further.

They went down fourteen levels and finally the stairwell leveled off and opened into a massive warehouse area. The team milled about, stunned, gazing with open mouths at the huge underground facility. Metal shipping containers were stacked twelve squared—twelve containers side by side, twelve high—on both sides of the cavern. Sasha immediately recognized them as the newest versions of his ice transport vehicles.

"Now, Sokolov, you know where your Spetsnaz rascals will start from," Bugyachev pronounced, his voice ringing back to them from the metal containers. "You go that way," he lifted an arm and pointed off into the dark distance of the warehouse, "and you come to the other entrance. From there are roads that lead up to the northern part of the island—all underground—and they come out close to the northern coast." Bugyachev led them past maintenance shops, huge stacked storage bins full of spare parts, and hundreds of bladders full of petrol. They walked through a large cafeteria, and then, in another cavernous space, almost as large, they came upon what was obviously the housing area. "I told them there was no need for this," Bugyachev said to those walking close to him, "that they should just let those Spetsnaz bastards sleep outside, on the ice, but no, the great men who make decisions felt that it would be too harsh for their tender and delicate constitutions, so they made this place." Those around him laughed dutifully.

"The walls ... they look like insulated concrete forms ... yet how can they withstand the temperatures?" the construction expert asked, staring upward where the concrete wall disappeared into the dark recesses of some unknown height.

Bugyachev turned to face him and spoke in a tone that lectured everyone around him. "Do you know what happened to the French, in Lorient, when sometime around, oh, when was it, around 1947 or 1948, after they put down their wine and cheese and got around to rebuilding their ruined country? The Germans had put in sub pens in the harbor, huge structures, and the French decided that since the glorious Red Army had kicked out the Germans from France, the French ought to at least get rid of what the Germans had built. And besides, the French didn't have any submarines and wouldn't know what to do with them if they had, right?" More laughter. "So they trundled up their demolition machines and swung their huge metal smashing balls, and—boom—hit the first wall. And guess what! Nothing happened ... nothing. The concrete wall of the sub pen didn't even shake. They smashed and swung and swung and smashed, and nothing happened. Then they thought to bring in explosives. So they planted dynamite at the base of the structures and set off the charges. When the dust cleared, the walls still stood, not even scratched. The French couldn't figure it out. Finally they found a captured German engineer who explained the mystery. When the Germans were pouring the concrete, they put a special mixture that contained ... can you guess ... no, well, I'll tell you. Sugar! That's right; they poured the concrete with a mixture of sugar in it. To this day they have not been able to take down the sub pens in France, which is why, eventually, the French decided instead to just build submarines. It was easier."

"So ... you poured these walls with sugar?" the construction expert asked.

"With the exact mixture the Germans used," Bugyachev explained. "Nothing is coming through those walls, and nothing will crack them—not even Mother Nature."

***

The Lyachovsky islands were named for the Russian explorer, Ivan Lyachov. There were two: 'Great' Lyachovsky, and 'Little' Lyachovsky. These are the southernmost islands in the New Siberian Island group, separated from the mainland of eastern Russia by the Laptev Strait, a mere 60 kilometers of freezing water distant. The highest point on Great Lyachovsky Island was only 270 meters in elevation (the Russians put a radar antenna on it). This much the guidebooks say (not mentioning the radar). What they don't report is the vast sense of aloneness; of bitter, snapping cold that cuts through cloth, flesh, and bone. There are calmer days when the wind is low and the sun shines and the temperature is relatively mild, but in mild weather, wherever one looks there is simply rock—black, crumbly, fine-grained, vesicular, looking like hard black sponges. When there was snow, it was everywhere, blotting out the sky, the sea, the land. Yet men—Russian men—came to the island, explored every inch of it, recorded the animal life, dodged the polar bears (or shot them), and in those days near the close of the age, carved great gouges in the volcanic rock, moving it with massive machines until they shaped the earth to support their war-making schemes.

When the team landed on Great Lyachovsky, snow covered the island. The runways, however, were cleared, awaiting the AN-72. Men stood around the white concrete blockhouse that seemed to be the standard airfield operations building Russians built at every arctic base, waiting for the fat airplane to come to a stop so they could roll out the moving stairway.

The officers and scientists came off the aircraft with practiced ease, accustomed to blowing wind, ice-covered steps, and the shock of freezing temperatures after landing at so many different bases. They were coming to look at something very different at Great

Lyachovsky, however. They were coming to inspect what would be the world's largest prison camp.

On Great Lyachovsky, the Russians had constructed a massive terminal designed to receive, process, store, and then distribute hundreds of thousands of prisoners—but they would be very different from the political prisoners Russia had sequestered in their Gulag Archipelago so many years previously. Today's Russia was dying for lack of people. They had made a plan, therefore, to prevent the loss of their country, and approached its execution in typical Russian fashion. They would conquer a foreign land, a land filled with vibrant, robust people, and take the best of those they captured back to Russia, giving them a choice—death, or life as a Russian citizen: truly, the 'Russian Way'.

The team gathered in a large auditorium—again, underground—and Bugyachev stepped to the podium to explain. He used a long wooden pointer against a massive map erected on the wall behind him, much as the old briefers would do in World War II.

"Look here," he began. "The Laptev Strait, just 60 kilometers. We are close to the mainland; this is why Great Lyachovsky was selected. The channel tunnel underneath the English Channel is around 50 kilometers; the Japanese have one about 53 kilometers. Now look at what has been built so far here on the island. You wouldn't have seen it coming in." A far wall illuminated, showing a projection of the field at which they'd landed. In the blowing snow on approach, they'd seen nothing. Now they saw the base layout. Bugyachev picked up the narrative. "Four runways: two that are 4800 meters long, running north-sout. In winter, the prevailing winds in the Laptev are from the south; in summer, they change, swinging to the north. Anything that flies can land on these runways—they are long enough. Here, though, on the western tip of the island, which you haven't been to, is the port. We'll bring specific packages into the airfield, but the vast majority will come in through the port. Sokolov, you were prescient enough to take a standard cargo container and make it a functional vehicle that can move over pack ice. Well, our Red Army engineers got busy—you must have motivated them. Here," and a picture flashed upon the wall of a small crate, "you see a crate that can turn a standard cargo container into a container capable of transporting up to 50 people. Unpack the crate and you get plumbing for a toilet, a portable floor-mounted heater, side heating pipes, materials for ventilation modifications, and other equipment necessary to convert a standard cargo container into a survivable compartment for 50 people for up to a week."

One of the social scientists raised a hand. "General, the containers look like cattle cars. Are we going to be importing Jews?" The crowd laughed. Bugyachev held up a hand. "You laugh, but we've had our Jewish problems in Russia. Do you know Lev Davidovich Bronstein? No? I'll tell you the name he took: Leon Trotsky—Jewish. You know Karl Marx—yes, Jewish. Leaders of the Menshevik faction, hey? Julius Martov and Pavel Axelrod—Jewish. Boris Pasternak, dwelling in the clouds ... right? Jewish as well. What do you think they made the Jewish Autonomous Oblast in Birobidzhan for, to take care of ailing Chinese? I'm telling you, scatter a bunch of Jews all over the place here and there in our country—Jews from America, no less—and you'll have nothing but problems."

"If they survive," someone quipped from the darkened auditorium.

"Good point, yes, these are American Jews we're talking about. There won't be places to get a blintz where we will put them. American Jews are soft, no question. But, comrade, to answer your question, yes, we will be importing Jews. And if you think these containers will remind them of cattle cars, wait until they get to where we are going to send them." There was even more gruff male laughter; there was little love for the Jew among upper segments of Russian military and social strata.

Colonel General Bugyachev went on with his briefing on the overall plan for importing, or 'patriating' millions of Americans. "We cannot say that we are re-patriating them now, can we? Truthfully, this will be a massive project, something only Russia would or could consider: importing the cream of almost half a nation's population, changing their nationality, making them into different people, teaching them Russian, prohibiting the use of English as a language, and completely eradicating their original culture. It will be a generational project, but it will ensure the survival of Russia. It will be complex, it will be costly, it will be bloody, and therefore it will be a combined arms operation led by the Red Army. So let us look at how we will go about it." He turned to the massive map on the wall with his pointer.

"The project has distinct segments, each of which operates simultaneously." Bugyachev rattled each segment off, ticking his fingers. "There will be intelligence, then collection, then transportation, then transition, then implantation, and then assessment. We start with our intelligence assets. Periotkin, come, tell the group about this segment."

Colonel Periotkin arose and walked up to the podium. Periotkin was a short, stocky man with wiry black hair somewhat longer than regulations permitted, but as he was in intelligence, it was expected. He had small black eyes under thick, beetling brows. He was known in the service—behind his back—as 'the Troglodyte'. Periotkin knew his appearance did not convey the impression of intelligence, but he played on this, and more than one opponent found themselves either out of position bureaucratically with their careers in tatters or, in more cases than most would admit, kneeling on a concrete floor, held at the arms by two guards, looking dully at a drain, wondering when the bullet would come—and it always did.

"We make lists," Periotkin started, "this is the first step." He looked up, not smiling. The team knew what he meant; no one laughed. "We have lists now of people in America we are considering. These are lists of both specific individuals and categories of individuals. For categories, we are looking for the young, the hardy, those in good physical condition, women of childbearing age. We will collect those with hard skills—farmers, cooks, machinists, engineers, and successful businessmen, mostly entrepreneurs. Individually, as an example, we are going to want this man," and here Periotkin showed a picture of a man in his twenties, and named him, giving the man's address. "This individual is a student at Boston University; he is studying political economics. He is working two jobs now, and intends to obtain an internship with a computer software firm to develop programs that predict national economic indicators based upon certain factors. This is another ..." and Periotkin showed a picture of a young woman. "She is single mother; she is a doctor currently practicing in Rhode Island, specializing in gynecology; she makes approximately two hundred and forty thousand dollars a year. She carries almost three million dollars of malpractice insurance; she paid almost one hundred and fifty thousand dollars in taxes last year. She currently has two outstanding lawsuits against her practice. And this is not an uncommon situation with American physicians ... at least those remaining in private practice."

One of the construction team members spoke up. "Excuse me, Comrade Colonel, but why would we want a capitalist doctor, especially one who makes so much money, who is independently employed? And you mentioned you wanted mostly entrepreneurs, who are the tip of the capitalist iceberg. I don't understand."

Periotkin looked up from his notes and blinked once or twice. They could see he was contemplating how to answer the question. General Bugyachev, however, saved him the trouble.

"This is a good question, Comrade Shaskavilik, and one that I should perhaps have answered before now, because the answer means a great deal to our plans, and everyone here needs to understand this point before you go further into this program." Bugyachev gathered himself, and the team sensed that he was going to communicate something of importance.

"The history of Russia has taken many turns," he began slowly, measuring each word, "and since the advent of the Party, our nation has prospered. The Party has come to the conclusion that there must be no possibility that in another hundred years, we will find ourselves facing this particular demographic situation again." The men in the room looked at each other, wondering. They knew the problem Bugyachev was talking about; the demographic disaster that had Russia on schedule to essentially disappear as a nation in a hundred years. Russian women were just not having babies; they were in fact slaughtering most of them in the womb. "Yes, Perevedentsev was right, even though we had him put away. They are bringing him out, now, you know, by the way,"—this to surprised looks again, with one social scientist smiling and nodding, "and he will be worked into the team's efforts." Viktor Perevedentsev, a social scientist studying Russian population, had, many years ago, predicted that the collapse of Russian society, due to the collapse of the Russian population, was not reversible, and he had warned of the problem. "Yes, he got himself arrested for stirring up trouble, but he was correct, and now he is being recognized as being correct, and instead of sticking him in some Gulag, we are going to make him part of the solution." Bugyachev looked down at his hands for a moment. "I am telling you people now, things are changing. We are embarking on very different ground. Why pick this single woman doctor? Because she is intelligent, she can make her way in the world, she is of child-bearing age, and she has a child that we can use as leverage to ensure she has others. And she is a gynecologist—you realize that this will be a discipline we want to foster to avoid future demographic emergencies due to low birth rates, yes?" The group politely laughed.

"Seriously," Bugyachev went on, "contributing to this issue, this birth rate problem, is that more men than we would like to admit drink themselves stupid; and most Russian men—yes, most all of us, we are Russians—smoke themselves into early graves, and though we like to rake America over the fire for their rampant homosexual population, HIV and AIDS are killing more Russians than we could possibly imagine ... today, comrades, not in the future. *Today*. These are problems that are killing Russians and no, I do not care what the nationalists say, this is not the work of the State's enemies. It is time to face up to the fact that when a Russian man lifts a bottle of vodka to his mouth, no one is forcing his elbow to bend. We—and I mean we in this room—are going to build upon a foundation that insists upon personal responsibility.

"And what seriously pisses me off," Bugyachev went on, looking at each one of the group intensely, "is that wherever there are Muslims in Russia, population is growing. The Chechens, the Ingush, the Dagestanis ... they will breed Russians into oblivion if we do not act. So, we are going to act. We are going to forcibly import at least 14 million

Americans into Russia—that is the target figure. That is something like ten percent of what we have now, and something less than five percent of the American population. Now this is the number we want to survive, comrades, so to hit this figure, we will plan to bring in ... what is it, Ryaltkev?"

The social scientist didn't bat an eye, knowing the figure by heart. "Twenty million, comrade General."

"Twenty million, right. That's twenty million people relocated. It makes Hitler's relocation and 'adjustment' of six million Jews seem pretty easy, doesn't it? But then they were just Germans; we are Russians.

"And let us consider another issue. In another hundred years, we do not want to find ourselves saddled with fear that causes us to bury problems we know exist—yes, yes, I know, this is something no one mentions, but if we are going to undertake this massive project which, if successful, will create a foundation for a new and modernized Russia, then we must take the best from the lands and peoples we conquer, and beginning with this team, we must not be afraid to speak of problems or difficulties. God knows we have buried enough Russians who have tried to speak of troubles and problems."

"Where is Solzhenitsyn when you need him?" someone piped up from the back, and the crowd burst out laughing again.

"You laugh, but this is a key point." Bugyachev countered. "We kicked him out in 1974, didn't we? Yes, we did—the KGB booted him into West Germany and we stripped him of Russian citizenship. He went into the West, and while he lauded their freedoms, he raked them over the fire for their debauchery and softness, and *then* what did he do?"

"He came home!" shouted someone from the crowd.

"He came home! Correct!" Bugyachev replied, with a sweeping hand gesture, then pounding the podium. "We gave him back his citizenship and he came home. And what does that tell us? It tells us that as long as we have a country that will admit its mistakes, we will, we *must*, survive into the future. It is Periotkin's job, and the job of the social science team working with him, to ensure that the people we take in will be those most likely to succeed in the transition, with a nature that will in the future benefit our country, of a character that will, in their seed, strengthen Russia to endure an uncertain future. This is what the first segment of our project is—identifying who we take—and Periotkin has been working on this now for five years."

Some wit spoke out from the darkened auditorium. "*This* is why he looks like he is in his seventies, yes?" Everyone laughed, including Bugyachev, looking directly at the intelligence colonel. "They have you pegged, Periotkin." The Colonel shrugged, his thick eyebrows working, and said nothing.

"Okay. So intelligence is the first segment of the plan. This segment identifies *who* we select; the next segment is gathering them—collection. This is a combined arms operation, most definitely. It will be the task of Admiral Valyutczech. Karentin, come, explain this segment."

Valyutczech was taller than Periotkin, tall and thin and spare, with sharp features, reminding Sasha of a bird of prey; ice-blue eyes, and thinning white hair. His uniform seemed too large for him, a thin neck poking out of a starched collar. Yet his mind had earned him enormous respect throughout the Russian armed forces, vaulting him into the General Staff of the Armed Forces of the Russian Federation at a relatively young age, and Bugyachev leaned on this submariner to plan and execute the complex organizational structures required for the project.

"Collection will take place in what we expect to be a rapidly changing, fluid environment," the Admiral began, in a high, glassy voice. "First there will be chaos and confusion, resulting from internal discord and the disruption of the target's infrastructure and general society. This we can expect and plan for. Our forces need to be capable of moving through this type of environment successfully—this means logistics preparations must account for little or no local support. But after this initial confusion, our goal will be to establish order. Americans very much respect law and order—or at least, the safety it gives, and will be willing to give up almost anything, including their freedom, to obtain that safety. So we leverage this. We will establish what we will call 'spheres of security'—these will be areas in which our forces completely control all elements of society. There will be food, water, shelter, the severest penalties for crimes among the people, and we will make sure that the population in these spheres is secure. These spheres will be located around American cities, and we will not waste resources trying to collect people from the outlying areas. We will instead strike quickly to control the food supplies, without which the vast majority of Americans outside of these zones will simply starve. We will also quickly seize control of all electrical power and water distribution. We will also commandeer all medical treatment facilities—hospitals, clinics, and pharmaceutical distribution elements—inside these zones. With control of the food, water, electricity, and medical services, the people will do what we tell them to do. Those that don't live within our spheres of security, those living out in the rural and suburban areas, will sooner or later just die off. We do not anticipate expending military assets or personnel resources to deal with the population remnants outside of our security spheres. Sooner or later they will die, which will save us significant time, money, and effort." Valyutczech paused and took a sip of water. The man had a reputation in the services as a cold fish, utterly unemotional, and nothing Sasha was seeing during this briefing disabused him of that impression. Thin-lipped, with a fish-like pallor one could only obtain from years under the ocean in a submarine, the man looked like death warmed over. He continued.

"Colonel Periotkin, as has been noted, will provide our forces with a list of individuals, or categories of individuals, who will be collected. Those who are not on Periotkin's list, or who do not fit his categories, we shall refer to as 'unlisted'. Individual Americans who are unlisted will be considered enemies of the Russian people and dealt with accordingly."

Valyutczech nodded to the projectionist, who put up a picture of the eastern half of the United States. "Here you see our area of operations. Essentially forces from the Western Military District will be charged with the main portion of intelligence, control, and collection. Forces from the Central Military District will be responsible for transportation, transition, implantation, and assessment. We will now look at some of the responsibilities of the Western Military District in the areas of control and collection."

Valyutczech put up the next picture, producing a collective gasp from the assembled group. The figures he projected for manpower were staggering. "Numbers for personnel may be somewhat of a surprise to most, but we have been implementing plans to radically restructure the Kontraktniki[48] process, and we have been ... satisfied ... with

48 'Contract soldiers', in the past typically of lesser quality. During Valyutczech's organizational reforms, they became a much more effective and professional force. These contract soldiers were similar to Gaius Marius' legionnaires, whom he obtained when he offered the citizenship to any Roman who would volunteer to serve in the legions. Marius saved Rome by doing this, and Valyutczech made a similar offer,

the results. Additional personnel have been distributed throughout the motorized rifle divisions, tank corps, artillery and rocket brigades, air defense troops, the various special corps units[49] and logistical establishments. Some, however, have been sequestered for this project alone. Each of these areas has been significantly restructured and embellished. For example, when we first began to plan for this project, we had then almost twenty motorized rifle divisions. Now we have forty." Several officers in the crowd blinked; where were these extra motorized rifle divisions? Twenty divisions were difficult to hide. Valyutczech brushed past their concerns. "When we first considered this effort, we had, as many of you may know, three tank divisions, after disbanding the 2nd and 21st divisions. Well, we have ten now." This was too much of a surprise to go without comment.

A Major General Zemeski, commanding the project's ground forces, one of the heroes of Russia's conflict in Georgia, considered to be a natural combat leader, spoke up. "Excuse me, Comrade Admiral, but ... but *ten* tank divisions? With the greatest respect, may I ask where they are hiding?" Valyutczech, surprisingly, cast a quick glance at Periotkin, who imperceptibly furrowed his brows. Valyutczech looked at the General. "Well," he said, taking another sip of water as if for dramatic effect, "you can ask. At this point, however, you do not need to know."

Bugyachev stood up from his place in the front row and turned to face the tanker. "Artyom, no problem, you will be told everything in due time." The tank officer looked from Bugyachev to the Admiral, unfazed, with a hard, stony face. It was known that Major General Artyom Zemeski was one of the bravest men in the Russian Army, having once withstood five days of constant assault by almost three companies of Turkish infantry with just five tanks during the attack on Batumi International Airport. Personally wounded three times, the final assault had degenerated into hand-to-hand combat, and later there were almost two hundred dead Turks around his tank. No one doubted his skill as a combat commander, and it was a known fact throughout the service that his men loved him. Yet only two men in the entire Russian Army knew Zemeski was Jewish, and both were dead. According to Artyom Zemeski, *that* was definitely something no one else needed to know. He'd miraculously evaded the spotty genetic tests that were just now becoming mandatory for the lower ranks in the Russian Army.

"I tip my hat to you, Admiral," Zemeski said brusquely, "that you could produce, man, arm, and then hide seven tank divisions."

"It is a matter of planning and organization," the Admiral replied, ignoring Zemeski's compliment.

"It's a Russian talent," Bugyachev put in. "Remember Stalingrad? Zhukov and Vasilevsky did the same conjuring trick."[50] Bugyachev waved a hand. "Go on, Karentin."

"So it is with the other force structure elements—the strategic rocket forces, the air defense forces, and the rest. They have increased to the point at which we are now ready to execute the intelligence and collection segments of the project, awaiting

promising contract soldiers land in the conquered provinces...again, copying Marius' offer, probably hoping to save Russia. As has been said, there is nothing new under the sun.

49 These special corps included reconnaissance, signals, radio-electronic warfare, engineering, radiation, chemical and biological protection, technical support, automobile, and rear-area security forces.

50 General Bugyachev refers to Generals Zhukov and Vasilevsky marshaling forces north and south of Stalingrad so that, during Operation Uranus, they could surprise and cut off the German 6th Army with a double envelopment, similar to what Hannibal did to Gaius Terentius Varro and Lucius Aemilius Paulus at Cannae. Come to think of it, the German general commanding the Sixth Army at Stalingrad was also named Paulus.

permission from the General Staff and the appropriate Central Party authority.

"Within the security spheres, at locations determined during the initial establishment phase, we will create collection points, most of which will be near transportation hubs. We will use whatever we can—apartment buildings, housing developments, even stadiums. We will staff these with my officers and those from Colonel Periotkin's team. We will collect and filter the population, separate those who meet Colonel Periotkin's conditions from those who do not, and then put those who do on transports out of the area. Those who we have used to cause internal dissent: the blacks, the media jackjaws, the celebrities, the homosexuals that so impressed our good comrade, Major Sokolov," and here the group again laughed politely, "and all the useful idiots—these people will all be eliminated. Those who do not meet the requisite conditions will be considered useless to Russia, either in our homeland or in the conquered territories, and to ensure the future security of the project, will be eliminated."

Regardless of how anyone felt personally about the announcement that Russia would be responsible for the murder of perhaps 200 million people, no one in the team voiced any objections. So, it might be remembered, did things go in Germany as plans for the industrialization of murder that became known as the first holocaust were made at Wannsee Conference in January of 1942. Only the muscles in Artyom Zemeski's jaw tightened, and no one saw that.

Bugyachev and members of his team went on to describe the transportation and transition elements of the project, and then described how the immigrants would be implanted into Russian society. The plans called for first a period of isolation so as to enable the transplanted immigrants to learn Russian—a critical necessity, everyone felt, since language is an essential element of, almost a carrier of, a culture—and to ensure they were politically and socially adapted. Most of the transplanted immigrants would spend this transition time in the many camps that in the past had comprised the Gulag Archipelago, now all again brought back on line and refurbished, readied to accept new occupants. Assessment teams would make their way into the camps and then, based on their recommendations, immigrants would be farmed out little by little into selected segments of Russian society, with a priority to areas of the country that were suffering from low population numbers and low birth rates.

"The basic principle, gentlemen, is that we cannot make these people feel like prisoners ... I mean, of course, once they get over the initial shock of being transported. Shock, anxiety, and the confusion of dislocation—all this will be natural, but to be a success, we cannot import 14 million prisoners into our society. It would be like injecting ourselves with cancer cells. No, to succeed, we need to convince these people that their only hope for a future lies in a revitalized, invigorated, modern Russia; that their only possibility to survive lies with us, and to become willing partners in making Russia their new home. We have been utilizing the American media for quite some time now to help us in this, and there have been a number of our agents, some of whom have attained to very high office in that country, who also have helped condition the populace to accept our ... solution. But whenever you are going about your activities in this, whenever you make plans, whenever you must decide on an execution strategy, remember, our goal is to make these 'immigrants' proud of Russia, to make them desperate to survive, and to convince them that their only hope for a bright future lies with us. They must believe that there is no future in America—and that, comrades, will not be as hard as it sounds.

"Have you heard of the explorer, Cortez? When he arrived on the shores of the Yucatan peninsula with 500 soldiers and 100 sailors, seeking to plunder the Aztecs, do you know what he did? Yes, many of you do. He burned his boats. There was nowhere else for his people to go then, so they worked with complete dedication to steal what they could from the natives, like the good capitalists that they were." The group of men dutifully chuckled. Bugyachev went on.

"So we too will burn their boats; we will burn their country down around their ears, and there will be nowhere else for them to go ... except to Russia ... with us."

At the completion of the meeting on Great Lyachovsky Island, and as this was the last meeting on the team's tour of Russian arctic facilities, Bugyachev tasked Sasha with drafting the final report of the team's reconnaissance, which took the form of a protocol. While Sasha drafted the document, the other team members went off to inspect the airfield and port facilities.

***

On the day Major Sokolov drafted the minutes that would become known in history as the Great Lyachovsky Protocol, seven thousand kilometers away in America, a demonically-possessed young man took two automatic pistols into an elementary school in New England and shot 25 children between the ages of five and ten years old. In a desolate farmhouse in Vermont, a serial killer, raised in a home whose parents adhered to the Christian Identity philosophy, which taught that Blacks and Jews were not really human beings, murdered his 35th victim. In San Francisco, the city council voted to permit nudity on the streets without any restrictions. In Chicago, a substitute teacher was dismissed for quoting a passage from the Bible to a student while at school. In Florida, a 51-year old transgender person made sports history as the first person to play college basketball as both a man and a woman. In Michigan, after the passage of a law giving workers the freedom to work without belonging to a union, union enforcers murdered the Governor's daughter as she played in a school soccer game. And in Washington DC, America's first gay president unilaterally ordered the routing of shoulder-fired anti-air missiles, artillery, and armored vehicles to Islamic rebels fronting for a coalition of ten Arabic nations bent on the destruction of Israel. After this order, he chaired a secret meeting that same day with top representatives from Russia, Syria, and Saudi Arabia. The meeting's objective was to plan for the orderly distribution of what Israeli population might remain after the invasion and destruction of the Hebrew nation.

***

Writing in a sequestered room on a laptop specifically set aside for top secret material and drawing heavily from published material supplied to him by Admiral Valyutczech, Colonel Periotkin, and General Bugyachev, Sokolov produced a report remarkably similar to a previous document generated at a meeting of highly-placed state bureaucrats who, in 1942, had also gathered together to plan the elimination of an entire people. Colonel General Bugyachev's remarks about the Jews chilled him, recalling what Ironbridge had said to him in the parking lot in Granite Sky.

So that such things will not be forgotten, we pause this narrative and reproduce the Great Lyachovsky Island Protocol that Major Sokolov drafted, taken from one of history's darkest pages, yet which in its uncanny resemblance to the Wannsee Protocol drafted in 1942, demonstrates the meticulous nature of the Great King's justice.

CLASSIFICATION: Top Secret

Distribution: As Specified/Controlled/non-electronic

Minutes of Discussion:

I. The following persons took part in the discussion about the final solution of the American and Jewish questions pursuant to support for the Russian Resurgence and Reclamation Project (R3P). The discussion took place in Great Lyachovsky Island on [date occluded].

Colonel General Fyodor Bugyachev – Commanding General, R3P
Admiral Karentin Valyutczech – R3P Plans and Operations
Lieutenant General Vitaly Borodin – Deputy R3P Plans and Operations
Vice Admiral Umytr Pelyusha – Director, R3P Logistics
Lieutenant General Pyotr Russilenko – Director, R3P Strategic Rocket Forces
Lieutenant General Saki Palentov – Commander, Western Military District
Lieutenant General Mikhail Selentovrya – Commander, Central Military District
Major General Zubrov Ducheskirova – Commander, Security Police Forces, Western Military District
Major General Mikhail Arenskiya – Commander, R3P Aviation
Major General Artyom Zemeski – Commander, R3P Ground Forces
Colonel Anatoly Periotkin – Intelligence
Colonel Yvgeny Makasy – Chief Administrator, Corrective Labour Camps
Colonel Illytch Ustinovich – Deputy Chief Administrator, Corrective Labour Camps, Arctic Region
Colonel Rastov Marichulski – Deputy Chief Administrator, Corrective Labour Camps, Siberian Region
Sergey Chiliskovich – Second Secretary, Russian Foreign Ministry
Colonel Alexi Badenova – Secretary, Central Transportation District
Sergei Lichinov – Deputy Secretary, Central Transportation District
Colonel Boris Traducholivitch – Director, R3P Construction

Dr. Lars Shaskavilik – Director, R3P Social Sciences
Dr. Fyodor Ryaltkev – Deputy Director, R3P Social Sciences
Dr. Tomar Tumaschevsky – Director, R3P Climatology and Geological Sciences
Dr. Seln Aronsk – Deputy Director, R3P Climatology and Geological Sciences

II. At the beginning of the discussion, Colonel General Bugyachev of the General Staff of the Armed Forces of the Russian Federation (hereafter, 'General Staff') established the team's mission, which was to establish appropriate protocols, procedures, policies, and regulations for the final solution of the American and Jewish questions in North America, and pointed out that this meeting had been convened for the purpose of clarifying fundamental questions. The wish of the Supreme Commander in Chief of the Russian Federation is to have a draft sent to him concerning organizational, factual, and material interests in relation to the final solution of the American question in North America. This requirement makes necessary an initial common action of all central offices immediately concerned with these questions in order to align their general activities under the authority of the General Staff. This report is intended to establish the prerequisites for that alignment.

A. The General Staff has been entrusted with the official central handling of the final solution of the American and Jewish questions without regard to geographic borders. The commander of all security forces in the Western Military District gave a short report of the main security objectives to be obtained upon control being established over American territories:

> *a) The detachment of American influence from every mechanism of information distribution—television, radio, Internet, newspapers, or other publications.*
>
> *b) The elimination of unlisted Americans from the living space in North America.*
>
> *c) The orderly and secure transport of listed individuals to distribution centers and thence to Transition and Resettlement Areas (TARAs)*
>
> *d) THE COMPLETE ELIMINATION OF ALL JEWS IN AMERICA, WITHOUT REGARD TO STATUS OR OCCUPATION. All Americans will be given an immediate scan using*

the Sorchesky Scanner[51] *to determine ethnic origin.*

By order of the Supreme Commander in Chief of the Russian Federation, an office to oversee and execute the R3P was set up on [date occluded]. The Commanding General of the General Staff was entrusted with the project's organization and execution. The project's main objectives are:

a) To make all necessary arrangements for the preparation of increased emigration of listed Americans into Russia;

b) To make all necessary arrangements for the elimination of unlisted Americans;

c) To direct and expedite the flow of emigration of listed Americans in each individual case out of North America;

d) To rapidly establish massive numbers of Russian citizens in the conquered territories of North America, in both geographic and societal positions of influence and/or leverage, behind and directing a 'shadow' government staffed with American puppets.

The aim of this effort will be to cleanse North American living space of Americans in a legal manner acceptable to the jurisdictional entities comprising extant World Courts.

All offices realized the inadvisability of importing unlisted Americans due to the particularly noxious yet contagious and virulent American culture. Drawbacks to permitting unlisted Americans to coexist in North America have compelled the General Staff to make plans for their final elimination.

The work concerned with emigration of listed Americans will be not only a Russian problem, but also a problem which the authorities of the countries through which the flow of emigrants will be directed would have to address. Internal opposition from the American military or paramilitary forces prevalent within America, demands by various foreign governments (specifically the Canadian government) for increasing sums of money for

51 This was a technology developed late in the final century of the Age of Man that permitted an instant determination of an individual's ethnic origins. Jews would no longer be able to pass for other ethnicities in this time.

costs of transportation through their northern provinces[52], *the lack of shipping space, austere or hostile living conditions during transport, and severely limited medical care, are expected to increase to an extraordinary degree the difficulties of emigration.*

The Americans themselves, or their coopted American liberal political organizations, will finance the emigration. In order to finance the infrastructure to eliminate unlisted Americans, the principle will be established that wealthy listed Americans, prior to their transport, will have their assets confiscated so as to finance the elimination of unlisted Americans. This will be effected by imposing an 'emigration tax' upon Americans, ostensibly to cover their emigration costs, yet the funds will instead be funneled to handle the costs of unlisted eliminations.

Anticipating these and other additional infrastructure costs, further confiscation of assets will be performed prior to the execution of the plan via American political agents we have in place, and, after the execution of the plan, wherever Russian authority is established and such financial measures may be required to effect ad hoc infrastructure creation or support. Measures have been put in place with cooperating members of American political leadership prior to this discussion for laws to be established that will make confiscation of personal assets or property an accepted form of social adjustment during turbulent economic times. To date, American contributions toward this project via cooperating American leadership sources—especially American law enforcement—have totaled slightly more than $9.5 trillion.

Plans in the R3P project are included to ensure that any functioning infrastructure element within the conquered areas pay a fee to the Russian government for their continued operation. Air carriers, individuals operating their personally-owned automobiles, passengers on busses and trains, will all pay a use fee to the Russian government. Any business that wishes to continue to operate in our Protectorate will pay a tax. Any communication or media company wishing to remain in business will pay a use tax to the Russian government. Americans will pay significantly less personal tax than they have been paying—our plan is to implement a flat 13% tax rate on all individuals—but they will pay it to the Russian government, not the American IRS.

52 The Russian General Staff expected (rightly, as it turned out) that Canada would cooperate fully with the Russians transporting captured Americans through their northern provinces, over the North Pole, and into Russia. The General Staff also anticipated (again, rightly) that the Canadians would charge for the service.

Until such time as the R3P commences, normal tourism and travel of Americans in Russia will be permitted to continue. After commencement, emigration of Americans to Russia will no longer be permitted, and Americans in Russia at the time of commencement will be transported to termination facilities and eliminated as enemies of the Russian people, unless they meet the qualifications of one or more of a number of 'listed' categories.

III. There are significant numbers of Jews in America. Regardless of what is promulgated for public dissemination, it is the desire of the Supreme Commander in Chief of the Russian Federation that those of Jewish blood be first identified, then isolated, and then eliminated[53]*. There will be no recurrence of the botched efforts made by Germany during the Second World War. Russia will complete what Hitler started regarding the Jews. However, it is of supreme importance that nothing of this initiative be publicized so as to avoid needless opposition as various public information outlets may liken this effort to the previous holocaust, and so generate misguided sentimentalist-based opposition. Consequently, all initiatives will be directed, structured, and conducted as though the objective was to isolate Jews for their own protection, and then place them into secure, sequestered locations. Jews have it in their blood to peacefully submit to authority—they would tie the hangman's noose for the hangman assigned to hang them if they thought it would buy them a reprieve—and therefore this sequestration must occur with both great dispatch and very visible authority. American officials in league with current Russian initiatives have already identified, with appropriate location data, millions of American Jews. All Russian forces in North America will be provided with locations of Jews in their sectors and will be required to identify and procure these individuals for transportation.*

The Germans only thought they were the Master Race. Russians know the truth.

There are currently approximately 6.6 million Jews in America, distributed through each state according to data provided in an appendix to this report (see Appendix A). In the past effort, Germany depended upon personal administrative records—all on paper. Not so now. Technology can now be employed that will make it easy to rapidly and instantly identify any Jew. According to Admiral Valyutczech, every effort will be made to eliminate

53 Here Sokolov noted the difference between what General Bugyachev had promulgated verbally during their meetings, and what he had provided in document form to make up the report. Such dichotomy did not unduly bother Sokolov, as he was quite well accustomed to duplicity within Russian political and military discourse.

100% of Jews in America. The number of Jews noted in this report includes those who adhere to the Jewish faith, who have converted to the Jewish faith, or who have Jewish grandparents (either side).

Handling the Jewish collection problem in individual states may meet with differing degrees of difficulty due to the attitude and outlook toward Jews that may exist in a particular state or location. Fortunately plans are being made that will cause massive dissatisfaction and opprobrium to adhere to American Jews in the same fashion that such emotions were attached to Japanese Americans immediately after the attack on Pearl Harbor.

Under proper guidance, in the course of the final solution the Jews are to be allocated for appropriate labor in the Arctic Construction Zone. Jews, separated according to sex, will be taken in large work columns to these areas, ostensibly to work on the trans-polar route. Once emplaced in transportation (air or ground vehicles), they will be transported to specific locations in the Arctic zone, deposited, and left to die. There will be no food, no water, no shelter, and no means of life support. There will be no need for guns, gas, or incinerators. They will all just freeze and die.

In the course of the practical execution of the final solution to the American problem, the continent will be combed through from west to east for Jews. America proper, including Alaska and Hawaii, will have to be handled first due to the housing problem and additional social and political necessities. Afterward, we will collect and transport Jews from Mexico and Canada. We expect those two nations to easily surrender what Jews they have in residence.

Along with listed Americans, evacuated Jews will first be sent, group by group, to so-called transit locations, from which they will be transported to alleged 'relocation / transition' settlements in the Arctic zone.

The beginning of the individual larger transportation actions will largely depend on military developments in particular locations throughout America proper. Regarding the handling of the final solution in those states occupied and influenced by Russian forces, it was proposed that the appropriate expert of the General Staff discuss the matter with the responsible official of the Russian Security Police.

In many northeastern states in America, the matter is no longer so difficult, since the most substantial problems in this respect have already been brought near a solution. In each American state, the provisional U.S. government will be directed to appoint a commissioner for Jewish affairs.

With regard to taking up preparations for dealing with the problem in Canada, Admiral Valyutczech considers it opportune to contact the chief of law enforcement in that Government with a view to these problems.

In occupied and unoccupied states or territories in America, Canada, or Mexico that may be Catholic, the registration of Jews for transportation will in all probability proceed without great difficulty as it will be arranged for the Holy Father to issue an edict clarifying that Jews are to be held in "Final and Infernal Opprobrium" by all true Catholics, and condemning any Catholic who opposes these measures.

Representatives from State Security who have had agents working in America called attention in this matter to the fact that in some states, such as those with a large percentage of fundamentalist Christians, opposition may arise. Expectations are, however, that such opposition will be minimal, as most fundamental Christian sects have already been coopted.

IV. In the course of the final solution plans, the Nuremberg Laws from past history should provide a certain foundation, in which a prerequisite for the absolute solution of the problem is also the solution to the problem of mixed marriages and persons of mixed blood.

Unlike the extensive regulations and policies attendant to mixed racial marriages or social contracts applied during the first aborted effort, DNA testing via the Sorchesky Scanner will reveal anyone possessing even the slightest tinge of Jewish ancestry. Anyone with Jewish ancestry will be eliminated—no exceptions. Should there be situations where a Jew is married to a non-Jew, the non-Jew may be offered the option of either dissolving the marriage or accompanying the partner during transport to their terminal destination.

With regard to the issue of those Jews working with our agents to support the R3P on the economy, Sergey Chiliskovich,

Second Secretary to the Russian Foreign Ministry, stated that Jews working in areas vital to the R3P effort, provided that no replacements are available, will not at first be transported. They will instead be told that due to their 'cooperation', they will not be handled as other Jews. This fiction will be maintained until such time as their usefulness to their portions of the R3P is concluded, at which time they will be transported and terminated.

Colonel Alexi Badenova, Secretary for the Central Transportation District, and Lieutenant General Mikhail Selentovrya, Commander of the Central Military District, jointly stated that the Central District would welcome it if the final solution of this problem could be started as close to the Protectorate's Central District boundaries as possible, since transportation will be a significant part of the R3P and it must be handled successfully from the first. Jews must be transported out of America as quickly as possible, since it is especially here that the Jew as a significant social destabilization force represents an extreme danger, and as well, the Jew is causing permanent chaos in the economic structure of America through continued behind-the-scenes control of most of the U.S. economy. Moreover, of the approximately 6.6 million Jews concerned, the majority are unfit for hard physical labor. Therefore it must be understood by both main parties (i.e. China and Russia) that holding facilities for Jews prior to transport must be located within the Joint Protectorate Area.

Admiral Valyutczech stated that the solution to the Jewish question in the overall structure of the R3P is essential to consider the project successful. Pursuant to this success, the Admiral revealed during discussions that there will be special units assigned particularly to the identification, collection, and transportation of Jews in America. These units would be charged with the full responsibility—and given commensurate authority and carry therefore the accountability—to comprehensively complete the final solution to the Jewish issue in America as quickly as possible. Most of these special units will be comprised of Muslim personnel, but in all cases commanded by Russian officers.

In conclusion the overall structure of the R3P was summarized, during which discussion both Colonel General Bugyachev and the Second Secretary from the Russian Foreign Ministry mentioned that certain preparatory activities for the final solution addressing Jews in America were already underway and results would be forthcoming—some very publicly. They stressed that these preparatory activities have been planned so as to minimize alarming the non-Jewish population.

The meeting was closed with the statement by Colonel General Bugyachev that the R3P was "perhaps the greatest initiative ever undertaken by Russia, or Russians, and if successful would most certainly put a 'stake in the ground' from which future Russian history would be measured and to which "all future generations of mankind would look with gratefulness to Russia for solving the historically irritating and dangerous problem of mankind's cancerous Hebrew race."

As Sasha finished the report, the memory of the warning he'd been given back in America again came to his mind—the warning about lifting his hand against the Jews. Ironbridge had said that things would go as they would go, that his senior officers would do what they were going to do, but he himself had been warned not to harm even one Jew. At the time, he hadn't believed what Ironbridge had been saying. But now, reading the report, noting the animosity the Russian General Staff had for the Jews, he was struck again with that same frisson of feeling he'd experienced talking with Ironbridge in the parking lot—a sense of the numinous.

He got up from his desk, closed the computer, turned off the light, and went to find something to eat. He would not sleep well that night.

END

Volume One – Book One

Biographies of Contributors to the Aeon Regis Historical Series

In this first century of the Age of the King, we are discovering that time is flexible. The King has enabled the Contributors to this historical series to reach back into time itself and view events as they occurred. This explains why there is a need for more than one perspective, for each contributor views their surroundings through not only their eyes but as well through a filter constructed of years of experience, emotions, knowledge, wisdom, and passions. The King could simply have provided a visual documentary of the times so that people in His Kingdom would know what happened, but the events only truly take on meaning when viewed through the eyes and hearts of others, and for this one needs words. A simple visual recounting would be gruel without garum[54].

Some Contributors died in conflict, some died in their beds, and some were taken up. All fought, and were fought; loved, and were loved; conquered, but were never conquered.

The Pastor: Daniel Steiner (1985-2017) was born in Grass Valley, California. After a misspent youth roaming the streets of Sacramento, Steiner submitted to the King at the age of 24. He studied to become a pastor in a non-denominational segment of the organized church of the day. He was for his entire life the pastor of a small church in Grass Valley, faithfully representing the King. He was a prolific writer, contributing articles and commentary to numerous publications, stridently opposing the merging of New Age philosophies and perspectives into the church. He opposed the Emergent Church movement, the "Purpose Driven Life" movement, and the various aberrations that sprang from the Latter Rain deceptions, such as Dominion Theology, the Manifest Sons of God, the Move, and the various health and prosperity perversions. Using the Internet, he published a number of newsletters and informational messages encouraging the faithful to resist these deceptions, He continued to preach against the false church up to the day he was killed. Members of the "church militant and triumphant" put him to death in Grass Valley, California. The theme of Steiner's work: *How the church was deceived.*

The Prophet: Arthur Kohn (1929-2007) was born in New York City.

54 Garum was a fermented fish sauce much prized by we Romans.

An angry, arrogant, highly intelligent, extremely abrasive intellectual, he was brought to his knees before He Who is the Spirit of Prophecy while on sabbatical in Europe during his 34th year. Intense and passionate in his devotion to the cause of the Messiah, he brought an extremely unpopular message that opposed prevalent doctrines of his time (Replacement Theology, Christian anti-Judaism, and a bankrupt, insincere, emotion-based form of worship originating in many Pentecostal and Charismatic denominations). He infuriated Jews by his message that the Holocaust was an act of judgment by God upon the Jewish people for their utter failure to recognize the time of their visitation; an act of judgment that was intended to awaken the Jews so as to avoid an even greater coming persecution. He taught throughout his life that the Jews would suffer during a time *after* their gathering back to the land in 1948, suffering beyond anything experienced in the Holocaust, that the gathering in 1948 was only so that God would get them in one place for nations to smite them again, putting them into the smelter prophesied by Ezekiel, only to be cast out again from Israel. In this last Diaspora, the nation would be crushed, and the exiles 'sifted through all the nations'[55], until only a remnant would be returned to the land, land that God would miraculously restore from its devastated condition. Kohn's prophetic message was that those known as Christians—whom Kohn referred to as 'true Jews'—would be called to provide a place of sanctuary and refuge for the ethnic Jews as they were globally persecuted, and in that place of refuge, show the Jew the love of Jesus so that Jews would become jealous. Kohn died in his sleep in 2007. The theme of Kohn's historical work: *How the Jews would face history's most intense persecution, the remnant seeing His face in the wilderness, and ultimately how they will bless the nations in the future.*

The Physician: Martin Svenson (1955-2015) was born in Fortitude, Wisconsin. He obtained his medical education in the United States military and went thence into private practice. After a failed marriage, he submitted to the Great Healer in his 28th year. He offered his talents as an obstetrician and gynecologist, specializing in maternity care. He suffered numerous crises of conscious as hospitals in America began to require abortions to be performed by staff physicians. He refused and lost position and status in the medical profession. He and his family moved to Chicago, where he found work in the emergency room of Cook County Hospital in the city of Chicago. He and his wife were killed by looters during the social instability that swept the United States in this time period. The theme of Svenson's work: *How men became animals.*

---

55 Author's note: I spoke with the prophet Amos about Kohn's interpretation of his book in preparation for writing this history. The shepherd prophet was not surprised so few had correctly grasped his meaning and intention, but was pleased that the King had graciously allowed someone possessing a monumental degree of persistence, stubbornness, and confidence to correctly interpret his message for the day in which his prophecy met its fulfillment. Those qualities of stubbornness and persistence were necessary to press home Amos' message to an unbelieving generation.

The Stonemason: Gruener Koenig (1870-1936) was born in Bavaria. A German Jew, Koenig became a master stonemason. Koenig fell upon a stone not cut by human hands and was broken to pieces in his 37th year and became what would come to be known as a Messianic Jew. He was the original stonemason contracted to build the Haus Wachenfeld in the Bavarian Alps in 1916. Called to renovate the home in 1935, he worked for a year improving the stonework. The supervising principality over that portion of Europe at the time had Koenig shot after he re-pointed the last stone. Koenig would fearlessly influence everyone with whom he came in contact on behalf of the King, even during that time of intense darkness in Germany. The principality had made significant investment in the new owner of Haus Wachenfeld (one Adolph Hitler) and wanted not even the tiniest whisper of Truth to interfere with the work being performed then in that dark and twisted human soul. The theme of Koenig's historical perspective: *How those people groups to be destroyed by the demonic 'world spirit' were first dehumanized prior to their destruction.*

The Artist: Ariella Yussefdotter (1990-...) was born in Haifa, Israel. Her early years were marked by a shallow, selfish, self-centeredness until a car accident confined her to a wheel chair for the rest of her life. She surrendered to He who is Beauty and Truth in her 28th year. Her character was deepened to such a degree that she produced some of the finest music the world has ever known. Her operatic suite depicting the ages of man, the love of God, and the intense heart of the Son have been assessed to be as complex as Mozart, more passionate than Beethoven, and as moving as Bach. In that time when no man could work, her music was banned. She took refuge in the American wilderness until she was taken up. The theme of Yussefdotter's history: *How beauty and truth died in the souls of men, choked by shallow character and callow selfish interest.*

The Engineer: Lucius Trennari Puentas (2BC-65 AD) was born in Rome and trained in the Roman army as an engineer specializing in the construction of aqueducts. Watching the early Christian martyrs die, he was so impressed that he sought—secretly—to discover more about the new sect. He submitted to the Ancient of Days in his 40th year and was martyred by Nero after the great Roman fire[56]. Puentas' historical theme: *How order fled from the world.*

The Olive Grower: Giuseppe Garratuzzo (1920-2018) was born in Reggio Calabria to Italian peasants. He became the Mediterranean's largest exporter of olive oil. He surrendered to the Root of Jesse in his 67th year, after reading a letter from his granddaughter. His life thereafter was marked by

56 Author's note: I knew and served with Lucius for many years. He was an exceptional engineer who supervised the construction of many aqueducts and other edifices Rome built in Spain, Gallia Comata, and Iudaea (Judea). In his 40th year he came to me in camp one evening outside of Iudaea. I spoke to him of my newfound faith in the Jewish Messiah. He left my tent deep in thought, and later gave his life to the service of the King. That decision eventually brought about his death, and afterward his life.

self-sacrifice, a mastery of the written Word, and a call to feed the poor. When the government of the time imposed controls on the world's food supply, he organized and led an underground resistance movement to bypass these restrictions and feed the hungry. He was arrested and martyred in 2018. The theme of Garratuzzo's work: *How the world's markets were put under the control of the evil one, whereby no man could buy or sell but that they had his mark.*

The Shepherd: Argus Weal (1824-1905) was a shepherd in Scotland, as was his father, and his father's father. He came to the true Shepherd in his 16th year. After trying his hand at preaching, he instead found his calling in writing, and when not working with his own (real) sheep, he wrote to encourage God's flock. Violently opposed to the unthinking Calvinism of his day, his message was that true children of the King will be marked by obedience; obedience and a deep, heartfelt love for God as opposed to a stale, dry, religious obligation or duty. He died in 1905, surrounded by his ten children and numerous grandchildren. The theme of Weal's historical perspective: *How the message of obedience to God was first diffused and then discarded in favor of individualism and a distributed "Christ-consciousness".*

The Fisherman: Lars Rorvaldson (1978-...) was born in the port city of Narvik, Norway. He came to the great Catcher of Souls in his 18th year among a hard-working community of Norwegian fisherman. When the Final Sifting came, he organized a network of sanctuaries and, using his fleet of three small fishing boats, lifted Jews from the coasts of England, the Netherlands, and Denmark and sequestered them in the mountains and forests of Norway. His network was one of the few to successfully survive the numerous assaults and attempts at infiltration perpetrated by the enemy during this time. Rorvaldson was taken up. The theme of his work: *How the global government pursued the Jews, and how the Jews became envious of true believers' faith in the wilderness.*

The Horse: Afanasy[57] (2020 -...), a Shire, was foaled on the Ironbridge's farm, and selected by the King in his fourth year to perform a number of services on His behalf, most notably pulling wagonloads of Jews to safety while running from the killing squads tasked with assassinating Jews in America during the Sino-Russian invasion of that country. He has in this first century of the new millennium been assigned as Steward of the great grassland plains of

57 It was a surprise to some upon their resurrection to find that animals have souls. The kingdom of beasts moved within a parallel but slightly different spiritual framework during the Age of Men, yet they did (and do) have souls. In the Age of the King, both beasts and men have been enabled in the King's spiritual frame of reference, and we are now able to freely communicate. One of the most important of the domesticated beast species (the other being the dog) used by God as symbology reflecting parallels with certain spirit realms, horses were renowned in the Age of Men for their ability to reflect the King's attributes of patience, deliberation, fortitude, endurance, inspiration, grace, dignity, majesty, and power, and the need for relationship before any useful work can be accomplished.

what was once northwest Russia. The theme of his perspective: *How believers learned patience, trust, forbearance, and fortitude.*

The Lion: Adili[58] (1985-2020) was born in the Sudanese veldt and became the king-lion of a small pride. The King asked him, and Adili agreed, to defend a village of Sudanese from an assault by Islamic troops bent upon genocide during the closing days of the end of the Age of Man. The troops themselves were driven by the principality ruling Northern Africa at the time. Adili and his pride kept the village safe for eight months. News of this miracle only reached the world after Northern Sudanese troops, supplemented by numbers of additional demonic entities, overwhelmed and slaughtered the pride and then decimated the village. A human survivor escaped and related the amazing story of a pride of lions that defended her village. The villagers considered the prowling cordon of defending lions to be a miracle of deliverance sent from the King, and there were many in that place who surrendered to the King because of this miracle. Adili is now the Steward of the great western veldt in Africa. The theme of Adili's contribution to this history: *How the beasts divided; some to defend righteousness, most to enlist on the side of evil to assault men.*

The Warrior Poet: Sartorius Crux Vita (0 BC-62 AD) was born in Moggio-Udenese, in the northern Italian Alps. He joined the legion in his 19th year as a rank and file soldier. He was promoted to Centurion in his 32nd year and stationed in the Roman province of Iudaea (Judea), with the *Cohors Secunda Italica Civium Romanorum* (the second Italian civic cohort from Rome). He was the Centurion who supervised the crucifixion of the King's Son. It was he who proclaimed that which was recorded in the Written Word: *"Truly this was the Son of God!"* After the crucifixion, he was sent to Rome to report on the event to several high-ranking Roman officials. These officials made no record of the Centurion's remarks, but judged that his experience had so changed him that it was necessary to remove him from his unit. He was assigned to the XII Legion and perished in the Battle of Rhandeia from a spear in the side wielded by a scabrous and monstrously ugly Parthian warrior mounted on an equally monstrous but quite regal bay charger—poetic justice for the warrior poet who himself had pierced the side of the King's son with his own spear. The theme of his contribution to this history:*How America met its end while the church lost its savor and was trampled underfoot in a time when understanding and discernment was dependent only upon faithfulness.*

58 Adili is Swahili for 'good or just'; 'honorable conduct'; 'righteous'.

Notes on the Protocols

The captured Protocols documented in this history come from a time just prior to the downfall of the world's most powerful nation in that day, America. I have not used the Adversary's own time references, as they cannot be relied upon; truth was never a staple in their realms. Prefacing each Protocol, I provide a brief introduction which confers upon the reader some level of background and context regarding the contents of the document.

***

From a warrior's perspective, I can confirm that a strategy of deceiving one's opponent as to one's true location, true scope, or true magnitude of power and resources, or best, as to one's very existence, is remarkably effective. I know, because we spoke of it many times over campfires, in the tents, and during training, of how Hannibal deceived Paulus and Varro at Cannae with the new tactic of envelopment which the overly proud, overly confident Roman consuls never considered. We know that Scipio Africanus' campaigns in Spain indirectly threatened Carthage, conducting surprise attacks on Carthage's armies, their bases, and their supply lines, and these efforts—unexpected as they were by Hannibal—were instrumental in the destruction of Carthage. Most people spoke about Caesar's foolishness in crossing the Rubicon with only one of his nine legions—the others were still in Gaul at the time—but they do not realize the power that comes from assaulting one's enemy rapidly, with forces that enemy does not think exist. Opposing Caesar were Pompey's ten legions in Rome, the seven in Italy, and a number of detachments throughout the countryside. But Caesar knew Pompey's mind—much as the adversary knew men's minds—and Caesar recognized that surprise and speed provided his greatest leverage. Wherever Caesar went after Pompey directly, he lost, for Pompey outnumbered his forces. When Caesar went after Pompey using an indirect strategy of deception or surprise, he won. Just so do we see the enemy of mankind, who was most certainly outnumbered by the King's forces, typically apply an indirect approach to their assaults, and sadly he was dramatically successful. The pattern repeats itself throughout mankind's history—in the Byzantine wars, medieval wars, the wars of Napoleon, the American Civil War, the European conflicts, and the conflict upon which this history focuses, which wrought America's downfall. The story is the same: surprise brought about by a preliminary period of deception, whether strategic or tactical, utilizing time-tested stratagems, typically results in a dislocation of the opponent's psychological and moral stability, and is prelude to the opponent's collapse.

I have included several captured sections, or *Protocols*, as the adversary referred to them, to provide the reader with a clear idea of how the principalities employed their strategies of deception and surprise so as to dislocate mankind's psychological and moral stability—particularly in the case of American psychological and moral stability—so as to effect the overthrow of the American nation by their own forces.

As a point of understanding, in our use of the word 'Powers', we mean to refer to demonic entities specifically imbued with authority to rule within or over a given geographical areas, termed a 'Principality'. The term 'Principality' may also refer to demonic authorities that were ranged within various hierarchical structures, similar to bureaucracies; the reader will be asked to determine the specific meaning by referencing the context. Powers trace their ascension from that time when the Adversary—known otherwise as Satan, their god and Man's nemesis—obtained his temporary deed to the earth and the control thereof, at the fall of Man in the Garden. Yet they operated in the realm of the spirit, and therefore were required to operate upon men through some physical means, and thereby were compelled to deceive men to do their bidding so as to affect events in the physical realm. And truly we have in this present Age come to realize that impacting nature was not their ultimate purpose; no, rather it was the destruction of mankind itself. Each principality referred to men using a different term based upon their perceptions and objectives. For example, the Zhongguo Principality referred to men as 'stones'[59], for they hated those whom the King loved. They could only achieve their objectives, however, by compelling flesh to do their will, for except in uncommon situations, only the natural was able to affect nature—only by flesh, or tooth, or claw, or by the hand of man could men be killed.[60]

From whence, therefore, came their power? In one of the greatest ironies, one of the greatest paradoxes still remaining, we have discovered that it was simply through men themselves, through each individual's spirit. Where men's spirits were directed toward truth and righteousness and justice and beauty and love, these powers or principalities withered like an unwatered, untended grape vine planted in a desert. Yet where men thought of power, or lusted, or hated, or murdered, or thought of ways to triumph over one another, to conquer one another, to defraud or cheat or bully or belittle one another, there it was that these entities would grow in strength and skill and power, and it was within such spiritual soil that they would obtain open access to controlling or compelling men given into their hands.

We can see, therefore, why such massive opposition throughout the Age of Man was thrown up against any theme, against any philosophy, any system or methodology that elevated truth, beauty, righteousness, peace, or love. We know too how much dark and evil power was arrayed against the King's Son when He came to sacrifice Himself for us, for it was this act which opened the floodgates to mankind, enabling every man to discern the truth of the world in which they lived. The Adversary came against this one supreme act of self-sacrifice with all the power he possessed. I know this experientially; I was there, at the foot of that very cross, and I can testify to the level of dark, intense spiritual influence, the hatred that compelled normally reticent,

59 We suspect, but do not know, that this term was a reference to the elements used in the game of Weiqi.

60 It is an interesting spiritual duality that the Adversary typically attempted to use flesh to kill flesh to produce death, while the King typically employed the Spirit to kill the flesh to produce life.

quiet, peace-loving passers-by to suddenly become enraged and to spit, to curse, to hurl insults at Him as He hung there. I know myself the anger, the dispassionate, illogical hatred, and the disdain that washed over me at the time, as my soldiers were called away from more productive duties and tasked to hammer in the nails, erect the crosses, and preside over the execution of common criminals. I can as I write these words still recall that overpowering stench, for there was a smell in the air then, too, though few speak of it. A smell of offal, of rottenness seemed to waft through the air on tendrils unseen, as though someone had slaughtered a dozen animals and left them in the heat to rot for weeks.

Every effort was made by these powers and principalities in the spiritual realm, and much in the physical realm, therefore, against a human being coming to understand the true nature of the world in which they lived. The powers and principalities would make enormous efforts to keep mankind unaware of their presence, and would only permit men to know of their existence when such men were too far established within their camp to resist.

In this effort they were greatly assisted by the churches themselves, whose various doctrines and rules were structured so as to create a thousand different ways for human beings to avoid the Cross—to avoid crucifying their own natures. To avoid the Cross they built all manner of schemes or doctrines or rule sets whereby man could instead retain his fleshly nature and yet, in his mind, conceive of himself as righteous and approved by God. In every religious system which conveyed to mankind the need to achieve one's righteousness and salvation by some man-made law or adherence to some list of activities one must perform or accomplish, mankind found themselves further deceived and so much clay in the hands of the Adversary. No amount of effort in the flesh could contrive to kill the fleshly nature and install a Godly nature; only the Cross could do that. Where man was encouraged to keep his own nature, there the Principalities and Powers flourished.

And so when a man harbored a thought of hatred toward his brother; when a man lusted; when a man schemed, or lied or murdered or leapt to grab power over his fellow men—in effect, when a man conformed to that which was simply his human nature—such actions formed in that man's spirit a certain quality which we know as spiritual death. In the spirit realm, a by-product of this quality—as a stench would be a by-product of a dead body—is power and authority conferred to these demonic principalities. However, when a man spoke the truth, or sacrificed for the good of others, or upheld righteousness and truth and justice—in effect, when a man worked to put his own nature to death and instead aligned himself with the Royal Law of Love in any or all its aspects, then a contravening exchange took place in the spiritual realms. A fragrance of life, of sweetness, of harmony was brought forth, and these powers and principalities—to whom this fragrance was the stench of death—were conversely denied power, influence, or dominion.

It is therefore clear now to the reader, one hopes, as to why and how such horrific excesses occurred throughout the Age of Man—horrible events where men starved or enslaved or slaughtered other men. How could such things happen? Simply because in a geographic area where such deeds were perpetrated, under which a particular principality ruled, men loved darkness rather than light; their deeds were comprised more of those things which fed the dark powers. The King had His own forces, true; forces arrayed to defend truth and righteousness and justice and love and beauty; but as it is a spiritual law, established by the King, that every man's will shall be done, so therefore do men create their own future for their nations and their lands by their deeds, by the power in spiritual realms they either strengthen or starve by the desires of their own will. The King structured the Age of Man upon a framework of nations, and in nations men lived, and over nations did these powers and principalities rule. The King permitted these powers and principalities to grow in strength and authority directly commensurate with the spirits in mankind within their areas of influence, and there were times throughout history when their power and influence was of such magnitude that they were enabled to break out against mankind in the most tragic of ways—in wars, in mass killings that stretched across hundreds or thousands of miles of territory, in subtle, dark manipulations that resulted in monumental death, sorrow, and horror. And in every way, every aspect of their exercise of power, they always sought to discredit the King's Son—He the True Source, Truth itself—for it was only through this one path shown to men by that Truth that the power of these demonic entities would be brought to an end, and by which men would be delivered from their clutches.

In many places the Adversary's strategy was to blame such killings primarily on race. A quick contemplation reveals how diabolically clever such a strategy truly was, for how can a man change his race? In ascribing these wanton butcheries to differences in race, the Adversary established a condition in which mankind came to believe that such things were inevitable and unchangeable, and in their zeal men then attempted to control such atrocities by applying their own laws—which was as futile as attempting to apply manmade law to alter the motion of the sun, moon, or stars.

It was the evisceration of Christianity in America that caused that nation's downfall, in no small part due to the Adversary's strategy of focusing men's attention on anything other than crucifying their human natures. As America sought ever more frantically for ever more ungodly solutions, the nation spiraled down further and further into the Adversary's enmeshing web, enabling the principalities which ruled over that geographic area a growing authority and power to command events, to influence culture and people and law, in such ways that eventually America succumbed in a welter of confused, bastardized pseudo-Christian ideologies contaminated by a combination of different heretical religious philosophies, Eastern influences, and, most prominently, the culture, mindset, and habits of the world itself. Thus did the last national bastion of Christianity pass from the world in the closing days of the age.

Sartorius Crux Vita
Diamond Gate, Jerusalem
Aeon Regis (AR) 40

www.ingramcontent.com/pod-product-compliance
Lightning Source LLC
Chambersburg PA
CBHW021846230426
43671CB00006B/283
9780982474952